THE HISTORY OF THE
UNIVERSITY OF OXFORD
VOLUME IV

Sir Thomas Bodley: wall monument in Merton College antechapel

THE HISTORY

OF THE

UNIVERSITY OF

OXFORD

VOLUME IV

Seventeenth-Century Oxford

EDITED BY

NICHOLAS TYACKE

CLARENDON PRESS · OXFORD

1997

Oxford University Press, Great Clarendon Street, Oxford OX2 6DP

Oxford New York

Athens Auckland Bangkok Bogota Bombay
Buenos Aires Calcutta Cape Town Dar es Salaam
Delhi Florence Hong Kong Istanbul Karachi
Kuala Lumpur Madras Madrid Melbourne
Mexico City Nairobi Paris Singapore
Taipei Tokyo Toronto
and associated companies in
Berlin Ibadan

Oxford is a trade mark of Oxford University Press

Published in the United States
by Oxford University Press Inc., New York

British Library Cataloguing in Publication Data
Data available

Library of Congress Cataloging in Publication Data
Data applied for
ISBN 0–19–951014–8

1 3 5 7 9 10 8 6 4 2

Typeset by Hope Services (Abingdon) Ltd
Printed in Great Britain
on acid-free paper by
Bookcraft Ltd., Midsomer Norton,
Nr. Bath, Somerset

Preface

THE idea of this volume was first conceived under the editorship of Hugh Trevor-Roper, Lord Dacre of Glanton. But by the time he left Oxford for Peterhouse, Cambridge, and handed over to the present editor, it was still at the planning stage. The opportunity was taken at that point to rethink matters, in discussions with the then general editor Trevor Aston who continued to play a supportive role right up to his untimely death; we were in fact due to meet to discuss the volume, at his suggestion, only a few days after he died in 1985. An exemplary model was by then to hand in the shape of volume iii of the series, covering the sixteenth century and edited by James McConica, and this has been followed with some adaptations. Among other changes to the original scheme of volume iv was the decision to commission a new author for the chapter 'University and Society', which in the event was written by Stephen Porter during his two-year appointment as research assistant; the other additions to the team were Alan Crossley, John Elliot, Kenneth Fincham, Penelope Gouk, Brian Levack, Paul Morgan, Ian Roy, and John Twigg. Unfortunately John Platt proved unable to contribute a chapter on theology to supplement that on 'Religious Controversy'. Extra burdens have also been shouldered, especially by Mordechai Feingold, whose scholarly labours have been massive, while Alan Crossley has kindly helped with chapters other than his own. The maps have been expertly drawn by Julian Munby.

Those writing about seventeenth-century Oxford are privileged to be able to draw on the work of a number of predecessors, notably that of the contemporary Anthony Wood and his subsequent editors. There are in addition many other relevant volumes published by the Oxford Historical Society, and despite the passage of time Falconer Madan's *Oxford Books* remains an indispensable bibliographical aid. In our task we have incurred numerous debts: to the staff of that jewel in Oxford's crown the Bodleian Library, to successive keepers of the university archives—especially Ruth Vyse and Simon Bailey—and to the college librarians and archivists many of whom are thanked individually in the various chapters. Like the other volumes in the series this volume has benefited from the generous funding provided by Oxford University, the individual colleges and the Nuffield Foundation. We are as well most grateful to the Scouloudi Foundation, for a grant to cover the illustrations. Ralph Evans, recently project co-ordinator, provided a vital link for a volume editor based in London. Anne Gelling, on behalf of the publishers, has always been a source of sound advice and practical help. During the editorial process, when only some of the chapters had been produced, I was able to draw on the skills of Adrienne Rosen. Latterly this task has been mine alone, but the copy-editor, Janet Moth, has saved me from frequent slips. We are also indebted to Mark Goldie, for allowing us to read work in advance of publication. Lastly William Davies, of Cambridge University Press, in an act of great magnanimity made available the typescript of the second volume of *A History of the University in Europe*—covering the period 1500 to 1800 and edited by Hilde de Ridder-Symoens. All have contributed to a truly collective enterprise.

N.T.

University College London
September 1996

Contents

Plates

Acknowledgements

Acknowledgement is gratefully made to the Ashmolean Museum, for permission to publish plates 24, 27, and 31; to B. T. Batsford Ltd, for plate 17; to the British Library, for plates 12, 25, and 28; to the Bodleian Library, for plates 1, 2, 3, 4, 5, 6, 7, 8, 10, 11, 14, 23, and 32; to the Museum of the History of Science, for plate 22; to the Oxfordshire Photographic Archive (Oxfordshire Council Leisure and Arts), for plate 18; to Mr J. Potter, for plate 30; to the provost and fellows of Queen's College, for plate 29; to the president and fellows of St John's College, Oxford, for plate 22; to Mr J. W. Thomas, for the frontispiece and plates 9, 13, 15, 16, and 19; to the warden and fellows of Wadham College, for plate 20; to the Wellcome Institute Library, London, for plate 26; to the York City Art Gallery, for plate 21.

Maps

Abbreviations

APC	*Acts of the Privy Council of England 1542–1631* (46 vols London 1890–1946)
ASA	All Souls College Archives
ASL	All Souls Library
BA	bachelor of arts
BCA	Balliol College Archives
BCL	bachelor of civil law
BD	bachelor of divinity
BL	British Library, London
Bloxam, *Reg. Magdalen*	J. R. Bloxam, *A Register of the Presidents, Fellows, Demies, Instructors in Grammar and in Music, Chaplains, Clerks, Choristers, and Other Members of Saint Mary Magdalen College in the University of Oxford, from the Foundation of the College to the Present Time* (7 vols Oxford 1853–81, index vol. by W. D. Macray Oxford 1885); cf Macray, *Reg. Magdalen*
BM	bachelor of medicine
BMus	bachelor of music
BNCA	Brasenose College Archives
BNCL	Brasenose College Library
Bodl.	Bodleian Library, Oxford
Brasenose Monographs	*Brasenose College Quatercentenary Monographs* (2 vols in 3 OHS lii-liv 1909)
CA	Christ Church Archives
CCCA	Corpus Christi College (Oxford) Archives
CCCL	Corpus Christi College (Oxford) Library
CJ	*Journals of the House of Commons*
CL	Christ Church Library
Collectanea i	*Collectanea*, 1st ser. ed. C. R. L. Fletcher (OHS v 1885)
Collectanea ii	*Collectanea*, 2nd ser. ed. Montagu Burrows (OHS xvi 1890)
Collectanea iii	*Collectanea*, 3rd ser. ed. Montagu Burrows (OHS xxxii 1896)
Collectanea iv	*Collectanea*, 4th ser. (OHS xlvii 1905)
Costin, *St. John's*	W. C. Costin, *The History of St. John's College, Oxford, 1598–1860* (OHS New ser. xii 1958)
CSPD	*Calendar of State Papers, Domestic Series, preserved in the Public Record Office, 1547–1704* (92 vols London 1856–1972)
CSPV	*Calendar of State Papers and Manuscripts relating to English Affairs existing in the Archives and Collections of Venice and in other Libraries of Northern Italy 1202–1675* (38 vols in 40 London 1864–[1947])
DCL	doctor of civil law
DD	doctor of divinity
Dean's Register of Oriel	*The Dean's Register of Oriel 1446–1661*, ed. G. C. Richards and H. E. Salter (OHS lxxxiv 1926)

DM	doctor of medicine
DMus	doctor of music
DNB	*The Dictionary of National Biography from the Earliest Times to 1900* (66 vols London 1885–1901, repr. in 22 vols London 1921–2)
ECA	Exeter College Archives
ECL	Exeter College Library
EHR	*English Historical Review*
Enactments	*Enactments in Parliament specially concerning the Universities of Oxford and Cambridge*, ed. L. L. Shadwell (4 vols OHS lvii–lxi 1912)
Foster, *Alumni*	Joseph Foster, *Alumni oxonienses: the members of the University of Oxford 1500–1714, their parentage, birthplace and year of birth, with a record of their degrees, being the matriculation register of the university arranged, revised, and annotated* (4 vols Oxford and London 1891–2)
Fowler, *Corpus*	T. Fowler, *The History of Corpus Christi College* (OHS xv 1893)
FRCP	fellow of the Royal College of Physicians
FRS	fellow of the Royal Society
HCA	Hertford College Archives
Hearne, *Collections*	*Remarks and Collections of Thomas Hearne*, ed. C. E. Doble, D. W. Rannie, H. E. Salter, *et al.* (11 vols OHS ii, vii, xiii, xxxiv, xlii–xliii, xlviii, l, lxv, lxvii, lxxii 1884–1918)
HLC	Huntington Library, California
HLRO	House of Lords Record Office
HMC	Historical Manuscripts Commission
HMC *Cowper MSS*	*The Manuscripts of the Earl Cowper, KG, preserved at Melbourne Hall, Derbyshire* (HMC 23rd ser. 3 vols 1888–9 as pts 1–3 of appx to 12th report)
HMC *De L'Isle and Dudley*	*Report on the Manuscripts of the Lord De L'Isle and Dudley, preserved at Penshurst Place* (HMC 77th ser. 6 vols 1925–66)
HMC *Downshire MSS*	*Report on the Manuscripts of the Marquess of Downshire, preserved at Easthampstead Park, Berks.* (HMC 75th ser. 5 vols 1924–88)
HMC *Egmont MSS*	*Report on the Manuscripts of the Earl of Egmont* (HMC 63rd ser. 2 vols in 3 1905–9)
HMC *Finch MSS*	*Report on the Manuscripts of Allan George Finch Esq., of Burley-on-the-Hill, Rutland* (HMC 71st ser. 4 vols 1913–65)
HMC *Hastings MSS*	*Report on the Manuscripts of the Late Reginald Rawdon Hastings Esq., of the Manor House, Ashby de la Zouche* (HMC 78th ser. 4 vols 1928–47)
HMC *House of Lords MSS*	*The Manuscripts of the House of Lords* (HMC 17th ser., new ser. 12 vols 1900–77)
HMC *Kenyon MSS*	*The Manuscripts of Lord Kenyon* (HMC 35th ser. 1894 as pt 4 of appx to 14th report)
HMC *Leyborne-Popham MSS*	*Report on the Manuscripts of F. W. Leyborne-Popham Esq. of Littlecote, Co. Wilts* (HMC 51st ser. 1899)
HMC *Lonsdale MSS*	*The Manuscripts of the Earl of Lonsdale* (HMC 33rd ser. 1893 as pt 7 of appx to 13th report)
HMC *Ormonde MSS*	*The Manuscripts of the Marquess of Ormonde, KP, preserved at Kilkenny Castle* (HMC 36th ser. 11 vols 1895–1920, 3 vols 1895–1909 as pt 7 of appx to 14th report, and new ser. 8 vols 1902–20)

HMC *Portland MSS*	*The Manuscripts of His Grace the Duke of Portland, preserved at Welbeck Abbey* (HMC 29th ser. 10 vols 1891–1931: 2 vols 1891–3 as pts 1–2 of appx to 13th report, 1 vol. 1894 as pt 2 of appx to 14th report, 1 vol. 1897 as pt 4 of appx to 15th report and 6 vols 1899–1931)
HMC *Reading Corporation MSS*	*The Manuscripts of the Duke of Leeds, the Bridgewater Corporation Trust, Reading Corporation, the Inner Temple etc.* (HMC 22nd ser. 1888 as pt 7 of appx to 11th report)
HMC *Salisbury MSS*	*Calendar of the Manuscripts of the Most Honourable the Marquess of Salisbury preserved at Hatfield House, Hertfordshire* (HMC 9th ser. 24 vols 1883–1976)
HMC *Wells Dean and Chapter MSS*	*Calendar of the Manuscripts of the Dean and Chapter of Wells* (HMC 12th ser. 2 vols 1907–14)
HMC *Second Report*	*Second Report of the Royal Commission on Historical Manuscripts* (1874)
HMC *Fifth Report*	*Fifth Report of the Royal Commission on Historical Manuscripts* (1 vol. in 2 1876)
HMC *Seventh Report*	*Seventh Report of the Royal Commission on Historical Manuscripts* (1 vol. in 2 1879)
HMC *Ninth Report*	*Ninth Report of the Royal Commission on Historical Manuscripts* (3 vols 1883–4)
HMC *Eleventh Report*	*Eleventh Report of the Royal Commission on Historical Manuscripts* (7 vols 1887–8)
HMC *Twelfth Report*	*Twelfth Report of the Royal Commission on Historical Manuscripts* (12 vols 1890–1)
HMC *Thirteenth Report*	*Thirteenth Report of the Royal Commission on Historical Manuscripts* (8 vols 1891–4)
HMC *Fifteenth Report*	*Fifteenth Report of the Royal Commission on Historical Manuscripts* (10 vols 1896–9)
JCA	Jesus College (Oxford) Archives
Late Medieval Oxford	J. S. Catto and Ralph Evans (eds), *Late Medieval Oxford* (History of the University of Oxford ii Oxford 1992)
Laud, *Works*	*The Works of the Right Reverend Father in God William Laud*, ed. W. Scott and J. Bliss (7 vols Oxford 1847–60)
Laudian Code, ed. Griffiths	*Statutes of the University of Oxford codified in the year 1636 under the authority of Archbishop Laud, Chancellor of the University*, ed. J. Griffiths, intr. C. L. Shadwell (Oxford 1888); the numbered titles into which the statutes are divided and the numbered sections and chapters into which titles may be subdivided are here designated respectively by upper-case roman, lower-case roman, and arabic numerals (for example VII. ii. 3 represents title VII, section ii, chapter 3; V. 2 represents title V, chapter 2)
LCM	Lincoln College Muniment Room
LJ	*Journals of the House of Lords*
LPL	Lambeth Palace Library
MA	master of arts
Macleane, *Pembroke*	D. Macleane, *A History of Pembroke College, Oxford* (OHS xxxiii 1897)
Macray, *Reg. Magdalen*	W. D. Macray, *A Register of the Members of St Mary Magdalen College, Oxford from the Foundation of the College* (new ser. 8 vols London 1894–1915); cf Bloxam, *Reg. Magdalen*

Madan, *Oxford Books*	F. Madan, *Oxford Books* (3 vols Oxford 1895–1931)
Magdalen and James II	*Magdalen College and King James II 1686–1688*, ed. J. R. Bloxam (OHS vi 1886)
MCA	Magdalen College Archives
MCL	Magdalen College Library
MCR	Merton College Record
NCA	New College Archives
NCL	New College Library
NUL	Nottingham Unviersity Library
OCA	Oriel College Archives
OHS	Oxford Historical Society
ORO	Oxfordshire Record Office
OUA	Oxford University Archives
PCA	Pembroke College (Oxford) Archives
PRO	Public Record Office, London
QCA	Queen's College (Oxford) Archives
QCL	Queen's College (Oxford) Library
Reg. Brasenose	[C. B. Heberden], *Brasenose College Register, 1509–1909* (2 vols in 1 Oxford 1909 and 2 vols in 1 OHS lv 1910)
Reg. Exeter	*Registrum Collegii Exoniensis*, ed. C. W. Boase (OHS xxvii 1894)
Reg. Univ. ed. Clark	*Register of the University of Oxford* ii, ed. A. Clark (4 pts OHS x–xii, xiv 1887–9)
Register, ed. Burrows	*The Register of the Visitors of the Univesity of Oxford*, ed. M. Burrows (Camden Soc. new ser. xxix 1881)
RO	record office
SA	*Statuta antiqua universitatis oxoniensis*, ed. Strickland Gibson (Oxford 1931)
SJM	St John's College (Oxford) Muniments
Stat. Coll.	*Statutes of the Colleges of Oxford* (3 vols Royal Commission 1853)
Statutes, trans. Ward	*Oxford University Statutes*, trans. G. R. M. Ward (2 vols London 1845–51); titles, sections, and chapters are cited in the same form as for *Laudian Code*, ed. Griffiths
Statutes of the Realm	*The Statutes of the Realm [1235–1713]: printed by command of his majesty King George the third* (11 vols London 1810–28)
STC	A. W. Pollard and G. R. Redgrave, *A Short-Title Catalogue of Books Printed in England, Scotland, and Ireland and of English Books Printed Abroad 1475–1640* (London 1926 [1927]); new edn by W. A. Jackson, F. S. Ferguson and K. F. Pantzer (2 vols London 1976–86)
TCA	Trinity College (Oxford) Archives
The Collegiate University	James McConica (ed.), *The Collegiate University* (History of the University of Oxford iii Oxford 1986)
The Early Oxford Schools	J. I. Catto and Ralph Evans (eds), *The Early Oxford Schools* (History of the University of Oxford i Oxford 1984)
The Eighteenth Century	L. S. Sutherland and L. G. Mitchell (eds), *The Eighteenth Century* (History of the University of Oxford v Oxford 1986)
The Flemings in Oxford	*The Flemings in Oxford*, ed. J. R. Magrath (3 vols OHS xliv 1903, xlii 1913, lxxix 1924)

TRHS	*Transactions of the Royal Historical Society*
UCA	University College (Oxford) Archives
VCH	*Victoria County History*
Venn, *Alumni*	J. and J. A. Venn, *Alumni cantabrigienses; a biographical list of all known students, graduates and holders of office at the University of Cambridge, from the earliest times to 1990* pt 1 *From the Earliest Times to 1751* (4 vols Cambridge 1922–7)
WCA	Worcester College Archives
WCM	Wadham College Muniments
West. CA	Westminster Cathedral Archives
Wood, *Athenae*	Anthony Wood, *Athenae oxonienses*, ed. Philip Bliss (4 vols London 1813–20)
Wood, *City of Oxford*	'*Survey of the Antiquities of the City of Oxford*' composed in *1661–6 by Anthony Wood*, ed. A. Clark (3 vols OHS xv 1889, xvii 1890, xxxvii 1899)
Wood, *Fasti*	Anthony Wood, *Fasti oxonienses*, ed. Philip Bliss (2 pts London 1815–20)
Wood, *History of the Colleges and Halls*	Anthony Wood, *The History and Antiquities of the Colleges and Halls in the University of Oxford*, ed. John Gutch (Oxford 1786)
Wood, *History of the University*	Anthony Wood, *The History and Antiquities of the University of Oxford*, ed. John Gutch (2 vols in 3 Oxford 1792–6)
Wood, *Life and Times*	*The Life and Times of Anthony Wood, Antiquary, of Oxford, 1632–1695, described by himself*, ed. A. Clark (4 vols OHS xix, xxi, xxvi, xxx 1891–5)

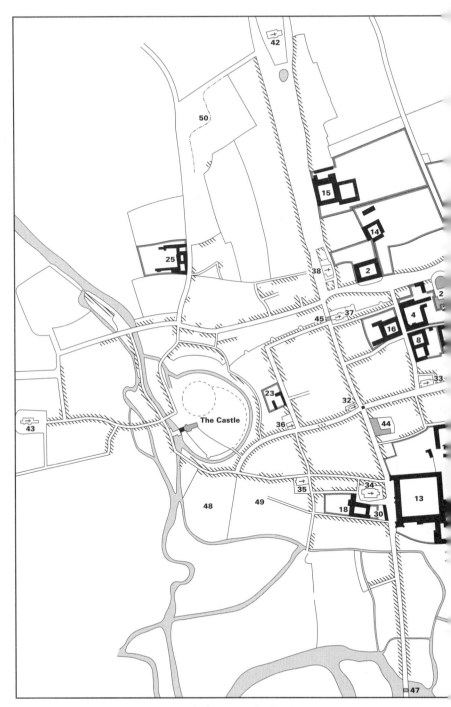

MAP 1. Oxford in 1675 (after David Loggan)

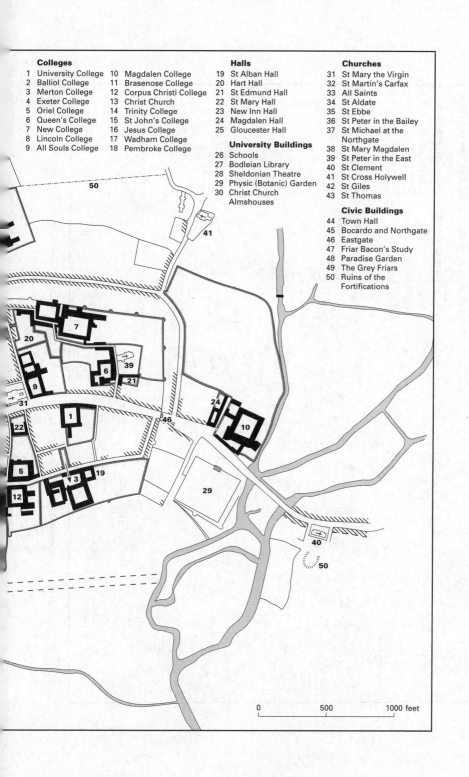

Colleges
1 University College
2 Balliol College
3 Merton College
4 Exeter College
5 Oriel College
6 Queen's College
7 New College
8 Lincoln College
9 All Souls College
10 Magdalen College
11 Brasenose College
12 Corpus Christi College
13 Christ Church
14 Trinity College
15 St John's College
16 Jesus College
17 Wadham College
18 Pembroke College

Halls
19 St Alban Hall
20 Hart Hall
21 St Edmund Hall
22 St Mary Hall
23 New Inn Hall
24 Magdalen Hall
25 Gloucester Hall

University Buildings
26 Schools
27 Bodleian Library
28 Sheldonian Theatre
29 Physic (Botanic) Garden
30 Christ Church
   Almshouses

Churches
31 St Mary the Virgin
32 St Martin's Carfax
33 All Saints
34 St Aldate
35 St Ebbe
36 St Peter in the Bailey
37 St Michael at the
   Northgate
38 St Mary Magdalen
39 St Peter in the East
40 St Clement
41 St Cross Holywell
42 St Giles
43 St Thomas

Civic Buildings
44 Town Hall
45 Bocardo and Northgate
46 Eastgate
47 Friar Bacon's Study
48 Paradise Garden
49 The Grey Friars
50 Ruins of the
   Fortifications

0   500   1000 feet

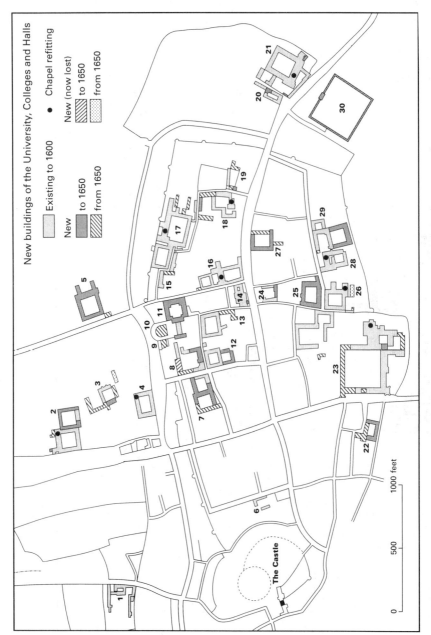

MAP 2. New buildings of the university, colleges and halls in Oxford during the seventeenth century

1 Gloucester Hall
No significant building

2 St John's College

1612	Kitchen
1615–21	▶Hall improvements
1619	Chapel improvements
1631–36	Canterbury Quadrangle
1642–43	Cook's Building
c.1670	Chapel screen
1676	Common Room

3 Trinity College

1618	Hall
1665	Common Room
1665–8	Garden Quadrangle N
1676–77	Kitchen
1682	Garden Quadrangle W
1687	Bathurst Building lost
1691–94	Chapel and Gate

4 Balliol College

1636	Chapel partly refitted

5 Wadham College

1610–13	Main buildings
1693–94	Parks Road building

6 New Inn Hall
Uncertain

7 Jesus College

c.1617	Hall and Kitchen
1619–21	Chapel
1620s	Principal's Lodging, S Range, and first Library
1636–7	Chapel lengthened
1639–43	Inner Quadrangle begun
1676–79	Library and Common Room completed
1690–1713	Inner Quadrangle completed

8 Exeter College

1616	Peryam's Building

9 Ashmolean Museum

1678–83	Ashmolean Museum

10 Sheldonian Theatre

1664–69	Sheldonian Theatre

11 Bodleian Library & Public Schools

1602–5	▶Duke Humfrey refitted
1610–12	Proscholium and Arts End
1613–24	Schools Quadrangle
1634–41	Selden End, Convocation House & Court
1668	▶Divinity School door

12 Lincoln College

1607–31	Chapel Quadrangle
1629–31	Chapel
1640–41	▶Hall cellar
1662	▶Common Room

13 Brasenose College

1605–13, 1635–6	▶Front Quadrangle, top storey
1656–63	Chapel and Cloister
c.1680	Hall oriel and cellar

14 St Mary the Virgin Church

1637	Porch

15 Hart Hall
Uncertain

16 All Souls College

1664	Chapel refitted
1670, 1675	Common Rooms and chambers over

17 New College

1637–8	Chapel refitted
1674	▶Front Quadrangle top storey added
1675	▶Warden's Lodging stair
1676	Warden's bridge
1678	▶Common Room panelled
1682–3	Garden Quadrangle

18 Queen's College

1622	North chamber block
1631–5	Chapel refitted
1671–2	Williamson Building
1692–5	Library

19 St Edmund Hall

1635	Front Quadrangle W, S end
1659	Front Quadrangle W, Hall
1680–88	Chapel and Library

20 Magdalen Hall
[Mostly uncertain]

1614	Rebuilding (Grammar Hall)

21 Magdalen College

1629–35	Gate [lost]
1631–7	Chapel refitted
1635	Rooms over Kitchen
1665	▶Almshouse range converted

22 Pembroke College

From 1626	Front Quadrangle S, W & E
1673–95	Quadrangle completed, with Tower and Master's lodgings

23 Christ Church

1610–12	▶Old Library restored
1631–3	Cathedral refitted
1640	Hall stair vaulting
c. 1640, 1660–70	Tom Quad completed
1669–73	Kill-Canon lodgings
c.1670	Chaplains Quadrangle rebuilt
1681–2	Tom Tower

24 St Mary Hall

1639–40	Hall and Chapel

25 Oriel College

1620–22	Front Quadrangle W then S
1637–42	Quadrangle N, Hall and Chapel

26 Corpus Christi College

1666–68	New Building (lost)
1675–76	Chapel refitted
c. 1690	President's Lodging, part

27 University College

1634–7	North and West ranges of Front Quadrangle
1639–42	South range
1639–41	Chapel and Hall built
1656–7	Hall roofed
1660–65	Chapel and Hall completed
1668–9	Kitchen and Library
1675–6	East range

28 Merton College

1608–10	Fellows' Quadrangle (inc Kitchen)
1671–3	Chapel refitted
1680	Common Room

29 Alban Hall
Uncertain

30 Physic (Botanic) Garden

1631–3, 1639	Garden wall and gates

Note that entries marked ▶ are not indicated on the map.

Introduction

NICHOLAS TYACKE

How should we regard developments at Oxford University during the seventeenth century and what, if any, unity does the period possess? At first sight indeed it looks like a tale best told in terms of discontinuities. For the civil wars and their republican aftermath mark a seemingly radical break, and certainly on one possible reading the old world collapsed during the revolutionary 1640s never fully to be restored. An alternative view would be that the first decades of the century witnessed a late Elizabethan flowering, the seeds of which, however, fell on stony ground. Either way the mid-seventeenth century appears to represent a watershed. Nevertheless, the events recorded in this volume are open to a very different interpretation. For almost everywhere there are signs of a long-term expansion, across the Interregnum, and one that despite the turbulent politics of the period was only beginning to falter late in the century.

The most obvious evidence for this being a time of growth lies in the extraordinary spate of building (map 2), itself witness to the burgeoning student numbers. Apart from the new colleges—Wadham (1610) and Pembroke (1626)—in many ways more impressive are the architectural additions to existing institutions, comprising rebuilding as well as extensions. New halls, chapels, libraries, ranges, and whole quadrangles proliferated. Brasenose, Lincoln, Merton, St John's, Exeter, Jesus, Trinity, Oriel, and Queen's were the colleges earliest in the field; they were followed by University College and St Edmund Hall in the 1630s. Despite the hiatus of the civil war, this impetus revived during the 1650s and gathered pace thereafter. 'In fact it is possible to see almost all that was done in the 1660s and 1670s as a continuation of initiatives taken in the pre-war period, or the implementation of what had proved impracticable then.'[1] This was especially true of Brasenose, University, Christ Church, and Jesus colleges, while fresh projects were undertaken at Trinity, Queen's, and New colleges. Much of the money was generated by elaborate fundraising schemes, such as at Jesus and Oriel, and involved the targeting of old members. The sense of corporate identity to which this witnesses extended, however, beyond the individual colleges and also embraced the university itself. While the entrepreneurial skills of heads of house were often crucial for collegiate expansion, it was the Mertonians Sir Thomas Bodley and Sir Henry Savile whose vision especially inspired the refoundation of the university library and the building

This introduction began life as a lecture given in Oxford, on 4 February 1995. I am grateful to the following for their comments on drafts of the enlarged text: Professor M. Feingold, Dr K. Fincham, Professor M. Hunter, Professor P. Lake, Professor J. McConica, Professor R. Porter, and Mrs S. Tyacke.
[1] John Newman, 'The architectural setting', pp. 171–2 below.

of the new university schools. Bodley, advised by Savile, provided much of the money, but the new schools were also in part funded by a nationwide appeal, which yielded in excess of £5,000. Half a century later Archbishop Sheldon, encouraged by Dean Fell of Christ Church, provided the university with a theatre for its more formal academic activities and a printing press. In so doing, moreover, Sheldon sought to fulfil the wishes of his predecessor William Laud.[2]

A great deal of this building activity was, of course, driven by an increase in the size of the undergraduate body, which began in the Elizabethan period, peaked during the 1630s, and recovered after a mid-century nosedive. 'The high numbers of student admissions to Oxford which characterized the middle decades of the century—from roughly the mid-1620s to the mid-1670s—were unprecedented and were not to be attained again for almost two hundred years.' Estimated admissions of students each decade, over these same sixty years, only fell below 4,000 in the 1640s.[3] Granted that until the 1650s national population was also rising, an explanation nevertheless of Oxford's demographic history exclusively in such terms appears unconvincing. For Oxford, like Cambridge, catered at this time for a national surge in demand from those seeking higher education. Thus it was becoming *de rigueur* for clergy to have at least a first degree, while a stay at university was increasingly regarded as desirable for the sons of the gentry—most of whom did not seek professional careers. Numbers attending university need in addition to be seen against a background of generally buoyant agricultural prices and rent receipts, until the later seventeenth century. We should bear in mind too the associated growth of secondary education, particularly in the number of schools which both prepared boys for university and required graduates as teachers. Although Oxford continued to draw 'its recruits from a broad social spectrum' during the seventeenth century, 'by the 1680s the combined intake of those matriculating as sons of gentlemen and clergy had come to outnumber the plebeians and paupers'. A majority of the latter were entered as battelers and servitors, often subsidizing their time at university by performing menial tasks for the fellows and commoners; some were also awarded scholarships and exhibitions, or had a patron. Among those intending to graduate, which included most of those below the ranks of the gentry, a statutory period of four years was required. Most matriculants were aged between 16 and 18 years. Certain colleges and halls had a strong regional bias, and they varied greatly in size; thus in 1634 Exeter College was the biggest with 230 persons—two-thirds of its students coming from Devon and Cornwall—and Corpus Christi College was among the smallest with seventy.[4]

Important as such matters are, this was also a golden age of academic endeavour at Oxford. Contrary to what is often claimed, ancient and modern studies coexisted there in harmony. Bodley's 'panbiblion', as a contemporary called it, was housed within the medieval shell of Duke Humfrey's Library, and, after its exten-

---

[2] John Newman, 'The architectural setting', *passim*. Dr R. Highfield has also kindly shared with me his knowledge of Bodley and Savile.

[3] Stephen Porter, 'University and society', pp. 33–4 below.   [4] Ibid. 54, 40.

sion east and west, the new library came virtually to envelop the old divinity school on the ground floor. Yet the latter remained the inner sanctum of the magnificent new schools quadrangle, which in turn was both a physical and intellectual extension of the library. This symbiotic relationship has been somewhat obscured by the fact that the library subsequently expanded into the schools buildings. The original connection, however, is clear from the monument erected after the death of Bodley in 1613, which provides a kind of coda to his achievement; Bodley's bust is flanked by pillars of books, with the seven liberal arts displayed in the background (frontispiece). What might have developed into a simply traditionalistic enterprise was saved from any such fate by the involvement of Savile, warden of Merton since 1585. More of an intellectual than Bodley, Savile ensured by his endowment of professorships in astronomy and geometry that 'science' would find a prominent place in seventeenth-century Oxford. The Savilian professors were assigned lecture rooms either side of the new schools tower, across the quadrangle from the library, and the tower itself doubled as an astronomical observatory (plate 1). But the inherently mixed nature of such activities can be further illustrated from another funeral monument, this time Savile's own: figures of Chrysostom and Ptolemy, Euclid and Tacitus stand either side, and on a southern hemisphere below is depicted the route of Magellan's circumnavigation of the globe (plate 9). As well as translating some of these personal interests into his own professorial endowments, Savile appears to have been partly responsible for the cluster of similar Oxford benefactions in the early 1620s.[5]

Yet early modern Oxford has rightly been characterized as a collegiate university, orientated towards the needs of undergraduates. While this system proved educationally quite flexible, it also imposed certain limitations on change. At the same time a sound financial infrastructure was basic, in a way that fundraising for specific projects was not. Although there existed great disparities in the endowment of individual colleges, and halls had none, a common problem during the first half of the seventeenth century remained coping with still increasing prices—especially of foodstuffs. But here, thanks to parliamentary legislation of the 1570s, colleges possessed what has been called a 'hedge against inflation' or 'form of index linking' in the guise of corn rents. Up to a third of their landed income was protected in this way. Despite some spectacular instances of mismanagement, as for example the incurring of £1,750-worth of debts at Brasenose during the 1620s and 1630s, other colleges can be shown accumulating healthy cash surpluses. Even the university itself, with a much smaller income than most colleges, had managed to build up a cash reserve of nearly £1,000 by 1641. This general prosperity, however, was abruptly terminated with the onset of the civil wars. Indeed it is in the realm

[5] Madan, *Oxford Books* i. 46; A. J. Bott, *The Monuments in Merton College Chapel* (Oxford 1964), 84–7; M. Feingold, 'Patrons and professors: the origins and motives for the endowment of university chairs—in particular the Laudian professorship of Arabic' in G. A. Russell (ed.), *The 'Arabick' Interest of the Natural Philosophers in Seventeenth-Century England* (London 1994), 111–12.

of finance that perhaps the greatest short-term dislocation can be detected. Thus in the years 1642–3 over £10,000 was loaned to Charles I, along with most college plate. (Neither loan was ever to be repaid.) Hard on the heels of this came the 'crippling effects' of internecine strife, as college rents fell rapidly away—leading in turn to a 'financial crisis'. Cut off by the war, many tenants were either unable or unwilling to pay their dues. Other sources of income were similarly affected, and the indirect burdens of being the royalist headquarters became increasingly onerous. The nadir was reached in the summer of 1646, when 'the discipline of the garrison soldiery, short of pay and provisions, appears to have broken down'. They mutinied and murdered their officers. Two years earlier, however, the parlous financial state of Balliol had actually led to its being 'dissolved', and All Souls was 'temporarily suspended'. Merton and Jesus seem to have been in scarcely better condition at this time. These were the years too when student numbers declined dramatically and academic life threatened to grind to a halt, with the university schools taken over as military stores and workshops. Nevertheless even as regards college finances signs of recovery are apparent during the 1650s, and most of the ravages had been made good by the time of the Restoration.[6]

On the other hand, the highly politicized nature of Oxford's external relations during the middle of the seventeenth century was more a difference of degree rather than of kind. For better or worse, the fortunes of Oxford and Cambridge were closely bound up with the regime of the day. Furthermore there are civil war analogies to be drawn with both the rapid religious changes of the Tudor period and the Catholic challenge posed by James II. Nor was the outwardly calmer reign of Charles I free from such tensions. Somewhat slow to embrace protestantism under Elizabeth, Oxford seemingly achieved a position of near religious equilibrium with the state in the first years of James I. 'A national institution in the public gaze', as the early Stuart university has been dubbed, a complex web of interdependence with the crown had developed since the fifteenth century, when the practice had arisen of electing a courtier as chancellor. This culminated during the reign of Elizabeth with a succession of lay grandees as holders of the office: Leicester, Hatton, and Buckhurst. Although still elected by convocation, they were effectively royal appointments. It was, moreover, during Leicester's period of office (*circa* 1570) that the vice-chancellor became the nominee of the chancellor, instead of being elected by congregation, and the candidates were confined to college heads and canons of Christ Church. The heads also increasingly emerged as the inner ring of university government and source of executive power, their position formalized by the Laudian statutes as the hebdomadal board in the 1630s. A contemporary account of this triumph of oligarchy dates from 1597, in which the author, Roger

[6] G. Aylmer, 'The economics and finances of the colleges and university c.1530–1640' in *The Collegiate University*, 536, 549–51; John Twigg, 'College finances 1640–1660', pp. 774–9 and *passim* below; Ian Roy and Dietrich Reinhart, 'Oxford and the civil wars', pp. 719–20 below; Blair Worden, 'Cromwellian Oxford', p. 750 below.

Jones of New College, traces the origins of Oxford's loss of 'academicall freedom' to interference by Henry VIII.[7]

Nevertheless, in return for loyal service to the state Oxford gained patronage and protection. A good illustration of the reciprocal nature of this relationship is provided by the conjunction of the royal charter and Laudian statutes in 1636. In requesting 'obedience' to the new code, Secretary Sir John Coke reminded the university of the recent grant of 'priveleges'. He went on to praise 'our greate chauncellor', Archbishop Laud, as the promoter of the 'glory' of Oxford: 'witnesse those preferments . . . dayly received' by 'the able men of our university', thanks to 'his power at the court', and the 'stately and magnificent buildings' erected.[8] Patronage, however, worked in both directions, college appointments offering tempting opportunities to outside, and especially royal, intervention. With the accession of James I, royal mandates initially rained down upon the university, threatening chaos by sometimes recommending multiple candidates for the same post although order was soon restored. College headships were among the greatest prizes, as well as being instruments of central government control—a function particularly apparent under Laud. 'Almost all the new heads of houses', during the 1630s, were either 'Laudian protégés or willing supporters'.[9]

Compared with Elizabeth, both James I and Charles I involved themselves more directly in university affairs, often staying at nearby Woodstock where such business could be transacted. Indicative of the increasingly close relations with the crown is the growing number of commemorative volumes of verses published by the university, in honour of various members of the royal family. Apart from the royal charter of 1636, the university had acquired the right to elect MPs in 1604. This was again linked with the question of privileges. Here the university most obviously required protection against the claims of its neighbour the city of Oxford, refusing to be 'subordinate to mechanical persons'. Litigation had now largely superseded the physical violence of the medieval period, but power relations between the two corporations remained regularly contested territory. The city's rapid growth of population and prosperity paralleled that of the university, but also compounded the problem by overcrowding. In the 1630s Oxford's total population numbered some 10,000 persons, of whom approximately a third were made up by the university. During the first half of the seventeenth century there developed a tug-of-war over their respective charters, which came to a head in 1642 when the city representatives withdrew from the annual oath-taking. The latter was

---

[7] Kenneth Fincham, 'Oxford and the early Stuart polity', p. 180 below; R. L. Storey, 'University and government 1430–1500' in *Late Medieval Oxford*; P. Williams, 'Elizabethan Oxford: state, church and university' in *The Collegiate University*, 401–3; Bodl. MS Wood d. 18, fo 7.

[8] Fincham, 'Oxford and the early Stuart polity', 179–80; NUL MS Cl. c. 73. We are indebted here, and elsewhere in the volume, to Dr R. Cust, for both drawing our attention to the Clifton papers at Nottingham University Library and providing xeroxes.

[9] Fincham, 'Oxford and the early Stuart polity', 191, 208.

abandoned throughout the Interregnum of the 1650s and only resurrected after the Restoration.[10]

Above all, however, it was the religious diversity spawned by the reformation that led to increasing state intervention in the life of the university, and this Tudor experience requires a brief recapitulation if subsequent seventeenth-century developments are fully to be understood. The beginnings of the process, it is true, are discernible earlier, notably with the suppression of Wycliffite teachings at Oxford during the late fourteenth and early fifteenth centuries. But the politically driven nature of the reformation in England, at the official level, meant that the two universities found themselves thenceforward in the ideological front line. Although the confessional allegiance might change, religious unity remained the goal of successive governments. Even more than in the past therefore the universities came to be conceived as founts of orthodoxy, purveying a body of religious truth to the nation at large. As early as 1521 Oxford theologians were marshalled to condemn Luther, but within six years a small group of sympathizers had emerged within the university itself. In the following decade matters became further confused, with Oxford having to be bullied into collectively approving Henry VIII's grounds for a divorce from Catherine of Aragon. Nevertheless the break from Rome was accepted without protest, being followed up by a royal visitation in 1535—the commissioners also lending their weight to the newly fashionable humanism, by setting up lectureships in Greek and Latin, at the same time as virtually abolishing the study of canon law.[11]

What in retrospect can be seen as the first tentative steps towards protestantism under Henry VIII gathered pace rapidly after 1547, with the accession of Edward VI. The death of the conservative Chancellor Longland, conveniently also in 1547, was followed by the appointment of Richard Cox, recently made dean of Christ Church and a suspected Lutheran back in the late 1520s. Under him Christ Church became a 'powerhouse of Edwardian protestantism', as well as a centre for foreign reformers. Thus, in the task of protestantizing Oxford, Cox was ably assisted by the exiled theologian Peter Martyr, who was appointed regius professor of divinity in 1548 on the deprivation of his predecessor. The next year saw a further royal visitation, accompanied by a formal disputation lasting four days in which the doctrine of transubstantiation was refuted. At Oxford doctrinal attention then shifted to the questions of justification by faith alone and unconditional predestination, paralleling similar debates in Cambridge fuelled by Martyr's opposite number as regius professor—Martin Bucer. But despite such efforts Catholicism remained deeply entrenched among the heads of houses and fellowship generally, making the Marian *renversement* of 1553 comparatively easy. On the other hand, the decision to stage the trial and burning of Cranmer, Latimer, and Ridley in Oxford is open to

---

[10] Alan Crossley, 'City and university', pp. 105–6 and *passim* below; Porter, 'University and society', 40.

[11] J. I. Catto, 'Wyclif and Wycliffism at Oxford 1356–1430' in *Late Medieval Oxford*; C. Cross, 'Oxford and the Tudor state from the accession of Henry VIII to the death of Mary' in *The Collegiate University*.

more than one interpretation. Certainly it seems to have frightened the future
Bishop Jewel, a close associate of Martyr, into subscribing to Catholic teaching on
the eucharist. Jewel subsequently fled abroad, as did Cox, Martyr, and some fifty
other Oxonians. Between 1553 and 1558 the universities were assigned a central
role in the Catholic restoration, Oxford coming under the eye of Cardinal Pole as
chancellor from 1556. Catholics were placed in the deanery of Christ Church and
regius chair of divinity, and colleges purged.[12]

Partly as a consequence of the religious upheavals of the reformation, the university population had dropped by the time of the accession of Mary to approximately 1,000. Continuity was required if confidence in English higher education
institutions was to be restored. Yet the death of Mary in 1558 threw everything
into turmoil once more. Even here, however, we should not exaggerate the extent
of discontinuity, because the type of protestantism which came back under
Elizabeth was essentially of the previous Edwardian variety. None the less the long
reign of the new queen and the smooth religious transition to that of her successor, James I, were at last to provide the conditions for sustained recovery and further growth. In the years 1559–62 it was the turn of Catholics to be purged—a
vital task if the university was to nurture a future protestant clergy, who would in
turn help to evangelize the nation. Perhaps inevitably it proved a slow business,
Catholics being weeded out well into the 1570s and even later. Central to the task
of protestant re-education was the returned Marian exile Laurence Humfrey,
installed in 1560 as regius professor of divinity. Along with Thomas Sampson, the
new dean of Christ Church, he ran into difficulties over conformity to the
Elizabethan ceremonial requirements. But unlike Sampson, who was deprived in
1565, Humfrey managed to accommodate his puritan scruples and remained in
office for almost thirty years. The theology that now came to dominate in Oxford
was 'firmly' Reformed or 'Calvinistic'. Such, at any rate, is the conclusion of the
late Canon Greenslade's investigation of the Elizabethan faculty of theology.
Greenslade also memorably comments that 'controversy . . . had in this period an
existential quality for theologians: it went to the roots of the Christian faith, it
determined the kind of church in which they lived and worked'.[13]

Up until the 1620s successive deans of Christ Church and regius professors of
divinity were all demonstrably Calvinist, and such views similarly found favour with
chancellors Buckhurst, Bancroft, Ellesmere, and Pembroke. The Calvinist trait of
divinity theses from the late Elizabethan period through to the early years of
Charles I is likewise very marked. Oxford puritans, by contrast, although a continuing presence, remained in the minority. At the same time the anti-Calvinist leadership of the 1630s, associated with the chancellorship of Laud, had demonstrable
Jacobean antecedents. From at least the 1590s, in fact, we can distinguish three

---

[12] Cross, 'Oxford and the Tudor state'; J. Loach, 'Reformation controversies' in *The Collegiate
University*, 368–80; Martin Bucer, *Praelectiones . . . in epistolam . . . ad Ephesios* (Basle 1562).

[13] Cross, 'Oxford and the Tudor state', 140; Williams, 'Elizabethan Oxford'; S. L. Greenslade, 'The
faculty of theology' in *The Collegiate University*, 324, 330.

factional groupings among Oxford protestants: avant-garde conformists, Calvinist episcopalians, and puritans.[14] For much of the reign of James I Calvinist episcopalians were in the ascendant. Explicit doctrinal differences, however, emerged relatively late and even under Charles I some of the most characteristic religious changes concerned forms of worship, notably the altarwise repositioning of communion tables and bowing towards them. Furthermore there appear to be affinities between Laudian churchmanship and the monarchical style favoured by Charles I, with the universities seen as microcosms of the required 'order and decorum' in both church and state. In this respect the Laudian statutes are the secular counterpart of the new ecclesiology. Analogies were drawn between reverence to the altar and that to the royal chair of state, the Oxford University orator, William Strode, going so far as to describe the king in 1636 as '*homo-deus*'. Preaching before Charles in Oxford the same year, Thomas Browne, a Student of Christ Church, castigated those who would have 'no altars or images, no kings or bishops'.[15]

During the second half of the sixteenth century the university population appears roughly to have doubled. But the new-found stability of the Elizabethan period is clearly, at best, only part of the story. We need as well to give due weight to the growing attractiveness of what the English universities had to offer by way of higher education. For the ideal which had begun to bear institutional fruit as early as 1517, with the foundation of Corpus Christi College, was fast becoming that of the governing class as a whole. They increasingly sought access for their sons to the 'latinate literary culture' of humanism, which although focusing on the classics also embraced mathematics. This latter aspect can be illustrated from the statutes drawn up for Christ Church during the mid-sixteenth century and those for the university in the same period, both of which provide for mathematical teaching. More generally, 'a vast shift of emphasis' had by this time occurred, away from the medieval scholastics of whom Duns Scotus was only the most famous. This humanist 'floodtide' has been documented especially from the surviving lists of books, particularly on logic, owned by individual scholars. While the 'Aristotelian framework remained more or less intact', it was 'increasingly used to support and accommodate new currents of thought'. Indeed as early as 1570 Savile can be found lecturing in the Oxford schools on Copernicus' *De revolutionibus*, describing the author as 'chief of modern mathematicians'.[16]

[14] Nicholas Tyacke, 'Religious controversy', pp. 570–4 below. N. Tyacke, *Anti-Calvinists: the rise of English Arminianism, c.1590–1640* (Oxford 1987, 2nd edn Oxford 1990), 58–81; Fincham, 'Oxford and the early Stuart polity', 188–9; for the concept of avant-garde conformity see especially P. Lake, 'Lancelot Andrewes, John Buckeridge and *avant garde* conformity at the court of James I' in L. L. Peck (ed.), *The Mental World of the Jacobean Court* (Cambridge 1991).

[15] Tyacke, 'Religious controversy', 584–6; K. Fincham and P. Lake, 'The ecclesiastical policies of James I and Charles I' in K. Fincham (ed.), *The Early Stuart Church, 1603–1642* (Basingstoke 1993), 48; NUL MS Cl. c. 8a.

[16] Porter, 'University and society', 33; J. McConica, 'The rise of the undergraduate college' and 'Elizabethan Oxford: the collegiate society' in *The Collegiate University*, 34–42, 701–8, 730; M. Feingold, *The Mathematicians' Apprenticeship: science, universities and society in England, 1560–1640* (Cambridge 1948), 23–44, 47.

Thanks to the ground-breaking work of Mordechai Feingold, we now know a great deal about the undergraduate curriculum as it emerged during the seventeenth century. Feingold is rightly sceptical of earlier portrayals of Oxford and Cambridge as intellectual backwaters, based as such views largely were on an uncritical reading of the statutes. Like James McConica writing on the Tudor period, he emphasizes the 'quintessentially humanistic' character of the curriculum, with the languages and literature of the classics at its heart. But university teachers also aimed to provide the undergraduates with an 'encyclopedic' survey or 'panorama of all knowledge', tailored in part to the needs of the sons of the nobility and gentry. The ideal was that of the erudite 'general scholar', and one fostered by a regimen of competitive oral exercises and disputations. Much even of the undergraduate curriculum, however, involved directed private reading, rather than attendance at lectures and tutorials. Those proceeding beyond the BA were left mainly to pursue their studies independently, although aided by the earlier inculcation of discipline at college and university level. Language was deemed the 'alpha and omega of the educational process', and above all the crucial vehicle of thought. The foundations were laid in the grammar schools, the universities taking over where they left off. After grammar came rhetoric and logic, with eloquence the goal. The medium was Latin and Greek prose, as well as poetry. Although this did not produce much in the way of scholarly editions of classical texts, the years 1610 to 1613 nevertheless saw the publication of Savile's edition of Chrysostom in eight folio volumes—a work of collaborative scholarship to which Oxford made a significant contribution. Similarly, from the other end of the century, one can instance John Mill's edition of the Greek new testament, published at Oxford in 1707. Modern European languages, notably French and Italian, and, as we shall see, oriental studies, also featured in the undergraduate curriculum.[17]

Logic had undergone a transformation at the hands of humanists, which was carried further during the seventeenth century. Partly this was a matter of simplification, but also of relative decline *vis-à-vis* rhetoric. Logic was now reduced to a 'strictly functional role in regulating thought and expression'. At the same time, it was seen as a 'gateway to all learning'. Feingold makes the very important point here that the attacks on logic by seventeenth-century contemporaries were largely confined to the realm of natural philosophy. Moreover the distinguished mathematician and Savilian professor John Wallis saw nothing incongruous either in writing a textbook on logic or in presenting it to the Royal Society as late as the 1680s. Nor should the sixteenth-century critique of Aristotle by Peter Ramus be misunderstood: what was useful was 'silently adopted'. After immersion in various introductory textbooks, the student still went on to study the *Organon* of Aristotle and further honed his logical skills in disputation. Victory in such verbal contests, however, was not privileged over the 'truth' concerning what contemporaries regarded

[17] McConica, 'Elizabethan Oxford'; Mordechai Feingold, 'The humanities', pp. 213, 216, 242, and *passim* below; Greenslade, 'Faculty of theology', 321; A. Fox, *John Mill and Richard Bentley: a study of the textual criticism of the New Testament 1675–1729* (Oxford 1954), pt 2.

as important matters. In some ways the pinnacle of this educational process was represented by the disputations at the annual Oxford Act, which attracted large numbers of visitors and where the masters and doctors demonstrated their knowledge across the range of academic subject areas.[18]

Ethics too was part of the undergraduate curriculum, but tempered after the reformation by the requirements of protestant Christianity. Although a distinction continued to be made between morals and faith, save by some puritans, the two spheres nevertheless needed harmonizing—especially when pagan texts were involved. As with the teaching of logic, undergraduates were introduced to the principles of ethics via a manuscript or printed epitome; they were then directed to read a combination of ancient and modern writers, including Aristotle. While the White professorship of moral philosophy had lapsed into being a 'sinecure' by the late seventeenth century, the Camden chair of history, which was similarly founded in the 1620s, served, among other things, to complement the teaching of ethics. History was indeed generally viewed as being a 'repository for literary, moral and political lessons'. English educators agreed with Jean Bodin, in his *Methodus*, that students of history should proceed from the general to the particular, on a broad chronological front. But the moral foundations had to be laid first, and 'politic' history was not really deemed suitable for undergraduates. Ancient history remained the staple fare, with stress on the literary and moral aspects of the texts. (More recent history was to be pursued after graduation.) The first Camden professor, Degory Wheare, clearly aimed his lectures at an undergraduate audience in explicating the text of Florus, which like Bodin before him he regarded as a good elementary introduction to Roman history. It was assumed, however, that students would go on to read Livy, Tacitus, and others. Thus no ideological significance should be read into the subject-matter of Wheare's lectures. Moreover the supposedly 'republican' Tacitus, as opposed to the 'royalist' Florus, had been partly translated into English by Savile and published in 1591.[19]

Mathematics, as we have already noted, was another important element of the undergraduate curriculum. But here, especially, it is necessary to peel away the layers of myth. Thus there was no real conflict between the mathematical sciences and classical humanism, apart from the constraints of a crowded syllabus and an emphasis on utility. Certainly over-specialization was discouraged at this stage of a student's career. Along with logic, mathematics was also seen as a means of training the mind. Mathematical lectureships proliferated in the early seventeenth century, both at college and university level. New College, Merton, and St John's all acquired such posts, and the two Savilian professors of geometry and astronomy catered in part for undergraduates. This period also witnessed the rise of the professional mathematical teacher, many of whom resided in Oxford. Far from university teaching being hostile to applied mathematics, the reverse was nearer the truth. Furthermore the famous anecdote about Savile rebuking the Oxonian

---

[18] Feingold, 'The humanities', 276–306.   [19] Ibid. 306–58; Madan, *Oxford Books* i. 31.

Edmund Gunter for a 'seemingly excessive preoccupation with instruments' needs reinterpreting. Like the eminent mathematician William Oughtred, Savile was concerned lest such 'shewing of tricks' became a substitute for a sound theoretical grounding. In fact Savile required his professors of geometry to include practical applications, such as surveying, in their teachings and students were generally expected to furnish themselves with mathematical instruments.[20] College libraries also began to accumulate collections of instruments, as for example St John's from the 1630s (plate 22). Astronomy teaching at the undergraduate level was similarly utilitarian in its orientation, and a limited range of textbooks for this and mathematical instruction was used. Nevertheless the Savilian professors of astronomy sought to incorporate the most recent discoveries in their teaching, from the 1620s onwards, as did some Oxford tutors even earlier. Study in depth had to be postponed until after graduation, the Savilian professors again playing a leading role. Among the multifarious activities of the first holder of the astronomy chair, John Bainbridge (plate 10), was the organization of expeditions to Latin America and the Near East in the 1630s, with the intention, among other things, of building up a series of simultaneous eclipse observations to establish accurate longitude values.[21] (Edmond Halley's voyage to St Helena in the mid-1670s therefore had clear Oxford antecedents.[22]) Related work was carried on throughout the seventeenth century, from a succession of observatories, with increasing numbers of Oxford men coming to train their telescopes upon the heavens. Links too with Gresham College, in London, were close, especially during the 1620s and 1630s. A further indication of Oxford's international reputation as a centre of astronomy by the mid-seventeenth century are the presentation portraits to the university of Galileo (1661) and Hevelius (1679). The holders moreover of both Savilian chairs furnish a list of famous names well into the eighteenth century. Nor did the building of the magnificent Radcliffe Observatory in the 1770s come out of an intellectual void.[23]

At the same time Oxford was singularly free from philosophical strife. As a natural philosopher, Aristotle came to be regarded as a 'past master' with little direct relevance to current debates. Matters were made easier by the conscious espousal of the principle of *libertas philosophandi*. In England, unlike other parts of Europe, Copernicanism was never condemned. Likewise there was little attempt to stop the spread of Cartesianism later. Rather, students were introduced to a variety of philosophical teachings, both old and new. The latter included the work of Francis Bacon, whose *Advancement and Proficience of Learning* was published at Oxford in 1640

[20] Mordechai Feingold, 'The mathematical sciences and new philosophies', pp. 368–74 and *passim* below.

[21] N. Tyacke, 'Science and religion at Oxford before the civil war' in D. Pennington and K. Thomas (eds.), *Puritans and Revolutionaries: essays in seventeenth-century history presented to Christopher Hill* (Oxford 1978).

[22] Little is as yet known about the undergraduate years of Halley at Queen's College, but on his return from St Helena it was Provost Halton who arranged for him to be created an MA: *CSPD 1678*, 517.

[23] Feingold, 'Mathematical sciences', 382–4; Tyacke, 'Science and religion'; Mrs R. L. Poole, *Catalogue of Portraits in the Possession of the University, Colleges, City, and County of Oxford* (3 vols Oxford 1912–25) i. 41, 66; G. L'E. Turner, 'The physical sciences' in *The Eighteenth Century*.

(plate 23), with a dedication to Charles I. Descartes, in turn, was already becoming fashionable by the 1640s. His popularity, however, was closely paralleled by that of Gassendi. Thomas Hobbes and John Locke both owed a debt to the new French philosophy, albeit reluctant to acknowledge it. Moreover the deteriorating relations of Hobbes with Oxford were, at least in part, his own fault. During the 1650s Hobbes launched a series of attacks on the university and some of its senior members, which led to him losing much of the respect which he had previously enjoyed. But in the case of Locke, after some initial alarums, the teachings of his *Essay concerning Human Understanding* (1690) were largely accepted, both author and book achieving quasi-canonization with the university portrait acquired in 1733 (plate 32). As early as 1696 an epitome of Locke's *Essay* was published for student use, by an Oxford tutor, and the full-length work soon came to be routinely recommended.[24]

Meanwhile an Oxford tradition of experimental philosophy had grown up since the 1650s, itself a development of the earlier Savilian scientific initiative, and such courses were to prove popular with both undergraduates and more advanced students. The later seventeenth century also saw the setting up of numerous laboratories, with a tendency to cluster in the vicinity of the High Street. Best remembered, perhaps, is the work of Robert Boyle and his use of the 'pneumatical engine' or vacuum pump. Boyle's assistant, the chemist Peter Stahl, gave lectures at Oxford in the early 1660s, and others followed in his footsteps. By the 1690s physics had joined chemistry as an experimental subject, under the influence of David Gregory, the then Savilian professor of astronomy, and his pupil John Keill. From the 1650s, however, there was talk of the university itself becoming directly involved in these developments. After the Restoration, the ubiquitous Dean Fell took an increasing interest in the matter, and it was he, among others, who persuaded Elias Ashmole to give his collection of specimens to Oxford, on condition the university provide a building. Apparently the scheme also early on involved a chemistry laboratory, and the appointment of Robert Plot as a professor. The building and laboratory were indeed provided by the university, but no endowment by Ashmole was in the event forthcoming. Despite Plot giving an initial course of lectures in 1683, and the setting up of an Oxford Philosophical Society, lack of money blighted the overall scheme. Yet one must guard against too readily describing the subsequent period in terms of 'decline'. With some intermissions, courses continued to be given in Oxford's *officina chimica*, in the Ashmolean basement, culminating with the establishment of the Aldrichian chair of chemistry in 1803. The Savilian professors of astronomy, notably James Bradley between 1729 and 1760, also helped keep alive the practice of lecturing in experimental philosophy; it has been calculated that over a third of all Oxford students attended Bradley's lectures in the middle of the eighteenth century. Furthermore

---

[24] My thanks to Professor B. Vickers for commenting on plate 23. Feingold, 'Mathematical sciences', 393, 395–8, 405–25; Madan, *Oxford Books* i. 217; Poole, *Catalogue of Portraits* i. 74–5; J. Yolton, 'Schoolmen, logic and philosophy' in *The Eighteenth Century*.

we do well to recall the pioneering balloon ascents made by James Sadler at Oxford in 1784, while a member of the Ashmolean staff.[25]

The efflorescence of oriental studies at Oxford during the seventeenth century is also linked with science, many of the early Savilian professors having related interests in Arabic mathematics and astronomy. The main impetus, however, seems to have come from biblical scholarship in which the study of Hebrew and, to a lesser extent, Arabic were both deemed essential by contemporaries. Such was the enthusiasm for Hebrew that it even came to be taught in certain leading grammar schools, for example at Westminster and Felsted. University teaching tended to focus on the regius professorship of Hebrew, founded by Henry VIII, reinforced by a 'mushrooming' of college lectureships in the subject during the first half of the seventeenth century. College tutors, in addition, provided at least elementary instruction. This interest also resulted in some editions and translations of Hebrew texts. At the same time it is refreshing to encounter John Prideaux, regius professor of divinity at Oxford from 1615 to 1642 and more usually remembered for his staunch defence of Calvinist orthodoxy, as a supporter of the innovative Hebrew scholar and Huguenot Louis Cappel, who 'argued forcefully against the antiquity of the vowel points and accents of the Hebrew text of the Old Testament'. Hebrew studies often went hand in hand with Arabic. Ironically it was Prideaux's religious rival Laud who founded a chair of Arabic in the mid-1630s, reflecting a growing preoccupation with the subject. The first and most distinguished holder of the post, Edward Pococke (plate 11), combined it with the Hebrew professorship from 1648 until his death in 1691. Under his joint oversight, and after a civil-war trough, the two subjects initially flourished, Pococke providing both basic and more advanced teaching as well as editing manuscripts. Nevertheless by the end of the century oriental studies generally were in trouble at Oxford, and elsewhere. There seems to have been a growing sense that this particular mine was worked out, and the necessary effort not commensurate with the reward. Arguably the editors and translators had done their work too well. Some further stimulus, however, was provided in the early eighteenth century with the foundation of the lord almoner's professorship, intended by the government to foster Arabic as a language of trade and diplomacy.[26]

The origins of the mid-seventeenth-century triumphs of Oxford medicine, like the rise of science more generally, are similarly to be located in the years before the civil wars. This can be illustrated by the decadal numbers admitted to the degrees of BM and DM, which more than doubled as between the 1620s and 1630s to approximately sixty. Later decades saw considerable fluctuation, but the figure was not exceeded until the 1680s. In the light of these statistics, and other evidence, it is possible to put a significantly different gloss on the tables produced many years ago by the sociologist R. K. Merton, who sought to link increasing

[25] Feingold, 'Mathematical sciences', 426–48; R. G. Frank, *Harvey and the Oxford Physiologists: a study of scientific ideas* (Berkeley 1980), 45–89 and *passim*; R. E. W. Maddison, *The Life of the Honourable Robert Boyle* (London 1969), 89–132; Turner, 'Physical sciences'.

[26] Mordechai Feingold, 'Oriental studies', pp. 452–8 below; P. J. Marshall, 'Oriental studies' in *The Eighteenth Century*.

recruitment into science with the stimulus allegedly provided by the rise of puritanism. Merton did not indicate the educational background of his scientists, their names derived from the *Dictionary of National Biography*, but subsequent reworking of some of the same material for the late seventeenth century suggests that there was a high preponderance of university graduates among them. Furthermore Merton's data appear to correlate with growing institutional support for science at Oxford University from the 1620s, at a time when Calvinists and, even more, puritans were under increasing challenge. If we are still to talk of the 'Merton thesis', it should rather be in terms of those two famous Merton College alumni Sir Henry Savile and Sir Thomas Bodley, who helped to provide an environment conducive to the emergence of early modern science. More generally, as Feingold has written, 'Oxford and Cambridge not only trained more students who made science their vocation, but provided a considerable proportion of the educated public with at least a modicum of scientific knowledge'.[27]

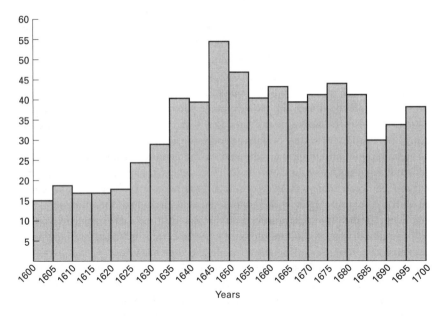

FIG. 1. The number of individuals recruited to science and medicine in each quinquennium between 1600 and 1700

Source: Data derived from Merton. C. Webster, *The Great Instauration: science, medicine and reform 1626–1660* (London 1975), 487. I am most grateful to Dr Webster for allowing me to reproduce this figure.

[27] Robert G. Frank, 'Medicine', pp. 513–14 below; R. K. Merton, *Science, Technology and Society in Seventeenth-Century England* (Bruges 1938, 2nd edn New York 1970); M. Hunter, *Science and Society in Restoration England* (Cambridge 1981), 62–3, 136–61; R. Porter, 'The scientific revolution and the universities' in H. de Ridder-Symoens (ed.), *Universities in Early Modern Europe (1500–1800)* (Cambridge forthcoming); Tyacke, 'Science and religion'; Feingold, 'Mathematical sciences', 426.

From 1612 to 1647 the regius professor of medicine at Oxford was Thomas Clayton senior, the 'most energetic and active' holder of the chair in the seventeenth century. It was Clayton who in 1623 secured the endowment of the Tomlins anatomy lectureship, which he exercised in person, using as a textbook Caspar Bartholin's *Anatomicae institutiones*. The new Savilian and Sedleian professorships, founded in the same decade, were in addition often held by medical men, as were an increasing number of college and hall headships; 'in the century after about 1620 fourteen physicians occupied university professorships other than that of medicine'. The most renowned seventeenth-century holder of the Sedleian chair of natural philosophy, Thomas Willis (1660–75), in fact devoted his lectures to medical topics. Willis combined these lectures with anatomical investigations of the brain during the early 1660s (plate 26). The Harveian theory of the circulation of the blood, from which flowed so much outstanding Oxford work in physiology, was maintained as an Oxford Act thesis as early as 1633. During the subsequent decade when Oxford was a royalist garrison, William Harvey himself can be found researching there on embryology; the results were included in his *De generatione animalium* of 1651.[28] It was during the 1650s, however, that Oxford science became more organized, on the basis of a 'club' with a set of rules, which in turn contributed to the founding of the Royal Society. Physicians 'composed the most important single segment' of this club and its Oxford successor of the 1680s. Some of the most remarkable experimental work carried out at Oxford, in the 1650s and later, involved injections and transfusions. The philosophical basis of medical understanding was moreover transformed at this time, by the new 'chemical–corpuscular approach'. Thus in 1654 Ralph Bathurst of Trinity College argued, in his *praelectiones* for the DM, that the purpose of respiration was 'to bring a nitrous particle-like vapour from the air into the blood'. This led on during the 1660s to the related experiments with a vacuum pump by Boyle, and an integrated theory linking air, lungs, and blood, culminating with the work of John Mayow published in the early 1670s. There was too, in these decades, a spate of publications by Oxford-trained physicians. But this dramatic upsurge of Oxford medicine was partly dependent on certain fortuitous circumstances which did not endure. The very upheavals consequent upon the civil wars had helped create an enlarged scientific community in the university, but one insufficiently 'anchored in institutional forms'. Hence a 'relative' decline in Oxford medicine has been noted from the 1690s, with a numerical falling away in the mid-eighteenth century. On the other hand the 1760s were to witness the foundation of a new anatomy school and lectureship in the subject at Christ Church.[29]

The one great exception to the signs of long-term expansion evident almost everywhere in seventeenth-century Oxford seems to be the faculty of civil law. Already weakened by the demise of canon law in the previous century, the civil law

---

[28] Frank, 'Medicine', 517, 524–5, 541–2; Tyacke, 'Science and religion', 84–5.

[29] Frank, 'Medicine', 548–58; C. Webster, 'The medical faculty and the physic garden' in *The Eighteenth Century*.

now offered only limited professional openings. The temporary abolition of the ecclesiastical courts during the civil wars and their aftermath made the situation much worse. Numerically speaking, however, the picture is less clear. Between the 1580s and the 1630s the combined total of BCL and DCL degrees per decade doubled, to 147. They then shrank back, totalling a mere forty-five in the 1650s, but in the 1670s rose to ninety-seven. Over time, such degrees came to be seen less and less as a vocational qualification. There is some suggestion as well that a BCL was academically undemanding compared to a BA, the same applying to a doctorate in the subject. But too little is still known about this to pronounce with confidence.[30]

We have already remarked on the dominance of Calvinism at Oxford until the 1620s. Although increasingly challenged thereafter, a strong Calvinist presence survived to the end of the century. The first unequivocally Arminian holder of the regius chair of divinity was probably Richard Allestree from 1663 to 1680. On the other hand, it is possible to trace a variety of anti-Calvinist influences dating back much earlier. Of published Calvinist theologians, Robert Abbot and John Prideaux are the most distinguished before the civil wars—between them spanning the years 1612 to 1642 as regius professors. In the opposite camp pride of place must go to Thomas Jackson, latterly president of Corpus, who died in 1640. Again judged by the criterion of publication, the Calvinist John Owen, dean of Christ Church, stands out in the 1650s. Paradoxically, however, the enduring strength of Oxford Calvinism meant that the vicissitudes of the Interregnum were the more easily survived, with the likes of Thomas Barlow of Queen's playing a not dishonourable role. Among pastoral theologians, two Oxford Arminians are especially notable: Henry Hammond, formerly of Magdalen College, in the 1640s, and Allestree after the Restoration. While, for those of a more 'rational' cast of mind, William Chillingworth's *Religion of Protestants* (Oxford 1638) remained a point of departure well into the eighteenth century.[31] A major battleground under Charles I was the doctrine of unconditional predestination, but in the reign of Charles II this switched to justification by faith alone. Moreover, despite a 'certain disengagement' thereafter on the part of the university, Bishop John Potter of Oxford, who was also the regius professor of divinity, can be found delivering a robust episcopal charge in July 1719 from the St Mary's pulpit, against an attempt to modify the terms of clerical subscription in favour of antitrinitarians.[32] Apropos the products of the divinity faculty, attention has been drawn to the very high numbers of BD degrees awarded during the early seventeenth century. Decadal numbers peaked at

---

[30] Brian P. Levack, 'Law', pp. 559–60 below; Brian Levack, *The Civil Lawyers in England 1603–1641* (Oxford 1973).

[31] Tyacke, 'Religious controversy'; for an example of the continuing influence of Chillingworth, see Arthur Ashley Sykes, *The External Peace of the Church* (London 1716), 11–13, 22–3.

[32] Tyacke, 'Religious controversy'; John Potter, *The Bishop of Oxford's Charge to the Clergy of his Diocese . . . July 1719* (London 1720); L. W. Barnard, *John Potter: an eighteenth century archbishop* (Ilfracombe 1989), 78–9.

217, between 1610 and 1619, but remained near to this mark in the 1620s and 1630s. The 1650s, however, saw an almost total collapse, with only ten BDs recorded. After the Restoration, numbers climbed back to about 100 per decade for the rest of the century. Such men comprised the élite of their profession, although a number of those taking the degree were already established parish clergy. (Many BDs, of course, went on to take a DD as well.) As well as compulsory chapel attendance, all students seem to have received regular religious instruction and approximately half of those who matriculated in the 'plebeian and pauper categories' during this period went on to be ordained.[33]

Integral to the successful functioning of Oxford's wide-ranging academic enterprise was the provision of libraries—above all the Bodleian, opened in 1602 and conceived by its founder on a heroic scale. Manuscripts as well as printed books came within the purview of the new university library from the outset, together already numbering some 16,000 items by 1620. During the next fifty years this figure more than doubled and the intellectual scope remained impressively broad. The library stock derived from a variety of sources: donations of books and manuscripts or money to buy them, copies of books printed by the London Stationers' Company, and an endowment provided by Bodley himself. This last, however, like university and college finances generally, was affected disastrously by the civil wars. Although some subventions were forthcoming from the university after the Restoration, the general financial position of the Bodleian remained very unhealthy and donations became the effective lifeline. Access was largely restricted to postgraduates, but users included 'a regular flow of students' from the continent. College and hall libraries complemented that of the university; dependent initially on regular donations by alumni, these were supplemented in the later seventeenth century by a share of admission fees. Most seem to have increased their holdings over the period. In the case of Queen's College this led to the building of a fine new library during the 1690s, its iconography illustrating the two complementary routes to knowledge through the reading of books on the one hand and the investigation of natural phenomena on the other (plate 29). Queen's in addition had a special library for the taberdars or senior scholars, the surviving catalogue of which includes works by Boyle, Descartes, Galileo, Gassendi, Gregory, Keill, Locke, Newton, Wallis, and Willis, as well as volumes of the *Philosophical Transactions* of the Royal Society. The copy of Newton's *Principia Mathematica* (1687) was donated by Provost Timothy Halton (d. 1704), who also contributed over a third of the building costs of the main library. While college libraries were sometimes open to undergraduates, from the end of the century their specific reading needs began to be

---

[33] L. Stone, 'The size and composition of the Oxford student body 1580–1910' in L. Stone (ed.), *The University in Society* (2 vols Princeton 1974) i. 21–2, and unpublished data kindly supplied by Dr J. Hill; Porter, 'University and society', 96. The question of how ordinands were trained at this time remains a historiographical 'black hole', but for some suggestive remarks see P. Collinson, *The Religion of Protestants: the church in English society 1559–1662* (Oxford 1982), 118–19.

catered for in separate rooms; evidence concerning Trinity College undergraduate library indicates a mix of books covering both classics and science.[34]

Oxford printing and publishing too played an increasingly important part in the intellectual life of the university. Between 1600 and 1630 an average of thirteen titles were printed each year. The average more than doubled during the 1630s, rising to twenty-eight. Crude as this measure is, the figure rose again in the 1670s to thirty-eight titles per year. The initial increase is clearly related to the letters patent secured by Laud in 1632, which allowed for three Oxford printers instead of the previous one. Although much of the output was religious, there was a leavening of other material. Nor, in fact, can the two categories always be simply distinguished. Thus George Hakewill's *Apologie of the Power and Providence of God in the Government of the World* the first edition of which was published at Oxford in 1627, argued, among other things, for supremacy of the moderns over the ancients. But the 1620s also saw the publication of a distinguished work on geography by Nathaniel Carpenter, a fellow of Exeter College, and we have already remarked on the Oxford reprint of Caspar Bartholin's anatomical treatise in 1633. Two years later, in 1635, the university syllabus itself was printed at Oxford in diagrammatic form. 'The resulting sheet, dedicated to Laud, shows the day and hour of each lecture, by means of a series of concentric circles with a sun in the middle; the moon, representing Monday, and a clock are so placed in relation to the sun as to indicate that the motif is Copernican' (plate 12). Leaving aside the untypical period of the civil wars, the 1650s registered a quickening of interest in mathematical publishing, with the Oxford production of various works by John Wallis. This interest continued after the Restoration, when Oxford established a near monopoly in the publications of William Oughtred. These decades also saw the Oxford printing of experimental results by Boyle and of anatomical investigations by Willis. Attempts to establish a 'learned press' in Oxford date back at least to the donation of Greek type by Savile, in 1619. With the encouragement of Laud, this began to bear fruit during the 1630s. Succeeding decades saw the publication of works involving extensive use of Hebrew and Arabic type, as well as Anglo-Saxon. Not until the 1670s, however, did the university come to play a more direct role, under the guidance of Dean Fell and with the support of Archbishop Sheldon. There resulted a remarkable series of works from the Sheldonian press, including items as diverse as William Beveridge's *Synodicon* (1672), an edition of the canons of the Greek Church, and John Mayow's *Tractatus quinque medico-physici* (1674), which contained a lengthy discussion of the chemistry of nitro-aerial particles.[35]

---

[34] I. G. Philip and Paul Morgan, 'Libraries, books and printing', pp. 659–78 below; J. R. Magrath, *The Queen's College* (2 vols. Oxford 1921) ii. 70–1; for iconographical advice, I thank Dr E. McGrath of the Warburg Institute; QCL Taberdars' Library Catalogue; QCL Sel. f. 41. I owe my knowledge of this Queen's College material to the kindness of Miss H. Powell; I. G. Philip, 'Libraries and the university press' in *The Eighteenth Century*, 751.

[35] Philip and Morgan, 'Libraries, books and printing', 678–85; Tyacke, 'Science and religion'; Madan, *Oxford Books* iii. 58, 71–2, 132–3, 216, 349, 123, 233, 265–6, 312, 221, 273–4, 262–3, 298–9; H. Carter, *A History of the Oxford University Press* (Oxford 1975), 25; Frank, *Harvey and the Oxford Physiologists*, 258–74.

There were, of course, other and less bookish sides to university life, which involved the making of music and staging of plays, as well as a range of sporting activities. Nor should we forget the recurring worries on the part of the authorities concerning the perils of drink, gambling, and sex. Music itself had both recreational and academic aspects. Comparatively few music degrees were awarded and of these virtually all were by creation, most recipients being 'practising organist-composers'. Nevertheless a new seriousness of purpose was injected by the foundation of the Heather professorship of music in 1627, which made provision for regular weekly instruction. The Oxford music school became a 'focus' for more 'informal groups' meeting elsewhere, with a penumbra of music teachers and dancing-schools. Among instruments played, from the mid-seventeenth century the violin came to compete with the viol. While secular music flourished throughout the period, the fortunes of sacred music were more varied; organists and choristers prospered in early Stuart Oxford but were suppressed during the 1650s, only coming into their own again after the Restoration. Links also existed between music and science, particularly as regards the theory of sound. More familiar, however, is the connection with drama, Oxford musicians performing for example at the plays staged for Charles I in 1636. A rich and diverse Oxford dramatic tradition dated from Tudor times, and one quite distinct from the professional theatre. Works in either Latin or English were regularly written and performed by members of the university but here, for reasons which remain obscure, the civil wars put an end to such activities both in the short and longer terms.[36]

For wealthy students there existed opportunities to ride and hunt in the Oxford neighbourhood. But 'tennis', whether played with hand or racket, appears to have been the popular sport *par excellence* in seventeenth-century Oxford, to the extent that Brasenose even went so far as to seek a reinterpretation, by the visitor, of the college statutes which ostensibly forbade all ball games. Many Oxford colleges now built ball courts although, unlike Cambridge, these do not normally seem to have involved the use of rackets and are perhaps more properly described as 'fives' courts. College provision was also increasingly made for various versions of the game of bowls. Tennis played with a racket was catered for by a number of specially built public courts, an indirect index of their vogue being the surviving tokens issued by the keepers and which feature a racket (plate 30). Dancing-schools too often doubled as gymnasia, teaching both the 'art of vaulting' and fencing. Proprietors of tennis courts were in addition sometimes licensed to sell ale, an occupation regarded rather less benignly by the university; in 1639 Vice-Chancellor Frewen, for example, suppressed 200 alehouses. Wasting of time and money featured high on the list of objections to alehouses, which were also feared as venues for gambling and possible sexual liaisons. Certainly a bewildering diversity of card and other games were played, often for money.[37] While much of the information

[36] P. M. Gouk, 'Music', pp. 621–40 below; John R. Elliott, 'Drama', pp. 641–58 below.

[37] Porter, 'University and society', 70–1; J. Potter, *Tennis and Oxford* (Oxford 1994), 28–81; P. Manning, 'Sport and pastime in Stuart Oxford' in *Surveys and Tokens*, ed. H. E. Salter (OHS lxxv 1920); Laud, *Works* v. 247.

about prostitution is anecdotal, a surviving diary kept by one of the proctors at the beginning of the eighteenth century records his regular efforts to get 'whores' expelled from the city. On the subject of pornography, Humphrey Prideaux, then a Student of Christ Church, reports a remarkable episode in 1675 when certain 'gentlemen' of All Souls were caught by Dean Fell, *in flagrante delicto*, attempting to print an edition of Giulio Romano's illustrations to the sonnets of Pietro Aretino.[38]

It might be assumed that such bastions of maleness as the early modern universities would have generated a set of fairly stereotypical gender attitudes. In reality, however, matters were more complex—at least as regards Oxford. Thus when, in 1608, the civil lawyer Thomas Gwynn, a fellow of All Souls, defended as an Act thesis the proposition that it was lawful for husbands to beat their wives, a rebuttal, by William Heale, a fellow of Exeter College, was published at Oxford the following year.[39] Later in the century Richard Allestree, in the preface to his book *The Ladies Calling*, which was printed at the Sheldonian press in 1673, questioned the 'received opinion' that women were 'naturally inferior to men; when tis considered how much of extrinsic weight is put in the ballance to turn it on the men's side'. He suggested instead that it might come down to a matter of educational opportunity. 'And truly had women the same advantage, I dare not say but they would make as good returns of it.' Although Allestree still taught that 'the mulct that was laid upon the first woman's disobedience to God' is 'that she (and all derived from her) should be subject to the husband', his was a patriarchalism with a difference.[40] But in the case of Charles Butler's *Feminine Monarchie*, published at Oxford in 1609, readers were presented with a radical inversion of gender roles based on the scientific observation of bees and their correct sexual identification. Contrary to general belief, 'the males heere beare no sway at al, this being an Amazonian or feminine kingdome'. A queen bee, not a king, rules over female workers and the only real function of the males or drones lies in 'breeding', after which 'they are all killed'. Yet, warns Butler, who had left Oxford for a Hampshire benefice in 1593, 'let no nimble tonged [female] sophisters gather a false conclusion from these true premisses, that they by the example of these may arrogate to themselves the like superioritie'. Or 'if they would so fain have it so, let them first imitate their singular virtues, their continuall industry in gathering, their diligent watchfulnes in keeping, their chastitie, cleanlinesse and discreete oeconomie etc'. Butler was also an investigator of bee 'musicke' (the sounds made by young queens at swarming time), composing a 'bees' madrigall' for the second edition of his book—published at London in 1623. The opening lines of the chorus of this madrigal run:

[38] Porter, 'University and society', 73; Crossley, 'City and university', 125; V. H. H. Green, 'The university and social life' in *The Eighteenth Century*, 339; *Letters of Humphrey Prideaux . . . 1674–1722*, ed. E. M. Thompson (Camden Soc. new ser. xv 1875), 30–2.

[39] *Reg. Univ.* ed. Clark, pt 1, 186; William Heale, *An Apologie for Women* (Oxford 1609).

[40] Richard Allestree, *The Ladies Calling* (Oxford 1673), sigs. b1ᵛ–b2, pt 2, 33. On the other hand Heale had earlier argued that the guilt of Adam was much greater than that of Eve, since he was the 'sole cause' of 'our first fall' and she merely the 'occasion': *An Apologie*, 62–3.

> As of all states the monarchie is best,
> So of all monarchies that feminine, of famous Amazons excels the rest.[41]

Clearly there was a considerable range of opinion on this whole subject, befitting an academic community.

It is a matter of historiographical dispute how far the religious policies pursued by Charles I, when 'Calvinist opponents were muzzled and marginalized', contributed to the crisis of the early 1640s. What we can say, however, is that, as with the upheavals of the previous century, Oxford was dragged in willy-nilly. Indeed both universities came under criticism almost immediately from members of the Long Parliament, partly because of their close ties with the Caroline regime. In June 1641 Laud resigned as Oxford's chancellor, to be replaced by Philip Herbert, fourth earl of Pembroke—a fairly obvious piece of political trimming on the part of the university. But as the prospect of fighting materialized during 1642, so Oxford provided generous financial aid to Charles I and subsequently became the royalist headquarters (plate 24). One consequence was that not until 1647 did the university experience a visitation by the representatives of the now victorious parliamentarians. This resulted the following year in the expulsion of nearly half the college fellows, mainly for refusing to acknowledge the authority of the visitors; nevertheless, the religious agenda of the latter involved the abolition of episcopacy and prayer book.[42] 'By 1652, when the five years of the parliamentary visitation ended, the resourceful and bitter resistance of Oxford's royalism had been worn down.' Oliver Cromwell was already chancellor, having been elected the previous year. The Independent John Owen served as vice-chancellor from 1652 to 1657, while another powerful figure in the university was the Presbyterian John Conant, appointed regius professor of divinity in 1654 and the successor to Owen as vice-chancellor in 1657. During the 1650s Calvinist theology, which had been in eclipse since the 1630s, came back. There was also a regular diet of 'godly' sermons, accompanied by an attempt at 'moral reformation'. Almost by definition 'the puritans were a community within a community, their friendships extending across the university and stretching too into the town, where the godly party among the citizens submerged their jurisdictional resentment against the university in the cause of common worship'. Similarly the sense of a 'common puritan cause' led to a 'truce' between Presbyterians and Independents. Among the colleges, Magdalen, Exeter, and Christ Church produced the highest numbers of dissenter clergy to be ejected in the 1660s. On the other hand, much of Oxford's puritanism seems to have been only skin deep. 'When puritan rule collapsed in 1659–60, it was among

---

[41] Charles Butler, *The Feminine Monarchie. Or a treatise concerning bees and the due ordering of them* (Oxford 1609), sigs. a3ᵛ, D5ᵛ, E2ᵛ (2nd edn London 1623), sig. L. Butler's book has been described by the leading entomologist E. O. Wilson as inaugurating the 'modern study of the honey-bee'. *Biophilia* (Cambridge Mass. 1984), 19.

[42] Fincham, 'Oxford and the early Stuart polity', 210; Roy and Reinhart, 'Oxford and the civil wars'.

young men that royalist enthusiasm was most widely noticed.' Likewise, they flocked in 1660 to the restored Anglican church services.[43]

The Restoration rout of Oxford puritans benefited, among others, those who followed in the religious footsteps of Archbishop Laud. (Here it is significant that Laud's collection of private prayers was published at Oxford in 1667, with imprimaturs by Archbishop Sheldon and Dean Fell.) Nevertheless, and unlike Cambridge, an important Calvinist presence also survived and even prospered in the university. Between them these groupings represented the two religious wings of the 'Cavalier Anglican' party. During the 1650s the Cavalier Anglicans had maintained a clandestine existence in Oxford, centred on the lodgings of the distinguished anatomist Thomas Willis—a further reminder of the lack of correlation between puritanism and science. After 1660 they defined themselves especially in opposition to the dissenters or 'fanatics', as they liked to call them. But the number of those who lost their fellowships between 1660 and 1662 was much smaller than in the late 1640s; the total comes to fifty-seven compared with 190 on the previous occasion.[44] Politically speaking, most of Oxford's Cavalier Anglicans were tories *avant la lettre* and in consequence closely identified with the regime. This alliance held despite attempts by Charles II to ease the lot of dissenters and Roman Catholics, and was subsequently reinforced by the Popish Plot and the emergence of whiggery. John Fell, successively dean and bishop of Oxford, epitomized Cavalier Anglicanism in both its religious and political aspects, whether writing in defence of diocesan episcopacy or helping in the House of Lords to vote down the attempt to exclude the Catholic James duke of York from the succession. Oxford played host to the third and final exclusion parliament, in 1681, and the university took a leading part in the subsequent tory reaction which culminated in the widely welcomed accession of James in 1685.[45]

Historians disagree about the political aims of James II, but there is no denying the alarm generated by his religious policies. Within less than a year the honeymoon period was over, and the monopoly position of the English Church threatened by the plans of the king to emancipate his co-religionists. The Catholic challenge in Oxford was mounted initially via a small group of converts, led by the master of University College—Obadiah Walker. Paucity of numbers was compensated for by royal support and an effective 'propaganda machine'. As well as opening a Catholic chapel at University College, served by Jesuits, Walker was authorized to publish the anti-protestant writings of his teacher the late Abraham Woodhead (plate 28). University vacancies were also filled by Catholics or fellow-travellers, including the deanery of Christ Church, by John Massey, where another new Jesuit chapel was created. Members of Christ Church made their opposition

[43] Worden, 'Cromwellian Oxford', 733, 758, 762, and *passim*.

[44] Madan, *Oxford Books* iii. 216; N. Tyacke, 'Arminianism and the theology of the Restoration church' in S. Groenveld and M. Wintle (eds.), *Britain and the Netherlands* xi (Zutphen 1994); R. A. Beddard, 'Restoration Oxford and the remaking of the protestant establishment', pp. 849–50 and *passim* below; Roy and Reinhart, 'Oxford and the civil wars', 729–30.

[45] R. A. Beddard, 'Tory Oxford', below.

most obviously felt in a series of published replies to Woodhead's tracts. The best-known incident, however, involved the Magdalen College fellows, who actively resisted royal wishes by electing a president of their own choice. They were in consequence expelled and replaced by Catholics, the college chapel being taken over for the celebration of mass. As previously the universities, and Oxford in particular, were seen by the crown as crucial for its religious purposes. Conversely the case of Magdalen College featured in the declaration issued by William of Orange, in October 1688, justifying his decision to invade England. The Williamite dénouement is not the province of the present volume, but there was to be no simple return to the Cavalier Anglican *status quo*. On the contrary, a gap thenceforward opened up between the pluralistic protestantism favoured by the regime and the more exclusive variety on offer in the universities. Moreover, under the early Hanoverians tory Oxford was to find itself seriously out of step with successive whig ministries.[46]

The incomparable chronicler of seventeenth-century Oxford, and half witness to it, was of course Anthony Wood. Often styled an antiquarian, he can also be seen as reflecting in part the Oxford ideal of a general scholar. For as well as his great interest in books and manuscripts, Wood was also an accomplished musician, a student of chemistry, and boon companion of the gifted medical man Richard Lower.[47] This very eclecticism helps to explain why the biographies contained in Wood's *Athenae Oxonienses* have proved so valuable to later historians of varying specialisms. Not a statistician in the modern sense, Wood none the less counted; thus the annual summations contained in his *Fasti*, of degrees granted, give some idea of change over time. Related institutional developments, at both university and college level, can similarly be deduced from his histories. Finally there is the wealth of more intimate detail recorded in Wood's autobiography or *Life and Times*, so meticulously edited by Andrew Clark. Introducing the second volume of the *Athenae*, published in 1692, the lawyer James Harrington (BA 1687) characterized the work as a collective memorial to the fourth 'Alfonsine or Medicean' age of learning, which 'first began in Italy' and thereafter 'diffus'd its influence into Britain'.[48] But it was Wood himself who sensed some of the forces which in his own lifetime were beginning to undermine the remarkable neo-humanist achievement of seventeenth-century Oxford, as the ideal of the general scholar degenerated into that of the gentleman scholar and erudition came to be regarded as pedantry or worse.[49] Such tensions had been present from the start, but the vast

[46] R. A. Beddard, 'James II and the Catholic challenge', pp. 917–47 below; Tyacke, 'Religious controversy', 609–15; G. V. Bennett, 'Against the tide: Oxford under William III' and P. Langford, 'Tories and Jacobites 1714–1751' in *The Eighteenth Century*.

[47] I am most grateful to Sir Keith Thomas for allowing me to read his unpublished Oxford Stanhope Prize essay on Anthony Wood. Related material is also to be found in M. Hunter, *John Aubrey and the Realm of Learning* (London 1975).

[48] Wood, *Athenae* i, pp. clxxii, clxxvi.

[49] Feingold, 'Humanities', 240.

increments of knowledge now made increasingly urgent a rethinking of educational goals and the means of achieving them. The problem, however, was Europe-wide, and if Oxford University appeared to flounder for much of the eighteenth century so did many other institutions of higher education.[50]

[50] For a comparative overview, see H. de Ridder-Symoens (ed.), *Universities in Early Modern Europe (1500–1800)* (Cambridge forthcoming).

I

University and Society

STEPHEN PORTER

AFTER a period of change and adaptation Oxford's role in the post-reformation order had been established before the beginning of the seventeenth century. The nature of its responsibilities was recognized in both government and ecclesiastical circles and in a much wider cross-section of society. Although there were those whose dealings with the university were primarily because its constituent colleges acted as landlords and impropriators, its greatest point of contact was, of course, through those who studied there. As one of the two universities in early modern England and Wales Oxford had an important function in providing an education for many members of the social élite, the future administrators of church and state, the clergy, the bureaucracy, and the burgeoning professions. The numbers who gained this experience were not especially large—a little over 1 per cent of the male population of England and Wales at the peak—but nor were they restricted to one social group, for throughout the century Oxford drew its recruits from a broad spectrum of the community.[1] Moreover, they came with varying intentions and prospects and this too considerably affected the character of the university.

Those who were well born were sent to the university with the intention that they should acquire sufficient knowledge to allow them to play their expected roles in national and local affairs and be able to converse in a learned and informed manner. By the seventeenth century it had become widely accepted that learning was 'an essential part of nobility' and one which conferred respect and status.[2] Thomas Isham thought that it was desirable even in a country gentleman, because it brought him 'a great reputation in the country'—all men having 'a great honour and respect for such a one'.[3] A grounding in social humanism meant paying

Professor Lawrence Stone generously allowed me to use the matriculation and degree statistics which were prepared for his study of the university; I am very grateful to him and to his research assistant Julian Hill. Dr Vivienne Larminie kindly supplied me with proofs of her edition of the Newdigate account book in advance of publication. I am also grateful to Mark Byford for allowing me to consult his thesis and notes on the university in the 1660s. See nn. 1 and 117 and appendix below.

[1] J. McConica, 'Elizabethan Oxford: the collegiate society' in *The Collegiate University*, 730–2; L. Stone, 'The size and composition of the Oxford student body 1580–1910' in L. Stone (ed.), *The University in Society* (2 vols Princeton 1974) i. 103. For revised population figures for England which slightly alter Stone's percentages see E. A. Wrigley and R. S. Schofield, *The Population History of England 1541–1871* (London 1981), 208–9, 576.

[2] Henry Peacham, *The Complete Gentleman*, ed. V. B. Heltzel (Ithaca NY 1962), 28.

[3] Northants. RO IC 928.

particular attention to the classical languages, rhetoric, logic, and mathematics. William Trumbull instructed his son to concentrate on Greek, Latin, and the 'liberal arts' and to 'learn to make a verse, a theme and an oration'.[4] A further requirement for younger sons was an education which would give them a suitable foundation for a career of an appropriate kind.[5] Noble and gentry families could employ a tutor to educate their sons to the required level at home, but the universities offered much more, for they introduced the young to a wider world than that of the household and their parents' immediate circle and one in which they could learn to conduct themselves in a manner befitting their status. They served as 'the first entrance into a publick, and more inlarged condition' for youths whose characters would, it was hoped, mature during their stay. In this respect they were regarded as providing a suitable preparation for those who were to go on the Grand Tour, but were as yet too young to embark upon it.[6] Furthermore, a youth was introduced to others of his generation during his time at university, enabling him to make contacts which would be useful, if not invaluable, in later life. John and Richard Newdigate became acquainted with Gilbert Sheldon, future archbishop of Canterbury, while they were at Trinity together between 1618 and 1620 and this was a connection which they maintained thereafter.[7] Some parents also hoped that life in a university environment would provide a stimulus that could not be given at home, to stir an interest in learning and counteract intellectual lethargy. Katherine Percival expressed the wish that the scholars which her son met in Oxford would make him 'bound in honoure to imittate som of them ... [and] make him ashamed of his slooth and ignorance'.[8]

Many of these requirements could also be satisfied by service in a great household or at the royal court, or some time spent on a continental tour.[9] The Inns of Court too provided a gentlemanly education where those who wished to spend some time in London, close to the centre of affairs, could acquire at least a rudimentary knowledge of the law which would be useful to them in the future.[10] They were regarded both as an alternative to the universities and as a supplement to them, for many youths of gentle or higher status attended one of the universities as well as one of the Inns. The relative merits of these courses of action and the virtues and shortcomings of a spell at university were debated by contempo-

---

[4] Berks. RO Trumbull Add. MS 46, letter 24 August 1622.

[5] As the proportion of heirs going to university was much greater than that of younger sons, among the landed élite at least, it may be that parents gave such a need a low priority: L. Stone and J. C. F. Stone, *An Open Elite? England 1540–1880* (Oxford 1984), 231–2, 264, 492–3.

[6] Christopher Wandesforde, *A Book of Instructions . . . to his son and heir*, ed. T. Comber (Cambridge 1777), 15; Stephen Penton, *The Guardian's Instruction or The Gentleman's Romance*, ed. H. H. Sturmer (London 1897), 58. For Sir Robert Southwell's views on the university's role, 1677, see BL Add. MS 46,954B, fo 217[r-v].

[7] V. M. Larminie, 'The lifestyle and attitudes of the seventeenth century gentleman, with special reference to the Newdigates of Arbury Hall, Warwickshire' (Birmingham Ph. D. thesis 1980), 321–7, 333.

[8] BL Add. MS 46,950, fo 227[r].

[9] R. A. Houlbrooke, *The English Family 1450–1700* (London 1984), 176–7.

[10] W. R. Prest, *The Inns of Court under Elizabeth I and the Early Stuarts 1590–1640* (London 1972), 21–4.

rary writers, although with uncertain influence upon the parents of prospective students.

Such considerations did not apply for those few youths whose education was of concern to the state. The university was employed as part of the policy through which the children of recusant parents of political significance were brought up within the established church.[11] In 1628 James Dillon, a member of a prominent Catholic Irish family, was sent to Oxford by the archbishop of Armagh and entered at Exeter College 'to reclaim him from the superstitions of the Romish Church'.[12] Almost fifty years later Lord Kingsale was sent to Christ Church by the privy council. He was then 10 and he remained there for six years under the watchful eye of the dean. His difficult, not to say obstreperous, personality and lack of intellectual accomplishments were the despair of his tutor, but he was instructed in the tenets of the Church of England and kept away from the influences of his Catholic Irish relatives during his formative years, which were the privy council's objectives.[13] The numbers who attended the university for this reason were small, but this was one of the functions which it served in this period.

Youths of lower social status went to the universities to obtain the training and qualifications required for them to develop a career, especially in the church. A university education provided them with opportunities which they could not otherwise have had. It also offered the widening of social horizons and increased geographical mobility. Although the levels of remuneration for teachers and the clergy in particular varied enormously the rewards to which a university entrant from a plebeian background aspired were partly economic. They were also social, for entry into the clergy endowed an individual with a status and respect in society which could only have been achieved with difficulty in another sphere. It was accepted that a graduate clergyman was entitled to gentle status and a Leicestershire rector's claim that his MA made him 'a gentleman and that a worshipfull one' was justified.[14] Few of the parochial clergy in the mid-sixteenth century were graduates, but the proportion steadily increased thereafter and by the early seventeenth century recruitment into the church was almost entirely from the universities.[15] There was a general complaint in the seventeenth century that private tutors and schoolmasters were neither highly regarded nor well paid, but many of them went on to obtain a benefice. For those whose fathers were farmers or artisans this represented

[11] J. Bossy, *The English Catholic Community 1570–1850* (London 1975), 162; L. Stone, 'Social control and intellectual excellence: Oxbridge and Edinburgh 1560–1983' in N. Phillipson (ed.), *Universities, Society, and the Future* (Edinburgh 1983), 9–10.

[12] *Reg. Exeter*, p. cii.

[13] G. E. Cokayne, *The Complete Peerage* (rev. edn 13 vols in 12 London 1910–59) vii. 287; HMC *Ormonde MSS* ii. 299–300, new ser. iv. 583–4, 586–8, v. 337–8, 522, 548, 554, vi. 76, 97; CA MS 426; BL Add. MSS 46, 953, fos 120ʳ, 160ʳ, 46, 956A, fo 7ʳ, 46, 956C, fo 153ʳ, 46, 957, fo 4ʳ.

[14] P. Styles, *Studies in Seventeenth Century West Midlands History* (Kineton 1978), 145; William Harrison, *The Description of England*, ed. G. Edelen (Ithaca NY 1968), 113–14; M. H. Curtis, *Oxford and Cambridge in Transition 1558–1642* (Oxford 1959), 270–1.

[15] R. O'Day, *The English Clergy: the emergence and consolidation of a profession 1558–1642* (Leicester 1979), 2–6; I. Green, 'Career prospects and clerical conformity in the early Stuart church', *Past & Present* no. 90 (Feb. 1981), 71–8; P. Collinson, *The Religion of Protestants: the church in English society* (Oxford 1982), 94.

a major social progression. Even for the sons of those who were successful in the professions or business a university education endowed further prestige.

Yet, despite these advantages, because of the difficulties involved in financing a further education only a small proportion of the plebeian population attended university. Many were unable to receive the degree of preparatory education required, either through lack of provision or parental unwillingness. The levels of basic literacy alone indicate the size of that part of the male population which did not receive even a minimal amount of schooling.[16] Those boys who had acquired the rudiments of an education at an elementary school faced the further problem of obtaining the necessary grounding in the classics. Some may have been able to receive the required tuition from a clergyman, but the majority had to get a place in one of the grammar schools, where such teaching was largely concentrated. Because most of the grammar schools were in towns children from rural families were at a disadvantage and such schools seem, moreover, to have come to provide largely, although not exclusively, for children from the upper and middling sections of society and from clerical backgrounds.[17] A great deal rested on the quality of the schoolmaster and his ability and willingness to prepare youths for university entrance. Not all masters were equally well equipped in this respect, or had the necessary enthusiasm. The schooling process, therefore, thinned out the number of recruits to the universities. On the other hand some boys whose parents were unaware of the opportunities may have been encouraged by a clergyman or schoolmaster to continue their studies to the standards needed for admission to university and perhaps have been introduced by him to members of his former college or hall.

Parental attitudes were indeed of great importance. We may assume that many parents of professional or clerical status were aware of the potential advantages of a university education for their sons and were willing, indeed solicitous, to support their attempts to obtain a place. This was presumably true of fathers from all backgrounds who had themselves studied at Oxford. Some were disappointed in their ambitions because of their sons' unsuitability or failure to obtain the necessary standards. William Woodhall had planned to send his son to Oxford, or an Inn of Court, but 'perceiving his tabackicall humor' he realized that neither course was advisable and in any case his son 'hath nott anie minde either to the one or to the other'.[18] Other parents may not have had a clear perception of the advantages, or their plans did not involve sending their sons to university. There were also those who intended that their children should succeed to the family farm or business and trained them with that end in view.[19] This commonly precluded a spell at univer-

---

[16] D. Cressy, *Literacy and the Social Order: reading and writing in Tudor and Stuart England* (Cambridge 1980), 72–177, 191–201; M. Spufford, *Small Books and Pleasant Histories* (London 1981), 19–37.

[17] J. Simon, 'Post-Restoration developments: schools in the county 1660–1700' in B. Simon (ed.), *Education in Leicestershire 1540–1940* (Leicester 1968), 32–3; D. Cressy, 'Educational opportunity in Tudor and Stuart England', *History of Education Quarterly* xvi (1976).

[18] H. F. Waters, *Genealogical Gleanings in England* (2 vols Boston Mass. 1901) i. 52.

[19] This applied to heirs and to younger sons: Houlbrooke, *English Family*, 172.

sity, although not invariably so, and Hugh Brown, a successful Bristol merchant, planned to send his son to Oxford for three years before he took him into his own business.[20] Many parents apprenticed their sons to other masters so that at the end of their term they would be qualified to follow a trade and be independent of them. This course of action had the further recommendation that once the premium had been paid to the master he undertook the costs of accommodation, food, clothing, and training. This did not apply when a son went to university, although some families could obtain help towards meeting the expense from relatives, friends, benefactors, and exhibitions.[21] The loss of a potential income was a further cost to be considered, however, for a youth who remained at home contributed to the family budget through his labour or earnings. The vast majority of parents must have been unable to undertake the expense of educating their sons at university, or could not be confident of being able to do so for a number of years ahead.

Those who had the means, perceived the benefits which could accrue and were able to secure a place for their sons sent them to university; between 1600 and 1690 approximately 35,000 students attended Oxford. It is impossible to provide a precise figure because of the nature of the records. This estimate is based upon the university matriculation registers, which are the principal numerical source for the size of the student intake, as the colleges' admission records are inadequate for the purpose.[22] The matriculation evidence also has a number of shortcomings. Until 1622 the matriculant's name, status, age, and county were given; thereafter his father's name and place of residence were also included and from 1650 the matriculation fee was entered. Some information was not recorded for the years 1648–60, however, because the intruded esquire bedel of law, Bernard Hore, was not allowed by his predecessor to see the earlier volumes and so had no guide on which to base his own record-keeping. His omission of the student's age, father's name and both place and county of origin means these are years for which the matriculation evidence is seriously deficient.[23] Even for the remainder of the period there is some degree of incompleteness in the recording of the required information, as the figures in table 1.1 for four sample groups of years show.[24]

The varying efficiency of the registrars and the differing ways in which they recorded matriculations also resulted in some inconsistencies. The practice of Thomas and John French, successive esquire bedels of law from 1608 to 1648, seems to have been to enter the matriculants' names only infrequently, producing

[20] P. McGrath, *Merchants and Merchandise in Seventeenth-Century Bristol* (Bristol Record Soc. xix 1955), pp. xxxi, 19.

[21] See pp. 76–81 below.

[22] Matriculations for 1567–1622 are printed in *Reg. Univ.* ed. Clark, pt 2, 48–405. Matriculation registers are OUA SP2, 1615–47, SP37, 1648–62, SP3, 1662–93.

[23] See Anthony Wood's notes in OUA SP37 (unfoliated).

[24] Hereafter referred to as the 'sample years'. The smaller proportion of omissions for 1605–7 reflects the fewer items to be recorded as well as the relative completeness of the record-keeping.

TABLE 1.1

Matriculation records in sample years

	Number of matriculation entries	% lacking one or more items of information
1605–7	870	1.0
1630–2	1,057	6.6
1663–5	1,161	2.1
1683–5	911	6.9
Combined	3,999	4.1

TABLE 1.2

Grouping of matriculations in sample years

	Number of days on which matriculation occurred	Number of matriculants	Mean number of matriculants per matriculation day
1605–7	91	870	9.6
1630–2	77	1,057	13.7
1663–5	153	1,161	7.6
1683–5	210	911	4.3
Combined	531	3,999	7.5

erratic numbers from year to year.[25] The numbers recorded at each session illustrate the regularity of the matriculation process.

During the period after 1660 students commonly, although not invariably, matriculated close to the date of their arrival at Oxford and admission to a society.[26] The regulations stipulated that the interval should be no more than fifteen days.[27] In fact some students who lived relatively near to Oxford travelled to the university to matriculate close to the end of a term and then returned home, coming into residence during the following term, having 'kept' the previous one by

[25] Standard deviations for the annual matriculation figures are 179 for 1610–39 and 65 for 1660–89, illustrating the comparative stability of the later period. See also Stone, 'Size and composition', 89.

[26] Of 139 identified entrants to Jesus 1680–8, 121 matriculated within twenty-eight days of admission to the college—seventy-two of them within seven days—and the longest interval between admission and matriculation was ninety-two days. Admission dates are taken from the college buttery books: Bodl. MSS DD Jesus College a. 26–33.

[27] *Laudian Code*, ed. Griffiths, 25–6.

virtue of completing the admission procedure and their matriculation.[28] Hence there is some clustering of matriculation dates towards the ends of terms and at the Act—which many parents attended and treated primarily as a social event— and the record of a student's matriculation may be earlier than the actual start of his period of residence rather than later, as it almost invariably was for the earlier period when the delays between admission and matriculation were often substantial ones.[29] The examples from the period of erratic matriculation shown in table 1.3 indicate that a minority of students matriculated during the year of their admission and that 8 per cent of the sample had been in the college for at least three years before they matriculated.

The negligence in matriculating students which these figures imply demonstrates that some could have avoided matriculation completely, not being compelled to do so by the college or university officers and not having a reason for going through the procedure if they did not wish to take a degree. Furthermore, a proportion of those who did go forward to a BA had not matriculated. They constituted 19 per cent of those graduating in the 1600s and, despite a subsequent fall, were still 5 per cent of graduates in the late 1630s.[30] Only when the matriculation procedure occurred close to the date of admission did the process come to encompass almost all students.

The incompleteness of the matriculation registers can be compensated for by numerical adjustment based upon a comparison of them with records of college admissions and of those students taking the BA degree—procedures which allow non-matriculants to be identified. The proportion of students not matriculating varied considerably, both from college to college and through time, and because suitable admission records are extant for only a minority of the colleges and for none of the halls the figures produced by this method can only be tentative ones, illustrative of trends in admissions, and they cannot be regarded as representing the actual numbers entering the university. The comparative completeness of the matriculation registers after the 1650s is in marked contrast to those of the earlier period when they failed to record between one quarter and one third of incoming students and an even higher proportion during the disruption of the 1640s.[31] The corrected figures for admissions for the first six decades of the century are consequently less secure than are those for the later ones. The numbers matriculating and the adjusted figures for admissions are given in table 1.4 and shown on figure 2.

[28] Bodl. MS top. Oxon. f. 31, pp. 11–14, 16; *The Life of Mr Thomas Hearne ... Written by Himself* (Oxford 1772), 4.

[29] For the Act as a social event see Penton, *Guardian's Instruction*, 73; *The Correspondence of John Locke*, ed. E. S. De Beer (8 vols Oxford 1976–89) i. 223; and Berks. RO Trumbull misc. corr. vol. L, no. 53.

[30] Stone, 'Size and composition', 12, 83–7, 90.

[31] The percentage corrections applied to the numbers of matriculations are: 1590s 41, 1600s 33, 1610s 31, 1620s and 1630s 25, 1640s 70, 1650s 28, 1660s 10, 1670s 7, 1680s 6, 1690s 7. See Stone, 'Size and composition', 83–7, 91. Stone's methodology and figures for admissions have been used throughout this section.

TABLE 1.3

Dates of matriculation and admission

College	Date of matriculation	Year of admission						Number in sample
		1628	1629	1630	1631	1632	Unknown	
Exeter	2 Dec. 1631	6	14	16	19	0	4	59
Brasenose	9 Dec. 1631	4	15	20	32	0	0	71
Balliol	15 June 1632	0	3	8	9	11	0	31

TABLE 1.4

Matriculations and estimated numbers of admissions by decade, 1590–1699

	1590–9	1600–9	1610–19	1620–9	1630–9	1640–9	1650–9	1660–9	1670–9	1680–9	1690–9	1590–1699
Matriculations	2,543	2,810	2,766	3,200	4,240	1,288	3,418	4,163	3,768	3,030	2,830	34,056
Estimated admissions	3,585	3,737	3,623	4,000	5,300	2,190	4,375	4,579	4,032	3,212	3,028	41,661

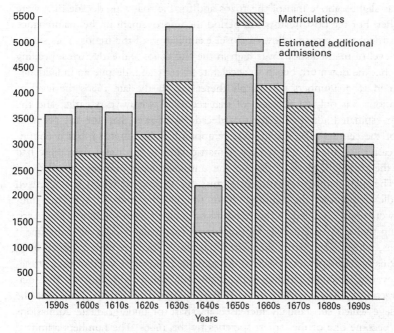

FIG. 2. Matriculations and estimated decadal admissions

The considerable variation in numbers admitted is at once apparent. There was an initial period of stagnation in the first two decades, with little sign of the rapid expansion to come, and indeed admissions were then only marginally greater than they had been in the 1590s.[32] The modest rise in numbers detectable in the 1620s was followed by a veritable boom in the 1630s, which saw the highest numbers of student admissions in any decade before the 1870s. Delays in registering matriculations during this period and the consequent fluctuations of the figures from year to year make it difficult to date the changes in the rate of growth precisely, but it seems that the considerable rise in numbers began in the late 1620s and that the high level in admissions continued throughout most of the 1630s before beginning to decline slightly in the years immediately preceding the civil war. The pre-war crisis, the civil war itself and the uncertain period that followed combined to produce several years of erratic record keeping and a low student intake. Recovery after the 1640s was fairly swift, however, and admissions during the 1650s were at a level

---

[32] Estimated admissions for the 1570s and 1580s are 4,130 and 4,450 respectively. Because of the enforcement of the university's requirements that students should live within a college or hall and be matriculated these figures are somewhat distorted and are less certain than those for the later decades. See. J. K. McConica, 'The rise of the undergraduate college' in *The Collegiate University*, 48–51; E. Russell, 'The influx of commoners into the University of Oxford before 1581: an optical illusion?', *EHR* xcii (1977), 723, 733–5, 741–3.

which was slightly above that of the 1620s and for the following decade they were even higher. For the post-Restoration period the improvement in the maintenance of the matriculation records allows a closer examination of the trends. This shows that the level of matriculations was high in the late 1660s and early 1670s, peaking in 1666, that the downturn began to accelerate in 1675 and, despite an individually high year in 1677, numbers fell sharply thereafter. By the late 1680s the level of matriculations was only 64 per cent of that recorded twenty years earlier and the figure for estimated admissions for that decade was lower than for any previous decade of the century. The decline was temporarily halted in 1689, but it continued thereafter and there were 200 fewer matriculants in the 1690s than there had been in the preceding decade, despite the unusually large number recorded for 1698.[33] The high numbers of student admissions to Oxford which characterized the middle decades of the century—from roughly the mid-1620s to the mid-1670s—were unprecedented and were not to be attained again for almost 200 years.

Ranking the colleges and halls by number of matriculants conceals subsequent migrations, which may distort the pattern, as those societies with relatively high proportions of foundationers' places drew students from those without such attractions. Nevertheless, such rankings remain generally stable, with most of the societies attracting a fairly constant share of the undergraduate intake. Jesus was the only college which substantially increased its share of undergraduate admissions and had become one of the largest societies by the 1660s. The numbers admitted to the halls were more volatile for they were without endowments and so were largely dependent upon the energies and abilities of their principals to attract students.[34] In the 1630s Gloucester Hall matriculated almost three times as many students as it had done in the previous decade and its popularity was attributed primarily to the ability and personality of the then principal, Digory Wheare, and its contrasting experience later in the century—it had only ten matriculants between 1675 and 1694—was certainly due to the conduct of Byrom Eaton.[35] Magdalen was the only hall to take in large numbers. It matriculated almost as many students as the largest colleges in the first six decades of the century, but its relative position declined thereafter.[36] The halls' combined share of total matriculations was generally between one fifth and one quarter until the 1680s when, with falling numbers in the university leaving spare residential capacity, students apparently were attracted by the colleges' extra teaching facilities, exhibitions, and scholarships, and the share of the halls fell quite sharply.[37]

[33] 336 matriculated in 1698, the mean for the other nine years of the decade was 277.

[34] HMC *Ormonde MSS* new ser. viii. 27.

[35] Wood, *Life and Times* ii. 304, 364, 398, iii. 1, 390; C. H. Daniel and W. R. Barker, *Worcester College* (London 1900), 113, 117–18.

[36] There were said to be 300 students resident at Magdalen Hall in 1624 and 240 in residence there was not uncommon: Bodl. MS Ballard 46, fo 97.

[37] This is reflected in the decision of the court of Christ's Hospital in 1685 to send its scholars to the colleges where they might obtain funds to supplement their scholarships: London, Guildhall Library, MS 12806/7, Christ's Hospital minutes 1677–89, p. 663.

TABLE 1.5

The five largest societies in the university, ranked by number of matriculants

	Five largest societies, ranked by number of matriculations, high → low	Matriculations in these five as % of total	Halls as % of total
1600s	Brasenose, Exeter, Queen's, Christ Church, Magdalen Hall	41	22[a]
1630s	Exeter, Magdalen Hall, Christ Church, Brasenose, Queen's	39	25
1660s	Christ Church, Exeter, Wadham, Brasenose, Jesus	38	21
1680s	Christ Church, Exeter, Trinity, Brasenose, Jesus	40	15

[a] Broadgates Hall, which became Pembroke College, is omitted from the 1600s figure to render it comparable with the later ones.

The figures derived from the matriculation registers indicate the size and dynamics of the student intake, but not the university's total population nor necessarily the relative size of its constituent parts. Evidence for these is available from seven enumerations and three other listings of members. That dated 1592 comprises only the heads of houses, fellows, and other foundationers. A census was compiled in 1605 for the visit of James I and another was drawn up six years later at the request of the prince of Wales. In 1612 'an exact account' was taken during the long vacation. John Scot's *The Foundation of the Universitie of Oxford* of 1634 provides a breakdown of numbers by colleges and halls for that year and a total for 1622. Langbaine's figures, ostensibly for 1651, are taken from Scot's enumeration with only minor alterations and can be discounted. The lists of members of the university who subscribed to the protestation oath of 1642 and to the oaths of supremacy and uniformity in 1661 and those who paid the poll tax in 1667 are available, but have to be adjusted to take account of exclusions. A further enumeration is undated but was evidently compiled as a contribution to the standing army debate of the 1690s. As with the matriculation registers these censuses and listings are an inconsistent source, compiled by different hands for different purposes at different stages of the academic year and varying in their content and degree of completeness.[38]

[38] The sources for 1592, 1611, and 1612 are Bodl. MS Twyne 21, pp. 513–14 and MS Twyne 2, fo 80; for 1661 OUA SP 129, fos 1–34; for the 1690s Bodl. MS Tanner 338, fos 203[r]–4[v]. Those for 1612 and the 1690s are printed in *Collectanea curiosa*, ed. J. Gutch (2 vols Oxford 1781) i. 191–203, those for 1605, 1611, and 1612 in Wood, *Life and Times* iv. 150–1. A copy of John Scot, *The Foundation of the Universitie of Oxford* (Cambridge 1634) is in Bodl. Gough maps 43, fos 139–40. The protestation returns are in *Oxfordshire Protestation Returns*, ed. C. S. A. Dobson (Oxfordshire Record Soc. xxxvi 1955), 100–19 and the poll-tax returns in *Surveys and Tokens*, ed. H. E. Salter (OHS lxxv 1920), 307–36. Thomas

The only one of the enumerations which does not separate the university into its component colleges and halls is that for 1622. The others do so and in some the memberships of the societies are further divided into their constituent parts. The number of houses, each with a head, had stabilized before the end of the sixteenth century and the only further addition was the foundation of Wadham in 1610 which brought the total to twenty-five.[39] The number of fellowships was increased by new endowments, although the statutory numbers were not always adhered to.[40] The 1592 list shows 471 fellows at fifteen colleges, a figure which was later increased as Jesus began to function fully after a sluggish beginning and with the foundation of Wadham and Pembroke. These colleges initially added forty-one fellowships to the total, and other endowments there and in other colleges further raised the number to 520 by the end of the period. There were considerable differences between the colleges in terms of the numbers of fellows provided for by their statutes, for there were 101 'students'—the equivalent status—at Christ Church, seventy fellows at New College, and fifty at St John's, but nine colleges still had fewer than twenty fellows each in the late seventeenth century. This also applied to the other members on the foundation, who included the canons, chaplains, clerks, choristers at five colleges, and the scholars. The well-endowed colleges of Magdalen, Merton, and Christ Church contained one third of the 362 foundationers who were not fellows in the 1690s. A century earlier the total figure for the same category had been put at 245. The overall number, including heads as well as fellows and other foundationers, was therefore 740 in 1592 and 907 by the 1690s, a rise of 22.5 per cent.

The most volatile section of the university, in numerical terms at least, was the student body, which consisted of those graduates and undergraduates who were not in receipt of emoluments from their colleges. It was divided into a number of groups according to the privileges to which their members were entitled and determined primarily by social status. The categories varied somewhat between the societies and were not static within each institution. Fellow-commoners were first permitted at Lincoln in 1606, at Balliol four years later, and at New College only in 1677.[41] Typically there were five groups of students besides the foundationers.[42] Noblemen's sons received the preferential treatment that was consonant with their social rank. Fellow- or gentlemen-commoners were the sons of the social élite,

Baskerville's figures for the 1680s were provided by Thomas Stevenson and do not give a total for any category within the university: 'Thomas Baskerville's account of Oxford, written in 1683–6', ed. H. Baskerville, *Collectanea* iv.

[39] Pembroke's foundation from Broadgates Hall did not alter the number of societies.

[40] In 1688 several fellowships of All Souls were vacant: Shropshire RO 3385/2/8.

[41] R. W. Hunt, 'Balliol College', *VCH Oxon.* iii. 83; A. H. M. Jones, 'New College' ibid. 161; M. R. Toynbee, 'Lincoln College' ibid. 171.

[42] The categories are described by V. H. H. Green, *The Commonwealth of Lincoln College 1427–1977* (Oxford 1979), 221–4. See also G. H. Wakeling, 'History of the college, 1603–1660', *Brasenose Monographs* ii pt 1, no. XI, pp. 16–17; *Reg. Exeter*, pp. xcvii–xcviii; *Registrum orielense*, ed. C. L. Shadwell (2 vols Oxford 1893–1902), i. pp. vi–xii; HMC *Lonsdale MSS*, 93–4 (Queen's); *The Moore Rental*, ed. T. Heywood (Chetham Soc. xii 1847), 7 (Brasenose).

defined at Lincoln as 'the sons of lords, knights, and gentlemen of good place in the commonwealth'.[43] They were allowed more elaborate dress than other students and they dined apart from them, at their own or at the fellows' table. At St John's, as elsewhere, it was expected that the fellow-commoners would 'goe some what better than the rest, and if they do not, they are little thought of and lyable to the censures of every malignante person'.[44] Below them in the student hierarchy were the commoners, who were entitled to receive the same quantity and quality of food as the foundationers and to dine at their own table. Henry Brougham was aware that, as a commoner, it was necessary 'for my credit's sake to live like a gentle-man'.[45] This involved paying another student of lower rank to carry out his menial tasks. It was the batelers and servitors who executed such chores for the fellows and higher grades of students. The distinction between batelers and servitors is not always entirely clear and seems to have been related to the amount and per-haps the nature of the work which they performed and the fees which they paid. Such students were entitled to less than full commons and dined off the 'broken meats', or left-overs, in hall. Their duties included serving at mealtimes. At New Inn Hall in the 1660s servitors waited on the commoners at dinner and supper, for which they received 1d per week for each name on the buttery book—in 1662 that produced 1s 4d weekly—and some of the commons of those who were absent.[46] By the end of the sixteenth century it had become customary for those who were commoners or of a higher status to employ servitors to carry out other domestic tasks which were regarded as degrading for students of their standing, such as bed-making, lighting fires, fetching wood and water, sweeping chambers, and buying provisions.[47] Some brought their own servitors to Oxford and they entered together, others had servitors assigned to them on their arrival. William Herrick described his servitor as 'a very honest and carefull fellow to doe any thing he is appointed, and so we use him, and he doth us much good service, and is very dili-gent to do those thinges which we appointe him'. He paid him 3s per quarter in 1613–15, and by the second half of the century a servitor attending a fellow-commoner normally received 1s per week, and a half of that if he was serving a commoner.[48]

[43] This statement implies that at Lincoln noblemen's sons were categorized as fellow-commoners: Toynbee, 'Lincoln College', 171.

[44] Bodl. MS Eng. hist. c. 481, fo 59ʳ. The privileges of fellow-commoners as defined at Lincoln in 1607 are in LCM register 2, fo 148. A more critical view of fellow-commoners was that they 'make little advantage there other than spend their moneys and come home less wise than they went': *Moore Rental*, ed. Heywood, 7.

[45] *The Flemings in Oxford* i. 114.

[46] Bodl. MS Rawlinson letters 52, fo 353ʳ. I am grateful to Dr Blair Worden for drawing my atten-tion to this item. This rate also applied at Hart Hall in the early seventeenth century: Bodl. MS Tanner 338, fo 413ᵛ.

[47] Bodl. MS Gr. misc. d. 2, fo 46ʳ; John Eachard, *The Grounds and Occasions of the Contempt of the Clergy and Religion Enquired into* (London 1670), 16–17.

[48] John Nichols, *The History and Antiquities of the County of Leicester* (4 vols in 8 London 1795–1815), iii. 165; HMC *Lonsdale MSS*, 94; *Chirk Castle Accounts, A. D. 1605–1666*, ed. W. M. Myddelton (privately published 1908), 79. Wage rates for servitors are also given in BNCA MS 85, fos 6ʳ⁻ᵛ, 43ᵛ⁻4ᵛ, 51ʳ⁻2ᵛ,

The common servants formed a further group within the colleges and halls as privileged persons. Their posts were stipulated in most of the colleges' statutes. At Trinity they comprised a manciple, a butler, two cooks, a barber, and a laundress; at Lincoln a manciple, a cook, a barber, and a laundress; at Wadham a manciple, two cooks, a porter, and a barber. The functions were sometimes combined, as at Brasenose, where the porter acted as the barber. At St Edmund Hall the bible-clerk was also the porter and the three common servants were the manciple, the cook, and the butler.[49] On this basis there would have been in all roughly 160 such servants within the university, a figure which is borne out by the 1661 returns.[50] It is not supported by the evidence for 1612 and the 1690s, however, which suggests a larger total. The number of *famuli* at thirteen of the twenty-four societies in 1612 was 128; assuming that the term was applied only to college and not to personal servants, and taking into account the size of the societies, the figure for the whole university can be put at approximately 250. In the 1690s enumeration the servants are not itemized by society and the total which it supplies was produced by allocating a notional fourteen to each college and seven to each hall, a total of 301.[51] In this enumeration it is clear that the figure does not include personal servants, who are assigned to another category. The totals for 1612 and the 1690s show a rise of 20 per cent between the two dates, although neither is derived from an exact enumeration. The number of servants engaged by the colleges and halls did increase as the size of the student body expanded, and as the earlier austerities were relaxed and a more self-indulgent regime became common. By the 1670s New College had two assistants to the butler and two to the cook, and a number of societies came to employ a gardener and a stable groom, presumably a reflection of the increasing tendency for the fellows to keep horses. The requirement that the servants should be bachelors had also come to be less strictly observed.[52] Although the student servitors carried out some of the menial duties there is evidence that servants were employed for many tasks, such as the scrape-trencher mentioned at Balliol in 1667, who assisted in the kitchen.[53] These were not necessarily college

55^v–6^v, 59^r–60^v, 63^{r-v}, 64^v, 67^{r-v}, 68^v, 72^r–4^v, 78^r–80^v, 87^v–92^r, 98^v–100^v; Bodl. MS Locke f. 11, fos 16^r, 26^v, 27^v, 53^v–4^r, MS Eng. hist. c. 481, fos 62^r, 65^r–6^r, 69^r–70^r, 81^r, 97^r–100^r, MS Film 743, item 283; Devon RO Z 1/53, box 9/2; *The Flemings in Oxford* i. 107–8, 111, 113, 115, 120, 122–3, 126.

[49] H. E. D. Blakiston, 'Trinity College', *VCH Oxon.* iii. 244; H. B. Wells, 'Wadham College' ibid. 280; Green, *Lincoln College*, 231–3; I. S. Leadam, 'The early years of the college', *Brasenose Monographs* ii pt 1, no. IX, p. 29; A. B. E[mden], 'The vice-chancellor's visitation of 1613', *St Edmund Hall Magazine* ii (1929), 62.

[50] A precise figure cannot be given for 1661 because of uncertainties of identity in the returns for three societies, but it was approximately 160. The figure for the early sixteenth century was 150: C. I. Hammer, 'Oxford town and Oxford University' in *The Collegiate University*, 77–8.

[51] The 1612 figure is produced by increasing the number of the 128 *famuli* identified at thirteen societies in proportion to the numerical size of those societies and that of the total for the university.

[52] Bodl. MS Tanner 340, fos 240^{r-v}, 243^r; NCA great register book, 1649–85, p. 106; Fowler, *Corpus*, 50.

[53] *Surveys and Tokens*, ed. Salter, 330; H. W. C. Davis, *A History of Balliol College* (Oxford 1899), rev. edn by R. H. C. Davis and R. W. Hunt (Oxford 1963), 88; *The Correspondence of John Locke*, ed. De Beer i. 208. In 1660 Christ Church attempted to reduce the number of bedmakers to twelve: CA D&C i. b. 3, p. 102. In 1678 Sir John Percival at Christ Church referred to his bedmaker, barber, laundress, and 'many others whom I employ': BL Add. MS 46,955B, fo 27^r.

residents or matriculated persons, but they were members of the university community.[54] The inclusion of such additional servants explains the discrepancy between the figure of 160 college officers and the numbers of servants estimated for 1612 and the 1690s.

The employment of college servants and student servitors did not preclude the retention of personal servants, although they were kept only by the heads of the houses and the wealthier fellows and students. In 1667 only three of the forty fellows at Magdalen had resident servants.[55] Duplication of the functions of a servitor rendered the maintenance of personal servants at Oxford an avoidable expense and it was also thought to be a potential distraction to an industrious student if his servant was less than fully occupied.[56] Some members of the élite did nevertheless keep their own servants with them while they were at the university. The Newdigate brothers were attended at Trinity by a family employee who seems to have acted as their valet and Lord Leigh had a personal servant, who handled his allowance, and a student servitor when he was at Christ Church in the 1660s.[57] Those at the top of the social pyramid were likely to bring a small entourage with them to Oxford.[58] Personal servants posed a problem for the authorities at Christ Church, for they were likely to be tempted to remain behind on their master's departure in the hope of finding another wealthy student who would employ them in the same capacity, hence the chapter's order in 1660 that they were permitted only as supernumeraries and were to depart when their masters left the college.[59] Although such servants were not members of the university they may be silently included in some of the enumerations. The 1667 returns indicate that the university then contained upward of 100 personal servants and for the 1690s a precise figure of 129 is given for this category.[60]

The censuses of 1605 and 1611 give the numbers of the members of each society, but do not indicate the categories which are included. The earlier one has a total of 2,254, with a high figure of 309 for Christ Church which suggests the inclusion of personal servants. If they were included throughout the university then 2,100 would be a more accurate figure for the academic population, students and college servants. The later census has a total of 2,409, representing a rise of 7 per cent in six years.[61] The rankings of the societies are broadly similar in the two sets of figures, the major discrepancies being Broadgates Hall, which appears to have

[54] Not being matriculated would account for such extra servants' absence from the 1661 returns.

[55] Surveys and Tokens, ed. Salter, 307.   [56] HMC Lonsdale MSS, 94.

[57] Larminie, 'Seventeenth century gentleman', 317. For Lord Leigh and his servant see Shakespeare Birthplace Trust RO DR 18/5/216, 218, 221, 225–6, 237, 243–4A, 261, 263. Both are listed in the 1667 returns: Surveys and Tokens, ed. Salter, 312, 314. For Lord Grey and his contemporaries at Christ Church in the early 1690s see Northants. RO FH 138.

[58] BL Add. MS 46,952, fo 185ʳ; HMC Ormonde MSS new ser. iv. 319, 326–7.

[59] CA D&C i. b. 3, p. 102. This had also been a cause for concern in 1636: ibid. i. b. 2, p. 241.

[60] The figure of 279 for 1667 includes college and personal servants and although the two categories are not always clearly distinguished in the returns perhaps 108 of these belonged to the latter category: Surveys and Tokens, ed. Salter, 216.

[61] Based upon the nominal total of 2,254 for 1605.

experienced an almost threefold increase in size within the six years—an expansion which is not confirmed by the numbers of matriculations—and Christ Church, for which an apparently more realistic population of 214 is given in 1611. The census for 1612 is much more detailed, itemizing and enumerating the constituent groups within each society. Unfortunately it is also unreliable. While the numbers for fellows and other foundationers are roughly correct, by analogy with the 1592, 1634, and 1690s figures, those for students are wayward at some colleges, notably at Queen's where the high numbers of batteders and commoners contribute largely to the apparent increase of 78 per cent in the size of the college since the previous year. The figures for eight other societies are more than 20 per cent higher than those given in 1611 and only that for Gloucester Hall shows a decrease.[62] The evidence suggests that it is the census of 1612 which is anomalous and its total of 2,920 must be regarded as inaccurate. The 1622 and 1634 censuses should be consistent because they are derived from the same authority—John Scot. They do not include 'divers young scholars that were relieved therein, which had no names in any of the colleges', which presumably refers to those who were not members of the university but lived in the town and sought to do tasks for those who were. For 1634 the categories of persons within the colleges and halls are mentioned and generally, although not invariably, a number is given for each one.[63] The total for 1622 is 2,850 and for 1634 it is 455 higher at 3,305. The 1634 census was taken roughly at the time when the university had reached a size that it was not to attain again until the nineteenth century. That there were 786 matriculations for that year partly reflects the vagaries of the record keeping, but also gives some indication of the scale of the university's intake at that period. Indeed 1634 was the peak year for matriculations in the seventeenth century.

Taking the census figures for 1605 and 1634 at face value the university had grown in numbers by almost 50 per cent in the intervening period. The expansion had been fuelled largely by the influx of students, and at the time of Scot's enumeration the proportion of members of the university who were students without a place on the foundation was higher than at any other period of the century. This is reflected in his census by the relative numerical decline of those colleges which restricted their intake of students, notably All Souls and Corpus Christi, and the increased relative size of other societies, such as New Inn Hall and Magdalen Hall, which had succeeded in attracting many more students than they had done in the early years of the century. By 1634 there were considerable differences in the sizes of the societies, with 230 persons at Exeter and only seventy at All Souls and Corpus. Christ Church, Magdalen Hall, and Magdalen College contained only slightly fewer members than Exeter, these four being much larger than the remain-

---

[62] These are All Souls, Brasenose, Jesus, Merton, Oriel, Magdalen Hall, New Inn Hall, St Mary Hall. See also Stone 'Size and composition', 88; Wakeling, 'History of the college, 1603–1660', 7.

[63] Comparison of Scot's figures for the constituent societies and the matriculation registers shows that the latter were not his source. A discrepancy between the aggregate of his figures for the constituent societies and his total throws some doubt upon his numeracy, if not his reliability.

der and together holding 27 per cent of the university's population. Almost a half of the colleges and halls had a membership of between 100 and 150. In table 1.6 the societies are ranked in order of size in 1634.

TABLE 1.6
Societies ranked by size in 1634

Number of members in 1634	Societies ranked highest → lowest
>200	Exeter, Christ Church, Magdalen College, Magdalen Hall
150–200	Brasenose, Pembroke, Queen's
100–49	New Inn Hall, Balliol, New College, Trinity, Wadham, St John's, Jesus, Lincoln, Oriel, Hart Hall, St Mary Hall
<100	St Alban Hall, St Edmund Hall, Gloucester Hall, Merton, University, All Souls, Corpus Christi

The figures for 1642, 1661, and 1667 are incomplete and require some adjustment to render them comparable with the earlier censuses. The protestation returns of 21–4 February 1642 record the names of those who swore to the oath to defend the protestant religion, as required by parliament. Some academics could only bring themselves to do so after appending elaborate qualifications to the oath.[64] Absentees, sick, and recusants are also listed. Those under 18 were not required to swear, although it may be that, given the nature of the oath, this age qualification was not strictly applied and some students younger than 18 are recorded. Eighteen college servants are identified in the returns and others are entered without being so described, but the precise number cannot be recovered because of difficulties of positive identification and it may be assumed, in the absence of more certain evidence, that the proportion of servants taking the oath was the same as for the remainder of the university population.[65] A comparison of the names of those taking the oath with those entered in the college buttery books provides an indication of the extent of under-registration.[66] Of the members of Balliol and Jesus 65 per cent are listed in the returns, and application of this proportion to the total of 2,038 produces a figure of 3,135 for the university, representing a fall of 5 per cent over the previous eight years.

[64] *Protestation Returns*, ed. Dobson, pp. v–vi, 104–5, 110, 112, 117; Wood, *History of the University* ii. 437–8.

[65] There is no list of college servants. Some of them who appear as privileged persons or servants in the matriculation register have been identified in the returns, where only surnames are given.

[66] Few societies have records for that term; only six months later the first troops arrived in Oxford as the civil war got under way and the preservation of such administrative material was presumably given a low priority.

The 1661 listing of members of the university had a similar origin, as it records subscriptions to the oaths of supremacy and uniformity imposed by the Restoration visitors. The returns were evidently drawn up independently for each society. That for Brasenose bears the date 28 January 1661 and comparison of the names included in the returns with admission and matriculation records shows that the lists were compiled during the first three months of that year. They provide a total of 2,176 names and indicate those who had taken the oaths, those who were absent, and also included six students who were minors. Those who were under 16 must have been under-recorded, for they constituted 11 per cent of matriculants at this date, which suggests that a further 125 students should be added to the recorded undergraduate population of 1,020.[67] There is no return for St Alban Hall, which had been virtually empty throughout the previous decade, with one matriculation in 1656 and a total of seven in 1659 and 1660, which may be taken to be the size of the omission. The figure of 275—midway between the figures for 1612 and the 1690s—can be substituted for the principal domestic officers who are listed. A corrected undergraduate body of 1,152, with the 973 foundationers and those of bachelor rank and above, and 275 servants produces a university population at this date of 2,400.

The returns for the poll tax levied in 1667 to help finance the Second Dutch War include the university. The assessments were made during February—the tax was paid in the weeks immediately following—and include members of the families of the heads of houses and personal servants, as well as college officers. Excluding these three categories from the nominal total of 2,067 produces a figure of 1,800. Absentees are identified at five of the colleges, but apparently are not given for the remainder. For the five colleges they constituted 17 per cent of the total membership and the addition of this proportion to the other societies raises the total by 270. There is no other obvious inconsistency in the returns. A correction has to be made to the figure of 1,035 undergraduates, however, to account for those under 16 years old and using the multiplier applied to the 1661 lists produces 130 additional students.[68] Again allowing for 275 college servants and officers and incorporating the additions for absentees and those under age provides a total university population of 2,475 and indicates a rise of just over 3 per cent since 1661, although matriculations for 1664–6 were more than 9 per cent higher than those for 1658–60.[69] This suggests that the 1667 figure may be too low, perhaps because it is derived from a source which, unlike the others used to estimate the size of the university, is a tax return and so subject to some degree of evasion. The extent of such evasion cannot be recovered, although it is unlikely that in the context of the university it was greater than 5 per cent, which would indicate a maximum population of 2,600.

[67] 79/723 matriculants in 1661 and 1662 = 10.9%. 1,020 × 100/89.1 = 1,145.

[68] 1,035 × 100/89.1 = 1,162, an addition of 127 undergraduates, rounded to 130.

[69] The total university population of 2,475 represents the nominal total of 2,067 reduced by the exclusion of the families of heads of houses, personal servants, and college officers to 1,800, plus 270 additional absentees, 130 undergraduates under 16, and 275 college officers.

The final source which supplies data for the size of the university in the seventeenth century is undated, but from the watermark and internal evidence it has been attributed to the years 1685–95.[70] A comparison of the numbers noted in the document and the numbers of matriculants, ranked in size order by society, suggests that it dates from the early 1690s. It was evidently drawn up with reference to the standing army debate—which rumbled on throughout the later part of the century and reached its height in the pamphlet war of 1697–9—for it compares the annual notional costs of the university with the expense of maintaining troops.[71] In addition to the heads of houses it includes 527 fellows, 362 other foundationers and exhibitioners, and 632 commoners, a term which in this context refers to 'Gentlemen, that live in Oxford on their own charges'.[72] The numbers of commoners are not precise, being given in multiples of five for all but two of the societies. Adding the figure of 301 which is supplied for college servants to the total of 1,546 for the four categories already specified produces a population of 1,847 for the university, 75 per cent of that estimated for 1667.[73]

The nine enumerations produce precise figures which suggest a degree of exactitude that is not a true reflection of the nature of the evidence or indeed of the level of numeracy prevailing in the seventeenth century. Nevertheless they do provide indications both of the university's population and of the fluctuations in its size. They support the conclusions drawn from the matriculation data, with which they can be compared by dividing each total by the sum of the matriculations for the three years preceding that of the enumeration, with the appropriate percentage adjustment.[74]

The waywardness of the index for 1612 is at once apparent, reflecting the inaccuracy of the census of that year. That for 1634 is also high, but this is perhaps explicable in terms of the erratic keeping of the matriculation register at that time and if the matriculations for 1634 are substituted for those of 1631 the index becomes 1.8. The remaining index numbers show a considerable degree of consistency. Indeed the enumerations confirm that the relatively slow growth rate of the early part of the century gave way to a period of more rapid expansion during which the university was growing at an average rate of roughly forty-five additional persons per year and that this phase was followed by a slight decrease in its population before the civil war. The enumerations suggest that the post-war recovery

[70] A. B. Emden, 'St Edmund Hall', *VCH Oxon.* iii. 330 n. 21.

[71] L. G. Schwoerer, *No Standing Armies! The antiarmy ideology in seventeenth-century England* (London 1974), 137–87.

[72] Presumably referring to all those who were not in receipt of college emoluments, hence the categories of foundationers and commoners include all students. The totals for fellows and commoners are incorrectly given in *Collectanea curiosa*, ed. Gutch i. 195.

[73] The 129 'servitors, Doctors' Servants' are taken to be personal servants and are excluded; see p. 39 above.

[74] Thus the index for 1605 is produced by dividing the census figure of 2,250 by the number of matriculations for 1602–4 plus 33%, a figure of 1,269. In the absence of a precise date for the 1690s enumeration the matriculation figure used is the annual mean of 1690–4 multiplied by three and increased by 7%.

TABLE 1.7

Comparison of censuses of the university with matriculations

Census date	Total population of university derived from census	Total divided by adjusted number of matriculations in three preceding years
1605	2,254	1.78
1611	2,409	2.05
1612	2,920	2.64
1622	2,850	1.78
1634	3,305	2.24
1642	3,135	1.82
1661	2,400	1.88
1667	2,475	1.77
1690s	1,847	2.09

was less complete than the decadal matriculation figures indicate, for although the lower secondary peak in the mid-1660s is apparent, the university appears to have been somewhat smaller in that decade than in the early 1620s and no larger in 1661 than it had been fifty years before. The lowest total of the century falls in its final decade, which also saw the lowest number of matriculations.[75]

The pattern of admissions to Oxford was not dissimilar from those of the other institutions of higher education—Cambridge University and the Inns of Court—which also experienced their highest admissions in the early seventeenth century, secondary peaks after the civil war and a steep decline in the last quarter of the century.[76] At Cambridge the increase in numbers came rather earlier than at Oxford, with highest numbers of admissions in the 1620s, a steady fall off thereafter until a revival in the 1660s, which continued into the following decade, and then a decline that, as at Oxford, produced lower figures in the 1680s than in the first decade of the century. The contrasting experience of the two universities during the 1640s largely accounts for the slight difference in total numbers of students admitted during the period 1600–89, in which Cambridge's intake was 5 per cent greater than Oxford's. Because of personal allegiances and the difficulty of access to Oxford while it was garrisoned as the royalist headquarters many parents were unwilling or unable to send their sons there. Some students went to Cambridge instead and some exhibitions normally tenable at Oxford and which were awarded by bodies beyond the royalists' control were allowed to them.[77] The numbers of

[75] See table 1.4 above.

[76] Stone, 'Size and composition', 5–6, 92; D. Lemmings, 'The student body of the Inns of Court under the later Stuarts', *Bulletin of the Institute of Historical Research* lviii (1985), 150–1.

[77] *CSPD 1645–7*, 327; London, Merchant Taylors' Company, minutes 9, 1636–54, fos 167[r]–70[v], 200[v], 203[v], 208[r], 213[r–v], 223[r], 231[r], 235[v]–6[v].

new enrolments at Oxford were very low as a result and the post-war conflicts between the existing and the new authorities also had a detrimental effect upon admissions. The situation regarding the Inns of Court, which have been described as a third university, was rather different, for time spent at them was seen as both a supplement and an alternative to a spell at Oxford or Cambridge, and a majority of youths attending the Inns also went to one of the universities. Admissions to the Inns show an even earlier peak than at Cambridge, with high numbers in the first two decades of the century, largely sustained until a trough in the 1640s, which was followed by a revival in the 1650s, with the number of entrants almost reaching the early-century peak. Numbers fluctuated thereafter until the 1680s saw the beginning of an unbroken thirty-year decline. Oxford's changing enrolments during the seventeenth century were not, therefore, simply a mirror of those at Cambridge and the Inns of Court.[78]

There was a similar, albeit less exaggerated, pattern of growth and decline in the population as a whole. England's population rose from a little over 4,000,000 in 1600 to a peak of 5,250,000 in the mid-1650s, but it fell thereafter and in 1690 stood at 4,900,000. Throughout the first half of the century the population grew at more than 0.5 per cent per annum and at twice that rate in the first decade. The later seventeenth century was marked by low levels of fertility, a number of years of high mortality, and declining life expectancy. A related trend was a fall in the proportion of the young in the population. The percentage of those under 24 years old began to decline in the mid-1620s and fell sharply after the mid-1650s until in the 1680s it reached a level which was the lowest in more than 300 years. There were, therefore, fewer males of university age in the population than there had been before the mid-century. The pattern of mortality shows that there were nine years with unusually high levels of mortality in the first fifty-seven years of the century, yet in the following twenty-eight years there were ten such years.[79] Parents' anxiety about epidemics in Oxford was reflected in their correspondence with both their children and the college tutors.[80] Epidemics certainly were disruptive and during the more severe outbreaks of plague or other infectious diseases the university

[78] A similar pattern of a sharp rise in student numbers to a peak which was followed by a decline and a subsequent period of stagnation has been found in other European universities, although with a different chronology. The increase in admissions began in the fifteenth century in Italy and rather later in Castile, where admissions peaked in the late sixteenth century. In France and Germany the peak came in the mid-seventeenth century, and in the Netherlands it was not reached until the 1690s. See R. L. Kagan, *Students and Society in Early Modern Spain* (Baltimore 1974), and his review in *Social History* viii (1983), 388–90 of W. T. M. Frijhoff, *La Société néerlandaise et ses gradués 1575–1814* (Amsterdam and Maarssen 1981).

[79] Wrigley and Schofield, *Population History of England*, 177–8, 183, 208–9, 212, 216–17, 229–39, 448–9, 528–9.

[80] Bodl. MS Eng. hist. c. 481, fo 30ʳ; Berks. RO Trumbull Add. MS 46, letter 30 April 1628, Trumbull misc. corr. vol. L, no. 58. For a tutor's reassurances to an anxious father see *Calendar of the Correspondence of the Smyth Family of Ashton Court 1548–1642*, ed. J. H. Bettey (Bristol Record Soc. xxxv 1982), 65, 74–5. The nature of the disease was not always specified, although in 1609 George Radcliffe reported that there was plague in Oxford: *The Life and Original Correspondence of Sir George Radcliffe*, ed. T. D. Whitaker (London 1810), 40, 44–5.

dispersed; some tutors took houses in the countryside and continued their teaching there, while many students returned home.[81] The plagues of 1603 and 1625–6 were especially bad in Oxford, but the town largely escaped the outbreaks of 1665–6.[82] Although there were fewer matriculations in the plague years there is no suggestion of any long-term reductions in numbers as a result of such epidemics. By the middle of the century smallpox was beginning to arouse concern. There were outbreaks in Oxford in 1649 and 1654 and they became increasingly common in the 1670s and 1680s, with particularly virulent ones in 1675 and 1683.[83] Plague epidemics had made most impact on the poorer sections of society, but such was not the case with smallpox, which acquired a reputation not only for attacking rich and poor alike but of actually causing greater mortality among the wealthier classes.[84] Deaths among the staff and students of the university and the periodic dispersal of members of the colleges and halls created considerable alarm. In the absence of dependable information from Oxford—there was a tendency to minimize the dangers to avoid deterring new students—parents may have estimated the risks of infection from conditions in their own area.[85] To that extent epidemics in Oxford only partly influenced their decisions on whether to send their sons to the university. Although parents could not keep their children in conditions of perpetual quarantine at home they were able to reduce the risks by withholding them from the densely populated colleges and halls temporarily, or even permanently. The increased incidence of smallpox after the mid-1670s did coincide with the acceleration in the rate of decline in matriculation; it is unlikely that this was entirely coincidental.[86]

[81] Costin, *St. John's*, 24–5; BNCA B2a. 40, pp. 3, 5–6. John Freind returned home in 1672 because of the 'spotted fever' and his parents were reluctant to let him return to Oxford until they had received news that there was no reported case of it there: Bodl. MS top. Oxon. f. 31, pp. 171–2, 177. For requests for dispensations for terms of absence because of smallpox see HMC *Ormonde MSS* new ser. iv. 608, 614–15, 617, 639–40, vii. 339, 356, 367, 420.

[82] *VCH Oxon.* iv. 76–7; Wood, *History of the University* ii. 279–80, 356.

[83] Smallpox caused less than 3% of deaths in London 1629–36, but in the early 1680s accounted for 8%. High mortality from the disease in the capital was generally followed by more widespread epidemics in the same or in the succeeding year. See C. Creighton, *A History of Epidemics in Britain* (2 vols Cambridge 1891–4, 2nd edn 2 vols London 1965) ii. 434–9, 444, 456–8. There were several outbreaks of the disease in post-Restoration Oxford: Wood, *Life and Times* ii. 74, 78, 124, 133, 205, 288, 317–18, 320–4, 330, iii. 67, 80–1, 83, 190, 195, 200, 209; *Letters of Humphrey Prideaux, sometime Dean of Norwich, to John Ellis, sometime Under-Secretary of State, 1674–1722*, ed. E. M. Thompson (Camden Soc. 2nd ser. xv 1875), 41, 47. There was an outbreak at Trinity in 1686: H. E. D. Blakiston, *Trinity College* (London 1898), 170. For the smallpox epidemic of 1675 see Northants. RO IC 919, 924, 936, 940.

[84] P. Slack, *The Impact of Plague in Tudor and Stuart England* (London 1985), 92–3, 118–19, 124–6, 133–43, 152–69, 187–95, 239–40, 304–10, 339–40; Creighton, *History of Epidemics* ii. 450.

[85] *The Correspondence of John Locke*, ed. De Beer i. 272–3. In 1652/3 Locke bought an antidote against smallpox: Bodl. MS Locke f. 11, fo 63. For letters to a student's father minimizing the danger of smallpox at Christ Church in 1674–5 see Northants. RO IC 842, 845, 850, 944, 947, 4784–5, 4787–8.

[86] The connection between smallpox and falling numbers was recognized in Oxford by the 1690s, if not before. The death from smallpox of a fellow and an undergraduate at Wadham in 1695 and the presence of 'the purples there had caused the numbers in the college to be very thin . . . and which for the same reason they are afraid will be for the future'. 'Some Wood family letters from Oxford, 1659–1719', ed. E. Wood, *Oxoniensia* li (1986), 132–3.

Population change had an indirect impact through its effect upon prices. The long-term rise in prices of agricultural produce during the period of population growth from the early sixteenth century to the middle of the seventeenth century increased the incomes of producers and landlords. Rents did lag behind rising tenant incomes during the early stages of this inflationary phase, but between 1600 and 1640 this was no longer the case and a doubling, tripling, or even greater increase in rental receipts was not uncommon during those years.[87] Agricultural prices continued to be buoyant in the 1650s and early 1660s. The years between 1664 and 1691, in contrast, saw a fall in prices and rents in both arable and pastoral regions and there is considerable evidence of farm tenancies being surrendered and rents postponed or reduced, with the result that almost all landlords suffered some loss of revenue, especially during the severe depression of the 1680s.[88] Some landlords and farmers had the cushion of alternative sources of income, but many had no such buffer against falling prices and this also applied to those members of the clergy whose receipts from tithes and from glebe land were similarly vulnerable. A slump in the farming economy also adversely affected those engaged in related services. During a period of falling agricultural prices these sections of society needed to economize and perhaps reduce non-essential spending where possible, with university education a likely target for such economies. In the more prosperous times of rising prices, expanding rent rolls, and competition for farms, on the other hand, parents whose income was thereby increasing would be more inclined to undertake this kind of expenditure, especially if it were perceived to have social and economic advantages. Rising food prices resulted in falling real incomes for those consumers whose earnings failed to maintain their purchasing power, while falling prices had the reverse effect and produced increasing disposable incomes. Consumers of agricultural produce were therefore better off during the latter part of the century, which also saw the recovery of the cloth industry from its earlier malaise and the expansion and diversification of overseas trade. The agricultural sector of the economy remained predominant none the less, and although the urban population doubled in the course of the century it was still only 20 per cent of the total by 1700.[89] The majority of Oxford's students were from a rural background and it follows that among the potential recruits to the university the numbers benefiting from low agricultural prices were much smaller than those who were adversely affected and that the reverse was the case during the earlier

[87] A. Everitt, 'Farm labourers' in J. Thirsk (ed.), *The Agrarian History of England and Wales* iv *1500–1640* (Cambridge 1967), 435; P. J. Bowden, 'Agricultural prices, farm profits, and rents' ibid. 594–609, 674–95.

[88] P. J. Bowden, 'Agricultural prices, wages, farm profits, and rents' in J. Thirsk (ed.), *The Agrarian History of England and Wales* v *1640–1750* (2 pts Cambridge 1984–5) pt 2, pp. 56–7, 75–8; C. Clay, 'Landlords and estate management in England' ibid. 176–7, 232; D. W. Howell, 'Landlords and estate management in Wales' ibid. 284.

[89] P. Clark and P. Slack, *English Towns in Transition 1500–1700* (London 1976), 11; P. J. Corfield, *The Impact of English Towns 1700–1800* (Oxford 1982), 7–9. One in three students gave a city or market town as their address when matriculating. This overstates the proportion from an urban background as boys were commonly sent from country schools to the town grammar schools before going to university and this was the place recorded at matriculation.

inflationary period. There was inevitably some lag between the onset of a shift in price levels and its impact upon expenditure patterns, until the trend became established and its effects began to be felt in terms of disposable incomes. Admissions of students to Oxford in the seventeenth century followed these fluctuations, with the pre-civil war boom, the post-war recovery in the 1650s and 1660s, and the subsequent decline broadly reflecting the pattern of price changes. There was a recovery in agricultural prices in the 1690s and also a check to the decline in admissions in the later years of that decade.

The educational background was also subject to change during this period, which was far from being one of uninterrupted progress. Even the levels of basic literacy varied. There was a downturn in basic educational provision in the last two decades of the sixteenth century which was followed by a revival after approximately 1610 that continued until the dislocation of the civil war years. The recovery which followed was itself succeeded by a period of stagnation in the 1680s and 1690s.[90] More pertinent to those sections of society which supplied the bulk of the university's recruits was a downturn in the quality of the education provided by the grammar schools. The beginnings of a decline in the teaching of the classics in such schools can be dated to the late seventeenth century and their intake became more socially restricted during the same period.[91]

A related cultural factor was the education of the clergy and the prospects for careers within the church. The transformation of the clergy into a profession manned predominantly by university graduates made it a necessity for those wishing to enter the church to attend one of the universities.[92] The connection was an indirect one, for the church had no control over the numbers or the educational or social standing of those who attended university with the aim of joining the clergy and very little over the forces within society which impelled youths to seek a clerical career. It was the awareness of the prospects and benefits of the profession among those with the opportunities and means to react to them which influenced the numbers who studied at Oxford as a stepping-stone to ordination. The sons of clergymen must have been aware of the nature and rewards of such a career and, through the network of contacts among the clergy, the opportunities which it offered. Although never more than 21 per cent of matriculants they could have passed on such information to the laity.[93] But knowledge and the circulation of information were less than perfect, and in the absence of any concerted attempt to influence recruitment in this way even the clergy's perception of the current position regarding prospects for a career in the church must have been incomplete and perhaps misleading.

Religious policy had a more direct influence through the tests which were imposed on members of the university and so reduced the numbers of those who

---

[90] Cressy, *Literacy and the Social Order*, 169–74.

[91] Stone, 'Size and composition', 11; Cressy, 'Educational opportunity', 309–13, 316–17.

[92] O'Day, *English Clergy*, 2–6, 132–43.

[93] The proportion of 21% was only achieved at the end of the century: see table 1.10 below.

were willing to seek admission. The measures of 1581 had had the effect of curtailing the numbers of Roman Catholics and similar restrictions were extended to protestant dissenters after the Restoration.[94] Neither group was thereby totally excluded from the university for the oaths of allegiance and uniformity and subscription to the Thirty-nine Articles were not required from those under 16 years old and noblemen were exempted, which allowed members of Catholic families such as Kenelm Digby, who was at Gloucester Hall in 1618, and the two sons of the Duke of Norfolk, who attended Magdalen College fifty years later, to spend some time at Oxford.[95] There were, too, those Catholics who conformed and matriculated. Charles Ingleby came from a Catholic Yorkshire family and was certainly a practising Catholic himself in middle and later life, yet he matriculated at Brasenose in 1662.[96] Similarly, some dissenters were prepared to modify their views sufficiently to take the oaths required at matriculation and so enable them to go forward eventually for a degree, although others took lodgings in the town, engaged tutors, attended disputations in the schools and debated with dons and students in the coffee-houses without becoming members of the university.[97] The sons of royalist gentry had acted in the same way during the 1650s. So many sons of Welsh gentry lodged in a house under the supervision of Francis Mansell, the displaced principal of Jesus, that it became known as the 'little Welsh-Hall', and they evidently kept themselves apart 'mixing as little as possible with those of the university'.[98] The dissenters' academies provided an attractive alternative to the universities, for conformists as well as nonconformists, and some dissenters chose to send their sons to universities in Scotland or on the continent, while many Catholic youths were also educated abroad.[99] The number of potential recruits lost to the

[94] McConica, 'Rise of the undergraduate college', 50–1; P. H. Williams, 'Elizabethan Oxford: state, church and university' in *The Collegiate University*, 427–8; Stone, 'Size and composition', 7; *Laudian Code*, ed. Griffiths, 25–6.

[95] M. Foster, 'Thomas Allen (1540–1632), Gloucester Hall and the survival of Catholicism in post-reformation Oxford', *Oxoniensia* xlvi (1981), 113–18; Wood, *Fasti*, 303; see also N. Briggs, 'William, 2nd Lord Petre (1575–1637)', *Essex Recusant* x (1968), 55.

[96] H. Aveling, 'The Catholic recusants of the West Riding of Yorkshire 1558–1790', *Proceedings of Leeds Philosophical and Literary Society* x (1963), 254.

[97] Edmund Calamy, *An Historical Account of My Own Life*, ed. J. T. Rutt (2 vols London 1829) i. 127–9, 221–4; A. Brockett, *Nonconformity in Exeter 1650–1875* (Manchester 1962), 76. For Henry and Peter Newcome's experiences at Oxford see *The Autobiography of Henry Newcome, M.A.*, ed. R. Parkinson (2 vols Chetham Soc. xxvi–vii 1852) i. 163–4, ii. 210–11, 217–19, 225–6, 232, 236–7. Thomas Martindale received private tuition at Brasenose but did not enter the college, and later his father withdrew him from Oxford and placed him with a tutor in Worcestershire: *The Life of Adam Martindale, Written by Himself*, ed. R. Parkinson (Chetham Soc. iv 1845), 187–8. Peter Birch was educated for four years by a private tutor in Oxford without being admitted to a college; then, on conforming to the Church of England, he entered Christ Church and took his BA and MA within a little over a year of matriculation. See 'Autobiography and anecdotes by William Taswell, D.D., sometime rector of Newington, Surrey, rector of Bermondsey, and previously Student of Christ Church, Oxford, A. D. 1651–1682', ed. G. P. Elliott, *Camden Miscellany* ii (Camden Soc. lv 1853).

[98] William Wynne, *The Life of Sir Leoline Jenkins* (2 vols London 1724) i, p. v. BL Add. MS 27,606 has letters of Sir Sackville Crow when he was a pupil of Mansell's.

[99] I. Parker, *Dissenting Academies in England* (Cambridge 1914), 46–8, 50–1, 56; H. McLachlan, *English Education under the Test Acts, being the history of the non-conformist academies 1662–1820* (Manchester 1931), 17–30; Bossy, *English Catholic Community*, 164–5.

university cannot be estimated, although students from puritan backgrounds had formed a significant part of the influx of the years before the civil war.[100] They can hardly have been so large a group that replacements could not be found from among the overwhelming majority of conformists within the population, assuming their willingness to take up any slack which had developed as a result of the extension of the religious tests. There was disillusion with the universities in some quarters, however, for when the causes of the political and religious upheavals of the 1640s and 1650s came to be examined the finger of culpability, if not of guilt, was pointed at them for training too many graduates, who were both puritan in sympathy and dissatisfied with the established order because such overproduction had caused poor career prospects in the church.[101] There was an inevitable reaction to this apparent cause of the troubles and the remedy was perceived to lie in a loyal, proficient, and respected clergy, preferably recruited from what were regarded as the more dignified sections of society.[102] How directly this ideal could or did affect recruitment to Oxford is uncertain, but it may have had some influence. By the 1680s the university had become associated with tory politics and high church sympathies, a reputation which was likely to deter parents of dissimilar views from sending their children there.[103] The whig families were presumably reluctant to expose their sons to such pernicious influences.[104] Indeed there was an underlying political dimension to Oxford's fluctuating recruitment. Wood regarded the political and religious tensions of James II's reign as a cause of the declining numbers of admissions. In 1687 he noted that scholars were 'frighted away for feare of popery' and the events of the following year produced a particularly small intake of matriculants.[105] As well as parental perceptions of the university's political and religious complexion, there had also been a change in the way in which the benefits of an education at Oxford were viewed. John Fell, the dean of Christ Church, was conscious of this changed attitude which had made a university education less popular and he identified the culprits who were likely to 'disparage and decry' it as 'papists, fanatics, travailed fops, witts, virtuosi, and atheists'. His peevish remarks manifested rather than explained a change that had certainly decreased the demand for an Oxford education.[106]

The relationship between the pattern of admissions to Oxford and these several influences was a complex one and the various sections of society were affected in

---

[100] Wood, *History of the University* ii. 384–5, 421, 424.

[101] Stone, 'Size and composition', 23, 53–5; M. H. Curtis, 'The alienated intellectuals of early Stuart England', *Past & Present* no. 23 (November 1962), 25–43. Curtis's views should be revised in the light of O'Day, *English Clergy*, 17–23, and Green, 'Career prospects and clerical conformity', 71–115.

[102] G. V. Bennett, 'Loyalist Oxford and the revolution' in *The Eighteenth Century*, 12–13; Stone, 'Size and composition', 38–9; J. H. Pruett, *The Parish Clergy under the Later Stuarts: the Leicestershire experience* (Urbana Ill. 1978), 38–9.

[103] Bennett, 'Loyalist Oxford', 9–16.   [104] Wood, *Life and Times* iii. 7.

[105] Ibid. 209. For the reaction of a student's father to the events of 1688 see *The Diary and Letter Book of the Rev. Thomas Brockbank 1671–1709*, ed. R. Trappes-Lomax (Chetham Soc. new ser. lxxxix 1930), 14; see also *The Flemings in Oxford* ii. 236, 241.

[106] Bodl. MS Rawlinson d. 850, fo 267ʳ.

different ways. Some indication of the social background of incoming students comes from the matriculation evidence, for the status at which a student matriculated was theoretically determined by his social rank, with the exception of the sons of the clergy, who constituted an occupational category.[107] No terminological uncertainties should have arisen for the sons of the élite and the similarity of nomenclature between the matriculation categories and the wider social rankings suggests that most students should have had little difficulty in selecting the appropriate grade if they had a clear perception of their father's standing in society. William Trumbull's father removed any possible doubts in his son's mind by sending him instructions about matriculation and a certificate proving his status as an esquire.[108] Others may have been less clearly directed by their parents and Henry Fleming was persuaded by 'some young men'—presumably other students—to enter himself as a pauper's son rather than as an esquire, so that his tutor had to cause the entry to be changed, although only to the still inaccurate status of a gentleman's son.[109] The term esquire was strictly applicable only to the heirs of noblemen's younger sons or of knights, but during the century it gradually came to have a wider usage, although not an indiscriminate one. The title of gentleman also had a theoretical application, to the younger sons and brothers of esquires and their male heirs, yet in practice landed wealth which was adequate to support a particular mode of life conferred gentility and a wider definition extended that rank still further to encompass those who could live without doing any manual labour— essentially the members of the professions. That there was some uncertainty over matriculation status is suggested by the alterations in a few students' rank after a short time at Oxford and the occasional practice of specifying his father's occupation in a student's matriculation entry.[110] The system even permitted clergymen's sons to matriculate under other titles and the clerical category is under-represented by at least 8 per cent as a result.[111] The choice of matriculation grade was evidently not as clear-cut as the terminology would suggest, presumably because the divisions used in society reflected a compound of ill-defined social and economic factors and their usage varied regionally as well as between rural and urban communities.

Some indication of the relationship between matriculation status and social rank is provided by an examination of the proportions of students who attended an Inn of Court. The ability and willingness to send a youth to an Inn as well as to provide for a spell at Oxford was partly a reflection of parental intentions for his future

---

[107] Matriculation status determined the fees payable, which at the end of the period were, for the sons of peers, dukes, marquises £3 6s 8d; earls, barons, bishops £2; baronets £1 6s 8d; deans, archdeacons, the eldest sons of knights £1; the younger sons of knights, esquires, holders of doctorates 10s od; gentlemen and clergymen 5s od; plebeians 2s 6d; for paupers' sons no fee was payable.

[108] Berks. RO Trumbull Add. MS 46, letters 24 August and 11 October 1622.

[109] *The Flemings in Oxford* i. 258.

[110] For example George Jackson, Magdalen College 1637, 'Pharmacop. Gen. Cond.' and James Ingram, All Souls 1625, 'mercatoris gen.': OUA SP2, fos 44ʳ, 67ᵛ.

[111] Based upon the sample years.

career, but it was also indicative of social standing, in being able to secure admission to an Inn, and wealth, given the extra costs involved. Table 1.8 shows that there was a distinct difference between those of esquire and higher rank and those who matriculated as the sons of gentlemen, and an even stronger contrast between those groups and youths from clerical and plebeian backgrounds.[112]

TABLE 1.8
Percentage of each matriculation group going to an Inn of Court

Peer, bt., kt.	Esq.	Gent.	Cleric.	Pleb.	[Paup.]
38	53	29	1	2	[0]

The example of the city of Worcester illustrates the way in which an urban community with a distinctive social profile was represented in the status of its matriculants attending the university. Worcester's economy was based to a great extent upon a thriving cloth industry, the prosperity of which was matched by a considerable growth in population from the late sixteenth century. Its society consisted of a small élite and a group of independent tradesmen, chiefly clothiers, of the middle rank, which together constituted perhaps 20 per cent of the population, and the lesser tradesmen, wage earners and poor, who comprised the remainder.[113] This was reflected in the choice of grades at matriculation, as table 1.9 shows. The correlation was only a relative one, however, for from those cases where the economic standing of the matriculant's father can be identified it is clear that although the plebeians and paupers were the less well-off groups within the student body, their parents were not from among the poorest members of society. Because of variable educational provision, economic means, career motivation, and admission opportunities, the university's intake was restricted to a small proportion of the male population of the city which was not representative of the whole.[114]

TABLE 1.9
Matriculants from Worcester, 1600–89 (%)

Peer, bt., kt.	Esq.	Gent.	Cleric.	Pleb. [paup.]	Total	Number in sample
0	3	20	7	70	100	154

[112] Based upon the sample years. See the tables in Prest, *Inns of Court*, 30 and in Lemmings, 'Student body of the Inns of Court', 152, 154.

[113] A. D. Dyer, *The City of Worcester in the Sixteenth Century* (Leicester 1973), 174–7.

[114] Seven of the twenty-five identified households from which plebeian and pauper students came had one or two hearths in the late 1670s. The proportion for the whole city was 70%. See *The Hearth Tax Collectors' Book for Worcester 1678–1680*, ed. C. A. F. Meekings, S. Porter, and I. Roy (Worcestershire Hist. Soc. new ser. xi 1983), 29.

Status chosen for matriculation determined an individual's standing in student society much less than did his rank within his college or hall where these divisions were of daily significance, marked by the differences in dress, accommodation, dining arrangements, and other privileges applicable to each grade. They were reflected in the charges borne by the students in both admission fees and recurrent expenses. The differences in costs had important attendant social implications; parents were more sensitive to the choice of status in college or hall than they were to the matriculation process.[115] Students were necessarily even more aware of the significance of the student hierarchy and objected if they were entered in a category which they felt undervalued their social rank. Peter Heylin was first entered by his father at Magdalen College as a batteler, not on the grounds of cost, but because his brother, as a commoner at Broadgates Hall, 'had been suffered to take too much liberty'. Peter later wrote that this was 'very much to my discouragement when once I understood the difference' and a year later he was pleased to migrate to Hart Hall as a commoner.[116] Such social sensitivities discouraged students from entering at a lower grade than was consonant with their assumed dignities, while considerations of expense deterred them from joining an unrealistically high one. As a result of the economic and social pressures on both parents and students, colleges' grades probably were linked in general terms to their members' notions of their relative standing in society.

Comparison of college grades and matriculation status shows a strong relationship between them.[117] Two thirds of those who matriculated at esquire or a higher status were fellow-commoners and none entered their society below the level of a commoner. The degree of correlation between commoners and gentlemen's sons was even greater, with 85 per cent of those joining at that status entering the ranks of the commoners. Only 8 per cent of gentlemen's sons lived at the lower grade of batteler and none as servitors. Some plebeians were commoners but the majority, 64 per cent, were battelers and only 10 per cent were servitors, a grade which was filled almost entirely by those who had matriculated as paupers. Indeed virtually all those who matriculated as paupers' sons were admitted to their societies at the lowest grade. Servitor status was generally avoided by clergymen's sons who, with very few exceptions, entered as commoners or battelers, the former slightly outnumbering the latter. Some of the students who passed their undergraduate years as servitors expressed their sense of the indignities and drudgery of such an existence, which suggests that few would have entered that grade if they could have afforded to live at a higher one.[118] That there was such a correlation between matriculation status and the grades in the colleges and halls strengthens

---

[115] *The Correspondence of John Locke*, ed. De Beer i. 201.   [116] Bloxam, *Reg. Magdalen* ii. 50.

[117] Based upon entrants to Balliol, Brasenose, Exeter, Oriel, and Wadham 1660–70: N = 1,061. This incorporates the findings in M. S. Byford, 'Restoration Oxford: a study of the composition of the student body 1660–1670' (Oxford BA thesis 1983), figures 2a and 2b for Oriel and Wadham.

[118] *Diary of Brockbank*, ed. Trappes-Lomax, 42; Eachard, *Grounds and Occasions*, 16–17; *The Flemings in Oxford* i. 235.

the impression that the matriculation categories did reflect real differences in the backgrounds from which the undergraduate population came.

The data shown in table 1.10 are inconsistent in one important respect, for the first four samples are taken from the period when a considerable proportion of the student body did not matriculate and many of those who matriculated did so in order to graduate. The categories of students which produced relatively high percentages of graduates are therefore presumably over-represented in the matriculation record before approximately 1660.[119] The 1663–5 and 1683–5 samples show that this applied to the sons of clergy, plebeians, and paupers and that a much lower proportion of the sons of gentlemen and those of a higher standing took a degree. Only the four samples from after 1660 can give a fairly realistic picture of the composition of the student population. This proviso also affects the interpretation of changes through time, with the further qualification that the matriculation terminology may not have been applied consistently over this period of 110 years; thus, for example, the decline of the plebeian and pauper categories towards the end of the seventeenth century could reflect a greater unwillingness to matriculate at those levels and not a real change in the social background from which the students came. This is suggested by the increasing frequency with which former pupils of Christ's Hospital entered Oxford as commoners rather than servitors, despite the financial hardship such a step entailed, and some of the beneficiaries of its scholarships matriculated as gentlemen's sons.[120] Such considerations alter the apparent pattern somewhat. Assuming that the true proportion of those of esquire and higher status is understated in the earlier samples then those categories experienced a greater relative decline than table 1.10 shows and that at a time when the term esquire was being more widely applied. Similarly, the low proportions of gentlemen during the years of high student admissions are perhaps illusory and reflect a comparatively low propensity to take a degree and their ability to avoid matriculation. The latter part of the century shows some stability between the various categories, although there was a steady increase in the proportion of those entering as sons of gentlemen and a sharp rise in the percentage of clergymen's sons by its close, with an apparently corresponding decline in those admitted as plebeians and paupers. By the 1680s the combined intake of those matriculating as sons of gentlemen and clergy had come to outnumber the plebeians and paupers. The samples for the period after the Restoration indicate that those classified as esquires and of higher status had ceased to decline relative to the size of the other groups.

Uncertainties respecting the matriculation evidence also occur in respect of the ages which were entered. Because of genuine doubts about their age, faulty memories, deliberate falsification in order to qualify for age-specific scholarships and exhibitions, or perhaps even to avoid the religious tests, 15 per cent of matricu-

[119] Stone, 'Size and composition', 13, 28.

[120] Ibid. 14, 37; Guildhall Lib. MS 12806/7, p. 127. By the early years of the eighteenth century it was said that those who would have entered as commoners a generation earlier were entering as gentlemen-commoners: Northants. RO D (CA) 354/51.

TABLE 1.10
Status at matriculation (%)

	Peer, bt, kt	Esq.	Gent.	Cleric.	Pleb. [paup.]	Total	Number in sample
1590–2	2	13	30	3	51	99	811
1605–7	11	17	30	10	32	100	869
1616–18	7	16	21	12	44	100	1,088
1630–2	7	11	18	18	46	100	1,054
1663–5	6	10	24	14	46 [22]	100	1,156
1674–6	7	9	28	13	44 [22]	101	1,118
1683–5	6	10	31	13	40 [20]	100	911
1697–9	6	9	32	21	32 [13]	100	892

lants gave ages which were in error by more than ± one year.[121] A further deficiency in the evidence arises because the age entered was that which was attained during the scholastic year of matriculation and so during the period when matriculation was delayed for a variable time after admission it does not represent a student's age when he entered the university. The median age for the years 1630–2 is therefore somewhat higher than it is for the other three sample groups of years, for which matriculation and admission ages may be taken to be generally synonymous.[122] A small and declining number of matriculants were aged under 13, half of them being of esquire or higher status. At the other end of the age-range only 2 per cent matriculated at 21 or over. Their subsequent careers at the university were similar to those of the student body as a whole and there is no reason to suppose that they were other than relatively mature students who had earlier lacked the opportunity or means to enter Oxford.[123] Table 1.11 shows that the greatest concentration was in the 16- to 18-year-old age-group and that the proportion of students matriculating in that range was three quarters in both of the samples from after the Restoration.

TABLE 1.11
Age distribution of matriculants (%)

Age	1605–7	1663–5	1683–5
<15	8.7	3.5	2.3
15	16.5	9.3	9.3
16	17.1	26.8	22.1
17	20.7	28.8	28.4
18	18.8	20.4	23.8
19	10.5	8.0	9.5
>19	7.7	3.2	4.6
	100.0	100.0	100.0
Number in sample	870	1,138	850
Unknown	0	23	61
Median age in years			
All students	16.9	16.9	17.2
Peer, bt, kt, esq.	15.9	16.4	16.9
Pleb., paup.	17.5	17.1	17.6

[121] Based upon a comparison of birth/baptism dates and matriculants' ages in 295 cases; two thirds of those in error underestimated their true age. See also *Bodleian Library Record* ii (1944), 93.

[122] The median age for 1630–2 is 17.9 years. Students gave their age at matriculation, not that at their admission to a college or hall.

[123] Clarendon alleged that 'those lubberly fellows, who come from great schools after they are nineteen or twenty years of age . . . bring their debauchery with them' and that youths should be no more than 16 when they went from grammar schools to university: *A Collection of Several Tracts of the Right Honourable Earl of Clarendon* (London 1727), 319, 323.

The median ages changed little during the period with only a modest rise by 1683–5.[124] The ages of students who matriculated as sons of esquires and of superior status were lower than the overall figure. A majority of the students from these categories did not intend to take a degree and could go to university with a lower level of intellectual attainment than those who planned to graduate. Moreover, students from wealthier families had access to a choice of educational facilities during childhood, both in terms of the schools available to them and perhaps instruction by private tutors, and so could achieve the standard expected of them while relatively young. For some parents it was a matter of pride that a son was equipped for university at an early age. John Evelyn was pleased to enter his eldest son at Trinity when he was barely 12 as one 'prompt to learne beyond most of his age'.[125] The practice of sending brothers to Oxford together—for companionship and to reduce the costs of accommodation by sharing a chamber—may have tended to lower the age of matriculation slightly because the younger ones were thereby entered comparatively early.[126] Overall 2 per cent of matriculants arrived at Oxford with an elder brother; almost two thirds of them were the sons of esquires of a higher rank, but less than 9 per cent were plebeians and none matriculated as paupers. Less well-off parents could not afford to prepare two sons to the required level of education at the same time or to maintain them at university simultaneously, whatever economies could be achieved. The median ages of those matriculating as plebeians and paupers were higher than the overall medians throughout the period. Youths from plebeian backgrounds commonly had to attend their local grammar school for two or three years once it had been established that they would be able to benefit from a university education and could find adequate support to go to Oxford. They were, therefore, somewhat older than the sons of wealthier parents by the time that they were ready for university. The example of Thomas Hollister, the son of a dairyman, suggests that they may also have had greater difficulty in gaining admission. His schoolmaster first attempted to enter him at St Edmund Hall in the spring of 1672 but only two or three servitors were taken in annually and no place was then available, nor could a vacancy be found for him at Hart Hall. Hollister was presumably unable to afford to enter at a higher status and lacked an introduction to the other halls and colleges and so was obliged to wait for two years before he was admitted at St Edmund Hall. He was then 18, although he had been suited for entry when he was 16. Similarly, enquiries about a place for John Glasbrook were first made in the summer of 1682

---

[124] Median figures have been calculated taking age at matriculation to be within ±0.5 of the given figure. For ages see Stone, 'Size and composition', 29–33, 57, 88–90, 97, 99. The median figures given there should be revised in the light of L. Stone, 'The age of admission to college in seventeenth-century England', *History of Education* ix (1980), 97–9.

[125] *The Diary of John Evelyn*, ed. E. S. De Beer (6 vols Oxford 1955) iii. 474. He was then too young to matriculate and hence was 13 when he did so fifteen months after his admission.

[126] Based upon the sample years. The median age for younger brothers of 15.3 years in the fifty-five cases indicates that this was the normal pattern, rather than a delay in sending the elder son.

but he did not enter Wadham as a servitor for another two years, matriculating in July 1684 as a pauper's son aged 17.[127]

Place of origin had a considerable bearing upon the selection of a college or hall, indeed on the choice of university. Oxford was the more convenient university for youths from counties on the western side of the country and connections of long standing had developed between such counties and the university. The south-west, southern England, the west midlands, Wales, and the area around Oxford supplied two thirds of the students who attended the university during the seventeenth century. Devon was the most important single county supplying recruits and was the origin of 9 per cent of matriculants. London was also a major source and was second only to Devon throughout the period. The London figures include those who had gone there to school or whose fathers lived partly in the provinces but also had residences in the capital for social or professional reasons. Movement away from a father's address to attend school or for another reason may cause a slight distortion in the figures for place of origin as it is inconsistently recorded in the matriculation registers. In the sample years 1630–2 it applied to only 6 per cent of matriculants and the information is not entered for the other samples. Comparatively few travelled far and such migration was generally over short distances, to a grammar school in a nearby market or county town and perhaps not outside the boy's own county; although a few would have gone further afield, to such schools as Eton and Winchester. Table 1.12 shows the regional distribution of matriculants and demonstrates that very few students arrived at Oxford from outside England and Wales. Scotland and Ireland had their own universities and supplied very few matriculants, and by 1683–5 these were outnumbered by those from the Channel Islands (all of whom went to Pembroke) and the West Indies.[128]

The connections between localities and the colleges had arisen chiefly through endowments. The terms by which some colleges had been founded and scholarships and fellowships endowed included the stipulation that some of the beneficiaries of the donor's generosity should be from a particular county, place, or school, perhaps with the additional qualification that preference should be given to their kindred or those with their surname. Thus two scholarships founded by Lewes Owen were tenable at Jesus by boys from Beaumaris school, preferably his own kin 'if any be found fit'.[129] Among the many such connections between schools and colleges were those between William of Wykeham's foundations at Winchester and New College, between Reading and the Merchant Taylor's school and St John's according to the terms of Sir Thomas White's gift, and between Abingdon school and Pembroke as established by Thomas Tesdale. Archbishop Grindal's endowment of two scholarships from the school which he had founded

---

[127] Bodl. MS top. Oxon. f. 31, pp. 19–20, 55, 146, 165, 167. Hollister matriculated 29 May 1674: Foster, *Alumni* ii. 733. Six servitors entered Wadham in 1684: *The Registers of Wadham College, Oxford*, ed. R. B. Gardiner (2 vols London 1889–95) i. 399–41.

[128] The Morley exhibitions at Pembroke provided for students from the Channel Islands: Macleane, *Pembroke*, 285–6.

[129] J. B. Squibb, *Founder's Kin* (London 1972), 141.

TABLE 1.12

Regional origins of matriculants (%)

	1603–5	1683–5
Local (Berks., Bucks., Oxon.)	9.7	9.8
South-west (Cornwall, Devon, Som.)	18.8	16.0
West midlands (Bristol, Gloucs., Herefordshire, Shropshire, Staffs., Warwicks., Worcs.)	15.8	19.4
South (Dorset, Hants., Wilts.)	13.8	12.1
South-east (Kent, Surrey, Sussex)	5.6	4.9
East Anglia (Beds., Cambs., Essex, Herts., Hunts., Norfolk, Suffolk)	1.9	2.0
East midlands (Derby., Leics., Lincs., Northants., Notts., Rutland)	6.1	6.3
North-east (Durham, Northumb., Yorks.)	4.2	3.3
North-west (Ches., Cumberland, Lancs., Westmorland)	7.1	7.5
Metropolitan (London, Middx.)	7.8	6.5
Wales (inc. Monmouth.)	8.5	10.2
Others (Channel Is., France, Ireland, Isle of Man, Scotland, W. Indies)	0.7	2.0
	100.0	100.0
Number	857	857
Unknown	12	54

at St Bees in Cumberland to Queen's is, like Owen's, an example of an attempt to give poor youths from a small town direct access to the university.[130] It was difficult to fill scholarships which were too specific because of the limited numbers from which suitable applicants could be drawn and so it was the normal practice for a donor to specify alternative schools or places from which the beneficiaries could be nominated. The Radcliffe scholarships at Brasenose were to be awarded to candidates from Steeple Aston School in Oxfordshire, Rochdale and Middleton schools in Lancashire, or any unpreferred undergraduates in the college, strictly in that order of priority.[131] In practice it was the final clause which was applied on each of the fourteen occasions when the scholarship was awarded before 1690 and only two Lancashire youths, and none from Oxfordshire, obtained the award. Regional concentration at colleges was, on the one hand, reinforced by the continued provision of such scholarships if suitable candidates could be found and by

[130] Andrew Willet, *Synopsis papismi* (London 1592, 5th edn London 1634), 1223.
[131] A. J. Butler, 'The benefactions bestowed on the college', *Brasenose Monographs* i, no. IV, pp. 23–4.

a parental inclination to send their sons to an institution where they would be with others from their own region while, on the other hand, it was weakened by those who wished to avoid this aspect for social reasons. Thus, although most Welsh students went to Jesus, there was an increasing tendency for the gentry families of Wales to send their sons to other colleges rather than to the one attended by their plebeian countrymen.[132]

For these reasons there were marked connections between, most notably, Jesus College and Wales, Exeter College and Devon and Cornwall, Queen's and Cumberland and Westmorland, Brasenose and Cheshire and Lancashire, University College and Yorkshire, and Lincoln College and that diocese.[133] Only in the first two of these cases did students from the region specified actually constitute a majority of the matriculants at the colleges concerned throughout the seventeenth century, although this also applied at Brasenose by the end of the period. Virtually the whole of Jesus's intake was from Wales and Monmouthshire, but fewer than 60 per cent of Welshmen at Oxford were at that college. Two thirds of the students at Exeter College came from Devon and Cornwall, representing slightly more than half of the students from those counties at Oxford. The proportion of Cheshire and Lancashire students who went to a single college—Brasenose—was rather higher; two thirds at the beginning of the period, when they were outnumbered within the college by matriculants from elsewhere, and almost three quarters at the end of it, by which time they constituted a slight majority of new admissions to Brasenose. Almost all students from Cumberland and Westmorland went to Queen's, but they were in a minority within the college. Other connections can be identified which were numerically less strong. Magdalen Hall was consistently popular with youths from Wiltshire, for example. New endowments brought about changes in local allegiances. Youths from the King's School at Worcester were sent to Christ Church until the late 1660s, but thereafter, by the terms of John Meeke's will, they went to Magdalen Hall.[134] In the early part of the century Exeter was the most popular college for students from Somerset, but after the foundation of Wadham that college became their commonest destination. Similarly, almost a half of Broadgate Hall's recruits in 1605–7 were from Devon, yet by the end of the period no matriculant at Pembroke, its successor college, was from that county. The matriculation records may not be an entirely accurate guide to the effect of regionalism because students who were already at the university could migrate to another institution to take advantage of geographically specific scholarships. Of all holders of scholarships at Brasenose between 1670 and 1689, 10 per cent had

[132] P. Jenkins, *The Making of a Ruling Class: the Glamorgan gentry 1640–1790* (Cambridge 1983), 224. Thomas Myddelton entered Oriel despite a plea that Jesus had 'the best gentry of south Wales' and that students from north Wales would 'faire the worse, if . . . the best of the country' did not go to the college: *Chirk Castle Accounts 1605–1666*, ed. Myddelton, 27–8.

[133] This discussion is based upon the matriculation evidence.

[134] *Documents illustrating Early Education in Worcester 685 to 1700*, ed. A. F. Leach (Worcestershire Hist. Soc. 1913), pp. lxxvi, 307–8, 314, 321. Between 1622 and 1689 Christ Church, Magdalen Hall, and Pembroke took just over half of the students from Worcester (80 out of 152).

matriculated at another society.[135] Such scholarships could be the objects of intense competition and even financial inducements. None the less some scholarships did reach the genuinely needy students for which they were designed. An example of the way in which the county–college link worked is provided by the case of Adam Parkinson of Leigh in Lancashire. His suitability for a university education was brought to the attention of some local gentry, presumably by his schoolmaster, and they sent him to Sir William Dugdale in Warwickshire, the grandson of a Clitheroe man, asking him to exploit his connections at Oxford on the boy's behalf. In April 1682 Dugdale directed him to Anthony Wood and he was entered at Brasenose in June, securing a Nowell scholarship, designed for Lancashire boys, the following November.[136]

In addition to those exhibitions and places that were specific to a particular school, place, or county and were tenable only at a nominated college, there were many which imposed no such restrictions upon their holders and could be held at any college, even at either of the universities. Students benefiting from such awards and those who did not require such financial support, at least at the outset, were theoretically free to choose their college or hall. Parents could make this choice by seeking a society of which they had some knowledge, either by repute or experience, or by taking the advice of clergy, schoolmasters, relatives, and friends. Penton recommended that parents should not elect to send their sons to a particular college or hall because its head was well known, or withhold them from another on the grounds that 'a vicious debauched person' had been there.[137] Some of the fluctuations in the numbers admitted at the colleges and halls can be attributed to changing perceptions of their relative merits both within the university and outside it. Although there was no shortage of those who were willing to offer an opinion the difficulty for parents was to obtain unbiased advice.[138] In many cases they already had a contact with a society through a relative, friend, or parish priest who was prepared to make an approach on their behalf, in others they personally knew someone at Oxford who they could ask or to whom they could entrust the placing of their son.[139] Some students were entered by their patrons at their own former college or hall, where their influence was naturally strongest. Sheldon, archbishop of Canterbury, and Dolben, when a prebendary of St Paul's, placed youths

[135] *Reg. Brasenose* i. 224–57.

[136] Bodl. MS Wood f. 41, fo 155ʳ; *Reg. Brasenose* i. 246; Wood, *Life and Times* iii. 12.

[137] Penton, *Guardian's Instruction*, 41.

[138] For Humphrey Prideaux's advice to his brother-in-law in 1696 in favour of Wadham see HMC *Fifth Report*, appx, p. 374. William Trumbull was advised to send his son to Merton although he had already decided to enter him at Magdalen and subsequently did so: Berks. RO Trumbull Add. MS 46, letter 21 June 1622.

[139] Nathaniel Freind had contacts with the principal and vice-principal of St Edmund Hall and so entered his son there in 1672 and later recommended it as a suitable society for his cousin's son, but the youth went to Wadham: Bodl. MS top. Oxon. f. 31, pp. 10–12, 193; Bodl. Ms Eng. letters e. 29, fo 173ʳ. Distant relatives approached Thomas Ellis at Jesus in 1662 and John Locke twenty years later for advice and help in choosing a college: *A Calendar of Letters relating to North Wales 1533—circa 1700*, ed. B. E. Howells (Board of Celtic Studies xxiii Cardiff 1967), 121; *The Correspondence of John Locke*, ed. De Beer ii. 520, 551–2.

at Trinity and Christ Church.[140] Others entered the societies of which their fathers had been members when they were at Oxford, although Penton thought that a college or hall should not be selected solely on the grounds that the prospective student's father had attended it.[141] In fact only one third of students whose fathers had themselves studied at the university entered their former college or hall and there was continuity over three generations in just over one fifth of identified cases.[142] The father–son connection was naturally strongest at the colleges with the most heavily regionalized intake, but only at Jesus was the proportion greater than a half. Those students whose brothers had preceded them to the university also had a contact with a society. Some brothers entered the university together or within a year of each other and in all but 8 per cent of such cases they were admitted to the same college or hall. Of the remainder, however, only 53 per cent of those whose brother or brothers had earlier been admitted at Oxford went to their society.[143] More distant family connections are harder to trace, but some indication of contemporary attitudes comes from the opinion of Julius Deedes in 1678 that it was desirable that his son and nephew should be at different colleges.[144] Previous attendance at a society by a close relative was apparently not an especially strong influence upon the choice of a college or hall.

One factor which influenced the choice of society for members of the social élite was that they constituted a small minority of students, fewer than 3 per cent of all matriculants between 1650 and 1689.[145] There was a desire among their parents for them to be with youths of their own quality for companionship, to avoid the isolation, loneliness, and boredom which their preferential treatment within the colleges was likely to engender and bearing in mind that they were commonly younger than the majority of students. There was also the need for accommodation of suitable quality and scale, perhaps with provision for personal servants.[146] The parents of the élite were in a position to exercise considerable control over the choice of tutor for their sons and were likely to seek the advice of others of their rank whose sons had attended the university in the recent past. For these reasons students from the élite were concentrated in relatively few colleges; between 1650 and 1689 almost 30 per cent of them matriculated at Christ Church and a further 27 per cent at

[140] Bodl. MS Add. c. 308, fo 23ᵛ; *The Correspondence of John Locke*, ed. De Beer i. 179–80.

[141] Penton, *Guardian's Instruction*, 41.

[142] Based upon initial letters AB, LMN, TUVW in Foster, *Alumni*. Figures from these samples and from the sample years suggest that only one in twelve of matriculants' fathers had also been to Oxford, but for 1663–5 and 1683–5 the proportion is slightly higher at one in nine. Because of the incompleteness of the matriculation record and the problems of positive identification these are certainly underestimates of the true proportions.

[143] Based upon the samples as in the foregoing note. John Evelyn's brother at Trinity persuaded their father to send John to another college, anticipating difficulties in obtaining a suitable tutor for him at Trinity, and so he was entered at Balliol: *The Diary of John Evelyn*, ed. De Beer i. 13.

[144] Bodl. MS Add. d. 105, fo 63ʳ.

[145] Élite is taken here to be the sons of peers, dukes, marquises, earls, barons, and bishops.

[146] HMC *Ormonde MSS* new ser. iv. 318. William Herricke, fellow-commoner at St John's in 1613, initially had nobody to converse with at table: Bodl. MS Eng. hist. c. 481, fo 34ʳ. See p. 39 above.

Trinity, Queen's, and Magdalen College.[147] Such concentration affected the profile of the student body of those colleges and especially that of Christ Church, which took 25 per cent of the élite who matriculated in the 1650s and 1660s and 33 per cent in the following two decades. In the 1670s such students constituted 14 per cent of its matriculants. This reflects the efforts of Dean Fell who assiduously cultivated his wide range of contacts among those members of the élite whose sons were almost ready for university, encouraging them to send the youths to Christ Church, reassuring them that suitable tutoring and accommodation were available and promising a personal interest in their sons' welfare.[148] In contrast, at eleven colleges and halls students from the élite constituted fewer than 1 per cent of matriculants.

TABLE 1.13

Members of the élite as a percentage of all matriculants, 1650–89

%	Ranked lowest → highest
0	Gloucester Hall, Hart Hall
0.1–0.9	Pembroke, New Inn Hall, St Alban Hall, All Souls, Balliol, Merton, New College, Magdalen Hall, St Edmund Hall
1.0–2.9	St Mary Hall, Exeter, Jesus, Lincoln, Brasenose, Corpus Christi, Wadham, St John's
3.0–4.9	University, Oriel, Queen's, Trinity
>5.0	Magdalen College, Christ Church

Other factors which served to attract or repel would-be students were those of cost, discipline, and religious orientation. The expense of a spell at Oxford varied between the student categories within the colleges and halls, but also among the various societies, and many parents may have been concerned to select as inexpensive an institution as possible for their sons. Nevertheless they could probably do no more than gain a general impression on the matter and accept whatever opinions were offered them, which may not have been particularly accurate. In 1690 Dean Aldrich claimed to the father of a prospective student that Christ Church was the cheapest college 'as to necessary expense' and a few years later Trinity was said to be the most expensive.[149] Another concern was the quality of the tutoring, both in respect of teaching and of discipline.[150] Riotous behaviour by the students of a college could gain it an unfavourable reputation which might deter

---

[147] This is roughly the same pattern as in the early seventeenth century although the deficiencies of the matriculation record preclude the production of comparable figures.

[148] HMC *Ormonde MSS* new ser. iv. 292, 318–19, 325; Northants. RO IC 842, 845, 850, 4777, 4785; *Letters of Prideaux*, ed. Thompson, 21.

[149] Surrey RO Guildford Muniment Room, Midleton MS 1248/1/233; Northants. RO D (CA) 354/51.

[150] Berks. RO Trumbull Add. MS 46, letter 21 June 1622.

some parents from sending their sons there and internal disputes within a society may have had a similar, albeit temporary, effect. Despite the activities of some of Exeter's students—such as their brawling with those of other houses—which caused the college to be regarded as an ill-disciplined one, it nevertheless maintained its position as one of the largest in the university.[151] Wadham, by contrast, had the reputation of being a well-governed society in the 1690s, with 'a very good sett' of fellows.[152] Opinions could be obtained respecting the relative merits of any society, but they were almost invariably partial and may not have been very influential. Some parents were at least equally concerned with a society's religious complexion. New Inn Hall and Magdalen Hall were regarded as having a strong puritan element in their character before the civil war, while Gloucester Hall contained a substantial minority of Catholics in the first quarter of the century.[153] Such reputations were often based upon the affiliations of the head and some senior members, rather than upon a unanimity of religious or ideological opinions within a society, and a student could be allocated to a tutor of amenable views if his parents so wished.[154]

Choice of tutor was agreed to be of almost paramount importance, for his role had become a crucial one, overseeing his students' instruction, finances, religious observance, and general conduct and deportment. He acted, indeed, *in loco parentis*.[155] Tutors were commonly, although not invariably, fellows of the college and at the halls the head, his deputy or others appointed by him, usually from among the members of MA rank.[156] For those parents who knew of a suitable man this was likely to be the determining factor in their choice of college and hall.[157] Others sought advice on the matter before sending their son to Oxford and perhaps asked intermediaries to try to secure the services of the recommended person.[158] This was not always successful and an alternative approach was to select a particular society and then to ask its head to allocate a suitable tutor, perhaps thereby plac-

---

[151] *The Correspondence of John Locke*, ed. De Beer i. 61–2 describes a battle between students from Christ Church and Corpus. For Exeter see W. K. Stride, *Exeter College* (London 1900), 71–2, 79–80; W. D. Christie, *A Life of Anthony Ashley Cooper, First Earl of Shaftesbury* (2 vols London 1871) i. 16–17; *The Diary of Thomas Crosfield, M.A., D.B., Fellow of Queen's College, Oxford*, ed. F. S. Boas (London 1935), 10.

[152] HMC *Fifth Report*, appx, p. 374.

[153] Wood, *History of the University* ii. 421, 424; C. M. Chavasse, 'St. Peter's Hall', *VCH Oxon.* iii. 337; Foster, 'Thomas Allen', 107–16; Wood, *Life and Times* i. 465; Daniel and Barker, *Worcester College*, 97–101.

[154] Societies regarded as representing a particular ideological stance attracted those whose views were contrary, in later life at least: Stride, *Exeter College*, 55–6; M. Stieg, *Laud's Laboratory: the diocese of Bath and Wells in the early seventeenth century* (London 1982), 80.

[155] Stone, 'Social control and intellectual excellence', 6–12; Penton, *Guardian's Instruction*, 41; *The Private Memoirs of John Potenger Esq.*, ed. C. W. Bingham (London 1841), 2; McConica, 'Elizabethan Oxford', 693–5.

[156] At Brasenose a decree of 1576 ruled that tutors had to be fellows: E. de Villiers, 'Brasenose College', *VCH Oxon.* iii. 209.

[157] Bodl. MS top. Oxon. f. 31, pp. 10–12.

[158] Bodl. MS Add. c. 308, fos 23ᵛ, 78ʳ, MS Eng. letters e. 29, fo 173ʳ, MS Ballard 3, fo 8ʳ; BNCA B2a. 38, pp. 8–12. HMC *Fifth Report*, appx, p. 374 provides examples of intermediaries assisting with students' admissions.

ing him under some obligation regarding the student's progress.[159] This course of action had to be followed by those without a contact at Oxford. The system gave the head a considerable degree of power within the society, for he could favour some tutors by allocating rooms and students to them and penalize the influence and incomes of others by not assigning pupils to their care.[160] Because of the patronage at the disposal of the parents of some students—and that which would accrue to such students in the future—the allocation of pupils to a tutor could also have long-term consequences for his career.[161] As a result of such considerations and promises made to reassure their parents the head or his deputy tended to undertake the supervision of the noblemen and fellow-commoners, leaving that of the other categories of student to the younger tutors.[162] For those who were to act as servitors the nature of the choice was rather different for their entrance to a society was a consequence of their arrangements with the students for whom they were to act and so they were not entirely free to choose which society they were to attend or the tutor who was to supervise them.[163]

A student's relationship with his tutor was, therefore, an important influence on his time at Oxford. First reactions to both the university and tutor were generally favourable. It was part of the tutor's role to provide a helping hand to youths who found themselves in the unfamiliar and perhaps bewildering situation of university life. The relationship between them may have been helped by the fact that tutors were commonly not a great deal older than their pupils and had themselves experienced life as a student in the relatively recent past. One third of students arriving at Oxford were assigned to a tutor who was under 25 years old and a further third to one who was aged 25 to 29; only 9 per cent had a tutor of over 40 at their first admission.[164] At Jesus in midsummer term 1684 five of the seven tutors were under 30 and they were among the six most junior fellows in the college.[165] Such relative inexperience may have made those tutors anxious to create a good

---

[159] At Christ Church in 1690 Dean Aldrich allocated Charles Boyle to Francis Atterbury: Surrey RO Guildford Muniment Room, Midleton MS 1248/1/233. For Thomas Barlow's promise to provide a suitable tutor at Queen's in 1670 see HMC *Lonsdale MSS*, 94.

[160] At Christ Church in 1650 it was ordered that 'none shall be tutors in this house but such as shall be approved of by the deane': CA D&C i. b. 3, p. 24. For the economic effects which Dean Fell's patronage had upon Taswell at Christ Church see 'William Taswell', ed. Elliott, 23–8. In 1690 John Hall, master of Pembroke, was alleged to have used his authority in this respect to deprive fellows of pupils: Bodl. MS Ballard 49, fos 137ʳ, 138ᵛ. See too Stone, 'Social control and intellectual excellence', 11.

[161] Lord Somers recommended his former tutor at Trinity as chaplain to the archbishop of Canterbury: W. L. Sachse, *Lord Somers: a political portrait* (Manchester 1975), 7.

[162] *Reg. Exeter*, p. ciii.

[163] Andrew Clark, writing about Balliol, distinguished between the admission of a student of independent means and the reception by the college of a student servitor: Bodl. MS top. Oxon. e. 124/7, fo 3ᵛ. Peter Foulkes entered Christ Church in 1668 as Sir Thomas Myddelton's servitor, but servitors were also admitted independently of other students to carry out general duties, as at Queen's in 1662: *Chirk Castle Accounts A. D. 1666–1753*, ed. W. Myddelton (Manchester 1931), 79; Bodl. MS Rawlinson letters 52, fos 353ʳ, 356ʳ.

[164] Based upon a sample of students for whom the tutor at first admission is known: N = 139.

[165] Bodl. MS DD Jesus College b. 103. College fellows are listed in E. G. Hardy, *Jesus College* (London 1899), 238–41.

impression, especially when dealing with youths from a higher social background than their own.[166] In many cases the initial rapport developed into a satisfactory relationship and the student benefited from the friendly supervision and teaching which his tutor provided.[167] Some personality clashes were inevitable, however, with the relations between tutor and pupil becoming strained as the latter matured and widened the circle of his acquaintances within the university. Some students found their tutors neglectful, perhaps preoccupied by college or incumbency matters, or suspected a degree of antagonism towards themselves, while tutors could become dissatisfied with a pupil's lack of discipline and endeavour, or dismayed by his limited intellect.[168] There was an increasing tendency for a few college fellows with good reputations for their tutorial ability to take charge of large numbers of pupils which may have left some of their students feeling isolated.[169] In 1682–5 Jonathan Edwards, vice-principal of Jesus, supervised between nine and twenty-two students each quarter, almost 38 per cent of the students who were in residence, although nine other fellows also acted as tutors during the period. By the beginning of the following decade John Wynne had become the most popular tutor in the college, taking 48 per cent of the students and frequently having more than twenty in his charge.[170] James Parkinson was such a popular tutor at Lincoln that he was said to have had 'many more pupils than all the rest of the fellows put together'. Ralph Eaton at Brasenose may be a more representative example, with an average of nine students in his care 1659–62 and never more than fourteen in one term.[171] Parents feared that a tutor who was in charge of too many students could not exercise proper supervision over his pupils, an anxiety expressed by one father who requested 'a tutor that is not over run with pupills' who would therefore be able to take 'an especiall care' of his son.[172] Feelings of isolation were enhanced by the practice of some tutors of assigning their teaching duties to young graduates who needed an income to tide them over the financially difficult period between their BA and MA—reducing the contact between them and their pupils

[166] See the reactions of Thomas Lynford (Corpus 1675) and Roger Altham (Christ Church 1676): Northants. RO IC 942; BL Add. MS 46,953, fo 72ʳ.

[167] John Freind, William Trumbull, George Radcliffe, and Edward Harley all had praise for their tutors: Bodl. MS top. Oxon. f. 31, p. 164; Berks. RO Trumbull misc. corr. vol. L, no. 36; *Life of Radcliffe*, ed. Whitaker, 48; *Letters of the Lady Brilliana Harley*, ed. T. T. Lewis (Camden Soc. lviii 1853), 54.

[168] For students' dissatisfaction with their tutors see: *Diary of Brockbank*, ed. Trappes-Lomax, 29, 31–2, 58–63; *The Diary of John Evelyn*, ed. De Beer i. 13, ii. 17; *Autobiography of Thomas Raymond and Memoirs of the Family of Guise of Elmore, Gloucestershire*, ed. G. Davies (Camden Soc. 3rd ser. xxviii 1917), 116; *Diaries and Letters of Philip Henry, M.A. of Broad Oak, Flintshire A. D. 1631–1696*, ed. M. H. Lee (London 1882), 12. For tutors' remarks on their pupils' intellectual failings see: R. Lodge, 'The college under the later Stuarts', *Brasenose Monographs* ii pt 1, no. XII, pp. 60–4; BL Add. MS 46,956A, fo 7ʳ; *The Letter-Book of Sir John Eliot (1625–1632)*, ed. A. B. Grosart (privately printed 1882), 171. Brian Twyne whipped and abused a pupil at Corpus, 1604–5: Bodl. MS Rawlinson d. 47, fo 55ʳ.

[169] Stone, 'Social control and intellectual excellence', 14–16.

[170] Bodl. MS DD Jesus College b. 103.

[171] Bodl. MS Add. d. 105, fo 79ʳ; Wood, *Athenae*, iv. 571; BNCA MS 85. For Thomas Chambers at Balliol see Henry Savage, *Balliofergus, or a commentary upon the foundation, founders and affaires, of Balliol Colledge* (Oxford 1668), 118.

[172] Bodl. MS Ballard 3, fo 8.

even more.[173] Towards the end of this period there was an attempt to formalize this practice and reduce the burden on busy tutors by introducing such students as under-tutors to assist in the task of supervision, but as their employment raised tuition costs by 50 per cent they seem to have been assigned only to the wealthier categories of students.[174] It was not unusual for an undergraduate to gravitate to another fellow or an older student within his society with whom he felt at ease to obtain advice, instruction, and companionship, even if he found his own tutor satisfactory.[175] In those cases where the relationship between pupil and tutor had seriously deteriorated the student could be assigned to another tutor. Such formal transfers sometimes followed complaints by the student, his parents, or perhaps by the tutor. Generally, however, they occurred because the tutor had left the university or had died.[176] Fellowships were held for an average of ten or eleven years and almost one fifth were retained for fewer than five years, which made it quite likely that a student would lose his first tutor for this reason, especially if he remained in residence to take a degree.[177]

During the sixteenth century the tutor's role in the instruction of undergraduates had gradually increased in importance until it had come to have a central place in their university education.[178] Tutors directed their pupils' studies and personally taught them in their rooms as additional instruction to the formal lectures and disputations. This made the choice of tutor all the more important because some tutors almost completely abrogated their teaching responsibilities. Thomas Hood recalled that his tutor 'sildome read to me' during his time at Trinity just before the civil war, and George Evelyn's tutor, a few years earlier, was 'more zealous and religious, than industrious to improve his pupils in academik studys'.[179] Others were conscientious, reading to their students in both morning and afternoon and perhaps accompanying them to the disputations.[180] The curriculum could be adapted to their students' needs. George Percival's studies were more or less of his own choosing and in his final undergraduate year his tutor was concentrating his reading entirely on his selected subject of anatomy.[181] The programme of study

---

[173] McConica, 'Elizabethan Oxford', 694; Bodl. MS Rawlinson d. 912, fos 4ʳ, 15ᵛ.

[174] Both Charles Boyle (Christ Church 1690–4) and Halliday Mildmay (Balliol 1690–1) were assigned under-tutors: Surrey RO Guildford Muniment Room, Midleton MSS 1248/1/233, 238; Hants. RO 15M50/1682, fos 3ʳ, 24ᵛ.

[175] BL Add. MS 46,956A, fo 23ᵛ; Berks. RO Trumbull misc. corr. vol. L, no. 43; *The Diary of John Evelyn*, ed. De Beer i. 13, ii. 17–18; *Diaries and Letters of Henry*, ed. Lee, 12. William Wake found congenial assistance when in 1675 his tutor at Christ Church became ill: N. Sykes, *William Wake, Archbishop of Canterbury 1657–1737* (2 vols Cambridge 1957) i. 10.

[176] *Autobiography of Newcombe*, ed. Parkinson ii. 211; BNCA B2a. 38, p. 11; *The Flemings in Oxford* ii. 257–8, 261; *Letters of Brilliana Harley*, ed. Lewis, 54–5. Daniel Finch's tutor, who left Christ Church in 1666, was permitted to nominate his successor: HMC *Finch MSS* i. 409, 414.

[177] Based upon fellowships commenced 1600–29 and 1670–99 at Brasenose, Exeter, Magdalen College, Lincoln, Oriel and Wadham: N = 1,014.

[178] Stone, 'Size and composition', 25–6; Stone, 'Social control and intellectual excellence', 6–12.

[179] Bodl. MS Ballard 49, fo 172r; *The Diary of John Evelyn*, ed. De Beer i. 13.

[180] *The Diary of Thomas Crosfield*, ed. Boas, p. 23; Bodl. MS Add. d. 105, fo 79ʳ; Berks. RO Trumbull misc. corr. vol. L, no. 13; *The Flemings in Oxford* i. 262.

[181] HMC *Egmont MSS* i pt 2, p. 589.

intended for those who planned to take a degree was not entirely appropriate for those who were destined for a shorter stay and required a social as well as a scholastic education. A tutor at St John's in the 1620s wrote to Sir Hugh Smyth, the father of a gentleman student: 'I know itt is not your intent to have him earne his bread by his books. When you left him here I tooke upon mee the charge of a gentleman, I shall blush to returne him you again a meere scholler.'[182] The evidence suggests that such students were required to give a certain amount of attention to their studies, although the extent to which this was enforced varied between the societies. In some houses they were compelled to attend academic exercises, while the authorities in others were not so strict. In the 1630s the gentlemen-commoners at Christ Church rarely went to the disputations in hall, but at University College the upper commoners were fined if they failed to do the same exercises as the poor scholars.[183] Such differences in academic discipline between the societies reflected the personality of their heads and so were liable to change. Among the heads who actively interested themselves in their students' academic work were Ralph Kettell at Trinity, John Bancroft at University College, and Thomas Tully, principal of St Edmund Hall from 1658 to 1676, who visited the scholars almost daily 'to observe whether they followed their studyes'.[184] Nevertheless some gentlemen students were able to avoid academic exercises, and it showed. William Powell's brother-in-law found him to be 'short even of that mediocrity which is tolerable in a graduate in the arts' and Christopher Guise later remembered 'Two yeares I hovered about Oxford, gayning little.' Thomas Hood's recollections were even blunter, for he later claimed that 'theither I came illiterate and soe departed, I neither studied or learnt anything', although this remark was made in an elegantly composed refusal to contribute to the building of a new chapel at Trinity and should be interpreted in that context.[185]

For those undergraduates who applied themselves assiduously to their studies the timetable imposed its own discipline. Insights into the daily routine are provided by the descriptions of four such students. William Trumbull entered Magdalen College as a fellow-commoner in 1622 and went on to take a BA and MA. He rose between five and six o'clock and after prayers, which were at six, he read a chapter in the Bible and then worked at his logic exercises. At eight o'clock he went to his tutor and they read Diogenes Laertius together for an hour. After a short break he went at about nine thirty to disputations, which lasted until eleven o'clock. After dinner he read Florus and it was his practice to go over and revise his day's studies after supper, reading some more biblical passages before going to

[182] *Correspondence of the Smyth Family*, ed. Bettey, 63.

[183] HMC *Finch MSS* i. 237; 'The Memoirs of Sir George Courthop 1616–1685', ed. S. C. Lomas, *Camden Miscellany* xi (Camden Soc. 3rd ser. xxxiii 1907), 104.

[184] *Brief Lives, chiefly of contemporaries, set down by John Aubrey, between the years 1669 and 1696*, ed. A. Clark (2 vols Oxford 1898) ii. 20–1; *Memoirs of Courthop*, ed. Lomas, 104; Bodl. MS top. Oxon. f. 31, p. 19.

[185] HMC *Cowper MSS* i. 76; *Memoirs of the Family of Guise*, ed. Davies, 117; Bodl. MS Ballard 49, fo 172ʳ.

bed soon after ten o'clock.[186] John Freind's timetable as a first-year commoner and prospective BA at St Edmund Hall in 1672 was a very full one and the 'method of study' was posted up in his room by his tutor. The day began with his own devotions and public prayers and his mornings were spent reading in English and Greek, with any time remaining before the midday meal devoted to philosophy. In the afternoons from one until five on Mondays to Wednesdays he was given philo-logical studies in Latin and on Thursdays and Fridays he looked at Greek authors. Saturday mornings in term time were set aside for exercises and in the vacations he studied Latin and Greek grammar. Every day after supper and on Saturday after-noons all spare time after 'lawful and honest recreations' had been allowed for was spent studying Latin poets and classical antiquities. He passed a part of each evening in private prayer and he and his chamber-fellow never sat up later than eleven o'clock.[187] Four years after Freind had arrived at Oxford John Percival was admitted at Christ Church. He was an orphaned younger son of a baronet, very aware that he would be expected to make his own way in the world and resolved to make a career in the law. His tutor tailored his studies accordingly and one of his chief aims was to improve John's ability to argue and express himself clearly. In the mornings they worked together at logic and Greek and in the afternoons concentrated upon mathematics and Latin orations. After he had been in Oxford for two years he was giving most of his attention to logic, trigonometry, rhetoric, philosophy, and—for his tutor was a sensible man—history, a subject that John recognized 'will be advantageous to me in whatsoever condition of life I shall be in'. By then his tutor's assignments took up six hours, three more were spent in reading material of his own choice and seven of the sixteen hours from six in the morning until ten in the evening were left for socializing and recreation.[188] John Harris's recollection of the routine at Trinity in the early 1680s was that during term time the day began with lectures in logic and natural philosophy to all the stu-dents at seven o'clock in the hall, with disputations there at ten and again at five, the latter by the BAs but with undergraduates also present. These disputations were performed on alternate days during the long vacation. At two o'clock there was an exposition on Greek and Latin authors in the hall. Tutors read to their pupils in the mornings between the opening lecture of the day and the disputations at ten o'clock and many did so again in the afternoon, setting weekly exercises which the students performed in the hall at the fellows' table on Saturday afternoons. The curriculum included courses in experimental philosophy, chemistry, and mathe-matics. Harris's impression of his college days was distinctly favourable. He took both the BA and the MA, followed a career in the church, and also pursued his interest in science and topography, being elected FRS in 1696, taking a BD at Cambridge in 1699, and returning to Oxford for his DD seven years later.[189]

[186] Berks. RO Trumbull misc. corr. vol. L, no. 29.
[187] Bodl. MS top. Oxon. f. 31, pp. 21, 258, 321.
[188] BL Add. MSS 46,953, fo 74ʳ, 46,955A, fo 50ʳ⁻ᵛ, 46,955B, fo 72ʳ.
[189] Blakiston, *Trinity College*, 172–3. For Trinity a generation earlier see *Aubrey on Education*, ed. J. E. Stephens (London 1972), 116, 120.

Many students had a great deal of potential leisure time. Servitors and battelers had less time to themselves than the other categories of student because they were occupied in carrying out their allotted tasks, but those of commoner and higher rank had many hours of leisure to fill and boredom was an obvious problem. Some continued their studies in their own time. Henry Hammond was said to have consistently worked for thirteen hours a day during his time at Oxford, John Percival spent some of his free time with a French tutor trying to improve his command of that language, and Brian Twyne carried a Hebrew grammar when he went for the customary walk with his fellow students in the afternoons, in case he was able to snatch a few minutes alone.[190] Those who had come to Oxford largely for a social education attended classes in dancing and fencing at the schools in the town, although these were relatively expensive, with an admission fee of £1 2s 6d and a monthly charge of 12s in the 1650s.[191] Music lessons were only marginally cheaper, but a student with a certain proficiency could enter a consort in his society.[192] In 1603 William Chafin was evidently pleased to report to his father that he had joined 'the society of a full consorte in this house [Exeter], all very worthie and kynde gentlemen, wch I hope wilbe a means somewhat to encrease my knowledge therin'. Some of Lord Kingsale's time was taken up with music and in 1676 it was reported that 'like one of his quality, he learns to sing and play on the virginals'.[193] There was a distinction to be made between spending a considerable amount of time and money on music in order to develop some degree of expertise, as George Stradling did, and treating it as an occasional pastime and acquiring the ability to play for recreation.[194] Drama provided a similar outlet for creative energies through the production of plays by students within the university, although these virtually ceased after the mid seventeenth century.[195] It was recognized that physical exercise 'availeth much for health after intermission from studie' and students engaged in tennis, fives, football, athletics, and, at a more leisurely pace, bowls and boating.[196] John Percival played against the walls of his chamber in Christ Church with a battledore and shuttlecock and his brother warmly recommended tennis and

[190] John Fell, *The Life of the Most Learned, Reverend and Pious Dr H. Hammond* (London 1661), 7; BL Add. MSS 46,953, fo 74ᵛ, 46,951A, fos 8ʳ, 49ᵛ; Bodl. MS Gr. misc. d. 2, fos 47ᵛ, 50ʳ. William Trumbull proposed to learn Spanish to avoid idleness: Berks. RO Trumbull misc. corr. vol. L, no. 8.

[191] These were the fees paid by Ralph Eaton's pupils: BNCA MS 85, fos 51ᵛ, 72ʳ, 73ʳ, 88ʳ⁻ᵛ, 100ʳ⁻ᵛ. In 1622 Poynings Moore entered the dancing-school for £1: *The Loseley Manuscripts*, ed. A. J. Kempe (London 1835), p. xix. William Taylor admitted to boredom but could not afford the fees at the dancing-school: Bodl. MS Eng. hist. c. 481, fo 54ʳ. See also P. Manning, 'Sport and pastime in Stuart Oxford' in *Surveys and Tokens*, ed. Salter, 116–24, 129–35.

[192] Figures for Eaton's pupils were £1 admission and 10s 0d per month: BNCA MS 85, fos 87ᵛ–8ᵛ. William Freke paid between 5s 6d and 6s 6d for his monthly music lessons: H. V. F. Somerset, 'An account book of an Oxford undergraduate in the years 1619–1622', *Oxoniensia* xxii (1957), 85–92. In 1610 George Radcliffe claimed that music lessons cost much less in Oxford than in London: *Life of Radcliffe*, ed. Whitaker, 52.

[193] Wilts. RO 865/501; BL Add. MS 46,953, fo 120ʳ.

[194] George Stradling, *Sermons and Discourses upon Several Occasions* (London 1692), preface (unpaginated). Cf. P. Gouk, 'Music', pp. 631–4 below.

[195] Manning, 'Sport and pastime', 129–35. Cf John Elliott, 'Drama', pp. 640–4 below.

[196] BNCA Al. 2, registrum B, 1594–1710, fo 24ᵛ; Manning, 'Sport and pastime', 102–16.

hunting.[197] In the middle and later years of the century especially it was not unusual for the wealthier students to keep one horse or more for hunting, although they could be hired in the town.[198] Only a few months after spending ten guineas on a horse Richard Ducie asked his uncle's permission 'to keep a man and a brace of geldings as some gentlemen of my quality here do: 'tis both creditable and very much for my health'.[199] The need to emulate other students of similar rank is apparent, as in so many aspects of university life. Birding was a less expensive pastime. William Herrick asked for a stone-bow to shoot at sparrows to help to pass the time.[200] Archery was another form of recreation. George Radcliffe thought that he should equip himself with a bow and arrows, for the master of his college was a keen archer.[201] Parental and tutorial opinion was that students should not indulge in such recreations too much in the early stages of their stay, that most of their pastimes should be carried out within their own society and that they should not occupy so much time that they were a diversion from studying. Sir Heneage Finch did not object that his son had spent some time with his dancing-master, but that he had done so during the morning when he ought to have been studying, and Sir Stephen Fox's directions to his grandson included the instruction that he should not go to the tennis courts during the mornings.[202] There was more hostility to some other student pastimes such as cards, dice, billiards, backgammon, and chess, which occupied the winter evenings but were also likely to lead to gambling and a waste of time and money.[203] That this was a danger is illustrated by the case of John Denham, who was an inveterate gambler when he was at Trinity and 'when he had played away all his money he would play away his father's wrought rich gold cappes'.[204] Most students were probably prudent or poor enough to engage in games and pastimes without getting into such difficulties, despite parental fears, and many leisure time activities were not expensive. The Newdigate brothers spent less than 3 per cent of their first year's outlay on recreation.[205]

One possible consequence of unsupervised free time was that boredom would lead students into unsuitable company. The pernicious influences to which their sons would be exposed in Oxford were a cause of parental anxiety throughout the

[197] BL Add. MSS 46,954A, fo 14ʳ, 46,954B, fos 110ʳ⁻ᵛ, 162ʳ. The fellows of Queen's also played at ball and shuttlecock in their chambers: *The Diary of Thomas Crosfield*, ed. Boas, 12.

[198] BL Add. MS 46,955B, fos 51ʳ, 117ʳ; Wood, *History of the University* ii. 635; Wood, *Life and Times* i. 423, ii. 212; Manning, 'Sport and pastime', 88–94. It was noted in 1640 that noblemen and gentlemen 'of the better sort' were allowed to keep horses: Laud, *Works* v. 260. Lord Brooke kept greyhounds at Magdalen in 1653: Warwicks. RO CR 1886/TN22, pp. 2, 12.

[199] Gloucs. RO D340a, C8/86.

[200] Manning, 'Sport and pastime', 95; Nichols, *County of Leicester* iii. 162; Wood recorded that a student had died after being accidentally shot during a birding expedition in 1687: Wood, *Life and Times* iii. 245.

[201] *Life of Radcliffe*, ed. Whitaker, 61.

[202] HMC *Finch MSS* i. 244; Bodl, MS Ballard 9, fo 101.

[203] Wood, *Life and Times* ii. 96. [204] *Brief Lives by Aubrey*, ed. Clark i. 217.

[205] Penton, *Guardian's Instruction*, 48, 54–5, 81; A. Bryant, *Postman's Horn: an anthology of the letters of latter seventeenth century England* (London 1936), 47; Gloucs. RO D340a, C8/42; Larminie, 'Seventeenth century gentleman', 311, 331.

period. There were fears that they would make friends too readily with youths of insufficient social standing, or consort with those who did little or no studying and whose conduct would distract them from their studies and tempt them with a dissolute lifestyle which they would be unable to resist. This would nullify their previous upbringing at home and at school and also increase the costs of their stay at Oxford.[206] Drunkenness, whoring, and gambling were seen as the chief threats in this respect, with the numerous alehouses and, later, coffee houses the means whereby young students were corrupted.[207] Parents were also concerned that their sons' religious observances should not be affected while they were at Oxford, for there were fears that they would be exposed to the influences of Catholicism, puritanism, and, especially after the Restoration, atheism, which would undermine their beliefs.[208] There was even a danger that a student would make a rash marriage while at the university. To guard against these hazards one anxious mother took lodgings in the town while her son was a student.[209] Many parents gave their sons a great deal of advice on their conduct, warning them to avoid bad company, especially their social inferiors, and to obey their tutors. They also instructed the tutors to exercise close supervision to protect the students against adopting bad habits.[210] Some fathers backed their advice with threats to withdraw their sons from the university if they were found to be wasting their time or mixing with unsavoury companions and William Trumbull went so far as to warn his son that he would be disinherited if he associated with 'lewd company' while at Magdalen College.[211] Yet

[206] *The Correspondence of John Locke*, ed. De Beer i. 220; *Letter-Book of Sir John Eliot*, ed. Grosart, 108; *Loseley Manuscripts*, ed. Kempe, p. xix. Contemporary writers warned of such dangers inherent in student life: Penton, 48; Wandesforde, *Book of Instructions*, 15–16, 27; D. Grenville, *Counsel and Directions Divine and Moral* (London 1685), 77; Jean Gailhard, *The Compleat Gentleman, or directions for the education of youth* (London 1678), 18.

[207] Laud thought alehouses 'the bane of a great many young men, which are sent to the university for better purposes'. In 1639 there were approximately 300 alehouses in Oxford and forty years later the figure was roughly 370. See Laud, *Works* v. 178–9, 201–2, 237–9, 245–7, 258–61; Wood, *History of the University* i. 298; Wood, *Life and Times* ii. 404; T. Warton, *The Life and Literary Remains of Ralph Bathurst, MD* (London 1761), 104. Penton admitted the uproar in the inns and taverns but attributed it not to the students but to the country gentlemen coming into Oxford: Penton, *Guardian's Instruction*, 42.

[208] Wood, *Life and Times* ii. 93, 96; Grenville, *Counsel and Directions*, preface (unpaginated) and pp. 148–9, 182–3; HMC *Finch MSS* i. 212, 444.

[209] *The Flemings in Oxford* ii. 89–90; BL Add. MS 46,956C, fo 11ʳ.

[210] Warnings to students about misconduct were common: Bodl. MS top. Oxon. f. 31, pp. 56, 64, 84; Berks. RO Trumbull Add. MS 46, letter 24 August 1622; *Loseley Manuscripts*, ed. Kempe, p. xix; *Moore Rental*, ed. Heywood, 8; *Trevelyan Papers*, ed. W. C. and C. E. Trevelyan (3 vols Camden Soc. lxvii, lxxxiv, cv 1857–72) iii. 176. Richard Ducie (matriculated at Queen's 1667) was bombarded with warnings as to his conduct by members of his family, and five years later Richard Myddelton was admonished by the vicar of his home parish on the basis of rumours of his misconduct while at Brasenose: Gloucs. RO D340a, C8/13–14, 16–17, 24, 42, 70; Nat. Lib. Wales, Chirk Castle MS F 6437. Sir Robert Harley cautioned his son about those who led dissolute lives and warned that Oxford 'do too much abound with such pigges': BL Add. MS 61,989, fo 7ᵛ.

[211] Berks. RO Trumbull Add. MS 46, letter 11 October 1622; *Letter-Book of Sir John Eliot*, ed. Grosart, 103, 106, 164; *The Life of Edward Earl of Clarendon ... by Himself* (3 vols London 1827) i. 8. In 1679 Thomas Newdigate had run up debts of £40 through keeping 'ill company' at Oxford and he was not allowed to return: Warwicks. RO CR 136/B 354A. John Vicars was withdrawn from Magdalen Hall by his father in 1635 and placed with a tutor in the country because he had 'by irregular courses broaken

the parents themselves did not escape criticism, particularly those who gathered at the Act in July and by their bibulous behaviour with the friends of their own student days set a bad example to their sons, newly enrolled as undergraduates.[212]

Such concern reflected the university's reputation for the unseemly conduct of some of its members, which was not entirely unfounded. Contemporaries such as Wood and Humphrey Prideaux made frequent references to the deplorable behaviour of students and, if they were somewhat jaundiced observers of the Oxford scene, there is also the evidence of the disciplinary action that was taken, the testimonies of visitors and the recollections of former students to confirm the impression which they give.[213] Christopher Guise admitted to having spent too much time drinking, 'beleeving itt a poynt of civility', and courting women in the alehouses; a student at Brasenose in the 1610s later remembered the drinking bouts which caused him to be repeatedly ill.[214] Others also had memories of time spent drinking, whoring, fighting—both among themselves and with the students of other houses—and raiding villages near to Oxford.[215] Some students were disciplined and others expelled for a variety of offences, even for attempted murder, and there were those who left the university prematurely to avoid expulsion.[216] Although the Restoration was followed by a year or so of especially high spirits such conduct appears to have been a feature of university life throughout the century and not just of its later decades.[217] Nor was it confined to undergraduates, for

out into much looseness and unthriftines of life': Guildhall Lib. MS 12806/4, Christ's Hospital minutes 1632–49, p. 54. One father advised the president of New College to 'cause a barber to cutt off my sonnes fansyefull long haire and locks . . . to take off part of his pride, humble him and make him keepe close to his studdy': NCA 1160, letter 23 February 1623.

[212] Penton, *Guardian's Instruction*, 73.

[213] Wood, *Life and Times* i. 455–7, ii. 2, 56, 95–6, 125, 300, 404, 429, iii. 241, 243; *Letters of Prideaux*, ed. Thompson, 2, 5, 13–14; HMC *Fifth Report*, appx, pp. 374, 377.

[214] *Memoirs of the Family of Guise*, ed. Davies, 115–16; 'The autobiography of Mr. Langley of Prestwich', ed. F. R. Raines, *Chetham Miscellanies* vi (Chetham Soc. ciii 1878), 113.

[215] Such events were among the recollections of Anthony Ashley Cooper, who entered Exeter College in 1637, of Thomas Hood, who was at Trinity in the early 1640s, and of Samuel Wesley, who matriculated at Exeter in 1683: Christie, *Life of Shaftesbury*, 16–18; Bodl. MS Ballard 49, fo 172ʳ⁻ᵛ, MS Rawlinson c. 406, pp. 100, 108. Philip Henry was following the example of others in requesting 'lord, forgive mee my University sins!': *Diaries and Letters of Henry*, ed. Lee, 33.

[216] For the attempted murder in 1677 of a fellow of Corpus by John Bradshaw, a student, see *The Flemings in Oxford* i. 228; Wood, *Life and Times* ii. 379. A student was expelled from Wadham in 1669 for disorderly behaviour and in 1610 two students left University College to avoid expulsion for drunkenness: Bodl. MS Add. c. 308, fo 145ʳ; *Life of Radcliffe*, ed. Whitaker, 64. Wood noted that discipline was strict in the 1650s and public drunkenness was severely punished: Wood, *Life and Times* i. 299–300. Of two undergraduates expelled from Christ Church in 1682 one had left the college and not returned and the second had been caught 'in a scandalous house, and in very bad circumstances'; as a result of the latter incident a bedmaker who 'used the trade of a procurer' was also dismissed. See *The Correspondence of John Locke*, ed. De Beer ii. 564; Bodl. MS Tanner 305, fo 141ʳ. John Russell, a gentleman-commoner, was removed from University College because of the fear that other young gentlemen might receive 'great damage' from his conversation: W. Carr, *University College* (London 1902), 128.

[217] For example there was a drunken riot at All Souls in 1632 and a battle between the students of Christ Church and Corpus Christi in 1658: E. F. Jacob, 'All Souls College', *VCH Oxon.* iii. 179; *The Correspondence of John Locke*, ed. De Beer i. 62. In 1636 Sir Christopher Wandesforde wrote that parents sent their sons to university 'with fear and trembling': Wandesforde, *Book of Instructions*, 15–16. Penton wrote that the behaviour which followed the Restoration was checked and that the university then

the relaxation of tutorial supervision following graduation gave some students the opportunity to carouse, and their behaviour was worse after they had taken their BA than it had been before.[218] The three young men whose boisterous behaviour in the Mitre tavern in the early hours of a winter morning in 1683 literally frightened the hostess to death were all fellows of All Souls.[219] This aspect of life in Oxford created a bad impression in some quarters. When Robert Woodford, the steward of Northampton, visited Oxford in 1639 he concluded that it was 'prodigiously profane ... for drunkennesse, swearinge, and other debauched courses, stage playes, etc'.[220] In the 1680s the leaders of the dissenters' community in London paid for Samuel Wesley to go to Oxford for a while so that he could see for himself what 'a perfect Sodom and Gomorrha' it was and so would not later regret having been unable to study there because of his religious beliefs. He was shocked by what he saw, but nevertheless entered Exeter College soon afterwards.[221] The university's reputation in this respect made some parents hesitate before sending their sons there and perhaps deterred others from sending them at all.[222]

Tutors found supervision of their pupils' conduct one of the most onerous aspects of their duties, for they could hardly keep an eye on all of their students all of the time and in any case some were incorrigible. Daniel Hill found that the 'hardest part of his office was the care of the behaviour and manners of his pupills' and yet he was a tutor at Christ Church when John Fell, a strict disciplinarian, was dean.[223] Other heads attempted to maintain firm discipline among the members of their houses, but some were quite ineffectual. Among the most ineffective was the bibulous Joseph Maynard, rector of Exeter from 1662 until 1666.[224] Much depended upon the attitudes of the tutors, the students themselves, and the deterrent effect of the punishments which were meted out. Those tutors who scarcely ever saw their pupils could exercise little or no control over their conduct. Others showed greater concern and did keep a check on their students. John Roswell went so far as to note the acquaintances which his pupil John Potenger made in the university, forbidding him to speak to those of whom he disapproved.[225] It was, however, difficult for tutors to deal with recalcitrant pupils from a superior social background to their own and their patience could be strained to the limit.[226] The

became 'sober, modest and studious', but this is not supported by the account of Clarendon written between 1666 and 1674 or that of Grenville, 1685: Penton, *Guardian's Instruction*, 41; *Tracts of Clarendon*, 322–3; Grenville, *Counsel and Directions*, 147–9.

[218] *Memoirs of Potenger*, ed. Bingham, 30–1.

[219] Wood, *Life and Times* iii. 83; Bodl. MS Tanner 340, fo 374ʳ.

[220] HMC *Ninth Report* ii. 498.   [221] Bodl. MS Rawlinson c. 406, p. 100.

[222] *Diaries and Letters of Henry*, ed. Lee, 182, 184, 249; *Memoirs of Potenger*, ed. Bingham, 3; Wandesforde, *Book of Instructions*, 15. John Fell attempted to dissuade Grenville from publishing his *Counsel and Directions* in case it should damage the university in this respect: Bodl. MS Rawlinson d. 850, fo 267ʳ⁻ᵛ.

[223] BL Add. MS 46,956A, fo 23ᵛ. For Fell see HMC *Finch MSS* i. 443–4.

[224] Wood, *Life and Times* i. 455–6, ii. 56.   [225] *Memoirs of Potenger*, ed. Bingham, 28–9.

[226] HMC *Ormonde MSS* ii. 286, new ser. v. 12–13, 46–8. For Thomas Good at Balliol in 1674 see *Letters of Prideaux*, ed. Thompson, 13–14.

statutes made provision for corporal punishment and it was employed from time to time, both formally within the structure of college discipline and inflicted by individual tutors. It seems to have gradually fallen into disuse during the period and the more usual and perhaps more effectual punishment was to withdraw a student's entitlement to commons.[227] Thomas Hood recalled that his name had been struck out of the buttery book at Trinity so frequently that he had 'allmost starv'd'.[228] Expulsion was also used as a threat and a punishment.[229] It was difficult to achieve any consistency in the enforcement of discipline, which varied between societies and also through time, with occasional bursts of activity aimed at achieving the recognized ideals of conduct, from which it was so easy to lapse.

Some control could be exercised over students' conduct by keeping their allowance on a tight rein. A tutor at Brasenose realized 'that some yonge gentlemen can hardly be kept in any order, let them but have an angell or two in their own purse' and that to permit his students to keep their own money would mean that he could no longer prevent them from going into the town, especially on Friday and Saturday evenings.[230] Many parents shared his point of view and directed their sons' tutors to restrict the amount of pocket money which they issued, although others were content that their sons should have charge of their own money, either from the outset or after they had been in Oxford long enough to have acquired some sense of financial responsibility.[231] The tutor's financial role usually came to an end at his pupil's graduation. The arrangement by which a tutor had charge of his students' money and so could exercise some restraint on their conduct was a common one, but had arisen for different reasons, for he was liable to the college or hall for payment of his pupils' residence costs and he made a private contract with parents so that he could discharge such debts and also cover their other expenses, including those which he charged for tuition.[232] Being the guarantor of the students' residence charges was an onerous liability, but one which was slightly eased by the introduction of caution money, a sum paid to the society on admission which could be offset against debts which remained outstanding on

---

[227] Stone, 'Social control and intellectual excellence', 9–11, 16. For college discipline see Fowler, *Corpus*, 53–4, 196, 223–4, 233, 359–64; R. W. Jeffery, 'History of the college, 1547–1603', *Brasenose Monographs* ii pt 1, no. X, pp. 36–7; Macleane, *Pembroke*, 185, 188.

[228] Bodl. MS Ballard 49, fo 172ᵛ. The duration of suspension from commons varied according to the nature of the offence. At St John's pernoctation was usually punished by loss of a week's commons, and there are also examples there (1636, 1668) of suspensions for twelve and fifteen days: W. H. Hutton, *S John Baptist College* (London 1898), 101–2; SJM register ii, fos 752–5. At Christ Church one undergraduate was suspended for two months in 1652, and two years earlier another had been sent home for one year for speaking 'gross and scandalous oaths': CA D&C i. b. 3, pp. 30, 53.

[229] For examples of expulsion see p. 73 n. 216 above.

[230] BNCA B2a. 40, pp. 19, 24–5.

[231] *The Correspondence of John Locke*, ed. De Beer i. 195, 221–3; NCA 1160, letter 23 February 1663; Bryant, *Postman's Horn*, 47. Penton recommended that a student should be allowed to keep any money which he saved from his allowance, to teach him the value of thrift: Penton, *Guardian's Instruction*, 49.

[232] Stone, 'Social control and intellectual excellence', 7–8, 11; McConica, 'Elizabethan Oxford', 693–5; Curtis, *Oxford and Cambridge in Transition*, 79. In 1611 a tutor at Brasenose pointed out to a father that he had given his 'word and strict bond' for students' expenses in college: BNCA B2a. 40, p. 25.

the student's departure. Costs of residence varied between the different student grades, reflecting the contrasting standards of fare which they received, and caution money varied in proportion. Most societies had introduced the system by the middle of the century, but it did not always function smoothly; at Brasenose, for example, it was begun in 1593, had to be revived in 1652, and was reintroduced ten years later.[233] A further restriction was to place an upper limit on the sums which the members of each grade were permitted to spend on their commons and battels. At St Edmund Hall in the Restoration period the weekly maximum for upper commoners was 7s 6d, for bachelors and commoners 6s, for semi-commoners 5s, and servitors were restricted to 2s.[234] Bills were presented at the end of each term and it was expected that payment would be prompt, for neither the society nor the tutor could risk letting a student's account accumulate such arrears that they exceeded his caution money and so might not be recoverable when he left. In 1670 Nicholas Martyn wrote home urgently for money, complaining that 'the college say they want monyes and are seveare to those that pay not their battell in a fortnight or 3 weeke time after the quarter'.[235] Most houses set a similar deadline and those who failed to meet it were liable to have their names struck out of the buttery book, effectively terminating their connection with the society.[236] Debts built up despite these precautions. Full payment of Thomas Brooke's expenses at Brasenose was not received until five years after his departure.[237] It was common for the societies to keep lists of unpaid debts. At Christ Church there were almost forty defaulters during the 1680s, mostly on small sums, and the thirty-one persons who were listed as debtors at Balliol from 1650 to 1670 together owed £253 3s 7d.[238] These were, however, a small proportion of the total expenditure on students' battels.

Students could receive financial support from a number of sources, the principal one being their family. Those parents who found it difficult to maintain a son

[233] Lodge, 'The college under the later Stuarts', 8. The system was introduced at Oriel in 1586, Christ Church 1599, University College 1612, Wadham 1614, and at Balliol apparently not before 1639: D. W. Rannie, *Oriel College* (London 1900), 94; CA D&C i. b. 2, p. 239; Carr, *University College*, 98–9; WCM convention book i, p. 6; BCA register 1514–1682, p. 225. For increases in caution money see *Dean's Register of Oriel*, 247, 313, 330. The system was enunciated in the Laudian statutes: *Laudian Code*, ed. Griffiths, 267.

[234] *Laudian Code*, ed. Griffiths, 274; A. B. E[mden], 'Orders for the butterie', *St Edmund Hall Magazine* ii (1930), 64. At Brasenose in the 1660s gentlemen-commoners batteled at no more than 8s per week: Bryant, *Postman's Horn*, 46. At Christ Church in 1653 the weekly limits were 5s for gentlemen-commoners, 4s for under-commoners, and 3s for scholars: CA D&C i. b. 3, p. 61.

[235] Devon RO DD 55, 978, letter 13 December 1670; I am grateful to Dr Stephen Roberts for drawing my attention to this item.

[236] At Balliol, St John's, and Magdalen College the period allowed was fifteen days: BCA register 1514–1682, p. 78; SJM register ii, fo. 324; Berks. RO Trumbull misc. corr. vol. L, no. 40. Such deadlines caused some apprehension among students: *Trevelyan Papers*, ed. Trevelyan and Trevelyan iii. 82–3. Those who could not pay had to leave the college: *Diary of Brockbank*, ed. Trappes-Lomax, 73–4; Bodl. MS Rawlinson c. 406, p. 101.

[237] BNCA MS 85, fos 87ᵛ–8ᵛ. Because of a spell of sickness a student at Trinity in the 1680s ran up a debt which far exceeded his caution money and after his recovery left the college without paying: Bodl. MS Ballard 49, fo 182ʳ⁻ᵛ.

[238] CA xxix, c. 4; BCA F. 11. 10, I.N.2; Davis, *Balliol College*, 139, 143–5. See Berks. RO D/EN F44/3 for a debt of £28 to a tutor at Merton in 1608.

at Oxford were sometimes helped by other members of the family and neighbours. It was a common practice for relatives to send students 'tokens' from time to time. These were usually of small value, perhaps 2s 6d or 5s, but for a poor recipient such occasional gifts represented a significant addition to his income.[239] Provision was also made in the form of legacies—some of which were specifically designed to assist a student while he was at Oxford—and more rarely in marriage settlements, such as that of Thomas Leigh of 1610 which provided £100 annually towards his maintenance while he was at the university.[240] Costs could be reduced if a student acted as a batteler or servitor and, if this did not eke out his allowance sufficiently, he could leave Oxford for a while and take a temporary job until he had earned enough money to allow him to return to his studies. Schoolteaching and private tutoring offered suitable employment.[241] It was by acting as a schoolmaster that Jonathan Jephcott was able to supplement his father's allowance sufficiently to maintain himself at New Inn Hall until he obtained a benefice in 1633.[242] Financial support from a patron could serve as a similar increment, or as an alternative, to family funds. In some cases the son of a tenant was sent to Oxford with his landlord's son, at the landlord's expense, to act as his servitor, but in others he may have received assistance without being put under such an obligation.[243] Nor was there necessarily such a direct connection between the patron and the beneficiary. Both laymen and churchmen, individually and collectively, were prepared to support youths without adequate maintenance who had been drawn to their attention as likely to profit from a university education and perhaps be suitable candidates for ordination thereafter.[244] Thomas Hearne benefited in this way. Hearne's

[239] *Diaries and Letters of Henry*, ed. Lee, 249; *The Flemings in Oxford* i. 14–15, 114, 231, 257, 490, 492–3, 496, 500, 503, 505, ii. 21, 47, 66, 95–6, 120, 130, iii. 53; HMC *Ormonde MSS* new ser. iv. 610; Bodl. MS Rawlinson c. 406, p. 101, MS top. Oxon. f. 31, pp. 120, 123, MS Gr. misc. d. 2, fos 57ᵛ, 62ʳ; 'The account-book of an Oxford undergraduate, 1682–1688', ed. E. G. Duff, *Collectanea* i. 253–5.

[240] Waters, *Genealogical Gleanings* i. 41, 366, 474, 613, ii. 868, 1061, 1120, 1186, 1351; Gloucs. RO will of Toby Read of Bitton, proved 9 June 1627; *Registrum Collegii Exoniensis* pt 2 *An Alphabetical Register of the Commoners of Exeter College, Oxford*, ed. C. W. Boase (Oxford 1894), 240. George Warburton of Trinity received a legacy of £25 in 1669: *Chirk Castle Accounts 1666–1753*, ed. Myddelton, p. 29. George Radcliffe used a legacy for lessons on the viol: *Life of Radcliffe*, ed. Whitaker, 52; BNCA B2a. 38, p. 9. For Thomas Leigh's marriage settlement see Shakespeare Birthplace Trust RO DR 18/13/1/9.

[241] This was a common reason for absence from Oxford: HMC *Ormonde MSS* new ser. iv. 601–2, 605–7, 609, 614, 622, 630, viii. 17; CCCL MS 390/1, fo 137ʳ.

[242] Edmund Calamy, *The Nonconformist's Memorial*, ed. S. Palmer (3 vols London 1802–3) i. 318.

[243] Larminie, 'Seventeenth century gentleman', 331; Bodl. MS Locke f. 11, fo 7ᵛ; *Chirk Castle Accounts 1605–1666*, ed. Myddelton, 25, 59, 64–5, 77–8, 82, 89, 115, 130; *Chirk Castle Accounts 1666–1753*, ed. Myddelton, 79, 85.

[244] Students received financial support from deans and chapters, borough corporations, and livery companies: HMC *Wells Dean and Chapter MSS* ii. 469; HMC *Reading Corporation MSS*, 207, 213; *Reading Records: diary of the corporation*, ed. J. M. Guilding (4 vols London 1892–6) iv. 217; Devon RO ECA B1/7, chamber act book 1611–34, p. 27; *Records of the Borough of Leicester*, ed. M. Bateson, H. Stocks, and G. A. Chinnery (7 vols London, Cambridge, and Leicester 1899–1974) iv. 495, 504, 530; *Extracts from the two Earliest Minute Books of the Dean and Chapter of Norwich Cathedral, 1566–1649*, ed. J. F. Williams and B. Cozens-Hardy (Norfolk Record Soc. xxiv 1953), 42, 61–2; London, Merchant Taylors' Company, minutes 5, 1601–11, pp. 308, 532, minutes 7, 1611–20, pp. 36, 46, 232, 237–8, minutes 8, 1620–36, fos 247ʳ, 432ᵛ, 451ʳ, minutes 9, 1636–54, fos 69ᵛ, 76ᵛ, 112ʳ. For the patronage of Sheldon and Dolben see pp. 61–2 above.

patron, Francis Cherry, paid for his education for seven years at St Edmund Hall, where Cherry had himself studied, until Hearne obtained his MA in 1703.[245] Some financial assistance of this kind was given in response to direct appeals from parents, perhaps seeking help in raising the extra funds needed for their son to take a degree.[246] Impecunious students were also likely to receive informal assistance from within the university. It was one of Ralph Kettell's practices when president of Trinity (1599–1643) to put money in at the windows of 'diligent boyes that he ghessed had but a slender exhibition from their friends', and other heads of houses befriended their students.[247] Nor was such generosity limited to senior members of the university, for in 1685 Samuel Wesley's outstanding battels at Magdalen College were paid for by a student at Exeter who also encouraged others to give him help. Wesley received more money for transcribing manuscripts in the Bodleian, and such casual employment provided supplementary income for other poor students.[248]

The universities benefited considerably from the spate of charitable giving which characterized the sixteenth and seventeenth centuries, receiving roughly 7.5 per cent of all donations during the period.[249] Much of this was in the form of endowments designed to provide exhibitions and scholarships for the support of students from a particular county, place, or school, those attending a nominated college or studying a specified subject.[250] In addition to the desire to support poor boys who were able enough to benefit from a spell at university, educational philanthropy after the reformation had the strong underlying motive of establishing protestantism and reducing Catholic influence. The flow of benefactions was probably at its greatest before the mid-seventeenth century, but if this slackened thereafter it certainly did not cease. Consequently the proportion of students receiving such funds rose during the century and especially after the number of admissions began to decline. Only 9 per cent of those entering Brasenose between 1610 and 1629 held a scholarship at some stage, but the proportion for the period 1670–89 was four times that level. By the later seventeenth century many students could reasonably expect to be beneficiaries. Slightly over half of all the youths from

[245] *Life of Hearne*, 2–8, 13; *DNB* s.v. Francis Cherry.

[246] Elizabeth Forster, a widow, appealed to Sir Nicholas Carew for help for her son, a batteler at Brasenose, to take a degree, 1669: Berks. RO D/ELI, C1/197. For appeals to the Merchant Taylors' Company see Merchant Taylors' Company, minutes 5, 1601–11, pp. 259, 334, 525, minutes 7, 1611–20, pp. 16, 495, 499–500, 502, 571, minutes 8, 1620–36, fos 451^r, 469^{r-v}, minutes 9, 1636–54, fo 258^v.

[247] *Brief Lives by Aubrey*, ed. Clark ii. 22–3. For example John Fell at Christ Church: 'William Taswell', ed. Elliott, 18, 23.

[248] Bodl. MS Rawlinson c. 406, p. 101; Calamy, *Nonconformists' Memorial* iii. 195; *Diaries and Letters of Henry*, ed. Lee, 11, 14; *The Bodleian Library Account Book 1613–1646*, ed. G. Hampshire (Oxford Bibliographical Soc. xxi 1983), 122, 126, 131, 135, 138–9, 144, 150.

[249] D. Owen, *English Philanthropy 1660–1960* (Oxford 1965), 347.

[250] Such donations are discussed in the various works of W. K. Jordan: *The Charities of London 1480–1660* (London 1960), 213–16, 231, 251, 255–61; *The Charities of Rural England 1480–1660* (London 1961), 58–60, 345, 355–6, 360; 'The forming of the charitable institutions of the west of England ... 1480–1660', *Transactions of the American Philosophical Society* new ser. 1 (1960), 66–7; *The Social Institutions of Lancashire* (Chetham Soc. 3rd ser. xi 1962), 32, 41, 45, 72–4, 94.

Worcester who studied at Oxford between 1668 and the end of the century received assistance from the Worfield charity, each exhibition being tenable for seven years.[251] Of course not all students were candidates for such assistance; some did not require or seek it and others did not qualify by the terms of the endowments. Such exhibitions also had their shortcomings. One was that they were generally for a fixed sum—rarely more than £10 per annum—and so their real value fell because of inflation and the rising cost of an Oxford education. Those donors who specified the value of their gifts in the sixteenth century could not have foreseen such a trend, but new endowments continued to make provisions of similar value even in the later seventeenth century. The Worfield exhibition was established by a will of 1650, yet was worth only £3 yearly to each recipient, and the Cartwright scholarships at Brasenose, which began in 1665, allowed £8 to be divided equally between two scholars. As many such low-value donations were given by senior academics within the university, who must have known that they were inadequate, it may be assumed that such financial assistance had come to be regarded as supplementing, rather than providing, student incomes. Some could be amalgamated to provide a more realistic sum, but this was sometimes precluded by the terms of the donation.[252] Their falling real values militated against the poorer students. A further drawback was that such funds were allegedly diverted to those whose families had adequate means. In 1604 the London Ironmongers' Company objected that Merton had nominated a student for a poor scholar's exhibition although his father was 'a wealthie man and of habilitie to maintaine his sonne himselfe', and a few years later it clashed with Magdalen College on similar grounds. Its major confrontation was with Oriel concerning the college's nominations for the Chapman exhibition, disbursed by the company. Amidst allegations of corruption and bribery on the part of Oriel's candidate the dispute went to chancery, where the company's case was dismissed. This may have been an unusual example because of the terms of that particular exhibition and the college was strictly speaking not in breach of them, although it was surely not complying with the spirit of the donation, for almost all of the beneficiaries were of MA standing, three quarters were fellows when they took up the exhibition, fewer than one quarter had matriculated as plebeians and it seems that a number of them had falsified their ages in order to qualify. The Ironmongers' Company was not alone in questioning the necessity of some candidates for such exhibitions.[253]

In the elections to places on the foundation a college could come under pressure from the crown, the visitor, or some other powerful figure to favour a

---

[251] *Reg. Brasenose* i. 113–59, 222–57; Worcs. RO Worcester city archives, charities A. 12.

[252] Worcs. RO Worcester city archives, A. 16; Butler, 'Benefactions', 23–6, 29 (Brasenose); Guildhall Lib. MS 12806/7, p. 697.

[253] Guildhall Lib. MS 16967/2, fos 10ʳ, 34ᵛ, 69ʳ, 117ᵛ–18ʳ, 126ᵛ–7ʳ, 128ʳ, 141ᵛ, 149ʳ–50ᵛ, 190ʳ⁻ᵛ, 194ʳ⁻ᵛ, 222ᵛ, 234ᵛ. Status and ages are from the matriculation record of those beneficiaries from 1665 identified in MSS 16,967/2–5. Christ's Hospital restricted its exhibitions to students below MA status: ibid. MS 12806/7, p. 596. See also Merchant Taylors' Company, minutes 5, 1601–11, p. 197, minutes 8, 1620–36, pp. 104, 106.

particular candidate.[254] The preferences which they expressed did not necessarily militate against poor students, but they could do so. John Fell's opinion that 'I think none poorer or greater objects of charity than the younger children of persons of condition' was given in respect of the, ultimately successful, attempts by him and the king to obtain an All Souls fellowship for one of Lord Winchilsea's sons. Fell's supporting statement that he had recently given a Student's place at Christ Church to a son of Lord Brereton reflected not only his design to influence the social composition of his own college, but also the then current view among many senior clerics that the dignity and prestige of the church could be increased only by preferring those from a superior social background.[255] This clearly had implications for the university places within their influence. Archbishop Sheldon pressed the provost of Queen's to elect as a scholar the son and heir of a Hampshire gentleman, writing repeatedly on his behalf.[256] A further difficulty for the son of poor parents who wished to obtain a fellow's place was the cost involved, especially as it had become a common practice for those resigning fellowships to nominate their successors on receipt of a suitable consideration. Brian Twyne wished to pass on his Surrey fellowship at Corpus to a relative if possible or, failing that, to any gentleman who was prepared to pay him 'some fee for gettinge the fellowes voices for his sonne'.[257] A graduate of the same college who in 1631 hoped to obtain a Kentish place there for his brother 'if it may bee had for love or monie' presented the college with a silver tankard worth £4 to further his application and George Austen agreed to lend £30 to a fellow of Magdalen College on the understanding that he would resign his fellowship to Austen's son at an agreed date, when a further £10 would be payable, although that arrangement apparently did not come off.[258] Yet there was some resistance to such practices.[259] Thomas Jeames became warden of All Souls in 1664 and set about tackling the problem of corrupt resignations with some success. When Robert Abbot was master of Balliol earlier in the century he made 'always choyce of the towardliest young men in all elections'.[260] There was opposition to Fell's policy even at Christ Church and his proposal to assign an exhibition to the son of a merchant with an annual income of £1,500 was defeated both on the grounds that the exhibition was

[254] Bodl. MSS Tanner 338, fos 318r–19r, 339, fo 182r, 340, fos 148r, 155r, 156r, 167v–9r, 222r, 281r, 423r; BL Lansdowne MS 960, fo 95r; HMC *Cowper MSS* i. 144; HMC *Salisbury MSS* xxiv. 47.

[255] Leopold William Finch, Lord Winchilsea's fifth son, who was to become warden of the college; ASA warden's MS 50, p. 318; Jacob, 'All Souls', 179.

[256] Bodl. MS Add. c. 308, fos 83r, 113v, 115v. In 1690 senior Studentships at Christ Church were regarded as 'not given by merit but . . . secured by friends': G. A. Aitken, *The Life of Richard Steele* (2 vols London 1889) i. 35.

[257] Bodl. MS Gr. misc. d. 2, fo 39v.

[258] *The Oxinden Letters 1607–1642*, ed. D. Gardiner (London 1933), 65–74. Austen's arrangement was for his son Ralph with Samuel German in 1616: Bodl. MS top. Surrey e. 4, fo 25r. For the example of William Lyford see Bloxam, *Reg. Magdalen* ii. 78–9. Wither referred to places which 'like offices in Court, are bought and sould': George Wither, *Abuses Stript, and Whipt, or Satirical Essayes* (London 1613), book II, satire 1, 'Of vanitie' (unpaginated); HMC *Ormonde MSS* new ser. viii. 4.

[259] At Balliol in 1676 there was an attempt to forbid them: Davis, *Balliol College*, 149.

[260] Jacob, 178–9; C. G. Robertson, *All Souls College* (London 1899), 141–8.

intended for orphans or the sons of poor parents and because of the precedent which would have been created.[261]

Whether exhibitions did reach the poorer students depended upon the terms of the gift, the right of nomination, the value of the award and the composition of the college. The case of the Chapman exhibitions at Oriel suggests that plebeians did not gain a substantial benefit from such awards, yet at the same college between 1670 and 1689 two other exhibitions were awarded exclusively to sons of clergymen, plebeians, and paupers and almost 80 per cent of them went to paupers. During the same period 77 per cent of beneficiaries at Brasenose were plebeians and paupers and 19 per cent sons of clergy. The Goodridge exhibitions at Wadham show a different pattern as they were reserved for commoners and scholars, and this is reflected in the fact that only just over one third of holders before the end of the century were plebeians or paupers, who were outnumbered by the sons of gentlemen and esquires.[262] Fellowships offered greater rewards for longer periods than the fixed-term and low-value exhibitions. They also required a longer period of residence and so greater financial resources before they could be obtained, for the statutes of most colleges forbade undergraduates to become fellows, quite unlike New College and Exeter where 36 per cent of fellows appointed during the century had no degree when elected.[263] It was much more usual, however, for those chosen as fellows to have a first degree at their election, and this applied to 60 per cent of those elected at six colleges. Comparison of tables 1.10 and 1.14 shows that a smaller proportion of plebeians and paupers were appointed to fellowships than matriculated and that the reverse was the case for the sons of gentlemen and clergymen. Only at Oriel, however, did gentlemen's sons and those of higher standing exceed a half of those entering the fellowship. Appointments to a fellowship did not necessarily reflect the social profile of the college, for they were not restricted to internal candidates. Only 64 per cent of elections were from within a college; the remainder came chiefly from another society in Oxford, just 4 per cent being drawn from Cambridge or elsewhere.

The costs which students had to cover were numerous.[264] The initial outlay included the cost of the journey to Oxford, fees to the college officers and the university, caution money, clothes, books, and the furnishings of a chamber. Admission fees varied with status. At Brasenose and Lincoln a fellow-commoner's fees were four times those payable by a batteler, for example.[265] Caution money

[261] 'William Taswell', ed. Elliott, 22.

[262] *Reg. Brasenose* i. 222–57; *Registers of Wadham*, ed. Gardiner i, pp. xxiv, 332–403; *Registrum orielense, 1500–1900*, ed. C. L. Shadwell (2 vols Oxford 1893–1902) i. 332–81.

[263] J. Buxton and P. Williams (eds), *New College Oxford 1379–1979* (Oxford 1979), 58; *Registrum Collegii Exoniensis: register of the rectors and fellows, scholars, exhibitioners and Bible clerks of Exeter College Oxford*, ed. C. W. Boase (Oxford 1879, 2nd edn Oxford 1893), 59–84.

[264] The students' accounts consulted for this and the following paragraphs are listed in the appendix to this chapter.

[265] Wakeling, 'History of the college', 18; Lodge, 'The college under the later Stuarts', 9; Green, *Lincoln College*, 223. For admission fees at Gloucester Hall in 1631 and New College in 1678 see Daniel and Barker, *Worcester College*, 112 and NCA 9655, pp. 82–4.

TABLE 1.14

Matriculation status of fellows, 1600–99 (%)

	Brasenose	Exeter	Lincoln	Magdalen	Oriel	Wadham	Combined
Peer, bt, kt	1	3	5	8	1	2	4
Esq.	12	9	5	3	7	4	6
Gent.	23	25	31	36	52	32	33
Clergy	21	24	22	25	19	26	23
Pleb./paup.	43	38	38	29	21	36	34
Total	100	99	101	101	100	100	100
Number in sample	145	181	87	252	104	113	882

Note. A further 136 cases are of unknown status.

was also levied according to rank; some societies exempted the poorest grades of students and others received only a comparatively small sum from them. Until 1650 a poor scholar at Exeter paid £2 and a fellow-commoner three times that sum, and by the end of the period the comparable grades at Balliol paid £4 and £10 respectively.[266] Caution money was recoverable at departure or was offset against the student's battels, but a further fixed cost of roughly similar value for commoners and those of higher rank was a silver tankard or piece of plate which was presented to the college at some point before the student left.[267] The minimum acceptable value appropriate for each category of student was laid down and was typically between £4 and £12. This was apparently a minor element in a student's university career, yet the choice of a suitable item and the optimum point at which to present it seem to have seriously exercised the minds of many students and their parents.[268] The cost of fitting out a chamber was also related to what a student could afford. It often included expenditure upon repairs such as to broken windows and other improvements. Wainscotting a room was a considerable expense but was perhaps worthwhile for those who anticipated a long stay.[269] Items such as furniture, linen, and hangings could usually be bought from the outgoing occupant or another departing member of the university at a generally accepted rate and the eventual expense could be further reduced by selling them when the student himself left Oxford.[270] Some students understandably preferred to bring their own bed and linen. The rent of a furnished chamber was perhaps 50 per cent higher than that

[266] ECA A. 1. 22, caution book, 1629–86; Bodl. MS top. Oxon. e. 124/7, fo 3ᵛ; BCA college register 1514–1682, p. 245; Blakiston, *Trinity College*, 117, 166. In 1668 a baronet's son paid £15 caution and £3 10s 0d fees at Christ Church and his servitor £2 and 2s 6d for the respective charges: *Chirk Castle Accounts 1666–1753*, ed. Myddelton, 79.

[267] At some colleges the requirement included books. For Sir John Williams, St John's 1662, and John Alford, Christ Church 1664, see Bodl. MS Rawlinson letters 61, fo 11ʳ, MS Locke f. 11, fo 52ʳ. See also Costin, *St. John's*, 74.

[268] It seems to have been a major concern for Richard Ducie, who matriculated at Queen's in 1667: Gloucs. RO D340a, C8/34–5, 38, 40, 42, 45, 53, 55, 57, 59, 64. Students were recommended to take their tutors' advice and follow the precedent set by those of similar rank: Nat. Lib. Wales, Chirk Castle MS F 6435; *Letters and Papers of the Verney Family down to the end of the year 1639*, ed. J. Bruce (Camden Soc. lvi 1853), 151. Examples of the prices of tankards donated to colleges include £5 4s 3d at St John's in 1613, £4 Corpus 1631, £12 St John's 1660, and, rather exceptionally, £33 5s 0d for an unspecified number for Lord Brooke and his brother at Magdalen College in 1653: *Oxinden Letters*, ed. Gardiner, p. 74; Bodl. MS Eng. hist. c. 481, fos 1ʳ, 20ʳ, 32ʳ, 48ʳ, 49ʳ, MS Rawlinson letters 61, fo 9ʳ; Warwicks. RO CR 1886/TN 21, lib. 11.

[269] Bodl. MS top. Oxon. f. 31, pp. 351–2; NCA 14753, winter quarters 1592–3, 1594–5; Berks. RO Trumbull misc. corr. vol. L, no. 29; *The Flemings in Oxford* i. 107. John and Richard Newdigate spent £6 10s 0d in 1618–19, their first year at Trinity, on repairs and furniture for their chamber: Larminie, 'Seventeenth century gentleman', 329. William Taswell (matriculated Christ Church 1670) wainscotted his chamber and lived in it for thirteen years: 'William Taswell', ed. Elliott, 15.

[270] The incoming occupant usually paid two thirds of the amount paid by his predecessor: *OED* under *thirds*; Bodl. MS Locke f. 11, fo 56ʳ–ᵛ, MS Add. d. 105, fo 41ʳ; *The Correspondence of John Locke*, ed. De Beer i. 195, 203, 273; Somerset RO DD/WO 55/8, account of Sir John Trevelyan, Wadham 1687; Berks. RO Trumbull misc. corr. vol. L, no. 68, letter of William Trumbull, Magdalen College 1628; 'Account-book of an Oxford undergraduate', ed. Duff, 254–5, 264. Nathaniel Clutterbuck noted in 1654 that the deduction on resale of chamber furnishings was 2d in the shilling: Gloucs. RO D149/F13, fo 316ᵛ.

of an unfurnished one.[271] It was not uncommon for wealthier students to buy such items as globes of the world or finely bound books to lend their chambers what they felt to be an appropriate ambience. They were also expected to mark their arrival by entertaining the fellows and they had to pay the musicians' fees if they were serenaded on their first evening in college.[272] Such items caused Charles Morgan, a fellow-commoner, to spend almost £50 by the end of his first day at Lincoln in 1673, which may not have been unusual for someone of his standing, but was more than many students needed to lay out in an entire year. One third of Morgan's expenses consisted of clothes, which were an important part of an undergraduate's initial outlay as the visible manifestation of his position within the university and society at large.[273] They were thereby also a potential source of anxiety as either unfashionable or unduly worn garments could cause social embarrassment. Requests for additional funds from home for a new suit were a frequent theme in students' correspondence. Brian Twyne's ploy, according to his indignant father, was to wear his oldest and most threadbare suit of clothes on his visits home, in order to impress his parents both with his need for a new set and his general poverty.[274] The poorer students could acquire academic garb second-hand and try to minimize their other expenses in clothing and footwear.[275] Similar considerations applied to books, which required an initial outlay and, if the student continued with his studies, occasional purchases thereafter.[276] Costs could be reduced if the student's family had copies of the required texts or a relative had already studied at the university. Many arrived with some necessary volumes in their baggage.[277] There was a thriving second-hand trade in Oxford, with Richard Davis's bookshop said to be the largest in Restoration England. Parents and friends took the opportunity of having a contact in the university to request copies of

[271] H. Owen, *Stanhope, Atkinson, Haddon and Shaw: four north country families* (privately published 1985). Furniture, furnishings, and linen for Halliday Mildmay, fellow-commoner at Balliol in 1690, cost £15 11s 1d: Hants. RO 15 M 50/1682, fo 3ʳ⁻ᵛ. At St John's in 1622 Thomas Smyth received bedding, napkins, tablecloths, and a carpet from home: *Correspondence of the Smyth Family*, ed. Bettey, 62.

[272] In 1603 William Chafyn bought a map of the world in four sheets from another member of Exeter for £1 6s 8d; William Roberts and John and Philip Percival furnished their chambers with books of maps and globes. See Wilts. RO 865/501; Bodl. MS Rawlinson d. 715, fo 218ʳ; BL Add. MSS 46,951A, fo 1ʳ, 46,953, fos 74ᵛ, 111ʳ⁻ᵛ. Charles Morgan's entertainment of the rector and fellows of Lincoln in 1673 cost £4 1s 1d: Bodl. MS Add. d. 105, fo 42ʳ. The 'Oxford music' serenaded Lord Brooke in 1653 and Sir John Williams in 1660 at their arrival at Magdalen College and St John's: Warwicks. RO CR 1886/TN 22, p. 1; Bodl. MS Rawlinson letters 61, fo 9ᵛ.

[273] Morgan's clothes 'considering the quality he is in, must be somewhat handsome and creditable': Bodl. MS Add. d. 105, fos 41ʳ, 42ʳ. Sir John Trevelyan's initial outlay at Wadham in 1687 was £38 19s 10d and Halliday Mildmay's was £24 12s 4d at Balliol three years later: Somerset RO DD/WO, 55/8; Hants. RO 15 M 50/1682, fo 23ʳ.

[274] Bodl. MS Gr. misc. d. 2, fo 56ʳ.

[275] 'Account-book of an Oxford undergraduate', ed. Duff, 254; BNCA MS 85, fos 82ʳ, 89ᵛ.

[276] In 1695 Robert Wood, a BA and fellow of All Souls, explained to his father that 'when a man is Batchelour of Arts t'is time for him to fix himself to some study which cannot be done without books' and that 'a few books consume a great summe of money': 'Wood family letters', ed. Wood, 129.

[277] Bodl. MS Eng. hist. c. 481, fo 44ʳ; R. Austin, 'Thomas Smyth of Lincoln College, Oxford', *Notes and Queries* 12th ser. ix (1921), 221–2; Nat. Lib. Wales, Powis Castle correspondence, MS 420; *Life of Radcliffe*, ed. Whitaker, 46, 52, 59, 61, 70–2; *The Flemings in Oxford* i. 124, 240–1, 294, ii. 1, 26–9, 49, 91.

books which they wanted.[278] Other occasional expenses included such items as fuel, candles, postage, ale, and tobacco, but these were minor, and leisure activities could be indulged according to the student's means. A greater and unforeseen expense was a bout of illness. William Freke's sickness in 1621 lasted three weeks and payments to the physician, apothecary, and nurse were almost 40 per cent of his expenses in that quarter; John Freind's short and fatal illness in 1673 cost £5 12s 6d.[279] A serious or prolonged illness such as smallpox could require a period of convalescence outside Oxford in addition to the costs of treatment and care.[280] Thomas Brockbank's sickness and recuperation in 1691 cost between £20 and £30. The majority of ailments were less serious and expensive and were cured by a period of rest and a concoction from the apothecary.[281]

The chief recurrent costs were for teaching and accommodation and were scaled according to status.[282] Tutors' fees were such an item: students of batteler status could expect to pay £2 or £3 yearly and a commoner £4. The highest grades of student paid proportionally much more. Fellow-commoners at Brasenose in the late 1650s and early 1660s paid £8 annually, and by the end of the period noblemen were paying £20 for a tutor and perhaps £10 more for an under-tutor. Not only were the charges for such students higher, but they seem to have risen more sharply during the century than those paid by commoners and others of lower status, whose tutor's fees remained almost static. This may reflect the greater amount of attention which those of the highest status demanded and received, for although Sir Charles Boyle's fee was £20 in 1690 his tutor claimed that this one student took up almost half of his time and Boyle also engaged an under-tutor.[283] The charges for chamber-rent were rather less than those for tuition and were related to the student's status and the accommodation which he occupied. A batteler's average annual rent was perhaps £1, a commoner's double that or slightly more and those of a higher status typically paid between £5 and £8 yearly. These sums covered only rental for the space occupied and the fees to the college servants were separate items which were usually more than the chamber-rent. The cost of employing a student-servitor had to be added to the fees, for those of commoner rank and

[278] Gloucs. RO D340a C8/36, 45, 75; *The Correspondence of John Locke*, ed. De Beer i. 210; *Journals of Sir John Lauder Lord Fountainhall . . . 1665–1676*, ed. D. Crawford (Scottish History Soc. xxxvi 1900), 169; *Life of Radcliffe*, ed. Whitaker, pp. 53, 76; *Diary of Brockbank*, ed. Trappes-Lomax, 15, 20, 33, 35, 40; *Letters and Papers of the Verney Family*, ed. Bruce, 152; *Letters of Brilliana Harley*, ed. Lewis, 20, 27, 31–2, 41, 43.

[279] Somerset, 'Account book of an Oxford undergraduate', 90; Bodl. MS top. Oxon. f. 31, pp. 354–5.

[280] For William Powell's recuperation after a bout of smallpox in 1692–3 see Nat. Lib. Wales, MS 17107, D1/C113, 117, 592.

[281] *Diary of Brockbank*, ed. Trappes-Lomax, 38–9; Bodl. MS Locke f. 11, fos 16ʳ, 23ᵛ–4ʳ, 26ᵛ, 29ᵛ, 61ʳ; BNCA MS 85, fos 6ʳ, 50ʳ–1ᵛ, 55ᵛ–6ᵛ, 59ʳ–60ᵛ, 64ʳ, 67ʳ–8ʳ, 72ʳ–3ʳ, 74ʳ–ᵛ, 76ʳ, 79ʳ–80ʳ, 82ᵛ, 87ᵛ, 89ʳ, 90ʳ, 91ʳ, 94ʳ, 99ʳ–ᵛ; Hants. RO 15M50/1682, fos 24ᵛ, 27ʳ; Somerset RO DD/SF 482; *The Flemings in Oxford* i. 314, ii. 68, 264, iii. 18, 35.

[282] See the appendix to this chapter.

[283] Surrey RO Guildford Muniment Room, Midleton MSS 1248/1/235, 238; *The Epistolary Correspondence, Visitation Charges, Speeches, and Miscellanies, of the Right Reverend Francis Atterbury, D.D., Lord Bishop of Rochester, with historical notes, and brief memoirs of the author*, ed. J. Nichols (4 vols London 1783–7) i. 10.

above who employed them. This was rated differently according to the student's society and may have related to the amount of work which was carried out by the servitor, which varied seasonally as it involved such tasks as carrying wood and lighting fires. At Brasenose servitors were paid 6*d* or 1*s* per week, depending on the student's standing, and at Christ Church John Percival, a gentleman-commoner, paid 10*s* quarterly. The highest payment contained in a range of students' accounts was the £4 yearly paid by Sir Charles Boyle.[284]

The largest recurrent cost in a student's outlay was that for food and drink from the kitchen and buttery. The fare varied according to the status, taste, and appetite of the individual. Some students were able to keep within the notional maxima laid down by their society, others were not, while seasonal price fluctuations and the availability of produce also affected the size of the bill. Costs could be increased by visits from acquaintances, other students, or relatives, so that a high-spending student at Brasenose attributed a week with particularly large bills to the good quality of his college's ales, which had prompted some of his friends to visit him there and imbibe at his expense. His battels for one quarter in 1698 were £10 8*s* 5*d*, which was twice the notional cost for a fellow-commoner in the second half of the century, while a commoner was expected to battel at under £4 each quarter and a batteler at £3 or a little more.[285] The fact that these targets were exceeded at a time when food prices had stabilized and even fallen is indicative of the self-indulgence in the university so deplored by some.[286]

That the pattern of expenditure varied considerably between the various undergraduate grades is borne out by the examination of a number of students' accounts. Sir Thomas Southwell's residence costs were only a quarter of his outgoings and were almost equalled by his outlay on leisure and miscellaneous items, including pocket money in excess of £11 yearly. His clothing took roughly 35 per cent of his annual expenses, which amounted to £200. Commoners could spend perhaps a quarter of that sum and their residence costs were a greater proportion of the whole at between 40 and 55 per cent, while clothing took between 20 and 35 per cent and their miscellaneous expenditure averaged 10 per cent. Tutor's and other teaching fees took 11 per cent of Southwell's outlay, which was a typical proportion for all grades of student. Books and paper absorbed about 4 per cent of a fellow-commoner's outgoings and twice that proportion was the most that a commoner would have to spend on such items. The pattern for William Dean, a servitor who entered Brasenose in 1659, provides something of a contrast, with 72

[284] BNCA MS 85, fos 44^{r–v}, 51^r–2^v, 55^v–6^v, 59^r–60^v, 63^r–4^v, 66^v–7^v, 72^r–4^v, 78^r, 79^v–80^v, 87^v–92^r, 98^v–100^v; BL Add. MSS 46,954A, fo 72r, 46,954B, fo 90^r, 46,955A, fo 106^r, 46,955B, fo 143^r; Surrey RO Guildford Muniment Room, Midleton MS 1248/1/235.

[285] Bryant, *Postman's Horn*, 45–6, 50; BL Add. MS 46,955B, fo 138^r.

[286] Bodl. MS Tanner 340, fos 93^r, 240^r, 243^r. Paradoxically the level and cost of living increased on fast days when, according to Taswell [1680], 'we commonly lived more sumptuously than usual, at inns or coffee-houses': 'William Taswell', ed. Elliott, 31–2. William Taylor found the diet 'sufficiente to contente any reasonable man that is far from gluttonye' but, ironically, because of Lent and Easter the winter quarter became known as the feasting quarter: Bodl. MS Eng. hist. c. 481, fos 54^r, 56^r.

per cent of his nominal outgoings spent on residence, 13 per cent on clothing, and 11 per cent on books; miscellaneous items, which included fees for examinations at the schools, took only 4 per cent. He was not charged for his tutoring, while his Mordaunt scholarship and serving up to four other students each quarter further reduced his costs, from a nominal £16 17s 8d yearly during the first two years to an actual outlay of roughly £9 12s 0d, or by more than 40 per cent. This annual expense was less than one bill which Sir Thomas Southwell received for buttons bought on his behalf in London.[287]

These examples indicate that the actual sums disbursed during a spell at Oxford varied a great deal. Few students can have exceeded Lord James Butler's expenditure of £1,100 during his first year at Christ Church in 1679–80, but as the grandson of one of the most powerful men in the state, who was also the university's chancellor, he did have to maintain an appropriate dignity and lifestyle. Even so his grandfather regarded such a level of expenditure as excessive and twice what should have been necessary. Lord Brooke's expenses in the mid-1650s had been at a more modest level equivalent to £450 yearly. These two youths were at the top of the expenditure scale, for even by the late 1680s noblemen at Christ Church were expected to exist on a yearly allowance of between £120 and £200 and only the sons of dukes were thought to require more. It is clear that such costs had risen a great deal during the century. In the 1590s the younger son of a knight living at the equivalent of fellow-commoner status spent between £30 and £35 annually; by the 1610s a comparable outlay was perhaps £35 to £45, but an allowance on that scale in Restoration Oxford would have been more appropriate to a commoner. A fellow commoner after the Restoration required double the amount which would have satisfied his predecessors in the 1610s and by the end of the period a student of that rank spending over £100 yearly was not unusual. The impression is of an accelerating rate of increase and a threefold rise in costs during the century. The lower grades of students were able to live more cheaply. Towards the end of the period an annual allowance of £20 was thought sufficient for those who lived frugally and a servitor at St Mary Hall apparently existed on an annual average of £10 in the 1680s.[288] The contrasts between the various grades are illustrated in table 1.15, which gives the costs of the first year of residence, excluding fees, of fourteen pupils of Ralph Eaton at Brasenose between 1658 and 1662 as entered in his own accounts and so directly comparable. If these cases were at all typical, fellow-commoners' expenses were roughly five times those of servitors and more than twice those of commoners.[289]

Costs were directly affected by the amount of time a student was in residence and could be reduced by periods of absence from the university while he was at

[287] CA MS 427; BNCA MS 85, fos 82ᵛ–3ᵛ.

[288] HMC Ormonde MSS new ser. v. 333; Surrey RO Guildford Muniment Room, Midleton MS 1248/1/235; Guildhall Lib. MS 12806/6, fos 297ᵛ, 332ʳ, 429ʳ, MS 12806/7, pp. 226, 663; 'Account-book of an Oxford undergraduate', ed. Duff, 255–63.

[289] BNCA MS 85.

TABLE 1.15

First-year expenses of fourteen Brasenose students, 1658–62 (£)

Fellow-commoners	74, 80, 90
Commoners	32, 32, 42, 50
Battelers	20, 25, 35, 38
Servitors	7, 14, 23

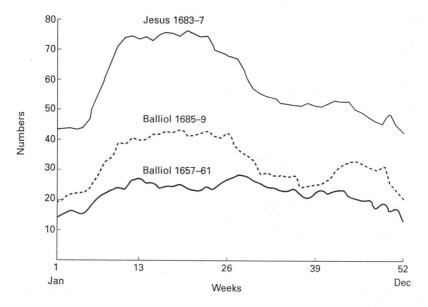

FIG. 3. Seasonal patterns of student residence (*a*) Balliol residence, 1657–61 (*b*) Balliol residence, 1685–9 (*c*) Jesus residence, 1683–7

home or elsewhere, perhaps earning money. This was an advantage for those students from counties close to Oxford, while those with further to travel were likely to make the journey home only infrequently.[290] Some fees had to be paid even when a student was absent and this was a source of irritation. Henry Townshend surely expressed the view of generations of parents when he wrote to his son's tutor: 'I do not understand why barbers, landresses and woman to make beds and swep chambers or such like should be paid for no service or work don by the quarter, when either one comes up in the middle of a quarter, or are absent a third part or half a quarter together, but proportionably for the tyme; I speake not of som

---

[290] Bodl. MS Rawlinson letters 52, fo 285ʳ.

few weeks.'[291] Even absence for a complete quarter required the payment of a fee for keeping the student's name 'on the books' of his college or hall. For both environmental and financial reasons the winter was the time of greatest absence among undergraduates, with lower numbers resident then than during the long vacation. Some tutors continued to teach their pupils throughout the summer. John Freind's tutor was reluctant to let his pupil, who had arrived the previous April, be away too long in August and September. John spent only three weeks of the long vacation at home, but he was aware that to stay in Oxford throughout the winter months would be 'a tedious thing' and was absent for eleven weeks between November and February.[292] His was a commonly held view and figure 3 shows the extent to which numbers fell during the winter. They increased again thereafter and the greatest concentration of student residence was in the spring and early summer. At Balliol in the period 1685–9 the second quarter contained almost one third of the total residence.[293] The Act in early July helped to maintain numbers until then, but there was a falling off thereafter. There was no wholesale return to Oxford after the long vacation and the Michaelmas term saw far fewer numbers in residence than the spring and early summer months. This feature was apparently becoming more accentuated, with a much more even pattern of residence at Balliol in 1657–61 than in 1685–9. At Jesus in the mid-1680s the rise in numbers following the long vacation was barely perceptible and there was a renewed thinning out in December. The peak periods saw undergraduate residence running at roughly twice the level of the winter months. Seasonality of admission followed a similar and related pattern, the majority of students first coming into residence during the late winter and spring (table 1.16). The six months February–July saw 76 per cent of new arrivals.[294]

The length of time which a student spent at Oxford was largely determined by his intentions. Those who planned to take a degree had to satisfy the residence qualifications, those who did not were free to leave whenever they had obtained such instruction as they required. The statutory period of residence for a BA was four years, or sixteen terms, including the two in which the student matriculated and graduated, which could be kept by spending only a few days in Oxford. Noblemen had been made a special case in 1591 when their requirement was reduced to three years, and dispensations of two terms could be granted to other students.[295] Very few students were able to shorten the time from admission to graduation to less than three years and the average duration was closer to the statutory four years, as the examples from Balliol and Jesus in table 1.17 show.[296]

[291] *The Correspondence of John Locke*, ed. De Beer i. 208.

[292] Bodl. MS top. Oxon. f. 31, pp. 82,83, 87, 90, 138–9, 172, 175.

[293] Measured in units of student-weeks, each week or part of a week during which a student was in residence being one unit: Bodl. MSS DD Jesus College a. 28–32; BCA bursar's books, series I/C, annual volumes.

[294] This is based upon the dates of first residence.

[295] *Laudian Code*, ed. Griffiths, 45. For an example of a student who was not allowed to proceed to a BA because he was three terms short of the requirement see BL Add. MS 46,956C, fos 90ᵛ, 110ᵛ.

[296] BCA bursars' books, I/C; Bodl. MSS DD Jesus College a. 26–33.

TABLE 1.16

Seasonality of admission at Balliol (1637–81), Exeter (1630–8), Jesus (1680–8), Lincoln (1673–89), St Edmund Hall (1658–82) (%)

Jan.	Feb.	Mar.	Apr.	May	June	July	Aug.	Sept.	Oct.	Nov.	Dec.	Total	Number in sample
3	12	18	12	12	10	12	3	2	9	5	3	101	1,858

TABLE 1.17

Length of residence at Balliol (1660–70) and Jesus (1680–8)

	Balliol		Jesus	
	BAs	Non-graduates	BAs	Non-graduates
Fellow-commoners	—	68 (69)	—	92 (87)
Commoners	199 (64)	79 (67)	181 (76)	96 (82)
Scholars	186 (77)	145 (64)	—	—
Battelers	208 (55)	157 (57)	203 (73)	118 (80)
Servitors	214 (67)	113 (68)	202 (80)	120 (52)
Combined	203 (64)	96 (66)	190 (79)	102 (80)
Number in group	40	37	26	54

Note: The figures show the number of weeks from first residence to departure/graduation; those in brackets show the percentage of that time spent in residence. These are the mean figures for each group.

Commoners were apparently able to take their BA sooner than the lower grades of student, some of whom waited for much longer than the statutes required before taking their degree, perhaps because they had difficulty in finding the fees—which were of the order of £10—and needed the extra time to raise the money.[297] Those not taking a BA spent, on average, roughly half as long between admission and final departure as those who graduated did between admission and graduation. A few students—10 per cent of the non-graduates—remained in residence for a long enough period to qualify for a BA without actually taking it. They presumably changed their intentions, either because they were able to obtain a post without

[297] *Life of Radcliffe*, ed. Whitaker, 56; Guildhall Lib. MS 12806/6, fos 223ᵛ, 344ᵛ, 396ᵛ; Costin, *St. John's*, 140; Berks. RO Trumbull misc. corr. vol. L, no. 42; Berks. RO D/ELi, C 1/197. William Hampton appealed for assistance in taking his BA on the ground that it would 'compleat and crowne the glory of a four yeares study': BL Add. MS 29,305, fo 33ʳ. The costs of taking a bachelor's degree varied somewhat and increased during the century. In 1694 Robert Wood, a commoner at Wadham, estimated the cost of his BA at £20: 'Wood family letters', ed. Wood, 124–5.

having to graduate or perhaps for purely financial reasons. There was little difference between graduates and non-graduates in terms of the proportion of time
which they spent in residence. At Balliol this was roughly two thirds of the period
until departure or graduation, at Jesus four fifths. The relatively frequent and
extended absences from Balliol made the patterns of attendance there more frag-
mented than at Jesus, where the periods spent in the college were longer. At both
colleges the first period of residence following admission was the longest one for
the majority of students. The aggregate figures for residence incorporate a wide
variety of patterns of behaviour, but none the less they point up the contrasts
between, for example, a typical commoner at Balliol who did not go on to a degree
and a servitor at Jesus who took a BA, for they were in residence for 53 and 161
weeks respectively. The gentleman student acquiring a social education had higher
costs than did a plebeian pursuing a degree, but he incurred them for a considerably shorter period.

The cost of living was apparently greater for students after graduation than
before, perhaps in part a consequence of the removal of tutorial control. James
Wilding's four undergraduate years as a servitor at St Mary Hall had cost less than
£40, yet his first year following graduation and migration to Merton cost £25 10s
0d. Similarly, Thomas Brockbank's expenses during the four years which he spent
at Oxford after graduating were 53 per cent greater than those of his four undergraduate years.[298] Many students obtained leave of absence after taking their BA
and earned money in various posts away from Oxford while waiting to take an
MA.[299] Others did not and remained in residence even after obtaining their MA,
perhaps awaiting ordination. At that point parental patience could grow thin and
pockets empty. Brian Twyne—later the university's first archivist—was in his
twelfth year at Corpus when he received a letter in which his father pointed out
that he did not have a 'mint to coyne monie to defray your charges' and compared
him to 'Hannibal that often overcame the Romanes, but still sent home to Carthage
for monie. I far prefer him that with a little learninge getteth his livinge, before
him that with much more must still live like an infant.'[300]

There were several reasons why students failed to graduate. According to critical contemporaries these did not include inadequate intellectual ability. The requirements for a BA were said to be so basic that any undergraduate who was in
difficulty could get through by memorizing the necessary exercises or receiving
extra, private, tuition from those former members of the university who still lived
in Oxford on the fringes of academia.[301] This may have been an unduly cynical
view, for there is evidence that students who were thought to be below standard

[298] 'Account-book of an Oxford undergraduate', ed. Duff, 255–66; *Diary of Brockbank*, ed. Trappes-
Lomax, 84.

[299] HMC *Ormonde MSS* new ser. iv. 601–30, vi. 381.

[300] Bodl. MS Gr. misc. d. 2, fos 56ʳ, 57ᵛ.

[301] Robert Burton, *The Anatomy of Melancholy* (Oxford 1621), 186; Eachard, *Grounds and Occasions*,
12–13; Berks. RO Trumbull Add. MS 46, letter 6 May 1625; Byford, 'Restoration Oxford', 41–2; Wood,
Life and Times i. 242–3.

were actively discouraged from continuing to graduation.[302] For those who were at Oxford purely for a social education there was little or no incentive to take a degree and a few who sought a career in the church were preferred to a living before graduating and so could avoid the expense. Moreover not all career-orientated students saw a professional advantage in taking a degree. John Percival apparently did not think one relevant to his planned career in law and he left after almost three years. On the other hand George Radcliffe, who went on to become a barrister, did take a BA, albeit after much vacillation and despite being persuaded by his friends at one point that 'The degree of bacchelour is a thing not neces-sary.'[303] Some students withdrew before graduating for financial reasons, changed family circumstances, or illness, and others died as undergraduates, from disease or in accidents.[304] For these various reasons fewer than half of the students admitted during the period 1590–1699 took a first degree, a little over a quarter an MA, and one in fourteen proceeded to a higher degree. Because of the time lag between a student's entrance and the stage at which he had satisfied the residence require-ments for each degree the chronology of degrees awarded as shown in table 1.18 imperfectly reflects the pattern of admissions. Nor were all students able to take a degree as soon as they had fulfilled such requirements. Roughly 2 per cent of grad-uates opted to take the BCL as a first degree despite the extra residence required, although they did not necessarily go into law after leaving Oxford.

The BA and MA degrees give no indication of their holders' specializations, if any, but this is suggested in the case of those who later took a further degree. The total number of higher degrees is uncertain because BCLs were taken as both first and higher degrees. The evidence of the sample years suggests that 236 of the 614 BCLs awarded between 1590 and 1699 were taken as higher degrees.[305] Fully 67 per cent of further degrees, other than MAs, were in divinity, with those in medi-cine and civil law accounting for 18 and 14 per cent respectively. The number of divinity degrees declined in both absolute and relative terms during the period, however, and there was a corresponding increase in those in medicine and civil law. Only 3 per cent of all degrees awarded were doctorates, which may reflect the level of seniority required, as well as the deterrent effect of the cost involved. When Claver Morris returned to New Inn Hall in 1691 to take a DM it cost him over £90, fees to the university taking £56 12s 2d of that sum.[306]

[302] Lodge, 'The college under the later Stuarts', 61–4; *Letter-Book of Eliot*, ed. Grosart, 139–42, 171. In 1690 Edward Wood's tutor at Wadham wrote in circumspect terms to his pupil's father: 'I cannot say, he is idle, as on the other hand I will not tell you, that he studies very hard'. Edward did not take a degree. 'Wood family letters', ed. Wood, 116.

[303] BL Add. MSS 46,954A, fo 5ᵛ, 46,954B, fos 128ᵛ, 217ᵛ, 225ʳ⁻ᵛ, 227ʳ⁻ᵛ, 235ʳ, 243ʳ⁻ᵛ, 46,956A, fo 23ʳ; *Life of Radcliffe*, ed. Whitaker, 65, 67, 83–4.

[304] Student deaths also included suicides: Nat. Lib. Wales, MS 17107 D1/C114; Wood, *Life and Times* iii. 424; Bodl. MS top. Oxon. c. 378, p. 261.

[305] In the sample years 61.5% of all BCLs were first degrees.

[306] *The Diary of a West Country Physician A. D. 1684–1726*, ed. E. Hobhouse (London 1934), 147–8; LCM A. 1. 2, medium registrum 1577–1739, fo 193ʳ.

TABLE 1.18
Degrees awarded

	1590s	1600s	1610s	1620s	1630s	1640s	1650s	1660s	1670s	1680s	1690s	1590–1699	%
BAs	1,328	1,666	2,095	2,535	2,325	950	1,282	1,661,	2,120	1,688	1,607	19,257	58
MAs	695	827	1,109	1,529	1,455	622	681	752	1,147	1,000	834	10,651	32
Other degrees	257	296	394	347	469	160	117	262	283	338	348	3,271	10
Total	2,280	2,789	3,598	4,411	4,249	1,732	2,080	2,675	3,550	3,026	2,789	33,179	100

TABLE 1.19

I. Higher degrees awarded as a percentage of all higher degrees, 1590–1699

BD	DD	BCL	DCL	BM	DM	BMus	DMus	Number
47	20	8	6	10	8	1	—	2,893

II. Higher degrees grouped by subject as a percentage of all higher degrees

	1600–19	1670–89
Divinity	83	60
Civil law	8	18
Medicine	7	22
Music	1	0
	99	100
Number	639	544

The degree statistics for the sample years are shown in table 1.20. That the earliest one is out of step with the other three samples both in respect of the comparatively small percentage of students taking a degree and the relatively high proportion of graduates who took an MA may reflect the unreliability of the estimated numbers of admissions and perhaps of the degree statistics too. Only for the final sample—when the numbers of matriculants and admissions were closely matched—can a breakdown by matriculation categories be meaningful. It is at once apparent that there is dissimilarity between them, the small proportion of those of esquire or higher status taking a degree contrasting with the relatively high percentages of the clerical, plebeian, and pauper intake. At the MA level, the most striking characteristics are that a high proportion of gentlemen's sons who graduated went on to take an MA and that there was a significant disparity between the plebeian and pauper categories in that respect. Such differences are surely explicable largely in terms of financial ability and provide confirmation that the choice of status at matriculation did reflect students' relative economic and social standing. A further characteristic to emerge from the four sample groups is that far fewer heirs took a degree than did younger sons, the latter being typical students, with 46 per cent of them graduating, while less than 18 per cent of heirs did so.[307]

Social background may also have had an influence upon the performance of the societies in terms of the proportion of students matriculated who took a first degree. Fell's policy of attracting the élite to Christ Church perhaps partly explains the relatively low numbers of its students who graduated, for example, and indeed

---

[307] For heirs N = 170, for younger sons N = 160.

TABLE 1.20

I. *Degrees taken by sample groups of students* (% of each group)

	First degree	MA	Higher degree
1603–5	37	28	5
1630–2	53	31	4
1663–5	44	24	4
1683–5	48	26	6

II. *Degrees taken by 1683–5 sample* (% of each group)

	Number	First degree	MA	Higher degree	MAs as % of graduates
Peer, bt, kt	53	17	6	7	33
Esq.	91	7	3	2	50
Gent.	268	45	31	9	70
Cleric.	119	70	39	12	55
Pleb.	177	68	37	3	54
Paup.	171	66	25	2	37

five of the six colleges with the highest proportions of matriculants from the élite produced fewer than average graduates.[308] On the other hand there was a positive correlation between the proportion of plebeian and pauper matriculants in a society and the percentage of its intake which graduated. The relationship was rather different at MA level, for the three societies with the fewest matriculants proceeding to that degree also had a high proportion of plebeian and pauper students and the correlation between the poorer grades in a society and the percentage of matriculants taking an MA was a negative one.[309]

No other strong relationship emerges from table 1.21. There was no correlation between the size of a society and the proportion of its matriculants who graduated. The new foundations of Pembroke and Wadham both produced high percentages graduating, as did All Souls and New College, and a higher than average number of matriculants from these four colleges subsequently entered the clergy. Wadham's late seventeenth-century reputation for the quality of its teaching seems to be borne out by the numbers of graduates and MAs which it produced, but Bathurst's regime at Trinity as described by John Harris was not reflected in the college's performance at first-degree or MA level.[310] Such influences were necessarily temporary ones given the rate of turnover of college fellows and the differing attitudes of

[308] Christ Church, Magdalen College, Trinity, Queen's, Oriel, University: see table 1.13.

[309] At first-degree level the correlation between the plebeian/pauper element and the percentage taking a degree is +0.206 and the corresponding correlation at MA −0.212, in a Spearman rank correlation test producing results between −1.0 and +1.0.

[310] See pp. 64 and 69 above.

TABLE 1.21

I. *Percentage of matriculants in 1683–5 sample taking a first degree*

%	Ranked highest → lowest
74–60	Pembroke, All Souls, Magdalen Hall, Wadham, New College, Hart Hall, Lincoln
59–45	Brasenose, Oriel, St John's, St Alban Hall, New Inn Hall, Merton, Trinity, University, Corpus Christi, St Mary Hall, Exeter, Jesus
44–30	Queen's, St Edmund Hall, Balliol, Christ Church, Magdalen College

II. *Percentage of matriculants in 1683–5 sample taking an MA*

%	Ranked highest → lowest
48–34	Magdalen Hall, New College, Queen's, Oriel, Lincoln, Wadham, Pembroke
33–17	Brasenose, St Edmund Hall, Trinity, Corpus Christi, All Souls, University, New Inn Hall, Merton, Christ Church, St John's, Exeter
16–0	Jesus, Magdalen College, Balliol, St Alban Hall, St Mary Hall, Hart Hall

successive heads of houses. Changing objectives among the undergraduates also led to fluctuations, for although the characters of the societies in terms of the social and regional composition of their student memberships were relatively stable, apparently no selectivity was exercised over their intake in terms of the intentions of their entrants. The numbers matriculating at a society over a period of three years were such that the decisions of relatively few individuals regarding graduation had a considerable effect upon the proportions of that generation taking a degree. Between 1663/5 and 1683/5 slightly over a half of the societies had moved more than five places in the rankings at first-degree level.

The church was the largest single outlet for Oxford's alumni in the seventeenth century and this had a considerable influence upon the character of the university, although it was perhaps an exaggeration to say, as did one disgruntled physician in 1667, that 'Theologie is the only thing that flourishes their'.[311] It was the prospect of a clerical career which drew most of the lower grades of matriculants and the sons of the clergy to Oxford and many of them achieved their objective. It was they who entered the church in greatest numbers with at least 45 to 50 per cent of the plebeian and pauper categories and 40 to 45 per cent of clergymen's sons taking holy orders. This contrasted with students from the other matriculation groups, for only approximately 20 per cent of gentlemen's sons and fewer than 5 per cent

---

[311] *Journals of Lauder*, ed. Crawford, 174; but see also O'Day, *English Clergy*, 133.

of those who entered as esquires or of higher standing joined the clergy.[312] The profile of the profession reflected this balance. One half of those members of the early Stuart clergy who had matriculated at Oxford had entered as plebeians and the other half was divided roughly equally between clergymen's sons and those who had registered their fathers as gentlemen or of a superior status.[313]

Some clergymen's sons had the certainty of a living before they entered university, for they were destined to succeed their father and perhaps form one generation of a clerical dynasty in a parish. Others could expect preferment from the patron who had supported them at Oxford. Such assurance belonged only to a minority and the competition for vacancies was a widespread cause for concern among students. It may be that in the introspective world of an Oxford society such anxieties became unduly exaggerated. The postponement of his ordination as deacon apparently caused the suicide of a young BA of Magdalen Hall at Christmas 1632.[314] Many expressed grave forebodings about their prospects of securing a satisfactory living and regretted that they had not followed a different course.[315] One MA was fearful that 'after all I might live to see my self an old Student of Christ Church than which nothing is more contemptible, or a threadbare curate than which nothing is more miserable'.[316] Contemporary writers also painted a gloomy picture of the career prospects of aspirant clergymen caused by the over-production of graduates and the low stipends which many livings offered.[317]

The disparity between the opportunities available in the church and the numbers of graduates seeking a clerical career may not have been as great as such sources imply. Temporary posts could be taken to fill the interval before an adequate living was secured. College fellowships were used in this way and provided stepping-stones on the way to a secure position in the church. The colleges increasingly acquired advowsons by purchase and bequests to provide for their members. One Magdalen College MA applied to his college for a living in Lincolnshire in competition with a candidate from Cambridge and supported his request partly on the grounds that 'the last man was a Cantabrigian, of whom the living yet smells'; his petition was granted.[318] Lectureships, chaplaincies, and parochial and perpetual curacies were other forms of employment, perhaps below the original expectations of their holders in terms of status and remuneration, but also likely to be held only

---

[312] Based upon the sample years.

[313] Green, 'Career prospects and clerical conformity', 76–7; Stieg, *Laud's Laboratory*, 69.

[314] Bodl. MS top. Oxon. c. 378, p. 261; Burton, *Anatomy of Melancholy*, 226. William Taylor admitted to periods of melancholy and tried to counter it by taking exercise: Bodl. MS Eng. hist. c. 481, fo 54ᵉ.

[315] *The Correspondence of John Locke*, ed. De Beer i. 410–11; Bodl. MS top. Oxon. f. 31, pp. 174, 175, 178; *The Flemings in Oxford* ii. 270; *Diary of Brockbank*, ed. Trappes-Lomax, 64, 70–1, 80. The Restoration was, however, a time of 'vacancye in many places': NCA 1160, letter 14 October 1661.

[316] Berks. RO Trumbull misc. corr. vol. LX, letter 18 April 1665.

[317] Burton, *Anatomy of Melancholy*, 177–85; Wood, *Life and Times*, i. 465; Eachard, *Grounds and Occasions*, 143; John Oldham, *The Works of Mr John Oldham: poems and translations* (London 1684), 139–42.

[318] Bloxam, *Reg. Magdalen* ii. 73. Figures compiled by Garry Lynch for the History of the University show that college patronage increased by 43% between 1585 and 1699, that is from 199½ to 273½ livings.

temporarily. The numbers of graduates who took such posts cannot be recovered, although some indication is provided by figures for Bath and Wells in the early seventeenth century which show that fewer than 30 per cent of 466 curates in the diocese held degrees.[319] Openings in Ireland and North America were also explored by some.[320] It was in their own areas that many graduate clergymen sought advancement, however, and between 39 and 50 per cent held a living in their county of origin at some stage of their careers.[321] The geographical distribution of Oxford-trained clerics was indeed much the same as that of its undergraduate entrants. Almost 80 per cent of ordinands in the west country dioceses after the Restoration were Oxford men, whereas in the east midlands incumbents trained at Oxford were greatly outnumbered by those who had been to Cambridge.[322] For a minority of graduates a parish was not the limit of their opportunities and 10 per cent of those known to have entered the church subsequently joined the ranks of the higher clergy. A favoured few reached the highest positions in the church and for them an Oxford education had paid handsome dividends. Rather more than a half of those who held bishoprics or deaneries in the seventeenth century had been to Oxford and 45 per cent of them had matriculated as plebeians. The career path for such matriculants could still lead to the top.[323]

Teaching provided an alternative and a supplement to a clerical post. Some alumni were engaged as private tutors. The complaints that it was difficult to get a good tutor reflect on the one hand the fastidiousness of parents in selecting someone worthy of instructing their children and on the other the abysmally low pay and inferior status associated with such positions.[324] They also suggest that able graduates could obtain other posts. Many such tutors seem to have been recent graduates or even undergraduates, perhaps using the position to raise money to take a degree or to buy an advowson from their employer with the intention of presenting themselves when the living became vacant. The nature of such positions

---

[319] Stieg, *Laud's Laboratory*, 83. For curacies in Leicestershire see Pruett, *Parish Clergy*, 55–7.

[320] *The Correspondence of John Locke*, ed. De Beer i. 181–2; *Calendar of State Papers Colonial . . . America and West Indies 1669–74*, 70–1.

[321] Based upon the sample years.

[322] Stieg, *Laud's Laboratory*, 55. In Winchester diocese the proportion of Oxford-trained ordinands 1676–84 was 69%: A. J. Willis, *Winchester Ordinations 1660–1829*, (2 vols Hambledon 1964–5) i. 5–7. See also Pruett, *Parish Clergy*, 7; K. S. S. Train, *Lists of the Clergy of Central Nottinghamshire* (3 pts Thoroton Soc. record ser. xv 1953–5) and *Lists of the Clergy of North Nottinghamshire* (ibid. xx 1961), *passim*; G. H. Carter, *The Norwich Subscription Books* (London 1937), 55–6 shows fewer than 2% were Oxford-trained 1663–89.

[323] That is 103 out of 189 bishops 1585–1700, 111 out of 217 deans 1600–1700, based upon a compilation by Garry Lynch. G. Holmes, *Augustan England: professions, state and society, 1680–1730* (London 1982), 91–2.

[324] Burton, *Anatomy of Melancholy*, 173; Peacham, *Complete Gentleman*, 87–8; Nichols, *County of Leicester* iii. 165; *The Correspondence of John Locke*, ed. De Beer ii. 491–2, 506–9; Bodl. MS Add. d. 105, fo 64r. Reflecting on the difficulties of obtaining a satisfactory tutor for their son, Mary Clarke wrote to her husband, Edward Clarke MP, that if they could find one they should value him as a great jewel: Somerset RO DD/SF 3833, letter 30 April 1687.

made them temporary ones.[325] Grammar schools offered greater security and remuneration and by the late seventeenth century their staff were recruited largely from among university graduates.[326] The statutes of some schools specified that this should be so and some imposed the further requirement that staff should be Oxford alumni, perhaps vesting the right of appointment with a college. Some teaching posts offered relatively low pay and were held for short periods, but others provided a sufficiently high income to attract and retain an able man. The amalgamation of livings in the late seventeenth century which raised the stipends of their holders was paralleled by the appointment of incumbent clergy to the masterships of grammar schools for similar reasons.[327] Some graduates taught in schools at a lower level or set up their own establishments because they had not found a suitable opening elsewhere or because they were disbarred from another career by the religious tests. It seems that a substantial, although indeterminate, proportion of Oxford's alumni taught at some level and that it was those who matriculated as plebeians that most commonly did so.

A university education was less of a requisite for entry into some other professions. This was the case in medicine, for a considerable proportion of country physicians not only had not been to university but indeed lacked any qualifications at all. The efficacy of a university training was itself in doubt and Thomas Sydenham, himself a graduate of Magdalen Hall, offered the opinion that 'one had as good send a man to Oxford to learn shoemaking as practicing physick'.[328] The universities could also be bypassed by aspirant lawyers. Only 55 per cent of barristers and 59 per cent of benchers called during the period 1590–1639 had attended university.[329] Consequently the number of those who joined the legal profession after leaving Oxford was only one sixth of the number of those who became clergymen. Even fewer went into medicine. There were anxieties none the less that by the second half of the seventeenth century the common law was becoming saturated by the increasing numbers of graduates going into it. Both medicine and law were primarily open to the sons of the gentry and their superiors, and the social status and financial resources which a young man required to

[325] Northants. RO Th 2575; HMC *Ormonde MSS* new ser. iv. 601, 606, 630; Styles, *Seventeenth Century West Midlands History*, 268.

[326] W. A. L. Vincent, *The Grammar Schools 1660–1714* (London 1969), 120–2.

[327] Bodl. MS Ballard 46, fo 87ʳ; HMC *Kenyon MSS*, 103; Oldham, *Works*, 139–40; Vincent, *Grammar Schools*, 160–1; *VCH Beds.* ii. 163–7; *VCH Gloucs.* ii. 370–4; *VCH Northants.* ii. 252–6; *VCH Surrey* ii. 201–3; *VCH Warwicks.* ii. 308–10, 337–8, 343–6, 350–3, 358–62; P. J. Orpen, 'Schoolmastering as a profession in the seventeenth century: the career patterns of the grammar schoolmaster', *History of Education* iv (1977), 183–8; Holmes, *Augustan England*, 57, 71–2.

[328] *Diary of the Rev. John Ward, A. M., Vicar of Stratford-upon-Avon*, ed. C. Severn (London 1839), 242; R. S. Roberts, 'The personnel and practice of medicine in Tudor and Stuart England' pt 1 'The provinces', *Medical History* vi (1962), 363–7; Holmes, *Augustan England*, 170–7, 181, 206–9.

[329] Of those who had been to a university, Oxford's alumni slightly outnumbered those of Cambridge: W. R. Prest, *The Rise of the Barristers: a social history of the English bar 1590–1640* (Oxford, 1986), 111–12.

make his way in those professions were a deterrent to many.[330] Those who entered them after a spell at Oxford came from a different background to those who pursued a clerical career. A majority of those who went on to practise medicine had matriculated as gentlemen's sons and barely a third had entered as sons of clergy or plebeians. The contrast was even more marked in those who entered the law; 35 per cent of them had matriculated as esquire or as of a higher status and only 15 per cent were from a clerical or plebeian background.[331]

The practice of the gentry and higher-status groups in educating some of their sons in the universities during this period was also reflected in the numbers of alumni serving in both central and local administration. Perhaps 35 to 40 per cent of the officials who were members of the civil service under Charles I and his sons had been to university, and the majority of them were Oxford men. Of the Oxford alumni who were officials in three departments during the years following the Restoration, three quarters had matriculated at a higher status than that of gentleman's son.[332] Oxford had also contributed to the educational experiences of 30 per cent of members of parliament, while Cambridge's representatives were rather fewer.[333] In the parliaments held between 1660 and 1690 30 per cent of the members of the house of commons were alumni of Oxford, but only 18 per cent had attended Cambridge.[334] This disparity is presumably explicable in terms of the geographical distribution of seats and especially the high numbers of members returned from the west country. An increasing proportion of local officials had also spent some time at one of the universities; more than 50 per cent of justices in a sample of six counties by the 1620s. In a west country county such as Somerset 54 per cent of those who acted as justices were university trained, and almost three quarters of them had been to Oxford. A similar proportion of the Devon justices had attended university, but there the Oxford connection was much stronger and Exeter College men predominated.[335]

[330] Holmes, *Augustan England*, 137; Prest, *The Inns of Court*, 29–31; W. R. Prest, 'The English bar, 1550–1700' in W. R. Prest (ed.), *Lawyers in Early Modern Europe and America* (London 1981), 70–1, 77–9; Lemmings, 'Student body of the Inns of Court', 152–5; *The Flemings in Oxford* ii. 262; Northants. RO D (CA) 354/51.

[331] Based upon the sample years.

[332] G. Aylmer, *The King's Servants: the civil service of Charles I, 1625–1642* (London 1961), 272–3; J. C. Sainty, *Office Holders in Modern Britain* (4 vols London 1972–5) i. 109–61, ii. 63–119, iii. 86–121, iv. 106–59 (the first three volumes, covering officials of the treasury, secretaries of state and the boards of trade, have been used for the analysis of status at matriculation). Rather fewer officials of the duchy of Lancaster, perhaps 21%, had been to university, Oxford alumni outnumbering those of Cambridge by two to one: R. Somerville, *Office-Holders in the Duchy and County Palatine of Lancaster from 1603* (Chichester 1972), 1–235.

[333] M. F. Keeler, *The Long Parliament 1640–1641: a biographical study of its members* (Philadelphia 1954), 27–8; D. Brunton and D. H. Pennington, *Members of the Long Parliament* (London 1954), 2, 5–7, 22, 27, 45–6; D. Underdown, *Pride's Purge: politics in the puritan revolution* (Oxford 1971), 401.

[334] B. D. Henning (ed.), *The House of Commons 1660–1690* (3 vols London 1983) i. 4.

[335] J. H. Gleason, *The Justices of the Peace in England 1558 to 1640* (Oxford 1969), 86–8; *Quarter Sessions Records for the County of Somerset* iv *Charles II: 1666–1677* (Somerset Record Soc. xxxiv 1919), pp. viii–xxi; S. K. Roberts, *Recovery and Restoration in an English County: Devon local administration 1646–1670* (Exeter 1985), 157–8.

This brief summary hardly does justice to the wide range of achievements of those who were educated at Oxford, not only in the professions but also in science and literature. Few can have remained impervious to the time which they had spent at Oxford during their formative years and the indications are that the experience was indeed a memorable one, reflected in the memoirs of former students and the donations and bequests which they subsequently gave to the university or their own society. Such gifts were received both from those whose purpose had been primarily to obtain a social education and those whose aim had been to use their period of study as the foundation for a career. The distinction between the two types of student was in any case not absolute, for not all of those who neither graduated nor subsequently entered one of the professions failed to use some of their time at Oxford in studying. The gentleman virtuoso was a characteristic figure of the period and a spell at Oxford can only have helped to stimulate the interests of such men as well as to provide the opportunity to join the circle of those with similar enthusiasms. The lives of some gentlemen alumni might have followed much the same course if they had not attended the university, but that does not mean that their education there had made no impression upon them. For the majority of those who pursued a career their time at Oxford had certainly opened up a range of opportunities which would not otherwise have been available. It was through their presence, especially in the parishes and schoolrooms, that Oxford's influence was most widely extended into society and succeeding generations of students were encouraged to enter the university.

Appendix

Examples of students' financial accounts are to be found in the following sources:

Robert Townsend, New College 1593–5, NCA 14753.

Christopher Trevelyan, Exeter 1605, and **John Willoughby**, Exeter 1630, *Trevelyan Papers*, ed. W. C. and C. E. Trevelyan (3 vols Camden Soc. lxvii, lxxxiv, cv 1857–72) iii. 83–4, 175–8.

Francis and Thomas Legh, Brasenose 1608–10, BNCA B 2a. 40, pp. 2–30.

William, Robert, and Richard Herrick, St John's and Christ Church 1613–20, Bodl. MS Eng. hist. c. 481, fos 41^r, 49^r, 52^r, 57^r, 62^r, 65^r–6^r, 69^r–70^r, 81^r, 97^r–9^r, 101^r–5^r.

John and Richard Newdigate, Trinity 1618–20, 'The undergraduate account book of John and Richard Newdigate, 1618–1621', ed. V. Larminie, *Camden Miscellany* xxx (Camden Soc. 4th ser. xxxix 1990).

William Freke, St Mary Hall 1619–22, H. V. F. Somerset, 'An account book of an Oxford undergraduate in the years 1619–1622', *Oxoniensia* xxii (1957), 86–92.

Walter Tuckfield, Exeter 1621–1626, Devon RO Z 1/53, box 9/2.

John and Richard Eliot, Lincoln 1630–1, *The Letter-Book of Sir John Eliot (1625–1632)*, ed. A. B. Grosart (privately printed 1882), 171–2.

Lord Brooke, Christ Church 1653–4, Warwicks. RO CR 1886/TN 22, pp. 1–22.

Martin Sanford, Oriel 1654–5, Somerset RO DD/SF 482.

William Roberts, Magdalen College 1655–7, Bodl. MS Rawlinson d. 715, fos 218^r–19^r.

Henry Brougham, Queen's 1657–9.

Henry Fleming, Queen's 1678–85.

George Fleming, St Edmund Hall 1688–92, *The Flemings in Oxford* i. 107–8, 110–13, 115–16, 120–6, 288–9, 314–15, 332–3, ii. 9–10, 15–17, 43–4, 67–8, 73–4, 80–4, 94, 99–100, 108–9, 117–19, 126–8, 131–3, 225–7, 244–5, 255–6, 265, 283–4, 289–91, 297–8, iii. 16–17, 25–6, 34–5, 49–50, 64–7.

Twenty-two pupils of Ralph Eaton, Brasenose 1658–63, BNCA MS 85, fos 11^v–101^v.

Sir John Williams, St John's 1660–2, Bodl. MS Rawlinson letters 61, fos 9^r–11^r.

Nine pupils of John Locke, Christ Church 1661–5, Bodl. MS Locke f. 11, fos 7^v–56^v.

William Moore, Queen's 1667–8, *The Moore Rental*, ed. T. Heywood (Chetham Soc. xii 1847), 7.

Sir Thomas Myddelton, Christ Church 1668, **John and Richard Myddelton**, Brasenose 1670–1, *Chirk Castle Accounts A. D. 1666–1753*, ed. W. Myddelton (Manchester 1931), 40–1, 78–9, 84–5.

Gerrard Gore, Trinity 1664, Somerset RO DD/GB 151.

Lord Leigh, Christ Church 1667–8, Shakespeare Birthplace Trust RO DR 18/5/197–261.

John Freind, St Edmund Hall 1672–3, Bodl. MS top. Oxon. f. 31, pp. 349–53.

Charles Morgan, Lincoln 1673, Bodl. MS Add. d. 105, fo 42.

Sir John Percival, Christ Church 1676–8, BL Add. MSS 46,954A, fo 72^r, 46,954B, fos 90^r, 93^r, 46,955A, fo 106^r, 46,955B, fo 143^r.

Sir Thomas Southwell, Christ Church 1681–3, CA MS 427.

James Wilding, St Mary Hall and Merton 1682–8, 'The account-book of an Oxford undergraduate, 1682–1688', ed. E. G. Duff in *Collectanea* i.

Thomas Molyneaux, Christ Church 1682–3, Surrey RO Guildford Muniment Room, 1087/2/3/1.

Sir John Trevelyan, Wadham 1687, Somerset RO DD/WO 55/8.

Charles Boyle, Christ Church 1690, Surrey RO Guildford Muniment Room, Midleton MS 1248/1/238.

Halliday Mildmay, Balliol 1690–1, Hants. RO 15 M 50/1682, fos 2ʳ–3ᵛ, 23ʳ–4ᵛ, 27ʳ.

John Stanhope, University College 1695–6, H. Owen, *Stanhope, Atkinson, Haddon and Shaw: four north country families* (privately published 1985), 51.

George Shakerley, Brasenose 1698–9, A. Bryant, *Postman's Horn: an anthology of the letters of latter seventeenth century England* (London 1936), 45–6, 50.

2

City and University

ALAN CROSSLEY

IN seventeenth-century Oxford, as in all centuries from the thirteenth to the twentieth, friction arose because two constitutionally separate but closely dependent communities occupied the same restricted space. The university's opinion of how the space should be apportioned was expressed in a petition to parliament in 1641: 'where two corporations live together, there is a necessity that one of them be subordinate to the other . . . as this very place hath found heretofore by bloody experience.' The university was a body 'more considerable in the church and state, consisting of the flower of the nobility and gentry . . . who will not endure to be subordinate to mechanical persons'.[1] Although sometimes willing to acknowledge the university as 'the stronger and more graceful' body, the mechanical persons of 'so eminent a city' were also capable of a different, insubordinate, stance.[2] For this was a litigious age, and as the city recovered its economic vigour it produced leaders who resented the implied humiliations of the burgesses' annual oath to the university or their annual obeisance at St Mary's church in expiation of the St Scholastica's day massacre. Seventeenth-century town–gown confrontations, though less violent than their medieval forerunners, were much more frequent, and litigation reached a peak as the various grants which had left the university in control of much of the city's government were repeatedly challenged.[3] At the same time the parochial town–gown debate began to be influenced by the social and political upheavals of a wider world: in the 1630s the university used the national influence of its chancellor Archbishop Laud to make gains over the city, later the city took advantage of the university's discomfiture in the aftermath of the civil war, and in turn the university sought revenge at the Restoration.

In an almost continuous sequence of disputes from the 1570s until the 1690s the crown, the privy council, and the central courts were assailed by claim and counter-claim touching most aspects of government and communal life in Oxford. Town–gown disputes frequently began as petty wrangles, but soon widened into

[1] OUA WP/Γ/26/1, pp. 442–3.

[2] Ibid. SP/D7/5. The second phrase was used by freemen in a petition of 1651: *Oxford Council Acts 1626–65*, ed. M. G. Hobson and H. E. Salter (OHS xcv 1933), 186.

[3] For the development of university privileges see H. Rashdall, *The Universities of Europe in the Middle Ages* (2 vols Oxford 1895, 2nd edn 3 vols Oxford 1936) iii. 79–113; *The Early Oxford Schools*, 133–47, 166; *The Collegiate University*, 86–94; *VCH Oxon.* iv. 53–7.

'omnibus' assertions of ancient rights derived from charter or prescription, backed
by laborious research and costly legal opinion. Sometimes there was little regard
for truth, as in 1598 when what the mayor reported as an unprovoked assault on
the city's trained band returning peaceably from exercises was seen by the university as the legitimate arrest of an armed mob, some dressed as women, carrying
into town a May queen, and indulging in morris dancing.[4] Such evidence tested the
patience of judges and privy counsellors, whose rulings occasionally revealed a note
of asperity, as in 1612 when the current town–gown quarrels were described by the
privy council as 'no little scandal both to religion and government'.[5]

Some general aspects of the city's development may be noted.[6] The town had
acquired the status of a city when the see of Oxford was created in 1542, and in
1605 the city's formal constitutional development was completed by a royal charter which, despite upsets in the later seventeenth century, survived effectively as
the city's governing instrument until municipal reform. The dominant theme of the
city's history from the later sixteenth century to the civil war was a rapid growth
of population and prosperity in response to the revival of the university. The small
and not wealthy town revealed in subsidy returns of 1523–4 became by 1662, on
the evidence of hearth tax assessments, eighth among English provincial centres,
with Cambridge significantly close behind. The town's total population, including
scholars, was probably fewer than 3,000 in the 1520s, fewer than 5,000 in the 1580s,
but probably 10,000 by the 1630s. The doubling of the city's population within a
few decades, achieved largely through immigration, inevitably caused tension
between the two communities, of which the most obvious signs were disputes over
the control of slum housing and vagrancy. The flood of newcomers put new pressures on existing institutions such as the traditional craft guilds, and, as they and
the corporation strove to protect the freemen's trading monopoly and to preserve
craft regulations, the university's claims to control guilds or to license craftsmen
re-emerged as central issues. At the same time that population growth began to
cause governmental problems new legislation made more government necessary,
increasing the strains on a magistracy shared between city and university. More regulation of the poor was ordained just as more paupers appeared, and concern over
standards of behaviour among scholars coincided with a legitimate increase in the
number of alehouses providing for a growing population. As the spacious city
depicted by Agas in 1578, set largely within the compass of its medieval walls,
turned into the crowded, overspilling city depicted by Loggan in 1675, the need to
improve water-supply, drainage, and other public services became intense.

A less obvious result of prosperity and growth was a change in the character of
the city's leadership. Although the traditional *cursus honorum* from constable to
mayor remained unchanged superficially, and although the large city council
retained its cumbersome, hierarchical structure, pressure for places caused a crucial

[4] HMC *Salisbury MSS* viii. 191, 201–3.

[5] *Royal Letters addressed to Oxford*, ed. O. Ogle (Oxford 1892), 345.

[6] For detailed discussion see *VCH Oxon.* iv. 74 ff.

transformation. As more and more successful men became established in the city their urgent need for the conciliar rank which adequately reflected their status made compounding for office commonplace; the rich or talented could move quickly up the hierarchy by buying chamberlains' or bailiffs' places instead of waiting to serve their turn in those annual offices. By the seventeenth century members of the inner council tended to be younger, wealthier, and better educated than their predecessors. Many were immigrants with the self-confident attitudes of new men: fewer than a third of the members of the inner council in the earlier seventeenth century were natives of Oxford.[7]

Close family and personal ties between townsmen and gownsmen were not uncommon in earlier periods, but by the seventeenth century there seems to have been a distinct narrowing of the educational and social gap between the leaders of the two communities.[8] Walter Payne, an early seventeenth-century mayor dismissed contemptuously as 'very weak of capacity and unable to read', was in no way typical.[9] By contrast Thomas Harris, mayor in 1603, although a woollendraper with no known formal education, was an able and arrogant man.[10] He rode roughshod over the 'dotards' of his own council, quarrelled with the city recorder, Thomas Wentworth, had the temerity to question the literacy of the high steward, William, Lord Knollys, and other privy counsellors, and corresponded on apparently equal terms with the formidable John King, vice-chancellor and later bishop of London. When Knollys secured Harris's dismissal from a council which regarded him as 'wholly at the dispose' of Bishop King and blamed him, above all, for selling the site for Wadham College too cheaply, Harris was astute enough to retain the university's backing in a prolonged but successful campaign for reinstatement as alderman.[11] Another notable mayor was John Davenant (died 1622), reputedly Shakespeare's friend and regular host at his tavern in Cornmarket Street. Davenant was earlier a warden of the Merchant Taylors' Company, and his children included a fellow of St John's College and the poet Sir William Davenant; he donated a manuscript to St John's and his own will provides a notable example of testamentary prose.[12] One beneficiary at least of the corporation's unsatisfactory deal over Wadham College was Alderman William Boswell, mercer, who secured a place for his son William as a foundation scholar and saw him become a fellow and a distinguished lawyer.[13] John Smith, brewer, son of an Oxford alderman, mayor in

[7] Ibid. 135–9.

[8] For the earlier periods see *The Early Oxford Schools*, 167–8; *The Collegiate University*, 108–16.

[9] PRO C 3/308/39.

[10] For his apprenticeship see Oxford City Arch. A.5.3, fo 272.

[11] Bodl. MS Twyne 5, p. 374; Oxford City Arch. F.5.2, nos 9, 11–12, 14–15; OUA NEP/H/4/3; ibid. SP/D/7/11, 14, 20, 29, 32–4, 36, 48; *Oxford Council Acts 1583–1626*, ed. H. E. Salter (OHS lxxxvii 1928), pp. l–liv, lvii, 255. For Wentworth, Knollys, and King see *DNB*.

[12] PRO PROB 11/140, fos 410–11ᵛ; Costin, *St. John's*, 52–3; W. H. Hutton, 'Shakespeare and Oxford' in *Catalogue of Shakespeare Exhibition in the Bodleian Library* (Oxford 1916), 73–90; H. O. Coxe, *Catalogus codicum MSS qui in collegiis aulisque Oxoniensibus hodie adservantur* (2 vols Oxford 1852) ii, St John's LVII.

[13] J. Wells, *Wadham College* (London 1898), 43; *The Registers of Wadham College*, ed. R. B. Gardiner (2 vols London 1889–95) i. 15.

1639, and MP in the Long Parliament, was also educated at Wadham College.[14] The family of Ralph Flexney, a butcher and the mayor in 1612, contained several graduates, including his son Thomas, registrar of the bishop of Oxford.[15] Later mayors with close university connections included Henry Silvester, father of a graduate and brother of Edward Silvester, a noted classics tutor, Walter Cave, mercer and brewer, son of an Oxford graduate, and Richard Hawkins, a heraldic painter and friend of Anthony Wood.[16]

Perhaps the most surprising town–gown connections were those between the young William Laud and several townsmen, possibly arising from Laud's own mercantile background. In 1602 he was friendly enough with a young mercer, William Chillingworth, to stand as godfather to his son William, later the controversial theologian.[17] The elder Chillingworth, a common councillor by 1606, only rose to the inner council in 1643 when Oxford was the royalist capital, but whether his career was hampered by his connections with Laud is not known.[18] In 1610 Laud wrote to the mayor on behalf of two other young tradesmen who wished to apply for the coveted city loan charity bequeathed by Sir Thomas White, founder of Laud's college; his intercession was successful, and one of the young men, Samuel Cockram, went on to become a leading city councillor.[19] Laud's personal contacts with townsmen provide an awkward reminder of how little is known of his private life.

Rising standards among the city's leaders, while altering the tone of the perennial town–gown debate, in no way introduced brevity or a spirit of compromise. By the early seventeenth century Oxford's town clerks, once fairly lowly figures in the corporate hierarchy, were efficient lawyers prominent in the inner council. Ralph Radcliffe, for example, appointed town clerk in 1614, evidently enjoyed a considerable London practice; earlier he had acted for the university in town–gown disputes, but in 1618 was allegedly instigator of a proposed city charter which seemed to threaten university privileges.[20] The city's recordership, usually linked with one of the city's two parliamentary seats, was held by men of the calibre of Thomas Wentworth (died 1627) who, like his father Peter, was an outspoken champion of parliament against the crown. Wentworth opposed the introduction of university representation in parliament in 1604 and became a 'most malicious and

---

[14] M. Toynbee and P. Young, *Strangers in Oxford* (London 1973), 142–3; M. F. Keeler, *The Long Parliament* (Philadelphia 1954), 340.

[15] Wood, *City of Oxford* iii. 162–3; Foster, *Alumni* ii. 509.

[16] For Silvester see Wood, *Fasti* ii. 34–5; Foster, *Alumni* iv. 1450. For Cave see Toynbee and Young, *Strangers in Oxford*, 150–1, 153. For Hawkins see *Catalogue of Oxford Portraits*, ed. R. L. Poole (3 vols OHS lvii, lxxxi–lxxxii 1911–26) i. 247–8; Wood, *Life and Times* v. indexes.

[17] C. Carlton, *Archbishop William Laud* (London 1987), 7, 127; *DNB*; Wood, *Athenae* iii. 81–94; *Brief Lives by John Aubrey*, ed. A. Clark (2 vols Oxford 1898) i. 171–4.

[18] For Chillingworth's council career see *Oxford Council Acts 1583–1626*; *Oxford Council Acts 1626–65*.

[19] Cf Laud, *Works* vii. 4–5, erroneously dating Laud's request 1619; cf *Oxford Council Acts 1583–1626*, 201 and *passim*.

[20] *Oxford Council Acts 1583–1626*, 279; OUA SP/D/7/32; PRO C 3/308/39.

implacable fomenter' of town–gown disputes.[21] The city could also look for support to its costly high stewards, usually influential courtiers such as the lord chancellor Thomas Egerton, Lord Ellesmere (steward 1601–10), his successor Sir William Knollys, later earl of Banbury (steward 1611–32), and George Villiers, duke of Buckingham (steward 1669–87); in the commonwealth period the high steward was Bulstrode Whitelocke.[22] All became involved in town–gown disputes, and indeed so assiduous was the duke of Buckingham in a dispute over noctivagation in 1677–8 that the council felt the need to bestow a grovelling accolade.[23]

In some respects, then, the city was better equipped than in the past for legal combat, and sometimes its leaders met the university on fairly equal and civilized terms: in 1650, for example, after a long debate in London before the lord commissioner, Whitelocke, the city delegation entertained the university representatives in a Fleet Street tavern.[24] It would be mistaken, however, to overstress the change, for there were many other occasions when the social and intellectual distances between town and gown were given full prominence. After all, most leading townsmen were craftsmen or shopkeepers, and Oxford shopkeepers, then as later, were suitable butts for university disdain: in 1628 a convivial conversation in Trinity College groves, which resulted in one of the participants being sentenced to lose his ears, included the remark that the king had wit enough to be a shopkeeper, 'to ask what do you lack, and that is all'.[25] In 1684 a university representative was not embarrassed to challenge the mayor's inclusion in the county magistracy on the grounds that 'it would not be grateful to the gentlemen of the county for a chandler or a baker (or such mean persons as sometimes their mayors are) to take precedence of them on the Bench'.[26] John King, as vice-chancellor, declared openly in 1609 that the city bailiffs were 'not fit for all services, and some of them at some times not fit for any', and a later vice-chancellor showed his contempt by boasting to Laud that 'to put an end to the town's snarling—I cast them out a bone which has set them at odds amongst themselves'.[27] Laud's own attitudes may be discerned in an ostensibly royal letter to the city referring to 'the liberties you use under our favour and goodness', and in his threat to make leading councillors 'come with their halters again', an allusion to a myth illustrating Oxford's medieval subjection.[28]

Even the city's more eminent protagonists were no real match for their university counterparts. In 1608 Thomas Wentworth was snubbed sharply by the

[21] Wood, *Athenae* ii. 414–15; *DNB* corrected by *Oxford Council Acts 1583–1626*, p. xlvi; *Oxford Council Acts 1626–65*, 7, 10; Wood, *History of the University* ii. 308.

[22] *DNB*; G. E. Cokayne, *The Complete Peerage* (rev. edn 13 vols London 1910–59). For the lavish entertainment of stewards see *Oxford Council Acts 1583–1626*, 139; *Oxford Council Acts 1666–1701*, ed. M. G. Hobson and H. E. Salter (OHS new ser. ii 1939), pp. xv, 102–5.

[23] *Oxford Council Acts 1666–1701*, 109.   [24] OUA NEP/H/5/9, pp. 109–13.

[25] Laud, *Works* vii. 17–18; *DNB* s. v. William Chillingworth.

[26] OUA WP/R13/4: notes probably by John Wallis, keeper of the archives.

[27] OUA SP/D/7/17; Laud, *Works* v. 252.

[28] Laud, *Works* v. 239; Bodl. MS Twyne–Langbaine 4, fos 187–90. For a discussion of the myth see Wood, *Life and Times* i. 373–6.

vice-chancellor John King, who warned him that as city recorder 'you neither have nor shall have to do with the proctors, or any the meanest member of the university'.[29] Soon the proud Wentworth was making humble submission to 'that noble mother in church and commonwealth to which I acknowledge myself for some part of my education'.[30] Likewise the city's high stewards, however eminent, were usually overshadowed by the university's chancellors. Thomas Howard, earl of Berkshire, steward from 1632, whose interest and reputation were described by Clarendon as 'less than anything but his understanding', could hardly compete with Laud.[31] Even the abler Lord Knollys was a half-hearted champion where conflict with the university was concerned: in 1611, perhaps mindful of his honorary degree, he felt the need to temper a protest to the vice-chancellor John King with the assurance that as steward he had always urged townsmen 'to acknowledge a superiority in the university'.[32] Lord Ellesmere in 1610 forsook the high stewardship of the city for the more attractive post of chancellor of the university and in 1650 Bulstrode Whitelocke was seriously tempted to do the same.[33]

Time and again the city's cause was frustrated by the university's influence. In 1618 the lord chancellor out of 'love for the university' raised the alarm about the city's covert progress towards a new charter, and during the critical disputes of the 1680s the university had the powerful support of the secretary of state, Sir Leoline Jenkins, 'our best friend'.[34] In king's bench in 1609 the city's legal arguments counted for little against the prejudices of judges who favoured the university: thus the lord chief justice, while acknowledging that the city bailiff had been arrested on a flawed warrant, still refused bail to avoid giving townsmen 'so much occasion of pride', while the lord chancellor ominously reminded the city's attorney how the king would thank him 'for being against the university which his majesty so highly favoured'.[35] Kings frequently expressed personal support for the university in town–gown struggles: in 1640 Charles I intervened in the university's favour during a privy council debate, in 1661 allusion was made to Charles II's 'very tender and peculiar care and regard' for the university, and in 1684 he personally rejected all the demands in a city petition.[36]

Most litigation in seventeenth-century town–gown disputes involved a search for precedents, and in this respect, too, the university was better served than the city. In 1636 the mayor gloomily predicted that the city's lawyers would be outmatched by 'the antiquary who maketh nothing else his study . . . one of the chiefest actors in causing these controversies'.[37] He was referring to Brian Twyne, first keeper of

[29] OUA SP/D/7/3.   [30] Ibid. SP/D/7/45.

[31] Cokayne, *Complete Peerage* ii. 150 n.   [32] OUA SP/D/7/29.

[33] *Oxford Council Acts 1583–1626*, p. lii; *Diary of Bulstrode Whitelocke*, ed. R. Spalding (British Academy Records of Social and Economic History new ser. xiii 1990), 254.

[34] OUA SP/D/5/9, no. 9; *Letters of Humphrey Prideaux*, ed. E. M. Thompson (Camden Soc. 2nd ser. xv 1875), 135.

[35] OUA SP/D/7/17.

[36] Bodl. MS Twyne–Langbaine 4, fos 187–90; *Royal Letters*, ed. Ogle, 371–3; OUA WP/R/13/6.

[37] Bodl. MS Twyne 9, p. 279.

the university archives (1634–44), drafter of the Laudian statutes and the university's great charter of 1636.[38] Twyne's work on the charter, involving extensive historical research and prolonged sojourns in London to see the charter through, was spurred on by violent antipathy towards townsmen.[39] His extreme view that they were 'too near engrafted into the university to be a body of themselves' caused him to reject even inconsequential city claims, and the fruits of his research sometimes provoked further needless litigation.[40] Twyne's obsessive volumes exemplify the tedium and the futility of most town–gown disputes, but, in preserving transcriptions of many archives subsequently lost, they represent also one of the few tangible gains from centuries of discord.[41] His work formed the basis of much that was later written about Oxford, particularly by Anthony Wood.[42]

Twyne's successors as keepers of the archives, Gerard Langbaine (1644–58) and John Wallis (1658–1703), remained in the forefront of town–gown disputes.[43] Langbaine, who enlarged Twyne's historical research, is credited with the university's printed reply to city grievances in 1649 and was prominent in the negotiations that followed.[44] Wallis, a distinguished and busy mathematician, was also an assiduous archivist and an aggressive proponent of university objections to the proposed city charter in 1684.[45] He, like Twyne, refused to yield an inch of ground to the city, even when legal opinion was against him.[46] In 1684, sensing that the university was weakening over the charter, he bluntly disassociated himself from any concessions.[47]

Probably the most crucial advantage of the university in town–gown confrontations was its importance to citizens as a captive body of consumers. In 1574 the city's high steward had described the university as the 'ground and cause' of Oxford's wealth, and when the city was ravaged by plague in 1603 the mayor, seeking financial aid from the university, commented sadly that the closure of colleges was 'most grievous and lamentable for us to hear', since the townsmen would soon be impoverished.[48] In 1641 the university was still able to claim, without too much exaggeration, that 'Oxford lies out of the road, and is in no way useful to the

---

[38] S. Gibson, 'Brian Twyne', *Oxoniensia* v (1940), 94–114; S. Gibson, 'The great charter of Charles I', *Bodleian Quarterly Record* vii (1932–4), 73–94, 121–32; C. E. Mallet, *A History of the University of Oxford* (3 vols London 1924–7) ii. 315–18.

[39] For Twyne's expenses see OUA WP/a/10/4–5.

[40] For example his concept of the 'partial leet' discussed below. The quote is from Bodl. MS Twyne 4, p. 466.

[41] His collections are listed in Wood, *Life and Times* iv. 202–22. For lost archives see for example *Munimenta Civitatis Oxonie*, ed. H. E. Salter (OHS lxxi 1920), pp. vi–xiii.

[42] Wood, *Life and Times* iv. 223–6.

[43] *DNB.*

[44] Ibid.; OUA NEP/H/5/9; ibid. SP/E/15; ibid. SP/E/2/20, printed as *The Answer of the University of Oxford* (Oxford 1649): copy in Bodl. G. A. Oxon. 4° 6 (28). For Langbaine's collections see Wood, *Life and Times* iv. 199–202.

[45] *DNB*; OUA WP/R/13.   [46] See for example OUA WP/β/15/9, nos 38–40.

[47] Ibid. WP/R/13/11.

[48] *Selections from the Records of the City of Oxford . . . [1509–1583]*, ed. W. H. Turner (Oxford and London 1880), 357; Wood, *History of the University* ii. 279–80.

public by any trade or manufacture. It serves only for the entertainment of scholars and the townsmen have no other possible means of subsistence'. In 1690 it was
argued that members of the university 'spend those revenues in the city which are
brought into them from abroad, and not only bring advantage, but almost the only
support to the city'.[49] Such arguments, of course, left out of account that Oxford
was also a market centre for a prosperous agricultural region, and that some of its
industries, notably leather and cutlery, served a much wider market than the city
itself.[50] Even so, despite remarkable growth, Oxford's economy was still characterized by small household enterprises heavily dependent on local consumption.
The wealthier and most influential townsmen were in the food and drink or the
distributive trades (chiefly mercers, drapers, and chandlers): over three-quarters of
the early seventeenth-century inner council were victuallers or distributors. Tailors,
shoemakers, and glovers, although numerically dominant, rarely acquired sufficient
individual wealth to rise high in the council. Some townsmen, the privileged persons discussed below, were so dependent upon the university that they found it
beneficial to matriculate, enjoy the university's privileges, and so stand aside from
the freeman body. Of the ordinary freemen there were few who did not regard the
supply of the university's needs as the basis of their livelihood.

Friction between consumer and supplier was inevitable, but at the same time the
economic link worked as a constraining force in town–gown disputes, since few
townsmen were prepared to withstand the university's ultimate sanction of discommoning. The penalty, usually declared in convocation and advertised in public
notices, deprived the victims of all trade or other contacts with scholars and privileged persons.[51] The 'thunderbolt' or 'heavy doom' of discommoning was used to
undermine the masons' company in 1609, to punish Thomas Wentworth and other
city officers in 1611, and to break the city's leading whigs in the 1680s.[52] In 1611
the citizens were particularly shocked at the treatment of Wentworth, a gentleman,
whose surname, 'though that of a house of honour and antiquity', was suddenly
made 'one of reproach' and set in large letters without Christian name on doors
and walls.[53] Lord Knollys argued that discommoning was appropriate only for
'great and enormous crime' and in 1612 the privy council agreed that it should be
used sparingly, being 'one of the severest censures' on men whose livelihood
derived from trade or professions within the city.[54] In 1640 the university claimed
that since 1612 only one townsman had been discommoned, a taverner who was
corrupting scholars with 'luxury and gaming', but the threat alone was probably a

---

[49] OUA SP/E/8/24; [James Harrington], *The Case of the University of Oxford* (Oxford 1690): copy in
Bodl. Gough Oxf. 105 (2), and MS version in OUA WP/Γ/28/8, nos 39–40.

[50] For a general discussion of the city's economy see *VCH Oxon.* iv. 101–21.

[51] Wood, *History of the University* ii. 303–4, 307–10; OUA WP/a/21/1: notices of discommoning
1635–1793; ibid. register of congregation and convocation 1595–1606, NEP/*supra*/11, register M, fo
28ª: submissions 1671–83.

[52] For the quotes see *Statutes*, trans. Ward, XVII. i. 2; OUA SP/D/7/27. For the use of discommoning see *VCH Oxon.* iv. 327; *Oxford Council Acts 1583–1626*, pp. xlix–lv; Wood, *History of the University*
ii. 299–305, 307–10; *Letters of Prideaux*, ed. Thompson, 83–4.

[53] Oxford City Arch. D.5.4, fo 373.   [54] OUA SP/D/7/29; *Royal Letters*, ed. Ogle, 348–9.

powerful deterrent.[55] Hence Wood's astonishment at the temerity of the Presbyterian mayor, Robert Pauling, who in 1679–80 defied the university's authority by
carrying out the night watch in person, 'whereas all mayors in memorie of man use
to be mealie mouthed and fearfull of executing their office for feare of loosing
trade'. The unfortunate Pauling, regarded in the university as 'our grand adversary'
was reported in 1681 to be almost broke because of discommoning. It was boasted
then that discommoning was a much more effective way of dealing with 'saucy'
(i.e. whiggish) townsmen than anything that Westminster Hall could offer.[56]

In 1571 an Act incorporating the university confirmed the discredited 'Wolsey's
charter' of 1523, beginning a series of town–gown disputes which continued into
the seventeenth century.[57] Townsmen were reported to 'scoff at and utterly con-
temn' Wolsey's charter, but it influenced the privy council in 1612 to favour such
university claims as the right to control manual occupations, was invoked in the
1620s to justify the university's interference with the tailors' company, and,
although largely superseded by the university's charter of 1636, was still cited in
1690.[58] The principal early seventeenth-century issues were carried over from the
sixteenth, notably the annual oath and St Scholastica's day ceremony, the control
of the market and of crafts and trades (including the related issue of privileged persons), the chancellor's jurisdiction, and the night watch. Among new issues achieving prominence were the licensing of alehouses and taverns, the taxation of
privileged persons, the right to felons' goods, the building of slum property, and
responsibility for street-cleaning and poor-relief.

The first major confrontation of the century, in 1609–12, illustrates the explosive potential of town–gown differences when uncompromising individuals were
involved.[59] The university was hostile to the masons' company, chartered in 1605,
and undermined its monopoly by admitting building workers as privileged persons
'by colour', that is by pretending they were *bona fide* college servants.[60] In 1609,
urged on by Thomas Wentworth, perhaps mindful of his rough treatment by the
vice-chancellor, John King, in the previous year, the corporation and the company
began a test case against a privileged slater.[61] The dispute soon became a wide-
ranging conflict inflamed by the personalities of King, Wentworth, the alderman

---

[55] OUA WP/a/21/1, no. 1; ibid. WP/Γ/26/1, fo 489.

[56] Wood, *Life and Times* ii. 463; *Letters of Prideaux*, ed. Thompson, 83–4.

[57] L. L. Shadwell, *Enactments in Parliament* i (OHS lviii 1912), 183–8. For Wolsey's charter see *Medieval Archives of the University*, ed. H. E. Salter (2 vols OHS lxx, lxxiii 1917–19) i. 255–72; *The Collegiate University*, 88; *VCH Oxon.* iv. 157.

[58] OUA register M, fo 24; *Royal Letters*, ed. Ogle, 349–50; *VCH Oxon.* iv. 323; [Harrington], *The Case of the University*.

[59] Summaries of the dispute in *Oxford Council Acts 1583–1626*, pp. xlix–lv; Wood, *History of the University* ii. 299–310; *Oxford Coroners' Inquests*, ed. H. E. Salter (Oxford 1912), 65–8. The chief manuscript mate-rials are OUA SP/D/7/1–48; ibid. WP/Q/29, fos 24–5; Oxford City Arch. D.5.7, fos 217–19; Bodl. MS Twyne 4, p. 101; ibid. MS Twyne–Langbaine 4, fos 85 ff.

[60] *VCH Oxon.* iv. 327.

[61] For King's correspondence with Wentworth see OUA SP/D/7/2–3.

Thomas Harris, and lesser figures such as a bailiff, Thomas Painter, whose challenge to university privilege by policing the town at night quickly supplanted the masons as the central issue. By the time the privy council adjudicated in 1612 the city was armed with a list of eight major grievances and the university thirteen. A measure of the breakdown in personal relationships was a malicious paper prepared (but perhaps not used) on the university's behalf against individual leading townsmen, which included accusations of immorality and popery.[62] A spate of discommonings quickly brought the masons to heel, but some leading townsmen only submitted on the privy council's orders, while Wentworth stayed out in the cold until a general amnesty in 1614.[63]

The privy council's comprehensive judgement of 1612 brought a lull in disputes until 1618, when the university demonstrated its power and a degree of paranoia by sabotaging the city's new charter, although it was concerned primarily with changes in the city's constitution. The university was perhaps peevish to quibble over the preamble's reference to Oxford as a free city, but it also raised more reasonable objections to clauses making the mayor and others JPs *ex officio*, granting the corporation all fines levied within the city, the probate of wills, the control of weights and measures, the power to make ordinances concerning victuals and an extension of the city's liberty beyond South bridge. The corporation's meek acceptance of defeat probably reflects its lack of unanimity over the proposed constitutional changes.[64]

In the 1630s town–gown relations worsened, partly because of Twyne's researches and Laud's personal interventions as chancellor, partly because of the city's continued growth, which revived tensions over cottage-building, alehouses, trading monopolies, food supply, and prices. Leet jurisdiction and the right to felons' goods were the chief subjects of an inconclusive arbitration in 1632, and in 1636 those issues and the right to market tolls were put to the judgement of Justice William Jones after a conference before Laud at Lambeth.[65] Characteristically both sides were dissatisfied with Jones's award, and later invoked only those parts which they found convenient.[66] The university's great charter of 1636 confirmed all existing privileges and added new ones, notably the right to appoint coroners, sole control of wine licensing, the right to make certain by-laws binding on all inhabitants, to search for corrupt victuals and suspect persons and to veto cottage-building and sports and pastimes, including feats of arms; the university was given greater market rights (including piccage, stallage, and toll), and scholars and privileged persons

[62] OUA SP/D/7/41. For the privy council ruling of 1612 see *Royal Letters*, ed. Ogle, 345–55.

[63] OUA SP/D/7/23–4, 45–6.

[64] *VCH Oxon.* iv. 122; Wood, *History of the University* ii. 331–2; OUA NEP/H/3/8; ibid. SP/D/5/9; ibid. WP/R/12; Bodl. MS Twyne–Langbaine 1, fo 122; PRO C 3/308/39.

[65] For the arbitration of 1632 see OUA WP/C/1; Oxford City Arch. D.5.4, fos 318–20; Bodl. MS Twyne 9, pp. 19–26, 61–9. For the 1636 conference see Bodl. MS Twyne–Langbaine 1, fos 144–5ᵛ; ibid. MS Twyne 9, pp. 51 ff, 277–8; OUA WP/C/44; Laud, *Works* v. 123–4.

[66] See for example Laud, *Works* v. 174–5; Bodl. MS Twyne 9, pp. 317–23; ibid. MS Twyne–Langbaine 1, fo 212.

were allowed additional rights and exemptions. Many clauses purporting to be exemplifications of ancient privileges contained glosses devised by Twyne which amounted in effect to new grants: thus the controversial right to felons' goods was said to apply to the whole university precinct, the university leet was said to embrace all inhabitants, and the chancellor's cognizance of pleas was extended to corporate bodies.[67] The extremism of the charter satisfied Twyne and Laud but stiffened the resistance of the corporation, which claimed that its privileges were so diminished that men were refusing to hold office.[68] Certainly most items in subsequent seventeenth-century compilations of city grievances were provoked by the new grants and interpretations of the great charter.[69]

In 1640 the privy council, in the king's presence and after a bullying cross-examination of the city deputation by Laud, gave judgement to the university over licensing and the night watch, and ordered a further report on cottage-building and on the observance of Justice Jones's arbitration of 1636.[70] At the beginning of the Long Parliament, when the university was already fearful of parliamentary hostility, the corporation petitioned the House of Lords on a wide range of issues.[71] The chancellor's proclamations were attacked as an assumption of royal power, and many of the great charter's grants were challenged, notably the university's right to appoint coroners, to issue by-laws, to interfere with the market and collect tolls, to have sole right of licensing taverns, and to veto feats of arms; recent privy council decisions were rejected implicitly in grievances over alehouse licensing, cottage-building, and felons' goods; the revival of arbitrary discommoning, presumably a reference to the university's recent campaign against the masons' company, was criticized as 'a plain way to set up a monopoly'.[72] The university's response expanded the usual, largely historical, arguments to include detailed censure of the environment in which it was obliged to live: it attacked the city's *laissez faire* approach to building and sanitation, and claimed that Oxford's prices were inflated by a closed shop operated by craft guilds and by local tradesmen's manipulation of the market. For the first time the university complained officially of the generous credit given to 'young gentlemen' against their tutors' wishes, 'to the extreme loss and grief of their parents'.[73] Later the citizens alleged that Laud, a man of 'predominant power and lofty spirit', had crushed their petition by deflecting it to a Lords' committee of his own choice; a compromise urged by the city's high steward in September 1641 came to nothing.[74] The city registered its dissatisfaction by

[67] Wood, *History of the University* ii. 399–402; Gibson, 'Great charter', 73–94, 121–32. Gibson states wrongly (ibid. 130) that the only new grant was the right to appoint coroners.

[68] Oxford City Arch. D.5.4, fo 377; Laud, *Works* v. 273–4, 277–80.

[69] See for example Oxford City Arch. D.5.4, fos 383–6.

[70] Bodl. MS Twyne–Langbaine 4, fos 187–90; *CSPD 1640*, 340; *Royal Letters*, ed. Ogle, 361–3.

[71] Laud, *Works* v. 291; *LJ* iv. 132, 178, 246; Oxford City Arch. D.5.7, fos 244–5.

[72] Oxford City Arch. D.5.7, fos 253–64; OUA WP/Γ/26/1, fos 435–7ᵛ. For the struggle over the masons see *VCH Oxon.* iv. 327; OUA WP/Γ/26/1, fo 454; ibid. SP/F/12; Bodl. MS Twyne–Langbaine 4, fo 87ᵛ.

[73] OUA NEP/H/3/10; ibid. WP/Γ/26/1, fos 438 ff, particularly 493–4.

[74] Oxford City Arch. D.5.7, fo 252; *Oxford Council Acts 1626–1665*, 102.

withdrawing from the annual oath and St Scholastica's day ceremony in 1642.[75] Laud, who boasted that in their petition the citizens had 'showed their teeth, but could not bite', soon found himself faced, when on trial for his life, with a selection of the same grievances.[76]

On the outbreak of the civil war the university's enthusiasm for the king was more evident than that of the townsmen.[77] In religion and politics, however, there was no straight town–gown division, and of those townsmen who favoured the parliamentary cause few were prepared to make personal sacrifices.[78] Alderman John Nixon fled when royalist forces entered Oxford in 1642, but the mayor, Leonard Bowman, was a confirmed royalist.[79] Most prominent citizens presumably followed the path of the recorder and MP John Whistler or the alderman Thomas Dennis, who claimed to have collaborated with the royalist occupiers only under duress.[80] In September 1642 Lord Saye's parliamentary troopers were given a luke-warm reception in Oxford, and it was not a townsman but a university puritan, Christopher Rogers, principal of New Inn Hall, who pressed for a parliamentary garrison, complaining that townsmen jeered at 'honest men' and called them roundheads. Lord Saye, moreover, failed to persuade the city to elect his candidate, Nixon, as mayor.[81] Even so, when the king and his army arrived in October 1642, they judged it prudent to disarm the citizens.[82] After the siege was lifted in 1646 the city's ruling group was split for a time between the returned parliamentarians and those who had remained in Oxford, but after an inevitable purge (which involved only four of the inner council and a dozen others) the city once more united against the university.[83]

Wood noted that the 'threatening ruin' of the university and the ejection of its 'most knowing and subtle men' made the citizens 'in a manner insolent, not knowing that the decay of the one must necessarily draw on the decay of the other'.[84] In 1649 the city's peremptory demands included the cessation of discommoning and of demands for the oath and ceremony, and the restriction of proctorial supervision to scholars and privileged persons.[85] Without waiting to negotiate the city then petitioned parliament, complained that it was in 'the same bondage' as when last it petitioned, and listed fifteen grievances which repeated or augmented those

---

[75] Bodl. MS Twyne–Langbaine 4, fo 302; *Oxford Council Acts 1626–1665*, 105, 112.

[76] Laud, *Works* iii. 447; iv. 174 ff.

[77] See for example HMC *House of Lords MSS* new ser. xi. 322–33; HMC *Portland MSS* i. 59–60.

[78] For the civil war and seventeenth-century religious life see *VCH Oxon*. iv. 78–85, 176–9.

[79] Wood, *History of the University* ii. 444–5; HMC *House of Lords MSS* new ser. xi. 324; *Calendar of the Committee for Compounding with Delinquents* (5 vols London 1889–93) ii. 1564.

[80] Keeler, *Long Parliament*, 387–8; W. R. Williams, *Parliamentary History of Oxfordshire* (Brecon 1899), 114–15; *Calendar of Committee for Compounding* v. 327; *Calendar of the Committee for Advance of Money* (3 vols London 1888) ii. 1120–1.

[81] Wood, *History of the University* ii. 450–4; *CSPD 1642–3*, 154; *VCH Oxon*. iv. 79.

[82] *Oxford Council Acts 1626–1665*, 369; Wood, *History of the University* ii. 456.

[83] *VCH Oxon*. iv. 122.   [84] Wood, *History of the University* ii. 631.

[85] Oxford City Arch. D.5.7, fos 248, 254–7; OUA register of convocation 1647–59, NEP/*supra*/26, register T, pp. 33–7; Wood, *Life and Times* i. 158.

of 1641.[86] The university's response, presented in lengthy sessions before the parliamentary committee for regulating the university, was surprisingly aggressive.[87] As 'the common nursery of religion and learning' it was 'the more noble corporation and more serviceable to the public'; all the city's grievances were rejected, and counter-charges made over such matters as neglect of poor-relief, the decline of local fairs, the inefficiency of city courts, and the tyrannical and greedy methods of the tailors' company.[88] The university was in a weak position, however, and by 1650, when Bulstrode Whitelocke became involved in the discussions, it was on the verge of major concessions.[89] Delaying tactics, and perhaps the acquisition as chancellor of Oliver Cromwell in 1651, ensured that proposed articles of agreement, still under discussion in 1652, were never signed.[90] Instead both sides preferred to avoid confrontation, and probably acted in line with the unsigned proposals.[91] Thus the annual oath and ceremony were ignored throughout the interregnum, townsmen were not discommoned, the proctors rarely patrolled except when called to a disturbance, and the chancellor's court, revived after closure in 1648, was frequented by townsmen but seldom used for the promotion of university privileges.[92] By 1658, however, the vice-chancellor was confident enough to proceed in the court against the city chamberlains, who had removed posts placed to inhibit traffic in certain streets.[93] In the university's court leet in 1658 the steward's charge reasserted many of the university's bolder claims in matters of licensing, felons' goods, control of streets, the night watch, and the market.[94] By then the scholars were back to their old ways, pelting the mayor and his brethren with vegetables as they proclaimed Richard Cromwell lord protector at the door of St Mary's church.[95]

At the Restoration the university immediately and successfully petitioned for restitution of its privileges; in 1661 the privy council confirmed the university's rights to the annual oath and St Scholastica's day ceremony and the night watch, and ordered the city not to interfere with any privilege enjoyed by the university in 1640.[96] A flavour of the bitterness of those times was given in negotiations preceding that decision, when the city's recorder tactlessly referred back to the concessions of *circa* 1650: he was sharply reminded that no advantage could come from

[86] Oxford City Arch. D.5.7, fo. 252, printed as *The Humble Petition of . . . the City of Oxon* (London 1649): copy in Bodl. G. A. Oxon. 4° 6 (28).

[87] OUA SP/E/2/20, printed as *The Answer of . . . the University* (Oxford 1649): copy in Bodl. G. A. Oxon. 4° 6 (28).

[88] OUA NEP/H/5/4. For the city's reply see Oxford City Arch. D.5.7, fos 307–13.

[89] For a diary of the negotiations see OUA NEP/H/5/9, pp. 1–114.

[90] Ibid. NEP/H/4/3; Oxford City Arch. E.4.3, fos 58–66ᵛ, 75–6ᵛ; for a printed version of the 1650 city proposals see *Oxford Council Acts 1626–1665*, 171–4.

[91] See for example OUA register T, p. 236; *Oxford Council Acts 1626–1665*, 182–3.

[92] OUA, TS reports on chancellor's court papers by W. T. Mitchell.

[93] OUA register T, pp. 321–2; cf *Oxford Council Acts 1626–1665*, 182–3; Wood, *Life and Times* i. 251.

[94] *Oxford Council Acts 1626–65*, 464–5.   [95] Wood, *History of the University* ii. 685.

[96] OUA register of convocation 1659–71, NEP/*supra*/27, register Ta, pp. 98–9; ibid. NEP/H/1; ibid. SP/E/2/1; Oxford City Arch. E.4.3, fos 81–90; *CSPD 1660–1*, 548–9; *CSPD 1661–2*, 14; *Royal Letters*, ed. Ogle, 371–3; Wood, *Life and Times* i. 370–6.

recalling 'what their carriage was at that time towards the university'.[97] For several years town–gown relations were conducted in a more temperate spirit, and in 1667–8, when several minor disputes seemed likely once more to develop into a serious conflict, both sides in a 'friendly meeting' before the bishop of Oxford made concessions over such matters as the night watch, privileged persons, and felons' goods; convocation in the end rejected the agreement, but the crisis passed.[98]

The changing political conditions of Charles II's reign drove an additional wedge between city and university. For the first time fairly clear political differences developed between the two bodies. A purge of the city council in 1662–3 had isolated several influential citizens who then returned to city government from 1667, beginning with such men as the former mayor John Lambe, 'a Presbyterian [and] an enemy of academicians'.[99] The university, although 'above such threats', was swift to enquire of Sir Joseph Williamson, then assistant to the secretary of state, whether corporations could thus restore men ejected by statutory commissioners.[100] The Presbyterian Robert Pauling, mentioned above, and John Bowell, 'a rank fanatic' purged in 1663, came to power at the height of the Popish Plot and exclusion controversy.[101] The dominant whig group on the council was led by Alderman William Wright MP, whose electoral majorities reflect the extent of whig sympathies among the citizens at a time when the university was regarded as a tory stronghold.[102]

In this period the freedom of the city was presented to Titus Oates, the duke of Monmouth, and the prominent whig, John, Lord Lovelace, and in 1681 the city launched another attack on the St Scholastica's day ceremony as 'a great relic of popery'.[103] In the volatile political atmosphere there were some unpleasant incidents, as in 1673 when scholars and 'townsmen of the meaner sort' engaged in sporadic fighting for about a week after the election as mayor of Anthony Harris, 'the only man of any note in the town true to the king'.[104] In 1683 a full-scale riot developed out of a tavern brawl between a handful of townsmen supporting Monmouth and a few scholars toasting the duke of York; the Monmouth supporters were predictably anti-university, and one of the ringleaders warned the proctor that 'he should see the hanging of all clergymen'.[105] The university looked on with distaste; although frustrated in its attempts to implicate the leading city whigs in the riots it gave enthusiastic support to the government's proposed purge

[97] Wood, *Life and Times* i. 371.

[98] Ibid. ii. 125; *Oxford Council Acts 1666–1701*, 307–8; Oxford City Arch. E.4.5, fo 150ʳ⁻ᵛ; ibid. F.5.9, fos 19–20ᵛ.

[99] Wood, *Life and Times* ii. 550; M. Toynbee, 'The city of Oxford and the Restoration of 1660', *Oxoniensia* xxv (1960), 75. For detailed discussion of late seventeenth-century city government see *VCH Oxon.* iv. 122–5.

[100] *CSPD 1667–8*, 589. For Williamson see *DNB*.

[101] *Letters of Prideaux*, ed. Thompson, 83–4.   [102] *VCH Oxon.* iv. 152–3.

[103] *Oxford Council Acts 1666–1701*, pp. xvi, 121, 126, 129, 134.

[104] Wood, *Life and Times* ii. 270; *Letters of Prideaux*, ed. Thompson, 90–1.

[105] PRO SP/29/424, fos 57–84; Wood, *Life and Times* iii. 510–12; *CSPD Jan.–June 1683*, 181, 186,192, 203–4, 211–13; *CSPD 1683–4*, 303–4; *CSPD 1684–5*, 64–5 (wrongly dated 1684).

of the city magistracy in 1683, advising that 'your reformation will mean nothing' without the removal of Wright, Pauling, and the duke of Buckingham (high steward).[106] Even before the city's charter was revised in 1684 Wright had been broken by a persecution campaign typical of the period, and Pauling by discommoning.[107]

The city surrendered its charters in 1683 at the behest of the influential local tory James Bertie, earl of Abingdon.[108] He promised that under a new charter any changes of personnel would be balanced by valuable concessions, notably additional markets and fairs, a boundary extension to include St Clements, additional aldermen, and the right for mayors to serve as county magistrates. The university, however, feared that the proposed charter would threaten its privileges over felons' goods and the night watch, and was determined to safeguard the full range of its privileges as extended by the charter of 1636. It therefore used its influence, particularly through the secretary of state, Sir Leoline Jenkins, to overturn all the city's proposals, greatly embarrassing the earl of Abingdon, who complained that this town–gown dispute had given him more trouble than any other matter in his ten years as lord lieutenant.[109] His irritation with the university raised his popularity among the citizens, who received the new charter in October 1684 with some rejoicing, although in the end it merely confirmed a purge.[110]

Reprisals from the city came in 1689–90 when the university was seeking parliamentary confirmation of its great charter of 1636.[111] By opposing the university's demands point by point the city raised for the last time the full range of issues which for so long had divided the two bodies; the city's case, drawn up by the recorder William Wright, son of the whig alderman, was argued effectively by the lawyer Sir Thomas Littleton, MP for Woodstock, who was made an honorary freeman.[112] The university's case, presented by the brilliant young lawyer James Harrington, was more moderate than its early seventeenth-century forerunners, disclaiming any pretence of governing the city but still arguing that the city corporation, because of anciently established oaths and agreements, was in some respects subordinate. The bill was only at the committee stage when parliament was prorogued in 1690, and an attempt to revive it in 1692 came to nothing.[113] According to some legal opinion the absence of parliamentary confirmation of university

---

[106] *CSPD July–Sept. 1683*, 325–6.   [107] *VCH Oxon.* iv. 124.   [108] Ibid. 123–4.

[109] The chief papers relating to the city's revised charter are OUA WP/R/13/2–14. Cf also PRO SP/29/437, no. 73; Bodl. MS top. Oxon. c 325, fo 32; *CSPD July–Sept. 1683*, 325–6; *CSPD 1683–4*, 309–11, 353; *CSPD 1684–5*, 4–5, 12–13, 67; *Oxford Council Acts 1666–1701*, 161. For the full list of the privileges which the university was protecting in 1683 see OUA SP/E/14/6.

[110] OUA WP/R/13/9; BL Add. MS 28,929, fo 108; Bodl. MS top. Oxon. c. 325, fos 27–8; Wood, *Life and Times* iii. 112.

[111] [Harrington], *The Case of the University*; [William Wright], *The Case of the City of Oxford* (Oxford 1690): copy in Bodl. Gough Oxf. 138(6).

[112] *Oxford Council Acts 1666–1701*, 216–17, 219; *DNB*.

[113] *CJ* x. 274, 301, 308, 336–7, 342; *Oxford Council Acts 1666–1701*, 239; Gibson, 'Great charter', 121, 124–30. For Harrington see *DNB*.

charters after 1571 left Wolsey's charter as the basis of university privileges into the twentieth century.[114]

It remains to examine in detail some of the principal issues dividing town and gown. Beneath most disputes, despite a succession of acts of parliament, privy council decrees and arbitrations, lay the unresolved question of who governed the city. Whether theoretical custody of the city belonged to the university or to the corporation was debated as persistently as any more practical points, and it would be unhistorical to dismiss such concerns as vain and trivial in a period when parliament itself debated the precedence of the two universities.[115] In 1609 the sheriff of Oxfordshire angered the corporation by implying that custody of the city lay with the university, but three years later the privy council concluded that custody belonged to the corporation and denied that the university could make by-laws binding the inhabitants.[116] The Laudian statutes of 1636 implied that the chancellor shared custody with the mayor, but the sheriff repeated his earlier mistake in 1668.[117] In commissions of the peace the vice-chancellor was usually named before the mayor, and in sessions the mayor customarily sat beneath the royal arms, with the vice-chancellor on his right and the recorder on his left.[118] In a farcical incident at the sessions in 1609 the mayor, Thomas Harris, failed to yield his seat at the right hand of a visiting judge to the vice-chancellor, John King.[119] After a prolonged dispute the privy council in 1612 ruled enigmatically that the chancellor's precedence should not be challenged, since the city lay entirely within the university's precinct where he had 'the most eminent jurisdiction', yet the mayor's authority was 'in his kind absolute also, and in no way subordinate to the other'.[120]

Given such guidance mayors continued to demand precedence over the vice-chancellor, but without much success.[121] During royal visits, for example, the university always played the major role from the outset, greeting the visitor first on the edge of its larger precinct, following a precedent of 1566 when Elizabeth I was met by the university at Godstow bridge, while the mayor and his party waited in the fields of St Giles.[122] Ill-feeling over such arrangements smouldered long after most of the principal seventeenth-century town–gown issues had been resolved or forgotten. In 1702 there was an unseemly brawl because neither body would yield precedence in the procession accompanying Queen Anne through the city; university men were forced to ride among the citizens, 'in the highest dishonour of good literature', fighting broke out, and visiting dignitaries were injured. Many

---

[114] *Medieval Archives*, ed. Salter i, pp. vii–viii; Gibson, 121–32.

[115] *LJ* iii. 52, 55, 66; Mallet, *History of the University* ii. 239.

[116] Oxford City Arch. D.5.4, fo 409; *Royal Letters*, ed. Ogle, 347–8.

[117] *Laudian Code*, ed. Griffiths, XVII. i. 2; *CSPD 1667–8*, 351.

[118] OUA NEP/H/4/17; Oxford City Arch. F.5.9, fos 45ᵛ–50ᵛ.

[119] Bodl. MS Twyne 5, p. 374ᶜ: printed in *Oxford Coroners' Inquests*, ed. Salter, 65–6.

[120] *Royal Letters*, ed. Ogle, 354.   [121] See for example OUA NEP/H/4/17.

[122] *Records of the City of Oxford*, ed. Turner, 314; *Elizabethan Oxford*, ed. C. Plummer (OHS viii 1886), pp. xviii–xxiv, 176, 198–204. For the definition of the university precinct see *Medieval Archives*, ed. Salter i. 361.

citizens were discommoned before the matter was settled with a complex written scheme to govern future processions. The university again contrasted the two corporations, the one 'engaged in the profession of the most noble and useful sciences; the other consisting partly of creditable retail tradesmen, but for the most part of the lower rank of mechanics'.[123]

The annual oath and the St Scholastica's day ceremony survived from the Middle Ages as the foremost symbols of the city's subjugation.[124] Each October the citizens swore the oath to observe university privileges, but, relying on a strict interpretation of a privy council order of 1575, they were represented at St Mary's by the mayor and bailiffs only, not by the sixty-three burgesses originally stipulated.[125] The requirement of the full complement of burgesses was confirmed by the privy council in 1612 and the oath was then sworn annually until 1642.[126] The oath featured prominently in the abortive negotiations of 1649–52, but was not sworn again until restored by a privy council order of 1661. Thereafter, despite occasional grumbling, it was not challenged seriously until the nineteenth century.[127] The St Scholastica's day ceremony, revised in 1575, was held regularly until refused in 1642 and 1643, when the council complained of jeering scholars taunting the mayor with wearing a halter on that day.[128] After the civil war the city continued to refuse attendance, and in negotiations suggested that its offering of 63d, matched by the same sum from the university, should be 'expended friendly between them' or given to the poor.[129] In 1661 the privy council restored the ceremony, which was duly observed until 1681 when the whig group on the council attacked it as popish and superstitious: when only twenty citizens attended the ceremony that year the vice-chancellor refused their oblations. The next year the whig alderman William Wright was so fearful for the city's charters that he advised full attendance.[130] In 1690, when the city vilified the ceremony as 'too great a badge of popery to be

[123] Oxford City Arch. E.4.4, fos 18–40; OUA register of convocation 1693–1703, NEP/subtus/30, register Bc, minutes at end; Oxford Council Acts 1701–52, ed. M. G. Hobson (OHS new ser. x 1952), 298–307; T. Wood, A Vindication of the Proceedings of the University of Oxford (Oxford 1703).

[124] For general accounts of the oath and ceremony see VCH Oxon. iv. 53–6, 159–60, 246; L. H. Dudley Buxton and S. Gibson, Oxford University Ceremonies (Oxford 1935), 153–5; Oxford Council Acts 1583–1626, pp. xxxvii–xxxviii. For varying forms of the oath see Medieval Archives, ed. Salter i. 362; OUA register of congregation and convocation 1535–63, NEP/supra/8, register I, fo 94ᵛ; ibid. register of congregation 1634–47, NEP/supra/16, register Q, fo 127.

[125] Reg. Univ. ed. Clark, pt 1, 295–313. For the order of 1575 see Records of the City of Oxford, ed. Turner, 369–70.

[126] Royal Letters, ed. Ogle, 353–4; Reg. Univ. ed. Clark, pt 1, 307–13; Bodl. MS Twyne–Langbaine 4, fo 302; OUA register Q, fos 127ᵛ–8ᵛ; ibid. SP/E/2/1, 6.

[127] OUA register Ta, p. 9 (separate pagination at end of vol.); Oxford Council Acts 1626–65, 272, 275; Royal Letters, ed. Ogle, 371–3; Wood, Life and Times i. 371. For nineteenth-century challenges see VCH Oxon. iv. 246.

[128] Bodl. MS Twyne 5, pp. 169–72; ibid. MS Twyne–Langbaine 4, fo 302ᵛ; OUA SP/E/2/1; Oxford Council Acts 1583–1625, pp. xxxvii–xxxviii; Oxford Council Acts 1626–65, 105, 112. For the revision of 1575 see Records of the City of Oxford, ed. Turner, 367–8.

[129] Oxford Council Acts 1626–65, 173, 399.

[130] OUA register of congregation 1659–69, NEP/supra/18, register Qb, fo 167ᵛ; Royal Letters, ed. Ogle, 371–3; Oxford Council Acts 1666–1701, 134, 276, 278, 282; Wood, Life and Times ii. 512, 517, iii. 4.

required in a protestant university', the university observed mischievously that an annual payment by the city of 100 marks for non-attendance, as agreed in 1357, would discharge the obligation entirely.[131] Thereafter there was no serious challenge until the late eighteenth-century.

The 'large and miscellaneous assortment of jurisdictions' acquired by the university in the Middle Ages, enlarged by Wolsey's charter and confirmed in 1571, continued to raise problems between town and gown.[132] Whatever grievances were voiced over the powers and procedures of the chancellor's court, citizens continued to use it since it provided the only (and a comparatively swift) remedy in debt actions involving privileged persons. There was continued dislike of the court's role, through office actions initiated by the vice-chancellor, proctors, or clerks of the market, in reinforcing the university's wide powers over the city, and in 1612 there was a half-hearted complaint concerning the chancellor's claim to exercise ecclesiastical jurisdiction over citizens in such matters as moral behaviour. The court's powers were confirmed by the privy council in 1612 and it was formally constituted a court of record with a common seal in 1636.[133] The number of actions entered in the court rose rapidly to a peak of over 300 in 1623, fell to about 100 in 1630, and recovered to over 300 before the civil war.[134]

Even so in 1649 the court appeared first in a long list of city grievances and was also attacked as arbitrary and tyrannical by the 'gentlemen of Oxfordshire' in a petition calling for its abolition.[135] The city challenged the court's cognizance of all pleas involving scholars and privileged persons (except for mayhem, felony, and freehold) and complained of the exemption of privileged persons from city courts, quarter sessions, and the central courts. The chancellor's court was criticized for its lack of a jury or of any 'certain law' (either civil, common, canon, or statute) for its use of ecclesiastical censure (i.e. excommunications for contumacy), and for the denial of adequate appeals. The university replied confidently that the court's cognizance derived from statute and that its procedures were swift and flexible, using 'the law proper for particular cases, mixt with equity'; civil law, the basis of the court's procedure, was employed in many countries and provided invaluable training for young jurists; the appeal system was fair and included a last resort to chancery; ecclesiastical censure had fallen into disuse and had now in effect been

---

[131] [Harrington], *The Case of the University.* For the agreement of 1357 see *Medieval Archives*, ed. Salter i. 168–71.

[132] For a general discussion of the chancellor's jurisdiction see W. S. Holdsworth, *History of English Law* (17 vols 1903–72, 7th edn 1956) i. 166–73; *VCH Oxon.* iv. 168–72; M. Underwood, 'The structure and operation of the Oxford chancellor's court', *Journal of the Society of Archivists* vi (1978), 18–27. For the sixteenth-century court see *The Collegiate University*, 100–3. For early eighteenth-century procedure see John Ayliffe, *The Ancient and Present State of the University of Oxford* (2 vols London 1714, 2nd edn 2 vols London 1723) ii. 312–34.

[133] Oxford City Arch. D.5.7, fos 218–19; *Oxford Coroners' Inquests*, ed. Salter, 65–8; *Royal Letters*, ed. Ogle, 351; Gibson, 'Great charter', 76.

[134] OUA calendars and index of chancellor's court papers, and TS reports by W. T. Mitchell.

[135] *The Humble Petition of . . . the City of Oxon* (London 1649); *The Humble Representation of diverse well affected Gentlemen of Oxon* (London 1649): copy in Bodl. Wood 515 (3).

abolished by act of parliament.[136] In 1649 Edward Carpenter, a privileged brewer who was well aware of the problems of debt recovery in Oxford, made vigorous and damaging comparisons between the courts of the chancellor and of the city, attributing the latter's inefficiency to the allowance of writs of error and the reluctance to imprison debtors; he noted that the law of the chancellor's court, far from being 'an arrow shot out of the pope's bow' was the same law used in many soundly protestant countries.[137]

The university was probably correct in claiming that only a few malcontents objected to the court: the corporation continued to negotiate for the right to sue privileged persons in its own or the central courts, and for an improved appeal procedure and the use of common law, but it was clearly as anxious as the university to preserve the chancellor's court. By September 1650 the only point of difference between the two sides was over appeals.[138] The court's business revived steadily thereafter, although it never achieved its pre-war volume, perhaps because the privileged community was smaller. Over 100 actions were initiated in 1662 and 1673, but by the end of the century the usual annual number was nearer fifty. Most actions were for small debts, and business was increasingly routine since many actions were uncontested. Excommunication, restored in 1661, was largely obsolete by the 1680s, although used once in a case of defamation. Office actions continued, mostly arising from the proctors' night walk or market and trading offences; in 1672–3 an office action was promoted by two privileged carriers against a third, unprivileged, carrier who was forced to matriculate after renouncing his freedom of the city. In the later seventeenth century the court continued to defend its monopoly over privileged persons: a mercer serving a writ on an MA was discommoned, a bedel's widow was deprived of privilege for suing in another court, and actions against privileged persons were removed from the city or central courts.[139] In 1690 the arrest of a city bailiff for serving a writ on an alleged privileged person was among a comprehensive list of city grievances from which the chancellor's court itself was notably absent.[140] By then the debate over the chancellor's jurisdiction was not so much between town and gown as between the university and the legal profession. There were increasing difficulties over pleading privilege in the central courts; several times when the chancellor's equitable jurisdiction was at issue judgement was given against him, and his criminal jurisdiction was regarded as even less securely based. An attempt to exercise leet jurisdiction

---

[136] *The Answer of . . . the University* (Oxford 1649); *Statutes of the Realm* v. 138. For the appeal system see Underwood, 'Oxford chancellor's court', 26–7.

[137] OUA SP/E/5/1, fos 61–2.

[138] OUA register T, pp. 33–7, 79, 112–15; ibid. NEP/H/4/3; ibid. NEP/H/5/9, pp. 109–13; *Oxford Council Acts 1626–65*, 174.

[139] OUA calendars and index of chancellor's court papers; Underwood, 'Oxford chancellor's court', 25–6.

[140] [Harrington], *The Case of the University*. For the arrested bailiff see Oxford City Arch. E.4.8, pp. 637–42; *Oxford Council Acts 1666–1701*, p. xxix.

in the vice-chancellor's court in 1700 was commented upon adversely by the solicitor-general.[141]

The controversy over the university's court leet illustrates some of the worst aspects of town–gown disputes in this period. The city's leet jurisdiction was exercised quite effectively in biannual courts for each of the four city wards, but certain 'cognizances' normally pertaining to leets had been transferred to the university during the Middle Ages.[142] The university therefore held a hybrid court, called by the sixteenth century a leet or view of frankpledge, which dealt with the assise of bread and ale, weights and measures, market offences such as forestalling, regrating and selling putrid victuals, street offences such as disrepair and obstruction, and even weapon-bearing and 'corrupt livers' (prostitutes). The university leet met in the city's guild hall and the bailiffs were expected to provide a jury of townsmen to serve alongside one of privileged persons; privileged persons, however, did not attend the city's leets.[143] Although the city and university leets were plainly complementary, the idea of a merger was never considered during the persistent disputes which began in the later sixteenth century and reached a peak in the 1630s.[144] Twyne, aware of the fortuitous origins of the university leet and of course unable to prove its antiquity by producing medieval court rolls, was undeterred by the attorney-general's opinion of 1633 that the grant of a leet by Wolsey's charter carried no weight; he argued that the court was not only ancient but was a full, not a partial leet, and that the amercements (which were usually trivial) belonged to the university. Twyne secured the grant of a full leet in the 1636 charter, but Justice Jones in the same year ruled that it was only a partial leet over townsmen, and that amercements for street offences and weights and measures belonged to the city.[145] Laud impatiently suggested that 'be they qualified leets or full leets', the vice-chancellor might just as well exercise the same jurisdiction 'in his private chamber without contradiction' as he was entitled to do.[146] In 1658 wide powers were still claimed for the university leet when it was revived after a long lapse, but it again fell into disuse after 1665.[147] Nevertheless the same arguments over leet jurisdiction were still adduced on both sides as late as 1690.[148] After an expensive and ineffectual revival in 1733 the university leet was finally abandoned.[149]

[141] Buxton and Gibson, *Oxford University Ceremonies*, 121–2; Holdsworth, *History of English Law* i. 172–3; OUA WP/a/34/3; ibid. NW/4/5. For difficulties with the central courts see ibid. WP/L/11b, and for the dispute of 1700 Bodl. MS Twyne–Langbaine 1, fos 114–17.

[142] For city leets see *VCH Oxon.* iv. 339.

[143] Ibid. 171–2, 339; I. G. Philip, 'The court leet of the University of Oxford', *Oxoniensia* xv (1950), 81–91. For the scope of the university leet in the early sixteenth century see *Medieval Archives*, ed. Salter i. 358–9, and for 'corrupt livers' ibid. 359–60, 370. The chief records of seventeenth-century university leets are OUA WP/C/7–16; ibid. WP/Q/1–19.

[144] For sixteenth-century disputes see *VCH Oxon.* iv. 171. For the arguments of Twyne and others see Bodl. MS Twyne 4, pp. 347, 353; ibid. MS Twyne 9, *passim*; ibid. MS Twyne–Langbaine 6, *passim*; OUA WP/C/11c.   [145] Gibson, 'Great charter', 77–8; OUA WP/C/44.

[146] Bodl. MS Twyne 9, p. 87; Laud, *Works* v. 244.

[147] *Oxford Council Acts 1626–65*, 464–5; OUA WP/Q/1–19.

[148] [Harrington], *The Case of the University*; [Wright], *The Case of the City*.

[149] OUA WP/Q/19; Hearne, *Collections* xi. 267, 270.

The policing of the city by the proctors after curfew (signalled by the tolling of Great Tom of Christ Church at 9 p.m. in winter and an hour later in summer) continued to provoke colourful disputes.[150] Confrontations between proctors and citizens in the darkened streets inevitably led to 'opprobrious words' and physical violence.[151] In 1640, when citizens attacked a proctor who was arresting a suspected prostitute, they 'rang their great bell at Carfax—as at the great slaughter'.[152] Forcible entry by proctors into the houses of 'well-demeaning citizens' in search of 'femmes putaines' and the standard fine of 40s levied on noctivigating citizens were potent sources of conflict, but the central issue remained the dividing-line between the policing powers of the proctors and those of the city officers.[153] Prolonged disputes in 1609–12 arose from the bailiffs' insistence on carrying out the night walk 'under pretence of taking felons' goods', and the issue was not settled by a privy council order of 1612 which acknowledged the university's ancient and sole right to the night watch while recognizing the right of city officers to pursue their reasonable business at night.[154] That business, under the statute of Winchester, included organizing the hue and cry irrespective of the curfew. In the 'troublous times' of 1640 the city watchmen clashed with the proctors and, after a constable had been tactlessly arrested by a proctor, the privy council concluded that bailiffs and constables might set watch at the gates but should only leave their posts 'to suppress a sudden tumult'.[155] There were further clashes between bailiffs and proctors in 1647, but even at the height of its power during the interregnum the city never fully denied the proctors' right to the night watch; instead it proposed that its officers should be free from proctorial interference when carrying out their duties at night, that proctors should restrict their searches to legitimate targets such as alehouses, tobacco shops, and bawdy houses, and that they should hand over arrested citizens in the morning to city officers (arrested scholars being similarly surrendered by city officers). A proposal in 1650 that all offenders should be dealt with according to the laws of the land (e.g. for drunkenness) constituted a rejection of the practice of fining citizens 40s merely for pursuing their legitimate business at night.[156]

In the latter years of the interregnum the city organized a night watch, with householders assisting constables on a rota system, and in 1660 the lord lieutenant asked the city rather than the university to provide a night watch 'in these times of great disturbance'.[157] The university quickly secured a privy council order in

---

[150] For the earlier history of the night watch see *VCH Oxon.* iv. 172; *The Collegiate University*, 104.

[151] See for example OUA WP/Γ/8/3; ibid. WP/R/11a, fo 23.

[152] Ibid. WP/Γ/26/1, fos 436, 442.

[153] For the two quotations see Bodl. MS Twyne 5, p. 365; OUA NEP/H/5/4, pp. 41–9.

[154] *Royal Letters*, ed. Ogle, 346–7. For the disputes of 1609–12 see above.

[155] Bodl. MS Twyne–Langbaine 4, fos 181–93; OUA WP/Γ/26/1, fos 435–41, 477–8; Laud, *Works* v. 274–6, 279–80; Wood, *History of the University* ii. 421; *CSPD 1640*, 340. For the privy council ruling see PRO PC 2/52, p. 654.

[156] Oxford City Arch. D.5.7, fo 30. For arguments of 1649–52 see OUA NEP/H/4/3; ibid. NEP/H/5/4, 41–9; ibid. NEP/H/5/8a; *Oxford Council Acts 1626–65*, 171–2; Bodl. G. A. Oxon. 4° 6 (28).

[157] *Oxford Council Acts 1626–65*, 462; Bodl. MS Twyne–Langbaine 4, fos 192–3, 306ᵛ; OUA SP/E/2/16–17.

1661 confirming its sole right to police the town at night.[158] Later disputes over noctivagation provoked major confrontations in the central courts.[159] The most serious challenge was offered in 1677–8 when a chandler, Philip Dodwell, allegedly with the city's backing, openly rejected the university's jurisdiction over citizens. He argued that as a freeman of Oxford he was exempt from university statutes and might pursue his 'lawful occasions at any houres by night or by day', and that under Magna Carta he was entitled to be tried by the law of the land and not by the vice-chancellor's civil law court. The university pointed out that if townsmen were allowed to wander at night unpunished 'the ancient quarrels and murders may be renewed to the hazard of the hopes of this nation placed here'. Having mishandled the suit, however, and recognizing that the city's high steward, the duke of Buckingham, 'a great crony' of Lord Chief Justice Scroggs, would be a formidable opponent in the disturbed atmosphere of the Popish Plot, the university submitted to a compromise.[160] The following year the whig mayor rekindled the quarrel by carrying out the night watch in person, and in negotiations over the revised city charter in 1684 the night watch remained an issue.[161] By then, however, the university knew that changed attitudes in the legal world to the implications of the petition of right and *habeas corpus* were undermining its claim to imprison and fine night walkers or to make forcible entries into citizens' houses; in 1690 it admitted reluctantly that it had no right to punish townsmen who broke the curfew with reasonable cause.[162]

The tensions inevitable between consumer and supplier were aggravated in Oxford because the principal consumer, the university, had considerable control over prices and supply in what was alleged to be 'the dearest place in all the land for food, clothes, and other necessities'.[163] The city complained that the university promoted unfair competition from privileged persons, interfered with the free market and set unrealistic prices; the university, complaining repeatedly of the citizens' avarice, depicted itself as the impartial proponent of 'an universal liberty of trading . . . most consonant to the native freedom of every subject'.[164] Accordingly it challenged the freemen's virtual monopoly of trade and the exclusivity and restrictive practices of the craft guilds, but was hardly *laissez faire* when it came to fixing commodity prices in the assises or condemning certain tradesmen for finding more profitable outlets in London. Thus in 1634 and later the vice-chancellor forbade

[158] *Royal Letters*, ed. Ogle, 371–3.

[159] See for example Wood, *Life and Times* ii. 125, 128; *Oxford Council Acts 1666–1701*, pp. x, 307; OUA WP/Q/29, fos 54–7; Oxford City Arch. F.5.9, fos 19–20ᵛ.

[160] For the Dodwell case see Wood, *Life and Times* ii. 381, 403; *Oxford Council Acts 1666–1701*, pp. xv, 106–7, 109; OUA WP/β/9/1; ibid. WP/R/11a, b; Oxford City Arch. E.4.4, fos 11–17. The reference to Buckingham and Scroggs is from OUA WP/R/11a, no. 20.

[161] Wood, *Life and Times* ii. 463; *CSPD 1684–5*, 67; OUA WP/Q/29, fos 72–3; ibid. WP/R/13/9, 11–12.

[162] OUA WP/R/13/9; [Harrington], *The Case of the University*.

[163] OUA NEP/H/3/10, no. 9.

[164] Ibid. NEP/H/5/4, pp. 75, 124. For university complaints see for example ibid. WP/Γ/26/1, fos 493–4.

the sale of tallow to 'foreigners' and ordered foreign butchers who sold meat in Oxford also to bring in their hides, fells, and tallow.[165] In 1639 the university, attributing high barley prices to engrossment of crops by the too numerous local maltsters, insisted that all of them, including the mayor, should submit to licensing and close regulation.[166] Similarly in 1640, perhaps influenced by a Star Chamber action against London butchers, the university launched an enquiry into the pasture holdings of the city's butchers, who were suspected of operating as graziers (taking advantage of the ban on royal purveyance within the five-mile area of Oxford) and either forestalling the Oxford market by holding cattle on local pastures until prices rose, or causing a shortage by selling off fatted cattle to London. The intense competition for local pasture was blamed for raising the price of dairy products and even, because of the cost of grazing visitors' horses, for the high price of Oxford inns. In fact most of the university claims seem to have been exaggerated.[167]

The university's control over trade derived from several sources. Under medieval grants it held the clerkship of the market and the assise or assay of bread, ale, wine, and weights and measures (plate 31); such rights conferred wide powers over the price and quality of goods but were used also to justify the licensing of bakers, brewers, and maltsters, the appointment of various testers and tasters and an extension of the jurisdiction of the university leet. The university by grant and prescription also controlled directly a group of privileged tradesmen and craftsmen whose numbers and immunities provided a constant irritant to the freemen. Under Wolsey's charter and a privy council order of 1575 the university even claimed the right to create and regulate its own craft guilds.[168]

The university's right to the clerkship of the market was never challenged, but there were disputes about what powers the clerkship conferred. The university's charter of 1636, for example, gave clerks the complete ordering of the market and the placing of stalls as well as the oversight of weights and measures and the quality of victuals; an arbitrator, Justice Jones, however, in the same year declared that the market and 'things incident thereunto' belonged to the city while the clerkship and its traditional fees belonged to the university.[169] Confusion continued over the city's right to levy tolls and pitching pence and the university's right to take toll corn in return for providing measures. The university regularly used public fasts or royal visits as an opportunity to proclaim an altered market day and so infuriate the mayor and corporation.[170] Although the university, surprisingly, claimed little control over the city's butchers beyond the appointment of flesh viewers and the

---

[165] O. Ogle, 'The Oxford market', *Collectanea* ii. 75–80, 89.

[166] OUA SP/E/7, fos 22–9.

[167] Bodl. MS Twyne–Langbaine 1, fos 148–58; OUA NEP/H/3/1, no. 7; ibid. SP/F/14; ibid. WP/Γ/26/1, fos 383–415; *VCH Oxon.* iv. 113–14.

[168] *VCH Oxon.* iv. 166–7. For general histories of the market and the clerkship see ibid. 305–10; *Collectanea* ii. 9–135. The leet is discussed above and privileged persons below.

[169] *Collectanea* ii. 80–1; Bodl. MS Twyne–Langbaine 1, fos 144–5ᵛ.

[170] See for example *Collectanea* ii. 38–9, 85–7, 90.

supervision of Sunday or Lenten observance, it sometimes used its powers over the market to interfere with the location of the shambles; in 1680, for example, the mayor and bailiffs on principle, as 'the only lords of the markett', countermanded a vice-chancellor's order temporarily placing the butchers in High Street, even though, because of expected congestion around Butcher Row in Queen Street during the king's stay, they evidently approved of the move.[171]

In general the university's direct intervention in trading matters diminished during the century, particularly after the civil war, reflecting a national trend away from the traditional commercial controls exercised by corporations and guilds. After the bitter disputes of the late sixteenth century, and much to Twyne's regret, the university failed to develop its claims to control guilds.[172] It renewed an ancient agreement with the tailors in 1604 and made half-hearted attempts to re-found companies of bakers and brewers in the early seventeenth century, but otherwise was content to operate negatively, crushing efforts by the masons to establish a company in 1604–12 and 1640, and by the tailors to acquire a royal charter in 1629.[173] Its continued regulation of guilds of privileged cooks and barbers was uncontroversial. The former university guilds of brewers and bakers, however, were allowed to lapse, while control of those crafts through licensing was gradually relaxed in the face of repeated challenges.[174] By mid-century most brewers and bakers were freemen; while brewers were keen enough to stress their strong links with the university whenever their trade was threatened by outsiders, notably by a crown monopolist in 1636 or by Abingdon men in 1643, their right to operate without university licences was prominent among the city's demands after the civil war.[175] The university defended its power over the victualling trades as an essential safeguard of the public interest, since the city's leaders were mostly victuallers.[176] In the later seventeenth century, however, licensing of brewers, bakers, and maltsters seems to have been largely abandoned and, although the vice-chancellor occasionally issued proclamations concerning the quality of ale, malt, or bread, most regulation was limited to the continuing assises, backed by courts leet held by the city, not the university.[177] By then the brewers, vintners, and bakers, instead of bringing in an assay of their products, recognized their obligations to the university by making small quarterly payments or giving a present to the clerks of the market.[178] Chandlers, already chafing at the university's control over them in

---

[171] See for example *Collectanea* ii. 38–9. For flesh viewers and Sunday observance see *Reg. Univ.* ed. Clark, pt. 1, 255, 339.

[172] Bodl. MS Twyne–Langbaine 4, fos 92ᵛ, 117ᵛ. For confirmation of the university's rights over guilds see *Records of the City of Oxford*, ed. Turner, 373.

[173] *VCH Oxon.* iv. 321–3, 327. For the university's continued hostility to the tailors' guild in the 1640s see OUA NEP/H/5/4, pp. 103–7.

[174] *VCH Oxon.* iv. 318, 321–2, 326. For early seventeenth-century licences see OUA SP/E/7, fo 5ʳ⁻ᵛ; *Reg. Univ.* ed. Clark, pt 1, 327–39.

[175] *VCH Oxon.* iv. 321; *Oxford Council Acts 1626–65*, 172; OUA NEP/H/5/4, pp. 51–6; ibid. SP/E/7, fos 15, 17; Bodl. MS Twyne–Langbaine 1, fos 136–41.

[176] OUA NEP/H/5/4, pp. 51–6.

[177] For proclamations and assises see OUA NEP/*supra*/14. For courts leet see above.

[178] OUA SEP/E/14/1, no. 1a; ibid. NEP/*supra*/14, fo 13.

1640, seem to have been less closely regulated in the later seventeenth century.[179] The university continued to set prices in the 1680s, not only for bread, ale, and wine, but also for meat, poultry, candles, and ostlery; in the 1690s it was particularly concerned with the allowable sizes of loaves, and it continued into the eighteenth century to assay all weights and measures used in the city and suburbs.[180]

Privileged persons were those who, while not scholars, were matriculated and enjoyed the university's privileges, including exemption from the city's jurisdiction and from many of the ordinary burdens of freemen; acquisition of privileged status allowed non-freemen to practise trades in the city, flouting the freemen's monopoly and the strict control imposed by guilds through the apprenticeship laws. To a large extent privileged persons formed a distinct community, standing aside from the government of the city, separately taxed, and answerable only to the vice-chancellor's court; there was a strong tendency, as in later times, for families to remain in the direct employment of the university or of colleges for generations, and the peculiarities of privileged status undoubtedly underlined the potentially divisive isolation of one segment of the city community.[181]

In 1609–12 the city was complaining that privileged persons were too numerous, that they operated trades to which they had not been properly apprenticed and that their trades were too diverse; a particular grievance was the building trade, in which the university had indeed made serious inroads by employing non-freemen and subverting the proposed masons' guild.[182] The claim that there were over 200 families of privileged persons was not too exaggerated, for by 1625 the number of individuals assessed for subsidy was 199, representing considerable growth since the beginning of the century although hardly keeping pace with general population increase in the city.[183] In 1612 the privy council had confirmed the university's right to 'set up' manual tradesmen, but ruled that they should pay 'scot and lot' with the citizens for their merchandise and should be appointed sparingly within guidelines first ordained in 1459.[184] In 1625 the trades of most privileged persons fell within the broad categories allowed in 1459. The city had long since accepted that certain tradesmen such as barbers, bookbinders, parchmenters, limners, and college cooks might be matriculated, and by 1625 the number of privileged tradesmen in categories to which the city still objected was smaller than in the sixteenth century; there were more privileged builders but fewer privileged victuallers and tailors, and

---

[179] Laud, *Works* v. 234–5, 239–40; Bodl. MS Twyne–Langbaine 4, fo 19ᵛ; *Collectanea* ii. 86.

[180] OUA NEP/*supra*/14, *passim*.

[181] For early seventeenth-century privileged persons see *Reg. Univ.* ed. Clark, pt 1, 381–406. The Carpenters, brewers of St Aldates, provide an example of a prominent Oxford family which took no part in city government: Toynbee and Young, *Strangers in Oxford*, 126–7.

[182] Oxford City Arch. D.5.7, fos 218–19; *Oxford Council Acts 1583–1626*, pp. xlix–li; *Royal Letters*, ed. Ogle, 349–51; *VCH Oxon.* iv. 327.

[183] For subsidies see OUA WP/R/1; ibid. WP/Γ/28/5–7; Oxford City Arch. F.5.8, pp. 451–4.

[184] *Royal Letters*, ed. Ogle, 349–51. For the agreement of 1459 see *Medieval Archives*, ed. Salter i. 243–7.

of those most held college posts such as rent-gatherer or manciple, which continued to be attractive to Oxford tradesmen, particularly victuallers.[185]

In 1654 the right of an unapprenticed baker to exercise that trade in Oxford because he was a privileged rent-gatherer for All Souls College was confirmed in the central courts.[186] Usually, however, the university was 'very tender' of the city's feelings over the qualification of tradesmen.[187] It adhered to the 1459 guidelines, arguing in 1689, for example, that a man it was defending was not a painter–stainer but a limner, and therefore entitled to the privilege.[188] There was the odd case of flagrant abuse, as in 1667 when a watchmaker, Joseph Knibb, having been refused the freedom, made clocks in Holywell as a privileged gardener.[189] The acquisition of privilege merely to gain access to the vice-chancellor's court or to escape action elsewhere seems to have become much less common, and in 1689–90 a city councillor's crude attempt to escape the burdens of office by matriculating as a scholar's servant ended in a victory for the city.[190] There continued to be movement between the ranks of the privileged and the free, and at least two seventeenth-century aldermen began their careers in the service of colleges.[191] There was even some tolerance of double status, despite express prohibition of it in the Laudian statutes.[192] The number of privileged persons declined in the later seventeenth century: in 1665 only 121, including sons and adult servants, swore the oath of allegiance. Few were employers, and few occupied trades outside the accepted guidelines.[193]

Throughout the period, despite occasional university claims, there were few 'privileged trades' in the sense of occupations restricted to privileged persons only. The book trades and occupations such as cook and surgeon came closest to that definition; in 1661, for example, a stationer and an apothecary were 'notoriously known by their trade to be privileged persons'.[194] Even so there were occasional freeman booksellers and numerous freeman apothecaries, and in other occupations such as barber and carrier, over which the university claimed considerable control, there was an even larger proportion of freemen.[195] In general the extent and nature of the privileged community was less contentious than in the sixteenth century, but there were continued wrangles over the exemption of privileged persons from city jurisdiction, from taxation, and from various civil and military obligations.[196]

---

[185] For the city's view of the acceptable categories of privileged person in 1650 see *Oxford Council Acts 1626–65*, 174.

[186] OUA WP/L/6.   [187] Ibid. SP/E/14/1, no. 4.

[188] *Oxford Council Acts 1666–1701*, p. xxix.

[189] Ibid. 19; Oxford City Arch. A.5.2, p. 91; ibid. F.5.9, fos 19–20ᵛ; C. F. C. Beeson, *Clockmaking in Oxfordshire* (Banbury Hist. Soc. 1962), 122–4.

[190] Oxford City Arch. E.4.8, pp. 637–42; *Oxford Council Acts 1666–1701*, p. xxix.

[191] *VCH Oxon*. iv. 163.   [192] Ibid.; *Laudian Code*, ed. Griffiths, II. 8–9.

[193] OUA WP/Q/15/21–4.

[194] Ibid. NEP/H/1, fo 16. For university statutes concerning medical practice see *SA* 41–2, 191, and for apothecaries see OUA SP/E/14/1, no. 4.

[195] For the university's control over carriers and barbers see *VCH Oxon*. iv. 289–90, 317–19.

[196] [Harrington], *The Case of the University*. For taxation and musters see OUA SP/D/5; ibid. WP/Γ/26/1, fo 487; Bodl. MS Twyne–Langbaine 1, fos 327 ff.

The university's claim to license alehouses derived from its ancient and undisputed right to hold the assise of ale, while the city magistrates issued licences under statutory provisions.[197] In the sixteenth century the magistrates of city and university acted together in annual licensing sessions, sending acceptable townsmen to register with the town clerk and privileged persons to the university registrar.[198] In the early seventeenth century the magistrates of both bodies by agreement restricted licences to seventy townsmen and twenty privileged persons. The consensus soon broke down, however; there were quarrels over the suppression of alehouses, which each body now licensed separately and the university was accused of failing to notify sessions of its licences.[199] The university's anxiety over the dangerous proliferation of alehouses reached a peak during Laud's chancellorship, when there were allegedly 300 houses, of which 100 were said to have been licensed by the brewer and alderman William Bosworth on condition that they sold his beer. A vigorous campaign by the vice-chancellor reduced the number of alehouses and culminated in a privy council order of 1640 making the university the sole licensing authority.[200] During and after the civil war that order seems to have been ignored; at the Restoration, when there were still some 250 inns, taverns, and alehouses in the city, the university failed to re-establish its sole right and quarrels continued as both bodies issued licences. In 1679 there were allegedly over 370 alehouses 'to create idleness and debauch scholars'.[201] In 1681, when the university was again challenged over its failure to notify sessions, its own legal advisers lacked confidence in its claims to license, arguing that although it had powers of supervision and suppression under the assise of ale it was not mentioned in statutes governing licensing.[202] Thereafter the university pressed its claims rather half-heartedly, but continued to issue licences to a few privileged persons.[203] The licensing of wine taverns, treated separately from alehouses, caused vehement town–gown quarrels throughout the century. The number of vintners in the city had been limited to three by an Act of 1553, but since both university and corporation claimed the right to grant the licences there were frequently six licensed taverns. Some vintners prudently acquired licences from both bodies, and additional complications arose when royal patentees attempted to operate in Oxford.[204] In 1661 the lord

[197] For licensing disputes see OUA SP/E/2/4; ibid. SEP/T/6, no. 21; *Collectanea* ii. 62 ff. For licences see *Reg. Univ.* ed. Clark, pt 1, 324–7; Oxford City Arch. D.5.4, fos 349–68; ibid. N.4.1–4. For papers concerning seventeenth-century alehouses see OUA WP/β/15/9.

[198] *Records of the City of Oxford*, ed. Turner, 399–400.

[199] Oxford City Arch. N.4.1; ibid. D.5.4, fo 370; ibid. D.5.7, fo 219; OUA WP/Γ/26/1, fos 438–41.

[200] Laud, *Works* v. 178–9, 239, 245–7, 252; *CSPD 1639*, 372–4 (date corrected by Laud, *Works* v. 277–80); OUA WP/Γ/26/1, fos 438–41. The number of public houses was usually below 250, including forty or fifty inns which escaped the usual licensing requirements: OUA WP/β/15/9, nos 8, 16; ibid. NEP/H/5/4, pp. 52–5; Bodl. MS Twyne–Langbaine 4, fos 184–7ᵛ; Laud, *Works* v. 269–70, 277–80.

[201] OUA WP/β/15/9, no. 31; ibid. SP/E/2/4; NEP/H/1, fo 28; Oxford City Arch. D.5.4, fos 324, 349–68; ibid. N.4.4; Wood, *Life and Times* ii. 404.

[202] OUA WP/β/15/9, nos 37–43. [203] Ibid. no. 45; [Harrington], *The Case of the University*.

[204] For accounts of wine licensing see OUA SP/D/6, no. 3; Oxford City Arch. E.4.3, fos 102–8; *Collectanea* ii. 62–8. For city licences see *Oxford City Properties*, ed. H. E. Salter (OHS lxxiii 1926), 347–52,

chancellor ruled in favour of the city over wine licensing, but the university continued to argue its case and to issue licences.[205]

Town–gown conflict over the physical environment ranged from squabbles over
street-repair and cleansing, over which the university had exercised considerable
control from the Middle Ages, to more illuminating arguments over the aesthetic
and social implications of the city's growth.[206] The corporation, as owner of the
waste, controlled encroachments on the central streets and on the important potential building land flanking the city's walls. Its policy of allowing encroachments in
return for a small rent called landgable was blamed by the university for unsightly
and obstructive jetties, chimneys, and shop signs.[207] The city protested that it never
allowed alterations to shops or cellars 'to the defacement of High Street', and city
leases frequently made aesthetic stipulations, indicating the council's reluctance to
countenance 'an eyesore to any man'.[208] Even so Thomas Wentworth, no friend
to the university, pointed out to the mayor that 'it were a pity those streets so beautiful by largeness should be more and more straitened by thrusting out buildings'.[209] In the 1630s the university badgered the privy council into ordering the
demolition of various encroachments, notably at Smith gate, Magdalen bridge, and
in the later Queen Street where an extension to the shambles was alleged to
obstruct traffic and to take light from the 'fair houses' on either side.[210] The city
council, itself watchful of undesirable encroachments, regarded university intervention as mere 'vainglory'.[211]

By the early seventeenth century the university was alarmed by indiscriminate
cottage-building on waste areas around the walls. The city argued that lack of space
in the central area and 'the wonderful great number of poor people' left no alternative, and that in any case privileged persons were deeply involved in the building activity.[212] In 1606 the two universities combined to seek an act of parliament
to remove cottages, which were thought likely to encourage plague and to harbour
'idle persons' who might debauch the scholars.[213] In 1612 the university claimed
that the city had allowed some 150 cottages to be built, but the city blamed its
lessees and insisted that many of the tenants were worthy labourers.[214] Similar disputes continued throughout the earlier seventeenth century. Privy council orders
to remove cottages in 1612 and 1626 seem to have been ineffective, but the city
reacted to at least part of the criticism over 'squab houses' by requiring its lessees

and for university licences see *Reg. Univ.* ii (1), 322–30; OUA WP/β/15/7, no. 13. On Oxford's wine
trade see J. Austin, 'Oxford taverns and the cellars of All Souls', *Oxoniensia* xxxiv (1969), 45–77.

[205] *VCH Oxon.* iv. 168.

[206] For street-repair and cleansing see ibid. 350–2.

[207] See for example OUA NEP/H/3/10. For landgable see *Oxford City Properties*, ed. Salter, p. xiii.

[208] Oxford City Arch. D.5.4, fos 330–2; *Oxford Council Acts 1583–1626*, 337.

[209] Oxford City Arch. F.5.2, fo 21.

[210] Ibid. D.5.7, fo 238; OUA WP/C/9; ibid. WP/R/10/2–6, 13b; *Oxford Council Acts 1626–65*, 53.

[211] Oxford City Arch. D.5.4, fos 387, 394; *Oxford Council Acts 1626–65*, 51–2.

[212] Oxford City Arch. D.5.4, fos 330–2.   [213] Wood, *History of the University* ii. 291–2.

[214] Oxford City Arch. D.5.4, fo 375.

to guarantee the city and parish against claims from poor inmates (or lodgers).[215] A survey made at the privy council's behest in 1640 revealed that in the previous two decades only some 180 new houses, by no means all 'squabs', had been built on formerly vacant ground; there were some 240 inmates in the city.[216] Despite repeated university allegations that the city was entirely to blame for cottage-building it was found that eighty-six of the surveyed houses were on college land, compared with only sixty-three on city land. Citizens had indeed built all but fifty-four of the houses, but privileged persons were also involved in speculative cottage-building, notably an apothecary, Thomas Broad, who was responsible for twenty squalid houses on Christ Church land in St Thomas's parish.[217]

Such evidence provides a rare and useful check on the reality behind the bold claims and intemperate language characteristic of town–gown disputes. Similar realities should be noted: despite incessant quarrelling over the control of the market it continued to be held twice weekly; despite wide-ranging complaints about the chancellor's jurisdiction his court was popular with the citizens; despite repeated allegations about the citizens' avarice it seems that Oxford prices compared favourably with those of Cambridge or London.[218] Although both bodies argued over control of street repair and cleansing neither was particularly keen to carry out those tasks. Over the whole range of town–gown disputes few substantial long-term gains were made by either side: certainly the expense of the interminable disputes, in professional research and advice, court fees, bribes, and travel, was out of all proportion to the benefits. In 1611–12, for example, the city spent nearly half its annual income on 'suits and controvercies', and litigation was the chief cause of its indebtedness before the civil war.[219]

Much evidence for town–gown relations derives from sources which, by their nature, reflect conflict rather than amity; yet for much of the time the university and city got on together perfectly well, co-operating at the official level in such matters as the relief of plague victims, the development of Thames navigation, or the appointment of common scavengers.[220] At a lower level the paucity of direct evidence of fraternization between citizens and scholars is balanced by the surprising rarity (except at times of political crisis) of trouble arising from their daily contacts in streets, shops, inns, coffee houses, and tennis courts. Moreover some town–gown dissension at the official level was actually provoked by excessive harmony at a lower level: taverners who frustrated the proctors by providing posterns

---

[215] *Royal Letters*, ed. Ogle, 345–55; Wood, *History of the University* ii. 291–2; *APC 1625–6*, 303–4; *Oxford Council Acts 1583–1626*, 313.

[216] OUA WP/β/15/8; ibid. WP/R/10/9, 15.

[217] For the condition of his cottages in 1637 see ibid. WP/Q/9.

[218] See for example J. E. T. Rogers, *A History of Agriculture and Prices* (7 vols in 8 Oxford 1866–1902), vi. 327 ff. For examples of high prices in Oxford see OUA NEP/H/4/11; Oxford City Arch. D.5.4, fos 121, 154.

[219] *Oxford Council Acts 1583–1626*, 404; *VCH Oxon.* iv. 142–3.

[220] *VCH Oxon.* iv. 76, 292, 352.

through which 'night rakes so often steal away', alehouse keepers who encouraged gaming and prostitution, and shopkeepers who granted easy credit were not generally unpopular with gownsmen.[221] University statutes forbidding scholars to haunt inns and eating-houses, to loiter with townsmen in the streets or visit their houses at night, or to participate with them in gambling, ball games, or cudgel play suggest that such practices were commonplace.[222] Townsmen prayed with gownsmen and listened to their sermons. They sent their children to such institutions as Magdalen College School.[223] The pages of Wood's diary illuminate a lively, divided, but not disintegrated community, and even in the political sphere, where passions were strongest, there were moments of communal rejoicing.[224]

[221] For posterns see OUA WP/a/21/1, no. 1; *Statutes*, trans. Ward, XV. 6; *VCH Oxon.* iv. 436.
[222] *Statutes*, trans. Ward, XV. 2–7; *VCH Oxon.* iv. 246.
[223] See for example R. S. Stanier, *Magdalen School* (OHS new ser. iii 1940), 101–2.
[224] Wood, *Life and Times* v. 206–7 under bells, bonfires.

3

The Architectural Setting

JOHN NEWMAN

BY 1600 a period of seventy years had elapsed during which no new university or college building had been erected. Of all the Tudor foundations only one, Corpus, had been provided with a complete set of buildings. At both Brasenose and Cardinal College (later Christ Church) work had stopped well before completion, leaving the one without proper chapel or library and the other with only half a quadrangle; the mid-century foundations of St John's and Trinity had taken over the buildings of suppressed medieval colleges not altogether suited to the new societies which occupied them; for Jesus College building work had never seriously started.

This inactivity is all the more surprising because the numbers of those living in many colleges were rising sharply, particularly of undergraduates after the matriculation statute of 1581. The most visible evidence of growing college populations was the rash of dormer windows bursting out from roofslopes where attic spaces were being brought into use as cocklofts for extra studies and even extra chambers.

At the very end of the century, however, there were signs of renewed activity. At St John's College a new range was constructed in 1595–1601, with a handsomely equipped library above and chambers below, the south range of a future second quadrangle.[1] At Christ Church the buildings of Peckwater Inn, which served as a second quadrangle, were repaired and modernized about 1599–1600.[2] At Merton in the same years part of the street range was reconstructed.

Then suddenly, from about 1607, building plans were under discussion on all sides. Some of these plans were destined to remain on paper for decades, but the array of evidence for a new determination to build is impressive. Among the medieval colleges the great episcopal foundations, New College, All Souls, Magdalen, remained content with their splendid edifices, but the early colleges and others less well endowed, financially dependent as they were on an ever-increasing body of fee-paying commoners, at last began to respond to the need to rebuild or extend.

I should like to thank Sir Howard Colvin, who commented on a draft of this chapter and suggested several improvements.
[1] *The Collegiate University*, 621.
[2] CA xii. b. 44, a rough building account inserted in the disbursement book for that year.

Chronologically the lead was taken by Lincoln College, where the west range of a second quadrangle was begun in 1607. Architecturally, however, the new quadrangle at Merton was much more important. Its foundation-stone was laid on 13 September 1608. Three months later at Oriel the first step was taken towards total rebuilding, when on 8 December timber sales of up to £100 from college lands were authorized to raise money to rebuild the college, the front part of which was becoming ruinous.[3] Nor was University College far behind in its preparations. On 12 November 1610 Dr John Browne, fellow, signed a contract for a new north range towards High Street with the masons who were then nearing the end of their work on the new quadrangle at Merton.[4] In the event neither college could proceed at once; Oriel delayed for a decade and it took almost a quarter of a century for benefactors to come forward to implement the plans at University College. At Balliol hopes raised in 1610 proved delusive, for the bequest of Thomas Tesdale, merchant of Abingdon, at first intended for its enlargement, was subsequently withdrawn after the college had begun to buy property to provide a site for a second quadrangle. Tesdale's bequest was used in 1624 to facilitate the transformation of Broadgates Hall into a new foundation, Pembroke College, where a first phase of new building began two years later.

From 1616 Exeter College was able to secure a series of benefactions which within a decade paid for a new range of lodgings, a new hall, and a new chapel. Last among the early colleges, Queen's, whose student numbers as recorded in 1611 were among the highest, built on the north side a new block containing eleven chambers, which came into use in 1622.[5]

The recent foundations with incomplete buildings also stirred into activity in the first decade of the new century. At Christ Church in 1610–12 the library in the monastic refectory was partly rebuilt and completely refitted at the expense of Otho Nicholson, a rich lawyer not previously connected with the college who a few years later erected Carfax conduit for the benefit of the town.[6] At Brasenose piecemeal works had been going on from 1603 and by 1610 had cost the substantial sum of £1,094. However, the gift of £140 in October 1614 'towards the erectinge of a chappell', a major initiative, was not followed up for over forty years.[7] At Jesus College a more positive attitude prevailed: in mid-1617 the college appointed agents to collect money in Wales 'towards the new erectinge buildinge and finishinge' of the college. Already by April 1619 a building had been erected on the site of Laurence Hall 'intended to bee used and employed as a chappell', and on 28 May 1621 it was consecrated as such.[8] Ralph Kettell, president of Trinity

---

[3] *Dean's Register of Oriel*, 224. For new Oxford university, college, and hall buildings during the seventeenth century, in general see map 2.

[4] UCA FAB 1/1.

[5] Wood, *Life and Times* iv. 151; QCA chamber rents recorded in the bursars' books.

[6] J. C. Cole, 'The painted roof of the Old Library, Christ Church. Pt 3: The execution of the work', *Oxoniensia* xxvi–xxvii (1963), 229–30.

[7] BNCA buildings 2, chapel 3.

[8] JCA shelf 17, register 1602–24, fo 35; and chapel consecration document.

College from 1599, erected *circa* 1615 a block of chambers for commoners which still bears his name and in 1618, after his attempt to excavate a cellar had brought down the medieval refectory, constructed a new hall with chambers above.[9] William Laud, while president of St John's College (1611–21), strained college finances almost to breaking-point in a sustained campaign to improve its facilities, as he recorded in a memorandum 'which the iniurious tongues of some men drove me to particularize for my owne contentment'.[10] In 1612 the college cook, Thomas Clarke, was encouraged to rebuild the kitchen and erect a block of chambers by it, but Laud soon got the college to buy out his interest. The hall was enlarged by one bay (1615) and given a new louvre (1619), wainscot, and a screen (1621). In 1616 major repairs were carried out to the entrance range of the quadrangle and the next year the ground level of the quadrangle was lowered and the internal walls battlemented. In 1619 Laud turned his attention to the chapel, making important improvements which are discussed below (p. 164).

Much more conspicuous than any of these were the two great contemporary constructions financed by individual benefactors. Sir Thomas Bodley, having refitted the university library in 1598–1602, went on in 1610–12 to pay for its extension with a new eastern wing, Arts End, and inspired the university to rebuild the schools, 1613–24, in three further ranges which thus formed a complete new quadrangle. Equally ambitious and splendid were the buildings of the new college founded and financed by Nicholas and Dorothy Wadham, erected with remarkable speed and determination in the years 1610–13.

By about 1620, then, much of the programme of Oxford building for the rest of the century had been adumbrated. In the years of Laud's chancellorship (1630–41), however, attention was focused on beautifying college chapels and on clearing the university's secular activities from the university church of St Mary's, a process only completed when the Sheldonian Theatre was opened in 1669.

Such an upsurge of building depended on the effective raising of funds. A good deal is known in many cases about the ways in which the necessary funding was put together; a general picture emerges which is familiar enough from the Middle Ages to the present day, the dogged soliciting of sums large and small, mostly the latter, from alumni and other well-wishers, with the occasional grand gesture of munificence from a benefactor whose name is immortalized in his (or her) building, as the Bodleian Library, the Sheldonian Theatre, and Wadham College preeminently illustrate.

Sir Thomas Bodley himself provided the great model, both by his generosity and in his understanding of the psychology of giving. The ruling passion of the last fifteen years of his life was the re-establishment of the university library on a permanent basis, with a continually growing stock of books and adequate accommodation for them for the foreseeable future. In a letter dated 23 February 1598 he reported to the vice-chancellor his intention to 'take the charge and cost

---

[9] *VCH Oxon.* iii. 241.   [10] Bodl. MS Tanner 338, fos 374–80.

upon me' of refitting Duke Humfrey's Library, 'to stirre up other mens benevolence, to helpe to furnish it with bookes'.[11] Bodley stressed to the university the
importance of thanking donors appropriately. He regularly sent lists of donors of
books and money for book-purchase, and with the first, 25 June 1600, gave instructions that members of the nobility and of 'honourable calling' should receive a formal letter of thanks, while for the rest members of convocation present when lists
of donors were read out should 'as they are acquainted and shall finde oportunity
to meete with any of those contributors, they would bee carefull to shew them with
what cheerfulnes and comfort their giftes are imbraced by the whole university'.[12]

He also provided a 'register booke' in which the university could record donations of books and money for the library. This spectacular volume with its brass
mounts and enamelled arms of Bodley in the centre of the front cover is eloquent
testimony to his seriousness of purpose. Until mid-1604 he retained the volume in
London, having the benefactors' names printed in it in a beautiful typeface, and
even when it was sent up to Oxford he expressed his anxiety that the university
should select a worthy scribe to continue the entries in manuscript.[13]

In 1609 Bodley redeemed a promise he had made at the outset, to provide an
endowment for the library. He purchased from Lord Norris the manor of
Maidenhead, the rent of which would produce £91 10s 0d a year, and tenements
in Distaff Lane, London, producing £40 a year, both of which he bequeathed to
the university. The rents from these properties were used for many years after his
death to cover the librarians' salaries and repairs to the fabric and fittings and for
book purchases.[14]

As the stock of books increased it became clear that Duke Humfrey's Library
would quickly become wholly inadequate to house them. During his lifetime
Bodley paid for the erection of Arts End and the proscholium, and in his will
(dated 2 January 1613, less than a month before his death) made provision that the
residue of his estate should be used to fund the building of a matching extension
towards the west which would form an impressive entrance to the library, and of
a third storey over the new schools, then about to begin construction.[15]

The rebuilding of the schools themselves, 'longe desired by the universitie and
as every man knowes upon urgent necessitie', Bodley could not fund from his
own pocket. But he took a vital step towards it late in 1611. On 5 November he
reported that he had approached Sir John Bennet to act in the dual capacity of
principal fundraiser and overseer of construction and advised the university to
secure his firm agreement by getting the chancellor (Lord Ellesmere), the arch-

---

[11] OUA register of congregation and convocation 1595–1606, NEP/*supra*/11, register M (reversed),
fo 31.

[12] Ibid. fo 45ᵛ.

[13] *Letters of Sir Thomas Bodley to Thomas James*, ed. G. W. Wheeler (Oxford 1926), 100, 134.

[14] OUA register M (reversed), fo 31; ibid. register of convocation 1606–15, NEP/*supra*/22, register
K, fo 36; Bodl. records, e. 8.

[15] Bodley's will is printed in W. D. Macray, *Annals of the Bodleian Library* (Oxford 1868, 2nd edn
Oxford 1890), 402–12.

bishop of Canterbury, and the bishop of London to urge him to it.[16] Bennet's formal letter of acceptance is dated 21 January 1612 and on 1 April he wrote again outlining his strategy for raising funds.[17] Letters, he recommended, should be sent to all diocesan bishops who were Oxford men requesting that they should themselves donate and should solicit donations from Oxford men, both clergy and laity, within their dioceses. Where the diocesans had been educated at Cambridge, approaches were to be made through some other suitable channel such as the chancellor. The money thus raised, Bennet proposed, should be transmitted to him in London, 'the fitte center (as I take it) for every parte of the circumference'. Only the diocese of Oxford should be managed by the university, through the agency of Anthony Blencowe, provost of Oriel. However, Bennet undertook to acknowledge all sums received and enter them in a 'faire booke of vellame prepared for that purpose', which was to be placed among the university's records. This volume records the success of the fundraising project in spite of a certain scepticism on Bodley's part, for in the seven years to 1619 no less than £5,012 17s 0d was received in donations.[18] Furthermore Bennet offered to provide out of his own pocket up to 10 per cent of the total cost.

The first stone was laid on 30 March 1613, the day after Bodley's funeral, when the benefactors' book showed donations of only £650. At the outset Bennet had predicted that the total cost would exceed £6,000, and as early as January 1615 convocation was discussing rates to levy on all BAs and MAs, while a proposal mooted at the same time to charge an admission fee on all new entrants to colleges and halls, on a sliding scale according to rank, from £3 6s 8d on an earl's son to 2s 6d on the son of a yeoman, was implemented the following November.[19]

The surviving dossier of copies of begging letters shows that they were mostly sent out in the name of congregation.[20] Several bright young college fellows, in particular William Lewis of Oriel College, but also, for example, Samuel Fell of Christ Church, were allocated the task of composing the individualized Latin letters to great men, but for mere gentlemen a 'generall English coppy' was prepared. The first date from as early as 23 November 1611, but most of these letters bear dates in 1612. Contributions were at first slow to come in. At the head of the list was George Abbot, archbishop of Canterbury, who in 1612 gave £100. Below him came thirteen heads of house, including the principal of Hart Hall, whose donations, ranging from £20 to £5, totalled £140. By the end of December 1613, however, £1,622 had been received, and thereafter annual totals remained fairly steady, averaging something under £600 a year until the end of fundraising in 1619.

Approaches to the episcopal bench had predictable results: in February 1613 100 marks were received from the archbishop of York and £40 from the bishop of

[16] OUA register K, fo 78.   [17] Ibid. fos 78ᵛ–9ʳ, 80ᵛ–1ᵛ.
[18] *Bodley to James*, ed. Wheeler, 220; Bodl. MS top. Oxon. b. 41. The details provided by this volume are analysed below.
[19] OUA register K, fo 156 and attached note; ibid. register of convocation 1615–28, NEP/*supra*/23, register N, fo 1.
[20] Bodl. Ms Add. c. 206.

London together with £70 from his diocesan funds reserved for pious uses. In July the bishop of Durham gave £50 and the bishop of Worcester £40, and by May 1614 the bishops of Rochester, Gloucester, and Carlisle had each donated £20, while two Welsh bishops had contributed £10 each. Among deans only those of Westminster and Winchester contributed. Begging letters to the dean and chapter of Bath and Wells, the dean of Chichester, and the chancellor of Lichfield all proved unproductive. Archdeacons plugged the gaps in some areas; an early donor, for example, was Philip Bisse, archdeacon of Taunton, who had already given money to the library and was to bequeath his own library to Wadham College. Contributions subsequently came in from the archdeacons of Buckingham, Winchester, Berkshire, Hereford, North Wiltshire, and Dorset, and the last two mounted local fundraising campaigns. There were also many donations from individual parish clergy as well as others *en bloc*, ranging from £37 contributed by the diocese of Exeter to £7 raised by Northumbria. The most startling gift is the £100 which the bishop of London forced his dying chancellor to make in 1619.

In financial terms members of the peerage were more worth courting than bishops. Among the earliest donors was Lord Spencer of Wormleighton, who gave £100. Those who responded to begging letters included the earls of Pembroke (£100), Dorset and Worcester (£50 each); further gifts of £100 came from Lord Petre of Writtle (Dorothy Wadham's brother) and Lord Danvers (who would later finance the creation of the physic garden). On the other hand, those who turned a deaf ear to invitations to contribute included the chancellor of the university himself, Lord Ellesmere, as well as the earls of Northampton and Montgomery and Lord Chief Baron Tanfield. Lower in the social hierarchy came fifteen baronets, knights, and other members of the gentry who each donated £20 or more, among whom Sir Richard Spenser (£50) and Sir George St Paul (£40) stand out. The latter's generosity was even dwelt on in his funeral oration.[21]

During the later phases of fundraising other types of potential donor were targeted. Lawyers, not surprisingly given Bennet's legal background, produced some big sums: Sir Julius Caesar gave £30 early on, in 1616 Hugh Hare of the Inner Temple gave £100, and in 1618 Edmund Meese of Grays Inn (a friend of Bennet's) bequeathed the same amount.[22] The Inner Temple and Grays Inn contributed £20 each. In 1617–19 eight London livery companies gave sums of £10 or more, headed by the Mercers' Company, which gave 100 marks.

Some colleges mounted collections among their members, notably Christ Church, which produced £80, and Magdalen, £74 17s 4d. Magdalen Hall, donating £65, came next. By the end something had come in from every college, down to the £3 17s 6d from Jesus College, and from four academic halls or their heads. Not surprisingly, by far the most generous single academic was Sir Henry Savile, warden of Merton and Bodley's particular friend, whose three separate gifts totalled £130.

---

[21] *Carmina funebria in obitum . . . Georgii de Sancto Paulo* (Oxford 1614).

[22] See Meese's will, PRO PROB 11/131, fo 148, proved on 20 February 1618 before Bennet in his capacity as judge of the prerogative court of Canterbury.

When we turn to consider how colleges fared in fundraising for their own building projects, it becomes apparent that the role of the head of house was vital, a corollary doubtless of the fact that the general financial fortunes of a college depended on the policy of the head. Savile, who had been elected warden of Merton as far back as 1585, illustrates this proposition even as he attempts to justify his prolonged absences from the college. In a letter to the visitor datable to 1601/3 he claimed that the college actually benefited financially by his absence:

And in the tyme of this great default through my absence that poore colledge hath bene able to bestow above a thousand markes in building one way and another, neare half so much more upon the library, mayntayneth at this day very neare twyse as many fellowes, as usually it hath done in our memory, and yet hath above a thousand pound in stocke, which about a yeare before my coming had not one peny in treasure, but was indetted to the bursars.[23]

Savile was justified in making this defence, for the college went on in 1608–10 to erect the shell of the fellows' quadrangle from its own accumulated funds.

The more normal role for a dynamic head of house who wanted to improve his college buildings was that of fundraiser. A particularly clear picture emerges at Jesus College where the erection of new buildings went hand in hand with the endowment of new fellowships to bring the foundation up to a viable size. The college was fortunate in being led by a succession of devoted principals, of whom Eubule Thelwall (1621–30) and Leoline Jenkins (1661–73) are only the most celebrated. Gifts and bequests of land or money to support fellows and scholars had begun with a bequest in 1602 from Herbert Westphaling, bishop of Hereford, and continued into the 1620s after Thelwall had obtained a new charter to increase the foundation from eight to sixteen. The building programme was initiated by Griffith Powell (principal 1613–20) by applying £100 of the money held in trust for the college by the warden and fellows of All Souls towards the construction of the hall, which was completed by Thelwall using £300 from the same source.[24] Meanwhile Powell established a building fund, stimulated by the bequest in 1615 of £100 from the widow of his predecessor. He thereupon initiated a programme of organized fundraising in Oxfordshire, London, and the ten counties of Wales, as well as among the clergy, bringing in a total of £744 before his death, at which 'the business was given over'.[25] In each Welsh county the college appointed an agent who, armed with a letter of attorney, was to approach 'knightes, esquires, gentlemen and others, men of good worth'. The letter appointing Sir Henry Williams agent in the county of Brecon was dated 10 May 1617. Eighteen months later he had raised £43 5s 0d.[26] It was Thelwall who applied these funds to building. Of him a college benefactors' book records 'before he came to be principall in the time of his predecessor Mr Powell he layd the foundation of the chappell, which shortly after he

[23] MCR D. 1. 23 (Garrard transcripts), letter xv.
[24] JCA shelf 17, rough benefactors' book, pp. 1–2.
[25] Ibid. benefactors' book 1626, pp. 67–76.   [26] Ibid. register 1602–24, fos 35ʳ–8ᵛ.

finished, and furnished.'[27] From 1626 he was raising money to build a library and the benefactors' book begun in that year records gifts amounting to £280, together with £175 donated in 1628–30 for books. According to Francis Mansell, Thelwall's successor, 'the college was near £5,000 the better for him'.[28] The splendidly panelled dining room in the lodgings which he built for the principal is his fitting memorial. Mansell himself kept up the good work. In 1636–7 the chapel was extended westwards at the expense of Sir Charles Williams.[29] The funds which the principal raised from Welsh clergy towards the building of a second quadrangle amounted by 1640 to £823, the pump primed by £100 of his own.[30] Thelwall's library had already made a beginning on this quadrangle, but unfortunately it had been raised on a colonnade insufficient to bear its weight, so Mansell had to dismantle it. This he did in 1639, storing the stalls and wainscotting for future reuse. On its site he began the north range of the new quadrangle; but the unsettled times soon stopped the work, and Mansell was ejected from his post. On his reinstatement in 1660 he was too old to pursue his scheme and it was left to Leoline Jenkins to complete the quadrangle and reinstate the library fittings. Since after his departure from Jesus Jenkins eventually rose to be secretary of state he could doubtless well afford the generous gesture which he made in 1676, when he paid for the new library and chamber range at a cost of £1,440. So at Jesus we find successive heads in both characteristic roles, as fundraisers and also as benefactors.

The head's role as benefactor was crucial at several colleges. At Oriel College, for example, Provost Blencowe had procured a charter of incorporation for the college in 1603, and initiated preparations for rebuilding five years later, but did not live to see work start. However, by his bequest of £1,300 in 1618 he set rebuilding in motion.[31] A sum of that size only primed the pump, and in order to complete the west and south ranges, the first phase of building, his successor William Lewis, exploiting his experience in the schools' fundraising campaign, sent out to eminent old members of the college 'letters, elegant, in a winning persuasive way' which retained their reputation half a century later.[32] When in October 1636 the college resolved to complete the rebuilding a benefactors' book was started and contributions were solicited from former fellows and fellow-commoners. Lewis himself contributed £100, but once again it was a donation from the reigning provost, John Tolson, which made it possible for work to recommence. At first he promised £500, or if necessary £600, although in the end he donated £1,150.[33] Yet as before money from other sources was required, and the college resorted to every

---

[27] JCA shelf 17, rough benefactors' book, p. 25.

[28] Wood, *History of the Colleges and Halls*, 581.

[29] JCA shelf 19, bursars' accounts 1631–50, p. 59.

[30] Ibid. shelf 17, benefactors' book 1626, pp. 77.

[31] *Dean's Register of Oriel*, 166, 224. By his will dated 14 September 1613, Blencowe bequeathed the residue of his estate to the college, desiring that 'it may be bestowed towardes the new buildinge of some part of those ruinous buildinges of the sayd colledge, which have most neede to be reedified, which I take to be, the west side': PRO PROB 11/131, fo 150.

[32] Wood, *History of the Colleges and Halls*, 527 n. 65.   [33] *Dean's Register of Oriel*, 251, 284.

conceivable device to squeeze cash out of its assets: first trees were to be felled on college farms and sold to the tenant farmers, then admission fees from fellows and fellow-commoners which normally paid for books or repairs were put towards the rebuilding. In June 1637 those tenants who refused to have trees felled on their land were requested to pay a year's rent by way of loan; in March 1638 £700 was raised by leasing the college property of Littleworth and in 1639–40 it was agreed to sell the next presentations to three of the college livings; finally in 1641 it was decided to sell all pieces of college plate donated by those who had not contributed to the building fund.[34] Only by these increasingly desperate and high-handed measures was momentum maintained.

At Brasenose the key figure was Samuel Radcliffe, principal from 1614 to 1648. During his long incumbency he seems to have discouraged benefactions towards the much-needed library and chapel.[35] Yet he paid £205 out of his own pocket in 1635–40 for the remaining cocklofts and battlements needed to make the quadrangle uniform.[36] At his death he bequeathed to the college the estate of Piddington Grange, the sale of which raised £1,850, enough to make it possible to embark on the second quadrangle. When in the spring of 1656 the college at last began construction, it referred to 'Dr Ratclifs new buildings'.[37] The basic structural costs to December 1658, when chapel, library, and cloister were all up and roofed, amounted to £2,341, leaving a shortfall which was bridged by means of a small bequest, gifts amounting to £170 from the principal and fellows and £123 borrowed from the college chest.[38] But of course substantial further sums were required for plastering, painting, glazing, and wainscotting, and when in June 1671 a list was drawn up of moneys from all sources provided for the new buildings the total amounted to no less than £4,775. Towards this figure benefactions of £315 were received after April 1663, including £120 from John Cartwright of Aynho; but the college clearly had to find a considerable sum from its own resources.[39]

Even where outside benefactors put up most of the money one may suspect that in many cases heads of houses played a vital role. This is certainly the case at St John's College where President Laud's improvements were largely paid for by benefactors, particularly members of the Merchant Taylors' Company, whom he had approached. Thomas and Benjamin Henshaw's gift of £150 in 1617 towards battlementing the quadrangle is acknowledged by their shield of arms on the east range. According to Laud's calculation, between 1615 and 1621 he raised £1,458, mainly for building works, almost entirely 'without anye counsell, helpe, or assistaunce of anye of the fellowes'. The college itself had only slender resources at this time and by the end of Laud's presidency had gone into debt.[40] The sequence of events at Exeter College is also suggestive. The college, even after its virtual refoundation in 1564 by Sir William Petre, was substantially under-endowed and

[34] Ibid. 255, 284, 286–7, 294, 296.
[35] *VCH Oxon.* iii. 216.
[36] BNCA MS A3/20, loose papers at end.
[37] Ibid. fo 1.
[38] Ibid. fo 78.
[39] Ibid. loose papers at end.
[40] Bodl., MS Tanner 338, fo 378.

experienced desperate overcrowding as hordes of commoners were admitted in the decades after the matriculation statute. In 1612, when the number of commoners in college had risen to 134, John Prideaux became rector. Over the next decade three major benefactors were found to fund the rebuilding of hall and chapel and the erection of a large new block of chambers. In 1622 a site for the chapel was obtained from the city of Oxford with royal support, through the good offices of the marquess of Hamilton.[41] George Hakewill, who provided £1,200 towards building the chapel, was a former fellow (and brother of Bodley's executor), and nephew of John Peryam, the alderman of Exeter who had put up £560 for the chamber block erected in 1616 and named after him Peryam's Mansions 'in regard of the firmenesse and magnificence of it'. Sir John Acland, who provided £800 towards the new hall built in 1618, was another Devon man, but is not known to have had any previous connection with the college. Rector Prideaux, in his sermon at the dedication of the chapel in October 1624, acknowledged the help of several former fellows who 'wrought on the pious dispositions' of Peryam and Acland, so he saw all three buildings as part of a single campaign of improvement.[42] One of the fellows he named, Isaiah Farringdon, is recorded later as collaborating with Prideaux in sending letters to the mayor and corporation of Exeter soliciting contributions.[43] All this suggests the operation of a master-mind, as does the limited financial commitment made by the college itself towards the cost of the three buildings, between £140 and £200 for each, an indication of planned funding such as is hardly met with elsewhere in Oxford at this period. In his survey of the college taken in 1631–2 Prideaux listed these and many other minor improvements, but he was still not satisfied, remarking sarcastically, 'In tyme perchance the cittye of Exceter will thinke uppon it to do some good to Exceter Colledg.'[44]

At University College the management of the rebuilding was in the hands of the master, Thomas Walker, but the chief supplier of funds was one of the fellows. Charles Greenwood not only put up £1,500 of his own money, but inspired his pupil, Sir Simon Bennett, to bequeath to the college at his death in 1631 an estate, Hanley Park near Towcester, enough to finance the new west and north ranges built in 1634–40. When building began the college indulged in wholesale asset-stripping and held three successive sales of the timber in Hanley Park, which raised £1,802 in all.[45] The completion of the rebuilding proved very protracted. When fundraising began again in 1655, the bursar, Dr Offley, raised £264 within the year from thirty-seven benefactors headed by the lord chief justice and the master of the rolls, but in the following year a mere £84 came in. It is not clear how all the money was found to erect the chapel, hall, kitchen, and library. As late as 1676–7, when the east range, the final element in the rebuilding, was nearing completion, the newly elected master Obadiah Walker was still sending out letters soliciting

[41] *Oxford Council Acts, 1583–1626*, ed. H. E. Salter (OHS lxxxvii 1928), 313; and see *Reg. Exeter*, 313.

[42] *Reg. Exeter*, pp. xcix–c.   [43] Ibid. p. cviii, citing *CSPD 1631*, 508.

[44] Ibid. 318.   [45] UCA FAB 1/3.

contributions.[46] He tackled those who had relatives at the college with predictable arguments, as for example: 'The present fellows labour with great industry for the publick benefitt . . . and are at considerable charges out of their own small revenues, without hopes of ever receiving any particular advantage to themselves by it . . . we expect that those whose posterity are most likely to be profited by it should also contribute.'[47] More novel was the project which he announced in 1677, 'the putting forth the life of our founder King Alfred', printed at the college's expense in the hope 'to make some advantage by it towards finishing our chappell and furnishing our library'.[48]

The costs of erecting many of the major buildings of the period are recorded, or can be deduced from surviving evidence, so that it is possible to appreciate the scale of the challenge fund-raisers faced. How much Bodley spent on erecting Arts End is not known, and the full building accounts for the rest of the schools quadrangle are no longer extant. However, a statement of Sir John Bennet, who had financial responsibility for the erection of the schools and the gallery over them from 1613, shows that in November 1621, when little of significance remained to be done, he had disbursed £13,269, a figure consistent with the several earlier partial statements of building expenditure which survive.[49] For the convocation house and the western extension of the university library over it a clear statement of cost survives: the purchase price of the site was £264 and building expenditure in 1634–41 amounted to £3,925, of which £1,000 went on the library joinery alone.[50] Thirty years later, between 1664 and 1669, it cost Gilbert Sheldon, archbishop of Canterbury, £12,239 to erect and fit out the Sheldonian Theatre, over and above which he gave £2,000 for a maintenance fund.[51] The actual cost of building the Ashmolean Museum in 1678–83 amounted to the relatively modest sum of £3,836.[52] For colleges less information survives, full accounts existing only for Wadham, but in two other cases a global figure is known. The grand total recorded in the building account book for Wadham College, 1610–13, amounts to no less than £10,918.[53]

Colleges embarking on rebuilding, however, will not have aimed to emulate the generosity of Dorothy Wadham, who provided what was patently too spacious accommodation for her fledgeling society. At Merton expenditure on building the fellows' quadrangle recorded in the bursars' books in 1609–10 totals £2,220, more than twice the round £1,000 of the basic estimates submitted by mason (£570) and carpenter (£430) in January 1609. That, however, omits all the costs of roofing and

[46] Ibid. Smith transcripts v. 184–92. [47] Ibid. 186. [48] Ibid. 192.

[49] See I. G. Philip, 'The building of the schools quadrangle', *Oxoniensia* xiii (1948), 40, for the partial figures, and OUA register N, fo 133, for Bennet's total expenditure.

[50] Wood, *Life and Times* iv. 53–5, quoting OUA vice-chancellor's accounts 1621–63 (Schools), NEP/pyx./C/1, fos 122^r–8^v.

[51] Bodl. MS Bodley 898.

[52] R. F. Ovenell, *The Ashmolean Museum, 1683–1894* (Oxford 1986), 21.

[53] WCM MS 8/1A. The figure bandied about at the time may have been the higher one of £11,360, wrongly entered by the accountant on the last page.

fitting out, which could have doubled the figure.[54] The new hall built in 1618 at Trinity College is reputed to have cost only £700.[55] In the same year Exeter College built its hall for £1,000, and in 1623–4 its new chapel for £1,400, the only Oxford college chapel to have a side aisle.[56] The building account book for the Canterbury quadrangle at St John's College shows that Laud spent £5,553 in 1631–6 on construction and fitting out.[57]

As for the two complete rebuildings, we have no figures for Oriel, but for University College it is possible to arrive at a reasonable approximation in spite of the extended history of construction. The full cost of the pre-war campaign from 1634, which comprised the west and north ranges and the walls of the hall and chapel range, was computed in 1647 at £4,934.[58] A rough estimate for finishing the hall and chapel and building the kitchen–library wing, probably made in 1641, came to £2,500.[59] How closely this was adhered to cannot be known in the absence of the relevant accounts. Recorded expenditure for the two-stage construction of the east range is £357 in 1668–9 (including demolition of the remaining medieval buildings) and £696 in 1675–6.[60] This produces a grand total of about £8,500—a very fair price, one would think.

Certain key initiatives mark the history of building, rebuilding, and refitting the colleges, which in so many ways revolutionized their appearance and functioning in the decades up to 1640. They are the refitting of the library at Merton College in 1589–90, the building of fellows' quadrangle there in 1608–10, followed immediately by the complete new Wadham College in 1610–13, and then in 1629–31 the new chapel with its fittings at Lincoln College. Together these embodied the new conceptions of library, chambers, and chapel in this period: all the main elements in colleges, that is to say, except the hall. New college buildings and those built for the university in this period also display redefined ideas on architectural style. This is not merely a stylistic change, from obsolete gothic to up-to-date classical, but a combination of continued adherence to certain medieval forms and a prominent display of the classical orders. Both function and style can be examined in the buildings associated with the two men who must be seen as the pioneers of change, Henry Savile, warden of Merton, and Thomas Bodley.

Of the medieval colleges, Merton possessed by far the most extensive accommodation for books. Its L-shaped library occupied the upper storey of two sides of Mob Quad, seven bays in the west range and ten in the south. Nevertheless, in the early years of Savile's wardenship a decision was taken to rehouse the books in a completely new way.[61] In place of the medieval lecterns, in 1589–90 the

---

[54] MCA liber rationarius bursariorum I (1585–1633), fos 127r–43r; registrum I. 3, fo 229. Since the college accounts do not include any payments for slating or fitting out the quadrangle, it may be that Savile, the warden, paid the £2,000 or so required out of his own pocket.

[55] *VCH Oxon.* iii. 241.   [56] Ibid. 116.   [57] SJM MS lxxxi. 2, fo 85.

[58] UCA FAB 1/6. Two variant figures in FAB 1/4 relating to the first phase, 1634–7, are respectively £65 and £125 higher.

[59] Ibid. FAB 1/4.   [60] Ibid. FAB 1/7, fos 19, 31.

[61] J. Newman, 'Oxford libraries before 1800', *Archaeological Journal* cxxxv (1978), 248–57.

Oxford joiner Thomas Key constructed and installed at least some of the surviving stalls in the west library. These are 5' 9" high under a shallow cornice, 7' 6" wide, divided front and back into two bays on each side, and give two shelves for folio volumes above a projecting reading-shelf. The existing readers' benches were retained. The point of this new design was to provide room for many more books standing on the shelves of the stalls than it had been possible to accommodate lying on the sloping tops of the medieval lecterns or on the shelves beneath them. In the new system as in the old all the books were chained, and they stood with their fore-edges outwards to facilitate chaining. Small and precious items which could not be chained were locked in cupboards at one end of the library. It soon became clear that the stalls darkened the library much more than lecterns had done, and in 1597–8 dormer windows towards the quadrangle were inserted in the west library. When in 1623 the south range was given similar stalls, dormer windows were inserted at the same time (plate 16). The entire library with its fittings survives virtually unaltered, except that the books have been unchained.

The new stall system quickly established its popularity. The new library at St John's College, begun in 1596, was designed for stalls with a considerably greater bay-width than in earlier libraries; in fact the stalls at St John's proved to be a little too widely spaced for readers' comfort. In the library at All Souls stalls providing shelves at three levels were erected in 1596–7 and the next year the room was much embellished and presumably made brighter by an enriched plaster ceiling.[62] At Queen's new stalls were erected before the turn of the century, at New College in 1602–6, at Corpus in 1604, and at Magdalen and Christ Church in 1610–11.

This is the background to the initiative of Sir Thomas Bodley, Savile's friend and former colleague at Merton, in refitting Duke Humfrey's Library with stalls on the new pattern for the benefit of the university as a whole. By 1598 the library had stood empty for many years, 'a great desolate roome'. On 23 February of that year Bodley wrote to the vice-chancellor offering to fit it up with 'seates, and shelfes, and deskes'. In response convocation set up a committee to assist in deciding on the 'fittest kinde of facture of deskes and other furniture'. By the middle of the year timber, the gift of Merton College, was being seasoned.[63] The stalls, the 'platforme' for which was based on notes supplied by Bodley and Savile, are stout plain pieces with little refinement, but, being as much as 7' 6" high, are crowned by a full entablature rather than a mere cornice. Books could be shelved at three levels above the reading-flap, and the stalls were 11' 6" long, far longer than in any college library. At the eastern, or inner, end of the library were the librarians' studies, called closets by Bodley and intended by him for 'lesser bookes' which could not be chained, and the 'grated places', lockable presses with pierced metal doors, for the most precious manuscripts and printed books.[64] For a library room Duke Humfrey was exceptionally lofty and well lit. Besides the two-light side windows lighting the reading-bays, great seven-light windows at east and west provided

---

[62] But there may have been an earlier plain plaster ceiling. Information from Professor J. McConica.
[63] *Bodley to James*, ed. Wheeler, pp. xi–xii.   [64] Ibid. 25.

general illumination.[65] More of a problem in the early years was the overheating of the room in midsummer.[66] Bodley's correspondence with his librarian, Thomas James, confirms that in July 1602 Thomas Key was working as joiner in the library, sawing and fitting wainscots supplied by Bodley from London.[67] As the number of volumes increased, first, in mid-1604, it was proposed to place chests for small books under the windows, but instead a gallery was constructed at the west end by August 1605.[68]

Bodley's policy of encouraging gifts of books was so successful that within a decade the physical extension of the library became a necessity. But before this was put in hand Savile had taken a new initiative, and it is necessary to turn back to Merton to examine this work, which not only set the course for new college building for the next half-century but also had an important bearing on Bodley's subsequent building.

Early in his wardenship (1589–91) Savile had rebuilt the north range of the front quadrangle between the fifteenth-century gatehouse and the thirteenth-century former warden's lodging. This provided six small chambers, the top two in cocklofts lit by fancy dormer windows.[69] By the first decade of the seventeenth century the number of fellows had risen to the high twenties, and although, with a total resident population in 1611 of seventy-three, Merton was by no means one of the most crowded colleges, there was a need for more accommodation.[70] Savile had doubtless been saving for years with this in mind, but the quadrangle which he erected in 1608–10 was more than the fulfilment of a practical need, rather it was an architectural statement of a new monumentality. The quadrangle was sited in the warden's garden, approached from the north through the splendidly vaulted gateway which Warden Fitzjames had put up a century before. In the west range a new two-storey kitchen was incorporated, aligned on the screens' passage of the hall. This may have been built ahead of the rest, in 1606, but its fenestration was arranged to disguise the fact that it differed in function from the rest of the new quadrangle. Built on an almost square plan, 102′ × 108′ fellows' quadrangle is as large as a complete medium-sized college. It provided twenty-three sets, and, for the warden, in the east range a first-floor long gallery (not now recognizable internally). The ranges are three full storeys high, each storey slightly loftier than the one below, so that the best chambers were on the top floor. At 20′ the internal depth of the ranges is 2′ more than the standard 18′ established at New College. The original layout of the chambers and their studies is uncertain; probably each chamber was a large, square room extending the full depth of the range and lit by a three-light window towards the quadrangle and at the back by two-light windows flanking the fireplace. Within each chamber were two studies, back to back, each

[65] J. N. L. Myres, 'Recent discoveries in the Bodleian Library', *Archaeologia* ci (1967), 159–60, for the east window. The west window is shown in Bereblock's woodcut.

[66] *Bodley to James*, ed. Wheeler, 9, 44, 139.   [67] Ibid. 49, 51.

[68] Ibid. 98, 135 n. 1, 138, 223.   [69] Well shown in Loggan's print.

[70] Wood, *Life and Times* iv. 151.

lit by a single two-light window, one towards the quadrangle, the other facing outwards. This maintained the study-to-chamber ratio established at Corpus nearly a
century earlier, though it need not imply that the chambers were intended to be
shared. There is evidence that throughout the sixteenth century it had been normal for fellows of Merton to occupy chambers singly.[71] Since at Merton, alone
among Oxford colleges, scholars had their own accommodation, Postmasters' Hall,
it is possible that the new chambers were intended for single occupation, and that
one of the 'studies' was really a bedroom, as gradually became the norm later in
the century at many colleges.

The arrangement of rooms is indicated by the fenestration pattern towards the
quadrangle, three-light chamber windows alternating with two-light windows which
alternately serve studies and staircases. On the outward façades the windows are
uniformly two-lighters. On the skyline a strong visual pattern is established by the
alternation of chimney-stacks and gables. Projecting bay windows at each end of
the south façade at first-floor level (the eastern one lighting the warden's gallery)
complete a visually satisfying composition as seen from Christ Church meadow.

Yet there is one alien architectural feature of the fellows' quadrangle, the tower-
like 'frontispiece of the orders' which fills the eye as one passes in under the
Fitzjames gateway. It consists of four storeys of paired fluted columns climbing up
through the orders from Doric, through Ionic and Corinthian to the crowning
Composite applied to a free-standing slab of masonry at roof level. Yet on all three
upper stages the columns frame gothic panelling. The large niches were empty by
Loggan's time (1675), but the diminutive heraldic panels, arms of the college and
of Savile, on the second stage, and the royal arms at the top, suggest that the missing statues must have represented James I above and Savile with, presumably,
Walter de Merton below. The frontispiece would then have formed a visible
memorial of benefactors and a statement of loyalty to the crown. Such displays of
superimposed columns, ultimately of French derivation, had been imported into
England by Protector Somerset, who gave his town palace in the Strand (1547–51)
a 'frontispiece of the orders' in place of a gate-tower. The idea quickly took root
(Burghley House, late 1550s; Kirby Hall, early 1570s) and lasted long (Cobham,
Kent, 1595; Stonyhurst, Lancashire, 1592–5). The earl of Salisbury's Hatfield House
(1608–12), exactly contemporary with the fellows' quadrangle, demonstrates the
still unflagging strength of the tradition. So at Merton Savile transplanted a palatial
and seigneurial motif into the academic world and gave it an appropriate symbolic
connotation.

One is probably safe in assuming that the overall conception of the fellows'
quadrangle was Savile's. He seems to have started without an adequate team of
craftsmen; when at the end of 1608 one third of the foundations had been laid,
work came to a halt because no local craftsmen could be found to undertake such
a big job. It must have been through Savile's connections in his native Yorkshire

[71] *The Collegiate University*, 628.

that craftsmen were recruited from Halifax, John Acroyd as master mason and John Bentley as his assistant, together with a master carpenter, Thomas Holt. Thus for the first, but by no means the last time in this period craftsmen had to be imported to realize the conceptions of Oxford patrons.[72]

Before long Savile's Yorkshire craftsmen were working for Bodley, whose ideas for extending the university library began to crystallize in 1608. By December he had prepared a 'plotte . . . for the lengthning of the librarie' and the following March sent a man down to survey the site.[73] Two months later he had acquainted the vice-chancellor with his plans and secured Acroyd's services.[74] The first stone was laid on 19 July 1610, the contract with Acroyd stipulating completion by Michaelmas 1611.[75]

The two-storey range which was built across the east end of the divinity school in 1610–12 provided a broad, shallow vestibule, the proscholium, and above it a substantial enlargement of the inner end of the library, Arts End (plate 2). The seven-light east window of Duke Humfrey, thus swept away, was reproduced in the new east wall, and similar four-light windows lit the north and south ends.[76] This made it impractical to continue with the stall system of shelving which had at first been proposed.[77] The cue was therefore taken from the overflow shelving at the west end of Duke Humfrey and a complete system of wall shelving devised, though Bodley may also have had in mind the royal library at the Escorial fitted up on this system for Philip II of Spain in 1584. This provided vastly increased space for smaller volumes on shelving fixed against the upper half of the walls. They are reached by galleries and secured by lockable doors and timber caging round the flights of steps up to the galleries. The joinery is quite plain, but employs classical forms: long, thin Doric columns to carry the galleries and short, thin Doric columns for seat backs and gallery rails.

Stylistically the fabric of the range is at variance with the joinery of Arts End, for the building itself was designed outside and in to harmonize as closely as possible with the divinity school and Duke Humfrey. The east front copies the close-set panelling of the east wall of the divinity school, and, as has already been mentioned, the main window there replicates the window which had lit Duke Humfrey. Even the crowning battlements and pinnacles are closely modelled on those on the north and south sides of the divinity school. Inside, the proscholium vault does not attempt to rival the spectacular display of the divinity school itself, but imitates instead the lierne vault of the Fitzjames gateway at Merton, but with

[72] VCH Oxon. iii. 102; J. W. Hanson, 'Halifax builders in Oxford', Transactions of the Halifax Antiquarian Society xxv (1928), 253–317.

[73] Bodley to James, ed. Wheeler, 178–80, 183–4.   [74] Ibid. 189.

[75] Ibid. 194 n. 1, 207.   [76] Myres, 'Recent discoveries', 164.

[77] Bodl. MS Wood F 27, fos 41ᵛ–2ʳ, reproduced in H. Colvin, Unbuilt Oxford (New Haven and London 1983), 7. See D. Sturdy, 'Bodley's bookcases: "this goodly magazine of witte" ', John Donne Journal v (1986), 280–1, for structural evidence that some of the wall shelving was made from dismembered stalls. However, it is difficult to accept the suggestion that stalls were ever actually erected in Arts End.

small pendants and shields of arms at the intersections of the ribs instead of the big figural bosses of the prototype.[78] In Arts End the timber roof is a refined variant of that in Duke Humfrey, set on a carved stone cornice, all completely convincing as an imitation of fifteenth-century work, and far superior to the crude supplementary struts and braces which Bodley's carpenter had inserted into Duke Humfrey a decade before.

Bodley, unable to visit the works during construction, was kept fully informed of progress by Thomas James and other Oxford friends—Nathaniel Brent, fellow of Merton, who acted as paymaster, John Hawley, principal of Gloucester Hall, the site overseer, and Thomas Gent also of Gloucester Hall. However, when there were problems to resolve, Bodley admitted, 'aboue many others, Sir Henry Sauiles is to me, as the iudgement of a mason'.[79] Bodley himself was concerned with practicalities and the quality of the workmanship: 'beautie and strength to the walle . . . are the very maine and principal pointes that I aime at in my building.' The finer points of design he happily left to others: 'For the fashion of the antickes and pendants, I referre my self wholy to the workman, together with your self, Mr Gent, Mr Brent, and Mr Principal, hauing heerewith returned your patterns againe: which I can like of well enough, if they be to your likinges.'[80]

Bodley's next project, the rebuilding of the schools (plate 1), he first mentions in a letter to the vice-chancellor dated 5 November 1611, but it is clear that the inadequacies of the existing fifteenth-century building, remodelled but not rebuilt in the late 1550s, had long been felt.[81] 'Those ruinous little roomes' Bodley called them, and Sir John Bennet, with whom he discussed his ideas, similarly stressed their deficiencies.[82] They formed a two-storeyed range longer but narrower than the divinity school facing it at right-angles not more than 40' to the east. With the construction of Arts End the two buildings confronted each other directly across the narrow lane called Schools Street. Changed teaching patterns in the university made it desirable to provide more schools as well as larger ones, so it was obvious that the site was wholly inadequate. The drastic but inevitable decision was soon taken to eliminate the north end of Schools Street by building the new schools to form a quadrangle, with Arts End as its western range, extending eastwards as far as Catte Street. Before the end of March 1612 the university, apparently acting on the instructions of Bodley and Bennet, had begun to take steps to buy out the inhabitants of Catte Street whose houses stood on the site.[83] This did not prove altogether straightforward and a whole year elapsed before the foundation stone of the new schools was laid.

By this stage, however, the plans had undergone major modification. In his will

[78] As was noted by J. Ingram, *Memorials of Oxford* (3 vols Oxford 1837) ii, 'Bodleian Library', 6. See also *An Inventory of the Historical Monuments in the City of Oxford* (Royal Commission on Historical Monuments, England: London 1939), pl. 3, where the two vaults are illustrated side by side.

[79] *Bodley to James*, ed. Wheeler, 210.   [80] Ibid. 212, 217.

[81] *The Collegiate University*, 599–600.   [82] OUA register K, fos 78[r–v].

[83] Ibid. fo 80[v].

of January 1613 Bodley decreed that the residue of his estate should be laid out in extending the university library over the new schools:

yf the intended present plott for buylding the newe schooles shall proseede in such sort as the same is all readie devised by publique consent, then ouer the tops of those two stories which are resolued to be the hight of the scholles there shall be contriued another third rome . . . to goe in compasse round about the scholes and so meete at each end in two lobies or passages framed with some speciall comlines of workmanshippe to make a faire enterance into the northe and southe corners of my late new enlargment estward, for there will be gayned by this means a very large supplement for stowage of bookes when the two libraries shall be fully replenished.[84]

In the light of this radically altered brief the foundations were increased by one quarter and the core of the walls by one fifth, in order to bear the weight of the third storey.[85] Nevertheless, the different functions of the two elements were not made architecturally explicit. The schools, being lecture rooms, needed maximum illumination, and so the big rectangular multi-light windows were functionally appropriate. By contrast, the top storey, its windows identical to those below, was poorly conceived for library use, the fenestration incompatible with the stall system of Duke Humfrey and needlessly sacrificing wall space if shelving to match that in Arts End was envisaged. Clearly the future library function seemed secondary. The top storey was at first referred to as the 'gallery', and the painted frieze running right round it—200 heads in medallions of the chief figures in secular and sacred learning, from the Greek and Roman philosophers to the divines of the early seventeenth century, alternating with still-lifes of books and other instruments of scholarship—suggests that the room was conceived as much in terms of a domestic long gallery, a place for edifying perambulation, as for the 'stowage of bookes'.[86]

The schools themselves consisted of twelve lecture rooms, four in the north range, four in the east, and four in the south. Those on the ground storey were entered by doorways direct from the courtyard, those above by means of the stairtowers set in the angles, the two western stairs giving access to one school each, the eastern stairs to two each. Since the upper schools were loftier and lit by larger windows than the lower, they were clearly better to lecture in, so were allocated to professors, while praelectors were to lecture below. The original allocation, made in the Michaelmas term of 1620, was as follows. The upper schools nearest the library, the only ones with separate staircase access, went on the north side to the professor of jurisprudence and on the south side to the professor of medicine, with below them the praelectors in moral and natural philosophy respectively. The other schools on the north side were allocated to the professor of Greek above and the praelector in grammar below, and the corresponding schools on the south side to the professor of Hebrew and the praelector in rhetoric. Finally in the schools at the eastern end the two newly established Savilian professors were to give their lec-

---

[84] Macray, *Annals of the Bodleian Library*, 406.   [85] OUA register N, fo 1ᵛ.
[86] J. N. L. Myres, 'Thomas James and the painted frieze', *Bodleian Library Record* iv (1952–3), 30–51.

tures, the professor of geometry to the north of the tower and the professor of astronomy to the south of it, with the praelector in metaphysics below the former, the praelector in logic below the latter.[87] The theology professors, of course, continued to lecture in the divinity school.

The new schools were designed to harmonize architecturally with the university library and the divinity school, as the continuation of identical battlements and pinnacles across the entire skyline emphatically proclaimed, although their plain ashlar walls contrasted with the decorative panelling, or 'mullet-work' as it is called in the accounts, carried on from the façade of the library over the two western stairturrets. But this was not thought of as a 'gothic' vocabulary stylistically at odds with the 'classicism' of the frontispiece of the orders on the entrance tower, for the sculptured bosses (plate 14) on the string course carried round under the battlements, another feature imitated from the medieval building, are referred to in the accounts as 'antickes', which relates them to the decorative vocabulary of 'antique work' introduced to England from Italy and France in the 1520s.[88]

The only approach to the schools quadrangle which was in the least dignified was from Catte Street, so the siting of the main entrance axially in the east range was predictable. Over the entrance, with equal predictability, a lofty tower was erected, though the pinnacles half absorbed into the root of the tower might suggest that it was an afterthought.[89] However, the series of superimposed columns on the inner face of the tower, since it starts from Tuscan at the bottom, must have been intended to rise through all five orders, taking it high above the three storeys of the quadrangle. In the account for the third storey (November 1615) the relevant (Ionic) tier of columns is itemized, but it is possible that the frontispiece of the orders was not in the original design. Structural examination of the fabric cannot elucidate this now, after the total renewal of the columns twice, in the 1870s and the 1960s. The siting of the frontispiece may well have caused some perplexity. Catte Street was too narrow for it to follow Somerset House in the Strand and stand on the external face of the gate tower; while the pre-existing proscholium and Arts End made it impossible to site it facing the entrance, the normal position in domestic architecture, already reflected in the fellows' quadrangle at Merton. Set as it is on the inner side of the entrance, it is properly seen only by those leaving the proscholium or looking out of the east window of Arts End. In all probability the latter viewpoint was considered the most significant. At any rate it is from this level that the sculptural group in the fourth storey of the tower can best be appreciated. The group represents symbolically James I's donation to the library in 1620 of the Latin edition of his writings, and, as Catherine Cole has demonstrated, the design of the tower was adapted to take the figures, which are set within the outer

[87] OUA register N, fo 94ᵛ. By 1675, when David Loggan published his print of the schools quadrangle, the distribution had changed somewhat. The present inscriptions over the doorways follow Loggan.

[88] The building account dated 6 November 1615 is entered in OUA register N, fo 1ᵛ.

[89] All three of Loggan's engravings of the schools show this peculiarity clearly.

frame of what had been a window.[90] In the same year Sir Clement Edmonds, elected in 1621 with Sir John Bennet member of parliament for Oxford University, presented to the library a pentagonal pillar faced with pilasters of the five orders. This alabaster object, which is quite small and serves to display a set of models of the five geometrical solids, perhaps intended as a visual aid for the new Savilian professor of geometry, survives in the university's Museum of the History of Science. It demonstrates an association between learning and the classical orders, just as the frontispiece of the schools quadrangle does on an infinitely greater scale. Roger North, writing in the mid-1690s, recognized the appropriateness of this learned architecture here when he wrote of 'the Scools at Oxford, where . . . are the 5 orders plac't in proper degrees . . . I must confess the designe was very suitable for an academy'.[91]

In Sir Thomas Bodley's mind, however, library and schools were not quite such an integrated entity as they were to become. The approach from the east through the quadrangle led only to the schools, with the divinity school at the far end beyond the proscholium. The library, on the other hand, was entered from the west, and in his will Bodley expressed his desire that the entrance from this direction should not be abolished but, on the contrary, enhanced by the 'raysinge of a faire staircase to make the ascent more easie and gracefull to the first great librarie' and 'some beautifull enlargement at the west end of the said librarie towards Exeter Colledge'. When, twenty years later, it at last became possible to implement this third stage of enlargement, Bodley's assumption no longer prevailed. At that point the shared approach to library and schools from the east was introduced.

Meanwhile, Savile's new quadrangle at Merton was exerting its influence. Nicholas Wadham was a rich but childless west-country landowner who decided to leave his fortune to foster education in some form. His first idea, apparently, was to found a college for English Catholics at Venice.[92] This highly provocative notion was perhaps the brainchild of his wife Dorothy, who as a Petre belonged to a recusant family and was herself presented as a recusant a few years after her husband's death. When Nicholas's thoughts turned to Oxford he first envisaged endowing Gloucester Hall or, failing that, Jesus College, very much as his father-in-law, Sir William Petre, had virtually refounded Exeter College. In October 1609, shortly before his death, this was still his plan, and he appointed as co-trustee with his wife Sir John Davis, a former member of Gloucester Hall who was expected to be able to 'compasse the procuringe of that house.'[93] Wadham had envisaged the expenditure of £2,000 in improving Gloucester Hall by means of a chapel, a

---

[90] C. Cole, 'The building of the tower of five orders in the schools' quadrangle at Oxford', *Oxoniensia* xxxiii–xxxiv (1968–9), 101.

[91] *Of Building: Roger North's writings on architecture*, ed. H. Colvin and J. Newman (Oxford 1981), 118.

[92] Wood, *Life and Times* i. 259, quoting information obtained from William Bull, fellow of All Souls, in 1658.

[93] T. G. Jackson, *Wadham College, Oxford* (Oxford 1893), 15; N. Briggs, 'The foundation of Wadham College, Oxford', *Oxoniensia* xxi (1956), 62–3.

buttery, cellar, and kitchen.[94] Greatly increased costs would be inevitable in the foundation and erection of a new college. But also, as a neighbour is said to have pointed out, greatly increased fame would accrue: 'Why, doe as Sir Thomas Bodley hath lately done. As he hath built a library, soe you build a college and you shall be remembred every day. It will last from generation to generation.'[95] Before he died Wadham had indeed decided to endow an entirely new college.

One of the last pieces of advice offered by Wadham was that his trustees should solicit royal support and the backing of the politically powerful.[96] Before the end of November 1609 his widow had sought help from the lord treasurer, the earl of Salisbury, in the dispute which soon arose between herself and her fellow trustee.[97] By February 1610 negotiations were under way for the purchase of the site of the Austin Friars immediately to the north of the city wall at the east end of Candich. When the city council, which had procured the site in 1587 for £610, demanded £1,000 for it, Dorothy Wadham must have appealed to the king himself. By 6 March 1610 the council was in receipt of letters from the king and from Lord Chancellor Ellesmere on the king's behalf and, after a vote, reluctantly agreed to sell it to Wadham's trustees for £600 plus the cost of buying out six tenants.[98] This was a bargain and in the opinion of the visitor, the bishop of Bath and Wells, preferable to the alternative site, eight acres belonging to Merton College, for which the trustees had decided to treat while negotiations with the city hung in the balance at the end of February 1610.[99]

If Dorothy Wadham was quick to claim the backing of the powerful when she needed it, she was also determined to keep control of the project in her own hands, as her letters to her brother Lord Petre make clear. As surveyor and master mason she chose William Arnold, 'an honest man, a perfectt workman, and my neere neighboure'. As clerk engrosser she proposed to employ 'a man of myne owne', and at the start of building twenty craftsmen with their apprentices arrived in Oxford from Somerset.[100]

In William Arnold Dorothy chose one of the outstanding architect-masons of the time, who in the 1590s had built Montacute House, Somerset, and in 1609–10 was making designs for Cranborne Manor, Dorset, for the earl of Salisbury. The strongly personal character of these two houses has made it possible to attribute other west-country buildings to Arnold.[101] Wadham College (plate 8) demonstrates Arnold's ingenuity as a planner, but it also shows how completely he both grasped the main issues in designing a modern college at Oxford and submerged his own personal style in adopting the vocabulary of the fellows' quadrangle at Merton. By 19 March 1610 he had been engaged on the project for five weeks and had drawn up a plan. What Dorothy Wadham refers to as 'the first modell' was considered by

[94] Jackson, *Wadham College*, 13.   [95] Wood, *Life and Times* i. 259.
[96] Jackson, *Wadham College*, 13.   [97] Ibid. 15.
[98] *Oxford Council Acts, 1583–1626*, 197; *Oxford City Properties*, ed. H. E. Salter (OHS lxxxiii 1926), 358–63.
[99] Briggs, 'Foundation of Wadham', 64–6.   [100] Ibid. 63–6; WCM 8/1A, fo 1.
[101] A. Oswald, *Country Houses of Dorset* (London 1935, 2nd edn London 1959), 25–9.

her brother and others as too 'spacious and sumptious' and was consequently 'suppressed', but she clearly reposed such trust in Arnold that it was only in the following October, when site works had been in progress for six months, that she instructed him to submit his revised plans to Lord Petre.[102]

The plan of Wadham College makes an arresting image on the page. That is typical of Jacobean architectural design, where formal ingenuity was highly prized. Symmetry dominates, at the expense of functional explicitness. Thus the doorway to the antechapel matches not the doorway to the hall but the doorway to the cellar beneath it; the hall itself is reached up an awkward dog-leg stair; and it is an oddly schematic idea to match the chapel with the kitchen. All these devices are produced by the overriding desire (not quite perfectly realized) for symmetry about the axis which runs from the entrance gateway to the frontispiece of the orders framing the hall doorway. This frontispiece is the most obvious borrowing from Merton fellows' quadrangle, but the conception of the three-storeyed elevations crowned by straight-sided gables, and the placing of oriel windows in the outermost bays of the entrance front, also derive from Merton. The chapel with its spacious antechapel forming a T-plan conforms to the Oxford pattern established by the chapel at New College and ensures correct orientation. The details of the piers and arches of the antechapel arcades are so close to those of the corresponding arcades at All Souls and Magdalen that one or other must have been deliberately taken as model.[103] In the elevation the only novel element is the tracery pattern, like buckled scrolls, of the 'hall' windows, as they are called in the building account, used to make the hall and antechapel uniform towards the quadrangle. Presumably it was felt to look suitably secular in contrast to the traditional, and hence ecclesiastical-looking, panel tracery in the windows of the chapel itself. Such a contrast, incidentally, was subsequently observed only at Jesus College, where the big east window of the chapel has full-blown gothic tracery but the hall has square-headed windows along the lines of those in the schools. At Exeter College both hall (1618) and chapel (1622–4) (plate 18) were given purely gothic panel tracery. Hall, antechapel, and chapel at Oriel College (from 1620) all employ the Wadham hall-window pattern, as do the windows in both the hall and the chapel at University College from 1634. The side windows at Lincoln College chapel (1629) are modified from the Wadham hall-window type.

The heating of the hall at Wadham was by the traditional brazier set on an open hearth, with a ventilation louvre in the roof ridge. The new halls at Exeter, Oriel, and University all followed suit, but at Trinity, where there were chambers over the hall, and at Jesus, the fireplace was set in an enclosed hearth, as the massive projecting chimney-breast at Jesus proclaims. Most colleges, nevertheless, delayed until the eighteenth century or even later before emulating this modernization. The timber roof of the hall at Wadham, constructed by Thomas Holt, the carpenter member of Sir Henry Savile's team of Yorkshire craftsmen, is of hammerbeam type,

[102] Briggs, 'Foundation of Wadham', 67, 72.
[103] *Inventory of Historical Monuments in Oxford*, pls 65, 151.

framed on precisely the same system as the roofs of a century earlier at Corpus Christi and Christ Church. Its coarse details, openwork pendants, and curved braces embellished with fleurs-de-lis and stylized dragon-heads mark it as a Jacobean production. The roofs of the halls at Jesus, Oriel, and University College (dated 1656) are all plainer and lankier versions of the Wadham roof, but the hall at Exeter in this feature too maintains its independence of local practice and employs an arched-brace system. It is in hall screens that the influence of Wadham is clearest. John Bolton, the Oxford joiner employed by Dorothy Wadham, devised for the hall screen a classical form new to the university (though it had been widely familiar elsewhere since the erection of the screen in the hall of the Middle Temple, London, in 1562–4), with Corinthian columns flanking the two entry arches and a panelled gallery front surmounted by pierced strapwork cresting. The screen and cresting in the hall at Exeter College are virtually identical, presumably also Bolton's work. At Jesus the screen has a balustraded top, but is otherwise similar in almost all respects; Magdalen's is designed on the same basic pattern, so Wadham's may have been stipulated as model, only differing in detail. The chapel at Wadham is also richly fitted up, with a lavishly crested screen by Bolton to separate it from the ante-chapel, and stained glass, inserted between 1613 and 1622 in all the windows.

The scale of Wadham College must have impressed contemporaries. The dimensions of all its parts are generous if not excessive for a foundation with only fifteen fellows and fifteen scholars. The quadrangle, 134' × 122', was surpassed only by those at New College, Magdalen, and Christ Church. The hall, 82' long, was longer than all but the monster halls of New College and Christ Church. In its chapel and antechapel, smaller admittedly than the most spacious of the medieval examples, Wadham almost exactly matched those of All Souls College. The chamber ranges, at 20' wide, followed the width of the ranges of Merton fellows' quadrangle, not the 18' norm of the medieval and Tudor colleges (though in this respect too Christ Church, and also Magdalen, had been laid out to incomparably more spacious dimensions). Only in the lodging for the head of the house might Wadham College have seemed underprovisioned. It was Dorothy Wadham's prejudice that the warden of her college should be celibate, so he was allocated no more than the traditional tower chamber and the three sets on the adjoining staircase to the north. The other thirty-nine chambers, reached by eight several staircases, each had two studies and the possibility of contriving a third under the staircase. There is no sign here of studies being used as bedrooms, for early chamber lists, which survive from *circa* 1620 onwards, show that a number of chambers were shared by three occupants during the 1620s and 1630s, one of the three invariably sleeping on a truckle bed and hence presumably a servitor or other junior member of the college.[104] However, it is clear that many chambers were not occupied at all, and in the early years the population of the college barely reached fifty.

[104] WCM 9/1.

Eighteen chambers are listed with occupants' names before 1623. The upper and middle chambers, rented at £5 a year, were more desirable than those on the ground floor at £3 a year. Cocklofts rented at 10s a year, but, judging by the early chamber lists, few of these were brought into use in the early decades.[105]

The extent and limitations of the influence of Wadham College in redefining ideas about Oxford collegiate architecture can be well studied in the two complete rebuildings, Oriel College (from 1620) and University College (from 1634). Nothing is known of the circumstances surrounding the design of the new buildings at Oriel, but for University College we have a complete series of preparatory plans and even a fragmentary model, the earliest English architectural model to survive.[106]

The site of Oriel College was awkward, bounded on three sides by public thoroughfares which did not meet at right-angles. Piecemeal rebuilding perpetuated the orientation of the college, with the entrance towards the west. Following Wadham, hall and chapel formed the east range, where there was barely enough space for them, especially as the east–west dimension of the quadrangle was maximized in order to provide adequate space for chambers for the eighteen fellows. Yet the chambers were largely confined to the south and west ranges, for more than half the north range was occupied by the provost's lodging, with the library in the top storey of the remainder. North of the lodging lay the provost's spacious garden, running up to the boundary of St Mary Hall; so the college was laid out in a way which benefited the provost at the expense of everyone else.

Architecturally the main accent is the three-sided porch over the hall steps above which three niches are squeezed in under a top pediment, providing for the statues of Edward II and, probably, James I below and, above, a statue of the virgin, to whom the college is dedicated. Doubtless, had there been room, all this would have been disposed within a frontispiece of the orders. Lack of space in the east range also forced the siting of the bursary in the old-fashioned position, within the entrance gate-tower. However the bursary was given a rich plaster ceiling and the gateway itself the first of Oxford's seventeenth-century fan-vaults. Oriel's most memorable innovation, the shaped gablets which punctuate the skyline within and without the quadrangle, may be a London idea, derived from some such recent building as Holland House, Kensington, *circa* 1606/7. The elevations of the chamber ranges look fussy, with their close-set two-light windows over which continuous hood-moulds jump up and down relentlessly. But they signal another significant change, for the differentiation between chamber windows and study windows, which had been preserved at Wadham, is here for the first time abandoned.

At University College (plate 5) these idiosyncracies—the gablets (in a variant form), the regular two-light fenestration, the busy hood-moulds, the fan-vaulted entrance—are all repeated, but in its plan the college shows a direct debt to

[105] WCM 9/2.   [106] Colvin, *Unbuilt Oxford*, pl. 10.

Wadham, particularly in the placing of the kitchen in a wing at the back with the library over it, but also in the (now realigned) dog-leg passage into the hall with the bursary behind. Here, on a regular site on the south side of High Street, a quadrangle 100' square was envisaged, with chamber ranges 18' wide to west, north and east, and hall and chapel end to end in the south range. The existing master's lodging on High Street east of the quadrangle was retained, so the eight staircases all lead to sets, thirty-six in all, each consisting of a chamber and two (in a few cases three) studies. The indication of room names on one plan, 'chamber', 'study', and 'bedroom', is the earliest clear evidence of the new way of occupying sets, already suspected for the fellows' quadrangle at Merton, and familiar from the post-Restoration period.[107]

The master, Thomas Walker, was closely involved with the rebuilding. The surviving accounts are in his hand and it was he who wrote on the first, over-ambitious rebuilding plan: 'This modell was refused as inconvenient.'[108] The other plans and the pasteboard model, which all relate to the executed design, show how it underwent a series of careful modifications and refinements, which doubtless represent the results of discussions between Walker and his surveyor.[109] The identity of the surveyor is not certain, but he was probably Richard Maude, master mason for the rebuilding from 1634; an almost identical vocabulary is used in the north elevation of the Canterbury quadrangle of St John's College, part of the range built by Maude in 1631–2 and for which he and his partners made 'drafts' and 'modells'; and a decade later, in 1643, Maude used the motifs once more, in the second quadrangle at Jesus College.[110] Some of the surviving plans for University College indicate a square cloister south of the chapel, which was never begun; but the main area of indecision was the centre of the south front of the quadrangle, with the entrances to hall and chapel and the through passage and staircase up to the library behind. Final decisions here may well not have been taken when work halted in the early 1640s. When it resumed in 1655 John Jackson acted as master mason, and he may have designed the bizarrely hybrid centrepiece recorded in the 1670s both by Loggan and in a college benefactors' book, but eliminated in 1802 in favour of something more purely gothic.[111]

In April 1630, less than nine years after leaving the president's lodging at St John's College, William Laud was installed as chancellor of the university. Thus arose his second opportunity for building improvement at his *alma mater*. His concern for his own college is well known and fully documented, but there is evidence that his ambition reached much higher and a case can be made that his influence on Oxford building in the 1630s was widespread.

[107] UCA P/6, and see for example A. H. Smith, *New College, Oxford, and its Buildings* (Oxford 1952), 94.

[108] UCA P/1. A redrawing of this plan is reproduced in Colvin, *Unbuilt Oxford*, pl. 11.

[109] UCA P/3–6, 12–14, 16.

[110] UCA FAB 1/2, fo 53; H. Colvin, *The Canterbury Quadrangle, St John's College, Oxford* (Oxford 1988), 44; JCA Shelf 17, account book for the second quadrangle.

[111] *University College Record* iii (1956–60), 110–11.

His most grandiose dream was 'to open the great square at Oxford between St Mary's and the schools, Brasen-nose and All Souls'.[112] This idea had probably emerged in August 1629, when the court was at Woodstock (without Laud, who fell seriously ill at the time). On 1 September 1629 the king himself wrote to the vice-chancellor recommending the demolition of the houses in this area, which 'take of from the lusture and dignity of our University of Oxford', and in response a hastily convened committee sent to Viscount Dorchester, the secretary of state, on 15 September a schedule of the properties on the site and the costs of buying out the occupants which demonstrated that 'the worke is very feisable'.[113] Nothing further was done, however, and Oxford had to wait until the building of the Radcliffe Camera, which began in 1737, for the realization of this dream. Laud himself was presumably attracted by the scheme because it would have enhanced the dignity and sacred functions of the university church, an objective which lay behind several of the building initiatives of the 1630s. In March 1639 he noted the decision that circuiting for degrees should henceforth begin not from the church but from the schools, adding 'We have now left only the Friday [vice-chancellor's] court in St Mary's church, and I hope that will not dwell there long.'[114]

The most striking improvement to the church itself was the rebuilding of the south porch in 1637, at the expense of Dr Morgan Owen, Laud's chaplain. The placing of a statue of the virgin and child on it formed one of the accusations against Laud at his trial; a witness stated that he had seen passers-by doing reverence to it.[115] Laud's defence that he knew nothing about the statue until it was set up may have been strictly true; but he was certainly acquainted with the proposal to erect the porch itself, for he knew the contract price of £230. The mason, John Jackson, who constructed the porch had the previous year completed the Canterbury quadrangle at St John's College. Furthermore the porch is crowned by the university arms, and it was the university which paid the workmen sums owed to them in excess of the contract price.[116]

Architecturally the most eloquent feature of the porch is the pair of monumental spiral columns which flank the entrance arch. The question arises whether they were meant to refer to the twelve spiral, vine-clad columns reverently preserved in St Peter's in Rome, one at least of which was believed to have come from the temple built by Solomon in Jerusalem.[117] Raphael had introduced such columns prominently into his *Healing of the Lame Man at the Beautiful Gate of the Temple*, one of the celebrated tapestry cartoons which had entered the British royal collection in 1623. One of Rubens's ceiling paintings installed in the Banqueting House in Whitehall Palace as recently as 1635 had depicted James I, the British Solomon, seated on a throne flanked by 'Salamonic' twisted (but not vine-clad) columns. At the entrance

[112] Laud, *Works* iii. 254.

[114] Laud, *Works* v. 217.

[116] Ibid. v. 174; cf Wood, *Life and Times* iv. 56.

[113] MCA President Frewen's papers, no. 2.

[115] Ibid. iv. 220, 229.

[117] J. B. Ward Perkins, 'The shrine of St Peter and its twelve spiral columns', *Journal of Roman Studies* xlii (1952), 21–33.

to a church, however, a pair of monumental columns might have been intended to provide a further reference to the temple in Jerusalem by recalling the two columns, Jachin and Boaz, which Solomon set up 'in the porch of the temple' (1 Kings 7. 21, AV). The new porch at St Mary's, it may therefore be argued, by means of its dominant spiral columns stressed the temple-like function of the church, a function which in the 1630s was still in competition with the various secular activities of the university which continued to take place there.

The completion of the convocation house in 1640 removed one of these secular activities, and in 1639, as we have seen, Laud expressed the hope that the vice-chancellor's court would soon go too.[118] Thirty years later the final stage was at last achieved, when in 1669 degree-giving ceremonies were transferred to the newly opened Sheldonian Theatre. But this too, it seems, had been conceived by Laud. When in June 1664 the university's thanks were conveyed to Gilbert Sheldon, archbishop of Canterbury, for the gift of the first £1,000 towards the new theatre, the resonant Latin letter made clear that the new building was intended to complete the removal of all secular functions from St Mary's church, where 'sacrifice is made equally to God and Apollo'. It continued: 'This great and altogether magnificent scheme only worthy of his doomed generosity, was projected not so long ago by that victim of piety, your noble predecessor, who, just as he deserved immortality by reason of his other virtues, so he especially laid just claim to it by his patronage of this academy'.[119]

Bodley's stipulation in his will that an entrance staircase should be built at the west end of his library was disregarded when in May 1634 construction began on a new convocation house on the site, with an extension of the library above. The circumstances of this change of plan are not made clear either in the university's records or in Laud's account of his chancellorship. Bodley's surviving executor, William Hakewill, had continued to press the university to construct the staircase until eventually on 19 April 1632 convocation appointed the first of several delegacies to set matters in train.[120] In November 1633 the project under discussion was still described as the new staircase (*nova graduum structura*).[121] The foundation-stone laid in May 1634 was however, as Laud records, for a new convocation house.[122] The following month Hugh Davies the mason was awarded £50, having sent in a bill for £89 for his time and expenses over a nine-year period in making one wooden and four pasteboard models for the staircase and for travelling to London to show the wooden model to Laud, to Hakewill, and to Sir Henry Vane, comptroller of the household.[123]

Abandoning the western staircase meant that the makeshift access to Bodley's library from the schools quadrangle had to be made permanent and the logic of a

---

[118] Laud, *Works* v. 217.
[119] OUA register of convocation 1659–71, NEP/*supra*/27, register Ta, pp. 189–90.
[120] Ibid. register of convocation 1628–40, NEP/*supra*/24, register R, fo 45ᵛ.
[121] Ibid. fo 72ʳ.
[122] Laud, *Works* v. 143; see also Wood, *History of the University* ii. 939–40.
[123] OUA accounts for the schools, N.W. 3/2.

western approach was lost. However, this consideration clearly weighed less than
the desire for a westward extension which would provide unimpeded space on both
levels. The chancellor's own interest in both these spaces is readily explained.
Convocation, which had traditionally met in the chancel of St Mary's church, had
more recently held its meetings in the congregation house on the north side of the
chancel. It is consistent with Laud's views on the function of St Mary's that he
should wish the university to have a purpose-built convocation house adjacent to
its new schools and library. Above the convocation house the library could be
extended to house the great collections of manuscripts which Laud was gathering.
As early as 1628 he had prevailed on his predecessor as chancellor, the earl of
Pembroke, to buy 240 Greek manuscripts for £700 from the Barocci library in
Venice and to present them to the university. In December 1634 he sent several
trunkfuls of manuscripts donated by Sir Kenelm Digby, and in the following May
over 450 on his own account, many in Greek and Arabic, some in Hebrew, Persian,
and Chinese.[124] When the library extension was completed in 1640 the names of
these three donors were inscribed there.[125] Only with the accession of John
Selden's great collection after his death in 1654 was this arm of the library given
its present name of Selden End. (plate 2)

In design the new range closely matched the rest of the library, with panel-
traceried windows of the simplest sort. The convocation house was given a remarkable plaster fan-vault, the earliest non-structural vault in Oxford, recreated in
masonry in 1758–9.[126] In the library the three west windows were at once reduced
to one when in 1639 Thomas Richardson shelved the room.[127] His joinery here,
modelled on that in Arts End but with improved proportions, and costing £1,000,
and the impressive seating of the convocation house below (plate 13), for which
he was paid about £325, constitute his *magnum opus*. For £73 18s od he fitted up
the square room at the north end of the lower storey known as the apodyterium,
to serve as the vice-chancellor's court and as a meeting-room for heads of
houses.[128]

Laud had been chancellor for only a few months when in August 1630 he proposed his first scheme for forming a second quadrangle at St John's College.[129] At
this stage he intended merely to lengthen the Elizabethan library range westwards
to link with the front quadrangle and to erect a matching north range which would
add to the president's lodging an extra upper and lower chamber and provide six
more fellows' chambers, thus freeing chambers in the front quadrangle to be occupied singly. Both ranges were to be battlemented and at the east end a blank wall

---

[124] Laud, *Works* iii. 209, v. 105, 112; OUA register R, fo 9ᵛ.

[125] Wood, *Life and Times* iv. 55.

[126] I. G. Philip, 'Reconstruction in the Bodleian Library and Convocation House in the eighteenth
century', *Bodleian Library Record* vi (1957–61), 419–21.

[127] Myres, 'Recent discoveries in the Bodleian Library', 158.

[128] OUA NEP/pyx./C/1, fos 125ᵛ–8ᵛ, printed in Wood, *Life and Times* iv. 54–5.

[129] Colvin, *Canterbury Quadrangle*, provides a definitive account of the design and building of the quadrangle.

was to run from one to the other with a 'cloister upon pillars' in front. An estimate prepared in March 1631 amounted to no more than £1,055, which was fully
covered by Laud's existing donations to the college.[130] The foundation-stone of
this relatively modest scheme was laid on 26 July 1631. When, five years later, the
Canterbury quadrangle was completed, it had become a showpiece of loyalty and
learning. Over the eastern cloister stood a room 111' long, soon to be fitted up as
a second, inner library, intended for manuscripts and printed books whose safe-
keeping was of special concern because of their rarity or small size, and also for a
collection of mathematical instruments, to encourage the study of mathematics,
hitherto neglected in the college. A matching western cloister supported a range
largely occupied by a new long gallery for the president. The north range was to
be used as originally planned, though the chambers were now to be allocated to
commoners and thus produce a revenue. Most spectacular were the frontispieces
placed to face each other as the central features of the eastern and western ranges.
In combination with the arcaded cloisters they gave the quadrangle a splendour
comparable with such Jacobean mansions as Audley End and Hatfield. However,
as Howard Colvin has pointed out, the design of the frontispieces was exalted yet
further during construction, by making two storeys of columns rise to a height
where the previous generation would have used three. Far more impressive and
sophisticated, too, than on any earlier Oxford frontispiece are the royal statues, life-
size bronze effigies of Charles I and Henrietta Maria by the court sculptor Hubert
Le Sueur. Sculpture plays an important decorative role as well, and the iconographical programme extends into the spandrels of the cloister arcades, filled with
busts in roundels symbolizing, on the library side, the seven liberal arts and 'learning' and on the gallery side the four cardinal and three theological virtues together
with 'religion'. This corresponded to the scheme of texts inscribed on the demolished schools building, familiar to Laud in his youth. The Canterbury quadrangle
eventually cost Laud £5,500.

Such a drastic change in conception was not achieved without mishap. Richard
Maude, the Oxford mason, was at first contracted for the north range. When the
scheme was enlarged to include both cloisters he took on as partners two other
local men, Hugh Davies and Robert Smith. In February 1633 John Lufton, the fellow charged with oversight of the building, made contact with some London
masons, for the Oxford partnership was becoming financially overstretched, and in
August replaced them by one William Hill. He soon proved equally incapable and
in June 1634 was dismissed in favour of another mason recruited by Lufton in
London, John Jackson. Jackson, unlike his predecessors, was employed not by contract but on a piece-work basis, and also received a weekly wage of £1 for acting
as overseer of the works just as William Arnold had done at Wadham College

---

[130] SJM lxxx. 2, fo 1, states that Laud gave £1,875 6s 8d to the college while he was still president,
which cannot be strictly true in view of the financial state of the college recorded by Laud himself at
the end of his presidency (Bodl. MS Tanner 338, fo 80). It must however represent a long-standing
benefaction which the college was to draw on from 1631.

twenty-five years before. Thereafter work went ahead without further difficulty. Jackson, about whose earlier career nothing is known, prepared templates for the great cornice and moulds for the open-work tracery vaults of the passage to the garden, so he must have been equally at home in classical and gothic vocabularies. Indeed his subsequent career in Oxford demonstrates that he revelled in both (see p. 171 below). He was also paid for executing the bulk of the carved stone-work, including the spandrel busts.

Laud himself was obliged to keep in touch with the progress of the work largely at long distance. In August 1631, when the king and council were at Woodstock, the college took the opportunity to send him a 'draft' of the initial scheme. In March 1632 President Juxon wrote recommending the enlarged scheme with two arcades 'of a form not yet seen in Oxford', which he estimated would cost £3,200. Adam Browne, Laud's London joiner, spent three days in Oxford in February 1633, helping Lufton to interview the London masons and 'drawing draughts and making moulds'. In May of that year Laud signed the contract with Le Sueur for the statues of the king and queen. On 3 September 1635, when work was drawing to a close, Laud was once more in the vicinity of Oxford, staying with the bishop at Cuddesdon. This gave him an opportunity 'to see my building there, and give some directions for the last finishing of it . . . staying there not two hours'. Finally, on 30 August 1636, in the great room which awaited fitting up as the inner library, he entertained the king and queen to a magnificent inaugural banquet on the occasion of their ceremonial visit to Oxford; and in the same room the following day presided over a meeting attended by the heads of colleges and halls, all other doctors of the university, and both the proctors. This summation of his roles as chancellor and bene-factor to his old college must have been deeply satisfying to the archbishop.

In Peter Heylyn's view Laud as chancellor gave an example in his own episco-pal and archiepiscopal chapels to the principal Oxford colleges, which 'beautified their chappells, transposed their tables, and fenced them with rails, and furnished them with hangings, palls, plate, and all other necessaries'.[131] In 1619 while he was still president of St John's College Laud had made major improvements to the chapel there which constituted the most coherent attempt to that date to beautify a college chapel and its services. He furnished the communion table with 'clothes of crimson and purple vellvett', and focused attention on it by painting the ceiling above. In the east window, at a cost of £120, he inserted painted glass illustrating the life of St John the Baptist, the college's patron saint. He set back the screen in order to provide more seating, and over a newly constructed vestry on the north side installed an organ which cost, with gilding, the very considerable sum of £280.[132] The intention to 'erect a choir', formed by 1622, was finally fulfilled by a bequest of Sir William Paddy in 1634 which endowed the post of organist, together with eight singing-men and four boy choristers.[133]

[131] Peter Heylyn, *Cyprianus anglicus* (London 1668), 294.
[132] Bodl. MS Tanner 338, fos 377ʳ, 379ʳ; Costin, *St. John's*, 67.
[133] Bodl. MS Tanner 338, fo 389; Costin, *St. John's*, 68.

Painted glass had already begun to be installed in Wadham College in 1613–14, on Dorothy Wadham's instructions, but the iconographically most significant window there is dated a little later, 1622. As for organs, even Christ Church spent less than St John's on the double organ which was installed in the cathedral in 1624–5 for £260, though it was set on a screen made by Thomas Richardson costing £50.[134]

The new chapel at Wadham College, consecrated in 1613, was not at first fully fitted up in modern fashion, for the black and white marble pavement was not laid until about 1670. At Exeter College the chapel consecrated in 1624 boasted a particularly eye-catching pulpit. It is neither of these, but rather the chapel built in 1629–30 at Lincoln College (plate 19), happily still surviving with little alteration, which one is tempted to admire as the beau ideal of a Laudian chapel. However, this was built for the college at the expense of its visitor, John Williams, bishop of Lincoln, who was Laud's great rival. Williams was as keen a proponent as Laud of aesthetic aids to devotion, their disagreement relating principally to the placement of the communion table, which the former preferred should be set 'table-wise', while the latter insisted that it should be 'altar-wise'. Bishop Hacket, in his biography of Williams published in 1693, described the chapel at Lincoln: 'The form of it was costly, reverend, and church-wise. The sacred acts and mysteries of our saviour, while he was on Earth, neatly colour'd in the glass-windows. The traverse and lining of the walls was of cedar-wood. The copes, the plate, the books, and all sort of furniture for the holy table, rich and suitable.'[135] Equally characteristic is the black and white marble paving of the chapel, emulated immediately by many other colleges and at the university church.

Laud was interested in the transformation of two college chapels in particular, those at Magdalen and Queen's, where the heads, Accepted Frewen and Christopher Potter, were two of his most faithful allies. In his history of his chancellorship he notes the various stages in the work at both.[136] Neither chapel survives in its Laudian condition—indeed at Queen's it has been completely rebuilt—but there is enough documentary evidence to attempt a mental reconstruction of both.

The chapel at Magdalen was the first at which the holy table was set altar-wise, in 1631.[137] By 1633 Richard Greenbury had executed a reredos of the last supper 'on blew cloth in *chiaro oscuro*'.[138] In that year the president gave a brass lectern, which still survives, and another donor a chandelier.[139] Two London masons, Andrew Marvin and Roger Cotes, laid a black and white marble pavement in 1635, the year in which Laud recorded the beautification as finished. However, the following year the visitor, Walter Curle, bishop of Winchester, commending what had

[134] CA xii. b. 69, *sub* first, third, and fourth terms.
[135] John Hacket, *Scrinia reserata* (2pts in 1 London 1693), pt 2, p. 35.
[136] Laud, *Works* v. 62, 84, 115, 143.   [137] Bloxam, *Reg. Magdalen* ii, p. xci.
[138] John Mennes and James Smith, *Wit Restor'd* (London 1658), 68–73.
[139] Bloxam, *Reg. Magdalen*, 281.

been done, urged the college to beautify 'the body of the church', presumably the antechapel, and the president and fellows duly undertook to raise £400 to this end.[140] Over half this sum was spent in 1637 on 'white glass drawne and shaddowed with figures' in the antechapel. In the main west window was a last judgement, executed by Greenbury for £117 12s 0d, and in the other six windows the still-surviving figures of forty-eight saints, which cost £112 14s 6d.[141]

The complete iconographical programme of the chapel and the deliberate visual contrast between the inner chapel and the antechapel are indicated by Peter Mundy's description written in August 1639: 'att the upper end off the quire is the birth, passion, resurrection and ascention off our saviour very largely and exquisitely sett forth in coullours . . . allsoe the windowes in scripture stories don artificially in lively coullours, onely att the upper end, in white and blacke, very largely representing the last judgementt [in the antechapel].'[142]

For these works at Magdalen College London craftsmen were called in. On the other hand Queen's College, as the bursars' account books show, obtained the best available local workmanship. Here the first phase of work, approved by the college on 3 December 1624, was carried out in 1630–1.[143] Thomas Richardson wainscotted the chapel for £50 and made a screen which cost £25 16s 0d. The roof clearly had a boarded ceiling divided into squares, like the surviving ceiling in the chapel at Lincoln College. This was painted blue by Edmund Wise, with gilt stars and 'great shields in the middle of the roofe, and the other smaller upon the ioyning of the battins', at a cost of £33. At the same time Robert Smith laid black and white marble paving.[144] In 1633–4 'the upper part, under the altar, and the steps to it' were paved with black and white marble and in 1635 William Harris, joiner, wainscotted here, provided two desks and set up rails (costing £13) 'before the communion table'.[145] Once again, an ambitious scheme of painted glass in the windows completed the programme. Abraham van Linge inserted a last judgement in the east window, for which he received £72 on 17 July 1635, and on 1 August 1636 agreed to make for £138 scenes from the life and passion of Christ for the six side windows (glass which survives reset in the eighteenth-century chapel).[146]

Meanwhile there was plenty going on elsewhere. In 1631–3 the cathedral of Christ Church was repaved by Nicholas Stone and Gabriel Stacey for about £330 and for £266 the choir wainscotted by Thomas Richardson and Thomas Wells.[147] In 1638 several painted glass windows by Abraham van Linge were inserted.[148] Of these one superb example, of Jonah seated under the gourd surveying Nineveh, has

[140] MCA miscellaneous college papers.

[141] Greenbury's contract dated 12 June 1637 and receipts dated 3 July 1639 and 7 June 1640 are in MCA miscellaneous college papers.

[142] *The Travels of Peter Mundy in Europe and Asia 1608–1667*, ed. R. C. Temple (5 vols in 6 Hakluyt Soc. 2nd ser. xvii, xxxv, xlv–xlvi, lv, lxxviii 1907–36) iv. 26.

[143] *The Diary of Thomas Crosfield*, ed. F. S. Boas (London 1935), 37.

[144] QCA 2/W/14, 2/W/28.   [145] Ibid. 2/W/14, 2/W/17.

[146] Ibid. 2/W/18, 2/W/27.   [147] CA xi. b. 35, fos 79ʳ–86ᵛ.

[148] *Travels of Peter Mundy*, ed. Temple, 27, gives the date.

escaped destruction. In 1636 Balliol repaved its chapel and completed the Tudor glazing programme of 1529–30 by inserting two van Linge windows (a scheme which still survives, reset in the nineteenth-century chapel), and in 1637–8 a major scheme of beautification of the chapel at New College was undertaken.[149]

At one or two colleges initiatives proved abortive. At All Souls, for instance, a proposal made in 1633 to establish a choir with an organ came to nothing.[150] At Merton resolutions were passed in March 1634 and August 1635 to pave the upper chapel with black and white marble, but presumably because of the hostility of the anti-Laudian warden, Sir Nathaniel Brent, nothing was done.[151] Enough, however, had been achieved throughout the colleges as a whole for George Garrard, visiting Oxford with the court in 1636, to exclaim:

> The churches or chappells of all the colledges are much beautifyed, extraordinary cost bestowed on them; scarce any cathedrall churches, not Windsor or Canterbury, nay not Pauls quire exceedes them; most of them newe glazed, richer glasse for figures and painting I have not seen, which they had most from beiond the seas; excellently paued theyre quires with blacke and whyte stone; where the east end admitts not glasse, excellent pictures, large and greate church worke of the best hands they cold gett from the other side, of the birth, passion, resurrection and ascension of our blessed sauiour; all theyre communion tables fayrely couered with rich carpetts, hung some of them with speciall good hangings . . . and rayld about with costly rayles.

The chapel which impressed him most was at Lincoln College: 'The communion table, pulpitt, and an excellent fayre skreene all of cedar, which giues such an odoriferous smell, that holy water in the Romish churches doth not exceede yt, lett them use what art they can to perfume yt.'[152]

At Oxford iconoclasm in the 1640s and 1650s, as reported by Anthony Wood, was primarily directed at the painted representations of the life of Christ and of the last judgement. Nevertheless it was the larger and more prominent chapels at Christ Church, Magdalen, and New College which suffered most, and so much survives of the painted glass inserted in chapel windows at this period that it deserves some further comment. There are, or were, coherent schemes of painted glass at Wadham College (1613–22), Lincoln College (1629–30), Queen's College (1635–7), Magdalen College (1637–40), and University College (1640–2). All include scenes of the life, passion, resurrection, and ascension of Christ, except for the unfinished scheme at University College, where they were also probably intended. In most there is also a strong element of typology, or parallelism between Old Testament episodes, 'types', and the New Testament events, 'antitypes', which they were believed to foreshadow. This interpretative device, used by Christ himself in his teaching, elaborately developed by the early church and the basis of numerous medieval illustrative schemes, inevitably fell foul after the reformation

---

[149] *VCH Oxon.* iii. 91, 146.   [150] Wood, *History of the Colleges and Halls*, 289.
[151] J. R. L. Highfield, 'Alexander Fisher, Sir Christopher Wren and Merton College chapel', *Oxoniensia* xxiv (1959), 71–2.
[152] A. J. Taylor, 'The royal visit to Oxford in 1636', *Oxoniensia* i (1936), 153–4.

of prohibitions against the depiction of Christ's person. A way round this difficulty is demonstrated in the chapel at the earl of Salisbury's Hatfield House, where in the east window dated 1610 eighteen Old Testament scenes are inscribed with the relevant Old Testament texts and also with typologically appropriate texts from the New Testament. At Oxford nothing so mealy-mouthed was employed, and late medieval schemes which had survived post-reformation iconoclasm, for example the windows at Balliol and New College, seem to have provided the basis for the seventeenth-century programmes.

At Wadham the north windows were filled first (1613–14) by Richard Rudland of Oxford, with fifteen figures of prophets in the lower lights, with a verse below each. In 1616 corresponding figures of Christ, the twelve apostles, St Paul, and St Stephen, each set over a verse of the creed, were executed by an unknown artist for the south windows. This confrontation, popular in English artistic representations in the fourteenth and fifteenth centuries, could be found in the antechapel windows at New College.[153] For the east window yet another artist was employed, Bernard van Lingé, brother of Abraham van Linge and a native of Emden in Friesland, who had been attracted to England by the prospect of work in St Paul's cathedral, but in 1621 when this did not materialize was recommended to the warden of Wadham.[154] Thus began the fruitful connection of the van Linge family with Oxford colleges. The east window (plate 20) has in the main lights ten scenes extending from Christ's entry into Jerusalem to the ascension, but the typologically matching Old Testament scenes are squeezed awkwardly into the tracery above. Thus the emphasis of Hatfield is reversed. It is possible that the east window at Balliol College, filled with glass of 1529–30 which included scenes of the passion, resurrection, and ascension may have provided the precedent for this arrangement.[155] The precise compositions of most of the New Testament scenes at Wadham derive from a volume which had entered the college library in archdeacon Bisse's foundation bequest, the *Evangeliae historiae imagines* (1596), published by the Jesuit theologian, Hieronymus Natalis, to accompany the second edition of his notes and meditations on the gospel.[156]

At Lincoln College an improved version of the Wadham scheme is employed. Twelve prophets in the north windows face the twelve apostles in the south, over verses from the prophetic books and from the creed respectively. The six-light east window contains the six fundamental scenes of Christ's life and passion: nativity, baptism, last supper, crucifixion, resurrection, ascension, and below, on the same scale, the six corresponding Old Testament 'types'. The windows at Lincoln appear to be all by a single glass-painter, and the signature of Abraham van Linge has recently been found on one of them. The colours are more subdued and the draughtsmanship less assertive than in his later work.

[153] C. Woodforde, *The Stained Glass of New College, Oxford* (Oxford 1951), 67–8.
[154] Jackson, *Wadham College*, 163–4.
[155] H. W. C. Davis, *A History of Balliol College* (Oxford 1963), 303–4.
[156] Hieronymus Natalis, *Adnotationes et meditationes in evangelia* (2nd edn Antwerp 1595) bound with the *Imagines*, Wadham College Library, pressmark A 2° 24, '*ex dono* D. Doctoris Philippi Bisse'.

At Queen's, in the next of Abraham van Linge's schemes, there were no Old Testament scenes at all. The six side windows were filled with the annunciation, nativity, last supper, resurrection, ascension, and pentecost, and the climax was the last judgement in the east window.

The elaborate programme at Magdalen College, which has already been described, may have incorporated medieval glass in the inner chapel, but its destruction in the 1650s makes it impossible to investigate further.

The last scheme, at University College where the master was Thomas Walker, Laud's kinsman and reserve executor, and Abraham van Linge again the artist, might seem like a reversion to the timidity of Hatfield. The three windows in what was formerly the antechapel contain three scenes presumably chosen for their suitability for that location, two—Jacob's dream and the cleansing of the temple—emphasizing purification, together with Christ in the house of Martha and Mary. The inner chapel windows are filled by a series of 'types', Old Testament subjects from the fall to the ascension of Elijah. In 1642, however, in view of the unsettled times, van Linge returned home to Holland cancelling his contract for the east window. So the college was deprived of the New Testament antitypes which must surely have been intended and would have made the whole programme coherent.

It has already become apparent that a deep sense of tradition conditioned much of the new building in Oxford in the early seventeenth century. Gothic forms and methods of construction continued to be employed, both out of unthinking conformism, and, as the schools quadrangle and convocation house most strikingly illustrate, by deliberate choice for visual consistency. Where conspicuous classical features were allowed to interrupt this gothic idiom they generally seem to have been introduced as carriers of symbolic meaning. It was not until 1632 that Oxford saw its first wholly classical building.

In 1621 Henry Lord Danvers, subsequently earl of Danby, had acquired five acres outside the city walls opposite Magdalen College and opened a physic garden there, which he intended to give to the university. A decade later he embarked on its enclosure with a high wall in which were set three handsome gateways, of which the main gateway faced north (plate 4). Here, free of any other building, though just across High Street from Magdalen tower, rose an elaborate rusticated composition, a pedimented triumphal arch, inspired by such recent works as the gateways built to Inigo Jones's design at Oatlands Palace and Arundel House in the Strand, or by the water gate to the duke of Buckingham's town palace, York House. The physic garden gateway was built by the sculptor and master mason, Nicholas Stone, whose first Oxford commission had been Sir Thomas Bodley's monument in Merton College chapel back in 1615, who had subsequently acted as Jones's master mason at the Whitehall Banqueting House, and who was combining this job in Oxford with work in Christ Church cathedral and with building Danby's country house at Cornbury, twelve miles to the north-west, where he certainly acted as designer too.[157] But the gateway he seems not to have designed. The confused and

[157] *The Note-Book and Account Book of Nicholas Stone*, ed. W. L. Spiers (Walpole Soc. vii 1919), 70.

ignorant way in which the rusticated banding is handled would not do credit to the executant of Inigo Jones's designs. Nor did Jones himself attribute the design of the gateway to Stone, but rather to 'sum mathematitians of Oxford that desined for a gate for ye garden of simples, lamly'.[158] Whether by 'mathematitians' Jones meant dons or master craftsmen is not clear; in either case his objection was to their misunderstanding of architecture as a disciplined art. A few years later, in 1639, Oxford dons were in a position to select some further designs for the physic garden. This may have been when the 'conservatory for evergreens', a sturdy up-to-date design as illustrated in Loggan's engraving, was about to be constructed. According to the president of Magdalen, Danby had sent 'outlandish workmen to enter upon the physic garden. They were directed to the dean of Christ Church [Samuel Fell], Dr Clayton [regius professor of medicine] and myself. We have perused divers models which they brought, and amongst them pitched upon one, which we think will be most proper for that place.'[159]

At Magdalen College itself there was a notable contemporary conversion to classicism when in 1635 a monumental Doric gateway with coupled columns and a commanding pediment was erected at the main entrance to the college. 'Mr Christmas', a member of the leading London mason family of that name, was paid for 'drawinge the modell [and] overseeinge the worke'.[160]

At Christ Church, by contrast, a remarkable display of traditionalism was taking shape. Samuel Fell's predecessor as dean, Brian Duppa, had initiated the building programme with the repaving and wainscotting of the cathedral in 1631–3, as noted above. This was a modernization deplored by that traditionalist of the next generation, Anthony Wood. Fell, as treasurer of the college, was probably already in charge of the works. His reputation in that capacity spread across Oxford: the provost of Queen's in December 1634, commending his 'skill in contrivance of building', remarked that 'the deane of Christ Church knew not how to have proceeded but for him'.[161]

It is probable that the main project, the completion of Wolsey's great quadrangle, did not get under way until near the end of the decade, after Fell's succession as dean in 1638. Here fidelity to the Tudor design was to be paramount. Before the outbreak of war Fell had erected the walls of two canons' lodgings, carefully copying the existing ranges, even to the extent of reproducing the wall shafts and springers for the cloister vaults which Wolsey had been unable to construct but which Fell, according to Wood, intended to add.[162]

The most spectacular work at Christ Church at this period, however, was the fan-vaulted staircase vestibule to the hall (plate 17). This is no mere imitation of a Tudor scheme, still less is it a sham like the contemporary plaster fan-vault of the

---

[158] Jones's marginal note in his copy, now at Chatsworth, of Daniello Barbaro, *I dieci libri dell' architettura di M. Vitruvio* (Venice 1567), 22.

[159] Laud, *Works* v. 248.   [160] See Loggan's engraving and Colvin, *Unbuilt Oxford*, 98 n.

[161] *Diary of Thomas Crosfield*, ed. Boas, 75.

[162] Wood, *History of the Colleges and Halls*, 447 and n. 158.

convocation house. On the contrary it is a complete masonry construction, but designed so that four vaulted cells spring from a lofty central pier, an arrangement more dramatic than in any known medieval fan-vault. According to Wood, Fell made it 'by the help of one . . . Smith, an artificer of London',[163] who has recently been persuasively identified as William Smith, a leading London mason and master of the Masons' Company in 1640.[164] His must be the credit for the constructive skill required for this daring feat; whether he was executing a design conceived by Wolsey's master masons or whether Fell, who had served on the committee for building the Bodleian Library staircase, took ideas from Hugh Davies's rejected design for that abortive project it is impossible to say.

The physic garden gateway, an independent structure on a new site, and the Christ Church staircase vault, part of a continuation of a late medieval scheme, represent the stylistic polarities possible in Oxford at this period. However, stylistic mixture remained a possibility too. Stylistically the most thoroughly mixed building of all is the second quadrangle at Brasenose College (plate 6), begun in 1656, only shortly before such mixtures went permanently out of fashion. This was to consist of the long-awaited chapel and library and a 'walk under cover, the great want of Brasenose'.[165] The 'overseer' was John Jackson, who had come to Oxford twenty years before to complete the Canterbury quadrangle at St John's College and had gone on to construct the new porch at St Mary's church, both of them buildings where a rich and bold classicism was combined with such gothic details as crenellation and miniature fan-vaults. At Brasenose Jackson was constrained by Principal Radcliffe's stipulation that the roof structure and stonework including window jambs from the dismantled medieval chapel of St Mary's college should be re-used. In its T-shaped plan and traceried windows the chapel was given a completely traditional internal effect, and in the plaster fan-vault which Jackson designed in November 1659 to mask the re-used roof timbers he demonstrated that new life remained in tradition. Externally, however, chapel, library, and cloister all exhibit a bewildering variety of stylistic clashes, columned doorcases under traceried windows, entablatures carrying cusped parapets, urns mutating into pinnacles, and much more in the same insouciant spirit. The new buildings at Brasenose were structurally complete in April 1663. Later that year Jackson received the commission to design a top stage to Tom Tower at Christ Church. One would like to know how he responded to that challenge; but before he could be paid for his model he was dead.[166]

After the hiatus of the war period, by the mid-1650s it was possible to think again of building, as the new works at Brasenose indicate. At University College fundraising began again in December 1655, and between March 1656 and April 1657 a total of £533 2s 0d was spent on the completion of the hall, under John

[163] Wood, *City of Oxford* i. 192.
[164] M. Batey and C. Cole, 'The great staircase tower at Christ Church', *Oxoniensia* liii (1988), 217.
[165] *Brasenose Monographs* iii. 15.   [166] *VCH Oxon.* iii. 32.

Jackson's direction.[167] But it was only after the Restoration and the reinstatement of the deprived heads that most pre-war projects were taken up again. In fact it is possible to see almost all that was done in the 1660s and 1670s as a continuation of initiatives taken in the pre-war period or the implementation of what had proved impracticable then. The erection of the Sheldonian Theatre in 1664–9 to provide a venue for the university Acts which had hitherto taken place in St Mary's church was the triumphant culmination of Laud's policy of the 1630s. Chapels once again became the focus of attention. At All Souls modernization at last began in 1664, and the long-delayed project at Merton was implemented in 1671–3. The painter Isaac Fuller, who was in Oxford in the early 1660s, had by 1664 executed a resurrection at the east end of All Souls college chapel, a last judgement in a similar position at Magdalen and a less ambitious painted altarcloth at Wadham.[168] In 1687 the east window of the chapel at University College was filled by Henry Gyles's scene of the adoration of the shepherds (plate 21).[169] Black and white marble paving was laid in the chapels at Wadham (1670), Corpus (1676–7), and Oriel (1677–8), and *circa* 1670 St John's acquired a new chapel screen. Other pre-war building programmes were completed. Tom quad at Christ Church was completed in 1661–72 and the great gate crowned with Wren's bell-stage in 1681–4. The rebuilding of the library at Jesus College and the completion of the east range at University College were both finally carried through in 1676–9. At a few colleges which had long been architecturally quiescent new projects to improve residential accommodation were set in motion, at Trinity College in 1664, at Queen's College in 1671, and at New College in 1682.

Probably the most significant change during this period was in the way fellows (and fellow-commoners) were accommodated. We have already noted a few earlier examples of studies becoming bedrooms, so that chambers could be devoted to daytime use. Wren's plans for new chambers at Trinity (1664) show an intermediate stage, whereby each chamber was equipped with a study and a bed recess.[170] The garden quadrangle at New College (1682–3) was the first building to employ the new system consistently throughout, for fellow-commoners sharing two to a chamber.[171]

This too was the period in which the fellows' common room became an institution. Anthony Wood noted the first to be established, at Merton College in 1661, 'to the end that the fellows might meet together (chiefly in the evenings after refection) partly about business, but mostly for society sake, which before was at each chamber by turns'.[172] By 1680 at least eight other colleges had formed senior common rooms. At All Souls a separate block was erected at the north-west end of the

[167] UCA CC fasc. 1/3/12, 13; bursar's account book for 1656.

[168] E. Croft-Murray, *Decorative Painting in England 1537–1837* (2 vols London 1962–70) i. 220b–1a.

[169] J. T. Brighton, 'Cartoons for York glass—Henry Gyles', *City of York Art Gallery Quarterly* (October 1968), 772–5.

[170] *Designs of Sir Chr. Wren for Oxford, Cambridge, London, Windsor etc.* ed. A. T. Bolton and H. D. Hendry (Wren Soc. v 1928), pl. IV, and unpublished drawing at Trinity College.

[171] *The Eighteenth Century*, 843.   [172] Wood, *History of the Colleges and Halls*, 528.

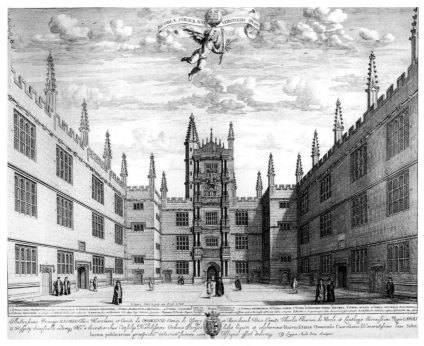

Pl 1. Schools Quadrangle (Loggan)

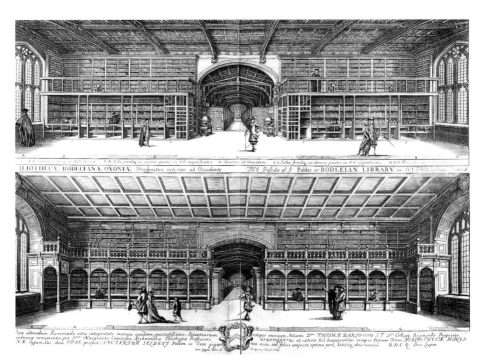

Pl 2. Bodleian Library (Loggan): interior, showing Arts End (above) and Selden End (below)

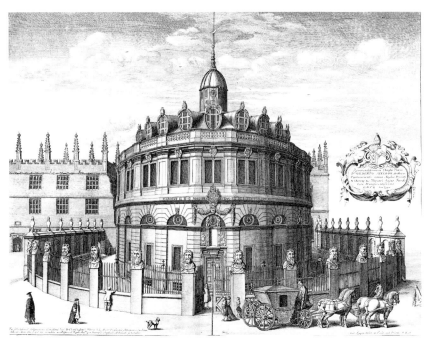

PL 3. Sheldonian Theatre (Loggan): from the north

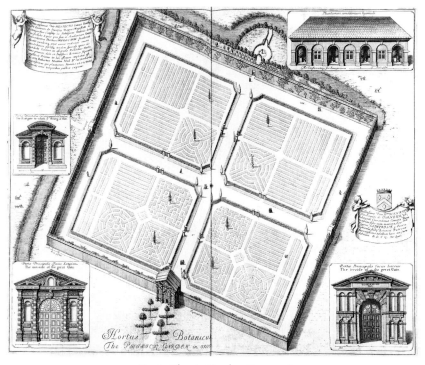

PL 4. Physic Garden (Loggan)

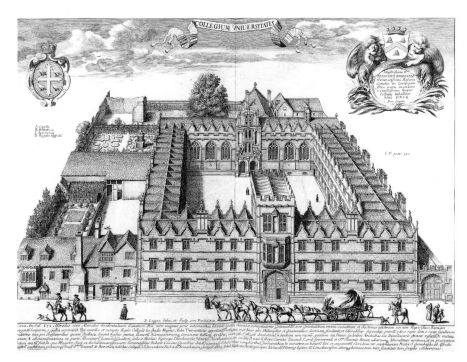

PL 5. University College (Loggan)

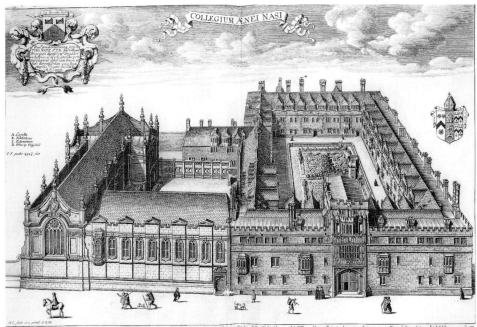

PL 6. Brasenose College (Loggan): showing chapel and library

PL 7. Trinity College (Loggan): showing Wren's new block

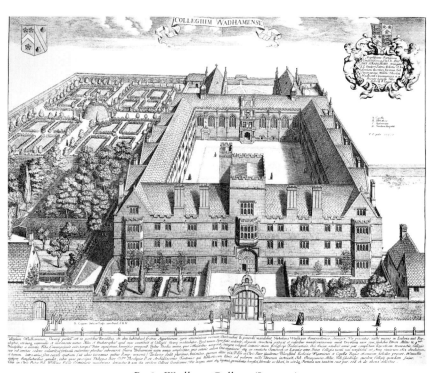

PL 8. Wadham College (Loggan)

garden, with two common rooms on the ground floor and chambers above.[173] When the new library was built at Jesus College in 1676–9 a senior common room, still in use today as such, was fitted up underneath it.

What gives the post-Restoration period its special interest, however, is the emergence of a young don, Christopher Wren, as a new kind of architect in Oxford, whose expertise in design was based on theoretical and scientific understanding rather than developed from a craft skill. Born in 1632, Wren had matriculated at Wadham College, been elected a fellow of All Souls College in 1653, and in 1661 was appointed to the Savilian professorship of astronomy. A founder member of the Royal Society, he established his reputation in the early 1660s as one of the outstanding scientific minds in Europe. Architecture attracted him both for its creative possibilities and because of the scope it provided for scientific problem-solving. His first architectural commission, to design the new chapel which his uncle, Bishop Matthew Wren, erected at Pembroke College, Cambridge, in 1663, demonstrated his commitment to the new classicism established by Inigo Jones, for he cast the chapel deliberately in the form of a classical temple. Contemporaneously Wren was developing his first architectural project at Oxford along equally antique-inspired lines.

According to Wood, after the Restoration various eminent former members of the university, in particular some of the bishops, urged that a new public building should be erected for the Act Exercises, the last university activity regularly performed in St Mary's church.[174] As early as mid-April 1663 it was reported that Wren had made a 'modell of a theater, to be built for the Oxonian Acts, and for playes also', and the model was exhibited at the Royal Society on the 29th of that month.[175] So at the outset the new building was conceived as a 'theatre', lending the university's degree-giving ceremonies an antique connotation and providing a venue better adapted to the production of plays than the college halls where they had hitherto been staged. Wren's model being lost, it is impossible to know how closely he adhered in this first design to the form and arrangement of antique theatres, which he could have studied primarily from Sebastiano Serlio's mid-sixteenth-century treatise on architecture, but which had also been a preoccupation of Inigo Jones.[176]

More than a year elapsed before the laying of the foundation-stone on 26 July 1664. In June Gilbert Sheldon, archbishop of Canterbury, had been formally thanked for his gift of £1,000 towards the cost of the new building (see p. 161 above). But his gift did not have the desired effect of stimulating generosity in others, and by September 1665, when according to the vice-chancellor's accounts £564 had been expended, Sheldon undertook to bear the whole cost of the building.[177]

[173] VCH Oxon. iii. 190. [174] Wood, History of the University ii. 795.
[175] The Correspondence of Henry Oldenburg, ed. A. R. Hall and M. B. Hall (13 vols Madison, London, and Philadelphia Pa. 1965–86), ii. 44; T. Birch, The History of the Royal Society of London (4 vols London 1756–7) i. 230.
[176] Colvin, Unbuilt Oxford, figs 14 and 16 are an attempt to visualize the model design.
[177] Wood, Life and Times, 125.

This forced the architect to scale down his design, in order to 'Confine the expence within the limits of a private purse'.[178] The Sheldonian Theatre as completed in 1669, and as it has been used from that time until the present day, undoubtedly bears the marks of compromise. In its D-shaped plan and in the use of superimposed orders enclosing arcading on the flat façade towards the divinity school it follows the Theatre of Marcellus in Rome, named by the architect's biographer as the basic source of inspiration.[179] But the curved, or rather faceted, front towards Broad Street (plate 3) is drastically simplified from the Marcellus model and hardly compatible with it, however ingeniously it is contrived to admit light above and below the various levels of seating inside the building.[180] The interior too has lost a vital ingredient of Wren's first conception, the stage. Indeed the internal arrangements have always been awkward, with the vice-chancellor seated among the tiers of spectators, and in place of the stage nothing but the door through which graduands enter, flanked by seating and with a loft above in which an organ was installed in 1671. The interior functions of the theatre were allocated by Wren and Dr John Fell, dean of Christ Church, who acted as accountant for the building construction. Cellar, roof-space, and the areas under the galleries were to house the learned press which was at last established by the university. The space in the galleries and in the semicircle of the floor was distributed in such a way that every element in the academic hierarchy of the university had its due place, together with Cambridge scholars and other visitors.[181] The functions of the new building were spelled out in the donation charter read at the ceremony on 9 July 1669 when Fell as vice-chancellor officially took possession of it on behalf of the university.[182]

There was a paradox in taking an antique theatre, open to the sky, as model for such a building. Wren's great triumph in the Sheldonian Theatre was the structural one of finding a way to roof a space of such exceptional dimensions, 80' × 70'. He did so by employing the geometrical flat floor devised by his friend Dr John Wallis, Savilian professor of geometry, the model of which was one of the sights of Oxford at the time.[183] The floor was incorporated into a trussed king-post roof which proved equal to its double task of spanning and load-bearing until its reconstruction in 1802.

Inside the theatre the roof-structure was hidden by the great painting on canvas executed by Robert Streater in 1668–9 (plate 15), the most ambitious illusionistic ceiling painting attempted in England at that date, not excluding Rubens's for the Whitehall Banqueting House. Streater's painting makes explicit the equation with an antique theatre or amphitheatre, where the seating could be shaded from the sun by means of awnings. Cherubs are shown rolling back the awnings, which appear to be supported on a lattice of gilded ropes, to reveal a heavenly vision of

[178] Stephen Wren, *Parentalia* (London 1750), 335.   [179] Ibid.

[180] See J. Summerson, *The Sheldonian in its Time* (Oxford 1964) for a witty analysis.

[181] Wood, *History of the University* ii. 796–7.   [182] Ibid. 799.

[183] Balthasar de Monconys in 1663 and Samuel Sorbière in the following year visited Wallis and in their travel books both reproduced an engraving of his model: *Iournal des voyages de monsieur de Monconys* (Lyon 1666), pt 2, fig. 8; *A voyage to England* (London 1709), 39.

allegorical import. In the centre Truth descends on the circle of figures representative of the arts and sciences studied at the university, while Prudence, Fortitude, and Eloquence, in the persons respectively of Minerva, Hercules, and Mercury, drive out Envy, Rapine, and Brutality.[184] The permanent validity of academic study is thus stated, together with the power that academic virtues had recently shown in reasserting themselves after the disruption of the civil war and Commonwealth. The interior of the theatre, inspiring and reassuring the academic community by these allegories, must have appeared wonderfully festive too, its columns simulating red marble, and its joinery painted stone colour and cedar colour, under the glorious polychromy of Streater's ceiling.

Wren's other Oxford works are of less significance, but they too display the independence of his mind. He argued in 1665 against his friend Dr Bathurst, president of Trinity, who wanted to extend his college in a conventional manner by means of a second quadrangle.[185] Instead, the college erected in 1665–8 to Wren's design a free-standing two-storeyed range set axially to the north of the first quadrangle, as classical in its sparing detail as in its sense of scale and proportion (plate 7).[186] Wood correctly noted its mansard roof as being 'according to a fashion received into England about twenty years before, and never seen in Oxon till this was finished'.[187] In 1682 a replica of Wren's range was erected at right angles, to link it to the front quadrangle, thus losing the formal effect of its original placement. Wren's concept of a formal block facing a pre-existing quadrangle was mooted in William Byrd's engraved design of 1682 for New College and implemented on a much grander scale at Magdalen College in the New Buildings begun there in 1733.[188] The range at Queen's College, built to Wren's design in 1671–2, and extending the frontage of the college northwards along Queen's Lane, was a larger and more floridly detailed version of the block at Trinity. In this situation the inappropriateness to a collegiate context of such a pedimented block, and especially of the enclosed, slope-ended roof, is apparent. Nor did Wren's ranges, with their third storey in the roof space, provide such good accommodation as the standard seventeenth-century chamber ranges: it is significant that at both Trinity and Queen's Wren's ranges have subsequently been heightened and re-roofed.

There is no evidence that Wren was involved in the design of the great new library at Queen's, constructed in 1692–5, though it is heavily dependent on his library at Trinity College, Cambridge, begun in 1676. Queen's Library, for all its size and magnificence (plate 29), is backward-looking in being fitted with stalls, in contrast with Wren's combination of stalls and wall shelving at Trinity, Cambridge. Ironically, the only new library in Oxford to follow the extensions of Bodley's

---

[184] Robert Whitehall, *Urania, or a description of the painting of the top of the theater at Oxon, as the artist lay'd his design* (London 1669), 3–7.

[185] Wren's letter to Bathurst, TCA miscellanea i, fo 82, is printed (in an inaccurate transcription) in Wood, *History of the Colleges and Halls*, 526 n. 59.

[186] Wren's executed designs are reproduced in *Designs of Wren*, ed. Bolton and Hendry, pl. V–VI.

[187] Wood, *History of the Colleges and Halls*, 526.   [188] Colvin, *Unbuilt Oxford*, fig. 19.

library in having exclusively wall shelving is that of 1680–8 at St Edmund Hall, the academic hall under the control of Queen's.

Wren's other contribution to classical design in Oxford concerned college chapels. A new chapel had been part of President Bathurst's plans for improving the buildings of Trinity College from 1665.[189] A fine drawing for the north elevation of the chapel, clearly the basis for what was built, survives among the Wren drawings at All Souls College, but when the chapel was finally erected in 1691–4 Wren seems to have been no more than a distant consultant.[190] Three colleges erected chapel screens to Wren's designs, All Souls in 1664, St John's *circa* 1670, and Merton as part of the refitting carried out in 1671–3. None survives in more than a fragmentary state, but it is clear that here too Wren set a new standard in his consistent use of monumental columns and pilasters and full entablatures, handled with a correctitude which had eluded the designer of even such a recent piece as the screen at Brasenose College chapel. Hereafter Oxford joiners such as Arthur Frogley had reliable models of modern design from which to work, and Wren-inspired screens can be seen, for example, in the chapels at University College and Corpus.

In this series of works Wren had familiarized Oxford with a properly understood classicism. Already in 1669 Corbet Owen in his *Carmen Pindaricum* on the inauguration of the Sheldonian Theatre had hymned Wren as the conqueror of gothic.[191] But that was to ignore the strength of conservatism within the university, and Wren himself for his last documented work at Oxford, the completion of the great gateway at Christ Church, decided that stylistic consistency demanded a gothic design.[192] In this he followed the college policy of the 1660s, whereby the great quadrangle had been completed uniformly on the model of the Tudor west range, but with the ground level within the walks sunk so that the surrounding ranges gained in apparent height and stateliness, and the cloisters had finally been omitted, increasing the sense of space. Style was thus maintained, but the visual effect of the quadrangle transformed.

Had Wolsey's great gateway been completed as intended, it would have been a large and highly enriched example of the type of college entrance tower established at Cambridge by the King Edward's tower of Trinity College as early as 1428, but unfamiliar at Oxford. Wren was, however, commissioned to combine the gatehouse with a bell-tower, so the deep oblong plan had to be converted to a square and the building crowned not by lofty angle turrets but by a central belfry. Wren also decided not to continue 'soe busy' as the founder began, so plain wall-surfaces on the bell-tower take the place of Wolsey's elaborate mouldings and wall-

---

[189] See his correspondence in TCA miscellanea i, fos 83–5.

[190] *Designs of Wren*, ed. Bolton and Hendry, pl. VI; *The Eighteenth Century*, 833.

[191] Corbett Owen, *Carmen Pindaricum in Theatrum Sheldonianum . . . recitatum Julii die 9° anno 1669* (Oxford 1669), verse 5 line 9.

[192] Wren's letters of 1681–2 to Dr John Fell, dean of Christ Church and bishop of Oxford, are printed in W. D. Caröe, '*Tom Tower*', *Christ Church, Oxford* (Oxford 1923), and reprinted in *Designs of Wren*, ed. Bolton and Hendry, 17–23.

panelling. However, the tower, crowned by a large ogee cupola, conformed to Wren's conception of the gothic manner 'which spires upward and the pyramidal formes are essential to it'. For this reason as well as on practical grounds he argued against adding an observatory room which would have necessitated a square top to the tower.

Great Tom, the bell which had formerly hung in the crossing tower of the cathedral, was recast in 1683 and Anthony Wood records that at 9 p.m. on 29 May 1684 it first rang out from its new position 'as a signal to all scholars to repair to their respective colleges and halls, as it did while it was in the campanile.'[193] With this reassertion of tradition we may fairly conclude our account of building works in seventeenth-century Oxford.

[193] Wood, *History of the Colleges and Halls*, 451.

4

Oxford and the Early Stuart Polity

KENNETH FINCHAM

ON 22 June 1636 the new university statutes, which were to govern Oxford for over two centuries, were delivered to convocation by four royal commissioners, headed by Sir John Coke, principal secretary of state to Charles I. Coke took the opportunity to outline the purposes and legality of the new statutes. No wise prince, he observed, ignored the health of his schools and universities, 'the noble and vital parts' of the body politic, capable of invigorating or enervating the entire realm. Oxford stood in need of reformation, and the new code aimed to foster peace, learning, and religion, 'for these three make a university'. Coke reminded his audience that the king was the fountain of honour and justice, from whom the university derived its privileges, preferments, and revenues. The university had lately received a new royal charter, protecting and extending its corporate privileges; now, in return for such benevolence, the king expected obedience to the new statutes. If Charles was a second Justinian, then the compiler of the statutes, 'their greate chauncellor' Archbishop William Laud, was another Trebonius. Coke praised his worth as equal to his honour, citing as evidence Laud's gifts of manuscripts and books to the Bodleian, his erection of the 'stately and magnificent' quadrangle at St John's and his preferment of Oxford men 'by his power at the court'. The oration ended with a command that the heads of colleges forthwith subscribe to the new statutes.[1]

Coke's speech serves as a convenient summary of the ties of interest and dependence which bound together crown and university in early modern England. Oxford looked to the crown to protect its jurisdiction and immunities, especially against challenges from the city corporation, to confirm its possessions and to grant licences of mortmain to extend them; similarly, it relied on crown and courtiers to provide major benefactions for its public library, teaching posts, and colleges, and advancement for its members within as well as beyond the university. In turn, the crown expected Oxford scholars to defend its claims, for example against Rome over the oath of allegiance controversy, or to collaborate in royal projects, most conspicuously the Authorized Version of the Bible.[2] The university

I am grateful to Jeremy Catto, Nicholas Tyacke and Conrad Russell for their comments on a draft of this chapter.

[1] NUL MS Cl. c. 73; Laud, *Works* v. 126–32.

[2] On licences of mortmain, see, for instance, *CSPD 1611–18*, 208, 209, 300; on the oath, see the writings of Sebastian Benefield and John Prideaux: STC 1871, 20344; J. P. Sommerville, *Politics and Ideology*

was also a useful reservoir of royal patronage with which to satisfy courtiers and their clients. More important, however, was Oxford's role in supporting monarchical authority in church and state: as a seminary of virtue and learning, its academics taught political obedience and religious conformity to their undergraduates, thereby equipping them to serve church and commonwealth. At the same time, Oxford itself served as a model of good government and protestant orthodoxy to the wider nation for, as Chancellor Buckhurst reminded the university in 1603, the eyes of the commonwealth were always on it. Contend over Christian doctrine, Buckhurst warned, and the common people will stagger in their faith.[3]

The university was not, therefore, a community of introspective scholars, but a national institution in the public gaze. Indeed, Oxford's proximity to London ensured that the worlds of court, capital, and university remained in close connection, as news and individuals travelled in both directions. Humfrey Leech's contentious sermon in favour of supererogatory works, preached at Christ Church, Oxford, in June 1608, was soon the talk of 'London, Lambeth and elsewhere'; likewise, the diary of Thomas Crosfield, fellow of Queen's, shows metropolitan politics being followed in Caroline Oxford. From the accession of the new dynasty it became increasingly fashionable for the university to produce verses to commemorate the births, marriages, deaths, and peregrinations of the Stuarts, with as many as eight collections being published in the decade after 1630. The university participated too in national days of mourning: at the funeral of Prince Henry in 1612, a funeral service and sermon was held at St Mary's, while the prince's college chapel of Magdalen was draped in black.[4] Senior academics served as chaplains to the crown, courtiers, and bishops, held cathedral canonries and sometimes deaneries, and were members of the High Commission meeting at Lambeth, while more junior colleagues preached regularly at Paul's Cross in London.[5]

Oxford pulpits also engaged with public affairs of the day, sometimes with widespread repercussions. In April 1622, at the time when James I was pressing ahead with a controversial marriage alliance with Spain while refusing military assistance to beleaguered protestants abroad, an Oxford MA, John Knight, defended the right of resistance against ungodly rulers. King and council reacted swiftly. Knight was imprisoned, convocation required to condemn his propositions, and later in the year directions to preachers were issued nationally, including a warning to avoid matters of state.[6] In 1630, Peter Heylyn, fellow of Magdalen College, used a uni-

in England 1603–1640 (London 1986), 10; on the translation of the Bible, see A. W. Pollard, *Records of the English Bible* (Oxford 1911), 37–64.

[3] OUA register of congregation and convocation 1595–1606, NEP/*supra*/11, register M, fos 74ᵛ–5ʳ.

[4] Humfrey Leech, *A Triumph of Truth* (Douai 1609), 58; *The Diary of Thomas Crosfield*, ed. F. S. Boas (London 1935); *STC* 19019–50; J. Nichols, *The Progresses, Processions and Magnificent Festivities of King James the First* (4 vols London 1828) ii. 504–5; Bloxam, *Reg. Magdalen* ii, p. lxxxvi.

[5] Between 1635 and 1641, fourteen of King Charles's sixty-one chaplains were resident academics (PRO LC5/134 fo 6); R. G. Usher, *The Rise and Fall of the High Commission* (Oxford 1913), 345–61; M. MacLure, *The Paul's Cross Sermons 1534–1642* (Toronto 1958), 225–56.

[6] Wood, *History of the University* ii. 341–7; PRO SP 14/132/85.i.

versity sermon to alert the authorities to the activities of the feoffees for purchasing impropriations, whom he branded as subversive puritans. The sermon demonstrated Heylyn's anti-puritan credentials and, it seems, won the approval of the new chancellor, Bishop Laud. Three years later the feoffees were disbanded by order of the court of exchequer, after their successful prosecution by William Noy, the attorney-general, who was probably armed with information supplied by Heylyn.[7] The latter's sermon had been preached on Act Sunday, during the ceremonies marking the end of the academic year, which ensured a large public audience. For the Act was also a social gathering, attracting country clergy and visitors from London and abroad. Its boisterous atmosphere is captured in a letter from one spectator attending the Act of 1640: 'I was mery ... amonge the doctors, in the midst of their disputations, where I was lyke to have my belly burst and my ribbs broken in the crowde, my shirt stucke to my backe, and sweate trickled down my cheekes, and yet I could have endured it to this day.'[8]

The web of university contacts extended far into the court. Prominent politicians filled the offices of chancellor and high steward, each non-resident at the university and expected to preserve Oxford's interests at the centre of power. Every college had its own visitor, sometimes the chancellor, but more often a prelate; between them, the archbishops of Canterbury and York, and the bishops of Winchester and Lincoln were visitors to twelve Oxford colleges, and, in an age of rising status for the episcopate, most enjoyed some influence at court. Visitors arbitrated in college disputes, sometimes after appeal to the crown,[9] and interpreted the ambiguities of local statutes. The lure of college patronage—leases, scholarships, and fellowships—drew other courtiers into Oxford affairs, while the demands of good government sometimes prompted the privy council to intervene.

Both the interdependence of court and university, and Oxford's role in national life, were well established at the accession of the Stuarts. The next forty years saw important developments within this broad framework. The most obvious of these was the greater direct involvement of James I and Charles I in university affairs, compared to their immediate predecessors, often in response to religious controversy—which was checked through royal instructions and demands for greater conformity. Each monarch inaugurated a new religious settlement which, though hardly as dramatic as the rapid changes in official policy between 1547 and 1559, nevertheless made its mark on theological debates and patterns of preferment

[7] G. E. Gorman, 'A Laudian attempt to "tune the pulpit": Peter Heylyn and his sermon against the feoffees for the purchase of impropriations', *Journal of Religious History* viii (1975), 333–49. Heylyn was already known to Laud, and had been appointed a royal chaplain earlier that year. George Vernon, *The Life of Dr Peter Heylyn* (London 1682), 35–6. For Laud's opposition to the feoffees, see Laud, *Works* iii. 216–17.

[8] *The Correspondence of Nathan Walworth and Peter Seddon of Outwood*, ed. J. S. Fletcher (Chetham Soc. cix Manchester 1880), 74. Distinguished visitors to the Act included, in 1617, the archbishop of Spalato, and, in 1633, James du Perron, the queen's almoner (PRO SP 14/93/29; Laud, *Works* v. 87).

[9] Thus, in 1622, a complaint to the king by President Anian of Corpus against one of the fellows, Robert Barcroft, 'for keeping conventicles' was referred to the visitor (OUA hyp/B/5, depositions 1619–27, fo 146ᵛ).

within the university. The four chancellors of Oxford between 1603 and 1630 (Lord Buckhurst, Archbishop Bancroft, Lord Ellesmere, and the third earl of Pembroke) were all active champions of the university's interests, but none was so influential or energetic within Oxford as William Laud, elected chancellor in 1630, which may be attributed to his high standing with Charles I and his determination to use royal authority to reinvigorate teaching and discipline within the university. Laud's rule as chancellor (1630–41) forms a distinct and important chapter in Oxford's relationship with the wider Stuart polity.

The Stuarts' favour towards Oxford was clear from early in James I's reign. The keen interest of the new king in university matters reflected, of course, his own donnish inclinations. On his first visit to the Bodleian in 1605, James declared that if he were not king he would be a university man and, if a prisoner, he would wish to be incarcerated in the library. He took much satisfaction in the elaborate ceremony with which the university received his published *Works* in 1620, in comparison to the more perfunctory attitude of Cambridge, and claimed that he had always preferred Oxford to Cambridge. He was also willing to settle rows between academics, as providing opportunities to debate theology and to confirm his cherished image as peacemaker. The favour of Charles towards the universities, as he acknowledged, was influenced by hereditary affection: not just for his father James I, but also his father-in-law, Henri IV, who had restored discipline in the University of Paris after ending the civil wars. Indeed, Charles may well have been very conscious of this parallel with Henri: he too had faced what he regarded as a malaise of disorder, in the later 1620s, and thereafter saw the two universities, purged of faction and heterodoxy, as key agents in the restoration of an ordered and peaceful society.[10]

Royal involvement in Oxford affairs was also more visible after 1603. Elizabeth I had made two state visits to Oxford in forty-five years; her successors each visited twice in half that span.[11] After 1603 there developed another and more regular point of contact between monarch and university. Despite her annual progresses, usually in southern England, Elizabeth had rarely stayed at the royal manor of Woodstock, quite possibly because she had been confined there for a time in her sister's reign. Her two successors, by contrast, were frequent visitors to Woodstock, usually staying for a week in late August, where they enjoyed the hunting and invariably received a university delegation. There would be a Latin oration, a sermon from the vice-chancellor, presents of gloves for the royal party, and even,

---

[10] D. H. Willson, *King James VI and I* (London 1956), 290; *The Letters of John Chamberlain*, ed. N. E. McClure (2 vols Philadelphia 1939) ii. 308; OUA register of convocation 1628–40, NEP/*supra*/24, register R, fos 125ᵛ–6ʳ. For royal interference in the internal affairs of the University of Paris after 1600, though slight by English standards, see L. W. B. Brockliss, 'The University of Paris in the sixteenth and seventeenth centuries' (Cambridge Ph. D. thesis 1976), 40–5.

[11] James I visited in 1605 and 1614, Charles I in 1629 and 1636. Both also passed through Oxford on their regular visits to Woodstock, as disclosed by city churchwardens' accounts (ORO DD Par. Oxford St Peter le Bailey b 3, fos 7–62).

on one occasion, the performance of a play.[12] These regular visits enabled university business to be transacted and views exchanged. The directions of James I to both universities, issued in the winter of 1616/17, required that an annual account of their observance be submitted each michaelmas when he was in the area—meaning his stay at Newmarket for Cambridge and at Woodstock for Oxford. It was there too, in August 1631, that Charles I spent six hours settling university disputes over preaching. Oxford's petition for a new charter was presented to Charles at Woodstock in 1635. Moreover the correspondence of Laud during the 1630s indicates that he used his time at Woodstock to keep tabs on his vice-chancellor and direct university matters.[13] The character of this outside intervention, from 1603, now deserves closer scrutiny.

In April 1603, on his journey from Edinburgh to London to take up the reins of power, James I received the millenary petition, supposedly signed by a thousand puritan ministers, requesting 'a due and godly reformation' of abuses in the English Church. Once James had agreed to convene a meeting to hear these complaints, a national petitioning campaign, in support of change, was organized by puritan activists. However, the authorities in both universities distanced themselves from this agitation and condemned the drive for reform. At the Hampton Court Conference, in January 1604, James offered a series of minor concessions to the puritan delegation, at the price of conformity within an episcopalian church. The following winter the bishops ousted those puritan ministers who refused either to conform or to accept the new requirement to subscribe to canon 36 of 1604. While the conformity of Cambridge University was closely scrutinized by a commission appointed by its chancellor, Robert Cecil, the experience of Oxford in 1604–5 prompts the question why, despite the presence of influential figures such as John Rainolds, president of Corpus Christi and the leading puritan spokesman at Hampton Court, it managed to escape a formal investigation of nonconformity.[14] The answer lies in an understanding of the row over preaching in the last months of Elizabeth I's reign, and the pivotal role of Lord Buckhurst, chancellor of the university since 1592.

Buckhurst's choice of vice-chancellor for 1602–3 had been John Howson, canon of Christ Church. Preaching the accession day sermon, on 17 November 1602, Howson censured the current preoccupation with the pulpit which, he claimed,

[12] E. Marshall, *The Early History of Woodstock Manor* (London 1873), 152–91; OUA vice-chancellors' accounts WP/β/S/1a/3, WP/β/S/1b; for a printed oration and a sermon, see *STC* 20343.7, 20359. The relative value of the gloves shows a fine sense of status and political influence: in 1621, for example, £7 was spent on a pair for the king, £6 on those for Prince Charles and Chancellor Pembroke, £4 10s od for the royal favourite, Buckingham, and £4 for other influential courtiers.

[13] Wood, *History of the University* ii. 324, 376; S. Gibson, 'The great charter of Charles I (3 March 1636)', *Bodleian Quarterly Record* vii (1932), 122; Bodl. MS top. Oxon. c. 326, fo 125 (Laud to Pincke, 6 September 1633); MCA MS 730(a), fo 93ʳ (Laud to the president and fellows of Magdalen, 16 October 1638).

[14] J. P. Kenyon, *The Stuart Constitution* (Cambridge 1986), 117–19; P. Collinson, *The Elizabethan Puritan Movement* (London 1967), 448–67; HMC *Salisbury MSS* xvi. 389–91.

overshadowed the proper worship of God as prescribed in the prayer book. This was an uncompromising attack on the evangelical practice of many Calvinists as well as puritans, and Howson was answered in the pulpit by several junior members of the university who were supported by a head of house, Provost Airay of Queen's. Howson had to appeal to the privy council for assistance in order to restore his authority. Submissions were extracted from offending preachers; one libeller, Darling of Merton, was condemned by Star Chamber 'to be whipt and to loose his ears', while all university preachers and ministers were required to subscribe to a version of Whitgift's three articles of 1583, upholding the royal supremacy, and the lawfulness of the prayer book and articles of religion.[15]

The defeat of Oxford puritans in 1602–3 helps to explain their quiescence the following summer during the petitioning campaign. Henry Jacob, organizer of the agitation, solicited the help of Proctor Christopher Dale of Merton, and hoped that Airay could be recruited. In the event, the only public response was *The Answere* to the millenary petition in the name of the vice-chancellor, the doctors, proctors, and heads of houses. This claimed that the real aim of the petitioners was a Presbyterian church-government which was incompatible with monarchy. Such a polemical position betrays the hand of Howson, although it was not actually printed until October 1603, after Howson had been succeeded as vice-chancellor by George Abbot.[16] *The Answere* itself split Oxford opinion. While some resident MAs evidently supported it, others suggested that it did not genuinely represent the university's views, since it had not been proposed to convocation, the assembly of regent and non-regent masters, and at least three heads were rumoured to dissent from it. Two of these were probably Rainolds and Airay, but a third was named as Thomas Singleton, principal of Brasenose, who was unhappy about the defence of non-residence, an issue which had been vigorously debated in the preaching disputes of the winter of 1602–3. Proctor Dale, it was reported, had opposed publication of *The Answere*.[17] Nevertheless, this discontent was effectively contained by the authorities.

We may assume that Chancellor Buckhurst had endorsed *The Answere*. Certainly he was perturbed by puritan petitioning in Sussex that summer, complaining to James I of their 'seditious and dangerous procedings'. Yet, staunch conformist as he was, Buckhurst may well have had misgivings about Howson's provocative actions as vice-chancellor in 1602–3. It is noticeable that in March 1603 Airay escaped without a public submission, and Howson himself felt obliged to clarify

---

[15] C. Dent, *Protestant Reformers in Elizabethan Oxford* (Oxford 1983), 208–18; *Letters of John Chamberlain* ed. McClure i. 186–7.

[16] C. Burrage, *The Early English Dissenters* (2 vols Cambridge 1912) ii. 146–7; *The Answere of the Vicechancelour, the Doctors, both the Proctors, and other Heads of Houses in the Universitie of Oxford: to the humble petition of the ministers of the Church of England* (Oxford 1604 edn), sigs Ev, E3iv; compare the tone and similar invocation of 'the puritans democracie' of Presbyterianism in Howson's *Certaine Sermons made at Oxford, Anno. Dom. 1616* (London 1622), 92–3, 159–63.

[17] BL Add. MS 28,571, fos 181–6, a reference I owe to Nicholas Tyacke. See the similar allegations of *The Answere*'s unrepresentative character in BL Add. MS 8,978, fo 17. N. Tyacke, 'Religious Controversy', pp. 573–4 below.

his own position as regards preaching in a second edition of his accession day sermon, published sometime in 1603. Moreover, at the end of Howson's term of
office, Buckhurst voiced fears that the university's reputation had suffered badly as
a result of the disputes, and he urged that the university's governors prevent such
contentions arising again. Though his explicit criticism was aimed at agitators such
as Airay, there was an implied rebuke to his deputy.[18] Confrontation was not the
only, nor the most desirable, way of governing the university. Howson's successor
was George Abbot, a more moderate figure and practitioner of that evangelical
Calvinism which Howson had so berated.

Two years later, in June 1605, Buckhurst wrote privately to Airay, urging him to
become vice-chancellor the following month. This letter has been long known, but
its significance has been overlooked. At the very time that puritan ministers were
losing their livings, Buckhurst attempted to win over an acknowledged puritan sympathizer. The letter is effusive in its promises of goodwill and respect, and represented, Buckhurst confessed, 'a sure pledge of my love towards you'. Buckhurst
stated that he had no doubts of Airay's conformity, whatever had been surmised
to the contrary, and promised his favour so long as Airay remained conformable.[19]
In the short term, Buckhurst was rebuffed: Airay declined to be vice-chancellor,
though he did serve the following year, 1606–7. No doubt Airay was unwilling to
take up the post while the fate of his close friend John Rainolds hung in the balance: indeed, two months later the new vice-chancellor acted as the king's agent in
pressing Rainolds to subscribe. By July 1606 attempts to extract subscription from
Rainolds appear to have failed, so that Airay could safely take office.[20]

Who prompted Buckhurst to make these overtures to Airay? One obvious influence was George Abbot, master of University College, vice-chancellor in 1600–1,
1603–4 and, in place of Airay, in 1605–6. Abbot was also chaplain to Buckhurst,
and closer to him than any other divine. Abbot was a committed Calvinist, but also
a moderate conformist. In his capacity as dean of Winchester he had attended the
Hampton Court Conference, and later wrote disparagingly of the puritan delegates
as 'refragatory persons'. As his rule as archbishop would demonstrate, Abbot was
anxious to avoid damaging disputes over nonconformity in favour of intensive
preaching and a joint front against the menace of Rome.[21] But Buckhurst's letter
to Airay also discloses that Richard Bancroft, newly appointed as archbishop of
Canterbury, had backed Airay's nomination as vice-chancellor. This suggests that
Bancroft, for all his hostility to the puritan case of further reform, had absorbed
the implications of James I's promise of patronage to 'moderates' who were

[18] BL Add. MS 28,571, fo 179 (Buckhurst to Whitgift, September 1603); Dent, *Elizabethan Oxford*,
211, 217; OUA register M, fos 74ᵛ–5ʳ.

[19] Bodl. MS Rawlinson a. 289, fo 76. This letter has often been misattributed to 1606, though the
date and internal evidence prove it was written in 1605.

[20] HMC *Salisbury MSS* xvii. 422–3, 431. Airay drew up Rainolds's confession of faith on his deathbed
and acted as his executor: CCCA MS 303, fos 122–5, 220ᵛ.

[21] George Abbot, *An Exposition upon the Prophet Ionah* (London 1600), sig. A3iv; PRO SP 105/95, fos
28ᵛ–9ʳ; K. Fincham, *Prelate as Pastor: the episcopate of James I* (Oxford 1990), 47–8, 226, 253, 255–6.

prepared to conform.[22] Airay's appointment as vice-chancellor would demonstrate clearly, in and outside Oxford, the benefits of conformity, and might heal divisions opened up during the subscription campaign.

It may also have been Abbot who persuaded Buckhurst that a minute inquiry into the conformity of Oxford colleges was not necessary. Chancellor Cecil had conducted such a survey at Cambridge, almost certainly in response to James I's concern about the prevalence of puritanism there. The nonconformity of Emmanuel had been raised at the Hampton Court Conference, and James remained suspicious of the college, and especially of its master, Laurence Chaderton. At Oxford, by contrast, the king may have been reassured by knowledge of the recent crackdown against puritans in early 1603, for royal attention was chiefly focussed on John Rainolds, who was urged to subscribe in the summer of 1605.[23] It is true that James planned to enforce full subscription to canon 36 of 1604 on graduates taking degrees in both universities, and a draft letter to Cambridge, dated April 1605, is extant. But at the time the instruction, if sent, was not acted on, although in 1613 James was under the mistaken impression that all Oxford graduands subscribed. In fact this was not adopted in either university until a fresh order was issued in 1616–17.[24]

Between 1603 and his death in 1608 Buckhurst relied chiefly on evangelical Calvinists to serve as his deputies: Abbot, Airay, and John King, dean of Christ Church, appointed vice-chancellor for 1607–8. The only exception was John Williams, principal of Jesus and vice-chancellor in 1604–5, who was close to Howson in his theological views. Nevertheless, there were no clear moves against puritan or indeed Calvinist practices during Williams's year in office. Yet, despite his favour to Calvinists, Buckhurst retained his own counsel. Though Abbot tried to blacken Howson in Buckhurst's eyes, the chancellor expressed respect for him; and when Airay attempted to use his authority as vice-chancellor against a controversial sermon preached by William Laud, enemy of the Oxford Calvinists, Buckhurst intervened to persuade Airay to settle the matter discreetly.[25]

Buckhurst died in April 1608. His successor was Archbishop Bancroft, the first clergyman to be chancellor of either university since the 1550s, a testimony to the growing status of churchmen after the accession of James I. Although Bancroft's tenure was brief (he died in November 1610), it was marked by frequent interventions to maintain discipline and above all protect religious orthodoxy at Oxford. Although Bancroft has a reputation as the unyielding opponent of puritanism, it is

[22] Fincham, *Prelate as Pastor*, 213–14.

[23] HMC *Salisbury MSS* xvi. 363, 367, 389–91, xvii. 422–3; R. G. Usher, *The Reconstruction of the English Church* (2 vols London 1910) ii. 338.

[24] PRO SP 14/13/63, 10A/68–9; C. H. Cooper, *Annals of Cambridge* (5 vols Cambridge 1842–1908) iii. 59–60; Wood, *History of the University* ii. 323.

[25] 'John Howson's answers to Archbishop Abbot's accusations at his "trial" before James I at Greenwich, 10 June 1615', ed. N. Cranfield and K. Fincham, *Camden Miscellany* xxix (Camden soc. 4th ser. xxxiv 1987), 335; Bodl. MS Rawlinson a. 289, fos 78ʳ, 80ʳ; Laud, *Works* iii. 262. The Calvinism of Buckhurst himself emerges clearly in his will, where he claimed to be an elect saint, which was cited in his funeral sermon: George Abbot, *A Sermon preached at Westminster* (London 1608), 19–20.

clear that in the years after 1606 he became increasingly alarmed at the threat from Catholicism at court, in the dioceses, and at Oxford. On the privy council Bancroft opposed the influence of crypto-Catholics such as Northampton and Worcester, and condemned attempts to exempt Catholics from the full weight of penal legislation. He was also concerned by several defections to Rome in 1607–9, first by Theophilus Higgons, a London lecturer and formerly at Christ Church, and then by Humfrey Leech, also of Christ Church. Both subsequently published a defence of their actions to the delight of Catholic observers. According to John King, Bancroft's deputy throughout his chancellorship, it was a time of 'generall apostasy from the gospell unto popery'. There are signs, too, that Bancroft was perturbed by the views of some anti-Calvinist divines, such as Richard Butler, an intimate member of the circle around Bishop Neile, which included Laud and John Buckeridge the president of St John's.[26]

His cancellarial authority enabled Bancroft to address these problems in Oxford. First, he reminded the university of its status as a protestant seminary: divine service and sermons should be attended, the sacraments administered, weekly catechizing of all undergraduates performed, and the Thirty-nine Articles read out in colleges once a quarter. But he also warned against controversial arguments which ran contrary to the accepted teaching of the English Church and, in a letter to convocation in January 1609, cited the case of Leech, whose preaching on works of supererogation had raised a storm of protest leading to his apostasy and the 'shipwrack of a good conscience.'[27] A month earlier Bancroft had sent private, and more specific, guidance to Vice-Chancellor King and Principal Williams of Jesus, who was also Lady Margaret professor of divinity, on the topics best avoided in academic exercises.[28] Doubtful questions which seduced some and scandalized others should not be permitted—nor those which criticized foreign kingdoms or universities. The 'apparent doctrine' of the fathers and 'ancient churches' should be preferred to any novel teaching. Though the Leech case no doubt influenced Bancroft, he may also have been mindful of the doctoral theses defended by Laud six months before, in June 1608, one of which maintained that only bishops could ordain ministers.[29] This was certainly controversial divinity, since it unchurched most foreign protestants, and struck a blow at the belief, cherished by many Jacobean divines, in their church's place at the heart of the community of reformed churches. Though we possess no direct evidence of contemporary reactions to Laud's proposition, it was unlikely to have been quickly forgotten. The imposition of the oath of allegiance on the university in the summer of 1610 was another

---

[26] A. J. Loomie, 'Sir Robert Cecil and the Spanish embassy', *Bulletin of the Institute of Historical Research* xlii (1969), 42, 46; *STC* 13452, 15363; Leech, *Triumph of Truth*, 60; West. CA (series A) viii. 549, ix. 94; 'John Howson's answers', ed. Cranfield and Fincham, 338.

[27] Wood, *History of the University* ii. 296–8.

[28] PRO SP 14/38/30. The document, dated 18 December 1608, is addressed to 'Vicecan Dr Williams principal Colleg Jesu Oxon', which I have taken to refer to Williams *and* the vice-chancellor, John King.

[29] *Reg. Univ.* ed. Clark, pt 1, 206.

precaution to safeguard Oxford's position as a citadel of orthodoxy.[30] Bancroft also insisted that discipline be imposed on the student body: academic dress should be worn at appropriate times and undergraduates warned off frequenting taverns and alehouses. Initially at least the vice-chancellor and proctors responded vigorously, so that a student could comment in December 1610 that the university was 'very much reformed about drinking, long hair and other vices'.[31]

The anxiety of Bancroft about doctrinal discord among Oxford academics was well founded, as developments under his successor were to prove. The new chancellor, elected the day after Bancroft's death, was the lord keeper, Baron Ellesmere, who already enjoyed close ties with Oxford, as steward to the city (1601–10) and who had much experience of college affairs .[32] His influence and expertise assisted the university in 1611–12 during a bitter struggle with the city over privileges and immunities, which was settled by the privy council in June 1612 after a three-day hearing. The rights of the university on a range of contentious issues such as privileged persons, noctivagation, and discommoning were vindicated, but it was cautioned to exercise them with moderation.[33]

In his first letter to the university, Ellesmere urged it to avoid the snares of popery and puritanism, echoing the pronouncements of his master, James I. His six years as chancellor, however, witnessed public and sustained disagreement among university divines. This was a direct consequence of the emergence of rival churchmen in positions of power at court, who were prepared to champion the cause of their university protégés, and who served a monarch willing to tolerate their intrigues and to mediate between them. Most important here was the appointment of Abbot as archbishop of Canterbury in 1611, a divine dedicated to eliminating backsliders from the English Church, and a professed enemy of Catholics and anti-Calvinists. It was Abbot who drew Ellesmere into these rivalries in 1610–11, persuading him to warn James I of the popish inclinations of Laud in an effort to block his election to the vacant presidency of St John's College. Laud's rival for the post was John Rawlinson, one of Ellesmere's chaplains. The events of the disputed election, which was eventually confirmed in Laud's favour, are well known and need not be rehearsed here.[34] But crown's own role is less familiar and worth exploring. The first intervention came after the defeated party had appealed to the visitor, Bishop Bilson of Winchester. A signet letter was sent to Bilson in support of Laud; a second followed, a month later, instructing Bilson to arbitrate between the two sides. In late July Laud and his supporters appealed to the king, claiming that Bilson was exceeding his powers, at which James took the matter into his own hands and spent three hours hearing the case at Tichborne on 29 August. Only on 23 September did a signet letter confirm that Laud's election should stand. The role

[30] OUA SP/E/6.   [31] *VCH Oxon.* iii. 65–6.

[32] HLC EL 1926, 1928, 1930; *Oxford Council Acts 1583–1626*, ed. H. E. Salter (OHS lxxxvii 1928), p. lii.

[33] *VCH Oxon.* iv. 155–73; *Royal Letters addressed to Oxford*, ed. O. Ogle (Oxford 1892), 345–55.

[34] Laud, *Works* iii. 134–5; H. R. Trevor-Roper, *Archbishop Laud 1573–1645* (London 1940), 42–3; N. Tyacke, *Anti-Calvinists: the rise of English Arminianism c. 1590–1640* (Oxford 1987), 68–9.

of Ellesmere and Abbot in this protracted process is obscure, although Sebastian Benefield, pro-vice-chancellor and chaplain to Abbot, certainly tried to weaken Laud's chances before the election. Thereafter, however, Laud saw the greatest threat as coming from Bilson. The latter, however, had no power-base at court, and was outmanœuvred by Laud's patron, Bishop Neile, who was evidently responsible for securing the signet letters on Laud's behalf.[35]

Abbot's allies at Oxford continued to pressurize anti-Calvinist divines. In 1612 John Howson preached a provocative sermon claiming that faulty translations in the Genevan Bible tended towards Arianism. He was warned by his old opponent Airay and Robert Abbot, the archbishop's brother, to preach another sermon, moderating his claims, but Howson defended his remarks and threatened to appeal to the king, as visitor of Howson's college. As a precaution, he sent a copy of his sermon to Bishop Neile. Both Abbot and William Godwin, dean of Christ Church, then condemned Howson's views from the pulpit, and Howson eventually appears to have been censured by the vice-chancellor.[36]

In June 1615 Laud and Howson each appeared before James I to clear their names. If, as seems likely, Archbishop Abbot was intent on securing royal authority for a crackdown on anti-Calvinist views, then these hearings represent a significant defeat for the Oxford Calvinists. In the case of Laud, the immediate cause was a sermon he had preached on Shrove Tuesday which contained soteriological doctrines subsequently denounced as popish by Robert Abbot. Neile secured Laud's acquittal, and Archbishop Abbot accepted that his brother had overreacted. We are better informed about Howson's interview with the king. Abbot attempted to brand Howson as a crypto-papist by raising disputes going back twenty-five years, while Howson retorted with the charge that Abbot and his university supporters were puritans. James I, displaying typical self-confidence in his powers as broker of a genuine peace, refused to back either Howson or Abbot. He accepted the professions of orthodoxy by Howson, but required him to preach more often against popery. This Howson did in a series of university sermons the following year, in the course of which he also lashed out at the 'puritans democracie' of Presbyterianism, adding that he feared that some of its advocates were amongst his audience.[37]

Less than two years later the king issued instructions to both universities. It was, as Bishop Montagu noted, unprecedented for 'a king, first with his own mouth, then with his own hand' to give such directions. Their immediate origins are unclear. However, the fact that they were drawn up at Newmarket in December 1616 in the presence of a Cambridge delegation, and were only conveyed to the Oxford authorities a month later, perhaps implies that they were in response to

---

[35] Bodl. MS Tanner 338, fos 326, 346–7, 365, 370; PRO SO 3/5 (19 May, 17 June, 3 August, and 23 September 1611); LPL MS 943, p. 59.

[36] 'John Howson's answers', ed. Cranfield and Fincham, 321–2, 329; West. CA xi. 370.

[37] 'John Howson's answers', ed. Cranfield and Fincham, 323, 328–41; Howson, *Certaine Sermons made at Oxford*, 92–3, 159–63.

events, not now recoverable, at Cambridge. Nevertheless, James may well have
been mindful of the Oxford disputes brought to his attention in 1615. The instructions themselves were adopted by convocation, and posted in halls and colleges.
The twin goals of conformity and order run through these instructions. Puritan
influences were checked by the requirement that henceforth all graduands were to
subscribe to canon 36, and that only conformable dons were to preach in the city.
Students were to attend St Mary's in preference to the city churches. Factious
preaching was forbidden, and divinity students were encouraged to use the writings of the fathers and schoolmen in preference to compendia and abbreviations.[38]
Since the latter were usually compiled by foreign protestants, this may have been
intended as a warning shot to leading Calvinists such as John Prideaux, appointed
regius professor of divinity in 1615, who regarded systematic catechisms as useful
primers in divinity and publicly warned against reading the fathers too soon.[39]

The part played by Ellesmere in the events of 1615–17 is not documented,
though he certainly remained a close political ally of Archbishop Abbot. Just a
week after the royal instructions had been issued, Ellesmere resigned as chancellor, and on the same day convocation elected William Herbert, third earl of
Pembroke, to succeed him. Pembroke proved to be a benign, though not noticeably active chancellor, intervening to settle academic disputes over dress, protecting the university against threatening moves from the city, and acting promptly on
royal initiatives. A typical example of Pembroke's benevolence was his agreement,
at the request of the university, to augment the stipends of the professors of civil
law and medicine by appointing them as principals of halls which lay in his gift.[40]
The theological quarrels of his predecessor's time temporarily died down, followed
by uneasy equipoise between Archbishop Abbot and his opponents, whose
stronger position in and beyond the court was signalled by Laud's promotion to
the deanery of Gloucester in 1616 and Howson's elevation to the bishopric of
Oxford three years later.

Pembroke took little discernible part in the events following John Knight's controversial defence of the right of resistance in April 1622. Both king and council
wrote to the vice-chancellor and heads of houses, requiring the university to condemn the published teaching of David Pareus on the Epistle to the Romans, the
source of Knight's argument, and to search for and confiscate copies of the offending commentary. These were burnt in St Mary's churchyard. Though the Oxford
authorities established that Knight was not, as had been feared, acting as a
spokesman for a wider body of opinion, they pushed through convocation a series
of propositions condemning his thesis. The royal instructions of 1617 were ordered
to be sent to every college, there to be read out once a quarter, and particular

[38] Cooper, *Annals of Cambridge* iii. 105; Wood, *History of the University* ii. 323–4, 326–8; Bloxam, *Reg. Magdalen* ii, p. lxxxvii. For a possible Cambridge link, see Tyacke, *Anti-Calvinists*, 40.
[39] PRO SP 16/27/46.
[40] Wood, *History of the University* ii. 331–2, 336–8; OUA register of convocation 1615–28, NEP/*supra*/23 register N, fo 65; OUA NEP/*supra*/44, fos 54ᵛ, 55ᵛ.

importance was attached to the clause directing students away from modern protestant writers and towards the study of scripture, the fathers, and the schoolmen. At the subsequent visitation of halls, the vice-chancellor added some new inquiries about conformity, including attendance at university sermons, in accordance with the royal instructions.[41]

Oxford had long experience of external involvement in the distribution of its patronage. The elections of heads of house, fellows, and scholars and the renewal of college leases were frequently accompanied by letters of recommendation on behalf of candidates from courtiers and churchmen as well as crown, chancellor, and college visitors. After 1603 this intervention intensified, with royal mandates showering the universities, until complaints resulted in a more selective choice of nominations. Even then, the scramble for place in Jacobean Oxford, involving large numbers of patrons, contrasts with the more orderly distribution of academic posts in the 1630s with the emergence of Chancellor Laud as chief patronage-broker under the crown.

Although the patronage of a few notables, chiefly Archbishops Abbot and Laud, discloses ideological motives, most university patrons were primarily concerned to demonstrate their influence and advance their protégés. Colleges, in turn, could secure powerful allies by succumbing to these importunities. Accept the nominee of Judge Whitelocke, the fellows of Wadham were told in 1628, and 'the judge wilbe reddy to acknowledge it, if you have any occacon hereafter to use him'.[42] Yet we should not regard outside intervention in college elections as unwarranted interference, since very often the prime movers were the rival candidates themselves, in a period of increasing competition for academic positions as university numbers steadily expanded. The royal prerogative was also prized as an enabling device to overcome inconvenient college statutes which might bar candidates on grounds of age or county of origin, and limit fellowships to a fixed number of years. Dispensations were not necessarily unwelcome to the college authorities, although they could be disputed.[43] The first warden of Wadham, Robert Wright, secured a royal dispensation to marry, notwithstanding the statutory requirement that the warden remain celibate. That he chose to resign shortly afterwards may owe more to the forthright opposition of the redoubtable foundress, Dorothy Wadham, rather than the inadmissibility of his dispensation.[44] Nor, as we shall see, was this an isolated incident of the crown's mandates being crossed in Jacobean Oxford.

---

[41] Wood, *History of the University* ii. 341–7. Pembroke did at least sign the privy council letter of 31 May 1622 (ibid. 344). OUA NEP/*supra*/45, fo 121ᵛ.

[42] WCM 7/10 (Laud to the warden and fellows, 2 February 1628).

[43] V. Morgan, 'Whose prerogative in late sixteenth and early seventeenth century England?', *Journal of Legal History* v (1984), 39–64.

[44] *The Statutes of Wadham College* (London 1855), ch. 2; PRO SO 3/5 (30 June 1613). Dorothy Wadham's character emerges clearly in N. Briggs, 'The foundation of Wadham College, Oxford', *Oxoniensia* xxi (1956), 61–81.

It has been suggested that from the 1580s crown and court began to play a substantial part in university patronage.[45] It was extended still further in the early years of James I as a result of the king's willingness to pass commendatory letters under the signet, the most authoritative expression of the royal command. Thus at Woodstock in September 1603, for example, James authorized five mandates: two to All Souls for candidates for fellowships, another to Magdalen for a demy's place, and two on behalf of prospective lessees to Oriel and All Souls respectively. A month later, Oriel and All Souls received further mandates in favour of two other lessees.[46] Such multiple requests produced some bewilderment. In June 1604 the fellows of Magdalen wrote to the king asking which of the two candidates whom he had backed for a single fellowship was his preferred nominee.[47] No college was immune from these letters, though the majority were directed to All Souls and Magdalen, each endowed with a larger fellowship than other colleges, with the exception of New. This rash of mandates clearly embarrassed some Oxford colleges which were not willing to comply with the crown's wishes: All Souls, for example, twice rejected Robert Gentili, son of the professor of civil law, on the grounds of ineligibility due to his youth, and he was only admitted to a fellowship on a devolution to the visitor.[48] It was Cambridge University, however, that lodged an effective protest, which led to a sharp reduction in the number of mandates bearing the signet. In July 1607 the vice-chancellor and eight heads wrote to their chancellor, Robert Cecil, drawing attention to the flood of royal letters, often procured, they claimed, by unworthy candidates, which led to elections against the 'statutes of foundations, oaths of electors and free choice of the fittest'. Cecil was also keeper of the signet, and evidently tightened procedures for issuing signet letters, with the result that from 1608 only three or four were authorized for Oxford fellowships or scholarships each year for the rest of the reign.[49] However, the steady stream of recommendations from courtiers and churchmen did not abate, and the crown itself sometimes backed candidates without using the signet, a famous example being Edward Hyde's application for a demy's place at Magdalen in 1623. Despite the king's support, Hyde was not elected.[50]

Such defiance was probably no more than an irritant to James I, who was much more concerned to secure suitable candidates for headships: men of learning, religious conformity, and judgement. The rise of the undergraduate college in Tudor Oxford had enhanced the importance of their heads, who enjoyed increasing authority over university affairs at the expense of congregation and convocation, a development formalized in 1631 with the establishment of the hebdomadal board,

---

[45] V. Morgan, 'Country, court and Cambridge University, 1558–1640: a study in the evolution of a political culture' (East Anglia Ph. D. thesis 1983), 333, 453, 458. This is an important study, drawing on material from both universities, from which I have profited enormously.

[46] PRO SO 3/2 (17 and 20 September, 19 and 30 October 1603).

[47] PRO SP 14/8/68.

[48] *CSPD 1603–10*, 159; PRO SO 3/3 (15 September and 1 November 1606); ASA, C. T. Martin, *Catalogue of the Archives of All Souls' College* (London 1877), nos 73, 80, pp. 307–8.

[49] HMC *Salisbury MSS* xix. 179–80: PRO SO 3/4–8.   [50] *CSPD 1623–5*, 8, 88.

a weekly meeting of the vice-chancellor and college heads to discuss university business. In 1608 the king severely reprimanded a group of Magdalen fellows for attempting to frustrate a royal mandate and install their own candidate in the vacant presidency, and reminded them of the eminence of that office, governing a college where 'a great part of his gentrie and nobilitie should learne the principles of obedience to God and himselfe'.[51] So James I, just as his predecessor had done,[52] intervened regularly in the elections to headships, often issuing mandates under the signet. Such letters helped secure the elections of Harding and then Langton to Magdalen (1608 and 1610), Laud to St John's (1611), Pincke to New College (1616), and Hood to Lincoln (1620).[53] The reversion of New College (1613) was promised to Arthur Lake, and the king's support trumped a rival claimant sponsored by the queen.[54] Behind these moves can be identified influential courtiers. Lake owed his elevation to his brother Sir Thomas, Latin secretary to the king, Langton was chaplain to Robert Cecil,[55] and Laud's suit, as we have seen, was advanced by his patron, Richard Neile, clerk of the closet. Fellows were customarily promised a free election, but the royal nominee was clearly identified, and usually elected.

Only at All Souls, and perhaps at Corpus, did the fellowship defy the king. In August 1618 the king wrote twice under the signet recommending Henry Beaumont, a former fellow and founder's kin for the vacant wardenship of All Souls. The real mover was the royal favourite, Buckingham, a relative of Beaumont, who had attempted to secure him a bishopric the previous year; and to Buckingham the fellows wrote after electing another, observing that they were bound by oath to choose the most sufficient and able candidate. Of Beaumont they knew little, since he had left the college years before, and they begged Buckingham to intercede with the king. Discreet pressure may also have been applied to the fellowship from another quarter. The successful candidate, Richard Astley, was chaplain to the visitor, Archbishop Abbot, who at the time was becoming disenchanted with his former protégé, Buckingham.[56] Four years earlier, at Corpus, the king's candidate was Robert Burghill, who secured the same number of votes as Thomas Anian, amid allegations that several fellows were ineligible to vote. The matter was referred to the visitor, Bilson of Winchester, who pronounced Anian to be elected. Since Bilson claimed that he did 'nothinge in this case, but what his majestie liketh and alloweth', it may be that James had switched his nomination to Anian, perhaps encouraged by Anian's patron, the university chancellor Lord Ellesmere.[57]

[51] *The Collegiate University*, 402–3; Macray, *Reg. Magdalen* iii. 73–9.

[52] Dent, *Elizabethan Oxford*, 72–3, 207.

[53] PRO SO 3/3 (10 and 18 February 1608), 3/5 (16 November 1610, 19 May 1611), 3/6 (12 August 1616), 3/7 (November 1620).

[54] Bodl. MS top. Oxon. b. 48, fos 11ʳ, 14ʳ.   [55] HMC *Salisbury MSS* xx. 297.

[56] PRO SO 3/6 (July 1618); ASA, Martin, *All Souls' College*, nos 134–5, 137, p. 312; *Letters of John Chamberlain*, ed. McClure ii. 48; C. G. Robertson, *Oxford College Histories: All Souls* (London 1899), 98; K. Fincham, 'Prelacy and politics: Archbishop Abbot's defence of protestant orthodoxy', *Historical Research* lxi (1988), 53 n. 91.

[57] PRO SO 3/6 (4 April and 23 May 1614); CCCA A/5/2/5; Fowler, *Corpus*, 175–7; BL Add. MS 39,353, fo 106ᵛ.

Where there was no royal nomination for a headship, other influences were brought to bear. Sometimes this was a matter of custom or prescription: thus the archbishop of Canterbury, as visitor of All Souls and Merton, chose the warden in each college from a slate of candidates proposed by the fellowship; Dorothy Wadham retained the power of nomination to all positions at Wadham during her lifetime, and the chancellor nominated principals of Oxford's dwindling number of halls, with the exception of St Edmund Hall, where the right lay with Queen's.[58] But the authority of the visitor was also evident elsewhere: thus successive chancellors, as visitors of University College, nominated successive masters: Buckhurst backing his chaplain Abbot (1597), Bancroft his nephew John (1610) and Laud his kinsman Walker (1632).[59]

With this extensive and established pattern of external involvement it is unsurprising to learn that at least one chancellor, Ellesmere, courted popularity by promising on taking office to permit free elections, a self-denying ordinance he appears generally to have observed.[60] Other chancellors were more assiduous patrons, but were not necessarily the most influential. In the middle years of the reign, Archbishop George Abbot was a key patron: his brother Robert became regius professor of divinity then master of Balliol, and his son-in-law, Nathaniel Brent, became warden of Merton; one chaplain, Parkhurst, succeeded Robert Abbot at Balliol, while another, Mocket, became warden of All Souls, and a third, Benefield, was appointed Lady Margaret professor of divinity.[61] Abbot, Mocket, and Benefield were all committed Calvinists intent on defending doctrinal orthodoxy against Arminianism, but their patron had to struggle to enlist royal support for his views and after 1618 lost influence at court. At about the same time, Buckingham emerged as a major patron in the university, as elsewhere, though his patronage in Jacobean Oxford, as in the national arena, was not marked by a commitment to any one ideological cause.[62]

For James I the universities had a significant role in promoting within the British archipelago that union of hearts and minds to which he was so attached. Prominent young Irishmen, such as the grandson of the earl of Tyrone, were dispatched to Oxford to learn civility and religion, and from 1618 James financed the education of poor students from Jersey on the recommendation of the three estates.[63] Oxford would inculcate political obedience and sound religion, and, it was hoped, eradicate Catholic or Presbyterian influences. Similarly, James expected the universities

[58] Robertson, *All Souls*, 19; BL MS Stowe 176, fo 221; *The Statutes of Wadham College*, ch. 31; OUA NEP/*supra*/44.

[59] W. Carr, *Oxford College Histories: University College* (London 1902), 92, 98, 104.

[60] Bodl. MS top. Oxon. b. 48, fo 27ʳ. See, however, his recommendation of a candidate for a fellowship of All Souls in 1614: ASA Martin, *All Souls' College*, no. 46, p. 329.

[61] For Parkhurst see *DNB* and Bodl. MS Rawlinson d. 47, fos 39ᵛ, 50ᵛ–1ʳ; for Mocket, LPL MS 1730, fo 14; for Benefield, his *Doctrinae christianae sex capita* (Oxford 1610), sig. *3v.

[62] N. Cuddy, 'The revival of the entourage' in D. Starkey (ed.), *The English Court from the Wars of the Roses to the Civil War* (London 1987), 218–19; PRO SO 3/6 (12 August 1616, July 1618, 13 August 1618), 3/7 (November 1620); C. Russell, *Parliaments and English Politics 1621–9* (Oxford 1979), 9.

[63] *APC 1615–16*, 308; *APC 1616–17*, 345–6; *APC 1618–19*, 192.

to open their doors to young Scotsmen. Probably the first to matriculate was a scion of the Anglo-Scottish aristocracy, Francis Stewart, orphaned son of James, second earl of Moray, who attended Christ Church after 1604 with a pension of 200 marks; then in 1606 John Young, son of James VI's tutor, was elected to a fellowship at Sidney Sussex, Cambridge. Both were to hold public office in England: Stewart as MP for Oxford and elsewhere in the 1620s, and Young as dean of Winchester from 1616 to the 1640s. Among the courtiers receiving MAs on the state visit to Oxford in 1605 were a bevy of Scots, including the duke of Lennox, Lord Erskine, and Sir Patrick Murray.[64]

But the university resisted electing Scotsmen to scholarships and fellowships, on the grounds that only those born in England and Wales qualified under college statutes. After failing to intrude a number of Scots into Oxford and Cambridge, in December 1609 James threatened a royal visitation to revoke what he regarded as hostile college statutes, but he was temporarily pacified by the intervention of Robert Cecil, chancellor of Cambridge. The issue resurfaced in February 1611 when the chancellors of both universities examined the restrictions attached to scholarships and fellowships funded by the colleges. They were informed that Scotsmen were ineligible by birth, and to support them as supernumeraries would reduce the emoluments of college fellows. Two examples from Oxford will suffice. The forty fellowships at All Souls were for those born or bred in the province of Canterbury, while the twenty fellowships at Corpus were tied to particular dioceses or counties: five from Winchester and two apiece from Bath and Wells, Exeter, Gloucester, and Lincoln dioceses, one from Durham, two from Kent, and one each from Bedfordshire, Lancashire, Oxfordshire, and Wiltshire; similar restrictions applied for the twenty college *discipuli*.[65] Remedial action was piecemeal. In 1612, the statutes of a recent Cambridge foundation, Sidney Sussex, were modified to allow Scots and Irish to compete for fellowships, provided they had studied at the university for six years;[66] in the same year, James I altered the statutes of the new Oxford foundation of Wadham, so that those nine scholarships not tied to Somerset and Essex might be open to all from 'Magnae Britanniae'; since fellows were elected from amongst the scholars, and the warden from the fellows, Wadham became the first constitutionally 'British' college at either university.[67] Similarly, the statutes of Jesus College, compiled in 1622, imposed no local conditions on the choice of fellows and scholars except where endowments specified otherwise. This would certainly have met with James's approval, but it primarily reflected the

---

[64] *CSPD 1603–10*, 31, 119, 368; *VCH Cambridge* iii. 483; *Reg. Univ.* ed. Clark, pt 1, 236–7.

[65] Robertson, *All Souls*, 104–5; *CSPD 1603–10*, 569, 571. HLC EL 1915–16, 1966–77; *The Egerton Papers* ed. J. P. Collier (Camden Soc. old ser. xii, 1840), 444–5.

[66] *VCH Cambridge* iii. 483. Morgan, 'Country, court and Cambridge', appx III, 'Scotsmen at Cambridge', argues that James made extensive use of the signet to intrude Scotsmen, a tactic which was neither regularly nor successfully used at Oxford.

[67] WCM 4/31 (a near-contemporary source on James's role), 1/4 chs 2 and 6 (where 'Anglia' is crossed out by the scribe and replaced by 'Magnae Britanniae' in one, but retained in the other, and tidied up in 1/6, a slightly later version of the statutes). I am grateful to Dr Cliff Davies for his help in elucidating this episode.

wishes of the founder, expressed in the charter of incorporation of 1571; it is ironic, therefore, that the steady stream of benefactions tied to Wales after 1622 gave Jesus its strong Welsh character by the later seventeenth century.[68]

In 1618 Wadham itself experienced some Jacobean bullying which demonstrates James I's impatience with restrictive college statutes. In October James wrote to the warden and fellows requiring them to elect the Scot Walter Durham, a graduate of St Andrews, to the next vacant fellowship, notwithstanding his ineligibility on three counts: he was already an MA, he was over-age, and he was not a scholar of the college. Durham vigorously pressed his suit, supported by John Young, by now an influential figure at court. The fellowship were worried that James would regard their resistance as contempt of his race, and as another manifestation of that hostility which he had checked a few years before by changing the statutes. The college itself felt peculiarly vulnerable, as a young and relatively poor foundation which had just lost both its foundress and its first visitor, Bishop Montagu; but its appeals to Chancellor Pembroke evidently worked, and the matter was eventually dropped.[69]

For all this interference, James I fulfilled his promise of favouring the university. He augmented the income of the regius chairs of divinity, law, and medicine, wrote under the signet to the city of Oxford to secure land for the erection of Wadham and, in his first parliament, gave the royal assent to a bill which allowed the universities to make presentations to livings in the gift of convicted recusants. This last was a valuable extension of ecclesiastical patronage for Oxford, which held the advowson of just three livings, and between 1603 and 1640 the university made forty-seven presentations to thirty-two livings.[70] Best known, however, was the crown's grant of university representation in parliament.

In March 1604, a week before his first parliament was due to open, James I issued letters patent authorizing the election of two burgesses from each university. Although the precise circumstances of this grant are obscure, James's consent was evidently secured by Sir Edward Coke in association with both chancellors and several well-connected lawyers and divines. Yet it also marked the culmination of repeated attempts since 1566 to win parliamentary representation for the universities, and fits well into the broader picture of the steady expansion of the house of commons throughout the sixteenth century. University MPs, so Coke and others argued, could assist with legislation touching Oxford and Cambridge generally, as well as individual colleges, each with their own set of statutes, and guard their immunities from incursions. This latter concern resurfaced time and again, so that protection of university jurisdiction dominates a list of points drawn up for Oxford MPs in 1621. In the event, university MPs were usually placed on appropriate com-

[68] E. Hardy, *Oxford College Histories: Jesus College* (Oxford 1899), 50–2.

[69] WCM 4/28–31.

[70] Nicholls, *Progresses* i. 552; OUA register M, fos 89ᵛ–90ʳ; PRO SO 3/4 (19 March 1610); A. D. Hewlett, 'The University of Oxford and the Church of England in the time of William Laud' (Oxford B. Litt. thesis 1934), 65, 70.

mittees considering bills such as those against married dons or for the incorporation of Corpus and Oriel (all 1606).[71]

No resident member of the university served as an MP between 1604 and 1640. Instead MPs were mostly Oxford graduates, often holding court or legal office, and generally with previous experience of the commons. They were elected by convocation, usually by acclamation, and sometimes supported by commendatory letters from patrons, but the course of 'parliamentary selection' did not always run smoothly, and three of the eight elections between March 1604 and April 1640 were contested.[72] On the first occasion, in 1614, one seat was assured for Sir John Bennet, an executor of Sir Thomas Bodley's will, and benefactor to the Bodleian, who had laid the foundation-stone of the schools quadrangle the previous year. The rivals for the other seat were two prominent civilians, Francis James and Sir Daniel Dunne: the latter had helped to procure university representation in 1604 and had served as one of the university's MPs between 1604 and 1610. Ellesmere had to write privately on behalf of Dunne to the vice-chancellor, who may have secured his election with the assistance of other senior members, rather than the 'multitude of voices'.[73] In 1626, some members of convocation offered the name of Sir Francis Stewart as an alternative to Sir Thomas Edmondes, who was comptroller of the royal household, one of the university's MPs the previous year and sponsored by both Chancellor Pembroke and Archbishop Abbot. Edmondes was not an Oxford graduate, though his son had recently attended the university, and there may well have been resentment at his nomination twice in two years; Stewart, in contrast, was himself an Oxford MA, but had evidently not pressed his case, possessing a safe seat under Pembroke's patronage at Liskeard. Indeed there is some suggestion that Stewart's name was proposed on the spur of the moment in order to challenge Edmondes. Nevertheless, the vice-chancellor declared Edmondes to be elected, a decision later overturned by the commons' committee of privileges.[74] Two years on, in 1628, a scrutiny of votes occurred in another contest, this time between Sir John Danvers and two candidates backed by Chancellor Pembroke: Sir Henry Marten and Michael Oldisworth. In the event, Danvers and Marten were elected.[75]

As this last case suggests, the view that convocation had 'less and less choice throughout the period' is not persuasive.[76] Instead the practice developed that the senior MP, named first on the returns, would be nominated by the chancellor, and the other, or junior, MP would be chosen by the university, an arrangement

---

[71] M. B. Rex, *University Representation in England 1604-90* (London 1953), 21-36; PRO SP 14/124/31; *CJ* i. 260, 278, 286. On the growth of the commons, see J. Loach, *Parliament under the Tudors* (Oxford 1991), 35-6. I also acknowledge the generous assistance of the History of Parliament Trust.

[72] Possibly a fourth contest occurred in 1621, when vote by scrutiny was used for the first time: Rex, *University Representation*, 356.

[73] Bodl. MS Tanner 74, fo 34ʳ; *Letters of John Chamberlain*, ed. McClure i. 525.

[74] Rex, *University Representation*, 75-7; and Bodl. MS Bodley 594, fos 133ʳ-5ʳ, printed ibid. 356-9. For Pembroke's extensive parliamentary patronage, see V. A. Rowe, 'The influence of the earls of Pembroke on parliamentary elections, 1625-41', *EHR* l (1935), 242-56.

[75] Rex, *University Representation*, 115.   [76] Ibid. 130.

mirroring the custom of many boroughs where the local patron nominated one candidate and the corporation the other.[77] This practice was acknowledged in 1625, when the chancellor openly assumed the right to nominate the senior MP, and may go back to 1614, when Bennet was evidently elected as the university's choice. In the 1620s the junior position was regularly filled by Sir John Danvers, who was elected after Bennet's expulsion from parliament for corruption in 1621, and who served as a university MP in 1625, 1626, 1628–9, and April 1640.[78] Danvers was the younger brother of the earl of Danby, founder of the university's physic garden in 1622, and once a student at Brasenose. Since Danvers was a fairly inactive MP, we must attribute his regular selection to personal standing in Oxford rather than to his parliamentary performance.[79]

With the accession of Charles I in March 1625, Oxford acquired a sovereign who quickly grew convinced that a thorough reformation of the university was imperative. The first request for reform in fact came from parliament in 1625. Reacting to unresolved charges of misconduct against the heads of Corpus in Oxford and of Trinity in Cambridge and allegations of simony in college elections, all aired in the parliament of 1624, this parliament petitioned that 'the ancient discipline of the two universities' should be restored. Charles promised to investigate the matter, and the following year wrote to the chancellors of Oxford and Cambridge to inquire about the grounds of complaint, warning that if the university authorities could not reform themselves then he would intervene.[80] Subsequent events suggested to Charles that, indeed, all was not well. At Cambridge the royal favourite, the duke of Buckingham, faced unprecedented opposition in his bid to become chancellor of the university in June 1626, and was eventually elected with a slender majority of five votes out of over 200 cast. At Oxford, Charles was 'highly offended' by the presumption of students who killed his game at Woodstock, and instructed Chancellor Pembroke to expel the offenders. In 1628, Pembroke's attempt to regulate the proctoral elections was opposed by a group in convocation, including the proctors themselves, a defiance of legitimate authority that roused Charles to anger. Such examples, he wrote to Pembroke, 'spread from such places are able to infect a whole state, and if they should continue in such courses, wee must be driven to be more severe than wee are willing to bee, to soe famous a university as that in former times hath bin'. Later that year, an Oxford student was accused of defaming the memory of Buckingham in the aftermath of his assassination. In the view of Charles's chief informant and assistant in Oxford affairs, William Laud, the university 'was extremely sunk from all discipline, and fallen into

---

[77] M. Kishlansky, *Parliamentary Selection* (Cambridge 1986), 37–48.

[78] OUA register N, fos 112ᵛ–13ʳ. In 1624 the university choice was evidently Sir Isaac Wake, diplomat and Oxford's public orator between 1604 and 1622.

[79] Rex, *University Representation*, 100, 111, 118.

[80] *CJ* i. 777a; Russell, *Parliaments and English Politics*, 198, 241; Fowler, *Corpus*, 177–81; *Proceedings in Parliament 1625*, ed. M. Jansson and W. B. Bidwell (London 1987), 157, 262; *CSPD 1625–6*, 558.

all licentiousness'; the project to reform its statutes, announced in June 1629, was the first step to revitalize the university.[81]

So disorders at Oxford were subsumed into, and reinforced, that sense of national malaise which the king saw behind his domestic political difficulties in the late 1620s. Both Charles and Laud believed that monarchical power, ecclesiastical authority, and social order were threatened by puritan activism, which had used parliament as a platform to frustrate royal projects and sow dissent between the king and his subjects, corrupted right religious practice through false teaching, neglect of ceremony, and an obsessive concern with preaching, and split parishes into warring groups of the godly against their enemies. Laud himself traced the causes of this back to the decay of university discipline.[82] The answer was to reimpose respect, order, and deference throughout society, and in this task the universities had a key role, as seminaries of virtue, learning, and protestantism, rather than as academies of disorder. Just as Charles feared that their tumultuous behaviour might be imitated across the nation, so universities could be influential models of discipline and piety, complementing the royal court as images of virtue, but also disseminating these ideals in the localities as gentlemen-commoners returned to their estates and graduate ordinands dispersed to take up benefices.

Laud was already the driving-force for change at Oxford before his election as chancellor in April 1630. It was he who helped devise the new proctorial cycle, presented to the university in December 1628, and Pembroke's instruction to begin the revision of the statutes was on his initiative.[83] Laud might long have continued to direct Oxford affairs at Pembroke's elbow had the earl not unexpectedly died on 10 April 1630. Two days later Laud was elected in his place. This was the only contested cancellarial election in early Stuart Oxford: Laud's opponent was the earl of Montgomery, Pembroke's younger brother and heir, and high steward of the university, whom he defeated by nine votes. What has hitherto been overlooked, however, is the fact that the king's candidate was not Laud but Lord Treasurer Weston, who apparently had Laud's formal support, but the royal nomination reached Oxford after the election had been completed. Laud nevertheless sought Charles's approval before accepting the office. He owed his election to a group of prominent academics in the university, led by Vice-Chancellor Frewen of Magdalen and Dean Duppa of Christ Church, who were acting independently of their candidate. Duppa later acknowledged to Laud that he knew of Laud's support for Weston, but referred to 'hinderances, which kept us from following your directions'.[84] Why did Laud endorse Weston? Perhaps Laud was meekly following the crown's lead, but he may have been happy to continue his supervision of Oxford affairs without the trappings of office. Power without formal responsibility would have provided Laud with some protection against his critics, were

---

[81] CSPD 1626–7, 402; CSPD 1628–9, 329, 338; Wood, History of the University ii. 360–4; Laud, Works v. 13–14.

[82] Laud, Works vi. 294. [83] PRO SP 16/119/34–5, 122/43–4; Laud, Works v. 14.

[84] PRO SP 16/164/41, 165/28; Laud, Works iv. 189, v. 3–5, vi. 275; The Court and Times of Charles I, ed. T. Birch (2 vols London 1848) ii. 74.

political circumstances to change. Such thinking certainly informed his conduct of ecclesiastical affairs, where he was anxious to associate the king with every controversial decision.[85] In any event, Laud's assumption of authority as chancellor was by no means inevitable, and it was subsequently disputed by some supporters of Montgomery, who petitioned the king that the conduct of the election broke university statutes, but the appeal was rejected.[86]

Laud's own control over the university was not consolidated until the following year. In May and June 1631 a series of university sermons criticized the new order: the path to preferment in and beyond Oxford lay, it was claimed, in embracing heterodox doctrine, a charge which breached the royal moratorium of December 1628 on discussing predestination, while the meetings of heads of houses to discuss the revision of the statutes were labelled as a conventicle, and the new ceremonialism, symbolized by the erection of an altar at Magdalen College, was denounced as popish. One preacher, Giles Thorne of Balliol, even dared to suggest that in matters of faith, Christians must obey God not the magistrate. Thorne and another preacher, Thomas Ford, resisted the vice-chancellor's intervention by appealing to the proctors, who took the matter out of the vice-chancellor's hands. Several participants in this preaching campaign had opposed Laud's election the previous year: Thorne and a sympathizer, Francis Hyde, had both appealed to the king against it, while John Prideaux, rector of Exeter and regius professor of divinity, condoned the preaching campaign of 1631 and apparently had also favoured Montgomery in 1630.[87]

These disputes were settled by the king at a lengthy hearing at Woodstock, on 23 August 1631. Two of the preachers were expelled, another eventually allowed to recant. The two proctors were replaced, and Prideaux and Wilkinson, principal of Magdalen Hall, were both severely reprimanded. The vice-chancellor's powers of investigation and imprisonment were strengthened and a weekly meeting of the vice-chancellor and heads of houses was instituted to maintain the peace and order of the university. The hearing represented an unqualified triumph for the Laudian interest, as Laud privately acknowledged in his diary by including it amongst the most decisive dates of his life. Opposition in the university had been cowed into submission, and for the rest of the decade criticism in Oxford was muted and piecemeal. Laud even had the satisfaction of interceding with Charles on behalf of Prideaux, which made Prideaux's dependence on Laud plain to all.[88]

There is no doubt that Laud supervised university affairs more closely than any

---

[85] K. Fincham and P. Lake, 'The ecclesiastical policies of James I and Charles I' in K. Fincham (ed.), *The Early Stuart Church 1603–42* (Basingstoke 1993), 45.

[86] PRO SP 16/165/18; Bodl. MS Bodley 594, fo 139.

[87] Wood, *History of the University* ii. 372–6; Laud, *Works* v. 49–56; PRO SP 16/499/46. A copy of Ford's sermon survives in Dr Williams's Library, London, MSS Quick, RNC 38.35, pp. 632–54.

[88] The fullest contemporary account is Bodl. MS Jones 17, fos 300ʳ–9ᵛ. See also Laud, *Works* v. 56–70; PRO SP 16/198/53. Crosfield's claim, which is often repeated, that it was Montgomery rather than Laud who interceded for Prideaux is contradicted by two more authoritative sources: *Diary of Thomas Crosfield*, ed. Boas, 56; Bodl. MS Jones 17, fo 308ᵛ; Laud, *Works* v. 57.

of his four Jacobean predecessors. *The History of his Chancellorship*, written by Laud
in the early 1640s during his enforced leisure as a prisoner in the Tower, testifies
to his involvement in routine academic affairs. The decision of Laud, from the outset, to require a weekly exchange of letters with his vice-chancellor ensured a constant flow of intelligence from his deputy and directives from himself. 'I trust by
your weekelie directions . . . never to bee without a sure and ready help' was the
reaction of one vice-chancellor.[89] The letters from his deputy provided the staple
diet of information, supplemented by letters from allies such as Peter Turner of
Merton or Brian Duppa of Christ Church, which enabled Laud to initiate change
and then monitor its effect.[90] Through such channels, Laud could proceed to build
his vision of a prosperous, privileged, and prestigious university, characterized by
academic discipline, political virtue, and protestant orthodoxy. It was to be constructed on the tripod of revised university statutes, a new charter, and the authority of metropolitical visitation.

The most important of these, upon which all else depended, was the reform of
the statutes. The inadequacies and ambiguities of the existing code, which Laud
described as 'broken, crossing and imperfect', had been demonstrated at the
Woodstock hearing of 1631 and prompted Charles to observe that the university
could not be well governed until the statutes were revised. This was a view that
Laud had long held: 'I did ever foresee that it was not possible to make a reformation, or settle that body, unless the statutes were first perfected.'[91] The revision
of the statutes, which had been periodically attempted but never completed since
Wolsey's day, took Laud a mere seven years from inception to final publication.
The task was initially entrusted to a group of fifteen delegates, but it was soon
found more convenient and expeditious to rely on a sub-delegacy of four members, the most prominent and industrious of whom were Richard Zouche, regius
professor of civil law, and Brian Twyne of Corpus Christi. In September 1633 convocation submitted the completed draft of the statutes to Laud for a final review,
and in July 1634 an amended version, newly published, was sent to the university.
These published statutes stood for a probationary year and, after further minor
changes, the Laudian code was finally promulgated in June 1636.[92] So from
September 1633 the perfecting of the statutes was taken out of the hands of the
university, and supervised by Laud at Lambeth, with the assistance of Peter Turner
of Merton. Laud himself admitted that he reserved to himself 'the last consideration of all' so there is good reason to accept Secretary Coke's simple statement, in
June 1636, that the compiler of the new university statutes was Laud. Certainly
Twyne was perturbed by the changes introduced in the first review of 1633–4, complaining of 'many innovations' that had crept in, and the substantial alterations to

[89] Laud, *Works* v. 13; Bodl. MS top. Oxon. b. 48, fo 35ʳ. Many of these letters are extracted in Laud,
Works v. *passim*.

[90] Laud, *Works* v. 49–50, 172, 212–13; *CSPD 1629–31*, 243; *CSPD 1637–8*, 316, 561–2, 601–2, 605.

[91] Laud, *Works* iii. 253, v. 14; Bodl. MS Jones 17, fo 303ᵛ.

[92] Wood, *History of the University* ii. 385–90; Laud, *Works* v. 14, 17–18, 83–4, 91–2, 101–3, 124–6. For
the text, see *Laudian Code*, ed. Griffiths.

his own preface. Nevertheless, he acknowledged that the Laudian code was 'alltogether and totally made up and grounded upon the old statutes of the universitie longe ago received'.[93]

It is also true that the statutes codified and clarified important changes in university life. First, the gradual extension of cancellarial authority over convocation and congregation during the previous century was formally recognized. The practice, since 1570, that the chancellor instead of convocation picked the vice-chancellor was given legal status; so too was his customary right to appoint principals of halls and the university's high steward. The rights of convocation had been further pared in 1628 when it lost the right to elect proctors; those of congregation were also reduced. After 1631 congregation could no longer accept appeals against the vice-chancellor; now in 1636 the choice of readers in grammar, rhetoric, logic, and metaphysics was removed from congregation and invested in the pair of colleges electing proctors each year. These moves reflected Laud's suspicion of congregation's capacity for disorderly conduct, and he urged his deputy to call fewer meetings. The statutes also vested extensive discretionary power in the chancellor and his deputy in the interests of peace and order. Since Elizabeth's reign the heads of house and the vice-chancellor had co-operated in monitoring university affairs and preparing the agenda for meetings of convocation, a process formalized in the royal statute of 1631 setting up hebdomadal council. The vice-chancellor was to meet the heads of colleges and halls every Monday, in and out of term, to discuss university business, an arrangement embodied as one of the *Statuta Carolina* of 1636. Though no formal records of the council survive for the 1630s, it is clear from Laud's *History*, as well as the comments of his critics, that it was an active body, working closely with the vice-chancellor, and capable of coordinating the enforcement of policy within the walls of colleges and halls. As a former head of house, Laud knew only too well that the observance of regulations on academic dress, student behaviour, and college tutoring depended on the active assistance of the heads.[94]

Many of the statutes, as Twyne had conceded, restated traditional requirements on discipline, teaching, and residence. A number of these regulations, such as those relating to academic dress, had already been revived following Laud's election as chancellor. Laud defended the enforcement of the gown and cap on the same grounds as that of ceremonies in the church: each was 'the hedge and the fence of those things which are of far greater consequence', each also a reminder of place and purpose. Thus for students, academic formalities were an encouragement to fulfil their task 'to grow in piety and good letters'. One celebrated change in teaching practice was the introduction of oral examinations in place of disputations as

---

[93] K. Sharpe, 'Archbishop Laud and the University of Oxford' in H. Lloyd-Jones, V. Pearl, and B. Worden (eds), *History and Imagination* (London 1980), 146–7; NUL MS Cl. c. 73; Bodl. MS Twyne 17, pp. 67–70, 72, 79.

[94] *The Collegiate University*, 401, 402–3; Bodl. MS Bodley 594, fos 140ʳ–45ᵛ; Laud, *Works* v. 25, 164 n. and *passim*. The proctors were added to hebdomadal council in 1634. For examples of its work, see PRO SP 16/385/26; Laud, *Works* v. 191–3.

the final hurdle for the arts degrees; this was introduced from Michaelmas term 1638 under the watchful eye of the vice-chancellor.[95]

A new charter was also required to confirm and amplify the university's privileges. Laud intended that this should express Oxford's status and importance, and match the rights secured by Cambridge in Henry VIII's reign. However, the king's willingness to issue such a charter seemed in doubt following the Woodstock hearing of 1631. It was reported that Charles I had questioned the existing privileges that the university enjoyed and threatened to recall their current charter, 'till he shall fynde you deserve them better and can tell how to use them in the advance and not the impayringe of government'. He was evidently dissuaded by Laud, and the relative peace of the university thereafter made Charles willing, in August 1635, to receive the petition for a fresh grant of rights. Less than a year later, in March 1636, a new charter was passed under the great seal, confirming the privileges of the university and enlarging its jurisdiction at the expense of the city. Felons' goods, for example, though awarded to the city in 1605, were now given to the university, which was also permitted for the first time to appoint two coroners. The predictable result was to provoke further disputes between town and gown.[96] The charter also included the letters patent of 1632 and 1633 which had given legal status to the university press in Oxford, by authorizing three printers to produce all kinds of books, including bibles. The charter of 1636 extended the privileges of the press still further. However, Laud's ambition to establish a Greek press at Oxford remained unfulfilled on his fall in 1640.[97]

Thus by the summer of 1636 new statutes regulated the internal affairs of Oxford, and a new charter defined its relations with external jurisdictions. There remained the matter of Oxford's role as a protestant seminary, which Laud wished to draw more closely into his orbit. At a hearing at Hampton Court on 21 June 1636 Charles upheld Laud's claim to visit both universities as metropolitan, an authority enshrined in letters patent issued the following January. Shortly afterwards Laud declared that he intended to begin with Cambridge. The fact that Laud never held a metropolitical visitation of either Oxford or Cambridge has obscured the importance of this project in his plans for university reform. The visitation would investigate religious not academic matters: 'I am to visit, as I conceive, the body of the university, and every scholar that is in it, for his obedience to the doctrine and discipline of the Church of England; and this is the extent I intend, and not to meddle with the statutes of colledges or university, or particular visitors of any colledge.' Since the majority of clergy received their education at the two universities, it was essential for Laud to ensure that they were not contaminated by false teaching and puritan practices, which would ultimately undermine order and

---

[95] Bodl. MS Twyne 17, p. 79; Laud, *Works* ii, p. xvi, v. 16 and 17 note a, 19, 200, 204, 207.

[96] Laud, *Works* iii. 254; PRO SP 16/198/64; Gibson, 'The great charter of Charles I', 73–94, 121–32; *VCH Oxon.* iv. 156–7, 170, 173; *CSPD 1635–6*, 168. Additionally, the Laudian statutes stated that the custody of the city, granted to the citizens in 1612, was to be shared between city and university: *VCH Oxon.* iv. 156–7.

[97] Laud, *Works* iii. 254, v. 79–81, 159–62.

discipline in the wider church. Indeed, when at the royal hearing counsel for Cambridge University alleged that Laud's claim amounted to erecting a concurrent jurisdiction with that of the king, Laud retorted that he wished only to curb sedition, an answer which more than satisfied Charles and effectively silenced his critics.[98]

Two questions, however, arise in this context. Why did Laud intend to visit Cambridge first, and why did no metropolitical visitation of either university take place? Laud was convinced that the case for religious reform was more pressing at Cambridge, whose chancellor, the earl of Holland, had little enthusiasm for Laudian ideals. In September 1636 Laud had received a dossier of evidence, probably compiled by John Cosin, of puritan nonconformity and 'common disorders' within the university.[99] At Oxford, by contrast, the need to correct religious disorders was less urgent in view of Laud's supervision of university affairs since 1630. As we shall see, conformity within the colleges could be pursued through the hebdomadal council and the authority of college visitors. Under the letters patent, more than one visitation to either university needed explicit royal sanction, so in Oxford's case Laud may well have been prepared to bide his time.

In a report to the king in January 1640 Laud wrote how he had intended to visit Cambridge, 'from performance of which duty, I have been bold heretofore to acquaint your majesty what hath hindered me'. Laud probably was referring here to the Scottish crisis behind which he saw an attempt by covenanters and English puritans to engineer his downfall. To proceed with an examination of Cambridge nonconformity in the midst of this would provoke further hostility towards him. What clinches this interpretation is the remark by Laud at his trial that in about 1637–8 'my troubles began then to be foreseen by me, and I visited them not'.[100]

The royal visit to Oxford in August 1636 has rightly been regarded as the apogee of Laud's chancellorship. The revised statutes were in place, a new charter secured, and the metropolitical right to visit both universities confirmed. Many Oxford chapels had been refurbished and the new Canterbury quadrangle at St John's was complete. Careful preparations and drilling ensured that the entertainment of the royal party proceeded smoothly as the university displayed that order and respect for authority that Charles I so prized. Indeed, on his entry to Oxford, the graduates lined both sides of the road, wearing academic dress to distinguish their degrees and show their conformity with the statutes, and standing in uncharacteristic silence, not, as Wood's *History* implies, from sullenness but from fear of breaking ranks.[101] The royal occasion indicates that in externals at least Laud had already stamped his ideals on the university. We may inquire, however, into the extent to

---

[98] PRO SP 16/345/39; John Rushworth, *Historical Collections* (8 vols London 1659–1701) ii. 324–32; NUL MS Cl. c. 73; Laud, *Works* v. 576, vii. 335.

[99] Cooper, *Annals of Cambridge*, iii. 279–83.

[100] Laud, *Works* iii. 230, iv. 193, v. 366. The second of these references I owe to Peter Yorke.

[101] Trevor-Roper, *Archbishop Laud*, 287–94; Sharpe, 'University of Oxford', 150–2; contrast Wood, *History of the University* ii. 408, with the account by Francis Cheynell in NUL MS Cl. c. 84a.

which they were disseminated throughout the university in its routine academic and religious life.

It has been argued that the ideal of a docile and disciplined university remained a pipe-dream. The attempt of Laud to enforce the full letter of the statutes was undermined by his dependence on university officers and heads of house whose loyalties, priorities, and private interests did not always dovetail with his agenda. So we find Laud criticizing the indolence of the proctors, accusing Vice-Chancellor Baylie of negligence, and fearing slack supervision within college walls. Samuel Fell, dean of Christ Church and a Laudian supporter, was rebuked in 1639 for conduct 'most unlike a man that understands government', while Laud's visitors to Merton in 1638 exposed widespread corruption and illegal practices under Warden Brent.[102] Such evidence warns against confusing statutory achievement with its punctilious observance.

The chief difficulty facing Laud was in supervising a collegiate structure relatively impervious to instant reform. However, we should acknowledge that it could be addressed more gradually through his influence over the selection of new heads. At Balliol, for example, the reform of the college had to await the appointment of a new master, Thomas Lawrence, in 1637.[103] Moreover, the visitorial system gave Laud an additional lever of control over the internal affairs of colleges. By 1637 Laud himself or a close ally was visitor of every Oxford college bar one. As archbishop, Laud was visitor of All Souls and Merton and, with the suspension of Williams of Lincoln, also visitor of Balliol, Oriel, Lincoln, and Brasenose; as chancellor Laud was visitor of University, Jesus, and Pembroke. His close colleague Curle of Winchester visited New, Magdalen, Corpus, Trinity, and St John's, his former patron Neile of York was visitor of Queen's, and his zealous subordinate Piers of Bath and Wells visited Wadham. The visitor of Christ Church was Charles I. Only Exeter, governed by John Prideaux and visited by Bishop Joseph Hall, was not already in Laud's pocket. At Queen's and Magdalen, as we shall see, the visitors prodded the fellowship into observing the new ceremonialism in chapel, while at Wadham in 1633 Bishop Piers conducted a thorough visitation of college discipline and issued a series of injunctions.[104]

Nor should the criticism that Laud directed at his subordinates conceal the swift and discernible impression he made on university discipline after his election as chancellor. Thomas Crosfield's diary makes it clear that the keen wind of reform was quickly felt: Provost Potter enforced proper academic dress in Queen's, and within the university old statutes were again observed and dispensations no longer granted. John Howson, visiting Oxford in November 1631, complimented Laud on the 'new reformation of my mother this worthy universitie'. At the other end of the decade, a letter from Brasenose in November 1638 reports the fears amongst the fellows that Laud's moves against beneficed academics would cost them their

---

[102] Sharpe, 'University of Oxford', 146–64; Laud, *Works* v. 224.
[103] *The Diary of John Evelyn*, ed. E. S. De Beer (6 vols Oxford 1955) ii. 18.
[104] See pp. 206–7 below; WCM 2/1, fos 61–7.

fellowships or their livings.[105] Here, at least, the chancellor's effectiveness was readily conceded.

For benefactions, as for discipline, Laud made his mark in Oxford during the 1630s. He augmented the income of the chair of Hebrew, founded a lectureship in Arabic, donated coins, books, and over a thousand manuscripts to the Bodleian, and chivvied Charles I into endowing three fellowships, at Exeter, Jesus, and Pembroke, for natives of Guernsey and Jersey 'that they may be the better informed of the doctrine and discipline of the Church of England'.[106] The 1630s was a decade of college building, as Laud noted with satisfaction in his *History*, the most magnificent of which was his own quadrangle at St John's. The university's internal reformation and international standing should, he felt, be mirrored in its external appearance, just as contemporary improvements to London and St Paul's cathedral were inspired by its metropolitan status.[107] Standing on the leads of the Bodleian in 1629, Charles I proposed the creation of a *piazza literaria* by clearing the houses between the library and the university church. A subsequent survey established that the cost would be over £1,500, prohibitive enough for the project to be shelved, though not forgotten, by Laud.[108]

Refurbishment of college chapels accompanied college building. Many choirs were repaved with black and white marble, rails erected to protect altars and carpets provided to adorn them, while pictures and new stained glass added colour and richness. A visitor in 1636 favourably compared Oxford glass to that at Windsor, Canterbury, and St Paul's. He was particularly impressed by Lincoln chapel, financed by Laud's enemy Bishop Williams, a reminder that beautification was no Laudian monopoly. Nevertheless, many of these alterations were carried out at the behest of Laud and his lieutenants—Frewen at Magdalen, Jackson at Corpus, and Potter at Queen's.[109]

New emphasis was now placed on reverent behaviour at divine service. Laud encouraged the canonical requirement of bowing at the name of Jesus, and the non-canonical practice of bowing to the altar. No doubt, as visitor, Laud was the inspiration for Warden Brent's order of 1637 that in future members of Merton should bow to the east on entering and leaving chapel. Laud's allies, Neile of York and Curle of Winchester, visitors respectively of Queen's and Magdalen College, required similarly devout conduct in chapel. At Queen's the fellowship were to wear the surplice, stand at the creed and gospel, and bow at the name of Jesus and to the altar, while at Magdalen Curle praised the redecoration of the chapel, but

[105] *Diary of Thomas Crosfield*, ed. Boas, 43–5, 48–50, 52; *The Correspondence of John Cosin*, ed. G. Ornsby (2 vols Surtees Soc. lii, lv, 1868–72) i. 209; BNCA B2 a 38, p. 50.

[106] Trevor-Roper, *Archbishop Laud*, 113, 273–7, 281–2; Laud, *Works* iii. 233, v. 19, 23; *CSPD 1631–3*, 368; A. J. Eagleston, *The Channel Islands under Tudor Government, 1485–1642* (Cambridge 1949), 142.

[107] Laud, *Works* v. 99, 115, 123, 143, 174. One notable omission from this record was Oriel, whose main quadrangle had been rebuilt by November 1638: BNCA B2 a 38, p. 52.

[108] *CSPD 1629–31*, 46–7, 50, 58; Laud, *Works* iii. 254. The original idea seems to have come from Secretary Dorchester.

[109] Laud, *Works* v. 62, 84, 115, 143; Fowler, *Corpus*, 358–9; MCR *Registrum 1567–1731*, p. 327; A. J. Taylor, 'The royal visit to Oxford in 1636', *Oxoniensia* i (1936), 153.

added it must be matched by 'an uniforme reverence in all parts of divine worship and service, according to the canonicall injunctions of our Church and the commendable and imitable practise of his majestie's chapell, that so God may be worshipped, not only in holinesse, but in the beauty of holinesse'.[110]

The religious temper of the university was changing. Neglected rites, ceremonies, and offices—such as confirmation—were now enforced.[111] Open discussion of predestination had been forbidden under the royal declaration of 1628. Three years later, at the Woodstock hearing, Charles ordered that his prohibition be re-read in every college and hall. He also insisted that it be applied to critics as well as supporters of Calvinism, and said that he had heard ('which I do not believe') that at Oxford his declaration was only enforced against Calvinists, and challenged Provost Potter of Queen's that he had preached against Calvinists and had not been censured. He was assured by Potter and Laud that this was incorrect, since Potter had not preached in the university since the declaration had appeared.[112] Indeed, even before this hearing, Laud had proceeded against Tooker of Oriel for attacking the five points of Dort, and amongst those convented between 1631 and 1640 for contravening the declaration were offenders on both sides. Laud was also prudent enough to warn the anti-Calvinist Thomas Lawrence, on his appointment as Lady Margaret professor of divinity in 1637, to avoid provocation and 'be very mindful of the waspishness of these times'. For all this, allegation of partiality against Calvinists persisted, resurfacing for example in a university sermon of 1634. This reflected the fact that though no formal treatises were published against Calvinist teaching on predestination, there was plenty of sniping against it in the Oxford press and pulpit.[113]

Defences of ritualism and attacks on evangelical piety formed the content of many visitation sermons and theological tracts by country ministers in the 1630s, which can be paralleled by Oxford preaching. Ned Harley, son of the godly Sir Robert, and a student at Magdalen Hall in the late 1630s, complained that he had 'not the word of God preached ... in a right manner'.[114] A good example of the sort of divinity which discomforted Harley is the sermon preached before Charles I in Christ Church on 30 August 1636. The preacher, Thomas Browne, took as his text 'Benedictus rex qui venit in nomine domini. Gloria in excelsis.' After establishing that kingship had divine sanction, Browne moved on to castigate

---

[110] Laud, *Works* v. 39, 204–7; MCR *Registrum 1567–1731*, p. 327; *Diary of Thomas Crosfield*, ed. Boas, 74; MCA MS 730(a), fo 91^r, printed in Bloxam, *Reg. Magdalen* ii, p. xcv.

[111] *Diary of John Evelyn*, ed. De Beer ii. 23.   [112] Bodl. MS Jones 17, fos 303, 309^v.

[113] Laud, *Works* v. 15–16, 186; Wood, *History of the University* ii. 382, 385, 395, 415–16, 422–3. Laud himself restrained the anti-Calvinist Thomas Jackson from printing his sermons in 1640, for 'no man should presume to print any thing there which might break the rule given in his majesty's declaration one way or another', but it is significant that he intended 'some delay' in their publication rather than their total suppression (Laud, *Works* v. 268); for anti-Calvinist comments, see Tyacke, *Anti-Calvinists*, 83–4.

[114] P. Lake, 'The Laudian style' in Fincham (ed.), *The Early Stuart Church*, 161–85; J. Eales, *Puritans and Roundheads: the Harleys of Brampton Bryan and the outbreak of the English civil war* (Cambridge 1990), 66.

contemporary errors: 'Some exalt God thorowe no organ but the nose, some are all for *pax* but they will have no *gloria*, no altars or images, no kings or bishops; others are for *gloria*, but it is *gloria in profundis* not *excelsis*, they who say God is glorifyed by the damned in Hell.' Browne's intention was to assimilate puritan scruples over ceremonies with the threat of Presbyterian democracy and Calvinist teaching on reprobation into a catalogue of false teaching which had no place in a bastion of orthodoxy such as Oxford. A hostile observer admitted that 'the sermon was commended by diverse'; Laud regarded it as 'excellent' and shortly afterwards appointed Browne as one of his chaplains.[115]

Religious divisions also permeated the distribution of university patronage as the number of patrons and the range of their theological interests contracted. While external pressures continued to be felt, the wishes of the chancellor were now usually decisive—a marked change from the position in James I's reign. College statutes of course continued to be flouted: at Magdalen in 1630 a signet letter from the king, who was acting on the wishes of the earl of Bristol, secured a fellowship for a commoner rather than a demy, for whom they were reserved. It is significant that the request was made after Laud's consent had been secured. In 1635 Laud used his visitorial authority to intrude a Cambridge man into All Souls, in breach of the statutes. His nominee was Jeremy Taylor, which, as Hugh Trevor-Roper has observed, 'shows the conscientious purposes for which he exercised these questionable powers'.[116] As part of the renovation of conciliar government in the late 1620s, grants were usually stayed at the signet until the chief office-holder of the relevant institution had been consulted. Thus the chancellors of both universities evidently vetted recommendations through the signet for fellowships and scholarships; but at Oxford, in contrast to Cambridge, very few mandates under the signet were issued after 1633, and none after 1637.[117] This suggests that university patronage was firmly under Laud's thumb and that the king was willing to follow his advice. The blunt instrument of a royal command was no longer necessary. Almost all the new heads of house after 1630 were Laudian protégés or willing supporters: Jackson at Corpus (1631), Walker at University (1632), Baylie at St John's (1633), Sheldon at All Souls (1635), Lawrence at Balliol (1637), Fell at Christ Church (1638), and probably also Mansell at Jesus (1630).[118] In addition, Walker and Baylie were Laud's kinsmen.[119] Similarly, those who served Laud well received ecclesiastical preferment outside the university. Bishoprics went to his 'ancient friend' Bancroft, his confidant Juxon, and his ally Duppa;[120] while deaneries were con-

---

[115] NUL MS Cl. c. 84a; Laud, *Works* v. 150.

[116] MCA CS/40/2/1–3; Trevor-Roper, *Archbishop Laud*, 280–1; ASA Martin, *All Souls College*, nos 174–7, pp. 315–16.

[117] Morgan, 'Country, court and Cambridge', 486–8; PRO SO 3/10–12. It is worth emphasizing how gradual this development was: in the autumn of 1630 a royal letter was dispatched to New College, without the knowledge of Laud but, after consultation with him, a revised version was sent under the signet: SO 1/2, p. 3; Laud, *Works* vi. 290.

[118] The one exception is Daniel Escott, the obscure warden of Wadham (1635–44).

[119] For Laud's links with Baylie and Walker, see Laud's will, in Bodl. MS Add. c. 304b, fo 25ʳ.

[120] Laud, *Works* iii. 215–16, v. 155.

ferred on Potter of Queen's, Frewen of Magdalen, Jackson of Corpus, and Baylie of St John's. Entries in the signet office books indicate that Laud was associated with nearly all these promotions.[121]

This patronage discriminated between Laudian enthusiasts and those who waited for better times. Its partisan character was quite evident to contemporaries. A skit circulating in the university in 1636 proposed appropriate names for ships financed by different colleges. St John's was the Triumph or Speed-Well, All Souls under Sheldon the Hope-Well and Christ Church, where Dean Duppa was Prince Charles's tutor, the Prince Royal. The heads of all three were staunch Laudians. Queen's ship was the Convert, a reference to Provost Potter's adoption of the anti-Calvinist cause, while Merton was the Rainbow, since amongst its fellowship were Laudian partisans such as Peter Turner and critics such as Francis Cheynell. Others were less favoured. Exeter was the Repulse since its rector, John Prideaux, would fail if he bid for a bishopric, while Brasenose was the Despair, since they were 'a college of anti-Arminians' with no hopes of preferment. Magdalen Hall, under John Wilkinson, was the Reformation, New Inn Hall under Christopher Rogers, the Whelp of the Reformation, comparisons which Laud, who saw the skit, particularly liked.[122] Such a satire pinpoints the discomfort of several Calvinist heads with Laudian rule in Oxford. Wilkinson was censured for his part in the preaching campaign of 1631, while Rogers suffered suspension from a city benefice for refusing to read the Book of Sports.[123]

For John Prideaux, a head of house, regius professor of divinity, and the chief spokesman for Oxford Calvinists, the 1630s were an especially uncomfortable decade. In both 1631 and 1633 he was before Charles I at Woodstock to account for his behaviour—on the first occasion, for supporting the appeal of Ford and Thorne against the vice-chancellor during the preaching controversies, and two years later for allegedly limiting the authority of the church in a confrontation at the Act with Peter Heylyn. The latter became Charles I's principal religious polemicist and delighted in embarrassing Prideaux. Another enemy was Thomas Lawrence, who was accused by Prideaux of favouring popery at the Act of 1629 and who became Lady Margaret professor of divinity in 1637.[124] It is no wonder that Prideaux complained that his support for the doctrine and discipline of the church went unrecognized and his students were 'countenanced in my declining age to vilify and vex me'. He was also passed over for the post of vice-chancellor and, it seems, was not selected as a pro-vice-chancellor, despite possessing

---

[121] PRO SO 3/10 (July 1631, April 1632, July 1633), 3/11 (April and December 1635, May and October 1638). Two of these seven promotions do not record Laud's involvement—namely Frewen's preferment to Gloucester deanery in 1631, procured by Secretary Dorchester, and Juxon's elevation to the bishopric of Hereford in 1633, signified and procured by Secretary Windebanke.

[122] NUL MS Cl. c. 84b. For Potter's 'conversion', see Tyacke, Anti-Calvinists, 79–82.

[123] Laud, Works v. 56; BL Add. MS 35,331, fo 56ᵛ; Diary of Thomas Crosfield, ed. Boas, 68.

[124] Laud, Works v. 56, 87–91; Peter Heylyn, Examen historicum (London 1659), sig. P2ᵛ, P3ʳ; LPL MS 943, p. 133. For Prideaux's role in licensing Chillingworth's The Religion of Protestants, at the behest of Laud, see Tyacke, 'Religious Controversy', pp. 588–9 below.

immense experience of university government, having served as vice-chancellor on four occasions between 1619 and 1626.[125] Prideaux vented his frustration in a number of ways. In convocation he opposed the fulsome tones adopted by the university in its correspondence with Laud, and criticized the decision to grant Robert Skinner, another anti-Calvinist, his DD without exercises or charges at the request of Laud; while in a court sermon of December 1634, he publicly rebuked Laud for failing to curb 'the great increase of papists within these late yeares'.[126]

Another malcontent was Francis Cheynell, fellow of Merton, whose letters reveal his distrust of official policy. William Strode, the public orator, addressed Charles I in 1636 as 'homo-deus', which Cheynell regarded as close to blasphemy. Cheynell also claimed that Laudians were as puritan as any for going beyond the canons with such ceremonies as bowing to the altar, and was deeply offended by the sermon Browne had preached before Charles I. Cheynell also ran into trouble for condemning the doctrine that heathens might be saved 'by conforminge their lives to the light of nature'.[127] Yet, like his senior colleague Prideaux, Cheynell could do little. Until the end of the personal rule, religious opposition in Oxford persisted, but it was ineffectual. As with much tacit disquiet during the 1630s, we should not mistake impotence for indifference.

Laud's chancellorship made a decisive impression on academic life and religious practice at Oxford. Calvinist opponents were muzzled and marginalized, a remarkable transformation from the position under James I. Thomas Triplet commented on this change in a letter to Laud in 1640. He recalled the days when 'puritanism' was 'the way to rise' and only Laud, Howson, and two or three others in the university opposed it.[128] That the tables had been turned was not just the achievement of Laud, of course, but his chancellorship consolidated the triumph of like-minded university men. His rule also intensified long-term trends evident in the reigns of both Elizabeth and James: greater outside control of religious teaching, more stringent demands for conformity, and the refinement of oligarchic government within the university. Laud's work in erecting a new brand of political and religious uniformity also contributed to the university's royalism in the 1640s, led by many Laudian appointees and graduates. Both the ideology and the men were to reappear forcibly at the Restoration.

---

[125] Laud, *Works* v. 90. Lists of pro-vice-chancellors exist for 1634–5 and 1636–41, and Prideaux's name is not among them: OUA register R, fos 94ʳ, 130ʳ, 150ʳ, 157ʳ, 167ᵛ, 180ʳ.
[126] NUL MS Cl. c. 73; OUA register R fo 131ᵛ; Bodl. MS top. Oxon. c. 378, p. 278, MS Carte 77, fo 388ᵛ.
[127] NUL Cl. c. 75, 84a; Laud, *Works* v. 205; see pp. 207–8 above. For Strode's language, see *CSPD 1640–1*, 253.
[128] *CSPD 1639–40*, 518–19.

5

The Humanities

MORDECHAI FEINGOLD

HISTORIANS, even those specializing in the history of higher education, have traditionally been reluctant to undertake an exhaustive study of the curriculum at Oxford and Cambridge. 'There should be too much wearisome detail to indicate the chief studies at Oxford', wrote Charles Mallet, in 1924, to justify his perfunctory treatment of the university curriculum. Nor did this rationale for neglect change much over the past century. Far more appealing was the concern with the religious and political culture at Oxford and Cambridge, its roots in the larger national setting and the varieties of its local manifestations. As for the institutional histories of the universities, they almost always tended to be prosopographical studies of heads of house and famous alumni, the assumption being that 'the chief interest ... of an educational institution must always lie in the sons whom ... it has given to serve ... in church and state'. What was generally true of historians of education was invariably true of other scholars, most particularly biographers. The possible course of studies followed by whatever 'great minds' these scholars set out to reconstruct was invariably ignored, either because it was believed to be inaccessible, due to lack of evidence, or inconsequential, owing to lack of bearing on later pursuits. To all these charges and their underlying assumptions it is still worthwhile quoting the virtually lone voice of Costello: 'The history of a curriculum may be dull in comparison with the detailing of events in the forum or in the field, but these events, from the Middle Ages on, are largely shaped by men who have themselves been formed in the microcosm of the university.'[1]

The following account seeks to dispel the impressionistic, often prejudiced, perceptions that have passed for evidence and in their place lay the groundwork for a measured study of the intellectual character of early modern Oxford. The

I have incurred many debts in the course of writing chapters 5, 6, and 7. Roger Ariew, Jeanny Ashworth, Peter Barker, Laurence Brockliss, Larry Green, Marjorie Grene, John Harwood, Michael Hunter, Lisa Jardine, James McConica, Gerald Toomer, Nicholas Wickenden, Dan Woolf, and Perez Zagorin all have read earlier drafts or shared with me their knowledge. I am grateful for the assistance of Valerie Jobling, Helen Powell, and Ruth Vyse, as well as to the library staff at the Bodleian Library, Brasenose College, Christ Church, and New College. Above all, I owe a special debt to Nicholas Tyacke who was unwavering in his patience and support.

[1] C. E. Mallett, *A History of the University of Oxford* (3 vols London 1924–7) i, p. x; D. Macleane, *A History of Pembroke College, Oxford* (OHS xxxiii 1897), p. vii; M. Feingold, 'Oxford and Cambridge histories: an outdated genre?', *History of Universities* i (1981), 207–12; W. T. Costello, *The Scholastic Curriculum at Early Seventeenth Century Cambridge* (Cambridge Mass. 1958), 2.

undergraduate curriculum will be the focus of this re-evaluation for two reasons. First it was shared by all students, irrespective of social background or length of stay. (As will be shown later, more advanced studies were carried on independently—and not necessarily at university—and in any case were intended to elaborate upon a shared general education.) Second, and even more importantly, the elementary course of study at Oxford (and Cambridge) has been the one most neglected. As Stone noted two decades ago, 'very little is known about either the contents and significance of the curriculum or the quality of the teaching provided'.[2] Since then such scholars as Charles Schmitt, James McConica, and John Gascoigne have indeed extended the pioneering, if somewhat contradictory, work of William Costello and Mark Curtis, and thereby shed additional light on the subject.[3] What follows, however, by demonstrating the dynamic nature of the Oxford curriculum in the seventeenth century and its far-reaching consequences for the tens of thousands of Englishmen educated there, aims to further advance our understanding.

Rather than attempting an exhaustive study, I have tried to offer an interpretation of the various ideals that animated the programme of study and their implementation. For obvious reasons, most of the illustrations are taken from Oxford sources, though occasionally the experience of Cambridge students has been cited—either because it better illuminated a particular issue or because an Oxford counterpart was lacking. Here one should note, in passing, the essential harmony of the undergraduate curriculum at both institutions, as evidenced by student notebooks and library catalogues. In the words of the Oxonian Nicholas Fitzherbert (m. 1572), Oxford 'so resembles Cambridge in the method of instruction that the two universities may reasonably be rivals'.[4]

The most pervasive misconception concerning the seventeenth-century curriculum is that it survived and flourished as a relic of medieval scholasticism. This tenacious body of thought, claimed Costello, 'retained three distinguishing marks: it was dialectical, Aristotelian, and highly systematized'. Moreover, so the argument continued, the construct proved impervious to new ideas:

The fault of scholasticism lay not in its building so towering a skyscraper, complete to the last bit of wiring and plumbing, but in its failure during the fifteenth, sixteenth, and early seventeenth centuries to produce teachers who could maintain the structure as a totality and forbear tinkering with the details. Instead of busying themselves in absorbing new evidence,

[2] L. Stone, 'The size and composition of the Oxford student body 1580–1910' in L. Stone (ed.), *The University in Society*, (2 vols Princeton 1974) i. 3. See also J. Twigg, 'Evolution, obstacles and aims: the writing of Oxford and Cambridge college histories', *History of Universities* viii (1989), 187.

[3] C. B. Schmitt, *John Case and Aristotelianism in Renaissance England* (Kingston and Montreal 1983); C. B. Schmitt, *The Aristotelian Tradition and Renaissance Universities* (London 1984); J. McConica, 'Humanism and Aristotle in Tudor Oxford', *EHR* xciv (1979), 291–317; J. McConica, 'Elizabethan Oxford: the collegiate society' in *The Collegiate University*, 645–732; J. Gascoigne, 'The universities and the scientific revolution: the case of Newton and Restoration Cambridge', *History of Science* xxiii (1985), 391–434; J. Gascoigne, *Cambridge in the Age of the Enlightenment* (Cambridge 1989).

[4] *Nicolai Fierberti oxoniensis . . . academiae descriptio* (Rome 1602, repr. OHS viii 1887), cited in Costello, *The Scholastic Curriculum*, 2.

in re-explaining old findings, and in thinking out a larger synthesis, which could embrace the discoveries of the new learning and harmonize it all with Aristotelian physics and, where necessary, with theology, the scholastics tragically entangled themselves in splicing wires and complicating circuits within the building. As a consequence, the seventeenth century mind was heir to a system so oversystematized that its only escape was either to attempt a new synthesis by incorporating the new discoveries, to give up the struggle, or to branch off in a new direction.

And as the third alternative eventually proved triumphant, the universities, clinging to an outmoded edifice, lost out.[5]

The above picture is predicated on a conception of the structure of higher learning seen exclusively in terms of the new modes of thought that originated in the seventeenth century. It postulates the curriculum to be philosophical in character and therefore a model that both compares with and offers a direct contrast to the competing philosophies of Bacon, Descartes, Locke, and Newton. This characterization of the Oxford and Cambridge curricula in the seventeenth century, however, is unfounded. It assumes that the chief studies at both universities were logic, physics, and metaphysics, and that the authors studied in the process were principally those indigestible commentators on the works of Aristotle. But in fact the curriculum was quintessentially humanistic in nature, though far more irenic and ecumenical than that envisaged by its Italian progenitors. McConica drew the broad lines of this expansive humanistic culture of learning when he described John Rainolds, president of Corpus Christi College:

Rainolds's mental world exactly demonstrated the flowering of the Oxford schools under Elizabeth: catholic and eclectic, sensitive to the whole of the tradition of learning in the past including the medieval achievement, widely read in contemporary continental thought, yet staunchly protestant and if anything Calvinist. It rested on the foundation erected by Fox and Wolsey, an erudite humanism in which the counsels of antiquity were dominated by the doctrines of Cicero and Quintilian on the formation of the wise and virtuous man who would strive for the common good, and by the scriptural and patristic learning that looked to Augustine's *De doctrina christiana* as its fountainhead.[6]

Of all the factors that contributed to the misinterpretation of the curriculum the most obvious, and most detrimental, have been the university statutes. The *Nova statuta* of 1564–5 were vague in the extreme when it came to delineating the order of studies. They simply stipulated that the undergraduate devote three terms to the study of arithmetic, two to music, four to rhetoric, two to grammar, and five to dialectic. Historians, therefore, have sought to gain guidance from the 1570 Cambridge statutes which, though brief, indicated a timetable: 'the first year shall teach rhetoric, the second and third logic, the fourth shall add philosophy.' The curricular requirements of the Laudian statutes seem to have introduced little change. Rhetoric was prescribed for the first year, dialectic for the second and third

---

[5] Costello, *The Scholastic Curriculum*, 8, 10–11. See also C. Hill, *Intellectual Origins of the English Revolution* (Oxford 1965), *passim*.

[6] McConica, 'Elizabethan Oxford', 713–14.

years, and moral philosophy—along with Greek and arithmetic—was studied by students in their third and fourth years.[7] This brief description of the prescribed course, taken on its own, might merit the oft-applied adjective 'trite', and the added prominence with which Aristotle figured in the statutes further substantiate the initial poor impression.

A fuller discussion of the actual position of Aristotle in the curriculum will be offered below. Here it is necessary to address a related confusion concerning the nature of the curriculum—the tendency to interpret common seventeenth-century abbreviations of the curriculum as descriptive of the actual content of the whole course. Anthony Wood related that when Walter Charleton arrived at Magdalen Hall in 1635 he 'was put under the tuition of Mr. John Wilkins ... by whose instruction he profited much beyond his years, in logic and philosophy'. But Wood did not intend to claim that Charleton was exposed only to Aristotelian logic and philosophy.[8] Such terms were simply current shorthand for the entire corpus of studies, corresponding to the binary division of all disciplines into arts and sciences. Robert Sanderson (MA 1607), for example, clustered the arts of discourse (grammar, rhetoric, and logic) under the rubric 'instrumental disciplines', while 'philosophy' (*scientia*) incorporated the remaining branches of learning with a further subdivision into the 'contemplative disciplines' (the mathematical sciences, physics, and metaphysics), and the 'active disciplines' of ethics, economics, and politics. An analogous classification was presented by the tutor John Cole. Corresponding with Sanderson's 'instrumental disciplines' (the arts), were the 'directive' subjects: they 'do not inform the intellect ... but "prepare its operation" and direct it according to certain norms'. The sciences, studies pertaining to knowledge, are 'objective'. They 'treat of things as we find them in nature, in so far as these things are the objects of the understanding'. The latter included not only philosophy—consisting of the mathematical sciences, physics, ethics, and metaphysics—but the three higher faculties as well.[9] It was common usage, then, to compress the multi-dimensional character of the course into a compact formula that intuitively evoked the two divisions of learning. But before elaborating on the encyclopedic composition of the curriculum we must backtrack somewhat and reiterate the humanistic character of the course.

While the statutes offer an insufficient indication of the centrality of classical languages and literature to the curriculum, the wording and content of the various manuals of advice leave little room for doubt. Richard Holdsworth, the noted Cambridge tutor and divine, plainly and emphatically presented the affinity of the classics to other disciplines. He defended the study of Greek and Latin authors as

---

[7] *SA* 390; G. Dryer, *The Privileges of the University of Cambridge* (2 vols London 1824) i. 164; *Statutes*, trans. Ward i. 21–2. Neither the *Nova statuta* nor the Laudian statutes included natural philosophy or astronomy in the undergraduate curriculum.

[8] Wood, *Athenae* iv. 752.

[9] Robert Sanderson, *Physicae scientiae compendium* (Oxford 1671), 1–2; BL MS Lansdowne 797, fo 2, cited in Costello *The Scholastic Curriculum*, 37–8. Costello was unable to establish the identity of Cole; several individuals with this name were students at both Oxford and Cambridge.

that 'without which all the other learning though never so eminent, is in a manner voide and useless; without those you will be bafeld in your disputes, disgraced and vilified in publicke examinations, laught at in speeches and declamations. You will never dare to appear in any act of credit in the university . . . The necessity of this studie above the rest is the cause that it is to be continued through all the four yeares in the after noons, wheras other studies have each a parcel of your time alotted to them.'[10] Other authors of students' guides took a similar line, privileging language and literature not only by singling them out for continuous and uninterrupted study, but by underscoring the pertinence of philological and literary concerns in the study of philosophy as well. Thus the students were instructed to read Aristotle (or Plato) in Greek and, in general, also encouraged to consider the style of those works they studied for content.[11]

Indeed, the Laudian statutes themselves made clear that the ultimate purpose of both the BA and MA courses was to ensure, above all, the acquisition of a mastery of language and literature. The stipulations governing the examinations of candidates of both degrees were unambiguous:

In order that the learning and progress in polite letters of all persons taking degrees in arts be more fully ascertained by the congregation of regents . . . it is enacted that every person, before his admission to supplicate for a grace, shall undergo an examination.

The examination is not to be on philosophical subjects merely, to which limits the narrow learning of the last age was confined, but also matters of philology; and a principal object of inquiry with the examiners will be what facility the several persons have of expressing their thoughts in Latin; for it is our will that no persons shall be admitted to the bachelorship of arts but those who can with consistency and readiness, and still less to the master's degree . . . but those who can with suitableness and aptitude express their thoughts in Latin on matters of daily occurrence.

The possession of such skills was to be demonstrated through *ex tempore* rendering into Latin of 'dialogues or familiar conversations written in English'.[12] Many other exercises, including at least some of the disputations, were also transformed into literary occasions, thereby revealing even further the humanistic character of the curriculum.

By the turn of the seventeenth century the undergraduate curriculum had become the staple offering of Oxford. Statutory prescriptions notwithstanding, it was during this period that the students received their grounding in the entire arts and sciences curriculum. Several factors contributed to this unofficial compression of the course. First the momentous transformation that took place in the grammar schools—which now produced scholars exceptionally well grounded in the

---

[10] Quoted in H. F. Fletcher, *The Intellectual Development of John Milton* (2 vols Urbana Ill. 1956–61) ii. 637.

[11] As Holdsworth put it, 'the reading of Aristotle will not only conduce much to your study of controversy, being read with a commentator, but allso help you in Greeke and indeed crown all your other learning, for he can hardly deserve the name of a scholar that is not in some measure acquainted with his works'. Fletcher, *The Intellectual Development of John Milton* ii. 643.

[12] *Statutes*, trans. Ward i. 65–7.

language and literature of Greece and Rome, and not infrequently in logic and rhetoric as well—diminished considerably the need for university teachers to inculcate incoming undergraduates with the rudiments of learning. In addition, the printing revolution rendered the time-consuming and tedious ancient practice of 'reading' obsolete, as inexpensive editions of textbooks could now be got by even poor students. Thirdly, a surge in the number of upper-class students who did not intend to graduate, let alone continue with the MA course, compelled educators to squeeze all instruction within the compass of the undergraduate course. And though this compression cannot be viewed as making the undergraduate course 'an end to itself', still it became a self-contained entity, common to all, and the strongest evidence against the argument that the vast majority of those who did not graduate were deprived of basic instruction in key areas.

Obviously educators were not deluded into believing that such a brisk survey would ensure mastery of all subjects or that all students were equally able to keep up the pace. Nor were they recommending a superficial grasp of learning. All they intended was to present a panorama of all knowledge, rooted in the interconnectedness of its various constituents, and thereby lay a solid foundation upon which the student could proceed to build, independently, for years to come. John Grandorge (MA 1692) prefaced his manual of student advice with a clarification: 'wherein are sett before him several of the most useful books in every particular art or science; which if they cannot all be read within the space of four years, must be pursued after the taking of his first degree, and before he can expect to take the degree of master of arts'. The Cantabrigian Daniel Waterland made a similar point:

I do not expect one and the same task should serve for all capacities: some may be able to do more, others less, than I have prescribed ... The former may read many other books besides these here mentioned, as they have leisure, and as their own fancy or judgment may lead them. The latter may be content with only some part of what is here set down; or, by the advice of their tutor, choose some shorter and easier way of getting a moderate share of learning, suited to their circumstances and capacities.[13]

Before elaborating on the innovative feature of independent study more needs to be said about the similarity of the curricular requirements for all undergraduates, irrespective of their social origins and future careers. Historians have often assumed that those destined for the church or a scholarly career followed the traditional statutory requirements for both BA and MA, with their heavy dose of scholasticism, while the gentry and nobility pursued a lighter, more varied (and modern) course. The bounds of scholarly interpretation range from the extreme position taken by Loomey—who argues for the existence of parallel systems of instruction

---

[13] Bodl. MS St Edmund Hall 72; Daniel Waterland, *Works* (4 vols Oxford 1843) iv. 406. Jean Gailhard endorsed this position as well: 'I do not expect youth should have the fruit of every art, science, language, or vertue I have named; only let them have the seeds of it, and let these be dispositions thereunto and foundations to build upon hereafter'. Jean Gailhard, *A Treatise Concerning the Education of Youth* (London 1678), 100.

for the two classes of students—and the more nuanced position taken by O'Day and McConica who emphasize the degree of overlap between the two groups, though they, too, ultimately endorse the existence of semi-divergent spheres. As McConica phrases it for the sixteenth century, 'statutory regulations were interpreted with great flexibility even within the degree programme ... while a commoner who eschewed a university degree might assemble almost any course of studies that he wanted and that his tutor would approve'.[14]

Though the extent to which commoners were exempted from the heavy philosophical studies—and would-be clergy denied the opportunity to pursue 'extra-curricular' studies—is open to question for the latter part of the sixteenth century, certainly after 1600 things were different. Tutors' manuals, library catalogues, and correspondences make clear that in principle a common education was advocated for all students. To quote Stone, 'never before or since—not even in the 19th century—has the social élite been so determined to give their children a truly academic education before they went into the world to take up their hereditary responsibilities'.[15] The compression of the course and the assimilation of a larger body of knowledge into the curriculum was sufficient to recommend itself to upper-class parents. When Sir Bevil Granville sent his son to Oxford in 1637 he told Degory Wheare that though the youth would remain there for just three years he 'desire[d] to have him a good scoller, and kept strictly to those courses that may conduce to that end'. A decade and a half later Francis Mansell (principal of Jesus College 1620–47) articulated the same aim of grounding commoners in the entire arts and sciences curriculum, though at an accelerated pace, when he described to Sir Sackville Crow 'the course I take with my charge that are gentlemen designed for the Inns of Court or travell, after 3 yeeres stay here'. Such a course sought 'to enable them in point of skill and readines in the Latin and Greeke tongues', as well as in the study of logic, natural and moral philosophy, history, civil law, and the mathematical sciences. For the same reason in 1677 Sir Robert Southwell instructed his nephew John Percival to inform his tutor that he intended to remain at Oxford for only a couple of years before proceeding to the Inns of Court, so that the tutor may put him 'forward' and provide him with a 'sufficient tincture' of each subject.[16]

This basic congruity between the educational needs of scholars and members of the ruling class was based on the classical ideal that posited the essential interconnectedness of knowledge and the necessity of acquiring it in its entirety. Such an ideal, in turn, derived from the legacy of Aristotle's unified cycle of learning as well as the expressed exhortations of Cicero and Quintilian to aspire to all arts and sciences. Cicero stated his intentions several times in *De oratore*: 'The orator must be

---

[14] J. Loomey, 'Undergraduate education at early Stuart Cambridge', *History of Education* x (1981), 9–19; R. O'Day, *Education and Society 1500–1800* (London 1982), 106–9, 115; McConica, 'Elizabethan Oxford', 722.

[15] Stone, 'Size and composition', 25.

[16] R. Granville, *The History of the Granville Family* (London 1895), 205; BL Add. MS 27,606, fos 9–9ᵛ; BL Add. MS 46,954B, fos 128ᵛ, 225.

accomplished in every kind of discourse and in every department of culture', he argued, and 'no one should be numbered with the orators who is not accomplished in all those arts that befits the well-bred'. In the absence of such universal knowledge 'oratory is but an empty and ridiculous swirl of verbiage'. Or again, 'no man can be an orator complete in all points of merit, who has not attained a knowledge of all important subjects and arts. For it is from knowledge that oratory must derive its beauty and fullness, and unless there is such knowledge, well-grasped and comprehended by the speaker, there must be something empty and almost childish in the utterance.' Quintilian paraphrased Cicero to the same end when he argued that in training the ideal student of literature [*grammaticus*], reading literary works alone was insufficient: 'every kind of writer must be carefully studied, not merely for the subject matter, but for the vocabulary ... Nor can such training be regarded as complete if it stop short of music, astronomy and philosophy.'[17]

Erasmus and Vives forcefully propagated such objectives in their educational writings. Nor did their endorsement fail to find a ready audience among English humanists. Thomas More, for example, expressed his approbation in a letter to Martin Dorp where he described his version of the humanist as one who was at once both an accomplished orator (*grammaticus*) and a well-rounded scholar: 'no one ... may be styled a man of letters who has not run through each and every one of the sciences.' Later in the century Roger Ascham further perpetuated the notion and it eventually became a commonplace among English scholars.[18]

THE EARLY MODERN IDEAL AND ITS CRITICS

By the seventeenth century the ideal of the general scholar had reached its apogee. 'I know the general cavil against general learning is this', wrote Thomas Fuller, 'that *aliquis in omnibus est nullus in singulis*; he that sips of many arts, drinks of none. However, we must know that all learning, which is but one grand science, hath so homogeneal a body, that the parts thereof do with a mutual service relate to, and communicate strength and lustre each to other.' Educators championed this model of education, insisting on the need to survey the vast boundaries of learning. 'How great a taske they have, how many leaves and volumes to be turned over, before they can justly deserve the name of a scholar', wrote Holdsworth. Isaac Barrow, master of Trinity College, Cambridge, concurred. The business of the scholar and the gentleman was 'to cultivate the mind with knowledge':

And if to get a competent knowledge about a few things, or to be reasonably skilful in any sort of learning, be difficult, how much industry doth it require to be well seen in many, or to have waded through the vast compass of learning, in no part whereof a scholar may conveniently or handsomely be ignorant; seeing there is such a connection of things, and depen-

---

[17] Cicero *De oratore*, trans. E. W. Sutton (2 vols Cambridge Mass. 1912) i. 13–14, 17, 53; Quintilian, *Institutio oratoria*, trans. H. E. Butler (4 vols London and New York 1920) i. 63–5.

[18] Thomas More, *In Defense of Humanism* in *The Complete Works of St Thomas More*, ed. D. Kinney (15 vols New Haven Conn. 1963–) xv. 12; Roger Ascham *The Scholemaster* in *English Works*, ed. W. A. Wright (Cambridge 1904, repr. Cambridge 1970), *passim*.

dence of notions, that one part of learning doth confer light to another, that a man can hardly well understand anything without knowing divers other things; that he will be a lame scholar, who hath not an insight into many kinds of knowledge; that he can hardly be a good scholar, who is not a general one.[19]

If the realization of such an ideal was not attainable by all, it was none the less aspired to by most educated men; and great was the reputation of those who succeeded, as seen in the eulogy of one of the founding members of the Royal Society, the physician William Croune, by the one time Oxford student John Scott (m. 1657):

As for his understanding, it was a very learned university of knowledge, wherein languages, and arts, and sciences flourished, and every thing almost was comprehended that deserves the name of learning. He was a general scholar, as all his learned acquaintance will testify, an accurate linguist, an accurate mathematician, a well read historian, and a profound philosopher, and in that laborious course he had run through the whole circle of learning. He contented not himself with a slight and cursory view of the several parts of it, but took a full prospect of them all, and was *aliquis in singulis*, as well as *in omnibus*.[20]

For much of the century the attainment of erudition was pursued by many scholars for whom no sacrifices were too formidable. John Milton's autobiographical account may serve as representative of the experience of many contemporaries: 'My father destined me in early childhood for the study of literature, for which I had so keen an appetite, that from my twelfth year scarcely ever did I leave my studies for my bed before the hour of midnight. This was the first cause of injury to my eyes.' However, neither this affliction nor his headaches could slacken his 'assault upon knowledge'. Likewise, Meric Casaubon (MA 1621) confessed he 'had some kind of apprehension' of becoming a general scholar in his youth, 'more than every bodie hath ... that pretends or aspires to learning'. He entertained such thoughts 'with great admiration, and as earnest longing, soe that it hath broken [his] sleepe many tymes, and made [him] forgett [his] meat, to the prejudice of [his] health'.[21]

Numerous examples can be found of students who spent all their time, as well as their meagre resources and health, in an unrelenting pursuit of erudition. John Greaves (MA 1628), 'having now read over all the Greek and Latin writers with great attention, he applied himself to the study of natural philosophy and mathematics'. John Freind (MA 1701), we are told by his biographer, spent his student days at Christ Church 'reading the ancient poets, orators, and historians, and by reading them, and forming himself upon their model, he polished his stile so

[19] Thomas Fuller, *The Holy and Profane State* (Boston 1864), 110; Fletcher, *The Intellectual Development of John Milton* ii. 624; Isaac Barrow, 'Of industry in general', *The Theological Works of Isaac Barrow* (8 vols Oxford 1830) iii. 230–1.

[20] John Scott, *A Sermon preached at the Funeral of Dr. William Croune* (London 1685), 26.

[21] *Complete Prose Works of John Milton*, ed. D. M. Wolfe (8 vols New Haven 1953–80) iv. 612; Meric Casaubon, 'Of learning', cited in M. R. G. Spiller, *'Concerning Natural Experimental Philosophie': Meric Casaubon and the Royal Society* (The Hague 1980), 195.

exquisitely in his academical prolusions, that every one, when he came to write upon physical subjects, was extremely charmed with its elegance, beauty, and spirit'. John Norris (MA 1684) also commented how, prior to his devoting himself to philosophical studies, he had made 'no small proficiency in classical learning, as 'tis called, and I have since plied it very hard, and run through all the criticisms of it'.[22]

It is of course possible to devalue the effort or mock the profundity reached by young scholars. The biographer of William King (MA 1688) concluded after inspecting the latter's *nachlas*, that 'before he was eight years standing in the university, he had read over, and made reflections on, twenty-two thousand and odd hundred books and manuscripts'. With understandable incredulity Samuel Johnson commented sarcastically on this amazing feat of intellectual activity: 'the books were certainly not very long, the manuscripts not very difficult, nor the remarks very large; for the calculator will find that he dispatched seven a day, for every day of his eight years, with a remnant that more than satisfies most other students.'[23] Still it would be a mistake to dismiss King's considerable accomplishments. His 'adversaria' and other classical writings (including his contribution to the war waged by Christ Church men against Richard Bentley) as well as his satires on the Royal Society show him to be no mean scholar. And King was hardly exceptional. Thus George Hakewill earlier described John Rainolds as 'a living librarie', who had committed to memory not only the entire corpus of Augustine's works 'but almost all clasicke authours' as well. Anthony Wood, among others, admired the great John Hales (MA 1609) who 'had turned over ... all writers, profane, ecclesiastical, and divine, all councels, fathers and histories of the church' and who was hence esteemed 'the best critic of the last age'.[24] The high reputation of John Selden (m. 1600) was likewise sung by Ben Jonson:

> Stand forth my object, then, you that have beene
> Ever at home: yet, have all countries seene;
> And like a compasse keeping one foot still
> Upon your center, doe your circle fill
> Of generall knowledge; watch'd men, manners too,
> Heard what times past have said, seene what ours doe.[25]

It fell to John Locke (MA 1658) not only to doubt the feasibility of such an ideal, but to condemn it vociferously. He couched his attack as a 'rational' argument. Since, he asked, the ideal of general scholar was a chimera that inevitably eluded

[22] *The Miscellaneous Works of John Greaves*, ed. T. Birch (2 vols London 1737) i, p. ii; John Freind, *The History of Physick* (4th edn 2 vols London 1750) i. 6; John Norris, *Reflections upon the Conduct of Human Life* (London 1690), 154.

[23] *The Original Works of William King*, ed. J. Nichols (3 vols London 1776) i, p. xxvii; Samuel Johnson, *Lives of the English Poets*, ed. George Birkbeck Hill (3 vols Oxford 1905) ii. 27.

[24] George Hakewill, *An Apologie of Declaration of the Power and Providence of God in the Government of the World* (Oxford 1627, 3rd edn Oxford 1635), 254; Wood, *Athenae* ii, 504; J. H. Elson, *John Hales of Eton* (New York 1948), 11.

[25] 'An Epistle to Master John Selden' in *Ben Jonson*, ed. C. H. Herford Percy and E. Simpson (9 vols Oxford 1947) viii. 159.

us, why then bother? Some men, he sneered in *The Conduct of the Understanding* 'that they may seem universally known, get a little smattering in everything'. Undoubtedly knowledge was valuable, but not for the purpose of displaying it in discussion. Only a handful of people were capable of attaining 'a real and true knowledge in all or most of the objects of contemplation' and 'the instances are so few of those who have in any measure approached towards it, that I know not whether they are to be proposed as examples in the ordinary conduct of the understanding. For a man to understand fully the business of his particular calling in the commonwealth and of religion . . . is usually enough to take up the whole time.' In a different context he was even more censorious of the very trait that constituted a general scholar—a wide and varied reading: 'There is nothing almost has done more harm to men dedicated to letters than giving the name of study to reading and making a man of great reading to be the same with a man of great knowledge, or at least to be a title of honour.'[26]

In disparaging the ideal of the general scholar and advocating in its stead a utilitarian, even vocational, education, Locke also blasted another cherished value of humanist education, that of non-specialization. For though the course of study advocated for all its beneficiaries was 'utilitarian'—in the sense of preparatory for, and applicable to, whatever calling was eventually followed—it certainly was not intended to be vocational. A few examples illustrating the widespread antipathy to specialization should suffice. While an undergraduate, Brian Twyne (MA 1603) was often forced to assure his father that he neither applied himself to the study of divinity nor medicine but assiduously spent his 'time in such sort as one of [his] standynge doth requyre it, [pursuing] good liberall artes'. A generation later, as a Cambridge undergraduate, John Milton complained bitterly of the impoverished intellectual horizons of his fellow students at the very puritan Christ's College who, in their zeal to train for a profession, lost sight of the study of good letters: 'There is really hardly anyone among us, as far as I know, who, almost completely unskilled and unlearned in philology and philosophy alike, does not flutter off to theology unfledged, quite content to touch that also most lightly, learning barely enough for sticking together a short harangue by any method whatever and patching it with worn-out pieces from various sources—a practice carried far enough to make one fear that the priestly ignorance of a former age may gradually attack our clergy.' Such was also the essence of William Laud's complaint against the single-minded preoccupation of the 'godly' at Oxford. 'A man would think those two [probationary] years', before Winchester scholars were elected fellows at New College,

and some years after, should be allowed to logic, philosophy, mathematics, and the like grounds of learning, the better to enable them to study divinity with judgement: but I am of late accidentally come to know, that when the probationers stand for their fellowships, and are to be examined how they have profited, one chief thing in which they are examined

---

[26] John Locke, *Of the Conduct of the Understanding*, ed. F. W. Garforth (New York 1966), 70–1, 82.

is, how diligently they have read Calvin's *Institutions* ... I do not deny but that Calvin's *Institutions* may profitably be read ... when they are well grounded in other learning; but to begin with it so soon, I am afraid doth not only hinder them from all grounds of judicious learning, but also too much possess their judgements before they are able to judge.[27]

In fostering the love of erudition educators made good use of competitiveness and emulation, mostly in the form of public oral exercises. Though the source for much of the misunderstanding surrounding the curriculum, such a pedagogical method, inherited from antiquity and rooted in the firm pairing of competition and academic excellence, was unanimously endorsed by renaissance educators. Thus to grasp the early modern commitment to exercises and contests, it is helpful to quote Quintilian, the first century Roman rhetorician, one of the main sources for renaissance educational thought, who based his argument in favour of formal schooling, in part, on the group dynamics of students: 'He will derive equal profit from hearing the indolence of a comrade rebuked or his industry commended. Such praise will incite him to emulation, he will think it a disgrace to be outdone by his contemporaries and a distinction to surpass his seniors. All such incentives provide a valuable stimulus, and though ambition may be a fault in itself, it is often the mother of virtue.' Quintilian's own experience had taught him that 'this practice did more to kindle our oratorical ambitions than all the exhortations of our instructors, the watchfulness of our *paedagogi* and the prayers of our parents'. Finding himself in a group, then, the student would 'desire first to imitate and then to surpass' his companions. And the moral Quintilian drew was simple: 'give me the boy who is spurred on by praise, delighted by success and ready to weep over failure. Such an one must be encouraged by appeals to his ambition; rebuke will bite him to the quick; honour will be a spur, and there is no fear of his proving indolent.'[28]

Early modern educators perpetuated such a conviction. 'Healthy emulation, between individual boys or sections of a class, is needful in the early stages of school life', insisted the celebrated Italian pedagogue Vittorino da Feltre. 'A desire for personal distinction may, in later years, be safely relied upon; and as the boy nears manhood the force of reason will supersede all forms of external stimulus.' For his part Erasmus also believed that the 'interest in the subject-matter may not be at first strong enough to survive'. Initially 'it must be nourished by associating pleasure with the actual teaching process. This is secured ... by encouragement of ambition' and emulation. He only cautioned that care be taken so that a quest for fame did not result in 'conceit and contempt for others'. Likewise, the didactic value in channelling the desire for fame and the fear of ridicule to instructional ends was emphasized by the Spanish humanist Vives, who added his endorsement to the various forms of oral contest as most conducive to learning—with the pro-

---

[27] H. G. Scott, 'Some correspondence of Brian Twyne', *Bodleian Quarterly Record* v (1926–8), 214; Milton, *Complete Prose Works* i. 314; Laud, *Works* v. 117.

[28] *Institutio oratoria* i. 49–53, 57.

viso that such exercises be aimed at the advancement of learning and not the display of brilliance or the pursuit of vain glory.[29]

English educational theorists adopted such common wisdom. John Brinsley recommended a well-regulated competitive regime that would inspire the students while at the same time breaking the monotony of a prolonged and arduous routine. The several exercises and disputations, he asserted, 'constantly observed, together with that strife and contention by adversaries, must needs provoke to a vehement study and emulation, unlesse in such who are of a very servile nature'. Milton, too, was a firm believer in the keen competitiveness that ambition and emulation usually aroused. When he portrayed the ideal teacher, for example, he underscored the latter's ability to draw the students to 'willing obedience, enflamed with the study of learning, and the admiration of vertue, stirred up with high hopes of living to be brave men, and worthy patriots ... That they may ... delight in manly, and liberall exercises: which he who hath the art, and proper eloquence to catch them with, what with mild and effectual perswasion, and what with the intimation of some fear, if need be, but chiefly by his own example, might in a short space gain them to an incredible diligence and courage, infusing into their young breasts such an ingenuous and noble ardor, as would not fail to make many of them renowned and matchlesse men.'[30]

No better testimony can be cited for the approbation accorded the principles of emulation and competitiveness by sixteenth- and seventeenth-century theorists than the praise showered on the course of studies of those who had brought such practice to perfection—the Jesuits. Sir Edwin Sandys (MA 1583) described with admiration what he had witnessed in various Jesuit colleges abroad where even 'in their bare grammatical disputations [they] inflame their scholars with such earnestness and fierceness, as to seem to be at the point of flying each in the other's face, to the amazement of those strangers which had never seen the like before, but to their own great content and glory, as it appeared'. John Aubrey (m. 1642) recognized similar advantages: 'The Jesuits do breed up their youth to oratory the best of any in the world. They have in their schools tribunes, dictators, etc., and do exercise their oratory daily, both studied and *extempore*, so that they must of necessity be better orators than others not so bred.' Small wonder that Francis Bacon, John Hall, and John Dury all 'recognized the superiority of the rigorous pedagogical discipline of the Jesuits' and sought to implement it in their proposed curricula.[31] Nor did such practices disappear later in the century. Gilbert Burnet still

[29] W. H. Woodward, *Vittorino da Feltre and other Humanist Educators* (Cambridge 1897, repr. New York 1970), 205; W. H. Woodward, *Desiderius Erasmus concerning the Aim and Method of Education* (Cambridge 1904, repr. New York 1964), 98–9, 208–9; *Vives: on education*, ed. F. Watson (Cambridge 1913, repr. Totowa 1971), pp. lviii–lx, 57–8, 116.

[30] John Brinsley, *Ludus literarius*, ed. E. T. Campagnac (Liverpool 1917), 280–6; Milton, *Complete Prose Works* ii. 385.

[31] Edwin Sandys, *Europae speculum* (London 1632), 81, quoted in F. Watson *The English Grammar Schools to 1660* (Cambridge 1908, repr. London 1968), 93; *John Aubrey on Education*, ed. J. E. Stephens (London 1972), 68; *Samuel Hartlib and the Advancement of Learning*, ed. C. Webster (Cambridge 1970), 59.

believed that 'emulation is that which presseth children most effectually to their studies in schools ... as also company makes all go most vigorously about their work'. Without it, he continued, 'I shall expect but small, and slow progress from all children'.[32]

In accordance with the prevalence of this pedagogical principle, the student was confronted at every stage of the educational process with the pressures and thrills that invariably accompanied exercises. Having already been exposed to contests and challenges in school, the undergraduate was taught to expect the same routine at university. From daily conversations in Latin (in the midst of an often discriminating and censorious audience) and the preparatory performances in tutorials and college exercises, to participation in university disputations and examinations as well as in the often strenuous competition for scholarships and fellowships, the educational structure revolved around the display of skills and their perfection. Through diligence and the observation of others, the student was expected to cultivate his own proficiency while at the same time himself serving as the model for others. To this end the Cambridge tutor James Duport exhorted his students: 'slubber not over your exercises in a slight and careless perfunctory manner ... but take paines about them, and doe them exactly for your owne credit and good example of others.'[33]

It is true that, especially at the early stages of their stay at college, the continuous routine of trial by fire extracted a certain toll. If their observation of others' performances inspired many a student to excel, the obligation to join in could intimidate with equal force. Holdsworth addressed this issue. 'Be over carefull to performe your acts well, that you may be encouraged by the applause, and not put out of conceit with your studies by discredit and reproche, for that causes many to throwe their studies quicke asyde, and seek for content in other things.' Many students undoubtedly shared the experience of Brian Twyne who prayed God to 'give [him] witte, dexteritie in disputchinge matters, [and] care in providing a strong and healthful bodie to beare the tediousness of n[ight] studies and daye studies'.[34] The glory in performing well and despondency at failure can be seen from the autobiography of Simonds D'Ewes of St John's College, Cambridge. Having met with success in his first disputation against senior sophisters the smug D'Ewes eagerly awaited his next opportunity the following day. This time, however, his opponents had the upper hand and the proud D'Ewes 'not finding so good success the second afternoon as [he] had done the first, and fearing also that this course would

[32] J. Clarke, *Bishop Gilbert Burnet as Educationist* (Aberdeen 1914), 21–3; O'Day, *Education and Society*, 52–3. Even in the middle of the eighteenth century David Hume concluded in one of his essays that 'a noble emulation is the source of every excellence'. One 'is animated with new force, when he hears the applauses of the world ... and, being aroused by such a motive, he often reaches a pitch of perfection, which is equally surprizing to himself and to his readers'. David Hume, *Essays*, ed. E. F. Miller (Indianapolis 1987), 135–6.

[33] G. M. Trevelyan, 'Undergraduate life under the protectorate', *Cambridge Review* lxiv (1943), 329.

[34] Fletcher, *The Intellectual Development of John Milton* ii. 653; Scott, 'Some correspondence of Brian Twyne', 214.

in time have engaged [him] in the society and acquaintance of some of the looser sort, [he] forebore going thither any more'.[35] Obviously the privileges enjoyed by a commoner like D'Ewes were not extended to the generality of students, and many had no choice but to endure as best they could public challenges and their attendant humiliation. John Potenger (BA 1668) took special care to protect his reputation when he first arrived at Oxford: 'I was forced to manage myself with great circumspection, that my fellows might not find my blind side, though they shrewdly ghessed at it. In discourse I seldom offered at anything I did not understand. At dinner and supper, it being the custom to speak Latin, my words were few, till I came to a tollerable proficiency in colloquial Latin.' Others found the disputations traumatic—often because they preferred (and excelled in) the more literary exercises. John Lightfoot, the great Cambridge Hebraist, hated disputations and 'could by no means fancy that contentious and quarrelsome study, it being very disagreeable to the quiet genius of this young student'. Lightfoot savoured his linguistic and literary exercises instead, and his tutor apprised various heads of house of the fact that his charge was 'the best orator of all the undergraduates'.[36]

A telling illustration of the manner in which a student was goaded to improve himself through observing others perform is provided in the verse autobiography of the poet George Wither (m. 1604). At first Wither neglected his studies but he soon perceived his shortcomings:

> asham'd to find my selfe still mute,
> And other little Dandiptats dispute;
> That could distinguish upon *Rationale*,
> Yet scarcely heard of *verbum personale*;
> Or could by heart (like parots) in the schooles,
> stand pratling; those (me thought) very pretty fooles.
> And therefore in some hope to profit so,
> That I like them (at least) might make a show;
> I reacht my bookes that I had cast about,
> To see if I could picke his meaning out.

Other students never forgot the admiration (or envy) they had felt when faced with the superior performance of their peers. Richard Carew (m. 1566) remembered how 'being a scholar at Oxford of fourteen years of age, and three years standing, upon a wrong conceived opinion touching [his] sufficiency, [he] was there called to dispute *ex tempore* (*impar congressus Achilli*) [no match in conflict with Achilles] with the matchless Philip Sidney, in presence of the earls Leicester, Warwick, and divers other great personages'. Just as invigorating were classroom competitions. Decades after he had been a student at Oxford Samuel Johnson still recalled how 'at the

---

[35] On another occasion, however, D'Ewes had disputed against his friend Richard Saltonstall 'with very good success to mine own content'. *The Autobiography and Correspondence of Sir Simonds D'Ewes*, ed. J. O. Halliwell (2 vols London 1845) i. 138, 140.

[36] *The Private Memoirs of John Potenger*, ed. C. W. Bingham (London 1841), 29; Fletcher, *The Intellectual Development of John Milton* ii. 245.

classical lecture in the hall, [he] could not bear [John] Meeke's superiority, and [he] tried to sit as far from him as [he] could, that [he] might not hear him construe'.[37]

Related student customs, derived from literary techniques acquired in school and replete with their distinctive punishments and rewards, evolved in most colleges. Thus Anthony Wood described those devised 'to initiate the freshmen', not only at Merton College but other colleges as well. Every night in December 'the senior under-graduates would bring into the hall the juniors or freshmen . . . every one in order was to speake some pretty apothegme, or make a jest or bull, or speak some eloquent nonsense, to make the company laugh. But if any of the freshmen came off dull, or not cleverly, some of the forward or pragmatical seniors would "tuck" them, that is set the nail of their thumb to their chin, just under the lower lipp, and by the help of their other finger under the chin, they would give him a mark, which sometimes would produce blood.' Another custom, 'salting', also called for the display of wit. The freshmen were brought into the hall where 'they were to speak their speech with an audible voice to the company; which if well done, the person that spoke it was to have a cup of cawdle and no salted drinke; if indifferently, some cawdle and some salted drink; but if dull, nothing was given to him but salted drink'.[38]

Among the most important instruments to inculcate competitiveness and emulation were the disputations and declamations. Given the didactic function of these exercises, it is important to understand that their perpetuation was not a determined effort by the university authorities to enforce a scholastic content of education. In fact, as we shall see below, by the seventeenth century the disputations were rapidly turning into literary occasions, the intention of which was neither to generate new knowledge nor to even determine its veracity. Unfortunately, the survival of the medieval format of disputations made them an easy target for critics who conveniently ignored the different function these exercises had now assumed. For example, Bacon's exhortation to the authorities of Cambridge University to put 'away all zeal of contradiction', is an instance of a reformer's disregard for the pedagogical objectives of university exercises.[39]

The prevailing ideal of scholarship also encompassed certain presuppositions concerning the proper means of acquiring learning. One such assumption was that

[37] George Wither, *Juvenilia* (3 vols Manchester 1871) i. 4; Richard Carew, *The Survey of Cornwall*, ed. F. E. Halliday (London 1953), 169; *Boswell's Life of Johnson*, ed. G. Birkbeck Hill and L. F. Powell (6 vols Oxford 1964) i. 272. In 1763 young Jeremy Bentham boasted that in his examination he 'had a very numerous audience' and 'was up for near an hour together, which was nearly as long again as the usual time. I hope I have acquitted myself tolerably well; and am pretty certain, if I have not gained credit, that at least I have not lost any.' L. S. Sutherland, 'The curriculum' in *The Eighteenth Century*, 475.

[38] Wood, *Life and Times* i. 133–4, 138–40.

[39] *The Works of Francis Bacon*, ed. J. Spedding, R. L. Ellis, and D. D. Heath (14 vols London 1857–74) iii. 326. Not inappropriately Costello likened the disputation to a Spanish bullfight: 'The maneuvers of the disputants were as technical as the veronica and half-veronica; the audience was as critically appreciative; the ceremonial was as elaborate. And success as sought for! Fame and fortune often depended upon the disputants' skill.' Costello, *The Scholastic Curriculum*, 15.

beyond the introductory level the acquisition of learning was accomplished not so much by passive attendance at lectures as by private industry on the part of students. Cognizance of such an expectation is important if we are to appreciate the structure of teaching. In his autobiography Edward Gibbon ridiculed the pretension of Oxford tutors to offer competent instruction in all branches of learning, 'instead of confining themselves to a single science'.[40] But as incontrovertible as the force of the argument may be for the late eighteenth century, it cannot be assumed to be equally compelling for the seventeenth. By the time Gibbon wrote his autobiography (c 1789) both the state of knowledge and the conscientiousness of Oxford tutors had changed dramatically. The commitment to the ideal of the general scholar that inspired seventeenth-century academics and which enabled them to offer at least competent instruction in the entire cycle of learning, had lost much of its force by the middle of the eighteenth century. Nor did the quality of teaching escape the general decline that afflicted both Oxford and Cambridge from the 1660s on. But, equally important, the rapid advances in most branches of knowledge during the previous two centuries made the task of tutors ever more formidable, the ability to be sufficiently versed in all subjects ever more rare. Issues of motivation and qualification aside, however, the seventeenth-century tutor had also been assisted in his duties by college and university lecturers, most of whom read regularly and offered competent instruction. In such an environment, the office of tutor was more to guide and supervise than to teach. Having made sure that the basic principles of the disciplines were grasped by the student, the tutor assumed the role of director of studies, overseeing the more or less independent consolidation of higher-level skills. Richard Holdsworth made the point explicit when he described the private studies of the young undergraduate: 'you will finde more content, and better retain that which you get out of your own industrie, than which you receave from your tutor'. John Wallis described the relations between student and tutor in similar terms. The latter served as a guide, 'directing them what books to read, explaining these authors to them and taking account of their proficiency therein'.[41]

The gradual growth towards self-sufficiency encouraged during the undergraduate course became the norm for the bachelor of arts. The expectation was that once graduated the student would relinquish both tutor and daily supervision. In the picturesque language of the critic of university education during the 1640s, John Hall, 'then they are turned loose, and with their paper-barks committed to the great ocean of learning'.[42] John Potenger's experience was typical: 'being a bachelour of arts', he recalled, 'I was free from the government of a tutor, and wholly left to my own management and freedom, as far as was consistent with the college and

[40] *Autobiography of Edward Gibbon*, ed. J. B. Bury (London 1962), 41.

[41] Fletcher, *Intellectual Development of John Milton* ii. 635; 'Dr Wallis's letter against Mr Maidwell', *Collectanea* i. 314. See also Joseph Mede, *Works* (London 1677), p. iv of 'The life of . . . Joseph Mede'.

[42] *The Advancement of Learning by John Hall*, ed. A. K. Croston (Liverpool 1953), 26. Hall, of course, disparaged the learning offered by the university.

university discipline.' As was expected of him, he 'spent most of [his] time in reading books'. In 1690, two years after he left Oxford, John Norris recounted his university career to date: 'I have now spent about thirteen years in the most celebrated university in the world; and according to the ordinary measures perhaps not amiss, having accomplished my self in a competent degree both with such learning as the academical standard requires, and with whatever else my own private genius inclined me to'.[43]

University officials soon formalized such practice. Already the 1570 Cambridge statutes distinguished between the undergraduate and graduate course; though ordered to attend various lectures, the bachelors of art were understood to be self-reliant: 'and that, which had been before begun, they shall complete by their own industry.' Four decades later a Cambridge interpretation of the statutes actually dispensed MA candidates from all residency requirements, reasoning 'that a man once grounded so far in learning as to deserve a bachelorship in arts is sufficiently furnished to proceed in study himself'. In practice such a ruling was translated into an increasing number of dispensations granted annually by both universities to those who, though not in residence, were nevertheless applying for the MA degree.[44]

The early cultivation of independent study was also justified on the grounds that formal schooling represented only a part of the actual educational process, which was expected to last a lifetime. As we shall see more fully below, at school and university one ideally received grounding in the constituents of language, arts, and sciences, acquired the habits of reasoning and judgement, and, perhaps most important, imbibed a love of literature that would last until one's dying day. Thomas Traherne (MA 1661), for example, intimated that the conspectus of knowledge he acquired at Oxford furnished him with the intellectual tools for a lifetime of study:

Having been at the university, and received there the taste and tincture of another education, I saw there were things in this world of which I never dreamed; glorious secrets, and glorious persons past imagination. There I saw that logic, ethics, physics, metaphysics, geometry, astronomy, poesy, medicine, grammar, music, rhetoric, all kinds of arts, trades and mechanisms that adorned the world pertained to felicity: at least there I saw those things, which afterwards I knew to pertain unto it.[45]

In his account of Abraham Cowley's education Thomas Sprat commented somewhat more indirectly on this philosophy of education:

The first beginning of his studies was a familiarity with the most solid and unaffected authors of antiquity, which he fully digested not only in his memory but his judgment. By

---

[43] *Private Memoirs of John Potenger*, ed. Bingham, 30–1; Norris, *Reflections upon the Conduct of Human Life*, 156.

[44] M. H. Curtis, *Oxford and Cambridge in Transition 1558–1642* (Oxford 1959), 91, 97.

[45] William Miller, *A Sermon preached at the Funerall of the Worshipfull Gilbert Davie Esquire* (London 1621), sig. C4ᵛ; Thomas Traherne, *Centuries, Poems, and Thanksgivings*, ed. H. M. Margoliouth (2 vols Oxford 1958) i. 132.

this advantage he learnt nothing while a boy that he needed to forget or forsake when he came to be a man. His mind was rightly seasoned at first, and he had nothing to do but still to proceed on the same foundation on which he began.[46]

The other objective of the formal stage of schooling, the inculcation of an almost intemperate love of the classics, was even more consequential. For contemporaries who believed in the constancy of human nature, the classics offered more than merely the foundations of knowledge. Students developed an emotional commitment to antiquity and its repository of useful knowledge, which illuminated the human condition and guided behaviour. Not that the study of Cicero or Horace or Terence was thought capable of turning students into wise and virtuous citizens all at once. But the cumulative effect of reading the classics over time was believed to ensure the formation of their character and make them upright and judicious.

Nor was the love of the classics considered any less dispensable in old age. Quintilian, among others, had claimed that 'the study of literature is a necessity for boys and the delight of old age, the sweet companion of our privacy and the sole branch of study which has more solid substance than display', and the educated élite of the seventeenth century subscribed to this axiom. Izaak Walton recorded that in old age Bishop Robert Sanderson 'could repeat all the *Odes* of Horace, all Tully's *Offices*, and much of Juvenal and Persius, without book; and would say "the repetition of one of the *Odes* of Horace to himself was to him such musick, as a lesson on the viol was to others, when they played it to themselves or friends" '. Likewise we are told by Obadiah Walker that William Oughtred 'in his old age, had Ovid and Virgil fresh in his memory'. Indeed, it was this quality that William Temple extolled at the close of his *An Essay Upon the Ancient and Modern Learning*: 'among so many things as are by men possessed or pursued in the course of their lives, all the rest are baubles, besides old wood to burn, old wine to drink, old friends to converse with, and old books to read.'[47]

Establishing early the habit of independent study as the key to a lifetime of learning also bore significantly on the nature of advanced studies at the university. As we shall see more fully below, in allowing bachelors and masters of art to carry on their studies privately, the university did not forsake its mission to offer graduate instruction and research facilities. Simply the students were now expected to assume full responsibility for what previously had been rigorously supervised. As John Wallis elaborated in 1700: 'I do not know any part of useful knowledge proper for scholars to learn, but that if any number of persons (gentlemen or others) desire therein to be informed, they may find those in the university who will be ready to instruct them, so that if there be any defect therein, it is for want of learners not of teachers'. In this context, it is wise to heed the modern observation that 'what [went] on outside the classroom, in private reading, conversation with fellow

---

[46] *Critical Essays of the Seventeenth Century*, ed. J. E. Spingarn (3 vols Oxford 1908–9) ii. 121.

[47] Quintilian, *Institutio oratoria* i. 65; Obadiah Walker, *Of Education* (Oxford 1673), 127; Izaak Walton, *The Lives of John Donne . . . and Robert Sanderson* (London 1973), 398; *The Works of Sir William Temple* (4 vols London 1814 repr. New York 1968) iii. 486.

students, informal discussion with the faculty, and extracurricular activity, may [have been] more important than what [went] on inside it'.[48]

The importance of discipline in the realization of such lofty educational goals weighed heavily on the minds of parents and educators alike. Although an in-depth appraisal of the role of discipline in university life cannot be attempted here, its centrality to the undergraduate curriculum must be stressed.[49] In this context, the emphasis on discipline as the prerequisite of good learning was predicated on the relative youth of the student body; while unruliness was viewed as the perennial temptation of all youth, such a temptation was deemed twice as dangerous for the well-to-do student. Without strict discipline, it was believed, such a student would abuse the privileges he had traditionally enjoyed, dispensing in due course with his more demanding studies and exercises. Therefore, as long as the expectations for members of the upper classes remained the same as for other university students, the prescription of discipline as an antidote for unruliness remained universal. Likewise, recurring complaints about university education concerned lax discipline and inattention by tutors which encouraged frivolity, if not downright vice, in undergraduates.

Faith in the power and necessity of discipline was absolute. As Archbishop Laud told Vossius, the decay of discipline in the universities is 'the cause of all our ills in church and state'. Even a cursory reading of the statutes he introduced at Oxford reveals that upholding discipline was a key feature of the Laudian code—order and authority as prerequisites for 'sound learning in the university and spirituality within the church'.[50] The enforcement of such a regime, however, was conditional on personal and continual supervision by university authorities as much as by individual tutors. For, as Vice-Chancellor Frewen told Laud, as long as he attended disputations they were performed properly, but they could be brought to a 'dead stand' if he were absent. For this reason a common routine of every incoming vice-chancellor was to warn scholars of the firmness with which he would enforce discipline and learning. In 1692, for example, Henry Aldrich announced that he would 'severely look after the discipline of the universitie, disputations in Austins, wall-lectures, examinations, Lent exercises'.[51]

Nor was the conviction that discipline advanced learning restricted to university authorities. Parents, including members of the upper class, never doubted the wisdom of such a premiss. Those who recalled their own shortcomings as students were perhaps the most adamant defenders of uncompromising observance of discipline. 'I do with griefe finde mine owne defects', wrote Sir Bevil Granville to Degory Wheare in 1637, 'and I feel an infinite mayme by the want of letters.' He

[48] *Collectanea* i. 317; L. Stone, *The Past and the Present* (Boston and London 1981), 212.

[49] See also McConica, 'Elizabethan Oxford', 652–66.

[50] Laud, *Works* v. 101; H. R. Trevor-Roper, *Archbishop Laud 1573–1645* (London 1940, 2nd edn London 1965), 117. These remarks have particular reference to Leiden University; K. Sharpe, 'Archbishop Laud and the University of Oxford', in H. Lloyd-Jones, V. Pearl, and B. Worden (eds), *History and Imagination* (London 1981), 161–2.

[51] Laud, *Works* v. 267–8; Wood, *Life and Times* iii. 404.

was 'desirous therefore to have it supplyed' in his son and requested the principal of Gloucester Hall to make the youth 'a good scoller, and have him kept strictly to those courses that may conduce to that end'. To his son, Sir Bevil wrote of the infinite benefits that the application to studies would confer and urged him not to 'let the view of other youths' liberty or mispending their time disquiett or ensnare you'. A generation later Sir Heneage Finch wrote to his son Daniel at Christ Church in much the same spirit:

It is a very great satisfaction to mee that you have not been discouraged from pursuing those studyes which I require of you, by any unkindnesse of those who desire not to see any better example then they themselves are willing to follow. It was my fortune there, as it is yours now, to meet with the same inconveniences, and for the same reasons. But you must look upon the university as the way to greater things, and therefore, however others divert themselves, bee you sure to keep on a constant and regular motion, and you shall quickly find yourself to gett ground of your fellowes.

On another occasion he pleaded with his son 'for though others who are less disposed to study may take your forwardness in ill part, yet I presume nothing shall weigh with you more then the satisfaction of my desires'.[52]

An emphasis on well-supervised conduct recurs in the correspondence between parents and heads of house. Writing in 1670 to Sir John Lowther, Thomas Barlow hoped to entice this father of a prospective student by assuring him that at Queens' College even the

upper communars, which usually are baronetts or knights sonnes, or gentlemen of greater fortunes . . . are not (as in all other houses generally) freed from any exercise the meanest gentlemen undergoe; soe we conceave, and (by experience find and) know it to be true, that to exempt them from any beneficiall exercise, is not a priviledge, but indeed an injury and losse to them; seeinge it is really a depriveinge them of the just means of attaininge learninge, which is the end they and we should aime att.

A few years later Sir Justinian Isham stated in a letter to John Fell that notwithstanding 'the usual libertie now given', he still favoured 'the ancient and severer way of education', and therefore wanted his son to 'bare a very great respect towards his governors and tutors, be constant at lectures and perform such exercises as shall be required'.[53]

Given the esteem for discipline, especially as regards the learning process, contemporaries understandably insisted that colleges either flourished or declined in direct proportion to the success of their heads in maintaining it. John Evelyn condoned retrospectively the severity of Thomas Lawrence (master of Balliol 1637–48) 'considering that the extraordinary remissenesse of discipline had (til his coming) much detracted from the reputation of that colledg'. In particular, the diarist continued, under his regime fellow commoners 'were no more exempted from

---

[52] Granville, *The History of the Granville Family*, 205, 207; HMC *Finch MSS* i. 217–18, 237.
[53] HMC *Thirteenth Report*, appx 7, 93–4; Northants. RO Isham correspondence, no. 845; *The Diary of Thomas Isham of Lamport (1658–81)*, ed. G. Isham (London 1971), 36.

exercise than the meanenst scholars there'. Edward Hyde, earl of Clarendon, shared Evelyn's disapproval of allowing noblemen to 'chuse whether they would be obliged to the public scholastick exercises' of their colleges. Writing late in life he expressed his delight in hearing that 'those abominable exemptions' enjoyed by the nobility from scholastic exercises 'are abolished, and that all men, of what quality soever, are obliged at least to be present at all disputations, and they will be ashamed to be long present without acting a part in them'. Indeed Stephen Penton, principal of St Edmund Hall (1676–84), argued on the eve of the Glorious Revolution that 'gentlemen in the university ought to doe more exercise than others, for they stay but little time there and ought to be accomplished in haste'.[54]

Anthony Wood often commented how the tenure of a learned and firm governor contributed to the flourishing of a college or hall—both numerically and intellectually—and vice versa. At Gloucester Hall, he noted, there were ninety-two students in 1634 during the principalship of Degory Wheare; after the Restoration there were scarcely any. Wood's approbation of stern administration led him even to praise the 'severe discipline' of the puritan and long-time principal of Magdalen Hall, John Wilkinson. Wood likewise attributed the success of Christ Church in attracting so many members of the upper class to the success of John Fell in maintaining high standards of discipline and learning. For this reason, Wood concluded, 'there were usually 35 or 36 gentlemen-commoners and 8 or 10 noblemen' at the college.[55] Wood was not alone in making such a connection. John Aubrey described in loving detail the care taken by that eccentric but 'excellent governor' of Trinity College Ralph Kettell (president 1599–1643) 'to keepe-downe the *juvenilis impetus*' there. In supervising studies, Kettell's 'fashion was to goe up and down the college, and peepe in at the key-holes to see whether the boyes did follow their books or no' and 'was constantly at lectures in the hall to observe them'.[56]

Other examples abound. Sir Henry Savile was known to be the 'very severe governor' of Merton College, whose 'scholars hated him for his austerity'. But he was also credited with establishing the college's reputation and transforming it into one of the most important centres of scholarship at Oxford. At Corpus Christi College the prosperity brought about by the firm rule of Thomas Jackson during the 1630s was commended even by William Prynne, while the popularity of Queen's College in the decade before 1640 was in large measure believed to be the harvest reaped from the industry of Christopher Potter.[57] During the Interregnum it was the strict

[54] *The Diary of John Evelyn*, ed. E. S. De Beer (6 vols Oxford 1955) ii. 17–18; *The Miscellaneous Works of . . . Edward, Earl of Clarendon* (London 1751), 326; Stephen Penton, *The Guardian's Instruction* (London 1688), 50. At University College in the 1630s John Bancroft, too, made sure that commoners attended exercises as did any poor scholar: 'The Memoirs of Sir George Courthop 1616–1685', ed. S. C. Lomas, *Camden Miscellany* xi (Camden Soc. 3rd ser. xxxiii 1907).

[55] Wood, *Athenae* i, p. lxxvi; iv. 285; Wood, *Life and Times* iii. 257.

[56] Kettle also made sure that the beer served at Trinity was the best to be had at Oxford so the student would have little incentive to seek it elsewhere. *Brief Lives chiefly of contemporaries, set down by John Aubrey, between the years 1669 and 1696*, ed. A. Clark (2 vols Oxford 1898) ii. 17, 20–1.

[57] *Brief Lives by Aubrey*, ed. Clark ii. 214; H. W. Garrod, 'Sir Henry Savile: 1549–1949' in. J. Jones (ed.), *The Study of Good Letters* (Oxford 1963), 101–19; T. Fowler, *The History of Corpus Christi College* (OHS

rule of John Conant that restored to Exeter College 'that ancient and wholesome discipline' made famous under John Prideaux. Conant habitually attended lectures and disputations and frequently entered the students' rooms to observe what books they read and 'reprove them if he found them turning over any modern authors', sending them instead to Cicero for language. Thomas Tully's manner of governance was credited with infusing St Edmund Hall with a new intellectual vigour. As described by John Freind in 1672, Tully made a habit of 'visiting the schollars chambers . . . almost every day to observe whether they followed their studyes', and in this way his scrupulous attention to the life of the hall assured its rapid rise in reputation. Andrew Allam declared that under his leadership (1658–76) the hall 'flourished in proportion to its bigness equall with any other in the university; and this was effected by means of the exercise of a strict, even and regular discipline'.[58]

But by the end of the seventeenth century belief in the necessity of keeping members of the upper classes on a tight rein had waned—in practice, if not in theory. Of course the cracks had begun to appear much earlier. Writing to the grandmother of Thomas Knyvett in 1612, the youth's Cambridge tutor Elias Travers was at pains to argue that it was not for lack of parts that Knyvett's initial application to study had faded away but 'for that fatall conceite gentlemen have taken up, they need not study so much, nor apply their time so frugally nor aspire to that sufficiency that other schollers doo, who meane to make a fortune out of their learning'. A few years later Sir John Eliot observed despondently from his confinement in the Tower how his son exhibited a similar attitude at Oxford. 'How is it varied from the intentions of your promise', he wrote, 'that makes you less affected to the college than the towne, and for acquaintance more studious than in books.' The younger John Eliot finally needed to be removed from Oxford.[59]

But it was only in the last quarter of the century that such laxness became endemic. Peter Drelincourt, Lord James Butler's guardian at Christ Church, was beside himself when he was forced to report in 1679 that his charge had lately

grown both very remiss in his studies and little observing of what I tell him for his good. He hath in his head (either through his own arguing or through some idle and pernicious persons suggesting) that being born of such illustrious a family, and to such great estate as he is, and being not intended for a doctor, he needeth neither much learning neither a governor, being both old and wise enough to govern himself, and to do what he pleaseth.

In a similar fashion Sir Robert Southwell wryly commented in 1684 that his nephew Thomas Southwell increasingly 'grew importunate to be removed from Oxford' rejecting her 'with scorn, calling it a place of pedantry, and murmuring that he

xxv 1893), 189–90; *The Diary of Thomas Crosfield*, ed. F. S. Boas (London 1935), pp. xix–xxiv, 44, 50, 74; Sharpe, 'Archbishop Laud and the University of Oxford', 157–8.

[58] W. K. Stride, *Exeter College* (London 1900), 61–2; Bodl. MS top. Oxon. f. 31, pp. 18–19; *VCH Oxon.* iii. 329; J. N. D. Kelly, *St Edmund Hall* (Oxford 1989), 43; Wood, *Life and Times* ii. 264.

[59] *The Knyvett Letters (1620–1644)*, ed. B. Schofield (London 1949), 20; J. Forster, *Sir John Eliot: a biography* (2 vols London 1864) ii. 569.

should not be trusted with a small allowance, who was in so short a time to handle the whole fortune'.[60]

Indicative of the changing atmosphere were the responses that the errant students produced—ingenious or impudent, depending on one's interpretation. Thus
when in 1700 Peter Shakerley rebuked his brother George, then at Brasenose, how
'the account I have of your neglect of study and expense of money, notwithstanding your repeated promises to the contrary, is what I thought I should not
have been troubled with any more considering the holy vows and resolutions you
made', he received the following response:

> That I have not followed my studies as I ought to have done I confess with shame. But
> who is he that has? Where is he to be found? *Numquis apud Parthes Armeniesve latet?* I would
> not by this argue myself comparatively studious, for such a way is odious to all, but really
> sir one of the greatest obstructions to my study has been your continual chiding of me. A
> man should sit to read a book as free from cares as from prejudice, for as the one biases
> the judgment, so the other distracts the thoughts. The concern I have always had upon me
> upon your account has made me sit in my study not a few hours every day without being
> able to set to anything cheerfully.[61]

There would seem to have been a growing number of such students, both
among the gentry who increasingly experienced pressure from their peers against
close application to study, and also among those who cheerfully emulated the wilful neglect of learning by the élite. In 1721, for example, a gentleman-commoner
of University College, 'alone among his "gown" in taking a BA, found his greatest
difficulty in the fact that gentlemen-commoners considered it beneath their dignity
to dispute in the hall. If he did so he would be "guilty of great singularity and be
accounted a person proud of his own performances" '. Such an attitude may also
account for the growing chorus of denunciations against the pedantic character of
the curriculum. Stephen Penton sardonically remarked that 'ill-natured, untoward
boys, when they find discipline sit hard upon them ... will learn to lie, complain,
and rail against the university, the college, and the tutour'.[62]

This in turn reflects the momentous shift in attitude now occurring on the part
of the nobility and gentry towards the universities. The passion for learning and
veneration of erudition that had prevailed since the days of Queen Elizabeth, and
which was shared by members of the social élite and scholars alike, was rapidly
losing its broad appeal. It has been said that 'what we see in the late seventeenth
century is a wholesale rejection of the value of a university education as a preparation for life as a member of the élite'. The sons of the upper class became 'cured
of that respect for classical learning as such which had been propagated with such

[60] HMC *Ormonde MSS* v. 194–5; HMC *Egmont MSS* ii. 142. Southwell had already written several
months earlier that Thomas's 'way of study is to have a taste of all things ... It is true this enables him
to appear gay and pleasant in company, and by some to be admired for much knowledge. But if this
humour should stick upon him in riper years, it would neither be so becoming or useful.' CL MS 427,
fo 18.

[61] A. Bryant, *Postman's Horn* (London 1936), 51–3.

[62] L. Sutherland, 'The curriculum' in *The Eighteenth Century*, 478–9; Penton, *Guardian's Instruction*, 55.

zest by the humanists. They were now demanding no more than an all-round training in the liberal arts, the shallower and broader education of the quintessentially
amateur virtuoso, which was something that the universities were ill-equipped to
offer.' A sharp decline in the number of upper-class matriculants was the result and
consequently, during the eighteenth century, Oxford and Cambridge reverted to
'where they began in the Middle Ages, as fairly small training schools for the professions, mainly the Church'.[63] The repercussions of this upper-class disenchantment with both erudition and the universities were significant in view of the pivotal
role played by the élite in effecting the 'educational revolution'. As they repudiated
learning and the institutions that professed it, their example was promptly emulated by others further down the social scale and hence before long the universities themselves were but a pale reflection of their former glory.

This is not to say that the advocacy of learning had ever completely swept the
board among the aristocracy. Even at the height of the humanist triumph, ingrained
prejudice against bookishness had lingered. Many were undoubtedly reluctant to
make the investment of time and energy necessary for the attainment of erudition,
believing it sufficient to take literally the advice of James I to Prince Henry: 'As
for the studie of other liberall artes and sciences, I would have you reasonablie
versed in them, but not preassing to be a passe-maister in any of them, for that
cannot but distract you from the points of your calling.'[64] Consequently educators
in the early seventeenth century still complained of the belittlement of learning by
members of the social élite, quite often adopting the same phraseology that had
been employed by their humanist predecessors a century earlier.[65] James Cleland,
for example, still believed in 1607 that a

> false and fantastical opinion prevaileth so against reason now a daies, that ignorance is
> thought an essential marke of a noble man by many. . . . Such is the miserie and blindness
> of this unhappie age, that manie growing in yeares professe nothing more then scoffing at
> learning and the professors therof, in calling them al clerks or pedants. If they perceive anie
> noble man better disposed to learning then themselves, presentlie after a scorning manner
> they will baptize him with the name of philosopher; have a compasse and a rule in his studie,
> then hee is an astrologian; can hee make halfe a sonnet, hee is a rimer.[66]

But even if the aristocracy did not rise fully to the scholarly heights advocated by
the humanists, there was nevertheless no questioning that the élite should pursue
learning and patronize erudition.

By mid-century, though, the climate was already changing. Henry Peacham, who
in *The Complete Gentleman* (1622) had recommended a well-rounded course of learning for members of the upper class, had by the eve of the civil war lost his earlier

---

[63] Stone, *The Past and the Present*, 209, 214.

[64] *The Basilicon Doron of King James I*, ed. J. Craigie (2 vols Edinburgh and London 1944) i. 151.

[65] See for example Richard Pace's response to a nobleman who would rather see his son hanged
than lettered for 'gentlemen's sons ought to be able to blow their horn skillfully, to hunt well, and to
carry and train a hawk elegantly, but the study of letters is to be left to the sons of peasants'. F. Caspari,
Humanism and Social Order in Tudor England (Chicago 1954, repr. New York 1968), 257–8.

[66] James Cleland, *The Institution of A Young Noble Man*, ed. M. Molyneux (New York 1948), 134–5.

faith in the prospects of converting them. 'Our nobility and gentry', he complained in 1638, do not 'so much affect the study of good letters as in former times, loving better the active than the contemplative part of knowledge.' Peacham then bade farewell to a career in education, 'having evermore found the world unthankful, how industrious soever [he had] been'. After the Restoration most observers grew nostalgic for a bygone golden age. The noted Anglican divine and canon of Christ Church Richard Allestree yearned in 1660 for the day when gentlemen would again 'lay aside that common error of thinking it more manly to be ignorant than to learn', while the veteran defender of learning, Edward Leigh (MA 1623), in 1671, likewise articulated the desire to see 'our gentry generally more studious'.[67]

The shift was particularly conspicuous because as late as the 1650s many believed that the patronage of learning had been a distinguishing feature of the English. James Harrington thought that the English people had 'or have had, a nobility or gentry the best studied . . . in the world', while Edward Waterhouse was convinced that 'the English nobility and gentry [were] now as learned as ever in any age they [had] been; and as the nobility and gentry of any other nation [was]'.[68] But as an aversion to learning set in, it was no longer possible to commend the general veneration of scholarship. One could only single out those few who still upheld the discarded ideal—as in Anthony Wood's portrayal of John Wilmot, second earl of Rochester (MA 1661), as 'thoroughly acquainted with the classic authors, both Greek and Latin, a thing very rare (if not peculiar to him) among those of his quality'.[69]

Much of the blame for this reversal in attitudes was ascribed to the deleterious effects of the growing influence of French culture. Hand in hand with the rise of France to political and military greatness was the ascendancy of French language, style, and fashion. The guiding principles now in vogue were sociability and decorum, the venue being the mixed company of the court and the salon, where speech, learning, and taste were all subordinated to the rules of 'politeness'. To please was far more important than to inform, and what mattered most was not what one did but how one did it. The new taste for refinement and elegance was most conspicuous in conversation. Here, as Abel Boyer depicted the mandatory 'art of pleasing in company', what was required of the polite man was 'a dexterous management of our words and actions, whereby we make other people have better opinion of us and themselves'. By the time of the eighteenth century, when courtesy was supplanted by etiquette, the serious literary content that was integral to the former was

---

[67] Henry Peacham, 'The truth of our times' in *The Complete Gentleman*, ed. V. B. Heltzel (Ithaca NY 1962), 185, 188; Richard Allestree, *The Gentlemans Calling* (London 1660), 53; Edward Leigh, *Three Diatribes or Discourses* (London 1671), sig. A2v. Jonathan Swift, too, saw the Restoration as auguring the 'corrupt method of education among us'. 'An essay on modern education' in Jonathan Swift, *Prose Works*, ed. T. Scott (12 vols London 1897–1908) xi. 50.

[68] James Harrington, *Political Writings*, ed. C. Blitzer (New York 1955), 132; Edward Waterhouse, *The Gentleman's Monitor* (London 1665), 349, quoted in L. Stone, 'The educational revolution in England, 1560–1640', *Past & Present* no. 28 (1964), 64.

[69] Wood, *Athenae* iii. 1229.

also discarded. Etiquette simply required the compliance with a code of manners and a set of 'exact rules of interpersonal behavior with a relative disregard for moral thought', and 'whereas courtesy treated man broadly in society, etiquette focused narrowly on sociability'.[70]

In 1855, when defending Oxford education, Mark Pattison excoriated French liberal education for being 'wholly subordinate to the purpose of shining in society; only so much of it is attained as shall serve as a qualification for conversation, and no accomplishment is so showy and dazzling as the easy and habitual use of the language of philosophical culture'. Such a verdict was the legacy, stretching back to the sixteenth century, of the English belief in the superficiality of French education and its deleterious influence on England. Already Roger Ascham (died 1568) had cited certain young gentlemen who 'count[ed] it their shame to be counted learned' simply because 'the ientlemen of France do so'. Thomas Overbury observed in 1612 that French aristocrats were 'good courtiers, good souldiers, and knowing enough in men and businesse, but meerly ignorant in matters of letters, because at fifteene they quit bookes, and begin to live in the world'. Evelyn in 1652 slighted the intellectual prowess of most French noblemen: 'I cannot affirm that the youth of the gentry and noblesse of France are bred altogether so literate as most of our English and Dutch are ... It is the field and court which the gentry affect as the best education.'[71]

By the second half of the seventeenth century many observers grew irate with the rapid spread of the French devotion to politeness which, in turn, gave rise to the ideal of the man *à la mode*, whose chief concern was the ease and graceful fluency of his conversation. 'One reason why learning hath decayed in these later times and now', wrote Anthony Wood in the late 1660s, 'is the nation of England her too much admiring the manner and fashions of the French nation.' Wood did not speak only for the constituency of professed scholars. Literary figures were equally concerned with the demise of the previous canons of learning which had resulted from the new fashion. Samuel Butler wryly described a situation in which

> Though to smatter words of Greek
> And Latin be rhetorique
> Of pedants counted, and vainglorious,
> To smatter French is meritorious.[72]

For his part Thomas Shadwell repeatedly denounced the triumph of French cultural imperialism, not least because 'the false instructions of ignorant, petulant, and conceited tutors, [along] with the French education, and the vicious examples of

---

[70] Abel Boyer, *The English Theophrastus* (London 1702), 106, 108, cited in Lawrence Klein, 'The third earl of Shaftesbury and the progress of politeness', *Eighteenth-Century Studies* 18 (1984–5), 190; Michael Curtin, 'A question of manners: status and gender in etiquette and courtesy', *Journal of Modern History* 57 (1985), 409.

[71] M. Pattison, *Essays*, ed. H. Nettleship (2 vols Oxford 1889) i. 436; Ascham *The Scholemaster*, 213; J. Lough, *France Observed in the Seventeenth Century by British Travellers* (Boston and London 1986), 95–6.

[72] Wood, *Life and Times* i. 422; T. B. Macaulay, *History of England* (4 vols London 1967) i. 310–11.

Paris' had debauched 'the heads and hearts, the intellectuals and morals of so great a part of our young gentry, that it can never be sufficiently bewailed by all sober men'. So it was that

> our good natur'd nation thinks it fit,
> To count French tops, good wares; French nonsense, wit.

Daniel Defoe scolded the prevailing opinion 'that universities make young men pedants; that to dance, fence, speak French, and know how to behave yourself among great persons of both sexes, comprehends the whole duty of a gentleman', and thought that the 'pernicious custom in rich and noble families, of entertaining French tutors in their houses' most contributed to the decline of learning. Not surprisingly, as Thomas Baker noted at the start of the eighteenth century, university life and manners were publicly ridiculed by the élite, the Oxford Act attracting 'men of fashion' who came 'to shew some new French cutt, laugh at learning and prove their want of it'.[73]

In practice, the demise of the ideal of erudition meant that already by the middle of the seventeenth century members of the élite, though still encouraged to follow their studies, were also advised against parading their learning in fashionable society. John Selden's reflection during the 1650s on the need for circumspection in the use of scholarship heralded the coming trend: 'He that comes from the university to govern the state, before he is acquainted with the men and manners of the place, does just as if he should come into the presence all dirty, with his boots on, his riding-coat, and his hat all daubed. They may serve him well enough in the way, but when he comes to court, he must conform to the place.' By the early 1670s such caution was routine. The former Oxford scholar Richard Lingard informed members of the social élite who went down from the university that 'there is a husk and shell that grows up with the learning they acquired, which they must throw away'. Therefore, a gentleman was advised that 'when you come into company, be not forward to show your proficiency, nor impose your academicall discourses, nor glitter affectedly in terms of art'.[74]

John Locke especially serves as a good barometer for the changing climate of opinion. Seizing upon the latent prejudices against erudition, Locke constructed a powerful anti-intellectual programme of education that appealed to the nobility not only through its elevation of decorum as the summit of education, but also through its sanctioning of superficiality in the formal course of study. When Locke argued that 'the business of education is not ... to make them perfect in any one of the

---

[73] Thomas Shadwell, *Some Reflections Upon the Pretended Parallel* (London 1683), 23–4; Thomas Shadwell, *The Miser*, in *The Complete Works of Thomas Shadwell* (5 vols London 1927) ii. 17 (I owe these references to Steven Pincus); Jonathan Swift, 'An essay on modern education', *The Prose Works of Jonathan Swift*, ed. T. Scott (12 vols London 1897–1908) xi. 52–31; [Thomas Baker], *An Act at Oxford* (London 1704), 2.

[74] John Selden, *Table Talk*, ed. S. A. Reynolds (Oxford 1892), 187; R[ichard] L[ingard], *A Letter of Advice to a Young Gentleman Leaving the University* (London 1670), 3, 11. See also Walker, *Of Education*, 249–50.

sciences, but so to open and dispose their minds as may best make them capable of any, when they shall apply themselves to it', he shrewdly appropriated the language employed by the humanists in their ideal of education only to strip it of the substantial scholarly content they had invested in it. Locke articulated his position in response to the earl of Peterborough's intention to raise his son a scholar: 'Your lordship would have a thorough scholar, and I think it not much matter whether he be any great scholar or no; if he but understand Latin well, and have a general scheme of the sciences, I think that enough. But I would have him well-bred, well-tempered [and] conversant with men and the world.'[75]

After 1700 a growing number of educators adopted, more or less willingly, Locke's relegation of learning to the bottom of the gentleman's educational experience. Advising Lord Roos of the manner in which he was to proceed with his education, Henry Felton (MA 1702), the future principal of St Edmund Hall, maintained that 'there is no necessity of leading you through these several fields of knowledge. It will be most commendable for you to gather some of the fairest fruit from them all, and to lay up a store of good sense, and sound reason, of great probity, and solid virtue.' Even in the study of the classics, Felton continued, it was important not to over-exert oneself with serious scholarship: 'the next direction I would give your lordship is that you would decline the critical part of learning as much as possible, for that will lead you insensibly from good sense, and good language, and it is below a person of your lordship's parts and quality to take notice of it.' The only thing to take care of was always to 'use the best and most correct editions . . . where the sense and language are complete' while the 'various readings will be only troublesome'.[76]

Felton, like Walker, Lingard, and Locke before him, charted a course of education that was informed by the necessity to avoid at all cost the semblance of that dread intellectual disease—pedantry. 'One word', wrote Meric Casaubon in 1668, approvingly paraphrasing the judgement of a friend of his, 'consisting of but two syllables, hath undone (or much damaged) good learning: it is . . . the word pedant.' The meaning of the term was made clear by John Aubrey who characterized the total output of sixteenth- and seventeenth-century scholarship as falling into this category. Pedantry for him meant 'criticall learning'—the 'conversation and habitts of those times' being as 'stiffe and starch't as their bands and square beards, their style pedantique, stuff't with Latin and Greek sentences, like their clothes'.[77]

---

[75] Locke, *Of the Conduct of the Understanding*, 73; *The Educational Writings of John Locke*, ed. J. L. Axtell (Cambridge 1968), 189 n. 3. 'Education in England', opined Johnson in 1778, 'has been in danger of being hurt by two of its greatest men, Milton and Locke. Milton's plan is impracticable, and I suppose has never been tried. Locke's, I fancy, has been tried often enough, but is very imperfect; it gives too much to one side, and too little to the other; it gives too little to literature.' *Boswell's Life of Johnson* iii. 358.

[76] Henry Felton, *A Dissertation on the Reading of the Classics and Forming a Just Style* (London 1713), 14–15, 40–2.

[77] Spiller, '*Concerning Natural Experimental Philosophie*', 197; M. Hunter, *John Aubrey and the Realm of Learning* (London 1975), 41. 'These are not times', lamented Henry Stubbe, 'wherein men who have will or leisure look into those antiquated studies; to be wits and agreeable company, to be poets, to see, and

Erudition was doomed once the French fashion, as well as the new science, made deep inroads into learned culture. Anthony Wood delineated some of the consequences for the decay of learning and the universities:

One that discourseth in company scolar-like (viz. by q[u]oting the fathers, producing an antient verse from the poets suitable to his discourse) is accounted pedanticall and pedagogical. Nothing but news and the affairs of Christendome is discoursed off and that also generally at coffee-houses. . . . Before the warr wee had scholars that made a thorough search in scholasticall and polemicall divinity, in humane authors, and natural philosophy. But now scholars studie these things not more than what is just necessary to carry them throug the exercises of their respective colleges and the universitie. Their aime is not to live as students ought to do, viz. temperat, abstemious, and plaine and grave in apparell; but to live like gentlemen, to keep dogs and horses, to turne their studies and coleholes in[to] places to receive bottles, to swash it in apparell, to weare long periwigs, etc.[78]

Both Meric Casaubon in the 1660s and Daniel Defoe half a century later saw the rapid decline in the veneration of erudition as the disastrous consequence of the vagaries of fashion. Casaubon drew an analogy between the fashionable horror of pedantry and what he 'had read in the histories of England of the word *nithing*; the imputation whereof was once so generally abhorred in England, that even the most coward (naturally) would choose present death, such operation it had then, and become resolute and valiant against their nature, rather than to undergoe the ignominie of it'. Defoe, too, drew a parallel when ascribing 'the reason of the generall ignorance, which we are so fond of in this age' to the power of fashion. Just as during the reign of Richard III courtiers wore humps under their clothes 'that so they might be in the fashion and look like the king', so at present 'glorious ignorance came to be the fashion so much among us . . . that we grow proud of this deformity'. Many parents 'look[ed] upon learning as a thing of indifference and of no great use to a gentleman' and forbore sending their sons to school, either because they assumed that leaving their sons 'a great estate [was] enough and [made] a full amends for all the pretended defficiencies of the head' or because they feared 'that making them schollars [would] but plunge them into politicks, embark them in parties, and endanger their being some time overthrown and ruined'.[79]

It is hardly surprising, therefore, that a new conception of the ideal intellectual and educator emerged—the gentleman-scholar—as the only one capable of serving as tutor to members of the élite. William Cavendish, duke of Newcastle and governor of the future Charles II, discouraged his charge from becoming 'too studious, for too much contemplation spoils action'. The youth was encouraged to

understand and write plays, to talk of and pretend to certain toyish experiments, these are cares of such high concernment, that all philology is but pedantry, and polemical divinity controversies with which we are satiated.' Henry Stubbe, *Legends no Histories* (London 1670), 11.

[78] Wood, *Life and Times* i. 423.

[79] Spiller, '*Concerning Natural Experimental Philosophie*', 197; Daniel Defoe, *The Compleat English Gentleman*, ed. K. D. Bülbring (London 1890), pp. xiv–xvi, 10–11.

emulate his tutor Brian Duppa, former dean of Christ Church, who 'hath no pedantry in him; his learning he makes right use of, neither to trouble himself with it or his friends'. Duppa 'reades men as well as books ... and in a word strives as much discreetly to hide the scholler in him, as other men's follies studies to shew it, and is a right gentleman, such a one as man should be'. Another paragon of such an ideal was Henry Aldrich of Christ Church who was highly commended in 1679 by John Percival as 'a gentleman born, well bred himself, and tho excellent both in ancient and modern learning, yet wholly free from all that can be interpreted as pedantry'. Thomas Taylor (demy of Magdalen College, 1689–95), described in similar terms his tutor Thomas Ludford: 'A person in whom the scholar and gentleman were so well met, that neither of them spoiled the other. He was learned without arrogance, genteel without vanity, witty without affectation, well bred, airy, gay and easy, yet never relaxed his mind so far as to abate in any part of its real improvement.'[80]

The new conventions, which profoundly affected the canons of learning and erudition, also transformed literary sensibilities. All that smacked of pedantry was condemned, not only *vis-à-vis* the prevailing literature, but also the literary output of former times, which was re-evaluated according to this new yardstick. The poet Richard Flecknoe, for example, ruled that Ben Jonson's 'fault' was that 'he was too elaborate, and had he mixt less erudition with his playes, they had been more pleasant and delightful then they are'. Dryden granted John Donne to be 'the greatest wit, though not the best poet of our nation', principally because Donne 'affects the metaphysics, not only in his satires, but in his amorous verses, where nature only should reign; and perplexes the minds of the fair sex with nice speculations of philosophy, when he should engage their hearts, and entertain them with the softness of love'. In turn Dryden himself was dispensed with by Henry Felton who admitted that 'Mr Dryden was indeed a gentleman, but he writ more like a scholar, and tho' the greatest master of poetry the last age could boast, he wanted that easiness and familiarity, that air of freedom and unconstraint, that gentle and accomplished manner of expression, which is more sensibly to be perceived, than described'.[81]

This radical change in the attitude towards learning troubled even such individuals as Sir William Temple who generally argued against 'pedantry'. Temple complained that the nobility no longer patronized learning, let alone thought it requisite to acquire it. In his retort to Temple, William Wotton thought such disaffection came not a minute too soon:

Pedantry which formerly was almost universal, is now a great measure dis-used; especially, amongst the young men, who are taught in the universities to laugh at that frequent citation of scraps of Latin, in common discourse, or upon arguments that do not require it; and

---

[80] H. Ellis, *Original Letters Illustrative of English History* (1st ser. 3 vols London 1825) iii. 288–9; BL Add. MS 49,956A, fo 36; Father Daniel, *A Voyage to the World of Cartesius*, trans. Thomas Taylor (London 1692), sig. A2ᵛ.

[81] *Critical Essays of the Seventeenth Century*, ed. Spinram ii. 94; *Essays of John Dryden*, ed. W. P. Ker (2 vols Oxford 1900, repr. New York 1961) ii. 19; Felton, *A Dissertation on the Reading of the Classics*, 74.

that nauseous ostentation of reading, and scholarship in publick companies, which formerly was so much in fashion. Affecting to write politely in modern languages, especially the French and ours, has also helped very much to lessen it, because it has enabled abundance of men who want academical education to talk plausibly, and some exactly, upon very many learned subjects.

Commenting in 1753 on the state of learning among the English aristocracy John Brown lamented the absence of 'a knowledge of books, a taste in arts, a proficiency in science, [that] was formerly regarded as a proper qualification, in a man of fashion. The annals of our country have transmitted to us the name and memory of men, as eminent in learning and taste, as in rank and fortune. It will not, I presume, be regarded as any kind of satire on the present age, to say, that among the higher ranks, this literary spirit is generally vanished'.[82]

THE IDEAL IN PRACTICE

As befitting the anterior system in which thought and expression were inextricably linked, language had been the alpha and omega of the educational process. Erasmus articulated this relationship at the outset of his *De ratione studii* wherein he insisted that

all knowledge falls into one of two divisions: the knowledge of 'truths' and the knowledge of 'words', and if the former is first in importance the latter is required first in order of time. They are not to be commended who, in their anxiety to increase their store of truths, neglect the necessary art of expressing them. For ideas are only intelligible to us by means of the words which describe them; wherefore defective knowledge of language reacts upon our apprehension of the truths expressed.[83]

The inseparability of language and thought as expounded by Erasmus was a dominant feature of renaissance culture, one that was challenged—though not yet rejected—only in the latter part of the seventeenth century. From the time of the early Italian humanists who regarded style as an 'indispensable condition of permanence, almost indeed of credibility, in a literary work', conviction of the necessary union between reason and eloquence had remained constant. Here the humanists summed up a tradition going back to the ancient orators. In the words of Isocrates, 'the right word [was] a sure sign of good thinking'. The self-evidence of this position was accepted by virtually all English educators for the next two centuries. To quote but one adherent, Thomas Barlow (MA 1633) wrote in the 1650s that 'wee must know wordes before wee can compasse the knowledge of thinges, all learning beeing lockd up in some language'.[84]

---

[82] *The Works of Sir William Temple* iii. 481–3; William Wotton, *Reflections upon Ancient and Modern Learning* (London 1694), 354; John Brown, *An Estimate of the Manners and Principles of the Times* (London 1757), 41–2, quoted in G. C. Brauer, *The Education of a Gentleman* (New Haven 1959), 55.

[83] Woodward, *Desiderius Erasmus Concerning the Aim and Method of Education*, 162.

[84] Woodward, *Vittorino da Feltre and other Humanist Educators*, 230; B. Vickers, *Classical Rhetoric in English Poetry* (London 1970), 92; 'A Library for Younger Schollers', ed. A. Dejordy and H. F. Fletcher (Urbana Ill. 1961), 12.

But the veneration of language transcended even such philosophical considerations. For humanists both on the continent and in England language exerted the authority of a moral force. On the simple level, it has been said, 'bad style and inferior vocabulary had come to imply not merely dulness but moral obloquy as well'. More profoundly, since language was considered the cornerstone of civilized society, 'a culture was in danger when its language [became] debased, blurred and vulgarized'. Roger Ascham was convinced that 'all writers, either in religion or any sect of philosophy, whosoever be found fond in judgment of matter, be commonly found as rude in uttering their mind'. Ben Jonson argued in a similar vein that 'wheresoever manners and fashions were corrupted, language is. It imitates the publicke riot. The excesses of feasts and apparell are the notes of a sick state; and the wantoness of language, of a sick mind.' And since it was the continuous reading of ancient poets, orators and historians that perpetuated language, humanists like Meric Casaubon were 'very confident that where the reading of such authors is out of fashion, barbarism and grossest ignorance [would] quickly follow'.[85]

By the late sixteenth century, however, the greater part of language training was expected to be acquired at grammar school and not, as had been previously the case, at university. Indeed, instruction in grammar at the university was now officially prohibited, fluency in Latin having effectively become 'the basic entrance requirement for Oxford and Cambridge'.[86] Such fluency included a command of Latin language and literature, both poetry and prose, as well as at least rudimentary Greek. And though the training imparted at school was predominantly geared towards mastery of language, in anticipation of university-level studies the upper forms placed increasing emphasis on 'matter' as well. The orientation was encapsulated by Osborne: 'their first travels being ended for language, whereby a possibility to understand all authors is gained, their minds would be wrought toward deeper contemplations'.[87]

This is not to say that once students ventured into the higher realms of education they were allowed to abandon the study of language. Further refinement was both needed and expected. Richard Holdsworth exhorted second-year students not to forget their grammars: 'it is now a yeare agoe or more since you came from schoole and unless you look over them now and then, you shall perceave them to slip out of your memory and now reading them over with a riper judgment, you shall see as it were with clearer eyes then before, and observe many things which you formerly passed over unregarded.' Stephen Penton, too, reminded the young

[85] B. Hall, 'Biblical scholarship' in *Cambridge History of the Bible*, ed. S. L. Greenslade (3 vols Cambridge 1963–70) iii. 39; Ascham, *English Works*, 265; *Ben Jonson*, ed. Percy and Simpson viii. 593; T. M. Greene, 'Roger Ascham: the perfect end of shooting', *English Literary History* xxxvi (1969), 609–25; Spiller, *'Concerning Natural Experimental Philosophie'*, 165.

[86] L. Jardine, 'Humanism and the sixteenth century Cambridge arts course', *History of Education* iv. (1975), 18–19.

[87] Francis Osborne, *Advice to a Son*, ed. Edward A. Parry (London 1896), 67. Thomas Fuller conveyed the same message: 'Our artist knowing language to be the key of learning, thus begins.' Fuller, *The Holy and Profane State*, 110.

undergraduate that 'philology is still improveable', and that 'speeches and theams will still deserve a good share of his thoughts, though logick, and philosophy must make the greatest noise in his head'.[88] To these ends tutors prescribed several grammatical treatises, lexicons, and dictionaries in the hope that a growing command of etymology and syntax would enable the student 'to understand the best authors in both languages', that is, Latin and Greek. In addition to increasing familiarity with words and idioms the students were expected to read a variety of works that introduced them to ancient religions, laws, customs, and institutions, thus setting the stage for the eventual study of textual criticism.[89] Almost needless to add, throughout the undergraduate course verse and prose compositions were assigned as a means to fluency.

Unquestionably, the emphasis on the rules and precepts of the various arts involved considerable amounts of drilling and memorization, which in turn could lead to tedium, if not outright bitterness, on the part of the undergraduate. Educators and parents, though aware of this danger, were nevertheless convinced that a rigorous and continuous routine of versification, memorization, translation, composition, declamation, and disputation was indispensable for a solid and enduring educational foundation. James Cleland articulated the common wisdom when he reasoned thus: 'it is hard matter to put out of minde that which we have learned in yonger years.' In one of his aphorisms on education Sir Henry Wotton propagated an identical moral. Under the heading 'he seldom speeds well in his course, that stumbles at his setting forth', Wotton drove home the message by citing approvingly 'a discreet censor lesson a young scholer, negligent at his first entrence to the elements of logick and philosophy, telling him that a child starved at nurse, would hardly prove an able man'.[90] Educators similarly attempted to soothe the student's anxiety, if not outright distaste, by emphasizing the higher purpose behind these exercises. 'Albeit the roots of learning be bitter', entreated Cleland, 'yet the fruit thereof is sweet ... At the beginning manie detest learning ... but after they have digested and felt the sweetnes thereof, they are allured therewith as it were with hony, or sweete new wine, that they cannot be satisfied before death cal up them.'[91]

Parental wisdom tended to affirm the wisdom of the schools. 'Apply your studies diligently', William Fleming advised his son Daniel at Queen's College, 'for now is the time to lay the foundation to all accomplishments thereafter.' John Evelyn wished his son to be 'as well furnished as might be for the laying of a permanent and solid foundation', a wish similarly expressed by Sir Bevil Granville who urged his son to disregard all hardships and the example of youths who misspent their time, and instead apply himself assiduously for a mere three years for the infinite

[88] Fletcher, *Intellectual Development of John Milton* ii. 641; Penton, *Guardian's Instruction*, 94.

[89] '*A Library for Younger Schollers*', ed. Dejordy and Fletcher, 14; Bodl. MS Rawlinson d. 188, fos 7–8.

[90] Cleland, *The Institution of A Young Noble Man*, 29; Henry Wotton, *A Philosophical Survey of Education or Moral Architecture and the Aphorisms of Education*, ed. H. S. Kermode (Liverpool 1938), 88.

[91] Cleland, *The Institution of A Young Noble Man*, 141–2.

benefit that would thence accrue. Nearly a century later even the earl of Chester-field was still using identical reasoning in preparing his son for university: 'These two years', he wrote, 'must lay the foundations of all knowledge that you will ever have; you may build upon them afterwards as much as you please, but it will be too late to lay any new ones.'[92]

In retrospect, it is easy to leap to the conclusion that the often tedious mastery of rules and precepts was advocated simply as an end in itself by defenders of an impoverished system of education, but this was not the case. In a culture that regarded Latin as a living language, command of the tongue was believed essential to the inculcation of proper habits of style and thought. As for the rules them-selves, they were but means intended to give way to practice—composition, decla-mations, and disputations. John Grandorge of St Edmund Hall emphasized that the learning of grammar and rhetoric was 'to lay down rules and directions for speak-ing', but one would hardly become an orator without 'some patterns to follow and similate'. Abraham Fraunce offered in 1588 a more elaborate view of this blend:

Neyther let any man thinke, that because in common meetings and assemblies the wordes and tearmes of logike bee not named, therefore the force and operation of logike is not there used and apparant. For, as in grammer wee name neyther noune, pronoune, verbe, nor any other parte of speech; and as in rhetorike, wee make mention neyther of *metonymia*, *synecdoche*, *exclamatio*, nor any other rhetorical figure or trope, yet use in our speech the helpe of the one in speaking grammatically, and the direction of the other in talking eloquently; so although in common conference wee never name syllogismes . . . and other words of art, yet do wee secretly practise them in our disputations, the vertue whereof is, to make our discourses seeme true to the simple, and probable to the wise.[93]

Such a view of grammar, rhetoric and logic, encapsulated the essentially utilitarian image of the arts of discourse held by educators and parents alike. These subjects were 'instrumental disciplines', the objective of which was unabashedly functional. As described by Obadiah Walker, the arts of discourse 'are but foundations, upon which all sciences are built, but themselves appear not in the edifice'.[94]

Evidently the study of classical languages and literature was nowhere near com-plete by the time the students embarked upon rhetoric and logic and, later, phi-losophy. The ideal of absorption of the entire corpus of Greek and Latin literature was to prove the business of a lifetime and not a one- or two-year excursion. Erasmus emphatically reminded his readers that 'we are not to be dubbed "begin-ners" because we have not yet mastered' the extant writings of the minor classical authors. Hence, while continuing his study of Latin and Greek language and liter-ature, the student ventured into contiguous fields: 'A method of investigation comes next to the study of language', explained Vives, 'a means whereby we can test the

[92] *The Flemings in Oxford* i. 17; *Diary of John Evelyn*, ed. W. Bray (4 vols London 1906) iii. 305; Granville, *The History of the Granville Family*, 205, 207; *The Letters of Philip Dormer Stanhope 4th Earl of Chesterfield*, ed. Bonamy Dobrée (6 vols New York 1932) iii. 1154.
[93] Bodl. MS St Edmund Hall 72; Abraham Fraunce, *The Lawiers Logike* (London 1588), 120.
[94] Walker, *Of Education*, 110.

true and the false by simple and well-arranged rules.' The student was intended to pursue the two concurrently, 'so that he goes on to the completion of the one whilst making progress in the other'.[95]

The harmony of the arts of discourse was recapitulated by the Oxford tutor Thomas Heywood. 'The business of this first year', he wrote, 'is to learn to think well, and to express our thoughts to others, so as to communicate to them the very ideas, judgments and reasons we have within ourselves, whenever we discourse or write. In other words 'tis to understand the nature of a composition in generall.' This was required in order 'to frame distinct notions' as well as 'a theme, a decla-mation, an oration, an epistle, a character, a dialogue, a discourse or treatise' or, in poetry, 'an epigram, a satyr, an ode, whether Sapphyick, Alcaick, or Pindarick, an epistolary poem . . . a pastorall, and an epick poem'.[96]

Latin and the Arts of Eloquence

Rhetoric and logic came first in the order of studies, both as the sister arts of dis-course and as the two general skills that 'offered techniques to all other arts'. Contemporaries viewed the two as inseparable and of equal worth. Logic and rhetoric 'cannot be parted asunder', warned Holdsworth. 'Logick without oratory is drye and unpleasing and oratory without logick is but empty babling.' John Selden's imagery was more colourful: 'Rhetoric without logic is like a tree with leaves and blossoms, but no root.' To Ben Jonson 'in all speech, words and sense are as the body and the soule' while Thomas Fuller impressed upon his readers that rhetoric 'gives a speech color, as logic doth flavor, and both together beauty. Though some condemn rhetoric as the mother of lies, speaking more than the truth in hyperboles, less in her miosis, otherwise in her metaphors, contrary in her ironies, yet is there excellent use of all these when disposed of with judgment.'[97]

Like logic, rhetoric claimed to be universal in application. As Farnaby phrased it, 'the material of rhetoric is any matter which may be the subject of persuasion'. Yet just as logic was conceived of as a means to regulate thought, but not in itself capable of determining true knowledge, so it was held that close application to rhetoric and the acquisition of style did not necessarily come 'at the expense of critical reflection on the subject matter'. In the words of Isaac Barrow rhetoric was 'the art of conveying our thoughts to others by speech with advantages of clear-ness, force, and elegancy, so as to instruct, to persuade, to delight the auditors'.[98]

The anti-rhetorical stance of modern scholarship makes it difficult to appreciate the centrality of eloquence to early modern culture and the vitality it once possessed. The subject-matter of rhetoric often proved seductive to teacher and

---

[95] Woodward, *Desiderius Erasmus Concerning the Aim and Method of Education*, 164; *Vives: on education*, ed. Watson, 163–4.

[96] Bodl. MS Rawlinson d. 40.

[97] Fletcher, *Intellectual Development of John Milton*, 643; Selden, *Table Talk*, 148; *Ben Jonson*, ed. Percy and Simpson viii. 621; Fuller, *The Holy and Profane State*, 112.

[98] R. M. Ogilvie, *Latin and Greek* (Hamden Conn. 1964), 37; Thomas Farnaby, *Index rhetoricus* (London 1633), 1; Barrow, *Theological Works* iii. 242.

student alike. C. S. Lewis has explained such allurement in these terms: 'Your father, your grown-up brother, your admired elder schoolfellow all loved rhetoric. Therefore you loved it too. You adored sweet Tully and were as concerned about *asyndeton* and *chiasmus* as a modern schoolboy is about cricketers or types of aeroplane.'[99] Not surprisingly such an attraction to modes of speech exposed rhetoric to critics, both then and now. Peter France, in his study of early modern French rhetoric, astutely observes that rhetoric 'was the object of much ingratitude, and was often spurned by those who had most profited from it, but this did not diminish its significance as a powerful force in the world of writing and speaking, reading and listening'. The message is reiterated by Brian Vickers, who warns against the hostility of modern scholars towards rhetoric, the early modern detractors of which have come to be viewed as the 'avant-garde élite' of the seventeenth century.[100]

The fact that the greatest among seventeenth-century philosophers censured language and rhetoric as detrimental to deep thinking is viewed as evidence of the impoverishment of rhetoric and the failure of neo-Latin culture in general. Yet, to quote Vickers again, in their zeal to undermine rhetoric these modern-day scholars have taken the 'calls for the banishment of rhetoric as proof that this duly took place'.[101] What is ignored in such criticism is the explicit polemical character of seventeenth-century critics. Substantively, they targeted simply the abuses of language; but so, too, did the humanists themselves. More to the point, the concentrated attack on language, rhetoric, and poetry by the proponents of the new philosophy was part and parcel of their advocacy of a competing programme, the success of which was contingent on the elimination, or at least abatement, of the interest in language.

As it turned out the deep-seated partiality to the literature of the ancients and the large allocation of student time to its pursuit was a cause of concern, not only to proponents of the new philosophy, but to educators as well. It will be argued below that much of the seventeenth-century complaint against logic and philosophy came as a result of a too successful training in the classics, which in turn made university students prefer poetry and rhetoric to the thornier philosophy. Indeed, some observers even believed that prolonged exposure to the beauties of language and poetry was potentially harmful to a career at the Inns of Court. According to Augustine Baker, students who lingered at university rarely adapted to the study of the law 'for to wits seasoned with these pleasant studies . . . the law is more harsh and barbarous'.[102] Analogously, not the least significant of the motives informing the harsh censure of language, poetry, and rhetoric by the likes of Bacon, Hobbes, Sprat, and Locke was prompted by similar considerations. Beyond their genuine

---

[99] C. S. Lewis, *English Literature in the Sixteenth Century* (Oxford 1954), 61.

[100] P. France, *Rhetoric and Truth in France* (Oxford 1972), 4; B. Vickers, *In Defence of Rhetoric* (Oxford 1988), 199, 201.

[101] Vickers, *In Defence of Rhetoric*, 201.

[102] *Memorials of Father Augustine Baker 1575–1641*, ed. J. McCann (London 1933), 65.

concern to dismantle wrong ideas and eliminate the scholastic philosophy of words, these philosophers complained bitterly of the propensity of their contemporaries for 'sweet rhetoric' and their concomitant disinclination to engage their minds with 'real' knowledge.

For Bacon, the 'first distemper of learning' occurred 'when men studie words, and not matter'. The great popularity of the lectures delivered at sixteenth-century Cambridge by Car and Ascham had tended almost to 'deifie Cicero and Demosthenes, and allure all young men that were studious unto that delicate and polished kinde of learning. ... In summe, the whole inclination and bent of those times, was rather towards copie, than weight.' Obviously Bacon—who wryly remarked that 'profoundness of wisdom will help a man to a name or admiration, but that it is eloquence that prevaileth in the active life'—realized that his programme stood little chance of success unless the taste for 'words' abated. Sprat also considered the real problem with 'easy vanity of fine speaking' to be its ability to snatch 'many rewards that are due to more profitable and difficult arts'. He attributed the cause of this preference to 'the present genius of the English nation, wherein the study of wit, and humour of writing prevails so much, that there are very few conditions, or degrees, or ages of men who are free from its infection'. The dilemma for Sprat was 'that, of all the studies of men, nothing may be sooner obtained than this vicious abundance of phrase, this trick of metaphors, this volubility of tongue, which makes so great a noise in the world'. Yet it was precisely such 'beautiful deceit' that the English preferred to 'undeceiving expressions'— principally 'because they have laboured so long after it in the years of their education that ever after they think kinder of it than it deserves'. As might be expected Locke, too, lamented that 'wit and fancy finds easier entertainment in the world, than dry truth and real knowledge'. Regrettably, he continued, 'the concern of mankind' was so little given to truth and knowledge because clearly it was 'the arts of fallacy [that were] endowed and preferred'. He concluded 'men love to deceive, and be deceived, since rhetorick, that powerful instrument of error and deceit, has its established professors, is publickly taught, and has always been had in great reputation'.[103]

The polemical stance of the critics aside, their descriptions convey the centrality of rhetoric in seventeenth-century culture. The lengthy and careful linguistic instruction at both school and university culminated with training in the mastery of eloquence. But this 'included much more than the mere parroting of precepts: the student who had read widely among the Greek and Latin masters necessarily acquired a *habitus* of style which reduced the precepts to practice'.[104] Only through the acquisition of such a disposition was Latin rendered a living and dynamic medium of speech and writing.

---

[103] *Works of Bacon*, ed. Spedding, Ellis, and Heath iii. 409; Thomas Sprat, *The History of the Royal Society* (London 1667), 111–12, 413; John Locke, *Essay concerning Human Understanding*, ed. P. H. Nidditch (Oxford 1975) 508.

[104] Costello, *The Scholastic Curriculum*, 61.

The rhetorical training was intended to be as comprehensive as possible, exercising the student in a variety of ancient and modern styles. This eclectic approach, premissed on the belief that the ability to master and appreciate style arose from sustained exposure to the full range of available models, was delineated in Thomas Farnaby's popular *Index rhetoricus*: 'I should not have the young and inexperienced youth diverted entirely to the lush fullness of Cicero, and I should not have him confined only to one very beautiful field. But as he matures, I would have him wander more freely through the fertile fields of the authors and, as an adult, I would have him rejoicing in open horizons.' After pursuing such rhetoricians and historians as Cicero, Pliny, Caesar, Livy, Sallust, Tacitus, Quintus Curtius, Suetonius, and Valerius Maximus, the student was expected to add Quintilian, Plautus, Terence, and then, as he advanced further, Agellius, Capella, Apuleius, 'and the other Africans'. Nor were more recent authors—Petrarch, Politianus, Lipsius, Strada, and the 'one who now inspires all the youth, Barclaius'—ignored.[105]

Throughout much of the seventeenth century this heavy eclecticism of styles was the staple recommendation of tutors. Richard Holdsworth offers a good example of how the mixture of the approved classical authors was integrated with other ancients as well as neo-Latin writers. After reading 'such authors in prose as write a plain easy and familiar style out of which it is proper to learn Latin'—Cicero, Terence, Ovid, Virgil, Martial, and Horace, as well as Erasmus, are specified—'now you come to some more raised and pollished [authors] the reading wherof will worke your fancy to such a kinde of expression when occasion is'. Here, Famiano Strada's *Prolusiones academicae*, John Barclay or Petronius Arbiter offered 'the same kinde of stile, that is such for Latine as Sir Philip Sydnie is for English'. Further works recommended by Holdsworth included the orations of Robert Turner and John Rainolds, both of which were intended to exercise the student 'in quaint style'. Later still Holdsworth recommended works of the more obscure Roman stylists such as Aulus Gellius, Macrobius, and Plautus, though he advised against imitating the latter's style. From Clement Barksdale's depiction of undergraduate studies at Oxford on the eve of the Restoration we get a similar picture. The student who read the classics 'must so honour the ancient writers, as not to neglect those of latter time'. Specifying Melanchton, Politian, Erasmus, Scaliger, Casaubon, Lipsius, Sarravius, and Grotius, Barksdale was convinced the student would 'find a great deal of pleasure and profit in those authors [and] especially get a good judgement in the affaires of learning and knowledge of good authors'.[106]

By the end of the seventeenth century, however, different conceptions of style and the introduction of new canons of correctness—not to mention the gradual decline in the vitality of Latin—effected certain changes in instruction. Though a tutor such as Thomas Heywood still recommended in 1704 to 'affect no stile, but be master of all', one cannot fail to detect a certain closure and narrowness in terms

[105] R. Nadeau, 'A renaissance schoolmaster on practice', *Speech Monographs* xvii (1950), 173–4.
[106] Fletcher, *The Intellectual Development of John Milton*, 644–5; Clement Barksdale, *An Oxford Conference of Philomathes and Polymathes* (London 1660), 4–5.

of the range of approved writers and styles—especially as regards neo-Latin authors. 'No modern writer compared with the ancients for patterns', was the opinion of John Grandorge in 1690, since 'for the most part they are but lame copies of those originals, and imperfect imitations of those greatest masters of antiquity'. Grandorge recommended the careful study of only 'the pure and unaffected Latin [prose] authors (which are commonly classicks) from Plautus to Plinius the younger'. The poets he listed were Terence, Virgil, Lucretius, Horace, Ovid, Catullus, Tibullus, Propertius, Lucan, Martial, Juvenal, and Claudian. Another contemporaneous author of a manual of advice thought only 'the best classical authors', needed to be mastered, citing by name a sample that included Cicero, Plautus, Terence, Virgil, Horace, Ovid, Lucan, Seneca, and Juvenal.[107]

The range of authors studied by Oxford undergraduates can be gleaned from surviving library catalogues and accounts. Once allowance is made for the limitations of our records—the inconsistent nature of even the best accounts listing individual book titles, and the tendency for poorer students to borrow far more books than they purchased—a remarkable similarity emerges. The purchases of the Newdigate brothers during 1618–19 included Horace, Juvenal, Persius, Pliny, Ovid, Ravisius Textor, Lucan, Martial, Theophrastus, Plautus, Seneca, Petronius Arbiter, and Aulus Gellius, in addition to a variety of historical works by Tacitus, Florus, Livy, Sallust, and Suetonius. The library catalogues of two recent Oxford bachelors of art in the 1650s were more detailed. John Hutton of New College, who died in 1653, owned Sallust, Pliny, Varro, Plautus, Martial, Caesar, Horace, Juvenal, Persius, Virgil, Catullus, Tibullus, Propertius, Quintus Curtius, Terence, Cicero, Macrobius, Statius, and Tacitus among the ancients, and Erasmus, Lipsius, Scaliger, Heinsius, Strada, Barclay, Budaeus, and Joseph Hall's *Mundus alter et idem* among the moderns. Edward Bernard's collection of Latin literature in 1658 included Cicero, Pliny, Apuleius, Petronius Arbiter, Virgil, Ovid, Horace, Martial, Juvenal, Persius, Prudentius, Terence, Seneca, Lucan, Claudian, Plautus, Silius Italicus, Ausonius, Lucretius, Livy, Caesar, Tacitus, Valerius Maximus, and Sallust.[108] Henry Fleming brought with him to Magdalen College in 1678 Horace, Juvenal, Persius, Virgil, Seneca, Florus, and Cicero. At Oxford he acquired Quintus Curtius, Suetonius, Terence, Quintilian, and, among the moderns, Polydor Vergil, Barclay, and Famianus Strada. The titles of other authors purchased by Fleming while an undergraduate can be gathered from the books he bestowed on his brother George when the latter came up to Oxford in 1689: Smetius' *Prosodia*, Caspar Barlaeus' *Poemata*, and Heinsius' *Orationes duae*.[109]

---

[107] Bodl. MS Rawlinson d. 40; Bodl. MS St Edmund Hall 72; Bodl. MS Rawlinson d. 188. Daniel Waterland's early eighteenth-century list included Terence, Cicero, Cornelius Nepos, Caesar, Sallust, Ovid, Virgil, Horace, Juvenal, Persius, and Livy. After graduation the student was advised also to read Pliny, Seneca, Lucretius, Plautus, Quintus Curtius, Suetonius, Tacitus, Aulus Gellius, Lucan, Martial, Catullus, Tibullus, and Propertius. Waterland, *Works* iv. 407–13.

[108] 'The undergraduate account book of John and Richard Newdigate, 1618–21', ed. V. Larminie, *Camden Miscellany* xxx (Camden Soc. 4th ser. xxxix 1990), 162, 163, 177, 178, 194, 195, 198–9; OUA chancellor's ct inventories s.v. John Hutton; Bodl. MS Lat. misc. f 11, fos 15–17.

[109] *The Flemings in Oxford* i. 250–4, 322–3, 326, ii. 16, 28, 83–4, 117, 276–7, 279, 280.

By the early eighteenth century, when erudition and breadth of knowledge were rejected as an ideal unworthy of emulation, the estrangement from renaissance models became complete; not surprisingly, the canon of ancient authors shrank too. In line with the prevailing dictates of neo-classical taste, the approved canon of classical authors was pared down to a choice list of masterpieces. Locke's gentleman, for whom good breeding was considered the essence of education, needed neither the application 'to the understanding of any language critically' nor the wide reading of books, but 'only the best authors on those subjects'. Henry Felton applied such principles of selection to the education of Lord Roos, who was urged to 'decline the critical part of learning as much as possible, for that [would] lead [him] insensibly from good sense, and good language'. Instead a reading-list aimed at the acquisition of the correctness and pure sense of language was advocated under the principle that 'good taste is to be formed by reading the best authors'.[110] By the middle of the eighteenth century the earl of Chesterfield enunciated and sanctioned the dramatic shrinkage in the range of approved authors:

I have always observed, that the most learned people—that is, those who have read the most Latin—write the worst; and this distinguishes the Latin of a gentleman scholar from that of a pedant. A gentleman has, probably, read no other Latin than that of the Augustan age, and therefore can write no other; whereas the pedant has read much more bad Latin than good, and consequently writes so too. He looks upon the best classical books as books for schoolboys, and consequently below him; but pores over fragments of obscure authors, treasures up the obsolete words which he meets with there, and uses them, upon all occasions, to show his reading at the expense of his judgment.[111]

The preferred taste of the eighteenth century and its partiality to certain styles and authors have been co-opted by historians ever since. Viewing the 'plain style' as the 'progressive' choice of both the adherents of the new philosophy and the opponents of monarchic ideas, they have been consistently dismissive of a rhetorical culture that cherished erudition and eclecticism, and instilled rhetorical training based on a proliferation of styles. Not surprisingly the universities were maligned for their alleged role in cultivating pedantry—or at least in propagating the cult of Cicero that supposedly did to language what the deification of Aristotle did to natural philosophy.

It should be borne in mind, however, that the several learned styles popular in the Elizabethan and early Stuart periods were promoted by scholars and courtiers alike. A case in point is the Euphuistic style that originated at Oxford *circa* 1570, around John Rainolds.[112] What is remarkable is that this 'jerky, highly patterned' style was as popular at court as it was at Oxford, and not least among women. Euphues, claimed the author, and former soldier, Barnaby Rich, 'combines courtliness and humanism in perfect balance, as one "who can court with the best, and

---

[110] Felton, *A Dissertation on the Reading of the Classics*, 40–2, 129.

[111] *The Educational Writings of John Locke*, ed. Axtell, 273, 421; Chesterfield, *Letters* i. 150.

[112] G. K. Hunter, *John Lyly: the humanist as courtier* (London 1962), 260, 263; W. Ringler, 'The immediate source of Euphuism', *Publications of the Modern Language Association of America* liii (1938), 678–86.

scholler it with the most, in whom I know not whether I should more commende his maners or his learnyng, the one is so exquisite, the other so generall" '. John Hoskins (MA 1592) also believed Euphuism was 'particularly apt "and prettie to play with amonge gentlewomen" and thus entirely appropriate for a *courtly* setting of recreation and entertainment'.[113]

While all fashions are transitory, rhetorical styles proved more transitory than most. Already in 1602 the diarist John Manningham recorded the following *bon mot* at the expense of John Rainolds: 'Though a fashion of witt in writing may last longer then a fashion in a sute of clothes, yet if a writer live long, and change not his fashion, he may perhaps outlive his credit. It were good for such a man to dy quickly'. Contemporaries were well aware of such transiency. Nor did they hesitate to move from one style to another. When John Hoskins wrote his *Directions for Speech and Style* in 1599, he freely admitted to 'have used and outworne 6 severall styles, since [he] was first fellowe of Newe Colledge' in 1579. Other examples abound. John Aubrey reported that 'in his younger yeares' John Selden 'affected obscurity of style which, after, he quite left off, and wrote perspicuously'.[114]

Euphuism was followed by a succession of similarly demanding styles, all pre-missed on erudition and the inventive wielding of language. Generally referred to as 'metaphysical', these styles consisted of 'intense verbal cleverness, allusive silences, striving after paradox; love of conceit; fondness for the jarring and unex-pected image'. Samuel Johnson offered an apt summary of the metaphysical mode in his depiction of metaphysical wit as consisting of 'the most heterogenous ideas ... yoked by violence together; nature and art are ransacked for illustrations, com-parisons, and allusions; their learning instructs, and their subtilty surprises; but the reader commonly thinks his improvement dearly bought, and, though he some-times admires, is seldom pleased'. Yet this mode, too, was widely popular outside the universities and owed its durability to court patronage. As Richard Flecknoe pointed out in 1653, when the mode was on the wane, just as style under Queen Elizabeth was 'flaunting and pufted like her apparell', so during the reign of James I it inclined '*regis ad exemplum* ... much to the learned and erudite'.[115]

The succeeding learned styles became 'pedantic' only after erudition lost its

[113] Barnaby Rich, *The Second Tome of the Travailes and Adventures of Don Simonides* (London 1584), sig. I3, quoted in C. Bates, ' "A large occasion of discourse": John Lyly and the art of civil conversation', *Review of English Studies* xlii (1991), 474 n. 18; *The Life, Letters, and Writings of John Hoskins 1566–1638*, ed. L. B. Osborn (New Haven 1937, repr. Hamden Conn. 1973), 130.

[114] *The Diary of John Manningham*, ed. R. P. Sorlien (Hanover NH 1976), 132; *The Life, Letters, and Writings of John Hoskins*, ed. Osborn, 152–3; *Brief Lives by Aubrey*, ed. Clark ii. 224. In 1665 Joseph Glanvill described his own 'present relish and genius, which is more gratified with manly sense, flowing in a nat-ural and unaffected eloquence, then in the musick and curiosity of fine metaphors and dancing periods. To which measure of my present humour, I had indeavoured to reduce the style of these papers, but that I was loth to give my self that trouble in an affair to which I was grown too cold to be much con-cerned in. And this inactivity of temper perswaded me I might reasonably expect a pardon from the ingenious, for faults committed in an immaturity of age and judgment that would excuse them.' Joseph Glanvill, *Scepsis scientifica* (London 1665), sig. C4^{r-v}.

[115] Ogilvie, *Latin and Greek*, 22; Johnson, *Lives of the English Poets* i. 20–1; G. Williamson, *The Senecan Amble* (Chicago 1966), 211.

appeal and a new decorous fashion measured language by its conformity to other rules of language. Gilbert Burnet summarized the trend:

The English language has wrought it self out, both of the fulsome pedantry under which it laboured long ago and the trifling way of dark and unintelligible wit that came after that, and out of the coarse extravagance of canting that succeeded this: but as one extream commonly produces another, so we are beginning to fly into a sublime pitch, of a strong but false rhetorick ... Yet it cannot be denied but the rules and measure of speech is generally taken from them; but that florid strain is almost quite worn out, and is become now as ridiculous as it was once admired.[116]

Poetry also occupied a central position in the study of language and literature at Oxford. Highly valued for its contribution to the learning process, it was equally cherished for the pleasure it imparted. Apart from enhancing philological studies, the relentless practice of verse composition also 'encouraged clarity of thought, elegance, eloquence, brevity of expression, versatility, and quickness of wit'. Obadiah Walker thus summarized the virtue of poetry:

It is better also, if he understand and practice (though not much, except he have a considerable dexterity in it) poetry; without which no man can be a perfect orator, but his fancy as well as expressions will be low and mean. Poetry warms the imagination, makes it active, and prompt to soar to the top of Parnassus; it emboldens to the use of a lofty metaphor, or confident *catachresis*. Besides accustoming the stile to measure [it] gives insight, judgement, and readiness also in oratoricall number. It teacheth also to chuse good words, to consider, weigh, and pierce better into what we read, to take notice of the most delicate artifice, and discern sparks of diamonds. So that it is observed that when poetry is despised other sciences also are in the wane.[117]

Nevertheless, the very pleasingness of poetry made it a double-edged sword in the education process. Even more than with rhetoric, it was feared that students brought up to admire poetry would carry their enthusiasm to an excess and end up evading the more demanding studies. Consequently, parents and educators habitually tempered their endorsement of poetry. Henry Peacham's chapter on poetry in *The Complete Gentleman*, for example, though a warm tribute to poetry, was none the less prefaced with the caveat that poetry should be pursued only 'to sweeten your severer studies'.[118] Certainly if an instructive example of the adverse result of the perils of taking poetry too seriously was needed it was provided by the Oxford career of Richard Granville. He was encouraged to admire poets and historians, 'the one sort for their witt and learned allegories, the other [for their] elloquence and glorious examples of courage, magn[animity and] all other virtues which may stirr up an ingenious and active [spiri]tt to imitation'. Richard took this advice literally, forsaking logic and philosophy for poetry, to the dismay of his

---

[116] Cited in Williamson, *The Senecan Amble*, 227.

[117] Walker, *Of Education*, 109. Grandorge concurred: poetry was 'requisite for an orator to raise his fancy and elevate his thoughts and to give a sprightlynesse and beauty of expression to them'. Bodl. MS St Edmund Hall 72.

[118] Peacham, *The Complete Gentleman*, 90–108.

father, Sir Bevil, who chastized him for foolishly neglecting 'those harder and more difficult artes' which could not be acquired elsewhere. 'If you once fixe upon the sweetnesse' of the classical poets, he warned, 'you will abandon all the harsher studies which would be most profitable for you.'[119]

Though parents and educators alike took measures to avert what was considered over-indulgence, the passion often proved irresistible. Not a few students followed the route taken by Francis Kynaston (m. 1601), who went down without a degree 'being then more addicted to the superficial parts of learning, poetry and oratory (wherein he excelled) than logic and philosophy'. Other one-time devotees lived to regret their former poetic indiscretions. Some, like John Norris, most regretted the loss of time that those 'unconcerning curiosities' involved. Others, who rose to scholarly and academic eminence, were embarrassed by the survival in the public domain of samples of their frivolous verse. John Mill, who in 1676 composed a Latin ode on the fire at Northampton—'a young man's compliment to the head of his college, sent by way of showing what he could do'—was evidently so keen to obliterate all records of this youthful production that he even tried to get Thomas Hearne to tear out the offensive pages from the Bodleian copy of the book.[120]

The many allurements of Oxford literary culture did more than simply tempt students away from the more difficult studies. The genuine passion for literature, poetry, and wit, and the reverence of those who were reputed to have acquired proficiency therein, also caused undergraduates to seek the company of these same university 'wits'. Unfortunately, not a few of these oracles interpreted literally Horace's maxim that 'no poems can please for very long, or even live at all, that water drinkers write',[121] and held their meetings in local taverns, thereby introducing the undergraduates who tagged along to more than just learning. Sir Bevil Granville hoped to steer his son away from such company, which had once proved to be his own undoing. He thus requested Degory Wheare to safeguard his son Richard

from the infection of that general contagion which hath spread itself not only over the university but the whole kingdom, and which I can with sad experience say was the ruin of divers hopefull gents there in my time. ... There was a nation of ancient seniors (and I doubt not but there is a succession of them unto these days) who, having gotten a convenient stock of learning in their youth to make them good company, did employ their parts to nothing but the encrease of good fellowship, and changed from the better study to the worse. They were my destruction and many others in my time.

---

[119] Granville, *History of the Granville Family*, 210, 223–4. To drive the point home Sir Bevil recalled the consequences of his own excessive devotion to 'so facile and pleasing studies' while a student: 'I was left to my owne little discretion when I was a youth in Oxford, and so fell upon the sweete delights of reading poetry and history, in such sort as I troubled no other bookes, and doe finde my selfe so infinitly defective by it, when I come to manage any occasions of waight.'

[120] Wood, *Athenae* iii. 38; John Norris, *Reflections upon the Conduct of Human Life* (London 1690), 157; Hearne, *Collections* iii. 462; A. Fox, *John Mill and Richard Bentley* (Oxford 1954), 8.

[121] *Horace's Satires and Epistles*, trans. J. Fuchs (New York 1977), 72.

Christopher Guise, too, attributed his untowardness at Oxford to the bad influence of good companions:

The vice of Oxford scollars is theyr frequenting tipling houses, and comonly that liberty most taken by the most ingeniouse. I was inclined to poetry and all ingeniouse studyes, the scrapps of which dropt in att our compotations. There we censur'd and extoll'd whom we pleas'd, and the title of ingeniouse was a sugred sop that gave a good relish to all concomitant qualityes and made us swallow licentiousenesse and, by consequence, idlenesse. For he who so begins to thinke well of himselfe from that time neglects to improve his stocke.

In the early eighteenth century it was young Samuel Johnson who 'was generally seen lounging at the college gate, with a circle of young students around him, whom he entertained with wit, and keeping them from their studies, if not spiriting them up to rebellion against the college discipline, which in his maturer years he so much extolled'.[122]

Notwithstanding the possible risks associated with poetry, by and large contemporaries continued to recommend it to students as well as to read and compose it in old age. Much of the poetry attempted may seem trivial if not outright insipid today. Certainly, from our perspective, the subject-matter of these compositions was often lethargic. Yet the educational value of such efforts was considerable. When Samuel Johnson came to comment on Joseph Addison's Latin poems on subjects 'on which perhaps he would not have ventured to have written in his own language', Johnson remarked: 'When the matter is low or scanty a dead language, in which nothing is mean because nothing is familiar, affords great conveniences; and by the sonorous magnificence of Roman syllables the writer conceals penury of thought and want of novelty, often from the reader, and often from himself.'[123]

But by the middle of the seventeenth century poetry found detractors as well. The pragmatic and often cynical Francis Osborne even believed the perils of poetry outweighed its utility. Consequently he cautioned his son not to be

frequent in poetry, how excellent soever your vein is, but make it rather your recreation, than business. Because, tho' it swells you in your own opinion, it may render you less in that of wiser men, who are not ignorant how great a mass of vanity for the most part coucheth under this quality, proclaiming their heads, like ships of use only for pleasure, and so richer in trimming than lading.

Far more damning was John Locke. 'Poetry and gaming', he wrote, 'which usually go together, are alike in this too that they seldom bring any advantage, but to those who have nothing else to live on.' Elsewhere Locke reasoned that, if one displayed

no genius for poetry, 'tis the most unreasonable thing in the world to torment a child and waste his time about that which can never succeed. And if he have a poetic vein, 'tis to me the strangest thing in the world that the father should desire or suffer it to be cherished, or

---

[122] Granville, *History of the Granville Family*, 206; *Autobiography of Thomas Raymond and Memoirs of the Family of Guise of Elmore, Gloucestershire*, ed. G. Davies (Camden Soc. 3rd ser. xxviii 1917), 116; *Boswell's Life of Johnson*, ed. Hill and Powell i. 74.

[123] Johnson, *Lives of the English Poets* ii. 83.

improved. Methinks the parents should labour to have it stifled and suppressed, as much as may be.[124]

This new breed of critic, however, was less concerned with the educational hazards of poetry and rhetoric than with the hold they exerted over the educated public. After all, most of these detractors were the architects of the new philosophy (or its propagandists), for whom the appetite for poetry was viewed as not only frivolous but a hindrance to the diffusion and acceptance of the new modes of thought. Thomas Sprat's approach was to argue that poetry was serviceable in antiquity when the poets, 'by the charms of their numbers, allured [the Greeks] to be instructed by the severer doctrines, of Solon, Thales, and Pythagoras. This was a course, that was useful at first, when men were to be delightfully deceived to their own good'. But now the members of the Royal Society—whose design Sprat promoted—'indeavored, to separate the knowledge of nature, from the colours of rhetorick, the devices of fancy, or the delightful deceit of fables'.[125]

Greek Studies

Though proficiency in Latin was certainly much more common among seventeenth-century educated Englishmen than proficiency in Greek, attainments in the latter should not be overlooked. By 1600 a fair number of students arrived annually at the universities from grammar schools throughout England (and not only from the few great schools in and around London), already well grounded in Greek. There they found a fully operational system of instruction that included, in addition to the regius professor of Greek, competent lecturers in every college as well as many tutors capable of providing some Greek teaching. A fundamental difference, however, existed between the pedagogy of the two languages; Latin was taught both as a living language and the language of scholarship, while Greek was taught almost exclusively as a foreign tongue. Hence, whereas the study of Latin was premised on the ultimate ability of the student to think, converse, and compose in Latin, as well as grounding him in the literary, philological, and philosophical doctrines of Roman culture, the study of Greek was geared predominantly towards the acquisition of erudition. Save for those school exercises that forced the student to try his hand at imitating the Greek poets and orators, or engage in double translation in order to enhance mastery, few were expected to resort to colloquial Greek, even though the university statutes allowed for Greek (and Hebrew) to substitute for Latin in public conversation. That fluency in Greek was not commonly expected may also be concluded from a brief survey of the many volumes of poetry that were published at Oxford throughout the seventeenth century. These rarely included instances of students who exhibited their skills in Greek verse, in contrast to their readiness to versify in Latin. Nevertheless, within these limits, the

[124] Osborne, *Advice to a Son*, 20–1; *The Educational Writings of John Locke*, ed. Axtell, 283–4.
[125] Sprat, *History of the Royal Society*, 6, 62.

study of Greek was advocated quite seriously by contemporary parents and educators.[126]

Indeed, the attainment of Greek had become an ideal that informed the programme of study for members of the upper class as well as for scholars. James
Whitelocke (BCL 1594) 'labored mutche in the Hebrew and Greek tongs' during
his undergraduate days at St John's College and Edward, Lord Herbert of Cherbury
(m. 1596) claimed many years later 'to have made in Greeke the exercises required
in . . . colledge oftner then in Lattaine', while Sir George Radcliff thought it 'necessary for a gentleman to learn Latine and French perfectly, [and] some Greeke'.[127]
Other examples abound. During 1622 William Trumbull admonished his son William
not to allow his desire to study modern language distract him from his 'principall
studyes'—Latin and Greek. The advice remained common enough throughout the
century. When John Evelyn asked Christopher Wren to recommend a suitable tutor
for his son, he specifically requested that the person 'be a perfect Grecian', especially because Evelyn's 'owne defects in the Greeke tongue and knowledge of its
usefulnesse' obliged him 'to mention that particular with an extraordinary note'.
Similarly Sir Justinian Isham insisted that his son pursue the study of Greek diligently while Nathaniel Freind counselled his son John to 'go on in your school
learning, never thinking you have enough until you have mastered all authors in
Greek and Latin'. Stephen Penton concurred. A gentleman, he thought, ought to
be 'very well furnished with skill in the Latin tounge, and no stranger to Greek'.
As late as 1693 Thomas Smith advised Theophilus Hastings, seventh earl of
Huntingdon, that when choosing a tutor and companion for his son attention
should be given to his being a competent Latin and Greek scholar, as well as proficient in French.[128]

Those who had not acquired an adequate grounding in the language before their
arrival at Oxford received such a foundation from their tutor or the college lecturer during the first year or two of the undergraduate course.[129] The rest were set
to work (for the most part on their own) on expanding and deepening their understanding. They were thus assigned new and more difficult Greek texts, and were
expected to continue with the routine drilling of double translation. In addition,

[126] It should be noted, however, that according to Wood during the Interregnum at least some philosophical and theological disputations were conducted in Greek, 'but since this restoration seldome or
never'. Wood, *Athenae* i. 297.

[127] *Liber Famelicus of Sir James Whitelocke*, ed. J. Bruce (Camden Soc. lxx 1858), 13; *The Life of Edward,
First Lord Herbert of Cherbury*, ed. J. M. Shuttleworth (London 1976), 15; *Wentworth Papers 1597–1628*, ed.
J. P. Cooper (Camden Soc. 4th ser. xii 1973), 325.

[128] Berks. RO Trumbull papers, MS 46 letter of 11/21 October, 1622; *Diary of John Evelyn*, ed. Bray
iii. 305; Northants. RO Isham correspondence, no. 860; Bodl. MS top. Oxon. f. 31, p. 55; Penton,
Guardian's Instruction, 93; Bodl. MS Smith 63, fo 67. It is therefore not surprising to find Charles Boyle,
future earl of Orrery, engaged in a translation of Plutarch's life of Lysander, a performance that moved
Dean Aldrich to request Boyle to prepare for publication the ill-fated edition of the Phalaris letters.

[129] Some students even availed themselves of private teachers. The Greek-born Christopher Angelus
came to Oxford in 1610, entered Balliol and 'did very good service among the young scholars in the
university that were raw in the Greek tongue, and continued among them till the time of his death' in
1639. Wood, *Athenae* ii. 633.

they were now expected to pay closer attention to the content of the works as well as to embark upon a study of the critical apparatus of Greek language and literature: lexicons and grammars, works pertaining to mythology and to the antiquities of Greece, and commentaries on the theory of Greek poetry and prose. Such independent study was closely monitored by the tutor who assigned students, according to their station and capacity, written exercises and examinations.

The manuals of advice again provide us with the opportunity to reconstruct the course followed by at least some of the better students. Richard Holdsworth's 'Directions for a student in the university' represents the minimalist view of a tutor having to begin from scratch. Every afternoon of the four-year undergraduate course would be devoted to the study of 'the Greek and Latine toungs, history oratory, and poetry'. In the first two years the student would follow the basic diet that could also be found in many of the grammar schools: the New Testament, Aesop, Hesiod, Demosthenes, Theocritus, Homer, and some of the minor poets. For the third and fourth years Holdsworth stipulated, as did most contemporaries, Aristotle in Greek, thereby enhancing at one and the same time the student's linguistic skills and his philosophical acumen. In addition for these years Macrobius and more poetry were also assigned. After graduating BA the student was expected to complete his reading of the Greek poets and pursue Plutarch, Xenophon, Herodotus, Thucydides, and Diogenes Laertius.[130]

A more detailed course of study was drafted by Thomas Heywood. For the first-year student he recommended Longinus, Plato's *Gorgias*, and Aristotle's *Rhetoric* for the theoretical part of prose writing, and the orations of Demosthenes and Isocrates for a model. In poetry, Aristotle, Scaliger, Casaubon, and Heinsius provided the theory while Homer, Theocritus, Pindar, Anacreon, Sophocles, and Euripides offered the illustrative material. During the second year, while the student continued with Sophocles, Aeschylus, and Euripides, he would add Andronicus Rhodius, Theophrastus, some chapters from Maximus Tyrius, and the commentaries by Arrian and Simplicius on Epictetus for prose, and Theognis and Phocyllides for poetry. The course was rounded off in the final two years with Macrobius and Plato, while still pursuing the poets. In keeping with the pedagogical assumptions underlying university education that envisaged the continuation of the educational process beyond the BA degree, whatever the student was unable to complete within the four years of the undergraduate course was to be completed while preparing for the MA degree.[131]

Another, anonymous, tutor, though less methodical in his presentation, offered much the same diet. In order to improve and deepen the knowledge of the Greek language he recommended Richard Franklin's *De tonis*, Posselius or Apollonius Alexandrinus' *De syntaxi*, and the contrasting accounts by John Cheke and Esternius concerning Greek pronunciation. He then assigned Longinus, Aristotle, Dionysius Halicarnassus, and Hermogenes among the rhetoricians, and several

---

[130] Fletcher, *The Intellectual Development of John Milton* ii. 625–47, *passim*.
[131] Bodl. MS Rawlinson d. 40.

ancient and modern authors for the better elucidation of Greek laws, religion, and customs. Among the recommended literary texts one finds the usual list: Homer, the minor poets, Aristophanes, Euripides, Sophocles, Demosthenes, and almost a complete run of the Greek historians, as this tutor put particular emphasis on the study of history. John Grandorge was equally concise. Having mentioned several grammars and reference works, he went on to enumerate those works that every-one agreed to be the best. For Greek oratory, Grandorge listed Demosthenes, Aeschines, Isocrates, Xenophon, Lucian, and Julian, 'to which may be added Plato and Aristotle for purity and style and Herodotus, Thucydides and other ancient historians and writers both in prose and verse', while for poetry he mentioned Aeschylus, Euripides, Sophocles, Aristophanes, Homer, Aratus, Hesiod, Pindar, Anacreon, and so on. Daniel Waterland's directions were similar. The undergrad-uate years were devoted to reading Xenophon, Lucian, Justin, Homer, Cornelius Nepos, Theophrastus, Isocrates, Demosthenes, Hesiod, Theocritus, Sophocles, Euripides, and Thucydides. Later, while he pursued his philosophical studies, the student was exhorted not to neglect his philological studies and to include, 'espe-cially', Aristotle's *Rhetoric*, Epictetus, Marcus Antoninus, Herodotus, Plutarch, Aristophanes, Callimachus, Herodian, Longinus, and Plato.[132]

Reading-lists and book accounts shed further light on common practices, although in most cases the lists remain incomplete. As Sackville Crow was but a beginner in Greek when he arrived at Oxford in 1654 his tutor, Francis Mansell, read Thucydides with him daily to facilitate his understanding. Three decades ear-lier William Trumbull at Magdalen College was pursuing Diogenes Laertius in a similar manner. Thomas Isham undoubtedly followed the course laid down for him by his father, which included Aristotle's *Rhetoric* and *Ethics*, Homer, Demosthenes, Sophocles, Aristophanes, and perhaps even Euclid. The library catalogue of Edward Bernard, from his student days, included Homer, Hesiod, the minor poets, Lucian, Aristotle, Isocrates, Aristophanes, Pindar, Sidonius Apollinarius, Silicus, Ausonius, and Herodotus. Henry Fleming brought with him to Oxford in 1678 Homer, the minor poets, a Greek Testament, Camden's Greek grammar, Cornelio Schrevelio's *Lexicon manuale graeco-latinum*, and Francis Gregory's edition of *Etymologicum parvum*. In the next four years he also acquired Sophocles, Lucian, Pindar, Xenophon, and Herodian, as well as the *Opus prosodicum graecum novum* by Petrus Cöleman, Vigerus' *De praecipuis graecae dictionis idiotismus*, and Martin Ruland's *Synonima latino-graeca*. Finally at the turn of the century we find Thomas Devey (BA 1699) in possession of the New Testament, a Greek catechism, Aesop, Isocrates, Lucian, and the minor poets.[133]

The doubling up of subject-matter and language was a common practice among

[132] Bodl. MS Rawlinson d. 188, MS St Edmund Hall 72; Waterland, *Works* iv. 413.

[133] BL Add. MS 27,606, fos 5v–6; Berks. RO Trumbull papers, misc. corr. vol. 1, no. 13, letter dated 25 January 1623; Northants. RO, Isham correspondence, no. 860; Bodl. MS Lat. misc. f. 11, fos 15–17; *The Flemings in Oxford* i. 250–4, 321–2, ii. 28–9, 44; J. L. Salter, 'The books of an early eighteenth-cen-tury curate', *The Library*, 5th ser. xxxiii (1978), 41, 43.

tutors in the seventeenth century. Thus Ralph Bohun assigned the *Rhetoric* and *Ethics* in Greek to John Evelyn the younger in 1668.[134] Other texts used by tutors included the Greek Testament, which was read by most students, and the inculcation of such religious lessons in the Greek tongue was reinforced in the college hall during meals as well as in chapel.[135] Some heads of house could make even further use of the religious services in the colleges, as did John Mill, principal of St Edmund Hall, who took advantage of such opportunities to read scripture and offer 'textual, archaeological, exegetical, and theological' explanations of the text.[136]

As became the custom in other disciplines, by the early seventeenth century the basic training in Greek was undertaken by tutors and college lecturers, while the regius professor gradually came to offer specialized, more advanced, courses. Unfortunately, very little evidence concerning the content of such lectures survives but, probably, most professors followed the statutory requirements to lecture on a Greek text of choice. From a couple of entries in Thomas Crosfield's diary, for example, we learn that Henry Stringer (professor 1625–50) was particularly fond of Pindar, on whom he lectured in 1626 as well as 1631. John Harmar, who was intruded as regius professor in 1650, commended in a preface he contributed to John Ailmer's *Musae sacrae* (Oxford 1652) 'the revival of classical studies, and especially of Greek, at Oxford'. Harmar also listed the Greek poets in vogue at the time—Homer, Pindar, Lycophron, Anacreon, Theognis, and Theocritus—indicative perhaps of his own teaching. The only regius professor who appears to have deviated from the statutory requirement to lecture on a Greek text of choice was Humphrey Hody (MA 1682, regius professor 1698–1705), who offered a course of lectures on the history of Greek scholarship during the renaissance.[137]

The general endorsement of Greek as a necessary accomplishment of all students, however, waned during the seventeenth century. Since such study was recommended as a mark of scholarship, once this ceased to be an ideal informing upper-class aspirations so too did the study of Greek. And once Greek went out of fashion, a general decline among those studying it followed. Partly in response to the new fashions arriving from the continent, learned commentators began to doubt the need for Greek, at least for gentlemen. By the mid-1650s, for example, Francis Osborne already counselled his son that 'the attaining to the Latin is most of use, the Greek but loss of time'. To the mind of Gilbert Burnet a few decades later, 'were it not that the New Testament' was written in Greek he would not have 'very earnestly presse[d]' the learning of it, 'since for noblemen it is no otherwise useful, all Greek books being exactly well translated in this late critical age. But

---

[134] CL Evelyn letters, no. 301.

[135] John Freind described a daily routine of 'morning prayers, both public and private, and the reading of a chapter of the bible in English and Greek'. Quoted in P. F. Hammond, *John Oldham and the Renewal of Classical Culture* (Cambridge 1983), 10 n. 18.'

[136] Fox, *John Mill and Richard Bentley*, 24.

[137] *The Diary of Thomas Crosfield*, ed. Boas, 3, 53; F. M[adan], 'Greek at Oxford in 1652', *Bodleian Library Record* ii (1917–19), 264, 270; H. Hody, *De Graecis illustribus linguae graecae literarum que humaniorum instauratibus* (London 1742).

since the treasure of our faith is in Greek, it should be pressed upon all, not to be willing to owe our knowledge of that to second-hand.' Against this background we can understand the dispensing by Locke with Greek. Though he granted that 'no man can pass for a scholar that is ignorant of the Greek tongue', yet he was not 'considering of the education of a professed scholar, but of a gentleman, to whom Latin and French, as the world now goes, is by every one acknowledged to be necessary'. Continuing in this vein, Locke recommended the difficult pursuit of Greek only to those few already exhibiting an inclination toward such study. As regards the rest a smattering of Greek would be labour lost. 'For how many are there of an hundred, even amongst scholars themselves, who retain the Greek they carried from school, or even improve it to a familiar reading, and perfect understanding of Greek authors?'[138]

Such sentiments resulted in a perceptible deterioration of the level of Greek studies at both Oxford and Cambridge by the latter part of the seventeenth century. Precisely at the time when England began to produce classical scholars of European reputation, it forfeited a relatively large and homogeneous community of skilled philologists and discerning amateurs, who now substituted for an intensive study of the classics the fashionable pursuit of *belles lettres*. The new trend was becoming visible by the Restoration. In 1660 William Sancroft lamented that the study of both Greek and Hebrew was rapidly growing out of fashion among students, a sentiment shared by Anthony Wood. Half a century later Archbishop Wake wrote to Arthur Charlett in even graver tone: 'I assure you, that part of polite learning which consists in the learned languages, Latin and Greek ... [has] much decayed.' And in 1729 Thomas Hearne concluded that 'learning is at so low an ebb at present, that hardly anything of that kind is sought after, except it be English, Scotch, or Irish history'.[139]

Graeco-Latin Scholarship

Recognition of the centrality of the classics to early modern English culture is, in itself, insufficient for gauging the profundity of such knowledge. Any evaluation of quality, however, is encumbered by a long tradition of scholarship that has anchored all assessment almost exclusively in terms of priorities that inform modern criteria of erudition—namely the commitment to a dispassionate examination (and publication) of ancient documents, irrespective of their ethical and aesthetic values, by scholars for whom such scholarship is a vocation. This yardstick was already articulated by Hallam a century and a half ago when he opined that though they were 'deeply read in ancient learning, our old scholars were not very critical in philology'. But while Hallam could still conceive of the existence of erudition among English scholars even if it failed to be translated into scholarly editions, later

---

[138] Osborne, *Advice to a Son*, 67; Clarke, *Bishop Gilbert Burnet as Educationalist*, 51; *The Educational Writings of John Locke*, ed. Axtell, 307.

[139] G. D'Oyly, *The Life of William Sancroft, Archbishop of Canterbury* (2 vols London 1840) i. 128; Bodl. MS Ballard 3, fo 125; Hearne, *Collections* x. 205.

commentators refused to accommodate such distinctions. They became increasingly censorious in their judgement as they became more inflexible in their understanding of what constituted erudition. Before the mid-seventeenth century, thundered Housman, Englishmen 'were learning Greek and were not yet in case to teach it'. Wilamowitz agreed: prior to Bentley 'England was still in the purely receptive stage' and save for 'a few isolated works which [could] conveniently be treated . . . under the heading of Dutch scholarship', it required little attention. What held for the better-known figures was doubly true for the university community. Mullinger summarily dismissed early seventeenth-century dons as owning 'little real acquaintance either with [Greek] language or its literature'. Further elaborating on Mullinger, Fletcher claimed that by the 1630s 'it was becoming more and more difficult to find scholars who knew Greek'.[140]

Since the criterion for evaluation was both the number and quality of editions of the classics, the fact that the English were reluctant to produce even editions for schools further substantiated the general argument. The few editions that were published before 1650, though useful, were largely derivative. John Bond (MA 1579), for example, published in 1606 an edition of Horace's *Poemata*, while his edition of Persius' *Satires* was published posthumously in 1614. Thomas Farnaby (m. 1590) produced in rapid succession editions of Juvenal and Persius (1612), Seneca's *Tragedies* (1613), Martial's *Epigrammata* (1615), and Lucan's *Pharsalia* (1618). A decade and a half later Farnaby added Ovid's *Metamorphoses* and Virgil's *Opera* (1634 and 1636 respectively). Even the more original and demanding choice by another learned Grecian, Gerard Langbaine, who published in 1636 the Greek text of Longinus' *Liber de grandi loquentia*, accompanied by the Latin translation of Gabriel de Petra published two decades earlier, was ultimately intended to serve students, not scholars. And though certain of these textbooks enjoyed some popularity and were often reprinted both in England and on the continent, in the eyes of contemporaries—and even more forcefully in the eyes of modern scholars—the sum total of these 'school editions' amounted to very little.

'I came from England', wrote Hugo Grotius in 1613, 'where there is little commerce of letters; theologians are there the reigning authorities. Casaubon is the only exception, and he could have found no place in England as a man of learning; he was compelled to assume [the role of] the theologian.' A decade later another visitor, Lucas Holsten, described how 'he had buried himself in the Oxford libraries, turning over Greek and Latin manuscripts, which no one in those parts thinks of troubling'. Casaubon often expressed himself in a similar vein: 'As long as I shall stay in England, I see that I must make up my mind to forego classical letters . . . [The] king is so fond of theology, that he cares very little to attend to any literary

[140] H. Hallam, *Introduction to the Literature of Europe in the 15th, 16th & 17th Centuries* (3 vols London 1873, repr. New York 1970) ii. 281; *The Classical Papers of A. E. Housman*, ed. J. Diggle and F. R. D. Goodyear (3 vols London 1972) iii. 1004; U. von Wilamowitz-Moellendorff, *History of Classical Scholarship*, trans. Alan Harris, ed. H. Lloyd-Jones (Baltimore 1982), 77; J. B. Mullinger, *The University of Cambridge* (3 vols Cambridge 1873–1911) ii. 420 n. 3; Fletcher, *The Intellectual Development of John Milton* ii. 275.

subject.' When Daniel Heinsius prodded him in 1612 to undertake 'a British edition of Aristotle's works at the expense of the crown', Casaubon replied that ' "if you were here, you would never indeed have thought of this", because the "deeply religious king" had no leisure for dallying in philosophy or philology. Rewards went only to the "t[heologiae] c[ultoribus]" while there were almost none for the "caeterarum disciplinarum amatoribus" '.[141]

It is therefore hardly surprising that the two most recent scholars to address the issue of classical learning generally in early modern England have viewed the period before the Restoration with jaundiced eyes. Binns extends the low estimation of the level of Greek scholarship to include Latin scholarship: 'The editions of classical Latin texts which were printed in England in the Elizabethan and Jacobean age', he concludes, 'call for little comment. To a very great degree they were simply unadorned reprints of earlier continental editions. The Elizabethan and Jacobean era was not a great age of English classical scholarship.' Brink, too, argues categorically that the English were wanting in Latin as well as in Greek scholarship. Though he recognizes the relevance of 'classical scholarship in education at universities and schools ... [and the] civilizing influence on society', what ultimately matters to him is classical scholarship 'viewed almost exclusively as critical learning'. In England one finds *bonae litterae*, not erudition; the practitioners are educators, not critics. Even more significantly, he interprets the readiness with which English scholars continued to perpetuate the tradition inherited by humanists and reformers—which subordinated scholarship to theological ends, thereby allowing religious needs to engross their attention and colour their perceptions regardless of the conclusions they arrived at—as detrimental to classical scholarship. Consequently, even those contemporaries of Bentley, both at Oxford and Cambridge, who published learned editions are judged to have demonstrated 'soundness and clarity rather than originality'; nor was their linguistic facility 'matched by appropriate powers of thought'. Brink and all earlier commentators seem to agree that there existed an inherent incompatibility between the vocation of a divine and the life of scholarship; hence they would no doubt readily endorse Richard Porson's famous assessment of John Pearson—that 'he would have been a first rate critic in Greek, even equal to Bentley, if he had not muddled his brains with divinity'— to encompass virtually all seventeenth-century scholars.[142]

However, this preoccupation with modern standards of classical scholarship as the sole criteria by which to evaluate earlier practitioners is not only anachronistic but also ignores the contribution of a large number of important figures, who failed to publish even a single work and yet were crucial in establishing the very foundations of the linguistic and literary culture that made possible the rise of Bentley

[141] M. Pattison, *Isaac Casaubon* (Oxford 1892, repr. Geneva 1970), 286–7, 362; F. J. Blom, 'Lucas Holstenius (1596–1661) and England' in G. A. M. Janssens and F. G. A. M. Aarts (eds), *Studies in Seventeenth-Century English Literature, History and Bibliography* (Amsterdam 1984), 29; P. R. Sellin, *Daniel Heinsius and Stuart England* (Leiden 1968), 80–1.

[142] J. W. Binns, *Intellectual Culture in Elizabethan and Jacobean England: the Latin writings of the age* (Leeds 1990), 194; C. O. Brink, *English Classical Scholarship* (Cambridge and New York 1985), 1–13, 102.

and his successors. Anthony Grafton indicates the consequences of such an approach when he criticizes the widespread tendency to assume 'that seventeenth-century scholars must be measured by a twentieth-century standard, in regard to both the tools they applied and the choice of objects to which they might apply them'. To concentrate on 'high-profile textual criticism of Latin poetry practised on the continent by Nicolaas Heinsius and J. F. Gronovius', Grafton argues, at the expense of paying sufficient attention to Savile's edition of Chrysostom or John Selden's *Marmora arundelliana*, presupposes that the latter two did 'not matter as much'; it also assumes 'that breadth of viewpoint cannot make up for lack of cutting edge'.[143]

The incontrovertible predisposition of the English to theological studies is not indicative of their lesser regard for, or attainment in, secular learning. Rather the public manifestation of their extensive learning was channelled toward religious ends. Such a choice was, in part, the consequence of the charged religious atmosphere in England during the reign of Elizabeth and the early Stuarts, as well as of the fervent polemics against Roman Catholics in general—and the Jesuits in particular—which resulted in a consolidated sense of mission, shared by all English protestants, to obliterate the popish threat. Thus, the scholarly rebuttal of the Catholic challenge was important not only in terms of the need to produce effective learned responses to their adversaries' claims, but also as a unifying force within the English Church. Second, the great patrons of learning were themselves participants in—or supporters of—those scholarly religious disputes. This entanglement, coupled with the fact that the church provided virtually the sole avenue of promotion, made the direction of a scholarly career obvious. Conscience and perception of calling thus combined with the dictates of the laws of patronage to harness the theological propensities of generations of English scholars.

Nor did the English universities enjoy many of the established professorships that proliferated in continental academies such as Leiden, which offered exceptional scholars the opportunity to pursue erudition without interruption. Finally, for various reasons, English scholars also failed to participate actively in the republic of European letters, thereby further contributing to the obscuring of their scholarship which, for the most part, became simply a matter of reputation. Individually, English scholars were regarded by their contemporaries on the continent primarily as divines; collectively, they were viewed as respected, if peripheral, members of that large community of letters. Casaubon indeed recognized these circumstances and sought to mitigate the low esteem in which his continental friends held for the marked theological propensity of English learning. 'You must not suppose that this people is a barbarous people', he cautioned Salmasius, 'nothing of that sort; it loves letters and cultivates them, sacred learning especially. Indeed, if I am not mistaken, the soundest part of the whole reformation is to be found here in England, where

---

[143] A. Grafton, 'Barrow as a Scholar' in M. Feingold (ed.), *Before Newton: the life and times of Isaac Barrow* (Cambridge 1990), 291–2.

the study of antiquity flourishes together with zeal for truth.'[144] Salmasius remained unconvinced,[145] as did other colleagues in the Netherlands. Consequently, when Isaac Vossius received a copy of John Milton's assault on Salmasius, the *Pro populo anglicano defensio*, he wrote to Heinsius of his amazement at the sight of that literary accomplishment: 'I had expected nothing of such quality from an Englishman.' A few years later Johann Hoornbeeck was still voicing the common view when he commented on the 'shortcomings of the English scholars' in comparison to the benefit yielded by their moralistic works.[146]

It is therefore important to recognize that what England wanted was not competent philologists, but rather the requisite environment that would have enabled her scholars—and their indubitably deep and wide erudition which in the event was channelled almost exclusively into theological learning—to embark freely upon the study of letters. This cognizance of the purpose of scholarship disposed English intellectuals towards a distinctive, virtually predetermined, course of study. A few examples will demonstrate the point. Patrick Young (incorporated MA 1605) was one of the foremost British Greek scholars in the first half of the seventeenth century; he was also exceptional in that he served as royal librarian between 1612 and 1649, which freed him from the need to become a churchman. Still, Young's love of classical scholarship and the assistance he bestowed freely on the literary enterprises of foreign and native scholars—especially Daniel Heinsius and John Selden—were never translated into publication. Whether through choice or at the behest of others, Young devoted his life to biblical scholarship and the study of the church fathers. As early as 1613 he contemplated an edition of Origen and Theodoret, and by 1628 he was entrusted with the task of preparing an edition of the famous Alexandrian codex of the Septuagint. Such an edition would undoubtedly have been the crowning achievement of his career had he completed it. However, despite intense labour for over a quarter of a century, only a portion of the eagerly awaited edition appeared: in 1633 the Oxford press issued *Clementis ad Corinthios epistola prior*, which was followed four years later by a London edition of Nicetas' *Catena graecorum patrum in beatum Job*. Additional material was incorporated into Walton's Polyglot Bible.[147]

That the resolve to apply their scholarship to sacred learning was perhaps as much a matter of choice as of necessity—the former albeit guided by the prevalent assumptions concerning the ends of knowledge—can be gathered from the example of two other eminent scholars. Sir Henry Savile, that proficient

---

[144] Pattison, *Isaac Casaubon*, 291.

[145] Though the English climate may be healthier than that of Holland, he told Jean Daillé in 1630, 'there is no comparison between the two countries when I consider the society and communication of men of learning that I would find, not to mention the greater liberty to be enjoyed in a republic as opposed to a kingdom'. Quoted in P. Dibon, 'Communication in the respublica literaria of the 17th century', *Res Publica Litterarum* i (1978), 46.

[146] D. Masson, *The Life of John Milton* (7 vols London 1881–94) iii. 317; H. Scherpbier, *Milton in England* (Amsterdam 1933), 79.

[147] Thomas Smith, *Clarissimi viri Patricii Junii . . . vita*, in *Vitae quorundam eroditissimorum et illustrium virorum* (London 1707); J. Kemke, *Patricius Junius* (Leipzig 1898).

mathematician and superb Grecian who, according to Aubrey, 'would faine have been thought to have been as great a scholar as Joseph Scaliger', abandoned both mathematics and the classics by the early 1590s and devoted the next two decades to the preparation of a magnificent edition of Chrysostom (1612), to his collaboration on the King James version of the Bible, and to an edition of Bradwardine's *De causa Dei* (1618).[148] John Selden steered a similar course. A distinguished philologist as well as an independent and wealthy lay scholar, Selden's early work on English antiquities and his edition of the *Marmora arundelliana* (1628) were followed not by further work on Greek or medieval antiquities but by a growing preoccupation with oriental learning. He became one of the foremost Hebrew and Arabic scholars of the day and his publications were devoted to the study of the languages, rites, customs, and institutions of ancient Judaism.[149]

Equally instructive is the case of Henry Jacob the younger, who returned to England in 1628 after having studied with, among others, Heinsius and Erpenius at Leiden. The former highly recommended the young scholar to Selden, who was instrumental in acquiring for Jacob a fellowship at Merton College. It was Heinsius' wish that his gifted protégé should produce an edition of Aeschylus, and to this end in 1629 he requested Selden to put pressure on Jacob. But though Jacob had done some work on Aeschylus—his notes would be used by Thomas Stanley a generation later—Jacob's patrons, Selden and Laud, diverted his studies to different and theological ends. Yet Jacob himself exhibited a similar inclination to redirect his philological skills. Thus he contributed his share to the popular genre of comparative Greek and Hebrew studies of the Bible, and exhibited such an eagerness to defend Daniel Heinsius' *Sacrae excercitationes* against the calumnies of Salmasius that both Heinsius and his son Nicolaas viewed his zeal for theology as excessive.[150]

In the light of the above, it is easier to understand the scholarly 'reorientation' that befell Isaac Casaubon following his arrival in England in 1610. Both the king and his bishops expected the great scholar to wield his pen on behalf of the protestant cause and, in particular, to confute Baronius' *Annales ecclesiastici*. But, as Pattison perceptively observed, more than simply following the dictates of his new patrons the great scholar was actually 'catching the infection from his environment'—a point that became evident in some of Casaubon's letters such as the one in which he informed a correspondent that John Barclay's forthcoming *Pietas* would 'squash' Bellarmine's *Responsio Matthaei Torti* 'as dead as a mouse in a trap'.[151]

Nevertheless, within such a framework the methodology and techniques utilized by the English scholars were as exacting as those of the best classical scholars any-

[148] *Brief Lives by Aubrey*, ed. Clark ii. 214; see *DNB* s.v. Henry Savile.

[149] For Selden, see *John Selden on Jewish Marriage Law*, trans. J. R. Ziskind (Leiden 1991); M. Feingold, 'John Selden and the nature of seventeenth century science' in R. Bienvenu and M. Feingold (eds), *In the Presence of the Past* (Dordrecht and Boston 1991), 55–78.

[150] Sellin, *Daniel Heinsius and Stuart England*, 114–15; Bodl. MS Selden *supra* 108, fo 166; Aeschylus, *Agamemnon*, ed. E. Fraenkel (2 vols Oxford 1950) i. 78; J. A. Gruys, *The Early Printed Editions (1518–1664) of Aeschylus* (Nieuwkoop 1981), 177–8.

[151] Pattison, *Isaac Casaubon*, 317.

where. In preparing his edition of Chrysostom, Sir Henry Savile availed himself of manuscripts in Oxford libraries (the Bodleian and the various libraries of Magdalen, New, and Corpus Christi colleges), in addition to requesting loans, copies, and collations of manuscripts from libraries in Cambridge and London, from public libraries on the continent such as Heidelberg, Vienna, Augsburg, and the Vatican, and from sundry private collectors and scholars across the Channel. During the second decade of the seventeenth century a major collaborative project was conceived by Thomas James, who assembled a group of some twelve scholars to collate fifty-six manuscripts—obtained from various university, college, and cathedral libraries in England—in a determined effort to confute the recently published 'popish' editions of St Gregory, St Ambrose, and St Cyprian and ultimately, it was hoped, to prepare accurate editions of these prominent church fathers.[152]

Constraints of space do not allow for a detailed discussion of the many talented classicists who were educated at Oxford but who, because of their failure either to publish at all or, more commonly, to produce any pure works of classical scholarship, have never been studied seriously by modern scholars. Still, in order to substantiate the claim that Richard Bentley did not emerge out of thin air but, rather, was a member—and a collaborator—of a large and active community of competent philologists, mention should be made of a few of such scholars. Edmund Chilmead of Christ Church (MA 1632) was highly regarded for his knowledge of Greek by, among others, John Selden and Meibomius. Unfortunately, his poverty forced him to undertake various time-consuming chores, such as cataloguing in 1636 the Baroccian collection of Greek manuscripts bestowed on the university by William Herbert, earl of Pembroke, five years earlier. Archbishop Ussher urged him to publish the *Chronicon* of Johannes Malalas, a manuscript of which was in the collection, and Chilmead had completed the transcription, translation, and annotation—as well as excerpts and a Latin translation of another Baroccian manuscript, the *Chronicon* of Georgios Hamartolos—when the civil war put an end to the project. Among other manuscripts transcribed by Chilmead, and perhaps prepared for publication, was Gaudentius' *Isagoge harmonica* that was eventually published, from Chilmead's transcript, in Meibomius' *Antiquae musicae auctores septem* (1652). Chilmead also lent invaluable assistance to Sir Henry Holcroft's translation of Procopius of Caesaria. As Holcroft admitted: 'And where the translator himself hath suffered any impair, or casually committed some mistakes, they are both relieved by the able pen of Mr. Edmund Chilmead, by his exact comparing of the English with the Greek.'[153]

[152] S. van der Woude, 'Sir Henry Savile's Chrysostom edition in the Netherlands', *Studia Bibliographica in honorem Herman de la Fontaine Verwey* (Amsterdam 1966), 437; N. R. Ker, 'Thomas James's collation of Gregory, Cyprian, and Ambrose', *Bodleian Library Record* iv (1952–3), 16–30. Brian Walton, the editor of the great Polyglot Bible, clearly recognized the indispensability of manuscripts to the establishment of the 'correct' version and in the preparation of the Greek text alone he used over forty manuscripts. Fox, *John Mill and Richard Bentley*, 48.

[153] Bodl. MS Selden *supra* 109, fos 302–13 *passim*; Procopius of Caesarea, *The History of the Warres of the Emperour Justinian*, Englished by Sir Henry Holcroft (London 1653), preface; M. Feingold and P. M.

Much of the work of the talented Grecian and orientalist John Gregory (MA 1631) was angled to theological ends. In addition to his various labours in biblical criticism, Grégory assisted Bishop Augustine Lindsell in the preparation of Theophylact's commentary on the epistles of St Paul; he also left unpublished observations on the *Chronicon* of Malalas and several translations that were later published by Sir Edward Bysshe under the latter's name.[154] Gerard Langbaine 'beloved of Dr. Ussher, Selden, and the great Goliaths of literature' never followed up on his edition of Longinus that he published as a young master of arts in 1636, partly because of his involvement in the stormy political life at Oxford after he was elected provost of Queen's College in 1644, and partly because he unselfishly assisted in the scholarly work of others. For example, Langbaine 'drudged much' in the completion of Ussher's *Chronologia sacra* as well as extending invaluable assistance to John Selden's scholarly work until the latter's death in 1654. Twenty-one notebooks containing material Langbaine gathered from numerous Greek manuscripts in various libraries for some major project still survive unstudied.[155]

Nor were the priorities different later in the century. John Mill's extensive Greek learning was channelled for thirty years into his edition of the New Testament. Theophilus Gale (MA 1652) devoted his life to demonstrating that all ancient literature and philosophy derived from Hebrew learning—the fruit of this labour being published as *The Court of the Gentiles* (1669–77). Humphrey Hody early exhibited his promise as a scholar when he published in 1684 his *Contra historiam Aristeae de lxx interpretibus dissertatio*, which he followed with prolegomena to the 1691 edition of Malalas. Thereafter, though, Hody applied his learning almost exclusively to religious ends, despite being regius professor of Greek. He became an energetic adversary of the non-jurors and applied his learning to contemporary religious issues—for example, his translation of a Greek treatise ascribed to Nicephorus, and published under the title *The Unreasonableness of a Separation from the new Bishops* (1691). Only his lectures on the history of Greek scholarship in the renaissance attest to his continued interest in secular learning. Even many of the famous New Year books—the occasion offered by John Fell, and later Henry Aldrich, to a promising youth to edit a classical text for publication by the Oxford press—exhibited this marked theological predilection. Of the thirty books of this sort published between 1666 and 1700, no less than thirteen were theological in content.[156]

Thomas Creech (MA 1683), the learned editor and translator of Lucretius, turned to theology, and at the time of his death in 1700 was 'upon an edition of Justin Martyr'. Thomas Milles (MA 1695, regius professor of Greek 1705–7) was the editor of Cyril of Jerusalem (1703) and never brought to fruition his projected edition

---

Gouk, 'An early critique of Bacon's *Sylva Sylvarum*: Edmund Chilmead's treatise on sound', *Annals of Science* xl (1983), 139–57.

[154] Wood, *Athenae* iii. 205–7, 1220. See also M. Feingold, 'Oriental studies', pp. 469–70, 482–3 below.
[155] Wood, *Athenae* iii. 446–9; see Bodl. MSS Langbaine.
[156] These included Clement, Faustinus Presbyter, Zosimus, Lactantius, Athenagoras, Clement of Alexandria, St Barnabas, Origen, Aristeas, and Tatian.

of Aristophanes. They were indeed following a now familiar pattern, whereby a learned master of arts in his twenties tried his hand at Greek or Roman scholarship, only to abandon the field shortly thereafter in order to dedicate his life to theology. It was articulated most explicitly by the editor of Lycophron (1697) and the author of *The Antiquities of Greece* (1697–8), John Potter (MA 1694). In his preface to Lycophron, Potter announced his intention of devoting himself in future to theological study and to the service of the church. He refused the offer of the professorship of Greek in 1707 on the grounds that he had 'turned his study wholly to divinity'.[157] Joseph Addison, by contrast, did not wish to pursue theology. But having graduated MA at Oxford in 1693 he found himself obliged to pursue divinity and was incepted in that faculty the following year. His desire to avoid such a course if possible is suggested by a poem he published at the same time, 'An account of the greatest English poets', the last six lines of which run as follows:

> I've done at length; and now, dear friend, receive
> The last poor present that my muse can give.
> I leave the arts of poetry and verse
> To them that practice 'em with more success.
> Of greater truths I'll now prepare to tell,
> And so at once, dear friend and muse, farewell.[158]

Addison eventually succeeded in his bid for a non-clerical career, but most of his contemporaries were not as fortunate. For a long time to come scholars found the church the only viable means of preferment if they were not to languish in poverty.

Modern Languages

By comparison with the classics, the place of modern languages in the Oxford curriculum was, on the face of it, much more tenuous. No reference to such subjects appeared in the statutes. Nor did the tutors' manuals of advice make them a requirement.[159] Nevertheless, by the early seventeenth century some members of the upper class, and not a few scholars, were becoming competent in at least one vernacular language. The statutory silence, however, was not the result of a negative official attitude towards modern subjects, but rather reflected the as yet incomplete recognition of modern languages as true academic disciplines, replete with a

[157] Hearne, *Collections* i. 305; M. L. Clarke, 'Classical studies' in *The Eighteenth Century*, 532 n. 3. A rare exception to the rule is John Hudson (MA 1684), who produced several editions including Thucydides, Velleius Paterculus, Longinus, Dionysius Halicarnassus, and Josephus Flavius. Ironically he was an unsuccessful candidate for the regius professorship of Greek in 1698 because of his political ideas. According to Hearne, Gilbert Burnet convinced William III to bestow the position upon Hody who 'had writt for the government', whereas Hudson 'was rather suspected to be no friend to it'. Wood, *Athenae* iv. 451–60; Hearne, *Collections* i. 98; see *DNB* s.v. John Hudson.

[158] Peter Smithers, *The Life of Joseph Addison* (Oxford 1968), 27–8. For the manner in which men of science attempted to resolve similar dilemmas see M. Feingold, 'The mathematical sciences and new philosophies', pp. 441–6 below.

[159] Such authors did, however, recommend French texts for those already conversant with the languages, as for example John Grandorge who assigned Malebranche's *Recherche de la vérité* and the *Journal des savants*. Bodl. MS St Edmund Hall 72.

distinctive theoretical component and consequential subject-matter. Certainly the idea that any vernacular literature formed a legitimate and serious body of know-ledge, on a par with classical literature, was alien to a contemporary attitude that still regarded French or Italian literary works as more diversionary than profound. With emphasis more on their utility than on their accompanying insights, then, seventeenth-century educators considered the acquisition of modern languages as a desirable accoutrement of the gentleman, who found them increasingly helpful for travel on the continent, for polite conversation and, later, for state service.

An increasing number of upper-class students arrived at Oxford already tolera-bly well grounded in French, and perhaps Italian too, and there their parents expected them to improve upon such knowledge. Early in the century Sir George Radcliffe expressed the common sentiment that it was 'necessary for a gentleman to learn Latine and French perfectly'. Several decades later Sir Justinian Isham pre-scribed French as one of the studies for his son Thomas at Oxford in 1674. The heads of house and many tutors quickly responded to the changing requirements by incorporating instruction in such languages into their teaching, or at least mon-itoring the progress made by their charges with private tutors. Francis Mansell assured Sir Sackville Crow in 1654 that he would take care to read French and Italian authors with young Sackville. Similarly, Benjamin Woodroffe complied with the wishes of Sir Robert Southwell concerning his nephew's instruction in French by utilizing French sources, such as Davila, in the teaching of history.[160]

A fairly well documented example of an early seventeenth-century undergradu-ate is that of William Trumbull, who came up to Magdalen College in 1622 already in possession of some French. A correspondent had sought to dissuade William Trumbull from sending his son to Magdalen, recommending Merton instead; the recently elected warden, Nathaniel Brent, as well as one of the fellows, Robert Symonds, were described as great travellers 'and well languaged' and their skill would allegedly ensure that young Trumbull would exercise his French.[161] But Sir William persisted and Magdalen proved adequate. The son's letters and accounts reveal that his tutor was versed in French and that during the first year he read with him French, logic, and history. Subsequently, the tutor merely supervised William's independent readings. By 1624 Trumbull had also engaged a young Frenchman to keep him company, thereby facilitating his skills in conversation; by this time he was also studying Italian and Spanish, though only as recreation and 'not as a distraction from Latin and Greek'.[162]

[160] *Wentworth Papers 1597–1628*, ed. Cooper 325; Northants. RO Isham correspondence, no. 845; BL Add. MSS 27,606, fo 5ᵛ, 46,951A, fo 1.

[161] Brent's predecessor, Sir Henry Savile, was himself proficient in French and Italian and he, too, cultivated foreign languages at Merton. In 1595 for example the college paid 6s 8d to a certain Italian who provided instruction in Italian and Spanish. J. R. L. Highfield, 'An autograph manuscript com-monplace book of Sir Henry Savile', *Bodleian Library Record* vii (1963), 73–83; J. McConica, 'The rise of the undergraduate college' in *The Collegiate University*, 61.

[162] Berks. RO Trumbull MS Add. 46 *passim*, Trumbull misc. corr. vol. 1, nos 13, 29, 36. The advo-cacy of the study of vernacular languages at the univesity was usually couched in terms of a pursuit for leisure hours. Claude Holyband's dedication of his *French Schoolemaister* to Robert Sackville of Hart Hall

Though the response of Oxford tutors to this increasing emphasis of members of the upper class on the study of French undoubtedly contributed to a corresponding improvement in their own facility in the language, for the most part their knowledge remained insufficient to inculcate purity of speech and expression. This goal could only be attained by way of frequent conversation with native Frenchmen. Thus, as was the case with William Trumbull, members of the upper class began to seek out native speakers. Some noblemen could afford to hire a constant companion. The duke of Ormond sent his grandson, James, Lord Butler, to Christ Church with instructions that 'he may have with him somebody that may take care that he lose not the French he has learned'. The Swiss Peter Drelincourt was chosen to serve as companion and tutor to the young lord and, since Drelincourt considered his position to be more elevated than that of Butler's college tutor, Henry Aldrich, a quarrel soon broke out between the two.[163] Those who could not afford the expense involved in keeping a constant companion could avail themselves of the services of a large number of private tutors who made Oxford their home and offered instruction, often in the college rooms of the students.

Among the many tutors who are known to have offered French instruction, mention can be made of Pierre Morlet who taught out of his rooms at Broadgates Hall from the end of the sixteenth century. Several of his students contributed complimentary verses to his *Junitrix* (1596). John Sanford (MA 1595) taught French, Italian, and Spanish at both Balliol and Magdalen colleges following his return from a long period of travel on the continent. Between 1604 and 1611 he published concise grammars of the three languages for the benefit of his students. Sanford's contemporary at Oxford was the French-born Robert Farrear who offered instruction in French during the second decade of the seventeenth century, publishing in 1618 *A Briefe Direction to the French Tongue* for the use of his pupils. A local talent, Wye Saltonstall of Queen's College, served as a private French tutor from 1625 to 1640. Another Frenchman was Peter Bense, a religious refugee who settled at Oxford where he earned his living during the 1630s by teaching French, Italian, and Spanish. He, too, published a book intended to assist his students—a concordance of the French, Italian, and Spanish languages, published in 1637.[164]

Bense's practice was continued by Gabriel Du Gres who taught at Cambridge for several years prior to his arrival at Oxford in the late 1630s. Du Gres continued to teach at Oxford until 1661 and, from the advertisement to the second edition of his *Dialogi gallico-anglico-latini* (Oxford 1652), it appears that during the Interregnum he charged 10*s* a month—a fee that included a daily hour-long

---

(MA 1579) recommended the youth should not 'leave off [his] weightier and worthier studies in the universitie, but when [his] mind is amazed and dazled with long readinge, [he] may refresh and disport [himself] in learninge this tongue'. Similarly, Henry Leighton's preface to his 1659 French grammar advertised the text as designed for students during otherwise spare time. K. Lambley, *The Teaching and Cultivation of the French Language in England During Tudor and Stuart Times* (Manchester 1920), 200, 204.

[163] HMC *Ormonde MSS* iv. 292, 318, 333–4.

[164] Wood, *Athenae* ii. 277, 471–2, 624, 676; Lambley, *The Teaching and Cultivation of the French Language in England*, 201; R. C. Simonini, *Italian Scholarship in Renaissance England* (Chapel Hill 1952), 68–71.

tutorial. After the Restoration the fee was doubled. One of Du Gres's rivals was the Scot Henry Leighton, who taught French in various Oxford colleges until his death in 1669, and published in 1659 his *Linguae gallicae addiscendae regulae*.[165]

During the latter part of the century we encounter Hippolytus du Chastlet de Luzancy, who resided at Christ Church in the second half of the 1670s while teaching French in several colleges as well as serving as the companion of Thomas Southwell once or twice a week, conversing with him in French in return for Southwell's contribution to Luzancy's conversation in English. Luzancy was also that 'little Frenchman' whom Benjamin Woodforde engaged in 1674 to sit with Sir Philip Percival after supper 'and so will either attend him in his reading' of some books 'or in his occasional discourses'. In 1703, William Brydges of Balliol offered some insight into the teaching of a 'Mounsieur Conniers' with whom he studied French and Italian. Conniers 'has been in Oxford 3 years', wrote Brydges, 'and is likely to continue much longer. He has abundance of schollars in our colledge. Mr Ottley learns French of him. He has 10 shillings entrance and 10 shillings per month, and to come 3 times a weeke, which is 12 times, but he is not to have his money till 12 times are finished.' After two months Brydges himself had made good progress in his studies and 'could turn French into Italian tolerably well', thus encouraging him to think that two more months of study would make him proficient in Italian as well. John Wallis, therefore, did not exaggerate when he stated in 1700 that at Oxford there were 'always teachers' of French, Spanish, and Italian, giving the example of the future benefactor of All Souls, Christopher Codrington (m. 1685), who learned those languages there.[166]

However, the study of modern languages was not confined to members of the upper class. Other students sought to acquire such knowledge, not only because of the prospect of becoming tutors to their social superiors, but in order to gain access to a growing body of religious and philosophical literature that was being published in the vernacular. Such study was usually conducted in private, mostly through reading, and its nature can be constructed only by piecing together bits of information. For those who arrived at Oxford without French or Italian and who were unable, or unwilling, to employ a tutor, the most common method of pursuit was simply to work through a well-known text, such as the Bible, in the relevant vernacular, with the help of a grammar and a dictionary. At the turn of the sixteenth century, for example, Edward Lord Herbert of Cherbury sought to make himself 'a citizen of the world' in just such a manner. As he recalled in his autobiography, he taught himself 'without any master or teacher' French, Italian, and Spanish 'by the helpe of some bookes in Lattaine or English translated into those idioms and the dictionaryes of those several languages'. Almost a century later John

---

[165] Wood, *Athenae* iii. 184; Wood, *Fasti* ii. 29–30; Wood, *Life and Times* ii. 150–1; Lambley, *The Teaching and Cultivation of the French Language in England*, 203–4. A later teacher, Jacques d'Abadie, published at Oxford in 1676 *A New French Grammar*. In the 1650s we also find Alesandro Amiedo, a Jew from Florence, teaching both Hebrew and Italian at Oxford. Macray, *Reg. Magdalen* iii. 74.

[166] Wood, *Fasti* ii. 350–1; BL Add. MSS 46,951A, fo 8, 46,953, fo 74v; HMC *Egmont MSS* ii. 32; Jones, *Balliol College*, 144–5; *Collectanea* i. 319.

Norris depicted a very similar method of self-instruction. He assured a friend that the study of French need not be painful at all 'if, omitting the tedious way of learning the grammar, you only read over twice or thrice the particles, next the verbs, and then proceed to go over the dialogues, and after that any plain book with a translation, by which you may be mistress of French so far so to read a book by the help of a dictionary in a month's time. I speak upon experience'.[167]

Certain colleges appear particularly to have encouraged the cultivation of modern languages. Queen's College was one such place, in part because of the long tradition of French there (the statutes allowed for discussion in French to substitute for that in Latin). The diary of Thomas Crosfield offers some interesting insights into his own conversance with the language, as well as that of some of his colleagues. Crosfield exercised his written French on several occasions in the diary: he mentions that he has conversed in French with one 'Mr Laurine', perhaps one of the many religious refugees who visited Oxford in the seventeenth century and provided local scholars with the opportunity to converse with them in return for hospitality. Yet the only reference to his study of modern languages is an entry of March 1627, where he records purchasing a French bible and Florio's Italian dictionary from his exact contemporary at Queen's, Thomas Whethereld.[168]

Another diary entry by Crosfield is instructive concerning the readings of the young Gerard Langbaine. Visiting the room of Langbaine in 1633, Crosfield records the former's ownership of John Florio's Italian dictionary and the *Dictionarie of the French and English Tongues* by Randle Cotgrave, a French translation of Diego d'Estella's *Meditations tres devotes de l'amour de Dieu*, a French translation of Bocaccio's *Decameron*, Philippe de Commines's *Memoires*, and an edition of Rabelais's works. Italian books included Pietro Bembo's *Nuove lettere famigliari*, Giovanni Botero's *Delle relationi universali*, and Camillo Capilupi's defence of the St Bartholomew's day massacre-*Lo stratagema de Carolo IX*.[169] Langbaine certainly became sufficiently proficient in French to translate in 1638 Guillaume Ranchin's *A Review of the Council of Trent*. Crosfield also sheds light on the fluency in French of the college's provost, Christopher Potter (provost 1626-46), to whom Langbaine dedicated his translation of Ranchin. In 1627, 'mr provost made a French epistle to the queene for 6 liveings and obteined them in the Isle of Wight'. Potter mastered Italian as well, and he published in 1626 a translation of Paolo Sarpi's *The History of the Quarrels of Pope Paul V with the State of Venice*.[170]

Christ Church, too, produced many competent linguists. Brian Duppa (dean 1628-38) was versed in French, judging by his reading of various French books during the 1650s. So too was Francis Atterbury half a century later, as evidenced by the considerable number of French books, as well as a few Italian and Spanish

---

[167] *The Life of Edward, First Lord Herbert of Cherbury*, ed. Shuttleworth, 16–17; Richard Acworth, *The Philosophy of John Norris of Bemerton: (1657–1712)* (Hildesheim and New York 1979), 341–2 n. 6.
[168] J. R. Magrath, *The Queen's College* (2 vols Oxford 1921) i. 47; QCL MS 390, fos 25ᵛ, 34–34ᵛ, 62.
[169] *The Diary of Thomas Crosfield*, ed. Boas, 68.　　　　　　　　　　　[170] Ibid. 11.

ones, in his library.[171] The orientalist John Gregory acquired a 'useful command' of French, Italian, and Spanish, in addition to a mastery of the classical and oriental tongues, while his younger contemporary, the dramatist William Cartwright (MA 1635), understood 'French and Italian, as perfectly as his mother-tongue'. Edmund Chilmead translated from the French Jacques Ferrand's *A Treatise discoursing of the Essence and Cure of Love* (1640), and after he was ejected by the parliamentary visitors he carried out several more translations in order to make a meagre living. In 1650 he translated Jacques Gafferel's *Unheard-of Curiosities concerning the Talismanical Sculpture of the Persians* from French, and from Italian Leo of Modena's *The History of the Rites ... of the Present Jews* and Campanella's *Discourse Touching the Spanish Monarchy*. A younger Christ Church contemporary, Henry Greisley (MA 1641), also resorted to translation after his ejection, translating from the French Balsac's *The Prince* and Senault's *The Christian Man*. At Christ Church, and elsewhere, the lighter literature available in French was as much an incentive for study as a means to its attainment. By 1668 Anthony Wood recorded that 'a little before Christmas, the Christ Church men, young men, set a library in Short's Coffee house in the study there, viz. Rablais, poems, plaies, etc'. Although not referring exclusively to Christ Church, Dean Fell's statement in 1672 that 'we have choice men who understand French perfectly' is certainly indicative of the attention devoted to that language in the college.[172]

The numerous translations from European vernaculars into English also offer invaluable testimony to the linguistic skills of other Oxford students. We earlier encountered Nathaniel Brent who was described in 1622 as 'well languaged'. He certainly mastered enough Italian as early as 1616 to carry out, at the behest of Thomas James, a translation of Sarpi's *History of the Council of Trent*. James himself mastered both Italian and French, publishing in 1598, while still a bachelor of arts, a translation of Antonio Brucioli's *Commentary upon the Canticle of Canticles* as well as *The Moral Philosophie of the Stoicks* by Guillaume Du Vair. John Heath, of New College, translated in the year he graduated MA (1613) Pierre du Moulin's *The Accomplishment of the Prophecies*.[173] William Pincke, of Magdalen College, probably translated from the French John Cameron's *An Examination of those Plausible Appearances which seeme most to commend the Romish Church* (1626), and Edward Chaloner (MA 1610) translated in 1619 Jean Bede's *The Masse Displayed*. Gilbert Watts, fellow of Lincoln College, who 'understood several languages well', translated from the Italian Davila's *History of the Civil Wars of France*, but never printed

---

[171] *The Correspondence of Bishop Brian Duppa and Sir Justinian Isham 1650–1660*, ed. G. Isham (Northants. Record Soc. xvii 1955) 139; *A Catalogue of the Library of ... Francis Atterbury* in *Poets and Men of Letters*, ed. H. Amory (London 1973), *passim*.

[172] Gerard Langbaine the younger, *An Account of the English Dramatick Poets* (London 1691, repr. 2 vols Los Angeles 1971) ii. 52; David Lloyd, 'The life and death of John Gregory' in Lloyd, *Memoirs of the Lives ... of those ... that Suffered for the Protestant Reformation* (London 1667), 87; Wood, *Athenae* iii. 350–1; Wood, *Life and Times* ii. 147; *CSPD 1671–2*, 72.

[173] Some twenty works of the popular Huguenot divine Pierre Du Moulin were published in the early seventeenth century, and among other Oxford translators who contributed to such enterprise mention may be made of John Sanford, Robert Stafforde, and John Verneuil.

it, having learned that Sir Charles Cotterell and William Aylesbury (BA 1632) 'had the start of him in that work'.[174] William King translated in 1690 Madam Dacier's *The Life of Marcus Aurelius Antoninus*, and Thomas Taylor (MA 1693) translated Father Daniel's *A Voyage to the World of Descartes* and Malebranche's *Treatise concerning the Search after Truth*, in 1692 and 1694 respectively.

The skills of other Oxford students may be deduced from the contributions in French verse made by several individuals to Oxford collections of poetry during the seventeenth century. Predictably, some contributors were members of the upper class, but a few were not. Thus we find William Seymour, eldest son of William earl of Hertford, featuring in a 1636 collection, and Edward and Charles Vane, sons of Sir Henry Vane, similarly contributed two years later. But also included were Frederick Tunstall (1630, 1633), Thomas Bowyer (1630), Thomas French (1633), Samuel Wilson (1636), Henry Lucas (1637), Thomas Tully (1643), and Joseph Williamson (1651, 1654).[175] The list could be expanded. Similarly we can quote instances when university officials addressed visiting dignitaries in one of the vernacular languages, as did John Younger of Magdalen College (MA 1662) in 1683 when he addressed the duchess of York in Italian.[176]

Finally, ownership of books offers another rich source of information for gauging the knowledge of Oxford scholars of foreign languages. Richard Fysher (MA 1583), who died in 1601, owned a volume of Italian dialogues, another of Italian comedies and tragedies, and a few Italian literary works including Tasso, Paolo Giovio, and Boccacio. A fellow of Corpus Christi, Walter Browne, owned grammars, dictionaries, and bibles in French, Italian, and Spanish as well as Comines in French, and Botero and Petrarch in Italian. His contemporary at Corpus, Brian Twyne, owned, in addition to several grammars and other linguistic aids for both French and Italian, Nicholas Bernaud's *Le Cabinet du roy de France*, Jerome Bignon's *De l'excellence des roys, et du royaume de France*, Pierre Boaistuau's *Le Theatre du monde*, Justus Lipsius' *Les Six Livres des politiques*, and, in Italian, Girolamo Razzi's *La balia*. The library of President Oliver of Magdalen College included eleven books in French, while that of John Hutton, a fellow of New College who died in 1653, included ten French and Italian books. By the end of the century some young students possessed far more considerable collections. Peter Wood of New College, who died in 1703, owned works by Boileau, Le Bruyere, St Evremont, Pascal, Bayle, Montaigne, La Rochefoucauld, Placete, Voiture, Fontenelle, and various theological writings. Equally instructive is that all these books were bequeathed to friends at Oxford—including Robert Shippen of Brasenose, John Woodford of New College, and Thomas Dobbs of Lincoln—who were presumably in a position to utilize such gifts.[177]

---

[174] Wood, *Athenae* iii. 433.

[175] Madan, *Oxford Books* ii. 113, 123, 125, 132, 135; A. Turner, 'French verse in the Oxford and Cambridge poetical miscellanies, 1600–1660', *Modern Language Quarterly* x (1949), 458–63.

[176] Macray, *Reg. Magdalen* iv. 109.

[177] OUA chancellor's ct inventories s.v. Fyssher, Browne, Hutton, Wood; F. Ovenell, 'Brian Twyne's library' (Oxford Bibliographical Soc. new ser. iv 1952), 1–42; Macray *Reg. Magdalen* iv. 237.

Given such instances Lambley was surely mistaken in assuming that the study of French was incompatible with a university education. She quotes an incident recorded by Samuel Pepys of an Oxford doctor of law whose inability to converse with the Spanish ambassador in French she generalizes into 'the inability of the young Oxford student to speak French when in polite London circles'. But even if many Oxford scholars failed to *converse* fluently in foreign languages, the available evidence certainly contradicts the conclusion that 'the universities, like the schools, failed to keep in touch with practical life by their neglect of the broader education necessary to persons of quality and fashion'.[178]

Logic

In a book published in 1606 Bartholomew Keckermann, that indefatigable author of textbooks, marvelled at the contemporary proliferation of works on logic: 'Never from the beginning of the world was there a period so keen in logic, or in which more books on logic were produced and studies of logic flourished more abundantly than the period in which we live.' As the seventeenth century drew to a close, an anonymous Cambridge tutor reflected far more gloomily upon an even greater body of such works, which he saw it as his duty to condense and synthesize:

We are burdened with a variety of dialectics, and unless God hears our cry Aristotle is likely to have more commentators than contexts. It will be our task to summarize these burdensome volumes, and, having grubbed-up the metals from the mine, to refine the gold from the iron, so that the very finest, having been carefully sifted out, may not only be compressly, unambiguously, briefly and clearly squeezed into the narrow limits of a compendious enchiridion, but even luxuriate and blossom.[179]

The tenor of these divergent expressions demonstrates not only the durability of logic as a discipline, but also the fundamental shift that occurred in its teaching during the roughly one hundred years that separated them. For although logic undoubtedly remained central to the undergraduate curriculum, the purpose, scope, and depth informing that study underwent a profound metamorphosis. This shift began with the humanist crusade against specialized, technical, and highly philosophical logic—which had reached its apotheosis in the late Middle Ages—and the substitution of a more balanced version of the trivium, one that harmonized the study of language and literature with an accompanying de-emphasis on logic. This process was intensified during the seventeenth century when discourse—a composite of language, speech, and the art of persuasion—became the focus and goal of higher education. Logic, in this new ordering, was now conceived of as a fusion of the arts of reasoning well and of ordering discourse, as an instrument for the better direction of the mind and the better organization of knowledge.

---

[178] Pepys, *Diary* ix. 544–5; Lambley, *The Teaching and Cultivation of the French Language*, 208–9.

[179] Bartholomew Keckermann, *Praecognitorum logicorum tractatus III* (Hanau 1606), 109, quoted in E. J. Ashworth, *Language and Logic in the Post-Medieval Period* (Dordrecht and Boston 1974), p. ix; Cambridge University Library, MS Dd. 6. 30, fo. 1 quoted in Costello, *The Scholastic Curriculum*, 45–6.

Unfortunately most modern scholars fail to perceive this subtle, yet momentous, transformation, assuming instead the persistence of medieval logic well into the seventeenth century, and hence an undergraduate course characterized by constriction and rigidity. Nor is this attitude towards university education limited to censure of the undergraduate curriculum. The very narrow-mindedness that informed the teaching of logic is seen to have guided the curriculum as a whole and, ultimately, the attitude towards all new ideas. Indeed, this perceived antagonism to 'modern' subjects is supported by a substantial body of evidence seemingly giving voice to widespread contemporary disenchantment with logic and its tenacious hold over higher education. Such evidence may be divided into roughly three sorts: unequivocal indictments by Bacon, Hobbes, Locke, and other key promoters of the new philosophy; jaundiced recollections of alumni; and a literature of satire that made the undergraduate's encounter with logic a favourite subject of ridicule. What emerges, at least at first glance, is a picture of a university saddled with a moribund curriculum, which encouraged exorbitant verbal wrangling at the expense of truth, thus creating an intellectual environment inimical to all new learning.

As for the previously noted outpouring of textbooks, historians of logic have interpreted this as a symptom of the very low ebb that characterized seventeenth-century logic. Their criticism, however, is directed less towards the scholastic content of the literature of logic than towards its emptiness. From their point of view, the discipline as taught at Oxford and Cambridge exhibited ignorance of Aristotle and represented a conspicuous decline compared to the vibrant medieval tradition. As long ago as the mid-nineteenth century, Sir William Hamilton conjectured a steady deterioration of standards among tutors, that in turn resulted in the preference for rudimentary treatises, like Robert Sanderson's *Logic*, instead of the more intricate treatises by Brerewood, Crakanthorpe, or Smiglecius. But even Sanderson's book, according to Hamilton, proved too difficult for tutors, as it necessitated numerous additional explanations, thus generating a need for a fresh textbook, one 'more accommodated to the fallen and falling standard of tutorial competency'. Such a text was found in Henry Aldrich's *Artis logicae compendium* which was 'far shorter than Sanderson's; written in a less scholastic Latin; adopted an order wholly independent of the Organon; and made no awkward demands upon the tutor'. Aldrich's compendium aroused Hamilton's indignation not only because he regarded its compiler as a scholar 'so indifferently prepared for the task', but because of the deleterious consequences that he believed the epitome augured for the subsequent study of logic: 'As a slender introduction to the after-study of logic (were there not a hundred better) it is not to be despised; as a full course of instruction—as an independent system of the science, it is utterly contemptible.' Hamilton concluded that the phenomenal success of that slim volume at Oxford well into the nineteenth century meant that 'the minimum of Aldrich ... remained the maximum of the "schools"; and was "got up", not to obtain honor, but to avoid disgrace'.[180] Even more sweeping in his denunciation of the impoverishment of

[180] W. Hamilton, *Discussions on Philosophy and Literature* (New York 1855), 126–7.

Oxford logicians of the seventeenth century was Ivo Thomas, who unequivocally asserted that Richard Crakanthorpe's *Logicae libri quinque* 'should certainly not have been written, let alone printed four times'. More generally, Thomas thought that even if an Oxford student had read the entire output of textbooks produced by local authors—with a few Continental ones thrown in—'he would understand virtually no logic'.[181]

An appraisal of the content of seventeenth-century logic is impracticable here, especially since this would have to be carried out within the context of an even larger evaluation of renaissance and early modern logic in general.[182] Instead, I will attempt to dispel certain misconceptions relating to the place of logic within the Oxford curriculum. Only marginally interested in formal logic, contemporaries instead endowed the discipline with a strictly functional role in regulating thought and expression. Logic continued to be a prerequisite course encountered early in a university career by all students but the amount of content deemed essential, as well as the intensity of the study, were increasingly curtailed as the seventeenth century progressed. Furthermore, this examination of the teaching of logic in its new 'circumscribed' form should assist in our later reappraisal of the alleged 'scholastic' nature of the seventeenth-century curriculum as a whole.

Perhaps the most damaging criticism of the way logic was taught at the university was voiced by the heralds of the 'new philosophy'. Scholars cite the many instances where Francis Bacon maintained the deficiency of logic as the foundation of true knowledge. Though intended to ameliorate the impoverished state of human intellect, the received logic, according to Bacon, failed and 'in offering at what it cannot master has done more to establish and perpetuate error than to open the way to truth'. Thomas Hobbes, a one-time Oxford undergraduate, was equally prone to malign the verbalism and emptiness of Aristotelian and scholastic logic. Most vehement in his criticism, however, was John Locke, himself a former Oxford tutor, who mercilessly assailed both contemporary logic and the universities that inculcated it. Though the brunt of his wrath was directed against what he saw as a pathetic obsession with disputations in which truth and knowledge played

---

[181] I. Thomas, 'Medieval Aftermath: Oxford logic and logicians of the seventeenth century' in *Oxford Studies Presented to Daniel Callus* (OHS new ser. xvi 1959–60), 307, 309.

[182] For the beginning of such a general re-evaluation see W. J. Ong, *Ramus, Method and the Decay of Dialogue* (Cambridge Mass. 1958); W. J. Ong, introduction to Milton's 'Art of Logic' in *Complete Prose Works of John Milton* viii. 144–205; W. S. Howell, *Logic and Rhetoric in England, 1500–1700* (Princeton NJ 1956); W. S. Howell, *Eighteenth-Century British Logic and Rhetoric* (Princeton 1971); W. Risse, *Die Logik der Neuzeit, I: 1500–1640* (Stuttgart 1964); Ashworth, *Language and Logic*; E. J. Ashworth, introduction to her edition of Robert Sanderson's *Logicae artis compendium* (Bologna 1985); E. J. Ashworth, 'Traditional logic' in Charles Schmitt and Quentin Skinner (eds), *The Cambridge History of Renaissance Philosophy* (Cambridge 1988), 143–72; L. Jardine, 'Humanist logic' ibid. 173–98; L. Jardine, 'The place of dialectic teaching in sixteenth-century Cambridge', *Studies in the Renaissance* xxi (1974), 31–62; L. Jardine, 'Humanism and the sixteenth-century Cambridge arts course', *History of Education* iv (1975), 16–31; L. Jardine, 'Humanism and dialectic in sixteenth-century Cambridge: a preliminary investigation' in R. R. Bolgar (ed.), *Classical Influences on European Culture A. D. 1500–1700* (Cambridge 1976), 141–54; G. Nuchelmans, 'Logic, language, and abstract objects' in M. Ayres and D. Garber (eds), *The Cambridge History of Seventeenth-Century Philosophy* (forthcoming).

little part, he excepted no aspect of logic from censure. That 'artificiall ignorance and learned gibberish' which was logic, he thundered in an early version of the *Essay concerning Human Understanding*, was conceived and perpetuated 'by the interest and artifice of the Church of Rome', and keeps 'even inquisitive men from true knowledge'. Nor 'hath this mischeife stopped in logical nicitys or curious empty speculations; it hath invaded the great concearnments of human life and society, obscured and perplexed the materiall truths of law and divinity and brought confusion, disorder and uncertainty into the affairs of mankinde'. Locke even challenged the utility of logic in rendering discourse more methodical, for he claimed he had 'seldom or never observed any one to get the skill of reasoning well, or speaking handsomly by studying those rules which pretend to teach it'. In the final analysis, those who were bred on logic and disputations may acquire 'a great deal of wit, and prompt memories', but not necessarily 'the clearest judgment or deepest reason'. This was so because of

wit lying most in the assemblage of ideas, and putting those together with quickness and variety, wherein can be found any resemblance or congruity, thereby to make up pleasant pictures and agreeable visions in the fancy; judgment, on the contrary, lies quite on the other side, in separating carefully, one from another, ideas wherein can be found the least difference, thereby to avoid being misled by similitude, and by affinity to take one thing for another.[183]

Tempting as it is to see such instances of 'progressive' rebuke as proof of the moribund nature of the curriculum, to do so is to ignore the restrictive nature of most such statements. With the exception of Locke—whose vehement critique of logic must be understood within the context of his wish to supplant the existing basis of the curriculum with a new one of his own making—most of these individuals intended their remarks to be understood only within the context of the 'new philosophy'. Neither their interest nor their censure extended to the general course of studies at the university, certainly not to the undergraduate curriculum.

Both Bacon and the early champions of the Royal Society clearly distinguished between advanced scientific knowledge and the knowledge of the schools; the latter was felt to be a prerequisite step in the proper education of the individual, though not a guarantee for the attainment of 'true' scientific knowledge. The case of logic was no exception. Bacon clearly enunciated the complementary, yet

[183] John Locke, *Drafts for the 'Essay concerning Human Understanding', and other Philosophical Writings*, ed. P. H. Nidditch and G. A. J. Rogers (3 vols Oxford 1990–) i. 195–6; *The Educational Writings of John Locke*, ed. Axtell, 296; John Locke, *Essay concerning Human Understanding*, ed. P. H. Nidditch (Oxford 1975), 203. A pleasant contrast is provided by Leibniz whose 1696 'Letter to Gabriel Wagner on the value of logic' should be seen as more typical of the experience of early modern intellectuals: 'I confess that in my early youth I was inclined to reject much of what had been introduced into the learned world. But with growing years and deeper insight I discovered the value of many things which I had before considered trivial, and I learned not to condemn anything too easily. . . . I must also confess, to stick to the truth and give everyone his due, that I also find much that is good and useful in the logic of the past. Gratitude as well compels me to say this, for I think I can truthfully say that even the logic taught me in school has been most fruitful to me.' Gottfried Wilhelm Leibniz, *Philosophical Papers and Letters*, ed. and trans. L. E. Loemker (Dordrecht 1969), 462–3.

disparate, function filled by logic in the domain of letters and the new logic he envisaged for the study of nature: 'The logic which is received, though it be very properly applied to civil business and to those arts which rest in discourse and opinion', he asserted, 'is not nearly subtle enough to deal with nature.'[184] As will be shown later, this observation was hardly intended as criticism of the under-graduate curriculum, the purpose of which was limited to preparing the foundation upon which specialized knowledge of, say, science and philosophy, could later be constructed.

Bacon's sentiments were reiterated by Thomas Sprat, fellow of Wadham College, who, in his defence of the recently established Royal Society was careful to empha-size that the membership wished neither to castigate (or radically alter) the univer-sity curriculum, nor to appeal to anyone but mature scholars:

Men are not ingaged in these studies, till the course of education be fully compleated, that the art of experiments is not thrust into the hands of boyes, or set up to be performed by beginners in the school, but in an assembly of men of ripe years: who while they begin a new method of knowledge, which shall consist of works, and is therefore most proper for men, they still leave to learners and children the old talkative arts, which best fit the younger age.

Even a far more vehement apologist of the Royal Society, Joseph Glanvill (MA 1658), made this distinction explicit when he argued that his censure of Aristotle and the ancients was intended neither 'to discourage young academians from apply-ing themselves to those first studies which are in use in the universities', nor to cast aspersion on the official requirements there, which he saw as 'requisite and fit' for undergraduates. Glanvill further admitted 'that those speculations raise, quicken and whet the understanding, and on that account may not be altogether unprof-itable, with respect to the more useful inquisitions'. Thus, provided that mathe-matics was taught concurrently, Glanvill proceeded to endorse the study of logic and philosophy, only requesting that they be protected from excess—'from being nice, aiery and addicted too much to general notions'.[185]

Bacon and his successors, then, ascribed a limited positive role to logic within the domain of knowledge. So long as it did not transgress its approved boundaries and presume to become an arbiter in advancing the knowledge of nature, its role as a prerequisite propaedeutic study—beneficial even in the domain of science and philosophy—went unchallenged. In upholding this notion, Sprat, Glanvill, and their contemporaries at Oxford were heirs to a distinctive humanist heritage that had realigned the role of logic within learned culture. Not only did the humanists dispense with much of the previous specialized and technical formal logic and its

---

[184] *The Works of Francis Bacon*, ed. Spedding, Ellis, and Heath iv. 17–18.

[185] Sprat, *History of the Royal Society*, 323–4; Joseph Glanvill, *Plus ultra* (London 1668), 127. In defend-ing his book against the invective of Henry Stubbe, Glanvill reiterated his claim that he intended no malice towards the university curriculum: 'academical education is not at all concerned in what I have said, and intended only for men who were past those preliminary studies'. *A Praefatory Answer to Mr Henry Stubbe* (London 1671), 73.

attendant speculative grammar, but they contrived a new harmonious balance in the trivium by consolidating language, eloquence, and logic under the unified banner of the art of discourse. An important consequence of this reorientation of the trivium was to remove demonstrative reason from the domain of logic, as being unfit to accommodate the primary function of discourse, namely persuasion, and to substitute probabilistic reason. Thus, while logic no longer owed its paramountcy to the supposed capability of generating new truths from given truths, it none the less acquired fresh pre-eminence because of a perceived applicability to all mental processes involved in the acquisition of knowledge.[186]

Crucial to this metamorphosis was the idea that logic lacked its own distinguishing subject-matter. Subservient to all disciplines and master of none, logic was nevertheless viewed as the essential gateway to all learning precisely because its entire purpose was to manage thought and regulate discourse. This utilitarian and subordinate function had already been articulated in the late fifteenth century by Rudolph Agricola, who asserted that 'dialectic does not arrogate to itself the role of judging, does not by its own resources clinch this or that dubious matter; it simply furnishes the wherewithal for such a judgment to be made by someone conversant with the subject-matter'. Among the many English scholars who concurred with Agricola was Thomas Spencer, who advertised in his elementary textbook of logic that the 'art of logick doth differ from all other arts whatsoever; for logick ends in speculation, and proceedeth no further than to judge whether one thing be truly affirmed by another'.[187]

This limited role for logic made it no less essential since it was believed that even a moderate proficiency would serve to dispel confused thoughts, help form sound judgement, prevent the mistaking of fallacy for truth, sharpen the mind, and generally prepare the ground for rational discourse and correct reasoning. Furthermore, even if logic could not be expected to generate new truths, no one in the seventeenth century doubted that existing truth was in need of defence, and that logic was particularly well suited to thwart error and heresy.[188] Hence followed the assumption that an early introduction to the art of logic would set the student on the right path: his thoughts would be rendered regular through the inculcation of rules and precepts, and his understanding of them sharpened by constant

---

[186] What is more important, asked Sir Henry Wotton, than the laying down of 'good logical foundations which must consolidate their discourse hereafter? For surely without it a man (be his witt never so pointedly) is but a floating and superficial thing.' Sheffield University Library, Hartlib papers 7/112/3.

[187] Rudolfus Agricola, *De inventione dialectica* (Paris 1534), bk II, 210, cited in C. J. R. Armstrong, 'The dialectical road to truth: the dialogue' in P. Sharratt (ed.), *French Renaissance Studies 1540–70* (Edinburgh 1976), 43; Thomas Spencer, *The Art of Logick* (London 1628), 7.

[188] The mathematician and wit John Arbuthnot (a student at University College in the early 1690s) conceded that the precepts of logic were 'absolutely necessary for a rule of formal arguing in public disputations, and confounding an obstinate and perverse adversary', even when, 'in the search of truth, an imitation of the method of the geometers will carry a man further than all the dialectical rules'. 'An essay on the usefulness of mathematical learning' in G. A. Aitken, *The Life and Works of John Arbuthnot* (London 1892, repr. London 1968), 411.

exercise. The undergraduate, in other words, would acquire a *habit* of mind regulating all thought.

Such was the reasoning of John Wallis when in presenting the manuscript of his textbook of logic to the Royal Society, in 1685, he took great pains 'to obviate a mistake' he found people running into, 'as if the whole business of logick were but to dispute or quarel' about terms, without any 'further use in humane life, and that, when they go from the university, they were to put off their gown and logick both together, and leave behind them, as being of no further use'. Indeed, he believed just the opposite to be true. Whether logic be taught by rules or learned through use, its business was 'to manage our reason to the best advantage, with strength of argument and in good order, and to apprehend distinctly the strength or weakness of another's discourse, and discover the fallacies or disorder whereby some other may endeavour to impose upon us, by plausible but empty words, instead of cogent arguments and strength of reason'. Logic is neither a picayune wrangling about words and terms, nor the art of 'useless canting'. Its duty is 'the whole management of reason' for without it 'it is not possible either to speak or judge aright of any rational discourse'. Thus, concluded the Savilian professor of geometry, those principles taught to students at the university were intended to lay the 'foundations of that learning, which they are to exercise and improve all their life after'.[189]

Indeed, such convictions survived well into the eighteenth century, even among faithful disciples of Locke. Isaac Watts, for example, was careful to emphasize in 1724 that though

> true logick is not that noisy thing that deals all in dispute and wrangling, to which former ages had debased and confined it, yet its disciples must acknowledge also that they are taught to vindicate and defend the truth, as well as to search it out. True logick doth not require a long detail of hard words to amuse mankind, and to puff up the mind with empty sounds and a pride of false learning, yet some distinctions and terms of art are necessary to range every idea in its proper class, and to keep our thoughts from confusion.[190]

Though the reinstatement of logic on a new footing helps explain the ease with which early modern scholars continued to advocate its centrality in the curriculum, some commentators articulated a predicament that has troubled educators in different guises ever since Aristotle. As Bacon stated in the *Advancement of Learning*, since logic and rhetoric were the 'arts of arts' and 'the gravest of the sciences', they naturally fitted better the capacities of 'graduates than children and novices'. Consequently, he doubted the wisdom of introducing these subjects too early to

---

[189] Royal Society, London, MS early letters W. 2. 39; see also Wallis's preface to his *Institutio logicae* (Oxford 1687). In 1700 Wallis offered another forceful defence of the necessity of teaching logic and metaphysics even to gentlemen: 'A gentleman that, in the university, is well instructed in the true use of logick (however that be despised by those who understand it not), and thereby taught to argue strongly, to discourse rationally, to discover the fallacies of an empty flourish ... shall be able to do his king and country better service ... than he that (without these) can ride the great horse, can dance, sing, play, etc., which are things that have in them more of the beau, but less of the man.' 'Dr Wallis's letter against Mr Maidwell', *Collectanea* i. 315.

[190] Isaac Watts, *Logick* (London 1725, 8th edn London 1745), dedication.

students whose 'minds are empty and unfraught with matter, and which have not gathered ... stuff and variety'. Otherwise, Bacon reasoned, the 'wisdom of those arts, which is great and universal, is almost made contemptible, and is degenerate into childish sophistry and ridiculous affectation'. It was absurd to expect a student to be able to acquire a firm understanding of 'things' before he had learnt what those were; nor could the student be expected to classify knowledge before he had been taught 'matter'. Milton, too, relegated instruction in logic and rhetoric, 'those organic arts which inable men to discourse and write perspicuously, elegantly, and according to the fitted style', to the final stages of education in the ideal institution he envisaged, and for similar reasons.[191]

Bacon's strictures, however, reflected a dated conception of the scope and quality of education provided by the English grammar schools, while Milton's proposed seminary represented a composite of school and university where, understandably, the teaching of logic followed the study of language. From the late sixteenth century, the great grammar schools in London, and quite a few provincial grammar schools that emulated their course of study, educated many of the future students of Oxford and Cambridge, with the consequence that these students were older than their predecessors and their proficiency in language and literature far superior.[192] In addition, as I have said, by 1600 the restructuring of the curriculum to embrace the grounds of all learning within the undergraduate course was well under way, and the problem facing educators was not whether incoming students were in possession of 'matter' sufficient to pursue the study of logic, but instead how to deal with the unanticipated consequence of the 'improved' grammar school education—the arrival of students all too well grounded in classical languages and literature.[193]

The new dilemma was that, as the study of 'good letters' became the ultimate goal of the educational programme, the rigorous and protracted preoccupation with language at the grammar school meant that many young undergraduates would find, by comparison, the study of logic and philosophy unappetizing. Bacon himself appreciated the problem when he pointed out that 'that part of human philosophy which regards logic is less delightful to the taste and palate of most minds, and seems but a net of subtlety and spinosity'. Indeed, he continued, the sciences

[191] *Works of Francis Bacon*, ed. Spedding, Ellis, and Heath iii. 326; Milton, *Complete Prose Works* ii. 401. Locke, however, argued somewhat disingenuously that the study of logic was too difficult for young students, while those ripe in years no longer needed it.

[192] Vives had already charted the humanist ideal that logic was always to be taught in conjunction with the imparting of 'matter'—classics, history, and moral philosophy. Since the accretion of language alone is not enough, 'a method of investigation comes next to the study of language, a means whereby we can test the true and the false by simple and well-arranged rules'. The student was required to pursue the two concurrently, 'so that he goes on to the completion of the one whilst making progress in the other'. *Vives: on education*, trans. Watson, 163–4.

[193] Other critics of the universities deliberately exaggerated the 'unreadiness' of students upon arrival. John Hall, for example, claimed in 1649 that students arrived at the university 'with a few shreds of Latine ... And then possibly before they have survayed the Greeke alphabet ... be racked and tortured with ... harsh abstracted logicall notions, which their wits are no more able to endure then their bodies the strapado'. Hall, *The Advancement of Learning*, ed. Croston, 25–6.

'best liked' were those 'which have some infusion of flesh and blood; such as civil history, morality, policy, about which men's affections, praises, fortunes, turn and are occupied. But this same "dry light" parches and offends most men's soft and watery natures. But to speak truly of things as they are in worth, rational knowledges are the keys to all other arts.'[194]

Small wonder, then, that many students arrived at Oxford not only proficient in—and addicted to—the classics, but also affected with a fallacious perception of the extent and depth of their knowledge. Clement Barksdale (MA 1632) elucidated the point on the eve of the Restoration:

Some of us, though we come rich in learning from the grammar school, prove but mean fellows in the school of philosophy: whether it be, because in confidence and pride of our forwardnesse above others, we neglect our studies here, or because our fine poetry and oratory steals us away from the more rough and crabbed study of logick.[195]

Students admitted as much in private. Samuel Woodforde (BA 1657) later lamented that 'coming pretty ripe from Paul's School, [he] was too good to learn, and was so proud as to think [himself] almost as good as [his] tutor'. Consequently, he followed his fancy and 'neglected other more serious studies'. The confession of Philip Henry (MA 1652) was similar: 'Coming from Westminster School, his attainments in school-learning were beyond what generally others had that came from other schools; so that he was tempted to think there was no need for him to study much, because it was so easy to him to keep pace with others'. John Potenger said that since he was not 'immediately enter[ed] upon logick and philosophy, but was kept for a full year to the reading of classical authors, and making of theams in prose and verse', he opted later to acquire 'just logick and philosophy enough to dispute in [his] turn in the hall, for [he] was addicted most to poetry and making of declamations, two exercises [he] desired to excell in'.[196]

Not surprisingly, both parents and educators were alarmed by the prospect that young students would elect to fend off the required, yet demanding, course of logic and philosophy in favour of the more pleasing studies they had formerly acquired. As a former student of Jesus College observed in 1600, 'but thou wilt say it [logic] is obscure, unpleasant, and therefore in no wise profitable. Oh how weake is the connexion of this argument? Admit that it is at first rough and irksome, yet notwithstanding when thou shalt enter farther into it, an insatiable desire of learning it foorthwith will cause thee to embrace it.'[197]

A close scrutiny of the sentiments expressed by alumni and other contemporaries would further substantiate the claim that far from deprecating logic these

---

[194] *Works of Francis Bacon*, ed. Spedding, Ellis, and Heath iv. 406.

[195] Clement Barksdale, *An Oxford Conference of Philomathes and Polymathes* (London 1660), 3.

[196] L. A. Ferrell, 'An imperfect diary of a life: the 1662 diary of Samuel Woodforde', *Yale University Library Gazette* lxiii (1989), 141; J. B. Williams, *The Lives of Philip and Matthew Henry* (London 1825), 17; *Private Memoirs of John Potenger*, ed. Bingham, 29.

[197] William Vaughan, *The Golden-Grove* (London 1600, 2nd edn London 1608), bk iii ch. 41 (unpaginated).

individuals actually endorsed the study of a difficult, yet indispensable, subject, the main point of difference being the order and length of such study. Some passages in Herbert of Cherbury's autobiography, for example, have frequently been interpreted as a criticism of the teaching of logic at his alma mater. Yet Herbert was neither troubled by the authority of Aristotle nor even averse to logic. Since his comments were part of his prescription for the proper course of study for a first-born member of the upper class, Herbert's concerns were understandably predominantly pragmatic—considerations of time and moderation. Within this context he objected to tutors at the university who 'comonly spend much tyme in teaching them the subtilityes of logicke which as it is usually practized enables them for litle more then to bee excellent wranglers'. Though sounding strikingly like an anticipation of Locke, Herbert's ensuing comments elucidate his antithetical views concerning logic: 'I approve much those parts of logicke which teach men to deduce theire proofes from firme and undoubted principles, and showe men to distinguish betwixt truth and falshood, and help them to discover fallasies, sophismes, and that which the schoolemen call vitious argumentations.'[198]

With the same objective of upper-class education in mind, Cherbury also asserted that a student who intended to spend some two years at the university could not be expected to attempt more than a modicum of learning in the various disciplines. Accordingly, the six months' study he thought was adequate for logic represented a considerable portion of the course, proportionally analogous to the time allocated to logic in the full undergraduate course. Nor did other contemporary educational theorists think differently. As early as 1605 James Cleland, while rejecting the mere cluttering of the mind with notions and subtleties, none the less argued that logic was 'an instrument . . . and therefore should be taught plainlie and breiflie, to be imploied in other sciences, in disputing of vertue and vice, of natural and supernatural things: tending to shew good and evil, and what is true and false'. A perceptive commentator and one-time chancellor of Oxford, the earl of Clarendon, who has often been portrayed as an opponent of the teaching of logic at university, was quite explicit about the necessity of teaching it to well-born students:

I wish they may, as soon as they come to the university, be instructed diligently in the art of logick, and engaged in the forms of disputations, and all other exercises of the college in which they are; in which there ought to be no difference or respect to quality, which hath used to be an unhappy privilege, which noblemen have had, that they might chuse whether they would be obliged to the publick scholastick exercises of the house . . . but I am glad to hear that those abominable exemptions are abolished.[199]

Oxford tutors expressed similar views to their upper-class employers. In 1652 Leoline Jenkins informed a certain 'Lady A' that 'in time' he intended to acquaint

[198] *The Life of Edward, First Lord Herbert of Cherbury,* ed. Shuttleworth, 19–20.
[199] Cleland, *The Institution of a Young Noble Man,* 89; Edward Hyde, earl of Clarendon, 'Concerning education' in *The Miscellaneous Works of . . . Edward, Earl of Clarendon* (London 1727, 2nd edn London 1751), 326.

her son 'with logick and philosophy (the chief learning of this place) which, if
understood, will be an excellent help to manage his reason and discourse, so as to
speak concludent to any purpose'. Jenkins's mentor at Jesus College, Francis
Mansell, communicated a similar design in 1654 to Sir Sackville Crow, who had
previously admonished his son to 'bee carefull of making your logick grounds perfect'. 'Though we mustn't spend too long on this part of learning, yet we must
labour hard to attain unto some exactness in it, in regard of its general usefulness.'
Two decades later, Thomas Smith of Magdalen College informed Lady Digby that
having secured the foundation of religion, her son now proceeded

> with greater ease and certainty in raising the superstructure of all true and useful learning,
> befitting his quality and birth. It was highly necessary at first to teach him a little logic, that
> he might understand the sure and strict laws of arguing and find out the defects of an ill
> consequence, and not be imposed upon by slights and plausibilities, and mere shows of rea-
> son.

Only after such a ground-work had been laid could the young Digby be 'diverted'
with more 'pleasant studies'.[200]

The proper method of acquiring proficiency in logic was articulated by Sir
Robert Southwell, in a letter he sent to his nephew John Perceval at Christ Church
in 1677. Expected to proceed to the Inns of Court after a brief university career,
Perceval was advised that after he had gone through the first six books of Euclid,
he should make himself 'master of the rules of logic and above all the use of it',
by pursuing Robert Sanderson's *Logic*. Next, continued Southwell,

> your business should then be to frame and spin discourses out of your own mind that may
> contain the operation and practice of these rules and to observe diligently the instructions
> given touching the topics or sources from whence arguments are raised, to have them all
> flying in your mind. To be powerful and ready in argumentation, to defend that which is
> just and to persuade others to believe it, such will be the great business of your life in the
> profession of the law.[201]

Even Thomas Sprat, concerned as he was to demarcate the newly contrived boundaries of knowledge, doubted neither the necessity of logic nor its use in science:

> Logic is the art of conceiving, arguing, and method. And, notwithstanding all the progress
> which may happen in natural knowledge, all the several parts of reasoning, which it teaches
> in all manner of business, will continue the same. The operations and powers of the mind
> will still be the same degrees of arguing from particular things, to propositions, and con-
> clusions, and therefore they will still require the same means, and exercises for direction. It
> is not the complaint of the promoters of experiments that men have bin wanting to them-
> selves, in regulating, disposing, or judging of their own thoughts. Nay they rather condemn
> them for being wholy imployd about the productions of their own minds, and neglecting all
> the works of nature that are without them.[202]

---

[200] *Register*, ed. Burrows, p. cxvii; BL Add. MS 27,606, fos 1, 6; Bodl. MS Smith 60, p. 23.
[201] BL Add. MS 46,954B, fo 128.   [202] Sprat, *History of the Royal Society*, 326–7.

The comments of seventeenth-century philosophers, alumni, and others concerning logic, then, cannot be construed as a denunciation of its teaching but only as a conscious delimiting of its application. Nor is it warranted to utilize the many instances of satire of logic as indicative of a widespread disillusionment with the undergraduate course of study. Clearly, to marshal the well-known witticisms of Pope's *Dunciad* or Sterne's *Tristram Shandy*, which deride logic and the curriculum in general, as representative of the climate of opinion a century earlier is anachronistic.[203] Nevertheless it remains the case that earlier, lesser-known wits contributed their own share of biting humour. It is tempting to interpret the 'plea' of one student to pulp those logic textbooks plaguing undergraduates as reflecting the prevalent mood of repugnance for a seemingly barren and useless subject:

> Hang Brirewood and Carter, in Crakenthorp's garter,
> Let Keckerman too bemoan us,
> I'll be no more beaten for greasy Iacke Seaton
> Or conning of Sandersonus.[204]

Indeed, the names of the chief textbook authors became synonymous not only with the study of logic, but with sophisms in general. The Merton wit and future bishop John Earle, for example, depicted the 'Old College Butler' as the one who could divide 'an halfpenny loaf with more subtelty than Keckerman',[205] while Sir Thomas Overbury (BA 1598), in his character of 'A meere scholler', mused about that 'intelligible asse', who 'is led more by his eares then his understanding, taking the sound of words for their true sense, and does therefore confidently beleeve that Erra Pater was the father of hereticks, Rudolphus Agricola, a substantial farmer, and will not sticke to averre, that Systema's *Logicke* doeth excell Keckerman's'.[206]

Inviting as it may be to interpret such jests as yet another indication of the critical dismissal of an outdated wrangling discipline, a closer look reveals a more complex situation. For one thing, the satire directed against logic can be seen as indigenous to the culture of wit which, by the first half of the seventeenth century, was rapidly becoming a prominent feature of English society. Certainly, the commonality of the experience—the fact that all educated persons had studied logic at the university—lent resonance to students' gripes. Seen in these terms, the stereotypical representation of the Oxford logician and one time master of Jesus College Griffith Powell, appears innocuous enough:

[203] *The Twickenham Edition of the Poems of Alexander Pope*, ed. John Butt *et al.* (11 vols London 1938–68) v. 361; *Sterne*, ed. Douglas Grant (Cambridge Mass. 1970), 66–7.

[204] Thomas Randolph, *Aristippus, or the Joviall Philosopher* (London 1631), 21, quoted in Curtis, *Oxford and Cambridge in Transition*, 100.

[205] John Earle, *Microcosmography*, ed. P. Bliss (London 1811), 46. Another of Earle's targets was the 'self-conceited man' who 'prefers Ramus before Aristotle', as he favours Paracelsus over Galen. Ibid. 30.

[206] *The Overburian Character*, ed. W. J. Paylor (Oxford 1936), 34. By the second half of the century Keckermann was replaced by Burgersdijk as the embodiment of logic and pedantry, and hence the target of satire. See M. Feingold, 'The ultimate pedagogue: Franco Burgersdijk and the English speaking academic learning' in E. P. Bos and H. A. Krop (eds), *Franco Burgersdijk and his World* (Amsterdam and Atlanta Ga. 1992), 151–65.

> Grifith Powell, for the honour of his nation,
>   wrote a book of Demonstration.
> And having little else to doe,
>   He wrote a book of Elenchs too.[207]

Furthermore, satire does not necessarily negate a deep-seated appreciation (even affection) for the very thing being parodied, as is evident in George Wither's *Juvenilia*:

> [My tutor] labour'd to impart,
> The hidden secrets of the *Logick* Art;
> In stead of Grammar Rules he read me then,
> Old Scotus, Seton, and new Keckerman.
> He shew'd me which the *Praedicabiles* be,
> As *Genus*, *Species*, and the other three;
> So having said enough of their contents,
> Handles in order th'ten *Praedicaments*;
> Next *Post praedicamenta* with *Priorum*,
> *Perhermenias* and *Posteriorum*.
> He with the *Topickes* open; and discries
> *Elenchi*, full of subtile fallacies:
> These, to unfold (indeed) he tooke much paine,
> But to my dull capacitie in vaine:
> For all he spake was to a little passe,
> As in old time unto the vulgar was
> The Latine masse, which (whether bad or good)
> The poore unlearned never understood.

Eventually, like many other students, Wither came to recognize the value of the subject and his own inadequacy as a disputant:

> I reacht my bookes that I had cast about,
> To see if I could picke his meaning out:
> And prying on them with some diligence,
> At length I felt my dull intelligence
> Begin to open; and perceived more
> In halfe an houre, than halfe a yeere before.

---

[207] Wood, *Athenae* ii. 283. Next to John Case, Powell was considered 'the most important Aristotelian in Oxford' at the turn of the seventeenth century: Schmitt, *John Case and Aristotelianism in Renaissance England*, 108. Certainly other authors and professors suffered similar puns. When John Bainbridge, Savilian professor of astronomy, posted a notice advertising that he would read '*Lecturus de Polis & Axis*', an unknown hand augmented the notice:

> Doctor Bambridge, came from Cambridge,
> To read *De Polis & Axis*.
> Let him go back again, like a Dunce as he came,
> And learn a new *Syntaxis*.

Walter Pope, *The Life of Seth Lord Bishop of Salisbury*, ed. J. B. Bamborough (Oxford 1961), 11.

And (which is strange) the things I had forgot,
And till that very day remembered not,
Since first my tutor read them; those did then
Returne into my memory agen.
So; that, with which I had so much to doe,
A weeke made easie, yea, and pleasing too.[208]

To interpret such satire as more than a cathartic exercise of the eternal student in a culture that esteemed wit—especially when as adults these same detractors endorsed the butt of their previous barbs—is to ignore its spirit. Only at the end of the seventeenth century when the position of logic in the curriculum was seriously challenged did satire become truly spiteful.

The counterpart of the received view of logic as an object of derision is the common interpretation of Ramism as the victim of scholastic narrow-mindedness. The firmness with which the university officials allegedly clung to sterile Aristotelian logic is said to be matched only by their tenacity in thwarting all efforts to introduce the novel and 'progressive' teaching of Ramus. This view is to a large extent the result of a preoccupation with the debates of the 1570s and 1580s, which has tended to confer unwarranted profundity on the ideas of Peter Ramus and to misconstrue the complexity of the critical response to them. More worrying, the conclusions many historians drew from these studies have been applied more or less uncritically to the seventeenth-century university as well. What is insufficiently recognized is that after 1600 those very elements of the Ramist programme that so endeared it to (mainly protestant) English and continental academicians, brought about its demise. Admittedly, the iconoclastic attack on Aristotle, and deliberate forging of a system that promised not only a short-cut to all knowledge but also reassured converts that the minimal knowledge they had acquired would be sufficient, the inherent dogmatism which lent itself to the conduct of polemics, and, last but not least, the 'martyrdom' of Peter Ramus at the St Bartholomew's day massacre, all conjoined to make Ramism especially attractive to protestants in the immediate aftermath of the Council of Trent.

Within two or three decades after Ramus' death in 1572, however, these very attractions lost much of their original appeal. Erudition and the study of good letters—themes not particularly prominent among the priorities of most protestant reformers—together with the old humanist spirit in general, were rapidly gaining ground. As a consequence the Ramist critique of the existing curriculum and the proposed reforms were now interpreted as arrogant, superficial, and injurious to learning. The emergent mood of intellectual confidence and respect for true learning among protestants found new exemplars in such scholars as Scaliger and Casaubon who, though nominally well disposed towards the reforming spirit of

---

[208] Wither, *Juvenilia* i. 31–3. O'Day and Todd mistook the copy of these lines, made by Thomas Newman in 1624, for an original composition by that Exeter College undergraduate: Bodl. MS top. Oxon. f. 39, fos 18–19; R. O'Day, *Education and Society 1500–1800* (London 1982), 117; M. Todd, *Christian Humanism and the Puritan Social Order* (Cambridge 1987), 76–7.

Ramus, could not condone what they regarded as an irresponsible and poorly informed assault on scholarship and antiquity, or the ominous sanction the Ramist fad lent to 'philistinism'.[209] As Sharratt has aptly stated the case, Ramus gravely offended the humanists by compounding his want of 'literary and aesthetic sensibility' with a deliberate depreciation of literature precisely 'at a time when it was beginning to have an independent existence, and by doing this he restricted its scope as well as that of philosophy'.[210] Furthermore, the new generation of scholars deprecated the fact that, while attacking Aristotle and the ancients, Ramus borrowed heavily from them without acknowledgement. Not surprisingly, his haughty claims for originality earned him the appellation *usuarius*, as one who lived 'off the increments of intellectual capital belonging to others'.

By the early seventeenth century Ramus' logic, too, was deemed unsatisfactory. Authors of textbooks and university tutors alike recognized what modern historians have only recently begun to appreciate, namely, to use Ong's phrase, that Ramist logic was 'based on ukase prompted by impatience and pedagogical convenience, rather than by any profound insight into the nature of thought and expression'. Even more forcefully, Ashworth points out the unfortunate fusion of residual logic and dogmatism in Ramus: 'It seems quite clear that there was no formal basis for his so-called reforms. His only apparent principle was one of random simplification.' Indeed, such principles 'would serve only to bolster the dogmatism of a mind already convinced that it perceived the truth in an orderly manner'. Seventeenth-century scholars were by contrast far more tolerant in appreciating good knowledge whatever its source, just as they were more discriminating than their sixteenth-century predecessors in maintaining standards. They were also suspicious of any argument in favour of natural reason, according to which 'the mind would recognize intuitively the one and only true valid logical proposition'.[211]

Most important, even before the full extent of the inadequacy of Ramism as a viable intellectual alternative to the traditional curriculum in general, and to logic in particular, had been recognized, it was already becoming evident that Ramism threatened religion and order no less than it jeopardized learning. The seductive appeal of Ramist dogmatism and simplicity to radical puritans is well documented. Less appreciated is the fact that the contentiousness bred by such a union through the constant and deliberate provocation of hot-headed disciples further discredited Ramism not only in the eyes of conformists, but among some puritans as well. It

[209] See for example J. Glucker, 'Casaubon's Aristotle', *Classica & Mediaevalia* xxv (1964), 274–96. Franco Burgersdijk's reproach of Ramus as 'audacious, indiscrete and how very hurtful to antiquity' was representative of the consensus among scholars of the following generation: Howell, *Logic and Rhetoric in England*, 310.

[210] P. Sharratt, 'Recent work on Peter Ramus', *Rhetorica* v (1987), 34. See also his 'Peter Ramus and the reform of the university: the divorce of philosophy and eloquence' in P. Sharratt (ed.), *French Renaissance Studies*, 4–20.

[211] Milton, *Complete Prose Works* viii. 159; E. J. Ashworth, 'Some notes on syllogistic in the sixteenth and seventeenth centuries', *Notre Dame Journal of Formal Logic* xi (1970), 20; Ashworth, *Language and Logic in the Post-Medieval Period*, 15–16; P. A. Duhamel, 'Milton's alleged Ramism', *Proceedings of the Modern Languages Association* lxvii (1952), 1038–9.

became a truism that many debates were concerned only marginally with genuine intellectual issues and that for most protagonists Ramism was a thinly disguised assault on the religious establishment and its educational seminaries. Here a little-known case study demonstrates the interchangeability of Ramism and puritanism. In 1574 John Barebone of Magdalen College was allowed to incept MA only after he apologized for the offensive remarks and pugnacious behaviour he exhibited while performing his public exercises. His endorsement of Ramus and attack on Aristotle was, however, only an extension of his militancy in college, where Barebone eagerly participated—and even provoked—the bitter controversies that plagued Magdalen in those years and that eventually resulted in his expulsion in 1578.[212] McConica is undoubtedly correct, therefore, to interpret a 1586 statutory injunction reiterating the obligation to adhere to Aristotle as an attempt to cope with this and similar dissensions that threatened to ruin the university.[213]

In fact, the institutional effort throughout Europe to rout Ramism was motivated primarily by the strife provoked by its adherents, and not necessarily by intellectual conservatism. Joseph Scaliger's opposition to the introduction of Ramism into Leiden, a by-product of his fear 'that the inevitable quarrels between Ramists and Aristotelians would destroy the institution', was matched by instances in Germany where 'wild-eyed and sputtering Ramists [were] dismissed from university faculties as troublemakers and frauds'. At Oxford, the puritan John Rainolds found the moral example set by Ramus' controversies repugnant. Like Scaliger, he valued Ramus' devotion to the cause of protestantism more highly than his scholarship, and consequently only reluctantly endorsed Ramus' teaching.[214] The perils of contentiousness and dissension were exacerbated by the fact that Ramus appeared to be the 'patron saint' of students, thanks to his celebrated short-cuts to knowledge and to the heated debates in the schools, which appealed to undergraduates endowed generously with passion but only scantily with judgement. The young students, it was feared, would not only be delighted to cheer any assault on authority but would refuse in consequence to follow their proper studies. The noted Oxford teacher and philosopher John Case referred to such a possible outcome of the Ramists' attack on Aristotle, when he wryly remarked that as 'beardless youth often does what white hair denies to have been rightly done' he expected that 'young men will hold [his] work the poorer because [he] name[d] in it the old interpreters of Aristotle'.[215]

Viewed in these terms, it is much easier to understand the rationale behind the resolute rejection of Ramism; it stemmed not from a reactionary cabal but from an

---

[212] Wood, *History of the University* ii. 176; C. M. Dent, *Protestant Reformers in Elizabethan Oxford* (Oxford 1983), 55–8.

[213] *SA* 437; McConica, 'Humanism and Aristotle in Tudor Oxford', 301.

[214] J. H. Overfield, *Humanism and Scholasticism in Late Medieval Germany* (Princeton 1984), 165; A. Grafton, *Joseph Scaliger* (Oxford 1983), 336 n. 160; McConica, 'Humanism and Aristotle in Tudor Oxford', 306–7.

[215] John Case, *Speculum moralium quaestionum* (Oxford 1585), fo 5, cited in Howell, *Logic and Rhetoric in England*, 191.

informed repudiation of a derivative, superficial, and highly rancorous body of teaching. Richard Hooker, fashioning his views on those of his mentor John Rainolds, contributed this often-quoted verdict on 'Ramystry':

> In the povertie of that other new devised ayde two things there are notwithstanding singular. Of marveilous quicke dispatch it is, and doth shewe them that have it as much almost in three dayes as if it dwell threescore yeares with them. Againe because the curiositie of mans wit doth many times with perill wade farther in the search of things then were convenient, the same is thereby restrayned unto such generalities as every where offering themselves are apparent unto men of the weakest conceipt that neede be. So as following the rules and precepts thereof, we may define it to be an art which teacheth the way of speedie discourse, and restrayneth the minde of man that it may not waxe over wise.[216]

His older contemporary John Case remarked on the arrogance of Ramus, who appeared to have felt 'that in a single lifetime, he has exceeded the learning of all who have gone before', while, many years after he had left New College, Sir Henry Wotton censured epitomes for the same reason that he recalled his contemporaries berated Ramus—the poverty of learning which was translated into irresponsible short-cuts: 'In brief, what I heard sometimes spoken of Ramus, I believe of those thrifty compendiums; they show a short course to those who are contented to know a little, and a sure way to such whose care is not to understand much.'[217]

In contrast to received opinion, the clamp-down on Ramus can be interpreted as a sign of intellectual integrity and broad-mindedness. This is not to imply that contemporaries viewed the contribution of Ramism to be totally without value, only that, as Bacon so eloquently stated it, 'the most precious things have the most pernicious keepers'.[218] The good that was to be had from Ramus was silently adopted: for example, the format of the compact epitome as the proper introduction to the study of logic or the inclusion of an extended discussion of method. But the movement as a whole scarcely retained intellectual respectability. True, one may detect the residue of the former debates in the early decades of the seventeenth century. Daniel Featley of Corpus Christi College, for example, delivered an oration in about 1604 'In laudem dialecticae Aristotelis' in which he gloated at the sight of the Ramists having to hide in the shadow of their master for 'they could not bear the clear sunlight of science'. A quarter of a century later, John Nourse of Magdalen presented to the college president as a new year's gift a work contrasting both systems of logic, *Differentiarum inter logicam Aristotelicam & Remisticam collectio*, a tribute that undoubtedly brought about Nourse's election a few months

---

[216] *The Folger Library Edition of the Works of Richard Hooker*, ed. W. Speed Hill (5 vols Cambridge Mass. 1977–90) i. 76.

[217] McConica, 'Humanism and Aristotle in Tudor Oxford', 300; Wotton, *A Philosophical Survey of Education*, ed. Kermode, 23.

[218] For this reason Bacon offset faint praise of Ramus with fierce denunciation of him as 'that most dangerous of all literary corroders who constricts and distorts reality with his narrow method and his summaries'. *Works of Francis Bacon*, ed. Spedding, Ellis, and Heath ix. 128, vii. 19.

later to the college lectureship in logic.[219] But such instances proved the exception. Generally, Ramus was relegated to the position of a name on a list of past commentators rather than promoted as an authority to follow.

The changing boundaries and purpose of logic were implied in the distinctive method of study that evolved during the seventeenth century. First, the conventional form of a lecture, in the manner of 'diting'—a dictation of a prescribed text—or commentary on an approved text, was rapidly rendered obsolete. This was a consequence of both the demise of the public university lectures in the arts and, more profoundly, the privatization of the study of logic. Increasingly, the supervision a student received from his tutor in the study of logic was confined to the 'reading' of introductory compendia, which outlined the domain of study and acquainted the student with the primary terminology.[220] The young undergraduate was then left to proceed on his own, and the function of the tutor became more supervisory, an 'oracle' available for further information or a watchman to monitor progress. During this stage of independent study the student acquired (or borrowed) a sizeable assortment of logic textbooks. Paradoxically, however, the swelling number of books was accompanied by shrinking expectations of what needed to be mastered. The chief purpose of these additional books was to augment the introductory text assigned by the tutor and serve as reference tools for further explication of issues only briefly covered in the initial compendium, or to furnish material for disputation. Moreover, although the statutes stipulated that the study of logic be carried on for the last three years of the student's undergraduate course, in reality students devoted the mornings of only a year or so to a sustained study of logic—a situation created as much by the growing consensus on the merit of reducing the required technical expertise as by the need to accommodate the entire curriculum within the undergraduate course.

The infiltration during the seventeenth century of a distinct condensed course of residual logic is demonstrated by the many 'Directions' for students that had begun to proliferate by the middle of the century. One of the earliest, most detailed, and best known was compiled by the Cambridge scholar Richard Holdsworth, whose method was endorsed, at least implicitly, by tutors at both universities. Holdsworth recommended that newcomers quickly be put to a close study of the grounds of logic through a compendium ('systema logicum brevius') which he preferred to be of the tutor's own composition rather than a printed textbook 'because

---

[219] Bodl. MS Rawlinson d. 47, fo 100, cited in Sanderson, *Logicae artis compendium*, ed. Ashworth, p. xxix; QCL MS 390, fo 54, cited in *The Diary of Thomas Crosfield*, ed. Boas, 49; Macray, *Reg. Magdalen* v. 119.

[220] By the second half of the seventeenth century, when fewer tutors engrossed all teaching duties, a hybrid of college lectures and tutorials came into existence in the form of 'logic tables'—a group lecture/discussion of the rudiments of the subject, the like of which could be found in other subjects as well. John Freind (a student at St Edmund Hall, d. 1673) informed his father that 'the schollars of that class [in] which Mr March intended to put mee went into the compendium of logick', while at Trinity John Harris received his introduction to logic in 1684 in a similar way: Bodl. MS top. Oxon. f. 31, pp. 37–8, cited in Hammond, *John Oldham*, 9; H. E. D. Blakiston, *Trinity College* (London 1898), 172.

those that are printed are most of them rather fitted for riper judgments, than for the capacitie and convenience of young beginners', and also 'because it is found by experience that a teacher is more carefull and earnest to inculcate his own notions ... [and] best understanding why and to what end every thing there is sayd'. This short manual was then to be followed by a fuller one. His favourite was Burgersdijk's *Logic*, which he considered not only 'commonly approved and received', but better than those of Keckermann, Molinus, or Ramus. The student was expected to study the book pretty much on his own, taking notes to serve his memory later. Following a couple of months' study of this 'positive logic', Holdsworth recommended the perusal of two or three texts of 'controversies', to be selected from a list that included Brerewood, Smiglecius, Mas, Eustachius, and the Coimbra commentaries, the main criteria being clarity and eclecticism. Following a review of another 'system' the nine-month sequence assigned to logic came to an end, except that during the next two years the student would intermittently refresh his knowledge of 'controversies' to assist his preparations for disputations.[221]

Even though Thomas Barlow's influential manual of advice was far more detailed than Holdsworth's (it was compiled for those headed for the ministry) the basic premises were the same. Barlow, too, suggested that the student be initiated into the study of logic by an easy compendium, in this case Du Trieu's *Manductio ad logicam* which he characterized as 'a short and rationall systeme of logicke'. This was to serve as the basis for studying Paul Vallius' *Logica* and Mas's *Logic*, works considered by Barlow to 'have the most and easiest arguments, and soe (by reason of their perspicuitie) best for begginers'. A list of other textbooks, 'more exact and rationall, and therfore fittest for persons of a little more maturitie' followed, including works by Smiglecius, Antonio Ruvio, Toletus, and Zabarella. Finally, Barlow listed additional authors who covered specific topics for advanced study.[222]

These two examples demonstrate that, in the absence of any authoritative text, personal taste determined the choice of textbooks. Though certain authors were more popular than others—notably Robert Sanderson and Franco Burgersdijk— none was considered canonical and hence the primary objective of tutors was to compile a list of approved authors from which students could select their texts. Before the civil war, Thomas Sixsmith of Brasenose College believed that the best authors were Smiglecius, Ruvio, Brerewood, Keckermann, and Crakanthorpe. Around 1690, John Grandorge of St Edmund Hall recommended Narcissus Marsh's edition of Du Trieu's *Logic* as the best introductory epitome, to be read in conjunction with the logic of Port Royal, Obadiah Walker's *Artis rationis*, and John Fell's *Grammatica rationis*. These were to be read scrupulously so 'that which is wanting in one may be supplied by another'. For the more advanced student, to 'con-

---

[221] Fletcher, *The Intellectual Development of John Milton* ii. 634–6, 641, 643.

[222] '*A Library for Younger Schollers*', ed. Dejordy and Fletcher, 1–2. At least six copies of this list are known to exist. See Kearney, *Scholars and Gentlemen*, 198; Sanderson, *Logicae artis compendium*, ed. Ashworth, p. xiv n. 17.

sult upon occasion, but not [to be] read quite over', Grandorge recommended *inter alia* Crakanthorpe, Brerewood, Smiglecius, Mas, and Scheibler as well as Ockham and Scotus. Equally detailed was the course recommended by Thomas Heywood of St John's a few years later. His preferred introductory text was Sanderson fortified with additions from Du Trieu, Wallis, Stier, Brerewood, and Smith. His students were further encouraged to consult on occasion the relevant work of Burgersdijk, Heereboord, Crakanthorpe, and Alsted, while Smiglecius and Wallis were suggested for disputations. Heywood also included a list of authors on the 'new logic' which included Descartes, Clauberg, Du Hamel, and the logic of Port Royal.[223]

Students' library catalogues and letters confirm the use of an assortment of textbooks in the study of logic. During the first decade of the seventeenth century John English owned works by Caesarius, Case, Goclenius, Augustinus Hunnaeus, Keckermann, Ramus, Pacius, John Sanderson, and Toletus. Thomas Cole of University College acquired his knowledge of logic during the 1620s from Mas, Zabarella, Robert Sanderson, Ramus, Scheibler, Aristotle, Pacius, and Scotus, while in the early 1650s John Hutton of New College owned Robert Sanderson, Ramus, Scheibler, Pacius, Seton, and Keckermann.[224] The accounts of John Locke's students in the early 1660s indicate that they were directed to Du Trieu, Sanderson, Smith, Smiglecius, and Zabarella. For his part, Henry Fleming arrived at Queen's College in 1678 armed with the works of Stier, Brerewood, and Sanderson, to which he later added Crakanthorpe, Mas, Flavel, Smiglecius, Scheibler, and Isendoorn. His brother George, who entered Queen's ten years later, followed much the same diet: Du Trieu and Sanderson as introductory texts, 'over and above which [he privately] read Aristotle's *Organon*, and Crakanthorpe's *Logick* with others of the same subject'. Finally, while at Merton College in the 1680s, James Wilding used Seton, Sanderson, Aristotle's *Organon*, Heereboord, Isendoorn, Smith, and Brerewood.[225]

Understandably, commoners who usually sojourned at Oxford for two or three years at most were assigned a reduced diet proportional to their length of stay. The Herrick brothers were assigned by their St John's tutor, Francis Wren, works by Keckermann, Scotus, Aristotle, and Toletus. A few years later, the Newdigate

[223] BNCL MS 80, unpaginated; Bodl. MS St Edmund Hall 72; Bodl. MS Rawlinson d. 40, p. 1. The logic of Port Royal, *La Logique, ou l'art de penser*, became very popular in England both in its French version and in the Latin translation, *Logica, sive ars cogitandi*, made by Charles Towneley. According to Ralph Thoresby 'the good reception [the latter] has found in our universities has procured several editions at London, and I scarce meet with a young sophister, that come from thence, who does not tell me that it has been put into his hands, as well as into others', by their respective tutors'. *Letters of Eminent Men Addressed to Ralph Thoresby*, ed. J. Hunter (2 vols London 1832) ii. 205. Henry Oldenburg reviewed the Latin translation in the *Philosophical Transactions*, judging it 'worthy to be recommended to all young students, as passing by what is useless and pedantique, and comprehending what is indeed sober and necessary to direct our reason in all sorts of ingenious and useful sciences'. *Philosophical Transactions* x (1674), 139.
[224] W. C. Costin, 'The library of John English, B. C. L., fellow of St John's College', *Oxoniensia* xi (1946–7), 118–19; OUA chancellor's ct inventories, s.v. Thomas Cole and John Hutton.
[225] Bodl. MS Locke f. 11, fos 8–11; *The Flemings in Oxford* i. 251, 295, 322–3, ii. 217, 251–2; 'The account-book of an Oxford undergraduate, 1682–1688', ed. E. E. Duff, *Collectanea* i. 267–8.

brothers entered Trinity College where they purchased the texts of Sanderson, Keckermann, and Zabarella, while Thomas Smith, who in 1638 spent a little over a year at Lincoln College, had time enough for only Smith, Sanderson, and Brerewood. At Christ Church in the mid-1670s, John Percival began with a manuscript compendium and the terse printed text by Stier, whence he proceeded to learn the 'rules' of Sanderson and finally to view Aristotle.[226]

Though these guides stipulated exclusively printed textbooks, many Oxford tutors evidently endorsed Holdsworth's recommendation and initiated their students into the study of logic—as well as other disciplines—by distributing manuscript compendia of their own making or by a well-recognized contemporary. John Aubrey, for example, recalled that the logic notes he used at Trinity College around 1641 were prepared by Bishop John Prideaux, and he regarded them 'as good perhaps as any . . . short and clear [and] we learned them by heart. In teaching it is the best and most delightful way for youth first to see a prospect (as from a mountain) of what the science is, and then they will be the better encouraged to take a long journey thither.'[227] Other examples abound. In 1631 John Crowther compiled various epitomes, including one of logic, for the benefit of his student Ralph Verney at Magdalen Hall, while Thomas Crosfield at Queen's lent his own notes on logic and ethics for students to copy. Many such compendia survive. The one compiled by (or for) Nehemiah Rogers of Queen's in 1677 was based on the textbooks by Sanderson and Heereboord. Francis Cherry completed his outline of the subject on 30 September 1686, appending to it a very impressive catalogue of authorities, including Smiglecius, Crakanthorpe, Isendoorn, Pacius, Burgersdijk, Sanderson, Brerewood, Stier, Derodon, Keckermann, Zabarella, Flavell, Scheibler, and Du Trieu.[228]

The utilitarian purpose of logic, the predilection for compendia and the limiting of the subject to the introductory level are all confirmed by the publication history

---

[226] Bodl. MS Eng. hist. c. 481, fos 41, 62, 101; 'The undergraduate account book of John and Richard Newdigate, 1618–1621', ed. Larminie, 189, 194, 198; R. Austin, 'Thomas Smyth of Lincoln College, Oxford', *Notes and Queries* 12th ser. ix (1921), 221; BL Add. MSS 46,953, fo 122, 46,955A, fo 50ᵛ, 46,954B, fo 128, 46,954A, fo 172ᵛ.

[227] *Aubrey on Education*, ed. Stephens, 120. Though some compendia may have been used by tutors other than their compiler—as Aubrey's testimony demonstrates—some tutors were protective of their compositions, which exemplified their distinctive style or the profundity they sought in students. A rare glimpse of such a case may be derived from a letter sent by Daniel Featley to Sir Walter Ralegh *c*.1607 in which Featley remonstrated against the campaign at Corpus Christi College to dismiss him from serving as tutor, to students including Ralegh's son. Featley feared that by taking the students away from him his labour would be lost, too: 'I have given them many notes and directions of mine own which I would be loath other teachers should oversee and, although peradventure they might direct them in a better course, yet that course being contrary to mine and altogether unknown to them, it is not likely they will so well go forward in it'. Bodl. MS Rawlinson d. 47, fo 57, cited in O'Day, *Education and Society*, 116.

[228] F. P. Verney, *Memoirs of the Verney Family During the Civil War* (2 vols London 1892) i. 123, 164; QCL MS 390, fos 38, 40; BL MS Harleian 5043; Bodl. MS Cherry 46, cited in Sanderson, *Logicae artis compendium*, ed. Ashworth, p. xv n. 24. Similar compendia include Humphrey Hody's compilation while at Wadham College (Bodl. MS Rawlinson d. 1221) and the anonymous compendium of a member of University College (Bodl. MS University College 111).

of logic textbooks by Oxford scholars. The first wave, about 1613–30, represented a response to the demand for brief and reliable textbooks, which resulted in the publication in rapid succession of four books in the 1610s, all of which were originally private tutorial notes or elementary lectures delivered in the college. Inaugurating the list was the *Aditus ad logicam* by Samuel Smith of Magdalen College, published in 1613 and reaching eight editions by 1667. The following year, Edward Brerewood's posthumous *Elementa logica*, representing his labour as a tutor at Brasenose College three decades earlier, was published by his nephew.[229] Next followed the most influential English textbook of the seventeenth century, Robert Sanderson's *Logicae artis compendium*, published in 1615. Originally delivered as lectures at Lincoln College the previous year, the book enjoyed at least ten editions during the seventeenth century.[230] Yet another aspiring executor was responsible for the publication in 1619 of *Tractatus de demonstratione* by John Flavel of Wadham College, which gained its third and final edition in 1651. Slightly more advanced textbooks were published by two members of Queen's College in the 1620s. The more formidable was Richard Crakanthorpe's *Logicae libri quinque*, originally published in 1622 and going through four editions by 1677.[231] Christopher Airay's *Fasciculus praeceptorum logicorum*, originally published in 1628, also achieved a fourth edition by 1660.[232]

Following this spate of publications, subsequent textbooks published at Oxford were usually the product of heads of house. Inaugurating the new trend was John Prideaux, rector of Exeter College, who decided to publish some of his popular notes on logic in 1629 under the title *Tyrocinium ad syllogismum legitimum contexendum & captiosum dissuendum, expeditissimum*—a terse, eighteen-page *vade mecum* of how to construct syllogisms and expose fallacies. This publication he supplemented a decade later with the *Heptades logicae*.[233] Equally industrious was Thomas Tully, principal of St Edmund Hall. In addition to compiling a manuscript compendium of logic for the use of his students, Tully was responsible for the publication in 1662 of the Oxford edition of Du Trieu's *Manductio ad logicam*, to which he

---

[229] Many of Brerewood's papers passed into the hands of Thomas Sixsmith of Brasenose College who published in 1628, at Oxford, another work composed by Brerewood in the 1580s, *Tractatus quidam logici de praedicabilibus et praedicamentis*.

[230] According to Izaak Walton, some 10,000 copies were sold by the time he wrote his biography of Sanderson: Sanderson, *Logicae artis compendium*, ed. Ashworth, p. xiv.

[231] Crakanthorpe made plans immediately after the publication of the volume to revise it extensively and to this end sought the expert advice of the Cambridge scholar Michael Honeywood. But Crakanthorpe's death in 1624 put an end to the project. See N. Linnel, 'A unique copy of Richard Crakanthorpe's Logic', *The Library* 6th ser. iv (1982), 323–6.

[232] Another product of the 1620s is Thomas Lushington's *Logica analytica* published in 1650, probably in an effort to alleviate the poor financial situation of the ejected prebendary of Salisbury.

[233] In 1648 Prideaux amalgamated the two texts into his *Hypomnemata logica . . .* (Oxford 1648). Mention may also be made of a collection of logical, rhetorical, and moral maxims, generally attributed to Richard Zouche, principal of St Alban Hall between 1625 and 1661, which was published in 1657 under the title *Eruditionis ingenuae specimen*.

appended Gassendi's *De natura demonstrationis* as well as his own brief *Logica apodictica*.[234]

A more concentrated effort was carried out by Oxford heads in the 1670s. In 1673 John Fell, dean of Christ Church, published his *Grammatica rationis* which, he informed the reader, meant to compete neither with Aristotle nor with Bacon, Descartes, and Gassendi, but merely to offer what he considered a more interesting compendium, one based upon grammar and its terms. In the same year Obadiah Walker (who declined the mastership of University College in 1667 but accepted it in 1676) published his *Artis rationis*, his effort to acquaint young students with the keenness and clarity of the medieval nominalists, principally for the purpose of common reasoning,[235] while in 1677 Thomas Good master of Balliol published the inconsequential *A Brief English Tract of Logick*, a pamphlet containing thirty-two pages of terms and elementary syllogisms. Undoubtedly, however, the most famous—as well as the most influential—of this second wave of textbooks was Henry Aldrich's *Artis logicae compendium* of 1691, which enjoyed numerous editions well into the nineteenth century.[236]

Even a cursory view of these books reveals that Oxford teachers intended to produce only introductory textbooks, and the animating guidelines were those of brevity and simplicity. The books usually ranged from 150 to 250 pages in length (Crakanthorpe's 350-page composition was a noted exception) and imparted only the bare minimum of formal logic, as much as was thought sufficient to acquaint students with the divisions of logic, the terms of art, and the manner in which logic could be put into practice. Sporadically Oxonians also promoted the reprinting of some mammoth continental textbooks in logic: Smiglecius' 819-page *Logica*, the near-750-page *Cursus logicus* by Isendoorn, and the more than 600-page work by Scheibler. These books, however, were clearly intended to serve as reference tools and were far less popular among students and teachers than the brief and compact compendia produced at Oxford.

The place of Aristotle within such a system is more difficult to determine. Though both the Elizabethan and Laudian statutes ordained Aristotle (and Porphyry) as the only approved authors, clearly the actual course was different. Pointing to the profusion of compendia and commentaries, recent historians have even doubted whether Aristotle was taught at all during the seventeenth century. Such an inference is unjustifiable. True, when confronted with the hostile attack of

[234] Kearney, *Scholars and Gentlemen*, 147; Madan, *Oxford Books* iii. 161–2. Immediately following the publication of the *Manductio*, Narcissus Marsh, tutor and later principal of the hall, began 'to revise, alter and adjust' the book and 'make it fitter for use'. The revised text was eventually published and became renowned as the 'Provost's logic', the chief logic textbook at Trinity College, Dublin: J. H. T., 'Abp Marsh's Diary', *The British Magazine* xxviii (1845), 2; M. Pollard, 'The provost's logic: an unrecorded first issue', *Long Room* i (1970), 38–40.

[235] Walker was, in addition, responsible for the publication in 1675 of Ockham's *Summa totius logicae*. Madan, *Oxford Books* iii. 281, 316.

[236] An exception to the rule was the ageing John Wallis's *Institutio logicae* (Oxford 1687), published perhaps because of his duty as Savilian professor of geometry to teach practical logic as part of the instruction in geometry.

John Webster, Seth Ward retorted that 'Aristotles *Organon* is not read to the youth of this university'. Yet Ward undoubtedly meant that no *public* lectures on Aristotle's logic were given.[237] The literature of advice and the practice of students certainly document that the Stagirite was studied by the students in private. Most tutors believed that after students had acquired some proficiency in logic by pursuing those introductory textbooks, the independent study of Aristotle should follow both to deepen their understanding of the subject-matter and, simultaneously, to expedite their knowledge of Greek.

In the early years of the century Cleland articulated the notion that 'compendiaries' were useful as they 'lighten much and prepare the pupils young wavering thoughts, and make his judgment more solide to understand Aristotle the better'. A generation later Richard Holdsworth informed his students that 'the reading of Aristotle will not only conduce much to your study of controversy, being read with a comentator, but allso help you in Greeke, and indeed crown all your other learning, for he can hardly deserve the name of a scholar that is not in some measure acquainted with his works. Gather short memorial notes in Greek out of him, and observe all his termes.' Other instances abound. Nathaniel Sterry, who was intruded fellow of Merton College in 1649, counselled his students to begin their study of logic by pursuing the textbooks of Ramus and Burgersdijk and from them to proceed with Aristotle's *Organon* 'which will both further your philosophy and the Greek tongue'. Equally indicative of the prevailing practice is the 'advice' Sir Matthew Hale (Magdalen Hall *c.*1626–8) penned for the edification of his grandchild in which he insisted that once the youth had 'read some systems' his tutor ought to proceed and exercise his charge with Aristotle himself.[238]

The correspondence and library catalogues of Oxford students corroborate the above impression. In 1613 William and Roger Herrick were directed to the study of the *Organon*, while in 1677 John Percival similarly wrote to his uncle, Sir Robert Southwell, for a copy, which his Christ Church tutor, Roger Altham, had instructed him to peruse. George Fleming informed his father in 1689 that 'over and above' his study of introductory textbooks in logic he was also made to read the *Organon*.[239] Evidence derived from the library catalogues of undergraduates—or young dons—further substantiates the widespread practice. John English of St John's College owned Pacius' edition of the *Organon* when he died in 1613, as did an anonymous student whose inventory was taken *circa* 1640. Additional inventories containing copies of Aristotle include those of Thomas Cole and John Hutton, both of whom died in the early 1650s. Finally, James Wilding's 1688 library

[237] Ashworth, 'Traditional logic', 146; [Wilkins and Ward], *Vindiciae academiarum*, 25.

[238] Cleland, *Institutions of a Young Nobleman*, 85; Fletcher, *Intellectual Development of John Milton* ii. 643; Bodl. MS Tanner 88, fo 5; Matthew Hale, *Letter of Advice to his Grandchildren* (Boston 1817), 120. Francis Mansell, too, informed Sir Sackville Crow that the course he followed with the young Crow was intended to convey the knowledge of logic in both Greek and Latin: BL Add. MS 27,606, fo 6.

[239] Bodl. MS Eng. hist. c. 481, fo 62; BL Add. MS 46,954A, fo 172ᵛ; *The Flemings in Oxford* ii. 252.

catalogue confirms a young undergraduate's study of the *Organon* at Merton College.[240]

While the study of logic itself occupied a relatively short period of the undergraduate course, the format of disputation continued to absorb the student for the entire course of study, regulating both discourse and examination. Small wonder, then, that contemporary as well as later assailants of the early modern universities viewed the disputations as obstacles to the attainment of true knowledge. Many would wholeheartedly have endorsed John Webster's depiction, in 1654, of the disputations as little more than

a civil war of words, a verbal contest, a combat of cunning craftiness, violence and altercation, wherein all verbal force, by impudence, insolence, opposition, contradiction, derision, diversion, trifling, jeering, humming, hissing, brawling, quarreling, scolding, scandalizing, and the like, are equally allowed of, and accounted just, and no regard had to the truth, so that by any means ... they may get the conquest, and worst their adversary, and if they can intangle or catch one another in the spider webs of sophistical or fallacious argumentations, then their rejoicing and clamour is as great as if they had obtained some signal victory.[241]

Not surprisingly, Locke's strictures were even more sweeping. In *Some Thoughts concerning Education* he admonished parents:

If the use and end of right reasoning be to have right notions, and a right judgment of things, to distinguish betwixt truth and falshood, right and wrong, and to act accordingly, be sure not to let your son be bred up in the art and formality of disputing, either practising it himself, or admiring it in others; unless, instead of an able man, you desire to have him an insignificant wrangler, opiniater in discourse, and priding himself in contradicting others, or, which is worse, questioning every thing, and thinking there is no such thing as truth to be sought, but only victory in disputing.[242]

---

[240] Costin, 'The inventory of John English', 115; OUA chancellor's ct inventories, s.v. anonymous *c.*1640, Cole and Hutton; 'The account book of an Oxford undergraduate', ed. Duff, 267.

[241] John Webster, *Academiarum examen* (London 1653), 33. By 1677, with reforming zeal behind him, Webster rethought his former position. Attacking the detractors of learning, and Joseph Glanvill in particular, Webster derided the latter as a 'person who pretends to such high parts', and censured others who cried down all learning under the guise of defending the new philosophy: 'Not many years ago the truth of philosophy lay inchained in the prisons of the schools, who thought there were no proficiency to be made therein, but only in their logical and systematical ways ... And now when philosophy hath gotten its freedom, to expatiate through the whole sphere of nature, by all sorts of inquiries and tryals, to compleat a perfect history of nature, some are on the other hand grown so rigid and peremptory, that they will condemn all things that have not past the test of experiment, or conduce not directly to that very point, and so would totally demolish that part of academick and formal learning that teacheth men method and the way of logical procedure in writing of controversies, and handling of disputes. Whereas what is more necessary and commendable for those that treat of any controverted point in writing or in other disputations, than a clear and perspicuous method, a right and exact stating of the question in doubt, defining or describing the terms that are or may be equivocal, and dividing the whole into its due and genuine parts ... Let experimental philosophy have its place and due honour; and let also the logical, methodical, and formal way of the academies have its due praise and commendation, as being both exceedingly profitable, though in different respects; otherwise, in writing and arguing, nothing but disorder and confusion will bear sway.' John Webster, *The Displaying of Supposed Witchcraft* (London 1677), 10, 20.

[242] *The Educational Writings of John Locke*, ed. Axtell, 296–7.

Certainly, the oral nature of the undergraduate course made disputations the pinnacle of accomplishment. To the modern observer they may well appear futile exercises in wrangling and an indication of what Ong termed 'the polemical climate of academic life',[243] but contemporaries valued them highly. Disputations, in any case, did not imply the abrogation of truth in favour of victory at all costs. The 'correct' position in matters that counted was usually agreed upon beforehand and the ensuing debate was meant only to challenge the students' skills and allow 'truth' to shine. Naturally, as will be shown later, the ability to perform well was important as one's career could be launched on such an occasion, yet virtuosity did not mean that any position was valid simply because a disputant ran out of opponents capable of proving him wrong. For most educators, therefore, the training in the art of disputations remained an important educational tool. Obadiah Walker explained the strictly propaedeutic nature of the exercise of disputation, by which he meant

not that arguing and discoursing which a student useth with his own self to find out truth, but that which comprehendeth both this and the assistance also of others, publick and open argumentation pro and contra. This is it which brings a question to a point, and discovers the very center and knot of the difficulty. This warms and activates the spirit in the search of truth, excites notions and, by replying and frequent beating upon it, cleanseth it from the ashes and make it shine and flame out the clearer. Besides it puts them upon a continual stretch of their wits to defend their cause, it makes them quick in replies, intentive upon their subject: where the opponent useth all means to drive his adversary from his hold, and the answerer defends himself sometimes with the force of truth, sometimes with the subtility of his wit, and sometimes also he escapes in a mist of words and the doubles of a distinction, whilst he seeks all holes and recesses to shelter his persecuted opinion and reputation.

It is precisely 'by these velitations and in this palaestra' that young students are 'brought up to a more serious search of truth'. For that reason, concluded Walker, he saw no fault in allowing 'to dispute for victory' and he marvelled at those tutors who forbade their charges to dispute on 'questions where the truth was of concernment' for the whole purpose of the exercise is 'that the youth might have their liberty of exerting their parts to the uttermost, and that there might be no stint to their emulation'.[244]

His contemporaries almost unanimously concurred in perceiving the benefits of these drills for the education of youth. John Aubrey endorsed the opinion of Robert Sanderson that 'no exercise does improve young men's wits so much as disputation'. Nor did Thomas Sprat deny that 'disputing is a very good instrument to sharpen men's wits, and to make them versatil and wary defenders of the principles which they already know'. Only he cautioned that 'it can never much augment the solid substance of science itself'. For his part, the earl of Clarendon, the former chancellor of Oxford, stated:

---

[243] Milton, *Complete Prose Works* viii 160–1.   [244] Walker, *Of Education*, 117–18.

And tho' I perceive this disputing faculty is out of credit in the court, it is a most precious ingredient into wisdom and to the more serious part of life. The art of logick, which none of our travellers return with who carried it not with them, disposes us to judge aright in any thing, and though we do not make our conversation in syllogisms, and discourse in the mood and figure, yet our conversation and our discourse is much the more reasonable and the better formed, by the experience we have had in that art, and in which we may have spent some time very merrily. And I must say again this most useful art was never well taught or learned but in our universities.[245]

Once acclimatized, and despite possible aversion to logic, students settled into an almost exhilarating routine where they prepared their own disputations, observed those of their colleagues (sometimes with impromptu participation) and were occasionally called upon to perform their own. It would not be an exaggeration to state that the disputations became a form of entertainment. Walks in Christ Church meadow, we are told by Francis Vernon (MA 1660), were often used by students to rehearse disputations by stealth. Joseph Glanvill left posterity with an illuminating autobiographical confession of how, in his 'younger and talkative age, [he] was much delighted with those subtilties that exercise the brain in the niceties of notion and distinctions, and afford a great deal of idle imployment for the tongue in the combates of disputations. In which [he] acknowledge[d he] was none of the most backward, but being highly pleased with those engagements [he] found as much diversion in them as in [his] dearest recreations.'[246]

The popularity of disputations is reflected by the high turnout usually accorded to the great annual Act. Attendance of 'above 2,000' at such events, as recorded by Wood in 1693, was not uncommon. Royalty and gentry, scholars and the fashionable, rubbed shoulders on such public occasions when disputations were staged—either for the purpose of examining degree candidates or honouring visiting dignitaries. When Cosimo de Medici visited Oxford in May 1669 he was so entertained by the disputations of Henry Smith and John Milne of Queen's that he disregarded the offers made by the vice-chancellor to leave before they ended.[247]

The reasons for this popularity must be seen in terms other than a simple confirmation of the disputatious nature of early modern culture. By the early seventeenth century the reinstatement of a fully humanistic character to the undergraduate course, together with the functional and circumscribed scope of logic, radically altered the purpose and structure of the disputations. As some scholars have recently indicated, the similarity between the disputations at Oxford from the late sixteenth century onwards and medieval practices is superficial at best. Ashworth suggests that gone was 'the late medieval emphasis on logical subtleties and the deft handling of sophisms; and in its place is an emphasis on the presentation of straightforward, clear arguments, intended to establish truth'.

---

[245] *Aubrey on Education*, ed. Stephens, 119; Sprat, *History of the Royal Society*, 18; Clarendon, 'Concerning education', 326.

[246] [Francis Vernon], *Oxonium poema* (Oxford 1667), 14–15; Glanvill, *Plus ultra*, 123.

[247] Wood, *Life and Times* iii. 427, ii. 161. Appropriately, the topics chosen for the occasion were *An stellae medicaeae sunt lunae Jovis?* and *An detur vacuum?*

Instead of technical virtuosity, notes McConica, emphasis was placed on 'public debate on public issues'.[248] Such a trend intensified during the seventeenth century, partly because of the reorientation of logic to accommodate discourse and its reliance on probable, rather than demonstrative, reason.[249] Thus, the disputations evolved into a practical forum intended to exercise the theoretical skills students had acquired in logic and rhetoric, with greater emphasis placed on linguistic, moral, and contemporary issues in the debates.

The notable transformation in the subject-matter of the disputations cannot alone account for the reinvigoration of these exercises during the seventeenth century. Equally important was the incursion of a new, lighter vein which helped perpetuate their popularity. The Terrae-Filius—the appointed varier on the philosophical question at the annual Act—is the best-known representative of this new trend. Intended to provide humorous relief during the public Acts, the Terrae-Filius was already a common fixture in the early years of the seventeenth century, his popularity and assumed pedagogical value confirmed by his codification into the Laudian statutes. The original aim was to allow a promising incepting master of arts to display a whimsical variety on the approved disputation topics in philosophy, exhibiting elegance of style in addition to wit and readiness. By mid-century, however, the speakers became notorious as they began to disregard the questions altogether, opting, instead, to employ their wit in assailing university officials and college dons. Equally important, however, is the fact that this humorous lighter tone was introduced into other exercises as well, though without the notoriety achieved by the Terrae-Filius. Thus, the disputations acquired a new lease of life. By cultivating the employment of language, wit, and quickness of parts instead of the virtuous (if dry) technical skills previously emphasized, the disputations helped inculcate the new objectives of learning while at the same time securing unprecedented popularity. Also, as the tone of these disputations was analogous to the new taste of a fashionable culture, individual success on such occasions continued to promise recognition and reward.[250]

[248] Sanderson, *Logicae artis compendium*, ed. Ashworth, p. xxxv; McConica, 'Humanism and Aristotle in Tudor Oxford', 294.

[249] A parallel to the English custom may be found among the Jesuits. Both systems of education employed the humanist joining of logic and rhetoric (perceiving that the deployment of oratory and language would render the disputes more agreeable) and both shared the humanist circumscribed view of logic: 'unlike the scholastic disputation, in which the participants aimed at displaying their ability at the incisive employment of logical rigor in support of a proposition, that of the Jesuits would have been conducted "*in utramque partem*", as Cicero put it; that is, on either side of the question. They did not intend simply to provide a *sic et non*, however; the participants attempted to show their virtuosity by rendering their position more probable, by persuading the audience toward a judgment in their favor.' P. Dear, *Mersenne and the Learning of the Schools* (Ithaca NY 1988), 21.

[250] The perception that urbane and cosmopolitan culture was from the start 'antipathetic to the pedantic scholasticism of the universities' is unwarranted. In fact, the 'witty repartee of coffee-shops replaced the verbal gymnastics of the disputations' only at the end of the seventeenth century, after it had proliferated for decades in the schools. V. Morgan, 'Approaches to the history of the English universities in the sixteenth and seventeenth centuries' in G. Klingenstein *et al.* (eds), *Bildung, Politik und Gesellschaft* (Vienna 1978), 152.

In view of the fact that quite a few Terrae-Filius speeches have survived[251]— and because historians have often utilized them in order to interpret the university's course of study—one important aspect of these speeches must be considered here. There is a tendency to mistake these facetious orations for expressions of earnest philosophical opinion. Yet the Terrae-Filius was the academic version of the lord of misrule and it was inevitable that young and clever scholars would use the opportunity to revenge themselves on authority and unpopular teachers. Thus, by seemingly varying the prescribed topic of disputation, they actually assailed individuals and institutions to the delight of their colleagues and guests, and to the dismay of those targeted for abuse and ridicule. Not surprisingly, a 'successful' performance occasionally resulted in the student being denied his degree, and even imprisoned, pending his repentance.

A few examples demonstrate how such exercises should be taken more as an indicator of student culture than as testimony to an antiquated and conservative educational system. When in the late 1650s Robert South denounced the 'absurdity' of Cambridge scholars for adopting Gassendi's theory of atoms, he was not reiterating Oxford's adherence to Aristotle and to scholasticism, but perpetrating the age-old fashion of scurrilous attacks on the sister university by Oxford men. Similarly, the sundry versions of the thesis 'An mundus confletur ex atomis?' clearly demonstrate a jocular exposition of that theme. Even a promising (and 'progressive') title, as expressed by the 1671 reply in the affirmative by John Rotherham to the question 'An terra sit mobilis?' demonstrates how the theme was manipulated for the purpose of abusing Oxford dons. One such target was Thomas Lamplugh, principal of St Alban Hall and a man notorious both for his desire for a preferment and neglect of his duties at the hall. Rotherham clearly relished the opportunity to lash out with witticisms to the effect, for instance, that even though the earth moves, Lamplugh cannot be removed from his office.[252]

Livening the disputations not surprisingly increased the prospects of disorder. The Laudian statutes and later decrees refer to rowdiness in disputations that arose not only from the participation of individual bachelors and masters of art among the audience, but from the growing practice of 'coursing'—the challenge of members of one college by those of another. These occasions often deteriorated into shouting-matches in the schools, subsequently spilling over into brawls in the streets. Small wonder that university authorities often attempted to temper high spirits and even put down coursing all together. In 1652 Vice-Chancellor Daniel

[251] See B. Smith and D. Ehninger, 'The Terrafilial disputations at Oxford', *Quarterly Journal of Speech* xxxvi (1950), 333–9; L. A. Holford-Strevens, 'Some seventeenth-century *Terrae Filii*: evidence in the Bodleian', *Bodleian Library Record* xi (1982–5), 260–3; W. T. Gibson, 'The suppression of Terrae Filius in 1713', *Oxoniensia* liv (1991), 410–13.

[252] Robert South, *Opera posthuma*, 61 ff., 123 ff.; Bodl. MS Rawlinson d. 258, fos 7–8; Bodl. MS Rawlinson d. 1111, fo 32ᵛ; Kearney, *Scholars and Gentlemen*, 147. A corresponding Cambridge example from the early seventeenth century is provided by Alexander Bolde, who used the occasion of his debating the topic 'nullum corpus agit, nisi moveatur' (matter does not stir unless it is moved) to play fancifully on the various idiomatic meanings of the verb *agere*. K. M. Burton, 'Cambridge exercises in the seventeenth century', *The Eagle* liv (1951), 248–58.

Greenwood, who did not hesitate the previous year to call in the army garrisoned at Oxford in order to keep 'raucous' scholars in check, issued an injunction that threatened with severe punishment all those who disturbed the Act with 'hummings and other clamorous noises'. Five years later Vice-Chancellor John Owen admonished the Terrae-Filius that

he should have liberty to say what he pleased, provided that he would avoid profaneness and obscenity, and not to go into any personal reflections. The Terrae-Filius began, and in a little time transgressed in all the foregoing particulars, upon which the doctor did several times desire him to forbear those things which reflected so much dishonour on the university. But notwithstanding he went on in the same manner. At length the doctor, seeing him obstinate, sent in his beadles to pull him down, upon which the scholars interposed and would not suffer them to come near him. Then the doctor resolved to pull him down himself; his friends dissuaded him for fear the scholars should do him mischief, but he replied 'I will not see authority trampled on', and hereupon he pulled him down and sent him to Bocardo.[253]

Obviously it was impossible to eliminate coursing while maintaining the resuscitated form of rigorous disputation, for it was only through the blending of therapeutic, educational, and entertaining elements that the delicate balance of the system of disputations could be sustained. Contemporaries readily acknowledged that putting down coursing did much to abrogate the system. Anthony Wood, for example, contrasted the rigorous disputations during the Interregnum, which were excellent with 'much zelous coursing', with the decay he attributed to the iron rule of Dean Fell who aggressively attempted to put coursing down. Indeed, Wood claimed in 1683 that the repercussions of Fell's injunctions were ruinous. Bachelors of art, he lamented, would not dispute unless their supervisors were there, while the few masters present 'stand silent, while their abbettors sneare and grin. This wee get by having coursing put downe by Dr Fell.'[254]

The study of logic and the practice of disputation in seventeenth-century Oxford should be seen, then, strictly in utilitarian terms. Logic was intended exclusively as a propaedeutic study to foster the primary mental skills of young students and was consequently assigned to the outset of the educational process. Pupils were generally taught in the manner of John Harris under Stephen Hunt at Trinity College in the early 1680s. When Harris told his tutor that he 'could not find he had gained any real knowledge' from either studying logic or attending the disputations, the latter smiled and told Harris he 'must as much study to forget that cant when he left the university, as now he took pains to acquire it'.[255] In the following decade

---

[253] Wood, *Life and Times* ii. 563 n. 4, i. 175; P. Toon, *God's Statesman: the life and work of John Owen* (Exeter 1971), 75.

[254] Wood, *Life and Times* i. 297, 353, ii. 402, iii. 37.

[255] Blakiston, *Trinity College*, 174. Samuel Butler nicely phrased the issue: 'A logician, grammarian, and rhetorician never come to understand the true end of their arts, untill they have layd them by, as those that have learnd to swim, give over the bladders that they learnd by.' Samuel Butler, *Prose Works*, ed. H. de Quehen (Oxford 1979), 128. This is the moral to be drawn from the experience of Thomas Hobbes who, Aubrey reported, 'did not much care for logick, yet he learnd it, and thought himselfe a

it was the turn of Stephen Penton to cheer up his student Robert Wood of Wadham with the thought that the study of logic was akin to a puberty rite and that now that he had 'passed through the briers of logick' he was ready to proceed 'into the fair fields of philosophy'. The lesson was well learnt by the young Wood, who wrote to his father a couple of years later of his logical studies that 'our mother Oxford ... yields the same fruits at all seasons of the year, her common entertainment is either a little crabbed logick to mump upon or the husky mathematicks enough to choak one'. Yet 'it makes an old proverb good, that he who will eat the cornel must take the pains to crack the shell'.[256] Perhaps the reflection of Roger North best expresses the qualified endorsement of this early pursuit of logic:

Logic is a very dull science, especially that which relates to disputation, and must be driven by a tutor well versed in it ... And to say truth an age more advanced than ordinary youths fresh in the university is most proper for the study of logic. But in regard that is a time when somewhat must be learnt, and the rules of logic regulate the mind and make it more just to weigh other learning, and although the person neither is delighted nor thoroughly understands the drift nor perhaps the force of what he reads, yet it is fit to be learnt early; for when the mind is more advanced, and comes to work critically upon points of other learning and hath need, memory brings into use the former dull rules, and they are a great help, which else would not at such pinch be at hand.[257]

Moral Philosophy

Ethics was another cornerstone of the undergraduate curriculum, though in the eyes of parents and educators, who viewed the study and practice of morality as the highest goal it often took precedence over any other discipline. Lord Herbert of Cherbury minced few words when he characterized 'the learning of morall philosophy and the practice of vertue as the most necessary knowledge and useful exercise of man's life'. In a similar manner, when Sackville Crow came up to Oxford in 1654 his father exhorted him to make 'practique learning' his 'cheefe ayme, and the rest to serve only for attendants, necessary for a gentleman, who ought nott to bee ignorant in any thing, but bent only to such things as give him emprovement in wisdom, grounded on knowledge made out by practice'. In 1688 George Fleming informed his father that he had 'read over the never too much to be praised moral philosophy; which [he would] as much as in [him] layeth practice as well as study'. John Locke's judgement was similar. In an unpublished fragment entitled 'Of ethick in general' he opined that morality, being 'the great business and concernment of mankind, deserves our most attentive application and study', and a year before he died he still asserted that a gentleman, 'whose proper calling is the service of his country ... is most properly concerned in moral and political know-

---

good disputant'. Hobbes himself related the same point in his autobiography where he recalled that he had studied logic, and came to master the art only in order to learn to reject it. *Brief Lives by Aubrey*, ed. Clark i. 329; 'The life of Thomas Hobbes of Malmesbury', trans. J. E. Parsons Jr and Whitney Blair, *Interpretation* x (1982), 1.

[256] E. Wood, 'Some Wood family letters from Oxford, 1659–1719', *Oxoniensia* li (1986), 120, 133.
[257] *The Lives of the Norths*, ed. A. Jessopp (3 vols London 1890) iii. 16–17.

ledge. And thus the studies which more immediately belong to his calling are those which treat of virtues and vices, of civil society and the arts of government.'[258]

Understandably the importance attached to moral philosophy arose in large measure from the intimate connection contemporaries made between moral philosophy and religion. While morality had always been an integral part of Christianity, the advent of humanism, with its preoccupation with the individual—in whom virtue was considered to be the height of perfection—and protestantism, with its fixation on matters of conscience, raised to a new intensity the discussion of the nature and scope of morality, particularly its relationship to religion and its teachability. With the reformation the centuries-old debate over the compatability of the classics with Christianity was also reinvigorated. In view of its subject-matter, the domain of moral philosophy was more susceptible than most disciplines to such controversy. Both Luther and Calvin were uncompromising in rendering the spheres of morality and religion inseparable; true moral rectitude, they postulated, would be a distinguishing mark of the faithful.[259] In contrast, Philipp Melanchton posited two mutually exclusive spheres of influence: moral philosophy, which 'was the explication of the law of nature by the use of reason for the purpose of establishing rules to govern behaviour ... had nothing to do with the will of God or the remission of sins; it was exclusively concerned with rules governing external action and civil society. Conversely, theology had nothing to do with these ethical rules: "For Christ did not come to earth in order to teach moral precepts which were already known by reason, but rather to remit our sins and deliver the Holy Spirit to those who believed in him." '[260] This careful demarcation between the two areas, as we shall see later, while presupposing morality as ancillary to faith, was nevertheless instrumental in creating a semi-autonomous field for the study of external actions.

Obviously, this optimistic appreciation of man was not universally embraced by English protestants. The strict Calvinist stand was most eloquently expressed by the puritan William Ames, who denied that moral philosophy could be an autonomous discipline distinct from theology since, in his words, 'every precept of universal truth pertaining to living well in either ethics, economics, politics, or law very properly belongs to theology'. The 'revealed will of God' he considered as the sole rule in 'all matters which have to do with the direction of life'. With this credo

---

[258] *The Life of Edward, First Lord Herbert of Cherbury*, ed. Shuttleworth, 25; BL Add. MS 27,606, fo 4; *The Flemings in Oxford*, ii. 257; John Locke, *Essays on the Law of Nature*, ed. W. von Leyden (Oxford 1965), 70; *The Educational Writings of John Locke*, ed. Axtell, 398.

[259] Calvin certainly agreed that 'some residue of intelligence and judgment' survived the fall, and he willingly acknowledged that 'nothing, indeed, is more common, than for a man to be sufficiently instructed in a right course of conduct by natural law'. Yet what survived was nothing more than a 'shapeless ruin' and 'if we would test our reason by the divine law, which is a perfect standard of righteousness, we should find how blind it is in many respects'. John Calvin, *Institutes of the Christian Religion*, trans. H. Beveridge (2 vols Grand Rapids 1964) i. 221–47.

[260] J. Kraye, 'Moral Philosophy' in Schmitt and Skinner (eds), *The Cambridge History of Renaissance Philosophy*, 323. For the flavour of Melanchton's views see *A Melanchton Reader*, trans. R. Keen (New York 1988), 179–238.

in mind, Ames emphatically rejected attempts by contemporaries to distinguish between ethics—the domain of 'external morals and uprightness', and theology—the province of 'the inner man and piety'—denying that a 'practical philosophy' of ethics could teach the civil good independently of grace.[261]

The implications of this position were rigid biblicism and the rejection of the writings of pagan philosophers, neither of which, however, transpired at Oxford. None the less, celebrated Oxonians expressed views analogous to those of Ames—even though they could hardly be categorized as being Ames's disciples—when reflecting on Christianity and morality. Robert Boyle is a case in point. It was a mistaken assumption, he thought, 'that a large system of ethics, dissected according to the nice prescriptions of logick' was 'requisite or sufficient to make men virtuous. Too many of our moralists write as if they thought virtue could be taught as easily, and much in the same way, as grammar'. Echoing Hobbes and anticipating Locke, Boyle proceeded, in about 1660, to chastise those who wrangled 'about the titles and precedencies of the parts of ethical philosophy, and things extrinsecal enough to vice and virtue' and who spent 'more time in asserting their method, than the prerogatives of virtue above vice'. These authors were more solicitous to the ordering of 'their chapters than their readers actions; and [were] more industrious to impress their doctrine on our memories than our affections, and teach us better to dispute of our passions than with them'.

Boyle insisted that 'the actual possession of one virtue is preferable to the bare speculative knowledge of them all' and that, in fact, 'but little theory is essentially requisite to the being virtuous, provided it be duly understood, and cordially put in practice'. The 'numerous little notions' that moral writers chance upon, 'though the speculations be not unpleasant, afford us very little peculiar light to guide our actions by'. Similarly, though books of morality may provide reasons to deter us from vice that may not be found in the Bible, 'yet may a dextrous reader find in that heavenly book many more invitations to virtue, and detriments from vice, than most men are aware of; and some of them of an importance, that renders one of them as much more considerable than many ordinary ones'.[262]

Elsewhere Boyle expressed more conciliatory views, but the ambivalence evident in his writings between the 'correct' theological stance *vis-à-vis* the issue of morality and an awareness of the merit of incorporating the writings of the ancient moralists was shared by many contemporaries. In his *Christian Ethicks*, Sir Thomas Browne unambiguously recommended to his readers: 'live by old ethicks and the

---

[261] 'Theology alone homogeneously delivers the whole revealed will of God for directing our morals, will, and life. This whole revealed will of God alone is that right reason—if absolute rectitude be looked towards, as it must be looked towards here—in which alone, by the consensus of all who are of sound mind, the norm or rule of honesty, law, and equity (and therefore of virtues) is constituted. Therefore, although there may be some usefulness and necessity of household economy and politics for jurisprudence, the principal usefulness and necessity is nevertheless theology's. Theology abundantly supplies most distinctly and most perfectly the general rules, the first principles, and all the foundations of law.' William Ames, *The Marrow of Theology*, trans. J. D. Eusden (Boston and Philadelphia 1968), 225–6; William Ames, *Technometry*, trans. L. W. Gibbs (Philadelphia 1979), 113–15.

[262] *The Works of the Right Honourable Robert Boyle*, ed. T. Birch (6 vols London 1772) ii. 287.

classical rules of honesty. Put no new names or notions upon authentick virtues and vices. Think not that morality is ambulatory; that vices in one age are not vices in another; or that virtues, which are under the everlasting seal of right reason, may be stamped by opinion.' Later in the same work, however, Browne incorporated a stern admonition:

rest not in the high-straign'd paradoxes of old philosophy supported by naked reason, and the reward of mortal felicity, but labour in the ethicks of faith, built upon heavenly assis-tance, and the happiness of both beings. Understand the rules, but swear not unto the doc-trines of Zeno or Epicurus. Look beyond Antoninus, and terminate not thy morals in Seneca and Epictetus. Let not the twelve, but the two tables be thy law. Let Pythagoras be thy remembrancer, not thy textuary and final instructor; and learn the vanity of the world rather from Solomon than Phocylides. Sleep not in the dogma's of the Peripatus, Academy, or Porticus. Be a moralist of the mount, an Epictetus in the faith, and Christianize thy notions.[263]

These examples demonstrate that, irrespective of their positions on the religious spectrum, English protestants agreed, in principle, on the intimate and essential bonding of religion and ethics. It is not surprising, then, that tutors and educators felt compelled to walk a careful tightrope between espousing publicly their duties and procedures for educating youth into faith and virtue and concurrently imple-menting a more or less 'secular' course of moral philosophy. Furthermore, given the singular congruity between the two domains, it was inevitable that at least part of the theological disputes that raged at Oxford during the first half of the seven-teenth century would be camouflaged as debates over moral philosophy. Such was the case because the vaguely charted zone between faith and ethics enabled godly tutors to engage in religious indoctrination under the guise of offering legitimate undergraduate instruction. If virtue was but an expression of godliness, they reas-oned, then insistence on careful study of scripture, catechism, and the 'right' prac-tical divines were indispensable for inculcating morality. And although puritans were not alone in insisting that no moral education could be carried out without faith, they certainly placed a greater emphasis on proper religious conditioning and more vocally slighted the teaching of the Greek and Roman moralists than did their conformist brethren.

A good example of such a religious education can be found in the case of John Oxenbridge, a tutor at Magdalen Hall, who routinely compelled students under his charge to enter into a 'sacramentum academicum' with him. When interrogated by the vice-chancellor in 1634, Oxenbridge admitted that he 'dehorted' his charges from the reading of anything that tended toward 'lasciviousness or atheisme', and that he assigned them rigorous readings from the Bible, the *Catechism* of John Ball, and the works of Richard Rogers. Furthermore 'many allso did beginne at once to

---

[263] *The Works of Sir Thomas Browne*, ed. Geoffrey Keynes (4 vols Chicago 1964) i. 247, 243, 284. In the *Religio Medici* Browne further warned that 'if we are directed only by our particular natures, and reg-ulate our inclinations by no higher rule than that of our reason, we are but moralists; divinity will still call us heathens'. Ibid. i. 71–2.

translate and analize Calvin's Institutions', which they followed by reading the
works of William Bradshaw and William Pemble. Two decades later, the blind
Presbyterian tutor at Pembroke College, Thomas Cheeseman, assigned George
Trosse some classical authors but, in particular, Trosse recalled that he improved
his Latin through the reading of 'especially divines, such as Zanchy, Camero[n],
Pareus, etc'.[264] Small wonder that Archbishop Laud, averse as he was to religious
disputes at every level, sought strenuously to instil among students the foundations
of learning before plunging them into the mysteries of religion—including Calvin's
Institutes.[265]

Naturally, the most bitter phase of the dispute came during the Interregnum. Many
Oxford dons sounded only marginally less ominous than the radical would-be reformers of the universities, in exhorting parliament and the Oxford authorities to propa-
gate true religion. In a sermon he delivered at St Mary's church in 1654 the fiery Peter
French admonished the students that 'the search after true wisdom' was to be found
in scriptures, not in 'the books of philosophers'. The timing of French's sermon was
noteworthy since it coincided with the forceful attack of radical sectarians on the universities. Six months earlier, one of the most effective of these antagonists, John
Webster, vigorously articulated similar notions when he blasted the universities for
preferring to follow 'the dark lamp of a blind pagan, before the bright-shining sun of
the prophets and apostles'. Contemptuously, he dismissed Aristotle's *Ethics* and disputes over the supreme good as teaching 'nothing at all that is practicable, whereby
vertue might be obtained' or but touching it 'very slenderly'.[266]

Royalists, and even moderate puritans at Oxford, were also attacked on similar
grounds. Seth Ward and John Wilkins, authors of the rebuttal to Webster, along
with other members of the 'Oxford experimental club', were castigated by the
godly 'who ceased not to clamour, and even to article against them, as cavaliers in
their hearts, meer moral men, without the power of godliness; for you must know,
that a moral and umblameable person, if he did not herd with them, was an abom-
ination to that party'. Indeed, Walter Pope claimed to have heard a sermon at St
Mary's in which an eminent member of 'that party' thundered: 'there's more hope
of a whoremonger, a common drunkard, a profane swearer, than of these moral
men.'[267]

With the Restoration such battles subsided. Partly because of the act of uniformity, which effectively excluded dissenters from the universities, and partly because
of the painful lessons on the consequences of religious zeal, the tenor of religion

---

[264] PRO SP 16/266, no. 43; *The Life of . . . George Trosse*, ed. A. W. Brink (Montreal and London 1974),
114.

[265] Laud, *Works* v. 117. Paradoxically, as if to substantiate the thrust of Laud's argument, Oxenbridge
himself admitted that the students who had made an early start on Calvin, *Institutes* 'scarce have made
any progresse in it, for it proves too hard or large for them who [are] streightned in time and understanding especially in serious matters'. PRO SP 16/266, no. 43.

[266] *The Diary of John Evelyn*, ed. De Beer iii. 104–5; Webster, *Academiarum examen*, 86–7.

[267] Walter Pope, *The Life of . . . Seth, Lord Bishop of Salisbury*, ed. J. B. Bamborough (Oxford 1961),
45–6.

and morals was perceptibly altered. Not that ethics was perceived to be less bounded by religion. Whichcote's famous aphorism that morality was 'nineteen parts in twenty all religion' is indicative of the greater affinity ascribed by contemporaries to the two domains, in the wake of the furore created by the writings of Thomas Hobbes. The change may be seen instead in the crumbling of rigid biblicism. Increasingly, what had hitherto been castigated became the norm; divines and dons, as Pattison aptly put it, 'adopted the language and ideas of the moralists. They spoke not of sin, but of vice, and of virtue, not of works'.[268] The road to sentimentalism and the theology of virtue was opened.

Nevertheless, despite the theological vicissitudes of the seventeenth century, contemporaries were in agreement that there existed a unique nexus between religion and ethics and that the chief purpose of education was to instil as early as possible the religious foundations upon which all knowledge—especially moral knowledge—must build. Such a conviction was expressed as forcefully by the crypto-Catholic Obadiah Walker—who insisted on cultivating sound religious principles betimes so that the individual shall not 'miscarry' in virtue and conduct throughout life—and by the Presbyterian tutor and then rector of Exeter College, John Conant, who saw it as his primary duty to 'plant the fear of God in the undergraduates who were placed under him'.[269]

Obviously the process of religious and moral education did not start at the university. The principles of piety and morality were to be laid down at home, continued in school, and perfected at Oxford or Cambridge. Lord Herbert of Cherbury was typical of parents and educators who believed that youth is most susceptible to vice; hence, when children go off to school 'they should have one to attend them who may take care of theire manners as well as the schoolmaster doth of theire learning'. For 'it being the fraile nature of youth as they growe to ripenes in age to bee more capable of doing ill, unless theire manners bee well guided and themselves by degrees habituated in vertue' they may succumb to evil.[270] The schoolmaster John Brinsley agreed. Unless one was well 'seasoned and trained up in God's true religion and in grace', he reasoned, 'all other learning is merely vaine, or to increase a greater condemnation'. In order that a schoolboy should 'learne to fear the Lord and walke in all his commandments' he was required to read the Bible, learn the catechism and, with varying levels of emphasis, attend and analyse sermons.[271] Later in the century the need to ensure the inculcation of religious and moral principles in school was no less urgently championed by Robert Huntington. Shortly after he left Oxford to assume the provostship of Trinity College, Dublin,

---

[268] Benjamin Whichcote, *Moral and Religious Aphorisms*, ed. W. R. Inge (London 1930), 68; Mark Pattison, *Essays*, ed. H. Nettleship (2 vols Oxford 1889) ii. 64.

[269] Walker, *Of Education*, 48; John Conant, *The Life of John Conant*, ed. W. Stanton (1823), 4, cited by J. T. Cliffe, *The Puritan Gentry* (London and Boston 1984), 91.

[270] *The Life of Edward, First Lord Herbert of Cherbury*, ed. Shuttleworth, 18–19.

[271] Brinsley added that 'religion will teach them manners: [and] as they grow in it, so they will also in all civil and good behaviour. The word of the Lord is the rule and ground of all, to frame their manners by.' John Brinsley, *Ludus literarius* (London 1612), 253, 255.

Huntington circulated to local Irish schoolmasters a letter exhorting them to ensure they instructed their 'scholars with all industry and prudence in learning, manners and religion, that they may come qualified not only as to their accomplishment in Greeke and Latin ... [and] a competent understanding of oratory and poetry in both languages, but also as to their good behaviour and deportment too'.[272]

At Oxford the twofold task of fostering proper religious principles among students and educating them in virtue was consolidated. In compliance with the wish of Sir Sackville Crow to raise his son into a 'just, good and godly' person, the youth's tutor at Jesus College implemented, in 1654, a rigorous routine that aimed at inculcating piety and the true principles of the Church of England through the close study of Grotius, Hammond's *Practical Catechism*, and Jeremy Taylor's *Rules for Holy Living*. Thomas Barlow, provost of Queen's College, was equally attentive to such issues. Writing to Sir John Lowther in 1670, Barlow assured him that his grandson's tutor would instruct the youth 'in the grounds of religion' as well as those of literature. Furthermore, Barlow promised that he himself would 'at convenient times (privately) read over the grounds of divinity to him, that soe he may have a better understandinge and comprehension of the reason of that religion, which alone is, or can be a just foundation of true comfort here, and of our hopes of a better life hereafter'.[273]

The intricate accord forged between faith and morals meant that for the humanists and their successors the writings of the ancient moralists were to be harmonized with Christian views. Pagan texts were thus rendered Christian-like by deliberately glossing over the differences of opinion among them and by interpreting such texts as if they contained the Christian message. As Kristeller has perceptively observed, the humanists obliterated all 'sharp boundaries between philosophical concepts and theories derived from different sources' since, unlike modern scholars, they were not concerned to emphasize

the distinctive traits of various periods, schools, and writers of antiquity or in playing up one against the other. They tended to admire ancient literature in all its periods and representatives ... and to be syncretistic as well as eclectic; that is, they liked to harmonize the views of various classical authors, and to extract from their writings a kind of common wisdom that could be learned, imitated, and utilized.

This eclecticism persisted throughout the early modern period, even following the revival of Stoicism in the latter part of the sixteenth century. Thus the moral philosophy encountered by Oxford undergraduates consisted of what one scholar has described as the 'Platonizing Stoic ethics of Cicero, which blended harmoniously and almost indistinguishably with the eclectic Platonic ethics of the almost equally popular Plutarch, and with the traditional Aristotelian ethics'.[274] Lord Herbert of

---

[272] T. C. Barnard, 'Provost Huntington's injunctions to schoolmasters in 1684', *Hermathena* xix (1975), 72.

[273] BL Add. MS 27,606, fos 1, 8–8ᵛ; HMC *Lonsdale MSS*, 94.

[274] P. O. Kristeller, 'The moral thought of renaissance humanism', Kristeller, *Renaissance Thought II* (New York 1965), 37. H. Haydn, *The Counter-Renaissance* (New York 1950), 55.

Cherbury recommended approvingly such a deliberately syncretic and eclectic approach to moral philosophy:

> Christians and the heathens are in a manner agreed concerning the definitions of vertues. It would not bee inconvenient to begin with those definitions which Aristotle in his Moralls hath given as being confirmed for the most part by the Platonique, Stoique, and other philosophers, and in generall by the Christian Church as well as all nations in the world whatsoever, they being doctrines imprinted in the soule in its first originall and contayning the principall and first notices by which man may attaine his happines here or hereafter.[275]

Such an attitude was only natural. After all, contemporaries were not interested in dwelling at length on abstractions or hairsplitting distinctions between the opinions of ancient moralists. Nor did they intend to establish a pure 'science' of ethics. The legitimacy of ethics was based upon its being a practical art, an immediately applicable guide to virtuous living through its capacity to inculcate principles of private virtue and public duty. This utilitarian approach further accounted for the wilful propensity of contemporaries to assume greater consensus among ancient moral texts than really existed, a tactic that further authenticated Christian morality. The pedagogic framework they created was one in which Aristotle, by virtue of his comprehensiveness and methodical arrangement of material, provided a useful basis for the teaching of ethics—albeit cleansed to Christian specifications (as with the removal of Aristotle's worldly definition of the supreme good), and with which the moral teachings of Plato, Cicero, Seneca, Plutarch, and Epictetus were harmonized.

Disposing of contemplative and speculative learning, however, did not mean that the attainment of abstract knowledge as a prerequisite for the acquisition of morals was also discarded. In fact, the reverse was true as both theologians and educators were convinced that faith was grounded upon knowledge. For them, ignorance was the mother of heresy and superstition just as it was the begetter of vice. The virtuous person, it was commonly held, was the wise person, though there existed conflicting notions over what precisely the nature of wisdom was.[276] Equally incontrovertible was the principle that choice was the foundation of morality, and of Christian ethics in particular. But choice was inconceivable unless a process of mature deliberation grounded upon knowledge had taken its course. Benjamin Whichcote could therefore conclude, that 'knowledge alone doth not amount to virtue, but certainly there is no virtue without knowledge'.[277]

The potency of ignorance to subvert religion and morals was repeatedly emphasized by former Oxford graduates and resident dons who maintained that the absence of knowledge was the root of depravity. In his letter of advice of 1580 to Edward Denny, Philip Sidney entreated his friend to study ethics precisely because 'oftentymes wee erre, thinkinge we doe well, as longe as we meane well; where

---

[275] *The Life of Edward, First Lord Herbert of Cherbury,* ed. Shuttleworth, 24.

[276] Obviously such a perception was congenial to the assimilation of the rationalist morality of the ancients.

[277] Whichcote, *Moral and Religious Aphorisms,* 1.

indeed want of knowledge, may make us doe as much wickedness (though not so wickedly) as they which, even pretensedly commit all naughtiness'. In 1630 two Oxford preachers imparted a similar notion. The first argued that 'the state of sin is a state of blindness', concluding that 'every sinner is a perfect ignoramus'; while the other stated that 'there bee 2 evils from whence all others doe proceed, ignorance in the understanding, and concupiscence in the will'. Lord Herbert of Cherbury concurred: 'wee commonly sinne through noe other cause but that wee mistook a true good for that which was onely apparent and soe were deceived by making an undue election in the objects proposed to us.'[278]

Partly in response to the need to eliminate ill-informed judgements and partly in order to instil moral criteria, contemporaries approved of the teaching of moral philosophy. Painfully aware of the cataclysmic consequences of the fall for human faculties, they conceived of education as potentially contributing to the amelioration of the moral and intellectual ruin visited upon mankind. Obviously not much faith was placed in natural faculties, since these consisted merely of those remnants of reason and volition that survived the fall. Thus, in order to fortify one's imperfect native faculties and render moral judgement regular, schooling was indispensable. Edward Waterhouse, who was studying at the Bodleian Library throughout the better part of the Interregnum, echoed Cicero when he voiced the prevalent view according to which 'virtue may receive some weak impulsions from nature; but the vigorous, the full seas, and high tides are from learning'.[279]

Morality was understood in terms of the capacity of the individual to will that which conformed with the dictates of right reason; by extension, within such a framework, moral philosophy was viewed as a direct and necessary corollary of right reason. Richard Hooker was one among many who believed that in the absence of reason there could be no virtue: 'goodnesse is seene with the eye of understanding. And the light of that eye, is reason.' And again: 'the lawes of well doing are the dictates of right reason.' A generation later the puritan-inclined tutor at Magdalen Hall, William Pemble, was of the same opinion: 'If reason be governesse, we apprehend true good. If lead by passion, we follow appearances.' Later he added that 'true felicity' stems from the 'uprightnesse of judgment'. And for Nicholas Hill, who was alternatively characterized as a papist and an atheist, virtue was 'the constant gift of right reason [and] the expression of right reason in customary actions. Reason is virtue implicit; virtue is reason explicit.' It is not surprising, therefore, that contemporaries—who invariably attributed vice to a failure to comply with the dictates of right reason—were partial to Ovid's famous adage

---

[278] J. M. Osborn, *Young Philip Sidney* (New Haven 1972), 538; Bodl. MS Eng. th. f. 17, pp. 24, 54, cited in S. A. Dippel, *A Study of Religious Thought at Oxford and Cambridge 1590–1640* (Lanham 1987), 5; *The Life of Edward, First Lord Herbert of Cherbury*, ed. Shuttleworth, 25. See also 'Richard earl of Carbery's advice to his son', ed. V. B. Heltzel, *Huntington Library Bulletin* xi (1939). 78: 'the greatest mischiefe to our manners doth proceede from a mistake of the nature of thinges.'

[279] Edward Waterhouse, *An Humble Apologie for Learning and Learned Men* (London 1653), 193.

of self-resignation: 'Video meliora proboque; deteriora sequor'—I see and approve the better way, yet I follow the worse way.[280]

The assumed centrality of reason to ethics was naturally reflected in the structure of the undergraduate curriculum. The Laudian statutes stipulated that students from the second year on should attend, both the lectures in logic and in moral philosophy. In practice, however, students usually proceeded with the latter only after they had spent at least a few months pursuing logic. Such a sequence was essential if the student was to exercise judgement wisely, to reason purposefully, to be able to distinguish between right and wrong, reality and appearance, and to arrive at a 'correct' moral choice.[281] The formal part of the instruction in ethics carried on with the tutor, however, was considerably shorter than the time devoted to the logic course. This was so partly because of the distinctively practical nature of ethics, which discouraged speculation and overburdening abstractions, and partly because the student was expected independently to read books and imitate people. Thus all textbooks, whether long or short, provided students with the basic definitions of the subject, the nature of individual virtues and of the passions, with detailed characterizations of each, and precepts and suggestions as to how virtue in general—the sure consequence of right reason—might be achieved.

The inculcation of this abstract knowledge about virtue was considered incomplete until knowledge was reinforced by habit. Francis Bacon expressed the widely shared view that 'mens thoughts are much according to their inclination: their discourse and speeches according to their learning and infused opinions, but their deeds are after as they have been accustomed. And therefore, as Macciavel well noteth . . . there is no trusting to the force of nature, nor to the bravery of words, except it be corroborate by custome.' He further thought that only custom can 'alter and subdue nature', and 'certainly custome is most perfect when it beginneth in young yeares'. An early start was recommended because as Henry Percy, earl of Northumberland exhorted his son Algernon (m. 1617), what was early planted would easier be followed on, so the practice 'begets an habit and aptness to incline to virtue and reason'. It was also feared that in the absence of a settled habit, wickedness—which was more difficult to eradicate than virtue was to inculcate—would set in.[282]

This view of the human condition was emphasized by many contemporaries. Richard Vaughan, second earl of Carbery, prompted his son to become a creature of habit and render his moral conduct regular so that it may become fixed:

[280] Hooker, *Works* i. 78, 79; William Pemble, *The Summe of Morall Philosophy* in *The Works of . . . William Pemble* (Oxford 1659), 2–3 (separately paginated); Nicholas Hill, *Philosophia epicurea* (Paris 1601), proposition no. 25, cited in G. McColley, 'Nicholas Hill and the *Philosophia epicurea*', *Annals of Science* iv (1939), 402; Ovid, *Metamorphoses* vii. 20.

[281] By the time students began their course in ethics they had also gone through a considerable body of classical literature, which was expected to furnish them with a stock of examples and practical illustrations of virtue and vice.

[282] Francis Bacon, *The Essays*, ed. M. Kiernan (Cambridge Mass. 1985), 119–21; Henry Percy, ninth earl of Northumberland, *Advice to his Son*, ed. G. B. Harrison (London 1930), 59.

accustome thyselfe betimes to entertayne right and sound opinions, that they may growe up with thee, and by using thy selfe to thinke well, thou maiest soone come to doe well, and by frequency of well doing, it may at last become soe naturall, as that thou canst not but doe well, thou canst not doe otherwise. Or if at any time thou doest ill, it may appeare to be by constraint or force, rather then inclination.[283]

A moral habit could also alleviate the continued need to employ reason prior to action. Once reason had judged correctly, habit would ensure spontaneous assent in similar situations. The goal was not to encourage a mechanical perpetuation of involuntary action, reasoned Joseph Addison (MA 1693), only that 'we may perhaps forget the arguments which occasioned our conviction, but we ought to remember the strength they had with us, and therefore still to retain the conviction which they once produced'. After all, he continued, 'considering the weakness and limitations of our intellectual faculties' we can scarcely act otherwise. Indeed, he thought the moral habit to be analogous to the manner of 'the mathematician [who] proceeds upon propositions which he has once demonstrated, and tho' the demonstration may have slipt out of his memory, he builds upon the truth, because he knows it was demonstrated'.[284]

Next to precepts, educators strongly advocated examples, as these were 'of more force to move and instruct than are arguments and proofs of reason or their precise precepts, because examples are the very forms of our deeds'. John Locke was emphatic on the subject: 'but of all the ways whereby children are to be instructed, and their manners formed, the plainest, easiest, and most efficacious, is to set before their eyes the examples of those things you would have them do, or avoid.' Moreover examples could immediately be translated into action, another advantage over precepts in the eyes of educators. Considered more powerful than reason because of their capacity to excite the passions into propelling the will into action, they were also, however, considered potentially dangerous. As Sir Thomas Browne warned, certain people would be 'led rather by example, than precept; receiving perswasions from visible inducements, before intellectual instructions. And therefore also they judg of human actions by the event; for being uncapable of operable circumstances, or rightly to judg the prudentiality of affairs, they only gaze upon the visible success, and thereafter condemn or cry up the whole progression.'[285] It was believed imperative to alert the students that precepts and examples needed to be wielded concurrently, and that only after the ability to distinguish right from wrong had been acquired would a person be skilful enough to adopt edifying examples while shunning others.

---

[283] 'Carbery's advice to his son', ed. Heltzel, 78–9.

[284] Addison concurred with Bedford that custom 'has a mechanical effect upon the body, at the same time that it has a very extraordinary influence upon the mind'. Repeated actions 'construct by degrees so strong an inclination' so that 'what was at first exercise, becomes at length an entertainment'. Ultimately, the mind would become so 'accustomed to a thing it had been aversed to' previously that it 'conceives fondness and affection toward it'. *The Spectator* iv. 141–2.

[285] *The Educational Writings of John Locke*, ed. Axtell, 182; *The Works of Sir Thomas Browne*, ed. Keynes ii. 26–7.

History, widely regarded as 'philosophy teaching by examples', was most often recommended as the fittest storehouse of moral and political case studies for the instruction of youth. 'There is no learning', wrote Sir Henry Savile, 'so proper for the direction of the life of man as historie.'[286] Naturally not everyone endorsed the moral example of history. Most vociferous in criticism was Thomas Hobbes, who complained that on account of 'reading of these Greek, and Latine authors, men from their childhood have gotten a habit (under a false shew of liberty) of favouring tumults, and of licentious controlling the actions of their soveraigns; and again of controlling those controllers, with the effusion of so much blood, as I think I may truly say there was never any thing so deerly bought, as these western parts have bought the learning of the Greek and Latine tongues'.[287] Most other commentators, however, highly approved. The dangers posed by the tender age of impressionable students could be guarded against, while there was no substitute for the powerful lessons—both positive and negative—of history. As William London expressed it, history, 'speculum mundi', offered 'the best prospect into humane affairs' because in it 'are many examples of virtues, as copies drawn for our imitation; as baits to allure us, and alas no few of vice, as sea-marks to warn us; as a glass to shew us the ugly deformity of sinne'.[288] The efficacy of historical examples derived, in large part, from the general consensus concerning the constancy of human nature—analogous to the universality and immutability of morality itself—which empowered past examples to instruct the present. According to Obadiah Walker,

it will not be amiss to take notice that as there is no new thing under the sun, so neither any new action, but the same are represented over again under varying circumstances; so that he, who intends to be a wise man, must endeavour to distinguish the action (as physicians do in judging diseases) from the circumstances, that he may be able to give a good judgment and prognostick, and afterwards to frame a generall rule, which may stand him in stead at other times and occasions.[289]

Nowhere was the emphasis on example stressed more than when advocating the importance of keeping good company. Parents and educators alike never tired of insisting on the need to associate with grave, pious, and learned individuals and, even more important, to avoid as much as possible bad company. Francis Osborne warned his son at Oxford: 'beware what company you keep, since example prevails more than precept.' Company, Locke agreed, 'does more than all precepts, rules and instructions'. The need to keep good company was felt to be particularly acute at the university because of the relative independence youth enjoyed there, as well as the multiplication of undesirable temptation. 'Wherefore', recommended Peacham, 'your first care, even before pulling off your boots, let be the choice of

---

[286] Publius Cornelius Tacitus, *The Ende of Nero and Beginning of Galba*, trans. Henry Savile (London 1591), preface.
[287] Thomas Hobbes, *Leviathan*, ed. C. B. Macpherson (London 1976), 267–8. See also p. 369.
[288] William London, *A Catalogue of the Most Vendible Books in England* (London 1658), sig. F4.
[289] Walker, *Of Education*, 175.

your acquaintance and company. For as infection in cities in a time of sickness is taken by concourse and negligent running abroad . . . so it falleth out here in the university.'[290] Great emphasis was placed on directing students to avoid corruption of manners by succumbing to such pernicious examples of profanity, drunkenness, lasciviousness, and the like. Thus, though in general educators emphasized the need to keep company and follow examples as an integral part of the didactic part of moral training, they were equally careful to accentuate the care with which companions and models should be chosen, lest the moral foundations that were already laid be wrecked.

The goal of virtue was not the upright, yet reclusive, individual but rather the family man, the good neighbour and citizen. The protestant reformers, no less than Aristotle and Cicero, emphasized the inherent sociability of the individual, the result being that more often than not private manners were translated into public virtues. Conduct, therefore, was also taken to be an integral part of ethics. During the seventeenth century, however, an increasing emphasis was placed on what Sir William Petty (at Oxford 1649–52) dubbed 'small moralls'[291]—civility, polite conversation, carriage and apparel. An example of such concern can be gleaned from John Heywood's manual of advice which was sent to George Smith, shortly after the young scholar entered St John's College in 1696. Smith was admonished that his business at Oxford was 'to accomplish' himself by his studies to serve God, church and country 'in whatever station divine providence may hereafter place you. The chief qualifications for such a performance are these two, goodness and knowledge. By goodness I mean such a probity of mind, as may produce in you piety towards God, sobriety in your self, and decency of behaviour towards superiours, inferiours and equals.'[292]

Not only did the attainment of these 'small moralls' become almost as important as the attainment of rectitude itself, but the manner in which they were inculcated was similar. Conduct, like other virtues, was believed to be acquired through learning, not endowed by nature. Richard Steele (m. 1690) expressed the principle thus: 'A good mien (a becoming motion, gesture and aspect) is natural to some men; even these would be highly more graceful in their carriage, if what they do from the force of nature were confirmed and heightened from the force of reason. . . . A man who has not had the regard of his gesture in any part of his education, will find himself unable to act with freedom before new company.'[293] The principle of habit was equally applicable to conduct. Civility, Obadiah Walker reminded his readers, 'as all other virtues, requires an early initiation, and continual practise to arrive at a perfect habit of it'. Finally, in the eyes of contemporaries civility, like virtue, was considered to be universal and absolute, a correspondence

[290] Osborne, *Advice to a Son*, 34; *The Educational Writings of John Locke*, ed. Axtell, 165; Peacham, *The Complete Gentleman*, 50. Both Locke and Peacham, not to mention a host of other authors, include extensive further discussion on the subject of company.

[291] *The Petty Papers*, ed. the marquis of Lansdowne (2 vols repr. New York 1967) ii. 188.

[292] Bodl. MS Rawlinson d. 1178.   [293] *The Spectator* iii. 235.

that implied an analogous routine of instruction.[294] It was, therefore, important to cultivate those 'garments of the mind' as Carbery (following Bacon) had styled good breeding: 'whether you stand, sitt, or move, let it be with such a becomming, pleasing gravity, as that your very behaviour may commend you.'[295]

The teaching of ethics was premissed in large part on the ability of the will to regulate the passions. A discussion of seventeenth-century views concerning the will would require extensive recourse to contemporary theology—an endeavour that lies beyond the confines of this chapter. Nevertheless, the role of the passions in this model of human behaviour needs some amplification. During the Middle Ages and much of the renaissance cognition, not emotions, dominated the interests of scholars and educators. By the late sixteenth century, however, a growing preoccupation with the passions was becoming evident, and much greater scope was allowed to the treating of the passions in discussions about ethics. Eventually, as a consequence of—and often as a reaction against—the teachings of Descartes and Hobbes, this preoccupation with the passions, and with human nature more generally, would lay the foundations for sentimentalism and the morality of feelings.[296]

Even in the early years of the seventeenth century—and notwithstanding the Stoic revival—it was generally agreed that the establishment of the moral sovereignty of reason demanded not the annihilation of the passions, but only their control. In fact, commentators increasingly came to appreciate the need to keep the passions vibrant, if in check, in order to guarantee proper action. Locke was thus hardly original in expressing the correlation between managing the passions and subjecting them to the dictates of right reason: 'The great principle and foundation of all vertue and worth, is placed in this, that a man is able to deny himself his own desires, cross his own inclinations, and purely follow what reason directs as best, tho' the appetite lean the other way.'[297]

Given the growing importance attributed to the passions and to human nature, it is not surprising that introspection came to be regarded as essential to understanding our actions and helping reason and will to regulate our passions. In his letter of advice, the earl of Carbery expressed the new convention of self-knowledge as a means of assuring the harmonious interaction of the faculties:

The most profitable and necessary knowledge in the world is to knowe and study thy selfe. Wherefore withall the plainnesse, sincerity and observation you can make in your best temper of mind and body, lay your selfe open to your selfe. ... By this meanes your growth or

---

[294] Walker, *Of Education*, 213. Walker also made a distinction between the universality of civility and the dependence of ceremonies on time and place: ibid. 212.

[295] 'Carbery's advice to his son', ed. Heltzel, 79.

[296] See for example R. S. Crane, 'Suggestions toward a genealogy of the "man of feeling"', *English Literary History* i (1934), 205–30; H. W. Sams, 'Anti-Stoicism in seventeenth- and early eighteenth-century England', *Studies in Philology* xli (1944), 65–78; N. Fiering, *Moral Philosophy at Seventeenth-Century Harvard* (Chapel Hill 1981).

[297] *The Educational Writings of John Locke*, ed. Axtell, 138. Locke added that such 'power is to be got and improved by custom, made easy and familiar by an early practice': ibid. 143; see also pp. 147–8.

decay in vertue wilbe discovered, and consequently waies for the increase of that growth, or for repayring those decayes and breaches in the soule will more readily be found out, more easily cured.[298]

Sir Thomas Browne, too, advocated continuous introspection: 'study thou the dominion of thy self, and quiet thine own commotions. Let right reason be thy Lycurgus, and lift up thy hand unto the law of it; move by the intelligences of the superior faculties, not by the rapt of passion ... They who are merely carried by the wheel of such inclinations, without the hand and guidance of sovereign reason, are but the automatous part of mankind, rather lived than living, or at least under-living themselves.'[299]

The contribution of introspection to the human ability to attain knowledge appealed to pessimists and optimists alike. The former student of Queen's College, Sir John Davies (m. 1585), composed a celebrated philosophical poem on the theme, in which he expressed his metaphoric inner retirement:

> My selfe am center of my circling thought,
> only my selfe I studie, learne, and know.

Thomas Hobbes, too, may have ridiculed the propensity of his contemporaries to boast of their ability to read men, not books, and their misunderstanding of the true meaning of *nosce teipsum*, but he none the less stressed what he considered to be the true significance of self-knowledge: 'to teach us that for the similitude of the thoughts and passions of one man, to the thoughts, and passions of another, whosoever looketh into himself and considereth what he doth, when he does think, opine, reason, hope, feare, etc, and upon what grounds; he shall thereby read and know what are the thoughts and passions of all other men, upon the like occasions.'[300] By 1694 the young Lord Ashley's manifesto, in a letter to Locke, that the comprehension of our nature was the only thing that mattered, is indicative of the new climate of opinion:

What I count true learning, and all that wee can profitt by, is to know our selves; what it is that makes us low, and base, stubborn against reason, to be corrupted and drawn away from vertue, of different tempers, inconstant, and inconsistent with ourselves; to know how to bee always friends with providence though death and many such dreadfull businesses come in the way; and to be sociable and good toward all men, though they turn miscreants or are injuriouse to us. Whilst I can gett any thing that teaches this, whilst I can search any age or language that can assist mee here, whilst such are philosophers, and such philosophy, whence I can learn ought from, of this kind, there is no labour, no studdy, no learning that I would not undertake.[301]

---

[298] 'Carbery's advice to his son', ed. Heltzel, 90.

[299] *The Works of Sir Thomas Browne*, ed. Keynes i. 252.

[300] Sir John Davies, 'Nosce teipsum', in E. H. Sneath, *Philosophy in Poetry* (London 1903 repr. New York 1969), 230; Hobbes, *Leviathan*, 82.

[301] *The Correspondence of John Locke* ed. E. S. De Beer (8 vols Oxford 1976–89) v. 153.

These views are indicative of the growing trend to emphasize the role of the passions and of introspection within the domain of ethics, which reached its height at the start of the eighteenth century in the writings of such Oxford alumni as John Norris, Joseph Addison, and Richard Steele.

Imparting the principles of ethics began in earnest during the undergraduate's second year at Oxford. Already by the middle of the seventeenth century it had become customary to initiate students into the study of moral philosophy by assigning them a manuscript manual, usually of the tutor's own making, as was also the convention in logic and natural philosophy. William Pemble's *A Summe of Morall Philosophy*, for example, served as such an epitome. (The published version owed its existence to a zealous executor who published, indiscriminately, anything he found among the papers of his deceased mentor.) Decades after he left Oxford, John Aubrey still recommended that 'well-digested, clear and short' epitome of moral philosophy prepared by John Prideaux, rector of Exeter College, which he had read at Trinity College and which, he believed, students would 'quickly get by heart'. Authors of letters of advice, like Richard Holdsworth and John Grandorge, encouraged this practice, which is further verified by the evidence of student notebooks that indicate such epitomes were either prepared especially for them or that they copied their tutors' composition.[302]

Usually the reading of the intial epitome—either in manuscript or in printed textbook—was carried out together with the tutor. Thereafter, the student was once more left to pursue additional texts independently on the assumption that his progress and understanding would be monitored by the tutor. 'At present', wrote George Fleming to his father in 1689, 'my study is moral philosophy, concerning which I have lecters from my tutor in Stierius Ethicks; along with which I read myself Aristotles Ethicks and Curcellaeus'.[303] Of the more advanced texts, we find again that authors of letters of advice offered lists of books out of which the students could pick and choose according to their needs. Thomas Barlow, for example, judged Franciscus Pavonius' *Summa ethicae* 'an ingenius summe of ethicks' on top of which the undergraduate could follow with such texts as John Case's *Speculum moralium*, Johannes Crell's *Ethices elementa Racoviae*, Jean Buridan's *Ethica*, Alessandro Piccolomini's *Della institutione morale*, Franciscus Suarez's *Opus de virtute et statu religionis*, and the Coimbra commentaries. For those interested 'in the

---

[302] Pemble, *A Summe of Morall Philosophy*; *Aubrey on Education*, ed. Stephens, 116; Fletcher, *The Intellectual Development of John Milton* ii. 637. It is noteworthy that the manuscript compendium of ethics which Edward Brerewood compiled while a tutor at Brasenose College during the early 1590s was used by Oxford tutors and students for decades before it was published in 1640. Daniel Featley of Corpus Christi College, for example, used it in the early years of the seventeenth century and Thomas Smyth, a Lincoln College undergraduate, acquired a copy in 1638. Austin, 'Thomas Smyth of Lincoln College, Oxford', 221. Students' commonplace books containing such compendia include Bodl. MS St Edmund Hall 72; BL MS Harleian 5043, fos 34–45 (Nehemiah Rogers of Queen's College); Bodl. MS Cherry 34, fos 100ᵛ–180ᵛ (Francis Cherry of St Edmund Hall 1682); Bodl. MS Rawlinson d. 1121 (Humphrey Hody of Wadham Hall 1675/6); Bodl. MS Rawlinson d. 1442, fos 70–80 (Charles King of Magdalen College 1682).

[303] *The Flemings in Oxford* ii. 252.

speculative and disputeing part of ethicks' Barlow recommended the schoolmen, and in particular such commentators on Aquinas as Gabriel Vasquez, Gregorius de Valencia, Didacus Alvarez, Johannes Malderus, and Gregorius Martinez, in whose writings 'all morall quaestions are fully, and acutely discusd'. This impression of an excessively heavy scholastic dose in an undergraduate course is somewhat tempered when one realizes that Barlow intended the schoolmen to be read only by advanced students, 'of ripe understanding' who could 'reade them with some judgement'.[304]

Other Oxford tutors were less exhaustive in their coverage but similar in their tastes. They invariably assigned Aristotle—often in the dressing of Johannes Magirus—along with the other ancient moralists and differed mainly in their pre-scription of accompanying manuals. Thomas Sixsmith of Brasenose College, for example, recommended in the 1620s Buridan, Piccolomini, Medina, and Dithmar as well as some commentary on Aquinas. Nathaniel Sterry, who was intruded fellow of Merton College in 1648, recommended Eustachius a Sancto Paulo and Aristotle, while Stephen Penton suggested, in addition to Aristotle, Cicero, and Epictetus, works by Crell and Whitby, and the commentaries by Gregory of Valencia and Cajetan on Aquinas.[305]

After the student had completed the study of an introductory manual, John Grandorge suggested, in 1690, that 'he may read' one or more books from a list which included Cicero, Plutarch, Epictetus, Theophrastus, and Marcus Aurelius among the ancients, and Henry More's *Enchiridion ethicum*, Johannes Crell's *Ethica Christiana*, Gualtruche, and Peter a St Joseph on Aristotle among the more recent authors. For disputations Grandorge recommended Colbert, Wendelin, Aquinas, and Heereboord's *Meletemata*. To these 'may be added' Sanderson's *De juramenti promissorii obligatione*, Grotius, Filmer's *Observations upon Aristotles Politiques*, the two works by Samuel Pufendorf, *De jure naturae et gentium* and *De officio hominis et civis*. Special attention, he urged, should also be given to the many rebuttals of Hobbes's works. Another author of advice opined that the best available 'compleat body' of moral philosophy was Aristotle, Pavonius, Crell, and More. After the student con-sulted 'one or more of these' he should embark upon other recommended books in order to elaborate particular topics. For the passions he recommended Descartes and Edward Reynolds, while Hugo Grotius, Richard Cumberland, Pufendorf, John Selden, Leonard Lessius, Suarez, and Sharrock were assigned for the mastering of natural law. The 'best heathen writers', Cicero, Plutarch, and Seneca, were not, needless to say, forgotten, nor did the anonymous compiler forget to recommend, for those interested, Aquinas as the best casuist.[306]

These manuals of advice reflect the transformation that the teaching of moral philosophy was undergoing during the last three decades of the century, in reac-tion to the challenge posed by Hobbes and as part of an increasing cognizance of

---

[304] *'A Library for Younger Schollers'*, ed. Dejordy and Fletcher, 2–3, 49.

[305] BNCL MS 80 unpaginated; Bodl. MS Tanner 88, fo 5; Stephen Penton, *Apparatus generalis ad the-ologiam* (Oxford 1688), 41.

[306] Bodl. MS St Edmund Hall 72; Bodl. MS Rawlinson d. 188, p. 7.

the new spate of writings on ethics. The new direction is even more clearly notice-able in the advice of Thomas Heywood. This St John's tutor allocated much of the second year to the study of ethics. The recommended course included, of course, the ancient moralists, but only Eustachius, Stier, and Alsted were suggested from among the 'scholastics'. Instead, Heywood recommended the works of Henry More, Pufendorf, Reynolds, De la Chambre, the moral essays of the Port Royalists, Bacon's *Essays*, and Clarendon's assault on Hobbes. He also suggested that after a student had graduated BA he should devote much of the following year to a thor-ough review of moral philosophy, adding to his foundation of law and politics through the reading of Cumberland, Grotius, Aristotle, Cicero, Justinian, and Zouch. Heywood also assigned a discrete Platonic component, recommending much of Plato as such together with Ficino, Plotinus, and a portion of the Hermetic corpus.[307]

For the most part, the reading of more recent textbooks was recommended as a gloss and a guide to the writings of the ancient moralists, who alone were revered by early modern scholars—once, of course, all the obligatory remarks concerning the pre-eminence of Christianity had been observed. While most undergraduates were expected to peruse carefully only one or two of the above-mentioned text-books, it was assumed students would read and master the foremost moral writers of antiquity—Cicero, Plutarch, Aristotle, Seneca, Epictetus, and, although less fre-quently recommended, Plato and Marcus Aurelius. The universally high esteem in which the ancient authors were held is evident from Francis Mansell's assurance to Sir Sackville Crow that his son would not be detained for long from the 'divine moralities' of Plutarch and Seneca. It was also evident in Thomas Barlow's special praise of those 'excellent authors' Cicero, Plutarch, and Seneca—pagan authors he had previously commended, with some other ancients, as 'very well worth the . . . perusall'—who, 'if they livd as they writt, they have shamed Christendome'.[308]

Cicero and Aristotle in particular exerted distinctive influence—though in dif-ferent ways—on the teaching of ethics. The former acquired the status of a 'cult figure' of sorts. Robert Sanderson once told an admirer that all his learning was built upon the study of Aristotle's *Rhetoric*, Aquinas's *Secunda secundae*, and of Cicero, 'chiefly his *Offices*, which he had not read over less than 20 times; and could at this [old] age say without book'. Contemporaries expressed their admiration in various ways. Some lamented, as did Brian Duppa, the tendency, especially among young-sters, to deprecate Cicero: 'because we begin with it in our youth, we cast aside in our age, when we have most use of it'. Henry Peacham concurred: 'let it not seem contemptible unto you because it lieth tossed and torn in every school, but be pre-cious as it was sometimes unto the old Lord Burghley . . . who to his dying day would always carry it about him, either in his bosom or pocket, being sufficient,

[307] Bodl. MS Rawlinson d. 1178, fo 3ᵛ.

[308] BL Add. MS 27,606, fo 9; *'A Library for Younger Schollers'*, ed. Dejordy and Fletcher, 3, 21. In the view of Clement Barksdale it was Seneca who 'among all humane authors . . . hath the preheminence for precepts of moral vertue': *An Oxford-Conference of Philomathes and Polymathes*, 6.

as one said of Aristotle's rhetorics, to make both a scholar and an honest man.'
Parents, who generally felt comfortable about leaving the choice of books to their
sons' tutors, nevertheless made it a point to recommend Cicero, as did the earl of
Carbery who exhorted his posterity: 'I will commend one booke to you. Wee
beginne with it when we are boyes, yet it will become the oldest and gravest man's
hand ... a most wise and usefull booke, where you shall have excellent philosophy excellently drest.'[309]

If Cicero enriched the soul, Aristotle expanded the mind while contributing at
the same time to the study of language. Analogous to the assignment of the *Organon*
to Oxford undergraduates for the dual purpose of instructing them in logic while
simultaneously advancing their linguistic skills, was their immersion in the
Nicomachean Ethics which was intended to acquaint them with the moral system of
Aristotle while at the same time improving their proficiency in Greek. Already in
the mid-sixteenth century this trend is made evident by Conrad ab Ulmis, a student at Christ Church in 1550–2, describing his course of study: 'I devote the hour
from six to seven in the morning to Aristotle's *Politics*, from which I seem to
receive a twofold advantage, both a knowledge of Greek and an acquaintance with
moral philosophy.' Seventeenth-century tutors further engrained this convention.
Holdsworth, Sterry, and Duport are among those who specifically assigned Aristotle
to couple together matter and language. John Aubrey carried into his projected
academy the fruits of his own Oxford education when he assigned the reading of
'Aristotle's *Ethics* in Greek, to improve their Greek together with the science'.
Echoing similar sentiments was Ralph Bohun of Trinity College, who served as
tutor to John Evelyn the younger in the mid-1660s. In one of his letters to Evelyn
pére, Bohun articulated the prevalent practice of assigning Aristotle because of the
Stagirite's rare ability to combine content, method, and language: 'I intend to read
in Greek to my young man the ethicks of Aristotle and the rhetoric, which has so
admirable a connexion with the former that I think never any man beside taught
us the right sympathy between passions and words, I look upon him as the greatest master of methodising our thoughts.'[310]

Once again, library catalogues are indispensable in documenting the practices of
tutors and educators. The large library of John English was furnished with the writings of Cicero, Seneca, and Epictetus, to which were added Luis de Granada's *Loci
communes philosophiae moralis*, Freigius' *Quaestiones ethicae*, John Case, and works by
Lipsius and Joseph Hall. English also owned a few rather uncommon books, like
Samuel Heiland's *Ethicorum libri X*, Celsus Mancinus' *De quatuor virtutibus*, Gulielmus
Peraldus' *Summa virtutum ac vitiorum*, and Nicholas Hanapus' *Virtutum vitiorumque*

---

[309] Isaac Walton, *The Lives of John Donne ... and Robert Sanderson* (London 1973), 407; *Correspondence of
Duppa and Isham*, ed. Isham, 94; 'Carbery's advice to his son', ed. Heltzel, 84; Peacham, *The Complete
Gentleman*, 57. Sir Justinian Isham's exhortation to his son Justinian in 1674, while the youth was at
Oxford, to 'be constant to Tully his Offices', was so perfectly taken that the devotion of the future
fourth baronet to Cicero was 'even recorded on his monument'! *The Diary of Justinian Isham*, 36.
[310] *The Collegiate Society*, 41; *Aubrey on Education*, ed. Stephens, 116; CL Evelyn correspondence, no.
301.

exempla.[311] An anonymous student who died in 1640 owned works by Buridan, Brerewood, Piccolomini, Case, and Seneca, while the library of Thomas Cole included works by Golius, Case, Donaldson, Dithmerus, Keckermann, Eustachius, Pavone, Aristotle, Epictetus, Lipsius, and Seneca. Finally, the libraries of two younger students deserve mention. John Hutton died in 1653, leaving a collection of books among which we find ethical works by Eustachius, Melanchton, Case, Buridan, Brerewood, Abraham Scultetus, Burgersdijk, Charron, Epictetus, and Aristotle, whereas the undergraduate library of James Wilding (BA 1687) included Seneca, Plato, Eustachius, Stier, and Brerewood.[312]

Library catalogues are usually indicative of a scholar's possession of books in mature age, and while they provide a fairly accurate picture of what books had been read previously by their owners, they offer little guidance in determining the exact sequence of acquisition. Such information, however, may be gleaned through the reconstruction of student accounts and letters, even in the fragmentary state in which they have come down to us. And, indeed, such sources contain the recommended routine of reading the ancient moralists in conjunction with more recent textbooks. Richard Herrick at St John's read Cicero and Seneca alongside Caspar Bartholin's *Enchiridion ethicum* and Pierre Charron's *De la sagesse,* while the Newdigate brothers purchased Seneca and John Case as part of their study of moral philosophy during their stay at Oxford between 1617 and 1618. Walter Tuckfield of Exeter College acquired in 1631 the works of Plutarch and Seneca, while three decades later Sir John Williams carried with him to Oxford Cicero and Scultetus.[313] Other instances exist. Francis, third Lord Brooke was furnished with copies of Burgersdijk and Reynolds, while at Magdalen College in 1653. Two decades later John Percival acquired De la Chambre while Thomas Isham requested his father to furnish him with the works of Cicero, Aristotle, and Seneca. These last two books, as well as Reynolds's *A Treatise of the Passions,* were also studied by Locke and his pupils at Christ Church.[314]

It should be clear by now that students acquired their training in moral philosophy at their respective colleges from their tutors and in-house lecturers. This can be attributed in part to the general trend already discernible in the second half of the sixteenth century, with college tutors and lecturers assuming a growing share of the education of undergraduates, particularly in those essential components of logic, the classics, and ethics. But other factors contributed to the enfeeblement of any university provision. The predominantly practical character of the teaching of moral philosophy at Oxford, coupled with the intimate connection between

---

[311] Costin, 'The inventory of John English'. English's commonplace book (Bodl. MS Rawlinson d. 1423) attests to his extensive readings among ancient and modern stoics.

[312] OUA chancellor's ct inventories s.v. anonymous (1640), Thomas Cole (1653), John Hutton (1653); 'The account-book of an Oxford undergraduate', ed. Duff, 267–8.

[313] Bodl. MS Eng. hist. c. 481; 'The undergraduate account book of John and Richard Newdigate', 194, 195, 198 ed. Larminie; Devonshire RO MS Z 1/53 box 9/2; Bodl. MS Rawlinson letters 61.

[314] Warwick. RO MS CR 1886/TN21; BL Add. MS 46,953, fo 122; Northants. RO Isham correspondence, no. 862; Bodl. MS Locke e. 6, fos 1–10, MS Locke f. 11.

ethics and religion in the minds of contemporaries—which was inimical to any effort to establish a 'professional' and 'secular' discipline of moral philosophy for purposes not directly related to virtuous training—doomed almost from the out-set the White professorship of moral philosophy. Founded in 1621 by Thomas White—who was also the founder of Sion College in London—the new founda-tion was expressly aimed at undergraduates, but little guidance was offered by either White or anyone else concerning the course the incumbent should take. The Laudian statutes simply stipulated that the professor lecture upon Aristotle's ethics, economics, and politics. However, whatever initial formal instruction in moral phi-losophy was required at the undergraduate level was provided by tutors and col-lege lecturers; a more thorough understanding of ethics increasingly became the domain of independent study. Thus, the function of the professorship as originally conceived became redundant from almost the very moment of its founding. Nor was rejuvenation possible as long as the consensus over the subservience of moral philosophy to religion persisted. Indeed, only a drastic change in favour of a sec-ular and autonomous discipline of ethics could possibly have established the posi-tion of this chair on a par with such other new foundations at Oxford as the Savilian or Laudian professorships.

The alternative to providing elementary lectures on Aristotle's ethics was to mor-alize, and it seems that at least some of the professors, most of whom were divines, took advantage of the congruity between ethics and religion to use the chair as a pulpit. Indeed, Nathaniel Hodges (professor 1668–73) saw so little difference between his duties as a professor and a preacher that, according to Humphrey Prideaux, after Hodges had been made a canon of Norwich 'once in a year he [would] offer to preach, but, his sermons being most on end the translation of his morall philosophy lectures at Oxford, as soon as the people see him in the pulpit they all get out of church'.[315] Thus, in the absence of guiding principles, in the probable absence of an auditory, and in the certain absence of distinguished incum-bents, by the early 1670s at the latest, the White professorship faded into oblivion. This was particularly unfortunate because precisely at this juncture the chair could have offered a fitting platform for the discussion and dissemination of the new trends in natural law and the recent notions concerning moral and political oblig-ation. Such material was discussed by various tutors and college lecturers, such as John Locke in his lectures on the law of nature delivered at Christ Church in 1664, or the anonymous lecturer who delivered a course entitled 'De lege naturali' at Magdalen College twenty years later.[316] But by then the professorship had sunk so

---

[315] *Letters of Humphrey Prideaux . . . to John Ellis*, ed. Edward M. Thompson (Camden Soc. new ser. xv 1875), 161. This congruity of subject-matter frequently resulted in the regius professor of divinity, or the Lady Margaret professor, covering some of the ground of moral philosophy. The best-known example of such a practice can be seen in Robert Sanderson's celebrated lectures in 1646–7 on obliga-tion, which were published as *De juramenti promissorii obligatione* and *De obligatione conscientiae* in 1647 and 1661 respectively, and which became standard textbooks at Oxford after the Restoration.

[316] See Locke, *Essays on the Law of Nature*, ed. W. von Leyden (Oxford 1965); Bodl. MS Rawlinson Q e. 21, fos 127–57.

low that it was turned into an acknowledged sinecure: 'In 1673 a practice began of electing one of the proctors, usually the senior, to the office; in course of time the lectures were entirely dropped; and at length the professorship was so far forgotten, that it was never mentioned in the Oxford Calendar before the year 1831, the practice having continued, with one exception only, till February 1829.'[317]

History

In view of the pronounced humanistic character of English education in the early modern period, surprisingly little attention has been paid to the role of history—arguably the single most important humanistic discipline by the end of the sixteenth century[318]—within the framework of the *studia humanitatis*. This neglect is even more puzzling in face of the rapidly expanding literature devoted to the emergence of local, national, and medieval history during the English renaissance, and to the increasing reliance on history as a political tool during the same period. For their part, historians have tended to dismiss this seeming contradiction by arguing that nothing resembling the organized teaching of history in the modern sense—let alone its practice—could be found at Oxford and Cambridge. To find practitioners and consumers of 'true' history, we would have to shift our attention instead to London, and to the parliamentarians, courtiers, lawyers, and antiquarians residing there. It is this type of polarization between the universities and the capital that leads John Kenyon to conclude in his survey of English historiography, that history, 'despite its great prestige, had no foothold in higher education'.[319] In a similar manner, Kevin Sharpe, the only relatively recent scholar to attempt an evaluation of the teaching of history at Oxford and Cambridge in the early seventeenth century, contends that 'despite evidence of interest among students and college tutors, the study of history as an independent discipline had no place in the curriculum of either university'.[320]

A scrutiny of this bleak view of the place of history in the universities reveals that it is based upon three pervasive perceptions concerning the nature of history in the early modern period. First, as Bietenholz correctly observes, most scholars of early modern historiography are less interested in the humanists' placement of history at the pinnacle of education than in their contribution towards 'impregnating the methods and techniques of historical writing'.[321] Understandably, compared

---

[317] *The Historical Register of the University of Oxford* (Oxford 1900), 55. Thomas Dixon's perception of the professorship that he hoped to obtain in 1681 is indicative of the low ebb it had then already reached. It was simply a boon 'worth £500 in 5 yeares time', which would have enabled him to stay in Oxford rather than search for a living elsewhere: *The Flemings in Oxford* ii. 3.

[318] D. R. Kelley, 'The theory of history' in Schmitt and Skinner (eds), *The Cambridge History of Renaissance Philosophy*, 759.

[319] J. P. Kenyon, *The History Men* (Pittsburgh 1984), 6. Curiously, Kenyon continues by arguing that 'if the sons of the seventeenth-century ruling class learned any history at all, it was at school or from the lawyers at the Inns of Court'.

[320] K. Sharpe, 'The foundation of the chairs of history at Oxford and Cambridge: an episode in Jacobean politics', *History of the Universities* ii (1982), 127.

[321] P. G. Bietenholz, *History and Biography in the Work of Erasmus of Rotterdam* (Geneva 1966), 9.

with the seeming accomplishment of renaissance Italian humanists or sixteenth-century French jurists, the more 'literary' types of seventeenth century history, whether as practised in England or on the continent, appear somewhat pedestrian.[322]

Second, the partiality of scholars today to 'history-writing' and to 'politic history' prompts them to direct what little attention they pay to the teaching of history to those aspects that are relevant to their own frame of reference. In terms of the early modern period this focus assumes present-day tenets concerning the cohesiveness and integral nature of the historical enterprise. However, in the renaissance the teaching of history and the practice of history, though related, nevertheless constituted two distinct aspects of an as yet amorphous discipline. Only an appreciation of the singularity of each domain will enable us to avoid anachronism and recognize the centrality of history in the early modern period.

Third, the preoccupation of modern scholars with 'progressive' aspects of renaissance historiography has led them to detect a change for the worse in the writing and teaching of history as a result of the radical religious and political transformations of the sixteenth century. According to Bouwsma's tidy model, post-Tridentine Rome launched 'a direct attack on the historical accomplishment of the renaissance', finding repugnant both 'the freedom with which historians treated ecclesiastical history' and 'their tendency to regard the study of the past as an autonomous science in which all phenomena are to be understood as a part of the natural order'. Expurgation and suppression were employed in 'an effort to make history "safe" through its diversion from research into rhetoric and through the revival of the Ciceronian cliché *historia magistra vitae*, which reduced history to ethics teaching by example'. Concurrently, in Florence, 'the imposition of princely despotism gradually converted a responsible citizenry into passive subjects who lacked the motive to cultivate a larger political understanding through the study of history. Historiography, therefore, like classical studies in the same period, moved from the *piazza* into the *studio*, detached itself from active politics and reflected a steady decline in human confidence.' In Venice, on the other hand, there developed a new and vigorous historiography by the end of the sixteenth century, owing to the 'close contact with vital issues of political and social existence'. The conclusions drawn from such analyses are plain: wherever the republican ideal had died out, and whenever history was alienated from politics, the discipline was taken over by professional pedants or confessed contemplative literary men.[323]

Cochrane takes this argument one step further by ascribing to the seventeenth century the dubious honour of separating

---

[322] The denunciation of renaissance 'academic history' by modern historians of historiography is not counterbalanced by efforts of historians of humanism, who invariably relegate the topic (at least implicitly) to the domain of the expert historians of historiography.

[323] W. J. Bouwsma, 'Three types of historiography in post-renaissance Italy', *History and Theory* iv (1964–5), 304–9.

the two chief aspects of historical writing that, in fact if not always in theory, had coexisted throughout the renaissance: history as literature and history as research. It consisted also in the complete detachment of either from the concrete political and moral problems of the age. *Utilitas*, in other words, gave way to *delectatio* alone as the purpose of history as literature, and it gave way to a combination of *distractio* and *companalismo*, local flag-waving, as the exclusive motivation of history as research.[324]

Huppert argues for a similar calamity in seventeenth-century France. The achievement of Bodin and La Popelinière in creating the 'new history' on the basis of a 'fragile alliance between the practice of erudition and the writing of general history' was destroyed, because it 'provoked the wrath of the libertine-hunters' who feared the potentially pernicious consequences of the blending of erudition and history. Their assault produced the desired effect of separating the two yet again, with the result that both were 'tamed': history reverted back to pleasant annals, while erudition turned into harmless antiquarianism.[325]

In view of this apparently negative metamorphosis in the nature of early modern historiography, modern scholars thus conclude it is a misnomer to apply the title of 'history' to the treatment of the past as practised in contemporary institutions of higher learning. On the continent the teaching of 'history' can be found only 'in the restricted sense of explicating on classical authors'. In this context, the example of the Jesuit order appears most revealing. To quote Bouwsma again, the virtual absence of historical studies from the Jesuit's *ratio studiorum* can be attributed to 'the negative attitude of the Counter-Reformation toward historical study'. Whatever discussion of history lingered was 'largely directed to the formulation of a rigid Ciceronian orthodoxy which made of it only a body of examples, illustrating the static principles of morality or politics'. Cochrane concurs, arguing that Jesuit pedagogy eliminated modern historians from its programme and prescribed the reading of ancient historians 'not for what they said but only for how they said it. History thus presented as literature by the Jesuits became the sole concern of the seventeenth-century successors of the *ars historica* writers.'[326]

Together, these perceptions have helped fortify a conspicuously and intrinsically positivist disposition towards the study of early modern historiography. Since no notable historiographers were associated with the institutions of higher learning, and no 'great ideas' took root on university soil, the state of history in the universities is judged simply pitiful. To add to this overall condemnation, the universities are faulted for failing to accommodate an autonomous discipline of history within the curriculum, for assigning historical texts to facilitate the acquisition of language, or simply for pleasure, but not for the 'truths' they conveyed, for making history subservient to ethics, and for teaching history for allegedly utilitarian purposes in

[324] E. Cochrane, *Historians and Historiography in the Italian Renaissance* (Chicago 1981), 489.

[325] G. Huppert, *The Idea of Perfect History* (Urbana Ill. 1970), 170–82.

[326] D. R. Kelley, 'Johann Sleidan and the origins of history as a profession', *Journal of Modern History* lii (1980), 579; Bouwsma, 'Three types of historiography in post-renaissance Italy', 310; Cochrane, *Historians and Historiography in the Italian Renaissance*, 489.

the worst sense of the term. Indeed, this utilitarian aspect, which posited history as something to be viewed for everything *but* its own sake, was perhaps the one most vigorously noted and castigated. As Dean puts it, the 'effort to make the past operative in the present', prompted early modern theorists to espouse 'an attitude towards history that tended to be reactionary rather than liberalizing'. MacCaffrey summarizes the common perception:

> Their interests in classical learning were not in its historical, but in its contemporary relevance. It was not curiosity about the past but concern for the present and future moral well-being of men which led them to their studies. They saw the works of the classical authors as authoritative and inspiring guides to the moral development of contemporary men, which was for them the raison d'être of all their labors.[327]

By clinging to the recognizable, and more appealing, features of history as it has since evolved, modern scholars fail to empathize with the multifarious concept of history in the seventeenth century or to comprehend the prevailing ideals of education regulating its study during that period. Instead, they are content to isolate the myriad foibles inherent in academic humanist history, and show how each of them, and all of them together, perverted 'true' history, or at least significantly impeded its growth.

Not surprisingly, this thrust towards positivism has also led to an explicit correlation between the new history and the scientific revolution. The new history, it has been argued, was considered by the political and religious authorities in the early modern period as dangerous and as potentially subversive as the 'new science'. For this reason it was subjected to repression, or at least to considerable taming, in a manner comparable to the alleged stifling of new cosmologies and the mechanical philosophy within the universities. In other words, these traditional strongholds of the establishment thwarted the introduction of modern history as an academic subject as bitterly as they attempted to avert the assimilation of the new science into the curriculum—and for the same reason.

It is precisely this notion that Kelley articulates in his critique of sixteenth-century continental universities which, he asserts, 'were not uniformly cordial to the new discipline', simply because for 'a theologically oriented educational establishment, history could be as threatening as innovative natural philosophy'. Equally forceful is Bouwsma, who maintains that the counter-reformation, cognizant of the inherent dangers of history, 'proposed to absorb history, even earlier than the physical sciences, into the larger structure of dogma'.[328]

Nothing comparable to the study of continental renaissance historiography has been attempted for England, partly because it produced few, if any, innovative theorists before the seventeenth century. Still, the bleak conclusions drawn by schol-

---

[327] L. F. Dean, 'Tudor theories of history writings', *University of Michigan Contributions in Modern Philology* i (1947), 15; William Camden, *The History of the most renowned and victorious Princess Elizabeth*, ed. W. T. MacCaffrey (Chicago 1970), pp. xv–xvi.

[328] Kelley, 'Johann Sleidan and the origins of history as a profession', 583; Bouwsma, 'Three types of 'historiography in post-renaissance Italy', 308.

ars of Italian, French, and German historiography have been reproduced—spontaneously—by historians investigating the emergence of 'politic history' in England as well. Dean, for example, claims that 'historical theory and composition in Tudor times were apt to reflect the desire of political and clerical officialdom to maintain the *status quo*', thus expressly making the institutions of higher learning 'a conservative force'. Fussner views the 'historical attack on authority' as 'scarcely less devastating than the scientific', since the discipline ceased to be 'the submissive servant of faith'. And Christopher Hill—who has been relentless in promulgating the guilty verdict concerning the conservative nature of the English universities and their opposition to change of any sort—likens the new history to the new science by comparing the status of the former at seventeenth-century Oxford and Cambridge to that of sociology in the 1960s: popular with undergraduates and suspected by dons.[329]

It is not my intention to assess here this common perception concerning the similarity between the reaction of religious orthodoxy to both science and history in early modern Europe, and the consequences for the mouthpieces of orthodoxy—the universities. It is questionable, however, whether the English Church had the same coercive powers possessed by the Catholic Church on the continent. Nor is the perception of a policy of intervention from above—subverting the open and disinterested practice of history—justified. Nevertheless, before this latter assumption can be tested, the ideals animating the study of history and the role of history within the universities must first be examined.

In the seventeenth century history was viewed as a repository for literary, moral, and political lessons; hence, the attitude of humanist theorists that history was both central to the curriculum and yet fraught with dangers for impressionable, unprincipled youth. To offset this potential harm, they developed strict rules regulating the manner in which history should be pursued and the sort of authors appropriate for each stage of education. In terms of the curriculum, this concept translated itself into a precise progression of historical lessons tailored to the age of the student, his mental and moral capacity, and his vocation. This pyramid vision of teaching history both accounts for the exclusion of key works from early stages of study and the repetitive diet of 'approved' historians. While new texts and authors were introduced at various stages of a student's education, texts previously examined in one context or as a means of inculcating a particular literary or moral lesson were studied once again in order to explore a different dimension. This diversity of roles assigned to history also explains the seeming contradiction in the writings of various theorists of education from Erasmus to Locke, who appear to condemn and condone history within the compass of the same treatise. In fact, however, these authors merely sanction or disapprove of certain authors or specific lessons of history within the limited context of educating youth.

---

[329] Dean, 'Tudor theories of history writings', 15–16; Hill, *Intellectual Origins of the English Revolution*, 175–6.

The principles guiding late renaissance perceptions of the appropriate schooling in history are recapitulated by Jean Bodin in the second chapter of his *Methodus ad facilem historiarum cognitionem* (1566), where he emphasizes the importance of the correct reading of histories: 'It is not enough to have a quantity of historical works at home, unless one understands the use of each and in what order and manner each ought to be read.' Bodin distinguishes clearly between the mature author of histories and the inexperienced reader. The former, he argues, should not be reproved for composing specialized histories, as 'not all subjects should be treated by every writer, nor can they be, since each with infinite labor and diligence collects only as much as he can gather'. It is the reader who should be discouraged from premature concentration: 'I believe that this reproach applies, not to the writing, but rather to the reading of histories, whose fragments, if they are torn apart, will not cohere to each other or to the whole.' Bodin then proceeds to delineate the conventional method to follow. The student should first acquaint himself with a brief chronological chart—nor does the chart need be wholly accurate since the reader will acquire a better one later—which he should follow up with a brief universal history. 'Then from the general we move on little by little to the details, still in the order in which they are arranged in the tables of chronicles.' Thus in a steady methodical and chronological manner the student would acquire knowledge of the succession of nations and empires until he arrived at the present. At all times Bodin recommends the pursuit of the general before the particular and, therefore, the reading of a short epitome as an introduction to a more detailed book; Florus should be read before Livy, Justinus prior to Diodorus Siculus—an approach productive of 'unparalleled advantage'.[330]

Bodin, of course, was not original in defining such a programme, but the prestige enjoyed by his *Methodus* in England[331]—and the predilection of modern scholars to use this book as a yardstick to measure early modern historical theory and practice—warrants a detailed description of Bodin's views. Moreover, his specifications were emulated across the channel by English theorists, who also began to advocate the continuous interplay between the general and the particular as well as the strict emphasis on an ordered time sequence.

By the seventeenth century, however, a different kind of historical manual had come to corner the educational market in England, treatises like Vossius' enormous *Ars historica* or Degory Wheare's more manageable, and better-suited to beginners, *De ratione et methodo legendi historias dissertatio* (1623). True, Bodin briefly addressed the proper method for reading histories, and succinctly evaluated the chief historians. Yet educational considerations were incidental to his chief aim, which was to appraise the theoretical foundations underlying historiography and the affinity of history and politics. Thus the *Methodus*, like most other treatises commonly grouped

---

[330] Jean Bodin, *Method for the Easy Comprehension of History*, trans. B. Reynolds (New York 1969), 20–7.

[331] For a preliminary survey, see L. F. Dean, 'Bodin's *Methodus* in England before 1625', *Studies in Philology* xxxix (1942), 160–6.

under the rubric of 'artes historicae',[332] was beginning to be seen as inadequate, since the concern of those involved with the education of youth was only with the *reading*, not writing, of history. While not the case today, contemporaries kept the two categories distinct within the educational process; history-writing was viewed as unsuitable for undergraduates and relegated instead to the domain of 'professionals'—those who had completed their formal education and were actively engaged in the affairs of state or the pursuit of erudition.[333]

Unlike the dense and difficult *Methodus*, Wheare's manual was straightforward in articulating its pedagogical aims. Wheare stated outright that he intended the course of lectures he had delivered during his first year as Camden professor of history at Oxford—and which metamorphosed into his *Method*—to serve as no more than an annotated reading-list of the best authors: 'I have made it my business to propose, especially to my young hearer, a thread of histories disposed in such a right order, as he may from it learn the distinct changes and varieties of times, and the series of the great transactions that have passed in the world, down to our own age.' In a similar commitment to pedagogy, Matthias Prideaux warned the reader of his own manual: 'Expect no more here (good reader) then the title promiseth; that is, an introduction, not to rest on as satisfied, but to lead thee to larger volumes.'[334]

The manuals of Wheare and Prideaux enjoyed immense popularity. Wheare's *Method* was printed at least ten times, in both Latin and English, between 1623 and 1700, a popularity that Wheare's English translator openly boasted about. Matthias Prideaux's *An Easy and Compendious Introduction for Reading ... Histories* rivalled the popularity of Wheare's *Method*. First published in 1648 by the son of John Prideaux—the former rector of Exeter College, who was said by Wood to have been the actual author of the text—the book had gone through five editions by 1672, the last of which tallied 1,500 copies as we learn from the inventory of the publisher, Ann Lichfield, who died shortly thereafter.[335]

Like Bodin before them, the English authors of manuals and writers of advice continued to stress the observance of strict guidelines, cherishing always the

---

[332] See in general J. L. Brown, *The* Methodus ad facilem historiarum cognitionem *of Jean Bodin: a critical study* (Washington DC 1939); G. Spini, 'The art of history in the Italian counter-reformation' in *The Late Italian Renaissance 1525–1630*, ed. E. Cochrane (New York 1970), 91–133; G. Cotroneo, *I trattati dell'Ars Historica* (Naples 1971).

[333] The intention is made clear not only from the title of Wheare's book—as well as various advice manuals for the study of history such as John Hales's 'The method of reading profane history' or Thomas Hobbes's 'Of reading history'—but by explanatory statements like the one also made by Hobbes. The latter did not aim, he wrote, to prescribe 'the best way to an historiographer, but onely to shew the meanes how by readinge them to reape the most benefit for a mans private instruction'. F. O. Wolf, *Die neue Wissenschaft des Thomas Hobbes* (Stuttgart 1969), 160.

[334] Degory Wheare, *The Method and Order of Reading both Civil and Ecclesiastical Histories*, trans. Edmund Bohun (Oxford 1685), 131; Matthias Prideaux, *An Easy and Compendious Introduction for Reading all sorts of Histories* (Oxford 1648), 'To the reader'. Given the fondness of Englishmen for 'advice literature', it is quite likely that Wheare published his manual, at least in part, since he did not want to be bothered with private requests. Prideaux's manual was originally composed for the private benefit of Sir Thomas Reynell.

[335] Wheare, *Method*, 4–5; Wood, *Athenae* iii. 268; OUA chancellor's ct inventories s.v. Ann Lichfield; Madan, *Oxford Books* iii. 40, 188, 270.

principle of the general before the specific. 'Before you come to read the acts of any people', wrote John Hales (fellow of Merton 1606–13), 'as those that intend to go to bowls, will first see and view the ground upon which they are to play; so it shall not be amiss to you, first, to take a general view of that ground which you mean more particularly to traverse.' In a similar manner, Wheare advised the use of a short overview before one entered the 'vast ocean', since it would allow the student 'to contemplate with ease the whole body' of history before the foundations of the subject had been firmly laid. Underneath Gilbert Burnet's colourful rhetoric is the same plain principle that animated contemporary thought: 'In discoursing of geography and history, the method of painters is to be followed, who first draw the ruder draughts, and mark the proportions; afterwards filling them up with their true colours.'[336]

Another principle delineated by English and continental theorists in their discussions of the proper method for studying history—and one generally glossed over by modern scholars—concerns timing and the requisite qualifications for each stage. As a large portion of the study of history was expected to be carried out independently by the student, such study was dependent upon sufficient mastery of the languages necessary to read the histories in the original and, even more important, a student's religious and moral readiness to encounter and digest the lessons of this 'teacher of life'. As Milton put it: 'He who would write of worthy deeds worthily must write with mental endowments and experience of affairs not less than were in the doer of the same.'[337]

This moral and religious component was particularly crucial in view of the many alternative and conflicting forms of conduct that history provided. For the advanced student of history, the sole arbiter between right and wrong was his own judgement. Indeed, since it was believed that not until students had already completed their course of studies could they be expected to discriminate on the basis of reason, not passion, the domain of politics was specifically excluded from the early stages of the study of history. As Gilbert Burnet cautions: 'Only politics he must not study, nor learne intrigues, except it be for mere information, for a young man is not capable of that discretion which is requisite for the management of affairs. Though he may be perhaps sufficiently able to contrive and suggest good councells, yet there is a certain subtleness, closenes, and *leger de main* requisite in a states man, which a young man cannot know how to practyse.'[338]

The predilection of youth to follow passion rather than reason became an overriding concern among humanists quick to realize the ease with which the Roman,

---

[336] John Hales, 'The method of reading profane history' in *The Works of the Ever Memorable Mr. John Hales of Eaton* (3 vols Glasgow 1765) i. 165; Wheare, *Method*, 38; Clarke, *Bishop Gilbert Burnet as Educationist*, 46.

[337] Milton, *Complete Prose Works* v, p. xxiv.

[338] Clarke, *Bishop Gilbert Burnet as Educationist*, 74–5. Burnet recollected a youthful reproach he received from Archbishop Sharp, after he had composed, as a young man, a letter suggesting reforms of ecclesiastical abuses. When Sharp interviewed Burnet, he chided him on how 'young men understood not government and ought not to meddle in it'. Cited ibid. 213 n.

and to a lesser extent the Greek, past were capable of evoking powerful, and not altogether desirable, emotions. Impressionable young students, Erasmus feared, could not be expected to draw the right lessons when confronted with the pernicious portrayals of wicked majesty among the ancients: 'Now I shall not deny that a great fund of wisdom may be gathered from reading the historians, but you will also draw out the very essence of destruction from these same sources unless you are forearmed and read with discretion.' To circumscribe the danger and prevent the student from being swept away when reading about those 'great raging robbers', Achilles, Xerxes, Cyrus, Darius, and Caesar, the prior inculcation of strict Christian principles, moral precepts, and proper judgement were deemed essential. Such a moral foundation would ensure that the discerning future statesman was not deceived by the feigned clemency of Caesar in 'preparing and bolstering up his tyrannical way', but drew the fitting lesson of how 'earnestly' he should win the love of his subjects.[339]

Even humanists who did not share Erasmus' celebrated aversion towards history advocated similar caution. Without exception they followed Aristotle and other ancients who held that young men were ill equipped for civic knowledge. As Vives maintained, 'practical wisdom, is born from its parents, judgment and experience' and, therefore, 'wisdom is not to be looked for in youth, nor in young men whilst they lack experience'. Judgement and wisdom were the fruits of a lengthy process involving both theory and practice—the knowledge of books as well as of men. Hence, the pursuit of the political dimension of history, even for noblemen, was relegated to the domain of the mature student, the culmination of the educational process. Inherent in such an attitude was the tenet that 'politics' (encompassing politic history as well as contemporary and national history) constituted a 'profession' forbidden to young students, as were theology, medicine, and law.[340]

The assignment of certain authors or portions of a historical work to students, therefore, had an immediate purpose, as did the initial exclusion of certain authors and texts. Hence, when Sir Thomas Elyot recommended Livy, Xenophon, Quintus Curtius, and Tacitus to the future governor, he specifically concentrated on the literary and ethical precepts to be extracted from these authors. Indeed, precisely because the more profound lessons afforded by history were not to be acquired hastily, Elyot deemed the reading of Caesar and Sallust inappropriate at an early age,

---

[339] Desiderius Erasmus, *The Education of a Christian Prince*, ed. L. K. Born (New York 1968), 201–2.

[340] *Vives: on education*, ed. Watson, 228. Elsewhere Vives also argued that histories should be read 'when men are of ripe age': ibid. 249. See also Woodward, *Studies in Education During the Age of the Renaissance*, 199–200. Almost two centuries later Bishop Burnet admonished: 'but never s[h]ould either boy or youth hear a word of policy; for this of all things makes them become most arrogant and vain. And woe to that land where the young nobility begin to think of policy, and mending the state: for their arrogant selfe conceit, together with their hardy forwardnes and violence, will not fail to subvert and ruine it, and to this among other reasons I do not stick to impute most of our late disorders'. Clarke, *Bishop Gilbert Burnet as Educationist*, 47.

for their compendious writynge to the understandynge wherof is required an exact and perfect iugement, and also for the exquisite ordre of bataile and continuinge of the historie
without any varietie, wherby the payne of studie shulde be alleviate, they two wolde be
reserved untyll he that shall rede them shall se some experience in semblable matters.[341]

Although humanist theorists were unanimous in their philosophy of education,
stressing the centrality of history while at the same time carefully monitoring its
allotment, they held divergent opinions concerning specific authors in accordance
to personal preferences of style and content. Thus Cleland, who forcefully argued
that the reading of history 'should be the chiefest study of a young noble man, *when
he commeth to any perfection of speech and understanding*', criticized even more emphatically than Elyot the use of ancient historians for the purpose of teaching Latin and
Greek. When reading Livy, Caesar, or Plutarch, Cleland exhorted, the emphasis
should be placed not on 'grammatical construction', but on the 'conjunction of
minds'—that is 'deeds, and not words, which the pupil should have for the cheife
object and subject in that study'.[342]

The prevailing wisdom, then, dictated that the mastery of language, the strengthening of memory, and the sharpening of reason should precede and set the stage
for the cultivation of judgement. This bias determined the recommended educational policy for noblemen and commoners alike. Francis Bacon argued in 1595
that 'young students are better satisfied with a flowing easy style than with excellent matter in harsh words', and his prescribed course of study for the earl of
Rutland was arranged accordingly. Similar principles animated Thomas Barlow,
who urged scholars and prospective divines to 'bestowe their time and paines getting the languages especially ... and inflexing in their memoryes the canons and
summes of sciences, and historie, and such other studyes as tend chiefely to furnish the memory, but not in studyes that require most judgement'.[343]

The strict correlation of age and judgement continued to command universal
respect in England. In one of his earliest pamphlets John Milton recollected that
he had read at Cambridge some of the best orators and historians, 'whose matter
me thought I loved indeed, but as my age then was, so I understood them'.[344]
Later, in *Of Education*, Milton further encapsulated the humanist ideal by making
politics and history the culmination of his prescribed curriculum, when

yeers and good generall precepts will have furnisht [students] more distinctly with that act
of reason which in ethics is called *proairesis*: that they may with some judgement contemplat
upon morall good and evill. Then will be required a speciall reinforcement of constant and
sound endoctrinating to set them right and firm, instructing them more amply in the knowledge of vertue and the hatred of vice.

[341] Sir Thomas Elyot, *The Boke Named the Governour*, ed. H. S. Croft (2 vols repr. New York 1967) i.
85–90. The quote is on pp. 85–6.
[342] Cleland, *The Institution of a Young Noble Man*, 83 (emphasis added).
[343] *Works of Francis Bacon*, ed. Spedding, Ellis, and Heath ix. 25; '*A Library for Younger Schollers*', ed.
Dejordy and Fletcher, 38.
[344] Milton, *Complete Prose Works* i. 889. The allusion is to 1 Cor. 13. 11: 'When I was a child, I spake
as a child, I understood as a child, I thought as a child.'

Only after such objectives had been accomplished could the student proceed with the study of politics and 'choise histories'.[345]

Towards the end of the century John Locke summarized the conventional wisdom: 'As nothing teaches, so nothing delights more than history. The first of these recommends it to the study of grown men, the latter makes me think it the fittest for a young lad, who as soon as he is instructed in chronology . . . should then have some Latin history put into his hand.' Despite his keen recognition of the pleasure principle at work in many a schoolboy's love of history, Locke none the less asserted that in the early stages of education the teaching of history ought to be subordinate to rhetoric, and that the choice of authors 'be directed by the easiness of the stile'. He dissented only marginally from other educators by endorsing a more extensive use of historical texts in the early stages of education for the better teaching of language. He further recommended that the easiest Latin historians, and not grammatical drilling, be introduced first: the 'pleasantness of the subject inviting [the student] to read, the language will insensibly be got.' The study of Justinus, Eutropius, and Quintus Curtius should, therefore, prepare the student for the subsequent pursuit of Cicero, Virgil, and Horace.[346]

Gilbert Burnet also joined language, morality, and history into a compact and orderly enterprise, in which the study of language was based upon, and accompanied by, 'vertuous documents' that 'must be a very proper exercise for the raw and unripened capacities' of young students:

But because a boy cannot be much taken with long lectures of morality, history s[h]ould be the frequentest object of his longest discourses, and by this meannes as a boy shall be often released from the drudging pennance of learning a language, which chequer work in his study cannot but much please him, so he shall also learne things, both plain, suitable to his capacities, and usefull. As likewise, since all boyes naturally love talking about histories, he shall be hereby much enamoured of his master's company, and made to preferre it to many of his idle games.[347]

Although utility and 'self-improvement' have thus far been singled out as the qualities underlying early modern theories of teaching history, the pleasure principle noted by Locke also played a role—albeit an ambivalent one—in the recommended pyramidal progression of historical lessons. Unanimous in their exclusion of the graver aspects of history from the curriculum, renaissance theorists were equally agreed in their insistence that the pleasure to be got from reading history, though important, should not outweigh and thus jeopardize the gravity of the lessons history offered. Hobbes articulated the concern that the captivating nature of the subject-matter might overwhelm the young man, especially in view of the propensity of youth to follow passion rather than judgement:

[345] Milton, *Complete Prose Works* ii. 396, 400.
[346] *The Educational Writings of John Locke*, ed. Axtell, 293–4.
[347] Clarke, *Bishop Gilbert Burnet as Educationist*, 45–7.

I saw that, for the greatest part, men came to the reading of history with an affection much like that of the people in Rome: who came to the spectacle of the gladiators with more delight to behold their blood, than their skill in fencing. For they be far more in number, that love to read of great armies, bloody battles, and many thousands slain at once, than that mind the art by which the affairs both of armies and cities be conducted to their ends.[348]

Understandably educators warned against reading history solely for its inherent pleasure. The concentration on 'the naked and simple relations of things, and the accounts of great actions', stated Wheare, would certainly entertain a student, yet such delight could be derived equally from reading fables: 'But the reader we are now forming, ought to go beyond these things; for our end is not pleasure, but improvement, and that which is the ultimate end of all histories, that we may be taught to live well and happily.' Locke carried the analogy a step further when he berated 'antiquity and history, as far as it is designed only to furnish us with story and talk. For the stories of Alexander and Caesar, no farther than as they instruct us in the art of living well, and furnish us with observations of wisdom and prudence, are not one jot to be preferred to the history of Robin Hood or the seven wise masters.'[349]

Despite this oft-repeated cautionary advice, students frequently succumbed to their passion for history, as they did for poetry, abandoning other studies on the way, to the concern of parents, the dismay of tutors, and to their own subsequent penitence. I have already had occasion to mention Richard Granville, but many other young Oxonians strayed from the straight and narrow path of moderation. Samuel Woodforde recalled how he idled his undergraduate years away at Wadham College in the late 1650s: 'Coming pretty ripe from Paul's School, I was too good to learn, and was so proud as to think myself almost as good a scholar as my tutor.' Consequently he followed his fancy by reading the Roman historians instead of pursuing more serious studies, and 'added justly' to his 'shame' when 'on the Sundays' he wrote his 'discourse *de triumpho romano*'. William Wake, the future archbishop of Canterbury, who matriculated from Trinity College in 1673, also lamented (retrospectively) how, during his first two years as an undergraduate, he lost a taste for the arduous tasks of logic and philosophy and applied himself 'more to the classic authors, which were much more easy to be understood and more pleasing to [him]'.[350]

Within this framework the seemingly irreconcilable argument between Bartholomew Keckermann and Gerard Johannes Vossius over the appropriate audience for the study of history may be better understood. The former emphasized the primacy of method and the need to inculcate precepts before exposing

---

[348] *Hobbes's Thucydides*, ed. R. Schlatter (New Brunswick 1975), 8.

[349] Wheare, *Method*, 308; *The Educational Writings of John Locke*, ed. Axtell, 409.

[350] Ferrell, 'An imperfect diary of a life', 141; E. N. Hooker, 'The early poetical career of Samuel Woodforde' in *Essays Critical and Historical dedicated to Lily B. Campbell* (New York 1950), 88–9; N. Sykes, *William Wake* (2 vols Cambridge 1957) i. 10.

the student to examples, which, he believed, constituted the essence of history. Hence, for Keckermann, it was 'absurd for one to desire to read seriously and professedly, and to observe histories, which are nothing but examples of morality and politicks, before he has learned the rules and method of morality and policy'. Vossius, for his part, retorted by arguing that just as it was possible to learn a language without first acquiring the rules of grammar, so there was no reason why examples could not be advanced before precepts.[351]

In this debate between two of the most influential educators of the seventeenth century Degory Wheare sided with Keckermann:

In the hearer of ethicks, or politicks, there is required in the first place judgment ... that he may judg well concerning the rules of actions. And in the next place is required a well-disposed mind, that he may with dexterity endeavour to bring into use the precepts he hath received. And in the self-same manner it is necessary for the reader of histories to have the faculty of apprehending whatever examples he reads, and judging well of them. And then, that he should have an inclination and propensity of mind to follow what is good, and to shun and avoid what is evil: and of turning all he meets with to his use and advantage. *For the principal of history is practice, and not knowledge or contemplation* ... And therefore there are some men of very great learning, who assert there is hardly any sort of study which seems to require more sagacity, judgment, experience and prudence, than the reading history, which is the best mistress of civil conversation.[352]

Yet the contrast between Keckermann and Wheare on the one hand and Vossius on the other is deceptive, since it did not centre on *whether* any historical authors should be read by young students. Nor did the theorists disagree about the inappropriateness of familiarizing neophytes with the ultimate goal of the study of history. Each side simply addressed a different distinctive aim of history. While Keckermann and Wheare concentrated on the application of history to politics as the culmination of the study of that discipline, Vossius was ultimately concerned with history writing. Nevertheless, just as the former two proscribed the study of politic history for undergraduates, so Vossius explicitly excluded history-writing from the domain of the novice. Furthermore, neither Keckermann nor Wheare doubted the wisdom of assigning ancient historians to undergraduates for purposes other than politic history.

The solemnity with which *utilitas* and *voluptas*, the twin purposes of history, were propagated during the early modern period is indicative of the thought given to the overall integration of history into the curriculum, an attitude that may be lost on the modern reader just as the renaissance fixation with rules and method may ring strange in the modern ear. Thus, comparing these humanist theorists with those who 'regarded history as an autonomous field', Kelley can find little of appeal

---

[351] Both opinions are quoted in Wheare, *Method*, 300.

[352] Ibid. 297–317; the quotation is from pages 298–9. For a meticulous study of Vossius' historical thought, see N. Wickenden, 'Early modern historiography as illustrated by the work of G. J. Vossius (1577–1649)' (Cambridge Ph.D. thesis 1963). I am grateful to Dr Wickenden for allowing me to consult a revised version of his dissertation, which has now been published.

in the 'especially artificial and conservative "methodisers" like Aconcio and Vossius, who hoped to reduce history to—or perhaps better, to dissolve it in—a logical system'.[353] Yet, as this scrutiny of the underlying assumptions of the theorists should demonstrate, the two objectives of history—scholarship and its ancillary position to rhetoric and ethics—were not necessarily incompatible: neither the employment of historical texts in the service of rhetoric nor the utilization of history to convey ethical values and promote prudence negate the concurrent perception of history as an autonomous discipline.

As in the case of philosophy and logic, both gentlemen and prospective divines were subject to the same statutes and the same education in history.[354] Ever since the middle of the sixteenth century, however, when gentlemen began to flock to Oxford and Cambridge in increasing numbers, their formal course of studies tended to diverge both in depth and breadth, proportionate to the length of their stay at the university. This sometimes gave an impression of superficiality and could become the butt of satire. John Earle's caricature of 'a young gentleman of the university', for example, is indicative of contemporary perceptions of the educational concerns of a fashionable youth: 'Of all things he endures not to be mistaken for a scholar'; his tutor reads 'some short history' with him, and his 'main loytering is at the library, where he studies arms and books of honour, and turns a gentleman critick in pedigrees'.[355]

Earle's caricature is lent substance by his older contemporary at Merton College, John Hales who, when a friend requested his advice on a method to instruct gentlemen in reading history, obliged by sending what he considered a modest reading-list. Hales assured his correspondent that the prescribed course would suffice since it aimed at bringing 'up a young gentleman, who in all likelihood [would] not be over-willing to take too much pains'. Half a century later, Humphrey Prideaux of Christ Church responded to a similar request by curtly stating that if the person for whom the advice was intended 'be a gentleman, Dr. Hoels Universal History in English [William Howell *An Institution of General History*] will be sufficient for him'. On the other hand, were he a scholar, Prideaux would have assigned a comprehensive reading-list of the best Greek and Latin historians, and in the original tongues.[356]

In general, however, the prevailing wisdom underlying the prescription of historical works by university tutors was similar to that underlying literary ones. Young students were encouraged to follow a protracted and reflective method in their reading of ancient historians. And the assignments of manualists from Richard

[353] Kelley, 'The theory of history', 760.

[354] See pp. 216–17 above. Louis Wright made this cogent observation concerning the cultural influence of the élite, apropos history: 'what was useful in aristocratic education was soon recommended as a means of inculcating good qualities in the sons of shopkeepers'. L. B. Wright, *Middle-Class Culture in Elizabethan England* (Chapel Hill 1935), 298.

[355] Earle, *Microcosmography*, 67.

[356] Hales, 'The method of reading profane history', 175–6; *Letters of Prideaux*, ed. Thompson, 63.

Holdsworth before the civil war to Daniel Waterland in the early years of the eighteenth century make it clear that tutors invariably instructed their charges to proceed from general surveys to particular authors, to devote several weeks to a careful reading of the assigned Greek and Roman historians and augment such study with some application to geographical and mythological works whenever appropriate.

Thus for the first three months of his university career Holdsworth's student was instructed to read Thomas Godwin's *Roman Antiquities* and Justinus' epitome of Trogus Pompeius which would have furnished him with a broad survey of Greek and Roman history, customs, and institutions. After applying the next fifteen months to the study of languages, the student resumed his reading of histories during the summer of the second year with a close study of Florus, Sallust, and Quintus Curtius. Then, during the first three months of his fourth year, he would be expected to dedicate his afternoons to reading Cluverius' history, alongside Livy and Suetonius. For the advanced student, Holdsworth assigned, among other authors, Plutarch, Xenophon, Herodotus, Thucydides, and Tacitus. The course remained virtually the same at the turn of the eighteenth century, except that Greek history was more fully integrated into the curriculum. Waterland's first-year student was assigned the reading of Xenophon's *Cyropaedia* during the months of March and April, while Justinus and Cornelius Nepos were to occupy his afternoon hours in September and October. The following year, Caesar and Sallust were his diet in July and August, while the first eight months of the fourth year were devoted to a close study of Thucydides and Livy. The advanced students were assigned Herodotus, Plutarch, Herodian, Quintus Curtius, Suetonius, Tacitus, and Florus.[357]

Such a pace may seem sluggish, but early modern scholars adhered wholeheartedly to the Baconian maxim concerning the proper method of reading, according to which a select few texts were carefully 'to be chewed and digested'. Nor did the already crammed undergraduate curriculum leave any room for additional authors. This point was made explicit in John Evelyn's temperate rebuke of his grandson when the precocious youth wrote from Oxford requesting a fresh supply of history books: 'For how soon can you have read Herodotus, Thucydides, Polybius, Xenophon, Diodorus, whilst you are learning and applying yourself to the learning of those arts and things proper for the university?'[358] A more important justification of this pace was the fact that the historical texts were employed concurrently to impart language and ethics. This coalescence of history, moral philosophy, and language was clearly articulated by Arthur Mansell when he informed Sackville Crow in 1654 that during the afternoons his son 'already looks into Tacitus in Latin and I talk to him of Thucydides in Greek. He must not and shall not be altogether a stranger to the divine moralities of Plutarch and Seneca.'[359]

---

[357] Fletcher, *The Intellectual Development of John Milton* ii. 624–48; Waterland, *Works* iv. 407–15.

[358] W. G. Hiscock, *John Evelyn and his Family Circle* (London 1955), 207; From a subsequent letter written by the diarist it is evident that his grandson read these books in Greek: *Diary and Correspondence of John Evelyn*, ed. Bray iv. 41.

[359] BL Add. MS 27,606, fo 6.

The homogeneity suggested by the various tutors' manuals and letters of advice concerning the close attention to be paid by undergraduates to only a handful of ancient historians is confirmed by student diaries, correspondences, and library catalogues. The more affluent undergraduates could certainly afford to purchase additional history books and some, indeed, acquired various contemporary historians.[360] However, the similarities between the actual course of studies taken by the undergraduates, regardless of their social background, are far more instructive. Nearly all owned a couple of universal or Roman histories and the approved ancient historians. Many also possessed a methodological manual on the study of history. George Trosse, for example, who entered Pembroke College in 1657, recalled in his diary that he read many volumes of the Latin authors and a few Greek historians, such as Thucydides and Herodotus, while John Potenger probably depicted his own course of studies during the 1660s when he advised his grandson to 'keep an intimate acquaintance' particularly with Livy, Caesar, Sallust, Quintus Curtius, Thucydides, Appian, and Herodian.[361] Edward Bernard of St John's recorded in his 1658 library catalogues the cost of the books he acquired while an undergraduate. The 1653 Leiden edition of Livy (in three volumes) for example cost him 4s, while for each of the other historians he purchased—including Florus, Justin, Caesar, Aelianus, Quintus Curtius, and Tacitus—he paid between 6d and 1s 6d.[362]

The pattern remained constant throughout the second half of the seventeenth century. Henry Herbert carried with him to Oxford in 1670 the same authors read by Bernard, save that Herbert brought Herodian instead of Aelianus. Henry Fleming, who entered Queen's College in 1678, brought along (or purchased in subsequent months), Florus, Godwin, Quintus Curtius, Suetonius, Sallust, and Eutropius, authors he read in his 'spaire hours from logick'. Hungry for additional readings, he urged his father in 1680 to send him 'some geography bookes with maps in, and some Latin histories ... for they are soe very dear, that [he] would buy as few of them as [he] could'. A slightly younger contemporary, James Wilding, of St Mary Hall, owned in 1682 a small collection of history books, including Florus, Livy, Suetonius, Sallust, Godwyn, Procopius, Justinus, Xenophon, Cornelius Nepos, and Tacitus.[363]

The persistence with which ancient history was prescribed for undergraduates

---

[360] Richard Myddelton, who came up to Brasenose College in 1671, bought, in addition to the ancient historians, Camden's *Annals* and *Remains*, Walton's *Lives*, Heylyn's *Help to History*, Heath's *Chronicle*, Castlemaine's *Dutch War*, Ralegh's *History of the World*, Milton's *History of England*, Bentivoglio's *The Wars in Flanders*, Spotiswood's *History of Scotland*, and various biographies and travel books. Nat. Lib. Wales, Chirk Castle MS 10,597.

[361] *The Life of ... George Trosse*, ed. A. W. Brink (Montreal and London 1974), 114; *Private Memoirs of John Potenger*, ed. Bingham, 3–4.

[362] Bodl. MS Lat. misc. f. 11, fo 20.

[363] BL Add. MS 37,157, fo 69; *The Flemings in Oxford* i. 253, 262, 290, 296, 318, 322–3; 'The account-book of an Oxford undergraduate', ed. Duff, 267–8. Locke's account books also indicate that his students purchased, in addition to the major historians, the epitomes by Florus, Justin, Eutropius, and Godwyn. See, for example, the various accounts in Bodl. MS Locke f. 11.

should not be understood by modern historians as disparagement of subsequent history. Since the intention of the consolidated curriculum was to lay the foundations for all ensuing studies, the study of ancient history not only facilitated the acquisition of language and the inculcation of moral principles, but also provided the essential framework for the subsequent study of medieval and 'modern' history. The latter were considered 'specialized' subjects, however, suitable for pursuit only by mature scholars. Consequently, any attempt to document the 'professional' career of a scholar in history and antiquities must necessarily deal with post-undergraduate education. Further limiting the students' contact with any history except ancient history (in addition to their crowded schedule) was their exclusion from public and college libraries. It was only in 1653, after he had graduated bachelor of arts, that Anthony Wood was first allowed to use the Arts End in the Bodleian Library and, 'being a constant student therein, he became acquainted with the places in the arts library ... where the books of English historie and antiquities stand.[364]

With this context of the aims and limitations of the undergraduate curriculum in mind, we can better understand the thinking behind the attempts to establish, on several occasions in the late sixteenth and early seventeenth centuries, an 'academy for the study of antiquity and history'. When the promoters (professional lawyers and antiquarians resident in or around London) sought to organize their meetings under royal charter, they felt the need to allay the fears of Oxford and Cambridge that the new society would harm the universities—much the same way as the trustees of Gresham College acted in the 1570s and the members of the Royal Society in the 1660s. To dispel any threat, the promoters promised that their 'society will not be hurtfull to eyther of the universities for yt shall not medle with the artes, philosophy, or other fynall studyes their professed. For this Society tendeth to the preservation of hystorye and antiquity of which the universities being busyed in the artes tak little care or regard.'[365] Such a manifesto, however, was not intended to imply that no history was taught at the universities. What the society of antiquaries intended to promote was medieval English history and antiquities—advanced studies that were not part of the undergraduate curriculum. As Woolf correctly observes, none of the papers read at the meetings were entitled 'history', not only because they dealt exclusively 'with things rather than men, with customs or institutions rather than with events', but also 'because they were devoid of moral or exemplary content' and the authors 'almost entirely unconcerned with the rhetorical conventions of form which applied to true history-writing'.[366]

Once the student had graduated BA, he was released from the vigilant supervision of a tutor and from the requirement to apply himself to the reading of select

[364] Wood, *Athenae* i, p. xxii.

[365] E. Flügel, 'Die älteste Englische akademie', *Anglia* xxxii (1909), 268.

[366] D. R. Woolf, 'Erudition and the idea of history in renaissance England', *Renaissance Quarterly* xl (1987), 21–2.

ancient historians; also liberated from the time-consuming obligation to apply himself to the study of logic and languages, he was now expected to expand significantly his range of studies by completing the reading of Roman and Greek historians as well as by paying increased attention to more recent history. Unfortunately, it is far more difficult to establish the exact course of study carried on independently by bachelors of art, who were not obliged to account for their studies in the manner prescribed for undergraduates. None the less, available commonplace books, letters, diaries, and library catalogues provide—through glimpses here and there—a reliable and uniform picture.

A Wadham student, in the early 1620s, for example, jotted down notes he had taken from Guicciardini, an author many young Oxonians read in the late sixteenth and early seventeenth centuries. Half a century later Alexander Pudsey of Magdalen College (MA 1661) can be found reading Camden's *Britannia*, Machiavelli's *Discorsi*, and Thomas Dempster's *Antiquitatum Romanonum.*[367] For other students more oblique references are available. In 1626 Thomas Crosfield recorded in his diary that he was reading the *Memoires* of Phillippe de Comines, a book Crosfield found seven years later in the library of the newly graduated MA Gerard Langbaine who also owned Giovanni Botero's *Delle relationi universali.*[368]

But it is from library catalogues that we derive the fullest account of the reading habits of scholars. Perusal of the surviving lists demonstrates how committed students were to the study of history. Thomas Tatham, for example, who graduated MA in 1573 and died a fellow of Merton College in 1586, had acquired Bodin's *Methodus*, Johann Carion's *Chronicorum libri tres*, Machiavelli's *Il Principe*, the *Loci communes de institutione principum* by Reinhardus Lorichius, three works by David Chytraeus—*De lectione historiarum*, the *Chronologia historiae Herodoti et Thucydidis*, and *De scribenda historia*, Paul Giovio's *Historiarum sui temporis*, Sleidan's *De quatuor summis imperiis*, Viperanus' *De scribenda historia*, and Henricus Pantaleon's *Chronographia ecclesiae christianae.*[369]

A quarter of a century later, the greater availability of books and the growing interest in English history was reflected in the library of Walter Browne (MA Corpus 1598), who died in 1613. Alongside the ancient historians—Thucydides, Herodotus, Xenophon, Plutarch, Herodian, Tacitus, Sallust, Suetonius, Livy, and

---

[367] QCL MS 438, fo 98ᵛ, cited in M. Todd, 'Seneca and the protestant mind: the influence of stoicism on puritan ethics', *Archiv für Reformationsgeschichte* lxxiv (1983), 188 n. 22; MCL MS 311, fos 5ʳ⁻ᵛ, 14, 54ᵛ.

[368] QCL MS 390, fos 20ᵛ, 66ᵛ. The Langbaine list is printed in *The Diary of Thomas Crosfield*, ed. Boas, 68. Comines could be found also in the library of John Hutton of New College, who died in 1653 when a BA of three years' standing. Hutton also owned historical works by Sleidan, Guicciardini, Contarini, and Busbecq: OUA chancellor's ct inventories s.v. Hutton.

[369] William Michell, who graduated MA in 1588 and died eleven years later, owned, in addition to a good collection of Greek and Roman historians, Machiavelli's *Il Principe* and *Discorsi*, Bodin's *République*, Stow's *Chronicle*, and Camden's *Britannia*. Robert Dowe, who died in 1588, owned Comines, Guicciardini's *History of Italy*, Kromer's *De origine et rebus gestis Polonorum*, Bembo's *Historia Veneta*, Giovo's *Commentario delle cose de Turchi*, Buchanan's *Rerum Scoticarum historia*, Stanihurst's *De rebus in Hibernia gestis*, and Camden's *Britannia*. OUA chancellor's ct inventories s.v. Michell, Dowe, and Tatham.

Quintus Curtius—Browne owned works by Bodin, Sleidan, Comines, Botero, and Guicciardini, as well as three works by Machiavelli. In addition, he purchased two works by Polydor Vergil, George Buchanan's *Rerum scoticarum historia*, John Selden's *Jani anglorum facies altera*, Samuel Daniel's *Historie of England*, a copy of the Magna Carta, John Norden's *Speculum Britanniae*, the *Mirrour of Magistrates*, Thomas Walsingham's *Historia brevis*, and John Hayward's *The first part of the Life and Raigne of King Henrie the IIII*. John English, who died the same year, had a more modest collection of history books but, in addition to such ancients as Sallust, Livy, Caesar, Tacitus, and Herodotus, English also possessed Carion, Pontanus, Dariot, Camden, and Stow.[370]

The foundation of the Camden professorship of history in 1622 was intended to augment the predominantly undergraduate-oriented teaching of history at Oxford—by elaborating on the guided tutorials received in the colleges—rather than to enhance 'research'. It was one of five chairs established at Oxford within a period of five years. Camden's motive in endowing the chair was to promote a subject close to his heart and, through remembering his alma mater, found a memorial to his name. He thus belonged to that distinguished lineage of devoted university men who, either having remained single or denied a male heir, proceeded in old age to assure themselves an alternative route to immortality through the endowment of such professorships.[371] Camden specifically intended the history professorship to cater for young scholars and concentrate on ancient history. Accordingly, it is against this background that the choice of Degory Wheare as the first incumbent and Florus as the author to be explicated should be seen.[372] From a modern point of view such choices may seem unfortunate, but they reflect contemporary ideals concerning the teaching of history. Moreover there is no reason to believe that had Brian Twyne been successful in his bid for the professorship, the course of study offered would have been fundamentally different.[373]

[370] OUA chancellor's ct inventories s.v. Browne; Costin, 'The inventory of John English', 120–1.

[371] For the general pattern see M. Feingold, 'Patrons and professors: the origins and motives for the endowment of new university professorships in seventeenth-century England' in G. A. Russell (ed.), *The 'Arabick' Interest of the Natural Philosophers in Seventeenth-Century England* (Leiden 1994), 109–27.

[372] See p. 333 above and, in general, W. H. Allison, 'The first endowed professorship of history and its first incumbent', *American Historical Review* xxvii (1922), 733–7; H. S. Jones, 'The foundation and history of the Camden chair', *Oxoniensia* viii–ix (1943–4), 169–92; Sharpe, 'The foundation of the chairs of history at Oxford and Cambridge'. From a letter sent to Camden by Henry Savile it appears that Camden initially referred to his projected chair as 'an humanity lecture', further testimony as to the intended audience. Thomas Smith, *V. Cl. Gulielmi Camdeni et illustrium virorum ad G. Camdenum epistolae* (London 1691), 314.

[373] Camden's conferring the reversion of the professorship on Twyne, so shortly after his selection of Wheare, need not be interpreted as reflecting any misgivings on Camden's part for not having selected a renowned antiquarian like Twyne in the first place. It seems more likely that Wheare was expected to retain the chair for only a short term *en route* to a more distinguished position. Certainly Twyne's somewhat inexplicable resignation from his living in 1623 may be interpreted in such a light, since by holding a living he was ineligible for the chair. Wheare was elected master of Gloucester Hall in 1626, but by then Camden was dead and, whatever his original intention had been, Wheare, to Twyne's chagrin, decided to keep both positions.

Evidence suggests that the Oxford authorities may have expected the incumbent of the chair to explicate ecclesiastical history and controversial divinity. Such an advanced course could be harnessed to the cause of protestantism, since many of the intense religious disputes with Catholics during the reign of James I turned on historical questions. Thus, when in 1615 Sir John Coke dispatched to Fulke Greville his advice concerning the history chair Greville was contemplating establishing at Cambridge, he had few doubts about the sort of history the professor should expound:

The chief use of this profession is now the defence of one church, and therein of one state. Our adversaries are alreadie worne out of scriptures and fathers and now hold at thier sheat anchor only by antiquitie and prescription: wherein if wee pursue them hard ... the verie view of times past wil so discover their ambition, covetousnes, impostures, tyrannies, treacheries and al the depths of hel in that Roman gulph that as by scriptures they lost us, so by stones they shall loose there own and shew there religion as now it standeth to be incompatible wth al free minds and estates ... Wherfore in my poore opinion it is now as necessarie to have diligent historians as learned divines.

When Greville ultimately founded his chair he opted for civil history, which he believed better suited the needs of the university.[374]

Camden certainly intended the auditors of the Oxford lecture to be younger scholars, an intention further codified in the Laudian statutes, which stipulated that all bachelors of art should attend the bi-weekly lectures on Florus 'or any other historians of ancient date and repute'.[375] The founder made his aim clear when he was informed that some misunderstanding had arisen concerning the responsibilities of the professor:

Whereas I understand there hath been some doubt and question made touching the subject of my lecture, and what kind of history I intended my reader should insist upon. I do hereby signify that it ever was and is my intention that (according to the practice of such professors in all the universities beyond the seas) hee should read a civil history, and therein make such observations *as might bee most usefull and profitable for the younger students of the university*, to direct and instruct them in the knowledge and use of history, antiquity, and times past.[376]

Camden wished largely to exclude ecclesiastical history and controversial divinity from the domain of the lectureship since he was convinced—as were all his contemporaries—that such topics were wholly inappropriate for young students, many of whom were the sons of gentlemen, and that they should be pursued only by mature scholars. For this reason Camden was satisfied with the 'laudable beginnings' of Wheare. From what he had heard of the lectures, they were 'well approved' of at Oxford. Yet, again, the university's hope for a professorship in ecclesiastical history indicates not an opposition to secular history but merely a dif-

---

[374] N. Farmer, 'Fulke Greville and Sir John Coke: an exchange of letters on a history lecture and certain Latin verses on Sir Philip Sidney', *Huntington Library Quarterly* xxxiii (1969–70), 217–36.

[375] *Statutes*, trans. Ward i. 23.

[376] Camden's letter of 6 January 1622/3 is quoted in Jones, 'The foundation and history of the Camden chair', 175 (emphasis added).

ferent order of priorities. Nor from Camden's point of view did his constraint on the duties of the professor reflect any significant hostility to ecclesiastical history. Rather, the former schoolmaster sincerely believed that the young members of the university would best benefit from a professorship of ancient history.

Although the lectures of the Camden professors were not intended for professional scholars, the auditors were presumed already to have acquired an adequate background knowledge of the ancient historians; for this reason the professor was called upon to deliver an advanced course of lectures on a chosen text. In the manner of the time, the assigned text served as a medium through which a comprehensive account of the life, milieu, and work of the selected Roman or Greek historian was given. Besides explicating both text and context and resolving omissions or discrepancies between texts, the lecturer was expected to summarize the entire corpus of ancient historians, orators, and poets. Thus, even if these lectures were not 'critical' in the modern sense of the word, a professor's profound knowledge of the classics ensured that an assiduous student could reap considerable benefit from attending them, assuming, of course, that the professors were diligent in their obligations, as was usually the case during the seventeenth century.

The qualifications of the first incumbent, Degory Wheare, are not easy to assess since, unfortunately, Wheare has been caught up in debates over modernity, which have produced sweeping judgements rather than conclusions grounded on evidence. Thus Christopher Hill's attempt to portray the first Camden professor as a 'modern' simply because he assumed Wheare to have been a puritan, a friend of John Pym (whose tutor he had been), and a lecturer on a 'modern' subject, has been matched by an equally unsubstantiated dismissal of Wheare as an intellectual and, more specifically, as a historian. Yet the evidence suggests that in both his capacity as professor and as principal of a hall at Oxford Wheare led the life of a pedagogue, not a scholar. His lectures and publications reveal a well-read man who was truly committed to the education of youth. Whether he was also interested in the study of medieval history and antiquities—as was Wheare's close friend Thomas Allen—cannot be determined. But there is no reason to assume that his knowledge was inferior to that of many of his contemporaries at Oxford who, though they published little, none the less left sufficient testimony of their erudition.[377]

The first Camden professor died in 1647. Four years earlier, following the death of Brian Twyne, Wheare attempted to procure a royal letter of recommendation that would have secured a reversion of the chair to his son Charles. Infuriated Oxonians foiled such an effort by advancing the names of more qualified candidates. The list included the names of John Gregory of Christ Church, Abraham

[377] H. R. Trevor-Roper, review of Hill's *Intellectual Origins of the English Revolution* in *History and Theory* v (1966), 67; Sharpe, 'The foundation of the chairs of history at Oxford and Cambridge', 130–3 (on those who belittled Wheare); H. A. Lloyd Jukes, 'Degory Wheare's contribution to the study and teaching of ecclesiastical history in England in the seventeenth century' in G. J. Cuming (ed.), *The Church and Academic Learning* (Leiden 1969), 193–203.

Woodhead of University College and Gerard Langbaine of Queen's. The latter was the ultimate choice, but by the time Wheare died Langbaine had already been elected provost of Queen's College. Charles Wheare stood as a candidate, yet convocation elected instead the 33-year-old Robert Waring of Christ Church, a good classical scholar and a wit who was serving at the time as a junior proctor. According to Wood, the election of Waring was secured thanks to a solid turnout in his favour by the Students of Christ Church. However, the new professor was given few, if any, opportunities to exercise his new responsibilities, as he was turned out by the parliamentary visitors on 14 September 1648.[378]

Already in 1646 Lewis du Moulin had petitioned parliament, hoping to obtain either a headship of house or a professorship, and on 4 August he was granted the Camden professorship. Two more years would elapse before he was installed. Du Moulin was French by birth, the son of the more famous Pierre du Moulin, and a staunch Calvinist who was described by Wood as 'a fiery, violent and hot headed Independent, a cross and ill-natur'd man'. He appears to have been unsuccessful as Camden professor for reasons only remotely related to his scholarly attainments. In 1662, when John Harmar was turned out of his Greek professorship, he published a pamphlet in which, *inter alia*, he attributed Oxford's decline to the appointment to lectureships of foreigners like Christian Ravius, Joshua Hoyle, and, above all, Lewis du Moulin, whom he vilified at length.[379] Du Moulin himself had elaborated extensively on this point a decade earlier in dedicating his inaugural oration to John Owen. Referring to the 'affronts and difficulties he had encountered on account of his foreign origin and accent', du Moulin insinuated obliquely that his lectures had scarcely been attended. However, he blamed the laziness of the students, rather than their difficulty in understanding his Latin accent, as the cause for the poor attendance. Du Moulin also complained that he was shunned because of the common English dislike of France and of foreigners in general. Regardless of the reasons, du Moulin certainly embarked upon his new position in the most inauspicious manner, for he obtained an initial dispensation from lecturing, after his inaugural lecture, presumably in order to attend to his medical practice in London, a practice he kept throughout his tenure as professor.[380]

Du Moulin is remembered today, if at all, as a polemicist. Whatever historical work he undertook was carried out to support his religious convictions. The closest du Moulin came to composing a historical work was an ecclesiastical history that he had apparently completed by the 1670s. The work seemed particularly pre-

[378] Jones, 'The foundation and history of the Camden chair', 178–9; Wood, *Athenae* iii. 453–4; Wood, *Life and Times* iii. 513; *Register*, ed. Burrows, 185–6, 236.

[379] Wood, *Fasti* ii. 128; John Harmar, *Vindiciae academiae oxoniensis* (Oxford 1662), 39–56. For Ravius see M. Feingold, 'Oriental studies', pp. 490–1 below. The Irishman Hoyle was appointed regius professor of divinity in 1648.

[380] *Lord's Journal* viii. 451; Wood, *Fasti* ii. 125–8; Lewis du Moulin, *Oratio auspicalis* (Oxford 1652), dedication, summarized in *The Correspondence of John Owen*, ed. P. Toon (Cambridge and London 1970), 51–2; F. N. L. Poynter, 'A seventeenth-century London plague document in the Wellcome Historical Medical Library', *Bulletin of the History of Medicine* xxxiv (1960), 365–72; *Register*, ed. Burrows, 202.

judiced and offensive to a churchman like Gilbert Burnet, who hoped that since he had been able to extract from the dying du Moulin a deathbed retraction of the latter's attacks on the English Church no one would publish the manuscript, a prospectus of which appeared in 1679.[381] Except for his inaugural oration, du Moulin's other publications were all controversial in nature. Certainly, had he carried his interests into the classroom he would have violated the terms of the professorship. But although no evidence survives to attest to his qualifications as Camden professor, du Moulin appears to have been a man of some parts, since Archbishop Ussher singled him out, as he did Thomas Barlow and Gerard Langbaine, for receipt of a presentation copy of the second part of the *Annales veteris testamenti* (1654). Also, according to Zagorin, du Moulin had as early as 1650 utilized Hobbes's doctrine of sovereignty, in his *The Power of the Christian Magistrate in Sacred Things*.[382]

Following Du Moulin's ejection in 1660, John Lamphire was elected professor. Like Waring, Lamphire had a reputation as a noted classical scholar and a wit, and was said by Wood to have been 'the natural droll' of that company of royalist wits residing in Oxford during the 1650s, where Lamphire practised as a physician following his ejection from his fellowship in 1648. In 1662 he was also elected principal of New Inn Hall, a position he exchanged the following year for the headship of Hart Hall, and for the next quarter of a century Lamphire led an active academic life, gaining the reputation of 'a good, generous and fatherly man, of a public spirit, and free from pharisaical leven, or the modish hypocrisy of the age he lived in'. Little is known of his scholarly attainments except that he was an avid collector of books and manuscripts. His publications consisted of various verses and 'other mens work', which he edited (with occasional emendation) from manuscripts he purchased. One such work was Thomas Lydiat's *Canones chronologici*, which Lamphire published in 1675.[383]

Lamphire's death in 1688 was followed by the election of Henry Dodwell as professor. Undoubtedly the most distinguished scholar to occupy the chair before the late nineteenth century—and the only professor before the twentieth century not to have been educated at Oxford—Dodwell owed his preferment to the machinations of John Mill and other Oxford friends who effected his election 'in their earnest desires to serve the interests of learning and religion'.[384] Dodwell was an exceptional classical scholar and highly respected chronologer, but his was not the sort of history that pleased the eighteenth-century taste. Even Gibbon, who appreciated Dodwell's immense erudition, remarked after reading the *Annales Quintilianei*

---

[381] *The Last Words of Lewis du Moulin*, ed. Gilbert Burnet (London 1680), 17; BL MS Harleian 3520B: article 5 contains the prospectus, 'Les Nouvelles Lumières pour le composition de l'histoire de l'église'.

[382] James Ussher, *The Whole Works*, ed. C. R. Elrington (17 vols Dublin 1847–64) xvi. 268; P. Zagorin, *A History of Political Thought in the English Revolution* (New York 1966), 71.

[383] Wood, *Athenae* i, p. xxv; Wood, *Fasti* ii. 235.

[384] *Biographia Britannica* (6 vols London 1747–66) v. 320–8; Wood, *Life and Times* iii. 263; Francis Brokesby, *The Life of Mr Henry Dodwell* (London 1715); A. B. Emden, 'The missing Dodwell papers', *St Edmund Hall Magazine* iii (1934), 87–93.

that 'the most minute fact or passage could not escape him, and his skill in employ-ing them is equal to his learning', yet the 'worst of this author is his method and style, the one perplexed beyond imagination, the other negligent to a degree of bar-barism'.[385]

Contemporaries, however, were more appreciative of Dodwell, and his brief tenure as Camden professor appears to have been overwhelmingly successful. James Gibson recalled that, as an undergraduate, he was taken by a friend to hear one of Dodwell's lectures, and 'the school was so thronged and crowded that he never either saw or heard of the like, so that there was no standing with ease, which made him get out (otherwise much against his will) before the lecture ... was ended'.[386] The refusal of Dodwell to take the new oaths following the Glorious Revolution—despite the immense pressure exerted on him from all quarters—finally resulted in his having to forfeit the chair in 1691. His place was taken by Charles Aldworth, a man noted more for political astuteness than for learning, who, if Hearne and Amhurst are to be believed, scarcely ever lectured.[387]

Besides Wheare, Dodwell is the only other seventeenth-century Camden profes-sor whose lectures have survived, and these enable us to discern the similarities, as well as significant differences, between the two lecturers. First, both utilized their respective texts in order to provide extensive general commentary on Roman his-tory. Wheare was undoubtedly inferior in his scholarship, and Florus a far easier text to explicate than the *Scriptores historiae augustae* opted for by Dodwell. More sig-nificantly, Wheare seems to have interpreted Camden's directions literally and pitched his course to the capacity of only a mildly sophisticated audience. Dodwell, on the other hand, was fully cognizant of the great improvements in undergradu-ate education during the seventeenth century and offered a course strikingly more intricate in content. In fact, his lectures paralleled the advanced course offered by Edward Pococke and the various Savilian professors. Thus in his inaugural lecture Dodwell addressed the issue of writing history and constructed the course along the lines of what may be considered a research seminar.

Beginning with a general introductory series of six lectures analysing the author-ship and time of composition of the *Scriptores historiae augustae*, Dodwell turned to an elaborate investigation of the life and times of the Emperor Hadrian. Nineteen numbered lectures—the last three of which were never delivered on account of his ejection from the professorship—were published by Dodwell in 1692. This hefty quarto of over 600 pages attests to both his erudition and his methodology. Extensive scrutiny of chronology, for example, was fitted into digressions on var-ious dates in Hadrian's life. Detailed discussions of Roman law, offices, and insti-

[385] *Gibbon's Journal to January 28th 1763*, ed. D. M. Low (New York 1929), 82. Gilbert Burnet voiced a different complaint about the great learning of the former professor. He grieved at Dodwell's 'extrav-agent notions, which have been too much drunk in by the clergy in my time, have weakened the power of the church, and soured men's minds more against it, than all the books wrote, or attempts made against it, could ever have done'. Burnet, *History of My Time* vi. 182.

[386] Hearne, *Collections* x. 154.

[387] Jones, 'The foundation and history of the Camden chair', 182–3.

tutions were interspersed throughout the course with regular resort to other historians and to literary texts. His enforced departure was indeed a sad loss for
Oxford.[388]

Thus far the discussion has sought to set out the ideals of humanist theorists concerning the teaching of history and show how such ideals translated into the undergraduate curriculum. Since politic history was believed to be inappropriate for the
younger scholar, it had a place only in the student's postgraduate education. Once
such ideals are properly understood we can dispel the prevailing misconceptions
about the state of history in early modern English universities and, in particular,
apropos the role of Florus and Tacitus within the system of higher education. For
most modern scholars, the prominence seemingly allotted to Florus—that 'elementary and miserable compiler'[389]—in the curriculum is indicative of the pedestrian (even pitiful) state of history at the English universities and, even more
important, of the conspicuous political conservativism reigning at Oxford and
Cambridge. Such an atmosphere, it is argued, precluded the teaching of politically
'dangerous' historians such as Tacitus, let alone the more recent 'subversive'
authors like Machiavelli and Bodin. The popularity of Florus in the seventeenth
century, however, cannot be attributed to political cautiousness or the trepidation
of university officials towards history. Nor was it confined to England.[390] The popularity of that second-century Roman historian can be explained predominantly in
terms of the educational concerns discussed earlier.

To begin with, since only a portion of Livy's *History* survived antiquity, it was
understandable that an author who had incorporated into his own epitome material derived from Livy's lost books was recommended. Far more significant, however, was the pedagogical function performed by Florus. Educational theorists and
tutors alike valued Florus not simply for furnishing the best introduction to Livy,
and to the study of Roman history in general, but as a most advantageous writer
for young scholars on account of his easy style and engaging narrative. In the words
of Vives, 'it would be impossible to imagine anything of that kind of writing more
clear-sighted or more charming' than Florus' epitome.[391] Despite such approval,
early modern theorists were equally explicit in prescribing Florus merely as an
introduction to more weighty authors. Bodin's method of proceeding from the
general to the particular, we may recall, was emulated by nearly all subsequent

---

[388] A summary of Dodwell's *Praelectiones academicae in schola historices Camdeniana* may be found in
Brokesby's *Life of Dodwell*, 180–217. For further estimates of Dodwell, see J. M. Levine, *Dr. Woodward's
Shield* (Berkeley and Los Angeles 1977), 200–15 and *passim* and H. J. Erasmus, *The Origins of Rome in
Historiography from Petrach to Perizonius* (Assen 1962), 91–2, 109–10, 112 n. 5.

[389] R. Syme, 'Roman historians and renaissance politics' in *Society and History in the Renaissance*
(Washington DC 1960), 10.

[390] Burke's initial survey has demonstrated that throughout the seventeenth century Florus shared
with Sallust, Tacitus, and Quintus Curtius the greatest popularity, meriting at least ninety-one separate
editions. P. Burke, 'A survey of the popularity of ancient historians, 1450–1700', *History and Theory* v
(1966), 135–52.

[391] *Vives: on education*, ed. Watson, 241.

theorists. In fact, Bodin not only believed that the mastery of a short epitome must always precede the study of the more profitable authors—Florus prior to Livy and Justinus before Diodorus Siculus—but he actually singled out Florus' epitome as the most appropriate introduction for those wishing 'to understand clearly and to commit to memory the history of the Romans'.[392]

It is within this context that the general assignment of Florus to both gentlemen and scholars by English theorists should be viewed, and the often misunderstood statement of Francis Bacon be interpreted. Though in general Bacon condemned 'the corruptions and moths of history, which are epitomes', the use of which 'deserveth to be banished', he was not oblivious to their usefulness. Bacon simply feared that such epitomes would supplant the pursuit of more significant books. He mentioned Florus by name only once, in his letter of advice to the earl of Rutland, who was preparing to go to Cambridge. Cognizant of the predilection of aristocrats for getting by with little learning, Bacon merely attempted to dissuade the young earl from mistaking a slight work for a substantial one: 'Let him that never read Livy tell me that he is the wiser for Florus's epitome.'[393]

Other recommendations to members of the upper class were similarly couched. Cleland emphasized the benefit of epitomes in presenting the student with a broad framework, and thus designated Florus as an introductory text to Livy; Gilbert Burnet also reiterated the necessity of viewing the broad picture first. Degory Wheare's advice, therefore, articulated a common convention: 'ere you read the Roman story . . . first read carefully L. Florus, who briefly continues the story from Romulus till Augustus shut the temple of Janus . . . This will give you a general taste of your business, and add light unto particular authors.'[394] Thus the assignment of Florus as the author upon whom the first Camden professor of history was expected to lecture should be viewed within a renaissance theory of education. The benefactor himself specifically selected Florus, as he regarded the text as most appropriate for the young auditors of the lecture. Nor was his intention that the professor *declaim* Florus' text; rather he wished him to use it as a framework into which additional material could be incorporated. And this is exactly what Wheare did. Indeed, so detailed were his lectures in exploiting the framework provided by Florus that after eight years he had scarcely covered even the first book of the Roman historian.

If additional proof is needed to reinforce the specific pedagogical role assigned to Florus, we may quote from the inaugural lecture of a scholar far more distinguished than Wheare. Upon his appointment as professor of history at Leiden in 1613, Daniel Heinsius explained to his auditors the reasons for using Florus: 'no one rightly comprehends the full grandeur of Roman history unless he has entered upon it from the beginnings. This, gentlemen, ye shall do with me in Lucius

---

[392] Bodin, *Method*, 26–7.

[393] *Works of Francis Bacon*, ed. Spedding, Ellis, and Heath iii. 334, ix. 23.

[394] Cleland, *Institution of a Young Nobleman*, 84; Clarke, *Bishop Gilbert Burnet as Educationist*, 45–6; Wheare, *Method*, 38–9.

Annaeus Florus.' He proceeded to elaborate a programme of studies: 'As in a picture, we shall behold the life of the Roman people, its manners, efforts, but especially its wars and battles. These our Florus has minuted with care, so far as his
concise brevity permitted.'[395]

When Camden assigned Florus as an introductory text, he did not intend that
he should be the sole historian treated by the professors, but that the entire range
of Roman and Greek history would be covered. Certainly this intention is made
explicit in the Laudian statutes, which stipulate that the Camden professors
expound on Florus 'and other ancient authorities', thereby allowing future lecturers the same freedom enjoyed by the Savilian professors in determining their
course. That such latitude was exercised is made clear from the lectures of Henry
Dodwell, who embarked on one of the most difficult texts in Roman history—the
Scriptores historiae augustae.[396]

The above analysis of the popularity of Florus in terms of pedagogical considerations can now be applied to the standing perception of the universities as institutions deficient in—if not outright void of—historical instruction. The exclusive
concentration on a select number of ancient historians (to whom Florus served as
an introduction) during the undergraduate years is no indication that antiquarian
studies or medieval history were ignored or devalued at Oxford. Rather, it suggests
only that a strict observance of cherished educational principles guided the course
of study. Equally important, the case of Florus may also be used to dispel the political significance many modern scholars ascribe to that Roman historian. Correlating
the popularity of Florus with an alleged conservative ideological preference by
university officials, modern historians assume that Florus has always been perceived as upholding the case for absolute monarchy—or at least as being politically
neutral—and that Tacitus has consistently been eschewed for his republican, or at
least anti-monarchical, connotations.

The most explicit political interpretation of the foundation and early history of
the Oxford professorship of history has recently been articulated by Sharpe. In
examining the endeavours of William Camden and Fulke Greville to endow history professorships at Oxford and Cambridge during the early seventeenth century,
Sharpe argues for a hidden agenda on the part of these two men, since these bids
represent a clear 'statement of their respective founders' attitudes to the immediate circumstances of the 1620s'. How else can we account for the fact that 'the
greatest Elizabethan antiquary and historian recommended . . . as a basic text for
the young students of Oxford a work inaccurate and inconsistent in chronology
and geography'? Had Camden been interested only in promoting scholarship, it is

---

[395] Heinsius further argued that his predecessor, Dominicus Baudius, had also expounded on Florus:
see Daniel Heinsius, *The Value of History*, trans. G. W. Robinson (Cambridge Mass. 1943), 18–20. Similar
opinions were expressed by Lipsius and Savile.

[396] *Statutes*, trans. Ward i. 23. On the other hand, as late as 1786 Thomas Warton felt obliged to apologize for not lecturing on Florus by stating that such an elementary course would be 'out of keeping
with the time'. *The Poetical Works of the late Thomas Warton* (5th edn 2 vols Oxford 1802) ii. 368, cited in
Jones, 'The foundation and history of the Camden chair', 188.

implied, he would not have selected Degory Wheare as the first occupant of the chair, since the latter seemingly knew little and cared less about the 'archival research' so close to Camden's heart. Similarly, if Camden merely intended to cultivate learning, he could not possibly have specified Florus as the text to be taught, for in so doing, 'all continuity with his earlier antiquarian studies ends'. The 'puzzling' selection of Wheare as the first professor—rather than someone like Brian Twyne—and the equally enigmatic assignment of Florus as the prescribed text, concludes Sharpe, can only be understood in terms of political subterfuge. At both Oxford and Cambridge, the endowment of history professorships was intended to inspire a political nation, not to benefit a small community of scholars: 'Faced with a decline of leadership and public virtues, Camden and Greville, towards the end of their lives, turned to the young gentlemen, the future counsellors of kings, as the hope for England's rejuvenation.' At Oxford, then, at 'a time when direct criticism was dangerous', only in a course of lectures on a seemingly unthreatening historian could 'the ills of the state and their remedies be safely aired'.[397]

The flaws of this interpretation are many. By fixing his sights solely on the presumed tactics of political subterfuge, Sharpe is indifferent to the true love of scholarship that characterized Camden and Greville, just as he is oblivious to the far more mundane motives that animated these benefactions. Second, Sharpe's curious reading of Florus' veiled censure of imperial Rome cannot be extrapolated to imply an indictment on the part of either Camden or Wheare of early Stuart politics. Sharpe produces little more than speculations about Camden's political views, while he uses a modern edition of Florus—and not the actual manuscript copy of Wheare's lectures—to validate the political tone of Wheare's lectures. Only from the vantage-point of the twentieth century can Camden's singling out of Florus be regarded as cunningly shrewd and prudent, in view of the fate of Greville's professorship at Cambridge. At the latter institution, after just two lectures, the first incumbent, Isaac Dorislaus, was silenced as a consequence of his exposition of Tacitus. Again, Sharpe and other scholars impute political significance to the choice of Tacitus. But, once more, the evidence scarcely sustains the interpretation. First, there is no direct evidence that Greville assigned Dorislaus the particular text he was to read.[398] Second, while it is true that Tacitus could be interpreted in a subversive manner, it is misleading to assume that educational theorists and tutors generally refrained from assigning him. What happened in 1627–8 was that the Caroline authorities overreacted, in a tense political atmosphere nationally—generated by the levying of the forced loan.[399]

---

[397] Sharpe, 'The foundation of the chairs of history at Oxford and Cambridge'.

[398] Bradford claimed that it was Greville's 'way of paying memorial tribute to both Essex and Bacon', that prompted him to assign Tacitus, and that his endowing the lectureship was 'a by-product of the Tacitean revival, and as such it met the full force of the anti-Tacitean reaction'. A. T. Bradford, 'Stuart absolutism and the "utility" of Tacitus', *Huntington Library Quarterly* xlvi (1983), 150.

[399] Sharpe, 'The foundation of the chairs of history at Oxford and Cambridge'; R. Cust, *The Forced Loan and English Politics 1626–1628* (Oxford 1987), 62, 66, 184 and *passim*. J. P. Somerville, *Politics and Ideology in England 1603–1640* (London 1986), 33, 72–3, 128.

To conclude from this episode, then, that Tacitus was deemed an inappropriate author for a university audience is mistaken. No 'official panic' or 'anti-Tacitean' reaction followed. In fact, after a brief investigation, Dorislaus was vindicated. The reason for the continued suspension of the lectures was not in observance of the king's instructions but owing, in the first instance, to Greville's indignation. As Trevor-Roper pointed out long ago, the lectures were discontinued 'not because Brooke approved the lectures which the illiberal Laudians of the university had suppressed. Far from it. After an inquiry, the university authorities were satisfied that Dorislaus had been misunderstood. So were the bishops; so was the king. As far as they were concerned, Dorislaus could have resumed his lectures. The man who was not satisfied was Lord Brooke . . . '. Finally, following Greville's death, it was the unwillingness of the new Lord Brooke to continue the funding of the chair that sealed the fate of the Cambridge professorship.[400]

It is only the obsessive preoccupation of historians with politic history, and the highlighting of republicanism, that creates the illusion that early modern educated men generally perceived Tacitus as an anti-monarchical writer. Although contemporaries were well aware that Tacitus, more than any other ancient historian, could be read, in specific contexts, in a subversive way, they found this no reason to expurgate the author of the *Annals* from the university curriculum. In fact, most educated men would have expressed the same attitude towards the study of Tacitus as was expounded by the heralders of the Tacitean movement in England. For example, when Sir Philip Sidney outlined the course of studies he wished his brother Robert to follow he specifically recommended Tacitus for his 'pithy opening the venome of wickednes'. Another committed Tacitean, Sir William Cornwallis, was nevertheless also attentive to the possibly dangerous political overtones of the Roman historian. Tacitus, the alpha and omega of history, was judged by Cornwallis to possess 'so grave a stile, so judiciall a censure, and so piercing an eye into the designes of princes and states'. Yet he also considered Tacitus as 'more wise than safe', while arguing concurrently that 'the painter is not to be blamed though his picture be ill favoured if his paterne were so, nor Tacitus thought ill because Tiberius was a tyrant, Claudius a foole, Nero vicious'.[401]

To reiterate, it was only within a tense political context that the study of history posed dangers. More commonly it was the English past—rather than Roman history—that was potentially explosive, and it is to this danger that Sir Walter Ralegh addressed himself when he commented in the preface to *The History of the World*: 'I know that it will bee said by many, that I might have beene more pleasing to the reader, if I had written the story of my owne times . . . To this I answere, that who-so-ever in writing a moderne historie, shall follow truth too neare the heeles, it may happily strike out his teeth.'[402] Within the usually non-political atmosphere of the

[400] Bradford, 'Stuart absolutism', 148; Trevor-Roper, review of Hill's *Intellectual Origins* in *History and Theory* v (1966), 69.

[401] Sidney, *Works* iii. 132; Sir William Cornwallis the younger, *Essayes*, ed. D. C. Allen (Baltimore 1946), 42, 201.

[402] Sir Walter Ralegh, *The History of the World*, ed. C. A. Patrides (London 1971), 80.

undergraduate curriculum, Tacitus was assigned by virtually every educational theorist, his writings present in most private libraries, for his significance as a historian, moralist, and a superb—if austere—stylist was never doubted.[403]

It was not political cautiousness, therefore, that prompted Camden to assign Florus rather than Tacitus or, for that matter, any other historian, but a calculated educational consideration. Nor can it be argued that Wheare 'understandably equivocated in that part of his Oxford lectures that dealt with Tacitus' or paraphrased the contrasting testimonies of Lipsius and Casaubon concerning Tacitus because 'the equivocal reputation acquired by Tacitus' English disciples persuaded him not to venture his own judgment . . . [on] the historian of Roman tyranny'. These lectures, which were published shortly after delivery, intended to provide—as the title indicates—a proper method of reading histories. As was quite common with such books, Wheare supplied the judgement of noted scholars on *each* historian he discussed, Tacitus being no exception.[404]

Lastly, the fact that in his unpublished lectures on Florus, Wheare occasionally drew parallels between his time and the Roman past does not warrant the imputation that he intended an anti-monarchical partisan political message. Only a careful study of the lectures can determine the extent to which Wheare utilized the past in the service of the present; the present author, for one, found nothing particularly subversive in them.[405] Yet this does not mean that classical texts (or the Camden professors) could not be utilized for political purposes. A revealing example to the contrary exists in a letter sent by William Sancroft to Henry Dodwell in December 1690. At the time Dodwell was contemplating resigning the Camden chair, to which he had been elected two years earlier, and the ejected archbishop of Canterbury was hoping to dissuade his friend from this course of action, hoping instead that Dodwell would further the case of the non-jurors from the history podium at Oxford:

In God's name boldly mount your chair . . . I cannot but think it more advisable for you to keep yourself within the strict terms of your foundation and to read publickly, and in your lectures too (for the same reason) not to interpret Irenaeus (as others advise; the counsell is good, but not now and here). No. But, if I might take upo[n] me to suggest to you a proper argument for your lectures, I would wish that either fro[m] the first periocha of Tacitus's Annals, or rather (if it suits better with Mr Camden's rules) from the very last in Florus's History, you would take occasion to clear the revolution of the Roman government made in Augustus's age, and prove that the Roman power in our lord's time, and in the time of his 2 great apostles, were not meerly *de-facto* and usurped powers (as all our revolution-

---

[403] See for example 'The undergraduate account book of John and Richard Newdigate', ed. Larminie, 189; Berks. RO Trumbull papers, misc. letters nos 13, 29; BL Add. MSS 27,606 fo 5 (Sackville Crow), 46,953, fo 122 (John Percival); OUA chancellor's ct inventories s.v. Abel Trefrie, John Hutton, and John Cole. Equally telling is Sir Thomas Overbury's depiction of 'a mere fellow of an house': 'if he hath read Tacitus, Guicchardine, or Gallo-Belgicus, hee contemnes the late lord treasurer for all the state-policy he had'. *The Miscellaneous Works*, ed. E. F. Rimbault (London 1890), 105.

[404] J. H. M. Salmon, 'Stoicism and Roman example: Seneca and Tacitus in Jacobean England', *Journal of the History of Ideas* l (1989), 199–225.

[405] For Wheare's lecture notes, see Bodl. MS Auct F.2.21.

ers, and particularly the last most scandalous revolter pretend) but legal governments ...
Nor shall you need to endanger yourself, or the liberty at present allowed you, by descending to the modern hypothesis and by applying it to our present case. But scene your whole
discourse still at Rome, and it will as effectually do our business; and all that hear you,
whether well or otherwise-affected, will perfectly understand you, and thereby the former
will be edified, and the others not know how to help themselves; and above all (which
brought me first upon this thought) your fear of giving scandal will be utterly obviated and
removed.[406]

Dodwell was not, however, to be dissuaded and his refusal to subscribe to the new
oaths cost him the professorship. The incident nevertheless demonstrates that,
although the past is and has always been susceptible to manipulation, historians
need to evaluate each case on its own terms. In the case of Tacitus, the Roman
historian could be taken to sanction a variety of purposes. He might serve as a
model for the historian and a paragon for the politician. His writings could be used
as a manual for absolute monarchy, as well as championing republicanism. Tacitus,
in other words, 'served as guide to success at court; he became counsel for the theory of divine right, yet he fended for parliament and the people and vindicated
tyrannicide'.[407]

Even Casaubon's celebrated invective against Tacitus can be attributed, at least
in part, to pedagogical concerns. As a scholar Casaubon admired the Roman historian. But in the celebrated preface to his edition of Polybius—an author who
paid particular attention to the didactic purpose of history—Casaubon articulated
the value of history in education as well as his misgivings about the possible harmful consequences of the raging Tacitean fashion upon unformed minds: 'For what
can be more pernicious (especially to a young man) than the reading of those
Annals?', he asked. In fact, the critique of Tacitus could be explained in the same
way as his denunciation of Ramus. Personally, Casaubon respected Ramus' scholarship and efforts on behalf of learning; the misgivings he had were directed at the
licence Ramus appeared to be giving to short-cuts to the acquisition of knowledge
and thus to shallow scholarship.[408]

[406] Bodl. MS St Edmund Hall 10, pp. 5–6.

[407] M. F. Tenney, 'Tacitus in the politics of early Stuart England', *The Classical Journal* xxxvii (1941),
155. D. Woolf, *The Idea of History in Early Stuart England* (Toronto 1992), 253; Levy stated the argument
in a similar manner: 'Tacitus was a weapon that could cut both ways, a guide to profitable servility or
a way of showing a carefully hidden antagonism to ruthless princes.' F. J. Levy, *Tudor Historical Thought*
(San Marino 1967), 250.

[408] Wheare, *Method*, 108.

6

The Mathematical Sciences and New Philosophies

MORDECHAI FEINGOLD

SHORTLY after turning 80, the Savilian professor of geometry John Wallis (MA 1640) penned his *apologia pro vita sua*, in the course of which he indicated that during his student days at Cambridge mathematics was hardly considered a proper university subject and experimental philosophy was nowhere to be found. Another octogenarian, Thomas Hobbes (BA 1608), recalled in his autobiography an Oxford system of education based on incomprehensible logic and sterile physics. For his part John Locke (MA 1658)—a mere septuagenarian—regaled his admirers with how he, too, had misspent his time at Oxford, the upshot of which was to lay the blame for his lack of application on the reigning tyranny of Aristotle. Thus to Jean Le Clerc Locke intimated he had 'lost a great deal of time, when he first applied himself to study, because the only philosophy then known at Oxford was the peripatetick, perplexed with obscure terms and stuffed with useless questions'.[1]

These and similar recollections need to be taken seriously in any historical study. Yet a certain caution is also warranted. As Patricia Reif remarked three decades ago, 'criticism of education—teachers, schools, requirements—has been the therapeutic sport of students through the ages, but it seemed to reach an all-time high in the seventeenth century'.[2] Most scholars, however, have fastened upon such censures as incontrovertible testimony to the lamentable state of scientific and philosophical studies at Oxford and Cambridge. In their haste to judge the universities as unenlightened institutions, incapable of contributing appreciably to the intellectual formation of great thinkers, these same scholars fail to realize that deprecatory expressions by aged alumni often recall events after a lifetime devoted to extending the frontiers of their respective fields. They make no allowance for either selective memory or the inevitable ignorance of youth when compared with the wisdom of old age, and, perhaps most important, for the marked tendency of such men toward self-aggrandizement. After all it is a truism that, given the opportunity, in old age most great thinkers cannot resist the temptation to envisage

---

[1] C. J. Scriba, 'The autobiography of John Wallis, F.R.S', *Notes and Records of the Royal Society* xxv (1970), 27, 29, 30, 40; 'The life of Thomas Hobbes of Malmesbury', trans. J. E. Parsons Jr and W. Blair, *Interpretation* x (1982), 2; Jean Le Clerc, *The Life and Character of Locke* (London 1706), 2.

[2] P. Reif, 'The textbook tradition in natural philosophy, 1600–1650', *Journal of the History of Ideas* xxx (1969), 17.

themselves as impatient youths, stubbornly rejecting all authority and single-handedly carving out for themselves an as yet unexplored territory.

Further to distort the historical record, the damning statements have often been read out of the context that even their authors provided. In fact, notwithstanding their subsequent reflections, while at university Wallis, Hobbes, and Locke diligently pursued the course of study then in fashion and thought themselves—or were reputed by those who knew them—to have excelled therein. Wallis, for example, boasted that he 'had the good hap all along (both at school and in the university) to be reputed (if not equal) not much inferior, to those of the best of [his] rank'. Hobbes not only admitted to have benefited from studying the allegedly crabbed logic, but also told John Aubrey he 'thought himselfe a good disputant' while at Oxford. James Tyrrell, who befriended Locke there in 1658, told Lady Masham that already then, before Locke had embarked upon a serious study of Descartes, he was 'looked upon as one of the most learned and ingenious young men in the colledge he was of'.[3]

The seeming discrepancy between the various sections of these autobiographical accounts implies less the existence of internal contradictions than the wilful refashioning of experience on the part of the narrators. As a young student Wallis, according to his own testimony, 'had an eye from the first' on a clerical career, and it was only his unexpected appointment as Savilian professor of geometry in 1649 that made 'mathematicks which had before been a pleasing diversion' his 'serious study'. Hobbes and Locke, on the other hand, like many of their contemporaries, were far more interested during their student days in literary studies than in philosophy. Hobbes arrived at Oxford already a good classical scholar, who 'had turned Euripidis Medea out of Greeke into Latin iambiques'. During his four-year stay at Magdalen Hall, Hobbes allowed his predilection for literature to take precedence over the tedium of logic and natural philosophy, and thus turned 'to more pleasant things and perused books, in which [he] had been previously instructed, though not well taught'. His obvious attainments in such studies were responsible for his recommendation by Principal James Hussey as tutor to the son of the earl of Devonshire, in whose service Hobbes continued to cultivate the classics for two more decades, culminating with the publication in 1629 of his English translation of Thucydides.[4]

Locke arrived at Oxford from Westminster School, arguably the most rigorous training-ground at the time in classical languages and literature, and though it is tempting to interpret at face value his later claim that 'he spent a good part of his first years at the university in reading romances, from his aversion to the disputative way in fashion there', the fact remains that what guided Locke's reading and

---

[3] Scriba, 'The autobiography of John Wallis', 27; *Brief Lives . . . set down by John Aubrey between the years 1669 and 1696*, ed. A. Clark (2 vols Oxford 1898) i. 329; 'Lady Masham to Jean Le Clerc', *History of Ideas Newsletter* i–ii (1954–6), 16.

[4] Scriba, 'The autobiography of John Wallis', 30; 'The life of Thomas Hobbes of Malmesbury', trans. Parsans and Blair, 2; *Brief Lives by Aubrey*, ed. Clark i. 328–9. Hobbes was also the first English translator of Aristotle's *Rhetoric*.

scholarly preferences during the 1650s was a desire to immerse himself in humanist culture and a predilection for polite society. Locke, in fact, may at that time have contemplated a literary, rather than a philosophical, career. In addition to his reading of romances, he composed one himself and appears to have sketched the outline of a play, 'Orozes King of Albania', as well. The preferences of Locke and his considerable literary and linguistic proficiency were fully appreciated at Christ Church and resulted in him being appointed, successively, as college lecturer of Greek and of rhetoric, and later as censor of moral philosophy. In contrast to Hobbes, however, Locke quickly outgrew his devotion to the classics and subsequently 'atoned' for his youthful 'indiscretions' by criticizing not only scholasticism, but humanist culture too—with its attendant emphasis on the study of ancient languages and literature.[5]

An awareness of the context in which seemingly disparaging remarks were levelled against scholastic, as well as humanistic, learning proves crucial to our understanding of their significance. Equally crucial is the need to refrain from evaluating the curriculum on the basis of either the propagandist positions advanced by its key detractors or the various documents stipulating the 'official' course of studies, as has been the case until now. Accordingly, the present chapter offers a more nuanced context for understanding the various documents that have been taken to indicate the conservative bent of the university with its supposedly glaring omission of mathematics and natural philosophy in the curriculum. My main objective, it should be stated at the outset, is not to analyse in any detail the contribution of eminent Oxford men to the development of science, but to survey the landscape of scientific and philosophical knowledge at Oxford, primarily at the undergraduate level. This concentration on the experience of the generality of students highlights both the educational goals of the curriculum and the range of opportunities available to those interested in the pursuit of the new science. Most important, it suggests the essentially liberal environment prevailing in seventeenth-century Oxford, which in turn facilitated the swift and largely unchecked dissemination of the new modes of thought among teachers and students alike.

To evaluate the reception of the new modes of thought, however, it is also necessary to extend the boundaries of natural philosophy as it is understood today. At the turn of the seventeenth century the Aristotelian encyclopaedic image of the unity of knowledge still prevailed. Within such a view 'science' was interpreted to embrace all studies pertaining to contemplation and action, including natural philosophy, moral philosophy (subdivided into ethics, politics, and economics), metaphysics and logic. By 1600, however, the latter had been universally designated an 'art'—that is, an instrumental discipline pertaining to reasoning and speech. The various components of such an established frame were not only inextricably linked, but shared the same methodological and epistemological foundations. Nor should

[5] Joseph Spence, *Observation, Anecdotes, and Characters of Books and Men*, ed. J. M. Osborn (2 vols Oxford 1966) ii. 560; *The Correspondence of John Locke*, ed. E. S. De Beer (8 vols Oxford 1976–89) i. 85 and *passim*; John Locke, *Essays on the Law of Nature*, ed W. von Leyden (Oxford 1965), 19.

it be assumed that such a cohesive image of knowledge was rejected by the new philosophers along with their rejection of the knowledge itself. Descartes, for example, likened 'the whole of philosophy' to a tree the roots of which 'are metaphysics, the trunk is physics, and the branches emerging from the trunk are all the other sciences, which may be reduced to three principal ones, namely medicine, mechanics and morals'. Hobbes underscored a similar interdependence when he sought to explain nature, man, and society strictly in terms of motion, delineating his version of the tree of philosophy in the dedication of *De cive*: 'for treating of figures, it is called geometry; of motion, physic; of natural right, morals; put altogether, and they make up philosophy'.[6]

Consequently, though such figures as Hobbes and Locke are regarded today primarily as political philosophers, their understanding of the aims and scope of philosophy as well as the sources upon which they drew also make them an intrinsic part of the intellectual context of the mathematical sciences and natural philosophy. As has been noted, 'friends like Petty and Du Verdus were less impressed by the conclusions that Hobbes drew from his political system than the geometrical method it utilized'. Similarly the poet Abraham Cowley celebrated Hobbes as that 'great Columbus of the golden lands of new philosophies', while Seth Ward informed the reader of the 1650 Oxford edition of *Human Nature* 'that Mr. Hobbes hath written a body of philosophy, upon such principles and in such order as are used by men conversant in demonstration: this he hath distinguished into three parts; *De corpore, De homine, De cive*; each of the constituents beginning at the end of the antecedent, and insisting thereupon, as the later books of Euclid upon the former'.[7] Antagonists also expressed analogous views. Thus Robert Boyle maintained in 1662 that the admiration of Hobbes's 'demonstrative way of philosophy' enticed 'divers persons' to espouse the pernicious religious ideas of the *Leviathan*. Three years later Joseph Glanvill likewise commented that 'the ingenious world being growne quite weary of qualities and formes, and declaring in favour of the mechanical hypothesis (to which a person that is not very fond of religion is a great pretender), divers of the brisker geniusses, who desire rather to be accounted witts, then endeavour to be so, have been willing to accept mechanism upon Hobbian conditions, and many others were in danger of following them into the precipice'.[8]

A further reason for including political philosophy and epistemology in any discussion of the new science is the profound interest of Hobbes and Locke, among others, in the problem of knowledge and certitude. In their attempt to defeat scepticism and establish new criteria of truth as well as the means to attain it, they

[6] *The Philosophical Writings of Descartes*, trans. J. Cottingham *et al.* (3 vols Cambridge 1985–91) i. 186; *The English Works of Thomas Hobbes*, ed. W. Molesworth (11 vols London 1839–45, repr. Aalen 1966) ii, pp. iii–iv.

[7] Q. Skinner, 'Thomas Hobbes and his disciples in France and England', *Comparative Studies in Society and History* viii (1966), 161–2; Abraham Cowley, *Poems*, ed. A. R. Waller (Cambridge 1905), 189; *English Works of Hobbes*, ed. Molesworth iv, p. xi.

[8] *The Works of the Honourable Robert Boyle*, ed. Thomas Birch (6 vols London 1772) i. 187; Joseph Glanvill, *Scepsis scientifica* (London 1665), sig. b^{r-v}.

helped establish a new way of philosophizing, and one that was equally prescriptive *vis-à-vis* the domains of natural and human knowledge. Ultimately, it was their contribution to the philosophy of science—as well as their relentless disparagement of Aristotle and the schoolmen—that made their names synonymous with 'modernity', thus warranting their inclusion in any appraisal of the reception of the 'new philosophy'.[9]

THE MATHEMATICAL SCIENCES

The distinctively humanistic colouring of the Oxford curriculum in the early modern period does not imply disregard of the mathematical and natural sciences. True, compared with the preoccupation of educators, tutors, and students with the arts of discourse and with classical languages and literature, the study of the mathematics, and even more of physics, was far less intense. Nevertheless, these latter disciplines were still regarded as integral branches of undergraduate education. As the seventeenth century opened, the importance of the mathematical sciences lay primarily in their being inextricably interwoven with other subjects that comprised the unified body of knowledge constituting the course of study. For example, geometry was often likened to logic for its capacity to train the minds of youth to reason well, while arithmetic, geometry, astronomy, and optics were considered not only prerequisites for the study of philosophy but essential for the study of geography and chronology—the 'two eyes' of the important humanistic discipline of history. In addition to its propaedeutic role within a unified and systematized body of knowledge, however, the mathematical sciences were also considered indispensable for the education of a 'gentleman' by virtue of their utility in matters of warfare, navigation, and the management of estates.

Constraints of space prevent a discussion of the attitude of sixteenth-century humanists to the function of mathematics in the curriculum; suffice it to say that their advocacy of the *studia humanitatis* did not require the elimination of the mathematical sciences from the course of study. As with their acquiescence in the teaching of philosophy, the humanists were now content to concede, and even advocate, the relevance and applicability of the mathematical sciences to the affairs of life— their only stipulation being that the link forged by their medieval predecessors between mathematics and metaphysics be severed. Thus Erasmus' seemingly contemptuous dismissal of the mathematical sciences, grudgingly granting the need to teach only a 'smattering of arithmetic, music and astrology', is essentially indistinguishable in its pedagogical message from the more elaborate and sympathetic discussion of the topic by Vives. The latter, having described at considerable length and with some warmth the variety of mathematical disciplines, ultimately advocated the teaching of these subjects for their practical application, not their intrinsic value: 'let scholars study the elements of mathematics indeed and even some more advanced work, greater for some, less for others, according to the ability of each

---

[9] See also I. B. Cohen, 'The scientific revolution and the social sciences' in I. B. Cohen (ed.), *The Natural Sciences and the Social Sciences* (Dordrecht 1994), 153–203.

pupil, to lead up to their application in the affairs of life and to the better understanding of philosophical subjects.'[10]

The attitude of the English humanists followed similar lines. With differing
degrees of conviction about the benefits of mathematics, authors invariably agreed
on the need to teach it. If Sir Thomas Elyot perfunctorily bracketed all the mathematical sciences under the heading of 'cosmography' and felt it sufficient to state
that the subject is 'to all noble men, nat only pleasant, but profitable also, and won-
derfull necessary', Sir John Cheke enthusiastically combined an inspired teaching
of Greek at Cambridge with an equally rousing instruction in mathematics.
Similarly, though historians have often viewed the attitude of Roger Ascham as predominantly antagonistic to the teaching of mathematics, in fact the message he
wished to convey was not dissimilar to the one articulated by an acknowledged proponent of these studies, Henry Peacham. Ascham merely exhibited a typical
humanist concern with priorities when he admonished the reader of his *Schoolmaster*
against an excessive preoccupation with the mathematical sciences for 'as they
sharpen men's wittes over much, so they change men's manners over sore, if they
be not moderately mingled, and wisely applied to som good use of life'. With this
issue of balance uppermost in his mind, Ascham continued to argue that those
addicted to such studies were solitary by nature, 'unfit to live with others' and
'unapt to serve the world'. Henry Peacham, for his part, though he praised at length
the dignity and utility of geometry, ultimately couched his advocacy in strictly utilitarian terms: 'I cannot see how a gentleman, especially a soldier and commander,
may be accomplished without geometry, though not to the height of perfection,
yet at the least to be grounded and furnished with the principles and privy rules
hereof.'[11]

But as regards the education of the well born in particular, the very endorsement
of mathematics in utilitarian terms inevitably tended to restrict the scope and depth
of the recommended instruction. Hubert Languet, the self-appointed mentor of Sir
Philip Sidney after the latter had left Oxford in 1580, made the point clear in advising him on his readings. While approving of his (moderate) study of astronomy,
and even believing geometry to be 'an excellent study, and particularly worthy of
a liberal mind', he nevertheless disapproved of any serious delving on Sidney's part;
the young gentleman needed to consider his 'position in life, and how soon [he
would] have to tear [himself] away from the leisure' he now enjoyed for reading.
Thus, concluded Languet, he 'must devote the brief time which remains [to him]
entirely to the most necessary studies'. That Sidney assented to such reasoning is
evident both from his immediate compliance with Languet's recommendation and

[10] W. H. Woodward, *Desiderius Erasmus concerning the Aim and Method of Education* (Cambridge 1905),
145; *Vives: on education*, ed. F. Watson (Cambridge 1913, repr. Totowa 1971), 202–3.

[11] Sir Thomas Elyot, *The Boke Named The Governour*, ed. H. H. S. Croft (2 vols London 1883, repr.
New York 1967) i. 79; P. L. Rose, 'Erasmians and mathematicians at Cambridge in the early sixteenth
century', *Sixteenth Century Journal* viii (1977), 47–59; *The Whole Works of Roger Ascham*, ed. J. A. Giles (4
vols London 1864–5) ii. 103; Roger Ascham, *English Works*, ed. W. A. Wright (Cambridge 1970), 190;
Henry Peacham, *The Complete Gentleman*, ed. V. B. Heltzel (Ithaca NY 1962), 89.

from his subsequent duplication, eight years later, of virtually this exact reasoning in his letter of advice to Edward Denny.[12] Nor would this widely accepted attitude towards educational priorities alter much over the next century, despite the profound transformation of the mathematical sciences as well as the perceptible effort on the part of professors and tutors to reorient the curriculum to accommodate such radical change. Notwithstanding his own wide acquaintance with the new philosophy, Lord Herbert of Cherbury (m. 1596) only approved of the acquisition of the rudiments of arithmetic, essentially for its 'being most usefull for many purposes and among the rest for keeping of accompt'. Like Languet, however, Cherbury doubted the utility of geometry in the education of a gentleman, except for possible military application. Likewise, when in 1654 Francis Mansell, the ejected principal of Jesus college, presented Sir Sackville Crow with an outline of the course of study he offered to those of his students who were gentlemen, he openly admitted that 'for the mathematiques I never invite any of my pupils to engage farther in them then the plaine and necessary doctrines of arithmetique and geometry, and the use of the globes. If theyr owne genius delights to wade deeper, I assist them what I can.'[13] Indeed, even such a true lover of mathematics as the master of University College, Obadiah Walker, did not doubt the approved wisdom; 'onely let it be remembered', he quickly appended to his recommendation to study mathematics, 'that I advise it here as a piece of education not a profession. I would not have a gentleman give up himself to it, for it makes him less fit for active life, and common conversation.' Significantly, John Locke was even more dismissive than most of his predecessors in his prescription of the mathematical sciences. Mere grounding in geography and arithmetic was sufficient; as for geometry, he advised that 'the first six books of Euclid' were enough for a gentleman to pick up, and he further doubted 'whether more to a man of business be necessary or useful'.[14]

Obviously such a utilitarian and restrictive attitude to the study of the mathematical sciences had significant implications for the course prescribed for members of the gentry and nobility. In the event, however, because of the profound metamorphosis of the curriculum in general, all students in effect followed a remarkably uniform course of mathematics during their undergraduate career. As has been argued above,[15] the compression of the entire range of the arts, sciences, and philosophy into the undergraduate course, done partly to meet the special needs of well-born students, meant that the sheer volume of learning led to undergraduates

[12] J. M. Osborn, *Young Philip Sidney* (New Haven 1972), 127, 136–7, 142, 539.

[13] *The Life of Edward, First Lord Herbert of Cherbury*, ed. J. M. Shuttleworth (London, 1976), 20; BL Add. MS 27,606, fo 9ᵛ. William Higford, formerly of Corpus Christi College, Oxford, recommended to his grandson only the study of arithmetic, and principally for the benefit it would render in keeping accounts and managing a frugal household. William Higford, *Institutions: or, advice to his grandson* (London 1658, repr. 1818), 89–91.

[14] Obadiah Walker, *Of Education* (Oxford 1673), 113; *The Educational Writings of John Locke*, ed. J. L. Axtell (Cambridge 1968), 291. In his shorter letters on education Locke does not even mention the mathematical sciences as necessary for a gentleman.

[15] M. Feingold, 'The humanities', pp. 216–18 above.

being provided primarily with only the broad outline and basic principles of each subject, and to early specialization being explicitly discouraged. This new approach must constantly be borne in mind when evaluating the nature of mathematical and philosophical instruction, precisely because so much of the surviving evidence concerning university studies (in the form of letters, commonplace books, and tutors' accounts), relates to that official and supervised portion of education in which profundity was neither expected nor encouraged. To pronounce on the basis of such evidence, without paying heed to the new rationale informing undergraduate education, concerning either the competence of teachers or the attitude of the universities towards the sciences, would be gravely to distort the picture.

This new circumscribed role of mathematics within the educational framework was the reason for the changes introduced into the wording of the Elizabethan university statutes concerning the teaching of the subject. Instead of setting aside the entire first year for mathematical study as was stipulated by the 1549 Edwardian statutes, the Oxford *Nova statuta* (1564–5) detailed a course consisting of four terms of rhetoric, three of arithmetic, two of music, two of grammar, and five of dialectics. No particular order was specified.[16] Presumably, the inappropriateness of the enthusiasm displayed by Sir John Cheke (the chief spirit behind the Edwardian statutes) in assigning such an elevated position to mathematics in the undergraduate curriculum was recognized by the compilers of subsequent statutes. They were undoubtedly aware of the influx of well-born students into the universities in increasing numbers. (From the 1590s nearly half of the matriculants each year at Oxford described themselves as gentlemen or above.)[17] As many of these students did not seek a degree and were not expected to remain in residence for more than two or perhaps three years, it would have been a mistake to give the impression that as much as half their time might be devoted to the study of the mathematical sciences. Parents would in fact have considered such a prospect not only excessive and unbecoming, but even perilous. As Francis Osborne recalled in his letter of advice to his son at Oxford, mathematics had but a dubious reputation as recently as the early decades of the seventeenth century:

My memory reacheth the time when the generality of people thought her most useful branches spels, and her professors limbs of the devil; converting the honour of Oxford, due to her (though at that time slender) proficiency in this study, to her shame. Not a few of our then foolish gentry refusing to send their sons thither, lest they should be smutted with the black art.[18]

Mathematics, however, remained an integral part of the curriculum of the average undergraduate, being taught within a year of their arrival, at the latest.

Here it is also important to emphasize the propaedeutic function of mathemat-

---

[16] *SA* 390.
[17] R. O'Day, *Education and Society 1500–1800* (London 1987), 90; M. Feingold, *The Mathematicians' Apprenticeship: science, universities and society in England, 1560–1640* (Cambridge 1984), 29–30.
[18] Francis Osborne, *Advice to a Son*, ed. Edward A. Parry (London 1896), 14.

ics. Long before mathematics superseded logic as the focus of undergraduate examinations—especially in the form of the eighteenth-century Cambridge tripos—educators both on the continent and in England were fully cognizant of the contribution of mathematics to the training of the minds of youth. Their only concern was that such instruction be delivered in conjunction with, and not in place of, training in logic, which was still believed to be independently important for the inculcation of correct habits of thought. Vives, for example, argued that 'the mathematical sciences are particularly disciplinary to flighty and restless intellects which are inclined to slackness, and shrink from or will not support the toil of a continuent effort. For they engage the minds and compel them to action, and do not suffer them to wander.' Bacon expressed like views concerning the pedagogical role of the mathematical sciences in rendering the mind subtle: 'If the wit be too dull, they sharpen it, if too wandering, they fix it, if too inherent in the sense, they abstract it.'[19]

This emergent attitude was codified in a section of the Savilian statutes, which instructed the geometry professor to teach practical logic once a week. *The Institutio logicae* of John Wallis, though drafted during his student days at Cambridge, undoubtedly represents his compliance with such a requirement.[20] Isaac Barrow, first Lucasian professor of mathematics at Cambridge and the person responsible for modelling the Lucasian statutes on the Savilian ones, expressed similar sentiments. Thus in his inaugural oration Barrow forcefully argued that study of the mathematical sciences 'effectually exercises not vainly deludes nor vexatiously torments studious minds with obscure subtilties, perplexed difficulties, or contentious disquisitions'; it 'triumphs without pomp, compels without force, and rules absolutely without the loss of liberty'. Besides, he asked rhetorically, 'who can play well on Aristotle's instrument but with a mathematical quill?' Obadiah Walker also ascribed this auxiliary role to mathematics in terms of

the practice of discoursing, or the seeking after truth by evidence, which is mathematicks, geometry especially. I mean not a superficial taking upon trust the propositions ... but the high road of demonstration. .... It fixeth the fancy, it accostometh to thinking, and enquiring after truth in all discourses. Analytica is the gage of a man's parts, and algebra the pinnacle of argumentation.[21]

John Arbuthnot, who studied at Oxford in the 1690s, articulated the idea more fully when he argued that 'mathematical knowledge adds a manly vigour to the mind, frees it from prejudice, credulity, and superstition. This it does two ways:

---

[19] *Vives: on education*, ed. Watson, 202; *The Works of Francis Bacon*, ed. J. Spedding, R. L. Ellis, and D. D. Heath (14 vols London 1857–74) iii. 360. Bacon voiced similar sentiments in his essay 'Of studies'. But, as noted earlier, what attracted Vives was a source of concern to Ascham who feared the too-successful conditioning of the mind by the mathematical sciences: Ascham, *English Works*, 190.

[20] *Statutes*, trans. Ward i. 274. John Wallis, *Institutio logicae* (Oxford 1687). Lord Herbert of Cherbury also esteemed geometry as 'a science of much certainty and demonstration': *The Life of Edward, First Lord Herbert of Cherbury*, ed. Shuttleworth, 20.

[21] Isaac Barrow, *The Usefulness of Mathematical Learning*, trans. J. Kirby (London 1734), pp. xxviii, xxvi; Walker, *Of Education*, 112–13.

first, by accustoming us to examine, and not to take things upon trust, secondly, by giving us a clear and extensive knowledge of the system of the world.' Hence, when John Locke stated that arithmetic was the 'first sort of abstract reasoning' he merely reiterated a long-standing tradition, except that his intense distaste for logic caused him to dispense with the latter altogether.[22]

Though most students usually began their mathematical studies a year or so after coming up to Oxford once they had satisfied the logic and ethics requirements, as did Henry Fleming in the late 1670s, some may have begun with arithmetic and geometry, like the interlocutor in Clement Barksdale's *An Oxford Conference*: 'I am, this my first year, to let logick alone, and employ my time in classick authors ... with a little mixture of arithmetick and geometry, and the use of the globe.'[23] In the manner customary to all subjects, the tutor personally initiated his charge into the rudiments of the discipline and then allowed him to proceed on his own, supervising progress and giving further instruction and clarifications when needed. Also in line with the practice in other disciplines, by the second half of the seventeenth century many tutors began composing their own introductory compendia for the mathematical sciences. The commonplace book of Robert South from his student days at Christ Church during the 1650s, for example, includes brief 'systems' of arithmetic, geometry, and cosmography. A similar course was followed at Wadham College in the mid-1670s by Humphrey Hody, who copied 'systems' of geometry, optics, and cosmography in addition to the more traditional ones in logic, ethics, and metaphysics. Thomas Dixon of Queen's College prepared a compendium of geometry for Henry Fleming in 1679 before the youth embarked on Euclid, while Charles King of Magdalen Hall received, in addition to geometry, compendia of cosmography and optics.[24]

The tutor, however, was not alone in teaching mathematics. In fact, owing to the developments that transformed the mathematical sciences, the teaching of these disciplines was increasingly shared with other college fellows who were particularly inclined this way, as well as with professional teachers of mathematics and college lecturers. The more promising of such students also attended the lectures of the Savilian professors. During the sixteenth century the Oxford colleges tended to be less 'professional' in their offering of mathematics than some of their Cambridge counterparts, assigning instruction to either the logic or the humanities lecturer (and usually during the vacations) instead of supporting designated lecturers. However, this practice changed in the early seventeenth century. In 1616 Arthur Lake founded a mathematical lectureship at New College, and his example was

---

[22] G. A. Aitken, *The Life and Works of John Arbuthnot* (Oxford 1892, repr. London 1968), 412; *The Educational Writings of John Locke*, ed. Axtell, 290. For greater stress on the role of mathematics in training students to reason well, see *John Locke's* Of the Conduct of the Understanding, ed. F. W. Garforth (New York 1966), 51–5.

[23] *The Flemings in Oxford* i. 304; Clement Barksdale, *An Oxford Conference of Philomathes and Polymathes* (London 1660), 4.

[24] BL MS Lansdowne 695; Bodl MS Rawlinson d. 1221; *The Flemings in Oxford* i. 304; Bodl MS Rawlinson d. 1442.

soon followed by Sir Henry Savile, who endowed a lectureship at Merton College in about 1620, and Archbishop Laud, who established a mathematical lectureship at St John's College in 1636. The initial intention of these founders was, to quote Laud, to encourage 'younger fellows and students . . . to give themselves more to those studies than they have formerly done'. Soon the pattern spread to other colleges, so that by the end of the century virtually every house supported at least one fellow to teach the mathematical sciences.[25]

The expansion of expert mathematical instruction in the colleges corresponded with the growing awareness of the rapidly changing boundaries of mathematical intelligibility and the realization that, notwithstanding the relatively narrow expectations of university undergraduates, the existing tutorial system was ill suited to provide mathematical training within the brief period allotted to such studies. This attitude can be detected in the tendency of early manuals of advice to students to gloss over mathematics, not because their compilers disapproved of such instruction, but because of their explicit intention to refer, and defer, to experts in this field. Already in the 1650s Thomas Barlow (MA 1633) had introduced a cryptic statement under the heading of mathematics in which he advised: 'for mathematicks, I referre you to the professors of those sciences, who, as their knowledge is more, soe (I am confident) their charitie will not bee lesse, in communicating their directions in this particular.' Similarly, when the anonymous author of a late seventeenth-century letter of advice came to deal with astronomy, he simply stated: 'that part which treats of celestiall bodeys belongs properly to astronomy, and is therefore to be referred to mathematicks.' Even John Grandorge of St Edmund Hall, who did prescribe a few basic mathematical texts, still suggested that if the student have in mind 'to make any further progresse in this science, he may consult those who teach mathematicks *ex professo*'.[26]

What these compilers in effect recommended was what had increasingly become the practice of most students who could afford it, which was to employ an additional tutor for the study of the mathematical sciences. This new trend, it is important to add, does not necessarily reflect adversely on the quality of the regular tutors. For though some relinquished with obvious relief the teaching of a discipline they showed neither inclination for nor great knowledge of, others no doubt did so for the opposite reason. The routine teaching of the elements of arithmetic or geometry could be as tedious to a mathematician as the teaching of grammar to a literary scholar. Whatever the reason, the trend of acquiring a separate tutor for mathematics caught on quickly. By the late 1680s Stephen Penton (principal of St Edmund Hall 1676–84) articulated what had became widespread practice: 'it will be very accomplishing to have some time set apart for the mathematicks', he

[25] Feingold, *The Mathematicians' Apprenticeship*, 38; Laud, *Works* vii. 192; J. Jones, *Balliol College* (Oxford 1988), 144.
[26] [Thomas Barlow], '*A Library for Younger Schollers*', ed. A. Dejordy and H. F. Fletcher (Urbana Ill. 1961), 4; Bodl. MS Rawlinson d. 188, 4; Bodl. MS St Edmund Hall 72, fo 522.

advised newcomers to Oxford, but that study requires 'a tutor particular, whose singular conversation in that study shall teach him much in little time'.[27]

Perhaps the first to become a full-time teacher of mathematics at Oxford was Richard Holland, who from the early 1620s taught 'geography and mathematics among the young scholars for about 50 years, grew wealthy and being always sedulous in his employment, several afterwards became eminent by his instruction'. Holland handed over his flourishing practice some time before his death in 1677 to John Caswell of Hart Hall, who carried on with equal success until his appointment in 1709 as Savilian professor of geometry. Other instructors included John Hulett (MA 1633), who taught at Oxford from the late 1630s until his death in 1663, and Thomas Edwards (m. 1686), who tutored Oxford students from the late 1680s to the end of the century.[28]

Naturally much of our evidence concerning the students of these teachers derives from occasional references in letters or tutors' accounts. John Robartes, future earl of Radnor, for example, was taught mathematics while at Oxford in 1626 by the visiting orientalist and mathematician Mathias Pasor. Francis Greville, third Lord Brooke, having arrived at Magdalen Hall in 1653, hired John Hulett to read mathematics with him. The young nobleman quickly proceeded to acquire copies of Edmund Wingate's *Arithmetic* (1652) and Henry Gellibrand's *Trigonometry* (1633), in addition to various mathematical instruments. A decade later, Ralph Bohun began teaching geometry to John Evelyn the younger, but before long responsibility for the youth's mathematical education was transferred to Richard Holland, who devoted himself to Evelyn for an hour each day. The rapid spread of this custom can be seen in other instances. In 1679 Henry Fleming studied mathematics with his tutor; but when his younger brother George came up to Oxford a decade later it was decided that one of the local mathematics teachers should be engaged.[29]

Instead of one of these teachers of mathematics, some of the greater noblemen employed a fellow of a college renowned for his mathematical expertise. In part, such a predilection may have been motivated by considerations of social status. In 1667 John Beale, though appreciative of Holland's talent, none the less commented that his 'presence is not so gracefull, as to give much lustre to those ingenious arts'.[30] And such a personal consideration—in addition to the usual considerations of talent—may have played a role in the selection of a mathematics teacher. Be this as it may, in 1672 the earl of Lauderdale's nephew was instructed by Edward Bernard, then substituting for Christopher Wren as Savilian professor of astronomy. For many noblemen who entered Christ Church, a natural choice was to engage the very talented (and very accomplished) Henry Aldrich. In 1674, for

[27] Stephen Penton, *New Instructions to the Guardian* (London 1694), 97.

[28] Wood, *Athenae* iii. 649, 1109, iv. 690, 737; E. G. R. Taylor, *The Mathematical Practitioners of Tudor and Stuart England* (Cambridge 1954), 205, 238, 254, 272.

[29] *The Theological Works of the Learned Dr. Pocock*, ed. L. Twells (2 vols London 1740) i. 2; Warwick. RO, CR 1886/TN21; CL Evelyn correspondence, nos 307–9; *The Flemings in Oxford* iii. 24.

[30] CL Evelyn correspondence, no. 88.

example, Aldrich was overseeing the mathematical instruction of Charles Fitzroy, earl of Southampton, and a couple of years later he was again engaged to serve in the same capacity to Lord James Butler, the future second duke of Ormonde.[31]

By the end of the century the even more 'modern' concept of a mathematics class came into being, witnessed by the course followed by John Evelyn the third who took a comprehensive course of lectures conducted by John Keill at Balliol College from 1699 to 1700. The course comprised both theoretical and practical mathematics, including arithmetic, geometry, trigonometry, astronomy, dialling, surveying, stereometry, and geography. In 1700 David Gregory, Savilian professor of astronomy, circulated a scheme offering to institute—if a sufficient number of students were interested, which he reckoned should be more than ten and less than fifteen—a comprehensive course for the teaching of the mathematical sciences, divided into seven 'schools': Euclid, trigonometry, algebra, mechanics, optics, the principles of astronomy and cosmology. Gregory reckoned that each could be completed within three months, assuming a rate of three one-hour meetings a week. Nothing came of the plan, but other, shorter, courses began to mushroom at Oxford as the eighteenth century progressed.[32]

Mathematics, then, seemingly turned into an expertise except that a seriousness of purpose and rigorousness never developed on the part of most students or teachers. Humanistic in conception, the aim and purpose of the undergraduate course of study remained restrictive. The study of mathematics, especially for the well born, became yet another 'accomplishment'. In a manner not fundamentally different from their study of French or dancing, undergraduates received mathematical instruction for a few weeks or months—often exhibiting far less enthusiasm for it than they did for their more pleasing studies—and then moved on. And so long as the animating conception behind the instruction of mathematics remained humanistic, the opportunity presented by this inadvertent specialization to transform the status of mathematical studies within the curriculum could not be taken advantage of.

Much of our knowledge of the textbooks used by students derives from library catalogues and probate inventories. In the case of mathematics these display a basic uniformity throughout the century in terms of the number of books assigned (no doubt because of the relative brevity of the course), though with time their quality improved. The instruction in arithmetic, for example, was often based on English texts. In the early decades of the century students used Robert Recorde's

[31] *James Gregory Tercentenary Memorial Volume*, ed. H. W. Turnbull (London 1939), 178; BL Add. MSS 46,952, fo 185, 46,956A, fo 36. For an example of the esteem in which Aldrich's learning was held see Sluse's comment to Oldenburg in 1673 on the young man 'whose kindness, learning and scholarship beyond his years I cannot sufficiently commend': *The Correspondence of Henry Oldenburg*, ed. A. R. Hall and M. B. Hall (13 vols Madison and London 1965–86) x. 179. John Percival also commented on Aldrich that he was 'a gentleman born, well bread himself, and tho excellent both in ancient and modern learning yet wholly free from all that can be interpreted as pedantry': BL Add. MS 49,956A, fo 36.

[32] CL Evelyn correspondence nos 692–702; *Private Correspondence and Miscellaneous Papers of Samuel Pepys 1679–1703*, ed. J. R. Tanner (2 vols New York n.d.) ii. 91–4.

The Grounde of Artes (1540) and Thomas Hill's *The Arte of Vulgar Arithmeticke* (1600), but by the 1650s these sixteenth-century manuals had been replaced with Wingate's *Arithmetick Made Easie*—a very popular text that continued to be prescribed until the early eighteenth century—or Sir Jonas Moore's *Arithmetick*. Geometry invariably began with a study of at least the first six books of Euclid's *Elements*, though tutors differed in their choice of edition, some preferring Barrow's and others opting for Fournier's. Some students also supplemented their reading of Euclid with Petrus Ryff's *Quaestiones geometricae*. By the second half of the seventeenth century some undergraduates began to delve further into algebra. For these students William Oughtred's *Clavis mathematica* proved attractive until the end of the century, as did John Kersey's *The Elements of . . . Algebra*. Finally, the transformation of teaching by the last two decades of the century meant that increasing numbers of students acquired, in addition to the basic arithmetic and geometry texts, also one of the larger compendia that became popular, such as the *Mathematicae totius . . . clara, brevis & accurata institutio* of the Jesuit Pierre Gaultruche, William Leybourne's *Cursus mathematicus* or Claude François Milliet Dechales's *Cursus seu mundus mathematicus*.[33]

As well as the limited nature of mathematics within the undergraduate curriculum, the other essential feature was its practical orientation. Here, however, it is first necessary to lay to rest a long-standing misconception concerning the alleged hostility of the universities towards applied mathematics and mathematical practitioners—the received view being that whatever attention was paid to mathematics was confined to abstract book learning. Thus it continues to be argued that the mechanical philosophy was much indebted to the mathematics pursued by London practitioners, for whom instruments were a hallmark.[34] Implicit in all such claims is the corollary that the universities were averse to 'base' practical sciences and the instruments used by the mathematical practitioners. The following anecdote related by Seth Ward to John Aubrey has often been used to illustrate such a supposedly contemptuous, élitist view on the part of university dons. Sir Henry Savile (plate 9), so the story went, wishing for an Oxford man to serve as his first professor of geometry, interviewed Edmund Gunter for the position. Gunter arrived 'and brought with him his sector and quadrant, and fell to resolving of triangles and doeing a great many fine things. Said the grave knight, "Doe you call this reading of geometrie? This is shewing of tricks, man!", and so dismisst him

[33] This paragraph is based on an extensive study of library catalogues and book acquisition records, in particular those of John English, Thomas Cole, Edward Bernard, Robert South, John Percival, Henry and George Fleming, James Wilding, Peter Wood, and John Evelyn: W. C. Costin, 'The inventory of John English', *Oxoniensia* xi (1946–7), 119; Bodl. MS Lat. misc. f. 11, pp. 15–17; Bodl. MS Rawlinson d. 258; *The Flemings in Oxford* i. 295–6, ii. 284, iii. 16; BL Add. MSS. 46,952, fo 52, 46,953, fo 122; 'The account-book of an Oxford undergraduate 1682–1688', ed. E. G. Duff, *Collectanea* i, 268; OUA chancellor's ct inventories s.v. Thomas Cole (1652) and Peter Wood (1703); CL, Evelyn correspondence, no. 701.

[34] J. A. Bennett, 'The mechanics' philosophy and the mechanical philosophy', *History of Science* xxiv (1986), 1–28.

with scorne, and sent for [Henry] Briggs, from Cambridge.'[35] In point of fact Briggs had been professor of geometry at Gresham College in London for more than twenty years, while Gunter at the time was a Student of Christ Church, Oxford. Nevertheless historians have found in this anecdote confirmation of Oxford's disdain for—and lack of interest in—the utilitarian spirit that prevailed in the capital and supposedly fostered the awakening of English science. As Christopher Hill has put it, science in the Elizabethan age was 'the work of merchants and craftsmen, not of dons; carried on in London, not in Oxford and Cambridge'. For him, as well as for other scholars, the anecdote is indicative of the different 'conceptions of lecturing' at Oxford and Gresham College, 'and the Oxford attitude towards handicrafts'. Building on Hill, O'Day has interpreted the episode as evidence of Savile's hostility towards innovative, practical approaches to teaching. With a similar dichotomizing tendency, Pattenden has attributed Charles Turnbull's departure from Oxford to the fact that 'practical applications of mathematics were frowned upon' there.[36]

As regards the Savile anecdote, an alternative explanation can be offered of his irritation with Gunter's seemingly excessive preoccupation with instruments. Savile feared not practical mathematics *per se*, but a toying with instruments that might mask a shaky grounding in the theoretical parts of mathematics. His vision in endowing the professorships of geometry and astronomy was extremely ambitious. He explicitly required the future professors to be solidly grounded in both mathematics and philosophy, believing that only such multi-faceted scholars would be suited for the position.[37] What Savile attempted to exclude was not instruments but an infatuation with them that would subvert the mathematical curriculum. Savile, it must be stressed, required his two professors to address practical mathematics. The professor of geometry was instructed, in addition to his regular lectures, 'to teach and expound arithmetic of all kinds, both speculative and practical, land surveying, or practical geometry, canonics or music, and mechanics'. Similarly, the astronomy professor was 'to explain and teach ... the whole science of optics, gnomonics, geography, and the rules of navigation in so far as they are dependent on mathematics'. In fact, Savile's fears were very similar to those expressed by William Oughtred a few years later during the priority dispute between Oughtred

---

[35] *Brief Lives by Aubrey*, ed. Clark ii. 215.

[36] C. Hill, *Intellectual Origins of the English Revolution* (Oxford 1965), 15, 54–5; O'Day, *Education and Society*, 111; P. Pattenden, *Sundials at an Oxford College* (Oxford 1979), 31. The recollections of John Wallis have also been widely interpreted as indicative of the low level of mathematics teaching at the universities and a concomitant disregard for its practical application: 'for mathematicks ... were scarce looked upon as accademical studies, but rather mechanical; as the business of traders, merchants, seamen, carpenters, surveyors of lands, or the like, and perhaps some almanack-makers in London. ... For the study of mathematicks was at that time more cultivated in London than in the universities.' Scriba, 'The autobiography of John Wallis', 27.

[37] 'I ordain, enact, and decree, that the professors or lecturers are, for all time, to be elected from among ... [those] who, after having in the first instance drawn the purer philosophy from the fountains of Aristotle and Plato, are very well versed in mathematics, with the addition of a fair knowledge, at least, of the Greek tongue.' *Statutes*, trans. Ward i. 277.

and Richard Delamaine over the invention of a slide-rule: 'It is a preposterous course of vulgar teachers, to begin with instruments, and not with the sciences, and so instead of artists, to make their schollers only doers of tricks, and as it were juglers.' Oughtred, like Savile, was convinced that it was the duty of the mathematics teacher to convey first the theoretical foundations of the art before embarking on the 'superficiall scumme and froth of instrumentall trickes and practises'. As Oughtred told one of his students, William Forster, he intended 'to commend to [him] the skill of instruments, but first he would have [Forster] well instructed in the sciences'.[38] The source of Savile's irritation, therefore, ought to be understood in terms of priorities, not as a reflection of his antagonism to instruments or applied science.

The distinctive practical orientation of the mathematical course at the university also assumed prior acquisition of a theoretical grounding. James Cleland, for instance, admonished the university-bound nobleman to acquire the rules underlying the design of instruments—as well as the knowledge of geometry, optics, and astronomy—and to master their use, whether they be simple instruments such as rule and compass, or more complex ones such as astrolabe, globe, and sphere. Likewise, in tutoring John Aubrey through correspondence, John Lydall of Trinity College (MA 1647) unambiguously conveyed his conviction of the need to join together 'the more scholastick and geometricall part of navigation' and related disciplines, together with a study of their practical applications.[39] The expression of surprise by Robert Frank at Lydall's letters because 'they indicate a familiarity with a range of "practical" mathematical subjects hardly to be expected in so academic an environment' is, of course, symptomatic of the misunderstanding of the nature of mathematical instruction at Oxford. Tutors saw no dichotomy between theoretical and practical learning. To adapt Frank, they also shared 'Lydall's catholicity' and 'in their mathematics they were self-consciously neither "abstract" nor "practical". Rather, they saw no division between the two.'[40]

Most students were expected to own at least a modest collection of the essential instruments required for the basics of arithmetic, geometry, and astronomy, both theoretical and practical. These included a scale and compass, slide-rule, maps, and often a quadrant. Some students brought such instruments from home, and consequently no record of their ownership survives, except perhaps when the instrument required mending, as was the case with James Wilding's quadrant in the 1680s. Other students acquired such instruments, new or second-hand, at Oxford,

[38] *Statutes*, trans. Ward i. 273–4; A. J. Turner, 'Mathematical instruments and the education of gentlemen', *Annals of Science* xxx (1973), 59–60. Decades later Gilbert Burnet advised in the same spirit: without grounding in arithmetic, geometry, and trigonometry 'one may be a mechanist, but a mathematician shall he never be'. J. Clarke, *Bishop Gilbert Burnet as Educationist* (Aberdeen 1914), 61. For an early illustration of practical teaching by the Savilian professors see *Astronomiae studiosis D D D I[ohn] B[ainbridge] Quadrantes isti fiunt et cum libello prostant venales apud W. W. Oxonii* (London 1622).
[39] James Cleland, *The Institution of a Young Noble Man*, ed. M. Molyneux (2 vols New York 1948) i. 91–3; R. G. Frank Jr, 'John Aubrey, F. R. S., John Lydall, and science at commonwealth Oxford', *Notes and Records of the Royal Society* xxvii (1973), 200, 216–17.
[40] Frank, 'John Lydall', 199–200.

as Thomas Crosfield did in 1626 when he purchased second-hand 'a little globe, a dyall, a pair of compasses for 4s', or George Fleming in 1689 when he acquired a pair of compasses and a quadrant for 3s 6d. The more affluent of the students, however, often had new and expensive instruments built to specification. One of Theophilus Gale's students at Magdalen College, for example, laid out £3 15s for a new pair of globes and their carriage to Oxford, and nearly half a century later John Evelyn spared little expense and effort in ordering from London a complete set of mathematical instruments for the use of his grandson at Oxford, even engaging John Arbuthnot to inspect them.[41]

Compared with London, instrument-makers were quite rare at Oxford, and their shops very meagre. Indeed, in 1671 Edward Bernard thought that the absence of 'a set of grinders of glasses, instrument makers, operators, and the like' was one reason why Oxford was prevented from becoming a major scientific research centre.[42] Obviously, the size of the university town and the rather limited (and specialized) needs of the student body could not support many professional instrument-makers. The proximity to London, and the fact that so many of the university members were able to construct their own instruments, alleviated some of the problem. Nevertheless, some instrument-makers did make Oxford their home. Christopher Brookes, manciple of Wadham College and William Oughtred's son-in-law, settled into the business in 1649 and sold a variety of instruments at the college until his death in 1665. His trade was picked up by John Prujean, who, from his shop near New College, dominated the Oxford trade in scientific instruments for the last three decades of the seventeenth century. Prujean constructed and sold a large variety of instruments—many of which were designed by Oxford dons—and from the catalogue he published in 1701 it is possible to deduce the kind of instruments that were likely to be in demand at Oxford:

Quadrants of Richard Holland's, Oughtred's and Gunter's patterns; Gunther's nocturnal, Imanuel Halton's quadrant, with Halley's notes; Orontia's sinical quadrant; John Caswell's nocturnal; Tomson's pantamerton; Thomas Edward's astrolabe, scales for fortification, double horizontal dial, and analemma; John Collins's quadrant; Napier's rods; Halley's nocturnal; James Pound's cylinder-dial; George Hooper's dialling scales.[43]

[41] 'The account-book of an Oxford undergraduate', ed. Duff, 266; *The Diary of Thomas Crosfield*, ed. F. S. Boas (London 1935), 5; *The Flemings in Oxford* ii. 284; Bodl. MS Rawlinson d. 715, fo 218; BL Add. MS 15,949, fos 38–9ᵛ. Evelyn was assured that if John Keill, the youth's teacher, 'misliked' the instruments, they would be replaced. See also CL MS 421, for an account of Thomas Southwell's instruments in 1683. Evelyn's younger contemporary at Balliol, William Brydges, wrote home in 1703 requesting mathematical instruments and announcing his intention to 'goe out a measuring', confident that with practice he would make himself a 'master of measuring and surveying'. Jones, *Balliol College*, 145.

[42] S. P. Rigaud, *Correspondence of Scientific Men of the Seventeenth Century* (2 vols Oxford 1841) i. 159.

[43] Taylor, *Mathematical Practitioners*, 234, 256; R. G. Frank Jr, *Harvey and the Oxford Physiologists* (Berkeley and Los Angeles 1980), 80–1. Prujean's advertisement was published as an appendix to Holland's *Globe Notes* (Oxford 1701). Many of the items sold by Prujean were 'inexpensive paper instruments, the sort of which an undergraduate could readily afford to buy'. See D. J. Bryden, 'Made in Oxford: John Prujean's 1701 catalogue of mathematical instruments', *Oxoniensia* lviii (1993), 263–84. Several cardboard versions of these instruments can be found in the Museum of the History of Science at Oxford (I am grateful to Dr N. Tyacke for this information.)

Naturally, most students could not afford the more expensive instruments, and only a handful, even among the wealthy, thought it necessary to purchase specialized items. However, the use of these tools—which included a variety of optical, astronomical, and surveying instruments—was still taught, with the students usually relying on the private collections of their teachers or on the instruments Oxford colleges had assiduously acquired ever since the late sixteenth century. The very impressive collection of instruments owned by the Savilian professors and utilized in their teaching will be discussed below; here it suffices to point out the availability of such instruments for undergraduate teaching in the colleges. Archbishop Laud, for example, acquired a small collection of instruments for St John's College, and these, together with a few more that were added later, were borrowed by the college's mathematical lecturers for teaching purposes (plate 22). Trinity College library, too, was endowed with a good collection of instruments, which were evidently used in the advanced scientific instruction that was given at the college throughout the second half of the seventeenth century.[44]

No less suggestive of scientific interest is the private ownership of instruments by various fellows, who most probably employed them in their tutorial instruction. Such use was certainly made of the 'great many mathematicall instruments' owned by Thomas Allen. In general, our knowledge of even the existence of such instruments is fragmentary, confined to probate inventories and wills. President Nicholas Bond of Magdalen College, for example, owned a pair of globes and various other instruments at the time of his death in 1616, while the inventory of the goods of William Willis of Trinity College in 1663 recorded his ownership of a quadrant, a pair of globes and nine maps. In his will Robert Burton bequeathed his instruments to two favourite young scholars of Christ Church whom he expected to benefit from such gifts: 'I give to John Fell [the future dean of Christ Church] ... my mathematical instruments except my two crosse staves, which I give to my lord of Doune if he be then of the house.' Similarly the inventory of another Student of Christ Church, Thomas Lockey, reveals his ownership of 'a telescope with some other mathematicall instruments'.[45]

Equally significantly all professional teachers of mathematics at Oxford were known for their expertise in the design and construction of instruments, as well as for their skill in communicating the abstract principles of the various mathematical sciences. John Hulett was expert in the construction and use of quadrants and dials, and author of a manual, *Description and Use of a Quadrant* (1665). Thomas Edwards, too, published a manual, *Dialling made Easy* (1692), as well as designing a few instruments that were sold by Prujean. Both Richard Holland and John Caswell

---

[44] J. Fuggles, 'William Laud and the library of St John's College, Oxford', *The Book Collector* xxx (1981), 33. In 1654 Evelyn thought the St John's collection was worthy of mention. *The Diary of John Evelyn*, ed. E. S. De Beer (6 vols Oxford 1955) iii. 108; *The Journeys of Celia Fiennes*, ed. C. Morris (London 1949), 65.

[45] *Brief Lives by Aubrey*, ed. Clark i. 27; Macray, *Reg. Magdalen* ii. 180; Frank, 'John Lydall', 199; R. L. Nochimson, 'Studies in the life of Robert Burton', *Yearbook of English Studies* iv (1974), 103; I. G. Philip, 'Inventory of the goods of Dr Thomas Lockey', *Bodleian Library Record* v (1954–7), 84.

taught the use of mathematical and astronomical instruments, and the latter also took part in the attempt at a geodetic survey of England between 1681 and 1684.[46] In addition college tutors instructed their students in the use of instruments: Thomas Brancker of Exeter (MA 1658), who published in 1662 *Doctrinae sphaericae adumbratio una cum usu globorum artificialium*, and Edward Wells of Christ Church (MA 1693), who at the end of the century began publishing the series of manuals he had utilized in teaching geometry, optics, astronomy, and dialling.[47]

Save for a few individuals who intended to pursue astronomy as a vocation, the subject, like the other mathematical disciplines upon which astronomy was grounded, was valued by early modern tutors and educators primarily for its practical usefulness. Consequently the undergraduate course in astronomy was designed to provide only a panoramic view of the field, not mastery of it. In fact, astronomy was studied in conjunction with cosmography, from which subject the students branched out to familiarize themselves with the frame and constitution of the visible world and delved into the study of the mathematical representation of the heavenly bodies. It was, then, predominantly a descriptive course, sharing with arithmetic and geometry a utilitarian orientation and grounding in the use of instruments. Within such a framework, discussion of cosmology and planetary theory was considered, for the most part, incidental. The expectation was that a detailed and considered estimation of such issues would be pursued after graduation, once the student had accumulated knowledge and judgement. Instead, students primarily acquired the basic principles of spherical astronomy; they learned to recognize the location of the various constellations and to understand the meaning of a host of concepts such as zodiac, meridian, horizon, equinoxes, ecliptic, longitude and latitude. These preliminaries were followed by a discussion of the apparent motions of the heavenly bodies, to which was joined basic instruction in observational methods. When discussion turned to consideration of stellar distances, the velocity of planets, eclipses, brightness, and like topics, teachers could raise cosmological issues but a detailed discussion of planetary theories as such was not considered essential to the undergraduate course.

The study of astronomy also shared with arithmetic and geometry a common pedagogical approach. To facilitate learning, by the second decade of the seventeenth century tutors began to prepare brief manuals which served as the basis for the initial tutorials as well as background material to the study of the prescribed textbooks that the student was expected to pursue largely on his own. Thomas Knightley of Lincoln College, for example, composed an 'introduction to astronomie' for John and Richard Eliot in 1629, and two years later John Crowther of Magdalen Hall diligently 'brought to a perfect and complete head' the 'astronomy notes' he had prepared for the benefit of Ralph Verney. The rapid spread of the custom is evident in many commonplace books such as Humphrey Hody's

---

[46] Taylor, *Mathematical Practitioners*, 205, 238, 254, 272, 373, 406.
[47] Wood, *Athenae* iii. 1086–87; see also *DNB* s.v. Edward Wells

notebooks, written while he was at Wadham in the mid-1670s and which included, as we have noted, a system of cosmography.[48]

The brevity and limited scope of the undergraduate astronomy course also account for the relative homogeneity of the textbooks. The expectation that only two or three books could be digested before it was time to move on meant that most textbooks were geared towards the treatment of the spheres. During the first half of the seventeenth century the most commonly used text was Sacrobosco's *De sphaera*, usually in Christopher Clavius' edition. Thomas Sixsmith of Brasenose was only one among many tutors who assigned 'Clavius and other commentators uppon Johannes de Sacrobosco' to their students. John Hutton, a student at New College (BA 1650), purchased Clavius together with Rembertus Dodonaeus' *De sphaera*, while Thomas Cole of University College (MA 1631) preferred Oronce Finé's *Sphaera mundi*. Whatever differences existed among tutors, these were evident only in the choice of the accompanying text. Sixsmith recommended Michael Maestlin's *Epitome astronomiae*, Hutton acquired Cornelius Gemma's *De principiis astronomiae and cosmographiae*, while Cole utilized the relevant section in Bartholomew Keckermann's encyclopaedic *Systema compendiosa totius mathematices*.[49]

Though the new textbooks that began to make their way into students' hands from the 1640s may have been more up to date, they none the less preserved the basic framework of what was considered the appropriate astronomy course, and thus served as introductions to spherical astronomy. Certainly the two most popular new texts, Pierre Gassendi's *Institutio astronomica* and Moxon's *A Tutor to Astronomie and Geographie*, admirably suited such a purpose both by virtue of their coverage of much the same subject-matter as Sacrobosco's *Sphaera* and their accommodation of the growing need to provide the student with a detailed discussion of the Ptolemaic, Copernican, and Tychonic systems. The popularity of these texts can be gathered from the frequency with which they were assigned. At least one of John Locke's students was asked to purchase Gassendi's *Institutio* in 1663; John Freind of St Edmund Hall bought a copy in 1672, and Henry Fleming was instructed to study it in 1681.[50] Such examples can be multiplied. Similarly, Moxon's textbook was read both by John Percival at Christ Church in the 1670s and by Thomas Devey of Magdalen Hall two decades later, while John Grandorge's letter of advice of 1690 recommended both Gassendi and Moxon to his students. In addition, as we saw earlier, by the last two decades of the seventeenth century, students were making growing use of the new genre of 'cursus mathematicus', which included extensive sections on astronomy and the globe. James Wilding, for example, acquired Pierre Gaultruche's *Philosophiae ac mathematicae institutio*,

[48] J. Forster, *Sir John Eliot* (2 vols London 1864) ii. 589; F. P. Verney, *Memoirs of the Verney Family* (4 vols London 1892–9) i. 119, 23; Bodl. MS Rawlinson d. 1221, see p. 368 above.

[49] BNCL MS 80; OUA chancellor's ct inventories s.v. Hutton and Cole.

[50] Bodl. MS Locke f. 11, fo 28; Bodl. MS top. Oxon. f. 31, p. 171; *The Flemings in Oxford* ii. 73.

while George Fleming studied his astronomy from William Leybourne's *Cursus mathematicus*.[51]

Much of what the textbook lacked in detail and profundity, especially in the early part of the seventeenth century, was furnished by the tutors. The teaching of both Richard Crackanthorpe and Brian Twyne demonstrates the manner in which recent discoveries were easily interspersed into the traditional Aristotelian framework. Richard Crakanthorpe of Queen's College (fellow 1598–1624) familiarized his students in the 1610s with Tycho Brahe's work on the nova of 1572 and the comet of 1577, and provided them with details of the telescopic discoveries of Galileo, while seemingly engaged in a straightforward discussion of Aristotle's *De coelo*. Crakanthorpe's exact contemporary at Corpus Christi, Brian Twyne, also introduced his students to the telescopic discoveries of Galileo and some of the astronomical and optical views of Kepler. Again, such examples can be multiplied.[52] The receptivity of the students to these ideas can be seen by the growing number of instances in which undergraduates incorporated in their exercises themes derived from the new astronomy. One such theme was whether the moon was inhabitable. Thomas Crosfield recorded the disputation of students in the college hall on that topic, and in 1651 another member of Queen's, Charles Potter, published six topics he had discussed, which included the habitability of the moon (which was answered affirmatively) and the fluidity of the heavens.[53]

Despite the growing awareness among undergraduates of astronomical and cosmological issues, the need to cover the entire arts and sciences curriculum within three or four years naturally precluded any great proficiency in such topics. It was, therefore, only after they graduated BA that students who were inclined to scientific studies could seriously apply themselves this way, and here the pedagogical function of the Savilian professors of astronomy became most important. Sir Henry Savile's statutes specified that the duty of the professor was

> to explain the whole mathematical economy of Ptolemy . . . applying in their proper place the discoveries of Copernicus, Geber, and other modern writers . . . provided, however, that he may lay before his auditors, by way of introduction to the arcana of the science, the sphere of Proclus, or Ptolemy's hypotheses of the planets, and teach, either publicly or privately, the arithmetic of sexagesimal fractions.

Also included in the purview of the astronomy professor was the teaching of optics, geography, and navigation; to his discretion was left the decision whether

---

[51] BL Add. MS 46,953, fo 122; J. L. Salter, 'The books of an early eighteenth-century curate', *The Library* 5th ser. xxxiii (1978), 38, 42; 'The account-book of an Oxford undergraduate', ed. Duff, 268; *The Flemings in Oxford* iii. 16.

[52] QCL MS 196, fos 118–33; QCL MS 224, fos 130–81ᵛ CCCL MS 254; M. H. Curtis, *Oxford and Cambridge in Transition* (Oxford 1959), 121–2; F. Ovenell, 'Brian Twyne's library', *Oxford Bibliographical Society* iv (1952), 3–42; Feingold, *The Mathematicians' Apprenticeship*, 66, 73.

[53] QCL MS 390, fo 177; Charles Potter, *Theses quadragesimales in scholis Oxonii* (Oxford 1651). According to Wood, however, the work was actually written by Potter's tutor, Thomas Severne. See Wood, *Athenae* iii. 649.

to teach 'the spherics of Theodosius and Menelaus, and the doctrine of triangles, as well plane as spherical'.[54]

For the most part the professors found it possible to dispense with the teaching of the introductory material, for such instruction was largely carried out within the colleges. Instead, they either opted for topics that were central to the discipline at the time or, as frequently happened, taught around their current research interests. Indeed, such a pattern was initiated by the first occupant of the Savilian chair, John Bainbridge (plate 10). The chance survival of Bainbridge's papers enables us to witness the admirable manner with which he carried out his responsibilities. During the two decades in which he served as Savilian professor, Bainbridge lectured on all the topics stipulated in the statutes. He addressed theoretical issues along with methods and techniques of observation, discussed cosmological issues as well as topics drawn from chronology and the history of astronomy, and did not neglect optics and applied astronomy. Most significant, his lectures reveal him to be a true convert to the new astronomy, and he must have been instrumental in introducing generations of Oxford students and dons to the Galilean and Keplerian theories. Bainbridge was probably the first at Oxford to lecture publicly on Keplerian astronomy, and by the late 1620s he had delivered a course of lectures on elliptical planetary orbits—which he accepted as real. Bainbridge also lectured on topics raised by Galileo's discoveries and Kepler's optics and physics, from lunar theory to comets or the transit of Venus. Undoubtedly his teaching inspired many students, some of whom, notably John Wilkins and Jonathan Goddard, would be instrumental in cultivating the advanced study of astronomy at Oxford during the 1650s.[55]

Less is known about the tenure of John Greaves as Savilian professor, although as Gresham professor he had earlier collaborated with Bainbridge in astronomical matters. Since he was elected in 1643, in the midst of the civil war, and as he was ejected six years later, the amount of teaching he was able to do was probably not extensive.[56] Consequently it is possible to view Seth Ward as the restorer of astronomical studies to Oxford, for, in addition to being a first-rate astronomer, he closely emulated Bainbridge's commitment and diligence. By his own account, during his tenure as professor Ward never missed a class and always enjoyed 'a good auditory'. Part of the reason for his success was his special talent for making difficult material palatable to students, so much so, in fact, that years after he left Oxford the reputation of his lectures still lingered. In 1667 Francis Vernon extolled the teaching of the professor who had inspired him a decade earlier, describing in

[54] *Statutes*, trans. Ward i. 273–4.

[55] Trinity College Dublin MSS 382–6; Bodl. MS Add. a. 380, fos 204–9ᵛ; N. Tyacke, 'Science and religion at Oxford before the civil war' in D. Pennington and K. Thomas (eds), *Puritans and Revolutionaries: essays in seventeenth-century history presented to Christopher Hill* (Oxford 1979), 78, 82–3; A. J. Apt, 'The reception of Kepler's astronomy in England: 1596–1650' (Oxford D. Phil. thesis 1982), 246–55.

[56] As late as 19 September 1644 Greaves informed Archbishop Ussher that he was still prevented from lecturing: James Ussher, *The Whole Works*, ed. C. R. Elrington (17 vols Dublin 1847–64) xvi. 74.

charming verse the enlivening manner in which Ward unlocked the mysteries of the heavens to his captivated auditors.[57]

Ward himself described his teaching method thus:

The method here observed in our schooles is, first to exhibit the phenomena, and shew the way of their observations, then to give an account of the various hypotheses, how those phenomena have been salved, or may be (where the aequipollency or defects of the severall hypotheses are shewn.) And lastly to shew how the geometricall hypotheses are resolvible into tables, serving for calculation of ephemerides, which are of quotidian use.

Certainly the appearance of a comet in December 1652 was an event that lent itself to a detailed discussion, and Ward duly delivered at least one lecture in 1653 that surveyed previous comets and weighed the variety of theories advanced to explain them, proceeding modestly to propose 'that it was much more probable they might rather be carried round in circles or ellipses ... so great that the comets are never visible to us but when they come to the perigees of those circles or ellipses'. It is also clear from remarks made by Ward in his response to John Webster's *Academiarum examen* that Ward also lectured more generally on elliptical astronomy, perhaps even delivering in some form the detailed criticism of Ismael Boulliau that he published in 1654 and 1656. In 1654 Ward also published an epitome of plane and spherical trigonometry aimed at preparing younger students to cope with the mathematics necessary to follow the astronomy of ellipses. Likewise, from some notes penned by Christopher Wren it is possible to deduce that *circa* 1656 Ward taught a course that centred on Galileo's *Discorsi*.[58]

Wren was elected as Ward's successor in 1661. He was undoubtedly the most original of the seventeenth-century astronomy professors and for this reason it is doubly unfortunate that his lectures do not survive. However, in view of his predecessors' practice of expounding their current research interests and of Wren's own such practice while serving as Gresham professor of astronomy between 1657 and 1661, it is not unreasonable to assume that Wren acted similarly at Oxford. Thus, he may have offered up the results of his work on Saturn as he had done at Gresham College in 1659, and perhaps presented his theory of comets following the appearance of one in 1664. Nevertheless, by the late 1660s Wren was often called away to London and his frequent absences prompted him to appoint Edward Bernard as his deputy; with Wren's resignation in 1673, Bernard became his official successor.[59]

[57] Tyacke, 'Science and religion at Oxford before the civil war', 83–4; Walter Pope, *The Life of . . . Seth, Lord Bishop of Salisbury*, ed. J. B. Bamborough (Oxford 1961), 25; Francis Vernon, *Oxonium poema* (Oxford 1667), 13–14.

[58] Robert Plot, *The Natural History of Oxford-shire* (Oxford 1677, 2nd edn Oxford 1705), 229–31; [John Wilkins and Seth Ward], *Vindiciae academiarum* (Oxford 1654), 29–30, repr. in A. G. Debus, *Science and Education in the Seventeenth Century: the Webster–Ward debate* (London 1970); Seth Ward, *De cometis . . . inquisitio in Ismaelis Bullialdi astronomia philolaicae fundamenta* (Oxford 1653); Seth Ward, *Idea trigonometriae demonstratae* (Oxford 1654); Seth Ward, *Astronomica geometrica* (Oxford 1656); J. A. Bennett, 'Hooke and Wren and the system of the world: some points towards an historical account', *British Journal for the History of Science* viii (1975), 38 n. 32.

[59] J. A. Bennett, *The Mathematical Science of Christopher Wren* (Cambridge 1982); Bennett 'Hooke and Wren and the system of the world'.

In 1671 Bernard 'apologized' to John Collins that the mathematics he possessed was 'but just enough to admire Dr. Wallis here, and yourself and some few other abroad, and the remain[der] of [my] study is literal'. Though Bernard was unduly modest, his tastes were indeed somewhat different from those of his two immediate predecessors. Bernard's chief interests lay in Greek mathematics and astronomy and his scholarly work consequently aimed at collecting and republishing ancient texts rather than composing new ones. Understandably his lectures, though competent, lacked the originality of those of Ward and Wren; likewise, he dealt more with mathematical astronomy than with cosmology. At any rate, already in 1678 Bernard sought to exchange the Savilian chair with a living, hoping to see Flamsteed or Halley succeed him. However, as no suitable position was offered him, he remained professor until 1691.[60]

The new tradition of adding research to teaching and of joining cosmological speculation with meticulous astronomical observation was initiated by Savile, who made such an intention explicit in his statutes:

I also enjoin the professor of astronomy, in imitation of Ptolemy and Copernicus, and following in their track, to take astronomical observations as well as by night as by day (making choice of proper instruments prepared for the purpose, and at fitting times and seasons), and after reducing them all into writing ... And I am in hopes that the university will liberally contribute all assistance and exertion towards this object, as it is the only true way of establishing or amending the ancient astronomy.

In fact John Bainbridge, the first incumbent, recalled that Savile had intended to build an elaborate 'musaeum mathematicum' that would have included a well-furnished observatory, but died before he could bring this plan to fruition; hence the task of implementing Savile's wish was left to Bainbridge.[61]

Bainbridge was uniquely qualified for the labour. Not only was he a competent astronomer, but he evidently shared Savile's conviction concerning the importance of observations. In the absence of a separate observatory, immediately after his arrival at Oxford Bainbridge refitted the top room of the schools' tower—which had been appropriated as early as 1614 for instruction in astronomy—into a serviceable observatory, which he also had furnished with the requisite instruments. By 1629 Bainbridge owned an impressive collection, which included various telescopes, quadrants, astrolabes, solid and armillary spheres, staffs, dials, a mesolabium, and surveying instruments. Concurrent with his assumption of professorial duties Bainbridge undertook an intensive and unremitting programme of observations that would span over two decades.[62] However, the scheme that he

[60] Rigaud, *Correspondence of Scientific Men* i. 158; F. Baily, *An Account of the Reverend John Flamsteed* (London 1835, repr. London 1966), 667–8.

[61] *Statutes*, trans. Ward i. 274; Trinity College Dublin, MS 385, fo 144.

[62] R. W. T. Gunther, *Early Science in Oxford* (14 vols Oxford 1923–45) ii. 78; a list of the instruments as well as the scientific books in Bainbridge's possession can be found in Trinity College Dublin MS 385, fos 142–3ᵛ.

particularly set his mind on was far more grandiose. A firm believer in the need for multiple simultaneous observations throughout the world, Bainbridge sought to co-ordinate, from Oxford, just such an ambitious enterprise. Already in 1626 he wrote to Archbishop Ussher:

I am very busy in the fabric of a large instrument for observations, that I may, *mea fide*, both teach and write; and here again I humbly entreat you to take in your consideration my petition at Oxford, that you would, as occasion shall be offered, commend to the munificence of some noble benefactors this excellent and rare part of astronomy.[63]

His plan was to finance expeditions to various parts of the world to carry out a series of simultaneous observations in order to improve the accuracy of astronomy as well as cartography and navigation. For various reasons the grand design faltered, producing few results; still, Bainbridge continued to carry out his own observations at Oxford and these were freely communicated to astronomers both in England and on the continent.[64]

When Seth Ward arrived at Oxford in 1648 he, too, quickly turned to the matter of furnishing himself with an observatory and instruments to carry out observations. For some reason, perhaps convenience, however, he found the room at the top of the schools' tower inappropriate and opted instead to fit out a room in the Wadham College tower. As he wrote to Sir Justinian Isham in early 1652, he had 'spent much of [his] time . . . in building a slight observatory for the matter of [his] profession and in procureing and fitting telescopes and other instruments for observations'. The university contributed generously to the building of this observatory, the construction and repair of instruments, and the acquisition of books, allotting £42 for that purpose, and it was mainly from this location that most of the astronomical observations carried out by members of the Oxford group during the 1650s took place.[65] After the Restoration, though Wren may for a while have kept the room at Wadham, observations returned to the schools' tower. It was there in 1664 that John Evelyn found Wallis, Wren, and Boyle 'with an inverted tube or telescope observing the discus of the sunn for the passing of [Mercury] that day before the Sunn'.[66]

The significance of the observations carried out by the Savilian professors went beyond the results they obtained; they served to encourage others to take part as well. Thus numerous observations were carried out by Ward, Wren, Wallis, Goddard, and Neile, using improved telescopes that they themselves designed. A

[63] Ussher, *Works* xv. 352.

[64] Tyacke, 'Science and religion at Oxford', 78, 82–4; Feingold, *The Mathematicians' Apprenticeship*, 144–5, 186–7. John Greaves attempted to co-ordinate a similar design during his sojourn in the middle east in the late 1630s: see *Miscellaneous Works of Mr John Greaves*, ed. T. Birch (2 vols London 1737) ii. 434–8; *The Theological Works of the Learned Dr Pocock*, ed. Twells i. 71–2.

[65] H. W. Robinson, 'An unpublished letter of Dr Seth Ward relating to the early meetings of the Oxford Philosophical Club', *Notes and Records of the Royal Society* vii (1950), 70; R. T. Gunther, 'The first observatory instruments of the Savilian professors at Oxford', *The Observatory* (July 1937), 191.

[66] *The Diary of John Evelyn*, ed. De Beer iii. 384–5; *The Correspondence of Henry Oldenburg*, ed. Hall and Hall ii. 246

less familiar member of the group was Richard Rawlinson of Queen's College. Rawlinson observed, together with Wallis and Wren, the solar eclipse of 1654 as well as engraving the plate that accompanied the published version of their observation (plate 25). Rawlinson sent ten copies to Samuel Hartlib, requesting him to distribute them among continental savants, naming in particular Hevelius, Boulliau, and Schooten. In 1664 Rawlinson continued his observations, for which purpose he built himself a small observatory at Queen's College.[67]

The extent to which individuals applied their instruments to observe phenomena unrelated to comets, eclipses, or a transit is unclear. Weeks and months could be spent in systematic collection of data, the latter only to be lost forever with the dispersal of the observer's papers. Consequently, it is usually the demand to communicate observations of those few spectacular celestial events that affords us a glimpse of such activity. Samuel Lee, for example, observed a solar eclipse at Oxford on 25 October 1649. Similarly, Seth Ward mentioned that John Lydall of Trinity was one of the individuals to observe the 1653 comet. When another comet appeared in December 1664, Wallis and 'divers more' spent at least one whole night at the schools' tower hoping to observe it, but without success. Wallis, however, spent many subsequent nights observing the comet with his naked eye, charting its path on a celestial globe. The correspondence between Edward Bernard and John Flamsteed includes not only information about the observations of the 1680 comet carried out by the Savilian professor—and a few years later of a lunar eclipse—but evidence that on at least one occasion Henry Pigot of Wadham (MA 1683) made observations on the comet as well. In 1684 both Bernard and John Caswell observed sunspots and a few weeks later the two were joined by John Wallis and William Rooke (MA 1677, lecturer in mathematics at Queen's College) in observing a solar eclipse.[68]

The teaching of the geometry professors was comparable in quality to that offered by the astronomy professors. Thomas Crosfield's notes indicate that Briggs taught both trigonometry and algebra, and evidently introduced his Oxford auditors to his work on logarithms. John Wallis held the Savilian chair for over half a century (1648–1703) and from the start he offered up-to-date instruction in mathematics, including his own work. Seth Ward wrote in 1654 that in Wallis's lectures 'arithmetick and geometry are sincerely and profoundly taught, analyticall algebra, the solution and application of aequations, containing the whole mystery of both these sciences'. Indeed, Wallis's many publications often reflect the content of his teaching, from the rather introductory discussion of arithmetic and notation of the *Mathesis universalis* (1657) to the highly original *Arithmetica infinitorum* (1656). During his long tenure Wallis also lectured on algebra, conic sections, and mechanics. To

---

[67] John Wallis, *Eclipsis solaris Oxonii visae anno ... 1654* in *Operum mathematicorum pars altera* (Oxford 1656), paginated separately; Sheffield University Library, Hartlib papers 10/9/1–2.

[68] T. Hornberger, 'Samuel Lee (1625–1691), a clerical channel for the flow of new ideas to seventeenth-century New England', *Osiris* i (1936), 345; Ward, *De cometis*, 38–9; *Correspondence of Henry Oldenburg*, ed. Hall and Hall ii. 339–40, 354; Bodl. MSS Smith 9, fo 3, 45; fos 11–14, 32–3, 45–7; Gunter, *Early Science in Oxford* iv. 78, 81.

alleviate his routine Wallis may have employed some of his more promising students to substitute for him. George Hooper, future bishop of Bath and Wells, related that he was one such deputy during the 1660s.[69]

But in mathematics the advanced teaching of the relatively few individuals who sought to pursue such studies was dependent less on the public lectures by the professors than on their provision of private guidance. The point was plainly stated by Hobbes:

even those men that living in our universities have most advanced the mathematics, attained their knowledge by other means than that of public lectures, where few auditors, and those of unequal proficiency, cannot make benefit by one and the same lesson ... the true use of public professors, especially in the mathematics, being to resolve the doubts, and problems, as far as they can, of such as come unto them with desire to be informed.[70]

One feature of Hobbes's matter-of-fact depiction of the training of mathematicians is familiar enough today as well. However, in the context of the early modern period the need for private instruction for those seeking specialized knowledge was even more acute, since the university supported only one professor of mathematics and another of astronomy, whose lectures were intended to appeal to audiences of diverse capacities. This required careful planning on the part of the professor but, more importantly for this discussion, frequently prevented him from exploring publicly the farthest limits of the field. Seth Ward once commented on the demanding task of addressing such a mixed audience, the gist of which was repeated and elaborated upon by Edmond Halley in the early years of the eighteenth century. In his introductory lecture to a series concerning the 'geometrical construction of algebraical equations', Halley explained:

I have oftentimes experienced, on several occasions, how difficult a thing it is to discourse, especially in mathematical matters, so as to please the learned therein, and at the same time to instruct such as yet want to be taught: the former require nothing but what is new and curious, nor are pleased but with elegant demonstrations, made concise by art and pains: the latter demand explications drawn out in words, at length, least any part of the reasoning not being clearly apprehended, should hinder the evidence of the whole argument, whilst those already versed in mathematics cannot endure such prolixity.

Ultimately Halley resolved 'to consult, not so much [his] own reputation, as the profit of the auditory: omitting therefore what might make a shew of deeper learning'.[71]

Sir Henry Savile was fully cognizant of the twin obstacles of mixed audiences and the special needs of advanced students, and sought to resolve the conflict in his statutes. The duty of the professors, he stipulated, beyond their public lectures

---

[69] QCL MS 390, fos 17ᵛ, 18, 21; [Wilkins and Ward], *Vindiciae academiarum*, 28; W. M. Marshall, *George Hooper 1640–1727* (Sherborne 1976), 199; Vernon, *Oxonium poema*, 17.

[70] *The English Works of Hobbes*, ed. Molesworth vii. 346.

[71] Ward, *Idea trigonometriae demonstratae*, preface; Edmond Halley, 'Lectures read in the school of geometry in Oxford' in John Kersey, *The Elements of that Mathematical Art commonly called Algebra* (London 1717), app x, p. l.

and informal teachings of practical astronomy and geometry to any who care to listen, was to make themselves 'of easy access to the studious who would consult them on mathematical subjects, and particularly to their legitimate hearers'. In this, as in all other respects, Savile was most fortunate with his professors throughout the seventeenth century. Both Henry Briggs and John Bainbridge, respectively the first geometry and astronomy professors, were exemplary in encouraging promising youth. Henry Briggs's few surviving letters attest to his keen desire to promote mathematical studies. In his 1625 letter to Thomas Lydiat, for example, he expressed his disappointment that Lydiat's inability to attend the annual Act deprived Briggs of the opportunity to confer with him 'about our common business, the furthering of such as desire to understand the mathematics'.[72] Both Briggs and Bainbridge were responsible for the promotion of the mathematical talents of, among others, Henry Gellibrand and John Greaves. Indeed, Bainbridge's letter recommending Gellibrand for the position of Gresham professor of astronomy apprised the Gresham trustees that Gellibrand diligently attended his astronomy lectures and 'hath by many private conferences given [him] occasion to take notice of his singular skill in the mathematicks'.[73] Succeeding Savilian professors were equally forthcoming. Walter Pope attested to the diligence with which Seth Ward 'taught the mathematics gratis to as many of the university, or foreigners, as desired that favour of him', numbering among such scholars both Robert Hooke and Christopher Wren.[74] As a mentor, Wallis tutored William, Lord Brouncker, Edward Bernard, George Hooper, and Edmond Halley.[75] A few years before his death Wallis also recollected how he and Ward, apart from their public lectures and publications, 'instructed gentlemen and others, in their private lodgings' in the various mathematical sciences.[76]

The difficulty of the subject compounded by the small size of the mathematical community was responsible for a growing camaraderie among like-minded individuals, which transcended college and university boundaries, as well as (often) ideological divides. For over six decades (1570–1632) Thomas Allen of Gloucester Hall unselfishly offered his time and knowledge to teach mathematics and encourage the subsequent studies of generations of Oxford scholars, including Robert Fludd, Sir Kenelm Digby, Sir Thomas Aylesbury, John Gregory, Robert Hegge and Brian Twyne. Other individuals likewise offered their services gratis to such as wished to learn. Henry Gellibrand, for example, emulated from the start the examples of Briggs and Bainbridge, and the testimonial the president and fellows of Trinity College sent on his behalf to the Gresham trustees attests to 'his very loving readi-

[72] *Statutes*, trans. Ward i. 274; *A Collection of Letters Illustrative of the Progress of Science in England*, ed. J. O. Halliwell (London 1841), 46.

[73] Tyacke, 'Science and religion at Oxford before the civil war', 79.

[74] Pope, *The Life of Seth*, 25; Richard Waller, 'The life of Dr. Robert Hooke' in Gunther, *Early Science in Oxford* iv. 10.

[75] Thomas Smith, *Vita clarissimi et doctissimi viri Edwardi Bernardi* (London 1704), 8; Marshall, *George Hooper*, 6; C. A. Ronan, *Edmond Halley: genius in eclipse* (London 1969), 29.

[76] 'Dr Wallis's letter against Mr Maidwell', *Collectanea* i. 320.

ness, and also dexterity, and facility, freely to communicate to any one among us his knowledge in those studies'.[77]

Following Thomas Allen's death, various Oxford students came to enjoy the hospitality and superb mathematical education offered, free of charge, by the former member of King's College, Cambridge, William Oughtred, who hitherto had catered primarily to the members of his alma mater, including the future Savilian professors Seth Ward and John Wallis. Many years later Thomas Henshaw recalled how after he had been at University College for two years (1634–6), where he profited more in conversation with Obadiah Walker and Abraham Woodhead than with his own tutor John Elmherst, the two, recognizing his marked scientific bent, sent him to Oughtred 'to bee introduced by him in the study of the mathematicks'. Henshaw remained at Albury, Oughtred's Surrey rectory, for nine months before returning to complete his university education. In the following decade Robert Wood of Lincoln College (MA 1649), as he told Hartlib some years afterwards, acquired his mathematical education 'under that admirable and deservedly famous mathematician, old Mr. Oughtred'.[78]

Instrumental as were the Savilian professors in contributing to the spread of the new astronomy at Oxford through their teaching and encouragement of participation in astronomical observations, the relative ease with which Copernicanism and, later, Cartesianism and experimental philosophy came to prevail at Oxford was due in part to the tradition of philosophical toleration within the university during much of the seventeenth century. Not that most people were immediately converted to the new ideas. Many dons were as reluctant to accept Copernicanism before 1640 as the new generation of fellows was to embrace Descartes or atomism after 1650. But throughout the period both proponents and antagonists of the new science somehow managed to keep their disagreements civil and confined to the domain of learning, thus largely avoiding acrimonious public debates. Promoters of the new science were aware of the sensitivity of their colleagues, and generally refrained from unnecessary rhetorical excesses in propagating their ideas. Likewise, opponents tacitly conceded, at least to a point, the need to preserve *libertas philosophandi*, and thus usually resisted the temptation—so often resorted to on the continent—to condemn as religiously heterodox the learning they opposed. Moreover, attempts were rarely made to silence someone who wished to express a novel philosophical opinion or to interfere with his teaching. In fact, both conservatives and neoterics often found it possible and beneficial to air their differences in a proper scholarly manner; not surprisingly, the ensuing intellectual dialogue helped defuse potential tensions as well as contributing occasionally to the process of conversion. Most important, however, were the effects of this irenic

---

[77] M. Foster, 'Thomas Allen (1540–1632), Gloucester Hall and the survival of Catholicism in post-reformation Oxford', *Oxoniensia* xlvi (1981), 99–128; Feingold, *The Mathematicians' Apprenticeship, passim.* For Gellibrand see John Ward, *The Lives of the Professors of Gresham College* (London 1740, repr. New York 1967), 82.

[78] *Brief Lives by Aubrey*, ed. Clark ii. 108; S. Pasmore, 'Thomas Henshaw, F. R. S. (1618–1700)', *Notes and Records of the Royal Society* xxxvi (1982), 178; C. Webster, *The Great Instauration* (London 1975), 416.

mood on the ability of students to transcend their tutors' opinions and pursue their interests without censure or interference. I shall have more to say on intellectual freedom below, but a few instances illustrating its relation to the new astronomy are in order here.

Before 1640, the opposition to Copernicanism at Oxford was strongest among the stricter sort of Calvinists. William Pemble, for example, who was credited by an admiring disciple with being an 'expert in the mathematicks both mixt, and pure' disputed the reality of Copernicanism and even attempted to prove 'scientifically' that the 'opinion of Copernicus and others that the earth should move round once a yeare . . . is most improbable and unreasonable. And rejected by the most.'[79] Yet as far as we know Pemble never made a public issue of his views which, though undoubtedly informing his teaching, did not prevent him from tolerating open discussion. We should also recall that Pemble's favourite student, John Tombes, was the tutor of John Wilkins. Even more revealing is the case of Nathaniel Carpenter, the very learned fellow of Exeter College, whose critical reading of Aristotle and receptivity to new ideas did not go so far as to allow him fully to adhere to the Copernican theory, principally because of its apparent contradiction of scripture. He gladly embraced a comforting disclaimer, propitiously employed by Sir Henry Savile. When Carpenter had questioned Savile on whether the Copernican or Ptolemaic systems were true, Savile retorted with a 'merry answer' that pleased Carpenter: 'he cared not which were true', as long as the appearances were solved. 'Is it not all one (saith he) sitting at dinner, whether my table be brought to me, or I goe to my table, so I eat my meat?' Half a century later Robert South produced a variant of Savile's answer:

What am I benefited, whether the sun moves about the earth, or whether the sun is in the centre of the world, and the earth is indeed a planet, and wheels about that? Whether it be one or the other, I see no change in the course of nature. . . . The day begins no sooner, nor stays any longer with Ptolemy than with Copernicus.[80]

Such comments indicate the latitude within which the new astronomy could flourish undisturbed. So long as cosmological beliefs were not made into a doctrinal and binding issue, acquiescence was forthcoming even from the unconverted. For that reason George Hakewill perceived in 1635 no contradiction between his own rejection of Copernicanism and his general advocacy of 'progressive' views—including his endorsement of Henry Briggs's judgement that Copernicanism accounted for the heavenly bodies more simply and more accurately than did any other theory. It was also along such lines that Seth Ward argued in 1654 for a nearly universal acceptance of the new astronomy at Oxford:

[79] The Workes of . . . William Pemble (Oxford 1659), 145, and William Pemble, A Briefe Introduction to Geographie in The Workes (separately paginated), 13.
[80] Nathaniel Carpenter, Geography Delineated Forth in Two Bookes (Oxford 1625), pt 1, 143; Robert South, Discourses on Various Subjects and Occasions (Boston 1827), 323.

there is not one man here, who is so farre astronomicall, as to be able to calculate an eclipse, who hath not received the Copernican system (as it was left by him, or as improved by Kepler, Bullialdus, our own professor [Ward], and others of the ellipticall way) either as an opinion, or at leastwise, as the most intelligible, and most convenient hypothesis.[81]

Some scholars, however, assume that although the Savilian statutes required the professor of astronomy to teach Geber, Copernicus, and other modern writers, Savile was actually

thinking of the more accurate observations and techniques of 'recent' astronomers, rather than of radically new theories. [The professor's] primary duty was to lecture on practical and mathematical astronomy. The theory of the heavens would have been dealt with, officially, by his colleague in the school of natural philosophy where the teaching throughout was based upon the works of Aristotle.[82]

Yet it is essential to recognize that during the 1620s instruction in cosmology was, to all intents and purposes, appropriated by the Savilian professors. Whether this was because the Savilian statutes proved more flexible for the teaching of physics and cosmology, or because the occupants of the Savilian chairs were not only more eminent scholars compared with most Sedleian professors of natural philosophy, but also powerful academic figures, who could trespass on the territory of their colleagues with impunity, or perhaps simply because as things turned out all Sedleian professors in the seventeenth century were physicians, who felt ill at ease with the physical sciences, the results are indisputable. For whatever reason, a silent split occurred in the domain of natural philosophy, with the Savilian professors assuming responsibility for teaching that part of the curriculum that dealt with physics and cosmology, while the Sedleian professors confined their teaching almost exclusively to those parts of natural philosophy that related to the bio-medical sciences and to natural history.[83] This inadvertent division of labour made it natural for the Savilian professors to introduce mathematics into the domain of physics and with equal ease to invoke physical causes when describing planetary motion.

NEW PHILOSOPHIES

The Role of Aristotle in the Curriculum

Before proceeding to the reception of new philosophies at Oxford it is necessary to address the position of Aristotle within the curriculum, and to determine whether the evidence confirms the iron grip which Aristotelianism purportedly exerted over the course of studies. Chief among the documents used to bolster

---

[81] George Hakewill, *An Apologie or Declaration of the Power and Providence of God* (Oxford 1627, 3rd edn Oxford 1635), 301; [Wilkins and Ward], *Vindiciae academiarum*, 29.

[82] J. L. Russell, 'The Copernican system in Great Britain' in J. Dobrzycki (ed.), *The Reception of Copernicus' Heliocentric Theory* (Dordrecht and Boston 1972), 146. See also J. Gascoigne, 'A reappraisal of the role of the universities in the scientific revolution' in D. C. Lindberg and R. S. Westman (eds), *Reappraisal of the Scientific Revolution* (New York 1990), 230–1.

[83] For the Sedleian professors see Robert G. Frank, 'Medicine', pp. 525–6 below.

such a position are the university statutes which, on the surface, appear to substantiate a literal reading of the views of Hobbes and Locke (see pp. 359–60 above). Thus, the Laudian statutes specified that the university lecturer in logic explicate 'some part of Aristotle's logic', while White's professor of moral philosophy was required to discuss Aristotle's ethics, politics, and economics. For his part, the Sedleian professor of natural philosophy was expected to handle the entire corpus of Aristotle's scientific writings, from the *Physica* and *De caelo*, through *De generatione et corruptione* and the *Meteorologia*, concluding with *De anima*. Moreover, the ordinances regulating disputations and ceremonies also emphasized the centrality of Aristotle to the corporate identity of the university. That on 'the form of creating general sophists', for example, stipulated that one of the four regent masters should exhort the candidates to pursue polite literature and then 'recount the merits and advantages' of Aristotelian dialectics. This was to be followed by the bestowal of a copy of Aristotle's *Logic* upon each undergraduate. Finally, the statutes regulating disputations specifically charged that the determining bachelors who 'propounded questions in logic for discussion' should defend these according to Aristotle, 'whose authority is paramount'. In disputing questions in rhetoric, moral philosophy, and politics Aristotle 'and the entire doctrine of the peripatetics' was to be followed as well, under the penalty of a fine.[84]

The language of the Laudian statutes (which remained unchanged until the nineteenth century) easily lent itself to misrepresentation by critics of the universities—Hobbes and Locke, as well as the puritan sectarians during the Interregnum. It could also colour the perceptions of foreigners, as was the case with Christoph Arnold, who visited England in 1654. With a mixture of amazement and contempt, Arnold recorded in his diary that 'it is said that in the Oxford colleges in private discussions the authority of Aristotle is so great that whoever keeps on opposing this authority, or speaks denigratingly about it, is expected to pay the huge sum of five shillings'. Then, in a display of his religious leanings, Arnold concluded: 'if in England the Holy Scripture had the same weight as Aristotle, it would not be attacked by so many sectarian slanderers.'[85]

The tenacity with which Oxford continued to impose the statutory requirement to follow Aristotle appears to be supported by the proclamations of the Oxford vice-chancellors—issued annually between 1669 and 1675—which 'reminded' students of their obligation to defend Aristotle in their disputations. An analogous decree was issued in November 1668 by the Cambridge vice-chancellor, Edmund Boldero, 'forbidding undergraduates and BAs from basing their disputations on Descartes' work and stipulating that Aristotle's writings be used instead'.[86] These decrees, however, reflect an exceptional climate of opinion in the late 1660s and

---

[84] *Statutes*, trans. Ward i. 20–3, 34–5, 43–4. The statutes for the halls stipulated the same routine: ibid. i. 323–4.

[85] F. Blom, *Christoph and Andreas Arnold and England* (Nuremberg 1982), 83–4.

[86] Bodl. MS Wood 276A, nos 356, 357, 361, 368, 371, 375; Bodl. MS Rawlinson. c. 146, p. 37, cited in J. Gascoigne, *Cambridge in the Age of the Enlightenment* (Cambridge 1989), 54.

early 1670s that rendered such irregular measures necessary. Specifically, the universities reacted both to the pugnacious denigration of university learning by over-zealous proponents of the Royal Society and to the perceived surge of Hobbism (a synonym for religious and moral depravity)—'evidence' of which was found in the case of Daniel Scargill at Cambridge in 1667.[87] None the less, these decrees were aimed, not at enforcing philosophical conformity, but rather at ensuring the preservation of law and order during public disputations. And with good reason. The unfolding polemic over the kind of knowledge most worth having, and over the presumed repercussions of the new philosophy on religious orthodoxy, was potentially explosive and apt to produce raucous scenes at the Oxford Act. For example in 1669 both the university orator, Robert South, and the two Terrae-Filii attacked the Royal Society and the new philosophy—with the latter carrying raillery to extremes by slandering not only various Oxford dignitaries but the king as well![88] The university authorities, for whom the preservation of law and order had always been paramount, resorted to means that had proved successful previously. In 1586, for example, their predecessors had attempted to curb the heated debates that engulfed students and dons over the teachings of Peter Ramus by restricting the topics of disputation to the teaching of Aristotle alone.[89] Eight decades later, Peter Mewes and Ralph Bathurst (the incumbent vice-chancellors 1669–76), undoubtedly hoped that similar measures would prove as effective in calming hot tempers and restoring order. And to a large extent they had the desired effect.[90]

One of the objectives of this chapter is to challenge the negative perception that has traditionally been evoked by a literal reading of the Oxford statutes. Elsewhere I have argued that any interpretation of the curriculum at either Oxford or Cambridge based on the assumption that the statutes represented a true reflection of the actual course of study is inadequate—and the claim will be further substantiated below. First, though, it should be emphasized that this attempt to re-evaluate the received views concerning the backwardness of the universities does not presume to suggest that Aristotle was not taught there or to deny the pre-dominantly scholastic structure of the curriculum. Nor is it my intention to argue that all or even the majority of the fellows and students were proponents of the new philosophy—only that all students received at least an elementary grounding in the mathematical sciences and in natural philosophy, and that the system encouraged the more advanced pursuit of scientific studies by whoever desired it.

[87] J. L. Axtell, 'The mechanics of opposition: Restoration Cambridge v. Daniel Scargill', *Bulletin of the Institute of Historical Research* xxxviii (1965), 102–11.

[88] *The Diary of John Evelyn*, ed. De Beer iii. 531–2; *Works of Boyle*, ed. Birch vi. 459; *The Correspondence of Henry Oldenburg*, ed. Hall and Hall vi. 129–30, 137, 189–90.

[89] *SA* 437; J. McConica, 'Humanism and Aristotle in Tudor Oxford', *EHR* xciv (1979), 301.

[90] Comparable measures were implemented in the United Provinces as well. During the 1650s the curators of Leiden University prohibited the public discussion of Descartes's ideas, not from hostility to Cartesianism so much as from an effort to curb the sharp disputes that had arisen. Similarly the 1656 decree of the States of Holland and West Friesland against various Cartesian principles was implemented because 'the states were seeking to quiet passions rather than to establish an official position in philosophy'. E. G. Ruestow, *Physics at 17th- and 18th-Century Leiden* (The Hague 1973), 61.

Undoubtedly, certain dons were cheerfully unaffected by either the new or the old philosophy, while others unquestionably championed 'antiquated' world views. Again, however, a proper context is required if we are to understand the true meaning of such 'conservativism'. The case of John Fell, dean of Christ Church and bishop of Oxford, is instructive. Fell was reported by William Wake (MA 1679) to have discouraged him from the study of Cartesianism, 'being wholly devoted to the old philosophy'. The dean was also reputed to have condoned (if he did not instigate) Henry Stubbe's attack on the Royal Society.[91] Yet Fell was not a stubborn, uninformed, opponent of the new science. He was a staunch supporter of scientific studies at Oxford, whose objection to Descartes and to the Royal Society must be carefully situated within the broader context of the Restoration debate over science. Nor were his personal philosophical predilections in any way obstructive to others. Though he attempted to discourage Wake, Fell none the less allowed his protégé to proceed with his study of Descartes, just as his esteem for John Locke was unaffected by the latter's pursuit of a similar course.[92]

An analogous institutional case is that of Queen's College which was reputed throughout the seventeenth century to be a stronghold of Aristotelian teaching—often eliciting disparaging comments as a result. In 1667, for example, Francis Vernon singled out the veneration for Aristotle as a distinguishing mark of the college. A quarter of a century later the perception still lingered, as is evident from Robert Wood's ridicule of Queen's men, who 'are so accustomed to Aristotle, that they make use of his terms in common conversation'.[93] But even if Queen's tutors were more prone to impart to their students a heavier diet of scholastic commentaries than did tutors in other colleges, such a predisposition hardly signified the extent of their teaching. Thus the brief compendia prepared by Richard Crakanthorpe for the use of his students demonstrates the ease with which this influential tutor incorporated information culled from the most recent scientific works into his manuals, which were themselves arranged along traditional Aristotelian lines. Similarly the diary of Thomas Crosfield (MA 1625) indicates that, irrespective of the prevailing philosophical orientation, during the 1630s Queen's College undergraduates were free to debate in public topics drawn from the recent optical and astronomical discoveries of Galileo and Kepler.[94] Furthermore, even at Queen's the passion for the ancients often proved to be more literary than scholastic. An American visitor to the college at the start of the eighteenth century described the students' exercises during dinner in terms that make it clear that it was the language of the ancients, rather than their natural philosophy and metaphysics, that appealed to the predominantly humanist community: eight bachelors of arts 'recited Aristotle in Greek or Latin ... till they were interrupted by the

---

[91] N. Sykes, *William Wake Archbishop of Canterbury 1657–1737* (2 vols Cambridge 1957) i. 10.

[92] M. Hunter, *Science and Society in Restoration England* (Cambridge 1980), 143 and *passim*.

[93] Vernon, *Oxonium poema*, 13; E. Wood, 'Some Wood family letters from Oxford, 1659–1719', *Oxoniensia* li (1986), 132.

[94] QCL MSS 196, 390; Feingold, *The Mathematicians' Apprenticeship*, 66, 103–4.

provost with some question upon the topic they were reciting, which they generally answered very smartly, and were obliged to go on 'till the provost said *sufficit*'.[95]

Contextualizing the statutes in order to gain a better understanding of the actual
course of study, however, is insufficient to prove that Aristotelianism simply served
as the old skin into which the new wine was poured. But before a more thorough
account is offered of the manner in which the new philosophy permeated the
course of study, a closer scrutiny of the actual role of Aristotle in the undergraduate curriculum is in order. This reveals the rather circumscribed position he was
accorded. Contemporaries were quite capable of distinguishing, correctly, between
those writings of Aristotle that retained their relevance and those that had served
their purpose. As a consummate expert on moral, political, and literary issues,
Aristotle was justly studied; as a natural philosopher, however, he was regarded by
Oxford professors and tutors simply as a past master with whom they openly
reserved the right to differ. In his polemic with John Webster and other sectarian
opponents of the universities during the Interregnum, Seth Ward made this point
clear. After praising Aristotle's contribution to humanist studies and to the 'his-
toricall parts of nature', Ward continued:

only his physicks is to be eliminated, it being founded upon either false, or not intelligible
principles, referring all things to that system, and modell of the world, which time and observation have manifested to be untrue. The astronomy depending thereon (upon that system
of foure elements, and a quintessentiall solid heaven) falls necessarily upon the removall of
his physicks, or rather the physicall part of that astronomy.[96]

Ward's position was not that of a hack defender of university privileges and learning against their detractors. Robert Boyle, who was a critic of Aristotelian natural
philosophy and metaphysics, reiterated Ward's important distinction more fully a
decade later, in the preface to his *Origine of Formes and Qualities*. Wishing to articulate the precise nature and scope of his criticism of Aristotle, Boyle said:

By which nevertheless I would not be understood to censure or decry the whole peripatetick philosophy, much less to despise Aristotle himself ... For I look upon Aristotle as one
(though but as one amongst many) of those famed ancients, whose learning about
Alexander's time enobled Greece; and I readily allow him most of the praises due to great
wits ... And I here declare once for all, that, where in the following tract, or any other of
my writings, I do indefinitely depreciate Aristotle's doctrine, I would be understood to speak
of his physicks, or rather of the speculative part of them (for his historical writings concerning animals I much admire) nor do I say that even these may not have their use among

---

[95] A. B. Forbes, 'Harvard on tour at Oxford, 1703', *Publications of the Colonial Society of Massachusetts*
xxviii (1930–3), 97.

[96] [Wilkins and Ward], *Vindiciae academiarum*, 45–6. Ward concluded 'when these things are laid aside,
that which remains deserves for him [Aristotle] the honour that ought to be given to one of the greatest wits, and most usefull that ever the world enjoyed'. More than three decades earlier John Bainbridge
referred to Aristotle as 'that great and witty, but often misleading peripateticke': *An Astronomical
Description of the Late Comet* (London, 1619), 12.

scholars, and even in universities, if they be retained and studied with due cautions and limitations (of which I have elsewher spoken).[97]

Ward and Boyle articulated the reasoned and, outside polemical contexts, generally acceptable position concerning the 'worth' of Aristotle. The Cambridge champion of the new science, William Watts, stated the position plainly during the 1630s: 'Aristotle (it must be confessed) hath made all learning beholden to him; no man hath learned to confute him, but by him, and unless he hath plowed with his heifer'. His younger Oxford contemporary, Thomas Browne (MA 1629), who was generally favourable to the assault on Aristotle's natural philosophy, concurred: 'while much is lacking in Aristotle, much wrong, much self-contradictory, yet not a little is valuable. Do not then bid farewell to his entire work; but while you hardly touch the Physics and read the Metaphysics superficially, make much of all the rest and study them unwearyingly'.[98]

The ability to honour Aristotle and yet forsake him whenever he was in the wrong was, to the mind of many Oxonians, the testimony of a truly liberated mind and the consequence of a generous dose of philosophical freedom at the university.[99] Such an atmosphere not only made possible the free pursuit of all studies, but rendered superfluous rhetorical excesses against Aristotle. Wilkins and Ward used this two-pronged argument in their counter-attack on Webster—emphasizing the vigilance with which philosophical freedom was guarded at Oxford, while branding Webster's claims about the enslavement of the university to Aristotle as those of an ignorant enthusiast. All new systems of thought have their 'strenuous assertours', insisted Wilkins in the preface to the *Vindiciae academiarum*. Indeed, intellectual pluralism at Oxford had reached such a propitious state that 'there is not to be wished a more generall liberty in points of judgment or debate, then what is here allowed'. As for Aristotle, despite 'his profound judgment and universall learning, yet are we so farre from being tyed up to his opinions, that persons of all conditions amongst us take liberty to discent from him, and to declare against him, according as any contrary evidence doth ingage them, being ready to follow the banner of truth by whomsoever it shall be lifted up.' For his part, Ward repeatedly emphasized the supremacy of 'liberty and variety amongst us'.[100]

This response to the charge that philosophical studies at Oxford laboured under the yoke of Aristotle is significant not only for its forceful rebuttal of a hostile critic, but for its illustration of the pride with which Oxford scholars throughout the seventeenth century championed philosophical freedom. An early example of

---

[97] *Works of Boyle*, ed. Birch iii. 9.

[98] William Watts, 'To the venerable artists and younger students in divinity, in the famous university of Cambridge', repr. in *A Collection of Voyages and Travels*, ed. J. Churchill (6 vols London 1732) ii. 464; *The Works of Sir Thomas Browne*, ed. G. Keynes (4 vols Chicago 1964) iii. 206.

[99] Already in the mid-1570s John Rainolds defended his criticism of Aristotle's ethical theory of the *summum bonum* by saying that he was 'enjoyned' as a 'publike teacher to deliver sound and true opinions, not errors in the expounding of authors': John Rainolds, *An Excellent Oration . . . very usefull for all such as affect the studies of logick and philosophie*, trans. J. Leycester (London 1638), 3.

[100] [Wilkins and Ward], *Vindiciae academiarum*, 2, 32, 39, 48.

such advocacy can be found in the publication at Oxford of Nathanael Carpenter's *Philosophia libera* in 1622. Carpenter, a fellow of Exeter College, designed the book to serve as a primer stressing the dignity and necessity of *libertas philosophandi*, and inviting his readers, students in particular, to cultivate such freedom. He emphasized the pitfalls of blind submission to the authority of the ancients and, subsequently, through a discussion of various illustrative instances, insisted on the need to apply sober judgement in philosophical studies. Thus, though he himself was not a proponent of Copernicanism, Carpenter none the less upheld an author's duty to present impartially the views of the 'moderns' as well as of the ancients, and thereby vest the reader with the ability to choose freely among alternatives. 'In nullius iuratus verba', he spiritedly paraphrased Horace, emphatically denouncing servility to the ancients when dealing with 'the business of nature'. Carpenter restated his position three years later in his *Geography Delineated*, where he occasionally returned to the theme of *libertas philosophandi*, for example in discussion of the heliocentric hypothesis. Again, though Carpenter rejected the theory on religious grounds, he none the less acted on his conviction that the reader should be presented with a fair and complete account of even those views rejected by the author: 'I would not willingly mangle it in any part', he declared, 'but shew it whole and intire to the view of the judicious; who herein may use their philosophicall liberty, to imbrace or reject what they please.'[101]

Indeed, Oxford authors often waved the banner of philosophical freedom, sometimes in unexpected contexts. When Francis Potter published in 1642 *An Interpretation of the Number 666*, he defended his advocacy of an original theory by quoting William Gilbert:

I know how hard it is to impart the air of newness to what is old, trimness to what is gone out of fashion, to lighten what is dark, to make that grateful which excites disgust, to win belief for things doubtful. But far more difficult is it to win any standing for or to establish doctrines that are novel, unheard-of, and opposed to everybody's opinions.

'But all truths which are now old', added Potter, 'were once new, and have had their severall oppositions. New truths are like new friends, worthy to be tried, though not to be trusted, and I propose these things to the wise and learned, as Martiall proposed himselfe to his friend, to be tryed and examined first, and to be believed afterward.'[102] On the eve of the Restoration Edward Bagshaw, Locke's predecessor as censor of moral philosophy at Christ Church, appended to a genuine encomium of Aristotle's contribution to ethics, a fiery denunciation of slavish adherence to authority, exhorting his young auditors to join him in resisting any infringement of philosophical freedom.[103]

---

[101] Nathaniel Carpenter, *Philosophia libera* (Oxford 1622); Nathaniel Carpenter, *Geography Delineated*, pt i. 76. For further discussion see R. F. Jones, *Ancients and Moderns* (St Louis 1961), 65–71, 288–9.

[102] Francis Potter, *An Interpretation of the Number 666* (Oxford 1642), 'The epistle to the reader', sig. **; William Gilbert, *On the Loadstone and Magnetic Bodies*, trans P. F. Mottelay (New York 1893), p. xlix.

[103] Edward Bagshaw, *Exercitationes duae ... altera academica, de philosophia veterum, ejusque usu* (London 1661); Jones, *Ancients and Moderns*, 141.

Locke himself imbibed such principles during his student days, as becomes evident from one of his early letters:

When did ever any truth settle it self in any ones minde by the strength and authority of its owne evidence? Truths gaine admittance to our thoughts as the philosopher did to the tyrant by their handsome dresse and pleasing aspect, they enter us by composition, and are entertained as they suite with our affections, and as they demeane themselves towards our imperious passions. [But] when an opinion hath wrought its self unto our approbation and is gott under the protection of our likeing tis not all the assaults of argument, and the battery of dispute shall dislodge it. Men live upon trust and their knowledg is noething but opinion moulded up betweene custome and interest, the two great luminarys of the world, the only lights they walke by.

A few years later, Samuel Parker publicly expressed his gratitude to Ralph Bathurst, president of Trinity College, who 'first rescue[d] him from the chains and fetters of an unhappy education', and who had introduced him into a society that valued most 'a true freedom and ingenuity of mind'.[104]

College disputations and other public exercises offered students a wealth of opportunities to express their own approving sentiments on the theme of philosophical freedom. At Merton College, for example, a long tradition—stretching back to the late sixteenth century—established the custom of explicitly requiring students to vary from the opinion of Aristotle. Joachim Hübner, who attended one such occasion in 1640, was full of admiration for what he had seen: 'One of the best exercises at Oxford', he told Samuel Hartlib, 'is their declamations against Aristotle, which are kept yearly at a certaine time. Their speeches for the most part are most accurately elaborated wherin Aristotle is mightily towsed.' Some instances of such orations can be found in Hugh Cressey's response in the affirmative, in 1632, to the question 'An scepticorum dubitantia praeferenda sit peripateticorum thesibus?', and in Edmund Dickinson's delivery, two decades later, of an oration in defence of the liberty to philosophize. More generally, as late as 1693 the theme still retained its popularity. That year the young Joseph Addison delivered a polished oration during the Act, in which he fastened on the stock battle-cry: 'How long, gentlemen of the university, shall we slavishly tread in the steps of the ancients, and be afraid of being wiser than our ancestors?'—a rhetorical question which Addison followed with an impassioned tribute to the contribution of Descartes and Boyle (with an allusion to Newton as well) to the consolidation of true philosophy on new and certain foundations.[105]

---

[104] *The Correspondence of John Locke*, ed. De Beer i. 123; Samuel Parker, *A Free and Impartial Censure of the Platonick Philosophie* (Oxford 1666), sig. A3ᵛ.

[105] Sheffield University Library, Hartlib papers, Ephemerides, 1640 F–G 1, 5; MCR Merton College Register, vol. 2, fo 310; Feingold, *The Mathematicians' Apprenticeship*, 103; Edmund Dickinson, 'Oratiuncula pro philosophia liberanda', appended to his *Delphi Phoenicizantes* (Oxford 1655), separately paginated; Joseph Addison, 'An oration in defence of the new philosophy', appended to Fontenelle's *A Conversation on the Plurality of Worlds*, trans. W. Gardiner (London 1777), 141–5. Such publicly sanctioned liberty was privately exercised by the student, as can be gathered from Walter Charleton's recollection of 'that quondam custome' he and John Evelyn shared 'when we were fellow-collegiates in Oxford, of discoursing

The finest testimony to the prevalence of English academic freedom is the fact that, in sharp contrast to what occurred elsewhere, there are no instances of official condemnation of new scientific ideas. While all Catholic, and some protestant, universities either banned or imposed severe restrictions on the teaching of Copernicanism, in England such an option was never even considered. Similarly, whereas at Paris, Geneva, Louvain, Uppsala, and the Italian universities the teachings of Descartes were condemned at various times from the 1640s onwards, at Oxford and Cambridge no official attempt to curb the rapid dissemination of such ideas was ever felt necessary. Not that everyone was receptive. Certain dons expressed an aversion to the new ideas—invariably motivated by their perceived religious implications—and even cautioned their charges against them. Nevertheless, the tradition of intellectual freedom was too firmly embedded in English academic institutions to be uprooted by anxiety over the possible subversive implications of natural philosophy. At most, during the strife between the universities and the Royal Society in the late 1660s, the vice-chancellor posted a flyer reminding students of their duties to defend Aristotle. But the intention was to calm hot spirits. Certainly no effort was ever made to enforce such 'advice'.

It is not surprising, therefore, that contemporary observers often commented on the intellectual freedom enjoyed by the English. John Barclay summarized this perception in 1612: 'In philosophy, and the mathematicks, in geography, and astronomy, there is noe opinion soe prodigious and strange, but in that island was eyther invented, or has found many followers, and subtile maintainers.' Three years later it was the turn of Johannes Drusius, who had taught Hebrew in Elizabethan Oxford, to contrast the persecution he suffered at home in the Netherlands with the freedom enjoyed by the English in their cultivation of all good learning.[106] Accustomed to the freedom of thought at Oxford, John Locke was surprised to find, when he visited France in 1676, that 'the new philosophie [was] prohibited to be taught in universitys, schooles and academies', while Newton reflected in the early eighteenth century on 'the happiness of [his] being born in a land of liberty where he could speak his mind—not afraid of [the] inquisition as Galileo ... not obliged as Des Cartes was to go into a strange country and to say he proved transubstantiation by his philosophy'.[107]

At the same time, contemporaries, and especially those who had joined teaching with research, firmly believed that, despite the undeniable contribution of various 'moderns' to the study of nature, none should be allowed to impose his views

freely and calmly of some argument or other in philosophy'. Walter Charleton, *The Immortality of the Human Soul* (London 1657), 3.

[106] *The Mirrour of Mindes, or, Barclay's icon animorum*, trans. Thomas May (London 1635), 117–18 quoted in F. R. Johnson, *Astronomical Thought in Renaissance England* (Baltimore 1937 repr. New York 1968), 248; J. E. Platt, 'Sixtinus Amama (1593–1629): Franeker professor and citizen of the republic of letters' in G. Th. Jensme, F. R. H. Smit, and F. Westra (eds), *Universiteit te Franeker, 1585–1811* (Leeuwarden 1985), 242.

[107] John Locke, *Travels in France 1675–1679*, ed. J. Lough (Cambridge 1953), 60; F. E. Manuel, *A Portrait of Isaac Newton* (Cambridge Mass. 1968), 267.

unchallenged to the exclusion of competing theories. After all, no matter how superior to the ancients a new theory may be, none thus far had managed to accommodate the totality of available knowledge; besides, to chain oneself to a new authority
would undermine the very concept of philosophical freedom that had just been
acquired. Contemporaries clearly recognized that while errors of fact and method
within Aristotelian natural philosophy had become manifest, the shortcomings of
the various new theories, though not yet apparent, might become so in the future.
Consequently, to accept them wholeheartedly on faith alone would be a mistake.
Also recognized was that the neoterics, such as Descartes, Hobbes, and Locke,
were in their own way quite dogmatic. They acknowledged neither the benefit they
derived from their predecessors nor from competing modes of thought, demanding instead total and immediate acceptance of their ideas. And if the previous century had taught seventeenth-century savants anything, it was how transitory were
all theories and systems. Only intellectual pluralism and the right to choose could
accommodate and guide the search for truth.

The crux of the matter was that though most scholars were cognizant of (and
even receptive to) the competing new natural philosophies, during much of the
seventeenth century none of these was ultimately capable of offering a comprehensive, non-controvertible interpretation of the observed phenomena. As has
been remarked, 'many assumptions about the behaviour of natural phenomena'
which 'Descartes deduced from his principles, such as the instantaneous transmission of light, proved just as wrongheaded on examination as traditional Aristotelian
sacred cows'. It was therefore believed essential to keep an open mind, retain the
good that the ancients had to offer as well as subject all new theories to careful
scrutiny.[108] The issue was articulated plainly by Obadiah Walker in 1673 when he
observed that although new scientific discoveries would continue to be made, 'to
lay new principles ... is a business of an higher difficulty'. There is nothing in natural philosophy that cannot be debated and, consequently, the greatest freedom
should be allowed in the university when discussing such matters. For 'even they
who most pretend to experiments will find it difficult to produce one new, or confute an old, universal proposition; and when they shall discover one, they will find
it disputed both with contrary reasons and experiments'. Walker's position was similar to that expressed by Robert Burton three decades earlier. Commenting on the
proliferating disagreements among natural philosophers, Burton mused on how
'the world is tossed in a blanket amongst them, [as] they hoist the earth up and
down like a ball, make it stand and go at their pleasures: one saith the sun stands,
another he moves; a third comes in, taking them all at rebound, and, lest there
should any paradox be wanting, he finds certain spots and clouds in the sun, by

---

[108] L. W. B. Brockliss, *French Higher Education in the Seventeenth and Eighteenth Centuries* (Oxford 1987),
75. Even the schoolmen had their use, as Henry Stubbe reminded Hobbes in 1656: 'That the schoolemen were a company of cheates as to the generality of their writeings, I easily grant; yet even in their
writings they have [good] intervalls many of them; and the new philosophy may well be confirmed out
of their reasons.' *Lettere di Henry Stubbe a Thomas Hobbes*, ed. O. Nicastro (Siena 1973), 10.

the help of glasses ... and thus they disagree amongst themselves, old and new, irreconcilable in their opinions ... [they] with their followers, vary and determine of these celestial orbs and bodies'. Even John Wallis, in the 1670s, admitted that, 'when all hath been sayd that can be on both sides', the verity of either the Copernican hypothesis or the circulation of the blood must 'be left at last to the readers pleasure' which 'side to join'.[109]

Partly for this reason, Wilkins and Ward lashed out at Hobbes's presumptions in unambiguous terms. The former's intimation that Hobbes was 'magisterial' in his writings[110] was further developed by Ward into a full-fledged indictment. 'It appears that the end he proposes to himselfe', Ward wrote in reference to the prescriptions of the author of *Leviathan*, is 'that the world should be regulated exactly by that modell which he there exhibits, and that his reason should be the governing reason of mankind.'[111] Hobbes's criticism of the universities, therefore, was not only inaccurate but disingenuous, for he faulted them simply for not teaching his views: 'From whence it is manifest, that the only thing which paines him is the desire that Aristotelity may be changed into Hobbeity, and instead of the Stagyrite, the world may adore the great Malmesburian phylosopher.' Ward was pleased to inform Hobbes that at Oxford he and his colleagues 'enjoy a liberty of philosophizing'; and, should Hobbes honour them with a visit, Ward was certain 'he would hardly find any other fault with [them], except that great unpardonable one, that the publick reading of his *Leviathan*, is not by a sanction of the magistrate imposed upon [them]'.[112]

A few months after the publication of *Vindiciae academiarum*, the former Student of Christ Church Meric Casaubon levelled a similar charge of arrogance against Descartes. In *A Treatise concerning Enthusiasme* Descartes was likened to Numa Pompilius—and Minos before him—who also sought 'to make their lawes received as oracles' by shrewdly dressing their opinions with the garb of novelty while imputing the source of their opponents' wisdom to 'the fruits of caves, and darknesse'. Casaubon elaborated on the theme a decade later when he branded both Descartes and Hobbes imperious: 'intolerable pride and arrogancie ... being the chiefest foundation of both.' Haughtiness and self-conceit were as conspicuous in Descartes as they were in Hobbes, who 'with no less confidence, though not soe

---

[109] Walker, *Of Education*, 118; Robert Burton, *The Anatomy of Melancholy*, ed. T. C. Faulkner *et al.* (5 vols Oxford 1989–) ii. 57–8; *The Correspondence of Henry Oldenburg*, ed. Hall and Hall xi. 37.

[110] Hobbes is 'a person of good ability and solid parts', wrote Wilkins, 'but otherwise highly magisteriall, and one that will be very angry with all that do not presently submit to his dictates. And for advancing the reputation of his own skill, cares not what unworthy reflexions he casts on others.' [Wilkins and Ward], *Vindiciae academiarum*, 6–7.

[111] Ward is referring to the passage where Hobbes, cognizant of the centrality of the universities in training the political and social élite, expressed the hope 'that one time or other, this writing of mine, may fall into the hands of a soveraign, who will consider it himselfe ... without the help of any interested, or envious interpreter; and by the exercise of entire soveraignty, in protecting the publique teaching of it, convert this truth of speculation, into the utility of practice'. Thomas Hobbes, *Leviathan*, ed. C. B. Macpherson (London 1976), 408; see also pp. 727–8.

[112] [Wilkins and Ward], *Vindiciae academiarum*, 51–2, 58–9.

great luck, doth take upon him to be the oracle of the world; who would make the world beleeve noe such thing was in the world, truly and really, as art, or science, or philosophie, till he was borne and began to wryte'. It is obvious, concluded Casaubon, that 'the designe of both is and hath beene, but of Cartesius particularly, that all other bookes and learning should be layd asyde as needless, but what came from him, or was grounded upon his principles'.[113]

The sincerity of these expressions of intellectual freedom and the light they shed on university learning are not diminished by the fact that the curriculum retained, at least superficially, its Aristotelian framework throughout much of the seventeenth century. After all, the durability of Aristotelianism, as Charles Schmitt has pointed out, was due in no small part to pedagogical convenience. If such sixteenth-century critics as Pico, Copernicus, Ramus, Telesio, and Bruno were able 'to show a few Aristotelian doctrines to be in error, they could in no way produce a comprehensive alternative system to replace the established one' and Aristotelianism, despite its many flaws, 'still covered such a wide range that no other system could challenge its cultural hegemony'.[114] Only during the first half of the seventeenth century did comprehensive alternatives to Aristotle become available, following the publications of the works of Bacon, Galileo, Kepler, Harvey, Hobbes, Gassendi, and Descartes. Yet although the new ideas were widely recognized as offering superior knowledge, another generation was to pass before they were digested into textbooks appropriate to neophytes. But even then the old learning was not immediately rendered obsolete, both because of the pedagogical function of the university to impart old as well as new learning and because the new learning could hardly be made comprehensible without at least some grounding in what it sought to replace.[115] Seth Ward commented in 1654 on the continued utility of the Aristotelian structure of knowledge. No reading of 'modern' rhetoricians, moralists, and politicians, he argued, could replace Aristotle, for even if the writings of various innovators 'did conteine things better in their kind than

[113] Meric Casaubon, *A Treatise Concerning Enthusiasme* (London 1655), 172; M. R. G. Spiller, *'Concerning Natural Experimental Philosophie': Meric Casaubon and the Royal Society* (The Hague 1980), 206. For an interesting analogous attitude towards Descartes expressed by Christiaan Huygens see R. S. Westman, 'Huygens and the problem of Cartesianism' in H. J. M. Bos *et al.* (eds), *Studies on Christiaan Huygens* (Lisse 1980), 97–9.

[114] C. B. Schmitt, 'Philosophy and science in sixteenth-century universities: some preliminary comments', in J. E. Murdoch and E. D. Sylla (eds), *The Cultural Context of Medieval Learning* (Dordrecht 1975), 489.

[115] A similar dilemma faced the Newtonians at the turn of the eighteenth century, as they were forced to convey the new ideas within the more traditional Cartesian text of Jacques Rohault until such time as proper textbooks became available. When Samuel Clarke asked William Whiston in 1697 whether he should publish a translation of Rohault, the latter replied: 'Since the youth of the university must have, at present, some system of natural philosophy for their studies and exercises; and since the true system of Sir Isaac Newton's was not yet made easy enough for the purpose, it is not improper, for their sakes, yet to translate and use the system of Rohault ... but that as soon as Sir Isaac Newton's philosophy came to be better known, that only ought to be taught, and the other dropped.' William Whiston, *Historical Memoirs of the Life of Dr Samuel Clarke* (London 1730), 5–6, quoted in M. A. Hoskin, '"Mining all within": Clarke's notes to Rohault's *Traité de physique*', *Thomist* xxiv (1961), 355.

Aristotle', these 'are not fit to be read in universities by way of institution'. The moderns, Ward continued,

have written diffusedly *stilo oratorio* . . . but have not given a briefe methodicall body of the things they handle. The businesse of such as have the institution of youth, is to give them, first a briefe and generall comprehension of the kinds and natures of those things, about which their studyes, and endeavours are to be employed, and so to excite and stirre them up to a deepe and more thorough consideration of them, to set them into a way of study and knowledge.

It is primarily for this reason that Aristotle is important and the reason why he 'hath been universally received as *magister legitimus*' in the schools: 'the universallity of his enquiries, the brevity and method of them, fitting them for institutions, and not the truth or infallibility of his workes' have all rendered the teaching of Aristotle irreplaceable.[116] Thus, speaking as an educator rather than as a professional scientist, the Savilian professor of astronomy advocated a position similar to one that Bartholomew Keckermann had expressed half a century earlier, when he frankly admitted that it was 'better to teach methodically ordered traditional positions, even if erroneous or questionable, rather than as-yet unmethodized new theories, even if true'.[117]

Moreover, whatever its shortcomings, the philosophy of Aristotle still provided an indispensable background for the comprehension of the more recent world views, just as the terminology utilized by Aristotle and his followers still remained an integral component of both new and old philosophy. In 1668 Ralph Bohun of New College articulated at length his method of education to John Evelyn, whose son was then under Bohun's care:

I begin with the philosophy of the schooles, which though I make it not my creed, and have often declared to your selfe how insufficient I believe the peripatetic hypothesis to solve the phaenomenas of nature, with any tolerable consistency to it selfe, yet since Aristotle has so universally obtained in all the universitys of Christendome for so many ages [and] thus insensibly crept into all modern writers by the use of his terms, it's almost impossible, as things stand, to be either divine, physician, or lawyer without him . . . how then can it be expected that we should understand the new philosophies without him, when the greatest part of their works consist only in confutation of his; so that I should advise Mr John to speak against Aristotle because he had read him, and not like the young gallants of the town that continually condemn his hypothesis only because they heard it censured in the last coffeehouse, or think it out of vogue in the Royal Society. . . . All that I admonish Mr John is that he should not be prejudiced too soon.[118]

Such efforts to avoid early bias in the minds of youths further testifies to the conscious attempt on the part of tutors and educators to inculcate among students the liberty of philosophizing by offering them a range of options. Gilbert Burnet's

---

[116] [Wilkins and Ward], *Vindiciae academiarum*, 39.
[117] P. Reif, 'The textbook tradition in natural philosophy, 1600–1650', *Journal of the History of Ideas* xxx (1969), 29.
[118] CL Evelyn Correspondence, no. 301.

views were typical. After the young student completed his course of mathematics, he was to 'be acquainted with the hypotheses of philosophy'. However, cautioned Burnet, 'I would not allow so many moneths as we give yeeres; and the youth is only to be acquainted with the several sects, and their chieffe grounds; but must not be byassed to any; but left at liberty to chuse, in a riper age, what shall seem most 'sutable to nature's operations, and not to poor pedantick sophistry'. Interestingly, the views expressed by Bohun and Burnet were basically those that informed Locke in his recommendation of the proper course of natural philosophy. In the company of contemporaries, Locke was convinced that none of the available systems offered either total or certain knowledge. Yet

> it is necessary for a gentleman in this learned age to look into some of them, to fit himself for conversation. But whether that of Des Cartes be put into his hands, as that which is most in fashion, or it be thought fit to give him a short view of that and several others also, I think the systems of natural philosophy, that have obtained in this part of the world, are to be read, more to know the hypotheses, and to understand the terms and ways of talking of the several sects, than with hopes to gain thereby a comprehensive, scientifical, and satisfactory knowledge of the works of nature. Only this may be said, that the modern corpuscularians talk, in most things, more intelligibly than the peripateticks, who possessed the schools immediately before them.

Burnet and Locke also agreed that, in the words of the latter, the writings of the chief experimental authors 'may be fit for a gentleman, when he has a little acquainted himself with some of the systems of the natural philosophy in fashion'.[119]

The conviction that the correct method of teaching philosophy necessitated a proper blend of old and new learning—and that the terminology of the former was indispensable for the comprehension of the latter—resulted in their study in tandem by all students, irrespective of social origins or career choices. Stephen Penton, for example, cautioned the well-born youth coming up to the university not to expect that 'the taylor should put on him philosophy with his gown'. Rather, at 'his first coming to Oxford, it is fit he should be made acquainted with some general knowledge of philosophy, of the original design, and several parts of it'. This meant familiarizing himself with the terms of art and, though such a course 'may be thought dry diet for a gentleman', yet no philosophical argument or learned conversation could be understood without it. 'After a short system of physick[s], in the old way', concluded Penton, 'a taste of the new philosophy would relish well, to understand the differing principles upon which it proceeds.'[120]

This broad consensus on the manner in which the study of philosophy was to proceed began to be codified in tutors' manuals by the early years of the seventeenth century. In the 1620s Thomas Sixsmith of Brasenose College divided the various branches of natural philosophy according to the titles of Aristotle's works;

---

[119] Clarke, *Bishop Gilbert Burnet as Educationist*, 61, 63; *The Educational Writings of John Locke*, ed. Axtell, 304–6.

[120] Penton, *New Instructions to the Guardian*, 94–6.

nevertheless, concurrent with his recommendation of some obligatory commentaries on the text, Sixsmith assigned other books as well. Thus, Pedro Hurtado de Mendoza and Antonio Rubio on the *Physics* were joined by Francesco Zabarella. In reading *De generatione et corruptione* the student was asked to pursue such commentators as Dominicus Báñez, Antonius Rubius, and Spigelius in the company of Jean Fernel 'with other physicians and anatomists', while when pursuing *De caelo* the student was to be guided not only by Ruvio and the Coimbra commentators, but by Clavius' commentary on Sacrobosco and Michael Maestlin's *Epitome astronomiae*. A generation later the trend was unmistakable. Thomas Barlow of Queen's College recommended in the mid-1650s that the student read some philosophical commentary from among a list that included such conventional authors as Ruvio, Franciscus Toletus, Benito Peirera, Aegidio Romanus, and Jacob Martini, as well as Libertus Fromondus' *Meteora* ('the best of that subject extant') and Joannes Chrysostom Magnen's *Democritus reviviscens*. 'You may adde to these', Barlow concluded, 'Gassendus, Des-Cartes, Digby, White, Bacon's Naturall History, or centuries of experiments.'[121]

The more detailed manuals of advice that proliferated at the start of the eighteenth century further elaborated on the practice. One anonymous tutor reasoned that 'as for naturall philosophy it is probable that an historical method in the study of it might be most scientificall, and that the best way would be to begin with the most antient authors of that sort, and so to follow them'. Thus, a flavour of the Pythagorean, stoic, Platonist, Epicurean, and Aristotelian world views was to be acquired before the student began study of the new philosophy, which commenced with the reading of Bacon, was followed by Descartes and some of his disciples, and concluded with Boyle and the transactions of the various scientific academies for experimental philosophy. John Grandorge thought that an adequate introduction to the 'old' Aristotelian philosophy could be got by a student reading Robert Sanderson's compendium and Adriaan Heereboord's *Meletemata*, 'after which he may read over' works by David Derodon, Daniel Sennert, Pierre Gaultruche, and Johannes Clauberg, with 'recourse' to Marcus Fridericus Wendelin, Jacopo Zabarella, and the Coimbra commentaries for disputation practice. The 'old and new Epicurean philosophy' was to be followed by the reading of Gassendi and Charleton, as well as by the 'several pieces of Mr Boyle who is a great promoter of the corpuscularian philosophy and has purged it from all the errors' of Epicurus. The study of the new philosophy commenced with the reading of Descartes's *Principia* to which Jacques Rohault, Jean-Baptiste Du Hamel, Boyle, and Willis were added. Henry More's philosophical works, Grandorge thought, would serve a dual purpose for these 'not only show the falsity of several of the Cartesian principles, but also may serve as an introduction to that philosophy'. Lastly came the experimental philosophy for which Boyle was again recommended, together with the apologetical writings of Sprat and Glanvill on behalf of the Royal Society, the

---

[121] BNCL MS 80; Barlow, '*A Library for Younger Schollers*', ed. Dejordy and Fletcher, 3–4.

Philosophical Transactions and, if the student understood French, the *Journal des savants* and Malebranche's *De la recherche de la vérité*. Thomas Heywood offered an even more meticulous diet of the several sects. Once the student had gone through 'a system of the peripatetick philosophy'—following Sanderson, Sennert, Wendelin, or Aristotle himself—he was expected to proceed with a system of the 'ancient corpuscular philosophy' (Gassendi's *Syntagma* was recommended) and then pursue Descartes and Rohault for the new philosophy without, however, neglecting to pay proper attention to the opponents of Cartesianism such as Henry More, Pierre-Daniel Huet, and the Jesuit Gabriel Daniel. This part of study out of the way, Heywood, too, directed the student to the study of experimental philosophy for which he recommended a wide range of (predominantly) English authors, from Bacon to Boyle, not neglecting to mention the *Philosophical Transactions* as well as the various works that had recently engaged the public attention on the theory of the earth—the treatises by Thomas Burnet, William Whiston, Woodward, and Keill.[122]

The prescriptions of tutors leave little doubt that the undergraduate curriculum was consciously balanced in order to acquaint the student with the divergent versions of natural philosophy, both ancient and modern. For this reason, if the university authorities were guilty of anything it was for their seemingly excessive veneration for the wording of the statutes, rather than for any attempt to enforce submission to Aristotelianism.[123] As has been observed of Restoration Cambridge,

in a university obsessed with devotion to the letter rather than the spirit of the statutes—and thus more concerned with the form rather than the content of the curriculum—the transition from the old to the new philosophy took place without any change in the university's official regulations which, in any case, were more concerned with disciplinary than intellectual issues. So long as students continued to study philosophy (and particularly natural philosophy) as required by statute and tradition the particular brand of philosophy was less a matter of concern, though there was a natural reluctance to abandon the order and pedagogical convenience of scholastic natural philosophy.[124]

That neither the wording of the statutes nor the tutors' insistence on the study of scholastic texts alongside modern ones inhibited the dissemination of new modes of thought at Oxford can be demonstrated by a study of the manner in which the new world views were received: the French philosophical traditions—represented by the teachings of Descartes, Gassendi, and Malebranche—and the native English contribution, in the form of Hobbes and Locke.

---

[122] Bodl. MS Rawlinson d. 188; Bodl. MS St Edmund Hall 72; Bodl. MS Rawlinson d. 40. Many tutors, however, and particularly those who were given charge of well-born youths, did not bother with too many textbooks, and recommended one or two texts for each subject. Thus Penton recommended Daniel Sennert's *Epitome naturalis scientiae* for the old peripatetic philosophy and Gassendi's *Syntagma* for the new. Stephen Penton, *Apparatus generalis ad theologiam* (Oxford 1688), 39.

[123] They had little choice in the matter anyway for the Laudian code intended to bind the university 'in perpetuity'. 'Not only was the university itself precluded from altering [the statutes], but it seems that neither did the crown intend under normal circumstances to intervene further': L. Sutherland, 'The Laudian statutes in the eighteenth century' in *The Eighteenth Century*, 190.

[124] Gascoigne, 'The universities and the scientific revolution', 396.

Descartes, Gassendi, and Malebranche

Scholars have often commented on the diffusion of Cartesianism in England. Although attention has been concentrated on such well-known figures as Henry More, John Locke, Robert Boyle, and Isaac Newton, it tends to establish that the English were highly receptive to Cartesian ideas—albeit while resisting Cartesian metaphysics.[125] What is less familiar is that knowledge of Descartes permeated scholarly circles in England prior to the publication of his *Discours* in 1637, and that by the early 1640s Descartes's reputation had become well established. The key intermediaries during this early stage were such Oxford alumni as Sir Kenelm Digby and Thomas Hobbes, as well as Sir Charles Cavendish and his brother the duke of Newcastle, Sir William Boswell, and Samuel Hartlib. Through the good offices of these individuals and their friends, copies of Descartes's works were made available in England even before booksellers imported them. Digby, for example, sent a copy of the *Discours* to Hobbes shortly after its publication. Likewise, during the 1640s the earl of Newcastle sent a copy of every new work by Descartes to Robert Payne at Oxford as soon as these became available on the continent.[126] Other former members of the university also studied Descartes. Brian Duppa, sometime dean of Christ Church, was familiar with several of Descartes's works by 1650, while Meric Casaubon recalled long after the event that he 'had read his method, in French ... many years before [he] mett any man, who eyther in print or by discourse tooke any notice of him'.[127]

The dissemination of the ideas of Pierre Gassendi ran parallel to that of the ideas of Descartes. In some ways indeed Gassendi may have exceeded Descartes in popularity since his version of the mechanical philosophy was more palatable to the taste of the English, who were ill at ease with the explicit metaphysical underpinnings of Descartes. Similarly, Gassendi was well served by the availability of his two influential textbooks: the *Institutio astronomica* (1647) and the *Philosophiae Epicuri syntagma* (1659). These were very popular among Oxford tutors and students during the second half of the seventeenth century, at a time when no comparable Cartesian textbook was available.[128] But during the 1650s and 1660s the more

---

[125] Relevant studies include M. Nicolson, 'The early stage of Cartesianism in England', *Studies in Philology* xxvi (1929), 356–74; S. P. Lamprecht, 'The role of Descartes in seventeenth-century England', *Studies in the History of Ideas* (New York 1935), 181–240; L. Laudan, 'The clock metaphor and probabilism: the impact of Descartes on English methodological thought, 1650–65', *Annals of Science* xxii (1966), 73–104; C. Webster, 'Henry More and Descartes: some new sources', *British Journal for the History of Science* iv (1969), 359–77; A. Pacchi, *Cartesio in Inghilterra* (Rome 1973); A. Gabbey, 'Philosophia Cartesiana triumphata: Henry More, 1646–1671' in T. M. Lennon *et al.* (eds), *Problems of Cartesianism* (Kingston and Montreal 1982), 171–249; G. A. J. Rogers, 'Descartes and the English' in J. D. North and J. J. Roche (eds), *The Light of Nature*, (Dordrecht 1985), 281–302.

[126] Bodl MS Rawlinson d. 1104, fo 12, printed in Nicolson, 'The early stage of Cartesianism', 358; BL MS Lansdowne 93, fo 179.

[127] *The Correspondence of Bishop Brian Duppa and Sir Justinian Isham, 1650–1660*, ed. G. Isham (Northants. Record Soc. xvii 1955), 23; Spiller, *'Concerning Natural Experimental Philosophie'*, 203.

[128] Only with the publication of Jacques Rohault's *Traité de physique* in 1671, and especially after its translation into Latin three years later, did Cartesianism obtain an effective textbook.

detailed expositions of Gassendi enjoyed wide popularity as well. Shortly after the publication of the massive three-volume edition of his *Animadversiones in decimum librum Diogenis Laertii* (1649), Robert Payne borrowed a copy of the first volume from an Oxford friend and after reading it wrote enthusiastically to Gilbert Sheldon that in his estimation Gassendi's 'reason is so cleare, and his modesty so great, that he winnes belief and love of all that read him; and seemes to have deserved the reputation he hath gotten, of the best philosopher in France'. In a subsequent letter Payne advised Sheldon that the three-volume set cost 48s and that he liked 'them so well, that were it not that some other necessaries call more importunely on [him] for money, [he] would buy them'.[129]

William Petty, who settled at Oxford in 1649, had earlier befriended Gassendi in Paris and acknowledged him to have been among those who greatly influenced his studies 'as well by their conversation as their public lectures and writings'. Subsequently Sir Charles Cavendish kept Petty informed of the progress of 'your worthy friend and myne Mr. Gassendi', in publishing the *Animadversiones*.[130] Within a few years many others were infected. In Norwich the Oxonian Sir Thomas Browne read Gassendi's *De vita et moribus Epicuri libri octo* (1647) soon after it was published and was sufficiently impressed to include a respectful reference to 'the learned pen of Gassendus' in his *Pseudodoxia epidemica* (1650).[131] In the same year that Browne's book was published Walter Charleton (at Oxford 1635–46) discovered the writings of Gassendi and Descartes, probably through his erstwhile Oxford friends John Evelyn and Sir Kenelm Digby. In Charleton's words, such reading changed his 'mode of thought almost entirely'. By 1652 he had acknowledged in the preface to his *The Darknes of Atheism Dispelled by the Light of Nature* a debt to Gassendi's *Animadversiones*—'the leaves of whose most learned works, we blush not to confesse ourselves to have been so conversant in, that we have sulleyed them by open revolution'. Two years later his enthusiasm matured into the formidable *Physiologia Epicuro-Gassendo-Charltonia*.[132]

Such rapid dissemination of Gassendi's Epicureanism elicited a chorus of comments. Robert Boyle, who arrived at Oxford in 1655, had already written three years earlier a short essay 'of the atomicall philosophy' which he felt compelled to undertake because that doctrine, 'revived and so skillfully celebrated in divers parts of Europe by the learned pens of Gassendus, Magnenus, Des Cartes and his disciples, our deservedly famous countryman Sir Kenelme Digby and many other writers, is now growne too considerable to be any longer laugh't at, and considerable enough to deserve a serious enquiry'. In the following decade Meric Casaubon

---

[129] BL MS Lansdowne 93, fo 179; W. N. Clarke, 'Illustrations of the state of the church during the Great Rebellion', *Theologian and Ecclesiastic* vi (1848), 171.

[130] E. Straus, *Sir William Petty* (Glencoe 1954), 28; Frank, *Harvey and the Oxford Physiologists*, 92.

[131] *The Works of Sir Thomas Browne*, ed. Keynes ii. 540. It was probably around 1650 that Browne also purchased Gassendi's *Animadversiones*. See J. S. Finch, *A Catalogue of the Libraries of Sir Thomas Browne and Dr Edward Browne, his Son* (Leiden 1986), 31, 43.

[132] L. Sharp, 'Walter Charleton's early life 1620–1659, and relationship to natural philosophy in mid-seventeenth century England', *Annals of Science* xxx (1973), 324, 327 n. 55.

grudgingly admitted that Gassendi was 'the most accomplished generall schollar we have had of late', yet the crucial role he played in the revival of Epicureanism greatly alarmed Casaubon who thought it 'most prodigious and incredible' that 'so many, professing Christianity, should entertain the attempt with so ready an assent and applause'.[133]

John Wilkins and Seth Ward did not exaggerate, then, when in the context of their polemic with the critics of the universities in 1654 they emphatically stressed the rootedness of the new French ideas at Oxford. Wilkins did so in the context of slighting Hobbes's pretence of novelty: 'there are here many men, who have been very well versed in those notions and principles which he would be counted the inventer of, and that before his workes were published'. Ward was more blunt. He dismissed John Webster's insinuation that Oxford men were ignorant of Descartes and Gassendi by pointing out that not only did many Oxford men study the French savants carefully, but their knowledge was such that they could easily detect someone who had plagiarized them: 'there is not one argument against Aristotle', thundered Ward, that Webster 'hath not taken entirely out of *Gassendis exercitations adversus Aristoteleos*, beside a little out of Helmont.' In less explicit terms Hobbes, too, was branded a plagiarist, when he was told that his theory (in *Leviathan*) 'explaining sence upon the grounds of motion, was almost generally received here before his book came forth. Being sufficiently taught by Des Cartes, Gassendus, Sir K. Digby, and others'.[134] Equally telling as to the wide diffusion of Cartesian and Gassendist ideas is the overall impression gained by Samuel Sorbière on his visit to England in 1663 that English savants were divided into two camps: 'whereas those who are meer mathematicians favour Descartes more than Gassendus, the literati on the other side are more inclined to the latter'. Sorbière also observed that neither party was dogmatic, despite their general allegiances.[135]

Oxonians read and discussed Descartes's ideas assiduously. John Aubrey was introduced to Descartes while an undergraduate at Trinity College in the late 1640s, and he discussed what he learnt with Edward Davenant who 'could not endure to heare of the new (Cartesian, or etc.) philosophy; "for", sayd he, "if a new philosophy is brought in, a new divinity will shortly follow" '. Robert Hooke, who arrived at Oxford in 1653, was three years later well advanced in his study of Descartes and, if Aubrey is to be trusted, he then made Boyle 'understand Des Cartes' philosophy' as well.[136] In 1656 Seth Ward made extensive use of the works of both Descartes and Gassendi in his attempt to refute the physics of Thomas Hobbes. The testimony of Locke that the first books to give him 'a relish

[133] R. S. Westfall, 'Unpublished Boyle papers relating to scientific method', *Annals of Science* xii (1956), 111–12; Spiller, *'Concerning Natural Experimental Philosophie'*, 82, 204.

[134] [Wilkins and Ward], *Vindiciae academiarum*, 7, 32–3, 53.

[135] Samuel Sorbière, *A Voyage to England* (London 1709), 38. The vehemence with which Thomas Sprat attempted to repudiate Sorbière's observation tends further to confirm the Frenchman's general impression.

[136] *Brief Lives by Aubrey*, ed. Clark i. 201, 411; Robert Hooke, *Micrographia* (London 1664), 44; Frank, *Harvey and the Oxford Physiologists*, 57.

of philosophical studys were those of Descartes' can be corroborated through a study of his 1659 notebook, which demonstrates the close examination he made of Descartes's philosophy.[137] Joseph Glanvill of Exeter College (MA 1658) was also engaged in a careful study of Descartes during the late 1650s, and his first book brims with such hyperboles as 'incomparable', 'great', 'most excellent', and the 'miracle of men' to describe the Frenchman.[138]

Nor was the situation different after the Restoration. Having graduated BA in 1676, William Wake, who had previously neglected his philosophical studies in favour of classical literature, embarked on a study of Descartes and other modern authors—notwithstanding the hostility of his benefactor at Christ Church, Dean Fell, to such study. Humphrey Hody read, in about 1680, Gassendi's *Syntagma* and Descartes's *Principia*, while Thomas Smith delivered in 1684 a series of lectures at Magdalen College, in the course of which he frequently referred to Descartes and Gassendi. Charles Boyle, the future earl of Orrery, devoted the better part of a month (mid-November to mid-December 1691) to a close reading of the *Principia*, assisted by his sub-tutor at Christ Church Robert Morgan (MA 1686). On the whole, the young nobleman was pleased with the book, informing his tutor Francis Atterbury that, to his mind, Descartes was 'the best philosopher, that, upon the most rational grounds, gives the most probable account of nature's operations'.[139] Other scholars left testimony to their study in the form of records of ownership. Samuel Lee, for example, a protégé of John Wilkins at Wadham College, purchased in 1651 a copy of Descartes's *Meditationes*, which joined his moderate collection of other works by Descartes and Gassendi, as well as many other scientific writings. Francis Vernon of Christ Church described in his 1667 verse depiction of Oxford life how young students pursued both Descartes's and Gassendi's Epicurean philosophy. William Smith of University College acquired the 1672 edition of Descartes's *Principia* and later donated it to the new Ashmolean library, where he was enrolled in a course of chemistry read by Robert Plot.[140] Henry Stubbe, John Wallis, and John Owen are just a few among many others who owned fairly complete runs of Descartes and Gassendi, books they almost certainly acquired during the 1650s.[141]

[137] Seth Ward, *In Thomae Hobii philosophiam exercitatio epistolica* (Oxford 1656); 'Lady Masham to Jean Le Clerc', 17; BL Add. MS 32, 554, cited in Rogers 'Descartes and the English', 300–1.

[138] Joseph Glanvill, *The Vanity of Dogmatizing* (London 1661), 32, 44, 48, 73, 87.

[139] Sykes, *William Wake* i. 10; Bodl. MS Rawlinson 1221; Bodl. MS Smith 128; *The Epistolary Correspondence of . . . Francis Atterbury*, ed. J. Nichols (4 vols London 1789–90) ii. 5, 7–9. Atterbury himself owned a copy of Descartes's *Le Monde* as well as a work by the Cartesian popularizer Antoine Dilly *De l'ame des bêtes*. He also owned two works by Spinoza. *A Catalogue of the Library of . . . Francis Atterbury* in *Sale Catalogues of Libraries of Eminent Persons* vii *Poets and Men of Letters*, ed. H. Amory (London 1973), 2, 15, 41.

[140] *Publications of the Colonial Society of Massachusetts* xxviii (1930–3), 402; *The Library of . . . Samuel Lee* (Boston 1693); Vernon, *Oxonia poema*, 16; R. T. Gunther, 'The chemical library of the university', *Bodleian Quarterly Record* vi (1929–31), 202.

[141] BL MS Sloane 35; Edward Millington, *Bibliotheca Oweniana* (London 1684); C. J. Scriba, *Studien zur Mathematik des John Wallis (1616–1703)* (Wiesbaden 1966), appx; Frank, *Harvey and the Oxford Physiologists*, 58, 93, 345, n. 82.

Evidence for the trickling down of such influence may readily be found by surveying the donations by students and dons of books by Gassendi and Descartes to their college libraries. Such information is particularly important, not only because college libraries relied primarily on this form of acquisition as the source of their holdings, but because these gifts also indicate the intellectual bent of the donors and their perceptions of the needs of their libraries. Thus, for example, Christ Church benefited in 1649 from Robert Payne's presentation of a copy of Descartes's *Meditationes* as well as from the joint gift by Henry Lowell and Henry Guy of the three-volume edition of Gassendi's *Animadversiones*. At Corpus Christi College it was the donation of two intruded fellows in 1652 that furnished the library with similar works: Samuel Byfield donated the 1650 Latin edition of Descartes's philosophical works, as well as works by Bacon, Torricelli, and Harvey, while Samuel Ladyman donated Gassendi's *Animadversiones*. New College benefited in 1656 from Thomas Tanner's gift of Descartes's *Opera philosophica*, two of Gassendi's works—*Exercitationes paradoxicae adversus Aristoteleos* and *Institutio astronomica*—and works by Gilbert, Thomas White, Digby, Kepler, and Galileo, as well as Hobbes's *De corpore*. A year later, John Gruter added Descartes's *Meditationes* and two additional works of Gassendi, *De apparente magnitudine solis* and the *Disquisitio metaphysica*.[142]

Echoing the new trends, all colleges, large and small, proceeded to augment these gifts through purchases of works by Descartes and Gassendi. In the 1640s St John's College acquired works by Descartes, Gassendi, Digby, Mersenne, and Torricelli. In the late 1680s and early 1690s New College expanded its collection of works by Descartes and Gassendi, which it had received from students, by selling duplicates and using the proceeds to acquire books by Cartesians such as Clauberg, La Forge, Spinoza, and Locke, as well as the *Philosophical Transactions*, the *Acta eruditorum*, and the *Journal des savants*. Significantly, the holdings of the smaller halls that catered primarily to undergraduates were also furnished with such works. The library of Magdalen Hall, which consisted of a choice 600 books purposely selected for the use of students in the 1650s by Principal Henry Wilkinson, included in 1661 Descartes's *Opera philosophica*, Gassendi's *Animadversiones*, and Charleton's *Physiologia Epicuro-Gassendo-Charltoniana*. Similarly the smaller, but more modern, undergraduate library of St Edmund Hall comprised *circa* 1695 some 400 books, including a complete run of the works of Descartes and Gassendi in addition to many other scientific works.[143] The availability of such books in college libraries made their reading far more common, benefiting fellows and even some students, who otherwise would have been unable to afford such books: for example, between 1666 and 1668 five students of St Edmund Hall—John March, Conyers Richardson, William Stephens, John Thomson, and Henry Chennel—borrowed the

[142] Hugh Kearney, *Scholars and Gentlemen* (Ithaca NY 1970), 83; CL benefactors book, 96; CCCL MS 303 (loose cancelled page of benefactors); NCA benefactors book, 89, 91.
[143] Kearney, *Scholars and Gentlemen*, 83; NCA 'catalogue of discarded books'; *Catalogus librorum in bibliotheca Aulae Magdalenae* (Oxford 1661), sigs A8, B3ᵛ; Bodl. MS Rawlinson d. 316, fos 13–43.

multi-volume edition of Gassendi's *Animadversiones*, either for their own study or in preparation for their tutoring of younger students.[144]

The swift and complete manner in which French ideas permeated the English universities may also be deduced from various polemical railings against the supposedly pernicious effects of the writings of Descartes, Gassendi, and their followers on religion, as well as from contemporary satires that alluded to their popularity. Already in 1654 Robert Baillie, the Scottish Presbyterian, had begged that eminent Dutch oracle of Calvinism (and staunch opponent of Descartes), Gijsbert Voetius, to compose a suitable protestant natural philosophy textbook that would arrest the rapid spread of Descartes's pestiferous ideas among young scholars at Oxford and Cambridge. Five years later, in his satiric attack on John Wilkins and the powers that be at Oxford, Henry Stubbe mocked the excessive preoccupation of members of the Oxford club with the doctrines of Descartes and Gassendi, scornfully 'calling' for the endowment of two professorships whose incumbents would teach the principles of the two Frenchmen.[145] Other examples illustrative of the diffusion of French ideas in the universities abound. When in 1665 the Cambridge physician Robert Sprackling attempted to rebut Marchmont Needham's attack on the Royal College of Physicians by, among other things, ridiculing Needham's ignorance, Sprackling advised his opponent 'to accommodate himself with some young gentleman of Cambridge or Oxford that may tutor him in Gassendus, and shew him such things as will put him into as high an extasie in seeing things so strange to his knowledge'. A more amiable satire, 'addressed to a friend, that is about to leave the university', was composed by the one-time student of St Edmund Hall, John Oldham (at Oxford 1670–4), who clearly recollected his own university experience when he cautioned the nameless friend not to presume he could 'live by systems of philosophy / [his] Aristotle, Cartes, and Le-Grand'.[146]

Best known, however, is John Eachard's biting indictment of prevailing intellectual fashions at the English universities, and their contribution towards undermining the foundations of the English Church as well as subverting learning in general. Specifically, he targeted the impudent young student who returns home from Oxford or Cambridge confident in the profundity and superiority of the 'knowledge' he has acquired. There

comes rattling home from the universities the young pert sophister with his atoms and globuli . . . full of defiance and disdain of all country parsons, let them be never so learned and prudent, and as confident and magisterial as if he had been the prolocutor at the first

[144] BL MS Lansdowne 697, fos 9–10.

[145] *The Letters and Journals of Robert Baillie . . . 1637–62*, ed. D. Laing (3 vols Edinburgh 1841–2) iii. 268–74; [Henry Stubbe], *Sundry Things from Several Hands Concerning the University of Oxford* (London 1659) in *Harleian Miscellany* (London 1810) vi. 91. I follow Charles Webster in viewing Stubbe's pamphlet as a satire. See Webster *The Great Instauration*, 175–8.

[146] Robert Sprackling, *Medela Ignorantiae* (London 1665), 74–5; *The Poems of John Oldham*, ed. H. F. Brooks (Oxford 1987), 226. Thomas Wharton, in 1673, criticized the virtuosi at the universities who adopted 'the "new fangled fopperies" ' of Descartes and Gassendi: Hunter, *Science and Society in Restoration England*, 138.

Council of Nice. And he wonders very much that they will pretend to be gown-men, whereas he cannot see so much as Cartes's *Principles*, nor Gassendus's *Syntagma* lying upon the table, and that they are all so sottish and stupid, as not to sell all their libraries, and send presently away for a whole wagon full of new philosophy.[147]

The significance of such evidence of the early and widespread influence of Cartesian and Gassendist ideas at Oxford transcends its relevance to the university curriculum. Such information also supplements our knowledge of those major thinkers whose intellectual development often preoccupies modern scholars and helps us to re-evaluate the extent and nature of the influence of earlier thinkers on the genesis of their ideas. John Locke's debt to Gassendi is a case in point. Scholars have often pointed out the congruity between the views of both philosophers; more contentious is their estimation of when, and to what extent, Locke was influenced by the Frenchman. This disagreement is in part the result of Locke's notorious unwillingness to admit any intellectual debt and in part the result of the disinclination of scholars—following Locke's own disparagement of the curriculum at his alma mater—to re-examine the course of study at Oxford Thus most scholars assume that Locke discovered Gassendi only during his visit to France in the second half of the 1670s (*after* he had drafted an early version of the *Essay*), when he met François Bernier and acquired the latter's *Abregé de la philosophie de Gassendi*. More recently, Kroll has offered another possible intermediary: Thomas Stanley's *The History of Philosophy*, which rendered into English much of Gassendi's *Syntagma*.[148] However, as the evidence presented above suggests, knowledge of the ideas of Gassendi was widespread at Oxford during Locke's student days; copies of Gassendi's works were readily available in Christ Church library, as well as in the libraries of scholars whom Locke knew well.

It has also been suggested that Robert Boyle introduced Locke to atomism—a theory not far fetched in view of Boyle's close association with Locke. Yet in his own published writings Boyle was equally reluctant to admit his own indebtedness to Gassendi. In order to establish his originality, it was important for him to argue, in 1661, for example, that he 'purposely refrained, though not altogether from transiently consulting about a few particulars, yet from seriously and orderly reading over' Gassendi's *Syntagma*, Descartes's *Principia*, and Bacon's *Novum organum*—so that he might 'not be prepossessed with any theory or principle, till [he] had spent some time in trying what things themselves would incline [him] to think'. Later, in 1666, although conceding he had derived some benefit from Gassendi's *Syntagma*, Boyle quickly added that this would have been greater 'if [he] had more seasonably been acquainted with it'. Such public disclaimers are not, however, borne out by

---

[147] John Eachard, *Some Observations upon the Answer to an Enquiry into the Grounds and Occasions of the Contempt of the Clergy* (London 1671), 142.

[148] R. I. Aaron, *John Locke* (Oxford 1937), 36–8; D. F. Norton, 'The myth of British empiricism', *History of European Ideas* i (1981), 331–6; R. W. F. Kroll, 'The question of Locke's relation to Gassendi', *Journal of the History of Ideas* xlv (1984), 339–59; F. S. Michael and E. Michael, 'The theory of ideas in Gassendi and Locke', *Journal of the History of Ideas* li (1990), 379–99.

Boyle's private papers. As early as 1647, for example, Boyle singled out Gassendi in a letter to Hartlib as 'a great favorite of mine' and, as we noted earlier, his 1652 essay 'of the atomicall philosophy' demonstrates a deep concern with the issue, and more than a passing knowledge of Gassendi and other writers on atomism.[149] Again, his own readings as well as the passionate pursuit by others at Oxford of Gassendist ideas during the years he spent there should warn historians against accepting at face value Boyle's public statements concerning the ancestry of his views.

The warm reception at Oxford of new philosophical trends entering from France was extended later in the century to embrace the ideas of Nicolas Malebranche. In fact, all the chief English proponents of Malebranchist ideas were educated at Oxford: John Norris, Thomas Taylor, and Arthur Collier. Norris received his BA degree from Exeter College in 1680, at which time he was elected fellow of All Souls, where he remained until he left Oxford in 1689. During this decade Norris embarked upon a serious study of Malebranche, publishing his first defence of Malebranche's doctrine that 'God is the "good in general" '.[150] Directly or indirectly, Norris introduced younger contemporaries to his idol. Chief among these was Thomas Taylor, a clerk of All Souls between 1688 and 1689 and demy of Magdalen College from 1689 to 1695. Taylor, considered by McCracken as the true founder of British 'idealism', inaugurated his publishing career in 1692 with a translation of the biting satirization of Descartes by Father Daniel, *A Voyage to the World of Cartesius*. This was followed two years later by Taylor's translation into English of Malebranche's *Treatise concerning the Search After Truth*.[151] Arthur Collier matriculated at Pembroke College in 1697 but, together with his brother William, removed to Balliol College the following year, and it was there that the two demonstrated an avid interest in natural philosophy and metaphysics. Arthur read the Latin version of the *Recherche* together with several works by Norris, thereby conceiving of 'a new inquiry after truth'.[152]

Malebranche appealed to many others besides this small group of philosophers, such as Christopher Codrington, who entered Magdalen College in 1685 and was elected fellow of All Souls five years later. While at Oxford Codrington acquired a considerable reputation for his literary skills as well as for his wit. He also developed an early passion for Malebranche and, upon visiting France, eagerly sought out the company of the philosopher. Indeed, his 'addiction' was widely recognized,

[149] *The Works of Boyle*, ed. Birch i, pp. xli, 302, iii. 9; Westfall, 'Unpublished Boyle papers relating to scientific method', 111–13; R. H. Kargon, *Atomism in England from Hariot to Newton* (Oxford 1966), 93–100; Frank, *Harvey and the Oxford Physiologists*, 92–5; J. J. Macintosh, 'Robert Boyle on Epicurean atheism and atomism', in M. J. Osler (ed.) *Atoms, Pneuma, and Tranquility: European and Stoic Themes in European Thought* (Cambridge 1991), 197–219.

[150] C. J. McCracken, *Malebranche and British Philosophy* (Oxford 1983), 156–79; John Norris, *The Theory and Regulation of Love* (Oxford 1688).

[151] A revised edition appeared in 1700 and this included Malebranche's *Short Discourse upon Light and Colours*, which Taylor published from manuscript. McCracken, *Malebranche and British Philosophy*, 8–9, 179–91.

[152] McCracken, *Malebranche and British Philosophy*, 9, 191–204.

eliciting a facetious remark from Matthew Prior following the death of Codrington's father: 'if you have not philosophy enough to sustain the loss, burn your Malebranche and wet your pocket handkerchief.' At Oxford Codrington befriended Richard Steele and Joseph Addison, who also shared his esteem for Malebranche. Addison, who may have acquired at least part of his knowledge from Taylor (the two became demies at Magdalen in 1695), also made Malebranche's acquaintance when he visited France in 1700. Writing to John Hough, bishop of Lichfield, Addison described his visit to the philosopher, noting that Malebranche had 'a particular esteem for the English nation' and rightly so, concluded Addison, for in England 'he has more admirers than in his own'.[153]

An even broader readership is evident from tutors' manuals such as the one by John Grandorge of 1690, which recommended those students versed in French to read Malebranche's *Recherche*. Likewise, the Christ Church collection books indicate that select students in the early eighteenth century were assigned to read the work. Ownership of the *Recherche* serves as our source of knowledge as regards other students: Francis Atterbury (MA 1687), who was a successful tutor at Christ Church until he left Oxford in 1695, or such obscure undergraduates as Thomas Devey of Magdalen Hall (BA 1699), who owned not only Malebranche but also a nearly complete collection of the works of John Norris.[154] Not everybody read Malebranche approvingly. John Keill of Balliol College, for example, in 1698 ridiculed the 'follies' of both Descartes and Malebranche, while exhibiting some familiarity with the latter: 'I would fain know what the author [Malebranche] meant by his seeing every thing in God by its idea', wrote Keill, 'for I must confess that the oftner I read his long illustration on this point, I understand it the less.' Indeed, he read and re-read Malebranche's doctrine of 'all things in God', yet had 'not so couragiously resisted [his] sense, as the philosopher advises, as to be able to penetrate such a solid piece of nonsense'.[155]

Thomas Hobbes

The reception of Hobbes's ideas was, by contrast, more intricate and complex. In the late 1640s and early 1650s, Hobbes's reputation was considerable; he was highly, and openly, regarded as a man of science by contemporaries in England as well as on the continent, though, as Malcolm noted, such a reputation was grounded 'on the basis of very little published work'.[156] Significantly, such renown was particularly evident among past and present members of Oxford, a fact that

---

[153] Nicolas Malebranche, *Œuvres complètes*, ed. A. Robinet (20 vols Paris 1958–68) xix. 978, 984, 1012, xx. 355; V. T. Harlow, *Christopher Codrington 1668–1710* (Oxford 1928), 91; *The Letters of Joseph Addison*, ed. W. Graham (Oxford 1941), 25; H. H. Campbell, 'Addison's "Cartesian" passage and Nicolas Malebranche', *Philological Quarterly* xlvi (1967), 408–12.

[154] Bodl. MS St Edmund Hall 172; J. Yolton, 'Schoolmen, logic and philosophy' in *The Eighteenth Century*, 584; *A Catalogue of the Library of ... Francis Atterbury*, 34; Salter, 'The books of an early eighteenth-century curate', *passim*.

[155] John Keill, *An Examination of Dr Burnet's Theory of the Earth* (Oxford 1698), 8–9.

[156] N. Malcolm, 'Hobbes and the Royal Society' in G. A. J. Rogers and A. Ryan (eds), *Perspectives on Thomas Hobbes* (Oxford 1988), 51.

can be attributed to Hobbes's being an alumnus of the university as well as to his intimate relations with several dons, who helped spread his fame. Most important among these was Robert Payne (MA 1617), the ejected canon of Christ Church, who had become a personal friend and an admirer of Hobbes during the 1630s while serving as chaplain to the duke of Newcastle. In addition to propagating Hobbes's views and circulating manuscript copies of his unpublished works at Oxford during the late 1640s, Payne also laboured indefatigably, though unsuccessfully, to abate the mounting hostility of Gilbert Sheldon and other episcopalian divines toward Hobbes.[157] Another member of Christ Church, Thomas Lockey, was in all likelihood one of Payne's converts, and it was Lockey's manuscript copy of Hobbes's *Human Nature* that was used by Francis Bowman in 1650 to print an unauthorized edition of that work.

The publication of *Human Nature* also provided an opportunity for two of the foremost natural philosophers in Oxford at that time, Seth Ward and Ralph Bathurst, to express their esteem for Hobbes. Ward was the actual author of the 'publisher's preface' to the book, wherein he asserted that Hobbes 'hath written a body of philosophy, upon such principles and in such order as are used by men conversant in demonstration'. Ward further expressed the hope that Hobbes would soon complete his intended trilogy (*De corpore, De homine,* and *De cive*) and thus succeed in satisfying 'the judgment and reason of mankind'. For his part, Ralph Bathurst contributed some enthusiastic Latin verses. But such manifestation of admiration by these two men of science did not stop here. Shortly after Hobbes's return to England in 1651, Ward travelled to London purposely to make his acquaintance, while Bathurst entered into a brief exchange of letters with Hobbes—who sent his two Oxford admirers complimentary copies of the *Leviathan* as a token of his gratitude for the labours they had taken with *Human Nature*. Bathurst thanked Hobbes for such a gift in a fulsome letter in which he expressed his hope that Hobbes would soon publish his work on optics, as well as *De corpore,*

especially since now the best wits, as well here as in other countries, are so greedy to listen after workes of that nature, and to vindicate themselves from the chimericall doctrines of the schools; under which, to the bane of true knowledge, they have for these many hundred years so miserably laboured. And thus much I am the rather bold to suggest to you, because if by your other workes already published, you have gained so high an esteem [even when almost a whole order of men thought it concerned them to cry downe your opinions], how much more shall those be received with honour, in whose argument no man's Diana will be brought into question.[158]

The rapid dissemination of Hobbes's ideas was noted by another member of Christ Church, Henry Stubbe, who urged Hobbes in late 1656 to 'speak favourably

[157] M. Feingold, 'An Early Translator of Galileo and a friend of Hobbes: Robert Payne of Oxford' in North and Roach (eds), *The Light of Nature*, 265–80.
[158] *The English Works of Thomas Hobbes*, ed. Holesworth vi, pp. xi–xii, xv–xvi, vii. 337–9; Thomas Warton, *The Life and Literary Remains of Ralph Bathurst* (London 1761), 48–9. The passage in brackets, omitted from the published version, was supplied by Malcolm from a copy of the original at Trinity College, Oxford: Malcolm, 'Hobbes and the Royal Society', 56.

of this university, wherein you have many favourers'. Stubbe reiterated the plea a few weeks later, again assuring Hobbes that 'very many' at Oxford greatly valued his work, 'even all that pretend to ingenuity'—a clear, though slighting, reference to the members of the Oxford scientific club. Stubbe also singled out Bodley's Librarian, Thomas Barlow, as a person who highly regarded Hobbes, and it was owing to Stubbe's intercession that Hobbes sent Barlow a presentation copy of his *De corpore* along with a courteous letter. Barlow returned an equally civil response to his 'honored friend Thomas Hobbes', in which he professed to have read all of Hobbes's works 'constantly as they came out', further intimating how he had often acknowledged in conversation his indebtedness to them 'in many particulars'. Barlow then proceeded to express a common reaction among contemporaries when faced with the more controversial aspects of Hobbes's views:

I confesse (at present) I doe not concurre with your judgement in every thinge, yet I have (as I think all sober men should) according to the principles of naturall reason and Christianity learned this much civility, as to be thankfull for those discoveryes of truth, which any man makes to me, and where I doubt or differ, to suspend my censure till more mature consideration.[159]

Highly ambivalent feelings about Hobbes were articulated as early as 1651 by the former dean of Christ Church, Brian Duppa. In a number of letters he wrote Sir Justinian Isham shortly after *Leviathan* was published, Duppa dubbed its author as the 'greatest monster' and 'daemonium hominis', adding that 'none ever was more gamesome in religion' than Hobbes. Yet Duppa also admitted that 'as in the man, so there are strange mixtures in the book—many things said so well that I could embrace him for it, and many things so wildly and unchristianly, that I can scarce have so much charity for him, as to think he was ever Christian'. Seth Ward, too, made it plain in the following year that even though Hobbes was deluded in his arguments, the pernicious implications of the *Leviathan* did not necessarily annul the power of the author's reasoning. He 'hath a very great respect and a very high esteem for that worthy gentleman', wrote Ward in the third person, 'but he must ingenuously acknowledg that a great proportion of it is founded upon a belief and expectation concerning him, a belief of much knowledg in him, and an expectation of those philosophicall and mathematicall works, which he hath undertaken, and not so much upon what he hath yet published to the world'. Despite the fact that Hobbes's book proceeded 'mathematically', Ward saw little 'reason from thence to recede from any thing upon his authority'. For not only did Hobbes injure mathematics 'and the very name of demonstration, by bestowing it upon some of his discourses, which are exceeding short of that evidence and truth which

---

[159] *Lettere di Henry Stubbe a Thomas Hobbes*, ed. Nicastro, 15–16, 19–20. An important member of the Oxford club, and a friend and collaborator of Hobbes in Paris during the mid-1640s, was William Petty, for whom see Skinner, 'Thomas Hobbes and his disciples in France and England', 160–1; L. G. Sharp, 'Sir William Petty and some aspects of seventeenth century natural philosophy' (Oxford D. Phil. thesis 1977), 39–47 and *passim*; F. Amati and T. Aspromourgos, 'Petty contra Hobbes: a previously untranslated manuscript', *Journal of the History of Ideas* xlvi (1985), 127–32.

is required to make a discourse able to bear that reputation', but he was 'only a negative witnesse, and his meaning in denying incorporeal substances, can rationally import no more' than his own inability to apprehend 'any such beings'. Like a person who observed Jupiter unaided by a telescope and then denied the existence of moons orbiting the planet, so was Hobbes comprehending 'with his fancy' that which others have apprehended 'with their minde'.[160]

Disenchantment with Hobbes came gradually, and its severity was owing, in part, to factors other than the understandable reaction to the implications of his religious and political teachings. Most important in this regard was the enmity that Hobbes generated among key figures of the Oxford philosophical club—a group whose members had hitherto proved the most receptive to his ideas. This was due not only to his persistent and unrelenting rebuke of the universities but, in addition, to the acrimonious dispute that had sprung up by the mid-1650s, and which continued for the next two decades, between Hobbes, on the one hand, and Seth Ward, John Wallis, John Wilkins, and Robert Boyle on the other. The first shots were fired in 1654 when, as we have seen, the genuine anxiety that permeated Oxford as a consequence of the radicals' concentrated attack on English institutions of higher learning prompted Wilkins and Ward to compose a powerful apologia for the universities. Their *Vindiciae academiarum* was ostensibly directed against John Webster's *Academiarum examen*, which had been published the previous year, but it was partially aimed also (as the title page explained) at what Hobbes, in the *Leviathan*, and William Dell 'have published on this argument'. It was the apparent affinity between the arguments of Webster and Hobbes (whom Webster had read with approval[161]) that caused Wilkins and Ward summarily to brand them both as enthusiasts who sought the destruction of Oxford and Cambridge. When Hobbes remained unrepentant and even retaliated—responding to Ward's insinuations that he [Hobbes] was both a plagiarist and mathematically incompetent, by adding a chapter to *De corpore* (1655) in which he claimed to have solved the problem of squaring the circle—the stage was set for total war. Wallis immediately seized the opportunity to expose several of Hobbes's more glaring mathematical errors, while Ward, prodded by Wilkins, followed suit by publishing a comprehensive and piercing critique of Hobbes's philosophy in general. Hobbes's vehement rebuttal— where a personal attack on the two Savilian professors was joined with a reassertion of much of his former censure of the university—elicited a derisive reply from Wallis to which Hobbes returned an equally abusive response. And so the dispute continued. This protracted controversy ensured that the most powerful group at Oxford during the late 1650s was mobilized against Hobbes. Moreover the conse-

---

[160] *The Correspondence of Bishop Brian Duppa and Sir Justinian Isham 1650–1660*, ed. Isham, 43, 41; Seth Ward, *A Philosophical Essay Towards an Eviction of the Being and Attributes of God* (Oxford 1652), 'To the reader'. John Owen thought the *Leviathan* 'was a booke the most full of excellent remarques of any, onely [that Hobbes] deify[ed] the magistrate, and spoyled all by [his] kingdome of darknese': *Lettere di Henry Stubbe a Thomas Hobbes*, ed. Nicastro, 28.

[161] John Webster, *Academiarum examen* (London 1654), 88, repr. in Debus, *Science and Education in the Seventeenth Century*, 170.

quences continued to be felt after the Restoration, as the stature of his antagonists was sufficient to counter Charles II's half-hearted patronage of Hobbes and to marginalize the philosopher of Malmesbury in the republic of English letters.[162]

On the heels of this clash by Hobbes with members of the Oxford philosophical club followed the war waged on him by the theologians. What concerned the latter as much as the subversive content of his work was the following that Hobbes appears to have generated. Such rapid spread of Hobbist ideas undoubtedly added some urgency to the need to refute Hobbes; in turn, the number and vituperativeness of such attacks further served to testify to the widespread study of Hobbes.[163] Already in 1657 George Lawson prefaced his important critique of Hobbes's political philosophy with the observation that 'many gentlemen and young students in the universities' considered the *Leviathan* 'to be a rational piece', and it was partly in order to disabuse them of such notions that Lawson composed his treatise. A couple of years later Meric Casaubon lamented the rapid spread of Cartesian and Hobbist ideas at the universities while Edward Hyde was hoping that John Wilkins's protégé, Matthew Wren (MA 1661), could be persuaded to refute the *Leviathan*, especially since Hyde had been informed that various tutors at Oxford preferred to read that book to their pupils rather than impart to them the more appropriate moral and political lessons of Aristotle and Cicero. Francis Osborne, who lived at Oxford during the 1650s supervising his son's education there, was a personal witness to the vogue for reading Hobbes. He commented with some bemusement on the fate of the latter, who, like other Englishmen that 'have imbellished this doting age with new notions', was rewarded for his genius with censure and by being branded an atheist.[164]

It would be a mistake, therefore, as Quentin Skinner properly pointed out several years ago, to view Hobbes as 'a complete outcast from intellectual society, a writer who was studied only to be refuted, whose impact was entirely "negative"'. Equally inaccurate is the view, most recently articulated by Rogow, that the 'Oxford luminaries accorded a cool reception' to both *De cive* and *Leviathan*. Skinner was opposing a school of thought that assumed Hobbes to be 'an isolated phenomenon in English thought, without ancestry or posterity'. Samuel Mintz, whom Skinner was criticizing, had put forward the claim for Hobbes's strictly negative influence on English thought, since he believed that Hobbes founded no school, left no disciples, nor exerted anything resembling even remotely the sort of

[162] John Wallis, *Elenchus geometriae Hobbianae* (Oxford 1655); Seth Ward, *In Thomae Hobbei philosophiam exercitatio epistolica* (Oxford 1656); Thomas Hobbes, *Six Lessons to the Professors of Mathematics of the Institution of Sir Henry Savile* (London 1656); S. Shapin and S. Schaffer, *Leviathan and the Air-Pump: Hobbes, Boyle, and the experimental life* (Princeton 1985); J. Prins, 'Ward's polemic with Hobbes on the sources of his optical theories', *Revue d'histoire des sciences* xlvi (1993), 195–224.

[163] Cf Q. Skinner, 'The ideological context of Hobbes's political thought', *Historical Journal* ix (1966), 294.

[164] George Lawson, *An Examination of the Political Part of Mr. Hobbs his Leviathan* (London 1657), sig. A2ᵛ; Spiller, 'Concerning Natural Experimental Philosophie', 61; Peter Barwick, *The Life of . . . Dr. John Barwick* (London 1724), 430; Francis Osborne, *A Miscellany of Sundry Essayes, Paradoxes, and Problematicall Discourses, Letters and Characters* (London 1659), sig. a2ᵛ.

influence Bacon, Newton, and Locke exerted over English thought.[165] However, what Mintz and more recent commentators, such as Mark Goldie, fail to realize, is that the charges of impiety and atheism that were habitually levelled against Hobbes after 1660 ensured that Hobbes's writing would go, not unread, but only unacknowledged.[166] To quote Skinner again: 'Hobbes's political works were to gain a sufficiently sinister reputation for any public or printed avowal of sympathy with their views to become very difficult'.[167] Oxford students and dons, then, like English scholars in general, continued to acquire and study Hobbes's books. However, they could not admit to any positive influence such writings may have exerted over them and, instead, felt it incumbent upon themselves publicly to renounce him.

The implications of such prudent 'silent' reading and reluctance to acknowledge indebtedness are far-reaching. A case in point is the issue of Locke's reading of Hobbes. Aaron, for example, argued that the latter's influence on Locke was 'primarily of a negative sort. He is aware of him and sometimes is obviously seeking to answer him. But in the positive sense the influence is slight.' Similarly, Laslett claimed that it could 'be quite confidently asserted that Hobbes did not interest Locke particularly, not as much as Machiavelli, not beyond the point where he felt that every good library should have *Leviathan*. Locke did not want Hobbes's literary company.'[168] However, Locke was a Student of Christ Church, many members of which were disciples of Hobbes. Indeed, by the late 1650s, Locke himself was carrying on an intellectual dialogue, if not a friendship, with two members of Christ Church who were influenced by Hobbes, Henry Stubbe and Edward Bagshaw. To the former, Hobbes's closest confidant at Oxford in the late 1650s, Locke addressed a letter in 1659, in which he criticized Stubbe's views on toleration as expressed in *An Essay in Defence of the Good Old Cause*.[169] Bagshaw was Locke's predecessor as censor of moral philosophy at Christ Church and it was during his term in that office, in 1658, that he wrote Hobbes a fulsome letter in which he depicted Hobbes as an oracle who was visited by many who came 'to seek from [his] per-

[165] Q. Skinner, 'Thomas Hobbes and his disciples in France and England', *Comparative Studies in Society and History* viii (1966), 154; Skinner, 'The ideological context of Hobbes's political thought', 286–7 (where Skinner quotes Trevor-Roper); A. A. Rogow, *Thomas Hobbes* (New York 1986), 55; S. L. Mintz, *The Hunting of Leviathan* (Cambridge 1970), 147.

[166] It is important not to argue, as Goldie does, that the 'polemic against Hobbes might be summarized as the last gasp of scholastic Aristotelianism'. M. Goldie, 'The reception of Hobbes' in J. H. Burns (ed.), *The Cambridge History of Political Thought 1450–1700* (Cambridge 1993), 594.

[167] Skinner, 'Thomas Hobbes and his disciples', 159. See also Skinner, 'The ideological context of Hobbes's political thought', 304: 'A man who had been named in parliament as the author of blasphemous and profane works was not a writer to cite idly or without very necessary reason as an authority on anything.'

[168] Aaron, *John Locke*, 33; J. Harrison and P. Laslett, *The Library of John Locke* (Oxford 1971), 23. Even von Leyden downplays the extent of Hobbes's influence on the young Locke. See Locke, *Essays on the Law of Nature*, 37–8.

[169] *The Correspondence of John Locke*, ed. De Beer i. 109–12. The two remained in touch for many years and Locke supplied Stubbe in 1672 'with legal arguments supporting the royal supremacy in religious matters'. See J. Jacob, *Henry Stubbe, Radical Protestantism and the Early Enlightenment* (Cambridge 1983), 117.

son the solution of all doubts'. In the following year Bagshaw published his *The Great Question concerning Things Indifferent in Religious Worship*, to which Locke composed a rebuttal in 1660.[170] Admittedly, far too little is known about the precise relationship between Locke and such elder members of Christ Church. Yet, because of the avid interest in Hobbes during the 1650s, a closer attention to such relationships is in order, despite the fact that Locke never quoted Hobbes nor acknowledged indebtedness to the *Leviathan* or any other of Hobbes's books—indeed, by the 1690s Locke was actually pretending that he had never read Hobbes.

Obviously Hobbes was not read by most undergraduates, whose curriculum was sufficiently crammed as it was. But once the students graduated they were left to pursue their own studies, and this period provided ample opportunities for the reading of Hobbes. John Potenger illustrates the point. Having graduated BA in 1668 Potenger 'spent most of [his] time in reading books, which were not very common, as Milton's works, Hobbs his *Leviathan*; but they never had the power to subvert the principles which [he] had received, of a good Christian, and a good subject'.[171] Other readers included Anthony Wood, who read the *Leviathan* and sundry of the works that aimed at refuting it, and Samuel Parker, fellow of Trinity College, whose ambivalent reading of Hobbes is discussed by Ashcraft. The Savilian professor of astronomy, Edward Bernard, perused Hobbes's writings as well. He thought Hobbes was but an indifferent philosopher or mathematician and that his best book was his translation of Thucydides. Though Bernard did not admire Hobbes, he still thought the latter to be an 'elegant writer and pleasing, besides his style, for the novelty of his affections'.[172] Ownership of Hobbes's works may also indicate readership. John Hutton of New College, for example, owned a copy of *De cive* when he died in 1653, while Francis Atterbury's library included both *Leviathan* and the *Opera philosophica*. Thomas Devey read *Behemoth* at Magdalen Hall in the mid-1690s, and Peter Wood (MA 1696 New College) owned *Leviathan*. Finally, the Oxford bookseller Anthony Stephens kept three copies of *De cive* and one copy of *Human Nature* in his shop during the 1680s.[173]

John Locke

The immediate reception of Locke was not unlike that which had greeted Hobbes half a century earlier: initial enthusiasm and attentive study of the *Essay concerning Human Understanding* accompanied by growing concern from various quarters over certain religious implications of the underlying philosophy. Ultimately, however—and in contrast to the long-term fortunes of Hobbes's philosophy—the ensuing

[170] Skinner, 'Thomas Hobbes and his disciples', 163; M. Cranston, *John Locke* (London 1966), 59–63; Locke, *Essays on the Law of Nature*, 23–7.

[171] *The Private Memoirs of John Potenger*, ed. C. W. Bingham (London 1841), 31–2.

[172] Wood, *Life and Times* ii. 472–3; R. Ashcraft, *Revolutionary Politics and Locke's Two Treatises of Government* (Princeton 1986), 42–55; Bodl. MS Smith 47, fo 39.

[173] OUA chancellor's ct inventories s.v. John Hutton and Peter Wood; *A Catalogue of the Library of ... Francis Atterbury*, ed. Amory 17, 22; Salter, 'The books of an early eighteenth-century curate', 42; D. G. Vaisey, 'Anthony Stephens: the rise and fall of an Oxford bookseller' in R. W. Hunt, I. G. Philip, and R. J. Roberts (eds), *Studies in the Book Trade in Honour of Graham Pollard* (Oxford 1975), 112–13.

debates over religious issues, though heated, only marginally impeded the spread of Lockian ideas.

Oxford scholars took notice of the *Essay* within days of its publication. By mid-December 1689 James Tyrrell was able to inform the author that local dons had been quick to purchase the book, which was being favourably received: 'it came downe to Oxford last week', he wrote, 'and many copyes are sold of it, and I hear it is well approved by those who have began the readeing of it.' Two months later Tyrrell further intimated: 'I must tell you that your booke is received here with much greater applause, then I find it is at London; the persons here being most addicted to contemplation, as there to action.' That the *Essay* was quickly read and discussed is evident. Edward Bernard had perused the book by mid-January 1690 (though he complained in one of his letters that he had found it difficult and over-contemplative) and later that year Richard Old solicited Locke for a presentation copy for Christ Church's library.[174] Another Christ Church tutor, Francis Atterbury, assigned the *Essay* to at least one of his charges, Charles Boyle, Lord Orrery, in the autumn of 1691. By 15 November Boyle informed his tutor that he had 'just made an end of Locke' and that he 'was extremely pleased with him'. Furthermore, continued the precocious student, 'I think there is a great deal of very good sense in him; and I believe a great part of it is his own. Besides, his language is sound, proper, and pure; and his instances so familiar, that any one may under-stand him. If he says the thing over and over, I think we are obliged to him; for he has nothing but what will bear reading twice at least.'[175]

Other tutors at Oxford read the *Essay* to, or discussed it with, their pupils and in 1695 John Wynne solicited Locke's sanction of his intended epitome of the *Essay*, which he hoped would benefit all undergraduates. In his first letter to Locke, Wynne conveyed his own enthusiasm for the *Essay*, which he had also detected among his friends: 'I have for some time made it my busines, in my little sphere, to recommend it to all those that I have any influence over. Nor did I ever meet with any, who after an attentive and diligent peruseal complained of being disap-pointed in their expectations; but on the contrary, they owned themselves to have been infinitly benefitted by it.' In a subsequent letter Wynne referred again to 'some others' at Oxford 'who entertain so high an opinion' of the *Essay*. It was this pos-itive attitude, he informed Locke, that encouraged him to contemplate composing an epitome that could be put into the hands of all newcomers to the university for, 'in all probability it would have the same effect upon us all, if it were but read and considered by all'. Armed with Locke's blessing and assistance, Wynne quickly compiled his *An Abridgement of Locke's Essay*, and that small book, accompanied by

---

[174] *The Correspondence of John Locke*, ed. De Beer iii. 763, iv. 10, 186–7; Bodl. MS Smith 47, fo 57. The *Essay* was published in December 1689 and another issue was published the following year. It was sold out by 1692. The second edition was published in 1694 and the third in 1695. See H. O. Christophersen, *A Bibliographical Introduction to the Study of John Locke* (Oslo 1930, repr. New York 1968), 26–7.

[175] *The Epistolary Correspondence of . . . Francis Atterbury* ii. 2.

Wynne's teaching, greatly contributed to the diffusion of Locke's ideas in Oxford.[176]

Such is the necessary background for a proper evaluation of the first attempt, made in November 1703 by several heads of house at Oxford, to curb the popularity of the *Essay*. As Tyrrell informed Locke during one of their meetings, it was

proposed by Dr. Mill, and seconded by Dr. Maunder, that there was a great decay of logical exercises in the university, which could not be attributed to any thing so much as the new philosophy which was too much read, and in particular your book [the *Essay*] and Le Clerc's philosophy, against which it was offred that a programma should [be] published, forbiding all tutors to read them to their pupils.

However, Tyrrell's report continued, Thomas Dunster of Wadham College not only commended the book but also objected to taking any official action against it. Such a move, the warden argued, would create 'too much noise abroad as if the university went about to forbid the reading of all philosophy save that of Aristotle'; equally to the point, 'instead of the end proposed it would make yong men more desirous to buy and read those books when they were once forbid then they were before'. As a result of such reasoning, at their next meeting the heads resolved only privately to advise tutors to refrain from teaching Locke and Jean Le Clerc. Most significantly, however, and to Tyrrell's obvious glee, no action was taken to implement even such a lukewarm resolution, not even by the heads of such staunch high church colleges as University, Magdalen, New, and Jesus. In fact, quite a few dons of that party actually read the book approvingly, even going so far as to 'allso encourage their pupils [to pursue it] after they have done with their logick'. Henry Sacheverell of Magdalen College (MA 1695) and William Percival of Christ Church (MA 1695) were specifically singled out by Tyrrell among those who encouraged their students to study the *Essay*.[177]

Though historians have traditionally construed this episode as denoting the conservatism of the Oxford curriculum and the hostile reaction to Locke and the new philosophy in general, closer examination reveals a more complex situation. Rather than demonstrating a concentrated effort on the part of the heads of house to defend the hegemony of Aristotle at Oxford, it should be viewed in the context of the growing concern among English scholars following the Restoration about the

---

[176] *The Correspondence of John Locke*, ed. De Beer v. 261, 272. Some of those who read and discussed Locke at Oxford during the 1690s include John Norris, who promptly proceeded to criticize certain of Locke's views in an appendix to his *Christian Blessedness* (London 1690), John Toland, who arrived at Oxford in autumn 1693, already an acquaintance and somewhat of a disciple of Locke, Christopher Codrington of All Souls, who carefully studied Locke while at Oxford, and Peter Wood of New College, who owned, in addition to the *Essay*, Locke's Two *Treatises of Government*, *Thoughts on Education* and *The Reasonableness of Christianity*. A younger student, Samuel Parker of Trinity College, read the *Essay* in the late 1690s, though in imitation of Locke he claimed to have desisted from such reading until he had completed his own philosophical discourses, 'wherein he resolved to quit all authority for the simple evidence of his own naked reason'. R. E. Sullivan, *John Toland and the Deist Controversy* (Cambridge Mass. 1982), 4–5; Harlow, *Christopher Codrington, 1668–1710*, 51; OUA chancellor's ct inventories s.v. Peter Wood; Samuel Parker, *Six Philosophical Essays Upon Several Subjects* (London 1700), sig. A4.

[177] *The Correspondence of John Locke*, ed. De Beer viii. 202, 209, 221–2, 269–70.

general decay of higher learning. Erudition, the apex of scholarly effort during the previous half-century, appeared to have suffered a major blow—not least because of the advent of the new philosophy. Most heads of house were actually well disposed toward the new philosophy. Of the two singled out by Tyrrell as instigating the move against Locke, Mill (as noted earlier) actually exhorted students such as George Fleming not to neglect their studies of the new philosophy, while under Mander a lectureship in mathematics was established in 1697 at Balliol with John Keill (who devised a rigorous syllabus as well as initiating the teaching of experimental science) as its first incumbent.[178]

What prompted the Oxford heads to act was a growing uneasiness not unlike that which had animated much of the antagonism towards the nascent Royal Society four decades earlier: that the new philosophy might so excite youths that they would lose their taste and regard for the more 'consequential' studies—linguistic, historical, and patristic learning. This concern for the fate of critical learning during the 1660s and 1670s was certainly genuine, heightened by the militant rhetoric employed by the proponents of the new philosophy—who attacked both the ideal and content of university education. Such rhetoric not only made imperious claims for science, but denigrated the universities and the learning offered within their walls. As Meric Casaubon said in 1669, Glanvill, Sprat, and their ilk devalued the learning of the ancients and cried 'down all other studies and learning, ordinarily comprehended under the title of humane learning, to be but umbratick things, verbal things, of little or no use', especially as compared with this alleged 'new light of true real knowledge'. Not that Casaubon opposed scientific studies. He was quick to emphasize that 'hitherto nothing hath been said to impair the credit or usefulness of natural or experimental philosophy'; only 'that we would not allow it to usurp upon all other learning, as not considerable in comparison'. For Casaubon was 'very confident that where the reading of such [classical] authors is out of fashion, barbarism and grossest ignorance will quickly follow'.[179]

Casaubon and others, such as Henry Stubbe, aimed not only at the preservation of humanistic learning. They also wished to defend the Church of England, whose doctrinal foundations were believed to depend on the cultivation of such scholarship. This conviction accounts for much of John Fell's 'hostility' toward the new science and also informed the remarks by Gilbert Sheldon to Henry More not long after the former's resignation as chancellor of Oxford in the summer of 1669.

---

[178] *The Flemings in Oxford* ii. 296–7; Jones, *Balliol College*, 144, 148–9. In 1698 John Keill dedicated his *Examination of Dr. Burnet's Theory of the Earth* to Mander, stating that 'the principles on which I have grounded my arguments in the following discourse being mathematical, it doth more peculiarly belong to you, whose prudence in so industriously promoting the mathematical sciences, both by your direction and encouragement I cannot sufficiently commend'. sig. A2ᵛ–A3.

[179] Spiller, *'Concerning Natural Experimental Philosophy'*, 155, 165, 180. A few years earlier William Sancroft had commented sadly on the demise of the 'old genius and spirit of learning' that he had detected in Restoration Cambridge, 'the Hebrew and Greek learning being out of fashion everywhere ... and the rational learning they pretend to being neither the old philosophy nor steadily any one of the new'. G. D'Oyly, *The Life of William Sancroft, Archbishop of Canterbury* (2 vols London 1821) i. 128. For the decline of erudition see Feingold, 'The humanities', pp. 234–42 above.

Personally, the archbishop intimated to the Cambridge Platonist, 'he was disposed to look upon the new "free method of philosophizing" with far from unfriendly sentiments, but provided always, he added, "that the faith, the peace, and the institutions of the Church were not thereby menaced" '.[180] By 1700 the menace to church and learning appeared even more threatening. In this atmosphere Locke's spiteful castigation of humanist learning was too reminiscent of the language previously utilized by Sprat and Glanvill, causing him to be viewed as much as a destroyer as a reformer of learning.[181] In their lukewarm criticism, therefore, the heads of house can be seen as making a last-ditch effort to preserve the pluralism and comprehensiveness of the undergraduate curriculum. Their aim was less to root out Locke's 'new way of ideas' than to ensure the continuous cultivation of the arts of discourse. Equally to the point, they sanctioned the study of the new science, only cautioning that it not be at the expense of moral philosophy and metaphysics. To such an end, they sought to prevent premature specialization, their abortive censure representing an effort to restore the former order of studies. The young Oxford scholar Samuel Parker of Trinity (not to be confused with the bishop of Oxford) was not alone, therefore, in articulating the prevalent fear of the encroachment of science when, in 1700, he boldly justified his deliberate and 'remarkable omission' from his *Six Philosophical Essays*:

I mean my neglect of mathematical arguments, of which the world is become most immoderately fond, looking upon every thing as trivial, that bears no relation to the compasses, and establishing the most distant parts of humane knowledge, all speculations, whether physical, logical, ethical, political, or any other upon the particular results of number and magnitude. Nor is it to be questioned, but the dominion of number and magnitude is very large. Must they therefore devour all relations and properties whatsoever? 'Tis plainly unreasonable. In any other commonwealth but that of learning, such attempts towards an absolute monarchy would quickly meet with opposition. It may be a kind of treason, perhaps, to intimate thus much; but who can any longer forbear, when he sees the most noble, and most usefull portions of philosophy lie fallow and deserted for opportunities of learning.[182]

Be this as it may, the fact that our knowledge of the attempt to limit the Oxford influence of Locke derives exclusively from members of the philosopher's own circle, and that no attempt was apparently made to implement the recommendation of the heads of house, is a strong indication that at the start of the eighteenth century no campaign was afoot against either the *Essay* or the new philosophy in general. The only context in which the *Essay* did come under censure was a theological one, and even here the criticism was often oblique. A few divines certainly entertained private misgivings about the religious implications of Locke's attack on

---

[180] M. Hunter, 'The origins of the Oxford University Press', *The Book Collector* xxiv (1975), 511–34; Henry More, *Enchiridion metaphysicum* (London 1671), sig. 3ʳ⁻ᵛ, quoted in J. B. Mullinger, *The University of Cambridge* (3 vols Cambridge 1873–1911) iii. 646. John Williams, bishop of Chichester, wrote to Arthur Charlett in 1705, commenting on how few among those ordained were proficient in the original tongues, and especially in oriental learning: Bodl. MS Ballard 9, fo 84.

[181] For Locke's assault on humanist learning see Feingold, 'The humanities', pp. 220–1. 238–9, 255–6, 278–9, 300 above.   [182] Parker, *Six Philosophical Essays*, sig. A3–A3ᵛ.

innate ideas and the book's seeming endorsement of materialism. But once again, our knowledge of their reaction derives primarily from reports transmitted to Locke by James Tyrrell, who seems deliberately to have provoked Oxford divines to address the religious implications of the *Essay*. Thus, in December 1689 Tyrrell conveyed to Locke the appraisal of a 'friend' who opined that the *Essay* was 'either extremly commended, or much decryed, but has ten enemies for one friend'. In his next letter Tyrrell told Locke that he found 'the divines much scandalized that so sweet and easy a part of their sermons, as that of the law written in the heart is rendered false and uselesse'—though he proceeded to dismiss such criticism by adding: 'but you know the narrownesse of most of their principles'. Significantly, it was also Tyrrell who first enunciated, to Locke's evident dismay, the notion that certain of Locke's ideas smacked of Hobbism.[183]

In themselves, though, such grumblings hardly constituted a campaign against the *Essay*. Except for John Norris, no public criticism of the book appeared prior to the publication in 1694 of James Lowde's *A Discourse Concerning the Nature of Man*, and only during the following two years did the writings of John Edwards and Edward Stillingfleet begin to generate interest in the religious implications of Locke's epistemology.[184] Indeed, Locke himself realized as much in 1697 when he observed that the growing chorus of complaint was only indirectly concerned with the *Essay*, which had 'crept into the world . . . without any opposition, and has since passed amongst some for useful, and, the least favourable, for innocent'.[185] What precipitated the campaign against Locke was the pouring off the press, following the lapsing of the licensing act in 1695, of an avalanche of pamphlets attacking the clergy, the church, and, it seemed, religion itself. Chief among these was Locke's own *The Reasonableness of Christianity*, which was hastily prepared in 1695 in anticipation of—and in an attempt to distance Locke from—John Toland's *Christianity not Mysterious*, published the following year. The predicament facing Locke was not only that Toland explicitly utilized Lockian principles to sustain an alarming deist position. Writing from Ireland in 1697, William Molyneux informed Locke that Toland 'also takes here a great liberty on all occasions to vouch your patronage and friendship, which makes many that rail at him, rail also at you'.[186] A few years later, Locke was to be implicated in the views of another of his confidants, Matthew Tindal. Yet again, even Tindal's critics were willing to admit that Locke's *Essay* became embroiled in the deist controversy only inadvertently. Responding to Tindal's inflammatory *Rights of the Christian Church*, in which Tindal expressed scorn for those who feared that Locke's works would 'let too much light into the world', Jonathan Swift retorted that it was not Locke's *Essay* 'but other works that people dislike, although in that there are some dangerous tenets, as that of innate ideas'.[187]

---

[183] *The Correspondence of John Locke*, ed. De Beer iii. 793, iv. 10, 101–2, 106–9.

[184] See n. 176 above. Curiously, with the exception of Norris, all of Locke's early critics were Cambridge men.

[185] *The Correspondence of John Locke*, ed. De Beer vi. 6.   [186] Ibid. 82–3, 132–3.

[187] *The Prose Works of Jonathan Swift*, ed. H. Davis (14 vols Oxford 1939–68) ii. 97.

Again, this is the requisite setting for a correct understanding of the second attempt to check Locke's influence at Oxford. What, however, is also significant here, beyond the obvious religious motivation, is that the crusade against Locke between 1706 and 1709 was orchestrated by William Lancaster, who took advantage of his position during these years as the university's vice-chancellor. According to Hearne, Lancaster was a bitter enemy of Locke, and his antipathy spilled over against the latter's popularizer at Oxford, John Wynne, whose appointment in 1705 as Lady Margaret professor Lancaster attempted to block, speaking of him 'very scurrily' and dubbing him a 'Lockist'.[188] Lancaster extended his campaign in 1706 by delivering a speech upon assuming the vice-chancellorship, in which he vigorously attacked Tindal's *Rights of the Christian Church* and Locke's *Essay*. His obsession with the supposedly poisonous implications of Locke continued unabated for the next three years, culminating in 1709 in his invitation to the seniors of the university to 'join with him in stiffling the mischiefs of ill and pernicious books, written on purpose to ruin both the Church and university' wherein, once again, the *Essay* was paired with Tindal's book as 'written to advance new schemes of philosophy and bring an *odium* upon ancient learning'.[189]

These sporadic efforts to curb Locke's influence were ineffective. Though frequently quoted by historians as indicative of the tenacity with which the university clung to Aristotle and scholasticism, they belie the generally favourable reception of Locke's philosophy at Oxford in the late seventeenth and early eighteenth centuries (plate 32). Naturally not everyone read Locke, and certainly some dons openly fulminated against him. But even among these latter, few, if any, opted to defend antiquated natural philosophy as an antidote to Locke. The absorption of Locke into the system of instruction proceeded uninterrupted. Most Oxford colleges acquired a copy of the *Essay* for their libraries during the 1690s,[190] and by the turn of the century manuals of advice indicate the routine referral of students to Locke. Thus, the use of the *Essay* as a convenient scapegoat during the acrimonious religious controversies in the early eighteenth century over such issues as deism and Arianism should not obscure its incorporation in the Oxford curriculum. As was the case with Descartes, Hobbes, and the new philosophy in general, Locke was read by tutors and students, his views discussed and debated, and his philosophy accepted or rejected according to individual choice.

---

[188] Hearne, who disliked the political principles of Locke, expressed Lancaster's position more moderately. Freely admitting that Wynne was an upright individual and extremely able scholar and philosopher, Hearne none the less doubted his qualifications for the position. To him also Wynne was 'a great Lockist' and though 'an ingenious man and a good scholar', yet he was 'better skilled in natural philosophy than in divinity'. Worse still, 'he is withall a man of republican principles, and a great defender of them in the coffee-house'. Hearne, *Collections* i. 134, 194.

[189] Ibid. 293–4, ii. 282–3.

[190] The librarian of Christ Church requested (and received) a complimentary copy of the *Essay* from Locke in 1692, while New College acquired a copy the same year and St Edmund Hall library also included a copy by c.1695. *The Correspondence of John Locke*, ed. De Beer iv. 186–7, 202–3; NCA MS of books exchanged; Bodl. MS Rawlinson d. 316, fo 15.

Experimental Philosophy

The evidence presented thus far demonstrates that by the middle of the seventeenth century the average Oxford undergraduate was provided with a solid grounding in the mathematical sciences and a competent entrance into philosophy, both old and new. Equally evident is the introduction of most students to these subjects by their second year at the university, the precise details and scope of the course being tailored to the specific needs of the individual students, particularly those well-born students who remained at Oxford for only two or three years. Such an educational agenda clearly confutes the often-held assumption that, since the statutes allocated most scientific instruction to the MA course, 'the sixty to eighty per cent [of all students] who did not stay on through the MA had little idea of even an outdated system of natural knowledge, much less a modern one'.[191] In fact, a cultural change of major proportions was effected by this typical instruction of most undergraduates in the principles of mathematics and natural philosophy. As Kearney noted in passing some years ago, 'more men attended the English universities [in the seventeenth century] than at any time until the nineteenth century. This meant that more men received a training in abstract thought, particularly in mathematics, than before.'[192] In this manner Oxford and Cambridge not only trained more students who made science their vocation, but provided a considerable proportion of the educated public with at least a modicum of scientific knowledge, thus contributing to a relatively sizeable community of 'virtuosi' who made possible the flowering of English science.

This is not, however, to imply that the undergraduate offerings in mathematics and philosophy signified a fundamental change in the general orientation of the course of study or the aims of university education. The venerated humanist ideal remained essentially intact, as did the conviction that the purpose of the undergraduate course was to provide a well-rounded training in the entire cycle of the arts and sciences—with specialization of any kind relegated to one's graduate career. Nor was the wisdom of this central tenet in the philosophy of higher education challenged by scientific practitioners. Even the most vocal champions of the Royal Society and of the new science conceded that advanced training in experimental philosophy was not the proper diet for undergraduates. As Thomas Sprat frankly stated, 'In this institution, men are not ingaged in these studies, till the course of education be fully compleated, that the art of experiments, is not thrust into the hands of boyes, or set up to be performed by beginners in the school; but in the assembly of men of ripe years.' It was this perception that restricted membership of the Oxford scientific 'club' of the 1650s to scholars of the rank of MA and above, a policy made explicit in the constitution of the Oxford Philosophical

---

[191] R. G. Frank, 'Science, medicine and the universities of early modern England: background and sources', *History of Science* xi (1973), 201.

[192] H. F. Kearney, 'Puritanism, capitalism and the scientific revolution', repr. in C. Webster (ed.), *The Intellectual Revolution of the Seventeenth Century* (London and Boston 1974), 241.

Society of the 1680s: 'No person of the university be elected into the society, that is under the degree of Art: M: or LL.B.'[193]

No less important for the orientation of the undergraduate curriculum was the disinclination of many parents to encourage their offspring to pursue chemistry and experimental philosophy which, they feared, would either distract them from more important studies or adversely affect their cultivation of good breeding. Indeed, even though many tutors concurred with John Wallis that the study of chemistry was 'a piece of knowledge not mis-becoming a gentleman', it was the hostility of the parents that often prevailed. Already in 1654 Seth Ward alluded to such an attitude when he criticized John Webster's motion to turn the universities into technical and vocational schools: 'Which of the nobility or gentry', asked Ward rhetorically, 'desire when they send their sonnes hither, that they should be set to chymistry, or agriculture or mechanicks?'[194] The reasons for such upper-class circumspection were social as well as intellectual. When Edmund Verney told his father in 1688 that he had not enrolled for a chemistry course because of the £3 expense involved, the latter was impressed less with his son's sudden display of frugality than with the fortuitous wisdom of the decision: 'I am gladd', replied the father, 'you didd not goe through with a course of chymistry. That sort of learning I do not approve of for you; it is only usefull unto physicians and it impoverisheth often those that study it, and brings constantly a trayne of beggars along with it.' Even Sir Robert Southwell, an avid natural philosopher and future president of the Royal Society, only gave his grudging approval to his nephew pursuing such studies in 1683: 'As for the course of chemistry', he wrote to Sir Thomas Southwell's tutor at Christ Church, 'I like it well enough, though I can hope for him no other benefit by it than an entertainment of the time, whereas to another it proves the directest passage into natural philosophy. It will but help him to talk at rovers, who is too guilty of that already.'[195]

The prevailing ideals of education, then, dictated a structure for the undergraduate curriculum that could scarcely accommodate advanced investigation—scientific or otherwise. Nevertheless, with the coming into vogue of experimental studies in the second half of the seventeenth century, some acquaintance with them was increasingly considered appropriate, even for undergraduates. For the most part, though, such knowledge was confined to an introductory and theoretical level, with the tutors encouraging their charges simply to read such books as expounded the principles—and related the results—of the new experimental philosophy. A few tutors, and some students, however, went further. One author of a student manual of advice specifically recommended his charges to join their introductory

[193] Sprat, *History of the Royal Society*, 323; Gunther, *Early Science in Oxford* iv. 46.

[194] 'Dr Wallis's letter against Mr Maidwell', *Collectanea* i. 316; [Wilkins and Ward], *Vindiciae academiarum*, 50. Cf also Francis Osborne's similar observation above p. 366.

[195] M. M. Verney, *Memoirs of the Verney Family* (4 vols London and New York 1899) iv. 405; CL MS 427, fo 21. Southwell proceeded to take the course and donated a copy of the textbook he used, Lemery's *Cours de chymie*, to the Ashmolean's library. R. T. Gunther, 'The chemical library of the university', *Bodleian Quarterly Record* vi (1929–31), 203.

study of anatomy with the observation of dissections. He also thought it fitting that the student add chemistry as well but, since such study was 'to be learned by going through a course in the laboratory', he desisted from elaborating further on the subject. Certain colleges even provided such instruction. The biographer of John Harris (student 1684–9) related that at Trinity College under President Bathurst 'lectures were . . . read in experimental philosophy and chymistry, and a very tolerable course of mathematicks taught'. Harris himself was entrusted by Bathurst to teach similar courses, 'to such as were inclined to learn' after graduation. Meanwhile, in 1701 John Evelyn the third apprised his grandfather that, in the company of other students, he regularly attended one of the experimental philosophy courses offered by John Keil.[196] Other students imbibed a taste for the new science more casually. In 1654 Francis Greville, third Lord Brooke, visited the botanic garden on several occasions, sampled an experiment, and even paid a shilling 'for a dog to anatomize'. Three decades later, James Wilding visited the Ashmolean at least twice in order to see 'the laboratory', and the larger expense he incurred the second time (1s 6d compared with 6d) may suggest he did more than simply tour the building.[197]

However, the particular educational ideals animating the structure and content of higher education were not in themselves sufficient to account for the subservient place of science in the curriculum. It is important to recognize that the number of people who aspired to profundity in mathematics or the natural sciences was, then as now, small. Again, the perceptive Seth Ward was fully cognizant of such limited appeal: 'It cannot be denied', he said, that 'the only way to perfect naturall philosophy and medicine' is through observations and experiments and 'that whosoever intend to professe the one or the other, are to take that course'—which, he had already pointed out, some indeed had done. Still, he continued,

of those very great numbers of youth, which come to our universities, how few are there, whose designe is to be absolute in natural philosophy . . . I am persuaded that of all those, who come hither for institution, there is not one of many hundreds, who if they may have their option, will give themselves to be accomplished naturall philosophers. Such as will, ought certainly to follow this course, [but] the paines is great, the reward but slender, unless we reckon in the pleasure of contemplation.[198]

[196] Bodl. MS Rawlinson d. 188, fos 4–5; Blakiston, *Trinity College*, 173; *Memoirs of Samuel Pepys . . . and a Selection of his Private Correspondence*, ed. R. Braybrooke (5 vols London 1828) v. 403. Benjamin Woodroffe's projected statutes for Worcester College (c.1690) intended to incorporate into the undergraduate curriculum there the type of education available in several Oxford colleges. The statutes included lectureships in mathematics and philosophy along with courses in anatomy, chemistry, and botany. The chemist was expected to deliver annually four lectures on the principles of chemistry and twelve on experimental chemistry. Similarly the botanist was required to offer four general and eight 'practical' lectures, as well as take his auditors' sampling. A fee of £5 was also budgeted for experiments: C. H. Daniel and W. R. Barker, *Worcester College* (London 1900), 159–60.

[197] Warwick. RO CR 1886/TN 21; 'The account-book of an Oxford undergraduate', ed. Duff, 258, 264. In 1697 George Fleming took a course with the 'bottanick professor', Jacob Bobart the younger: *The Flemings in Oxford* iii. 350.

[198] [Wilkins and Ward], *Vindiciae academiarum*, 49–50.

Accordingly, John Keill's lament at the start of the eighteenth century—that at Oxford 'mathematical learning was not as prized as a good Latin style'—was not a disparaging remark about the backwardness of Oxford, but rather an envious reflection by a practising scientist on current scholarly taste.[199] Yet despite the unmistakable predilection of most advanced students to specialize in topics other than science, it remains the case that, proportionately, compared with the present, a far greater segment of the educated public in the seventeenth century was exposed to natural philosophy. Anthony Wood's attitude is illustrative of contemporary scholars who placed scientific studies within a broader scholarly perspective. Having gone through one of Peter Stahl's chemistry courses in 1663, Wood admitted that he had gotten thereby 'some knowledge and experience', and yet, he continued, 'his mind still hung after antiquities and musick'.[200]

In this context, it is also important to reiterate the individualistic structure of the course of studies. As we saw in an earlier chapter, even undergraduates were left to pursue much of their reading independently, with the tutors serving primarily as guides. After graduation, supervision ended and the BA's had to proceed on their own. It was now that, unaccompanied, they were expected to build on the broad foundations they had previously acquired, and to pursue more specialized courses. In practice, therefore, advanced study of natural philosophy was a matter of personal choice. The point was made explicit by John Wallis in 1700: 'I do not know any part of useful knowledge proper for scholars to learn, but that if any number of persons (gentlemen or others) desire therein to be informed they may find those in the university who will be ready to instruct them: so that if there be any defect therein, it is for want of learners not of teachers.'[201]

Wallis was alluding here to a decline in the number of students eager to pursue advanced scientific studies by 1700 compared with the situation at Oxford four or five decades earlier. Yet the causes for such an ebb cannot simply be attributed to prevailing social or intellectual fashions which, after all, remained fairly constant throughout the seventeenth century, or be explained as a consequence of the considerable expense involved in taking experimental philosophy courses.[202] Nor can the university be faulted for having neglected to consider 'research' an integral part of its mission simply because advanced courses in experimental science were not specified in the statutes. I will attempt below to offer a general explanation for the relative decline of scientific studies at Oxford, but first it is necessary to document

[199] John Keill, *An Introduction to Natural Philosophy* (London 1726), p. x. John Arbuthnot, who regarded mathematics as the best medium to inculcate reason, found it 'surprising to see what superficial, inconsequential reasonings satisfy the most part of mankind. A piece of wit, a jest, a simile, or a quotation of an author, passes for a mighty argument.' 'An essay on the usefulness of mathematical learning' in Aitken, *The Life and Works of John Arbuthnot* 411.

[200] Wood, *Life and Times* i. 475.

[201] Feingold, 'The humanities', pp. 227–30 above; 'Dr Wallis's letter against Mr Maidwell', *Collectanea* i. 317.

[202] The sum of £3 that Edmund Verney was asked to pay for a course of chemistry appears to have been the standard fee throughout the period. Such also was Peter Stahl's fee earlier. See Wood, *Life and Times* i. 475.

the advent of experimentalism as a way of life at seventeenth-century Oxford and the positive attitude of the university towards the study of science and the provisions made for its encouragement.

When John Aubrey declared several years after the event that 'the searching into naturall knowledge began but since or about the death of King Charles the first', and that John Wilkins, who organized the Oxford scientific club, was 'the principall reviver of experimentall philosophy' at Oxford, he was describing not the sudden introduction of scientific studies *per se* after a long period of neglect, but rather the role Wilkins played in catalysing a new style of scientific practice that had only just been conceived.[203] For though empiricism and simple forms of experimentalism had been practised for some time, it was only following the publication of the works of Bacon, Galileo, Harvey, Descartes, and Gassendi during the second quarter of the seventeenth century that a new framework, which made experiment and observation its basis, became available. The mechanical philosophy, corpuscularianism, and the new biology all required that theories and hypotheses should be tested and demonstrated experimentally before they were proposed (ever so tentatively) as 'matters of fact'. Furthermore, this new form of experimental philosophy involved the invention and appropriation of various instruments which also started to become available during the second quarter of the century. Thus if experimental philosophy denotes the exciting new research being carried out in mechanics, statics, and pneumatics, as well as anatomy, physiology, and chemistry, it can be dated not much earlier than 1650.

Of course, the early decades of the seventeenth century had witnessed a burgeoning interest in all facets of natural philosophy and the mathematical sciences. Such a surge had also made itself felt in Oxford, where scholars contributed their share to the earlier, less systematic, forms of experiment. The Savilian professors often engaged in observations and demonstrations, and not only in astronomy and applied geometry. In 1632, for example, Peter Turner lectured on the magnetical philosophy of the Jesuit Niccolo Cabeo, and it is unlikely that he did not elucidate his topic by demonstration.[204] More often, though, these activities were conducted privately, alone or in the company of like-minded naturalists. Thomas Allen at Gloucester Hall regularly employed his 'great many mathematicall instruments and glasses' for experiments, frequently in the company of others, while his younger contemporary from Trinity College, Francis Potter, was engaged in a continuous process of invention and experimentation until he left Oxford in 1637.[205] Many scholars derived inspiration as well as practical hints about experiments from printed books. The works of Francis Bacon were particularly stimulating. In 1669 Meric Casaubon wrote that he had always had 'a great inclination' towards exper-

---

[203] Frank, 'John Lydall', 205; *Brief Lives by Aubrey*, ed. Clark ii. 301.

[204] QCL MS 390, fo 61ᵛ. Cabeo's *Philosophia magnetica* (1629), though modelled on Gilbert's *De magnete*, 'contained many new and clever experiments, and challenged Gilbert's view on the nature of magnetism'. J. L. Heilbron, *Electricity in the 17th and 18th centuries* (Berkeley and Los Angeles 1979), 181–3.

[205] *Brief Lives by Aubrey*, ed. Clark i. 26–9, ii. 161–70. For Potter see C. Webster, 'The origins of blood transfusion: a reassessment', *Medical History* xv (1971), 387–92.

imental philosophy: 'when I was young, I was well acquainted with Sir Francis Bacon his workes, and made tryall of divers of his experiments', though, he modestly admitted, 'seldome (for want of more judgement and dexteritie, perchance) with any success'. More successful was William Gilbert of Gloucester Hall (MA 1623), who was portrayed in 1634 by Hartlib as one who 'spends himselfe in a Verulamian philosophy for the natural part. Hase many brave experiments et if any understands Verulam.'[206] During the late 1640s many individuals derived pleasure (and information) from another storehouse of experiments, Athanasius Kircher's *Ars magna lucis et umbrae*. Robert Payne perused the book in 1649, extracting from it several examples for the benefit of Gilbert Sheldon. John Lydall of Trinity College, who also used in 1649 the description provided in John Wells's *Sciographia* in order to construct a glass dial, got hold in 1651 of the *Ars magna*, 'a booke much cried up for rare curiosities', and promised John Aubrey that if he found there 'any secret either of art or nature worth imparting [he would] not faile to do it'.[207]

Analogous with the introduction into Oxford of the new modes of investigation and the contemporaneous organization of English savants into informal groups, was the private lecture–demonstration. For some time after such courses were introduced in the mid-1640s they related principally to chemistry and the life sciences—and were an extension of the format of traditional medical lectures now transformed into a smaller setting. Here, individuals who had already acquired the new techniques served as initiators to both students and colleagues. Thus in 1647, when Gerard Langbaine (soon to be made provost of Queen's College) considered pursuing medicine as a career, he thought to avail himself of the instruction of 'a young man from Paris who gives a private cours of anatomy three times a week, four hours each'. The person may well have been William Petty, recently returned from the continent and visiting Oxford around this time. Shortly thereafter, Thomas Willis, in the company of seven other men, spent £27 4s 8d on 'chemicals, apparatus and building works' for a laboratory, and proceeded collectively to experiment and teach each other that science.[208] In this manner, several interlocking small groups of like-minded scholars eventually came together during the 1650s to form the Oxford scientific club.[209] The rapid assimilation of the new form of science into the private format of graduate studies bears out Seth Ward's indignant rebuttal of John Webster to the effect that chemistry was not neglected at Oxford—'there being a conjunction of both the purses and endeavours of severall persons towards discoveries of that kind, such as may serve either to the discovery of light or profit, either to naturall philosophy or physick'.[210] The carrying

---

[206] Spiller, *'Concerning Natural Experimental Philosophie'*, 212; Feingold, *The Mathematicians' Apprenticeship*, 74. Christopher Wren, dean of Windsor (MA 1613), also used Bacon and other books as his source for experiments. See R. Colie, 'Dean Wren's marginalia and early science at Oxford', *Bodleian Library Record* vi (1960), 541–51.

[207] BL MS Lansdowne 841, fos 21ʳ⁻ᵛ; Frank, 'John Lydall', 215.

[208] Ussher, *Works* xvi. 79; Sharpe, 'Life of Petty', 51; Webster, *The Great Instauration*, 165; Frank, 'John Lydall', 213, 215.

[209] For these see Webster, *The Great Instauration* and Frank, *Harvey and the Oxford Physiologists*.

[210] [Wilkins and Ward], *Vindiciae academiarum*, 35.

on of such endeavours in private, however, should not be viewed as a consequence of an underlying hostility on the part of the Oxford authorities towards the new science. As we shall see, within its limited resources the university supported the scientific work of its members.

The arrival of Peter Stahl in 1659 gave a great boost to experimental lectures in general, and to chemistry in particular. The German-born chemist, who had been brought by Boyle to assist him, quickly settled down in Oxford, built a laboratory, and began offering a series of courses that were received enthusiastically by the members of the university. We possess information about at least five classes given by Stahl between 1660 and 1663 to audiences of various sizes. Included among his auditors were John Wallis, John Locke, Christopher Wren, Ralph Bathurst, and Richard Lower. By 1664, however, Stahl had apparently exhausted the local market. According to Wood he left Oxford 'for want of disciples', offering instead lectures in London and the provinces, but he resurfaced at Oxford in November 1670 'and had several classes successively'.[211] Whatever the reasons for the scarcity of students for Stahl, some demand still persisted. Oxonians made up for his absence in various ways, importing foreigners to conduct courses or using local talent. Stahl had trained a number of people who were then able to continue on their own. John Locke and David Thomas, the latter of New College, combined their resources in 1666–7 to furnish a small laboratory, replete with instruments and working library, at a cost of £40. For a year they collaborated and carried out experiments. At the same time the Oxford physician and chemist William Wildan was also available to offer courses in laboratory chemistry, and in 1667 John Mayow, Robert Plot, and John Ward took a course with him.[212]

However, doubt has been expressed concerning the efficacy of such experimental chemistry courses in initiating 'anyone (other than the operator's apprentice) into practical laboratory work'.[213] The point is well taken. Nevertheless, the intention of most who enrolled in these classes was not to become professional chemists, but rather to acquire the basic principles of laboratory work and the application of chemistry to medical practice. For the next few decades we find references to a variety of lectures given by local individuals as well as visitors. In 1667, for example, Cressy Dymmock arrived at Oxford and offered a condensed course in experimental philosophy where, Ralph Bohun commented dryly, he 'decrys Aristotle and pretends as it were to inspiration in philosophy'.[214] Many Oxford fellows, recalled Wallis in 1700, periodically performed private experiments or offered

---

[211] Stahl's lectures are in BL MSS Sloane 499, 1625; Wood, *Life and Times* i. 290, 472; Gunther, *Early Science in Oxford* i. 22–4; G. H. Turnbull, 'Peter Stahl, the first public teacher of chemistry at Oxford', *Annals of Science* ix (1953), 265–70; Frank, *Harvey and the Oxford Physiologists*, 51, 53, 243; C. Brooks, 'Experimental chemistry in Oxford 1648–c.1700: its techniques, theories and personnel' (Oxford honour thesis, 1985), 18.

[212] Bodl. MS Locke, fo 25; Frank, *Harvey and the Oxford Physiologists*, 51, 225; Brookes, 'Experimental chemistry in Oxford', 19.

[213] A. V. Simcock, *The Ashmolean Museum and Oxford Science 1683–1983* (Oxford 1984), 32–3 and n. 77.

[214] CL Evelyn Correspondence, no. 301.

courses 'for their own satisfaction, and for the information of such others that desired it'. Among such individuals he named William Musgrave, Thomas Willis, and Richard Lower, as well as Plot 'and others successively to this time' who followed in the tradition of Stahl, and went through chemical courses 'with one company after another from time to time'.[215]

This supply of local talent was frequently augmented by foreign visitors. In 1681, for example, the Italian Giovanni Luca taught at least one *cursus chymicus* at Oxford and in April 1692 Wood jotted in his diary a note concerning 'an Italian . . . who takes classes of scholars to read to them anatomy'. This person may well have been one Doctor Baccio who boarded the previous year with Locke's friend, James Tyrrell, at Oxford. Tyrrell described him as an Italian anatomist 'of great worth' who, following the death of Locke's friend, Matthew Slade, performed a dissection of Slade's brain.[216] Another visitor who spent a few months at Oxford in the spring of 1695 was the Irishman, Bernard Connor, recently arrived in England after serving as physician to the king of Poland. Connor offered a course of lectures on 'a new plan of animal oeconomy'—a comprehensive foray 'into the knowledge of the fabrick, natural functions, and distempers of the human body' as well as 'the *materia medica*', which incorporated theoretical and experimental discussion of matter theory, as well as the principles of motion and chemical experiments. The course proved very successful, and procured for Connor invitations to offer similar courses in Cambridge and London. Connor was fulsome in his praise for his auditors at Oxford: 'I assure you', he wrote to a correspondent who invited him to Cambridge, 'that I have not met with better discipline, nor with persons more universally learned in any university of Europe.'[217]

By this time also experimental physics had come to prominence at Oxford. The arrival in 1692 of David Gregory as Savilian professor of astronomy infused new life into the study of the mathematical and physical sciences, both through his own teaching and research and because he was followed by his former Edinburgh students, the brothers John and James Keill. Gregory's astronomical and optical lectures presented his auditors with a sophisticated exposition of ancient and modern theories, including Newtonianism. In 1700 Gregory also devised an elaborate scheme for establishing 'collegia' for the private teaching of small groups of students in the various mathematical sciences, the subject-matter of which was to be

---

[215] 'Dr Wallis's letter against Mr Maidwell', *Collectanea* i. 316. See also Robert G. Frank, 'Medicine', pp. 548–54 below.

[216] BL MS Sloane 1243; Frank, 'Science, medicine and the universities of early modern England', 244. Wood, *Life and Times* iii. 387; *The Correspondence of John Locke*, ed. De Beer iii. 790–1, iv. 11.

[217] Bernard Connor, *History of Poland, its Ancient and Present State* (2 vols London 1698) ii. 289–322; S. Szpilczynski, 'Bernard O'Connor from Ireland: aulic physician to the Polish King Jan III Sobieski. A contribution to the development of medical thinking at the turn of the seventeenth century', *Proceedings of the XXIII International Congress of the History of Medicine* (2 vols London 1974) i. 762–71. I am grateful to Professor Davis Coakley who brought this article to my attention, and for his providing me with photocopies of both this article and the relevant pages of Connor's book.

thoroughly illustrated by observations and experiments.[218] John Keill began to lecture privately on mathematics and experimental physics at Balliol College in 1694. His criticism of Thomas Burnet's theory of the Earth in 1698 procured him the post of deputy to the Sedleian professor Thomas Millington the following year. The course of lectures he delivered in his new capacity, in which he set himself the task of deriving Newton's laws experimentally, was published in 1701 as *Introductio ad veram physicam*. Both this and other of Keill's courses were specifically tailored to the needs and background knowledge of 'the youth of this university', who had but a moderate knowledge of mathematics. His brother James appears to have begun offering medical and chemical lectures at Oxford in 1698, the year he published translations of Nicholas Lemery's *Course of Chymistry* and Amé Bourdon's *Anatomy of the Humane Body Abridged*. Both works served as texts in his courses, which continued until he left Oxford in 1703.[219]

That the university was willing to accommodate the new modes of thought is evident both from official legislation and material action. Concurrent with the opening of the Sheldonian Theatre, the heads of house met on 24 May 1669 and decreed that the grand new building should serve as the forum where all learning, including 'mathematical, critical, and chronological problems, and in a like manner all kinds of experiments, may be propounded and discussed . . . by all persons of whatever degree'. The resolution was codified into statute and enabled incepting masters of art who so desired to substitute such scientific performance for the customary rhetorical declamations. In 1704 at least one scholar, James Milnes, took advantage of this licence and, on the merit of a treatise on conic sections that was praised highly by the two Savilian professors, was awarded an MA degree.[220]

Financially, the university supported scientific studies throughout the century. Of course, Oxford had always relied on private benefactors to endow large-scale ventures and it was in this manner that it had acquired in the decades before the civil war the new schools, eight professorships or lectureships, and a botanic garden. In addition, however, and despite its meagre resources, the expenditure incurred by the university in order to ensure the provision of suitable scientific facilities was considerable. Observational astronomy was first to benefit. Even before the Savilian professorships were founded, a room at the top of the newly built schools' tower was fitted in 1614 to serve as an observatory; later, further expenditure was approved. In the early 1650s, as we saw above, the university disbursed the funds

---

[218] *Private Correspondence of Pepys*, ed. Tanner ii. 90–4. For Gregory's career see C. M. Eagles, 'The mathematical work of David Gregory, 1659–1708' (Edinburgh D.Phil. thesis 1977); P. D. Lawrence and A. G. Molland, 'David Gregory's inaugural lecture at Oxford', *Notes and Records of the Royal Society* xxv (1970), 143–78.

[219] A. Guerrini, 'Newtonian matter theory, chemistry, and medicine, 1690–1713' (Indiana Ph. D. thesis 1983), 145–69; A. Guerrini and J. R. Shackelford, 'John Keill's *De operationum chymicarum ratione mechanica*', *Ambix* xxxvi (1989), 138–52; F. M. Valadez and C. D. O'Malley, 'James Keill of Northampton, physician, anatomist and physiologist', *Medical History* xv (1971), 317–35.

[220] Wood, *History of the University* iii. 797–8; *Statutes*, trans. Ward ii. 73–4; OUA register of convocation 1704–30, NEP/*subtus*/31, register Bd, 15 January 1704.

necessary for Seth Ward to build another observatory at Wadham College. Half a century later, following the election of Edmond Halley as Savilian professor of geometry, the university paid for the repair of the house designated to be his residence—one of three houses bestowed on the university for the use of the Savilian professors in memory of John Wallis—and also bore the cost of adding a modest observatory on its roof for the benefit of the incumbent.[221]

More spectacular was the university's willingness to undertake the huge expenditure needed to transform Oxford into a major scientific centre. Nevertheless, the outlay on the building of the Ashmolean also represented the culmination of three decades of unsuccessful efforts by the practitioners themselves to institutionalize experimental studies at Oxford. As early as 1653 Samuel Hartlib was informed that 'they are now erecting a college for experiments et mechanicks at Oxford, towards which Dr. Wilkins hath given 200 lib. It is over the schooles or in the long gallery.' Wilkins undoubtedly expected his initiative and generosity to inspire other benefactors—a point elaborated on by Seth Ward in 1654, when he wrote 'how it is a real designe amongst us, wanting only some assistance for execution, to erect a magneticall, mechanicall, and optick schoole, furnished with the best instruments, and adapted for the most usefull experiments in all those faculties'. But in the short term his conception failed to materialize. Fortunately, for a season the widespread enthusiasm for the new science was sufficient to sustain the activity of Oxford men on a voluntary basis, but after the Restoration and following the foundation of the Royal Society—an undertaking towards which the contribution of Oxford alumni was particularly significant—new hopes were raised at the university as well. On 13 July 1664 the New College naturalist Robert Sharrock confided in Robert Boyle: 'I am not without hope that wee shall have some endowment for a society to study experimentall philosophy att Oxford, which I am very glad of both for the sake of the university, which I doubt not by this meanes may further increase its reputation and for the sake of knowledge in general which I doubt not will bee by this meanes promoted.' But this otherwise unknown scheme also failed to materialize. Undaunted, Oxonians made another concentrated effort six years later to institutionalize scientific studies, in the midst of the strife between the universities and the Royal Society. At that time, John Evelyn was told that at Oxford 'they talke already of founding a laboratorie, and have begged the reliques of old Tradescant, to furnish a repositary'.[222]

Evelyn was alluding to the anticipated benefits for scientific studies that would come from the concentrated effort, masterminded by the powerful dean of Christ Church (and university vice-chancellor) John Fell to promote the reputation of Oxford. Partly in an attempt to offset, and compete with, the Royal Society, Fell

[221] I. G. Philip, 'The building of the schools quadrangle', *Oxoniensia* xiii (1948), 39–48; Bodl. MS Ballard 24, fo 43; Bodl. MS Lister 37, fo 89; H. E. Bell, 'The Savilian professors' houses and Halley's observatory at Oxford', *Notes and Records of the Royal Society* xvi (1961), 179–86; Ronan, *Edmond Halley* 186.

[222] Webster, *The Great Instauration*, 171; [Wilkins and Ward], *Vindiciae academiarum*, 36; Royal Society, London, Boyle letters v. 98; Hunter, *Science and Society in Restoration England*, 146.

conceived of several ventures that aimed at bolstering scientific studies at the university. For example, one of the most ambitious enterprises projected by the new printing press established by Fell was the publication of nearly the entire corpus of 'ancient mathematicians Greek and Latin in one and twenty volumes', as well as various other scientific works. Botany, however, was first to benefit.

The foundation of the Oxford physic garden in 1621 by Henry Danvers, earl of Danby, was followed by a protracted period of construction (plate 4). In 1641 Danby granted Jacob Bobart the elder 'a ninety-nine-year lease of the site, with the "benefit of fees and fruits", and subject to good behaviour, promised him an annuity of £40 for life for caring for the garden'. This private arrangement terminated following Danby's death in 1644, and the income from the rectory of Kirkdale, Yorkshire, was hardly sufficient to cover the cost of the garden's upkeep—let alone pay the salary of a projected professor of botany. None the less, for several decades Bobart was able to draw a handsome profit from the sale of the fruits and vegetables that he grew, though after the Restoration such proceeds declined considerably as a result of the rapid expansion of private gardens.[223] At this point the university was spurred to act, appointing in 1669 Robert Morison as professor of botany and, conditional on his teaching, providing him (out of the university chest) with the salary of £40 a year. A further expenditure of £92 was approved for the building of a greenhouse and the shipment of plants. Morison delivered two series of lectures annually, in May and September, lecturing thrice weekly for five weeks in the middle of the garden, with tables of specimens set in front of him.[224] Initially the lectures proved most successful, but by the mid-1670s harder times set in, perhaps owing to difficulties in payment. Certainly in 1675 Morison attempted to better himself, applying, unsuccessfully, for the position of Sedleian professor of natural philosophy;[225] and in 1681 he submitted a pathetic application to Archbishop Sancroft stating that he was 'ruined'.[226] But the university's financial involvement was not restricted to the support of the professor and the physic garden. Far greater investment was made in the publication of Morison's *Plantarum historia universalis Oxoniensis*, for in 1693 it was reckoned that the university's expenditure on the book totalled £2,153.[227] Following Morison's death in 1683 Jacob Bobart the younger assumed his teaching duties, though without the title, delivering botany lectures intermittently even after his name ceased to appear in the vice-chancellor's accounts.

[223] OUA SEP/2/15; OUA WP 60 (3); C. Webster, 'The medical faculty and the physic garden' in *The Eighteenth Century*, 713.

[224] D'Arcy Power, 'The Oxford physic garden', *Annals of Medical History* ii (1919), 115; R. T. Gunther, *Oxford Gardens* (Oxford 1912), 4.

[225] In justifying to the university chancellor, the duke of Ormonde, why Morison was not elected, Ralph Bathurst admitted that Morison was, indeed, 'a knowing herbalist, and very well deserving encouragement in that way. But natural philosophy is of a farre larger extent; and its late improvements have been so great, that now no ordinary things are expected from the professor of it.' Warton, *Life of Bathurst*, 138.

[226] Bodl. MS Tanner letters 36, fo 216.

[227] H. Carter, *A History of the Oxford University Press* (Oxford 1975), 237–8.

By 1677 progress was finally made towards effecting the more ambitious design of an institutionalized scientific centre, when John Fell managed to persuade Elias Ashmole to bestow his important collection of rarities and manuscripts on the university, with the understanding that his munificence would be matched by the university. Writing to John Ellis in June or July of that year, Humphrey Prideaux divulged that they were 'now on a designe of erecting a lecture for philosophical history' to be read by Robert Plot and, as soon as a proper site was found, the work on building the house for Ashmole's gift 'with a laboratory annext' would also commence. In December John Evelyn warmly recommended Plot to Ashmole and the university authorities, confident in their success, swiftly proceeded to discharge their part of the bargain.[228] By the time the Ashmolean opened in 1683, the university had disbursed the staggering sum of £4,540 in total costs—£225 of which was devoted to the furnishing of a fine chemistry laboratory.[229] By making such an investment, the university sought more than simply to ensure its proprietorship of a coveted collection; it expected Ashmole to bestow on Oxford 'a professor of natural history and chemistry', thereby converting the new building into a leading research and teaching centre as well as an outstanding museum. In anticipation, it unilaterally conferred on Plot the rank of professor of chemistry. Ashmole, however, failed to fulfil these expectations. He viewed Plot's position primarily as keeper of the museum and was convinced that visitors' fees would be sufficient to support both Plot and his staff. So, to the chagrin of Plot, and, as we shall see shortly, to the eventual detriment of the professorship itself, Ashmole failed to endow the chair.

Such lavish expenditure on Oxford's part is as significant as it was unprecedented, given the university's perpetually penurious state and its habitual dependence on external support. Indeed when he resigned his position as Bodley's Librarian, in 1701, Thomas Hyde vindicated his tenure by claiming that he 'should have left the library more compleat and better furnished but that the building of the elaboratory did so exhaust the university mony, that no books were bought in severall years after it'. Hyde, who also served as Laudian professor of Arabic and regius professor of Hebrew, exaggerated somewhat, for in the last two decades of the seventeenth century the university spent nearly £2,500 in purchasing oriental books and manuscripts—at least in part at the behest of Hyde himself—and, in at least one case, from him.[230] None the less, the statement is indicative of the extent to which the university authorities had made a concerted effort to equip Oxford with the proper facilities for scientific research.

[228] *Letters of Humphrey Prideaux . . . to John Ellis*, ed. E. M. Thompson (Camden Soc. new ser. xv 1875), 60–1; *The Diary of Elias Ashmole, 1617–1692*, ed. C. H. Josten (6 vols Oxford 1966) iv. 1482, 1500–1.

[229] Gunther, *Early Science in Oxford* i. 45, 50–1; R. F. Ovenell, *The Ashmolean Museum 1683–1894* (Oxford 1986), 21, 25–7.

[230] W. D. Macray, *Annals of the Bodleian Library* (Oxford 1868, 2nd edn Oxford 1890), 170; I. G. Philip, *The Bodleian Library in the Seventeenth and Eighteenth Centuries* (Oxford 1983), 60–1, 125 nn. 51–2. See also Feingold, 'Oriental studies', pp. 478–9 below.

Initially the future seemed bright. Plot delivered his first official course of lectures in mid-September 1683, his auditors including John Massey of Merton College, Stephen Hunt of Trinity, William Smith and Nathaniel Boyse of University College, and Charles Harris, who was not a member of the university. He was assisted by Christopher White, the operator, 'who by the direction of the professor, shews all sorts of experiments'. The content of the course, which lasted a month, was described by Chamberlayne as

> concerning all natural bodies, relating to, and made use of, in chymical preparations, particularly, as to the countries, and places where they are produced, and found, their natures, their qualities and virtues, their effects, and by what marks and characteristicks they are distinguisht one from another, natural from artificial, true from sophisticated, with their several mixtures and preparations in tryals and experiments.[231]

Furthermore, in the general euphoria that accompanied the inauguration of this major scientific centre, Plot (one of the two secretaries of the Royal Society since 1682) and a few other scholars who for some time had held private gatherings to discuss scientific matters, decided in late October 1683 to formalize their meetings and thereby establish the Oxford Philosophical Society.

More than good intentions, however, were needed to secure the prosperous future of the Ashmolean as a centre of scientific teaching and research, and the home of a dynamic philosophical society at Oxford. The unfortunate failure of the Ashmolean to fulfil the expectations it initially inspired may be attributed, to some extent, to the actions (or, more appropriately, lack of actions) of both Ashmole and Plot. The former was interested in the museum almost exclusively as a monument to his lifelong preoccupations and a testament to his largesse. Thus, despite his earlier pledge to support a broader vision in which the edifice was only the first step in fostering scientific life at Oxford, Ashmole resisted repeated solicitations that would have furthered such a goal. More particularly, he failed both to endow the chemistry professorship and to supply the funds needed to institute a second lectureship. In contrast, the responsibility of Plot for the foundering of the plan lay in his negligence, induced by the failure of the Ashmolean to conform with his grandiose expectations. With his obvious talents, the grasping Plot was scarcely one to be satisfied by a keepership of a museum, or even a chemistry professorship, especially when it became increasingly clear that a generous remuneration would not accompany either position. Almost from the start the actions of Plot substantiate his contemporary reputation for acquisitiveness. A couple of months after the Ashmolean was officially opened, for example, Plot offered a chemistry course but, as the visiting Thomas Molyneux noted, the professor 'reads lectures to all that goes through a course of chymistry with him, and to those only, till there a public salary be settled upon him for it'. At about the same time Plot also concocted an elaborate scheme to enrich himself through the sale of a certain elixir, 'the alka-

---

[231] *Elias Ashmole*, ed. Josten iv. 1730; Edward Chamberlayne *Angliae notitia: or the present state of England* (London 1684), 327.

hest', the precise details of which have not survived.[232] One even wonders whether Plot was ever seriously interested in the positions he was to fill, for as early as 1681, at the time when the Ashmolean was still being constructed, the designated keeper and professor stood as a candidate for the principalship of Magdalen Hall—then the richest hall in Oxford. Unfortunately for Plot, notwithstanding the support of John Fell and the majority of the fellows of Magdalen College the position went to another.[233]

In the years immediately following the opening of the Ashmolean, Plot came to realize not only that Ashmole had no intention of endowing the chemistry professorship at all, but that the income derived from visitors' fees fell short of even the meagre remuneration Ashmole believed should suffice to cover the salaries of the museum staff. As a consequence Plot became even more resentful of the tedious daily routine of the keepership, especially the need to attend to visitors, not to mention the disparity, in his eyes, between his worth and the lowly dignity accorded the unsalaried professorship. Not surprisingly, the rift between Plot and Ashmole widened in the second half of the 1680s as Plot's interests swerved increasingly away from science and he became grossly inattentive to his duties at the Ashmolean. Certainly indicative of Plot's disenchantment with his position at Oxford as well as his shifting interests was his appointment in 1687 as registrar of the court of chivalry, followed the next year by his appointment as historiographer royal (perhaps as consolation for his failure to obtain the wardenship of All Souls). By 1689 the rift between Plot and Ashmole had become irreparable, with the latter complaining openly that Plot 'does no good in his station but totally neglects it, wandering abroad where he pleases'.[234]

In fact, by the time Plot resigned his professorship in 1689 he had already ceased to teach regularly, and in the following year he relinquished with equal readiness the keepership of the Ashmolean in favour of Edward Lhuyd. Unfortunately, the chemistry lectures failed to increase in either frequency or distinction following the election of Edward Hannes of Christ Church as Plot's successor. Only twenty scholars attended Hannes's inaugural lecture on 7 July 1690, and though he did offer several courses (charging the students as Plot had before him) the unendowed professorship provided little inducement to its incumbent. When Hannes left Oxford around 1695, the professorship was terminated.[235]

Significantly, these events coincided with the disintegration of the recently created Oxford Philosophical Society, which came into existence concurrently with

---

[232] See *DNB* s.v. Robert Plot; *Elias Ashmole*, ed. Josten iv. 1728; F. S. Taylor, 'Alchemical papers of Dr Robert Plot', *Ambix* iv (1949–51), 67–76.

[233] HMC *Ormonde MSS* vi. 60–2.

[234] *Elias Ashmole*, ed. Josten iv. 1865. Some teaching may actually have been carried out by Christopher White, the 'operator', who was trained by Stahl and served as Boyle's technician, being given the title 'university chemist'. Simcock, *The Ashmolean Museum and Oxford Science*, 8.

[235] Wood, *Life and Times* iii. 333. Hannes left Oxford after a long period of commuting, which made him 'so fatigued with frequent and long journeys, that, if they had not been made easier with good fees, must ere now have exhausted his spirits'. John Nichols, *Illustrations of the Literary History of the Eighteenth Century* (8 vols London 1818) iii. 260.

the opening of the Ashmolean and to whose early proceedings Plot had made an important—though short-lived—contribution. No doubt the other occupations of Plot and his drift away from scientific studies at Oxford in the second half of the 1680s affected the regularity of the society's meetings and the rigour of its activities—perhaps so much so that the two-year interruption brought about by the turmoil of the Glorious Revolution was all that was needed to provide a final death-blow.

While the fate of both the professorship and the Oxford Philosophical Society cannot be attributed solely to Plot's growing indifference, the fact remains that the Ashmolean did not live up to the great expectations it had raised among Oxford men of science. Certainly the impressive edifice never became the Oxford version of the Baconian 'Solomon's House' that had been envisaged. The dashing of such hopes was neither immediate nor total. But before attempting to determine the extent of the failure of the Ashmolean to galvanize Oxford science—and other factors contributed to the demise of the once-spirited Oxford scientific tradition—it should be noted that any such discussion should be couched in relative terms, as it inevitably prompts comparison with the glorious period 1640–85. During the 1690s and for a few decades afterwards, Oxford remained the home of several distinguished scientists, who both taught there and offered to those that were inclined superb opportunities for research. As we have seen, David Gregory arrived at Oxford in 1692 as Savilian professor of astronomy and was joined later by his former Edinburgh students John and James Keill. Together they contributed to the introduction of Newtonian science in Oxford and to the institutionalization there of the teaching of experimental science.[236] Though John Keill failed in 1704 to succeed Thomas Millington as Sedleian professor of natural philosophy—despite acting as deputy for the previous four years—Keill returned to Oxford as Savilian professor of astronomy in 1712, and upon his resignation nine years later was succeeded by the distinguished astronomer James Bradley. The Savilian professors of geometry were even more eminent. John Wallis continued to teach until his death in 1703 when he was succeeded by Edmond Halley, who held the position until 1742. Furthermore, the private courses in experimental philosophy that Keill delivered at Oxford until 1709 were taken over that year by John Theophilus Desaguliers and, following his move to London four years later, by John Whiteside, who added such teaching to his keepership of the Ashmolean.[237]

Yet the fact that such prominent men of science held positions at Oxford was no longer sufficient to ensure the flourishing of scientific research there. For one thing the incumbents proved, for the most part, to be absentees. After he was elected one of the secretaries of the Royal Society in 1713 (a position that he continued to hold until 1721) and even more conspicuously after he was elected

---

[236] For Gregory see Lawrence and Molland, 'David Gregory's inaugural lecture at Oxford'; Eagles, 'The mathematical works of David Gregory', 257–86 and *passim*.

[237] A. G. MacGregor and A. J. Turner, 'The Ashmolean Museum' in *The Eighteenth Century*, 648–51; G. Turner, 'The physical sciences' *ibid.* 671–4.

astronomer royal in 1719, Halley spent much of his time away from Oxford. In a similar manner, James Bradley passed the first decade after his election as Savilian professor of astronomy in 1722 at Wanstead, Essex, journeying to Oxford only to deliver his lectures. Then, after he was elected in 1742 to succeed Halley as astronomer royal, Bradley moved to Greenwich, again returning to Oxford only for the purpose of delivering his lectures.

What accelerated the process of decline, strangely enough, was the return to 'normalcy' after 1660, at which time various institutional constraints combined to contribute to the inhibition of scientific activity. Contemporaries noted from the start that the burgeoning of the Oxford scientific club of the 1650s was somewhat of an aberration. Already in 1657 Walter Charleton attributed the sudden fermentation of scientific activity in England, and at Oxford in particular, to the paradoxical repercussions of the tragedy of the English revolution: 'our late warrs and schisms', he wrote, 'having almost wholly discouraged men from the study of theologie, and brought the civil law into contempt, the major part of young schollers in our universities addict themselves to physick; and how much that conduceth to real and solid knowledge, and what singular advantages it hath above other studies, in making men true philosophers, I need not intimate to you.' Thomas Sprat put it more eloquently a decade later. In his narrative, the coming into existence of the Oxford scientific club was analogous to the phoenix rising from the ashes:

For such a candid and unpassionate company, as that was, and for such a gloomy season, what could have been a fitter subject to pitch upon then natural philosophy? To have been always tossing about some theological question would have been to have made their private diversion the excess of which they themselves disliked in the publick, [and] to have been eternally musing on civil business, and the distresses of their country, was too melancholy a reflexion. It was nature alone, which could pleasantly entertain them, in that estate. The contemplation of that draws our minds off from past, or present misfortunes, and makes them conquerers over things, in the greatest publick unhappiness.[238]

After the Restoration it was no longer necessary to seek refuge in scientific studies,[239] while quite a few of the formerly more active participants resumed careers they would otherwise have followed in church, state, or medicine. The consequent impact on Oxford was momentous. Less than a quarter of the hundred scientists and virtuosi who participated in the work of the various Oxford groups in the 1640s and 1650s were still in residence when Robert Boyle left for London in 1668.[240] By the 1680s nearly all of the twenty or so private chemical laboratories that were situated on or around the High Street had disappeared. This phenomenon was not the result of a repressive policy against the new science which, some

---

[238] Walter Charleton, *The Immortality of the Human Soul Demonstrated by the Light of Nature* (London 1657), 50; Sprat, *History of the Royal Society*, 55–6; B. J. Shapiro, 'Latitudinarianism and science in seventeenth-century England' in Webster (ed.), *The Intellectual Revolution of the Seventeenth Century*, 299–301.

[239] The pursuit of science by dissenters, who were barred from enrolling in the universities and participating in public life, was a mainly eighteenth-century phenomenon.

[240] Figures are based on the data provided in Frank, *Harvey and the Oxford Physiologists*, 64–89.

historians argue, set in after 1660, or of a sudden cessation of interest. Even such a hostile commentator as John Beale acknowledged in 1671 that Oxford enjoyed a considerable number of 'fit, capable, and hopeful persons, addicted to the design of the Royal Society, and willing to entertain correspondencies, and to assist in them'. They seemed to him 'by their qualifications and number very considerable—some in every college, and in every hall', with 'excellent professors, some lecturers, and very many students of useful arts amongst them'.[241] Rather, the number of new recruits could not keep pace with the drainage of talent to London. Moreover, precisely at this critical juncture, when, even under the best of circumstances, it would have been difficult for a new generation to rival the brilliance of its prede-cessors, inspired leadership was lacking and devotion to science was eclipsed by the promise of more lucrative careers. The departure of Wilkins, Ward, Boyle, Willis, Wren, and Hooke created a void which the Ashmolean ultimately, and despite initial hopes, failed to fill. Equally disappointing, the example of such fig-ures as Halley, Bradley, and their colleagues was insufficient to arouse emulation. Linked to this tapering off in the number and quality of new recruits was the vex-ing issue of the relationship between scientific and sacred learning.

For the committed scholar, it was generally believed that the proper end of knowledge was divinity. Analogously, the pursuit of secular studies, and of scien-tific studies in particular, was believed to be incompatible with the pursuit of theology as one's vocation. There survived from the Middle Ages a pattern of relin-quishing of 'profane' learning as part of the transition to one's 'higher calling'. In 1666 John Locke explained his refusal to be ordained (upon which his ability to keep his Christ Church Studentship was contingent), and his turning down of sev-eral good livings, by the 'difference of [his] studys'. For, as he wrote to John Parry, future bishop of Ossory, shortly after obtaining a royal dispensation from the need to take holy orders, 'should I put my self into order[s] and yet by the meanesse of my abilitys prove unworthy such expectation . . . I unavoidably loose all my former studys and put my self into a calling that will not leave me . . . and from whence there is noe desending without tumbleing'.[242] In presenting the dilemma in such a fashion, Locke offered an illuminating insight into the sort of deliberations faced by countless scholars who were confronted with the need to make career choices. In 1522, shortly after he had reluctantly accepted the bishopric of London, Cuthbert Tunstall (student at Balliol in the early 1490s) published his arithmetic treatise *De arte supputandi*. In the dedication to Thomas More, Tunstall publicly bids farewell to his former studies:

I not only resolved that I would devote what is left of my life to sacred literature putting all wordly writings entirely aside, but at first I thought it fitting that those papers . . . should be thrown away. For I did not consider them worthy to come into the hands of learned men, nor did I think it right that any part of my life should for the future be filched from sacred studies to polish them up.[243]

---

[241] *The Works of Boyle*, ed. Birch vi. 434.   [242] *The Correspondence of John Locke*, ed. De Beer i. 303–4.
[243] C. Sturge, *Cuthbert Tunstal* (London 1938), 73.

Such reasoning is repeated through the centuries, both by individual scholars and by family members, biographers, and other contemporaries. Thus, on his deathbed, Nathaniel Carpenter 'did much repent ... that "he had formerly so much courted the maid instead of the mistress", meaning that he had spent his chief time in philosophy and mathematics, and had neglected divinity'. Hannibal Potter, president of Trinity, was quite willing to tolerate his brother Francis's scientific studies while the latter was a fellow of the same college, but around 1643, six years after Francis had substituted a living for the fellowship—without any perceptible diminution in his scientific studies—Hannibal rebuked him on the basis of the essential incompatibility between his vocation and his scientific pursuits; for 'all mathematical inventions are far below the saving of one poor soul'.[244] John Janeway, discovered to be a mathematical prodigy at the age of 11, was retained at Eton College by Francis Rous until 1649, when he was sent for a few months to Oxford to be taught by Seth Ward. A few years later, however, Janeway, now a fellow of King's College, Cambridge, underwent a religious conversion and rejected his former studies not because 'he looked upon humane learning as useless, but when fixed upon any thing below Christ, and not improved for Christ, he then looked upon wisdom as a folly, and upon learning as madness, and as that which would make one more like unto [the] devil'. Isaac Barrow's resolve to resign his Lucasian professorship of mathematics at Cambridge in 1669 was grounded on like motives. As his first biographer recorded, 'he was afraid, as a clergyman, of spending too much time upon mathematics; for ... he had vowed in his ordination to serve God in the gospel of his son, and he could not make a bible out of his Euclid, or a pulpit out of his mathematical chair'.[245]

It should be remembered, moreover, that the lion's share of all college fellowships required their holders to enter holy orders within a few years of their taking the MA degree, and proceed in the faculty of theology. Indeed, this was the first step that Locke and many like him sought to avoid. Locke was fortunate in acquiring as a patron Anthony Ashley Cooper, the future earl of Shaftesbury, who was instrumental in getting him dispensed. His older contemporary at Christ Church, Thomas Willis, was not as fortunate, being forced to relinquish his Studentship for refusing to take orders. Earlier in the century Thomas Lydiat (MA 1599) was faced by a similar predicament. Seeking patronage that would deliver him from the need to take orders and assume a living, he pinned his hopes on Prince Henry, but the

---

[244] Wood, *Athenae* ii. 422; Bodl. MS Aubrey 13, fo 162; M. Hunter, *John Aubrey and the Realm of Learning* (London 1975), 57. A typical attitude from the puritan side is Edward Bagshawe's reflection on the proficiency of Robert Bolton (MA 1602) in mathematics and philosophy while a student: 'But all this while (or for the most part) though he was very learned, yet he was not good, hee was a very meane scholler in the schoole of Christ, he drew no religious breath from the soyle he came and his master like an ill seeds-man sowed the tares of popery in most of his schollers. This manner of education made him more apt to tread in any path than that which was holy'. Edward Bagshawe, 'The life and death of Robert Bolton' in Robert Bolton, *Workes* (London 1641), 10–11.

[245] Samuel Clarke, *The Lives of Sundry Eminent Persons in this Later Age* (London 1683), 61; M. Feingold, 'Isaac Barrow: divine, scholar, mathematician' in M. Feingold (ed.), *Before Newton: the life and times of Isaac Barrow* (Cambridge 1990), 80–1.

death of the young heir to the throne in 1612 put an end to his aspirations, and he accepted his family's living of Alkerton, where he still continued to pursue his scientific studies. Nevertheless, it is telling that when Henry Briggs sought to encourage Lydiat to publish some of his writings so that he might find the recognition he deserved, Briggs couched his entreaty in traditional terms: 'If your calling, being of so high a nature, would give you leave seriously to intend other business, I should intreat you to strive to get out your meditations and great pains ... But we that have no such eminent business may be busied about these trifles in respect, though in themselves they deserve to be of good account.'[246]

Evidence corroborating the claim that many men of science felt acutely the conflict between their expected conduct as churchmen and their continued desire to practise science can be found in the cases of those who ultimately managed to reverse the course on which they had unwillingly embarked. In 1613 Edmund Gunter failed in his first effort to obtain the Gresham professorship of astronomy, a position that was given instead to another member of Christ Church, Thomas Williams. Following this setback, Gunter proceeded BD two years later, at which time he was presented to the living of St George's, Southwark. Gunter, however, had not abandoned his hope of making mathematics his profession, and by 1618 he was regularly visiting Henry Briggs at Gresham College, perhaps even residing there, since William Oughtred mistook him for one of the Gresham professors. It was almost certainly owing to the influence of Briggs that, upon Williams's resignation the following year, Gunter was elected to replace him without competition. Gunter's successor as Gresham professor of astronomy, Henry Gellibrand, travelled a similar route. Having taken holy orders after receiving his MA in 1623, he became curate of Chiddingstone, Kent, until Gunter's sudden death created a vacancy that enabled his influential Oxford patrons, Briggs and Bainbridge, to intrude him into the Gresham professorship. The appointment of Gellibrand was subject to the condition that 'he [would] not hereafter take any other calling or course upon him, but apply himself wholly to this, or else wholly leave the place'.[247]

The need to be ordained to retain a fellowship proved detrimental to many budding scientific careers. Aware of just such a dilemma, Savile, in his statutes, dispensed with the need for his professors to take orders. But for the majority of would-be practitioners, unless they were able to enter into the one or two medical fellowships available in some colleges, the statutory requirements signalled the need

---

[246] Halliwell, *A Collection of Letters*, 46–7.

[247] I. Adamson, 'The foundation and early history of Gresham College London, 1596–1704' (Cambridge Ph. D. thesis 1975), 142–4. Nor was the situation different in the eighteenth century. James Bradley sought for two years after he graduated MA for a position commensurate with his marked scientific interests, but in vain. Consequently he was ordained in 1719 and appointed to several benefices. However, John Keill's death in 1721 provided him with 'an early opportunity to extricate himself from a position in which his duties were at variance with his inclinations', and through the intercession of powerful patrons on his behalf Bradley was elected; he immediately resigned his ecclesiastical preferments. See *DNB* s.v. James Bradley.

to seek their fortunes elsewhere. Other restrictions attached to fellowships also influenced the departure of their incumbents. Many of the fellowships could be held only for a limited duration, usually eighteen or twenty-one years. Thus, if it is borne in mind that election usually occurred when a scholar was in his early twenties, at the latest, such an individual could face the prospect of forced resignation around his fortieth birthday. Furthermore, the prohibition against marriage and the holding of an office or living that carried a remuneration above a specific (relatively low) income prompted scholars to seize opportunities elsewhere as soon as they became available. In retrospect, it is invariably to one, or a combination, of these factors that the departure from university of men of science may be attributed.

Not only was the university's ladder of preferment still erected upon the assumption that theology was the end of learning, but spokesmen drawn from across the religious spectrum continuously hammered away at this theme. In a 1658 sermon intended to defend human learning against the censure of radical puritans, the Presbyterian Edward Reynolds praised profane learning, including mathematics and philosophy, as contributing to the knowledge of God's 'works of creation'. However, he was careful to caution that 'we must get our learning seasoned with holiness, else it will not serve us to repress any temptation. Great learning will coexist with monstrous wickedness.'[248] In a similar vein Edward, Lord Herbert of Cherbury, esteemed the mathematical sciences to be 'the most undoubted and certain of all others', yet 'the end of this mathematical doctrine was but ignoble in respect of others, as tending only to the measuring of heights, depths and distances, and the making of some excellent engines, and the like; all which are of so mean consideration, that they can be no ways esteemed end objects adequated or proportioned to the dignity of our souls, whose speculations reach much further'.[249] The 'memorable' John Hales agreed. 'Much study in the mathematicks', he told John Beale some time in the 1630s, 'would tempt a man, that stood engaged to give [a] full account of the foundation of the Christian religion. For, saith he, the authentical portion of the Holy Text, and many mysteries will not come under the clearness of mathematical demonstrations.' As late as the start of the eighteenth century even Locke concurred: 'some men have so used their heads to mathematical figures that, giving a preference to the methods of that science, they introduce lines and diagrams into their studies of divinity or political enquiries, as if nothing could be known without them.'[250]

Granted the religious considerations and the restrictions associated with college fellowships in determining career trajectories or the length of stay at university, these perennial factors are insufficient in themselves to account for the corrosion of the scientific spirit at Oxford that set in at the turn of the seventeenth century.

[248] Edward Reynolds, *A Sermon Touching the Use of Humane Learning* (London 1658).

[249] Edward, Lord Herbert of Cherbury, *A Dialogue Between a Tutor and His Pupil* (London 1768), 2.

[250] John Worthington, *Diary and Correspondence*, ed. J. Crossley (2 vols in 3 Chetham Soc. xiii xxxvi cxiv 1847–86) i. 185–7; *Locke's* Of the Conduct of the Understanding, ed. Garforth, 78.

Changing intellectual fashions were also responsible for the declining interest in science. By their very nature, mathematics and the new science in particular required a degree of aptitude, dedication, and specialization not yet common in other disciplines. Such characteristics made it far more difficult, if not impossible, for most general scholars to pursue them concurrently with other studies. Nor was there any burning ambition to do so and by the 1690s the intellectual vogue had turned away from matters of 'erudition' (a retreat which would hurt classical studies and oriental learning as well), and the average student came increasingly to care for only a smattering of polite knowledge—a trend which was both observed and decried by the dwindling minority who still opted to pursue such studies.

Even in the 1640s the mathematician John Wyberd (at Oxford 1638–40) expressed a deep sense of isolation from his contemporaries who slighted mathematical learning in preference for frivolous speculations; and it is partly in such a context that we should interpret John Wallis's autobiographical statement on the desolate state of mathematics in pre-war Cambridge with which this chapter began. Certainly, as we have also seen, both Hobbes and Locke on various occasions castigated the disinclination of the educated public to devote itself to 'serious thinking'—science and philosophy. Looking back over the seventeenth century John Wallis recounted nostalgically how the exciting discoveries of a few individuals had inspired many students to take up the new science. 'But when it was no longer a new thing, this new ardor wore out', concluded Wallis. The first generation of enthusiasts was nearly spent, and now only a few replacements were forthcoming: 'and hence it is, as the nature of mankind is variable, that severer studies are neglected. Nay, it may happen ... that the sloth of the next age may succeed the industry of the present.' Several years later John Arbuthnot voiced similar sentiments. Responding in 1703 to Arthur Charlett's premature prediction of a new dawn for mathematical studies at Oxford, Arbuthnot put a damper on the enthusiasm of the master of University College: 'I am glad to hear from you that the study of the mathematics is promoted and encouraged' among Oxford youth, he wrote. Yet, despite their utility and reputation the mathematical sciences

have not been taught nor studied so universally as some of the rest, which I take to have proceeded from the following causes: the aversion of the greatest part of mankind to serious attention and close arguing; their not comprehending sufficiently the necessity or great usefulness of these in other parts of learning, [and] an opinion that this study requires a particular genius and turn of head, which few are happy as to be born with.[251]

Finally, this move away from scientific studies came at the time of change in the university structure more generally. The eighteenth century witnessed a Europe-wide decline, often sharp, both in the number of students and the quality of studies. To a certain degree Oxford and Cambridge fared better than most of their

---

[251] S. E. Morison, *Harvard College in the Seventeenth Century* (2 vols Cambridge Mass. 1936) i. 213; John Lowthorp, *The Philosophical Transactions and Collections . . . Abridged* (5th edn London 1749) ii. 2; Arbuthnot, 'An essay on the usefulness of mathematical learning', 409–10.

counterparts; for though matriculations, at their lowest during the 1750s and 1760s, were half of what they had been a century earlier, both universities still retained their position as stewards of higher learning and conduits to preferment in church and state. This was accomplished, in part, through the perpetuation of the established undergraduate liberal arts curriculum, which professed to shape character and train the mind through the study of the classics and the arts of discourse, and in this way lay the necessary foundations upon which any career choice could be constructed. Consequently, Oxford remained an institution that catered predominantly for undergraduate education, the assumption being that the best preparation for life was accomplished, through a survey of knowledge as a whole.

Historians still debate whether such a broad curriculum was suitable for the training of scientists. What is incontrovertible is that though the university was not inimical to scientific studies, and the course of study sought to provide a grounding in the mathematical sciences and natural philosophy, the specialized nature of the various scientific disciplines (just as much as of Greek and Latin criticism) prevented all but a few tutors from offering an adequate grounding in every discipline. As Gibbon pointed out in a memorable passage of his autobiography: 'instead of confining themselves to a single science ... [college tutors] teach, or promise to teach, either history or mathematics, or ancient literature, or moral philosophy; and as it is possible that they may be defective in all, it is highly probable that of some they will be ignorant.'[252]

The absence of specialized instruction was compounded by the fact that Oxford was devoid of any meaningful higher faculties, with the exception of theology. Significantly, it was precisely the flourishing medical and legal faculties in the Dutch republic, and later in Scotland, which attracted large numbers of students and around which a core of distinguished professors formed to offer specialized instruction in science and philosophy. Thus, in the early years of the eighteenth century Edinburgh abolished its system of regents and inaugurated instead the professorial system. Even more important, 'any person of any age and training could attend any of the classes in whatever number and order best suited his particular preferences and prospects' without the need to undergo either an admission examination or an examination at some later date, since relatively few individuals sought a degree. Edinburgh and the other Scottish universities also abolished all oaths, thereby contributing to their attractiveness to students of all denominations.[253]

The success story of Scottish science and philosophy in the eighteenth century was grounded upon a thriving professorial system, supported by students' fees and closely linked to the flourishing graduate faculties. These faculties, in turn, helped generate a variety of professors both in the medical area and in subjects related to medicine, such as chemistry, botany, and experimental natural philosophy. Equally important, the medical school and the various professorships served as

---

[252] *Autobiography of Edward Gibbon*, ed. J. B. Bury (London 1962), 41.

[253] J. B. Morrell, 'The University of Edinburgh in the late eighteenth century: its scientific eminence and academic structure', *Isis* lxii (1971), 158–71.

both magnet and catalyst, attracting individuals engaged in the sciences and spark-
ing, by their very proximity, a community of scientific enthusiasts. Oxford, by contrast, failed to follow a similar route, not only because its officials still believed in
the efficacy of liberal education, but because the statutes imposed by Archbishop
Laud on Oxford, and which intended 'to bind it in perpetuity', could not allow
such a fundamental structural change. Thus the Oxford curriculum, like the
Cambridge one, remained oriented towards undergraduate education, the beneficiaries of which were still obliged to reside in a college, be supervised (and taught)
by tutors, and follow a fixed course. This relative homogeneity proved far more
consequential for the future of both universities than the curricular emphasis that
distinguished them—namely the more mathematically oriented and rather narrowly
defined Newtonianism of the Cambridge undergraduate course compared with the
predominantly humanist orientation of Oxford. Hence, despite the presence of several professorships in both universities, their collegiate systems with their ingrained
tutorial instruction proved ruinous to their ability to focus research and to their
ultimate prosperity.[254]

The absence of a 'professional' group of scientific teachers and of an important
medical school, then, meant that virtually all scientific teaching would be introductory by nature. It is telling that though James Bradley's courses of experimental philosophy during the period 1746–60 drew a significant portion of the
undergraduate student body—1,221 of the estimated 3,000 students who matriculated during this period[255]—few opted to pursue science as a vocation. Nor was
there any effort on the part of students and dons to form scientific or philosophical clubs as their seventeenth-century predecessors had done. What occurred
instead was the dissipation of the scientific spirit, which, eventually, led to the
growing demands for drastic reform during the nineteenth century.

---

[254] For the situation at Cambridge see Gascoigne, *Cambridge in the Age of the Enlightenment*, 178–84,
270–84.

[255] Turner, 'The physical sciences', 673–4.

7

Oriental Studies

MORDECHAI FEINGOLD

IN his appraisal of the English political, religious, and cultural scene following the Restoration, Gilbert Burnet singled out the esteemed state of learning at Oxford, and 'chiefly the study of the oriental tongues'. More than a century later, this perception still lingered. When the young Edward Gibbon arrived at Oxford, his ambition was to master oriental learning. Although this was not to be, many years later Gibbon recalled that what had fired his youthful enthusiasm was the fact that 'since the days of Pocock and Hyde, oriental learning has always been the pride of Oxford'.[1] These two acute observers did not exaggerate. The seventeenth century was, indeed, the heyday of such studies at Oxford. During this period the university became a truly major centre for Hebrew and Arabic, drawing from all over Europe students and visitors eager to study with local scholars or use the rich resources of the Bodleian Library. In fact it was in the domain of oriental studies alone that Oxford competed on equal terms with the major philological centres of Europe.

The pursuit of Hebrew and Arabic studies at Oxford should be addressed concurrently, for as disciplines they were coupled in the minds of seventeenth-century scholars, both advocates and foes. The principal incentive for the study of both languages was their application to scripture and their contribution towards the bolstering of Christianity. Unlike Greek and Latin, which were also harnessed to such ends, Arabic, and especially Hebrew, were rarely commended for the intrinsic merits of their language, literature, and history.[2] Not surprisingly, the overlap among practitioners was close; virtually all English Arabists of the period were also at least tolerable Hebrew scholars (though there were more Hebraists who did not bother to pursue Arabic). This scholarly affinity between the two languages is epitomized by the fact that, for the period between 1648 and 1770, the regius professor of Hebrew and the Laudian professor of Arabic were usually one and the same.

Both languages were also linked in the battles that raged over the application of oriental learning to Christian theology. Owing to their 'exposure' to the blasphemous writings of Jewish or Muslim authors, scholars of Hebrew and Arabic were subject to suspicion concerning the sincerity of their religious convictions. As a

---

[1] Gilbert Burnet, *History of his own Time* (2 vols London 1724–34) i. 192; Edward Gibbon, *Memoirs of my Life*, ed. G. A. Bonnard (London 1966), 53.

[2] The partial exception of Arabic will be discussed below.

consequence, the rhetoric of censure employed by the opponents of these studies and the rhetoric of defence with which their practitioners responded were almost identical.

A similar affinity between the disciplines existed in the domain of scholarly publication. Since the audience for learned books in Hebrew and Arabic was limited and publishers were reluctant to risk capital, virtually all orientalists were compelled either to seek out prospective patrons willing to bear the considerable expense of publication, or else carry the cost themselves. As will become clear, this unfortunate dependence on patronage created a situation in which patrons of both Hebraists and Arabists could—and did—apply considerable pressure on their protégés to apply their skills to those theological concerns that engrossed the patrons themselves.

HEBREW STUDIES

Curiously, despite the position of prominence to which the study of Hebrew had been elevated by Christian scholars in the sixteenth century, this immersion in rabbinic literature did not bring about a corresponding tolerance in attitudes towards Jews. Just the opposite was the case. Unlike the study of Arabic which could at least in part be justified by virtue of its preservation of a large body of Greek literary and scientific writings—not to mention the major original contribution made by Islamic scholars to mathematics, medicine, and philosophy—the study of Hebrew could be validated only in so far as it remained ancillary to Christian theology. From the point of view of the Christian scholar, rabbinical texts could hold no value—literary or aesthetic—apart from their usefulness in interpreting the Old Testament and in providing a more accurate assessment of the culture that gave birth to Christianity. Indeed, to prove the distinctiveness of Christianity, Christian scholars reiterated their contempt for Jews. The Jews' obstinacy in rejecting Christ, they argued, was compounded by their post-biblical writings, which were riddled with blasphemies, follies, and assaults on Christianity.

Owing to the sensitive nature of their scholarship, Hebraists felt called upon to justify at some length their study of the Talmud and Jewish commentators. This they did by reference to the single-minded Jewish preoccupation with the Old Testament, which had resulted in a considerable body of portentous rabbinical commentaries. Since Christians had just embarked on the serious study of Hebrew and the Old Testament, they were in need of these very same interpretative commentaries. Nor did their relevance end here. A knowledge of the Talmud and other rabbinic glosses was also a prerequisite for the study of the New Testament for, in the words of the Cambridge puritan and Hebraist John Lightfoot, 'all the books of the New Testament were written by Jews, and among Jews, and unto them'. Hence the 'paradox' facing those scholars who immersed themselves in rabbinical authors:

There are no authors do more affright and vex the reader; and yet there are none who do more entice and delight him. In no writers, is greater or equal trifling; and yet in none is greater or so great benefit. The doctrine of the gospel hath no more bitter enemies than they; and yet the text of the gospel hath no more plain interpreters. To say all in a word—to the Jews their countrymen they recommend nothing but toys, and destruction, and poison; but Christians, by their skill and industry, may render them most usefully serviceable to their studies, and most eminently tending to the interpretation of the New Testament.[3]

Symptoms of such a deep-seated ambivalence had been explicit ever since the rediscovery of Hebraism by Christian scholars, most notably Pico della Mirandola and Johannes Reuchlin. The ensuing surge of Hebrew studies in Europe has been given increasing attention of late.[4] As recent scholars have demonstrated, the early debates over such studies—as exemplified by the Reuchlin affair or by the burning of the Talmud—were eventually eclipsed by post-reformation controversies, when the interpretation of scripture and its auxiliary apparatus became a fundamental issue of contention between protestants and Catholics. In particular, as a consequence of the reformers' setting far greater store on the study of the Old Testament (in the original languages) and of their advocacy of the binding nature of certain customs and injunctions delineated in it, the need to re-evaluate the contribution of the Jewish sources to Christianity assumed new urgency. Moreover, accusations of 'Judaization' were no longer confined to Catholic condemnations of their protestant foes, whom they accused of adopting Jewish blasphemies as their cardinal rules of faith. Now, fervent debates arose among protestants as they argued about the nature of Jewish sources, their relevance for Christianity, and the extent to which they should be used.[5]

Clearly underlying the protestant attitude to Hebrew was the conviction that impressionable young students should not be exposed to anything but the biblical text. Thus, at the start of the eighteenth century, Bishop William Lloyd of Worcester reacted indignantly when he was informed that the Jewish scholar he maintained at Oxford for the purpose of teaching Hebrew was using as his textbook the *Pirke avot*. Lloyd subsequently sent instructions that in the future Levi should confine himself to the text of the Old Testament.[6]

The debate over the 'inordinate' use of rabbinic sources waxed hot among orientalists themselves, and many a talented Hebrew scholar was attacked by fellow Hebraists for making excessive use of Jewish commentators. A good example is the celebrated separatist Henry Ainsworth—exceptional among zealous puritans for his open-mindedness to scholarship—who was castigated by the less tolerant William Pemble of Magdalen Hall for his 'lik[ing] too well this rabbinical blasphemy [the Talmud], as he doth in his annot[ations] dote on the rabbins too often'.[7] Nearly a century later, in his survey of ancient and modern learning, the Cambridge

---

[3] *The Whole Works of the Rev. John Lightfoot*, ed. J. R. Pitman (13 vols London 1822–5) xi, pp. iii–vi.

[4] See C. Wirszubski, *Pico della Mirandola's Encounter with Jewish Mysticism* (Cambridge Mass. 1989); J. Friedman, *The Most Ancient Testimony: sixteenth-century Christian Hebraica in the age of renaissance nostalgia* (Athens Oh. 1983); L. Jones, *The Discovery of Hebrew in Tudor England* (Manchester 1983).

[5] For a discussion of 'Judaization' see A. L. Katchen, *Christian Hebraists and Dutch Rabbis* (Cambridge Mass. 1984), 9–12; I. N. Rashkov, 'Hebrew Bible translation and the fear of Judaization', *Sixteenth Century Journal* xxi (1990), 217–33.

[6] Bodl. MS Ballard 9, fo 47.   [7] William Pemble, *The Workes* (Oxford 1659), 361.

non-juror Thomas Baker resorted to the same criticism when he fiercely inveighed against those who 'have gone too great a length' in utilizing Jewish sources. Some men, he wrote,

have studied the Talmud so long as to draw contagion from thence, and almost become rabbins themselves. A countryman of our own has exceeded in this, who, tho' he has only commented upon one book, has had such faith in the Talmud, as to believe, 'that many of its traditions were divinely deliver'd to Moses in Mount Sinai, which it was not lawful for Moses to divulge in writing; but being transmitted down orally to his posterity, they are related to us in the talmudic books'.[8]

If reliance on rabbinical sources was not peril enough to the Christian theologian, a whole new range of issues—generated by the rapid assimilation of the rigorous standards of textual criticism bequeathed by Valla and Erasmus to biblical exegesis—came to plague seventeenth-century scholars and divines, particularly protestants. Moreover, to these exacting methods of interpretation were added more recent branches of criticism: the contextualization of scripture within historical frameworks and the development of comparative religion. The combined effect of all these trends was to raise some profound challenges to the most fundamental tenets of protestantism, ranging from the inspiration of scripture and biblical infallibility to the authorship and integrity of the biblical canon.

During the sixteenth century English and European protestants, though willing to accept the existence of certain copying errors in the transmission of the biblical text, were, nevertheless, fully committed to the doctrine of scriptural inerrancy. However, a major furore erupted among protestants following the publication in 1624 of Louis Cappel's *Arcanum punctuationis revelatum* in which the French Calvinist author (resuscitating the controversial analysis of the sixteenth-century Jewish scholar Elijas Levita) argued forcefully against the antiquity of the vowel points and accents of the Hebrew text of the Old Testament.[9] In 1650 Cappel provoked a new storm with the publication of his *Critica sacra*, which not only elaborated upon the issue of the Masoretic pointing, but also initiated a new line of scholarship concerning the 'autographic' nature of the existing biblical texts, the relative merits of the Hebrew and Septuagint versions of the Old Testament, and the large number of variant readings he detected in divers versions of the scriptures, which added weight to the claim that the Hebrew text was faulty. To aggravate the controversy, Cappel's book was printed through the combined efforts of a Jesuit, an Oratorian,

---

[8] Thomas Baker, *Reflections upon Learning* (London 1699, 7th edn London 1738), 253–4. Baker was paraphrasing from Robert Sherringham's Latin translation of the Mishnaic codex *Joma*, against which Baker further exclaimed: 'And least this should not be enough, he is of opinion "There are many allegorical and pious sayings contain'd there, that [were] uttered by the ancient rabbins, when heated with the divinity, and moved by God." Could any Jew have said more? Or could it be imagined, a Christian would have said so much? If these be the fruits of rabbinical enquiries, surely they are better let alone'.

[9] A long and acrimonious debate between Cappel and the Johann Buxtorfs, father and son, ensued. For details, see Georg Schnedermann, *Die Controverse des Ludovicus Cappellus mit den Buxtorfen* (Leipzig 1879). See also R. A. Muller, 'The debate over the vowel points and the crisis in orthodox hermeneutics', *Medieval and Renaissance Studies* x (1980), 53–72.

and a Minim—Denis Petau, Jean Morin, and Marin Mersenne respectively—after all protestant presses refused to publish it. For the protestants this served as a further confirmation, if one was needed, that the fruit of such biblical scholarship played into the hands of their Catholic foes, who were only too delighted to use it to cast doubt on biblical inspiration and reinforce reliance on church and tradition for the interpretation of scripture.[10]

The significance of Cappel's 'contribution' to higher criticism was rapidly made apparent to protestants. Even before taking part in the Catholic venture to publish Cappel's work, Jean Morin had used Cappel's work to discredit the antiquity and superiority of the Hebrew text of the Old Testament, especially when compared with the newly discovered Samaritan Pentateuch, or even the Septuagint. Such a forceful and highly alarming critique was only the beginning. Within months of the publication of the *Critica sacra*, Thomas Hobbes's *Leviathan*, which included a devastating assault on the Mosaic authorship and integrity of the Pentateuch, was published in London. Matters worsened during the following three decades with the publication of Isaac La Peyrère's *Prae-Adamitae* in 1655, Benedict Spinoza's *Tractatus theologico-politicus* of 1670, Richard Simon's 'critical histories' of the Old and New Testaments in 1678 and 1682 respectively, and Jean Le Clerc's *Sentiments* in 1685. The rows that occurred over such publications had ramifications for Hebraic studies generally, which were increasingly viewed as a liability rather than an asset. Small wonder, then, that even Brian Walton's edition of the Polyglot Bible was attacked as 'affording a foundation for Mohammedanism, as a chief and principal prop of popery, [and] as the root of much hidden atheism in the world'.[11]

Naturally, many protestants resisted such new scholarship. Thus, for example, even though most experts came to accept Cappel's view concerning punctuation by the end of the seventeenth century, the puritans of Old and New England continued to defend the antiquity of the Hebrew vowel points. At Oxford, John Owen launched a massive attack on the revisionists and the entire Polyglot.[12] Even Lightfoot remained opposed—though silently—to this particular line of scholarship. Across the ocean, occasional commencement exercises at Harvard College included a defence of the divinely inspired origins of Hebrew punctuation, such as Cotton Mather's 1681 response in the affirmative to the thesis: 'Are Hebrew points

---

[10] Significantly, Cappel was virtually the only protestant to maintain the superiority of the Samaritan Pentateuch, and his *Diatriba de veris et antiquis Ebraeorum literis* (Amsterdam 1645) bolstered Morin's far stronger polemical argument expressed in the latter's *Exercitationes ecclesiasticae in utrumque Samaritanorum Pentateuchum* (Paris 1631), which so outraged protestant scholars. Thomas Barlow, who recommended Morin's book to young scholars, felt the need to caution the reader that Morin 'was a Jesuite, and sworne champion of their idolized vulgar Latine, against the original text, and therfore it will bee convenient to reade with him Henricus Hottingerus his *Exercitationes anti-morinianae*, who confutes him, where hee endeavors to confute the truth'. *'A Library for Younger Schollers'*, ed. A. Dejordy and H. F. Fletcher (Urbana Ill. 1961), 31.

[11] H. T. Norris, 'Professor Edmund Castell (1606–85), orientalist and divine, and England's oldest Arabic inscription', *Journal of Semitic Studies* xxix (1984), 161.

[12] Owen's relevant writings on the antiquity of the Hebrew vowel points, all published in 1659, can be found in *The Works of John Owen*, ed. W. H. Goold (24 vols London 1850–5) xvi. 281–476.

of divine origin?' Even more revealing, as late as 1767 a learned Hebraist, John Gill, could still publish a lengthy and forceful defence of the same argument.[13]

Nevertheless, despite this continuing opposition, an exceptional group of Hebraists was established at Oxford during the seventeenth century. Though hardly remembered today, a close scrutiny of its membership allows us to reconstruct a scholarly community that made Oxford renowned as a major centre for oriental studies.

A succession of well-qualified regius professors of Hebrew contributed greatly to the general dissemination of Hebraic studies at Oxford. Their passion for the language was infectious. Indeed, in view of the widespread suspicion, only unfailing support could have led to the establishment of a following. The requisite dedication (no doubt exaggerated somewhat) was voiced by Robert Wakefield, future Hebrew and Arabic lecturer at Oxford, in 1524: 'I would be prepared, day and night, to teach everything, and to communicate to those eager to learn whatever secrets I have extracted from the most recondite sources of the Hebrews and from their traditions.'[14] Unfortunately, none of the regius professors of Hebrew prior to Edward Pococke's appointment in 1648 published in their discipline and, consequently, our knowledge of their attainments is sometimes scanty in the extreme, even in terms of biographical details.

William Thorne (regius professor 1598–1604) was reputed to be a skilled linguist, and his Hebrew learning was highly respected not only by English scholars but by the great John Drusius, who dedicated to Thorne two books: *De litteris Mosche vechaleb libri duo* and the *Opuscula quae ad grammaticam spectant*, published in 1608 and 1609 respectively. Johannes Drusius the younger also paid high tribute to Thorne, addressing to him two Hebrew letters during his brief visit to England in 1605.[15] Even more obscure was John Harding, who served two terms as regius professor (1591–8 and 1604–10). Apart from his inclusion among the Oxford group of bible translators, little else about him is known and he was even conspicuously absent from among contributors of verses.[16]

Richard Kilbye, Harding's successor (1610–20) and also one of the bible trans-

[13] S. E. Morison, *Harvard College in the Seventeenth Century* (2 vols Cambridge Mass. 1936) ii. 611, 616; John Gill, *A Dissertation concerning the Antiquity of the Hebrew-Language Letter, Vowell-Points, and Accents* (London 1767). See also Simon Ockley's *Introductio ad linguas orientales* (Cambridge 1706) for another defence of the Buxtorfs' position, though the eighteenth-century biographer of the Cambridge orientalist hastened to add 'but the reader may be pleased to know, that he afterwards changed his opinion and went over to Capellus, although he had not any opportunity of publicly declaring it'. R. H. 'An account of Simon Ockley', *The European Magazine* xxxi (1797), 11.

[14] Robert Wakefield, *On the Three Languages*, trans. G. Lloyd Jones (Binghamton NY 1989), 68. Following a career on the continent and at Cambridge, Wakefield moved to Oxford in 1530 where he lectured in oriental languages and was made canon of Henry VIII's college two years later.

[15] Wood, *Athenae* ii. 480; H. J. Todd, *Memoirs of the Life and Writings of . . . Brian Walton* (2 vols London 1821) i. 124; L. Fuks, 'Het Hebreeuwse brievenboek van Johannes Drusius jr. Hebreeuws en Hebraisten in Nederland rondom 1600', *Studia Rosenthaliana* iii (1969), 21–4, 31; *Academiae Oxoniensis pietas erga . . . Iacobum . . . Regem* (Oxford 1603), 17.

[16] For Harding see Macray, *Reg. Magdalen* iii. 72–80.

lators, was apparently a far better Hebraist, arguably the most learned Hebrew scholar Oxford had produced to that date. He was one of the very few English scholars singled out by Isaac Casaubon as a 'man of learning'; certainly, the five surviving letters Kilbye addressed to Casaubon confirm his character as 'a man of some reading beyond the common'. Save for a single sermon and a few obligatory verses, however, Kilbye also published nothing. According to Anthony Wood, the regius professor intended to publish a continuation of Jean Mercier's commentary on Genesis, but this project never bore fruit. Mercier, whom Erpenius extolled as 'of all the Christians . . . the most distinguished in Hebrew philology', utilized rabbinic works extensively in his commentary. No doubt Kilbye's project, had it materialized, would have involved him in similar sources. Fortunately, a chance survival of another work by Kilbye, a manuscript commentary on Exodus—which judging by its look may have also been intended for publication—confirms Kilbye's firm grasp of Jewish learning. This commentary is based on nearly 100 Hebrew sources, including various biblical commentators, both the Jerusalem and Babylonian Talmud, the codes of Maimonides and Joseph Karo, a few Midrashim, and even the *Zohar*. Kilbye's ownership of some of the sources is confirmed by the list of Hebrew books he bequeathed to Lincoln College. Such books, representing the more expensive of his Hebrew possessions, included the magnificent eight-volume edition of Arias Montano's Polyglot Bible, valued at £20, the 1524–5 edition of Bomberg's great rabbinic bible in four volumes, valued at £8, and the 1514–16 Venice edition of Maimonides' *Mishneh Torah*, valued at £5. The Kilbye bequest also included various commentaries on the Pentateuch—those by Levi ben Gerson, Nachmanides, and Abraham Saba—David Kimhi's lexicon, Samuel Yaphe's explication of Aggadic passages in the Jerusalem Talmud, the *Yepheh Mareh*, Nathan ben Yechiel's Hebrew dictionary, the *Midrash Rabba*, and Genebrard's Hebrew and Latin edition of the *Seder Olam Rabba*.[17]

Kilbye's successor, Edward Meetkerke (1620–6), is another figure about whom little is known. The son of a former Dutch ambassador to England, Meetkerke—like the proficient Hebraist Nicholas Fuller some years earlier—was taught Hebrew while at Westminster School by Adrian Saravia, whose death Meetkerke lamented in 1613. Meetkerke also contributed some mediocre Hebrew verses to various Oxford poetical collections, but published nothing else in the language. Nevertheless, he had a reputation as a diligent tutor and teacher. The visiting Dutch student of oriental languages, Sixtinus Amama, for example, noted with respect the private instruction in Hebrew Meetkerke provided to sundry doctors and masters even before he was elected regius professor.[18]

---

[17] Wood, *Athenae* ii. 287; M. Pattison, *Isaac Casaubon* (London 1875, 2nd edn Oxford 1892), 366–7; Bodl. MSS Lincoln College, 51, fo 121; A. Schper, 'Christian Hebraists in sixteenth-century England' (London Ph. D. thesis 1944), 159–67; Madan, *Oxford Books* ii. 64, 70, 73, 84; Thomas Erpenius, 'On the value of the Arabic language', trans. R. Jones, *Manuscripts of the Middle East* i (1986), 22. For the list of books see OUA box of transcripts of inventories mentioning books (arranged alphabetically); V. H. Green, *The Commonwealth of Lincoln College 1427–1977* (Oxford 1979), 677–8.

[18] Madan, *Oxford Books* ii. 75, 91, 94, 101–2; J. E. Platt, 'Sixtinus Amama (1539–1629): Franeker

According to Anthony Wood, however, it was during the tenure of John Morris (1626–48) that the 'Hebrew and Chaldaic tongues which few in Oxford understood some years before . . . became to be so cheerfully studied that it received a wonderful proficiency, and that too in a shorter time than a man could easily imagine; so great a spur the hope of honour and preferments give to art and languages'.[19] Wood was undoubtedly referring to Laud's furthering of Hebraic studies by annexing in 1630 a prebend at Christ Church to the office of the regius professor of Hebrew. Again, we know very little of Morris himself, save for his reputation and three modest bequests: the first for the purchase of Hebrew books and the second (of £5 p.a.) for a student to deliver an annual sermon in praise of Thomas Bodley and of Hebrew studies. The third bequest established seven exhibitions, 'worth up to £3 a year in order to encourage students of Christ Church to study the Hebrew language and to attend the lectures of the professor of Hebrew'.[20]

Morris's death in 1648 coincided with the parliamentary purge of Oxford. However, the proficiency of the royalist and Anglican Edward Pococke (plate 11), who had been Laudian professor of Arabic for over a decade, was so universally admired that the regius professorship in Hebrew was conferred on him. Even though the reputation of Pococke today rests chiefly on his publications in Arabic, he was arguably the greatest scholar to occupy the Hebrew chair in the early modern period. His commitment to laying solid philological foundations for the benefit of theology—as advocated by Drusius and Erpenius—was complete. His edition of Maimonides' *Porta Mosis*—important for Hebrew as well as Arabic studies—as well as his commentaries on the four minor prophets, contain an immense store of learning and attest to Pococke's extraordinary grasp of rabbinic sources. As a teacher, too, Pococke was devoted and conscientious, as will be shown in a later discussion of his teaching methods.

Given the inseparable nature of Hebrew language and theology, it was only natural that Hebrew instruction of students was buttressed by the lectures of the regius and Lady Margaret professors of divinity, as well as the sermons and instruction of preachers and catechists. Such additional instruction in Hebrew could take the form of either exegesis on a selected passage of scripture or lectures devoted to specific topics. Thus it was during his tenure as Sir Francis Walsingham's divinity reader in the late 1580s and early 1590s, that John Rainolds delivered his extremely learned lectures on the Apocrypha, which included a wealth of material pertinent

professor and citizen of the republic of letters' in G. Th. Jensme, F. R. H. Smit, and F. Westra (eds), *Universiteit te Franeker, 1585–1811* (Leeuwarden 1985), 242, 247.

[19] Wood, *History of the University* ii. 850. During the 1630s George Hakewill proudly boasted that 'Hebrew and Greeke are now as common as true Latine then was . . . this last centenary having afforded more skilfull men that way then the other fifteene since Christ'. G. Hakewill, *An Apologie or Declaration of the Power and Providence of God in the Government of the World* (Oxford 1627, 3rd edn Oxford 1635), 268.

[20] Laud, *Works* v. 19; for Morris's effusive letter of thanks see ibid. 23–4; H. Thompson, *Christ Church* (London 1900), 246; E. G. W. Bill, *Education at Christ Church Oxford 1660–1800* (Oxford 1988), 303; W. Macray, *Annals of the Bodleian Library Oxford* (London 1868, 2nd edn Oxford 1890), 150; E. Craster, *The History of All Souls College Library* (London 1964), 63–4.

to the study of Hebrew. During the first half of the seventeenth century, John Prideaux, the regius professor of divinity, carried on this mission. His long tenure as regius professor (1615–42) was outstanding in terms of the frequency with which pertinent Hebraic material was explicated by him for the benefit of both students and dons. In 1627, for example, Prideaux provided, in the form of an Act lecture, the first public reaction at Oxford to the fierce debate between Louis Cappel and the two Buxtorfs of Basle. Prideaux not only offered his audience a solid introduction to the issue, but also judiciously and discreetly expressed his support for Cappel's position published three years earlier. The topic in general, and Prideaux's careful explication of it in particular, reverberated at Oxford. Some months after Prideaux delivered his lecture, the diarist Thomas Crosfield opined that Cappel (whom Crosfield did not mention by name) had proved 'invincibly or unanswerably' that the vowel points 'were not from the beginning: yet noe advantage given to the adversary or derogation from the scriptures authority'.[21] In 1631 Crosfield noted that Prideaux, this time in weekly divinity lectures, was indefatigably 'vindicating the Hebrewe text from corruption', through an analysis of selected passages in the prophet Micah.[22]

The early seventeenth century also marked the time when many Oxford colleges proceeded to emulate the model set by Laurence Humfrey, who in about 1566 established a public Hebrew lectureship at Magdalen College. At New College, Warden Arthur Lake endowed such a lectureship in 1616, allocating to its incumbent a stipend of £5 a year. Two decades later, in 1637, Sir John Maynard settled £12 annually on a lectureship in the oriental languages established by him at Exeter College. At approximately the same time, John Branston provided a similar post at Brasenose College.[23] Even some colleges that were not fortunate enough to receive an external endowment still sustained a lectureship in Hebrew. One such position was created at Merton College in the 1630s specifically to accommodate the genius of Henry Jacob. By the late 1650s, another had been created at Queen's College and Thomas Hyde appointed the incumbent; it was to this position that the orientalist Thomas Smith succeeded in the following decade. Surprisingly, Christ Church had to wait until after the Restoration before a lectureship in oriental languages was established by a gift from Richard Busby.[24]

Though most such foundations were made possible through external financial

---

[21] John Prideaux, 'De punctorum Hebraicorum origine' in *Viginti-duae lectiones* (Oxford 1648), 180–98. See also Prideaux's *Fasciculus controversiarum theologicarum ad juniorum* (Oxford 1649), 19–22; QCL MS 390, fo 164.

[22] QCL MS 390, fo 59ᵛ.

[23] Arthur Lake, *Sermons* (London 1629), 'A short view of the life and vertues of the author'; David Lloyd, *Memorials* (London 1668), 91; H. Rashdall and R. Rait, *New College* (London 1901), 240; *Registrum Collegii Exoniensis*, ed. C. W. Boase (OHS xxvii 1894), p. cvii n. 2.

[24] Negotiations over the endowment were set in motion as early as 1667 but it seems that Prideaux was the first lecturer—with Taswell as the first examiner—and that both these men were only appointed in 1675. The lecturer was expected to deliver twenty-five lectures a year. Bill, *Education at Christ Church*, 205–6; William Taswell, 'Autobiography and anecdotes', ed. G. P. Elliot, *Camden Miscellany* ii (London 1852), 18.

support, the mushrooming of Hebrew lectureships in the first half of the seventeenth century attests to the widespread enthusiasm for Hebrew studies at Oxford. Through the efforts of heads of house and a few professors, the required foundation for a flourishing community of Hebrew scholars was laid. This task was accompanied by an even more crucial aspect of Hebraic scholarship, the rise of a generation of students inculcated with the love for such an arduous subject. And here the list of supporters is long.

The 'wise and acute' William Langton, president of Magdalen College (1610–26), was a competent linguist and avid promoter of the study of Hebrew at Oxford, and the person entrusted with the younger Johannes Drusius, who arrived in England in 1605. A few years later, the elder Drusius recommended to Langton another disciple, Sixtinus Amama, whom he sent to study in England. The close bond that developed between Langton and Amama may be gathered from the latter's dedication to Langton, on 12 March 1617, of his manuscript translation of Ibn Ezra's commentary on Ecclesiastes. Three years later both Langton and Arthur Lake were the recipients of another dedication by Amama, this time of his edition of Johannes Drusius the elder's posthumous *De sectis Judaicis commentarii* (Arnhem 1619.) Amama explicitly expressed his gratitude to the two heads of house: 'From my arrival in Oxford you surrounded me with kindness and goodwill for which I shall be gratefull until my dying day. When I was with you you bestowed all manner of benefits upon me, on my departure you loaded me with gifts and, absent from you, you have sent the kindest letters.'[25]

Lake, too, was an important promoter of Hebrew. Not only did he establish the Hebrew lectureship at New College, but he also donated a choice collection of Hebrew books for the use of both lecturer and students. During the second decade of the seventeenth century, moreover, his house at Oxford became an important centre for Hebraists, and it was here that Amama met the veteran Hebraist Nicholas Fuller. Lake, as we shall see below, was also instrumental in securing a teaching position at Oxford for Jacob Barnett, whom Lake hoped to convert from Judaism.[26] Similarly, John Prideaux was not only a diligent and learned regius professor of divinity, but also rector of Exeter College for three decades (1612–42). Owing to his efforts Sir John Maynard endowed a Hebrew lectureship at the college, and it was in order to be taught by Prideaux that a large number of foreign scholars, including Louis Cappel (*c.*1610–13), came to Oxford. Thus, when Stephen Nettles dedicated to Prideaux his learned criticism of John Selden's *History of Tithes*, he justified the dedication to a person unknown to him with the claim that he had been encouraged to do so in view of 'the love [Prideaux bore] to the Hebrew studies'.[27] In the second half of the century, a comparable promotional function was

---

[25] L. Fuks, 'Het Hebreeuwse brievenboek van Johannes Drusius', 31; Platt, 'Sixtinus Amama', 239–40; Bodl. MS Rawlinson d. 1343. Langton was most probably the unnamed fellow referred to by the dissenter Samuel Clarke as one of Robert Harris's fellow students in Hebrew *c.*1600. See p. 468 below.

[26] Platt, 'Sixtinus Amama', 243; NCL benefactors book, pp. 53–64; see also p. 460 below.

[27] Stephen Nettles, *An Answer to the Jewish Part of Mr Selden's History of Tithes* (Oxford 1625), dedication.

PL. 10. John Bainbridge: Savilian professor of astronomy (1621–43)

PL. 9. Sir Henry Savile: wall monument in Merton College antechapel

PL 11. Edward Pococke: Laudian professor of Arabic (1636–91) and regius professor of Hebrew (1648–91)

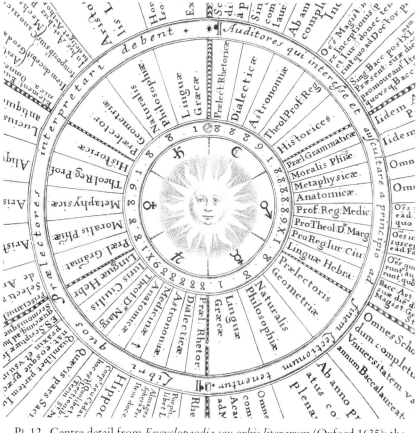

PL 12. Centre detail from *Encyclopaedia seu orbis literarum* (Oxford 1635): the Oxford University syllabus in diagrammatic form

PL 13. Convocation House: south end interior, showing vice-chancellor's canopied seat

PL 14. Carved grotesques ('antiques'): original outside wall of Arts End, preserved within schools quadrangle south staircase-tower

PL 15. Sheldonian Theatre: painted ceiling

PL 16. Merton College library: interior, south range, looking east

PL 17. Christ Church: hall staircase vault

PL 18. Exeter College chapel: exterior (pre-1856)

Pl. 20. Wadham College chapel: interior, east window

Pl. 19. Lincoln College chapel: interior, looking east

PL. 22. William Oughtred's 'Circles of Proportion' and 'Horizontall Instrument':
given to St John's College, Oxford, by George Barkham in 1635

PL. 21. University College chapel: design for east
window (*circa* 1687)

Pl. 23. Title-page of Francis Bacon's *Advancement and Proficience of Learning* (Oxford 1640)

Pl. 24. Silver crown coin of Charles I: struck at Oxford in 1644

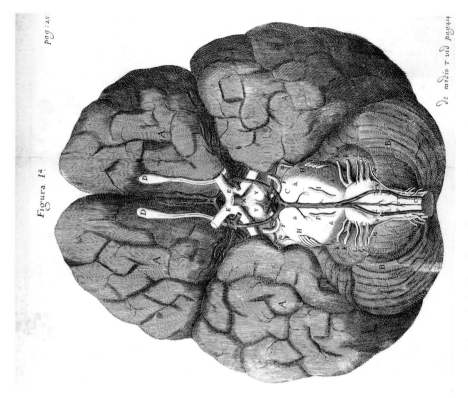

Pl. 26. The 'Circle of Willis': Thomas Willis, *Cerebri anatome* (London 1664)

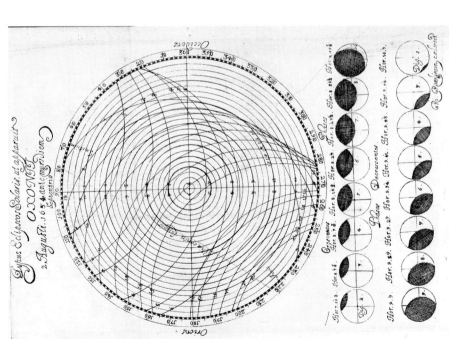

Pl. 25. Observation of a solar eclipse at Oxford, in 1654: John Wallis, *Operum mathematicorum pars altera* (Oxford 1656)

TWO DISCOURSES.

THE FIRST,

Concerning the SPIRIT of

MARTIN LUTHER,

and the ORIGINAL of the

REFORMATION.

THE SECOND,

CONCERNING THE

CELIBACY

OF THE

CLERGY.

by Abr. Woodhead.

Printed at OXFORD. An. 1687.

PL. 28. Title-page of Abraham Woodhead's *Two Discourses* (Oxford 1687): showing the King Alfred's head imprint

Donum Episcop Briff
Now Hereford Gloucest
Confecratorū kan o Ssam̄
Ďni 1660 Concionatori
Dr Alleftree.

PL. 27. Silver tankard, presented to Richard Allestree in 1660: on the occasion of the consecration of bishops Ironside, Monck, Nicholson and Reynolds

PL 29. Queen's College library: interior, pediment over the doorway

PL 30. Tokens issued by Oxford tennis court keepers

PL 31. Bushel measure, used by the clerk of the market:
Oxford University, 1670

PL 32. John Locke and the *Essay concerning Human Understanding*

filled by Dean John Fell of Christ Church and Arthur Charlett of University College.

Thus the general enthusiasm for the study of Hebrew initiated by the reformation was further stimulated by the efforts of many influential heads of house who helped foster at Oxford the requisite atmosphere for it to thrive. Notwithstanding the merits of the regius professors and the zeal of various dons, however, Oxonians increasingly realized that without personal contact with a native speaker of Hebrew their efforts to master the language would remain incomplete. And since only a handful of Jews were to be found in England after their expulsion in 1290, any opportunity to employ one was eagerly seized. John Rainolds, for example, was instrumental in securing the converted Jew, Philip Ferdinand, to teach at various Oxford colleges during the mid-1590s. Given the favourable atmosphere at Oxford for such studies, Ferdinand perhaps fared better there than he did a few years later at Cambridge where, as one of his students later recalled, most of his auditors 'soon got weary and left him'. Ferdinand himself also grew weary and left England for Leiden, where he was received with enthusiasm by the great Scaliger.[28]

It may have been Rainolds, or perhaps his successor as president of Corpus Christi College, John Spencer, who 'of his owne charge procured a Jewe to reade an Hebrew lecture' at the college. This lecturer appears to have been very popular, his teaching spreading beyond the walls of Corpus, for undoubtedly it was he whom Sir Thomas Bodley was hoping to engage in the cataloguing of the Hebrew books of his newly founded library. In late December 1607, Bodley instructed Thomas James to 'gette the helpe of the Jewe, for the Hebrewe catalogue. For it can not be done without him, and either by your self, or by your friends in authoritie, yow shall be able to procure, that for so short a time, his auditours wheresoever, will be willing to spare him, for so good a publicke purpose'. In all likelihood the person in question was, as Roth speculated, Jacob Wolfgang, a converted German Jew who registered as reader at the Bodleian Library on 22 May 1608, matriculating the following week.[29]

That Wolfgang attracted quite a following is made clear by the reminiscence of one auditor, although a hostile one:

And I remember one Wolfgangus a Jew, a teacher of the Hebrew tongue in my time, in Oxford; who (as both my selfe and others, who were his schollers with mee, easily observed), had but little learning, either in divinity or humanity, and so little acquaintance with the Latin tongue, that hee could not (without much difficulty) dictate two lines in that language with congruity.[30]

Between 1609 and 1613 another Jew, Jacob Barnett, taught Hebrew at both Oxford and London. In the capital he acted as private tutor to Isaac Casaubon,

[28] Wood, *Athenae* i. 667–8; S. Stein, 'Phillipus Ferdinandus Polonus' in I. Epstein, E. Levine, and C. Roth (eds), *Essays in Honour of . . . J. H. Hertz* (London 1942), 397–412; Samuel Clarke, *The Lives of Thirty-two English Divines* (London 1677), 397.

[29] Bodl. MS Rawlinson d. 47, fo 54; *Letters of Sir Thomas Bodley to Thomas James*, ed. G. W. W. Wheeler (Oxford 1926), 172–4, 187; C. Roth, 'Jews in Oxford after 1290', *Oxoniensia* xv (1950), 64–5.

[30] John Ley, *Sunday a Sabbath* (London 1641), 56–7.

while at Oxford he 'read Hebrew to divers young students'. Both Richard Kilbye, the regius professor of Hebrew, and Arthur Lake of New College were involved in supporting Barnett. Their support, which was intended to promote the study of Hebrew among Oxonians, was further inspired by the prospect of the imminent conversion of the Jewish exile, a prospect that eventually miscarried.[31] During the 1650s a few Jews were again to be found in and out of Oxford—Paul Isaiah, Alesandro Amiedo, and Jacob ben Asher—offering both individual and collegiate instruction.[32] Finally, in the late 1680s and through the last decade of the century, we find Isaac Abendana, who taught at Magdalen and Trinity Colleges as well as providing private tutorials. In the early years of the new century Abendana was succeeded by Philip Levi, who was supported financially by Bishop William Lloyd.[33]

Such converts and practising Jews usually remained at Oxford for only brief periods, and their teaching was supplemented by a whole regiment of Christian visitors to Oxford. Mention has already been made of Sixtinus Amama, who taught Hebrew at Exeter College in the mid-1610s, following in the Oxford footsteps of his own teacher, Drusius, during the 1570s. A decade before Amama's arrival, however, Drusius had sent to England his own precocious son, Johannes Drusius the younger, already a promising orientalist. Thomas Bodley, a close friend of the elder Drusius, wrote to Thomas James: 'The bearer hereof is the sonne of Drusius the Hebrician of Friseland. He purposeth a while to sojorne in Oxon, and withall upon liking, to teach either privatly or publickly (as he shall be sette a worke) the Hebrewe tongue, wherin, as likewise in the Chalday and Syriacke, his skill is extraordinarie.' Drusius did indeed provide instruction in Hebrew, commenting in one of his letters that his pupils included established scholars like Langton as well as younger students.[34]

In the 1620s Amama's place was taken by John Daniel Getsius, who resided at Exeter College and taught Hebrew for some years after 1624.[35] Between 1635 and 1643, and again after 1651, Victorin Bythner, also a foreigner, was to be found at Oxford offering tutorials in Hebrew.[36] These visitors were joined by some graduates of Oxford. Samuel Yerworth, for example, entered Oriel College in 1607 and after his graduation he remained at Oxford, providing instruction in Hebrew to

[31] Pattison, *Isaac Casaubon*, 413–16; Wood, *History of the University* ii. 316; Roth, 'Jews in Oxford', 65.

[32] Roth, 'Jews in Oxford', 66–7; W. S. Samuel, 'The strayings of Paul Isaiah in England, 1651–1656', *Transactions of the Jewish Historical Society of England* xvi (1945–51), 77–87. Ben Asher was teaching in London as well, and was hired by Richard Busby, while Isaiah received in 1656 a stipend of £3 from Magdalen College.

[33] D. Katz, 'The Abendana brothers and the Christian Hebraists of seventeenth-century England', *Journal of Ecclesiastical History* xl (1989), 43–4; H. E. D. Blakiston, *Trinity College* (London 1898), 173 n. 1; Bodl. MS Ballard 9, fos 47–8; D. Patterson, 'Hebrew Studies' in *The Eighteenth Century*, 542–3.

[34] Fuks, 'Het Hebreeuwse brievenboek van Johannes Drusius jr.', 31 and *passim*; *Letters of Bodley to James*, ed. Wheeler, 141.

[35] Wood, *Athenae* iii. 975.

[36] Ibid. 675–6. The account books of Magdalen College indicate a payment of £1 to Bythner in 1650. Macray, *Reg. Magdalen* iv. 4. Bythner's *Tabula directoria in qua totum to texnikon linguae sanctae, ad amussin delineatur* (Oxford 1637), which condenses the Hebrew forms into a single sheet, was probably published for the use of his students. I owe this reference to Professor Gerald Toomer.

young scholars, for whose benefit he prepared a brief Hebrew grammar, *Introductio ad linguam Ebraeam, brevissima,* published in 1650. In it Yerworth argued that 'two hours a day for six weeks will suffice to enable a man with moderate wits to study the Hebrew Old Testament with a lexicon and a fuller grammar at hand'.[37]

College tutors supplemented the weekly lectures of the regius professors and college lecturers as well as the teaching of private instructors. By the early seventeenth century most tutors were capable of providing instruction in all subjects, and the evidence indicates that the teaching of Hebrew became an integral part of their duties as well. At the very minimum, most tutors were able to provide their students with a rudimentary knowledge of the Hebrew alphabet and grammar and supervise their reading of the Old Testament. Even a cursory survey of students' accounts, or manuals of advice compiled by tutors, confirms this practice. For example, the 'directions' composed by Thomas Sixsmith of Brasenose included the instruction to purchase Buxtorf's Hebrew grammar and Schindler's lexicon, a recommendation echoed in virtually every manual of advice during the century.[38]

In fact, there existed a nexus between the teaching of the college tutor and the offerings of the private instructor that suggests that the proliferation of the latter may be explained not only by the general enthusiasm for the language, but also as a response to the tutor's desire—whenever financial considerations allowed or when he himself was deficient in Hebrew—to delegate the drudgery of grammatical instruction to others. When George Fleming, for example, notified his father in 1691 that his tutor insisted he should study Hebrew in the coming term, he added that such a course of study 'will be chargeable', meaning that he intended to hire a private tutor for the Hebrew, as he had done the previous term when he retained a private teacher of mathematics.[39] In this case, Fleming's resort to a private teacher was certainly not because of the tutor's ignorance, for the tutor in question was the celebrated biblical scholar John Mill. However the custom of referring students to specialists for training in selected topics—particularly those demanding much drilling—was becoming increasingly common.

Not surprisingly, as Hebrew became more firmly entrenched in the universities its teaching rapidly percolated down to the grammar school. Many seventeenth-century scholars advocated that students acquire a modicum of Hebrew grammar

---

[37] Wood, *Athenae* ii. 276; Madan, *Oxford Books* ii. 489–90. Yerworth was hardly original in such boasting. As early as 1524 Wakefield had argued that 'in only one month it can be learned from a very experienced man who is really outstanding in this field', assuring his auditors later that he could prove to them 'that you can get to know the language thoroughly in a short time without working'. Likewise, Bellarmine claimed his *Institutiones linguae Hebraicae* could enable any man to learn the language in eight days. Wilhelm Schickard went even further by boasting on the title-page of his *Horologium Ebraeum* that one could acquire the basic rules of Hebrew within twenty-four hours—obviously spread over a period of a few days. Yerworth himself appears to have been engaged in compiling a much larger text by the time his small manual was published.

[38] BNCL MS 80 (unpaginated).

[39] *The Flemings in Oxford* iii. 24. In the late 1650s George Trosse, too, engaged a private tutor who instructed him daily in the rudiments of the Hebrew language. *The Life of . . . George Trosse,* ed. A. W. Brink (Montreal and London 1974), 114–15.

even before their going up to Oxford and Cambridge. As Charles Hoole wrote emphatically: 'I may say it [Hebrew] is rarely attained there by any that have not gotten (at least) the rudiments of it before hand, at a grammar schoole.' And John Postlethwayte, formerly of Merton College (MA 1678) and now headmaster of St Paul's, maintained in 1697 that the main reason for the then impoverished state of Hebraic studies was the dwindling attention given to the subject in the grammar schools, so that it was becoming scarce, taught only in a few schools, and even in these 'only a little before boys were sent to the university'.[40] The repercussions of this decline, however, were only just becoming apparent by the 1680s and 1690s; the previous century, which witnessed the golden age of the English universities in oriental learning, had initiated the cultivation of Hebrew—and sometimes even Aramaic and Arabic—in a large number of schools throughout the country. From the second half of the sixteenth century, such schools as Westminster, Eton, Merchant Taylors', St Paul's, Felsted, Rotherham, Rivington, St Alban's, East Retford, and Blackburn all included Hebrew teaching. Following the example of these better-known institutions, Hebrew was increasingly taught in the smaller grammar schools, especially once a sufficient number of university graduates who had mastered Hebrew were available to hire as teachers and schoolmasters. Although the intention in most cases was only to teach the rudiments of Hebrew grammar and engage in simple translations from the Old Testament, the linguistic foundations laid in the schools enabled a few generations of English students to arrive at Oxford and Cambridge with a solid Hebrew background to build upon.[41]

When we turn to evaluate what was actually taught by tutors and professors at Oxford, the university statutes provide little help. Officially the study of Hebrew was prescribed only for bachelors and masters of art, who as part of their theology course were required to attend twice weekly the lectures of the regius professor of Hebrew. In practice, however, the auditors of the regius professor's lectures were advanced students, regardless of their university standing. Consequently, although most undergraduates relied on their tutors, college lecturers, and private teachers for their primary instruction in Hebrew, the more proficient and committed among them would also have attended the lectures of the regius professor, a fact that certainly contributed to the quality of the lectures.

However, the instruction received by most students was probably not very different from what many of them had received at school. They would continue drilling their grammar, reading selected passages from the Old Testament, especially psalms; and practising translation from Hebrew to Latin and back again.

---

[40] C. Hoole, *The New Discovery of the Old Art of Teaching Schoole* (London 1660), 192; Bodl. MS Ballard 34, fo 86.

[41] Examples include Henry Hammond, who arrived at Magdalen College from Eton in 1618 (J. W. Packer, *The Transformation of Anglicanism* (Manchester 1969), 16) and Edward Bernard who arrived at St John's from Merchant Taylors' School, 'not unacquainted with Hebrew'. Much information on Hebrew instruction may be obtained from a perusal of the histories of individual schools. In general, see F. Watson, *The English Grammar Schools* (London 1908); T. W. Baldwin, *William Shakspere's Small Latine & Lesse Greeke* (2 vols Urbana Ill. 1944).

Their mastery of Hebrew was intended to remain restricted—to allow access to the original texts of scripture—and consequently little attempt was made to acquaint them with the rich original sources of ancient Jewish culture, save perhaps for Josephus' *Antiquitates Iudaicae* or Cunaeus' *De republica Hebraeorum*. Purchases by Henry Fleming during 1679–80 are representative of the average student. Fleming acquired the Hebrew grammars of Bythner and Buxtorf as well as a psalter; no doubt he also owned a dictionary. Having made some inroads into the language, he added Bythner's more elaborate production, *Lyra prophetica Davidis regis*, which included the Septuagint, the Aramaic Targum, and a Hebrew and Aramaic guide.[42]

Nor was the study of Hebrew confined to students intended for the ministry. Both tutors and parents insisted that young undergraduates be able to read the Old Testament in the original. When Francis Gardiner sent his son to Cambridge in 1646, he wrote to the designated tutor William Sancroft: 'I hope therefore you have, besides the common task, appointed him some select Greek author to converse with, and that he hath your assistance to make some progress in the Hebrew bible.' Such a directive was echoed by many who sent their sons to Oxford. When Sackville Crow arrived at Oxford in 1654, his tutor, having described the course he took with his charges 'that are gents designed for the Inns of Court or travell', added: 'some of them have gained the Hebrew to boote, but I shall not trouble Mr Crow with that unlesse your lordship or Mr Crow desire itt.' In 1674 Zaccheus Isham assured his uncle Sir Justinian Isham that he would instruct his cousin Thomas in Hebrew, if Sir Justinian so desired. Two decades later John Mill, George Fleming's tutor at St Edmund Hall, insisted that his charge, then in his second year at Oxford, learn Hebrew too. Fleming, however, managed to evade such study for six years, relenting only when he decided to enter the ministry.[43] In the American colonies, the tradition survived longer. As late as 1759, the first president of King's College (later Columbia University) Samuel Johnson, still argued that Hebrew was a 'gentleman's accomplishment'.[44]

More difficult to evaluate is the actual teaching offered by the regius professors of Hebrew. Given the theological tenor of Hebraic studies and the proclivity of contemporaries to publish biblical exegesis, it should come as no surprise that the professors most commonly engaged in explicating selected passages of the Old Testament. Thomas Crosfield, for example, recorded that on 15 April 1630 John Morris expounded upon Exodus 32. 13.[45] Such a method not only catered to the future needs of the students, but also allowed the professor to elucidate the text through elaborate grammatical and etymological illustrations, at the same time acquainting his auditors with the appropriate Hebrew biblical commentators, the Talmud, and sundry other rabbinic authors.

During Pococke's long reign as regius professor, both the quality and level of

[42] *The Flemings in Oxford* i. 322–5, ii. 16.
[43] H. Cary, *Memorials of the Great Civil War*, (2 vols London 1842) i. 151; BL Add. MS 27,606, fo 8ᵛ; Northants. RO Isham correspondence, no. 856; *The Flemings in Oxford* iii. 18–19, 24, 350.
[44] Morison, *Harvard College in the Seventeenth Century* i. 200.
[45] QCL MS 390, fo 49.

teaching improved. Judging by the extant library catalogues of some students and by the publications of others, Pococke offered a comprehensive and distinct course of study, comprised of a balanced diet of scripture, Talmud, and, to break the monotony of biblical and legalistic instruction, a diversion to more pleasing literary works. In addition to a small army of dictionaries and lexicons, his most common texts included the Mishnaic tractates of *Sanhedrin* and *Makkoth*, which had been made available in a facing Hebrew–Latin edition by Johannes Cocceius, as well as the tractates *Middoth* and *Baba Kamah*, prepared by Constantin l'Empereur. The more pleasing texts were the two twelfth-century Hebrew classics, Judah Halevi's *Kuzari* and the *Itinerary* of Benjamin of Tudela. The former, written in the engaging form of a dialogue between a Christian, a Muslim, a Jew, and an Aristotelian, all vying to convert the king of the Cossars, also offered the reader a superb view of Jewish history, law, and rituals. The *Itinerary*, on the other hand, would have appealed to the fondness of the English for travel and exotic places.[46]

An excellent illustration of such a course of study can be gleaned from the catalogue Edward Bernard compiled of his books in 1658, to which a few titles were added a year or two later. On the whole, the books were purchased before Bernard graduated BA, and obviously reflect Pococke's teaching. Bernard owned a Hebrew Old Testament and the Hebrew grammars of Wilhelm Schickard and Johann Buxtorf, together with the latter's grammar for Syriac and Aramaic. More advanced texts included Cocceius' Mishnaic editions, the *Kuzari*, and Benjamin of Tudela's *Itinerary*, Buxtorf's valuable bibliography of rabbinic authors, and Petrus Cunaeus' treatise on the Hebrew Republic. Such a modest Hebrew collection cost Bernard less than £2. Though a far cry from the magnificent library he later amassed, it was nevertheless more than adequate for an undergraduate at Oxford.[47]

The conscientious manner and progressive nature of Pococke's teaching are corroborated by the various Hebraic publications undertaken by his students in the second half of the seventeenth century. The principal productions were the translation of, and commentary on, various sections of the Mishna as well as Maimonides' commentary on it. Pococke himself contributed only indirectly to the former. Although Pococke used the Mishna extensively in his various writings and taught from it, he never edited or translated a Mishnaic text, leaving that to his students and colleagues. Thus, in 1667 Samuel Clarke published an edition (with Latin translation) of the Mishnaic tractate *Berakhot*. Clarke intended this Hebrew pointed version, a slim volume of thirty-two pages, 'for the use of Talmudic students at Christ Church', and no notes were added to the text.[48] Far more impressive, how-

---

[46] Halevi's book had been edited and translated by the younger Johan Buxtorf as *Liber cosri* (Basle 1629), while Constantin l'Empereur published Benjamin of Tudela's *Itinerarium* four years later (Leiden 1633).

[47] Bodl. MS Lat. misc. f. 11, fos 13ᵛ–17. For a list of Bernard's Arabic books, see p. 489 below.

[48] *Massecheth berakoth*, trans. Samuel Clarke (Oxford 1667). Wood's attribution of the translation to both Clarke and Pocock in his respective biographies of the two suggests, perhaps, the close association between such fine scholars: Wood, *Athenae* iii. 883, iv. 320. See also Madan, *Oxford Books* iii. 214.

ever, was William Guise's edition of the tractate *Zeraim*. Published posthumously in 1690 following Guise's sudden death in 1683, this Latin version (without the Hebrew text), accompanied by an extensive commentary, illustrates the high point of Hebrew studies at Oxford. Guise's accomplishment, discussed more fully below, made him second only to Pococke at Oxford.

Equally significant was the role of Pococke in conveying to his students and colleagues the high esteem that seventeenth-century Hebraists accorded Moses ben Maimon (Maimonides). Scholars commended Maimonides not only because his writings were considered 'the most accessible and appropriate source of primary information on the religious and civil traditions and institutions of the Jews', but because the twelfth-century theologian and philosopher was conceived to be fundamentally different from other rabbis.[49] In holding such a view, Pococke and his English contemporaries merely followed in the footsteps of their contemporaries across the Channel. 'The *More nevukhim*', argued Scaliger, 'can not be commended enough. I rate not only that book but also all the works of that master so highly that I would say that he alone among the Jews has given up talking nonsense.' Gerhard Johannes Vossius quoted the famous saying about Maimonides 'from Moses to Moses there was none like Moses [*a Mose usque ad Mosen non fuisse similem Mosi*]', while Georgius Gentius styled him as the 'wisest of the Jews'. In particular, Maimonides was viewed as being remarkably free of 'fabulizing'. Johannes Buxtorf the younger praised Maimonides, in the preface of his translation of the *More nevukhim*, for having 'given over very little to talmudic fables and traditions'. Instead, 'out of a confused and very entangled order, out of a vile and varied language, [he] forced the [rabbinic] sayings into a perspicuousness, into a fixed order, with a pure Hebrew language, and in a facile and elegant style'.[50]

English scholars expressed similar sentiments. Maimonides was John Selden's preferred Jewish commentator, the object of such tributes as: 'Moses Maimonides was an exceptional master, equally of physics and mathematics as of Jewish theology and jurisprudence.'[51] The source of such esteem is not difficult to detect. The English, after all, were no more enthralled with Jews than were continental Hebraists. But Maimonides was viewed as a 'rationalist' in a fashion more Christian than Jewish, and this attitude endeared him to Christian scholars, especially since many Jewish scholars had criticized Maimonides on those very grounds. As Thomas Baker put it in the late seventeenth century, 'by mixing philosophy and reason with his comments, in order to make their books speak sense, [Maimonides] thereby gave such offence, that he was continually persecuted for it by his brethren, and hardly escaped being branded for a heretick'.[52]

Through his writings and teaching, Pococke contributed significantly to the perpetuation of the Maimonidean tradition. Most important was the publication in

[49] Katchen, *Christian Hebraists and Dutch Rabbis*, 12. I have greatly benefited from Katchen's lucid account of Maimonides' reception on the continent.

[50] Ibid. 35, 39, 95–6, 180, 248.

[51] John Selden, *Opera omnia*, ed. David Wilkins (3 vols in 6 London 1726) i. 437.

[52] Baker, *Reflections upon Learning*, 251.

1655 of his *Porta Mosis*, the Arabic text (in Hebrew characters) of the six prefatory sections to Maimonides' commentary on the Mishna, to which he appended a Latin translation and an extensive commentary, abundant with cross-references to the entire Maimonidean corpus and much else besides. In addition to his desire to draw attention to the existence of a considerable body of Jewish literature in Arabic, Pococke had undertaken this edition specifically because he believed that it was his duty as professor to promote rabbinic and oriental studies through such publications, and Maimonides served this purpose best. Pococke made equally extensive use of Maimonides in his commentaries on Hosea, Joel, Micah, and Malachi, and shortly before his death he also sent through the press a Latin translation of Maimonides' introduction to the Mishna prepared by his son.

The example set by Pococke was soon followed by other Hebraists. Humphrey Prideaux published in 1679 a Latin translation and commentary on the Maimonidean explication of the laws governing alms and the treatment of strangers. Like his master, Prideaux claimed that his purpose in preparing that part of the *Mishneh Torah*—in the aftermath of his appointment as the first Busby lecturer in oriental languages at Christ Church—was to assist beginners and to 'introduce young students in the Hebrew language into the knowledge of the rabbinical dialect, and to teach them to read it without points'.[53]

A few years later a group of three young undergraduates from Christ Church who had studied with Prideaux—and perhaps with Pococke too—produced a translation of an additional selection from the *Mishneh Torah*. George Smalridge, Edward Hannes, and Robert Morgan had arrived together from Westminster School in late 1682, and the manuscript translation was completed some time before the death of John Fell, dean of Christ Church, in July 1686. In their effusive dedication to the dean, the three not only expressed gratitude for his well-known encouragement of the study of philology, but also made it evident that the study of Maimonides had become seminal for advanced students of Hebrew in the Oxford of Pococke and Prideaux.

You sent us, reverend father, as explorers to the holy land. The journey thither is as it were by a road thorny with brambles, long and winding. But the hardships we endured in the sand, and the weariness we suffered have been repaid by the fruitfulness of that blessed land, and will be more amply repaid by your approval. We are indebted to our Jewish guide for our admittance to Jerusalem; our Jewish guide we owe to you. His care led us through the desert, by the hand as it were; it was your patronage of us that aroused and prompted that care.[54]

[53] Maimonides, *De jure pauperis et Peregrini apud Judaeos* (Oxford 1679), preface; *The Life of the Reverend Humphrey Prideaux* (London 1748), 7–8; S. Levy, 'English students of Maimonides', *Miscellanies of the Jewish Historical Society of England* iv (1942), 68–9.

[54] Bodl. MS Jones 36; Levy, 'English students of Maimonides', 69–70. Only Smalridge is known to have continued the study of Hebrew seriously, and in 1694 he was appointed to deliver the sermon, founded by John Morris 'in honour of Sir Thomas Bodley': Macray, *Annals of the Bodleian Library*, 151. As a tutor to Walter Gough in the early 1690s, Smalridge was undoubtedly also responsible for the latter's mastery of Latin, Greek, Hebrew, and Chaldaic: J. Nichols, *Illustrations of the Literary History of the Eighteenth Century* (8 vols London 1817–58) iii. 236.

Finally, although he arrived at Oxford after Pococke's death, Robert Clavering's publication of still further selections from the *Mishneh Torah* ought to be viewed as belonging to the tradition established by the late regius professor. Clavering arrived at Lincoln College in 1693, having already graduated BA from Edinburgh; his Hebrew studies would be rewarded by his appointment as regius professor in 1715. Ten years earlier, Clavering published the *Hilkhot Talmud Torah* and *Teshuba*, in the introduction of which he expressed his opinion that the fame of Maimonides would continue to flourish for ever.[55]

By its very nature, the study of Hebrew—as of other Semitic languages—was a hard and lonely road. Though by the seventeenth century the availability of appropriate texts removed one obstacle for Hebrew scholars as opposed to Arabists, someone wishing to read more than the Old Testament in Hebrew would still have to embark on a prolonged and solitary course of study. Recounting his own persistence in pursuing the oriental languages during the first two decades of the sixteenth century, Robert Wakefield depicted some of the toils of many subsequent scholars who pursued the study of Jewish learning and culture:

I have gained this knowledge by reading their language regularly and persistently. Such study required unflagging zeal, and involved much sweat, time and daily effort. It was done to the considerable detriment of my disposition, sight and health ... I, the one who is *automathes kai autodidaktos* and has availed himself only of the help of so-called silent teachers which do not answer questions.[56]

A diligent and caring instructor was obviously an additional boon; but it was chiefly the private drudgery of the student that mattered in the end. As Thomas Fuller phrased it, 'more pains then quicknesse of wit is required to get it, and with daily exercise he continues it. Apostacy herein is usual to fall totally from the language by a little neglect.'[57] Francis Osborne argued along similar lines that: 'a prosecution of the oriental tongues (beyond an ability to understand them) is like musick or fencing, unable to requite the time they consume: Hebrew being observed to grow for the most part in soils apter to produce roots than flowers.' At the end of the century, John Postlethwayte, undoubtedly recalling his own studies in Hebrew at Oxford during the 1670s and 1680s, stated that 'generally speaking such persons as have attained to any excellency in it, have been very little owing to any body but themselves, and to their books in it'.[58]

---

[55] *R. Mosis Maimonidis tractatus duo: 1. De doctrina legis, sive educatione puerorum; 2. De natura et ratione poenitentiae apud Hebraeos* (Oxford 1705); A. Altmann, 'William Wollaston (1659–1724): English deist and rabbinic scholar', *Transactions of the Jewish Historical Society of England* xvi (1945–51), 206; Levy, 'English Students of Maimonides', 74. Clavering had also compiled a short guide for the study of Hebrew, and consented to its publication by the Jewish teacher of Hebrew, Philip Levi, under Levi's own name: *A Compendium of Hebrew Grammar compos'd for the use of beginners* (Oxford 1705).

[56] Wakefield, *On the Three Languages*, 68.

[57] Thomas Fuller, *The Holy State and the Profane State*, ed. M. G. Walten (2 vols New York 1938) ii. 73. Elsewhere he added: 'Skill in Hebrew will quickly go out, and burn no longer then 'tis blown': ibid. 33.

[58] Francis Osborne, *Advice to a Son*, ed. E. A. Parry (London 1896), 110; Bodl. MS Ballard 34, fo 86.

If the aspiring Hebraist needed to be self-motivated and highly disciplined, he nevertheless had recourse to like-minded individuals who, in a manner reminiscent of Latin and Greek instruction, could form some sort of mutual support group. Two examples from the end of the sixteenth century make the point clear. In 1596 the young Brian Twyne described to his father how he had joined a group of fellows at Corpus Christi College who were drilling their Hebrew 'by stelth, walkinge whole afternoones'. This atmosphere of both dedication and seclusion is confirmed by Twyne's contemporary at Oxford, Robert Harris (BA 1600), who was said by his biographer to have studied Hebrew with his tutor Stephen Goffe of Magdalen College 'in which study some other of the fellows joyned with them, whereof one afterwards was president'. Somewhat later, John Gregory was said to have 'travelled through twelve languages without any guide, except Mr Dod the decalogist, whose society and directions for the Hebrew tongue he enjoyed one vacation near Banbury'.[59]

Naturally, those colleges or halls housing forceful proponents of oriental studies—either as heads of house or tutors—were the centres that produced generations of Hebrew scholars. The joint example of Magdalen College and Magdalen Hall illustrates this point. The college, we saw earlier, was not only endowed with a Hebrew lectureship, but was also blessed with a series of presidents who supported Hebrew, even when they themselves were not distinguished scholars. During the early 1620s, for example, under President Langton two students excelled in the oriental languages. Henry Hammond (MA 1625) turned out to be not only an eminent champion of the English Church in its darkest hour, but his voluminous publications amply attest to his scholarship in general and knowledge of Hebrew in particular.[60] His less well known colleague, Sampson Johnson, was a remarkably talented orientalist who numbered John Bainbridge and Archbishop Laud among his patrons but who failed to publish anything.[61]

The Magdalen College lecturer in Hebrew for over two decades in the early seventeenth century was John Wilkinson, who would also serve as principal of Magdalen Hall for forty years (1605–43, and 1646–8).[62] Indeed, it was during his long tenure that the hall produced a series of talented Hebraists. Thomas Godwin, author of *Moses and Aaron*, for example, graduated MA in 1609, staying on for a while as a tutor. There he was joined in 1614 by William Pemble, who had just graduated BA from Magdalen College, and who would remain tutor in the hall until his death in 1623.[63] Pemble turned out to be a key figure in encouraging the cultivation of Hebraic studies. In 1615 William Pincke matriculated from the hall. Highly regarded for his considerable skill in both Greek and the oriental languages, Pincke died prematurely at 30, thus—according to his literary executor—putting an

[59] H. G. Scott, 'Some correspondence of Brian Twyne', *Bodleian Quarterly Record* v (1926–8), 214; Clarke, *The Lives of Thirty-two English Divines*, 315, 89.

[60] For Hammond see Packer, *The Transformation of Anglicanism*.

[61] For Johnson, see p. 484 below.

[62] For Wilkinson, see Bodl. MS Ballard 46, fo 97ᵛ; Macray, *Reg. Magdalen* iii. 117–21.

[63] Wood, *Athenae* iii. 51–3, ii. 330–1.

end to 'some master-peece ... he attempted in the Greek antiquities, and observations on the Hebrew text'. Thomas Coleman, whose proficiency as a Hebraist
was commended by John Selden, also entered Magdalen Hall in 1615.[64]

Although it is not certain that Pemble served as the official tutor for either
Pincke or Coleman, he would undoubtedly have encouraged their study of Hebrew
and theology, since he also served as the hall's catechist. More easily confirmed is
Pemble's tutorship of two other Hebraists, Edward Leigh and John Tombes, who
arrived at Oxford in 1616 and 1617 respectively. The former, who graduated MA
in 1623, became a prolific author, whose knowledge of Hebrew is demonstrated by
his *Critica sacra* (1638) and *Treatise of Religion and Learning* (1656). Tombes became a
noted tutor, numbering John Wilkins among his students, and succeeded Pemble
as the hall's catechist. He eventually turned Baptist and, as a result, little of his early
promise as a learned classicist and Hebraic scholar was translated into scholarly
publications.[65] In view of such extensive and concentrated effort by both principal and tutors to cultivate oriental learning at Magdalen Hall, it is not surprising
that the hall was also the first home of Edward Pococke, who had been a student
there between June 1618 and December 1619, at which time he carried his love for
such learning to Corpus Christi College.

Space does not permit a detailed study of the content and depth of Hebraic studies among Oxford scholars in the seventeenth century. Nevertheless, a sampling of
the sources used by six such scholars, both before and after the civil war, indicates
the diversity of their interests and the scope of their knowledge of rabbinic literature.

John Viccars (MA Lincoln College 1625) produced in 1639 his learned *Decapla
in psalmos*, which included variant readings of the biblical text, derived from Greek,
Syriac, and Arabic manuscripts he had obtained from various English and conti-
nental libraries. To this work Viccars appended a translation of the twelve major
Hebrew commentaries on the Psalms, including the Targum, Rashi, Kimhi, Ibn
Ezra, Obadiah Gaon, and the Midrash Tehilim, with his own observations and
learned notes. Less original, but equally useful, was Edward Leigh's *Critica sacra*,
running quickly through four editions in seven printings between 1646 and 1664.
Perhaps the subtitle of this lexicon of some 1,500 radices best indicates its content:
'Observations of all the radices or primitive Hebrew words of the Old Testament,
in order alphabetical, wherein both they (and many derivatives also issuing from
them) are fully opened out of the best lexicographers and scholiasts.'[66]

With the possible exception of Pococke, John Gregory was perhaps the most
talented Hebraist at Oxford before the civil war. His biographer relates that on

---

[64] Ibid. ii. 475–6; William Pincke, *The Triall of a Christians Sincere Love Unto Christ* (Oxford 1631, 3rd
edn Oxford 1636), sig. A2ᵛ. For Coleman, see Wood, *Athenae* iii. 211–13; Selden, *Opera omnia* i, pt ii.
1075.

[65] Wood, *Athenae* iii. 926–31, 1062–7.

[66] It is notable, however, that Leigh relied considerably on the labours of Christian Hebraists and
only intermittently on Jewish sources.

account of his knowledge of the oriental languages Gregory was considered an 'oracle' among his contemporaries and consequently sought out twice a week by a group of scholars who desired his guidance; 'none communicated his notions more readily, none expressed himself more satisfactorily' than Gregory. Wood, for his part, styled Gregory 'the miracle of his age for critical and curious learning'.[67]

The profound, if eccentric, knowledge of this Christ Church scholar can be gathered from his notes on select passages of scriptures. In a series of relatively short explicatory chapters on such topics as the name of God, the mark of Cain, the religious significance of the 'east', the upper chamber of the Temple, the separation of milk and flesh, and *theom rabba* (the great deep), Gregory makes free use of a massive body of rabbinic literature. He is well versed in the standard commentaries on the Old Testament available in any edition of the rabbinic bible, including those of Rashi, Ibn Ezra, David Kimhi, Isaac Abravanel, Bahya ben Asher, and Nachmanides. But he is also versed in sources less well known among Christians, such as Isaac ben Arama's commentary on the Pentateuch, the *Akedat Itzhak*, and Joseph ben David ibn Yahya's *Perush Hamesh Megillot u-Ketuvim* (Bologna 1538). Of the Halakhic and other rabbinic sources, Gregory displays effortless ease in quoting from both Talmuds and various Midrashim; he is at home with the Maimonidean corpus, and he is acquainted with Joseph Karo's code, the *Shulhan Arukh*.

Gregory is also unusual among Oxford Hebraists for his awareness of the mystical stream in Judaism. Owing to the condensed nature of his writings, however, we cannot easily evaluate his knowledge of the kabbalah. Noteworthy is his occasional invocation of the *Zohar*, which he treats with apparent familiarity, and his use of the *Sefer ha-Musar*, a kabbalistic and ethical treatise by the sixteenth-century Spaniard Judah Kalats as well as Moses bar Cepha's *De paradiso explicatio* in Andreas Massius' Latin edition. His brief treatment of the legend of the she-devil Lilith is a good illustration of his gloss on a passage lending itself to mystical explication. Within a page and a half Gregory exhibits his familiarity with various sources of the legend, referring specifically to the *Alphabetum Ben Sira* in the 1519 Constantinople edition, the *Tosafot* to the tractate *Niddah*, and Azariah de Rossi's *Me'or Einayim*, with whose interpretation he takes issue.[68]

Equally revealing is the youthful production of Thomas Smith. Nicknamed both 'Rabbi Smith' and 'Tograi Smith' on account of his passion for oriental learning, he published, in 1662, his *Diatriba de Chaldaicis paraphrastis*, which is significant not for its novelty (it was hardly original) but for the wide range of sources that a young bachelor of arts of two years' standing was able to marshal.[69] As a matter of fact, this small dissertation documents the ability of Christian Hebraists to trace the

[67] Clarke, *The Lives of Thirty-two Divines*, 88; Wood, *Athenae* iii. 205.

[68] John Gregory, *Notes and Observations upon some passages of Scripture* (Oxford 1646, 2nd edn London 1650).

[69] When Smith proceeded BA in 1660, 'he was dispensed with two terms by the chancellor, to whom he was recommended by Provost Barlow for his progressive learning far beyond his age and standing': J. R. Magrath, *The Queen's College* (2 vols Oxford 1921) ii. 57. For a sample of his Hebrew learning by 1660, see the notes of Smith on Hebrew grammar: Bodl. MS Smith 99, fos 11 ff.

Hebrew original from translations and secondary literature. A detailed examination of the sources used by Smith enables us to evaluate the scholarly standards of the more committed Hebraists.

The *Diatriba* represents a critical discussion of the sundry Aramaic translations/paraphrases of different parts of the Old Testament—the Targums—the antiquity, authorship, and authority of these translations, and their relationship to the Hebrew text of the Bible and their employment for the elucidation of scripture and the Talmud. The route pursued by Smith had been well charted by Christian scholars ever since the study of the Targums had been strongly advocated by Johannes Reuchlin. Sebastian Münster, for example, regarded the Targum as often more explicit than the Hebrew original, and in his influential Latin translation of the Bible he often followed the appropriate Aramaic text. Another celebrated Hebraist, Paulus Fagius, contributed to the Christian appreciation of these sources both through his translation into Latin of the most important of the Aramaic texts, the *Targum Onkelos*, and his publication of Elijas Levita's important dictionary *Meturgeman*, including a Latin translation of Levita's introduction, which contained a detailed account of the various Targums.

The attention accorded to the Targums, particularly by Calvinist scholars, originated in an appreciation of the light such texts might shed not only on difficult Hebrew passages, but also on the 'true' meaning of the Old Testament. In this context, the perceived antiquity of the Aramaic translations was particularly appealing. The composition of the two major Targums, those of Onkelos and Jonathan, were believed to have predated, or at least been contemporaneous with, the birth of Christ and the composition of the Talmud. Many Hebraists therefore argued that the Aramaic paraphrases were uncluttered by rabbinic fables and, in view of the overall harmony between the Aramaic and Hebrew texts of the Old Testament, inviolable testimony that the Jews had not deliberately corrupted the text of the Old Testament as part of their anti-Christian polemic.

Various Oxford scholars perpetuated this view. Henry Hammond gave primacy to the Aramaic over both Greek and Syriac:

> Of these three, the Chaldee [Aramaic], which is not so literal as the others pretend to be, but owns the liberty of a paraphrast, is yet as commodious as any to direct to the literal sense, the very designe of a paraphrast being truly this, to render that fully in more words which an equal number could not sufficiently express. Yet hath not this made so full a provision for us, but that all other aids have sometimes been little enough to stear us through the difficulty.

The sentiment was expressed equally forcefully by Smith's patron and provost of Queen's College, Thomas Barlow, for whom the Targums facilitated not only an understanding of the Old Testament but also 'how the Ancient Jews interpreted it', adding that 'As for antiquity, so for authority and sobriety, they are more significant than ... all the rabbins.'[70]

[70] Henry Hammond, *A Paraphrase and Annotations upon the books of the Psalms* (London 1659), preface; T. Barlow, *Autochediasmata, de studio theologiae* (Oxford 1699), 9–10. Brian Walton included a discussion

That Smith was aware of such a tradition is obvious. His most frequently quoted source is the introduction to Levita's *Meturgeman*; Smith was also a beneficiary of the recent completion of that mammoth accomplishment of Anglican scholarship, Walton's edition of the Polyglot Bible, which provided him with a convenient translation of the various Targums—based on the previous efforts of Paulus Fagius, Conrad Pellican, and Francis Taylor—and the variant readings provided by Samuel Clarke for the same edition. Smith was equally conversant with the contributions of Christophorus Helvicus[71] and Christopher Cartwright.[72] In fact, in the *Diatriba* Smith often emerges as engaged in a dialogue, at times critical, with his predecessors. *Inter alia*, he also contributed his modest share to the continuing polemic with such Catholic detractors of the Hebrew Masoretic text of the Old Testament as Nicholas Serarius and Jean Morin.[73]

In addition to such immediate sources, Smith also benefited from a different source—Jewish–Christian polemical literature. Naturally, he utilized the famous (or infamous) *Pugio fidei*, composed by the thirteenth-century Dominican Raymundus Martini and published for the first time by Joseph de Voisin in 1651. Voisin added to the volume a wealth of additional material and commentary, thus making it an indispensable source for future Hebraists. Compared with the well-known *Pugio*, the other fiercely anti-Jewish polemical source used by Smith was almost obscure. This was the *Shevilei Tohu*, a vicious denunciation of Judaism written by the apostate Gerard Veltwyck and published in 1539 by Bomberg at Venice.[74] For good measure, Smith also used the effective Jewish polemic, *Sefer Nizzahon*, written in 1390 by the learned Bohemian scholar and kabbalist Yom Tov Lipmann Muelhausen, and published in 1644 by Theodore Hackspan.

As noted earlier, by the time Smith published his *Diatriba*, a great body of literature existed in Latin—both translations from the Hebrew and original works of generations of Christian Hebraists—and of such literature Smith made full use. In addition to the *Meturgeman*, Smith freely availed himself of the other important dictionary of that *doctissimus rabbinus* Elias Levita, *Tishbi*, a lexicon of Hebrew words in the Talmud that was available to him in Fagius' Latin translation. Another valuable Hebrew and Aramaic dictionary was the *Tsemah David*, compiled by David de

on the Targums in his prolegomena to the Polyglot Bible, which was used by Smith: *Biblia sacra polyglotta*, ed. B. Walton (6 vols London 1655–7) i. 81–7. See also Pococke's endorsement of the Targums in the preface to his *A Commentary on the Prophecy of Micah* (Oxford 1676).

[71] Christophorus Helvicus, *Tractatus historicus et theologicus de Chaldaicis Bibliorum paraphrasibus* (Giese 1612).

[72] Cartwright's *Electa Thargumico-Rabbinica, sive annotationes in Genesin* (London 1648) included a succinct explication of the various Targums in its long preface. Both in this book and its sequel, *Electa Thargumico-Rabbinica, sive annotationes in Exodum* (London 1653), Cartwright utilized extensively the Aramaic paraphrases for his commentaries on the first two books of the Pentateuch.

[73] The relevant books of the prolific Jesuit Serarius included *Rabbini et Herodes, seu de Tota Rabbinorum gente, partitione, creatione, auctoritate, pluribusque rebus aliis et sacris et profanis, maxime de Herodis tyranni natalibus, Judaismo, uxoribus, liberis et regno, libri tres* (Mainz 1607) and *Prolegomena Biblicae* (Mainz 1612); Jean Morin, *Exercitationes ecclesiasticae in utrumque Samaritanorum Pentateuchum* (Paris 1631).

[74] A Latin translation entitled 'Itinera deserti' was prepared by Conrad Pellican in 1545 but never published.

Pomis and published with facing Latin and Italian translation. To complete the list of Smith's lexicographical tools, the great dictionaries of the Buxtorfs were all available to him.

In addition to these lexicographical tools in Latin dressing, other sources were also available in Latin translation. Thus, many of Smith's references to the Mishna were to those tractates that had been translated by Johannes Cocceius and Constantin l'Empereur, while the great Midrashic chronology of the world, *Seder Olam Rabba*, was made easily accessible by Genebrard's Latin edition of 1578. Of the works of Maimonides, the *More nevukhim* had been rendered into Latin as the *Doctor perplexorum* in 1629 by the younger Johann Buxtorf; the *Halikhot Olam*—a study of the composition of the Mishna and Gemara, and formation of the Halakha, written by the fifteenth-century talmudist Jeshua ben Joseph Ha-Levi— had been translated by Constantin l'Empereur as *Clavis Talmudica* in 1633.

Obviously, the availability of a text in Latin translation does not necessarily imply that Smith could not—or did not—use the original. His ability to do so can be evaluated through the competent treatment he made of rabbinic sources available only in Hebrew, particularly post-medieval Jewish writings.[75] Noteworthy are the references to *Sefer ha-Yuhasin* by Abraham ben Samuel Zacuto, which provided a detailed account of the development and transmission of the Jewish oral law, and to the important *Me'or Einayim* by the sixteenth-century Italian scholar Azariah ben Moses de Rossi. The latter was banned by contemporary rabbis for its application of renaissance textual criticism to the study of the Talmud, and the assimilation of pagan and Christian sources for the purpose of elucidating the Jewish text. Such a methodology and its ensuing censure undoubtedly added to the book's popularity among Christian Hebraists.[76]

Smith's introduction to the *Diatriba* and the notes accompanying it enable us to glimpse the network of teachers and colleagues who participated in furthering his studies. Chief among them was Samuel Clarke, *architypographus* to Oxford University since 1658, and the person to whom Walton entrusted the section on the Targums in the Polyglot Bible. Clarke was not only able to guide Smith through the maze of literature on the Targums, but he also made available to Smith his own translation of the Targum of the Chronicles, which he made from a manuscript in the

---

[75] It goes without saying that Smith availed himself of the biblical commentaries of Rashi and Ibn Ezra—available to him in any edition of a rabbinic Bible—and of the most popular Midrash of all, the Midrash Tehilim.

[76] Smith's younger colleague at Oxford, Humphrey Prideaux, would some years later cover much the same ground—and refer to much the same sources—in a long digression on the subject which he inserted into his most famous book. The Aramaic paraphrases, argued Prideaux, 'vindicate the genuineness of the present Hebrew text' of the Old Testament 'by proving it the same that was in use when the Targums were made', so the Jews could be proved innocent of the accusation that they corrupted the holy text after the rise of Christianity. He also claimed that the Targums could serve a polemical purpose against the Jews, who valued them highly, if the Aramaic text were used to interpret 'correctly' the many prophecies of the Messiah he believed were to be found in the Old Testament. See Humphrey Prideaux, *The Old and New Testament Connected in the History of the Jews and Neighbouring Nations* (2 vols London 1716–18, 16th edn 4 vols in 2 London 1808) iv. 618–45.

Cambridge University Library.[77] Also supportive were Edward Pococke and Thomas Barlow as well as our author's namesake, the recently deceased librarian of Cambridge University, who had been a talented orientalist and an associate of various members of Queen's College, Oxford, since the late 1640s.[78]

Also important are the lectures delivered by Smith in the 1660s, while serving as Hebrew lecturer at Magdalen College. *Praelectiones de modo divini cultus respectu loci deter-minati* displays the fascination of many Europeans with the the 'esoteric' topic of worship 'towards the east' practised by Jews and early Christians.[79] Smith uses many of the same sources as before—the two Talmuds, various Midrashim, Maimonides, and various rabbinic commentaries—adding some more recent liter-ature such as the relevant writings of Leon Modena and Menasseh ben Israel, per-tinent Arabic sources mostly derived second-hand from Pococke's *Porta Mosis* and Golius' Arabic lexicon, and the various tomes of John Selden.[80]

Smith's *Diatriba* invites comparison with the scholarly accomplishment of Humphrey Prideaux's edition of Maimonides' *De jure pauperis et peregrini*, published at Oxford in 1679. The latter text represents the learning of a scholar slightly senior to Smith at the time of composition (Prideaux received his MA in 1675), who had recently been appointed the first Busby lecturer in oriental languages at Christ Church.[81] Prideaux's correspondence makes clear the reverence in which he held his ageing mentor Pococke, as well as the great assistance he derived from him. For example, in September 1675, when the regius professor fell dangerously ill, Prideaux wrote to John Ellis:

My greatest affliction now is the sicknesse of my worthy friend Dr Pocock, who hath his old distemper returned upon him, which, if it doth prevaile, must necessaryly kill him and deprive me of the best friend I have in this place, and utterly spoile me for a linguist; since the greatest encouragement I have to follow those studys is the more then ordinary helpe which I hope to receive from him.

---

[77] Clarke completed the translation in 1662 but it was not published until 1715 by David Wilkins. See Clarke's correspondence on the subject with Lightfoot, who assisted in the task: *Works of Lightfoot*, ed. Pitman xiii. 401–21. For Clarke's notes on the Polyglot's edition of the Aramaic paraphrases see *Biblia sacra polyglotta*, ed. Walton vi. 17–72. Clarke intended to add a seventh volume to the Polyglot Bible, publishing from various manuscripts Arabic and Syriac versions of several books of the Old Testament. He published a prospectus soliciting subscribers, but the project never materialized. Bodl. Θ fo, 663 no. 36. I owe this information to Gerald Toomer.

[78] For Smith see Paul Hammond's good, if partial and incomplete, study, 'Thomas Smith: a belea-guered humanist of the Interregnum', *Bulletin of the Institute for Historical Research* lvi (1983), 180–94.

[79] A similar, though much shorter, exposition was made by John Gregory two decades earlier; see p. 470 above.

[80] Bodl. MSS Smith 113–14.

[81] Following Prideaux's death in 1724 Hearne entered the following 'eloge' into his diary: Prideaux was 'a person who, besides all the services he hath done to the world as a scholar, hath eminently dis-tinguished himself in his writings, as a man that had religion truly at heart. He hath left behind him the character of a great and good man.' Ten years later Hearne somewhat tempered his praise: 'Prideaux's chief skill was in orientals, and yet even there he was far from being perfect in either, unless in Hebrew, which he was well versed in.' Hearne, *Collections* viii. 292, xi. 382.

Pococke, for his part, was confident of Prideaux's learning. Earlier that year Prideaux had informed Ellis that he had been entrusted with the manuscript of Pococke's commentary on the prophet Micah—published in 1677—'the doctor haveing thought me worthy to peruse it before it goe to the presse'.[82]

As mentioned earlier, Pococke was undoubtedly the inspiration behind Prideaux's translation of Maimonides, its structure, and the adjoining commentary. We may further conjecture that the regius professor had also personally supervised the execution of the task. As was the case with Smith, a survey of the sources utilized by Prideaux establishes the qualifications of the young scholar. A reliable translation of a didactic nature, the work contains only a modest scholarly apparatus that is intended primarily to clarify the language rather than elucidate the text. Nevertheless, the notes of Prideaux demonstrate how fully conversant he was with the Maimonidean corpus as a whole; they provide extensive cross-references to other parts of the *Mishneh Torah*, relying not only on existing partial Latin translations and commentaries—executed by Dionysius Vossius and Guglielmus Vorstius—but also on Joseph Karo's commentary on the Maimonidean text, the *Kesef Mishneh*, and Moses ben Jacob (of Coucy), *Sefer ha-Mitzvot ha-Gadol*, which was based on the *Mishneh Torah*. Prideaux also invoked Karo's own code, the *Shulhan Arukh* and, of course, included many references to both the Jerusalem and Babylonian Talmuds. Other rabbinic sources consulted included Abraham ben David's *Sefer ha-kabbalah*, an explication of the chain of rabbinic tradition, and Joseph Ha-Levi's *Halikhot Olam*.

ARABIC STUDIES

The growing realization by the second half of the sixteenth century of the affinity between Hebrew and Arabic and especially the relevance of Arabic in elucidating scripture prompted increasing numbers of Oxford scholars to acquire at least a smattering of Arabic. Indeed, some of the translators of the King James version of the Bible were reputed to have obtained considerable skill in oriental languages. Miles Smith, one of the two general editors of this masterpiece, was supposed to have been proficient in Hebrew, Syriac, and Arabic, while his friend Richard Brett had somehow added Ethiopic to his arsenal of oriental tongues.[83] Unfortunately, owing to the scarcity of evidence, we cannot determine either the extent and depth of their knowledge or the manner in which it had been obtained.

By the early seventeenth century, however, scholars aspiring to Arabic could have had recourse to William Bedwell, who drew English and foreign students alike

---

[82] *Letters of Humphrey Prideaux . . . to John Ellis*, ed. E. M. Thompson (Camden Soc. new ser. xv 1875), 42–3. From another letter we gain a glimpse of Prideaux's 'apprenticeship' in Hebrew. In 1676 he commissioned Ellis to purchase for him in Amsterdam the *Kaf Nahat*, Isaac ben Gabbai's commentary on the Mishna, and Zacuto's *Sefer ha-Yuhasin*—for which he was willing to spend 18s or more. Prideaux also boasted of the fine collection of Hebrew books Christ Church had recently purchased from a sale of Bodleian duplicates, a collection that would greatly enhance his studies. Ibid. 54.

[83] Wood, *Athenae* ii. 359, 611. Smith befriended the Egyptian Abudacnus who taught Arabic at Oxford: A. Hamilton, *William Bedwell the Arabist 1563–1632* (Leiden 1985), 37, 100.

to his Tottenham house for instruction.[84] Occasional opportunities may also have
been available at Oxford. Quite possibly Johannes Drusius taught elementary
Arabic while teaching Hebrew and Syriac at Oxford in the 1570s. Other visitors to
Oxford could also have offered Arabic instruction. The erudite Danish scholar
Lauge Christensen arrived at Oxford *circa* 1596, after having studied theology at
Franeker, where Drusius had supervised his studies of the oriental languages. The
Arabic and Syriac verses he contributed to the *album amicorum* of William Bedwell
attest to both his competence and the warm friendship he contracted with the
English Arabist. Similarly, Peter Kirsten's visit to England in 1602 may have
afforded an opportunity for some Oxford men to take advantage of the German
Arabist's rapidly expanding knowledge of the oriental languages.[85]

More positive evidence can be found with scholars of the next generation of
Oxford Hebraists. Richard Kilbye, whom we encountered as a learned Hebraist,
appears to have been a student of Arabic as well; Isaac Casaubon noted seeing in
his rooms in 1613 one of the only two copies of Raphelengius' *Lexicon Arabicum*
he believed were then to be found in England. (The other was owned by Lancelot
Andrewes.)[86] Casaubon was perhaps unaware of another keen student of the oriental tongues, Arthur Lake. In 1617, Lake, having been elevated to the bishopric
of Bath and Wells, donated to New College—in addition to many Hebrew books—
his small, but important, private collection of Arabic books for the further encouragement of these studies. They included a copy of the Koran, Raphelengius'
lexicon, the grammars of Kirsten and Erpenius, and sundry Arabic editions of
scriptural texts.[87]

Quite probably there existed a correlation between this display of interest in
Arabic and the first attempt since the days of Wakefield, in the early sixteenth century, to institute the teaching of the language in Oxford. Yusuf Ibn abu Daqan, or
Josephus Abudacnus (Barbatus) as he was commonly known, arrived at Oxford in
1603, but left for France shortly thereafter to teach Arabic in Paris, where he numbered the young Erpenius among his students. In 1610 he returned to England and,
having procured a letter of recommendation from Richard Bancroft, archbishop of
Canterbury, 'to the end he might read the Arabian tongue', he went back to
Oxford. Sir Thomas Bodley added his own commendation of the Egyptian-born

[84] An excellent study of the 'father' of Arabic studies in England is provided by Hamilton, *William Bedwell*.

[85] For Christensen, see ibid. 14–15, 20–1, 122; for Kirsten, who would contemplate emigrating to England during the Thirty Years War with his Arabic printing press, see ibid. 19–20, 50, 104–5, 122–3.

[86] Pattison, *Isaac Casaubon*, 367. Kilbye bequeathed the book to Lincoln College.

[87] For Lake's endowment of lectureships, see p. 458 above. His donation of books is enumerated in NCA benefactors book, pp. 53–64. The Arabic books he donated are: *Liber psalmorum Davidis*, ed. Victor Scialac and Gabriel Sionita (Rome 1614); three titles by Erpenius: *Proverbiorum Arabicorum centuriae duae* (Leiden 1615), *Grammatica Arabica* (Leiden 1613), and his edition of *Novum D. N. Jesu Christi Testamentum Arabice* (Leiden 1616); three works by Peter Kirsten: *Vitae evangelistarum quatuor* (Breslau 1608), *Grammatica Arabica* (Breslau 1608), and *Deras sacra canticorum et carminum Arabicorum* (Breslau 1609); Franciscus Raphelengius, *Lexicon Arabico-Latinum* (Leiden 1613); and Anon., *Alphabetum Arabicum* (Rome 1592).

Barbatus, entreating Thomas James to help install him at Oxford not only for the advantage of local scholars but also 'lest Cambridge should endevour, as I make account they would, to draw him unto them'. Bodley's first librarian apparently complied, for a month later Bodley thanked James for his efforts. Barbatus remained at Oxford until 1613, teaching Arabic and other oriental languages and studying in the Bodleian Library where he composed his *Historia Jacobitarum*, published by Thomas Marshall in 1675.[88]

No direct information exists to identify Barbatus' Oxford students. Yet, in view of the enthusiasm that usually accompanied the arrival of such teachers, it would be safe to assume that Lake and Kilbye, as well as other known orientalists such as Thomas Jackson and John Prideaux, were among his auditors. Barbatus may also have been Louis Cappel's teacher of Arabic during the latter's sojourn at Oxford in the early 1610s.[89] Certainly the arrival of Sixtinus Amama at Oxford shortly after Barbatus' departure was propitious. As noted earlier, Amama is known to have provided instruction in Hebrew, but he may have provided lessons in Arabic as well, since he himself had studied the language with Erpenius for a few months prior to his arrival to England.[90]

The most formidable obstacle to the study of Arabic in the seventeenth century was the dearth of books. Aware of this problem, Sir Thomas Bodley, as early as 1603, contemplated the dispatch of a scholar well versed in Hebrew and Arabic to the near east solely for the procurement of oriental manuscripts. Unfortunately, nothing came of this scheme and the problem persisted. Half a century later, John Worthington, master of Jesus College, Cambridge, forcefully expressed conventional wisdom concerning the scarcity of appropriate books, 'without which the pains and time spent upon grammar will not receive a due recompense'. He further commented that his own 'pursuit of those languages was cooled by that very consideration, that there were no printed books, none but MSS which are kept close, and are not for the common use'. Even as late as 1720 Humphrey Prideaux still maintained that the study of Arabic 'cannot, without long and sedulous application, be attained unto; and it adds to the difficulty, that most of the books, to be made use of in this matter, lie in manuscript, which cannot be easily come at, or easily read'. To illustrate his case, Prideaux pointed out that he knew of only three printed Muslim histories—that of Erpenius and the two volumes edited by

---

[88] Wood, *Fasti* i. 301–2; Hamilton, *William Bedwell*, 34–7; *Letters of Bodley to James*, ed. Wheeler, 193–4, 196. In 1612 Barbatus contributed four poems (in Arabic, Chaldaic, Syriac, and Turkish) to a volume lamenting Prince Henry's death, *Eidyllia in obitum fulgentissimi Henrici Walliae Principis*, parading, no doubt, his erudition in the languages he was offering. In the absence of suitable founts, however, Hebrew characters were used in printing such verses: Madan, *Oxford Books* i. 62.

[89] Cappel probably accompanied Bedwell on his trip to Leiden in 1612, and he contributed verses in Latin, Greek, and Arabic to Bedwell's *Album amicorum*: Hamilton, *William Bedwell*, 122–3. Jackson, the future president of Corpus Christi College, was said to be a competent student of the oriental languages: Wood, *Athenae* ii. 665.

[90] Platt, 'Sixtinus Amama', 239, 242.

Pococke—'but these are only jejune epitomees, containing no more than the bare bones of oriental history'.[91]

The library catalogues of those who made an attempt to master Arabic confirm the poor assortment of printed books available to them. The collection of John Smith, the Cambridge Platonist who died in 1652, may be considered typical of the generality of Englishmen who had mastered Hebrew and who now sought to embark on Arabic. The dozen or so Arabic books in Smith's library included Erpenius' two Arabic grammars, Pococke's *Specimen historiae Arabum*, Raimondi's *Liber Tasriphi*, Ravius's sample translation of the Koran, Thomas a Novaria's *Thesaurus Arabico-Syro-Latinus*, and various biblical texts in Arabic.[92]

In contrast to the paltry number of Arabic printed books in general, and the lamentable meagreness of oriental manuscripts in most English public and private libraries, the relatively rich manuscript holdings of the Bodleian Library stand out. No doubt these holdings contributed as much to Oxford's growing prominence in oriental studies as such scholars as Pococke or Hyde. The chorus of excitement over the Bodleian's oriental treasures began as early as 1613 with Robert Burton's verse lamenting the death of Sir Thomas Bodley. A decade later the visiting German orientalist Matthias Pasor, attempting to entice public spirits to endow an Arabic chair at Oxford, also commended the oriental treasures of the Bodleian Library. But, important as the early collections were, they paled in comparison with the bequests and acquisitions that followed. First to arrive were the manuscripts presented by Archbishop Laud during the 1630s. This donation of some 600 oriental manuscripts fired the imagination of contemporaries, including that of the eccentric Oxford orientalist Henry Jacob, whose oration in 1636 effusively praised the archbishop and his gifts. Nor did John Worthington exaggerate when in the 1650s he referred to the Bodleian Library as the 'great magazine of oriental books'.[93]

After the Restoration the Bodleian holdings in Hebrew and Arabic manuscripts continued to grow. For the first time, too, the library laid out considerable sums for the procurement of such manuscripts. The purchase of the oriental manuscripts of Samuel Clarke and Thomas Greaves, in 1670 and 1678 respectively, was merely the beginning. Nothing could compare with the opulent acquisitions of the 1690s—the Bodleian's glorious decade of oriental mania. The year 1692 marked the library's purchase—for £800—of 420 manuscripts from the estate of Edward Pococke. A few months later the princely sum of over £1,100 was disbursed to Robert Huntington for his important collection of some 600 manuscripts. Another substantial expenditure occurred in 1697, when the Bodleian paid £340 to Edward Bernard's widow for a collection of mostly oriental books and manuscripts. This

[91] *Letters of Bodley to James*, ed. Wheeler, 88; John Worthington, *Diary and Correspondence*, ed. J. Crossley (2 vols in 3 Chetham Soc. xiii, xxxvi, cxiv 1847–86) ii. 26; *Life of Prideaux*, 277–8.

[92] Queens' College, Cambridge, benefactors book.

[93] *Justa funebria Ptolemaei Oxoniensis* (Oxford 1613), 45; Matthias Pasor, *Oratio pro linguae Arabicae professione* (Oxford 1627), sig. B7[r-v]; Henry Jacob, *Philologiae anakalupterion* (Oxford 1652), 40–2; Worthington, *Diary and Correspondence* ii. 104.

unprecedented and aggressive policy of oriental acquisition was truly exceptional; the only comparable expense for western manuscripts during the entire second half of the seventeenth century was the purchase of the Hatton manuscripts in 1671 for £156.[94]

Indeed, this determined policy demonstrates that Oxford scholars were fully cognizant of the widespread reputation of the Bodleian's oriental holdings and, totally out of character, were willing to deplete both library and university funds in order to increase these holdings even further.[95] Conveniently, Bodley's Librarian since 1665 was the orientalist Thomas Hyde—who occasionally sold his own manuscripts to the library[96]—but he was obviously supported by many others. So it was with some justification that in 1692, following the acquisition of Pococke's manuscripts, Thomas Smith boasted that now the Bodleian surpassed the French Royal Library. The Bodleian Library thus became a Mecca to orientalists.[97] Already in 1639 Archbishop Ussher had sent Dudley Loftus to study there and for two years bore his expenses, while Simon Ockley also carried out most of his research in the library 'which [was] without question, the best furnished with oriental manuscripts of any in Europe'.[98]

This accumulation of manuscripts was clearly a by-product of the enthusiasm for the study of Arabic during the seventeenth century. Such enthusiasm was fanned in part by a line of foreign visitors to Oxford capable of offering instruction in the oriental languages. And none of these visitors proved to be more consequential for Arabic studies than Matthias Pasor. Escaping from the Thirty Years War, the German scholar arrived in England in late spring 1624, having spent the previous year at Leiden where he perfected his knowledge of Arabic and mathematics by conferring with Erpenius and Snel. At Oxford Pasor was sponsored by John Prideaux and Henry Briggs, and in June of that year he was incorporated MA. Shortly thereafter he left for Paris, where he studied for a few months with the Maronite Gabriel Sionita. However, in 1625 Pasor was back at Oxford. He took up residence at Exeter College and became, in the words of Henry Briggs, 'a very painfull and diligent reader for Arabicke and Chaldee', providing instruction both through public lectures and private tutorials. His public lectures were delivered

---

[94] Macray, *Annals of the Bodleian Library*, 134–5, 147–8, 161, 165–6; I. G. Philip, *The Bodleian Library in the Seventeenth and Eighteenth Centuries* (Oxford 1983), 60–1, 125 nn. 51–2.

[95] Obviously the enormous expenditure on manuscripts gravely affected the purchase of printed books. Hyde, however, preferred to put the blame on the building of the Ashmolean that 'so exhaust the university mony, that no books were bought in severall years after it': Macray, *Annals of the Bodleian Library*, 170.

[96] In 1692, for example, Hyde sold the library thirty-eight Arabic and Persian manuscripts for £50: ibid. 160.

[97] Bodl. MS Smith 47, fo 249. It is also important to note that the Bodleian's reputation in this field encouraged donations as well. John Selden bequeathed his oriental manuscripts to the library in 1654 and Narcissus Marsh also preferred to give his precious collection of oriental manuscripts—which included a great portion of Golius' manuscripts—to the Bodleian, instead of to the library he himself built in Dublin.

[98] G. T. Stokes, 'Dudley Loftus: a Dublin antiquary of the seventeenth century' in G. T. Stokes (ed.), *Some Worthies of the Irish Church* (London 1900), 37–40; A. J. Arberry, *Oriental Essays* (London 1960), 16.

twice a week during term and the cost shared by his auditors as well as by contributions from various colleges. Merton College, for example, contributed £2 in 1626 and £1 in 1627, while Magdalen College paid £5 in 1627.[99]

In 1627 Pasor published the inaugural lecture he had delivered the previous year, in which he made a passionate plea for the endowment of a lectureship for the oriental tongues at Oxford. Consciously perhaps, the lecture emulated in both structure and content the oration delivered by Erpenius at Leiden 'On the value of the Arabic language'. Like Erpenius, but with less fervour, Pasor noted the positive contribution of Islam to learning—not to mention the preservation of a large corpus of Greek writings in Arabic—in such subjects as mathematics, astronomy, medicine, history, and poetry. Fully aware of the English predilection for theology, however, Pasor dwelt more than his mentor on the value of Arabic for the study of scripture and, more particularly, for the confutation of Catholicism. He argued explicitly that both the Greek and the Hebrew tongues had been bountifully provided for in recognition of their indispensable contribution to the 'true' elucidation of the Old and New Testaments. Likewise, argued Pasor, other oriental languages needed endowment; the study of Arabic and Syriac would not only help illuminate the Hebrew text, but would also enable the proper study of various oriental texts of scripture—in a manner reminiscent of the important Latin translation of the Old Testament by Emanuel Tremelius and Franciscus Junius. Such a concentrated application to Arabic, concluded Pasor, would bring about the purging of the 'Augean stable of papistical superstitions, and wash away the filth of the school-men's sophistry'.[100]

Whether Pasor's eloquence or instruction actually contributed to the foundation of the Laudian professorship of Arabic in the following decade is not clear. Evident, however, is the warm welcome Pasor received at Oxford. By the end of 1627, Henry Briggs wrote to his friend Samuel Ward, master of Sidney Sussex College, Cambridge, that the Arabic lecture 'findeth diverse constante hearers, so that I hope we shall have some here able to interpret our Arabicke Euclide or any ordinarie booke written withe pointes. I hope your chancellor will set forwarde the like lecture withe you, and not permitt Erpenius his bokes to be spoiled for lacke of use.'[101] One among such 'constante hearers' appears to have been Thomas Crosfield, who attended Pasor's inaugural lecture on 19 October 1626 and at least a few subsequent lectures, for in his diary he recorded that the German started with the basics by providing elementary instruction in Arabic grammar.[102]

---

[99] Pasor's knowledge of Arabic was far from profound, as he himself admitted in his autobiography. Yet his presence at Oxford certainly contributed to the interest of many local scholars in the language. *Parentalia in piam memoriam reverendi & clarissimi D. Matthiae Pasoris* (Groningen 1658); Wood, *Fasti* i. 416; Wood, *Athenae* iii. 444–6; Bodl. MS Tanner 72, fo 228; Macray, *Reg. Magdalen* iii. 49; *The Theological Works of the Learned Dr Pocock*, ed. L. Twells (2 vols London 1740) i. 2.

[100] P. M. Holt, 'The background to Arabic studies in seventeenth-century England' in G. Russell (ed.), *The 'Arabick' Interest of the Natural Philosophers in Seventeenth-Century England* (Leiden 1994), 26.

[101] Bodl. MS Tanner 72, fo 211. Briggs referred to the purchase of Erpenius' manuscripts by the duke of Buckingham, which were presented to Cambridge University Library by Buckingham's widow following the duke's assassination.   [102] QCL MS 390, fos 20–1.

To a large extent, Oxford Arabists during the seventeenth century belonged to two distinct clusters: those who were undergraduates—or acquired their entrance into Arabic—during the 1620s; and those who came up to Oxford between 1655 and 1670. These two groups roughly corresponded, on the one hand with the period of pioneering enthusiasm prior to the foundation of the Laudian chair, and on the other with the most energetic phase in Edward Pococke's career as Arabic professor. It is important to remember, however, that with the exception of Pococke the first generation of Oxford Arabists amount to little more than names. Except for reputation, most have left little or no trace of their studies. Despite the paucity of sources, however, an attempt will be made to reconstruct what must have been a lively community of like-minded scholars and to determine the importance and scope of their achievement.

Pride of place undoubtedly goes to Edward Pococke. Having obtained his MA in 1626, the young linguist from Corpus Christi College proceeded during the next year or two to learn all that Pasor could teach him before applying himself in about 1628/9 to William Bedwell for further instruction. Bedwell was also the person to recommend Pococke to Archbishop Laud, and he may also have been responsible for Pococke's appointment as chaplain to the Levant Company merchants at Aleppo, a post Pococke took up in 1630. Pococke stayed in the east for six years, vastly expanding his knowledge of Arabic and Hebrew and purchasing numerous manuscripts both for Archbishop Laud and for himself. By 1634 Laud also had appointed Pococke as his first professor of Arabic at Oxford, and in 1636 the young orientalist made his leisurely way back to England. At Oxford, Pococke busied himself with preparations for his inaugural oration, scheduled for August 1636, and with inspecting and arranging the manuscripts Laud had dispatched to the Bodleian Library. Nevertheless, Pococke wished to return to the east, and within a year his Oxford friends Peter Turner and John Greaves were able to persuade the archbishop to consent. Pococke left England in the summer of 1637, returning only in 1641. For the next fifty years, dividing his time between Oxford and his living at Childrey, Pococke devoted himself to teaching, writing, and encouraging English orientalists.[103]

During Pococke's second journey to the east, Thomas Greaves deputized for him at Oxford. Greaves had been admitted scholar at Corpus Christi College in 1627 and, even if Pococke was not his tutor, the elder scholar soon came to appreciate the oriental learning of Greaves, even naming him his literary executor before leaving Oxford for his second voyage. Moreover, in 1636, when Pococke envisaged that Laud might procure a preferment for him that would necessitate his permanently relinquishing the Arabic chair, Pococke warmly recommended Greaves to the archbishop. His 'chamber fellow', Pococke informed Laud, was so thor-

[103] *Works of Pocock*, ed. Twells i. 2; H. R. Trevor-Roper, *Archbishop Laud 1573–1645* (London 1940, 2nd edn London 1962), 282; Hamilton, *William Bedwell*, 53; PRO SP 16/329/30, 16/381/75; P. M. Holt, 'An Oxford Arabist: Edward Pococke (1604–91)' in his *Studies in the History of the Near East* (London 1973), 3–26.

oughly initiated into Arabic, both by his own industry and through his brother John's help, that he would be the most obvious candidate to succeed him. The previous year Greaves had already been circulating his 'excellent notes' on an unspecified 'Arabique dialogue', which he hoped to publish. But, despite Selden's exertions with a publisher, the venture never materialized. Nevertheless Laud acceded to Pococke's recommendation to the extent of appointing Greaves to act as a substitute. For the next four years Greaves carried on lecturing at Oxford, and in 1639 he was consulted by the archbishop on the state of Arabic learning at the university and the course Laud should follow in endowing the chair in perpetuity.[104] Also, in 1639, Greaves published his own inaugural oration of two years before. Without attempting to be original, he contributed his share to what by then had become a well-trodden course of commending the study of Arabic for the access it promised to Greek treasures, lost in every tongue but the Arabic, to Muslim scientific and medical contributions, and, above all, for its pertinence to theology.[105]

John Gregory's attainments as a Hebrew scholar have already been discussed. But Gregory was equally well versed in Arabic, and at least knowledgeable in Syriac, Persian, Ethiopic, and Armenian. His various commentaries on scriptural texts included citations to a large number of Arabic manuscripts, both in the Bodleian Library and elsewhere. Naturally, he used various Arabic copies of scripture—he refers to the Arabic Pentateuch and Arabic versions of the Apocrypha in the Bodleian—but he also used manuscript copies of the Koran and various of its commentators. Gregory was also well versed in the authors of Muslim rituals, and on a few occasions he relied on Joseph the Egyptian's *codex conciliorum* from among the Roe manuscripts in the Bodleian. Among the histories he consulted, mention can be made of Ibn Hishām's history and the ecclesiastical history of Eutychius. Geographies included the so-called *Geographia Nubiensis*, as well as the manuscript geography of Abū Ishāq al-Istakhri and divers Arabic astronomical tables. Sometimes the magnitude of his reading is glimpsed by accident. Thus, in order to demonstrate the prevalent use among Muslims of 'If God will', he cited al-Tūsī's commentary on Euclid; elsewhere he quoted from an Arabic manuscript of Ibn Rushd's commentary on Aristotle.

Gregory was indefatigable in searching out oriental manuscript collections. Although the Bodleian Library, and especially the Laudian collection, provided him with much of the material he needed, he constantly sought additional sources. Thus, Eutychius' history was located in the Cambridge University Library, the Kitāb al Burhān at Balliol College, and a scriptural manuscript was consulted at Queen's College, Oxford. Private collections were also used. A certain Arabic theological manuscript was consulted in the library of Henry King, bishop of

[104] Wood, *Athenae* iii. 1061–2; PRO SP 16/329/39; Holt, 'An Oxford Arabist', 23 n. 10; *Miscellaneous Works of Mr John Greaves*, ed. T. Birch (2 vols London 1737) i, p. lxvii; Laud, *Works* v. 176–7, 237.

[105] Thomas Greaves, *De linguae Arabicae utilitate et praestantia* (Oxford 1639). Two decades later Greaves contributed the notes to the Persian text in Walton's Polyglot Bible.

Chichester. But the best private collection in England during the first half of the seventeenth century was the one amassed by John Selden, to which Gregory had free access. The few surviving letters between Selden and Gregory attest not only to the assistance Gregory provided to Selden's oriental studies, but also to his borrowing of manuscripts from the great scholar.[106]

William Seaman was a Balliol man who graduated MA in 1626. A keen orientalist, Seaman's strength lay in Turkish, a language he had studied since youth. In 1628 Seaman travelled to Constantinople in order to cultivate further his knowledge of the language, and stayed there for several years. On his return to England he settled at his living at Upton Scudamore in Wiltshire, where he diligently pursued his studies. In 1652 he translated into English Hojah Effendi's *Reign of the Sultan Orchan*, and shortly thereafter he began, at the urging of Robert Boyle, to translate the New Testament into Turkish, a work finally published in 1666. Four years later Seaman published his important Turkish grammar, a project in which he was assisted by Pococke.[107]

Henry Jacob, son of the English separatist of the same name, arrived at Oxford in 1628, having previously studied Arabic with Erpenius. Armed with Bedwell's letter of recommendation to the university's chancellor, he was admitted a member of Merton College and, in the words of Wood, 'having not so much logic and philosophy to carry him through the severe exercises of that society, the warden and fellows tacitly assign'd him philological lecturer'. The linguistic skills of Jacob quickly endeared him to Oxford and London scholars. In 1629 he was engaged in compiling the long-overdue catalogue of Hebraica at the Bodleian, at the same time assisting various Oxford scholars with advice and instruction in the oriental languages. Thomas Crosfield, for example, obtained directions from Jacob for the study of Greek and the oriental tongues, and Samuel Hartlib noted in his diary that Jacob had 'done most in *did[actic]a linguarum* in the Greeke ... In short tables hee would bring all the languages esp[ecially] the orientals.' By 1628 Jacob was also acquainted with Selden and became the most important of the many Oxford scholars to assist him in his oriental studies.[108]

Selden's intercession with Archbishop Laud, accompanied by the similar solicitations of Peter Turner and Henry Briggs, procured Jacob a fellowship at Merton College in 1636. To make amends for the intrusion, Laud informed the warden and fellows that Jacob, without any further charge to the college, would deliver a weekly public lecture 'upon some title of antiquity, in which he shall compare the Roman, Greek and oriental antiquities one with another'. Save for the inaugural address and

---

[106] The correspondence, revolving around astronomical, astrological, and chronological matters, is in Bodl. MS Selden *supra* 108, fos 52, 74, 243, 278a, 278e. Gregory was assisted in carrying out transcriptions for Selden by the veteran scholar Brian Twyne.

[107] *DNB* s.v. William Seaman; *The Works of the Honourable Robert Boyle*, ed. T. Birch (6 vols London 1772) vi. 511–12; Madan, *Oxford Books* iii. 122, 204–5, 247; *Works of Greaves*, ed. Birch i, p. xxxiv.

[108] Wood, *Athenae* iii. 329–33; G. W. Wheeler, 'Bibliotheca rabbinica (1629)', *Bodleian Quarterly Record* iii (1920–2), 144–6; QCL MS 390, fo 165; Sheffield University Library, Hartlib papers, 'Ephemerides', 1634, A5; Bodl. MS Selden *supra* 108, fo 17.

a few annotations upon it—hinting at the erudition to which his audience is likely to have been treated—none of his lectures or major writings survive, probably because he was ejected from his fellowship in 1648, his library confiscated and many of his papers scattered.[109]

Richard Busby, who arrived at Christ Church in 1624, acquired his knowledge of oriental languages at Oxford. After he became headmaster of Westminster School, he personally guided the systematic cultivation of Hebrew and Arabic there. Following the Restoration, as we have seen, he also established a lectureship in oriental languages at Christ Church. He was the author of a short Hebrew grammar, compiled for students and published at Oxford in 1708—said by Gagnier 'to be the best that has been yet made, and that 'tis preferable both to Buxtorf's and Schickard's'—as well as an Arabic grammar, which does not survive. His library was particularly rich in Hebrew and Arabic books, and the fruits of his own oriental compositions were circulated among such scholars as Samuel Clarke, Edmund Castell, and Edward Pococke, all of whose criticism he solicited.[110]

We have already mentioned Sampson Johnson, who was elected demy at Magdalen College in 1622. His assiduous pursuit of Hebrew and Arabic won him the recommendation of John Bainbridge to Archbishop James Ussher, in 1629, for the vacant post of chaplain to the Aleppo merchants. Johnson, wrote the Savilian professor,

> hath spent some years in the oriental languages, and being desirous to improve his knowledge therein, is content to adventure himself in the voyage; he would take the pains to preach once a week, but not oftener; being desirous to spend the rest of his time in perfecting his languages, and making such other observations as may tend to the advancement of learning.

If Ussher interceded on behalf of that 'learned gentleman of fair hopes', he was unsuccessful, for ultimately the position was given to Pococke.[111]

Two other renowned linguists were exact contemporaries at Queen's College—Gerard Langbaine and William Burton. Langbaine arrived at Oxford at the beginning of 1626 and quickly distinguished himself as a Grecian and oriental scholar. His considerable linguistic skills won him the provostship of Queen's College in 1644, as well as the high esteem of such scholars as Ussher and Selden. The former regarded Langbaine as 'the only man, on whose learning as well as friendship he could rely, to cast [his *Chronologia sacra*] into such a form, as might render them fit for the press'. Meanwhile the intimate collaboration of Langbaine and Selden

---

[109] Laud, *Works* vi. 461–2; Jacob, *Philologiae anakalupterion* (Oxford 1652), 1–45. The volume, published shortly before Jacob's death, was edited by Henry Birkhead, whose introduction provided much of the biographical detail for Wood's account, as well as the list of works written by Jacob.

[110] P. M. Holt, 'The treatment of Arab history by Prideaux, Ockley and Sale' in B. Lewis and P. M. Holt (eds), *Historians and the Middle East* (London 1962), 291 n. 3; Hearne, *Collections* ii. 307–8. For Busby see G. F. R. Barker, *Memoir of Richard Busby* (London 1895).

[111] Macray, *Reg. Magdalen* ii. 110, iii. 164–5, iv. 188; James Ussher, *The Whole Works*, ed. C. R. Elrington (17 vols Dublin 1847–64) xv. 447. In 1630 Johnson was hired to compile the list of Hebrew books given to the Bodleian by Henry Fetherstone: Macray, *Annals of the Bodleian Library*, 68 n.

had repercussions beyond Langbaine's contribution to Selden's scholarly work; time and again Langbaine called on his friend to use his considerable political influence in London. Selden's patronage proved crucial for the preservation of learning in Oxford under parliamentary rule. During the 1640s and 1650s Langbaine was the most important supporter of oriental studies at Oxford, promoting the career and publications of such scholars as Edward Pococke and Samuel Clarke.[112]

Langbaine died on 10 February 1658, some six weeks after the death of his friend William Burton. Burton had matriculated from Queen's College in 1626 and, like Langbaine, was an excellent Grecian as well as an esteemed orientalist. Shortly before his death Burton published a small and curious book, *Veteris linguae Persicae historia*, which, though not a profound contribution to oriental learning, nevertheless demonstrated the erudition of Burton and his taste for the abstruse comparative philology then in fashion.[113]

Lesser-known figures who belonged to this flourishing community of orientalists included James Lamb, who graduated MA in early 1620 as a member of St Mary Hall. A dedicated student of Arabic, he compiled a large Arabic grammar in three volumes, which remains in manuscript, as does his collection in four volumes towards an Arabic lexicon.[114] John Viccars entered Lincoln College in 1624 with a Cambridge BA. His *Decapla in psalmos* proves his considerable knowledge of Hebrew and Arabic.[115] William Pincke, also mentioned earlier, was not only a competent orientalist, but was one of those at Magdalen College from whom George Digby, earl of Bristol, received instruction in Arabic.[116]

All the scholars discussed thus far pursued oriental studies as an integral part of their theological or philological interests. A few additional members of the community, however, were exceptional in their pursuit of Arabic in order to further their mathematical and astronomical studies. Such individuals included all four Savilian professors appointed before the civil war, and a few of their students. Their importance for the larger community of Oxford orientalists can be gauged not only by the extent of their participation in the common philological pursuit; far more important, their close association with such influential figures as Laud, Ussher, and Selden allowed them to exploit the networks of patronage for the benefit of oriental studies in Oxford generally.

The senior member of this group of mathematicians was Henry Briggs. A friend of William Bedwell since their Cambridge days, Briggs was reunited with him in London after his election to the Gresham professorship of geometry in 1597. Undoubtedly, Briggs was assisted by Bedwell in his investigation of Arabic astronomical and chronological texts—a study he carried out with James Ussher. In 1619 Briggs moved to Oxford and Merton College as the first Savilian professor

---

[112] Wood, *Athenae* iii. 446–9, 438–40. For Langbaine's patronage see pp. 490 and 499–500 below.

[113] Wood, *Athenae* iii. 438–40. Marcus Boxhorn reprinted the *Historia* in 1720, adding elaborate notes to Burton's text.

[114] Lamb's manuscripts were given to the Bodleian in 1669: Wood, *Athenae* iii. 668; Macray, *Annals of the Bodleian Library*, 135.

[115] Wood, *Athenae* ii. 657.   [116] Macray, *Reg. Magdalen* iii. 166–8.

of geometry. As noted earlier, Briggs shared the enthusiasm of many Oxford men for Matthias Pasor's sojourn at Oxford and expressed his willingness to lobby for an Arabic lectureship at Cambridge. Nothing came of the latter, but, until his death in 1631, Briggs helped to encourage both mathematical and oriental studies at Oxford.[117]

Even more enthusiastic about Arabic was John Bainbridge, first Savilian professor of astronomy. Another collaborator of Ussher, Bainbridge wrote to the archbishop in 1626 that, having purchased an Arabic astronomical book, he could follow the tables

but the canons [the rules explaining the use of the tables] annexed are more difficult, and yet do so much the more incite me to find out that particular meaning, which is not possible without knowledge in the Arabic; wherefore I have made entrance into the rudiments thereof, and hope, *labore et constantia*, at length to be able to translate any Arabic book of mathematics. It is a difficult thing which I undertake, but the great hopes I have in that happy Arabia to find most precious stones for the adorning and enriching my *syntaxis mathematike*, do overcome all difficulties, besides the great satisfaction to see with mine own eyes . . . and not to be led hoodwinked by others, who though they may be expert in that tongue, yet without special skill in these particular sciences, cannot truly translate the Arabic; besides that every one hath a special purpose in his study of that language, taking no delight to follow another's course.

Bainbridge was not a person to proceed piecemeal. Having decided to undertake the study of Arabic, he demonstrated full appreciation of the best course to pursue by entreating Ussher to supply him with a good copy of the Koran, 'the only book whereby that language is attained'. The enthusiasm of Bainbridge, fired perhaps by Pasor's lectures, was also motivated by his study of ancient astronomy and chronology. Like Briggs, Bainbridge assisted Ussher's chronological studies and, in addition, by 1624 he had initiated a correspondence with Erpenius, attempting to take these topics further, but the sudden death of the Leiden professor cut short any such exchange. Bainbridge continued with his studies of Arabic astronomy and chronology, collaborating with both Selden and Ussher, and seeking William Bedwell's assistance as well. He also used the fruits of such studies in his Savilian lectures. In 1632 Bainbridge made another attempt to obtain information on various oriental astronomical manuscripts at Leiden by contacting Jakob Golius, Erpenius' successor and a notable mathematician, using the good services of Griffin Higgs, a former Mertonian and now a resident in Holland. Bainbridge never published his studies on ancient astronomy and chronology. After his death, however, his former student and friend John Greaves edited one small work, the *Canicularia* (Oxford 1648), which demonstrates the extensive use made by Bainbridge of oriental astronomical sources.[118]

[117] For instances of the exchange of books and information between Briggs, Ussher, and Bedwell, see Ussher, *Works* xv. 64, 89; Bodl. MS Rawlinson c. 849, fo 5.

[118] Ussher, *Works* xv. 351–2; Thomas Smith, 'De vita . . . Joannis Bainbridgii' in his *Vitae quorundam eruditissimorum et illustrium virorum* (London 1707), 11; Trinity College, Dublin MS 382, fos 86–7, 91–2, 101–2ᵛ; Bodl. MS Selden *supra* 108, fo 230.

Of Peter Turner little is known. Wood described him as a universal scholar who excelled in Hebrew and Arabic as well as in Greek and the mathematical sciences. Such erudition explains the respect Archbishop Ussher expressed for his learning, as well as Turner's intimacy with both Selden and Laud. At any rate, Turner succeeded Briggs as Savilian professor of geometry in 1631. Thanks to his great familiarity with Archbishop Laud, he was in a good position not only to promote Arabic studies at Oxford, but to entice Laud into supporting the eastern travels of both Pococke and Greaves during the 1630s.[119]

Our knowledge of John Greaves is far more extensive. Having been elected to a fellowship at Merton College in 1624, Greaves was greatly encouraged in his study of the oriental languages—as well as of mathematics and astronomy—by Briggs, Bainbridge, and Turner, and he grew to be an extremely competent linguist. Like Bainbridge, Greaves was absorbed with the study of ancient astronomy and chronology, and came to appreciate the importance of collecting and studying a wide variety of Arabic and Persian manuscripts. It was for the further pursuit of such studies that Greaves left England in 1635, travelling to Leiden for the sake of Golius' lectures and the manuscripts in the university library. From here he proceeded to Paris where he met another keen mathematician and orientalist, Claude Hardy, then on to Italy, before returning to England the following year. Between 1637 and 1639 Greaves embarked on his great journey to the east, intending to carry out Bainbridge's ambitious scheme of astronomical observations and to purchase manuscripts.

After his return to England, Greaves commenced a major project of editing and translating into Latin various Persian and Arabic astronomical and geographical tables. He may also have composed commentaries to such editions—the title-page of some of his publications stated as much—but none were ever published. Among Greaves's extant works mention can be made of parts of Ulugh Beg's astronomical tables, which Greaves appended to his edition of Bainbridge's *Canicularia*, Shah Cholgi's astronomical tables, an edition of the geographical tables by Ulugh Beg and Nassar Eddin, and a chronological treatise based on Persian and Arabic tables. The skill of Greaves in Persian also prompted Selden to request him before the civil war to publish a Persian grammar. Owing to the lack of the correct fount, however, publication was delayed until 1649. But the intention to publish a Persian lexicon, for which Greaves collected some 6,000 words, never bore fruit.[120]

The culmination of the passionate interest in Arabic studies at Oxford during the 1620s and 1630s was the establishment of the Laudian professorship. The sources of Laud's own interest in oriental languages are, however, somewhat obscure. In general, as Trevor-Roper has suggested, the archbishop believed in the 'divine and infallible revelation by which the originals of scripture were first written'. Such a

---

[119] Wood, *Athenae* iii. 306; John Ward, *The Lives of the Professors of Gresham College* (London 1740), 133.
[120] Thomas Smith, 'De vita ... Joannis Gravii', in his *Vitae*; Ward, *Lives of the Professors of Gresham College*, 135–52; *Miscellaneous Works of Greaves*, ed. Birch.

conviction, however, did not preclude the endorsement by Laud of the recent fruits of higher criticism, nor an unwillingness to accept any manuscript as infallible. Rather, he believed only a close scrutiny and collation of sundry manuscripts could establish a 'true' text. Given this outlook, his patronage of both Greek and oriental studies is understandable.[121]

During the presidency of Laud, in 1617, St John's College had purchased an Arabic dictionary. Laud may also have been influenced by the general enthusiasm for Arabic learning that swept England in the late 1620s, when pressure was put on influential individuals actively to support such studies. Thus Laud's own former patron the duke of Buckingham, having been appointed chancellor of Cambridge University in 1626, was induced to donate to the university library the manuscript collection of Erpenius which he had purchased the previous year. As chancellor of Oxford University, Laud probably came under pressure to do something similar. Regardless, by November 1630 Laud, then bishop of London, drew a catalogue of 'acts of bounty' he projected to effect, and amongst these he resolved to 'erect an Arabick lecture in Oxford, at least for his life-time, his estate as he supposed not being able for more, that this may lead the way'.[122]

In accordance with Laud's wishes, Pococke was to lecture every Wednesday during vacation and during Lent for one hour, and then make himself available to students between 1 p.m. and 4 p.m. In his lectures, the professor was required to explain 'the work of some approved and ancient author, in which the proprieties of the language and the elegance of expression are remarkable'. Laud further stipulated that the professor's lectures should provide 'a clear explanation of the words and grammatical meaning of the author, and point out all that has a reference to the grammar and peculiarities of the language; and shall also show, whenever occasion offers, the agreement of the Arabic language with the Hebrew and Syriac'.[123]

Pococke delivered his inaugural oration on 10 August 1636, and immediately proceeded 'with a course of lectures upon the proverbs ascribed to the Caliph Ali'.[124] In contrast to what has been argued above was not the duty of the regius professor of Hebrew, the Laudian professor was entrusted with the basic grammatical drilling of many of his auditors, which required him to devise a two-tier system of instruction, for beginners and for advanced students.

The text with which Pococke launched his teaching career was the edition of Ali's proverbs published by Golius in 1629.[125] As Holt has demonstrated, Pococke used the text in conjunction with the two grammatical works compiled by

[121] Trevor-Roper, *Archbishop Laud*, 273–84; H. R. Trevor-Roper, 'The Church of England and the Greek Church in the time of Charles I' in D. Baker (ed.), *Religious Motivation: biographical and sociological problems for the church historian* (London 1978), 213–40.

[122] SJM computus annuus 1617, fo 41 (I owe this reference to Dr N. Tyacke); John Rushworth, *Historical Collections* (4 pts London 1659–1701, another edn London 1721) ii. (1), 74. Laud subsequently recorded, apropos this item, 'Done. I have now settled it forever': Laud, *Works* iii. 255. An Arabic professorship was established at Cambridge in 1632, by Thomas Adams.

[123] *Statutes*, trans. Ward i. 295; *Works of Pocock*, ed. Twells i. 9–10.

[124] Holt, 'An Oxford Arabist', 6.

[125] *Proverbia quaedam Alis Imperatoris Muslemici, et Carmen Tograi*, ed. Jakob Golius (Leiden 1629).

Erpenius: *Rudimenta linguae Arabicae* and the *Grammatica Arabica*. By the late 1650s Pococke had also added, mainly for the use of the more advanced students, Golius' *Arabicae linguae tyrocinium*, basically a reworking of Erpenius' larger grammar that Golius had augmented with fresh material. By this time Pococke was already lecturing on another Arabic text published by Golius, the *Carmen Tograi*, a text that Pococke republished with an extensive commentary in 1661.[126]

The *Carmen Tograi*, as well as the manuscript lecture notes discovered by Holt, attest to the diligence and thoroughness that animated Pococke's teaching of Arabic. As was his custom with Hebrew, Pococke assigned his students a short, pleasing, and relatively simple text; his lecture consisted of a meticulous analysis of nearly every word and concept in the text, accompanied by extensive etymologies and frequent comparisons with words and concepts in both Hebrew and Syriac. Occasionally Pococke would digress by providing copious explanatory notes setting out the historical and cultural context, or would explicate matters pertaining to the theological concerns of his auditors—most commonly in terms of scriptural exegesis.

The ownership of Arabic books by Oxford students enables us not only to corroborate the information derived from Pococke's lecture notes and publications, but also to discern the divergence of motives that animated the various auditors. Most of the students who bothered with Arabic did so as an extension of their Hebrew studies; most probably these students were furnished with grammar and vocabulary, and their reading material confined to scripture. Henry Stringer's donation of books to New College library in 1654 is perhaps representative of the holdings of an amateur Arabist: an Arabic grammar, the lexicons of Raphalengius and Golius, Erpenius' Arabic New Testament, and Gabriel Sionita's edition of the Psalms.[127] The more ambitious students went further. Edward Bernard's 1658 catalogue of books demonstrates the full range of Pococke's teaching. Besides Golius' Arabic grammar, Greaves's Persian grammar, and two Syriac grammars, Bernard owned the *Proverbia quaedam Alis*, Ravius's edition of a particular Surah of the Koran, Pococke's *Specimen*, and Erpenius' *Historia Saracenica*.[128]

In sharp contrast to the vibrant atmosphere of the 1620s and 1630s, during the next one and a half decades, for obvious reasons, oriental studies languished. The major interruption created by Charles I's removal to the university, the siege and eventual fall of Oxford in 1646, and, finally, the protracted process of replacing royalist fellows with 'loyal' ones, took a heavy toll on learning at Oxford. By the time the dust had settled, almost the entire first generation of orientalists and their patrons were gone. By 1658 John Bainbridge, John Greaves, John Gregory, Henry Jacob, William Burton, John Selden, Gerard Langbaine, and James Ussher had all

---

[126] *Works of Pocock*, ed. Twells i. 58–9; Holt 'An Oxford Arabist', 6–7.

[127] NCA benefactors book, p. 84; Samuel Lee (MA Magdalen Hall 1648) owned an Arabic Testament and Golius' lexicon.

[128] Bodl. MS Lat. misc. f. 11, fos 13ᵛ–17.

died. Within ten years Samuel Clarke and James Lamb would also be dead, while Thomas Greaves would have retired to the country. Thus it was left to Pococke to train, almost single-handedly, a new generation of Arabists at Oxford. This he did with remarkable success, principally between 1655 and 1675. In this task he was aided by the equally successful efforts of Richard Busby at Westminster School to equip his students with the rudiments of Arabic before they headed to Oxford.

The few exceptions to the rule, those orientalists who came to Oxford during the 1640s, ought to be mentioned first. Samuel Clarke, 'right famous for oriental learning', arrived at Oxford in 1640, but left four years later. He graduated MA upon his return in 1648 and was immediately designated by Gerard Langbaine as *architypographus* of the university, a position he would secure only a decade later. In the meantime Langbaine obtained for Clarke the mastership of a boarding school at Islington, a position that enabled him to participate in Walton's edition of the Polyglot Bible. His knowledge of the oriental languages, Clarke acknowledged later, he owed to Pococke. His accomplishments in Hebrew and Aramaic have already been noted; to Arabic studies he contributed a small treatise on Arabic prosody—appended to Pococke's *Carmen Tograi*—which was edited and published by Clarke. Among his papers in the Bodleian Library are a few manuscript compositions he had hoped to publish. For example, he seems to have contemplated a new edition of Abulfeda's *Geography*, for which purpose he collated the available printed text with various manuscripts; he compiled a Persian and Turkish lexicon, and left unfinished collections for an Arabic vocabulary.[129]

Zachary Bogan—who graduated BA from Corpus Christi College in 1646 and continued his studies at Oxford until his death in 1659—was reputed to be a skilled orientalist, second only to his friend and mentor Pococke. Unfortunately, only allusions to such learning are to be found in his extant writings.[130] More obscure still was the orientalist Henry Chapman (created MA in 1649 as a member of Magdalen Hall), the compiler of the index to Pococke's edition of *Porta Mosis*.[131]

The sad state of learning in general, and of oriental studies in particular, during the 1640s and early 1650s may be illustrated by the Oxford career of that eccentric and crafty orientalist, Christian Ravius. This wandering German, who was employed by Ussher to procure manuscripts during the 1630s, had hoped that the ascendancy of the puritans would provide some opportunities for him. He taught oriental languages in London in 1647–8 and the support of Samuel Hartlib (and perhaps Selden too) resulted in Ravius's intrusion in March 1649 as fellow, librarian, and lecturer in oriental languages at Magdalen College. The ambition of Ravius, however, reached higher, and he conspired to succeed Pococke as professor during the bleak days when the royalist Pococke faced—in addition to being ousted

---

[129] Wood, *Athenae* iii. 882–5; Clarke's correspondence is in BL Add. MS 22,905. In 1659 Thomas Cawton, who was instructed in oriental languages by Robert Sherringham in Holland, arrived at Merton College in order to study with Clarke, and remained at Oxford for some three years: Wood, *Athenae* iii. 1108.

[130] Wood, *Athenae* iii. 476–7, 331; John Prince, *Worthies of Devon* (Exeter 1701), 107.

[131] Wood, *Fasti* ii. 121; *Works of Pocock*, ed. Twells i. 45.

from his Christ Church canonry—ejection from his chairs. Ravius undoubtedly antagonized not a few Oxonians by this attempt. John Greaves who, like Edward Bernard later, had little regard for Ravius's scholarship, wrote to Pococke that Ravius had proposed to dedicate one of his works to him, the very thought of which sent Greaves into a 'cold sweat'. Wood recalled that Ravius found only a few students at Oxford and within a few months he resigned his Magdalen appointments and set sail for Sweden where he was given a professorship in the oriental languages.[132]

Nearly all the distinguished Arabists arrived at Oxford during the 1650s. Edward Bernard was elected scholar at St John's College in 1655 and rapidly mastered Hebrew, Arabic, and Syriac, to which he later added Coptic as well. The genius of Bernard in the mathematical sciences made him the only scholar among the second generation of Oxford Arabists to pursue vigorously those studies that had animated Bainbridge and Greaves three decades earlier. Thus in early 1669 Bernard travelled to Leiden to consult the Arabic manuscripts bequeathed by Joseph Scaliger and Levinus Warner, in particular the Arabic manuscript of Apollonius' *Conics*,—which included books v to vii missing in the Greek original. He planned an edition and translation of the text, but as would be the case with nearly all his grand ventures, the project failed to materialize in his lifetime. In due course Bernard also envisaged the ambitious project of publishing a multi-volume edition of ancient Greek and Arabic mathematicians, to be printed by John Fell's newly invigorated Oxford press. But save for a prospectus nothing came of the project. Until his death on 12 January 1697, Bernard busied himself in assisting the philological publications of other scholars—one project would have been a joint publication with Pococke of Arabic proverbs on which Pococke had laboured since 1635—in addition to publishing short works of his own, such as a treatise on ancient weights and measures. But the extent of Bernard's knowledge of oriental languages can only be deduced from a scrutiny of the extensive manuscript collection and the annotated printed books eventually purchased by the Bodleian Library. There one may find a lifetime's labour of transcripts and notes on Greek and Arabic mathematical, chronological, and scriptural texts. It was, perhaps, appropriate that the death of such a devoted philologist was hastened by his desire to attend, despite his ill health, the celebrated sale of Jakob Golius' manuscripts in Holland.[133]

Robert Huntington entered Merton College in 1652, graduating MA a decade later. A retiring scholar and dedicated orientalist, Huntington obtained the chaplainship at Aleppo, where he arrived early in 1671. For the next ten years he travelled extensively in the near east, perfected his knowledge of the oriental languages, and engaged in massive purchases of manuscripts both for himself and for his

[132] Macray, *Reg. Magdalen* iv. 78–9; Wood, *Athenae* iii. 113–33; *CSPD 1649–50*, 564; *Works of Pocock*, ed. Twells i. 33; K. M. Pogson, 'The wanderings of Apollonius', *Bodleian Quarterly Record* iii (1920–2), 152–3.
[133] Thomas Smith, *Vita Edwardi Bernardi*, appended to his *Roberti Huntingtoni ... epistolae* (London 1704); *Biographia Britannica* (6 vols London 1747–66) ii. 263–7.

Oxford friends, Edward Pococke, Edward Bernard, and Narcissus Marsh. He returned briefly to Merton in 1682, but within two years he left for Ireland, where Marsh was instrumental in securing for him a string of preferments. Like most orientalists of this Oxford group, Huntington published very little. Our knowledge of his learning has to be derived from his correspondence, part of which was published by Thomas Smith, and from his great collection of manuscripts.[134]

Bernard's and Huntington's lifelong friend, Thomas Smith, entered Queen's College in 1657, graduating MA in 1663. His early application to oriental studies, particularly Hebrew and Aramaic, has been discussed above, along with the lectures he delivered in the early 1660s on the subject of the 'worship towards the east', which incorporated the early fruits of his Arabic studies. In 1668 Smith went as chaplain to the English ambassador at Constantinople where he pursued both his oriental studies and his researches on the Greek Church. His observations were published in Latin, then in English translation as *Remarks upon the Manners, Religion and Government of the Turks* (1678). Although a prolific author, Smith published little else on oriental learning. Nevertheless, interspersed in his many writings and among his numerous letters is abundant evidence of his wide reading and immersion in such studies.[135]

Both Bernard and Smith were befriended at Oxford and later by Narcissus Marsh, who entered as a commoner at Magdalen Hall in 1654. By his own admission, while an undergraduate Marsh applied himself to 'old philosophy, mathematicks, and oriental languages', and before graduating BA in 1658 he 'had made a good progress in them all'. Marsh published little, and nothing at all on oriental studies. He did assume the role, however, of patron to oriental scholars—in particular Robert Huntington and Edward Bernard—and amassed an important collection of oriental manuscripts, comprised mostly of manuscripts which Huntington had purchased for him in the east, and the Golius manuscripts purchased for Marsh by Bernard.[136]

Among the lesser-known students of Arabic, mention should be made of George Hooper, who was elected a Westminster student at Christ Church in 1657. Having laid the foundations of his Hebrew and Arabic scholarship under Richard Busby, Hooper proceeded to pursue Hebrew, Arabic, and Syriac under Pococke. He graduated BA in 1661 and, according to his daughter, used his languages extensively in his unpublished commentary on the Old Testament.[137] Hooper's intimate friend

---

[134] For Thomas Smith's life of Huntington see *Roberti Huntingtoni . . . epistolae*, pp. i–xxxvi. A partial rendering into English is 'The life and travels of . . . Robert Huntington', *Gentleman's Magazine* xcv pt 1 (1825), 11–15, 115–19, 218–21.

[135] *DNB* s.v. Thomas Smith (1638–1710)

[136] 'Archbishop Marsh's Diary', *British Magazine* xxviii (1845), 18. The most recent account of Marsh and the library of printed books he founded in Dublin is M. McCarthy, *All Graduates and Gentlemen: Marsh's library* (Dublin 1980).

[137] Copies of the textbooks used by Busby, including Erpenius' *Grammatica Arabica*, are still to be found among the books given by Hooper to the cathedral library of Wells. Hooper was one of Busby's favourite pupils, and subsequently a trustee of Busby's will. W. M. Marshall, *George Hooper 1640–1727* (Sherborne 1976), 2–3, 5.

and fellow student of Arabic at Oxford was Thomas Ken, the future bishop of Bath and Wells, who arrived at New College in 1656. Our knowledge of his studies at Oxford is confined to the books he acquired, which included Erpenius' grammar, Golius' lexicon, Erpenius' *Historia Saracenica*, and Pococke's two editions of Bar Hebraeus.[138]

Two younger orientalists, Humphrey Prideaux and William Guise, have been discussed above in connection with their Hebrew studies. Prideaux's mastery of Arabic is, however, not easy to ascertain. When in 1701 William Byrd the younger met that 'master of abundance of learning', he noted that Prideaux 'valued himself particularly upon his skill in Arabique, by virtue of which he has conversed more with the Alcoran and the comments upon it, than some other doctors have with the Bible'.[139] Yet Prideaux's qualifications as a prominent Arabist are debatable. He was predominantly a Hebrew scholar whose most important Islamic publication, as will be seen below, was derivative. Nevertheless, Prideaux serves as a fitting illustration of the general calibre of students trained by Pococke.[140]

William Guise, on the other hand, who graduated MA from All Souls in 1677, was an exceptional orientalist and undoubtedly would have been the natural successor to Pococke had he not died aged 30. 'The greatest miracle' in the knowledge of oriental languages, Guise displays in his posthumous Latin translation and elaborate commentary on the Mishnaic order *Zeraim* (the Hebrew part of which has been discussed earlier) his mastery of Arabic and his facility with Syriac, Samaritan, Persian, and Armenian—all in an exemplary Pocockian manner. Naturally, many of his references are to Arabic lexicographers. The great Arabic dictionary *Qāmūs* by al-Fīrūzābādī and the equally famous *Sahāh* by al-Jauharī are the most often cited. Given the nature of the Mishnaic text, Guise makes good use of Islamic literature relating to medicine, botany, zoology, and veterinary medicine in his meticulous explication of the Hebrew text. Among his sources were: Ibn al-Baytār's great pharmacopoeia *Al-Jāmi* (Guise also refers to al-Baytār's commentary on Dioscorides); Muhammad ibn Musa al-Damīrī's *Hayāt al-Hayawān* (Life of animals); al-Zahrāwī's (Abulcasis') great medical encyclopedia *Al-Tasrīf li-man ajiza an al-talīf*, and Abū Hanīfa al-Dīnawarī's *Kitāb al-Nabāt*. In addition he quotes from the geographies of al-Idrīsī and Abulfeda. Such extensive knowledge of printed, and especially manuscript, sources can be further corroborated by Guise's unpublished writings.[141] One represents the young scholar's transcription and collation of the

---

[138] E. H. Plumptre, *Thomas Ken* (2 vols London 1888) ii. 296.

[139] *The Correspondence of the Three William Byrds of Westover, Virginia 1684–1776*, ed. M. Tinling (2 vols Charlottesville Va. 1977) i. 211.

[140] For Prideaux see *Life of Prideaux*; R. W. Ketton-Cremer, 'Humphrey Prideaux' in his *Norfolk Assembly* (London 1957), 63–91, 228; Holt, 'The treatment of Arab history', 290–4; for an affectionate letter from Prideaux to Busby see Nichols, *Literary History of the Eighteenth Century* iv. 395–6.

[141] Wood, *Athenae* iv. 114–15; *Letters of Prideaux to Ellis*, ed. Thompson, 44, 103; Bodl. MS Marsh 533; *Epicedia universitatis oxoniensis in obitum illustrissimae principis Annae Ducissae Eboracensis* (Oxford 1671); Madan, *Oxford Books* iii. 249–50; T. Hyde, *Syntagma dissertationum quas olim auctor doctissimus Thomas Hyde*, ed. G. Sharpe (2 vols Oxford 1767) i, p. vii. See also p. 465 above for Bernard's publication of Guise's translation of *Zeraim* (Oxford 1690).

Koran, while others include his extensive collections from Arabic historians and geographers.

Mention ought also be made of the younger Edward Pococke, who was groomed to be an orientalist by his father. In 1671 he published the Arabic text and Latin translation of Ibn Tufayl's *Risalat Hayy ibn Yaqzan* as *Philosophus autodidactus*, though no mention was made of the manuscript translation carried out by the elder Pococke as early as 1645. Edward Pococke the younger continued his oriental studies at Oxford, gaining some eminence therein, but failed in his bid to succeed his father as Laudian professor of Arabic. As a consequence, the younger Pococke aborted his projected edition of Abd-al-Latîf's account of Egypt.[142]

Pococke's death on 10 September 1691 marked the end of an era. A resident of Oxford for over seven decades, the venerable regius professor of Hebrew and Laudian professor of Arabic epitomized not only the conscientious teaching and committed scholarship that distinguished Oxford in the seventeenth century, but also the zeal for philology that characterized most students during this period. By the time the 87-year-old Pococke died, young scholars were no longer being roused to difficult and esoteric studies. As for the old guard, their numbers were rapidly dwindling.[143] Initially, though, the future still appeared promising. The Oxford electors were determined not only to prefer the best available candidates, but, sensibly, they resolved to separate the two chairs. The choice of the Laudian professor of Arabic was relatively simple. Thomas Hyde was the most obvious candidate both in terms of scholarship (the only other serious contender was the younger Edward Pococke) and political support, and he was duly elected on 22 December 1691.[144]

The regius professorship of Hebrew, on the other hand, proved more difficult to fill. Even before Pococke's death, Edward Bernard, who was known to have contemplated for some time surrendering his Savilian professorship in astronomy in return for a theological position, was approached; but, as Bernard indicated to Thomas Smith, he had small ambition for the chair.[145] Humphrey Prideaux was also offered the chair, but he too declined, partly because of his antipathy towards

---

[142] Holt, 'An Oxford Arabist', 14.

[143] An instructive parallel is provided by the case of Edinburgh. As in Leiden, it was the town elders who paid the salaries of the professors and fluctuation in interest could affect the salaries attached to each chair. Thus in 1640, at the height of oriental mania, Julius Conrad Otto was appointed to teach Hebrew and oriental languages for 1200 merks p.a. (c. £65). By 1674 the professor's stipend was reduced to 700 merks 'in consequence of the few students of divinity that attend him', and by 1701, following the resignation of Alexander Rule, an open search failed to produce candidates—not surprising since by then the remuneration had been further reduced to 500 merks (c. £27). A. Grant, *The Story of the University of Edinburgh* (2 vols London 1884) i. 200–1, 254, 296, ii. 11–12, 404.

[144] Wood, *Life and Times* iii. 373, 379. Hearne stated years later of the younger Pococke ''tis said he understands Arabick and other oriental tongues very well, but wanted friends to get him into the professorships of Hebrew and Arabick at Oxon': Hearne, *Collections* ii. 63. For an exceptionally warm remembrance of Pococke senior written by Locke in 1704, see *The Correspondence of John Locke*, ed. E. S. De Beer (8 vols Oxford 1976–89) viii. 37–42.

[145] Bodl. MS Smith 47, fo 90.

his former colleagues at Christ Church, but more significantly because of his grow-ing weariness of Hebrew. As he wrote to John Ellis on 12 October 1691: 'I nau-seate that learning, and am resolved to loose noe more time upon it.'[146] At the same time, rumours began to circulate in London that Friedrich Spanheim the younger, the Leiden professor of theology, was seriously being considered for the position. In fact, the process of electing a new regius professor had apparently come to a halt until the king returned to England from Flanders.[147] Nevertheless, the rumours persisted to the day of election, 14 November 1691, at which time Roger Altham of Christ Church was elected. The choice proved unfortunate. According to Wood, Altham did not lecture 'because he is no Hebritian. Yet being a Christ Church man he was admitted canon. Partiality! Others of other houses were fit for it; but the place is reserved for a Christ Church man.' This time Wood did not exaggerate. Already in 1675 Prideaux had expressed his opinion that Altham was 'a very mean scholar', while the day after the election Bernard wrote to Thomas Smith that the choice of Altham would prove to be a great check to the study of Hebrew at Oxford. Bernard's prophecy was fulfilled. In the wake of Altham's inaugural oration, Bernard informed Smith that the address took the form of a long sermon on the tongues of Babel, largely 'plagiarizing' Walton's prole-gomena to the Polyglot Bible and painfully demonstrating that the new professor understood little of his profession.[148]

Altham would retain the professorship until his death in 1715, save for the period 1697–1703 when, following his refusal to take certain oaths to the new monarchy, he was forced to resign. Thomas Hyde seized the opportunity to add yet another position to the many he already held, thus reuniting the two chairs once again. Nevertheless, matters hardly improved. Hyde, it seems, cared as little for the toil of teaching as he did for the inherent 'drudgery' involved in his post as Bodley's Librarian. Hyde's letter of resignation as librarian in 1701 gave a clear indication of his sentiments: 'I may have my time free to myself to digest and finish my papers and collections upon hard places of scripture, and to fit them for the press; seing that lectures (though we must attend upon them) will do but little good, hearers being scarce and practicers more scarce.'[149] Hence, despite his greater suitability for the position, compared to Altham, Hyde's short tenure as regius professor of Hebrew did not augur well for Hebrew studies. Leaving aside the issue of com-mitment, however, even in terms of Hebrew scholarship Hyde was far inferior to Pococke. Oddly—and suspiciously—all his Hebrew writings were composed (or advertised) just prior to the death of Pococke, whom he aspired to succeed. His

---

[146] *Letters of Prideaux to Ellis*, ed. Thompson, 150. According to his biographer, Prideaux lived to regret his decision: *Life of Prideaux*, 89.

[147] Bodl. MS Smith 59, fos 57, 59; Bodl. MS Smith 57, fos 229, 231.

[148] Wood, *Life and Times* iii. 375; *Letters of Prideaux to Ellis*, ed. Thompson, 28; Bodl. MS Smith 47, fos 96, 104. Thomas Hearne asserted in 1706 that Altham procured the professorship 'by the interest that Dr Radcliff the physitian had at that time with the earl of Portland', and that he was 'a good scholar, and a most excellent preacher, but as yet has done nothing remarkable in the way of his profession': Hearne, *Collections* i. 228.

[149] CL MS Wake 16, fo 50, printed in Macray, *Annals of the Bodleian Library*, 170.

most celebrated Hebrew publication, the translation of Abraham Farrisol's *Itinerary*, was said by Edward Bernard and Thomas Hearne to have been greatly indebted to the assistance of Abendana—assistance that went unacknowledged, as did Abendana's composition of a small treatise on chess which Hyde printed under his own name. In addition, Hyde's design to publish a new edition of the *More nevukhim*, a project he announced in a 1691 prospectus, never materialized. Indeed, one suspects that the alleged dearth of financial backing claimed by Hyde as reason for the miscarriage served as a convenient pretext for a scholar who was predominantly interested in the Persian and Arabic languages.[150]

Whether the attitude of Hyde discouraged students, or whether the apathy of students confirmed his indifference, the fact remains that he produced few—if any—orientalists. This dearth certainly worried various government officials, who feared that his death would deprive England of those translating and interpreting skills Hyde had provided for the government for decades. This concern was in large part responsible for the foundation in 1699 of the lord almoner's lectureships in Arabic at both Oxford and Cambridge, intended to train young scholars for government service. Hyde was appointed as instructor. But once again his concern was more with remuneration than with students and, as he found the proposed salary of £20 'insulting', he searched for a way out: 'I shall desire to be excused from medling in it', he wrote to John Postlethwayte on 4 May 1702,

not so much for the value of a little money, but because the thing is undecent and by everybody laughed at and ridiculed, as we have found by experience already: and therefore this I would avoyd. I suppose the queen will as easily grant the pension to be a little larger, if it's so proposed to her. Though after all, I had rather be wholly excused from both trouble and profit.[151]

As for Hyde's mastery of oriental languages, a careful study of his scholarship is still a desideratum. For the present, however, it may be safe to argue that despite his frequent pretensions, Hyde was a rather mediocre orientalist, except for Persian in which he excelled. Prideaux, even if biased, scoffed in 1682 that Hyde 'doth not understand common sense in his own language, and therefore I cannot conceive how he can make sense of anything that is writ in another'. The correspondence between Thomas Smith and Edward Bernard substantiates such sentiments, though with less bluntness. After the professor's death in 1703, Hearne recalled that, Hyde's reputation on the continent notwithstanding, 'he was disrespected in Oxford by several men, who now speak well of him'.[152]

---

[150] Bodl. MS Smith 47, fo 92; Hearne, *Collections* iii. 76. Hyde's Hebraic publications during his *anni mirabiles* are Abraham Farissol, *Itinera mundi* (Oxford 1691) and *De ludis orientalibus libri duo* (Oxford 1693). We may add that of some thirty-one books that Hyde 'designed for the press if he lives to finish them, he having already done something towards all of them', only three would have involved the application of Hebrew language in a serious manner; see the list in Wood, *Athenae* iv. 525–7.

[151] L. S. Sutherland, 'The origin and early history of the lord almoner's professorship in Arabic at Oxford', *Bodleian Library Record* x (1978–82), 168–9.

[152] *Letters of Prideaux to Ellis*, ed. Thompson, 133; Hearne, *Collections* i. 235. John Wallis, Hyde's successor as Laudian professor, argued that Hyde was ignorant of Turkish: Bodl. MS Smith 54, fo 67.

The example set by Hyde was carried to the extreme by his successor John Wallis (professor 1703–38) who, remarked Hearne, 'if ever he understood the language may be supposed now to have forgott it, he having the character of one that keeps much company and few books, intirely neglecting his studies'. As Marshall has aptly summarized the career of this Laudian professor: 'Not only did John Wallis give no lectures for most of his long tenure, but he did nothing to advance knowledge either.'[153]

The events surrounding the appointment in 1738 of Wallis's successor as Laudian professor, Thomas Hunt, provide additional confirmation of how little regard was attached to the study of Arabic—beyond its application to theology, and its intimate affinity with Hebrew—in the first half of the eighteenth century. Lancelot Blackburne, archbishop of York, advised Hunt to deliver Hebrew lectures, notwithstanding his election to the Arabic professorship. Hunt complied to the extent that both in his inaugural oration and in private he was at pains to show 'how much the knowledge of the Hebrew may be improved by the study of the Arabic, Syriac and the other oriental languages, but especially the Arabic'.[154]

The ensuing lack of inspired teaching and of genuine concern for the recruitment of disciples contributed to the waning of interest in oriental studies. By the early years of the eighteenth century, Oxford scholars almost uniformly lamented this development. When William Wake received from Arthur Charlett what appeared to him to be an overly sanguine representation of the state of humanistic learning at Oxford, the archbishop retorted: 'I assure you that part of polite learning which consists in the learned languages, Latin and Greek (for Hebrew I shall except as belonging to divines alone) has much decayed.' Indeed, the very exception of Hebrew indicates the demise of the previously cherished trilingual ideal. And this was precisely what Robert Clavering, the future regius professor of Hebrew, was referring to when he wrote to Charlett in 1703: 'I am glad to find some people sensible of the great decay of that sort of learning which our ancestors prized so much and we value so little; it is to be hoped that some time or other a genius may arise that will revive the repute of eastern literature: but when that will be I cannot tell.' Two years later, Bishop Williams of Chichester wrote to Charlett in a similar vein: 'I will assure you that of late years we find a great defect in [oriental learning], amongst those that repair to us for orders.' This situation was again alluded to in 1710 by Bishop William Lloyd of Worcester, who personally maintained a few private teachers of Hebrew at Oxford in the early years of the eighteenth century: 'I am sorry to see how this sort of learning is neglected, and even contemned, by too many of the divines of our church.'[155]

The decline of Hebrew and Arabic cannot, of course, be attributed solely to the decline in the quality of the professors. In some respects the waning interest was

---

[153] Hearne, *Collections* ii. 63; P. J. Marshall, 'Oriental studies' in *The Eighteenth Century*, 554.
[154] Bodl. MS Rawlinson letters 96, fos 38, 288.
[155] Bodl. MS Ballard 3, fo 125; Bodl. MS Ballard 9, fos 139, 84; *Letters written by eminent persons in the seventeenth and eighteenth centuries*, ed. J. Walker (2 vols London 1813) i. 208.

merely the symptom of a decline in scholarship in general. As early as 1660 William Sancroft lamented that the study of both Greek and Hebrew was rapidly going out of fashion among Cambridge students,[156] and although the impact of such a trend was not felt fully for some decades, the signs became clearer as more and more such studies became the private domain of a few individuals rather than the province of a large community.

Paradoxically, signs of impending difficulty were becoming conspicuous even when the community of orientalists was growing and flourishing. Already during the 1650s some of the original champions of Arabic were losing their enthusiasm— for reasons that are not easy to explain. Perhaps the fruits that theologians had hoped to reap had not materialized. Perhaps the Polyglot Bible—which made available all the necessary scriptural texts in the oriental languages—made access to the original superfluous. Whatever the reason, a noticeable disenchantment set in. John Evelyn, for example, recorded his conversation with Archbishop Ussher not long before the latter's death when, among other topics, the subject of oriental studies was raised. The archbishop, reported Evelyn, 'told me how greate the losse of time was to study much the eastern languages, that, excepting Hebrew, there was little fruite to be gathered at exceeding labour, that, besides some mathematical bookes, the Arabic itselfe had little considerable'. A few years later, another great promoter of oriental learning—but mainly for Hebrew purposes—John Worthington, also conceded that he did not 'much care for to trouble [himself] about the keys [to orientals] when there was no treasure of things to be come at'.[157]

This shift in attitude alarmed practitioners. By 1663, when Pococke finally published the complete edition of Bar Hebraeus' *Historia dynastiarum*, he evidently felt, to use his biographer's words, that 'the love of Arabick learning was now waxed cold'.[158] Comparing the reception of this latter work with the enthusiastic reception of the *Specimen* nearly a decade and a half earlier, the disillusioned scholar wrote to his friend Thomas Greaves: 'The genius of the times, as for these studies, is much altered since you and I first set about them; and few will be persuaded, they are worthy taking notice of.'[159] Nor had the winds shifted only in England. In Leiden, another great centre of Arabic, a like change of attitude set in. Following Golius' death in 1667 no Arabist of comparable stature was elected until 1729,

[156] G. D'Oyly, *The Life of William Sancroft, Archbishop of Canterbury* (2 vols London 1840) i. 128. A corresponding concern was expressed in 1663 by Samuel Pepys. Having attended the annual examination at St Paul's School he was grieved to see that the new generation of boys did not 'answer in any [of the three languages] as well as we did': *The Diary of Samuel Pepys*, ed. R. Latham and W. Matthews (11 vols Berkeley and Los Angeles 1970–83) iv. 33.

[157] *The Diary of John Evelyn*, ed. E. S. De Beer (6 vols Oxford 1955) iii. 156; Worthington, *Diary and Correspondence* ii. 26.

[158] *Works of Pocock*, ed. Twells i. 60. In a letter to Boyle, Pococke expressed his fear that contempt would greet the publication of the book: *Works of Boyle*, ed. Birch vi. 325.

[159] *Works of Pocock*, ed. Twells i. 60. Greaves could not but agree: 'How these studies are esteemed in the universities, I know not; in these parts [he resided then in Fulham], for ought I observe, they are not much followed or regarded, and receive small incouragement from those, who, I thought, would have been fautors and promoters of them.' Ibid.

when Albert Schultens was appointed professor of oriental languages. Hieronymus Harderus—who was to have been appointed in 1675 as *extra ordinarius linguarum orientalium professor*, but who never assumed office—described in a letter to Pococke as early as 1671 the lamentable state of Arabic studies at Leiden; he railed against the 'avarice of the age, which gave no attention to any sciences, that were not greatly lucrative', even censuring Golius himself who 'did not exercise the students, not even those that were maintained at the publick expence, in these studies, nor use his authority to make them take pains therein'.[160]

Such a situation evidently affected Pococke. The *Historia dynastiarum* was his last important Arabic publication, and during the closing twenty-eight years of his life he devoted his full attention to producing learned commentaries on the minor prophets. After all, for Pococke, too, Arabic was ancillary to his theological concerns. Still, even in this sphere of studies he commented on the dwindling support. When dedicating his commentary on Micah to Seth Ward, bishop of Salisbury, Pococke reflected on 'the need of patronage and protection that this work hath, in regard that there is in it much stress laid on such part of learning (the oriental I mean), which of late, if not all along, both had that unhappiness, as to be scarce able to keep itself, not only from neglect, but contempt, as needless [or] at least of no great use or necessity'.[161]

Indeed, nothing better illustrates the peculiar state of oriental learning during the seventeenth century than the publication record of its most distinguished practitioners. The esoteric nature of such scholarship and the formidable obstacles that confronted those who sought to master it, were compounded by its restricted audience. Consequently, oriental learning was dependent on patronage to a greater degree than all other disciplines, and it was precisely this total reliance that made the pursuit of oriental languages so precarious. Even when patrons for these studies could be found, the orientalists, and particularly the Arabists, were rarely free to pursue an independent course of study. Their scholarship was often not of their own choosing, but was instead regulated according to the requirements of their patrons; similarly, their publications were tailored to the specifications of these same individuals.

Here the case of Edward Pococke is particularly illuminating. During the 1640s and 1650s, it was the urging of John Selden and Gerard Langbaine that prompted—sometimes even forced—Pococke into publication. Most notable was the work the Laudian professor carried out on the *Annals* of Eutychius, the tenth-century patriarch of Alexandria. Selden 'assigned' Pococke the publication of the text, while Langbaine reinforced the pressure. Selden also assumed all costs while

---

[160] J. Brugman, 'Arabic scholarship' in Th. H. Lunsingh Scheurleer and G. H. M. Posthumus Meyjes (eds), *Leiden University in the Seventeenth Century: an exchange of learning* (Leiden 1975), 214; *Works of Pocock*, ed. Twells i. 67. For Golius see W. M. C. Juynboll, *Zeventiende-eeuwsche Beoefenaars van het Arabisch in Nederland* (Utrecht 1933), 119–83; J. J. Witkam, *Jacobus Golius (1596–1667) en zijn Handschriften* (Leiden 1980).

[161] *Works of Pocock*, ed. Twells i, dedication.

he was alive, and in his will he left the sum of £50 for the completion of the project, which eventually appeared in 1656.[162]

Pococke's next major publication, his edition of *Porta Mosis*, owed a great deal to the prodding of Langbaine, even though in this instance Pococke may have been a more willing editor. The printing of the Maimonides volume was assured following Langbaine's extensive purchase of Hebrew fount in the early 1650s, and his ability to persuade his fellow delegates at the Oxford press to carry out such a project.[163] No sooner did Pococke complete his edition of the *Porta Mosis* than Langbaine began pressing him to carry out the complete edition of Bar Hebraeus. But the provost of Queen's College died in 1658, before Pococke was ready with the text, and a different task was laid on the shoulders of the double-barrelled professor. This time it was the growing missionary zeal of Robert Boyle that drove Pococke into action. A year or so before the Restoration Boyle began urging Pococke to publish an Arabic translation of Hugo Grotius' *De veritate religionis Christianae* in order to distribute it among Muslims. Pococke produced the desired translation in 1661, while Boyle took charge of the entire cost of printing.[164]

The Grotius translation out of the way, Pococke resumed his work on his edition of Bar Hebraeus. With Langbaine dead, it was Samuel Clarke who assumed the role of prompter. The two, in fact, had just collaborated in publishing the *Carmen Tograi*, a publication Pococke had carried out as part of his duties as Laudian professor—and which was financed and seen through the press by Clarke, the university's *architypographus*. For the much more costly edition of Bar Hebraeus, however, Clarke was able to secure a subvention of £140 from the delegates of the Oxford press, and the *Historia dynastiarum* was finally published in 1663.[165]

Obviously, the symbiotic relationship between patron and client was not as crude as might first appear. In most cases Pococke was not averse to pursuing those projects suggested to him by Selden and others; the issue is only that he might have wished to follow a different path. For example, Pococke proposed editing the Arabic Old Testament commentary of Rabbi Tanchum from a manuscript in his possession, but abandoned the idea when no encouragement was forthcoming. Instead, he laboured for almost three decades on his elaborate commentaries on the minor prophets, a task laid on him by John Fell and underwritten in full by the Oxford press, which published the four treatises between 1677 and 1691.[166]

---

[162] In his introduction to the *Contextio Gemmarum, sive, Eutychii patriarchae Alexandrini annales* (Oxford 1656), Pococke stated that it 'was not undertaken by him from his own inclination, but upon the persuasion and importunity' of Selden: *Works of Pocock*, ed. Twells i. 53. Selden, *Opera Omnia* i, p. lvi; Madan, *Oxford Books* iii. 51–2. It was also Selden who had recruited Pococke to contribute his share to Walton's Polyglot Bible.

[163] *Works of Pocock*, ed. Twells i. 44; C. Roth, 'Edward Pococke and the first Hebrew printing in Oxford', *Bodleian Library Record* ii (1948), 216–17. Langbaine became a delegate in 1653; he had already expressed to Selden his intention to support oriental publishing.

[164] Worthington, *Diary and Correspondence* i. 161; *Works of Pocock*, ed. Twells i. 57, 60; *Works of Boyle*, ed. Birch vi. 118, 131, 323–5; Madan, *Oxford Books* iii. 127–9.

[165] *Works of Pocock*, ed. Twells i. 59–60; J. Johnson and S. Gibson, *Print and Privilege at Oxford to the Year 1700* (London 1946), 37. Pococke himself was made a delegate in 1662: ibid. 40.

[166] *Works of Pocock*, ed. Twells i. 45–6, 72.

In contrast to the protracted, but at least continuous, stream of publications by Pococke, the publishing career of Thomas Hyde was less impressive. Writing to Thomas Smith in 1696, Hyde bluntly stated that he had printed a specimen for a projected new edition of Maimonides' *More nevukhim*, and proposed to the delegates of the Oxford press 'to have done the whole work, but they would not allow any thing for my pains, and so there is an end to that design. For I would not labour three or four years for nothing. If I could see the coin in a better condition, and money more plenty, I would propose the printing of my *History of the Religion of the old Persians and their Magi.*' But if Hyde hoped that a Latin treatise on such a topic would fare better, he was sadly mistaken. When his *Historia religionis veterum Persarum* was in the press, both he and his friends found it difficult to find subscribers. In fact, Hyde complained that not only was he unable to convince the booksellers to carry the book, but even Oxford college libraries refused to buy it. Hyde's venture indeed proved something of a fiasco. In addition to his need to peddle his own books, the book was sold below cost, fetching only 5*s* a copy. Half a century later, when John Cleland mused over the lack of encouragement that befell Edward Lhuyd, he digressed to reminisce about the similar fate of the former Laudian professor: 'Need I mention the celebrated Dr Hyde's boiling his tea-kettle, with almost the whole impression left on his hands of that profoundly learned treatise of his, "De religione veterum Persarum", admired by all literary Europe, and neglected at home: so low was the taste for literature in this country already sunk!'[167]

The increasing frustration orientalists faced in publishing their works was stated plainly by Thomas Smith when he lamented that those precious manuscripts on the Mandaean Gnostic sect that had been procured by Robert Huntington would remain unpublished, as

these books are and will be rather an amazment than useful to the beholders, no interpreters yet being found, which are and must be wanting until the pristine glory of these studies, which are now decayed by the negligence of sluggish and illiterate men, and which by the most unjust and partial censure of many are accounted empty and unprofitable, shall be recovered by the liberality of princes, potentates, and prelates.[168]

Such frustration of prospects for publications coincided with an increased lethargy in Pococke as a teacher. Pococke, now in his eighties, lost much of his former energy and rigour, not to mention an active interest in recruitment—qualities that had made him such a successful and beloved teacher. Indeed, this change in Pococke, the result of disillusionment as well as age, probably proved cataclysmic for oriental studies at Oxford. By the 1680s, proficient and dedicated students eager to embrace the oriental languages had become few and far between. And as no one at Oxford was able (or willing) to offer that special relationship that had always

---

[167] Hyde, *Syntagma dissertationum*, ed. Sharpe ii. 487–9; I. G. Philip, 'Advice on advertising publications, 1701', *Bodleian Library Record* xi (1984), 263–4; Hearne, *Collections* ii. 235; J. Nichols, *Literary Anecdotes of the Eighteenth Century* (9 vols London 1812–15) ii. 457. See also John Toland, *Nazarenus* (London 1718), 2–3.

[168] Smith, 'The life and travels of . . . Robert Huntington', 117–18.

characterized mentor and disciple, the pursuit of oriental studies declined further.[169]

The rapid deterioration in oriental studies during the eighteenth century, therefore, is attributable to a variety of causes. As argued earlier, the study of Hebrew and Arabic was validated almost exclusively by their theological ends. Yet by 1700 the theological ideals and motives that had animated many scholars since the reformation had dissipated, partly due to the realization that excessive preoccupation with oriental learning actually resulted in irrevocable damage to previously held convictions concerning the authority and inerrancy of scripture. Equally important, by the start of the eighteenth century, the mammoth output of a century and a half of Christian Hebraica made the need to master the oriental languages obsolete. The bookshelves of private scholars and public libraries alike were adorned by Latin editions of all the oriental knowledge deemed worthy of mastery by Christian scholars, and the English contribution during the second half of the seventeenth century alone was imposing. The six huge volumes of Walton's Polyglot Bible were joined by the two folio volumes of Edmund Castell's *Heptaglotton*, the nine folios of John Pearson's collection of the best biblical commentaries in the *Critici sacri* and the equally valuable collection of Matthew Poole's *Synopsis criticorum aliorumque sacrae scripturae interpretum* in five folio volumes. There were also the collected works of John Selden, John Lightfoot, John Spencer, Edward Pococke, and James Ussher, which together set out in Latin a wealth of information on almost every aspect of ancient laws, customs, and culture. To the English contribution can be added the equally impressive editions of continental counterparts. Most notably, Christian Knorr von Rosenroth's translation of the *Zohar* and related material, the *Kabbalah denudata*, had appeared in 1677, and between 1698 and 1703 Wilhelm Surrenhuis produced the long-awaited complete translation of the Mishna in six sumptuous volumes.

In Arabic, too, by the start of the eighteenth century enough sources had been translated into Latin to give rise to the misconception that the study of the original was no longer necessary. Not only had the various oriental versions of scripture been incorporated into Walton's Polyglot Bible, but during the 1690s the Koran, too, had been published in an Arabic–Latin edition. In addition, a plethora of Latin and vernacular books on matters oriental—most notably the compendia compiled by Hottinger and D'Herbelot—were made available.

---

[169] Some instances from Cambridge further illustrate this point. In about 1647 two young students from Trinity College, Isaac Barrow and Samuel Sprint, approached Abraham Wheelock, the first Adams lecturer in Arabic 'to discourse with him about the Arabicke language, which they were desirous to learn. But upon hearing how great difficulties they were to encounter, and how few books there were in that language, and the little advantage that could be got by it, they laid aside their design'. Whether such an attitude was owing to Wheelock's age or infirmity, or the simple wish not to be bothered, it no doubt put off many prospective students. Only in 1668, four years after he had been appointed to the Adams lectureship, could Edmund Castell boast that thanks to his efforts the founder of the chair 'is not a little glad when he hears his donation to be now at last entertained with good respect'. E. Calamy, *An Abridgment of Mr Baxter's Life and Times* (London 1702, 2nd edn 2 vols London 1713) ii. 340; M. Feingold (ed.), *Before Newton: the life and times of Isaac Barrow* (Cambridge 1990), 17; *Works of Lightfoot*, ed. Pitman xiii. 392.

Two examples may illustrate the manner in which oriental publications could now be produced without resort to the original language. As Holt demonstrated, Prideaux's publication of *The True Nature of Imposture fully display'd in the Life of Mahomet* benefited little from Arabic. The material from the Koran had been gathered from the poor 1543 Latin edition by Bibliander—which Prideaux himself disparaged—while virtually all his references to Muslim historians derived from the footnotes to Pococke's *Specimen historiae Arabum*. Prideaux did not even make use of the printed Arabic edition of the Koran published in 1694 by Abraham Hinckelmann. Again, although Simon Ockley was a genuine Arabist, his *History of the Saracens* was much indebted to D'Herbelot's *Bibliothèque orientale*.[170] Clearly, then, since virtually all the requisite primary sources (from the point of view of eighteenth-century observers) were now readily available in translation—not to mention a massive body of accompanying scholarly apparatus—there seemed little incentive to indulge in the arduous, solitary, and possibly 'dangerous' pursuit of orientalism.

Not surprisingly, the study of oriental languages in the eighteenth century underwent fundamental changes. In terms of Hebrew, William Wotton's directions for the study of theology and the role of such a language within it contrasts with the advice given by his seventeenth-century predecessors. Although Wotton (died 1726) 'often wished, that, at least, a competent skill in Hebrew were a necessary qualification for orders with us . . . because then students in divinity would not be obliged at every turn to take things upon trust', he nevertheless took it for granted that his readers would be, to a large extent, ignorant of Hebrew. Thus his prescription for the books necessary for a divine were limited exclusively to Latin and English editions.[171] As for the study of Arabic and other oriental languages, the growth of the British empire would create new opportunities and open new avenues for such study. But here, too, the motives and ideals that had animated the studies of Pococke and his contemporaries would vanish and give way to new justifications.

---

[170] Holt, 'The treatment of Arab history', 293–4; Arberry, *Oriental Essays*, 45.

[171] William Wotton, *Some Thoughts concerning a Proper Method of studying Divinity*, ed. H. Cotton (Oxford 1818), 3, 30–1, and *passim*.

8

Medicine

ROBERT G. FRANK Jr.

IN early 1657 Henry Oldenburg, an itinerant German scholar then living in Oxford as tutor to the nephew of Robert Boyle, wrote to Thomas Coxe, DM, that 'Oxford is indeed a city very well furnished with all the things needed for the grounding and cultivation of learning: among which rich libraries, fat revenues, convenient houses, and healthy air easily hold first place'. It was a place where men weary of 'disputations and wordy learning', and who wished to 'bend their minds to more solid studies' could 'penetrate from nature's antechamber to her inner closet'. At Oxford, he had written a few months previously to the young medico Thomas Sherley, there were chemists attempting to advance their art, and 'philosophers and seekers into nature who are trying to bring natural science to a greater certainty and usefulness than in the past. Until now physicians have pronounced many diseases to be incurable, and confessed that they very often failed to cure others.' Medicine, Oldenburg clearly felt, was entering a new age.[1]

The embedding of innovative science and medicine into the university's rich physical and institutional fabric was a phenomenon remarked upon by many a visitor from the 1650s to the 1680s. John Evelyn, when at Oxford in the summer of 1654, met virtuosi like John Wilkins and Christopher Wren, heard disputations in medicine, viewed the anatomy school and physic garden and wrote with forgivably near-sighted pride that this 'is doubtlesse the noblest universitie now in the whole world'. Balthazar de Monconys saw the same sights in 1663, and also had an interview with Oxford's internationally renowned physician, chemist, and anatomist Thomas Willis, who was also the Sedleian professor of natural philosophy. Lorenzo Magalotti visited in 1669, noting the splendid colleges and libraries, and hearing lectures in geometry by John Wallis, in anatomy by John Paris, and in experimental philosophy by Willis, 'the most distinguished of all the learned men in the university'. He recorded the names and salaries of Oxford's twelve professors (not including music), of whom five were in science and medicine, and of whom five were physicians. Oxford was, he said, the most celebrated university in Europe next to Paris.[2]

---

[1] *The Correspondence of Henry Oldenburg*, ed. A. R. Hall and M. B. Hall (13 vols Madison, Wisconsin and London 1965–86) i. 96–8, 112–14.

[2] *The Diary of John Evelyn*, ed. E. S. De Beer (6 vols Oxford 1955) iii. 104–10, 140; Balthasar de Monconys, *Iovrnal des voyages* (3 vols Lyons 1665–6) ii. 48–55; Lorenzo Magalotti, *Travels of Cosmo the Third, Grand Duke of Tuscany, through England, during the Reign of King Charles the Second (1669)* (London 1821), 251–76, especially 260 and 265–6.

Other evidence supports this picture of medicine, linked with science, con-tributing to the brilliance of mid-seventeenth-century Oxford. William Harvey, the discoverer of the circulation of the blood, was resident from 1642 to 1646, and was briefly warden of Merton. Anatomists of later fame, like Charles Scarburgh, Nathaniel Highmore, George Joyliffe, and Thomas Wharton, started their work there in the 1640s, some of them with Harvey's direct encouragement. At Oxford during the 1650s a sequence of clubs for experimental philosophy included med-ical men like Willis, Ralph Bathurst, George Castle, Timothy Clarke, Edmund Dickinson, Jonathan Goddard, Nathaniel Hodges, Thomas Millington, and William Petty, as well as non-practitioners such as Wren, Boyle, and Robert Hooke, who interested themselves in clinical medicine and in the medical sciences of anatomy, chemistry and botany. After the Restoration these were joined by younger physi-cians such as Walter Needham, John Locke, Richard Lower, and John Mayow to carry out epoch-making researches on the structure and function of the brain and heart, on the meaning of respiration, and the physiological role of an oxygen-like analogue in the air. Oxford medical men had a key role in founding the Royal Society of London in 1660, and during the Restoration period they were unusually prominent in London's Royal College of Physicians. By the 1670s the writings of English physicians, and of Oxford men in particular, enjoyed a reputation that was Europe-wide.[3]

This meteoric rise of Oxford medicine to prominence in the seventeenth cen-tury took place against a background *circa* 1600 that had promised little. Although the university itself was in a flourishing state, the medical faculty, never prominent in Oxford's affairs, had dwindled away to almost nothing. In the decade 1590–9, when the university admitted an estimated 3,585 students and awarded 695 MAs, there were only three BMs and five DMs conferred, and three men incorporated on the basis of foreign DMs. In 1605 there were no doctors to act as opponents in the disputations planned to entertain King James, so two local BMs, Henry Ashworth and John Cheynell, were created on the spot; they and one other in the same year were the first DMs to be admitted since 1598. The regius professorship of medicine was held in 1600 by Bartholomew Warner, an amiable time-server, and the senior Linacre lectureship by a Merton fellow who had occupied it since 1558 and who had most likely ceased to lecture; the junior Linacre lecturer had been suspended from his fellowship in 1598 for insubordination. There were no institu-tions for teaching anatomy by dissection—or at all, for that matter—nor were there facilities for learning medical botany or chemistry. There were no university pro-fessors for the other sciences that supposedly undergirded medicine, such as math-ematics, astronomy, and natural philosophy. No medical man was a head of house, or occupied a professorship other than that of medicine. For access to medical books, the few practitioners or students in the faculty received little or no help

---

[3] For an overview of the blossoming of Oxford medical research, see R. G. Frank Jr., *Harvey and the Oxford Physiologists: a study of scientific ideas and social interaction* (Berkeley and Los Angeles 1980).

from either the decayed university library or local booksellers. Little wonder convocation could find no one to dispute before the king.[4]

Just over a century later, at the beginning of the eighteenth century, Oxford medicine was once again entering into somnolence, a long, quiet prelude to a period when medicine at both ancient universities lost relevance in the face of new developments in medical education and practice at Leiden, in the London hospitals, and at the University of Edinburgh. If medicine at tory Oxford was, as Webster has shown, perhaps not as damnable as later reformers would have it, it was certainly a pale shadow of its seventeenth-century self.[5]

How and why did Oxford medicine rise and fall? To answer that question entails only in small part recounting the brilliant work of a handful of medical scientists whose investigations and writings gained the fame that enthralled Oldenburg, Evelyn, and visiting foreign dignitaries. The mid-seventeenth-century efflorescence was grounded in a series of more fundamental institutional and social changes that (1) drew vastly increased numbers of university men into the study and practice of medicine, (2) provided entry into a spectrum of medical career paths for acquiring a medical education and using it to establish practices in London and in the provinces, (3) created new opportunities for Oxford men to learn anatomy, botany, and chemistry as medical sciences and (4) opened up within Oxford new places for physicians as fellows of colleges, heads of house, professors, or simply as resident practitioners. Yet the distinguishing characteristic of these favourable alterations was their contingent nature: dependent upon political events, personal influence, and informal mechanisms, they failed to bind medicine as a subject to the essential structure of the university enterprise. Indeed, what links there were soon fell prey to the recurrent Oxford evils of non-residency and neglect of office, such that the university as a whole was little prepared or inclined to respond to the further changes in medicine that occurred in the eighteenth century.

STUDENTS, PRACTITIONERS, AND MEDICAL CAREERS

It has been the persistent, if forgivable, tendency of historians of Oxford medicine to concentrate their attention upon those physicians whose study and later practice of medicine followed a particular path: BA and MA, perhaps a fellowship in a college, then BM and DM, and on to London to become a fellow of the Royal College of Physicians in due course and, possibly as a capstone to one's career, a court or royal physician. Richard Lower, quite apart from his scientific accomplishments, admirably exemplifies what might be taken as the paradigm sequence. He was born in 1632 into the Cornish gentry, educated under Richard Busby at Westminster School, and elected to a Studentship at Christ Church in 1649. He took his BA in February 1653, and MA in June 1655. Lower came gradually into the study of medicine, eventually accumulating his BM and DM in 1665, a few years

---

[4] The figures for admissions and MAs are taken from S. Porter, 'University and Society', pp. 32, 92 above; for medical degrees see p. 514 below.

[5] C. Webster, 'The medical faculty and the physic garden' in *The Eighteenth Century*.

after he had lost his Studentship at Christ Church for failing to be ordained. In 1666 Lower married a widow possessed of a neighbouring manor in Cornwall, and in 1667 settled in London. That same year he became FRS and a candidate in the Royal College of Physicians. Lower's admission as FRCP in 1675 coincided with his growing practice in aristocratic circles, and, in Wood's phrasing, 'no man's name was more cried up at court than his'. The strong whig sympathies of Lower lost him practice in the early 1680s, but he re-emerged as a favourite after the Glorious Revolution, and remained prominent until his relatively early death in January 1691.[6]

Lower's medical study reflected the standard course envisaged by the ancient statutes of the university, which were little changed when they were revised in 1565, and which were then recodified under Laud's aegis during the 1630s. Four years of reading and disputation in grammar, rhetoric, logic, mathematics, moral philosophy, and some Greek led to the BA; a further three years of philosophical studies brought the young scholar to the MA. Only then, at least according to the statutes, could he commence studies in one of the three higher faculties of theology, law, or medicine. The *studiosus medicinae* was required to attend the lectures of the regius professor of medicine and to take part in disputations in the schools. After three years he could petition to be admitted BM and, after an additional four, to be admitted DM. To complete the degree, the incepting doctor had to read a course of either three long or six short lectures on a 'Galenic' subject.[7]

This full statutory course, taking a minimum of fourteen years and leading in an orderly academic way to the DM, was in fact completed only by a minority.[8] During the seventeenth century more than 950 men can be identified who received medical degrees at Oxford, or who became medical practitioners. Slightly more than 100 of the medical degrees were incorporations on the basis of non-Oxford DM degrees by individuals who had no previous or later association with Oxford; such birds of passage included eminent practitioners who had taken their degrees at Cambridge or abroad, but they formed no real part of Oxford medicine. Of the remaining approximately 850 Oxonians, only 32 per cent actually received an Oxford DM according to the usual statutory prescriptions. Another 13 per cent received the degree by creation, a procedure that served partially to honour distin-

---

[6] Frank, *Harvey and the Oxford Physiologists*, 64–5, 179–80, 208–10, 283, 299, 341; Wood, *Athenae* iv. 297.

[7] *SA*, pp. cii–cv, 346, 378–9; *Reg. Univ.* ed. Clark i. 123–9; *Laudian Code*, ed. Griffiths VI. v. 1–4, pp. 62–3.

[8] The following figures about career paths at seventeenth-century Oxford are based upon a prosopographical analysis of a total population consisting of: (1) all recipients of BM or DM degrees as listed in Wood, *Fasti* and Richard Peers, *A Catalogue of all Graduats in Divinity, Law and Physick, and of All Masters of Arts, and Doctors of Musick: who have regularly proceeded, or been created, in the University of Oxford* (Oxford 1705); (2) all Oxonians who studied or took degrees abroad, in so far as those are determinable by published lists; (3) Oxonians known to have practised medicine because they sought a licence from the Royal College of Physicians, the bishop of London, etc., in so far as those have been published. Because the foregoing omit some degrees and licences, totals have been corrected from data found in a page-by-page search of a 60% sample of Foster, *Alumni*.

guished intellectuals like William Viscount Brouncker or Robert Boyle, or to laureate older practitioners who had stepped out of the academic course, but which
could also be used by the nimble medical student to obtain his degree without waiting the statutory time, or performing the statutory exercises. In 1643, for example,
Walter Charleton, Nathaniel Highmore, and Christopher Merret, all later to be distinguished physicians in their various ways, used the king's presence to be created
DM, rather than having to wait for their degrees. Once the parliamentarians took
charge of the city, medical students of a different political stripe, such as Thomas
Wharton, John French, and William Petty, received their degrees in a similar way.
All that was needed were plausible credentials and friends in power.[9]

Another extremely popular way of receiving a DM was to be laureated abroad.
Over 150 Oxford physicians, approaching 20 per cent of the total, came into practice in this way. Some actually spent a considerable time in foreign universities, but
most were simply obtaining certification for their Oxford studies, a fact that can
be seen in the few days or weeks that often elapsed between matriculation and DM.
Another group of approximately 115 practitioners, about 13 per cent, studied
abroad without actually taking a degree there. By far the most frequent goal of such
travellers was the University of Leiden, where about 170 Oxonians went to study
medicine, and where forty-five took their DMs. About a third as many travellers,
almost sixty, found their way to Padua, where forty-one received their degrees.
Smaller numbers were laureated, in declining order of frequency, at the other
Dutch universities of Utrecht, Harderwyck, Franeker, and Groningen, as well as at
various French universities including Caen, Montpellier, Angers, and Bourges.[10]
Thomas Browne (MA 1629), later to become the famous literary doctor of
Norwich, provides a well-documented example. After study at Padua and Montpellier he received his DM from Leiden at the end of 1633. There he could see dissections in a well-appointed anatomical theatre, simples in one of Europe's best
botanical gardens, and hear lectures by such eminent scholar–practitioners as Otto
Heurnius, Adrian Valckenburgh, and Adolph Vorstius. As an additional benefit
Browne received his degree aged 28, at least three years sooner than he could have
at Oxford; about a third of those taking degrees abroad were 25 and younger, considerably younger than the average age of 33 for regular Oxford DMs. In order to
be set upon an equal footing with his colleagues, and thereby also to be qualified
for fellowship in the Royal College of Physicians, a foreign graduate needed only
to be incorporated upon his degree at Oxford, which Browne did in 1637.[11] Taking
a degree abroad, and then incorporating upon it at Oxford, remained popular until

[9] Wood, Fasti ii. 48–9, 106, 115, 156.

[10] For Leiden and other Dutch universities see R. W. Innes Smith, English-Speaking Students of Medicine
at the University of Leiden (Edinburgh 1932); for British visitors who enrolled at Padua during this period
see H. F. Brown, 'Inglesi e Scozzesi all'Università di Padova dall'anno 1618 sino al 1765' in Monografie
storiche sullo Studio di Padova (Venice 1922); Smith's manuscript lists of English-speaking matriculants at
continental universities are in the Royal College of Physicians, London.

[11] C. W. Schoneveld, 'Sir Thomas Browne and Leiden University in 1633', English Language Notes xix
(1982); Wood, Fasti i. 498.

the end of the 1660s, after which most Oxonians with foreign DMs simply did not bother.

The two lower medical qualifications, the BM and the licence to practice (ML), were in most cases simply taken as stages on the way to the DM. But some practitioners could, and sometimes did, content themselves with these. In all, perhaps 175 or so Oxford physicians, about 20 per cent of the total, stopped at this stage. Such qualifications were not ideal for launching a career in London, since the holder could, for example, rise no higher than a licentiate of the College of Physicians; fewer than ten even bothered to obtain its approval. It is therefore not surprising to find that such physicians were intending to practise in the provinces, were uninterested in the organized medical hierarchy, or could foresee practising medicine only as a kind of sideline. After being a student of medicine for six years, Robert Wood (MA 1649 and fellow of Lincoln College), was licensed to practise in April 1656; he seems to have done so for a while in Dublin before seeking other preferments, and eventually ended up as accountant-general of the revenue in Ireland. Thomas Sydenham studied medicine at Oxford for a few years in the period after the king's surrender, got himself created BM in 1648, and for three decades practised in London on the basis of this and a licence from the College of Physicians. Perhaps the most famous in this category was John Locke. His large collection of surviving manuscript notebooks shows that he began studying medicine shortly after his BA in 1656 and that he practised occasionally during the 1660s while continuing to hold his Student's place at Christ Church; he took the BM as his only medical degree in 1675, long after his interests had begun to shift.[12]

The last class of Oxford medical practitioners is the most difficult to characterize because its members are the most difficult to identify. It consists of those with an MA, or merely a BA, or perhaps even no degree whatsoever, but who practised in rural areas, in county towns, and provincial cities, and sometimes even in London. Many made careers simply on the basis of an academic education, attending some lectures and reading. Others supplemented these Oxford studies with some other kind of medical qualification: a sojourn at Leiden or Padua, a certificate as a licentiate or extra-licentiate of the Royal College of Physicians, or an episcopal licence to practise. John French (MA 1649) was a servitor at All Souls, who served first as rector of Wenvoe, Glamorgan, until he was ejected in 1662, whereupon he practised physic in Cardiff until his death in 1691. David Barton had something of the reverse career. After taking his BA from Magdalen Hall in 1641, he studied medicine at Leiden and presumably went into practice. Upon the Restoration he took his long-delayed MA at Oxford and was preferred rector of St

---

[12] Foster, *Alumni* iv. 1673; K. Dewhurst, 'Thomas Sydenham (1624–1689): reformer of clinical medicine', *Medical History* vi (1962), although for the purposes of his argument Dewhurst is at pains to play down the significance of Sydenham's studies at Oxford. Locke's medical side is treated in K. Dewhurst, *John Locke, Physician and Philosopher* (London 1963). On his manuscript notebooks see P. Long, *A Summary Catalogue of the Lovelace Collection of the Papers of John Locke in the Bodleian Library* (Oxford 1959); J. W. Gough, 'John Locke's herbarium', *Bodleian Library Record* vii (1962); P. Long, 'The Mellon donation of additional manuscripts of John Locke from the Lovelace Collection', *Bodleian Library Record* vii (1964).

Margaret's, New Fish Street, London in 1662, where he remained until his death. John Etwall took his BA from Trinity in 1685, his MA from St Mary Hall in 1688, and in the same year was examined as an extra-licentiate of the College of Physicians for practice in Bristol. John Curteyne, a fellow of Lincoln College ejected in 1660, and boon companion of Richard Lower and Anthony Wood, practised among his fellow scholars during the 1660s with no other qualification, as far as the evidence allows us to suppose, than his MA, private study, and, presumably, attending medical lectures.[13]

Although one can, from printed sources, identify over 125 of these graduate practitioners, constituting about 15 per cent of the total number of known Oxford physicians, it is certain that such figures underestimate their numbers by a factor of at least three or four. The university registers that form the basis of collective biographies such as Foster's *Alumni Oxonienses* are very frequently silent on men's medical interests, and we know of their roles as practitioners only through totally adventitious evidence: a licence to practice granted by a bishop or archbishop, their inscription as a medical student in a foreign university for which a matriculation register has been published, a chance comment of biographers or historians like Anthony Wood, remarks in a letter, or the totally arbitrary survival of manuscripts. John Ward is a good example of the last. As a Student of Christ Church in the 1650s he read medical books, collected recipes, learned medical botany in the physic garden, attended anatomical lectures and post-mortems, and prepared chemical medicaments in a laboratory. In 1662, after investigating the costs of a Leiden DM (£16 'besides feasting the professors') and a Lambeth licence (not above 30s), he finally decided for the Church, and was preferred to the vicarage of Stratford-upon-Avon. From then until his death in 1681 he continued none the less to be interested at least as much in the bodies of his parishioners as in their souls; for some years he stayed in contact with his medical friends at Oxford, bought and read medical books and prescribed for his flock. Ward's life and medical career are traceable in exquisite detail because he wrote and preserved sixteen manuscript diaries/commonplace books that chronicle his intellectual evolution, and which have survived because someone in the eighteenth century noticed that they contained a few items of unique information about the bard of Stratford, William Shakespeare.[14] One can only guess for how many other graduate practitioners the evidence of their medical interests lies yet undiscovered, or has been lost completely.

It was no accident that medicine and the church intertwined in the careers of practitioners such as French, Barton, and Ward. For the great majority of Oxford scholars beyond their teens, staying on to take a BA or MA, and getting a fellowship, were stations on the route to a clerical position. When, for a variety of

[13] Foster, *Alumni* i. 80, 363, ii. 467, 534; Smith, *English-Speaking Students*, 16; W. Munk, *The Roll of the Royal College of Physicians of London* (2 vols London 1861, 2nd edn 3 vols London 1878) i. 477.

[14] R. G. Frank Jr., 'The John Ward diaries: mirror of seventeenth-century science and medicine', *Journal of the History of Medicine* xxix (1974).

reasons, prospects in the church diminished, significant numbers were deflected into a medical career. The number of those taking medical degrees more than doubled in the 1630s, reflecting a decreased number of new graduate openings in the church, as well as perhaps the reduced opportunities for a puritanically inclined cleric to compete for them under the Laudian order. The outbreak of civil war and the triumph of the parliamentary party also turned numerous scholars to medicine. Wood notes that Ralph Bathurst was chaplain to Bishop Robert Skinner of Oxford before the war, 'but when he saw little hopes of rising by divinity, studied physick'. He became an especially close friend of his Oxford contemporary, Willis, and by the late 1650s the two physicians were 'eminently known in the university'. After the Restoration Bathurst reverted to a church career, becoming president of Trinity, a royal chaplain, and dean of Wells. The king's return caused an opposite, and perhaps even larger, set of changes for the opposing party. Francis Crosse, MA and sometime fellow of Wadham, was ejected from the rectory of Charlinch, Somerset, in 1662, returned to Oxford to study medicine, and was at Leiden for most of a year before taking his DM there in 1664. Afterwards 'retiring to the city of Bristol', Wood notes, Crosse 'practised there with good success among the precise party'. He did not, however, totally forget his former career; in 1672 some west country Presbyterians requested and were granted a licence for Francis Crosse of Bristol, DM, to preach in Thomas Ford's house at Pensford, Somerset. Similar stories of the mixing of medical and clerical careers could be multiplied by the dozen, and reflect changes that probably affected hundreds of Oxford physicians.[15]

These four broad categories of Oxford-educated physicians—home-grown DMs, foreign DMs, BMs, and MLs, and graduate practitioners—show the spectrum of qualifications that seventeenth-century practitioners might hold. The notion prevalent in Europe and America over the past century, that there is essentially one kind of medical education that serves as the foundation for all practitioners, would not only have been foreign to earlier centuries, but puzzlingly irrational. The illnesses of a court aristocrat were thought to demand a physician highly subtle, learned, and experienced, while those of a merchant in a country town, or of a yeoman farmer, were deemed to be less complicated and could well be treated by someone who had the benefit of a university education, even if the practitioner had not put himself to the time, trouble, and expense of acquiring degrees or licences from one of the learned corporations.

Looked at from this viewpoint, one can see the Oxford medical faculty and its students as considerably larger and much more diverse than simply that body of men who were on a statutory seven-year road from the MA to the DM. It included not only the handful of those who had already acquired a doctor's degree, and were in residence in Oxford, but those who were studying and learning to practise medicine in any of its aspects. One could start even before the BA, and leave at any

---

[15] Wood, *Life and Times* i. 365; W[illiam] D[urham], *The Life and Death of ... Robert Harris* (London 1660), 50; Foster, *Alumni* i. 356; Smith, *English-Speaking Students*, 59; Wood, *Fasti* ii. 287; *CSPD 1672*, 10, 41.

time, dependent only on an individual titration of future locus and type of practice against the costs, personal and financial, of continuing in the university town.

As the nature of medicine, and the perceived opportunities for careers in other fields, changed in the course of the seventeenth century, so did recruitment of physicians. A rough measure of this recruitment is the decennial total of DM and BM degrees admitted, plus DMs incorporated from other universities. From the thirteen medical degrees granted in this way during the entire decade of the 1590s, the numbers rose to eighty-one for the 1630s, peaked at 128 in the 1640s, remained above 100 in the 1650s and 1660s, and settled into a range between about fifty-six and ninety-four for the last three decades of the seventeenth century. Even more remarkable are the numbers of degrees calculated first as a percentage of the total admissions at Oxford in the preceding decade, and second as a percentage of MAs admitted in the same decade (see table 8.1). Thus, by the middle of the century the career of medicine was attracting eight to fifteen times as many Oxford men as it had during the late Elizabethan period.[16] Nor was this due to some kind of hidden shift from Cambridge to Oxford. The sister English university seems in fact to have produced more physicians throughout the century than Oxford.

Such an enormous increase in the demand for university-educated physicians has not been adequately analysed. In part it came about because London continued to grow throughout the century—attracting physicians disproportionately to its growth in population, not to mention the opportunities provided for increasing numbers of surgeons and apothecaries. But only about 20 per cent of Oxford-trained physicians ended up in London, most of the demand coming from elsewhere. Some was provided by the university and town, where another 15 per cent seem to have stayed on and practised. This was not an unreasonable decision, given the large population of intelligent, reasonably prosperous, and medically conscious potential patients. The remaining 60–65 per cent of Oxford physicians scattered primarily over the south and west of England and the midlands. Oxonians practised in cities such as Chester, Bath, Bristol, Gloucester, and Exeter, in larger county and cathedral towns like Leicester, Worcester, Northampton, Salisbury, Southampton, and Canterbury, and were even to be found in smaller towns such as Daventry,

[16] One can gauge the usefulness of this measure by assessing the extent to which the total of *degrees* (BMs + DMs + incorporated DMs) represents accurately the number of *persons* entering medicine in a given decade. It overestimates the number of medical practitioners because (1) 35% of BM and DM degrees were taken by the same person; (2) 7% of DMs by incorporation were never Oxford men; (3) 3% of DMs by creation were not nor ever became practitioners. It underestimates because (1) about 20% of graduate practitioners did not acquire a qualification for which printed evidence survives; (2) 15% of Oxford doctors took a DM elsewhere which they never incorporated at Oxford; (3) 10% of Oxford medical men practised solely on the basis of a medical licence (ML) from the university, without taking a medical degree, and therefore are not listed in Wood, *Fasti* or Peers, *A Catalogue of all Graduats*. Creations are included because for twenty-four created BMs and ninety-three created DMs whose careers are well known enough to characterize, 83% and 75% respectively seemed to have practised on the basis of their degrees. Numbers of BMs and estimates of university entrants have been generously provided by Professor Lawrence Stone and his research assistant Julian Hill from matriculation and degree statistics prepared for his study of the university.

TABLE 8.1 *Decennial numbers of medical degrees granted at Oxford, 1590–1699*

| | BM | | DM | | Number incorporated | Total | % entrants preceding decade | % MAs same decade |
	Admitted	Created	Admitted	Created				
1590–9	3	—	5	1	4	13	0.3	1.9
1600–9	9	—	5	2	10	26	0.7	3.1
1610–19	14	—	11		9	34	0.9	3.1
1620–9	19	—	7	2	13	41	1.1	2.6
1630–9	50	28	13	3	15	81	2.0	5.6
1640–9	15	28	17	49	19	128	2.4	20.6
1650–9	24	3	31	7	36	101	4.6	14.8
1660–9	20	2	17	28	38	105	2.4	14.0
1670–9	23	—	17	9	7	56	1.2	4.9
1680–9	51	—	25	9	5	90	2.3	9.0
1690–9	48	—	42		4	94	2.9	11.3

Tonbridge, Truro, Barnstaple, Newbury, and Weston-under-Edge, just to name a few.

Oxford practitioners could spread out over the country because, from the 1630s on, there is clear and increasing evidence that a physician practising outside London, if he were skilled both professionally and socially, could carve out for himself a highly respected and very remunerative position. By 1667, at the age of 46, Thomas Willis had accumulated £300 in savings from his Oxford medical practice, and was earning at the rate of £300 per year. Peter Eliot, his slightly older contemporary in Oxford medicine, left an estate of £200 a year upon his death in 1681. Yet another Oxford physician, Edward Exton, married a rich widow after he was ejected from his fellowship at Magdalen College in 1648; his wife conveniently died so that he could be restored to it in 1660. During the 1650s William Petty earned £400 a year from his practice in Dublin, above and beyond his medical work for the army at £1 per day, and in addition to his profits from trading in confiscated Irish lands. Even before he had received his medical degrees, Ralph Bathurst received £100 from parliament for less than four months of his services in the summer of 1653 helping Daniel Whistler care for sick seamen at Ipswich and Harwich. Perhaps the most spectacular example of financial advancement through medicine is the case of John Bidgood, a fellow of Exeter College, who was BM in 1648, DM at Padua, and incorporated upon it in 1660. He practised at Exeter for thirty years, and died there in 1691 possessed of £25,000–£30,000. This fortune was 'all of his own getting', and came to him quite simply because he was an excellent clinician, with extraordinary diagnostic skills, who, in the words of his memorial inscription, 'by education, study, and travel rendered himself one of the most accomplished and beneficial physicians of his age'. By the mid-seventeenth century the ambitious physician did not need to make his way to London to rise in the world.[17]

With prominence and wealth came an ascent in social class. One scholar has argued that, at least in the first third of the century, physicians were not quite gentry.[18] Even if this were true then, for Oxford it had certainly changed by the 1660s. Over the entire century, the matriculation rank of 'gentleman' or above accounted for 57 per cent of the Oxonian physicians for whom we have evidence of social status. Given that there was a financial disincentive to declare a high social class at matriculation, the numbers of actual gentry were probably higher. Another 13 per cent came from clerical families. This was in a period when 32–52 per cent of Oxford matriculants gave their family origins as 'plebeian'.[19] That this

---

[17] 'The poll tax, March, 1667' in *Surveys and Tokens*, ed. H. E. Salter (OHS lxxv 1920), 233; Wood, *Life and Times* iii. 8, 76; will of Sir William Petty, 2 May 1685 (copy): BL MS Sloane 2903, fo 16ᵛ; *CSPD 1653* , 507; Foster, *Alumni* i. 122; Munk, *Roll* i. 348–50; J. Prince, *The Worthies of Devon* (London 1810), 74–7.

[18] W. Birken, 'The social problem of the English physician in the early seventeenth century', *Medical History* xxxi (1987).

[19] On matriculation rank see *Reg. Univ.* ed Clark, pt i, pp. xxiv–xxv; distributions of social rank at matriculation are given in L. Stone, 'The size and composition of the Oxford student body 1580–1909' in L. Stone (ed.), *The University in Society* (2 vols Princeton 1974) i. 93.

gentry-dominated profession was not filled entirely from the ranks of the 'mere' or 'parochial' gentry is suggested by the fact that 14 per cent of Oxford physicians came from armigerous families or were sons of knights. A similar process of social ascent can be seen in the careers of practitioners. William Paddy was one of the first Oxford-educated physicians to be knighted in 1603, a process of recognition—sometimes unwelcome, because of the fees involved—that accelerated in the 1630s and 1640s, becoming relatively widespread after 1660. Edward Greaves was the first medical baronet to be created (1645), and Thomas Clayton junior the first medical professor to be knighted (1661). Other Oxford physicians in London were knighted for diplomatic or political services to the state (John Finch, William Petty) or medical advice to the crown (John Baber), but perhaps a truer index of social status comes late in the century when provincial physicians like Thomas Browne and John Floyer came to be knighted as well.

REGIUS PROFESSORS, MEDICAL LECTURES, AND ACADEMIC EXERCISES

As the new century began, Leiden had four professors in the medical faculty and Padua had seven. Oxford, like Cambridge, loaded almost all teaching and supervisory responsibilities in medicine upon the shoulders of one man, the regius professor of physic. The chair had been founded in 1540 as part of a two-pronged reform: to bring regularity to medical lecturing by replacing the moribund custom of new degree-holders teaching as part of their necessary regency, and to create a place for a senior scholar knowledgeable in the Greek medical classics, who could teach the texts of Galen and Hippocrates according to the rigorous demands of the new medical humanism. He was enjoined by statute to lecture on these twice a week in term, on Tuesdays and Fridays at 8 a.m. He was also responsible for certifying, presumably after some kind of examination, that candidates for the licences to practise medicine or surgery, as well as those for the degrees of BM and DM, were fit to receive the licence or degree for which they supplicated. Although one might assume that the regius professor would also preside at disputations, in the early seventeenth century there were recurring difficulties in finding any DM, much less the regius, to serve as the moderator in the *vesperies* and as the respondent in the *comitia*; BMs and MA students in medicine were often dispensed to stand in. For these duties of lecturing, certifying, and occasionally presiding at disputations, the regius professor received £40 a year from the king, in whose gift the appointment lay.[20]

The century opened with Bartholomew Warner (1556–1619) in the chair. He had matriculated at Lincoln in 1575, but soon translated to St John's, where he took his arts degrees in due order—BA in 1576 and MA in 1579. In 1583 he married the step-daughter of the famous Oxford philosopher and pedagogue John Case, so it seems likely that he started practice some years even before he took his BM in

[20] Wood, *History of the University* ii. 859–61; *Reg. Univ.* ed Clark, pt i, 123–9; for the regius professorship in the sixteenth century see G. Lewis, 'The faculty of medicine' in *The Collegiate University*, 224–38.

1586. The DM came at a leisurely pace, in 1594, and may in part have been to qualify him for the regius chair, to which he was appointed in 1597. About his medical interests we know little beyond the titles of the questions on putrid fevers and
purging that he disputed *in vesperiis* for his doctor's degree; otherwise he wrote no
books, left behind no manuscripts, and was associated with no changes in the
nature of his office. The only item of note about him was his success in marrying
off three of his four daughters to Oxford doctors: Thomas Clayton, DM of
Gloucester Hall, in 1611, and John Speed and William Taylor, both DMs of St
John's, in 1628.[21]

Such relationships are of more than passing interest, because it was to his son-
in-law, Thomas Clayton senior (1575–1647), that Warner resigned the chair in 1612,
while retaining the reversion of it. Clayton was born in London and matriculated
gen. fil. at Balliol in 1591, whence he was admitted BA in 1594. He took his MA
from Gloucester Hall in 1599, and most likely was a student in medicine, and perhaps even in practice, long before he supplicated for a medical licence in 1610, and
accumulated his BM and DM in 1611. As in the case of his predecessor, he may
have taken the degrees with an eye towards the chair. It would have been about
this time, or perhaps even earlier, that he married Warner's daughter, for their son
Thomas junior was born in late 1611 or early 1612. His tenure of the regius professorship was extremely long: almost exactly thirty-five years, until his death in
July 1647.[22]

Clayton senior was also the century's most energetic and active 'king's professor
of physic'—as the position was commonly called. Over 120 BMs, almost ninety
DMs, and numerous licentiates in medicine or surgery were admitted during his
tenure, many with his *testamur*. These recommendations have survived in the convocation registers because, as Clark notes, 'the registrar about 1590 became alive
to the fact that he could secure a fee from candidates by registering the certificate
given by the professor'. Clayton testified in 1618, for example, that the surgeon
Bernard Wright had demonstrated his proficiency with 'many patients, where he
hath showed good skill, rare judgment, and dexterity; as also by his dissection of
many bodies for anatomy'. A later instance involved rather better known figures;
Clayton and William Harvey testified in June of 1646, just a few days before the
surrender of the Oxford garrison, on the fitness of Charles Scarburgh to be created DM. In 1623 Clayton solicited the establishment of the Tomlins readership in
anatomy, and until his death carried it out in his own person. An anonymous manuscript of the 1680s recalled that Clayton was also 'a good linguist, to whom great
Avicenne might speak and be understood without an interpreter, a good divine too;
and this his skill he did so seasonably exercise towards his patients, that it rendred
him worthy of double honour'. These humanistic gifts were expressed in a rather

21 Foster, *Alumni* iv. 1573; Wood, *Athenae* i. 687; *Reg. Univ.* ed Clark, pt i, 190.
22 *CSPD 1611–18*, 118; Foster, *Alumni* iv. 288.

different way through the medieval and renaissance medical manuscripts that he bequeathed to the Bodleian.[23]

Clayton was also solicitous for the institutional position of the regius chair. The annual royal fee of £40 had been adequate in the mid-sixteenth century, but its value had been badly eroded by the intervening inflation. As part of a general augmentation of stipends, Clayton prevailed upon King James in 1617 to annex the mastership of the hospital of Ewelme to the regius chair. In the next year the king declared his intention further to improve the situations of the regius professors by appropriating from the university the power to appoint principals of halls, and to use those positions as additional benefactions. Clayton was given the reversion as principal of Broadgates Hall, and came into the office in 1620. When the hall was refounded as Pembroke College, he became its first master, remaining in office until his death. In presiding over the college he seems also to have given special encouragement to the study of medicine. In the 1620s, for example, disputations were held there under the 'lecturer in medicine'. In addition, an unusually large number of Broadgates and Pembroke men took medical degrees, especially in the 1630s; these included Thomas Browne.[24]

The regius professorship changed hands upon Clayton's death in 1647 in the same way it had in 1612—in the family. John Speed, son-in-law of Bartholomew Warner and brother-in-law of Clayton senior, had originally been granted the reversion of the office, but after his death in about 1640, Thomas Clayton junior (1612–93) petitioned for, and was granted this. He was 35 when he came into the professorship, having taken all of his degrees at Pembroke (BA 1629, MA 1631, BM 1635, DM 1639). He, like almost all of his predecessors, published nothing; the questions he discussed *in vesperiis* for his degree were standard Galenical items, so they too shed little light upon his medical interests. The younger Clayton held the chair until 1665, but evidence for his attention to duty is rather hard to find. Unlike his father, he was no lover of anatomy, and very soon after acquiring the regius chair, he separated off the Tomlins readership, to be held by a series of deputies. As did his father, Clayton junior also gave *testamurs* for admission to degrees or licences, but this was also done by other resident DMs in the town. Wood records that immediately after the Restoration the lectures in medicine were neglected, but on Clayton he is hardly an unbiased source. Perhaps more damning is the singular fact that over the two decades from the late 1640s to the late 1660s,

---

[23] *Reg. Univ.* ed. Clark, pt i, 123–4; OUA register of convocation 1641–7, NEP/*supra*/25, register Sb, fo 113; Bodl. MS Rawlinson d. 810, fo 44; his gifts are noted in F. Madan and H. H. E. Craster, *A Summary Catalogue of Western Manuscripts in the Bodleian Library at Oxford* ii pt 2 (Oxford 1922), nos 2363, 3474, 3500, 3541, 3547, and 3637.

[24] *CSPD 1611–18*, 490; the statutes of the hospital at Ewelme are UCA MS 145; on Clayton as head of house see Macleane, *Pembroke*, 213–15, 219–20, and D. Macleane, *Pembroke College* (London 1900), 95, 102–6, 110–14; medical men educated there during his tenure include Richard Gardiner (ML 1621), Henry Herne (BM 1630), William Ford (DM 1631), Thomas Clayton junior (BM 1635, DM 1639), Leonard Traherne (BM 1635), Nathaniel Chamberlaine (BM 1635), Joseph More (BM and DM 1638), and George Joyliffe (MA 1643).

when Oxford was host to numerous clubs and smaller groups pursuing the medical and physical sciences, Clayton's name is never mentioned as even a passive participant.[25]

What the younger Clayton inherited from his father in all too great measure was an obsession with collecting honours and offices, and the remunerations that went with them. Within a few weeks of his father's death one finds Clayton junior asserting his 'patent to succeed my father in the professors place of physicke', and asking Langbaine about how he might be admitted to the 'mastership of the hospitall of Ewelme annexed to it'. He submitted to the parliamentary visitation in 1648—Wood said he 'cringed to the men of the intervall'—thereby retaining his office. In 1655 he asked friends to appeal to the protector for payment of three years' arrears, in 1658 he petitioned for an augmentation of his salary to £80 per annum, and in 1659 he tried for even more. The scramble began in earnest after the Restoration. In April 1660 Clayton was elected one of the two burgesses from the university to sit in parliament, and in the autumn served as a commissioner in the Restoration visitation. In September, when it seemed clear that the wardenship of Merton would become vacant through the promotion of Reynolds to the bishopric of Norwich, Clayton petitioned for a royal letter ordering the sub-warden and fellows to name him as one of the three candidates presented to the visitor, the archbishop of Canterbury, for election as the new warden. When the fellows failed to co-operate, and only one of seven gave him a second-place vote at the election in March 1661, Clayton went up to London and got a royal letter directing Juxon to nominate him. This the archbishop did on 26 March; Clayton was knighted on 27 March, and attempted to take possession of the warden's lodgings on 30 March 1661. He succeeded only after several weeks of vituperative exchange, thereby beginning a long and rancorous rule as warden that lasted until his death in 1693. There were clashes with the fellows about the alleged extravagances of Lady Clayton, undue influence and bribery in the election of fellows and postmasters, and a particularly tragic incident in 1681 when Clayton seems to have badgered a mentally unstable fellow into suicide. Oxford's medical faculty and students may well have breathed a sigh of relief in 1665 when Clayton, his financial status assured, vacated the regius professorship.[26]

The next incumbent, James Hyde (1618–81), fitted well into the rising social status of the chair; he was most junior son of Sir Lawrence Hyde of Salisbury, a barrister and former attorney to the wife of James I. The youngest Hyde had taken his degrees in arts at Hart Hall (BA 1635, MA 1639), was created BM in late 1642, a year after being elected a fellow of Corpus Christi, and took his DM in June 1646, days before the royalists surrendered Oxford. Hyde was ejected from his

---

[25] *CSPD 1640–1*, 341; Foster, *Alumni* i. 288; OUA register of congregation 1634–47, NEP/*supra*/16, register Q, fos 178[r–v], 180[v]; Wood, *Life and Times* i. 361.

[26] Clayton to Langbaine, 19 July 1647: OUA WP/g/10 fasc. 2, 'Dr. Tho. Clayton's letter about succeeding his father in the physick professor's place 1647'; Wood, *Life and Times* i. 312, 318–36, 361, 383–98; *CSPD 1655*, 172–3, *CSPD 1658–9*, 263–4, *CSPD 1660–1*, 262, 525; G. C. Brodrick, *Memorials of Merton College* (OHS iv 1885), 110–14, 118.

fellowship in due course (1648), was imprisoned in the Tower for a time in 1651, and seems to have spent at least part of the decade in *émigré* circles on the continent; after the Restoration he claimed that at Cologne in 1655 he had been promised a place as physician in ordinary to the royal household. He returned to Oxford and in 1661 became Tomlins reader of anatomy as Clayton's deputy. This, with the help of Hyde's good family connections—his brother was the bishop of Salisbury and his cousin Edward Hyde, earl of Clarendon, was chancellor of Oxford—led to his appointment as regius professor in 1665, albeit at the pre-civil war salary of £40 a year. One of his first duties after his inaugural lecture in June was to give a laudatory speech presenting Robert Boyle to convocation so that the eminent philosopher could be created DM, an honour that pleased Boyle inordinately. In 1662 Hyde was appointed principal of Magdalen Hall, which headship he held until his death in 1681.[27]

If Hyde's tenure was less stormy than Clayton's, it was equally unmarked with signs of accomplishment. There are random references to his lecturing in the schools, for example on the occasion of the visit of the duke of Tuscany in 1669, and he made out the usual testimonial certificates, so he seems to have carried out his duties as expected. But he devolved the Tomlins readership to a deputy in 1666—almost as soon as he decently could—and seems to have had no significant contacts with the circle around Willis, Lower, Boyle, and others who were so active in medical investigations in the 1660s.[28]

John Luffe (*c.*1646–98) was on several counts even less noteworthy than his predecessor. The son of an Aylesbury minister ejected in 1662 for nonconformity, he had originally matriculated at Magdalen Hall, took his BA from Trinity College during Bathurst's time as president, and then his remaining degrees from St Mary Hall (MA 1668, BM and DM 1673). Luffe defended some mildly innovative questions as an inceptor *in vesperiis*, including the chemical notion that 'concoction' in the stomach is carried out by an acid ferment. A year later, in 1674, he was appointed Tomlins reader, and in 1681 succeeded Hyde in the regius chair. Like Clayton and Hyde before him, Luffe soon relinquished the duties of anatomical lecturer attached to the professorship, turning them over in 1684 to Robert Pitt, but retained the regius chair until his death at the relatively young age of 53. Luffe published nothing, was a member of no scientific clubs, had no discernible reputation as a clinician, and even an inveterate gossip like Wood found almost nothing to say about him.[29]

The five regius professors spanning almost exactly a century are united in a number of traits. The most notable is their lack of literary productivity. In an age in which news and knowledge circulated ever faster via the printed page, they wrote

[27] Foster, *Alumni* ii. 781; *CSPD 1651*, 104, 107; *CSPD 1661–2*, 29; Wood, *History of the University* ii. 884; *CSPD 1664–5*, 343, 389; Wood, *Life and Times* ii. 35, 38, 57.

[28] Wood, *Life and Times* ii. 160–1; Wood, *History of the University* ii. 884.

[29] Foster, *Alumni* iii. 949; OUA register of congregation 1669–80, NEP/*supra*/19, register Bd fo 204ᵛ; Wood, *History of the University* ii. 861, 884–6.

nothing. Were they guardians, rather, of an oral teaching tradition, one of honourable ancestry in the university? Except for a few years in the tenure of the younger Clayton, there is no hint that any of the five was a non-resident or a non-reader. Yet there survive no manuscripts or students' notes of any of those exegeses of Hippocrates and Galen, presumably so dutifully delivered at 8 a.m. on Tuesday and Fridays in term. Contrast that with the dozens of surviving notebooks kept by Englishmen of medical teaching at Leiden,[30] and one is forced to conclude that perhaps the regius professors did their jobs too well. They continued to purvey a teaching conceived as commentary on classical texts, rather than focusing on the human body and its ills. Of the five, only Clayton senior seems to have been comfortable in the long term with teaching over the cadaver; and although all five practised in the town, only he seems to have had any considerable reputation as a clinician. Added to this was the inherent institutional weakness of an academic office at the disposal of the crown. Rather than being chosen by a committee of electors who, when filling for example the Sedleian or Savilian chairs, had to debate with each other about the merits and deserts of candidates, the regius professorship was negotiated with a patron as a kind of plum that could be passed down through the family, engrossed by a reversion, or distributed as a reward for political loyalty. Correspondence speaks tellingly of the professorship as an office, like many distributed by the Stuarts, to be 'enjoyed'. Little wonder that the last regius elected in the century, Thomas Hoy in 1698, was a notorious non-resident for years on end.

Although the regius professorship was the only university-wide provision for teaching in medicine, from the 1510s onwards Thomas Linacre's generosity to Merton supported medical fellows of the college to 'expound and read in the public refectory' daily 'out of the books of Galen and Hippocrates', to 'any of the university that would please to be their auditors'. Such appointments had been intended by the founder to reform medical education at Oxford according to the ideals of medical humanism, and in a manner later duplicated in the regius professorship, by creating teaching positions and financial rewards for learned practitioners who were capable of bringing clinical expertise to bear on the philological exposition of works such as Galen's *De sanitate tuenda, Methodus medendi, De alimentis,* and *De simplicibus.* In the 1510s and 1520s these lecturers were paid for by Linacre himself, and after his death in 1524 by his feoffees, until a regular endowment was established in the late 1540s, and the power of appointment settled on Merton. The senior and junior Linacre lecturers, with stipends respectively of £12 and £6 a year, were to be elected every three years by the college from among its members, or in the absence of a suitable candidate, from any other college or hall. Inevitable modifications arose in practice: the senior position soon became tenable for life or until leaving Oxford, by the 1630s the junior lecturer was elected with the informal expectation of promotion, and already by the 1590s the duties had

---

[30] There is a large collection of such notebooks in the Sloane MSS in the British Library.

been scaled back to some twenty to thirty lectures per year. None the less it appears that, well into the 1670s, the Linacre lecturers in almost all cases carried out their duties of public teaching on the classical texts or—if one reasons analogously from the practices of other university lecturers—on topics of diet, pathology, and therapeutics arising from them.[31]

Although it is now impossible to judge what auditory such lectures had, it is much easier to assess what quality of men occupied the positions in the seventeenth century—and it was high. Theodore Goulston held the junior Linacre lectureship from 1604 to 1611, well before he took his BM and DM in 1610, but Wood says that he was already 'much in esteem for his knowledge' of physic. He went on to become FRCP and to practise in London, edited and translated the *Rhetoric* (1619) and *Poetics* (1623) of Aristotle, wrote a volume of commentaries on Galen's *Opuscula* (1640), gave £200 to endow an anatomy lecture at the College of Physicians, and left a large and excellent medical library to Merton.[32] The movement away from the ideal of the classical humanist is represented by Edward Greaves (junior lecturer 1640–3, senior lecturer 1643–7). He had studied at Padua before taking his DM in 1641, and afterwards at Leiden. From the experience of his Oxford practice he wrote a perceptive pamphlet, *Morbus epidemicus anni 1643*, describing a typhus outbreak in the Oxford garrison. For his adherence to the royalist cause he was created a baronet in 1645, the first medical man to be so honoured, and travelled with Charles II until 1653, when he began a highly successful London practice. Daniel Whistler (senior lecturer 1647–53) was by contrast an ardent parliamentarian, but no less astute a clinician. After a BA at Merton he had taken his MD at Leiden in 1645 with a thesis that gave the first printed description of what was called 'the English disease', rickets. He was later Gresham professor of geometry in London, FRCP and very active as one of the Royal College's examiners (censor), as well as a founding fellow of the Royal Society. Chemistry, yet another direction of seventeenth-century medicine, was represented by Edmund Dickinson (junior lecturer 1653–*c* 1663, senior lecturer 1664–9). A DM from Merton of 1656, he practised in Oxford until 1684, devoting money and time to chemistry, for which purpose he kept an operator. His obsession was shared by Charles II, whose physician Dickinson became, and who built him a laboratory under the royal bedchamber. After about 1670 the incumbents of the Linacre lectureships were generally rather less distinguished than their predecessors, although even in that period there were some active authors. Thomas Alvey (junior lecturer 1679–85) wrote a short treatise on the blood and urine (1680), and William Coward (senior lecturer 1685–9) was a prolific publisher of tracts on medical chemistry,

---

[31] Wood, *History of the University* ii. 862–3; a full and expert account of the foundation and its endowments is given in J. M. Fletcher, 'Linacre's lands and lectureships' in F. Maddison, M. Pelling, and C. Webster (eds), *Essays on the Life and Work of Thomas Linacre c.1460–1524* (Oxford 1977), 107–97; an excellent analysis has been done by R. G. Lewis, 'The Linacre lectureships subsequent to their foundation' ibid. 223–64, especially 231–43 and 247–53. Her dating of incumbency in the two lectureships is followed below.

[32] Wood, *Fasti* i. 339; Lewis, 'Linacre lectureships', 241.

poetry, and on the human soul—the latter work so controversial that in 1704 the house of commons ordered it to be burnt. The two also exemplify another increasingly frequent pattern; both seemingly held their positions as non-residents, and hence are unlikely to have lectured.

The link between the Linacre lectureships and Merton points to a more general relationship between college and medical man that strengthened in the course of the century. For one, an increasing number of physicians were, when the statutes allowed, elected to fellowships, although it was still the case throughout the century that the majority had to finance their medical studies without such benefits. At the higher level it was certainly true that positions as heads of house became much more available to medical men. Although Merton had a long tradition of physicians as warden, in the renaissance university a place as head was almost exclusively reserved for a divine. In the early part of the century the only physicians in such positions were Robert Pincke (BM 1612) as warden of New College (1617–47) and Thomas Clayton senior first as principal of Broadgates Hall (1620–4) and then as master of Pembroke (1624–47), the one more by virtue of his DD and support of Laud, and the other because he carried over when a hall was refounded as a college. Beginning in the 1630s halls started electing—or having imposed upon them—a disproportionate share of physicians. The principal's place at St Mary Hall was held in almost unbroken succession by John Saunders (1632–44), Nicholas Brookes (1644–56), and Martin Llewellyn (1660–4). Gloucester Hall had Tobias Garbrand (1647–60) and John Maplet (1660–2), and then much later the cleric–physician Benjamin Woodroffe (1692–1711). The principal's role at Hart Hall was exercised by Philip Stephens (1653–60) and for many years by John Lamphire (1663–88). Magdalen Hall similarly had two physicians as long-term heads, James Hyde (1662–81) and Richard Adams (1694–1716). Positions as heads of college, which were choicer plums, often went to cleric–physicians whose degree in divinity helped meet statutory requirements. Ralph Bathurst held the record for longevity with four decades as president of Trinity (1664–1704); among his fellow virtuosi were William Levinz as president of St John's (1673–98) and Henry Clerke in the like office at Magdalen College (1672–87). Merton continued its tradition of medical wardens with William Harvey (1645–6), Jonathan Goddard (1651–60), Thomas Clayton junior (1661–93), and Richard Lydall (1693–1704). Indeed, from the early 1650s through to the late 1680s there were almost always between four and six colleges and halls with physicians at the head, a pattern of support that greatly enhanced the local medical community.

For a period of about a quarter of a century the incumbents of the Linacre lectureships also coincided significantly with those of the new university chairs in the sciences that had been founded around 1620. Edward Lapworth was the senior Linacre lecturer from 1619 to 1636, while also being the first Sedleian professor of natural philosophy. Peter Turner held the junior lectureship from 1628 to 1631 before becoming Savilian professor of geometry, while his fellow Savilian in the astronomy chair, John Bainbridge, was junior lecturer from 1631 to 1636 in succession to Turner, and senior lecturer from 1636 to 1643 after the death of Lapworth.

Such overlaps of chair-holders reflect the more widespread phenomenon that medical study, with its attendant emphasis on Latin and Greek, mathematics, natural philosophy, chemistry, and botany, provided a broad education suitable for a professorship generally. Certainly it proved so throughout the seventeenth century, to a degree unmatched either before or since; in the century after about 1620 fourteen physicians occupied university professorships other than that of medicine.

On the arts side, the regius professorship of Greek was held from 1650 to 1660 by John Harmar, an ordained minister and former teacher at Westminster School, who had supplicated for his BM in 1632. In addition to numerous Latin orations and primers and translations of Greek, he may have been the author of a small tract on venereal disease. William Levinz, also in orders and a long-time fellow of St John's, held the same chair from 1665 to his death in 1698; he accumulated his BM and DM in 1666, shortly after his election, and amassed a remarkable library that included numerous works in medicine and science.[33] Throughout almost exactly the same period the Camden professorship of ancient history was held by physicians. Lewis du Moulin was a French protestant and Leiden DM who settled down to practise in Oxford in the 1640s. His staunch puritanism led the parliamentary visitors to appoint him to the Camden chair in 1648, and he incorporated on the strength of his Leiden degree the following year. In addition to producing a steady stream of controversial literature, his manuscripts show that he continued to practise medicine.[34] Du Moulin's successor in 1660, John Lamphire, had a mirror-image career. Ejected from his fellowship at New College, he had practised physic in Oxford in the 1650s, associated himself with the scientific virtuosi who met at a coffee-house, and was Anthony Wood's doctor. He proceeded DM in 1660 just six weeks after being elected to the chair, which he held until his death in 1688.

The Savilian professorships of geometry and astronomy, founded in 1621, were frequently used to support and further the scientific interests of learned physicians. John Bainbridge, a Cambridge DM who had studied at Padua, incorporated upon his degree at Oxford in 1620, moved into Merton, and held the Savilian professorship of astronomy from 1621 to his death in 1643; he continued to practise at least through the 1620s, and lectured on the Linacre bequest for long after that. Peter Turner, the son and grandson of eminent London physicians, fellow of Merton for more than forty years and former Linacre lecturer, was Savilian professor of geometry from 1631 to 1648; in keeping both with his heritage and with his early interests, he was created DM during the king's visit in 1636. At the end of the century, and into the following one, the Savilian chairs continued at times to be occupied by a DM. David Gregory, an Edinburgh geometrician and writer on optics, was elected to the astronomy chair in late 1691, and took his MA and

---

[33] *Bibliotheca Levinziana* (London 1698).   [34] BL MS Sloane 2014.

DM from Balliol in early 1692. On the latter occasion he delivered 'Tres lectiones cursoriae' that treat, as one might have predicted, medical aspects of optics; the manuscript for these show that statutory provisions were still enforced, and they constitute, along with the lectures of Bathurst and Petty, the few remaining exemplars of such exercises.[35] Although famous primarily as a Newtonian physicist, Gregory continued to prescribe for patients until his death in 1708 and became an honorary fellow and councillor of the Royal College of Physicians of Edinburgh. His protégé, John Keill, followed Gregory from Edinburgh to Oxford, took arts degrees from Balliol, and lectured on experimental physics at Hart Hall and Christ Church; in 1712 he was elected Savilian professor of astronomy, and took his DM in 1713.

But of all the chairs, it was the Sedleian professorship of natural philosophy that provided the closest link to medicine. Edward Lapworth, the son of a Warwickshire physician, was master of Magdalen College School from 1598 to 1610, began to practise shortly after 1600, took a medical licence in 1605, and accumulated his BM and DM in 1611—probably because he wished to marry. He was appointed Sedley's first reader in 1618, was elected to the senior Linacre position a year later, and held both posts until his death in 1636. Lapworth lectured regularly and saw patients in Oxford during term-time, while tending an upper-class practice in Bath during the summer. His successor, John Edwards, had a similar career trajectory. A fellow of St John's and sometime headmaster of the Merchant Taylors' School, he held the chair from 1636 to 1648, when he was ejected. He had accumulated his BM and DM in 1639, an indication of a practitioner's life that he seems to have continued in Oxford until his death in the late 1650s. By far the most eminent of the Sedleian incumbents was Thomas Willis. His tenure from 1660 to his death in 1675 coincided with a period of remarkable scientific and medical productivity that made him perhaps the most well-known physician in Europe. Unfortunately, in his latter years he taught by deputy. This custom, with its ultimately insidious effect of lowering standards, was continued by Willis's friend and medical colleague, Thomas Millington, who held the professorship from 1675 to his death in 1704. An All Souls BM and DM of 1659, when elected Millington had already established a flourishing London practice that lead to a knighthood in 1680, a post as royal physician to William and Mary and later to Queen Anne, and the presidency of the Royal College of Physicians. His inaugural lecture as professor in 1676 was, according to Wood, 'much commended', but, with the exception of John Keill, who lectured from *circa* 1699 to 1704, Millington's deputies have left no trace in the Oxford medical or scientific community. The professorship was thus held by physicians for all but twelve of the eighty-six years from its founding to Millington's death.

Although the statutes enjoined the Sedleian professor to read on works of Aristotle such as *De physica* and *De anima*, Willis's tenure provides us with unique

[35] David Gregory, 'Tres lectiones cursoriae', Aberdeen University Library, MS 2206/8, fos 1–48, cited in A. Guerrini, 'Archibald Pitcairne and Newtonian medicine', *Medical History* xxxi (1987), 73.

evidence of how such lectures, regulations notwithstanding, might be used to teach medical subjects. Soon after his election, most probably in the academic year 1661–2, Willis delivered a series of lectures whose contents partially survive because they were transcribed by Richard Lower, who sent parts of them on to Robert Boyle, and loaned others to John Locke for abridging into a medical commonplace book. The lectures make almost no reference to Aristotle, treating instead such general topics as life, sensation, movement, and nutrition, before going on to neurological subjects like pain, epilepsy, hysteria, sleep, coma, paralysis, delirium, frenzy, melancholia, mania, and stupidity. Then came more focused discussions of the parts of the brain that Willis held responsible for these manifestations—the cerebrum and cerebellum. He attempted to give his own synthesis on each topic; he referred hardly at all to Galenic works, sparingly to medical writers of the sixteenth and seventeenth centuries, but rather extensively to his own scientific and clinical experience in Oxford. He lectured in this way because he viewed his statutory charge rather broadly: to teach, among other subjects, 'the offices of the senses, both external and also internal, and of the faculties and affections of the soul, as also the organs and various provisions of all these'. In carrying out these duties Willis became dismayed by the excessively hypothetical nature of his teaching and resolved, with the anatomical help of Lower and in discussions with Millington and Christopher Wren, to explore the anatomy and pathology of the brain. This investigative enterprise led to four major works on neuroanatomy and pathology, beginning with the *Cerebri anatome* (1664): more than 1,400 quarto pages that formed the largest part of an *œuvre* that went through twelve editions between 1676 and 1720. Throughout the whole can be traced the major ideas, and sometimes even the specific medical cases, that arose in the Sedleian lectures.[36]

The academic obligations of the *studiosus medicinae* were not limited merely to attendance at lectures; the statutes also demanded an occasionally more active role, embodied in the disputations undertaken during term and for degrees, and in the *praelectiones* required for taking the DM. Ordinary disputations within the faculty were to take place in order of seniority *in schola medicinae*, from 1 p.m. to 3 p.m., twice each year in Hilary and Trinity terms. All students and bachelors in the faculty were to attend, with the disputants fined for failure to appear. Opposing once and responding once pro forma, with the usual requirements for posting advance notice, were demanded by the statutes before a medical student could propose a grace to be admitted BM.[37] A rather more formal set of disputations took place most years in early July. *In vesperiis*, on a Saturday from 1 p.m. to 5 p.m. in the school of medicine, the incepting doctors would each dispute as respondent a set of three questions or theses of their own choosing. At the Act (*comitia*) on the fol-

---

[36] On the duties of the Sedleian professor see *Laudian Code*, ed. Griffiths IV. i. 9, pp. 36–7. Lower's autograph notes from some of Willis's lectures were sent to Boyle, and are now in the Royal Society of London: Boyle Papers, vol. xix, fos 1–35; about 1667 Locke made extracts from Lower's notes in Bodl. MS Locke f. 19, pp. 1–156 *passim*, and both were edited and translated by K. Dewhurst in *Thomas Willis's Oxford Lectures* (Oxford 1980); Thomas Willis, *Cerebri anatome* (London 1664), sigs a1ᵛ–2ᵛ.

[37] *Laudian Code*, ed. Griffiths VI. v. 2, VIII. 1, IX. vi. 2, pp. 62–3, 81, 116.

lowing Monday the senior inceptor would propound a different set of three questions, usually with a bachelor as respondent, and each inceptor would discuss one
of them until all had had an opportunity to dispute. In part to curb a 'passion for
innovating', but probably also to avoid embarrassment on a public occasion, the
questions to be disputed in all faculties had to be approved by congregation in
advance.[38] For the seventeenth century the titles of almost 300 such disputations,
the *quaestiones in vesperiis* and *in comitiis*, have been preserved, providing a remarkable and detailed picture of the shifting content and emphasis of Oxford medical
education.[39]

A few topics dealing with popular medicine or the medical profession remind us
that disputations, especially those at *comitia*, could occasionally be displays of eloquence aimed at a lay audience. Inceptors in 1637, 1652, and 1669 solemnly denied
the mildly titillating proposition that love potions could induce love.[40] In 1640
Edward Greaves castigated 'marketplace empirics' and asserted the dignity of the
physician's life.[41] John Speed declared in 1628 that the whole man was the subject
of medicine; not only could human life be extended by this art, but even the very
day and hour of death might be predicted by the physician. Astrologers, Arthur
Acland argued in 1653, had no such knowledge of the future.[42] Such confidence
was further reflected in the twice-asserted proposition that in the cure of diseases
it was preferable for the patient to have several physicians at the bedside.[43] It is
noteworthy that such overtly propagandistic and rhetorical subjects essentially disappeared after the early 1650s, an attitude perhaps ironically reflected in the negative answer Charles Twysden gave in 1677 to the question 'whether eloquence was
necessary in a doctor'.[44]

Since Hippocrates, physicians had given advice on diet and regimen in relation
to health, a subject abundantly represented in the disputations of the first four
decades of the century. Supper, it was affirmed in 1608, and then again in 1639 by
the Sedleian professor John Edwards, ought to be more copious than dinner.[45]

---

[38] *Laudian Code*, ed. Griffiths VII. i. 7 and 15, pp. 70, 73–4.

[39] Titles of disputations are to be found in the Oxford congregation registers. Those up to 1622 are
printed in *Reg. Univ.* ed. Clark, pt i, 189–94. For the years after 1622 see: OUA register of congregation
1622–30, NEP/*supra*/14, register O, fos 240–4; OUA register of congregation 1630–4, NEP/*supra*/15,
register P, fos 274–9; OUA register of congregation 1634–47, NEP/*supra*/16, register Q, fos 178–81;
OUA register of congregation 1647–59, NEP/*supra*/17, register Qa, fos 150–4; OUA register of congregation 1659–69, NEP/*supra*/18, register Qb, fos 174–6; OUA register of congregation 1669–80,
NEP/*supra*/19, register Bd, fos 203–9; OUA register of congregation 1680–92, NEP/*supra*/20, register
Be, fos 202–5ᵛ; OUA register of congregation 1692–1703, NEP/*supra*/21, register Bf, fos 183–4ᵛ.
References below list the occasion (*vesperies* (v) or *comitia* (c)), name and college of the disputant, and
the year. Note that for inceptors, the year of defending theses *in vesperiis* was not always the year of
admission to the DM.

[40] (c) Edward Lenton, Magdalen Hall, 1637; (c) Richard Jackson, St Mary Hall, 1652; (v) Peter
Gerard, Brasenose, 1669.

[41] (c) Edward Greaves, All Souls, 1640.

[42] (c) John Speed, St John's, 1628; (c) Arthur Acland, Oriel, 1653.

[43] (c) Richard Spicer, Exeter, 1622; (v) Charles Bostock, Christ Church, 1640.

[44] (c) Charles Twysden, Christ Church, 1677.

[45] (v) William Turner, Balliol, 1608; (v) John Edwards, St John's, 1639.

Other inceptors argued that more than a single meal per day was necessary for well-being, that a feeling of lethargy after eating was a sign of health, and that a moderate diet was most conducive to longevity.[46] Disputants agreed, further, that a variety of foods was preferable to a simple diet, that leavened bread was more healthful than unleavened, and that wine ought not to be diluted or forbidden to women.[47] Nevertheless, Robert Vilvaine, who was to become a prominent Exeter physician, argued in 1609 that intemperate drinking was more destructive to the human body than immoderate eating.[48] Remarkably, such topics disappeared entirely after mid-century; only one is to be found after 1640.

The civil war, which brought a suspension of the Act from 1641 to 1650, also marked a divide in thinking about the nature and causes of diseases. Disputations in this category made up slightly more than a fifth (22%) of the total, distributed proportionally throughout the century. In the decades before 1640, however, such origins were most often sought in the traditional qualities, elements, humours, and temperaments inherited from classical medicine. Inceptors defended such propositions as that excess heat and liquid were the cause of stones and gout, that wind in melancholia arose from a hot cause rather than from a cold one, that black bile conduced to wisdom, or that women were more tormented by melancholia than men.[49] Several, including Thomas Clayton junior in 1635, declared that an innate complexion could be changed by medical art.[50] Many diseases were disputed which, later in the century, would not even be considered to be such. Love was affirmed to be a disease, as was old age.[51] Charles Bostock asserted in 1632 that a small heart was optimal for health, and that anger could produce disease and death.[52] Theodore Goulston, whose mastery of the Greek classics was exemplary, no doubt felt himself qualified to argue in 1610 that there had been no new varieties of disease since the beginning of human time, and that recurring diseases were the same as the originals.[53] One might be tempted to say that also of recurring *quaestiones;* the old chestnut of classical medicine, 'Whether the essence of fever is heat?', received an affirmative answer from no fewer than six disputants from 1620 to 1683.[54]

But from 1651 the discussion of causes of disease began to change in important ways. For one, disputants treated a much greater variety of diseases. Stones, gout,

---

[46] (v) William Turner, Balliol, 1608; (c) John Goodridge, Wadham, 1618; (v) Anthony Nourse, Wadham, 1651.

[47] (c) Thomas Grent, New College, 1615; (v) John Edwards, St John's, 1639; (c) Thomas Johnson, Oriel, 1608; (v) [no name given], 1609.

[48] (c) Robert Vilvaine, Exeter, 1609.

[49] (v) William Barker, St Mary Hall, 1608; (v) Andrew Bird, Merton, 1618; (c) Charles Bostock, Christ Church, 1632.

[50] (c) George Beard, Exeter, 1622; (c) Thomas Clayton junior, Pembroke, 1635.

[51] (c) [no name given], 1620; (v) John Speed, St John's, 1628.

[52] (c) Charles Bostock, Christ Church, 1632.   [53] (v) Theodore Goulston, Merton, 1610.

[54] (v) Francis Banister, Trinity, 1620; (v) Thomas Simpson, Christ Church, 1632; (v) Jonathan Maud, Brasenose, 1652; (v) Thomas Hayes, Brasenose, 1669; (v) Charles Twysden, Christ Church, 1677; (v) David Williams, Oriel, 1683.

phthisis, scurvy, epilepsy, pleurisy, melancholia, and fever occurred as topics before the civil war. To these were added rickets, dropsy and anasarca, hysteria, catarrh, plague, arthritis, measles, typhus, yellow jaundice, and hypochondria; fever was more closely discussed in its intermittent, hectic, pestilential, putrid, and malignant forms. Beginning also during the 1650s was a clear inclination to trace diseases back to specific organs and physiological processes, many of which were themselves newly recognized or discovered around the middle of the century. Robert Fielding of Balliol did both in 1654 when he attributed the 'new' disease of rickets to an impeded circulation of the blood and a deficient fermentation of the same liquid; the notions of circulation and fermentation had only been widely current since the 1640s.[55] Also in 1654 Fielding rejected the traditional explanation that catarrh came to the lungs from the brain, and his fellow disputant Richard Lydall denied that such catarrh caused thoracic diseases in any case.[56] In 1661 George Castle traced hypochondria to the spleen, although two decades later several others, including John Radcliffe in 1682, were inclined to deny that organ, widely seen as a source of ferments, a role in either hypochondriacal or melancholic affections.[57] Edward Jones in 1669 used the chemical phenomenon of tartaric dregs cast down by fermenting liquids to account for the origin of bladder calculi.[58] Francis Eedes thought in 1674 that intermittent fevers originated in a depraved stagnation of the newly discovered pancreatic juice, but a year later Radcliffe rejected the speculation that such fevers resulted from a fermentation caused by mixing pancreatic juice and bile.[59] From a modern standpoint, many such explanations that proliferated after mid-century are no less 'wrong' than the humoral pathologies they were attempting to replace. The point, rather, is that they represented a vigorous rethinking of the causes of disease in reaction to the perceived explosion of new anatomical and physiological knowledge; real debate replaced an endless re-posing of traditional questions.

Medical therapy was a category which maintained its popularity throughout the century, constituting overall one quarter (25%) of the subjects of disputation. As might be expected, bloodletting by venesection was the therapy most often discussed, although it tended to be proportionally of more interest before 1640. Disputants asserted that bloodletting was appropriate in syphilis, 'morbilis' (probably typhus), itching, 'putrid' and 'purple' fevers, and at the beginning of measles; indeed, Goulston argued in 1610 that venesection was to be used in any acute disease whatsoever after four days.[60] Several inceptors agreed that pregnant women

[55] (v) Robert Fielding, Balliol, 1654.
[56] (v) Robert Fielding, Balliol, 1654; (c) Richard Lydall, Merton, 1654.
[57] (c) George Castle, All Souls, 1661; (v) Thomas Rose, Exeter, 1681; (v) John Radcliffe, Lincoln, 1682.
[58] (v) Edward Jones, Merton, 1669.
[59] (v) Francis Eedes, Christ Church, 1674; (c) John Radcliffe, Lincoln, 1675.
[60] (v) Edward Lapworth, Magdalen, 1611; (v) Francis Banister, Trinity, 1620; (v) John Speed, St John's, 1628; (c) Thomas Clayton junior, Pembroke, 1635; (v) Simon Baskerville, Exeter, 1611; (v) Tobias Venner, St Alban Hall, 1613; (v) Theodore Goulston, Merton, 1610.

could be bled,[61] but there was disagreement about whether the method should be used on boys under the age of 14.[62] After the acceptance in the 1640s of the circulation of the blood there were fewer discussions of the absolute usefulness of blood letting, and in 1669 Peter Gerard even denied that there could have been a good reason for ligaturing in venesection before Harvey's discovery.[63] Disputants in 1676 and 1682 none the less continued to recommend phlebotomy at the beginning of measles in order to draw off malignant blood, although in 1680 Joshua Lasher, much later to be regius professor, denied emphatically that the positions of the moon and stars were of any importance whatsoever in bloodletting.[64]

The other pillar of medical therapeutics, purging, was also much debated, although here again most such disputations occurred before mid-century. Robert Fludd asserted in 1605 that purging did not accelerate the feebleness of old age, and subsequent disputants affirmed the appropriateness of purging at the beginning of disease, especially gout and pleurisy.[65] Inceptors in the 1650s emphasized that purging was sound procedure for pregnant women and even for dysenteries, although an emetic was preferred for eruptive diseases like measles.[66] One clear shift in this aspect of therapy was away from the traditional idea that purging could act selectively, drawing off only a particular humour; this Galenic conceptual foundation of therapy was uniformly rejected by five disputants from the 1650s to the 1680s.[67]

The general trend in therapies after mid-century was away from classical notions and towards new and specific remedies. The doctrines of critical days and astrological influences were rejected, as were the notions that the powers of drugs could be known by signatures, or that there was any such thing as a universal medicament.[68] Indeed, the traditional basis for such prescribing, diagnosis by urinoscopy, was repeatedly rejected as insufficient.[69] Instead, cooling regimens for measles, such as that recommended by Sydenham, were espoused by, among others, Locke's close medical associate David Thomas in 1671, and by John Radcliffe in 1682.[70] In

---

[61] (v) Ralph Bayley, New College, 1618; (v) William Denton, Magdalen Hall, 1635.

[62] (v) John Saunders, Oriel, 1628; (v) Peter Fiott, Exeter, 1657.

[63] (c) Peter Gerard, Brasenose, 1669.

[64] (v) Ralph Harrison, New College, 1676; (c) Stephen Fry, Trinity, 1682; (v) Joshua Lasher, St John's, 1680.

[65] (v) Robert Fludd, Christ Church, 1605; (v) Edmund Deane, St Alban Hall, 1608; (v) Tobias Venner, St Alban Hall, 1613; (v) Bridstock Harford, Lincoln, 1640.

[66] (v) Alan Pennington, Queen's, 1652; (v) Peter Fiott, Exeter, 1657; (v) Timothy Clarke, Balliol, 1653.

[67] Variants on the proposition 'An cathartica humores elective attrahant?' were affirmed by (v) George Raleigh, New Inn Hall, 1618, and (v) William Ford, Pembroke, 1632. It was rejected uniformly thereafter: (v) Thomas Waldron, Balliol, 1653; (c) John Ludwell, Wadham, 1672; (c) Joshua Lasher, St John's, 1676; (v) John Bateman, Merton, 1682; (c) Samuel Desmaistres, Oriel, 1683.

[68] Respectively: (c) Charles Twysden, Christ Church, 1677, and (v) William Gibbons, St John's, 1683; (v) Joshua Lasher, St John's, 1680, and (v) Thomas Rose, Exeter, 1681; (c) John Ludwell, Wadham, 1672; (v) William Warner, St John's, 1676, and (c) Charles Twysden, Christ Church, 1677.

[69] (v) John Luffe, St Mary Hall, 1673; (v) William Warner, St John's, 1676; (c) Francis Smith, Magdalen, 1680.

[70] (c) David Thomas, New College, 1671; (v) John Radcliffe, Lincoln, 1682; (c) Henry Southcot, Exeter, 1684.

the same year Radcliffe affirmed that the newly discovered Peruvian bark (containing quinine) could be employed without danger in every kind of intermittent fever (which included malaria).[71] In the same period one inceptor argued that chemical medicaments were to be employed in place of the old Galenicals, and another specifically recommended volatile salts to treat pleurisy.[72] The rise of specifics, like the declining theoretical interest in venesection and purging, reflected a fundamental shift in the content of academic medicine in response to new discoveries.

Exactly such a watershed in medical knowledge can be seen most clearly in the overwhelming attention that Oxford disputants paid after the civil war to anatomy and physiology. Overall there were more than 120 disputations on such subjects, representing 43 per cent of the topics discussed throughout the century; 109 of these fell in the period 1650–85. Disputants examined the detailed characteristics and possible actions of organs such as the brain, nerves, heart, lungs, liver, spleen, pancreas, stomach, glands, lymphatics, kidneys, and muscles. More abstract physiological principles were also subjected to scrutiny: the circulation of the blood, respiration, the making of chyle from food (chylification), excretion of urine, the nourishment of the parts, and the secretion of fluids such as bile, pancreatic juice, milk, and saliva.

One such physiological process, sanguification (the creation of blood from foodstuffs), was the subject of intense debate. The Galenic view had held that food products (chyle) were carried by veins from the intestines to the liver, which converted them into the blood that was subsequently passed on to the venous system. In 1627, however, the Italian anatomist Aselli had shown that chyle was drawn off from the intestines via separate vessels, the lacteals. Further, the French savant Jean Pecquet had announced in 1651 that these lacteals drained first into a lymphatic reservoir, the *receptaculum chyli*, whence the chyle was carried via another new structure, the thoracic duct, to empty into the venous blood flow just before it entered the heart. The liver was therefore bypassed entirely. Where, then, and how did sanguification take place, and what was the new role of the liver? The disputant quickest off the mark was Timothy Clarke, who in 1653 was the first to deny that the liver was the 'manufactory' of the blood, and he was followed in this opinion by others.[73] Richard Lydall suggested a year later that heat might be the true cause of sanguification, and Edward Stubbe argued in 1657 that this faculty was established in the heart.[74] Disputants in the succeeding decades examined the possibility that the spleen might be responsible before finally settling, in the late 1670s, on the formulation that 'blood forms blood'.[75]

[71] (v) John Radcliffe, Lincoln, 1682.

[72] (v) William Warner, St John's, 1676; (v) Charles Lybbe, Magdalen Hall, 1682.

[73] (v) Timothy Clarke, Balliol, 1653; (c) Sherrington Sheldon, Oriel, 1663; (v) Charles Lybbe, Magdalen Hall, 1682; (v) David Williams, Oriel, 1683.

[74] (c) Richard Lydall, Merton, 1654; (v) Edward Stubbe, Pembroke, 1657.

[75] Spleen: (c) Thomas Jeamson, Wadham, 1664; (v) Francis Eedes, Christ Church, 1674. Blood forms blood: (c) William Coker, All Souls, 1673; (v) Samuel Izacke, Exeter, 1675; (c) Joshua Lasher, St John's, 1676.

Overall, the focus after mid-century on blood and its properties is nothing less than astounding, a tribute to how profoundly Harvey's discovery had influenced the scientific part of medicine. Before 1640 but one disputation had been concerned with the composition or function of blood; between 1650 and 1685 there were no fewer than thirty-seven. Disputants dealt with every aspect of the blood conceivable to seventeenth-century medicine: whether it contained humours and spirits; its role in nourishing the parts; how it was cleansed in respiration; how it picked up ferments from organs such as the spleen; how it was the source of secretions such as milk, urine, and catarrh; whether and if so where it was 'enkindled' to create the heat that it brought to all parts of the body.

Particularly striking is how disputations on anatomy and physiology reacted rapidly to some new book or idea. In 1651 Ralph Bathurst denied that the foetus was nourished by the maternal blood, and in 1653 William Page asserted that all animals originated from an egg—propositions that derived from William Harvey's *De generatione animalium* (1651).[76] In 1657 William Quartermaine defended the new idea that the lymphatics distributed nutriments against Francis Glisson's even more recent concept, proposed in *Anatomia hepatis* (1654) of a 'nutritive juice' distributed by the nerves.[77] Thomas Willis's concept of an 'enkindling' of the blood had been adumbrated in passing in his three published works of 1659–67, but its discussion in lectures at Oxford no doubt formed the background to Thomas Jeamson's assertion in 1669 that such a process took place in the heart.[78] Willis himself argued in detail precisely the same point in a tract published in the following year. The issue was in turn disputed with vigour over the next fifteen years, Willis's protégé John Master and the budding clinician John Radcliffe being among the participants.[79] Such rapid and vigorous reactions to new discoveries were possible because there prevailed a supreme optimism that detailed knowledge of body organs, fluids, and their functions would in general only serve to extend, consolidate, and perfect learned medicine. As Quartermaine affirmed in 1657, *methodus medendi* was by no means changed by recent anatomical discoveries, a sentiment echoed in almost precisely the same words by Jeamson in 1669.[80]

The richness of theme and treatment found in the disputations *in vesperiis* and *in comitiis* are reflected with less strength and clarity in the ordinary disputations *in schola medicinae*. For these exercises little evidence survives before the Restoration. Thomas Crosfield's diary, for example, records that he attended 'disputationes in medicina' on 17 November 1626, but contains no further particulars.[81] Beginning in 1663, the congregation registers for the next forty years contain the titles and participants for seventy-six such theses, involving in all fifty-four medical students. Although these exercises were supposed to take place twice a year, in January and

---

[76] (c) Ralph Bathurst, Trinity, 1651; (v) William Page, St John's, 1653.

[77] (v) William Quartermaine, Pembroke, 1657.   [78] (v) Thomas Jeamson, Wadham, 1669.

[79] (v) John Master, Christ Church, 1672; (c) John Radcliffe, Lincoln, 1675; (v) Edward Wrigglesworth, St John's, 1679; (v) Richard Adams, All Souls, 1684.

[80] (c) William Quartermaine, Pembroke, 1657; (v) Thomas Jeamson, Wadham, 1669.

[81] *The Diary of Thomas Crosfield*, ed. F. S. Boas (London 1935), 6.

June, the one in winter was frequently dropped, and over the forty-year period fewer than half the disputations actually did take place. None of the recorded participants, either respondents or opponents, had yet taken a doctor's degree, and for most it was an exercise done either immediately before the BM, or *en route* between the BM and DM. Among the group of participants are nine for whom there is no other evidence of medical studies, reminding us once again that medical students, and even medical practitioners, did not always take degrees.[82]

The topics discussed in these ordinary disputations leaned very heavily (54%) towards questions of anatomy and physiology. Some were typical set-pieces, arguing that blood nourished,[83] that blood made blood,[84] that the brain was the seat of sense and motion,[85] that respiration was necessary to life, or that the heart was a muscle.[86] Others were more sophisticated in asserting the anti-Galenic proposition that the liver's sole function was to secrete bile, the mechanistic thesis that animal secretion depended upon the diverse shapes of the glands, and the finding of Lower and other Oxonians that inspired air did indeed enter into the blood.[87] The Harveian propositions that all animals were generated from an egg and that there could be no spontaneous generation both made what one might call an anniversary appearance in 1702, slightly more than fifty years after they were first published.[88]

Theses on the causes of disease and the effectiveness of therapies were almost as popular. Here again disputants sometimes brought out old chestnuts, affirming that imagination could cause disease,[89] denying that medicaments purged selectively,[90] and affirming that fevers were rooted in the heart.[91] Scurvy drew particular attention. Thomas Jeamson had argued in 1668 that it differed from syphilis only in degree, whereas by the early 1680s Richard Blackmore, Samuel Derham, and Thomas Mundy all asserted that it was due to a dyscrasia in the blood.[92] Medical

---

[82] I am grateful to Dr N. Tyacke for drawing my attention to these ordinary disputations in medicine, which are to be found in OUA register of congregation 1659–69, NEP/*supra*/18, register Qb, fos 39, 48, 73ᵛ, 78, 81, 85; OUA register of congregation 1669–80, NEP/*supra*/19, register Bd, fos 15ᵛ, 51, 56, 79, 98, 109ᵛ; OUA register of congregation 1680–92, NEP/*supra*/20, register Be, fos 5, 9ᵛ, 16ᵛ, 20, 26, 29ᵛ, 39ᵛ, 50, 56, 59ᵛ, 66ᵛ, 87ᵛ, 93ᵛ, 111; OUA register of congregation 1692–1703, NEP/*supra*/21, register Bf, 3, 12ᵛ, 20ᵛ, 51, 58ᵛ, 62, 67, 70ᵛ, 77, 81, 91, 97. References for individual disputations are given below by name, college, and year.

[83] Stephen Napleton, All Souls, 1698; John Beeston, New College, 1699; William Thorp, New College, 1701; [Francis?] Smith, Magdalen College, 1702.

[84] James Marwood, Exeter, 1684; John Beeston, New College, 1699; William Thorp, New College, 1701; [Francis?] Smith, Magdalen College, 1702.

[85] Norton Bold, Corpus, 1669; William Bridges, St John's, 1700.

[86] Stephen Napleton, All Souls, 1698; [Francis?] Smith, Magdalen College, 1692.

[87] John Manship, Corpus, 1694; Andrew Crispe, Oriel, 1699; Stephen Napleton, All Souls, 1700.

[88] Brune Bickley, New College, 1702.

[89] Richard Blackmore, St Edmund Hall, 1680; Samuel Derham, Magdalen Hall, 1681 and 1686.

[90] Edward Fettiplace, Christ Church, 1663; George Barbor, Oriel, 1677; Robert Whitehall, Merton, 1677; John Walker, Lincoln, 1692;

[91] Thomas Alvey, Merton, 1671.

[92] Thomas Jeamson, Wadham, 1668; Richard Blackmore, St Edmund Hall, 1680; Samuel Derham, Magdalen Hall, 1681 and 1686; Edward Forde, Wadham, 1682;

students showed that they were abreast of new ideas by attributing hysteria to the nerves and denying that the spleen caused hypochondria.[93] On the whole, however, the term disputations on pathology and therapy, like those in anatomy and physiology, showed less breadth of knowledge and cognizance of recent discoveries than those argued by inceptors at the Act—understandably so, both because the participants were on average younger, and because the disputations had more of an instructional intent.

Although the titles—and thereby subjects—of hundreds of medical disputations are recorded in the congregation registers and in the fugitive sheets printed for the Act, detailed content is more difficult to recover because so few full texts have survived. Ralph Bathurst's extant three disputations at the Act in 1651 would each have lasted about fifteen to twenty minutes; they contain a few classical references but are constructed largely on the basis of modern anatomists like Pierre Bellon, Girolamo Fabricio, Johann Vesling, Jean Riolan, Pierre Gassendi, Jan van der Wale, and William Harvey, as well as medical or scientific writers such as Julius Scaliger, Pietro Castelli, Jan Baptist van Helmont, and even Thomas Browne. If the questions were being disputed by an incepting doctor *in vesperiis*, as was true for Bathurst in 1654, they might be extracted from topics that the new DM had treated in the three or six *praelectiones* delivered separately for the degree. Certainly in Bathurst's case, the lectures *De respiratione* were an admirable critical synthesis of modern opinions, to which Bathurst added his own ideas and interpretations.[94] In many ways, then, disputations are, especially after mid-century, more significant than their brief length and life might imply; they provide one of the few systematic insights into the changing outlook and preoccupations of the Oxford community of practitioners.

MEDICAL BOOKS, MEDICAL APPRENTICESHIP, AND THE PHYSIC GARDEN

The topics of disputations show, especially between 1650 and 1685, a medical community changing its ideas of disease and therapy, and reacting to diverse currents of innovation in anatomy and physiology. But if the formal medical lectures of the university could provide only a rather sketchy framework for the theoretical knowledge and practical experience expected of an university medical practitioner, where and how were such knowledge and experience acquired? The answer is from books and from colleagues. More than before or since, seventeenth-century Oxford offered medical students an informal curriculum broader and richer than the statutory one.

To judge from surviving manuscripts, the would-be physician began his medical education, sometimes when he was only a BA or even an undergraduate, by collecting recipes and almost random bits of medical information. John Ward and John Locke both started to do so when they were about 21, and young Students

---

[93] William Coward, Merton, 1686.

[94] Thomas Warton, *The Life and Literary Remains of Ralph Bathurst, M.D. . . . Dean of Wells, and President of Trinity College in Oxford* (London 1761), 211–36 (*quaestiones*), 127–210 (*praelectiones*).

of Christ Church. The early prescriptions in Locke's notebook, begun in 1652, were rather simple: recipes for stone and colic, stomach-ache, heat in the face, ague, measles, gout, consumption, fistula, cancer, sore throat, toothache, rheum, and so on. Several, such as those for gout, colic, fluxes, and to 'heale a wound or hurt in ye eye', are attributed to his fellow student, Richard Lower. Others came from friends whose later careers were clerical. A few even derived from physicians in town, such as 'Dr Bathurst's method of cureing a gentlewoman of the scurvy'. Such collections were not at all confined to prospective doctors; most of the dozens of recipe books in Oxford libraries were kept by non-physicians.[95]

Self-education by reading began in earnest when the notebook-keeper began to supplement family and college recipes with prescriptions from published collections. Ward extracted copiously from Jean de Renou's *Dispensatorium galenico-chymicum* (Paris 1608), Thomas Johnson's *Mercurius botanicus* (London 1634), Johann Schröder's *Pharmacopoea medico-chymica* (Ulm 1641), and the chemical works of Angela Sala. Locke went further, and began to interlard his recipes with short extracts about disease conditions from Jacobus Hollerius, Pierre Paschal, Pierre Borell, Lambert van Velthuysen, Leonhard Fuchs, Pietro Castelli, and Jan Baptist van Helmont. A few from among scores of such entries give a flavour: epilepsy, hydrops, asthma, calculi, 'haemmorhagia vulvus', scrofula, cramp, ophthalmia, consumption, gonorrhoea, rickets, diarrhoea, podagra, glaucoma, cancer, and a multi-page extract on plague, as well as a long one, with recipes, on 'female diseases'. In another notebook Ward used a manuscript loaned to him by his Christ Church contemporary, Robert Lovell, to extract a series of headings of illnesses and symptoms, each with a list of the medicaments used in treatment. In the seventeenth century diseases were considered to be autonomous species with real identities that could be combated with the appropriate remedies. The commonplace book, with its pragmatic distribution of disease by an alphabetically keyed scheme, was a perfect reflection of the structure of medical knowledge.[96]

A common next step was to master several systematic compendia of medicine. Locke did exactly that around 1659 to 1660 when he filled a notebook with extracts from Daniel Sennert's *Opera omnia* (1656), which contained a multi-volume system of medicine based on the new corpuscular philosophies that had emerged on the continent from the 1620s. Another favourite among university physicians was Lazare de Rivière's *Observationes medicae* and *Praxis medica*, which Locke had in editions of 1656 and 1658 respectively. Ward also read de Rivière's works, which were

[95] Bodl. MS Locke e. 4 [c 1652–9], pp. 1–26, 69, 136, 138–9, 141–4. The following recipe books from the period 1550–1700 are typical: Balliol College MS 339 (Nicholas Crouch, c 1663–4); ECL MS 78 (John Sheffield, c 1650), MS 79, MS 80, MS 81, MS 82, MS 84, MS 85; CCCL MSS 168, 169, 173, 174, 177, 265 (Brian Twyne); Bodl. MS Rawlinson a. 369 (Oxford physician c 1589–1614), MS Rawlinson c. 10, 275 and 497.

[96] The diary-like commonplace books of John Ward, in sixteen volumes, are in the Folger Shakespeare Library, Washington DC; for a description see Frank, 'John Ward diaries', 174–9. The following citations of Ward's diaries give volume number, approximate date, and folios. His early collections of recipes are in Ward diaries iii [c 1652–8], *passim*, and v [1659], fos 1–32; similar notes of Locke are Bodl. MS Locke e. 4, pp. 26–156, especially 86–95, and in MS Locke f. 20 [c 1654–7].

notable for the large number of cases they contained. His friend Lovell recommended these to study for the examinations of the Royal College of Physicians, and Ward duly noted the advice in his commonplace book: 'Riverius his Institutions much admired by the Colledg; they usually examine their candidates out of itt.' Other works serving a similar purpose were older ones like Jean Fernel's *Universa medicina*, Santorio Santorio's *De statica medicina*, and van Helmont's *Ortus medicina* of 1648; all were read and abstracted by Ward and Locke.[97]

The rapid progress of late renaissance anatomy, especially in the works of Paduan teachers and their students, culminated in Harvey's revolutionary discovery announced in *De motu cordis* (1628); beginning in the late 1630s both traditions found a clear and marked reflection in Oxford medical reading. As a medical student and young practitioner Nathaniel Highmore (Trinity BM 1641, DM 1643) filled a notebook with anatomical extracts from Colombo, Fallopio, and Caspar Bauhin. He read Spigelius' book *De humani corporis fabrica* (Venice 1627) especially closely, and copied out extracts *de corde* and *de pulmonibus*. These in turn launched him into a series of essays on respiration, the circulation, and the functions of the heart and arteries—with numerous references to Harvey's arguments and experiments. In about 1643 Highmore showed some of these writings to Harvey, at that time living in Oxford, who urged him to publish. The result, Highmore's *Corporis humani disquisitio anatomica*, was the first anatomical textbook to be organized explicitly around the concept of the circulation, an honour it shared with Thomas Bartholin's *Anatomia* (Leiden 1651).[98]

These works opened the floodgates of the new anatomy. Francis Glisson's *Anatomia hepatis* (1654), with its new views on functions of the liver, soon appeared in notebooks like those of Ward and Locke. By the 1660s and 1670s a broad stream of anatomical literature flowed forth from the continent: Thomas Bartholin on the lymphatic vessels, Lorenzo Bellini on the microscopic structure of the kidneys, Anton Deusing on nutrition, Regnier de Graaf on the reproductive organs, Marcello Malpighi on the lungs and brain, Nicholas Steno on muscles and glands, and Jan Swammerdam on respiration. Added to these were works by Englishmen who, following the lead of Harvey and Glisson, brought forth a profusion of works in anatomy and physiology: George Ent's defence of the circulation (1641), Thomas Wharton on glands (1656), Thomas Willis on fermentation and fevers (1659), neuroanatomy (1664), and neuropathology (1667), Robert Hooke on microscopy (1665), Walter Needham on the foetus (1667), John Mayow on respiration (1668), Richard Lower on the heart (1669). All were abstracted by that omnivorous reader John Locke in the years after 1660—although one freely admits

---

[97] Bodl. MS Locke f. 18 [*c* 1659–60]; J. Harrison and P. Laslett, *The Library of John Locke* (Oxford 1965), 221; Ward diaries ix [1662–3], fo 57ᵛ.

[98] BL MS Sloane 577, *passim*; Nathaniel Highmore, *Corporis humani disquisitio anatomica* (The Hague 1651), sig. A1ʳ; on Highmore's Harveian stance see Frank, *Harvey and the Oxford Physiologists*, 27–8, 97–100.

that he was probably a great deal more systematic and interested than his fellow students of medicine.[99]

Such a feast of the accumulated—and fast accumulating—knowledge of European medicine was possible because in the course of the seventeenth century Oxford had very rapidly become both a book repository and a centre of the book trade. Starting from essentially nothing in 1598, the Bodleian Library had, by 1620, grown into a collection of 16,000 books and manuscripts. Through the deposit agreement with the Stationers' Company and through purchases and donations, it had further expanded by the 1670s to over 40,000 items, including almost every work of interest to a natural philosopher or physician. If the medical student did not have authors like Schröder, Sennert, de Rivière, Harvey, Glisson, and all the rest on his shelf, he could find them a short walk away.[100] Should he wish to buy such books, the number of booksellers had, by the 1630s, more than doubled since the beginning of the century. Many of the twenty-five were of course small, but a giant like Richard Davis had, in the late 1680s, a stock of well over 30,000 volumes in his shop on High Street near what is now the front quadrangle of Oriel College. This included over 2,000 volumes in philosophy and mathematics and about 3,000 titles on medicine and the medical sciences.[101] In addition booksellers like Davis occasionally published medical books, such as Highmore's tracts on hysteria (1660), Lovell's herbal (1659), Mayow's physiological treatises (1668 and 1674), Willis's works on neuroanatomy (1667 and 1672) and therapy (1674 and 1675), and William Cole on animal secretions (1674).

Many an Oxford medical scholar made good use of these booksellers. John Locke's library, by no means large in comparison to some, comprised over 3,600 volumes, about 40 per cent of them medical. This library was accumulated in London and abroad as well as in Oxford, while that of William Levinz shows what could be gathered in a lifetime just on the Isis. The latter contained just over 2,400 books, of which 20 per cent were medical and scientific, including the continentals de Renou, Sennert, Schröder, Bartholin, de Rivière, Pecquet, Malpighi, Sylvius, de Graaf and the Englishmen Harvey, Ent, Highmore, Glisson, Wharton, Willis, Sydenham, Needham, Mayow, Lower, Cole, and many others. Henry Stubbe's collection was rather smaller, slightly less than 1,700 volumes, but was even richer in medical and scientific works (65%), including sixteenth- and seventeenth-century anatomists such as Vesalius, Fabricius ab Aquapendente, Fallopius, Coiter, Riolan, and Vesling, plus all the continental and English 'moderns' that one would expect. Nor did one even have to be an avowed medical practitioner to sample such wares. Joseph Williamson of Queen's, whose later career was as a secretary of state, had

[99] BL Add. MS 32, 554 [1660–4], passim; Ward diaries iii [c 1652–8], passim; Harrison and Laslett, Library of John Locke, 80, 83, 123, 130, 144–6, 157, 179, 183, 187, 195, 239, 242, 263, 265.

[100] The Bodleian Library in the Seventeenth Century (Oxford 1951), 7–13; estimates of numbers and proportions based on Thomas Hyde, Catalogus impressorum librorum Bibliothecae Bodlejanae in academia Oxoniensi (2 vols Oxford 1674).

[101] Frank, Harvey and the Oxford Physiologists, 46; Catalogi variorum in quavis linqua & facultate insignium tam antiquorum quam recentium librorum Richardi Davis bibliopolae (3 pts London 1686–8).

about sixty medical books in his collection. These included the complete works of Hippocrates and Fernel and the medical compendium of Sennert, anatomical texts by Colombo, du Laurens, Riolan, Bartholin, Vesling, and Pecquet, medical works by Oxonians such as Willis, Highmore, and Hodges, and numerous collections of recipes and chemical protocols, such as Ashmole's *Theatrum chemicum Britanicum* (1652) and the inevitable Schröder. John Owen, DD, dean of Christ Church during the Commonwealth, had a tidy collection of medical works, including those by Paracelsus, Fernel, Spigelius, Sennert, Bartholin, Pecquet, Diemerbroeck, Harvey, Highmore, Glisson, and Charleton.[102]

Medical training at the early modern English universities has often been disparagingly characterized as 'literary'—as if there were some better 'practical' education available. In fact, education through the book exposed a practitioner to a spectrum of knowledge unobtainable solely through an apprenticeship: normal human anatomy and physiology, the symptoms and diagnosis of disease, gross post-mortem changes as a result of illness, chemical medicaments, and herbs, the comportment of a physician, and the management of cases. Moreover, the dismissive appellation 'literary' implies that would-be physicians spent years poring over texts of Galen, Hippocrates, and their followers in antiquity. Certainly by the 1620s this was no longer so. At any time throughout the century the medical student had access to a more than sufficiently rich variety of books that had been published in the previous thirty years, to constitute a solid core of medical learning. It was by mastery of this learning, rather than through lectures, that the student became a physician.

More practical experience was seen as properly erected upon this scholarly foundation, and came through friends and colleagues in the Oxford community. When in 1658–61 Ward began, as a senior MA in his late twenties, seriously to prepare himself for medicine, he seems to have attached himself to William Conyers, a DM of 1653 from St John's, who was six years older and already established in practice. Scores of Conyers's treatments, cures, and recipes are described in the diaries, many introduced with phrases like 'I saw Dr Conyers prescribe . . .'. Towards the end of his Oxford medical education Ward even helped Conyers with the autopsy of an Oxford woman 'who died of a kind of dropsie'; he spent several pages in his diary describing the state of the visceral organs. Ward had more distant relations with Willis, who none the less provided dozens of recorded recipes and dicta, ranging from Willis's use of blister plasters and smelling-salts of 'spirits of hartshorne' to his treatment of a fellow Christ Church Student for scurvy. The practice of the entire community supplied material for the student's education. One reads in Ward's diaries of Dr Maplet making 'issues in the braine,' of Dr Meadford evacuating 'hydropick humor,' of digitalis used for 'falling sickness', of a sore throat treated by Dr Bathurst, of *mercurius dulcis* 'much used by Dr Lydall', that Robert

---

[102] Harrison and Laslett, *Library of John Locke*, 11, 15; *Bibliotheca Levinziana*, 12, 16–17, 29–35; BL MS Sloane 35 [Stubbe]; QCL MSS 42, 44(1) and 44(2) [Williamson]; Edward Millington, *Bibliotheca Oweniana* (London 1684), 24, 27, 31.

Boyle had found a *balsamum sulphuris* to treat the king's evil, of Dr Lamphire using bloodletting, of a hand fistula treated by Dr Bates, and of Dr Millington's use of the Jesuit's bark in fevers. Similar items were gleaned from the practice of Drs Edmund Dickinson, Henry Clerke, Thomas Janes, Henry Yerbury, James Hyde, and Philip Stephens. From such contacts, some close and some more passing, the established Oxford medical practitioners could then testify, as they regularly did from the 1630s on, that a given student had practical knowledge worthy of being admitted to the DM. Clearly by mid-century the medical community at Oxford was large, active and diverse enough to provide such training, should the student show sufficient initiative to seek it out.[103]

If the young would-be physician was particularly talented, one of the local practitioners might even take him on as a kind of junior partner. Ralph Bathurst seems to have so served Willis *circa* 1648–51, and they became lifelong friends. Bathurst thereafter went on in 1653 to serve as an assistant to Daniel Whistler in Portsmouth, tending sick sailors during the first Dutch war. Richard Lower, ten years younger than Willis, seems to have acted in a like capacity of partner/assistant from about 1660. In 1662 the two doctors treated one of John Locke's tutees during a serious illness, for which the senior physician received £1 and the junior 10s. In April 1664 the two were on horseback visiting patients in Northamptonshire when Lower discovered by accident the medicinal virtues of a spring at Astrop; they recommended it to patients and the village developed a local reputation as a spa. Lower's letters to Boyle in this period are full of treatments and investigations he did with and for Willis.[104]

Another option for the budding physician, one whose partial appeal might have lain in avoiding the high costs of living in the university town without a college fellowship, was to read and gain experience in a rural practice, perhaps in conjunction with an older doctor. Thomas Browne studied and practised medicine in rural Oxfordshire in the period after making his medical grand tour and taking a DM at Leiden in 1633, and before incorporating at Oxford in 1637. Browne later recommended a course of reading to Henry Power, a Cambridge graduate starting in the provinces, and served as mentor to his own son Edward before the latter took his DM at Merton. Joseph Williamson, who had dabbled in medicine and chemistry while a fellow at Queen's, was later asked to find a place for a scholarly Edinburgh MA where the young man 'might gain experience in the practice of physic'.[105]

To be a physician meant to prescribe, and would-be physicians could and did gain experience from close contacts with apothecaries. Ward seems to have spent

[103] Ward diaries v [1659], fos 29ᵛ, 32, vii [1658–60] *passim*, especially fos 28ᵛ, 49, 50ᵛ, 60ᵛ, 95ᵛ, viii [1660–2] *passim*, especially fos 64–8, 96ᵛ.

[104] *CSPD 1653–4*, 104, 507; Bodl. MS Locke f. 11, fo 23ᵛ; Wood, *Athenae* iv. 297; *The Works of the Honourable Robert Boyle*, ed. T. Birch (6 vols London 1772) vi. 462–81.

[105] F. L. Huntley, *Sir Thomas Browne: a biographical and critical study* (Ann Arbor 1962), 90–8; Wood, *Athenae* iv. 56–9; *The Works of Thomas Browne*, ed. G. Keynes (4 vols Chicago 1964) iv. 26, 255–6. On Williamson see *CSPD 1656–7*, 127, *CSPD 1660–1*, 551, *CSPD 1661–2*, 319.

much time with the Oxford apothecary Stephen Toone, a younger man but like him a minister's son who came from the same part of Northamptonshire. Toone was the source of dozens of recipes and was also a helpmeet in investigations. During his last year at Oxford, Ward and Toone did a dissection of a dog in which they 'came to the lower belly and so to the breast, and opend . . . blew up the lungs, and so ended not finding what wee lookd for, to wit the passages of the chyle'. Such anatomical and physiological interests also concerned the two on Ward's long return visits to Oxford in 1664 and 1665. Toone had 'a dog which they call "Spleen" because his spleen is taken out'. After the dog died, Ward wrote out in his diary some queries on splenic function 'to be inquired into in dissecting Mr Toon's dogge, call'd "Spleen" '.[106]

A student's relations with local surgeons could be equally close and fruitful. One such, Francis Smith, became a close companion of Ward's; others, such as the older surgeon William Day, and the hybrid physician/surgeon John Gill, appear in his diaries more as sources of surgical and pathological information. Smith passed on chemical procedures, a description of a deformed birth, news about opening the 'head of one that died of an apoplexie' and finding 'nothing in the ventricles', and of an experiment on arterial blood carried out with Lower, as well as the information that 'some doctors especially in Oxford now are of opinion that histerical fits are caused by the indisposition of the braine'—as against the traditional medical view that hysteria was an exclusively female complaint caused by the uterus. In 1661 Ward recorded details of a splenectomy performed by Day, and that 'the same spleen and the dog was stoll after by Mr. Hartford, and brought up to London and there dissected'. Ward also discussed anatomical research with Gill, who told him 'very many pretty stories' of the surgeon's 'enquisitions' in dissecting bodies. When Conyers directed an autopsy, it was Gill who opened while Ward and the senior physician looked on. Such contact and co-operation among Oxford's medical practitioners was more commonplace than the typical picture of three separate healing orders—physician, surgeon, apothecary—would lead us to believe, and explains how a student could, with persistence, gain a broad exposure and even some experience in all aspects of medicine.[107]

Furthermore Browne, Bathurst, Lower, Ward, Locke, and others were in varying degrees of practice often long before they actually took a medical degree or obtained a licence. The supplications for admission in fact frequently contain testimony to a candidate's clinical skills. It therefore makes little sense to speak in twentieth-century terms of a person before the BM being 'not yet qualified'. The path from collector of recipes, to onlooker, to informal apprentice, to assistant, and perhaps even to partner represented the gradual acquisition of experience melded with scholarly knowledge, enabling the budding physician to master cases of

---

[106] Ward diaries v [1659] *passim*, vii [1658–60] *passim*, viii [1660–2] *passim* and fo 43, x [1663–5], fo 56ᵛ, and iv [1665], fo 35ʳ⁻ᵛ.

[107] Ibid. vii [1658–60], fos 24–5, 30ᵛ–1, viii [1660–2], fos 32, 40, 65–8ᵛ, ix [1662–3], fo 123, iv [1665], fo 25ᵛ–7.

increasing seriousness and complexity. Being 'qualified' was not a legal status, but a set of capabilities assessed by society on a sliding scale. The MA and college fellow considered well able to treat a serious 'malignant fever' in a farmer's family or the headache of a young gentleman-commoner would never be called to cure the dropsy of a local squire's wife. Possession of the BM, and most especially the DM, simply made the practitioner 'fully' or 'unconditionally' qualified.

TEACHING AND LEARNING ANATOMY

If institutions for the endowed professorial exposition of classical texts had brought late-renaissance Oxford into line with the most progressive methods of continental Europe, by the early seventeenth century the university had once again fallen behind. At Padua, Basle, and Leiden—the universities most favoured by Oxford sojourners around 1600—there were professors to teach anatomy by lecture and dissection; at Oxford there was none. A provision of the Edwardian statutes of 1549 had made attandance at two anatomical dissections necessary for degrees, but this requirement was silently dropped from the *Nova statuta* of 1565, most probably for the very good reason that there were no dissections to attend. *De usu partium* was among the Galenic texts introduced in the *Nova statuta* as possible subjects of lectures to be read for the DM, but that scarcely meant that anatomy was intended to be studied practically and concretely.[108] Before the 1620s there seems to be very little evidence of interest in, or the perceived necessity of, anatomy as a basis for medical study and practice; a DM disputation *in vesperiis* by Francis Banister in 1620 on whether the spleen is nourished by black bile, and Brian Twyne's collectanea on vision and anatomy nearly exhaust the list.[109] Nor can one identify any medical graduates educated before about 1610 whose later distinction in anatomical subjects might be traced back to Oxford.

This lack seems to have concerned Thomas Clayton senior, for we can only assume that it was at his instigation that an otherwise little-known Westminster merchant, Richard Tomlins, wrote to convocation in the autumn of 1623 with an offer to found a lectureship in anatomy. The governing statutes were drawn up and adopted in the autumn of 1624, prefaced with an assertion that 'the knowledge and true understanding of man's body and the partes and faculties of the same' was necessary not only for the 'artes of phisicke and chirurgery', but also to those who studied 'divinitie, philosophy and all other good literature'. The reader of the lecture was to be the regius professor of physic, for which duties he was to have £25 per annum. Each spring, immediately after the Lenten assizes, he was to claim the 'sounde body of one of the executed persons', or some other body if that were not possible. The cadaver was to be dissected and prepared by a 'skilfull chirurgian', with whose assistance the reader was to give four complete lectures, from 9 a.m. to 11 a.m. and from 2 p.m. to 4 p.m., in the course of two days. In these he was to 'shewe, teach and deliver the scituation, nature, use and office, of the partes of

---

[108] *SA* 346, 378–9.   [109] *Reg. Univ.* ed Clark, pt i, 194; CCCL MS 263.

the body'. The first two lectures were to be on the 'natural parts', such as the liver, spleen, stomach, and intestines, the third on the 'vital parts' such as the heart and lungs, and the last on the animal parts seated in the brain. The lectures were to be public, that is without fee, and all students in medicine and all surgeons in the university were 'necessarily bound to attend', upon forfeiture of 2s. The sum of £3 was to be allowed to the surgeon, and £2 for the decent burial of the body. In addition to the spring dissection, the reader was obliged to read publicly three times in Michaelmas term on the bones of the skeleton, and could give other lectures on anatomy as he wished. To ensure that the reader read, and that students attended, the statutes contained provision for the vice-chancellor and proctors to appoint a paid deputy, and stated that supplicants for a licence in medicine or surgery had to produce testimony that they had been present at one entire anatomical dissection and at 'one whole reading of a sceleton'. As a place for the lectures, a large room on the first floor at the south-west corner of the schools quadrangle was assigned; throughout the seventeenth century this also served as the school for lectures in medicine. Clayton, with Bernard Wright serving as surgeon, inaugurated the endowment with a lecture on 12 March 1625.[110]

For the first decade and a half, Tomlins seems to have paid Clayton directly, but that in no way impeded the development of anatomy as a subject, and the growth of a broad appeal, even among those not intending medicine as a profession. When Clayton performed his second dissection in the following spring of 1626, he had among his auditors the diarist and theologian Thomas Crosfield, an MA of the year before, and not yet a fellow of Queen's. The Tomlins reader seems to have felt the need for a good anatomical vade-mecum, for he arranged in 1633 for an Oxford printer, William Turner, to bring out a duodecimo edition of a favourite continental dissecting manual, the *Anatomicae institutiones corporis humani* by Caspar Bartholin. At the Act in the same year, one of Clayton's students, the inceptor Edward Dawson, gave an affirmative answer to the question 'Is the circulation of the blood probable?', just five years after Harvey had published his discovery and when the circulation of the blood was accepted by almost no one. Responding to Tomlins's continuing generosity in support of such studies, the vice-chancellor spent £19 17s 10d over the period 1634–40 in fitting out the anatomy school with panelling, 'pewes', new glazing, and assorted other woodwork. Thomas Trapham, the Oxford surgeon who was later to embalm the body of the executed Charles I, gained both experience and a fee when he prepared a skeleton for the university in 1634. In the same year a 'Mr Camden, enginer', began a tradition of gifts of *naturalia* by 'bestowing the dodar (a blacke Indian bird) upon the anatomy schoole'. The whole enterprise was put on a firm financial footing in 1638–9 when Tomlins settled £500

---

[110] OUA register of convocation, 1615–28, NEP/*supra*/23, register N, fos 194–8ᵛ; the regulations for the Tomlins lecture are to be found in *SA* 550–5, and summaries are printed in Wood, *History of the University* ii. 883 and in Hearne, *Collections* ii. 379–80, 400; the plan of the schools quadrangle in the seventeenth century is given in Wood, *Life and Times* ii. 62–5.

upon the university to endow the lecture, and the usual trust for its administration was approved by convocation.[111]

For the remainder of the century there are recurring bits of evidence that the Tomlins readers carried out their tasks very much as intended, even though not usually in the person of the regius professor. Thomas Clayton junior, who according to Wood 'could not endure the sight of a bloody body' and never actually lectured in this capacity, began the custom in 1650 by formally resigning the readership in favour of William Petty. From that point on, it became *de facto* a separate appointment, albeit in the gift of the regius professor.

TABLE 8.2 *Tomlins readers in the seventeenth century*

Thomas Clayton senior	1624–47	as regius professor
Thomas Clayton junior	1647–50	as regius professor
William Petty	1650–*c.*1652	deputy for Clayton
Henry Clerke	*c.*1652–61	deputy for Petty
James Hyde	1661–5	deputy for Clayton
	1665–6	as regius professor
John Paris	1666–9	deputy for Hyde
Thomas Jeamson	1669–74	deputy for Hyde
John Luffe	1674–81	deputy for Hyde
	1681–4	as regius professor
Robert Pitt	1684–6	deputy for Luffe
Stephen Fry	1686–*c.*1695?	deputy for Luffe
James Keill	*c.*1695–*c.*1700?	deputy for Luffe and Hoy?

By 1710 the system of deputies appointing deputies reached the point of low comedy when the antiquarian Thomas Hearne clashed with James Monro, deputy for Charles Tadlow, in turn the deputy of Thomas Hoy, a notorious non-resident by then living in Jamaica. Hearne objected in part to the fact that Monro read privately rather than publicly, thereby receiving 'large fees of every person he reads to'. More materially, Hearne disliked the smells that drifted from the anatomy school into the adjacent Bodleian, and feared possible losses from the library's collection of medals and 'curiosities', which by that time was stored there.[112]

Easily the most famous of the Tomlins readers was William Petty. He had gone to sea at the age of 15, learned Latin and Greek at Caen, and in 1643 had enrolled as a student of medicine at Utrecht. After spending the years 1644–6 in further

[111] *Diary of Thomas Crosfield*, ed. Boas, 2, 71, 135; OUA vice-chancellor's accounts 1621–66, WP/21/4, 32–3, 37, 39, 41; Hearne, *Collections* ii. 374; OUA register of convocation 1628–40, NEP/*supra*/24, register R, fos 155ʳ⁻ᵛ, 161ᵛ–4.

[112] Wood, *History of the University* ii. 883–6; OUA register of convocation 1647–59, NEP/*supra*/26, register T, 124–5; Hearne, *Collections*, ii. 380–1; H. M. Sinclair and A. H. T. Robb-Smith, *A Short History of Anatomical Teaching in Oxford* (Oxford 1950).

studies of medicine, anatomy, and chemistry at Leiden and Paris, and becoming acquainted with anatomists like Jan van der Wale and the philosophical group around Thomas Hobbes, he returned to England in late 1646 and resided in the area of Reading and Oxford as a medical practitioner.[113] In the subsequent few years of political upheaval he was in contact with London projectors like Samuel Hartlib and John Pell, and tried to secure his future by means of such innovations as a machine for duplicating writing and a proposal for a teaching and research hospital, the 'nosocomium academicum'. The latter was to encompass a 'house, garden, library, chymicall laboratorie, anatomicall theater [and] apotheca, with all the instruments and furniture belonging to each of them'. A chief physician with a salary of £120 a year would 'visite and examine all the sick' twice each day, supervise a staff of other physicians, surgeons, and apothecaries as they took care of patients and recorded their observations, and from such 'histories' he would 'collect a systeme of physick and the most approved medicinall aphorisms; taking notice by the way where those of Hippocrates are deficient or true, and by how many severall experiments he hath so found them'. As an important part of this research, the physician in charge 'shall either dissect or overlook the dissection of bodies dying of diseases'.[114]

After the trial and execution of Charles I such visionary new institutions may well have appeared less promising to Petty than the vacancies then being created at Oxford by the parliamentary visitation. In October 1649 he proceeded DM by virtue of testimonial letters from Lieutenant-Colonel Kelsey, the commander of the Oxford garrison. At the same time Petty wrote to his cousin of his intention of once again undertaking 'chymistry and anatomy', and offered him 12d a day for helping with such tasks as making a 'sceleton'.[115] Petty completed his degree the following March by reading the statutory six lectures, and in April, May, and June of the same year he was examined for admission as a candidate at the Royal College of Physicians.[116] After appointment as Tomlins reader in December 1650, he gave an 'oratio inauguralis anatomica' in the schools on 4 March 1651, and shortly thereafter his lectures over the cadaver.[117] Petty followed this with a more general 'lec-

---

[113] Lord Edmund Fitzmaurice, *The Life of Sir William Petty, 1623–1687* (London 1895), 1–21. Volume iii of the Petty Papers at Bowood, Calne, Wiltshire, labelled 'Sir William Petty's Medical Studies and Other Papers', is divided into thirty-one numbered items dating from the period 1645–53, each paginated or foliated separately; these are cited below as 'Petty papers'. They constitute unique evidence for anatomical teaching at Oxford, as well as for the exercises performed for a medical degree. No. 21 is a medical diary kept during May–June 1647, with names of patients living in London, Reading, Oxford, and Bath.

[114] William Petty, *A Declaration Concerning the Newly Invented Art of Double Writing* (London 1648); [William Petty], *The Advice of W.P. to Mr. Samuel Hartlib for the Advancement of Some Particular Parts of Learning* (London 1647[/8]), 9–17, quotations from pp. 9 and 13.

[115] OUA register T, 73, 75; Fitzmaurice, *Life of Sir William Petty*, 14.

[116] Petty papers, iii. (1) [24 pp.] and (7) [79 fos]. Petty referred to these in a catalogue of his own writings as 'Six physico-medical lectures read at Oxford 1649[/50]': see Fitzmaurice, *Life of Sir William Petty*, 317. London, Royal College of Physicians, 'Annals' iv, fo 27^{r-v}.

[117] Petty papers, iii. (27), 'Oratio inauguralis anatomica scholis publicis publico habenda. 4to Martij, 1651/50 Oxonii' [12 pp.]. The anatomical lectures are ibid. (4) [57 fos], where the notes are divided into

tio anatomica proemialis' delivered at the Act in July 1651, and then performed the required three osteological lectures in the autumn. To help him carry out his duties, he persuaded the vice-chancellor to spend £2 8s 8d for instruments and materials, the first such expenditures for the physic/anatomy school in over a decade.[118] In the same year he got himself appointed to a fellowship at Brasenose, was chosen vice-principal there, and was elected professor of music at Gresham College in London. Petty certainly proved himself an ambitious young man to accumulate so many offices by the age of 29, but it was that very ambition that founded the Lansdowne line, and thereby preserved a record in manuscripts of an anatomical teacher at work in Oxford.

It is ironic that after such assiduous, if brief, attention to his Tomlins duties, Petty's anatomical interests should be best remembered through a rather more private dissection: the 'resurrection' of Anne Greene. This young woman, aged 22 and living in the household of Sir Thomas Read, had become pregnant by Jeffrey Read, the knight's grandson. In desperation and confusion she drowned the baby at birth, and for this she was condemned to hang on 14 December 1650. After she had been suspended from the noose for half an hour, she was cut down, put in a coffin, and conveyed to a private house 'where some physitians had appointed to make a dissection'. When Petty and Thomas Willis arrived, they found her still breathing, and set to work to revive her. Soon joined by Ralph Bathurst and Henry Clerke, the four used the tools of contemporary medicine—cordials, bleedings, heating clysters, plasters on her breast, rubbing of her extremities, anointing of her neck, temples, and feet with comforting oils—to bring about a recovery within a week. One onlooker lauded the generosity of 'those gentlemen that freely undertook and so happily performed the cure', that 'whilst they missed the opportunity of improving their knowledge in the dissection of a dead body, they advanced their fame by restoring to the world a living one'. Such an astounding event called forth the usual quickly printed narratives adorned with undergraduate poetry, including one in praise of the university's physicians:

> Oxford (The Arts Metropolis) ner'e knew
> A rarer feat then was performed by you
> Brave Æsculapian friends! whose Art could give
> After the Execution a Reprieve.
> Others can by their Chymistry reduce
> A Plant or flower from its dust or juyce;
> But your sublimer Art hath done much more
> Whilst humane soules you from their Urnes restore.

five sections and deal with strictly anatomical matters; they are in a rough, hasty hand and have been heavily corrected by Petty himself.

[118] Petty papers, iii. (26), 'Lectio anatomica proemialis habenda in actu publico, Oxonii Annj 1651' [13 pp.]. Lectures on bones are ibid. (28) and (30) [c.49 pp.]. These seem to correspond to the second and third of the 'Three ostiological lectures 1651' mentioned in his catalogue of writings: see Fitzmaurice, *Life of Sir William Petty*, 317. Supplies are mentioned in OUA vice-chancellor's accounts, 1621–66, WP/21/4, 54, and inventoried in OUA SEP/L/2/21.

Yet though your skil and pity could dispence
More daies to her beguiled Innocence:
No Act removes a ruin'd Virgins shame,
Unlesse revived she, be not the same.
Thus 'tis more easy to recall the Dead
Then to restore a once-lost Maidenhead.

Petty was rather less lyrical when he described the events in a letter to Hartlib, and concluded: 'my endeavours in this businesse have bettered my reputation'.[119]

The Tomlins foundation, however, had a weakness: it supported an annual two-day dissection, but no extended and detailed teaching of human anatomy. That seems to have been provided by informal instruction, for which evidence exists from the 1650s onwards. Ward recorded in the spring of 1662 that 'Dr Stephens went over a bodie of anatomie 16 termes to schollars; hee read Vestlingius. Mr Burnet was his scholler. Hee had 5 pounds of him for itt.' This was Philip Stephens, whom the visitors had put in as fellow of New College in 1649; he became principal of Hart Hall in 1653, DM in 1656, and moved to London in early 1659. It is unlikely that he taught four terms a year, so his classes must have extended over five or six years, beginning in the early 1650s. His text, Johann Vesling's *Syntagma anatomicum*, was a straightforward explication of the human body as encountered in dissection, but with the unusual twist that the book accepted the Harveian discoveries, while placing them within an Aristotelian natural philosophy that would have been congenial to a traditional university setting. By the 1660s such anatomical teaching was taken over by Willis, and especially Lower, so much so that when Samuel Sorbière visited Oxford in 1663 he noted that their informal anatomy classes were more popular than the official instruction. Edward Tyson of Magdalen Hall seems to have played a similar role in the 1670s, as did William Musgrave in the 1680s and James Keill in the 1690s. As a textbook for his teaching, Keill translated Bourdon's dissecting manual, *The Anatomy of the Human Body, Abridged* (1698), that went through fifteen editions in seventy years. Each of the four last-named informal teachers—Lower, Tyson, Musgrave, and Keill—was at the time in his late twenties or early thirties, tended only a small university and town practice, and had not yet taken a final medical degree—the perfect colleague or teacher.[120]

Although resurrections did not occur often, the scene of Oxford physicians and medical students gathered informally over a body for a dissection or autopsy was repeated with increasing frequency after 1650. Only in this way could the normal human anatomy as described in books be made three-dimensional. In 1658 William

---

[119] [Richard Watkins], *Newes from the Dead* (Oxford 1651), 1–8, 14–15; this poem was written by Kingsmill Lucy, a gentleman-commoner of Christ Church; other poems were penned by such future scientists and virtuosi as Joseph Williamson, Robert Sharrock, Christopher Wren, and Walter Pope. Sheffield, Sheffield University Library, Hartlib Papers, bundle viii (23), Petty to Hartlib, 16 December 1650.

[120] Ward diaries ix [1661–3], fo 76ᵛ; Johann Vesling, *Syntagma anatomicum* (Padua 1651), sig. +4v, pp. 117–21; Samuel de Sorbière, *Relation d'un voyage en Angleterre* (Paris 1664), 105–6.

Conyers led a group of would-be anatomists to dissect a young woman hanged at Greenditch, only to find that she too was revivable. Another group went as far afield as Aylesbury, in 1663, to dissect an executed criminal. Such opportunities were worth the travel because only then could practitioners carry out a full anatomy of all parts. It is ironic that the metropolis, with its huge population, offered only slightly better opportunities. Ward recorded in 1662 after his arrival in London that there 'are but 2 publick anatomies in a year, att Barbers Chirurgions Hall, besides private ones'.[121]

Autopsies, limited to searching out the cause of death, were more frequent because they did not depend upon executions. None the less they were comparatively rare at Oxford in the first half of the century; Lapworth attested to a monstrous birth in 1633, apparently on the basis of a post-mortem, and Highmore records two autopsies at Oxford, one in 1640.[122] Active pathological inquiry began only after mid-century. In May 1650 Willis recorded in his casebook a post-mortem on a patient dead of 'dropsy of the lungs'. Through the 1650s he became a regular performer of autopsies. By the time of his Sedleian lectures of 1661–2 Willis could adduce post-mortem findings on newborns that had died of epilepsies, three or four men 'whose heads we dissected', an academic who suffered from pleurisy, another with an encapsulated abscess in the diaphragm, and a young woman dead from apoplexy whose cerebral ventricles were filled with a yellowish humour. He referred in passing to similar kinds of autopsy findings in his *Cerebri anatome* and *Pathologiae cerebri* relating to convulsives, paralytics, hysterics, and asthmatics.[123] Lower was even more active as an investigator of anatomical pathology, especially in the period from 1661 to 1667. In 1663 he described to Boyle a post-mortem case in which the right carotid artery was completely occluded, a finding that led Lower and Willis to investigate the functions of the carotid and vertebral arteries in supplying blood to the brain—which set of structures is still known eponymously to anatomists and neurologists as the 'circle of Willis' (plate 26). A single long letter to Boyle in June 1664 reported in detail on five autopsies: a senior fellow that had succumbed to dropsy, a townsman who had died of an apoplexy, a 'very able and healthy' young scholar stricken with 'a lethargy' and a young gentleman and fellow of All Souls whose thorax was almost completely filled with fluid, as well as another in the same condition. Lower, Willis, and Millington did a particularly spectacular post-mortem two years later, in May 1666, when they examined the body of a young Wadham scholar who had been struck by lightning while aboard a rowing-boat on the Thames; it was such an event, John Wallis reported, that despite the hot weather and close room, there were seldom fewer than forty

---

[121] Wood, *Life and Times* i. 510, 250–1; Ward diaries ix [1662–3], fo 15ᵛ.

[122] QCL MS 121, p. 302; Highmore, *Corporis humani disquisitio anatomica*, 60, 178–9.

[123] K. Dewhurst, *Willis's Oxford Casebook* (Oxford 1981), 118; Dewhurst, *Thomas Willis's Oxford Lectures*, 86, 120, 141; Willis, *Cerebri anatome*, 152; Thomas Willis, *Pathologiae cerebri, et nervosi generis specimen* (Oxford 1667), 60, 84, 107, 121, 158, 199.

observers.[124] The pace of autopsy inquiries seems to have slackened in the 1670s and 1680s, but one can still find references to Edward Tyson autopsying someone who had died from inflammation of the gall-bladder, or to William Musgrave and Nicholas Crouch reporting in 1685–7 before the Oxford Philosophical Society of post-mortems on patients who had died of consumption, of pleurisy, of dropsy, and of stomach cancer.[125] By then the tradition of holding autopsies was clearly established; how frequently they took place depended upon having one or more anatomically inclined physicians in the university town.

Surgeons, too, regularly conducted post-mortems, with the medical community privy to the results. In early 1660 Ward and Boyle looked on as a surgeon con-ducted the autopsy of Edmund Gwynn, a servitor at Christ Church recently deceased. Ward's diary similarly records results of post-mortems by Francis Smith, William Day, John Gill, and Roger Fry. When Day died in late 1665 Fry conducted the autopsy, and Ward recorded that the dead surgeon 'had a hole in one kidney so large yt one might turne ones finger in itt; he died of a dropsie'. Fry's own demise was ironically tied to his interests in pathology; he was killed by a fall from his horse on his way into the countryside to conduct an autopsy.[126]

SCIENTIFIC CLUBS, MEDICAL INVESTIGATIONS, AND BOOKS

Co-operative and informal self-instruction in medicine and the medical sciences at Oxford reflected more widespread seventeenth-century patterns of awakening interest in new natural philosophies and the investigation of nature by experiment. Indeed, Oxford science in the 1650s was known by subsequent generations primarily for its contribution to the founding, in 1660, of the Royal Society of London, the greatest of English institutional memorials to this shift in approach. Revisionists of this hoary historiographic tradition have recently succeeded in draw-ing a more complex and nuanced picture of seventeenth-century English science, of the origins and character of the Royal Society and of the changing groups and clubs at Interregnum and Restoration Oxford, such that it is now easier to see the role that physicians played in these enterprises.[127]

Although Harvey had carried out embryological observations with colleagues during the siege of Oxford, and Willis and Bathurst had joined together for chem-ical experiments at least as early as 1648, the first self-conscious 'club' was orga-nized in late autumn 1649 by William Petty. It met in his lodgings in Buckley Hall (107 High Street), and it was there that Petty, Willis, Bathurst, and Clerke gathered

[124] Lower to Boyle, 4 June 1663: *Works of Boyle*, ed. Birch vi. 467, Lower to Boyle, 24 June 1664: ibid. 470–2; Wallis to Oldenburg, 12 May 1666: *The Correspondence of Henry Oldenburg*, ed. Hall and Hall iii. 122–5.

[125] *Philosophical Transactions* no. 142 (December–February 1678–9), 1037; *The Philosophical Society*, ed. R. T. Gunther (Oxford 1925), vol. iv of *Early Science in Oxford* (14 vols Oxford 1923–45), 133, 154, 171, 188, 209.

[126] Ward diaries vii [1658–60], fo 52, xi [1665–6], fo 17ᵛ; Bodl. MS Rawlinson d. 810, fo 21.

[127] For an overview of these Oxford clubs see especially C. Webster, *The Great Instauration: science, medicine and reform, 1626–1660* (London 1976), 153–78, and Frank, *Harvey and the Oxford Physiologists*, 25–30, 51–7.

to dissect Anne Greene. It was also suitable, Wallis recalled, because it was the house of an apothecary, John Clarke, where the members could 'view, and make use, of drugs and other like matters'. Clarke was a well-known chemist, and had formerly been Harvey's apothecary. By October 1651 the group had acquired the *sine qua non* of a club: a set of rules governing admission and conduct of the Thursday afternoon meetings, emphasizing especially experiments. Upon Petty's departure from Oxford in late 1651 or early 1652, the club transferred its venue to John Wilkins's lodgings in Wadham College. There it flourished and became known to visitors such as Evelyn, Oldenburg, Walter Chartleton, and Robert Boyle—the latter made so welcome that he moved to Oxford in about February 1656. Meetings seem to have lapsed later that year, or in early 1657, as Wilkins became increasingly involved in Cromwellian politics. They began again, probably in late 1657, at Boyle's lodgings in Deep Hall (88 High Street), next to University College and opposite the entrance to All Souls; in February 1658 Petty wrote to Boyle from Ireland that he had not, amongst all his intelligence, 'heard better news, than that the club is restored at Oxford'. In addition to Boyle's collection of chemical and physical apparatus, Deep Hall also housed the apothecary shop of John Crosse, a knowledgeable botanist and well-connected virtuoso; it was there also that Peter Stahl taught chemistry classes from 1660 to 1663. The meetings continued at Boyle's lodgings, and were particularly active in 1664–8, so much so that the botanist Robert Sharrock entertained the hope 'that wee shall have some endowement for a society to study experimentall philosophy att Oxford'. When Boyle was absent in London, as he frequently was from early 1660 to mid-1664, the virtuosi, and especially the physicians, seem to have congregated at Willis's house, Beam Hall, in St John Street opposite Merton College. The now-eminent physician moved permanently to London in 1667, and Boyle did the same in 1668, thereby completing an exodus of many of the group's members that had begun at the Restoration and accelerated about 1665.[128]

The club lapsed thereafter, and regular gatherings seem not to have resumed again until late 1682, when a group coalesced around Robert Plot and found a fixed abode in 'the natural history school' at the Ashmolean building that opened in the spring of 1683. The multifarious scientific activities of this 'Oxford Philosophical Society' from October 1683 to November 1687 are traceable in a remarkable set of minutes, supplemented by the correspondence that the group conducted with the Royal Society and with a similar society in Dublin. Medical and physiological topics were regularly on the agenda: injecting dyes to tincture the lacteals, dissection of a boar's testicles, injecting water into the thorax of a dog, excising portions of lung, tying the external jugulars and cutting a ureter, as well as receiving

---

[128] John Wallis, *A Defence of the Royal Society* (London, 1678), 8. The rules of 1651 are Bodl. MS Ashmole 1810, transcribed in D. McKie, 'The origins and foundation of the Royal Society of London', *Notes and Records of the Royal Society of London* xv (1960), 25–6. Petty to Boyle, 17 February 1657[/8]: *Works of Boyle*, ed. Birch vi. 139; London, Royal Society, Boyle letters, v. fo 98, Sharrock to Boyle, 13 July 1664.

discourses on digestion and reports on interesting post-mortems.[129] Overall, the range and type of medical inquiries probably reflect quite accurately the experimental investigations carried out in previous incarnations of the club.

Fate has preserved details of two of these successive groups, one dating from late 1651 and the other from early 1684.[130] They show that the clubs at those two dates were of roughly equal size, with twenty-five and thirty-two members respectively. There were twelve (48%) medical practitioners in the first and ten (31%) in the second. Clearly physicians composed the most important single segment of each club, a fact also confirmed by the minutes of the later Oxford Philosophical Society. Also noteworthy is the comparative youth of the physicians. In the Petty club all twelve were between 18 and 33 years old. In the OPS Bathurst was a grey-beard at 64, and William Gibbons, a fellow of St John's, was rather older than average at 35; the other eight physicians ranged between 23 and 29 years old. In each case the medical practitioners were on average six to seven years younger than the other members. Such a distribution is understandable. Oxford offered many more opportunities for doctors in training than for those who hoped to make a career there. In addition, relatively few college fellowships were tenable in the long term by physicians, creating yet another pressure on the practitioner to leave by his early thirties. The informal organizations of Oxford encouraged medico-scientific investigations, while at the same time the formal institutional structure of the university placed limits on an interest in them.

Unfortunately, the Royal Society did not prove, in the long run, to be a framework within which large numbers of Oxford physicians could further pursue their scientific inquiries. In the 1660s virtuosi–physicians such as Jonathan Goddard, Daniel Whistler, Ralph Bathurst, Henry Clerke, Thomas Willis, Robert Wood, William Petty, Timothy Clarke, Richard Lower, Walter Needham, John Locke, and George Castle joined the Royal Society with alacrity. But only Goddard, Whistler, Petty, and Clarke were active for more than a short period, and even proven experimenters like Willis and Lower did not find themselves sufficiently attracted to come to Gresham one afternoon a week. The situation became worse after the mid-1670s. Of the ten physicians in the OPS in 1684, only Bathurst and Musgrave were ever members, and neither lived in the metropolis. Overall, more than 250 medical practitioners were educated at Oxford from 1665 to the end of the century; a mere fifteen joined the Royal Society, and only Edward Browne and Edward Tyson were active there. In part this coolness may have reflected a body of opinion within the College of Physicians after 1670 that viewed the Royal Society as a rival organization for interpreting nature. It may also have stemmed in part from the increasing ridicule that witty circles directed against the Royal Society from the

[129] *The Philosophical Society*, ed. Gunther, especially 8–15, 22–3, 29, 31, 36, 67–9, 76, 82–4, 87, 101, 105, 109, 111, 133, 154, 164–5, 171, 187–9, 196, 209–10.

[130] In mid-1651 Gerard Langbaine organized about two dozen members of the club to index books in the Bodleian Library for scientific facts: lists of assignments in Bodl. MS Wood donat. 1, pp. 1–3. The articles adopted by the Oxford Philosophical Society in March 1684 contain the names of thirty-five member–subscribers, thirty-two of whom can be identified: *Philosophical Society*, ed. Gunther, 44–8.

mid-1670s onwards. Some of this disdain was perhaps warranted, for by the end of the century it had become clear that the human body and disease would not yield up their secrets as quickly as had been assumed fifty years earlier. Finally, the greater distances a doctor had to travel and the press of patients in a busy metropolitan practice made it more difficult for a London physician to attend meetings than in the smaller and less bustling milieu of Oxford.

Investigations of injecting drugs into blood vessels, leading to the development of the first blood transfusion, provide an illuminating example of how such associations spurred Oxford physicians and scientists to carry out medical research.[131] Ovid's retelling of the Aesop fable—rejuvenation through filling old veins with new blood—had prompted many proposals for transfusion, but it was Harvey's observation in *De motu cordis* (1628) on the rapid spread of poisons via the circulation that provided the stimulus. While discussing such questions in a group at Boyle's lodgings at Oxford in about March 1656, Christopher Wren ventured that he could 'easily contrive a way to convey any liquid poison into the mass of blood'. Boyle provided the dog and, with 'the assistance of some eminent physitians', Wren used a syringe with a slender pipe to infuse an opium solution into a vein in the leg. The dog was stupefied for a time, but recovered, and its exploits, Boyle recounted, 'having made him famous, he was soon after stoln away from me'.[132] Repeated experiments in succeeding years refined the technique and tested the effects of other drugs, such as emetics. Meanwhile Wren, appointed to a Gresham professorship, showed the procedure to Timothy Clarke (DM 1653), who became its leading investigator in London. In the early 1660s Willis and Lower at Oxford developed techniques for injecting inks and coloured fluids to trace the path of blood vessels, and to follow physiological processes such as digestion. Indeed, the 'circle of Willis', discovered in a post-mortem, was confirmed by such injection experiments. As Lower noted in a letter to Boyle, without syringes 'anatomy is as much dificient, as physic would be without laudanum'.[133]

Such successes, as well as the resort of many London physicians and virtuosi, including Wilkins and Clarke, to Oxford in the plague summer of 1665, occasioned discussions of the possibility of injecting blood into veins. These led Lower and Boyle to try transfusion of blood from one dog's jugular vein into another dog via pipes. The first attempts in August failed. In February 1666, after the departure of the visitors, Lower finally succeeded in leading blood from the cervical artery of one dog to the jugular vein of another. He repeated the operation, calling in Wallis, Millington, and other Oxford physicians as witnesses, as well as spreading the news by post to Boyle in Stanton St John and to Hooke in London. Lower's Christ Church crony, John Ward, visited Oxford not long after, and jotted the news down in his diary: 'Dr Lower let one doggs blood into the bodie of another by opening

[131] A full account may be found in Frank, *Harvey and the Oxford Physiologists*, 169–78.

[132] Robert Boyle, *Some Considerations touching the Usefulnesse of Experimental Naturall Philosophy* (Oxford 1663) pt ii, 'postscript', 62–5.

[133] Lower to Boyle, 4 June 1663 and 24 June 1664: *Works of Boyle*, ed. Birch vi. 467, 474.

the veins of one and the arteries of another, and putting in a quill into each and so letting one blood on the other side; the one died, the other lived'.[134] Using a written account of Lower's procedure, a group at the Royal Society duplicated the feat later that year, and the subsequent publication by Oldenburg in the newly founded *Philosophical Transactions* prompted trials on humans in London and Paris during 1667 and 1668—in some of which Lower participated, as part of a brief flurry of activity in the Royal Society before he lapsed into absence. The decade-long path from injection to transfusion, whose story is here much abbreviated, proceeded along lines of club membership and co-operative investigation that characterized Oxford science and medicine from the 1640s to the 1680s.

Injection and transfusion were in turn part of a much larger enterprise, Oxonian in its themes and participants, for reconstructing the essentially Galenic medical sciences of anatomy and physiology that had endured for over a millennium and a half.[135] The starting-point again was Harvey's *De motu cordis*. Its experiments and reasoning demonstrated that the heart acted like a pump to circulate blood across the lungs and throughout the body, but gave few reasons *why* this should be the case. Accepting the circulation meant casting other traditional explanations into doubt. If arterial blood was continuously becoming venous blood, why was one bright red and the other dark? Was there an innate heat residing in the heart? Did respiration serve to moderate that heat, and vent its waste vapours? Were vital spirits generated in the heart from air brought there from the lungs? How and why did the *foetus in utero* breathe? Did muscular action need respiration? Why did the adult body need food, and how was nutrition carried out? By the late 1630s, as English physicians came slowly to accept Harvey's discovery, they also saw the need to grapple with its implications.

In the first phase, during the 1640s and 1650s, Oxford physicians rejected old physiological explanations, proposed as yet unproven new ones, but most of all changed the very nature of explaining. Harvey himself gave impetus to this questioning during his enforced sojourn in besieged Oxford from 1642 to 1646. He gathered a circle of colleagues, including Charles Scarburgh and Nathaniel Highmore, who were privy to embryological observations later published in his *De generatione* (1651); these cast doubt on the Galenic vital spirits and emphasized the primacy of the blood, and its heat, over that of the heart. Highmore, in his anatomical text of the same year, took the process further. He explicitly denied that air entered the heart to generate vital spirits, stressed the primacy of the blood and how the circulation distributed heat and nutriments, and accepted the respiratory functions of cooling and depuration, but argued that they were related to the blood, not the heart.

Harvey was a staunch Aristotelian, but, beginning with Highmore, Oxonians came to believe that the solids and fluids of the body were corpuscular in nature, and that their properties were to be understood through a very anti-Aristotelian

---

[134] Ward diaries xi [1665–6], fo 32.
[135] The following account is condensed from Frank, *Harvey and the Oxford Physiologists*.

science: chemistry. Highmore, Petty, Bathurst, Willis, and their circle all saw chem-istry and the atomical philosophy as the necessary new basis for reconstructing the medical sciences. Bathurst, in his *praelectiones tres de respiratione* for the DM in 1654, provided what was to prove an influential example of the power of the chemical–corpuscular approach. Respiration, he argued, was not to cool the heart or the innate heat. It took place rather to bring a nitrous particle-like vapour from the air into the blood, a chemical substance that enabled the blood to serve the vital functions of the body. Willis proposed explanations of a similar chemical–corpuscular structure in the treatises on fermentation and fevers that made up his *Diatribae duae medico-philosophicae* (1659). Animal heat, he argued, was not an innate entity, but was rather generated in the ventricles of the heart from food and air particles by an 'inkindling'—a fermentation that produced heat by increased intes-tine motions of the constituent particles of spirit, sulphur, salt, water, and earth.

The second phase of investigation, from 1659 to 1669, was marked by increas-ing sophistication, bringing experiments with new physical apparatus and vivisec-tional techniques to bear on theories about respiration, the heart and the blood. In late 1658 Willis's quondam chemical assistant, Robert Hooke, by then working for Boyle, constructed for his mentor a vacuum pump into whose receiver he could put experimental animals. Through experiments performed at Oxford in 1659, and published by Boyle in *New Experiments Physico-Mechanical, touching the spring of the air, and its effects* (1660), they could prove that an animal, such as a lark or a mouse, sickened and eventually died when the receiver was evacuated. Such experiments, Boyle reflected, clearly showed that disposing of wastes could not be the sole func-tion of respiration; rather, the trials suggested that some substance was needed *from* the air, and/or that the air had to be of a requisite 'spring'. Further experiments from 1660 to 1665, both at the Royal Society in London and at Oxford when Boyle was there, not only confirmed these aspects of respiration but suggested that a sim-ilar lack of an aerial substance caused a flame to go out in an evacuated receiver. Hooke even suggested, as an aside in his *Micrographia* (1665), that this missing sub-stance was a nitrous saline particle necessary for combustion.

In a parallel set of inquiries from 1664 to 1667, Willis, Lower, Boyle, and others in Oxford investigated the chemical properties of blood. As Ward recorded in his diary for April 1665: 'Dr Willis and Dick Lower opened a dogg and they first let him blood in the jugulars to discover whether arterial blood and venal did differ in colour and constitution'. Locke further speculated in his notebook that 'it is the nitrous salt in the aier that gives it [blood] the tincture and volatilizes it', thereby accounting for the bright red colour, which was in turn lost after the blood circu-lated through the body.[136] Such speculations were confirmed in a brilliant series of vivisectional experiments in London in 1667–8. Hooke and Lower showed that if fresh air was pumped continuously through the lungs of a dog, and allowed to escape through holes punctured in the pleura, the animal could live without the

[136] Ward diaries iv [1666], fo 25ᵛ; Bodl. MS Locke f. 19, p. 227.

normal reciprocating mechanical motion, and that the blood entered the lungs venous dark red, and came out an arterial bright red. What had it absorbed? Lower, in publishing these experiments in *Tractatus de corde* (1669), used the term *pabulum nitrosum*, and framed his explanation in phrases that leave no doubt that he was greatly influenced by reading Bathurst's still-unpublished lectures on respiration.

In the third phase, from *circa* 1667 to 1674, one can trace how Willis, Boyle, and a much younger medico from All Souls, John Mayow, integrated this experimental evidence on air, lungs, and blood into a chemical–corpuscular system that linked the chemical nature of respiration with that of combustion, and explained both on the basis of nitro-aerial particles that we can in retrospect recognize as functioning like oxygen. Boyle contributed primarily by publishing, in an article in 1670 and further in *Flame and Air* (1672), a diverse series of air-pump experiments on respiration and combustion dating from the mid-1660s. Willis's ideas were elaborated in his *Pathologiae cerebri* (1667), in short tracts on the inkindling of the blood and the motion of the muscles in 1670, and in *De anima brutorum* (1672). Mayow's were sketched out in his *Tractatus duo* (1668) on respiration and muscular motion, and in grand and expanded form in the *Tractatus quinque* (1674). The two argued that respiration served to bring nitro-aerial particles into the blood, changing its colour. There the particles inkindled the nutrients and generated heat just as such particles did when a combustible material burned in the air. Mayow emphasized that as respiration or combustion removed nitro-aerial particles from an enclosed space, the elasticity of the air was also reduced, and neither mouse nor candle could survive. Nitro-aerial particles served further, he believed, to fuel an 'explosion' in muscles that inflated them into contraction; they also accounted for why the foetus could 'breathe' *in utero*. Mayow supported these and numerous related propositions with ingenious experiments that showed an equal facility with chemistry and physiology.

The ideas, experiments, and discoveries of the Oxford Harveians constitute one of the most important episodes in the development of medicine in early modern Europe, and they are intimately tied up with the community of scientists and physicians active there from the 1640s through to the 1670s. A shortened narrative perforce suppresses the rich detail of interrelationship that bound this community together, and which was the essential prerequisite of its scientific success. Unfortunately, it was also a community whose brilliant investigations were not anchored in institutional forms. Unlike Padua or Leiden, Oxford had few career places in the colleges or university explicitly designed for medical teaching and research. By the late seventeenth century inflation had rendered the Linacre stipends increasingly inadequate, and the positions increasingly marginal. The regius professorship devolved through court intrigues. Non-residence and teaching by deputy were increasing problems after about 1670. Even where medical men occupied other professorships, such as those of Greek, history, natural philosophy, or astronomy, a learned physician was being supported in Oxford at the cost of directing his efforts elsewhere.

Yet despite such shaky university foundations, the century had marked a signal change in the status of Oxford medicine *vis-à-vis* the international intellectual community—from nonentity to brilliant innovator and then to solid citizen. Those physicians educated before about 1630 had continued the unambitious and marginal scholarly activities of their sixteenth-century forebears. They included one representative of the classical line: Theodore Goulston (DM 1610) and his editions of Aristotle and Galen dating from 1619. Beginning in 1616 Robert Fludd (DM 1605) also published prolifically, but these were theosophical books attempting to ground a new science in biblical texts. Essays and poetry found exponents in Robert Vilvaine (DM 1611), Edward Lapworth (DM 1611), and John Harmar (BM 1632). Protestant theology was explicated by the likes of Richard Capell (MA 1607), William Denton (DM 1634), and Lewis du Moulin (DM Leiden, incorporated 1649). The only prominent books of medical content were those of the Oxford and Bath practitioner Tobias Venner (DM 1613), such as the *Via recta ad vitam longam* (1620) and *A Briefe and Accurate Treatise concerning the taking of the Fume of Tobacco* (1638), both of which were in the venerable tradition of popular health guides.

Beginning with the generation educated in the 1630s, and extending well into the 1660s, the intellectual and scientific productivity of Oxford physicians expanded to take a place inferior to none in Europe. In addition to the usual categories of *belles-lettres*, occasional theology, and even political tracts, Oxford authors expanded into new territories. One such was natural history. Jacob Bobart produced a catalogue of the Oxford physic garden in 1648, which was expanded greatly by Philip Stephens (DM 1656) and William Browne in their *Catalogus horti botanici oxoniensis* (1658). Other Oxford-educated practitioners wrote natural histories for England and the wider European realm: the *Phytologia britannica* (1650) of William Howe (MA 1644), *The Art of Simpling* (1656) by William Cole (BA 1656), the *Compleat Herball* (1659) and *Compleat History of Animals and Minerals* (1661) of Robert Lovell (MA 1653), and the *Pinax rerum naturalium britannicarum* (1667) of Christopher Merret (DM 1643).

Anatomical and physiological works of importance written by Oxford-trained physicians began with Highmore's *Disquisitio anatomica* (1651), and marched through the next quarter century: Thomas Wharton's *Adenographia* (1656), Walter Charleton's *Oeconomia animalis* (1659), Willis's neurological trilogy, the *Cerebri anatome* (1664), the *Pathologiae cerebri* (1667), and *De anima brutorum* (1672), Timothy Clarke's papers on injection and the anatomy of glands, Walter Needham's *De formato foetu* (1667), Mayow's *Tractatus duo* (1668) and its brilliant successor, the *Tractatus quinque* (1674), Lower's *Tractatus de corde* and John Betts's *De ortu et natura sanguinis* (both in 1669), and William Cole's *De secretione animali cogitata* (1674).

Building upon these basic investigations, and occasionally separate in method and intention, were a series of widely respected, and sometimes seminal, works on health and disease: Edward Greaves's description of typhus (1643), Whistler's account of rickets (1645), Christopher Bennet's investigation of consumption (1654), Willis's widely influential *De febribus* (1659) and his more massive and practical *Pharmaceutice rationalis* (2 volumes, 1674–5), Nathaniel Hodges's description of the plague (1671), Richard Morton's excellent further account of consumption in *Phthisiologia* (1689), and, beginning in 1666 with the classic *Methodus curandi febres*, Thomas Sydenham's five major works of clinical medicine, which appeared over the next two decades. Finally, as one might have expected, Oxford authors made their contributions to the more polemical literature of the profession of medicine, with works by Jonathan Goddard, John Twysden, George Castle, Christopher Merret, Daniel Coxe, Henry Stubbe, Gideon Harvey, and Richard Griffith, just to name a few who plunged into the debates that raged from the mid-1660s to the early 1680s.

Those educated in Oxford medicine from about 1670 to the end of the century were less productive than their immediate forebears, while still producing a moderate stream of works similar in type. Edward Tyson was perhaps the finest anatomist of his period; he published most of his numerous dissections as articles in the *Philosophical Transactions*, with only his excellent anatomy of a chimpanzee appearing in book form as *Orang-Outang, sive homo sylvestris* (1699). Humphrey Ridley's *The Anatomy of the Brain* (1695) built usefully upon the foundations erected by Willis, and James Keill's textbook, a guide to his Oxford teaching, became the standard anatomical vade-mecum of the early eighteenth century. Clinicians were not of the earlier stature of Willis or Sydenham, but Walter Harris gained a reputation for his *Pharmacologia anti-empirica* (1683) and *De morbis acutis infantum* (1698), and Sir John Floyer's *The Physician's Pulse Watch* (2 volumes, 1707 and 1710) was merely one of his numerous works purveying sound common sense in treatment. There were fewer medical controversialists, although Robert Pitt, in *The Crafts and Frauds of Physick expos'd* (1702) and later works, was effective as a protagonist for restrained treatment. Noteworthy, finally, is the declining portion of belletrists, although one of them, Thomas Hoy, managed to get himself appointed Oxford's regius professor of medicine in 1698.

FROM DYNAMISM TO STASIS

The 'decline' in Oxford medicine that set in during the 1690s and continued for almost two centuries was, like many such, only relative to changes around it. The number of BMs and DMs granted in the half-century after 1690 totalled on average about eighty per decade, representing about 2.6 per cent of those who entered Oxford. From the 1730s onwards these totals decreased consistently. Overall, therefore, the number of medical degrees remained on roughly a plateau from the 1660s through to the 1730s, below the abnormally high numbers of the 1640s and 1650s, but well above those in the sixteenth century. The great surge in numbers of Oxford physicians, eight- to fifteenfold, had taken place from about 1600 through to the 1650s. Yet, while numbers of Oxford medical degrees remained approximately static after 1660, the numbers of medical practitioners in English society continued to grow at an ever-accelerating rate. Over the period 1605–19 there were thirty-two English physicians wealthy enough to have their wills probated in the Prerogative Court of Canterbury; for 1657–70 the total was eighty-one, and in 1686–1700 the same court probated 120 physicians's wills.[137]

---

[137] Numbers of degrees from Webster, 'The medical faculty and the physic garden', 685; numbers

The learned practitioner, one educated in arts at Oxford or Cambridge, found himself competing with non-scholars on many different fronts. At the highest level, admission to the circle of graduate physicians could much more easily and cheaply be obtained by taking a DM outside England. Leiden, Utrecht, and other Dutch universities were increasingly popular throughout the 1730s, after which the numbers of Englishmen at Edinburgh began to swell. Medical travel abroad grew in part because London's Royal College of Physicians ceased in actuality to demand an Oxford or Cambridge medical degree, whether gained in course or by incorporation, as a precondition for admission. Of Oxonians alone, sixty-four are traceable who took foreign DMs between 1660 and 1699, and only four bothered to incorporate, even though fifteen ultimately became candidates or fellows of the Royal College of Physicians. Numerous others simply bypassed the ancient universities entirely, going directly to the continent or Scotland for medical degrees.

At the lower levels of practice, Oxford or Cambridge practitioners without a BM or DM were increasingly outnumbered on their home turf, in the provinces, by apothecaries, surgeons, and barber–surgeons. Systematically gathered data on numbers and types of medical practitioners are lacking before the late eighteenth century, but selected vital records suggest the outlines of change. Between the two periods 1605–19 and 1686–1700, the number of physicians' wills recorded in the Prerogative Court of Canterbury increased fourfold, to be sure, from thirty-two to 120; but the number of other practitioners swelled from seventy-two to 632— almost ninefold. In the city of Chester, whose population was growing certainly no faster than that of the country as a whole, a total of seven apothecaries, surgeons, and barber–surgeons were admitted as freemen in the three decades beginning in 1600; for the period 1670–99 the analogous figure was seventy-one. The archdeaconry of Nottingham issued marriage licences in the same two periods to, respectively, eight and fifty-one of these non-physician practitioners. Even in the town and university of Oxford, with its plethora of physicians, apothecaries and surgeons made headway; wills for six were probated in the period 1600–39, and for twenty-four in the decades 1670–1709. Clearly a growing portion of the population was entrusting more of its medical problems to those who claimed expertise more specifically in medicaments and manual operations; the surgeon–apothecary was beginning his transformation into the British general practitioner.[138]

Overall, medicine had flourished in seventeenth-century Oxford because its predominating characteristics in this era fitted well with those of the university. It was still an essentially learned profession, and Oxford provided books and a long-term resident scholarly community. Medicine at this time was stamped by anatomical

of entrants from Stone, 'Size and composition', 91. Evidence about the wills of physicians proved in the Prerogative Court of Canterbury is taken from the volumes published by the British Record Society Index Library.

[138] *The Rolls of the Freemen of the City of Chester*, ed. J. H. E. Bennet (Lancashire and Cheshire Record Soc. li 1906), 83–115, 157–205; *Abstracts of Nottinghamshire Marriage Licences*, ed. T. M. Blagg and F. A. Wadsworth (British Record Soc. Index Library lviii and lx London 1930), 15–114, 259–514; J. Griffith, *An Index to Wills Proved in the Court of the Chancellor of the University of Oxford* (Oxford 1862).

discovery, and the best Oxford physicians responded so vigorously to the challenges of the age that men such as Harvey, Highmore, Wharton, Willis, Lower, and Mayow made discoveries still appreciated centuries later. Even the scores of medicos who scrutinized these anatomical findings by means of such an antiquated form as the schools disputation testified thereby to the invigorating sense of innovation that reigned in the university. Medicine was seen as closely related to natural philosophy, and for four decades Oxford was home to a galaxy of 'scientists' and virtuosi whose interests overlapped and meshed with those of the university's physicians, a symbiosis expressed in numerous private collaborations and public clubs. Clinical skill was still learned in a haphazard way, through friends, recipe-collecting, and casual experience. Oxford, with its physic garden, small geographical compass, and concentrated community of physicians, surgeons, and apothecaries, offered as good an opportunity for training as many a larger city. And despite its age-old reputation for atheism, medicine was often a fall-back profession for those finally unwilling or unable to pursue a cleric's career; for most of the century, many a puritan and crypto-Catholic benefited from an Oxford education before veering off into one or another level of medical practice.

In the eighteenth century medicine continued to change, but the ancient universities failed to change with it. Formal lectures by a coterie of well-paid professors became more important. Oxford's professors in medical subjects, when unsupplemented by DMs occupying chairs in the sciences, remained few in number, and lectured less rather than more. More medical students, reacting perhaps to the increasingly prevalent custom of non-residency among fellows, left after the arts course and merely came back to take the BM and/or DM after waiting out the statutory period. Clinical instruction at the bedside began to crystallize elsewhere around large urban voluntary hospitals; Oxford had neither hospital nor teaching clinicians. Continental and Scottish university instruction brought elements of surgery and materia medica into medical training; Oxford did not. Anatomy emerged from a period of discovery into one of consolidation and application; its increasingly surgical nature failed, in part because of social snobbery, to find enthusiastic devotees at the English universities. In the eighteenth century dissenters became important in medical practice and medical science; they were of course excluded by statute from even coming up to Oxford or Cambridge. In sum, during the seventeenth century the university's physical fabric and statutory framework, enriched with strong personalities and informal mechanisms for learning, had functioned well in training a vastly increased number of scholarly physicians for London, Oxford, and the countryside. Bereft of such personalities, and confronted with a profession that continued to change, the bare fabric and framework proved to be largely incapable of further transformation.

9

Law

BRIAN P. LEVACK

THE SURVIVAL OF THE FACULTY

THE seventeenth century was a difficult time for the faculty of law at Oxford. Hostility towards the civil law, coupled with bleak employment prospects for graduates in law, threatened the future of legal studies at the university, first during the reign of James I and again during the civil war period. On both occasions the faculty managed to recover its earlier strength, but in the process its character underwent significant change.

During the first decade of the century it was widely rumoured that 'the civil law should be put down and quite exterminated the kingdom'. Whether there was any substance to these rumours, which arose because of the alleged 'designs of evil men about the king', cannot be determined.[1] There is no question, however, that the profession of the civil law had fallen on hard times, and civilians were apprehensive that both their profession and the university faculty with which it was closely tied would be destroyed. The main problem that civilians faced was intense competition from the common lawyers, who were encroaching upon their jurisdiction and also gaining some of the judicial appointments which had traditionally been reserved for civil lawyers. Since many of the students studying law at Oxford did so in order to prepare for careers as proctors, advocates, and judges in the ecclesiastical and admiralty courts, an attack of this sort upon the sources of the civilians' livelihood threatened the faculty itself. As one contemporary predicted, if the civilians were to be deprived of their customary judicial fees, 'they and that whole faculty must needs fall to the ground'.[2]

The dire predictions of professional and academic destruction did not come to pass. The beleaguered civilians not only gained verbal reassurances from the university convocation that their discipline was one of the 'four chief heads or ornaments of this university' but they also won the active support of the king.[3] James, who frequently expressed his admiration for the civil law, came to the assistance of the civilians by defending their jurisdiction from the encroachments of common lawyers on a number of occasions. As a further, more symbolic gesture of

---

[1] Wood, *History of the University* ii. 281. [2] BL Cotton MS Cleo F II, fo 230.
[3] Wood, *History of the University* ii. 281; OUA register of congregation and convocation 1595–1606, NEP/*supra*/11, register M, fo 77.

support he increased the salary of the regius professor of law.[4] Charles I took even more decisive action on behalf of the civilians by appointing them to judicial positions from which they had gradually been excluded.[5] With the ecclesiastical courts becoming extremely active during the archiepiscopate of Laud, who was himself a member of Doctors' Commons,[6] the civilians appeared to be well on the road to recovery by the late 1630s.

One sign of the restored health of the faculty was an increase in the number of law degrees that the university awarded. In each of the first two decades of the seventeenth century, when the civilians were experiencing the worst phase of their crisis, the total number of BCL and DCL degrees recorded in the registers of congregations barely exceeded fifty, a much lower figure than the seventy degrees conferred in the 1580s. By the 1620s, however, the number of degrees had climbed back to seventy-two. This figure did not represent a full recovery, since the number of all university degrees increased dramatically in the 1620s, so that the proportion of law degrees remained lower than it had been in the 1580s. But there can be no question that in the 1630s, when the number of law degrees reached an extraordinarily high 147, the faculty was once again in very good shape.

The recovery of the 1630s was short-lived. Once the civil war began, the number of degrees declined dramatically, totalling a mere thirty-nine during the 1640s and forty-five during the following decade. These figures, which represent a far steeper decline than occurred in the number of all degrees, suggest that a second crisis, more profound than the first, afflicted the faculty of law during these years. The main source of the difficulty was the destruction of the criminal jurisdiction of the ecclesiastical courts in 1641 and the abolition of the entire episcopal structure of church government in 1646. Under these circumstances civilians could find employment only in those courts which continued the probate and marriage jurisdiction of the church and in the admiralty courts. Since there were only limited employment opportunities in these areas, especially for recent graduates, enrolment in the faculty declined.

A further problem for the faculty of law developed when the visitors of the university attempted to reduce the number of legal fellows in New College and All Souls College in the early 1650s. Both colleges offered fellowships which had originally been endowed for canonists and civilians. When the formal study of canon law was abolished in the 1530s the canonist fellowships were reassigned to civilians, who by the beginning of the seventeenth century were able to evade their traditional obligation to take holy orders. The visitors, hoping to encourage the study of divinity, ordered that the canonist fellowships be given to divinity students.[7]

Shortly after the visitors had begun their assault upon the civilians in these two colleges, Dr Gerard Langbaine, the pro-vice-chancellor and keeper of the university archives, encouraged convocation to ask parliament to provide assistance for

---

[4] Bodl. MS Tanner 211, fo 231ᵛ.   [5] BL Add. MS 34, 324, fo 282.

[6] G. D. Squibb, *Doctors' Commons* (Oxford 1977), 175.

[7] *Register*, ed. Burrows, 362, 363 note a, 397–8.

the faculty of law, which he claimed had been 'languishing for some years' and was 'all but dead'.[8] Following the example of the doctors of law residing in London, convocation approved a petition which emphasized the crucial role civilians played in the conduct of diplomacy, the probate of wills, and both matrimonial and maritime litigation. Even more important, it drew attention to the distinction between the civil law and the canon law—an effort by the civilians to distance themselves from the highly unpopular and allegedly 'popish' ecclesiastical law.[9] Three years later the university directed a similar petition to Oliver Cromwell.[10]

The petitions of the 1650s did nothing to alleviate the plight of the civilians, but after the Restoration the faculty once again regained some of its numerical strength. During the 1660s the university awarded seventy-four law degrees, while in the 1670s it granted ninety-seven, and in the 1680s seventy-eight. The reasons for this late seventeenth-century recovery are not readily apparent. The Restoration did not revive the fortunes of either the ecclesiastical or admiralty courts, which now entered a long and gradual decline. Nor did it result in the appointment of civil lawyers to lucrative judicial or administrative posts. The university petitioned Charles II to bestow such positions on worthy civilians, but the king disappointed them.[11] It is unlikely, therefore, that the renewed interest in legal studies at Oxford in the late seventeenth century reflected greater optimism among students regarding careers as practising civil lawyers, ecclesiastical judges, or royal servants.

The decline of professional interest among civilians after the Restoration can best be seen in the career decisions made by the students who took the degree of DCL. Among the legists at Oxford, the doctors of civil law were traditionally the most likely to embark upon a professional career.[12] In the second decade of the seventeenth century, when the civil law was in decline, thirteen Englishmen took doctorates in law at Oxford.[13] Of these, eight became advocates in the court of the arches (all but one of them joining Doctors' Commons), while four pursued clerical careers and one, John Hawley, remained at Oxford to serve as principal of Gloucester Hall and judge of the vice-chancellor's court. In the 1670s a full twenty-three Englishmen received doctorates, but only six of them became advocates and joined Doctors' Commons.[14] Of the remainder, only four engaged in any legal activity whatsoever, serving for different periods of time as chancellors of dioceses. Two of the doctors, somewhat surprisingly, practised medicine, while four entered the church and no fewer than seven elected to remain at Oxford in various capacities. One civilian, Robert Plot, became a fellow and secretary of the Royal Society and was appointed both keeper of the Ashmolean Museum and historiographer royal.

---

[8] Wood, *Life and Times* i. 187.
[9] Ibid.; see also Bodl. MS Tanner 51, fo 8.
[10] *CSPD 1657–8*, 271–2.
[11] Wood, *Life and Times* i. 332.
[12] J. Barton, 'The faculty of law' in *The Collegiate University*, 281–3.
[13] OUA register of congregation 1606–11, NEP/*supra*/12, register, Я fo 130ᵛ; ibid. 1611–22, NEP/*supra*/13, register Sa, fo 294ᵛ.
[14] OUA register of congregation 1669–80, NEP/*supra*/19, register Bd, fo 236; Squibb, *Doctors' Commons*, 181–3.

The high proportion of non-lawyers taking law degrees at Oxford after the Restoration suggests that the purpose of an education in the civil law was changing. Previously regarded as training for a legal career and as an avenue to preferment in church and state, it was now beginning to be viewed as a form of more general, less professional education or simply as a means of acquiring an additional academic degree. Two developments may have encouraged this change in attitude. First, the faculty of law in the late seventeenth century gained a reputation for being academically undemanding. This not only enticed some students to take the BCL in lieu of the BA[15] but also made it possible for graduates in the arts to obtain a degree in a higher faculty without great effort. Second, the political reputation of the civil law began to improve after the Restoration. With Anglicanism triumphant, the civil law was less vulnerable to the persistent puritan claim that it was popishly affected, and with the common lawyers in a secure position, the charge that the civil law represented a continental threat to English liberty appeared less frequently. For the first time in more than a century legists could pursue a course of study that was not subject to hostile criticism.

THE REGIUS PROFESSORSHIP

During the first half of the seventeenth century, when there was much talk about the abolition of legal studies at Oxford, the scholarly reputation of the faculty of law stood higher than at any time in its history. In Alberico Gentili, who served as the regius professor of law from 1587 to 1608, Oxford had a legal scholar of genuine international distinction. An Italian immigrant, Gentili was not universally popular at Oxford, especially with the godly faction, but he was regarded as the 'grand ornament of the university in his time'.[16] His writings cover a wide range of legal, religious, and political topics, including a treatise written in 1605 on the absolute power of the king.[17] His scholarly fame, however, rests mainly on his contribution to the field of international law. His greatest work, *De jure belli* (1598), which originated in a lecture given at Oxford in the year of the Armada, and his study of embassies, *De legationibus* (1585), have established his reputation as the founder of the secular school of international law.[18]

Gentili was identified very closely with the *mos italicus* or Bartolist tradition of legal scholarship, rather than with the *mos gallicus* or humanist tradition, which had been developed by such legal scholars as Cujas, Budé, and Alciato. The humanists used philological techniques to discover the most accurate version of ancient Roman legal texts, and the comparative work they undertook in this regard made possible a genuinely historical approach to studying the law and governmental institutions.[19] With this approach Gentili had little sympathy. 'There is no reason', he

[15] J. L. Barton, 'Legal studies' in *The Eighteenth Century*, 595.   [16] Wood, *Athenae* ii. 90.

[17] Alberico Gentili, *Regales disputationes tres* (London 1605), 5–38.

[18] G. van der Molen, *Alberico Gentili and the Development of International Law* (Amsterdam 1938); A. Nussbaum, *A Concise History of the Law of Nations* (New York 1947, rev. edn New York 1962), 94–101.

[19] J. G. A. Pocock, *The Ancient Constitution and the Feudal Law* (Cambridge 1957), 1–29.

wrote, 'why an interpreter of the law should read or know history.'[20] It is true that he did make frequent reference to ancient and modern historians in much of his work, but his purpose was to provide support for the position he was advocating, not to illuminate the original context in which the law was written.

Although Gentili's successor, John Budden, never achieved great distinction as a legal scholar, he did leave a mark on legal studies at the university. When Gentili departed from Oxford in 1605 to serve as advocate for the Spanish government in the admiralty court, Budden assumed the duties of reader in civil law,[21] and in 1611 he was named regius professor. Budden, who had earlier served as a reader in philosophy at Magdalen College, wrote biographical sketches of Archbishop Morton and Bishop Waynflete and translated both Bodley's 'Statutes of the public library' and Sir Thomas Smith's *Commonwealth of England* into Latin. It appears that Budden, who never established a legal practice, approached the law from a humanistic stance, just as Smith had done. Certainly Budden's two great pupils, Richard Zouche and Sir Arthur Duck, gave evidence of viewing the law in that way.[22]

Zouche, who succeeded Budden as regius professor in 1620, is clearly the most distinguished civilian that Oxford produced in the seventeenth century. He was also the last of his kind: an English civil lawyer whose writings acquired a durable European reputation. His scholarly achievement consisted of a series of legal treatises that served as textbooks for students. The most famous of these, *Elementa jurisprudentiae* (1629), presents a broad outline of legal science. It provides an introduction to the basic categories and principles of all legal systems, which Zouche illustrates with quotations from the maxims of the law found in the last title of the *Digest*.[23] Zouche's approach to the civil law resembled that of Duck, who in *De usu et authoritate iuris civilis romanorum in dominiis principum christianorum* (1648) showed how all countries relied upon Roman law in matters of equity.[24] By identifying common denominators in all legal systems Zouche and Duck helped to illustrate the compatibility of the civil law with the common law, an enterprise which William Fulbecke and John Cowell had begun in the first decade of the seventeenth century by conducting point-by-point comparisons between the two legal systems.[25]

Following *Elementa jurisprudentiae* Zouche produced books on feudal, ecclesiastical, military, maritime, and international law, in each case providing a clear and comprehensive treatment of his subject. The last of these, *Juris et judicii fecialis, sive juris inter gentes* (1650), has established Zouche as an important figure in the history

---

[20] *Latin Correspondence by Alberico Gentili and John Rainolds on Academic Drama*, trans. and ed. L. Markowicz (Salzburg 1977), 61; Alberico Gentili, *De juris interpretibus dialogi sex* (London 1582), 629–35.

[21] *CSPD 1603–10*, 489.

[22] On the extent of Zouche's humanism see H. F. Jolowicz, 'Some English civilians', *Current Legal Problems* ii (1949), 149.

[23] *Digest* 50. 17.

[24] P. Stein, 'Continental influences on English legal thought', *La formazione storica del diritto moderno in Europa* (Atti del III congresso internationale della società italiana di storia del diritto 1977), 1109–10.

[25] William Fulbecke, *A Parallele or Conference of the Civill Law, the Canon Law and the Common Law of England* (London 1602); John Cowell, *Institutiones juris anglicani* (Cambridge 1605).

of international law.[26] Building upon the work of both Gentili and Hugo Grotius, Zouche provided a systematic treatment of the entire field. His most significant contribution to the development of this branch of law was the treatment of peace as a topic separate from war and not merely incidental to it. Unlike Gentili and Grotius, Zouche can be regarded as an early legal positivist who eschewed concepts of natural law and based his scholarship on contemporary legal practice.[27]

With the appointment of Sir Giles Sweit upon the death of Zouche in 1661, the regius professorship began to lose some of its lustre. On the surface, Sweit was not much different from Zouche. Both served as principal of St Alban Hall, a position which during the seventeenth century appears to have been under the control of the chancellor of the university and was later assigned to Sweit's two successors as regius professor.[28] Both Zouche and Sweit also became active in the administration of the chancellor's court—serving as its first two assessors under the terms of the Laudian statutes.[29] The two men also spent much of their time in London, where they served as advocates of the court of arches and had chambers in Doctors' Commons.[30] There, however, the similarities end. Sweit was not, like Zouche, a legal writer, and he therefore had no scholarly reputation, either in England or abroad. In this respect he was the first of a long line of undistinguished professors that stretched well into the eighteenth century. Sweit was also much less visible than Zouche at Oxford. Whereas Zouche had managed to discharge his duties as both professor and chancellor of the diocese of Oxford with regularity, Sweit found himself increasingly burdened with his work in London, especially after he became dean of the arches. In 1661 he named a deputy to perform his duties as regius professor, and in 1664 he was forced to abandon the principalship of St Alban Hall.[31]

In 1672 Thomas Bouchier, who had served as Sweit's deputy, succeeded him as regius professor. Bouchier was by no means unlearned, and he also spent more time at Oxford than his predecessor, but he was incapable of preventing the continuing decline in the intellectual stature of his faculty. In fact, Bouchier did great harm to the study of law at Oxford by arranging for his son James, also a civilian, to succeed him as regius professor in 1712.[32] The younger Bouchier, who in Thomas Hearne's opinion was a 'proud, vain, conceited, impudent, and ignorant coxcomb', knew very little civil law and was considered to be 'utterly unqualified' for the position.[33] His appointment only accentuated the decline in the quality

[26] Richard Zouche, *Iuris et judicii fecialis*, ed. T. E. Holland and trans. J. L. Brierly (2 vols Washington DC 1911).

[27] Nussbaum, *Law of Nations*, 164–7; W. S. Holdsworth, *Sources and Literature of English Law* (London 1925), 227–8.

[28] J. R. L. Highfield, 'Stubbins', *Postmaster* i (1956), 13–14.

[29] M. Underwood, 'The structure and operation of the Oxford chancellor's court, from the sixteenth to the early eighteenth century', *Journal of the Society of Archivists* vi (1978–81), 21–2. See further I. Roy and D. Reinhart, 'Oxford and the civil wars', pp. 691–2 below.

[30] B. P. Levack, *The Civil Lawyers in England, 1603–1641* (Oxford 1973), 274, 282.

[31] Wood, *Life and Times* i. 402; Wood, *History of the Colleges and Halls*, 658.

[32] Hearne, *Collections* viii. 74   [33] Ibid. iv. 177, viii. 95, ix. 85; HMC *Portland MSS* vii. 92.

of legal scholarship at Oxford which had set in during the late seventeenth century.

LEGAL STUDIES

At the core of legal studies at the university were the lectures of the regius professor. Candidates for the BCL degree were obliged to attend these lectures for either three or (if it was a first degree) five years, while those who took the doctorate were expected to attend for yet another four or five years.[34] Since the primary function of the law faculty was to train men for service in courts which followed civil law procedure, the lectures were supposed to have a bearing on English practice. There were obvious limits to such a requirement. The civil law had been received in England only in areas of special jurisdiction, and even in those restricted areas large portions of the *Corpus juris civilis* had little applicability. Much of what legists studied at Oxford had only jurisprudential value. Nevertheless, the lectures could focus on those sections of Roman law dealing with wills, legacies, marriage, and certain forms of contract, all of which came within the jurisdiction of either the ecclesiastical or the admiralty courts. With the development of international law as a field of study and practice, the lectures could also deal with those aspects of Roman law that touched upon international relations.

The main drawback of the civil law curriculum from the point of view of the prospective lawyer was that it did not provide instruction in English ecclesiastical law. Since the great majority of practising civil lawyers held posts in the ecclesiastical courts, there was a great need for training in this area. Before 1535 students had the option of taking a degree in canon law, but with the abolition of that branch of legal studies at the time of the reformation they had to find new ways to acquire such knowledge. There is little doubt that canon law studies continued in one form or another throughout this period. In 1659 Nicholas Stoughton was, by authority of the vice-chancellor and the whole university, allowed to incept *in facultate utriusque juris, tam civilis quam canonici*,[35] and as late as 1708 Thomas Wood, himself a civilian, wrote that 'the canon law is also read and practised within the universities'.[36] Some ecclesiastical law may have been discussed when the regius professors gave lectures on matters which concerned both laws. It was more common, however, for students to learn this law through a programme of private study. In addition to the standard medieval sources, legists had access to William Lyndwood's fifteenth-century collection of provincial constitutions,[37] Sir Henry Spelman's *De conciliis et decretis ecclesiasticis* (1639), Henry Swinburne's *A Brief Treatise of Testaments and Wills* (1590), and Francis Clerke's *Praxis*—a guide to the procedure

---

[34] *SA* 380; *Laudian Code*, ed. Griffiths VI. iv. 1, p. 3.

[35] OUA register of congregation 1647–59, NEP/*supra*/17, register Qa, fo 181.

[36] Thomas Wood, *Some Thoughts concerning the Study of the Laws of England in the Two Universities* (London 1708), 5.

[37] *Constitutiones provinciales Ecclesiae Anglicanae* (London 1496).

of the church courts.[38] In 1636 Zouche published his *Descriptio juris et judicii ecclesiastici*, which offered students a systematic introduction to the subject.

In addition to English ecclesiastical law, some civilians required knowledge of maritime law for their work as advocates and judges in the admiralty courts. We do not know whether the regius professor included any aspects of this law in his lectures. Zouche did, however, write a general treatise on the subject, *Descriptio juris et judicii maritimi* (1640), mainly for the benefit of students, just before he became judge of the high court of admiralty. It is possible that some civilians waited until they became advocates in London to develop expertise in this area.

One indication of the content of civilians' education in the seventeenth century is the questions or theses which prospective doctors of law disputed at the annual Act. Since the inceptors formulated these questions themselves, subject to the ratification of congregation, it is likely that the questions reflected both the content of the lectures they attended and the subject of their reading. In many instances the questions dealt with such matters as wills, legacies, and marriage—the parts of the law that had a bearing on English practice. In fact, the Laudian statutes required that at least one of each prospective doctor's questions should relate to such practical matters.[39] In 1605 Hugh Barker, who was about to embark upon a long career as an advocate in Doctors' Commons and as an ecclesiastical judge in the diocese of Oxford, centred all three of his questions on legacies, while in 1622 Martin Aylworth, who served as an advocate in the court of arches from 1622 to 1642, concerned himself exclusively with points of marriage law.[40] Some of the questions dealing with matrimony reflected a concern with ecclesiastical as well as civil law. One of John Edisbury's questions in 1672, for example, was whether natural children were legitimized by the subsequent marriage of their parents, a question to which both the civil law and canon law provided an affirmative answer.[41]

The Act questions also reveal a strong emphasis on international law, especially during the first part of the century. In 1612 Nathaniel Harris debated questions regarding the rights of princes to prohibit fishing in their territorial waters, the right to declare war against infidels, and the legality of reprisals, while in the same year Arthur Duck denied the proposition that an ambassador who had committed a crime in the country to which he had been sent could be punished by the prince of that country.[42]

Not all questions disputed at the Act touched on areas in which civilians could have become professionally active. Some, such as whether duelling was legal, whether the status of women in law was inferior to that of men, and whether it was permissible to kill to defend one's property, were designed mainly to demonstrate a general understanding of the civil law.[43] Others were of a constitutional

---

[38] Francis Clerke, *Praxis tam jus dicentibus quam aliis omnibus qui in foro ecclesiastico versantur appime utilis* (Dublin 1666). This work had been widely available in manuscript for fifty years before publication.

[39] *Laudian Code*, ed. Griffiths VII. ii. 2.   [40] *Reg. Univ.* ed. Clark, pt. i, 185, 189.

[41] OUA register Bd, fo 204.   [42] *Reg. Univ.* ed. Clark, pt. i, 187.

[43] Ibid.; OUA register Bd, fo 203; OUA register of congregation 1659–69, NEP/*supra*/18, register Qb, fo 174^v.

nature. The civil law contained a large amount of public law, and it had much to say regarding the powers of the prince and his relationship to the law. It is not too surprising, therefore, to find Peter Mews, in the year after the Restoration, defending the proposition that the prince is free from the law, or Edward Masters, two years later, denying that the people can make laws by themselves.[44] In these positions we have some tangible evidence that the study of the civil law had the potential of turning legists into royal absolutists, even if a significant number of them subscribed to different political views.[45]

Disputations regarding such matters as duelling and the powers of the prince remind us that, although legists took degrees in order to prepare for careers in the ecclesiastical and admiralty courts, much of their education was not immediately relevant to their future occupation. Indeed, it was precisely this feature of the civil law that made it attractive to students who had no intention of becoming civil lawyers. During the seventeenth century a number of prospective divines, as well as students with no apparent professional ambition, acquired a knowledge of the civil law. Some of these students attended the lectures of the regius professor and took degrees in the faculty of law, but most of them appear to have gained their knowledge of the civil law through private study. In some cases they were responding to concerted efforts to promote the study of the civil law outside the civilians' profession.[46]

The informal education of divines in the civil law owed much to Thomas Barlow, Bodley's Librarian from 1652 to 1660 and provost of Queen's College from 1657 to 1677. During the 1650s Barlow drafted an extensive guide 'for attaining some convenient knowledge of the civill law as far as it may be necessary for a divine'.[47] In the introduction to this work he explained that he would 'say nothing of the practicall part of it, which is the lawer's trade and benefit'.[48] The core of Barlow's guide is a list of more than ninety titles of the civil law which were relevant to the study of divinity. These include titles on marriage, adoption, usury, and the crime of sacrilege. Barlow also singled out the last title of the *Digest*, since it contained 'the very foundations and principles of morall right and equity'.[49] The final pages of the manuscript include a description of the canon law, a series of instructions on its use, and a list of books on both the canon law and English ecclesiastical law.

Barlow's view of the civil law as a source of moral principles influenced another guide that was drafted for university students in the late seventeenth century. This manuscript, which bears the title 'Some directions for young students in the

[44] OUA register Qb, fos 173ᵛ, 174ᵛ.

[45] Levack, *Civil Lawyers*, 86–121, 201–2.

[46] See Richard Zouche, *Cases and Questions Resolved in the Civil Law* (Oxford 1652) for an early effort in this regard.

[47] Bodl. MS Rawlinson c. 945, pp. 503–16; another copy of this work is in QCA MS 478, fos 49–58.

[48] Bodl. MS Rawlinson c. 945, p. 503.

[49] Ibid. p. 510. Thomas Wood, *A New Institute of the Imperial or Civil Law* (London 1704), p. xv, argues that his book 'may not be useless to young divines . . . to determine cases of conscience'.

university,' offers a general scheme of humanistic education for artists and bears no reference to the specific needs of either lawyers or clerics. It discusses the civil law only under the general heading of moral philosophy. The author includes Francisco Suárez's *Tractatus de legibus* (1612), Samuel von Pufendorf's *De jure naturae et gentium* (1672), and Hugo Grotius' *De jure belli ac pacis* (1625) among the works that the student should consult, and then recommends Barlow's manuscript for 'the part of moral philosophy which relates to or concerns the civil law'.[50]

The assimilation of the civil law to the study of philosophy and its inclusion in a liberal arts education received further reinforcement from John Aubrey, who in 1684 drafted a plan for educating young gentlemen between the ages of 9 and 18. According to Aubrey the study of the civil law should take place after the student has been trained in logic and rhetoric as well as in ethics. He should begin with Pufendorf and then study John Jacob Wisenbach's *Disputationes ad instituta imperiala* (1648), which Aubrey considered 'the best author for a beginner' that he had ever seen, and M. Pelisson's *Parephrase des institutions de l'Empereur Justinian* (1664). The purpose of this training would be to teach the young student 'how to drawe consequences ... and to detect paralogisms or fallacies'.[51]

Aubrey did not recommend that young gentlemen should continue their education at the English universities. There, it was feared, they would be 'debaucht by their idlenesse and luxurie' and learn very little. Rather, they should attend the university of Leiden, where they could improve their knowledge of the civil law and their proficiency in foreign languages.[52] But even if Aubrey thought little of English university education, his remarks on the civil law reflect an important change in English attitudes towards the law that was studied there. Instead of being regarded as a suspect body of professional knowledge, the civil law was now being recognized as a branch of philosophy and a commendable form of general intellectual training. This perception provides a further explanation why at Oxford in the late seventeenth and eighteenth centuries the civil law was spared the hostile criticism to which it had been subjected during the reign of James I.

---

[50] Bodl. MS Rawlinson d. 188, fos 6–7.   [51] Bodl. MS Aubrey 10, fo. 68.
[52] Ibid., fo. 70.

10

Religious Controversy

NICHOLAS TYACKE

Two spectres, often indistinguishable, haunted many English theologians during the seventeenth century. They called one popery and the other by the names of Arminianism and Socinianism, seeing their embodiment in particular individuals or groups. Those so accused sometimes replied in kind, but more usually they resorted to a counter-charge of puritanism. Truth, half-truth, and falsehood were all involved in this labelling. Although the focus of concern altered with circumstances, most of the ingredients can be found present in Oxford from the late Elizabethan period onwards; broadly speaking, an obsession with Roman Catholicism was increasingly paralleled by alarm about a novel rationalizing tendency in religion. An important milestone in this development was the Oxford publication, in 1638, of *The Religion of Protestants*, by William Chillingworth. An ex-Catholic, Chillingworth was widely suspected of both Arminianism and Socinianism.[1] Although they were, strictly speaking, antitrinitarians, Socinians were also deemed guilty, even more than Arminians, of subverting Christian orthodoxy through an exaggerated emphasis on the powers of both human reason and spiritual free will.

By contrast the character of Oxford divinity, until the reign of Charles I, was militantly protestant, generally Calvinist, in the sense of adhering to the Reformed theology of grace,[2] and strongly evangelical. This tradition had been established in the later sixteenth century, thanks especially to the shared outlook of successive deans of Christ Church and regius professors of divinity, whose names provide an impressive roll-call of Calvinists, continuing in unbroken succession from the 1570s to the 1620s. Deans Toby Matthew, William James, Thomas Ravis, John King, and William Godwin soldiered side by side with Laurence Humfrey, Thomas

I am most grateful to my former colleague Professor P. Lake, now of Princeton University, for commenting extensively on a draft of this chapter. Dr F. Trott has similarly given me the benefit of his advice on the Interregnum section, as has Professor J. H. Burns on political thought.

[1] William Chillingworth, *The Religion of Protestants: a safe way to salvation* (Oxford 1638); Francis Cheynell, *The Rise, Growth and Danger of Socinianisme. Together with a plaine discovery of a desperate designe of corrupting the Protestant religion, whereby it appeares that the religion which hath been so violently contended for (by the Archbishop of Canterbury and his adherents) is not the true pure Protestant religion, but a hotchpotch of Arminianisme, Socinianisme and Popery* (London 1643), 28–31, 34–5, 72–3; see pp. 588–90 below.

[2] Seventeenth-century contemporaries called this body of predestinarian doctrine 'Calvinist', yet the sources were multifarious—including the writings of the early Luther. In a specifically English context, the teachings of Martin Bucer and Peter Martyr were especially important.

Holland, Robert Abbot, and John Prideaux as regius professors of divinity. Prideaux, regius professor from 1615, was also a canon of Christ Church and the son-in-law of Dean Godwin. Other leading Calvinist evangelicals were George Abbot, Henry Airay, Sebastian Benefield, and John Rainolds.[3]

Some of these men were undoubtedly puritans. Thus Rainolds emerged as the champion of nonconformity at the Hampton Court Conference in 1604, while earlier, during the 1580s, he had advocated the institution of lay elders. Puritan sympathies also got Henry Airay into trouble in 1602.[4] But they also included in their ranks two future archbishops, George Abbot and Toby Matthew, and five future bishops, Robert Abbot, William James, John King, John Prideaux, and Thomas Ravis. We need in fact to distinguish here between episcopalians, who were basically satisfied with the polity and forms of worship of the English Church, and puritan critics of the establishment. The similarities, as well as the differences, can be illustrated by a comparison of the writings of George Abbot and Henry Airay, dating from the turn of the century. (Abbot and Airay were chosen master of University College and provost of Queen's College in 1597 and 1598 respectively.)

Both Abbot and Airay assumed that salvation came via preaching. Abbot defined this as a 'commission to be executed in God's name' for 'saving the soules of men', and Airay similarly spoke of it as the 'ordinarie meanes whereby the Lord worketh faith in the hearts of his children'. In addition they exhibit a shared belief in what has been called experimental predestinarianism, teaching that the elect should strive for personal certainty of their salvation. According to Abbot, 'either youth or age, life or death, in him that is elected, shall apprehend the promises. Be it the ninth houre, or the eleventh houre, yet there shal be a time.' This 'it is which bringeth comfort unto the wounded soule and afflicted conscience—not that Christ is a saviour, for what am I the better for that, but a saviour unto me' and 'mine inheritance [is] with the saints'. Similarly Airay maintained 'our labour and endevour must be that we may know ourselves to be the sonnes of God . . . elect and chosen in Christ Jesus before the foundation of the world'. For 'howsoever wee can helpe nothing unto our election . . . yet may wee know whether we be elected . . . by the fruits of the spirit'. Opponents of such doctrine were branded by them as 'papists'. Furthermore each took it as axiomatic that the pope was Antichrist.[5]

But Airay combined these views with a much harsher judgement than Abbot of the religious *status quo*. Referring to disputes between 'puritans' and 'protestants',

---

[3] N. Tyacke, *Anti-Calvinists: the rise of English Arminianism, c.1590–1640* (Oxford 1987, 2nd edn Oxford 1990), pp. ix, 18–19, 21–3, 59, 61–2, 72–4, 115. For the views of William Goodwin, see a Paul's Cross sermon preached by him on 5 November 1614: London, Dr Williams's Library, MS 12.10, fos 7ᵛ–8.

[4] P. Collinson, 'The Jacobean religious settlement: the Hampton Court Conference' in H. Tomlinson (ed.), *Before the Civil War* (London 1983), 38–44; John Rainolds, *The Prophecie of Haggai interpreted and applied in sundry sermons* (London 1649), 4–5, 16–18; C. M. Dent, *Protestant Reformers in Elizabethan Oxford* (Oxford 1983), 213–17.

[5] George Abbot, *An Exposition upon the Prophet Jonah* (London 1600), 231, 267, 632, 635; Henry Airay, *Lectures upon the Whole Epistle of Saint Paul to the Philippians* (London 1618), 265, 294–5, 431–2; George Abbot, *The Reasons which Doctour Hill hath brought for the upholding of papistry* (Oxford 1604), 9 and *passim*.

about 'ceremonies' and 'discipline', Airay concluded 'let us no longer halt betweene God and Baal, Christ and Antichrist, religion and superstition'. Meanwhile Abbot professed 'I do not yet find anything, either expressly or by consequent, directly to be drawne throughout the whole booke of God for the leaving or refusing of this or that garment, and so of other circumstances'. Again, when attacking separatists, Airay did not seek to extenuate the faults of the English Church. Abbot, however, countered separatism by arguing that 'the spouse is blacke while she remaineth on earth'. Accordingly a degree of ecclesiastical imperfection was inevitable, and a few years later he expressed his own ceremonial ideal in terms of 'seemely conformity'. Furthermore the two disagreed on the subject of bishops, Abbot holding the office to be apostolic whereas Airay could discern no trace of it in the New Testament. Any temptation therefore on our part simply to conflate puritanism and Calvinism must be resisted, because conformity especially remained a divisive issue.[6]

Yet conformity itself came in different guises. A much more abrasive variety than that of Abbot was purveyed by John Howson, a Student and latterly canon of Christ Church, for whom three sermons survive preached between 1597 and 1602. In these sermons Howson attacked what he saw as an undue stress on preaching among fellow English protestants. 'The end and use of churches is the publike service and worship of God', being 'comprehended under the name of prayer' which 'excels all other religious actions'. But nowadays *oratoria* are turned into *auditoria*, oratories into auditories' and 'the chief place' is 'given to preaching'. Howson associated himself with those slandered under the name of 'formalists', for 'diligently' observing 'the rites and ceremonies commanded by the Church and received from all antiquity', and complained bitterly of the state of parish churches. The latter, in country districts, were 'little better than hog-styes', and in towns merely 'white-limed' or 'at the best wainscotted'. His indictment of the current religious scene also included instances of judaizers, 'which wil see their neighbour perish before they wil relieve him on the sabboth day'. Nevertheless even Howson was still a doctrinal Calvinist at this time, as emerges from his remarks, in 1602, limiting the extent of Christ's atonement. The 'general and admirable benefite of our redemption . . . was sufficient for the whole world, but efficient to al the elect of God'.[7]

Between them, Abbot, Airay, and Howson exemplify the three main schools of religious thought present in Oxford, at the beginning of the seventeenth century. Moreover, as holders of the vice-chancellorship between 1600 and 1607, all three were involved in university politics at the highest level. In terms of age a mere five years separated the eldest, Howson, from the youngest, Abbot. Howson was only a canon of Christ Church when he was appointed vice-chancellor in 1602, although

[6] Airay, *Lectures*, 4, 17, 292–5; Abbot, *An Exposition*, 36, 240; Abbot, *The Reasons* 102; George Abbot, *Quaestiones sex* (Oxford 1598), 187–8. The editor of Airay's lectures, Christopher Potter, dedicated them to Abbot, by then archbishop, in 1618.

[7] John Howson, *A Sermon preached at St Maries in Oxford, the 17 Day of November, 1602* (Oxford 1602), 5–6, 17, 25; John Howson, *A Second Sermon preached at Paules Crosse, the 21 of May, 1598* (London 1598), 23, 39–40; John Howson, *A Sermon preached at Paules Crosse, the 4 of December, 1597* (London 1597), 7.

good precedent existed for this.[8] The choice of Howson was officially that of the chancellor, Lord Buckhurst, but it may well be that it was on the recommendation of Archbishop Whitgift. For since the death of Chancellor Leicester in 1588 there had been a series of attempts at enforcing a more rigorous conformity in the university; the firm views of Howson on such matters would have been widely known because of his published sermons. Announcing his appointment as vice-chancellor, in July 1602, Buckhurst wrote

I hartely pray and requier you all in generall, but especially you the proctors and heades of houses, unfeinedly to be assistinge and obedient unto him therein, whose good example whilst the inferiour sort and such as under your severall governments shall behold they doubtless will the more easely subscribe, and be conformed unto all good orders.

The terms subscribe and conform, as used by Buckhurst, seemingly have a religious connotation. Certainly by November Howson was involved in conflict with Oxford puritans, and early the following year he persuaded congregation to adopt a stiffer form of clerical subscription.[9]

Tension is also likely to have been heightened at this time by the fact that George Abbot was under a temporary cloud, and therefore not in the best position to mediate between the Oxford parties. Although chaplain to Chancellor Buckhurst, he had fallen out with Bishop Bancroft of London over the proposed renovation of Cheapside Cross. Wittingly or not, Abbot was sucked into a quarrel between leading London puritans and their diocesan—itself part of a long-running saga going back at least twenty years. Periodic instructions concerning Cheapside Cross had been issued to the London corporation, in the name of Queen Elizabeth, to make good the ravages of time and vandalism, the latter perhaps ideologically motivated. Resistance came to a head in 1601, with the puritans wanting to replace the now ruinous cross with some secular emblem. As in the past, they sought to exploit differences within the highest ranks of the established church over what constituted idolatry. Asked for his opinion Abbot, in his capacity as Oxford vice-chancellor, condemned Cheapside Cross because it incorporated representations of the holy spirit and of God the father, as well as being a 'crucifix'. He was supported in his judgement of January 1601 by the Oxford puritans Henry Airay and John Rainolds—a further instance of intellectual affinity.[10]

The death of Queen Elizabeth in March 1603 was the signal for a renewed national campaign by the puritans on behalf of a further reformation of the English Church. It was crucial to their strategy to win the sympathy of King James, first with a fairly

---

[8] Apart from Howson, six Elizabethan canons of Christ Church became vice-chancellors: J. Le Neve, *Fasti Ecclesiae Anglicanae*, ed. T. D. Hardy (3 vols Oxford 1854) iii. 476.

[9] Wood, *History of the University* ii. 237–8, 242, 258–9, 261; OUA register of congregation and convocation 1595–1606, NEP/*supra*/11, register M, fo 70; Dent, *Protestant Reformers*, 209–12, 217–18.

[10] London, Corporation of London Record Office, Repertories 20, fos 216ʳ⁻ᵛ, Repertories 25, fos 2ᵛ, 24, 262ᵛ; *APC 1599–1600*, 27, ibid. *1600–1601*, 44; George Abbot, *Cheapside Crosse censured and condemned* (London 1641), 2–3, 12; M. Aston, *England's Iconoclasts* (Oxford 1988) i. 294–342.

detailed statement of grievances and then by more general lobbying. What is known to history as the millenary petition, presented to the king that April, appeared to achieve the first of these aims. Pressure was thereafter kept up by soliciting support on a country-wide basis. The puritan leader Henry Jacob wrote to Oxford on 30 June, seeking signatures to a petition in the name of members of the university, a development which seems finally to have provoked a response from the university authorities. They were probably already aware of a grace passed by Cambridge University, on 9 June, threatening with suspension anyone who publicly opposed the 'doctrine or discipline' of the English Church. But the Oxford *Answere*, a point-by-point reply to the millenary petition, was not published in print until October, after George Abbot had succeeded Howson as vice-chancellor.[11] Thus Abbot was closely associated with this public rebuff to the puritans, which no doubt also helped in restoring him to the favour of Bishop Bancroft. Nevertheless there are grounds for thinking that the alliance between Abbot and Howson was at best an uneasy one, although they had not yet openly quarrelled. In addition one of the proctors involved, his 'zeal against the millenary petition' still remembered twenty years later, was William Laud, then a fellow of St John's College, and the first known religious disagreement between Abbot and Laud occurred in about 1603— concerning the visibility of the true church.[12]

The Oxford *Answere* assumes that the authors of the millenary petition have Presbyterian ambitions. Attention is first drawn to the form of local petition proposed by Henry Jacob, 'that the present state of our Church may bee farther reformed in all things needefull' and 'agreeable to the example of other reformed Churches, which have restored both the doctrine and discipline as it was delivered by our saviour Christ and his holy apostles'. The deduction made from this is that 'they wil never have an end, till they have set up the presbitery'. Again, commenting on the millenary petition itself, the *Answere* describes the real aim as 'the utter overthrow of the present church government and in steed thereof the setting up of a presbitery in every parish'. The case for reform, however, is dismissed as groundless in terms reminiscent of Howson rather than Abbot. For example Bible-reading, set forms of prayer, and printed homilies are recommended in lieu of sermons, as 'ordinarie effectual meanes to continue and increase ... true faith'.

[11] *The Stuart Constitution, 1603–1688*, ed. J. P. Kenyon (Cambridge 1966, 2nd edn Cambridge 1986), 117–19; P. Collinson, *The Elizabethan Puritan Movement* (London 1967), 452–9; C. Burrage, *The Early English Dissenters in the Light of Recent Research (1550–1641)* (2 vols Cambridge 1912) ii. 146–7; C. H. Cooper, *Annals of Cambridge* (5 vols Cambridge 1842–1908) iii. 2; *The Answere of the Vicechancelour, the Doctors, both the Proctors, and other the Heads of Houses in the Universitie of Oxford ... to the Humble Petition of the Ministers of the Church of England* (Oxford 1603). Subsequent editions of *The Answere* incorporate a letter from Cambridge University, dated 7 October and said to have been received 'immediately after' the first printing.

[12] 'John Howson's answers to Archbishop Abbot's accusations at his "trial" before James I at Greenwich, 10 June 1615', ed. N. Cranfield and K. Fincham, *Camden Miscellany* xxix (Camden Soc. 4th ser. xxxiv 1987), 335. John Hacket, *Scrinia reserata: a memorial offer'd to the great deservings of J. Williams ... archbishop of York* (London 1693), pt 1, p. 64; Peter Heylyn, *Cyprianus anglicus: or the history of the life and death of ... William [Laud] ... archbishop of Canterbury* (London 1668), 53–4.

A concluding reference to sacrilege also has the mark of Howson about it. It would appear, therefore, that the hard-line conformists were in the ascendant within the university at this point.[13]

A veil of secrecy, however, shrouded the making of the Oxford *Answere*, through which two members of Corpus Christi College, Ralph Barlow and Henry Mason, attempted to pierce in advance of publication. According to their subsequent depositions, they had heard rumours that some such work was in the press and went to see for themselves at the printing house. Barlow admitted that he succeeded in reading the title and 'heare and there in the treatise itselfe'. Related discussions also took place at Corpus, as to how far the university seniors had been unanimous in condemning the millenary petition. Some said 'all saving twoe' approved the *Answere*, probably referring to Airay and Rainolds. Others named 'a third'—Thomas Singleton, the principal of Brasenose College, who had allegedly refused his consent because the *Answere* defended clerical non-residency. More generally the Barlow group impugned the *Answere* as unrepresentative, disliking 'that anie such thinge shold be sett forth by a few men in the name of the whole universitie'. One of the sources of their information was Laud's fellow proctor, Christopher Dale, of Merton College, who had reportedly seen and read the *Answere* but 'did not think it shold come publicklie in printe'. Dale had in fact been the recipient of Henry Jacob's letter of 30 June, canvassing puritan support in Oxford. Jacob assumed that Dale was 'well affected' to the cause of further reformation, and added as a postscript 'I could wishe you to conferre with Dr. Airay about this matter'. Either Jacob was misinformed or Dale lost his nerve. At any rate no Oxford puritan campaign developed.[14]

Our knowledge of the activities of Barlow and Mason, and the conversations at Corpus Christi College, derives from an investigation launched this same October 1603 by the pro-vice-chancellor and dean of Christ Church, Thomas Ravis. It is unlikely to have been mere coincidence that the president of Corpus was also the puritan leader John Rainolds. His name does not occur in the depositions, although the latter indicate the existence of two factions within the college. John Boate and Henry Hindley are to be found siding with Barlow and Mason, against Walter Browne, Gilbert Hawthorn, and George Seller. The subsequent careers of the first group, however, do not suggest that any of them were strong puritans: Ralph Barlow, for instance, became archdeacon of Winchester in 1609. On the other hand Browne was probably already a member of the Howson–Laud circle, and soon to be defamed as a 'papist'.[15] Despite the evident worries of the university authorities, Oxford puritans kept a low profile at this time. Indeed of the three probable puritan heads in 1603 Airay was a conformist by 1606, when he was appointed vice-chancellor, Buckhurst writing privately to him the previous year that he understood him now to be 'conformable to the ecclesiastical discipline established in this

[13] The Answere, sigs ¶¶–¶¶2, pp. 15–16, 23, 31.
[14] BL Add. MS 28,571, fos 181–6; Burrage, *The Early English Dissenters* ii. 146–7.
[15] BL Add. MS 28,571, fos 181–6; Tyacke, *Anti-Calvinists*, 65–6.

land . . . whatsoever heretofore hath been surmised or suggested to the contrarye'. Singleton had already served as vice-chancellor in 1598–9, and did so again in the years 1611 to 1614. Only Rainolds may have remained obdurate, still refusing full subscription in 1605. George Abbot's successor as vice-chancellor, in 1604, was John Williams, principal of Jesus College and someone in the same religious mould as John Howson.[16] But it was churchmen of the type of Abbot who occupied the Oxford middle ground in these years, Abbot himself serving as vice-chancellor three times between 1600 and 1606, by the end of which period the Calvinist evangelicals had regained the initiative in the university and Howson's reputation was in eclipse.

Moreover anti-Catholic polemic continued to be *de rigueur* and it remained a Jacobean commonplace that the pope was Antichrist. The latter thesis was from time to time maintained by doctors of divinity at the annual Oxford Act, and conformists such as Gabriel Powell published whole treatises to the same effect. Nevertheless the point has been well made that puritans tended to dwell with special intensity on the subject. The same preoccupation with popery which led puritans to criticize the English Church as insufficiently reformed impelled them to attack with greater force the Roman seat of Antichristian error. Paradoxically this also had the effect of narrowing the gap between puritans and many of their protestant opponents.[17] Here a good illustration is provided by John Terry's book *The Trial of Truth*, the first part of which was published at Oxford in 1600. It is subtitled *A plaine and short discovery of the chiefest pointes of the doctrine of the great Antichrist*. Terry, a graduate of New College, had left Oxford in the 1580s. Dedicating the work to his diocesan, Bishop Henry Cotton of Salisbury, he refers to Antichrist as the 'capitall enemy' and urges his fellow ministers to sink any disagreements with the bishops, about 'government and ceremonies', in their fight against the common foe. At the same time he asks those in 'higher place' not to 'hastely adjudge' as 'factious and mutinous' all who 'differ a little' from them.[18]

The heads of Antichristian doctrine, as listed by Terry, included the denial of assurance on the part of the faithful that they are justified, prayer to saints as mediators between God and man, the teachings that God 'in no respect willeth sinne' and that free will concurs 'with God's grace in our conversion', transubstantiation, justification by works, the lawfulness of images, the continuing occurrence of miracles, works of supererogation, the perpetual visibility of 'the church of Christ' and the inclusion within it of the reprobate as well as the elect, the possibility of fulfilling God's law, and belief in purgatory and the papal supremacy. Terry has a final

[16] Bodl. MS Rawlinson a. 289, fo 76; HMC *Salisbury MSS* xvii. 422–3, 431; Tyacke, *Anti-Calvinists*, 64. I am grateful to Dr K. Fincham here for advice on dating.

[17] *Reg. Univ.* ed. Clark, pt i, 195, 199–200, 204, 213; Bodl. MS Wood 276 A, fo 414; OUA register of congregation 1622–30, NEP/*supra*/ 14, register o, fo 240[v]; Gabriel Powell, *Disputationum theologicarum et scholasticarum de Antichristo et eius ecclesia* (London 1605); C. Hill, *Antichrist in Seventeenth-century England* (London 1971), 3–33; P. Lake, 'The significance of the Elizabethan identification of the pope as Antichrist', *Journal of Ecclesiastical History* xxxi (1980).

[18] John Terry, *The Trial of Truth* (Oxford 1600), sigs a2–a3.

section identifying biblical allusions to Antichrist with the 'bishop of Rome'. His account is informed throughout by generally Calvinist assumptions. This becomes even clearer in *The Second Part of The Trial of Truth*, published at Oxford in 1602 and dedicated to the warden of New College, George Ryves. Here Terry writes that 'the certainty of our election to eternall life, and the assurance that we are the children of God and have our names written in Heaven', is traduced, by 'the servants of Antichrist', as 'the mother of pride and presumption and of carnal security'.[19]

Not everyone, however, endorsed such an anti-Catholic stance. Many years later William Laud recalled his distaste on reading the claim by Gabriel Powell, published in 1605, that he was 'as certain that the pope is Antichrist as that Jesus Christ is the son of God and redeemer of the world'. Powell was a member of St Mary Hall in Oxford and his book *De Antichristo*, which described the various notes of Antichrist and his church, apparently had the approval of the regius professor of divinity, Thomas Holland. There is, however, evidence that John Williams, Lady Margaret professor of divinity as well as principal of Jesus College, dissented. During an acrimonious exchange with John Howson in 1615, George Abbot said that the late Williams 'was popishly affected ... and defended that the pope was not Antichrist'. Such chance remarks enable a picture to be built up of those in Jacobean Oxford who now came increasingly to question the dominant religious views of the day.[20]

Anti-Calvinists at Cambridge had, in the mid-1590s, challenged current teaching on predestination. But they had elicited no support from the sister university. Rather, Oxford theologians had rallied to the Calvinist cause—asserting the unconditional nature of election and reprobation, the limited extent of Christ's atonement, and the inevitable perseverance of the saints. The first datable case of unequivocally anti-Calvinist views being entertained at Oxford is that of Thomas Jackson, then a fellow of Corpus Christi College. Even in this instance, however, we are dependent on later personal testimony. Writing more than twenty years afterwards, Jackson stated that it was about 1605 when he decided, still as a young man, against the doctrine of 'absolute' predestination. Yet, because he did not air his opinion in print until 1628, historians have assumed that he was a Calvinist throughout the Jacobean period. Humfrey Leech, a chaplain of Christ Church, was probably an earlier anti-Calvinist. His suggestion that true believers could finally fall from grace emerged only incidentally during 1607, when he was in trouble for advocating works of supererogation. The next year he became a Roman Catholic, which is likely to have had an inhibiting effect on any sympathizers. Nevertheless the latter, by Leech's own account, included John Buckeridge, president of St John's College, John Howson, and John Williams.[21]

---

[19] John Terry, *The Trial of Truth* (Oxford 1600), sigs a2–a3, pp. 8–31, 35–40, 42, 49–59, 66–8, 76–8, 88–108, 114, 127–8, 150–9; John Terry, *The Second Part of the Trial of Truth* (Oxford 1602), sig. C. The third part of Terry's *Tryall of Truth* was published at Oxford in 1625.

[20] Laud, *Works* iv. 309; Powell, *De Antichristo*, 341; 'John Howson's answers', ed. Cranfield and Fincham, 336.

[21] Tyacke, *Anti-Calvinists*, 60–4, 66–7; Dent, *Protestant Reformers*, 234–7; *The Responsa Scholarum of the*

Serious opposition to Calvinism in fact developed relatively late at Oxford, and the first decade of the seventeenth century was mainly taken up with other disputes which did not follow clear party lines. Two such questions concerned Christ's descent into hell and the right to remarry after divorce. The first revolved around the meaning of this article of the creed. In what sense had Christ 'descended into hell'? During the later sixteenth century, particularly under the influence of Calvin, a metaphorical interpretation had gained wide acceptance. Archbishop Whitgift, for example, sanctioned the view that the 'worde Hel ... signifieth not the place of everlasting torments' but 'the terrors and torments of the bodie and soule which Christ suffered'.[22] On the other hand a literalist interpretation also had its advocates. This was the position defended by Richard Parkes, in a pamphlet published at Oxford in 1604. Parkes, a graduate of Brasenose College, had left Oxford in the 1580s. In an expanded version of his argument, published at London in 1607, he identifies his opponents as 'puritans'. The lines of division, however, remained blurred because of a third and linguistic interpretation, which rendered the Greek *hades* and the Hebrew *sheol* as the place of the dead, not the damned. This last won continuing support across a wide religious spectrum, including the puritan Henry Jacob in the 1590s and the Arminian Henry Hammond in the 1650s.[23] Likewise the question of remarriage after divorce was not a straight party issue, despite John Rainolds arguing in favour and John Howson against. Howson's views were propounded as a doctoral thesis at the Oxford Act in 1602 and published the same year. But a reply to Howson was licensed for the London press in June 1603 by John Buckeridge, who later emerged as a leading anti-Calvinist and is generally regarded as having had a formative influence on William Laud. The latter in 1605 conducted a marriage service between the earl of Devon and the *divorcée* Lady Penelope Rich, while her former husband was still living.[24] Rumblings of a further controversy more directly involving Laud are detectable in 1608, when for one of his Act theses he argued that only bishops could ordain ministers and by implication unchurched most continental protestants. Two years later Ralph Barlow, who had been under suspicion of puritanism in 1603, can be found at the Act defending

English College of Rome pt 1 *1598–1621*, ed. A. Kenny (Catholic Record Soc. liv 1962), 212. Examination of a xerox of the original manuscript confirms that 'Hensonum' should read 'Housonum'. I am grateful to Dr Kenny for his help on this subject.

[22] Thomas Rogers, *The English Creede consenting with the true, auncient, catholique and apostolique Church* (London 1585), pt 1, p. 10. This work was licensed by Archbishop Whitgift: *A Transcript of the Registers of the Company of Stationers, 1554–1640*, ed. E. Arber (5 vols 1875–94) ii. 436.

[23] Richard Parkes, *A Brief Answere unto Certaine Objections and Reasons against the descension of Christ into hell* (Oxford 1604); Richard Parkes, *An Apologie of Three Testimonies of Holy Scripture, concerning the article of our creed, 'he descended into hell'* (London 1607), pt 2, sig. Aa3; D. D. Wallace, 'Puritan and Anglican: the interpretation of Christ's descent into Hell in Elizabethan theology', *Archiv für Reformationsgeschichte* lxix (1978), 274–5, 282.

[24] A. R. Winnett, *Divorce and Remarriage in Anglicanism* (London 1958), ch. 6; John Howson, *Uxore dimissa propter fornicationem aliam non licet superinducere* (Oxford 1602); John Rainolds, *A Defence of the Judgement of the Reformed Churches. That a man may lawfullie not onlie put awaie his wife for her adulterie, but also marrie another* (n.p. 1609); Thomas Pie, *Epistola ad ornatissimum virum D. Johannem Housonum* (London 1603): *A Transcript*, ed. Arber iii. 238; Tyacke, *Anti-Calvinists*, 67–8, 70, 174, 266–7.

the legitimacy of the 'Reformed' ministry as well as that of the English Church. Laud's views on this issue, however, would appear to have been thoroughly untypical at the time.[25]

As regards the development of anti-Calvinism, the writings of the Dutch theologian Jacobus Arminius were more important as a defining label than as a direct source. In his *Declaratio* or *Verclaringhe*, published posthumously in 1610, Arminius provided a classic anti-Calvinist statement. Rejecting unconditional election and reprobation, whether before or after the fall of Adam, he affirmed that God 'decreed to receive into favour those who repent and believe ... but to leave in sin, and under wrath, all impenitent persons and unbelievers'. Grace, both 'sufficient and efficacious', can be resisted, and perseverance is not guaranteed. Clearly it was unnecessary to have read Arminius in order to hold such views—witness the Cambridge anti-Calvinists of the 1590s. Similarly Thomas Jackson almost certainly came to reject Calvinist predestinarianism quite independently of any Dutch religious influence. Nevertheless Walter Browne, Jackson's mentor, owned four books by Arminius at the time of his own death in 1613. Indeed by 1611 the university authorities were taking note of Arminianism as such. Two years later Robert Abbot, the recently appointed regius professor of divinity, denounced the new phenomenon at the Act—the most public academic event of the Oxford calendar. His target on this occasion was the teaching of the Dutch Arminian Petrus Bertius, apropos falling from grace. Abbot spoke too of the corrupting influence in England of Arminian doctrine. He countered with an orthodox Calvinist exposition, maintaining that 'God's election cannot be frustrated'. Apart from the Bible, the main source cited is St Augustine. In 1614 and 1615 Abbot broadened his attack to encompass Arminian teachings on grace more generally. True grace, he maintained, is neither universal nor resistible, being the gratuitous gift of God to the elect and the cause of belief. At least one fellow Calvinist, Richard Field, was 'much offended' by Abbot making 'matters of opinion into matters of faith', adding that 'Oxford hath hethertoo bin free from these disputes, though Cambridge hath bin much disquieted with them'.[26]

By early 1615 Robert Abbot had identified Laud as in effect an Arminian. This particular accusation, however, was incorporated within a more all-embracing charge of popery, a charge which Abbot also levelled against Howson. Laud and Howson responded by suggesting that both Abbot and his brother George, now archbishop of Canterbury, were puritan fellow-travellers. According to Howson Oxford could only boast three or four 'suspected' Roman Catholics, whereas puritanism had 300 'supporters'. Ten years later Laud and Howson were indeed to join in condemning the teaching of the Synod of Dort, having by then clearly broken

---

[25] *Reg. Univ.* ed. Clark, pt i, 206–7; N. Sykes, *Old Priest and New Presbyter* (Cambridge 1950), 101.

[26] *The Writings of James Arminius*, trans. J. Nichols and W. R. Bagnall (3 vols Grand Rapids 1956) i. 247–8; Tyacke, *Anti-Calvinists*, 65–7, 72; Robert Abbot, *De gratia et perseverantia sanctorum* (London 1618), 1, 4, 18–20, 25; Nathaniel Field, *Some Short Memorials concerning the life of ... R. Field*, ed. J. Le Neve (London 1717), 22.

with the Calvinist beliefs which they had both once held. But no evidence is known to exist that either of the Abbots ever inclined towards nonconformity although Robert, like George, was a Calvinist evangelical, who characterized preaching as 'the very aire whereby we take the breath of spirituall and heavenly life'.[27] Nevertheless, such name-calling is indicative of a growing polarization of views. Moreover puritanism in Jacobean Oxford had been at best contained and certainly not eliminated. The strategy adopted by John Ley of Christ Church, appointed to a college living in 1616, was probably not untypical. He was willing to conform to 'the ceremonies' of the English Church 'if I may not enjoy my ministry without them', while respecting the conscientious scruples of others. Apparently more radical was William Crompton, who left Brasenose College for a Buckinghamshire lectureship in 1623. Two years later he was in trouble for maintaining the 'parity' of ministers and casting aspersions on the sign of the cross.[28]

Another Brasenose puritan, more similar to Ley than Crompton, was Robert Bolton, who was presented to a Northamptonshire benefice in about 1609. His biographer, writing in the early 1630s, remarked that he tempered 'zeale' with 'discretion', but it is to Bolton that we owe a remarkable account of an Oxford puritan deathbed. Thomas Peacock, a fellow of Brasenose, had been instrumental in Bolton's own religious conversion, although when he was dying in 1611 came to believe himself a reprobate. Those who wrestled for the soul of Peacock included John Dod, the deprived rector of Hanwell in Oxfordshire, and Henry Airay, telling him that 'whom God loveth once he loveth to the end'. Peacock's 'patron', Sir Robert Harley, also sent messages of encouragement and their combined spiritual ministrations were finally successful. This account, preserved by Bolton, is a practical essay in experimental predestinarianism, yet the prominent part played by Dod, who paid the dying man at least four visits, as well as the role of Harley, entitles us to label the episode puritan rather than simply Calvinist. On the other hand Bolton's supporters included John King, who became bishop of London in 1611.[29] Similarly the following year John Ley found a theological ally in James Ussher, the future archbishop of Armagh. Even Crompton, after being admonished in person by King James, was dismissed with a bag of gold.[30]

[27] Tyacke, *Anti-Calvinists*, pp. xi, 70, 266–71; 'John Howson's answers', ed. Cranfield and Fincham, 322–7, 330; Robert Abbot, *The Exaltation of the Kingdom and Priesthood of Christ* (London 1601), 26. In 1612 Howson had also preached a notorious Oxford sermon, accusing the annotators of the Genevan Bible of inculcating antitrinitarianism: Bodl. MS Rawlinson d. 320, fos 46ᵛ–7.

[28] John Ley, *Sunday a Sabbath* (London 1641), sigs b2ʳ⁻ᵛ; Daniel Featley, *Cygnea Cantio or learned decisions and . . . pious directions for students in divinitie, delivered by . . . King James, at White Hall a few weekes before his death* (London 1629), 12–14, 16–21.

[29] Edward Bagshaw, *The Life and Death of Mr Bolton* (London 1639), 17, 27; Robert Bolton, *The Last Conflicts and Death of Mr Thomas Peacock* (London 1646), sig. A2ᵛ, pp. 4–6, 21, 30–1, 36, 44, 54. A postscript notes that this tract was refused a licence for printing during the 1630s, as being 'too precise for those times': ibid., sig. D4ᵛ; J. Eales, *Puritans and Roundheads: the Harleys of Brampton Bryan and the outbreak of the civil war* (Cambridge 1990), 50.

[30] Ley, *Sunday a Sabbath*, sig. b; Wood, *Athenae* iii. 570; Tyacke, *Anti-Calvinists*, 69–70; Featley, *Cygnea Cantio*, 9.

A puritan of an earlier generation who maintained close links with Oxford, after his departure for a Cheshire lectureship in 1603, was William Hinde. The protégé of John Rainolds at Queen's College, he arranged for the Oxford publication in 1613 and 1614 of two works by his former teacher, dedicating them to Airay whom he described as the 'nearest and dearest friend' of Rainolds. Hinde was also the leading puritan in the diocese of Chester by the time of Bishop Morton's appointment in 1616. His nonconformity emerges from a published refutation by Morton, Hinde objecting to wearing the surplice, to using the sign of the cross in baptism, and to kneeling at communion.[31] The spirit of Rainolds lived on in Hinde, yet the patronage of the now conformist Airay lent a measure of respectability to his radicalism. Airay in turn was intimately associated with his predecessor as provost of Queen's College, Bishop Henry Robinson of Carlisle. On his memorial brass Airay is likened to Elisha hastening after Elijah (Bishop Robinson), the two both dying in 1616.[32]

An Oxford puritan tradition also survived at Corpus Christi College, where Rainolds had been president between 1598 and 1607. The ringleader within the college by the early 1620s was Robert Barcroft, who had graduated BA from Corpus in 1605. About the year 1616 he got into serious trouble for teaching that it was 'lawfull to excommunicate the king and to deprive him of his royall authority'. Barcroft was forced to recant and was suspended from his fellowship for a year. That he also failed to conform to the 'rites and religious ceremonies' of the established church emerges from a presentment made in 1621, by some of the parishioners of Warborough, near Dorchester in Oxfordshire. Barcroft had allegedly refused to wear a surplice when administering communion and had allowed some of those receiving to remain in their pews. More remarkably he had altered the words of the communion service, holding up the communion cup to the 'publique view of the congregation' and saying 'this is a token and signe of the blood of our Saviour Jesus Christ'. He similarly described the communion bread. His 'disciples' at Corpus included Thomas Norwood, Richard Thompson, and Benedict Webb— all much younger men. In addition the group was apparently in touch with John Sprint, an Oxford puritan from late Elizabethan days, who had finally announced his decision to conform in a published work of 1618. Sprint argued that it was better to conform than to be deprived, while confessing 'my unwillingness thereto if by any means I might avoide it'. The preaching ministry had, in the last resort, to take precedence over such scruples of conscience. 'For as it pleaseth God to save them that beleeve by preaching, so where no vision is the people perish.' Barcroft, who proceeded to the degree of DD at Oxford in 1623, may well have employed

---

[31] John Rainolds, *The Prophecie of Obadiah opened* (Oxford 1613), sig. A4; John Rainolds, *The Discovery of the Man of Sinne* (Oxford 1614); Thomas Morton, *A Defence of the Innocencie of the Three Ceremonies of the Church of England* (London 1618); R. C. Richardson, *Puritanism in North-West England: a regional study of the diocese of Chester to 1642* (Manchester 1972), 23–4, 30–1.

[32] Collinson, *The Elizabethan Puritan Movement*, 459; K. J. Höltgen, 'Richard Haydocke: translator, engraver, physician', *The Library* 5th ser. xxxiii (1978), 26–7; K. C. Fincham, *Prelate as Pastor: the episcopate of James I* (Oxford 1990), 195.

a comparable casuistry; for one of his doctoral theses he also maintained that the pope was Antichrist. As for Sprint, he dedicated his book to Dean Godwin and the canons of Christ Church—an act in part of filial piety towards the college where he had originally studied.[33]

The continuance of this broad alliance of Calvinist evangelicals was, however, threatened by the growing influence of anti-Calvinists at the royal court, dating from the later years of King James. The brothers Abbot in fact failed to curb the Oxford activities of Laud and Howson, or to hinder their ecclesiastical promotion. Laud, who was already president of St John's College, became dean of Gloucester in 1616 and bishop of St David's in 1621. The fortunes of Howson underwent a more dramatic improvement. After many years in the wilderness, he was consecrated bishop of Oxford in 1619. His predecessor was the staunchly Calvinist John Bridges. The deanery of Christ Church also fell to an Arminian, Richard Corbett, in 1620. The changing climate manifested itself most obviously in the royal directions sent to Oxford in January 1617. These involved a tightening up of subscription and conformity, but they also attempted to alter the basis of university religious teaching. 'Young students in divinity' were 'directed to study such books as be most agreeable in doctrine and discipline to the Church of England, and excited to bestow their time in the fathers and counsels, schoolmen, histories and controversies, and not to insist too long upon compendiums and abbreviators'. The compilers of this clause seemingly had in mind Calvinist commentaries, including Calvin's own *Institutes*. It is probable that one consequence was the effective abandonment from this date of the Oxford catechetical statute, of 1579, which had specified the Heidelberg Catechism and the *Institutes*, among other works, as yardsticks of orthodoxy.[34]

The ethos of the anti-Calvinist movement now gaining ground in Oxford can be inferred from the poems of Richard Corbett, which circulated in manuscript during the second decade of the seventeenth century. Much of this verse evinces a nostalgia for the pre-reformation past combined with hostility to modern 'puritans', and by extension Calvinists, who are convicted of irrationality. Corbett's poem 'The Distracted Puritane' has a stanza attacking Calvinist teaching on reprobation. Laud was later to write of this same doctrine that it made God into 'the most fierce and unreasonable tyrant in the world'. An associated anti-Calvinist hermeneutic can also be deduced from a sermon preached before the university, by John Hales, at Easter 1617. Hales, who at the time was regius professor of Greek, alluded to the recent royal directions, advising 'young students' not 'to think themselves sufficiently provided upon their acquaintance with some *notitia* or systeme of some technicall divine'. His general theme concerned 'the abuses of obscure and difficult places of

[33] Lincolnshire Archives Office MS Ciii/13/2/24, pp. 1–4, 9, 11–13: I owe my knowledge of this Barcroft material to Dr K. Fincham, who kindly provided me with a microfilm of the original manuscript; OUA register o, fo 240ᵛ; John Sprint, *Cassander Anglicanus* (London 1618), sigs ¶3, *3.

[34] Tyacke, *Anti-Calvinists*, 108–9, 113–14; P. Lake, *Anglicans and Puritans? Presbyterianism and English conformist thought from Whitgift to Hooker* (London 1988), 103; 121; Wood, *History of the University* ii. 323–4; *SA* 412–13.

holy scripture', particularly the epistles of St Paul, Hales laying down the rule that the meaning of a biblical passage should be self-evident if it was to bind dogmatically. Silence constituted his remedy for the proliferation of controversy on such subjects as 'predestination', disputants often raising questions which were both unnecessary and incapable of human resolution.[35]

Yet Calvinism at Oxford was not in fact dethroned until the end of the 1620s. Partly this was because of the Dutch Arminian dispute and the decision of King James to intervene on the Calvinist side, culminating with the sending of a British delegation to the Synod of Dort in 1618. This gave fresh momentum to the English Calvinist cause. At the Oxford Act between 1612 and 1617 eleven doctors of divinity handled the predestinarian question, all from a Calvinist viewpoint. Thereafter there was some lessening of interest, although no fundamental alteration occurred until the chancellorship of Laud. Moreover in January 1623 Gabriel Bridges of Corpus Christi College was forced to make a public recantation of Arminian positions which he had taught in a university sermon concerning predestination, grace, and free will. Calvinism indeed would appear still to have been strongly represented in the university.[36] Meanwhile, however, religious change was beginning on other fronts. In the wake of the royal declaration of sports in 1618, strict sabbatarian views were subjected to increasing criticism. At the theoretical level the debate centred on the extent to which the fourth commandment—to keep holy the sabbath day—was still morally binding. The practical issue concerned Sunday recreation. Hostility towards sabbatarianism was to be a marked feature of the Arminian ascendancy during the 1630s, but leading Calvinists were themselves not agreed on this issue. Thus for his Act oration of 1622 John Prideaux claimed that the fourth commandment was now in large measure abrogated. As a consequence, 'wee are permitted recreations of what sort soever, which serve lawfully to refresh our spirits and nourish mutuall neighbourhood amongst us'. On the other hand Prideaux did not cite the declaration of sports or specify what he meant by lawful recreations. This Latin oration was to be republished in English translation, by the Arminian Peter Heylyn, in 1634.[37]

The early 1620s also saw a striking new departure in church décor, with the glazing of the east window of Wadham College chapel. Completed in 1623, this depicted the crucifixion and other scenes from the life of Christ (plate 20). Indeed a series of side windows, portraying the apostles and prophets, had been begun in 1613. By contrast, during the Elizabethan period such glass was the target of offi-

---

[35] *The Poems of Richard Corbett*, ed. J. A. W. Bennett and H. R. Trevor-Roper (Oxford 1955), 13, 24–5, 33, 36, 46–7, 52–9; Laud, *Works* vi. 133; John Hales, *A Sermon preached at St Maries in Oxford upon Tuesday in Easter Weeke, 1617* (Oxford 1617), 3, 6, 9, 19, 24–5, 32–3, 39–40. On the evidence of this sermon, Hales was already in process of bidding Calvin 'good night' even before the Synod of Dort: *Golden Remains of the Ever Memorable Mr John Hales, of Eton College* (London 1673), sig. A4ᵛ.

[36] Tyacke, *Anti-Calvinists*, 72–5, 87–105.

[37] *Constitutional Documents of the Reign of James I*, ed. J. R. Tanner (Cambridge 1930), 54–6; Thomas Broad, *Three Questions Answered* (Oxford 1621); John Prideaux, *Orationes novem inaugurales* (Oxford 1626), 135, 147; John Prideaux, *The Doctrine of the Sabbath* (London 1634), 13, 39; cf K. L. Parker, *The English Sabbath* (Cambridge 1988), 164–7.

cially sponsored iconoclasm and the genre had effectively died out. For example Archbishop Abbot recalled the taking down of a picture of Christ from a window in Balliol College chapel during the 1580s, and at the Act as late as 1614 his chaplain William Westerman maintained that 'images should not be set up in churches'. The Wadham east window was the work of Bernard van Linge and paid for by Sir John Strangeways, a co-heir of the founder. Clearly a section of Oxford opinion was becoming less concerned about the perils of idolatry, although this revived fashion for religious painted glass would contribute to an iconoclastic reaction in the 1640s.[38]

Much more explosive at the time, however, was an Oxford sermon preached in April 1622 by John Knight, formerly of Broadgates Hall, who argued that inferior magistrates might take up arms against their ruler in the cause of 'true religion'. His remarks need to be understood in the context of the Thirty Years War which had broken out in 1618, and the attempt to involve England on religious grounds. When subsequently interrogated, he cited as his authority the exposition of Romans 13 by the Heidelberg divine David Pareus and also instanced the support of King James for the French Huguenot rebels. Knight was imprisoned and his propositions condemned by the university authorities, while the works of Pareus were publicly burnt. The topic of Knight's sermon was a highly sensitive one given the current negotiations for an Anglo-Spanish marriage treaty and the likelihood that toleration of Catholicism would be a condition. Moreover the resulting furore was especially embarrassing for Calvinists, since Pareus was an editor of the Heidelberg Catechism. Significantly King James took the opportunity to reiterate his directions concerning the course of divinity studies, and Pareus was branded a 'puritan'.[39]

Protestant anxieties intensified during 1623, with the journey to Spain of Prince Charles in pursuit of a Spanish bride. A volume of Oxford verse published that April, in celebration of the prince's safe arrival in Spain, illustrates the delicacy of the situation; all the contributions were anonymous and the place of publication was London. When Charles came home empty-handed in October, there was a return to normalcy, *Carolus redux* being published at Oxford with every contributor of verse identified by name or initials. Moreover there were at least three times as many authors involved in the latter volume. Nevertheless the continuing potential for disagreement is indicated by a university sermon preached the following April 1624. Parliament was now sitting and members of the House of Commons were pressing King James to intervene militarily against Spain. The preacher Thomas Lushington was, like Knight, a graduate of Broadgates Hall but his stance was very different. He referred to 'the peasant' who 'under pretence of his priviledge in parliament . . . would dispose of kings and commonwealths', and went on

---

[38] T. G. Jackson, *Wadham College, Oxford* (London 1893), 163–70; M. Archer, 'English painted glass in the seventeenth century: the early work of Abraham van Linge', *Apollo* ci (1975); Abbot, *Cheapside Crosse*, 6–7; *Reg. Univ.* ed. Clark, pt i, 210; Wood, *Athenae* ii. 142; Aston, *England's Iconoclasts*, 74–95.

[39] Wood, *History of the University* ii. 341–7. Wood gives Knight's Christian name as William, but cf *CSPD 1619–23*, 400.

to say that 'nothing now contents the commonalty but war and contention'. In the event Lushington was censured for these words and made to preach a recantation sermon. That August John Randol of Brasenose College returned to the question of foreign policy. His sermon was largely taken up with the domestic repercussions of diplomatic alliances, especially with regard to religion. Randol warned of 'matrimonially' dividing the nation against itself and stated that there was no 'excuse for tolerating two religions in one kingdome'. The sermon proved sufficiently acceptable to be published at Oxford the same year.[40]

James I died in March 1625. Thomas Crosfield, a fellow of Queen's College, noted in his diary that 'immediately' after the accession of King Charles the 'cancer of Pelagianism', that is to say extreme free will doctrine, began to spread. Crosfield particularly had in mind the Arminian views of Richard Montagu, published in the years 1624–5, and the fact that these appeared increasingly to have the support of the supreme governor of the English Church. Allowing for hyperbole and a certain foreshortening of perspective, his assessment was broadly correct: revolutionary religious changes were in the offing. A younger contemporary at Queen's, Thomas Barlow, elaborated in retrospect that 'the Church of England and all her obedient sons till 1626 or 1628' did 'approve' the teachings of the Synod of Dort. Up until then, that is to say, the English Church was doctrinally Calvinist. On the basis of a royal proclamation of June 1626 and a further declaration in late 1628, prefacing the Thirty-nine Articles, Calvinism was curbed nationally.[41] Preaching in February 1629 John Doughty, a fellow of Merton College, said that 'the orthodox religion stands now betwixt papistry and semi-Pelagianism'—the latter being an ancient equivalent of modern Arminianism. At the same time he spoke of 'schismaticks' who 'whilst they labour a breach in Christianity . . . make shew of a desired unity and peace', an allusion to the declaration of 1628. Thus 'Arminius, even then when hee was forging those opinions upon which such endlesse troubles have ensued, compos'de a treatise touching a generall reconcilement . . . at once hee offers embraces to the Church and stabs it'. Doughty dedicated his remarks to Nathaniel Brent, warden of Merton. Barlow, Crosfield, and Doughty can none of them meaningfully be called puritan. Indeed Doughty, in this same sermon, attacked those who while orthodox on 'doctrinal grounds' nevertheless dissented from the established church concerning 'externall rites'. Of course Laud, and those who thought like him, saw matters differently. They distinguished between the 'lit-

---

[40] *Votiva, sive ad serenissimum, potentissimumque Jacobum, Magnae Britanniae, Franciae et Hiberniae regem etc. De auspicato illustrissimi Caroli, Walliae principis etc. in regiam Hispanicam adventu, pia et humilis Oxoniensum gratulatio* (London 1623); *Carolus redux* (Oxford 1623); Thomas Lushington, *The Resurrection of our Saviour Vindicated* (London 1741), pp. viii, 19; John Randol, *A Sermon preach't at St Marie's Oxford, the 5 of August 1624, concerning the kingdome's peace* (Oxford 1624), 7–11; T. Cogswell, *The Blessed Revolution: English politics and the coming of war, 1621–1624* (Cambridge 1989), 273–6.

[41] QCL MS 390, fo 19; Tyacke, *Anti-Calvinists*, 48–50, 147–63; John Goodman, *A Serious and Compassionate Enquiry* (London 1674), 7: Bodl. press mark 8°. A. 43. Linc., annotated by Thomas Barlow. I owe this last reference to Dr J. Spurr.

eral' meaning of the Thirty-nine Articles and their 'exposition'. Calvinism was opposed by them as being both divisive and without legal authority; in less guarded moments, they also categorized Calvinist teaching as positively erroneous.[42]

Doughty's sermon was printed not later than March 1629, and was one of the last such Calvinist statements to pass the Oxford censor until the 1640s. As far as the university was concerned the election of Laud as chancellor, in April 1630, was a very important religious watershed. Calvinism completely disappeared from the Act after 1631, and by 1634 Arminian views were being both preached and printed at Oxford. The reversal was not total, however, the preferred method of Laud being silence rather than counter-assertion. Thus Arminianism was never maintained at the Act itself and Arminian preachers still had to tread carefully, for it was always possible to overstep the permitted bounds. Moreover, the demise of Calvinism was only part of a complex of religious developments occurring at this time; in 1627, for example, Peter Heylyn maintained during a university divinity disputation that the visible succession of the English Church derived from that of Rome, thereby reviving on a more public stage Laud's teaching of twenty-four years earlier.[43] It was probably in 1628 that Gilbert Sheldon, the future archbishop, created something of a sensation at Oxford by denying that the pope was Antichrist.[44]

In 1630, William Prynne, a graduate of Oriel College and already on a collision course with the Caroline regime, published under the title *Anti-Arminianisme* a second edition of his book claiming that historically the English Church under Elizabeth and James I had been Calvinist in doctrine. He now included 'an appendix concerning bowing at the name of Jesus', which elaborated on his interpretation of Philippians 2. 10—'at the name of Jesus every knee shall bow'. According to Prynne this was 'onely meant of a universall subjection and obedience of all creatures' to 'the irresistable all-subduing scepter of Jesus Christ', and 'not of any corporall genuflexion'. From this point of view, it was to be understood as a Calvinist proof text for the 'irresistibility of God's grace in the hearts of the elect'. But Prynne went on to reject the practice of genuflexion as such, and in so doing revealed his puritan sympathies. For the 1604 canons had laid it down that when the name of Jesus was mentioned during church services 'due and lowly reverence shall be done by all persons present'. What seems to have made the subject particularly topical by 1630 was the growing fashion for converting communion tables into altars and doing reverence towards them. Indeed Prynne explicitly recognized

---

[42] John Doughty, *A Discourse concerning the abstruseness of divine mysteries* (Oxford 1628/9), pt 2, pp. 8, 15–16, 22; Tyacke, *Anti-Calvinists*, pp. x–xi, 266–70.

[43] Tyacke, *Anti-Calvinists*, 78–83, 248–9, 263–5; Peter Heylyn, *Examen historicum* (London 1659), pt 2, appx, sigs P3ᵛ–P4. The relative novelty of the position adopted by Heylyn in 1627, concerning ecclesiastical visibility, can be gauged by comparing it with his own published views of the same year, where he locates 'our church before the time of Luther' among the Albigensians: Peter Heylyn, *Microcosmos* (Oxford 1627), 113. I owe this last reference to Dr A. Milton.

[44] Heylyn, *Cyprianus Anglicus*, 126: Bodl. press mark NN. 118. Th., annotated by Thomas Barlow; Thomas Barlow, *The Genuine Remains* (London 1693), 192. I owe these references to Dr R. Beddard.

the connection when he wrote that 'bowing to idolized altars' is 'a practize much in use of late among some Romanizing protestants'. He also witnessed to the emergence of a specifically English Arminian synthesis whereby the grace of the sacraments, especially as conveyed via the eucharist, effectively replaced that of predestination. Moreover this changing scenic apparatus of worship and its attendant ceremonial marked the culmination of criticisms voiced from the 1590s onwards, by John Howson and others, concerning English church practice. One of the earliest such altars to be set up in Oxford was at Magdalen College, in 1631—an event which helped spark a series of university sermons against Arminianism that summer. The preachers were all disciplined as a result, and John Prideaux was threatened with the loss of his regius chair for encouraging them. That an establishment figure like Prideaux should be associated with such a challenge to higher authority is indicative of the profound religious alteration now under way; two years earlier, at the Oxford Act, he had been provoked into exclaiming that 'wee are concluded under an anathema to stand to the Synod of Dort against the Arminians'.[45]

As well as the new altar at Magdalen the chapel itself was elaborately refurbished at this time, with Christ's 'birth, passion, resurrection and ascension . . . very largely and exquisitely set forth in colours' at 'the upper end of the choir'. The relationship, however, between aesthetics and theology remained a complex one. That there was no necessary connection is clear from the chapel-building activities of Bishop John Williams at Lincoln College, which included the installation of an east window depicting the crucifixion (plate 19). Certainly Williams was no Arminian. On the other hand Richard Corbett, now bishop of Oxford, turned the Lincoln consecration ceremony of September 1631 into an Arminian occasion, speaking out against Oxford preachers who condemned 'reverence' to the altar as 'apish cringing'.[46] The early 1630s also saw a revival of the sabbatarian question, with the publication at Oxford of two treatises by Edward Brerewood. The author was long dead and his writings had remained in manuscript for almost twenty years. Brerewood sought to exonerate servants who worked on Sunday from any personal blame, and this was evidently now deemed grist to the anti-sabbatarian mill. In 1633 the Jacobean declaration of sports was reissued and moreover generally enforced, which had not been the case earlier.[47]

Among the arguments deployed against sabbatarianism was that the Sunday round of sermons, bible study, and discussion represented a covert form of puritan organization at the parish level. The allegation was an old one but acquired new

[45] William Prynne, *Anti-Arminianisme or the Church of England's old antithesis to new Arminianisme* (London 1630), 183, 192, sig. qq*3; E. Cardwell, *Synodalia* (2 vols Oxford 1842) i. 255; Tyacke, *Anti-Calvinists*, 78, 82, 84; Wood, *History of the University* ii. 372–80; E. Calamy, *The Nonconformists Memorial* (3 vols London 1802–3) ii. 27.

[46] Bloxam, *Reg. Magdalen* ii, p. xcvi; Archer, 'English painted glass', 31; Tyacke, *Anti-Calvinists*, 209–10; *Collectanea* iv. 147–8.

[47] Edward Brerewood, *A Learned Treatise of the Sabaoth* (Oxford 1630); Edward Brerewood, *A Second Treatise of the Sabbath* (Oxford 1632); Parker, *The English Sabbath*, 154–60, 191–214.

force with the demotion of preaching and its replacement with a more sacrament-centred form of piety. This same alteration in perspective helps to explain the attack launched by Peter Heylyn against the 'feoffees for buying in impropriations', during an Oxford sermon, on Act Sunday 1630. Rightly grasping that a prime objective of this London-based group of clergy, lawyers and merchants was the funding of stipendiary lectureships, the purpose of which was the provision of sermons, Heylyn claimed that a puritan plot was involved to 'undermine' the English Church. His diagnosis was accepted by Laud, now bishop of London, and the Caroline government proceeded to suppress the feoffees in the years 1632-3. Heylyn also said that part of the money collected by the feoffees had been used 'for the support of silenced ministers during their lives' and 'of their wives and children also after their decease'. Other evidence exists which tends to bear him out on this point, and thus confirms the genuinely puritan nature of the enterprise. Calvinist episcopalians, however, had they still been in a position to influence events, might well have been prepared to give the feoffees the benefit of the doubt. As it was, such clerical leaders were obliged to adapt themselves to the new situation.[48]

Between 1616 and 1622 Prideaux, as regius professor, had lectured regularly at the Act against Arminianism and these lectures were published at Oxford in 1625, during his second period as vice-chancellor. (He had been rector of Exeter College since 1612.) For the remainder of the 1620s, however, his main preoccupation was with Roman Catholicism. A further shift occurred in 1632 and from then to 1637 Prideaux, in his Act lectures, was chiefly concerned with Socinianism. 'What will it profit us', he asked, 'to have relinquished popery only to fall into Socinianism?' Faustus Socinus himself had died in 1604 and the views of his co-religionists can be most readily gathered from the Racovian Catechism, which was published the following year. Socinianism, narrowly defined, was a form of anti-trinitarianism: God is 'but one person'. At the same time Socinian teaching on predestination overlapped with that of the Arminians, while elevating spiritual free will to new heights. 'The predestination of God in the scriptures signifieth no other thing than such a decree of his concerning men, before the foundation of the world, that to those who would believe in him and be obedient to him he would give eternall life; and punish them with eternal death and damnation, who would refuse to believe him and be obedient to him.' Therefore the decision of Prideaux to lecture against Socinianism at this time was partly tactical, since refuting Arminianism as such had become taboo. However, his lecture of 1636, concerning original sin, made clear the link—implicating as it did Dutch Arminian authors. Yet there are grounds too

---

[48] Peter Heylyn, *The History of the Sabbath* (London 1634), pt 2, pp. 250-9; G. E. Gorman, 'A Laudian attempt to "tune the pulpit": Peter Heylyn and his sermon against the feoffees for the purchase of impropriations', *Journal of Religious History* viii (1975), 342-3; Heylyn, *Cyprianus anglicus*, 198-200; N. Tyacke, *The Fortunes of English Puritanism, 1603-1640*, Friends of Dr Williams's Library, 44th lecture 1990 (London 1990), 5-7, 14-16.

for thinking that Socinianism was now beginning to make some genuine inroads. For example John Webberley, a fellow of Lincoln College, seems by 1642 to have become a Socinian.[49]

People had been burnt in England for denying the trinity as recently as 1612. All the more startling then to find William Page, in 1639, urging a common Christian accord between protestant, papist, Grecian, Lutheran, Calvinist, Arminian, *and* Socinian. Such 'differences of opinion', he said, should be contained within the bounds of 'charity'. Page was now chaplain to Bishop Walter Curle of Winchester, and these remarks come from the preface to his Oxford edition of *The Imitation of Christ* by Thomas à Kempis. But it does not follow that Page was a Socinian; rather, he belonged to what has been called an 'Oxford school of rational theologians', whose other members included William Chillingworth, John Hales, and Christopher Potter. Like Page, they all made the point that antitrinitarians were fellow Christians. Their recipe for religious harmony, and one which they shared with Socinians, involved a minimal Christian creed and the rational discussion of doctrinal differences in the light of scripture. The latter trait is particularly evident in Chillingworth's book, *The Religion of Protestants*, published at Oxford in 1638. 'Naturall reason', Chillingworth wrote, 'is the last resolution, unto which the Churches authority is but the first inducement.' This sounds very similar to Prideaux's description, in 1637, of Socinians who 'make reason their tribunal' for deciding controversies of faith. Moreover in the closing pages of *The Religion of Protestants* Chillingworth indicated his Arminian sympathies, as regards the doctrine of predestination. An imprimatur by Prideaux is nevertheless to be found at the front of the book.[50]

This seal of approval by Prideaux puzzled many contemporaries and requires an explanation. Thomas Sixsmith, a fellow of Brasenose College, read *The Religion of Protestants* soon after publication. He described it, in a private letter, as 'an od booke, some things very well done but at others I cannot but boggle'. Chillingworth 'overthrowes the popish cause but [on] grounds which indanger the shaking of our owne ... I conceive him to smell too much of the Socinian, to talke of natural reason for grace, [and] never to mention originall sinne, nor grace neither (havinge so often occasion) in the true notion of it'. Sixsmith also 'had much parlee' with Prideaux, as to why he licensed the book. He reported that Prideaux 'now much dislikes it' and 'his best excuse is that they have dealt fouly with him in printinge passages which he expunged'. Under pressure from Laud to license Chillingworth's book, Prideaux seems to have agreed on condition that certain changes were made in the manuscript. His stipulation, however, would appear not to have been observed. Furthermore there are signs that Prideaux may even have

[49] John Prideaux, *Lectiones novem de totidem religionis capitibus* (Oxford 1625); John Prideaux, *Viginti-duae lectiones* (Oxford 1648), 299, 330; *The Racovian Catechisme* (London 1652), 18, 146–7; H. J. McLachlan, *Socinianism in Seventeenth-Century England* (Oxford 1951), 103–7.

[50] McLachlan, *Socinianism*, 31–2, 72, 85–7; Thomas à Kempis, *The Imitation of Christ*, trans. William Page (Oxford 1639), sigs *11, ***2; Chillingworth, *The Religion of Protestants*, 65, 406–7; Christopher Potter, *Want of Charitie* (Oxford 1633), 113–16; Prideaux, *Viginti-duae lectiones*, 347.

been blackmailed into acquiescence. A document survives among the English state papers, endorsed as 'Exceptions to Dr. Prideaux his sermons', which comprises passages extracted from Prideaux's collected sermons, published at Oxford in 1636. Most of the extracts consist of generalized remarks about the failings of clerics and courtiers, but in one of these passages Prideaux had linked the growth of puritanism to 'the statelinesse of some, so different from apostolicall humility'. Such talk was decidedly dangerous in the wake of William Prynne's attacks on bishops as 'lordly prelates', published the same year. No formal proceedings were instituted against Prideaux, although their possibility is likely to have influenced his conduct.[51]

By the late 1630s Prideaux was a rather isolated figure in Oxford. On probation ever since the sermon campaign of 1631 against Arminianism, he had been reported to Laud in 1633 for allegedly making derogatory remarks about the nature of the church. Prideaux had indeed described the definition of the church propounded by Heylyn, for one of his DD theses, as a 'mere chimera'. Three years later, in 1636, Prideaux can be found attempting to tone down some of the more fulsome praises in an official letter from the university to Laud, about the new statutes. Among much verbal sparring in convocation, Prideaux said 'we do not recognise any legate a latere'—an allusion to Cardinal Wolsey which was probably not lost on his audience. In addition a satire circulating at this time, which likened the individual Oxford colleges to ships, labelled Exeter College the 'Repulse' because Rector Prideaux 'shall suffer the repulse if hee sue for bishoprickes'. Prideaux's position was made even more difficult by the appointment as Lady Margaret professor of divinity, in 1638, of the Arminian Thomas Lawrence.[52]

Thanks to surviving letters from Francis Cheynell, fellow of Merton College, we are thus able to penetrate behind the outwardly civil relations obtaining between Laud and Prideaux during the 1630s. Cheynell also reveals the avant-garde nature of Oxford theology in these years. In October 1636 he preached a fast sermon before the university which 'displeased' many of his hearers,

because I touched upon a doctrine which hath beene often preached at Saint Maryes with equall confidence and blasphemy, that the heathens might bee saved by conforminge their lives to the light of nature, without the knowledge of Jesus Christ our only Lord and Saviour. I told them that it was a doctrine condemned by Fathers, censured by Councells, cursed by our Church [and] confuted by Scripture.

Elsewhere it emerges from his correspondence that Cheynell probably had especially in mind Christopher Potter, the provost of Queen's College, who was now regarded by Calvinists as a turncoat for embracing Arminianism. Potter touched briefly on 'charitable' assumptions concerning the salvation of heathens in his book

[51] BNCL MS B2. a. 38, p. 35; PRO SP 16/406, fos 167–8; William Prynne, *A Looking-Glasse for All Lordly Prelates* (n.p. 1636) and *The Unbishoping of Timothy and Titus* (Amsterdam 1636).
[52] Laud, *Works* v. 87–8; NUL MS Cl. c. 73, MS Cl. c. 84b; Tyacke, *Anti-Calvinists*, 83.

Want of Charitie, published at Oxford in 1633 as a reply to the Jesuit Edward Knott.[53] *The Religion of Protestants* was a continuation of this protestant–Catholic exchange, Knott having replied to Potter. Chillingworth's book was, of course, first and foremost directed against Roman Catholicism—especially the doctrine of papal infallibility. As such it was greatly admired by Edward Hyde, the future earl of Clarendon, who graduated from Magdalen Hall in 1626. The book promoted the Bible, interpreted by reason, as an alternative authority to the pope. This new-style protestant propaganda, however, was equally subversive of Calvinist orthodoxy, for Chillingworth argued, like Hales earlier, that Christians are only bound to believe things 'evidently contained' in scripture. The reaction of Thomas Sixsmith, discussed above, was mild compared to that of Cheynell; indeed Sixsmith would remain in Oxford until ejected in 1648, by Cheynell and his fellow parliamentary visitors. Looking back on the 1630s, Cheynell described the religion patronized by Laud as 'a hotchpotch of Arminianisme, Socinianisme and popery'—yet one in which the appeal to 'reason' was a significant ingredient. At the time Cheynell had been prominent among those opposed to the new practice of bowing towards the altar, while moving in definitely puritan circles.[54]

But without events in Scotland the likes of Cheynell or Prynne, the latter locked up in the Channel Islands from 1637, might well have remained impotent. In June 1638 the Oxford vice-chancellor Richard Baylie, an Arminian protégé of Laud, allowed as an Act thesis the question 'Do the additions and alterations in the Scottish liturgy give just matter for scandal?'. Naturally the official answer was in the negative. Any public discussion of this matter, however, struck Laud as unwise and the thesis was subsequently withdrawn on his order. None the less the escalation of the Scottish prayer book rebellion into open war almost certainly lies behind two theses maintained at the Act in 1639. Thomas Weekes, a chaplain of Bishop William Juxon, there denied that 'temporal dominion is founded in grace', while Bruno Ryves, formerly of Magdalen College, rejected the view that 'an impious person forfeits dominion'. Both theses, which are without known precedent at the Act, allude to possible Calvinist justifications for rebellion. That such fears had some substance is illustrated by Prynne's interpretation, in 1642, of Psalm 105. 15—'Touch not mine anointed'— as a resistance text. The 'anointed' are, Prynne argued, the 'elect' and have the right to defend themselves by force of arms. By this latter date the Calvinist alliance, which had been so characteristic of the English Church under both Elizabeth and James I, was manifestly in ruins; cracks in the edifice already detectable during the 1590s had so widened as to bring bishops themselves tumbling down, amidst rival and mutually reinforcing accusations of popery and puritanism.[55]

[53] NUL MS Cl. c. 75, MS Cl. c. 84b; Tyacke, *Anti-Calvinists*, 79–81; Potter, *Want of Charitie*, 44–5. John Prideaux had argued the same case as Cheynell in his Act lecture of 1624: Prideaux, *Lectiones novem*, 192.

[54] *The Life of Edward Earl of Clarendon* (3 vols Oxford 1827) i. 48; McLachlan, *Socinianism*, 83; Cheynell, *The Rise, Growth and Danger of Socinianisme*, 28–9, 40–1; Laud, *Works* v. 205–6; NUL MS Cl. c. 78, MS Cl. c. 84b.

[55] Laud, *Works* v. 198–9; Tyacke, *Anti-Calvinists*, 183; OUA register of congregation 1634–47, NEP/*supra*/16, register Q, fo 180; William Prynne, *A Vindication of Psalm 105. 15* (London 1642).

*   *   *

For Oxford University the meeting of the Long Parliament, in November 1640, involved a realignment of religious groupings. More specifically John Prideaux was able to come in from the cold, as King Charles sought to woo the moderates among his critics. The following October 1641 Prideaux again became vice-chancellor, the fourth earl of Pembroke having replaced Laud as chancellor, and in November he was elected bishop of Worcester. This latter promotion gratified an episcopal ambition on his part dating back to the 1620s. At the same time Prideaux and his former ally the puritan John Wilkinson, principal of Magdalen Hall, now drew apart. During the anti-Arminian disturbances of 1631 Prideaux and Wilkinson had been the two seniors chiefly involved. Wilkinson, however, was to abandon Oxford in the early 1640s, only returning after the civil war in 1646.[56] But this should not blind us to certain underlying continuities. Thus the collected Act lectures of Prideaux, in which he berated Arminians, papists, and Socinians, were published at Oxford in a handsome folio edition of 1648—under parliamentary rule. Moreover, as we shall see, the old doctrinal divisions were to surface again after the Restoration and theological battle was to be resumed, albeit over the relationship of faith and works rather than grace and free will, with Thomas Barlow as the standard-bearer of Oxford Calvinism and George Bull cast in the role of a latter-day Richard Montagu.

In the short term, however, episcopalians of every hue banded together in defence of the institutional being of their church. They did so the more easily because Prideaux was succeeded as regius professor by Robert Sanderson, a man of moderate Calvinist credentials. Yet the most extreme defence of episcopacy published at Oxford was that by the Arminian Jeremy Taylor, in 1642. According to Taylor, late fellow of All Souls, the apostleship instituted by Christ is 'all one' with episcopacy, and thus the power of bishops over presbyters has 'divine' origins. He also argued in the strongest terms against the validity of non-episcopal ordinations, dismissing the traditional argument advanced in their defence: 'Necessity may excuse a personall delinquency, but I never heard that necessity did build a church.' Other apologists tended to omit the argument for the 'immediate divine institution' of episcopacy, treating the apostles as effective originators. That various shades of Oxford opinion in fact existed on this issue emerges most clearly from the *Reasons* adduced by the university in 1647 for refusing to subscribe to the solemn league and covenant. These *Reasons*, which were approved by Oxford convocation, comment rather tortuously on episcopacy that

it is if not *iure divino* in the strictest sense, that is to say expressly commanded by God in his word, yet of apostolical institution, that is to say was established in the Churches by the apostles according to the mind and after the example of their master Jesus Christ, and that by vertue of their ordinary power and authority derived from him as deputed by him gov-

[56] Le Neve, *Fasti* iii. 66, 469, 587; Wood, *Fasti* pt 2, p. 2; *The Correspondence of John Cosin*, ed. G. Ornsby (2 vols Surtees Soc. lii, lv, 1868–72) i. 96, 98, 100; Laud, *Works* v. 56.

ernors of his Church. Or at least that episcopal aristocracy hath a fairer pretention, and may lay a juster title and claime to a divine institution, then any of the other forms of church-government can doe; all which yet do pretend thereunto, viz. that of the papal monarchy, that of the presbyterian democracy and that of the independents by particular congregations or gathered churches.

Such apologists assumed that the fortunes of episcopacy and monarchy were linked, along the lines of 'no bishop, no king'.[57] Nevertheless a similar diversity of not always strictly compatible claims on behalf of kingship can be found in Oxford publications of the early 1640s. Thus Griffith Williams, the exiled bishop of Ossory, argued, in a treatise of 1644, that 'the institution of kings is immediately from God' and 'Adam the first king of all men'. On the other hand Henry Ferne, another refugee, had written in 1643 that monarchy is '*ductu naturae*, by nature leading men from paternall to regall government, and *exemplo divino* . . . by divine example, but not *iure divino*, by divine precept commanding all nations to be so governed'. Patriarchy and monarchy therefore are not the same. But Ferne was also concerned to deny the existence of any 'agreement or contrivement of the people'. Here a different case was advanced by Dudley Digges the younger, a former fellow of All Souls and apparently a layman. Digges accepted a contractualist origin of government, while arguing that no residual right of resistance remained. This was the price which subjects paid to escape from a state, 'wherein each single person look't upon the world as his enemy'. The same view can also be found in the writings of Henry Hammond, appointed a canon of Christ Church in 1645.[58]

This plurality of voices, raised in defence of church and king, did not, however, extend to the doctrinal sphere. Nor did power swing back to the Oxford Calvinists. The true nature of the situation is revealed by Hammond's *Practicall Catechisme*, which was published at Oxford in 1645 and, significantly, found favour with Charles. For this catechism is demonstrably based on Arminian premisses. Under the second covenant, grace is granted 'sufficient to perform what is necessary'. Providing 'we make use' of these 'talents', God promises 'more grace' and a final 'crowning'. Hammond goes on to argue that 'faithfull actions' are 'the condition of justification'. But 'if I doe repent no power of heaven or earth, or hell, no malice of Satan, *no secret unrevealed decree* shall ever be able to deprive me of my part in the promise'. In late 1646, after the surrender of the Oxford garrison, Francis Cheynell took up with Hammond, among other points, his teaching on justification. He alleged that Hammond was guilty of 'confounding faith and works', and saw cor-

---

[57] Apparently Sanderson did not take up his Oxford post until 1646: P. Lake, 'Serving God and the times: the Calvinist conformity of Robert Sanderson', *Journal of British Studies* xxvii (1988), 108–9 and *passim*; Jeremy Taylor, *Of the Sacred Order and Offices of Episcopacy, by divine institution, apostolicall tradition, and catholike practice* (Oxford 1642), 12–15, 38, 193; *Reasons of the Present Judgement of the University of Oxford, concerning the solemne league and covenant* (Oxford 1647), 8, 13–14.

[58] Griffith Williams, *Jura majestatis, the rights of kings both in church and state* (Oxford 1644), 14; Henry Ferne, *Conscience satisfied that there is no Warrant for the Armes now taken up by Subjects* (Oxford 1643), 7–8; Dudley Digges, *The Unlawfulnesse of Subjects taking up Armes against their Soveraigne, in what case soever* (Oxford 1643), 2–4; R. Tuck, *Natural Rights Theories: their origin and development* (Cambridge 1979), 103, 108.

rectly that a prior assumption was involved here about how grace operates in 'the elect'. According to Cheynell, 'God doth by his free and effectuall grace worke the hearts of his elect to receive Christ that they may be justified; not by their own obedience, or vow of obedience, but by the obedience of Christ alone, freely imputed by God and rested on by faith only'. Hammond replied that God requires of 'the unregenerate man . . . a readinesse to obey his call, not to resist but receive his grace when hee bestows it on him, and having received it, what degree soever it be, to cherish and make use of it'. Cheynell was now a Presbyterian, but the Calvinist episcopalian Thomas Barlow later claimed that Hammond's was the first English work to corrupt the doctrine of justification by faith alone, through introducing the condition of 'obedience'.[59]

Arguably, however, a book such as the *Practicall Catechisme* conceals as much as it reveals about the nature and range of the author's views. Any attempt, indeed, to reconstruct a body of thought simply from what was published is subject to a number of disadvantages, hence the importance of private papers, where they survive. Such material, it transpires, exists in abundance for one forgotten member of the group of royalist and Arminian divines driven out of Oxford by the parliamentary visitors in the late 1640s. Tristram Sugge was expelled from his Wadham College fellowship in 1648, at the age of about 37. He returned at the Restoration, only to die in 1661. Nothing from his pen apparently got into print, save some verses celebrating the birth of a daughter to Charles I. Nevertheless a number of his manuscript notebooks are to be found in the Allestree Library at Christ Church. Their authorship was long lost to view and has had to be recovered from the volumes themselves. Some of these can be dated internally to the 1650s, after Sugge's expulsion, and all were probably bequeathed by the author to Richard Allestree, who became Oxford regius professor of divinity in 1663.[60]

Sugge covers a wide range of questions, exhibiting throughout an unusual frankness. Moreover his alienation from the official religion of the Interregnum was profound. Thus he writes that 'the Church of England may recover again; it may be all this while that the carpenter's son is making a coffin for Julian [the Apostate]'. Yet this alienation sprang from deeper sources than simply the defeat of the episcopalian cause. For Sugge had serious reservations about the English reformation itself, commenting that 'as the Church of England hath been disobedient to her parent [Rome] so hath shee met with disobedient children'. In England, 'our first reformers' were 'lustfull, ambitious and sacrilegious persons'. Therefore, 'if the lust of Henry 8 or the impotencie of Edward 6, or the interest of Queen Elizabeth did

[59] Thomas Herbert, *Memoirs of the Two Last Years of the reign of that unparallell'd prince of ever blessed memory, King Charles I* (London 1702), 43, 131; Henry Hammond, *A Practicall Catechisme* (Oxford 1645), 8, 12, 47, 56 (my italics); Henry Hammond, *A Copy of Some Papers past at Oxford, betwixt the author of the Practicall Catechisme and Mr. Ch.* (London 1647), 20, 68–9, 118; QCL MS 266, fo 27; the Arminianism of Hammond is further confirmed by his *Severall Tracts* (London 1646), 37–70, and below p. 599.

[60] Madan, *Oxford Books* ii. 136; CL MS M.3.13 [fo 2], MS M.3.15 [fo 167]: I identified Sugge's notebooks during the summer of 1986, and must thank Mr H. J. R. Wing and Mrs J. Wells for all their help in this connection.

transport us too far, it is fit that we recede to a mediocritie'. This 'mediocritie', or *via media*, involved recognition of the pope as 'lieutenant-general of the churches in the west'. Sugge wanted the pope restored to his original primatial 'right' of calling general councils, receiving appeals from bishops, and determining controversies. Historically the Roman Church has 'usurped' beyond its rights, but 'our reformers' are open to the charge of 'schisme' by their 'utter refusall' of papal authority. One might well jump to the conclusion from these passages that Sugge was a crypto-papist. That, however, would be mistaken as his own use of party labels makes clear:

The name of protestant was rashly imposed and unadvisedly received by us, we being none of those Lutherans who protested against the edict of Charles the emperor and the Diet at Spires *anno* 1529. A Reformed Catholike, or a Catholike of the English Reformation had been a name more agreeable and more honourable.

Sugge in fact rejected Roman Catholic teaching on both the eucharist and purgatory. Nevertheless he defended prayer for the dead, on the grounds that there are 'sins remissible' at the day of judgement, and went on by extension to criticize the dissolution of the monasteries.

Whereas religious houses were built and endowed with this proviso that the inhabitants should pray for the soules of their founders and benefactors, the demolishers of those houses, and the impropriators of those revenues, did first perswade the people that prayer for the dead was superstitious and vain.

There are some similarities here with the thought of Herbert Thorndike, although this does not seem to have been a major influence.[61]

Sugge also emerges from his notebooks as a thorough-paced Arminian, with no time at all for 'absolute' predestination: 'St Paul saith of his fellow labourers that their names were written in the booke of life. Philippians 4. 3. Of these fellow labourers Demas was one. Colossians 4. 14; Philemon 24. Yet Demas proved an apostate. 2 Timothy 4. 10.' God makes 'them that beleeve vessels of honour and mercie', whereas 'them that beleeve not' are made vessels of wrath as a consequence of their 'demerit'. Grace is 'universall' and 'all men have grace ... not to offend, otherwise their offences were no sins'. His treatment of the seemingly opposite teaching of Romans 9 recalls that of John Hales: 'it is altogether unequall that this obscure passage should be alleaged against so many clear texts that evince the contrarie'. In addition Sugge identifies with Jeremy Taylor on the subject of original sin. 'The name of originall sin was never heard of till St. Austin's tyme.' Moreover, like Henry Hammond, he argues for the role of works in justification. 'Justification by faith is but conditional, and the condition is this that in due season wee also bring forth the fruit of good life.' Sugge goes on to make quite explicit the relationship between justification and predestination:

[61] CL MS M.3.6, fos 10, 19–22ᵛ, 90, 97ᵛ, 137–40, 144–5; *The Theological Works of Herbert Thorndike* (6 vols Oxford 1844–56) iv. 440–2, 722–3, 815, v. 380.

Faith and the purpose of good life doe precede our justification, and so long as we beleeve and live accordingly wee are in a justified condition. But if then wee put away a good conscience, or make shipwrack of this faith, wee are no longer justified but . . . wee are made reprobates untill wee do repent.

Given too the tendency to link accusations of Arminianism with ones of Socinianism, it is intriguing that Sugge admits to doubts about the trinity. The 'doctrine of a personall trinitie in a numericall unitie doth imply a contradiction: for it implyeth that there are but three persons and yet a fourth person, as also that there are three persons and yet but one person'. Again, Sugge points out that God the father is said to be 'unbegotten', whereas God the son is 'begotten'.[62]

In his political thought Sugge was influenced by the views of Sir Robert Filmer. Thus he can be found making excerpts from 'a manuscript intitled *Patriarcha*, borrowed of Mr. Ashwell'. What appears to be the same copy of *Patriarcha* still survives in the Allestree Library. The 'Mr. Ashwell' concerned was almost certainly George Ashwell, who like Sugge was a former fellow of Wadham College. Sugge, however, combined patriarchalism with a defence both of remarriage after divorce, for adultery, and the practice of usury. On these issues he was in agreement with Hammond. Moreover as regards charitable giving, Sugge reveals an even more unexpected radicalism. 'There is a kind of justice that we should be liberall to the poore [person], because our riches are an occasion of his povertie; for were the blessings of God but proportionably divided there would be enough for all. But one ingrosseth so much that another is in want.' The conventional view, by contrast, was that poverty is God-given rather than man-made. None the less it is as a Christian eirenicist that Sugge deserves especially to be remembered, and there survives what looks to be a draft title-page of his projected Latin treatise on this subject. As translated, it reads 'the kiss of peace and truth, by the mediation of Tristram Sugge of Wadham [College], Oxford: renovation not innovation, unity in fundamentals, liberty in matters doubtful, and charity in everything'. Yet we should also note that this was an eirenic which seemed to leave no room for Calvinists.[63]

After his expulsion from Wadham College, Sugge may well have continued to reside in the Oxford area. As we have seen, he probably borrowed a copy of Filmer's *Patriarcha* from his fellow collegian George Ashwell. In the 1650s Ashwell came to live at Hanwell in Oxfordshire. So too did Richard Allestree, who subsequently acquired Sugge's notebooks. This would appear to link Sugge with the famous trio of Allestree, John Dolben, and John Fell, three expelled members of Christ Church who continued to hold clandestine prayer book services in Interregnum Oxford—their act of defiance later immortalized in a painting by

---

[62] CL MS M.3.8 ('Analecta ad loca Scripturae difficiliae': Acts 13. 48, Romans 9. 11, 22), MS M.3.15, fos 21, 88–9, MS M.3.6, fos 77–8, 116, 131–2ᵛ, 149ʳ⁻ᵛ. For the views of Jeremy Taylor concerning original sin, see especially his *Deus justificatus* (London 1656).

[63] CL MS M.3.6, fos 62, 183ᵛ, MS M.3.20 ('Patriarcha'), MS M.3.15, fos 126ᵛ–8, [167]; Hammond, *A Practicall Catechisme*, 192–5; Henry Hammond, *Large Additions to the Practicall Catechisme* (London 1646), 9–10; R. B. Schlatter, *The Social Ideas of Religious Leaders, 1600–1688* (Oxford 1940), 146–7.

Peter Lely.[64] Expulsion, however, was by no means the general fate of erstwhile Oxford royalists. During the war all had advocated non-resistance to the monarch, but with the surrender of the king issues of conscience became less clear. What measure of obedience was owed to usurpers now emerged as a leading question, and in the event many college fellows managed to survive.[65] It is difficult to generalise about those who remained; nevertheless, Oxford University during the 1650s was to prove a relatively congenial place for Calvinist episcopalians like Thomas Barlow.

The position of such episcopalians was in addition made easier by the effective stalemate between Presbyterians and Independents. Plans to Presbyterianize the Oxford colleges, in 1648, were overtaken by the increasing role of the military in politics and the consequent need to accommodate Independency. As early as March 1650 the Presbyterian Francis Cheynell can be found urging a 'union' between 'godly Presbyterians and Independents'. Any remaining hopes of imposing Presbyterianism on Oxford were further dashed by the election of Oliver Cromwell as university chancellor in 1651. Cromwell appointed as his vice-chancellor the Independent John Owen, who held office continually from 1652 to 1657. There was the additional challenge of the sects. Cheynell himself had clashed at Oxford in late 1646 with the Seeker William Erbery, who denied the need for an ordained ministry. A more formidable threat, however, was posed by the Baptists. In 1652 John Tombes learnt that Henry Savage, the master of Balliol College, was due to defend infant baptism at the forthcoming Act. Tombes, a Baptist and former member of Magdalen Hall, managed to wangle his way into the position of opponent and thereby injected an element of unwelcome realism into the disputation.[66] Two years later Quaker missionaries began to arrive in Oxford. One of them, Elizabeth Fletcher, 'went naked through the streets ... as a sign against that hypocritical profession they then made there, being then Presbyterians and Independents, which profession she told them the Lord would strip them of'. Fletcher and her companion also interrupted church services, for which they were arrested and taken before the vice-chancellor and city magistrates. The two Quakers were sentenced to be whipped out of town, although the mayor of Oxford, who was himself a Baptist, opposed their punishment.[67]

In these circumstances, respectable puritans and Calvinist episcopalians tended

---

[64] Wood, *Athenae* iii. 1270, iv. 396; R. L. Poole, *Catalogue of Portraits in the Possession of the University, Colleges, City, and County of Oxford* (3 vols Oxford 1912–25) iii. 30–1.

[65] Robert Sanderson, *De juramenti promissorii obligatione praelectiones septem* (London 1647); I. Roy and D. Reinhart, 'Oxford and the civil wars', pp. 728–31 below.

[66] Francis Cheynell, *The Divine Triunity of the Father, Son, and Holy Spirit* (London 1650), sigs B4–B5ᵛ; *Truth triumphing over Error. Or a relation of a publike disputation at Oxford ... between Master Cheynell a member of the assembly and Master Erbury the Seeker and Socinian* (London 1646); Henry Savage, *Quaestiones tres, in novissimorum comitiorum vesperiis Oxon discussae* (Oxford 1653), sig. A2ᵛ, p. 24; John Tombes, *Refutatio positionis ... ab Henrici Savage ... proposita* (London 1653), sig. A2ᵛ.

[67] W. C. Braithwaite, *The Beginnings of Quakerism* (London 1912, 2nd edn Cambridge 1955), 158; Richard Hubberthorne, *A True Testimony of the Zeal of Oxford Professors and University Men, who for zeal persecute the servants of the living God* (London 1654), 1–4; *VCH Oxon.* iv. 417.

to rediscover important things in common. Here one of the most striking Oxford features of the 1650s, is the re-establishment of Calvinist orthodoxy. The same thing happened at Cambridge, both universities reverting to a situation which had obtained prior to the accession of Charles I. This can be seen particularly clearly from the divinity theses maintained at the Oxford Act and the Cambridge Commencement. Conscious continuity was also provided by the life and writings of the Oxonian John Prideaux. Thus in 1648 the newly appointed Oxford regius professor of divinity, Joshua Hoyle, spoke in glowing terms of him during his inaugural address. The following year saw the Oxford publication of the *Fasciculus controversiarum theologicarum* by Prideaux. I have already remarked on the publication at Oxford in 1648 of his collected Act lectures, including those against Arminianism. Similarly in the *Fasciculus* Prideaux maintains that election and reprobation are both 'absolute', and denies that 'grace sufficient to salvation' is granted to everyone. But the latter book also comments, at considerable length, on the questions of church government and liturgy. Furthermore the episcopal status of Prideaux is made quite explicit, the *Fasciculus* being prefaced with a dedication by him to his Worcester diocesan clergy in which he exonerates bishops from the charge of being Antichristian and invokes the memory of Cranmer, Latimer, Ridley, Jewel, and Whitgift. In the body of the book Prideaux argues that episcopacy is 'a distinct and superior order to presbytery', deriving from 'the institution of Christ or of the apostles'. He also defends the English prayer book as being in conformity with the Bible, albeit going on to gloss its doctrinal teaching in Calvinist terms. Thus the reference to baptized infants as being 'regenerate' is a 'charitable' assumption, not a statement of fact, for neither is grace granted universally nor can it be lost. In addition Prideaux denies that 'subjects' have any right to resist their 'king'. A second edition of the work was published at Oxford in 1652.[68]

But given some of the views contained in the *Fasciculus*, how are we to explain its original publication at Oxford? Had the work been published at London there would have been no real problem, because censorship in the capital was in a state of almost total collapse. Yet this was not the case at Oxford. In 1649 the vice-chancellor—the official licensing authority—was Edward Reynolds. Reynolds was a moderate, who resigned from Oxford in 1650 and shortly after the Restoration accepted a bishopric. The *Fasciculus* seemingly reflects the enduring significance of Calvinist episcopalianism, despite the rise of Arminianism having in the eyes of many served to discredit bishops by the eve of the civil war. For those unhappy with the subsequent experiments of the 1640s, Prideaux stood for an alternative tradition of church government which was nevertheless impeccably orthodox in doctrine. The relevance of this latter consideration is clear from the general tenor of Oxford divinity during the Interregnum. At Oxford the Act had been in abeyance

---

[68] Tyacke *Anti-Calvinists*, 37–49, 62–81; OUA register of congregation 1647–59, NEP/*supra*/17, register Qa, fos 150–4; BL MS Harleian 7038, pp. 108–9; Wood, *History of the University* ii. 607; John Prideaux, *Fasciculus controversiarum theologicarum* (Oxford 1649), sigs ¶2–¶4, pp. 136–9, 204–17, 221–30, 235–44, 273–6.

throughout the 1640s but was revived in 1651. That year John Conant, the rector of Exeter College, maintained three related Act theses. First, 'Grace sufficient to salvation' is not granted to 'everyone'. Secondly, God's grace in the conversion of a sinner is 'irresistible' and, thirdly, it cannot thereafter be 'utterly forfeited'. Next year Obadiah Grew, formerly of Balliol College, denied that Christ had died 'equally' for all. In 1654 Conant, this time as an incepting doctor of divinity, argued that 'the decree of election and reprobation' was 'absolute', while John Wallis, Savilian professor of geometry, opposed the view that election depended on 'foresight'. The same year George Kendall, late fellow of Exeter College, maintained that 'neo-Pelagian doctrine' was inimical to Christian faith, piety, and consolation. The views of Conant are particularly to the point, because he became regius professor of divinity in 1654.[69]

A similar Calvinist picture emerges from the theological works printed at Oxford in this decade. Indeed some of the Act material itself ended up in print—for example John Wallis's thesis of 1654. The previous year had seen the publication of *The Riches of God's Love*, by William Twisse. This was a posthumous work from an Oxford-educated Calvinist and constitutes a reply to an English Arminian treatise of 1633. Twisse's book, which defends Calvinist teaching on reprobation, is prefaced with a testimony by John Owen, the vice-chancellor. In 1654 Owen produced an anti-Arminian treatise of his own—*The Doctrine of the Saints Perseverance*. A response to the Independent John Goodwin's *Redemption Redeemed* of 1651, it witnesses to the development of a small Arminian minority within Puritanism.[70] George Kendall also wrote two books against Goodwin, which appeared in 1653 and 1654, concerning the doctrines of election and perseverance. Although printed in London, both these books by Kendall are dedicated to his alma mater Oxford University and contain references to the 'learned' and 'illustrious' John Prideaux. In addition they each have an imprimatur by Owen, as Oxford vice-chancellor, and by the two Oxford professors of divinity: Joshua Hoyle and Henry Wilkinson. (Wilkinson succeeded Cheynell as Lady Margaret professor in 1652.) Not content with this endorsement the publisher of the second volume included an 'attestation' from Bishop Joseph Hall, lest Kendall's views be dismissed as 'puritanicall'. Hall was the last surviving English delegate to the Synod of Dort, and provided an important plank in the Calvinist case for historical legitimacy.[71]

The full text of the Act theses maintained by Kendall in 1654 is extant in print.

---

[69] OUA register Qa, fos 150–2ᵛ.

[70] John Wallis, *Mens sobria serio commendata: concio ... accederunt eiusdem exercitationes* (Oxford 1657), 110–35; William Twisse, *The Riches of Gods Love ... consistent with his absolute hatred ... of the vessels of wrath* (Oxford 1653); Samuel Hoard and Henry Mason, *God's Love to Mankind, manifested by disprooving his absolute decree for their damnation* (n.p. 1633); John Owen, *The Doctrine of the Saints Perseverance, explained and confirmed* (Oxford 1654); D. D. Wallace, *Puritans and Predestination: grace in English protestant theology, 1525–1695* (Chapel Hill 1982), 144–57.

[71] George Kendall, *A Vindication of the Doctrine commonly received in the Reformed Churches concerning God's intentions of special grace and favour to his elect in the death of Christ* (London 1653), sigs aa, *****3; George Kendall, *Sancti sanciti: or the common doctrine of the perseverance of the saints* (London 1654), sigs A2, *4ᵛ; Tyacke, *Anti-Calvinists*, 212–13.

He there brackets John Goodwin and the episcopalian Henry Hammond as the two leading English neo-Pelagians or Arminians. Kendall singles out Hammond's treatise *Of Fundamentals*, published that same year. This work does indeed contain a most forthright condemnation, by Hammond, of 'the irrespective decrees of election and reprobation', as hindrances to the 'superstructing of Christian life'. Kendall published his Act theses, as part of a larger work, at Oxford in 1657. Two years later Edward Bagshaw the younger and Henry Hickman broadened the Calvinist counter-attack to include the Arminian episcopalians Thomas Pierce, Jeremy Taylor, and Laurence Womock. Bagshaw was a former member of Christ Church and Hickman a fellow of Magdalen College. Interestingly Hammond, Pierce, Taylor, and Womock were all published at London by the royalist bookseller Richard Royston. Both parties invoked the past, Hickman for instance transcribing the Oxford recantation of Arminianism, in 1623, by Gabriel Bridges.[72]

The 1650s also witnessed an analogous Oxford concern with Socinianism, in its antitrinitarian aspect. Francis Cheynell, as Lady Margaret professor of divinity, and John Owen each produced works on this subject in 1650 and 1655 respectively. Cheynell was particularly concerned with the writings of John Fry whereas Owen directed his fire against the more formidable John Bidle. Fry was a member of parliament, but had not apparently attended university. Bidle on the other hand was a graduate of Magdalen Hall and an ex-schoolmaster, who both translated Socinian works, including the Racovian Catechism, and wrote a series of antitrinitarian tracts. Bidle and Fry belonged to the world of puritanism, yet a section of episcopalian opinion continued to be suspected of Socinian sympathies in these years. Owen's answer to Bidle included a 'vindication of the testimonies of scripture, concerning the deity and satisfaction of Jesus Christ, from the perverse expositions and interpretations of them by Hugo Grotius', contained in his *Annotations* on the Bible. The previous year, 1654, Henry Hammond had defended Grotius on precisely this issue. Now Owen took up that challenge. At about the same date John Conant, as newly appointed regius professor of divinity, similarly devoted his lectures to 'critical exercitations' on the *Annotations* of Grotius, 'in which he vindicated the scriptures from such of his expositions as the Socinians had taken any advantage'.[73]

Grotius, and to a lesser extent Hammond, were practitioners of a new style of biblical criticism in the post-reformation context. They approached their subject-matter philologically and historically rather than regarding it as an arsenal of dogmatic truths, and the results were decidedly alarming to more fundamentalist

---

[72] George Kendall, *Fur pro tribunali ... accesserunt oratio de doctrina neo-Pelagiana* (Oxford 1657), pt 2, pp. 1–60; Henry Hammond, *Of Fundamentals in a notion referring to practise* (London 1654), 108, 126–8; Edward Bagshaw, *A Practicall Discourse concerning Gods decrees* (Oxford 1659); Henry Hickman, *A Justification of the Fathers and Schoolmen: shewing that they are not selfe-condemned for denying the positivity of sin* (2nd edn Oxford 1659), sigs b4–b5ᵛ; Wallace, *Puritans and Predestination*, 120–30, 140–2.

[73] Cheynell, *The Divine Triunity*; John Owen, *Vindiciae evangelicae, or the mystery of the gospel vindicated and Socinianisme examined* (Oxford 1655), sigs A–A3, pp. 152–347, 521–56; McLachlan, *Socinianism*, 163–217, 239–49; Henry Hammond, *An Answer to the Animadversions on the Dissertations touching Ignatius's Epistles* (London 1654), 125–37; John Conant, *The Life of the Reverend and Venerable John Conant, D.D.* (London 1823), 20.

minds. This, incidentally, helps explain Owen's hostility to the Polyglot Bible, completed in 1657, the final volume of which drew on the work of Grotius. How far the eirenical Grotius finally advanced beyond his earlier Arminianism is unclear. But while pursuing the elusive goal of Christian reunion he can be found corresponding amicably with both Socinians and Roman Catholics, and by the early 1640s had come to pin his hopes on a Gallican oecumenical initiative. Grotius died in 1645, still a protestant but of doubtful orthodoxy. Inevitably he was a suspect figure to Oxford's theological leaders in the 1650s, not least because of a continuing strain of virulent anti-Catholicism. Thus for example Thomas Tully of Queen's College maintained as an Act thesis in 1655 that the 'pseudo-Catholic Roman Church' is not 'truly Christian'.[74] Unlike Owen and Conant, however, Tully was to survive the upheavals of the Restoration and emerge as an important Calvinist voice within the re-established church.

The political undoing of the Interregnum in 1660 is a familiar story. So too, at one level, is the religious settlement which followed. An uncompromising episcopalianism triumphed over attempts at 'comprehension' and 'indulgence'. These developments are, to some extent, reflected in Oxford publications between 1659 and 1662. Hence in 1659 there appeared *Monarchy Asserted* by Matthew Wren—a layman although the son of his namesake the bishop. The work, which is dedicated to John Wilkins the warden of Wadham College, represents the culmination of a long-running debate between Wren and the republican James Harrington. Like the earlier treatises by Digges and Hammond, Wren's defence of monarchy assumes an original but irrevocable contract. Harrington is criticized for deriving 'empire' from the 'balance of dominion in land', since there are many other sources of wealth. For Wren governmental 'perfection' consists in a 'supream' monarch ruling through an hereditary nobility and backed up by a militia, and he looks forward to such an English outcome. In 1662 John Barbon's defence of the prayer book was also published at Oxford. Among other things it explicitly rejects the type of Calvinist reading earlier provided by Prideaux, on the subject of baptismal regeneration. The regenerate and justified can indeed finally fall from grace.[75] Barbon was a product of Exeter College in the 1640s and his rebellion against Rector Prideaux's teaching is particularly striking. Meanwhile Richard Allestree, recently restored as a canon of Christ Church, delivered a sermon at Westminster Abbey, in January 1661, on the occasion of the episcopal consecrations of Gilbert Ironside,

[74] H. J. de Jonge, 'Hugo Grotius: exégète du Nouveau Testament' in *The World of Hugo Grotius (1583–1645)*, Royal Netherlands Academy of Arts and Sciences (Amsterdam and Maarssen 1984), 97–115; John Owen, *Of the Divine Originall, Authority, Self-Evidencing Light and Power of the Scriptures ... Also a vindication of the purity and integrity of the Hebrew and Greek texts of the Old and New Testament, in some considerations on the prolegomena and appendix to the late Biblia Polyglotta* (Oxford 1659); H. R. Trevor-Roper, *From Counter-Reformation to Glorious Revolution* (London 1992), 48, 73–8; OUA register Qa, fo 153.

[75] Matthew Wren, *Monarchy Asserted, or the state of monarchicall and popular government in vindication of the considerations upon Mr. Harrington's Oceana* (Oxford 1659), 19–20, 77, 91, 107; John Barbon, *Liturgie a Most Divine Service* (Oxford 1662), 125–8.

Nicholas Monck, William Nicholson, and Edward Reynolds (plate 27). All four of these new bishops were Oxonians and, moreover, represented a wide variety of theological opinion. Addressing them as 'holy fathers', Allestree described Christ as the 'founder and God of your order'. He also spoke of the miraculous 'resurrection' of the English Church.

And truely 'twas almost as easie to imagination how the scattered atomes of men's dust should order themselves and reunite, and close into one flesh, as that the parcels of our discipline and service that were lost in such a wild confusion, and the offices buried in the rubbish of the demolisht churches, should rise again in so much order and beauty.[76]

But how was the ambiguous legacy of the English Church now generally to be interpreted, and after what image was episcopacy to be remade? More specifically in which of the two rival traditions, Arminian or Calvinist, was the restored ecclesiastical regime effectively to follow? With a different king and an almost completely new bench of bishops since the 1630s, the answer was not immediately obvious. At Oxford Thomas Barlow, provost of Queen's College, rapidly emerged as a leading figure among the surviving heads of house. Appointed Lady Margaret professor of divinity in 1660, from then until his departure for the bishopric of Lincoln in 1676 he wielded considerable religious influence. Barlow had lived through all the Oxford changes since the 1620s, but there is no question of his essential loyalty to episcopacy and prayer book. He regarded the former as 'iure apostolico' and described the latter as 'the best liturgy in the world', going on to speak of the 'fanatique zeale', of those who rejected it as 'unsound and superstitious'. At the same time, however, Barlow was a committed Calvinist. The fullest statement of his views on the predestinarian question is to be found in a manuscript notebook dating from the 1660s. 'Election and reprobation' are not 'from foresight of faith or infidelity'. Christ did not die 'for each and everyone'. The 'operation of grace' is 'irresistible' and 'the truly faithful' cannot 'fall away finally and totally'. Barlow also notes that 'the Arminians did not, durst not appeare in Kinge James his time'.[77]

In September 1661 Barlow wrote a critique of the prayer book, which was probably prepared for the committee of bishops discussing liturgical reform at this date. He argued that no human document is perfect, and one of his main suggestions was to bring the wording of the baptismal services more closely into line with Calvinist teaching. What this implies about the original Edwardian framers of the prayer book is not something which Barlow here tackles. Nevertheless he does say that the logical implication that children 'really regenerated' in baptism afterwards 'fall away', and 'eternally perish', is a doctrine which 'in all the time of Queen Elizabeth and King James was believed to be erroneous, and condemned as such

[76] Richard Allestree, *A Sermon preached in St. Peter's Westminster on Sunday Jan. 6, 1660* (London 1660/1), 35–7.
[77] QCL MS 340, p. 1, MS 279 ('Considerations concerninge the Common Prayer Booke'), p. l, MS 260 ('Controversiae Arminianae, Pelagianae [et] Socinianae'), pp. 2, 90, 158, 324, 411.

by the reverend bishops [and] the publique professors in both the universities'.
According to Barlow the prayer book ascribes too much to baptism, which is 'not
necessary to salvation'. Nor is the Bible correctly cited in its support. Barlow also
made a number of other suggestions for change, but all proved stillborn as regards
the revised prayer book of 1662.[78]

That members of the government were aware of the danger of renewed
Arminian–Calvinist conflict is clear from a passage in the royal directions to
preachers, issued in October 1662. They were 'admonished not to spend their time
and study in the search of abstruse and speculative notions, especially in and about
the deep points of election and reprobation, together with the incomprehensible
manner of the concurrence of God's free grace and man's free will'. The justifiable
complaint in the past had been that such rulings were not applied even-handedly,
to the resulting detriment of Calvinists.[79] Yet this earlier pattern was not repeated
in Restoration Oxford, both Arminian and Calvinist preachers enjoying there a
degree of practical toleration. An illustration of the new situation, drawn from
among the Oxford Calvinists, is provided by John Wallis. Puritan seems not too
strong a term for Wallis, who had been secretary of the Westminster Assembly
before his appointment to the Savilian chair of geometry in 1649. At the
Restoration he conformed and retained his various Oxford posts. Among his surviving sermons, two preached before the university in 1676 and 1681 are particularly revealing. They were published together at London in 1682 and entitled *The
Necessity of Regeneration*. Wallis dedicated them to the earl of Radnor, lord president
of the council, 'being made acquainted that they would not be unacceptable to your
lordship'. (Radnor is better known as Lord Robartes, who fought for the parliamentary cause in the civil war and had studied at Exeter College during the 1620s.)
Wallis went on to claim that 'I have therein purposely waved, as I alwaies do, all
nice disputes of speculative subtilties in controversal points . . . as more tending to
disturb the peace of the Church than to promote piety'. Nevertheless the sermons
themselves indicate the Calvinist bias of their author. 'To become the sons of God
by regeneration is the beginning of our sanctification.' Whom God 'designed to be
happy he designed to be holy, and whom he did thus predestinate them he called,
them he justified and them he glorified'. Wallis also clearly distinguishes between
regeneration and baptism. 'Our Church presumes of infants that they be at least
some of them regenerate when baptised', but 'nor is the Holy Ghost less able to
work effectively afterwards.'[80]

Another and even clearer example of Calvinist preaching in Restoration Oxford
is afforded by the sermons of Robert South. Educated at Oxford in the 1650s,
South became a Student and then, from 1670, a canon of Christ Church. He was

---

[78] *The Life of Edward Earl of Clarendon* ii. 118; QCL MS 279 ('Considerations concerninge the
Common Prayer Booke'), pp. 1–18: this manuscript is dated 23 September 1661.

[79] *Concilia Magnae Britanniae et Hiberniae*, ed. D. Wilkins (4 vols London 1737) iv. 577; Tyacke, *Anti-
Calvinists*, 50–2, 81–3, 181–5, 263–5.

[80] John Wallis, *The Necessity of Regeneration* (London 1682), sig. A, pp. 18–19, 35.

also public orator of the university, between 1660 and 1677. During the Interregnum he is said to have used the prayer book, and in 1698 publicly identified himself with those described as 'high-churchmen'. None the less he remained a Calvinist. Preaching at Christ Church in March 1668 South spoke of an 'eternal covenant made between the Father and the Son, by which the Father agreed to give both grace and glory to a certain number of sinners'. On this 'alone ... is built the infallibility of the future believing, repenting and finally persevering of such as Christ from all eternity undertook to make his people'. In the same venue, some ten years later and handling the subject of 'preventing grace', South asked rhetorically: 'doe we not sometimes see in persons of equal guilt and demerit, and of equal progress and advance in the ways of sin, some of them maturely diverted, and took off, and others permitted to go on without check or controll, till they finish a sinful course in final perdition?' Such grace, if vouchsafed, works 'by main force'. Both these sermons were published at London, during the 1690s.[81]

Similar bending of the rules, this time by an Oxford Arminian, is apparent in the preaching of Richard Allestree, who became regius professor of divinity in 1663. Most of his sermons were posthumously printed at Oxford in a collected edition of 1684, prefaced with a life by John Fell—now bishop of Oxford. Fell writes of Allestree as 'never intermedling with the unfathomable abyss of God's decrees, the indeterminable five points [of Arminianism], which in all times and in all countries, wherever they have happen'd to be debated, past from the schooles to the state and shock'd the government and public peace'. Allestree, however, made plain his Arminian sympathies when preaching. In a sermon at Whitehall, probably dating from the early 1660s, he described the sinner whose

will is grown too strong for the Almightie's powerful methods and frustrates the whole counsel of God for his salvation, neglects his calls and importunacies whereby he warns him to consult his safety, to make use of grace in time, not to harden his heart against his own mercies and perish in despight of mercy.

Such 'persevering obstinacy does deserve Hell and make it just'. In December 1665 Allestree returned to the theme of God's 'everlasting council', as regards sinners. This sermon was preached at Christ Church, where the pulpit clearly provided a variety of doctrinal fare. 'O do not thus break decrees, frustrate and overthrow the everlasting counsel of God's will for good to you. He set, ordain'd this child [Christ] for your rising again. Do not throw yourselves down into ruin in despite of his predestinations.' In another, undated, sermon Allestree remarked that 'the inheritance of the kingdom of God' is not 'entail'd'. An heir can be disinherited and 'we read of many that were cast off'. For God's 'promises' are 'conditional', on repentance and belief.[82]

The rules, however, could only be bent so far. Thus at Oxford in April 1679

---

[81] G. Reedy, *Robert South (1634–1716): an introduction to his life and sermons* (Cambridge 1992), 11–13; Robert South, *Sermons* (6 vols London 1692–1717) i. 498, 501, 508–10, iii. sig. A3, p. 450.

[82] Richard Allestree, *Forty Sermons* (Oxford 1684), sig. e^v, pt 1, pp. 61–2, 161–4, pt 2, pp. 93–4.

Thomas Smart of St John's College was censured for preaching 'very unadvisedly ... concerning God's decrees, contrary to the king's commands in that case, and in irreverent and unseemly language'. According to Anthony Wood, Smart's sermon was a 'bold and desperat' one 'against the Calvinists'. In the case of Oxford religious teaching more generally, after 1660 it seems to have been assumed that Charles I's declaration of 1628, silencing the predestinarian dispute, still applied. Such questions again disappear from the Act; they are also absent from the run-of-the-mill disputes in the divinity school, records of which survive in the congregation registers from the 1660s onwards.[83] Nevertheless two other recurring Act topics appear to reflect divergent emphases in Oxford theology during the later seventeenth century. On the one hand the Roman Catholic Church was branded as simply 'idolatrous', while on the other a distinction was drawn between 'the ancient practice of prayer for the dead' and belief in 'Romish purgatory'. First to maintain these respectively intransigent and meliorist theses, *vis à vis* Catholicism, were the Calvinist Thomas Barlow and the Arminian Richard Allestree, both in 1661.[84]

There were comparable limitations on airing the Arminian–Calvinist dispute in print at Oxford, although not apparently as regards previously published works. Thus the *Fasciculus* of John Prideaux was reprinted at Oxford in 1664 (we have already remarked on Prideaux's unremitting Calvinism). Similarly in 1671 *A Correct Copy of Some Notes Concerning God's Decrees, especially of reprobation* by Thomas Pierce, now president of Magdalen College, was also reprinted at Oxford. Pierce makes his Arminian stance abundantly clear throughout: election and reprobation are both 'conditional' and grace, which is 'universal', can be resisted. By contrast, in terms of new publications, nothing really equivalent to these two works was produced in Restoration Oxford.[85] The religious balance of forces, however, remained a delicate one. For example in January 1673 William Richards, chaplain of All Souls College, preached at the university church and is said, by Wood, to have 'insisted much on the Arminian points'. According to the same source, Richards was questioned for this by Thomas Barlow, as pro-vice-chancellor. Yet no record of any official censure survives.[86]

Oxford did, however, produce a more united front against Cambridge Platonism. This might seem surprising, given the earlier Platonist sympathies of the Arminian Thomas Jackson, but the arguments advanced by Henry More and his circle provoked hostile reactions across a wide theological spectrum—not least because they claimed to cut through the Arminian–Calvinist disputes.[87] Here More's use of the

[83] OUA register of convocation 1671–83, NEP/*supra*/28, register Tb, fo 3ᵛ; Wood, *Life and Times* ii. 448.

[84] OUA register of congregation 1659–69, NEP/*supra*/18, register Qb, fo 173.

[85] Thomas Pierce, *A Correct Copy of Some Notes concerning God's Decrees, especially of reprobation* (Oxford 1671), 32, 75, 78, 82. London publishing in these same years, however, was much more of a doctrinal free-for-all.   [86] Wood, *Life and Times* ii. 258.

[87] S. Hutton, 'Thomas Jackson, Oxford Platonist, and William Twisse, Aristotelian', *Journal of the History of Ideas*, 39 (1978); S. Hutton (ed.), *Henry More (1614–1687): tercentenary studies* (Dordrecht 1990), 7–9, 62–5.

patristic writer Origen, concerning the pre-existence of souls, proved especially controversial, being refuted in a divinity disputation at Oxford as early as 1663. This was followed up with a two-part contribution by Samuel Parker, published at Oxford in 1666 and with the imprimatur of the vice-chancellor, Robert Saye. Parker rejected Platonic 'metaphysical theologie' as a whole and Origenism in particular, with its attempt to explain sin in terms of the fall of free pre-existent souls as opposed to that of Adam. Parker was probably already an Arminian, yet the Calvinist Barlow found the teaching of Origen on this subject equally objectionable.[88]

Barlow himself left a mass of manuscript theological writings which are still extant—mainly at Queen's College, Oxford. The two posthumously published volumes of his occasional pieces barely begin to tap this reservoir of material. He also had a tendency to annotate his printed books, many of which are now in the Bodleian Library.[89] From these sources it is possible to reconstruct his views on a great variety of issues, and thereby also to recover a neglected strand in Restoration religious thinking. For Barlow Socinianism posed a comparable threat to Arminianism. Indeed, at the Act in 1661 he argued that Socinian teachings were 'destructive alike of church and state'. Barlow was in addition a sabbatarian, who deplored the Caroline declaration of sports, and he unhesitatingly identified the pope as Antichrist. He claimed too that communion tables had anciently stood in the middle of chancels, rather than at the east end, and that the English Church had rightly reverted to this practice after the Reformation; as bishop of Lincoln Barlow appears to have operated on the same principle, while furthermore revealing his opposition to all images whatsoever in churches. He was widely regarded as an oracle on such questions, and many of his writings originated as letters in reply to correspondents. A notable example of this genre is his 'answere to some queries proposed by Mr. W.A.', in 1671, on the subject of lay baptism. Barlow concluded that such baptism is invalid, and where it was known to have occurred the ceremony should be performed again by an ordained clergyman. Commenting on the fact that until the Jacobean revision of 1604 the prayer book had permitted lay baptism, he wrote that Archbishop Cranmer and his assistants had 'lived in the twilight and dawn of learninge and reformation, and 'tis much more to be wondered at that they saw and reformed soe many errors then that they oversaw this one'. Such views earned Barlow the title of 'puritan' in some quarters.[90] But he remained

---

[88] OUA register Qb, fo 39; Samuel Parker, *A Free and Impartial Censure of the Platonick Philosophie* (Oxford 1666), 52–115; Samuel Parker, *An Account of the Nature and Extent of the Divine Dominion and Goodnesse, especially as they refer to the Origenian hypothesis concerning the pre-existence of souls* (Oxford 1666), 18–22, 44–112; Wallace, *Puritans and Predestination*, 167; George Rust, *A Letter of Resolution concerning Origen and the Chief of his Opinions* (London 1661), 21, 58, 60: Bodl. press mark A. 4. 9. Linc., annotated by Thomas Barlow.

[89] Thomas Barlow, *Several Miscellaneous and Weighty Cases of Conscience* (London 1692); Thomas Barlow, *The Genuine Remains* (London 1693). I am most grateful to Miss H. Powell for all her help concerning the very important Barlow papers at Queen's College, Oxford. Mr P. Morgan has similarly helped me with Barlow's printed books in the Bodleian Library.

[90] OUA register Qb, fo 173; Heylyn, *Cyprianus anglicus*, title-page, pp. 77, 126: Bodl. press mark NN.

personally opposed to the schemes for toleration and comprehension which emerged in the late 1660s; moreover when toleration was finally achieved, in 1689, Barlow vented his impotent fury in pen and ink on a printed copy of the act.[91]

Fascinating though the views of Barlow are, we should nevertheless note that some of them were now becoming deeply unfashionable in episcopalian circles. Thus, for example, in 1683 Anthony Wood recorded that Exeter was unique among Oxford college chapels in not having its communion table set altarwise. Furthermore, despite Calvinism remaining influential at Oxford, research has revealed that at Cambridge Arminianism was in process of sweeping the board.[92] As regards Restoration Oxford, however, the rival camp to that of Barlow was probably led by Richard Allestree and John Fell, regius professor of divinity and dean of Christ Church respectively. Fell was the biographer of both Allestree and Hammond, which certainly appears to identify him with the Oxford Arminians. At national level the Barlow group looked for support from Bishop George Morley of Winchester, whereas the Allestree–Fell group had a similar patron in Archbishop Gilbert Sheldon, and these alignments provide the background to the great religious *cause célèbre* of the early 1670s, stemming from the published teachings of George Bull on the doctrine of justification. Bull's *Harmonia Apostolica* was licensed in April 1669, from 'Lambeth House', by a chaplain of Sheldon; a subsequent defence by Bull was likewise licensed in October 1675. Conversely two of the replies to Bull, published in 1674 and 1676, were dedicated to Morley. Each of these latter books, by Thomas Tully and John Tombes, the Baptist, was published at Oxford. According to Bull's biographer and younger contemporary, Robert Nelson, Morley also issued a 'pastoral charge' to the clergy of his diocese forbidding them even to read the *Harmonia*.[93]

Bull's book was published at London in 1670. Among the surviving copies is one heavily annotated by Barlow, and judging from his remarks there had been an earlier attempt to publish at Oxford, during the vice-chancellorship of Robert Saye, between 1664 and 1666. Saye, who was provost of Oriel College and another sur-

118. Th., annotated by Thomas Barlow; Barlow, *The Genuine Remains*, 191–3; QCL MS 278 ('De templis, eorum antiquitate et fabrica etc.') [fos 19–21], MS 278 ('An answere to some queries proposed by Mr W.A. 1671'), p. 6 and *passim*; Barlow, *Cases of Conscience*, pt 6; J. H. Pruett, *The Parish Clergy under the Later Stuarts: the Leicestershire experience* (Urbana Ill. 1978), 26.

[91] '[Tracts] for and against toleration anno 1667, 1668', pp. 71, 84, 86: Bodl. press mark B. 14. 15. Linc., annotated by Thomas Barlow; Bodl. MS Eng. lett. c. 328, fo 509; QCL MS 280, fo 251ᵛ. The *DNB* claim that Barlow 'endorsed' plans for comprehension in 1667–8 confuses a narrative account of these events written by Barlow with his own personal views: '[Tracts] for and against toleration anno 1667, 1668', pp. 4–14. Previously, however, in the peculiar circumstances of 1660, Barlow *had* adopted a more tolerant stance: Barlow, *Cases of Conscience*, pt 1.

[92] Wood, *Life and Times* iii. 53; N. Tyacke, 'Arminianism and the theology of the Restoration church' in S. Groenveld and M. Wintle (eds), *Britain and the Netherlands* xi (Zutphen 1994).

[93] George Bull, *Harmonia Apostolica, seu binae dissertationes* (London 1670), sig. Aᵛ; George Bull, *Examen censurae: sive responsio ad quasdam animadversiones* (London 1676), sig. Aᵛ; Thomas Tully, *Justificatio Paulina sine operibus ex mente Ecclesiae Anglicanae* (Oxford 1674), dedication; John Tombes, *Animadversiones in librum Georgii Bull, cui titulum fecit Harmonia Apostolica* (Oxford 1676), dedication; Robert Nelson, *The Life of Dr George Bull, lord bishop of St David's* (London 1713), 102.

vivor from the 1650s, had apparently refused a licence.[94] Bull himself had very briefly attended Exeter College in 1648, but is likely to have acquired his mature views subsequently. The *Harmonia Apostolica*, as the title implies, is an attempt to reconcile the apparently contradictory teaching of St Paul and St James on faith and works. At the outset Bull made quite clear that his target was 'solifidianism'. He argues that 'faith and works are jointly prescribed as the only condition of justification'. Those who deny this, like 'Luther and most of our own divines after his time', are in error. Moreover their teaching leads to 'libertinism'. The core of Bull's case is that St Paul and St James use the term 'works' in different senses. The works which St Paul 'excludes from justification' are those required under Mosaic and natural law. By contrast, 'moral works arising from the grace of the Gospel' are 'absolutely necessary' to justification. This, claims Bull, is the true meaning of the eleventh of the Thirty-nine Articles, and therefore St James is correct in saying that 'by works a man is justified and not by faith only'. He also indicates that his solution to the problem is incompatible with 'the irresistible operation of grace'. A person once justified can indeed fall from grace and be damned, because there is no 'absolute' decree of predestination.[95]

Bull wrote in Latin, yet it is not difficult to understand the shock waves generated by his book. Among fellow Church of England clergy the task of replying in print was undertaken by Thomas Tully, principal of St Edmund Hall. In his *Justificatio Paulina* of 1674 Tully reasserted the doctrine of justification by faith alone. Among other arguments, he maintained that St Paul spoke of a 'living' faith and St James of a 'dead' one. Tully claimed that Bishop Morley had read and approved *Justificatio Paulina* in manuscript. He also sent a copy of the published version to Sir Joseph Williamson, one of the two secretaries of state and a colleague at Queen's College during the 1650s.[96] Behind Tully, however, loomed the figure of Thomas Barlow, with whom he had almost certainly planned his public response to Bull. Previously the involvement of Barlow has been known mainly from Nelson's biography of Bull, where it is recorded that he lectured at Oxford against the *Harmonia Apostolica*. In fact four stout volumes of related lectures survive in Barlow's holograph. They are collectively entitled by Barlow 'De conciliatione Pauli et Jacobi', and cover a period of almost five years. The opening shots were fired in the form of an Act lecture, on 8 July 1671. Barlow described his task as both 'arduous' and 'full of danger', in clearing the subject from the misinterpretations of Socinians and papists. Bull's book is identified by name as an English Socinian product, because of the role it assigns to works in justification. (The Socinians did indeed so teach, but there was also an antitrinitarian smear involved here.) Barlow argues at length that the works rejected by St Paul are indeed those performed

---

[94] Bull, *Harmonia Apostolica*, sig. a: Bodl. press mark B. 7. 11. Linc., annotated by Thomas Barlow.

[95] George Bull, *Harmonia Apostolica: or two dissertations*, trans. (Oxford 1842), pp. ix–x, 20–1, 34, 71–6, 178, 194, 196–7, 213, 218–19; A. E. McGrath, *Iustitia Dei: a history of the Christian doctrine of justification* (2 vols Cambridge 1986) ii. 107–11.

[96] Tully, *Justificatio Paulina*, sig. a3ᵛ, p. 138; *CSPD 1673–5*, 400.

under the Christian gospel. They are the fruits of obedience not the cause of justification, and it is to these necessary fruits that St James refers. This intervention by Barlow came not a moment too soon. Two days previously, on 6 July, William Thornton of Wadham College had, for one of his divinity school theses, denied that 'faith alone justifies'. Given that Thornton's topic would have been approved in advance, the at least tacit support of Richard Allestree, in his capacity as regius professor, seems highly probable.[97]

Barlow returned to the subject of justification, in his ordinary lectures, on 19 October 1671. But not until November 1673 was Bull again mentioned directly, being bracketed then with Faustus Socinus. Barlow took his stand on the Thirty-nine Articles, going on to invoke by name John Davenant, Richard Hooker, John Jewel, John Rainolds, and William Whitaker, as well as all other English protestant writers on the topic—up to the 1640s. He again attacked Bull in the following December, exclaiming 'good God that we should live to see such times'. Further hostile references to Bull occur in February 1674, when the *Harmonia* is described as an act of 'parricide' against the Church of England, and also in the ensuing October, November, and December. Apart from a few mentions in January and February, however, Barlow apparently fell silent during 1675 on the subject of the 'Harmonist'. Finally there are some brief references to Bull in January and April 1676.[98] By this last date Barlow had already been bishop of Lincoln for over nine months, having received consecration at the hands of Bishop Morley the previous June. Among those gracing the associated festivities was the university chancellor, the duke of Ormonde. Sir Joseph Williamson seems to have played a major part in Barlow becoming a bishop and the original plan was that Thomas Tully should succeed him as Lady Margaret professor of divinity, but in the event this was prevented by Tully's death. The year 1676 also saw the publication at Oxford of a further reply to Bull, by John Tombes. His *Animadversiones*, as I have noted, were dedicated to Morley and they also bear the official imprimatur of Ormonde—a most unusual feature.[99]

The Bull affair sheds a fresh light on the nature of religious faction within the Restoration church, not least because Morley and Sheldon are normally thought of as being on the same side. In terms of the history of English religious ideas, however, perhaps the most remarkable aspect was the published response by Bull to Tully. This was appended to Bull's *Examen censurae*, which appeared in 1676. Although printed at London, the work was undertaken on behalf of the Oxford bookseller Richard Davis. Bull describes his opponents as Calvinists, who subscribe to the canons of the Synod of Dort. Against them, he identifies with the most forthright defenders of the Arminian Richard Montagu during the 1620s—the

[97] Nelson, *Life of Dr George Bull*, 102–3; QCL MS 239, fos 140, 148–9; OUA register of congregation 1669–80, NEP/*supra*/19, register Bd, fo 15ᵛ.

[98] QCL MS 240, MS 233, pp. 6–7, 116, 119, 229–33, 437, 489, MS 234, fos 2, 14, 26, 38. Barlow's surviving lectures may well be incomplete.

[99] W. Stubbs, *Registrum sacrum Anglicanum* (Oxford 1897), 127; *The Diary of John Evelyn*, ed. E. S. De Beer (6 vols Oxford 1955) iv. 66–7; *CSPD 1675–6*, 78–9, 138; Tombes, *Animadversiones*, title-page verso.

Oxonians Buckeridge, Howson, and Laud. According to Bull, it was all part of the same battle for the mind of the Church of England—conditional justification and conditional predestination going together. 'In truth, for the first four centuries no Catholic ever dreamed about that predestination which many at this day consider the basis and foundation of the whole Christian religion.' We should also recall here Morley's complaint back in the 1630s that all the best bishoprics and deaneries were held by Arminians. Yet unlike Montagu earlier, Bull did not earn preferment by his anti-Calvinist writings. The rewards went instead to his opponents, Tully becoming dean of Ripon and Barlow a bishop.[100]

This, combined with the fact that most of the controversy about justification was conducted in Latin, helps explain why the orthodoxy of the English Church did not become a major political issue during the increasingly stormy 1670s, despite the hostile comments of dissenters such as Lewis du Moulin. The latter's pamphlet about the 'several advances the Church of England hath made towards Rome' was published in 1680, at the height of the attempt to exclude James duke of York from the succession. Du Moulin was an Independent who lost his Oxford post as Camden professor of history at the Restoration, but had clearly kept up with religious developments in the university. Thus he singled out recent events at Oxford, mentioning both Bull and Tully by name, to illustrate the threatened inundation of 'Pelagianism, Socinianism and popery'.[101] Accusations of popery, however, were uncomfortably close to the mark in this context, given the publication at Oxford in 1675 of an anonymous volume of annotations on St Paul's epistles. As Barlow pointed out in his lectures, they adopt an essentially similar line to Bull—defending 'justification by works of the law, performed by the assistance of God's grace'. Often ascribed to Obadiah Walker, fellow and subsequently master of University College, these annotations were in significant part the work of Abraham Woodhead who was a Roman Catholic by the mid-1660s. Walker, the long-standing collaborator and close personal friend of Woodhead, was probably mainly responsible for the second half of the volume. Richard Allestree and John Fell also played a role, perhaps largely editorial.[102] Both Walker and Woodhead had come to entertain grave doubts about protestantism, in any form, during the 1650s at latest. Although restored to his University College fellowship in 1660, Woodhead was thereafter granted regularly renewed leaves of absence. His college emoluments were forwarded to him in London, apparently by Walker, where he spent much of

---

[100] I. M. Green, *The Re-establishment of the Church of England 1660–1663* (Oxford 1978), 23, 93, 97, 213; George Bull, *Examen censurae: or an answer to certain strictures*, trans. (Oxford 1843), 230–3, 342–3; *The Life of Edward Earl of Clarendon* i. 56; Tyacke, *Anti-Calvinists*, 161–2, 266–8; *CSPD 1673–5*, 527, 532.

[101] Lewis du Moulin, *A Short and True Account of the Several Advances the Church of England hath made towards Rome* (London 1680), 31; see also William Jenkyn, *Celeusma seu clamor ad theologos hierarchiae Anglicanae* (London 1679), 66–7, 83, 97.

[102] *A Paraphrase and Annotations upon all the Epistles of St Paul*, ed. W. Jacobson (Oxford 1852), pp. iii–iv, 3–6; QCL MS 234, fos 72ᵛ–73ʳ; Leeds, Yorkshire Archaeological Society, Woodhead papers, MS 51, fos 100ʳ⁻ᵛ; M. Slusser, 'Abraham Woodhead (1608–78): some research notes, chiefly about his writings', *Recusant History* xv (1981), 409, 412. I am grateful to Dr A. Davidson for bibliographical advice concerning Woodhead.

his time in composing Roman Catholic apologetic until his death in 1678.[103] Walker meanwhile remained at University College, and only declared himself a Roman Catholic after James II came to the throne.

The religious evolution of Obadiah Walker is indeed difficult to fathom, but some clues lie embedded in his edition of John Spelman's life of King Alfred. Published at Oxford in 1678, this was ostensibly part of a fundraising exercise for rebuilding University College—Alfred being claimed as founder both of the college and of the university. Nevertheless in the context of the time, with the Roman Catholic James as heir to the English throne, the story of Alfred's relations with the papacy also had considerable relevance. Most importantly, at least in this account, Alfred was 'anointed' by the pope and yet remained 'supreme' over the English Church. Walker subsequently erected statues at University College of Alfred and James II.[104] His religious position may originally have approximated to that of Tristram Sugge, although the association with Woodhead suggests the early adoption of a more extreme stance. Walker arranged for the Oxford publication of another work by Woodhead in 1680, but the more avowedly Romanist writings had to await the changed circumstances of James II's reign. Even then, however, it proved necessary to set up a special printing press in University College. During 1678 Walker had been named in the house of commons as a suspected papist, and in July 1680 Francis Nicholson, a former member of University College, was ordered to recant an Oxford sermon 'tending to establish the popish doctrines of purgatory and penance'. Nicholson at the time was preaching in Walker's stead.[105]

However, the failure of the parliamentary attempts to exclude the duke of York from the succession between 1679 and 1681 was followed by a rallying of royalist ranks. At Oxford this first manifested itself in reaction to an exclusionist tract by Samuel Johnson, entitled *Julian the Apostate* and published in London in 1682. The author was a beneficed Church of England clergyman and chaplain to the Whig Lord William Russell. Not content with advocating exclusion, Johnson had gone on to defend active resistance and even tyrannicide: quoting a comment on the supposedly Christian assassin of Julian that 'you can hardly blame him who shews himself so couragious for God and for that religion he approves'. The reader was clearly meant to draw an analogy here between the cases of pagan Julian and Catholic James. During 1682 *Julian the Apostate* was rebutted in a series of Oxford sermons. Henry Aldrich, canon of Christ Church, John Mill, principal of St Edmund Hall, George Royse, fellow of Oriel College, and William Wyatt, the university orator, were among those who preached against it. At the Act Mill also

[103] Leeds, Yorkshire Archaeological Society, Woodhead papers, MS 45, pp. 54, 60, MS 51, fo 47ᵛ; UCA registrum i (1509–1722), fos 40–51ᵛ; UCA general account B (1668–1706). I am indebted to Dr D. Sturdy for help concerning the relations of Walker and Woodhead with University College.

[104] John Spelman, *Aelfredi magni Anglorum regis invictissimi vita tribus libris comprehensa* (Oxford 1678), sig. aᵛ, pp. 4–6, 70–1; *VCH Oxon.* iii. 177.

[105] Abraham Woodhead, *Of the Benefits of our Saviour Jesus Christ to Mankind* (Oxford 1680); Slusser, 'Abraham Woodhead', 413–14; Wood, *Life and Times* ii. 421, 488; HMC *Twelfth Report*, appx vii, p. 150; OUA register Tb, fos 19ʳ⁻ᵛ.

maintained the thesis that 'confederacies entered into under the pretext of religion, and without the consent of the supreme magistrate, are clearly repugnant both to the practice of the primitive church and the principles of the reformed faith'.[106]

Yet this response was as nothing compared to that elicited by the revelation of the Rye House plot the following June 1683. An apparent attempt to assassinate both Charles II and the duke of York, the plot was seemingly predicated on the kind of teaching to be found in *Julian the Apostate*. That July twenty-seven propositions were formally condemned by Oxford University as 'destructive of the kingly government, the safety of his majestie's person, the public peace, the laws of nature and bonds of humane society'. Instead there was inculcated a 'submitting to every ordinance of man for the Lord's sake', and this to be 'absolute and without exception'. The mixed collection of propositions rejected include: the popular origin of 'civil authority', the idea of a 'mutual compact', that 'the soveraignty of England is in the three estates', the right of resistance to 'tyrants' and religious persecutors, the denial of hereditary right of succession to the crown, the lawfulness of making religious 'covenants', 'self-preservation' as the 'fundamental law of nature', no obligation passively to obey commands 'against the laws', 'possession and strength give a right to govern', 'the state of nature is a state of war', the right of self-defence 'against force', the unlawfulness of oaths, 'dominion is founded in grace', 'the powers of this world are usurpations upon the prerogative of Jesus Christ', 'presbyterian government is the scepter of Christ's kingdom', and that 'wicked kings and tyrants ought to be put to death'. This list was mainly the work of William Jane, the regius professor of divinity. Various books were also ordered to be burnt, among them the *Leviathan* of Thomas Hobbes and Johnson's *Julian*. At the Act in 1684 Arthur Charlett, fellow of Trinity College, identified patriarchalism with monarchy, while denying any contractual basis for sovereignty.[107]

Nevertheless there were those even in Oxford who dared to take a contrary view. In June 1682 Strange Southby, now of Magdalen Hall, was denied his master's degree for arguing *inter alia* that 'it is lawfull to take arms against the king'. A better-known case is that of James Parkinson, fellow of Lincoln College, who was expelled for his 'whiggisme' in September 1683. Parkinson was accused of defending the teachings of *Julian the Apostate*, as well as many of the other propositions condemned by the university. Interestingly he was initially protected by the rector of Lincoln College, Thomas Marshall. But Parkinson and Southby were small fry compared with John Locke, who was expelled from his Christ Church Studentship in November 1684. A draft of his *Two Treatises of Government* was almost certainly now in existence. Although nothing was directly proved against Locke, he had in

---

[106] Samuel Johnson, *Julian the Apostate: being a short account of his life, the sense of primitive Christians about his succession, and their behaviour towards him* (London 1682), 59–61; Wood, *Life and Times* iii. 18–19; OUA register of congregation 1680–92, NEP/*supra*/20, register Be, fo 202ᵛ.

[107] D. J. Milne, 'The results of the Rye House plot and their influence upon the revolution of 1688', *TRHS* 5th ser. i (1951); *The Judgement and Decree of the University of Oxford . . . July 21 1683* (Oxford 1683); OUA register Be, fo 205ᵛ.

fact already left England for Dutch exile.[108] At the same time royalism itself came in a variety of strengths. Timothy Halton, provost of Queen's College and pro-vice-chancellor, having in October 1683 licensed an English translation of *The Lives of Illustrious Men* by Cornelius Nepos, forbade its sale in January because of additional matter 'against the late parliaments'. Leopold Finch, in a dedication to the earl of Abingdon, had denied the 'power of parliament' to alter 'the lineal succession' and described the exclusionists as republican 'fanaticks'. In 1687 Finch, a younger son of the earl of Winchilsea, was to be appointed warden of All Souls, on the basis of a royal mandamus from James II.[109]

By the early 1680s a widespread assumption seems to have been that the accession of James would make little religious difference, and in particular that he would not seek markedly to improve the position of his fellow Catholics. Charles II died on 6 February 1685, and the first months of the new reign reinforced the impression of business as usual. Indeed as late as March 1686 James II reissued his brother's directions to preachers, with the clause about avoiding the 'deep points of election and reprobation'. For Oxford University at least the predestinarian question was still a live issue, because the regius and Lady Margaret chairs of divinity were both now occupied by Calvinists—albeit of very different kinds. William Jane had succeeded Richard Allestree as regius professor in 1680. According to Edmund Calamy, 'though fond of the rites and ceremonies of the Church', Jane was 'a Calvinist with respect to doctrine' and 'plainly showed this in his public lectures'. Like the Calvinist Robert South, however, he was also a high churchman in his ecclesiastical politics and played a leading part in the rejection of comprehension by convocation in 1689.[110] John Hall, master of Pembroke College, had followed Thomas Barlow as Lady Margaret professor in 1676. Calamy, who attended his lectures, recalls that 'he could bring all the catechism of the Westminster Assembly out of the catechism of the Church of England'. In 1689 Hall actively co-operated with the Williamite regime as a member of the commission on prayer book and related reforms, aimed at winning back dissenters. He became bishop of Bristol in 1691 and his position appears similar to that of John Wallis, who also is said to have harboured episcopal ambitions.[111]

This Calvinist monopoly of the divinity chairs at Oxford had its dangers, not least because of the rapidly growing strength of Arminianism in the English Church at large. Yet, in the short term, the challenge posed by Roman Catholicism came

---

[108] Wood, *Life and Times* iii. 19–20, 68–72, 117; P. Laslett, 'The English revolution and Locke's *Two Treatises of Government*', *Cambridge Historical Journal* xii (1956); R. Ashcraft, *Revolutionary Politics and Locke's Two Treatises of Government* (Princeton 1986), 430–5.

[109] Wood, *Life and Times* iii. 86, 208 (Halton had conducted the proceedings against James Parkinson); *The Lives of Illustrious Men. Written in Latin by C. Nepos and done into English by several hands* (Oxford 1684), dedication; *CSPD 1686–7* no. 1358.

[110] *CSPD 1686–7* no. 227; *Directions concerning Preachers* (London 1685/6); Edmund Calamy, *An Historical Account of my own Life*, ed. J. T. Rutt (2 vols London 1830) i. 272; G. V. Bennett, 'Loyalist Oxford and the revolution' in *The Eighteenth Century*, 27–9.

[111] Calamy, *An Historical Account of my own Life* i. 275; T. J. Fawcett, *The Liturgy of Comprehension 1689* (Alcuin Club liv 1973), 29, 160–76; Wood, *Life and Times* ii. 489.

to overshadow all else. On 26 July 1685 Nathaniel Boyse, fellow of University College, preached a thanksgiving sermon for the defeat of Monmouth's rebellion. According to his subsequent recantation of 1 August, his sermon had included certain remarks 'tending to popery'. The following autumn Obadiah Walker himself attracted attention by the publication of a further work by Abraham Woodhead, concerning the life of Christ. William Jane had censored some passages in the manuscript, 'savouring of popery', but Walker went ahead and published the original version. On 13 October Anthony Wood records an interview at Whitehall between Boyse and James II, in which the king commended both his sermon and the recent Woodhead publication—wondering 'how anyone shall find fault'.[112]

In May 1686 Walker, Boyse, and Thomas Deane, another fellow of University College, received royal permission to withdraw from Church of England worship and set up a Roman Catholic chapel instead. They were joined by John Barnard, fellow of Brasenose College. This was a propaganda *coup* out of all proportion to the small numbers actually involved. At the same time Walker also obtained a royal licence to print Woodhead's remaining unpublished manuscripts.[113] Moreover, restraints were now imposed on anti-Catholic preaching, a special example being made of George Tullie whose Oxford sermon of 24 May, against the 'idolatrous practices of the Romish communion', led to his suspension after Walker complained. Tullie, a former fellow of Queen's College and currently sub-dean of York, had sought to refute the 'modern palliators and expositors' of 'image worship' such as Bishop Bossuet. His reference to the 'worship of babies', by which he presumably meant representations of the infant Jesus, may particularly have angered Walker because this was the subject of the recently commissioned east window of University College chapel (plate 21). Although Walker had ceased to attend the protestant services of the college chapel, he wrote to the benefactor in 1687 that 'we there salute the morning light ... meditating on the shepherds and the angells adoring the true son, and that holy service and prostration, by your singular favour, is continually proposed as to our sight and consideration'.[114]

Successive editions of *An Exposition of the Doctrine of the Catholic Church* by Bossuet were printed at London in 1685 and 1686. His moderate explanation of Tridentine teaching was calculated at least to mollify protestant critics. Whether it achieved any success in this respect is difficult to know. Most of the protestant fellows of University College apparently dissociated themselves from Walker's letter about the new chapel window. On the other hand, the alacrity with which the dean and chapter of York agreed to suspend George Tullie may in part reflect a distaste for his

---

[112] OUA register of convocation 1683–93, NEP/*subtus*/29, register Bb, fo 3; Abraham Woodhead, *An Historical Narration of the Life and Death of our Lord Jesus Christ* (Oxford 1685); Wood, *Life and Times* iii. 164–6.

[113] Wood, *Life and Times* iii. 182–3, 198; *CSPD 1686–7* nos 342, 492–3, 899; *Collectanea curiosa*, ed. John Gutch (2 vols Oxford 1781) i. 288–9.

[114] Wood, *Life and Times* iii. 186; *CSPD 1686–7* no. 679; George Tullie, *A Discourse concerning the Worship of Images* (London 1689), sig. A2ʳ⁻ᵛ, pp. 13–14, 35; UCA, copy of letter from Obadiah Walker to Dr John Radcliffe [1687]; *VCH Oxon.* iii. 68, 79.

aggressive brand of protestantism. Again, as we have seen, there looks to have been a strand of protestant religious thought at Oxford loath to label the Roman Catholic Church 'idolatrous'.[115] But whereas during the reign of Charles II a mere trickle of anti-Catholic works was published at Oxford, in the years 1687 and 1688 this turned into a small flood. The renewed polemic was almost entirely directed against the writings of Abraham Woodhead, as published by Obadiah Walker at his University College press and many of them with the distinctive King Alfred's head imprint (plate 28).

Henry Aldrich, Francis Atterbury, and George Smalridge produced replies to Woodhead in 1687. They were reinforced in 1688 by James Harrington, who is not to be confused with the republican of the same name, and George Tullie. Aldrich, Atterbury, Harrington, and Smalridge were all members of Christ Church, and were no doubt outraged by the installation of the Roman Catholic John Massey as dean in 1686. (Massey was Walker's former pupil.) Short of a similar appointment to the regius chair of divinity, it is difficult to conceive of a greater affront to the Oxford religious establishment. Matters were subsequently compounded by the transformation of Magdalen College into a Roman Catholic seminary under Bonaventure Gifford. Such actions rendered ineffective the plea of James II, at Oxford in September 1687, for 'love and charitie' among Christians.[116] The fact that both Atterbury and Smalridge were later to become Jacobites further underlines the inept tactics of the king. An attack on vested interests was guaranteed to unite the Church of England against him.

One of the polemical techniques employed by Woodhead was, in Walker's words, 'to shew the incertitude and inconstancy of the Church of England in her doctrine and practices'. This is particularly evident in his *Two Discourses concerning the Adoration of our Blessed Saviour in the Holy Eucharist*, which sought to demonstrate the existence of alternative schools of eucharistic thought in the various English prayer books. At the same time Woodhead very much played down the Roman Catholic doctrine of transubstantiation. Part of the object of the exercise was to indicate a common middle ground shared by moderate protestants and Catholics. Henry Aldrich, however, would have none of this. There was, he said, no English 'Zwinglian' tradition; the essential distinction remained between the protestant 'real' as opposed to the Roman Catholic 'corporal' presence of Christ in the eucharist.[117]

[115] Jacques Bénigne Bossuet, *An Exposition of the Doctrine of the Catholic Church in matters of controversie ... Done into English from the fifth edition in French* (London 1685, 2nd edn London 1686); UCA, copy of letter from Obadiah Walker to Dr John Radcliffe [1687], endorsed: 'this letter not being much approved of had another from the fellows that privately accompanied it'; Wood, *Life and Times* iii. 186; see p. 604 above.

[116] Wood, *Life and Times* iii. 197–8, 201, 239; *CSPD 1686–7* nos 1203, 1427; *Magdalen and James II*; L. Brockliss, G. Harris, and A. Macintyre (eds), *Magdalen College and the Crown: essays for the tercentenary of the restoration of the college 1688* (Oxford 1988).

[117] Abraham Woodhead, *A Compendious Discourse on the Eucharist, with two appendixes* (Oxford 1688), 191; Abraham Woodhead, *Two Discourses concerning the Adoration of our Blessed Saviour in the Holy Eucharist* (Oxford 1687), pt 1, pp. 1–4, 16–20, 32; Henry Aldrich, *A Reply to Two Discourses. Lately printed at Oxford concerning the adoration of our blessed saviour in the holy eucharist* (Oxford 1687), 26, 37.

In his discourse *Concerning the Spirit of Martin Luther*, Woodhead similarly suggested that English protestants disagreed over the doctrine of justification. To which Francis Atterbury countered that the teaching of Luther on justification by 'faith alone' is 'now the Church of England's doctrine'. 'Good works are inseparable attendants upon this justifying faith, but they contribute nothing to the act of justification: they make not just, but are allwaies with them that are made so.' Even more striking is the claim by Atterbury that Luther's view of what Woodhead calls the 'servitude of man's will and inability to do good even in the regenerate' is 'when fairly expounded, the same' as that of the English Church.[118] The expression of such views confirms the powerful position of Oxford Calvinism at this juncture. Meanwhile it fell to George Smalridge to rebut *A Relation of the English Reformation* by Woodhead, which characterized the Henrician supremacy as a usurpation of state over church and had remarkably little to say about the pope. As with the issue of transubstantiation, Woodhead's keynote here was moderation.[119]

The following year, 1688, James Harrington and George Tullie replied to Woodhead on the subjects of charity and clerical celibacy. Roman 'sodalities', or confraternities, were weighed in the balance with the English poor law, and the pros and cons of a married clergy debated.[120] Although the protestant pamphleteers generally derided the arguments advanced by Woodhead, he was far from being the puny opponent that they liked to claim. Furthermore the protestant Samuel Parker, who in 1686 succeeded John Fell as bishop of Oxford, took much the same line as Woodhead in his *Reasons for Abrogating the Test*, published in 1688. Transubstantiation was an 'Aristotelian' formulation, about which laymen especially should not bother their heads. By contrast, both the patristic writers and 'the true old protestants . . . unanimously asserted the corporeal and substantial presence' of Christ in the eucharist. Again, argues Parker, it is the Zwinglians who are the exception. But by the time his tract appeared in print Parker was dead and the regime visibly crumbling.[121] Clearly the issue of religion was one of the reasons for the unopposed invasion of William of Orange in November 1688. That same month John Massey and Obadiah Walker both decamped from Oxford. Yet the flesh-and-blood realities of Roman Catholicism in the mid-1680s had served to mask the

---

[118] Abraham Woodhead, *Two Discourses. The first, concerning the spirit of Martin Luther, and the original of the reformation. The second, concerning the celibacy of the clergy* (Oxford 1687), pt 1, pp. 13, 100; Francis Atterbury, *An Answer to Some Considerations on the Spirit of Martin Luther and the Original of the Reformation* (Oxford 1687), 10–11, 60.

[119] Abraham Woodhead, *Church-Government Part V. A relation of the English reformation and the lawfulness thereof examined by the theses delivered in the four former parts* (Oxford 1687); George Smalridge, *Animadversions on the Eight Theses laid down and the Inferences deduced from them, in a discourse entitled* Church-Government Part V (Oxford 1687).

[120] Abraham Woodhead (ed.), *Pietas Romana et Parisiensis, or a faithful relation of the several sorts of charitable and pious works eminent in the cities of Rome and Paris* (Oxford 1687); Abraham Woodhead, *Two Discourses . . . The second concerning the celibacy of the clergy* (Oxford 1687); James Harrington, *Some Reflexions upon a Treatise called* Pietas Romana et Parisiensis (Oxford 1688); George Tullie, *An Answer to a Discourse concerning the celibacy of the clergy* (Oxford 1688).

[121] Samuel Parker, *Reasons for Abrogating the Test, imposed upon all members of parliament anno 1678* (London 1688), 10–23, 36–7, 51–2.

beginning of a new upsurge in protestant heterodoxy, especially as regards the doctrine of the trinity.[122] This latter question now rapidly took the religious centre stage, as can be seen from William's directions of 1696 for 'preserving of unity in the Church, and the purity of the Christian faith, concerning the trinity'. By then Oxford University itself had been racked by controversy on this issue, following in the wake of Arthur Bury's notorious book *The Naked Gospel*, first published in 1690. The title echoes that of an earlier work by Bishop Herbert Croft of Hereford, *The Naked Truth*, which appeared in 1675 and was also designed to advance the cause of reconciliation with dissenters. But whereas Croft had been mainly concerned with the question of conformity the goal of Bury, rector of Exeter College, was doctrinal comprehension. On the face of it, the sexagenarian Bury, who had fallen victim to the parliamentary visitors back in 1648, came from an impeccable episcopalian and royalist background. Moreover, in a sermon of 1662 he had accused English Presbyterians of being at least indirectly responsible for the death of Charles I. Among the very few recent authorities cited in *The Naked Gospel* is *The Religion of Protestants* by William Chillingworth, which helps locate its intellectual pedigree; nevertheless, both the appeal to 'reason' and the sheer theological daring on the part of Bury are far greater. Bury argued that much of what passed for orthodoxy was in fact the imposition of clerics living in the centuries after Christ. Therefore the completion of the sixteenth-century Reformation required that these theological accretions be stripped away, so that the 'primitive gospel' could shine forth. 'Simplicity of mind is its beauty, as was Eve's nakedness in her innocency, and simplicity of doctrine is the glory of the Gospel, as is the nakedness of the sun in its brightness.'[123]

For Bury the doctrine of the trinity was a prime example of later obfuscations of religious truth, although he also claimed to resolve the perennial dispute about the relationship of faith and works: 'they are both the same under different aspects, and in their comprehensive latitude either containeth the other'. Faith in Christ as a saviour, however, did not require belief in the 'eternity of his Godhead'. Thus the dispute between Arius and Athanasius on this issue was 'fruitless', and so too were the subsequent ramifications. The man who believes in Christ

as the traveller doth in the light shall in the end as certainly attain eternal life, as the traveller doth his journey's end; though concerning our Lord's person he may be as much mistaken as the ignorant but industrious traveller, who knoweth nothing of the greatness of the sun's body or the nature of its light.

---

[122] Wood, *Life and Times* iii. 282, 285; George Ashwell *De Socino et Socinianismo dissertatio* (Oxford 1680), dedication to Bishop Barlow.

[123] Wilkins, *Concilia* iv. 625–6; Herbert Croft, *The Naked Truth. Or the true state of the primitive church* (London 1675); Arthur Bury, *The Bow: or the lamentation of David over Saul and Jonathan, applyed to the royal and blessed martyr King Charles the I* (London 1662), 44; Arthur Bury, *The Naked Gospel. Discovering i. what was the gospel which our lord and his apostles preached, ii. what additions and alterations latter ages have made in it, iii. what advantages and damages have thereupon ensued* (London 1690), preface and p. 17.

It was necessary, Bury claimed, to break through the tangled web spun by theologians, to the simple gospel message which had originally swept the world. This reborn Christianity would serve both to heal internal divisions among believers and win new converts.[124]

Bury was inspired to his ultimately Icarian attempt by the prospect of prayer book reform in 1689, because the most potentially offensive statements concerning the trinity were to be found embedded in the English liturgy—notably the Athanasian creed. The reform commission set up by King William did indeed discuss the matter and recommended a new rubric. In the event, however, any hope of change was blocked in the Canterbury convocation, and *The Naked Gospel* became the victim of a conservative backlash. The book was burnt by the Oxford authorities in August 1690, and various statements extracted from it were formally condemned. As for the author, his alleged heterodoxy featured among charges contemporaneously levelled against him by the visitor of Exeter College, Bishop Jonathan Trelawney. Bury was deprived of his rectorship but won a reprieve by going to common law. Hence he can be found preaching before the university on New Year's day 1692, about the 'danger of delaying repentance'. As well as rebutting the charge of Socinianism, Bury maintained, apparently against Calvinists, that 'the question is not concerning God's secret but his declared will', and 'that ordinary rule whereby he professeth to judge the world'. The 'day of grace is shorter than the day of life' and 'there is a measure of iniquity beyond which God's spirit will not strive with man, but leave the reprobate to his own ways wherein he must certainly perish'. God woos, threatens and 'at last' deserts 'the obstinate and therefore perishing fool' (Henry Hammond had argued similarly in a tract published over forty years earlier). Not until 1695 did Bury finally leave Exeter College, the house of lords having upheld his original deprivation by Bishop Trelawney.[125]

Meanwhile the reverberations from *The Naked Gospel* continued to be felt, producing a series of related trinitarian defences including one by William Nicholls of Merton College. Conversely Bury's book was enthusiastically received in the radical intellectual circles frequented by John Locke. On the continent the Arminian Jean Le Clerc reviewed Bury sympathetically in his *Bibliotheque universelle* and the Calvinist Pierre Jurieu wrote against him, the latter provoking a Latin reply from Bury entitled *Latitudinarius orthodoxus* and published in 1697.[126] Amidst all the clamour of controversy, however, a remarkable sea change had by now occurred—silent and largely unremarked. Calvinism might still survive in Oxford, but elsewhere

[124] Bury, *The Naked Gospel*, 9, 20, 40.

[125] Fawcett, *The Liturgy of Comprehension*, 66, 200–1; *Judicium et decretum Universitatis Oxoniensis . . . contra propositiones quasdam impias et hereticas, exscriptas et citatas ex libello quodam . . . cui titulus est* The Naked Gospel (Oxford 1690); James Harrington, *An Account of the Proceedings of . . . Jonathan Lord Bishop of Exeter in his late visitation of Exeter College in Oxford* (Oxford 1690), 22–3, 32, 55; Arthur Bury, *The Danger of Delaying Repentance* (London 1692), 7, 13, 16; Henry Hammond, *Several Tracts* (London 1646), 37–70; *Registrum Collegii Exoniensis*, ed. C. W. Boase (OHS xxvii 1894), pp. cxxix–cxxx.

[126] William Nicholls, *An Answer to a Heretical Book called* The Naked Gospel (London 1691); *The Correspondence of John Locke*, ed. E. S. De Beer (8 vols Oxford 1976–89) iv. 12, 22, 150–1; Arthur Bury, *Latitudinarius orthodoxus . . . contra ineptias et calumnias P. Jurieu* (London 1697).

Arminianism had emerged supreme. During the 1660s an aggressive brand of anti-Calvinism had rapidly become established at Cambridge University, and Archbishop Sheldon increasingly lent his authority to such views in the English Church more generally. Meanwhile the public affirmation of the English Calvinist heritage was left almost exclusively to dissenters, such as the Oxonian Henry Hickman. The apotheosis of this long-term development was achieved in the 1690s with the triumph of a religious 'latitudinarianism' which was clearly Arminian in its theological emphases. In this context Bishop Gilbert Burnet's *Exposition* of the Thirty-nine Articles, published in 1699, both outlined the rise and fall of English Calvinism and set a seal on the new Arminian dispensation.[127]

Yet Oxford too contributed to this transformation in a very important and practical manner, by means of a body of popular Arminian devotional literature. This emanated from the Allestree–Fell group and its best-known product is *The Whole Duty of Man*. First published in 1658, with a prefatory letter from Henry Hammond, by 1700 the book had run through twenty-five recorded editions. Still bearing the scars of the Interregnum, *The Whole Duty of Man* calls for religious renewal in terms of an Arminian reading of the prayer book. The sacrament of communion and works of charity are held forth as the twin poles of the Christian life, which is to be led along lines later made famous under the label of the 'protestant ethic'.

For there is a husbandry of the soul as well as of the estate, and the end of the one as of the other is the increasing and improving of its riches; [and] when it is remembered how great a work we have here to do, the making our calling and election sure . . . it will appear our time is that which of all other things we ought most industriously to improve.

But this 'husbandry' was premissed on the free co-operation of the will of man with the grace of God; the basic requirement was 'an honest and hearty endeavour to do what we are able'. Thus, having flown the academic nest, Arminianism was already well on the way to establishing a significant following among the English laity.[128]

Much of the earlier anxiety was also now ebbing out of the religious situation. Despite the *frisson* engendered by the policies of James II his reign had exposed as myth the idea of a mass of secret papists, merely waiting for an opportune moment at which to emerge. Similarly the growing institutionalization of dissent served gradually to exorcize the threat of puritanism, a process advanced by the toleration act of 1689 which ushered in a new age of denominational pluralism.[129] For over

---

[127] Tyacke, 'Arminianism and the theology of the Restoration church'; Henry Hallywell, *Deus justificatus. or the divine goodness vindicated and cleared, against the assertors of absolute and inconditionate reprobation* (London 1668): this anti-Calvinist work was licensed by a chaplain of Archbishop Sheldon; Henry Hickman, *Historia quinq-articularis exarticulata, or animadversions on Dr Heylyn's quinquarticular history* (London 1673); Gilbert Burnet, *An Exposition of the Thirty-nine Articles* (London 1699), 148–52.

[128] *The Works of the Learned and Pious Author of the Whole Duty of Man* (Oxford 1684), sig. A3, pp. 63, 77; P. Elmen, 'Richard Allestree and the *Whole Duty of Man*', *Library* 5th ser. vi (1951); C. J. Sommerville, 'The anti-puritan work ethic', *Journal of British Studies* xx (1981).

[129] N. Tyacke, 'The "rise of puritanism" and the legalising of dissent, 1571–1719' in O. P. Grell, J. I. Israel, and N. Tyacke (eds), *From Persecution to Toleration: the Glorious Revolution and religion in England* (Oxford 1991), 40–9.

a century Oxford and Cambridge had found themselves in the front line, as successive English regimes struggled to contain the rivalries unleashed by the reformation, but the civil war and its aftermath had marked the beginning of the end of that role. Paradoxically, however, the tolerance which was thenceforward increasingly forced upon the nation turned the English universities into more rather than less exclusive institutions—many of the potential misfits simply going elsewhere. Greater peace of mind had been bought at the price of a certain disengagement from the intellectual challenges of the coming era.[130]

[130] The growing threat of antitrinitarianism, however, generated a series of Oxford responses from the 1690s onwards.

Music

P. M. GOUK

MUSIC in Oxford flourished throughout the seventeenth century, revolving about both the university and the city. The degree of BMus was granted from the end of the fifteenth century at latest; the earliest recorded recipient of the DMus was the celebrated composer Robert Fayrfax in 1511.[1] There was a newly revived tradition of performing sacred music in Oxford in the seventeenth century, following an earlier period of decline. Except during the Interregnum, services and anthems were performed in the colleges which had choral foundations, namely New College, Christ Church, Magdalen College, and St John's College, as well as in the university church of St Mary's. Secular musical celebrations also took place on various occasions in the college and university calendar. Regular events included the annual Act ceremonies, while exceptional occasions, notably royal visits, provided an opportunity to produce stage plays and lavish musical entertainments. Official university activities of this kind were paralleled by the public ceremonial and religious rites of the city, and indeed 'town' and 'gown' music overlapped.

The city waits and university musicians who were employed on such public occasions appear to have been closely connected to each other and in some cases were no doubt the same people. Such professionals also played a more informal role in the musical life of the city. Sons of the nobility and gentry coming to the university for a gentleman's education required training in instrumental and vocal techniques in order to acquire sufficient skill to participate in musical performances. A number of musicians ran music and dancing schools, often in conjunction with taverns, in order to meet this demand, which increased throughout the century. Tastes in musical style and practice, which usually originated in London, were naturally followed in Oxford. The increased popularity of concerted instrumental music (i.e. with several parts) in the seventeenth century is particularly noticeable. Generally there was a great deal of music-making among members of the university. In addition to these more obvious aspects of musical

I am particularly grateful for the bibliographical information and advice of Mr W. R. Loosemore, Professor J. R. Elliott, Dr J. Wainwright, Mr P. Ward Jones, and Mr P. Trevelyan. I would also like to thank Mr S. Tomlinson, formerly of the University Archives, for his assistance, and also the staff of the Music Library and Duke Humfrey.

[1] C. F. A. Williams, *A Short Historical Account of the Degrees in Music at Oxford and Cambridge with a Chronological List of Graduates in that Faculty from the Year 1463* (London and New York 1893), 16.

activity, there were a number of other ways in which interest in music was expressed, notably in the developing experimental philosophy of the period. Oxford was an important centre for investigation into the nature and properties of musical sound at this time.

Given that there was so much musical activity in seventeenth-century Oxford, it may seem surprising that there was no formal education in music provided for those taking the BMus or DMus degrees. This did not prevent the statutory requirements for these degrees, first outlined in the sixteenth century and formalized in the Laudian code, from including skills in both the practical and theoretical branches of music.[2] For the BMus it was (theoretically) necessary to have spent seven years in the study or practice of music. Knowledge of Boethius' *De musica*, the chief source on music since the Middle Ages, was also mandatory. A vocal work (*canticum*) of five parts had to be produced which was performed both in the music faculty and at the annual *comitia* or Act when the degrees were awarded. Anyone with the BMus degree was entitled to lecture on Boethius. The DMus required a further five years' study and the composition of a piece in six or eight parts.

The number of music degrees awarded in the seventeenth century was very small.[3] During James I's reign a total of fourteen bachelor's degrees were awarded, with another two supplicated for where the outcome is not known. Four doctorates were given in the same period of twenty-two years. These doctors of music were William Heather (1622), a gentleman of the Chapel Royal and founder of the Heather professorship of music, Nathaniel Giles (1622), gentleman of the Chapel Royal and master of the choristers, Orlando Gibbons (1622), gentleman of the Chapel Royal and organist of Westminster Abbey, and John Mundy (1624), organist of Windsor chapel. Between the years 1625 and 1644 seven bachelor's degrees were given, and only two doctorates. No degrees in music were awarded during the Interregnum, and even after the Restoration only a small number were conferred. One bachelor's degree and three doctorates were given between 1660 and 1682, after which none were given until 1707.

Those who received music degrees in the seventeenth century were usually practising organist–composers, not necessarily from the university. Few, if any, would have completed the requisite period of study and were instead awarded degrees by creation. The doctors of music were nearly all members of the Chapel Royal or servants of the king and distinguished professional musicians; it is likely that it was this royal connection which led to the award of the higher degree. The same pattern of organist–composers can be found among the bachelors of music. Degrees

---

[2] *Laudian Code*, ed. Griffiths VI. iii, IX. iii. 4.

[3] For the full list of those awarded music degrees at Oxford, see Williams, *Degrees in Music*, 75–83. Additional biographical details may be found in Wood, *Fasti* and *New Grove Dictionary of Music and Musicians*, ed. S. Sadie (20 vols London 1980). For the musical context of the period see P. LeHuray, *Music and the Reformation in England 1549–1660* (London 1967, 2nd edn Cambridge 1978).

in music, then, were awarded to established musicians who had received their training at either collegiate or cathedral schools of music and who usually became
organists, members of the Chapel Royal or some other royal ensemble. No credit
for the quality of its music graduates and doctors can be given to the university.
Candidates only visited the university for the purpose of performing their exercises
and receiving their degrees. The music lectures which were given in the sixteenth
and early seventeenth centuries were not part of a music faculty but were for the
benefit of those taking the Arts degree.

According to the Elizabethan statutes of 1564–5, the BA course lasted four years
and consisted of two terms of grammar, four of rhetoric, five of dialectic, three of
arithmetic, and two of music. The MA course involved a further three years' study
of geometry, astronomy, natural philosophy, moral philosophy, and metaphysics.
New MAs were expected to lecture on Boethius, and all undergraduates were
required to attend.[4] As in the case of most university statutes of the time, it is likely
that those for music were often ignored. Music lectures were regularly cancelled
due to lack of attendance or for some other reason. It seems that music was valued more for its social and recreational benefits than as an academic discipline.

The fact that the university offered no real training in either the theory or practice of music was clearly recognized as grounds for reform by the early seventeenth
century. It was for this reason that William Heather gave an endowment in 1627
which was to provide training in both the practical and speculative branches of
music. There had already been an attempt to revive the status of theoretical music
when the Savilian professorships were founded in 1619 with the intention of promoting the study of all the quadrivial disciplines.[5] The chair of geometry (first held
by Henry Briggs) did much to increase interest in mathematics among members of
the university. Another precedent for Heather's benefaction was the anatomy lectureship endowed by the Westminster merchant Richard Tomlins in 1624.

According to the Laudian statutes of 1636, the Heather endowment provided
both practical and speculative instruction.[6] In the first place, a choragus was
appointed to preside over weekly music practice sessions in term and to care for
the instruments and music practice books Heather gave to the music school. The
choragus had to provide musical instruction at the music school (located in the
new schools quadrangle) every Thursday, bringing with him two singing or musical boys. If nobody turned up to these sessions, the choragus and boys were to
rehearse pieces for three voices. The men who held this post during the seventeenth century (who later came to be called professors of music) were Richard

[4] *SA* 389–91; J. Caldwell, 'Music in the faculty of arts' in *The Collegiate University*, 201–12; N. C.
Carpenter, *Music in the Medieval and Renaissance Universities* (Norman Okla. 1958), 153–88.
    [5] *Laudian Code*, ed. Griffiths IV. i. 6, appendix statutorum, 244–53; M. Feingold, *The Mathematicians'
Apprenticeship: science, universities and society in England, 1560–1640* (Cambridge 1984), 31–2. The quadrivium
included astronomy, geometry, arithmetic, and music.
    [6] *Laudian Code*, ed. Griffiths IV. i. 6. appendix statutorum, 262–3. For Heather's negotiations with
the university during 1626–7 and the endorsement of convocation 26 February 1627, see OUA register
of convocation 1615–28, NEP/*supra*/23, register N, fos 222ʳ, 233–4ʳ, 236ᵛ–7ʳ; OUA SEP/C/8; Wood,
History of the University ii. 358–9.

Nicholson, organist at Magdalen (1626–39), Arthur Philipps, who followed Nicholson as organist at Magdalen (1639–56), John Wilson (1656–61), Edward Lowe, organist at Christ Church (1661–82), and Richard Goodson, another Magdalen organist (1682–1718).[7] Apart from Lowe, all the professors had Oxford music degrees. In view of his contribution to Oxford music, it is surprising that Lowe was never granted a formal qualification.

The Heather endowment also provided for a music lecturer who was appointed to read a lecture on the 'theory of the art' once a term in the music school. The lectures were to be in English 'because divers skilfull musitians are not so well acquainted with the Latin tongue as university men'. The first and only person to take up this position was John Allibond, MA of Magdalen College. The post lapsed in about 1632 when he left and no one was found to replace him.[8] The stipend was later assigned to the person who gave the annual music lecture at the Act. The bantering tone of the lecture in 1640 given by Richard West, MA of Christ Church, suggests that the event was already regarded more as an entertainment for the ladies than opportunity for a learned discourse: 'the sweet harmonie of your beautie (ladies) is the loadstone drawes them (the scholars) to this place.'[9] The convention that amusing banter, and even bawdiness, should set the tone of the annual lecture was continued after the Restoration.

As already indicated, candidates for music degrees were required to compose a vocal work in five parts for the BMus and a piece of six or eight parts for voices or instruments for the DMus. These exercises were apparently played first at the music school and then repeated as part of the entertainment at the Act ceremonies. The statutes were not necessarily strictly followed, however; when Heather and Giles received their degrees at the Act of 1622, an anthem by Orlando Gibbons was performed, rather than any work by the two candidates.[10] Since music degrees were awarded so infrequently after the Restoration, it became common for music to be commissioned for performance at the Act. Most of the surviving Act music dates from the period between 1669 and 1710. For example, in 1678 John Blow was commissioned to compose a work for the Oxford Act. His anthem 'Awake, my lyre' was performed a year later at the ceremony. Henry Aldrich, dean of Christ Church from 1689, also provided Act music on several occasions.[11]

[7] Williams, *Degrees in Music*, 35; for further details see *New Grove*. The post of choragus was re-established with that of professor in 1848.

[8] OUA register N, fo 236ᵛ (16 December 1626). According to Thomas Crosfield, Allibond gave music lectures—including jokes for the ladies—at the Act on 8 July 1626 and 9 July 1631: *The Diary of Thomas Crosfield*, ed. F. S. Boas (Oxford 1935), 5, 54, 107.

[9] Bodl. MS Tanner 88, fos 9–10. Other surviving music Act speeches include Bodl. MS Add. a. 368, fos 21–6 (Richard Torless, 1661); ibid. fos 6–12ᵛ (Thomas Laurence, 1669). References to music lecturers between the years 1661 and 1684 are found in Wood, *Life and Times* ii. 165, 490, 547, 564, iii. 24, 59–60, 105, iv. 77.

[10] *Laudian Code*, ed. Griffiths VII. i. 1, 2, 14, ii. 5, 8, IX. vi. 2; Wood, *Fasti* i. 842; Carpenter, *Music in the Medieval and Renaissance Universities*, 162–6.

[11] F. Madan, *A Summary Catalogue of Western Manuscripts in the Bodleian Library* (7 vols Oxford 1895–1953) v. 251–5; J. Westrup *et al.* (eds), *New Oxford History of Music* (11 vols Oxford 1954–) vi. 14. On Aldrich see n. 62 below.

After its completion in 1669 the Sheldonian Theatre provided an ideal venue for degree celebrations. Anthony Wood reports, perhaps with some exaggeration, that on 10 July 1680 over 2,000 people heard the music lecture in the Sheldonian given by Edmund Norden of Christ Church. Referring to this occasion Wood lamented the fact that 'antient and solid learning decayes, as it appeares by the neglect of solid lectures to heare an English one in the theater and musick'.[12]

The music school itself was initially located on the first floor of the schools quadrangle, next to astronomy and above the rhetoric school. Heather's original gift included a collection of portraits of musicians, stools, a harpsichord, a chest of viols, and two sets of partbooks. The 'Forrest–Heather' set, comprising six manuscript partbooks, contains the masses sung at Cardinal College *circa* 1527–30 and a similar royal repertory of the period 1553–8. This body of Catholic music would have had a purely historical value. Of more practical use was the second set, made up from over forty printed collections of madrigals, devotional polyphony, and other vocal works. These were originally in separate parts, the normal format of the time. The parts were subsequently bound together (soprano with soprano, bass with bass, etc.) so that the collection now comprises six bound volumes. Among the most important items are Nicholas Yonge's *Musica transalpina* (1588), John Ward's *First Set of English Madrigals* (1613), four sets of madrigals by Michael East (1604, 1606, 1610, 1624), and psalms, sonnets, and songs by William Byrd.[13]

During the civil war the schools were used as a magazine for the supplies of the king's troops, but the description given by Hawkins of the damage and losses inflicted on the music school is now thought to be something of an exaggeration.[14] In 1656/7 the school was moved, changing places with rhetoric, to the ground floor in the south-east corner of the quadrangle, where the doorway still bears the legend Schola Musicae. One reason for this move, undertaken by Wilson at the beginning of his tenure of the chair of music, was the structural weakness of the upper floors of the schools building. Accounts for these alterations and repairs still survive. An organ and harpsichord were repaired, four viols mended, and six new bows made. New locks were put on the doors, chairs were bought, paper and ink were purchased. Thomas Jackson was commissioned to copy music for use in the school.[15]

The process begun by Wilson of building up the collections of the music school and making it a centre of musical activity was continued under the direction of his

---

[12] Wood, *Life and Times* ii. 225, 248, 490, iii. 24, 59–60, 105.

[13] Bodl. MS mus. sch. e. 376–81. Two copies of the Heather endowment survive: OUA SEP/C/9; Bodl. MS mus. sch. C 203*(R). The latter is transcribed in M. Crum, 'Early lists of the Oxford music school collection', *Music and Letters* xlviii (1967), 23–34, together with a transcription of a catalogue of the music school collection dated 1682 (Bodl. MS mus. sch. C 204*(R)).

[14] J. Hawkins, *A General History of the Science and Practice of Music* (5 vols London 1776, 2nd edn 2 vols London 1853) ii. 699; Crum, 'Early lists', 27.

[15] Details of these repairs are in OUA vice-chancellor's bills and acquittances 1652–7, NW/3/4, fos 168, 171, 173, 175, 179, 185, 204, 225–7, 232. Thomas Jackson was probably the bass-viol player (later a singing-man at St John's) mentioned by Wood as one of the music masters who played at Ellis's meetings. See n. 43 below.

successors Lowe and Goodson.[16] Lowe was aided by an association which set up a subscription in 1665 to promote the study and practice of vocal and instrumental harmony in the university. The subscription (which ended in 1675) provided the music school with a new organ by Robert Dallam, a harpsichord, two violins with bows and cases, a theorbo given by Henry Lawes, and instrumental music books. John Hingston gave the school a set of partbooks containing his own works. In 1667 Lowe bought a collection of consort music from Anthony Wood, which originally came from the household of Baron North at Kirtling, Cambridgeshire. Another set of instrumental music was given by William Isles to Dr Fell in 1673 for the use of the music school. These collections include consort music by composers such as John Jenkins, Orlando Gibbons, Benjamin Rogers, and Thomas Baltzar. The books in the music school represent only a fraction of the enormous amount of instrumental music which was copied and arranged for use by a number of loosely knit groups of professional and amateur musicians who met regularly, usually on a weekly basis, at various colleges and lodgings.[17]

A special music lecture was given in the music school after the Restoration, in late May 1660, to celebrate the return of Charles II to his kingdom. Apart from the lecture itself, there were musical interpolations performed by singers and instrumentalists (including Wood on the violin). In 1665 the composer Matthew Locke visited Oxford and performed one of his own compositions at the music school. That same year John Bannister, then master of the king's music, came to the school with other royal musicians and performed on the flageolet. Cosimo de' Medici, grand duke of Tuscany, also visited the music school when he came to Oxford in May 1669.[18]

During the first decades of the seventeenth century there was a new flowering of sacred choral music in Oxford, as there was throughout the English cathedrals. William Laud, archbishop of Canterbury from 1633, played a key role in the support of the movement which encouraged the use of music in the liturgy. The positive attitude towards music among leading Stuart churchmen contrasts with that of the more puritan divines who had attempted to impose their reforms on the

[16] On the music school's early holdings see Crum, 'Early lists' and R. L. Poole, 'The Oxford music school and the collection of portraits formerly preserved there', *Musical Antiquary* iv (1912–13), 143–59. For later developments see B. Bellingham, 'The musical circle of Anthony Wood in Oxford during the Commonwealth and Restoration', *Journal of the Viola da Gamba Society of America* xix (1982), 6–71, especially 57–61; W. K. Ford, 'The Oxford music school in the late seventeenth century', *Journal of the American Musicological Society* xvii (1964), 198–203. The instruments of the music school were dispersed and sold in the nineteenth century, while the music books were formally transferred to the Bodleian in 1885 where they are now referenced MSS mus. sch.

[17] Descriptions of these music collections are found in Crum, 'Early lists', 27; Ford, 'Oxford music school', 199; R. Rastall, 'Benjamin Rogers (1614–98): some notes on his instrumental music', *Music and Letters* xlvi (1965), 237–42; A. Ashbee, 'John Jenkins's fantasia suites', *Chelys* i (1970), 3–15; M. Crum, 'The consort music from Kirtling, bought for the Oxford music school from Anthony Wood, 1667', *Chelys* iv (1972), 3–10. See also n. 44 below.

[18] Wood, *Life and Times* i. 316, ii. 69, 158, 161; Bellingham, 'Musical circle of Anthony Wood', 65–8.

Elizabethan church. In the second half of the sixteenth century the position of music and musicians in the English Church at times seemed precarious. In Oxford a low point in the fortunes of the choral foundations was reached in the 1570s and early 1580s, though this seems to have been brought about by impoverishment rather than any deliberate religious policy.[19]

Since its foundation in 1379, New College had provided for sixteen boy choristers and an organist for services in the chapel. Musical instruction is known to have been given to the choristers there as early as 1394. The 1483 statutes of Magdalen College provided for eight singing clerks, sixteen choristers, and an organist who was responsible for the boys' musical education. They received a training in plainsong, pricksong (reading musical notation), and the playing of instruments, usually given by the organist. A similar pattern was followed at the younger colleges of Christ Church and St John's. From its re-establishment in 1546 Christ Church had a choir consisting of between seven and eight choristers, eight and ten clerks, and an organist. St John's College statutes of 1562 refer to three chaplains, six choristers, and four singing-men.[20]

The earliest reforms in liturgical practice which threatened choral music were implemented under Edward VI. In 1548, for example, an organ was removed from New College, but it was restored under Mary. An organ was removed from the college for the second time in 1572. At Magdalen College the organ was damaged in 1549 or 1550 but was soon restored.[21] At the beginning of Elizabeth I's reign a small but vociferous group of radical protestant divines attempted to bring about a series of reforms which would have abolished 'all curious singing' (elaborate vocal polyphony) and the use of organs in church altogether. These and similar proposals were defeated in national convocation during 1563, but Thomas Sampson, dean of Christ Church, was among those who voted for them.[22]

Economic factors played a more important part in the decline of college and cathedral choirs. Inflation was particularly acute in the 1570s. Stipends for musicians remained static while the cost of living increased dramatically, a situation which led to absenteeism and a decline of musical standards in many cathedrals. It seems to have been financial difficulties which forced St John's College to abolish its choir in 1577, due to 'lack of funds'. No payments had been made to choirboys or singing-men of the college during the period 1568–72. After 1578 the choir at

---

[19] On the impact of the reformation on musical practice in the cathedrals and churches of England, see LeHuray, *Music and the Reformation*, 1–55; N. Temperley, *The Music of the English Parish Church* (2 vols Cambridge 1979) i. 1–99.

[20] *Stat. Coll.* i (5) 76–7, ii (8) 22–3, (11) 13, 49–51, iii (12) 41–2; C. E. Mallet, *A History of the University of Oxford* (3 vols London 1924–7) ii. 23, 37, 158, 177; W. H. Stevenson and H. E. Salter, *The Early History of St. John's College, Oxford* (Oxford 1939), 148, 169. The histories of individual Oxford colleges generally contain only scattered references to music; the exception is the chapter by P. R. Hale, 'Music and musicians' in J. P. Buxton and P. Williams (eds), *New College Oxford 1379–1979* (Oxford 1979), 267–72, on the chapel and choir school.

[21] Hale, 'Music and musicians', 268; Bloxam, *Reg. Magdalen* ii, pp. xcviii, 272, 275.

[22] LeHuray, *Music and the Reformation*, 35–7.

Christ Church cathedral was apparently no longer active until the end of the century, although the reasons for this are not known.[23]

A new attitude towards music and its place in worship was first signalled by John Case's *Apologia musices* (1588) and Richard Hooker's *Laws of Ecclesiastical Polity* (1593–1662). Both Whitgift and Bancroft were active in reforming the ministry and improving the conditions of service for church employees. By the end of the sixteenth century the general climate of opinion in the church favoured choral music and the use of organ accompaniment. Cathedrals and colleges alike were now willing to spend large sums of money on organs, refurbishing chapels and employing organists and musicians. Organs were installed by John Chappington in Magdalen and New College in 1597, while Thomas Dallam supplied a small portable organ to Christ Church in 1608.[24] The importance of choral services gradually increased to the extent that larger instruments were required. A new, fixed organ was installed in the Christ Church loft by Dallam in 1624–5. In the same year the dean and chapter of Christ Church gave an organ to the university for installation at St Mary's church. The coincidence between these two events suggests that the college passed over its old Dallam organ of 1608. Another new organ, also thought to be by Thomas Dallam, was bought by Magdalen College in 1635.[25]

In the case of St John's College it was largely due to the efforts of William Laud and William Juxon as successive presidents that a programme of refurbishment and adornment of buildings, together with the restoration of ceremonial and music, was undertaken. The rebuilding of the chapel began in 1619, when the old organ case was removed and a new organ loft installed. Sir William Paddy apparently gave the college a 'pneumatic organ of great cost' in 1618, and evidence for the use of a new organ dates from 1620. In this year John Frith (BMus 1626, died 1635) was appointed organist, and Mr Dallam (either Thomas or Robert) was paid for tuning the organ, which was probably built by the Dallam family. In 1637 the first eight singing-men and four choristers were appointed out of funds Paddy left in his will for this purpose. The organist, at this time Robert Lugge, was to be paid £20 a year. Lugge later resigned his post and converted to Catholicism. William Ellis was appointed organist in April 1639 and was paid a stipend up to 1642.[26] He was among those ejected from the college after the visitation in 1649 and about the same time obtained a licence to operate as a victualler and common alehouse-keeper, which he renewed until his reappointment as organist in 1660. By 1656 at

[23] Stevenson and Salter, *St. John's*, 169; Caldwell, 'Music in the faculty of arts', 208; CA cathedral act book A, *passim*.

[24] LeHuray, *Music and the Reformation*, 45–8; Bloxam, *Reg. Magdalen* ii, pp. xcix, 278; Hale, 'Music and musicians', 268; CA MS xii.b.52.

[25] CA MS xii.b.69; OUA WP/β 21/4; A. Freeman, 'Renatus Harris', *The Organ* vi (1926–7), 165. For further information about the Chappington and Dallam families and the organs they built see A. Freeman, 'Records of British organ-builders 940–1660' in *Dictionary of Organs and Organists* (Bournemouth 1912, 2nd edn London 1921), 31–7, 45–8.

[26] Costin, *St. John's*, 67–71.

the latest, Ellis was running a series of weekly music meetings described more fully below.[27]

Ellis's career reflects the dislocation that took place in the lives of chapel musicians in the middle of the century. As long as the king was resident in Oxford during the civil war the four choral foundations, which were all strongly royalist, continued to function. Several members of the king's private music (part of the royal band of musicians) followed the king to Oxford and contributed to the musical life of the city. But it was not long before they and Oxford chapel musicians lost their jobs. Following the surrender of the king in 1646 and the parliamentary visitations from 1647, the chapel choirs were disbanded and the musicians dismissed from their posts. The abolition of the choral foundations forced the musicians to find employment in the city or further afield. Some college organs were also either dismantled or removed entirely.[28] Although the organs which survived could not be played for worship, it seems that they could be used for secular entertainment. During his visit to Oxford in 1654 Evelyn heard Christopher Gibbons play on the organ at Magdalen College. This organ was later moved to Hampton Court by Oliver Cromwell.[29]

Once Charles II had been restored in 1660 choirs and organists were reinstated in the various colleges from which they had been removed, and organs were once more allowed to be used in worship. Organs were restored almost immediately at Christ Church, Magdalen College, New College, and St John's College.[30] In 1661 Edward Lowe, organist of Christ Church, published *A Short Direction for the Performance of the Cathedrall Service*, to instruct those who had forgotten or who had never learned the traditional service. A new organ was built for St Mary's church in 1676. Wood records that the inauguration of the new organ built by Bernard ('Father') Smith for the Sheldonian Theatre was celebrated in 1671 with vocal and instrumental music.[31] Following the Restoration, the musical life of Oxford continued once more in the churches and cathedral as well as in public and private secular entertainments.

[27] Oxford City Arch. N.4.1., N.4.2. (victuallers' licences 1578–1653, 1653–61). For other musicians who were alehouse-keepers, see below, p. 631.

[28] The organist 'Mr Jennings jun.' (i.e. Robert Jennings) was expelled from St John's in October 1648, when choral services ceased there: *Register of the Visitors of the University of Oxford 1647–1658*, ed. M. Burrows (Camden Soc. new ser. xxix 1881), 47, 91, 198. The organ was dismantled in 1651: Costin, *St. John's*, 108. At New College the organist Simon Coleman was expelled in 1649 together with many chaplains and fellows: Hale, 'Music and musicians', 270. Latin services continued in Christ Church up to Christmas 1648: Wood, *History of the Colleges and Halls* ii. 613. Edward Lowe continued to receive his allowance as Christ Church organist for another year, after which no further payments are recorded until 1659. Mr Loosemore has drawn my attention to the fact that Lowe also received remuneration as university organist throughout the whole period: OUA register of convocation 1647–59, NEP/*supra*/26, register T.

[29] *The Diary of John Evelyn*, ed. E. S. De Beer (6 vols Oxford 1955) iii. 109 (12 July 1654). The previous day Evelyn was entertained at All Souls with 'music, voices and *Theorbes* perform'd by some ingenious scholars': ibid. 106.

[30] W. G. Hiscock, *A Christ Church Miscellany* (Oxford 1946), 215–16; Bloxam, *Reg. Magdalen* ii. 285; Hale, 'Music and musicians', 269; Costin, *St. John's*, 124.

[31] Wood, *Life and Times* i. 316, 347, ii. 223, 358.

Another important group of musicians in Oxford was the professionals paid by the city and university for their services. References to waits in the city records date from the sixteenth century.[32] Waits were originally appointed by towns and cities as night-watchmen to guard their boundaries and to act as keepers of the peace. As a secondary duty they played wind instruments to mark the hours of the day and night. By the late sixteenth century these musical activities had become more important than any other duties, and there was increasing demand for the waits to provide their services at civic entertainments.[33]

In 1603 Oxford city council passed an act which awarded six waits the sole right to practise music in the city and its suburbs; all other musicians were to be treated as vagrants. The university musicians were formally exempted from this act in 1673. The waits were expected to perform on public holidays and civic occasions; any payment received at private functions by some of them was supposed to be shared equally among all. As freemen of the city (entitled to wear a silver chain as a badge of office) they had to be properly trained as apprentices and pay their dues. Their role as time-keepers and performers of 'loud music' meant that they chiefly played wind instruments, but some did play stringed instruments as well. Normally there were six waits, but the number could vary: in 1661 there were as many as eight but by 1673 there were only four. It appears that their duties continued throughout the Interregnum.[34]

A band of university musicians with similar functions was formed somewhat later. Around 1630/2 a series of proposals was put to the vice-chancellor, William Smyth, to form a new group. The proposal by the petitioners John Jarrett (or Gerard), John Polley, and Thomas Halwoode was accepted by the university. They were authorized to recruit four more musicians, bringing the total to seven, and a number of apprentices. One of these latter, Francis Jones, was employed by the first professor of music, while another, Thomas Curtis, later became assistant organist at Magdalen. A number of colleges contributed towards the cost of the musicians' badges of office.[35]

The duties of the university musicians were similar to those of the city waits. They had to perform 'loude musicke' using wind instruments both for time-keeping and at public events at colleges and halls, and 'low musicke' for indoor entertainment. There was a tradition of annual 'music nights', benefit occasions at which the musicians played at particular colleges in return for money. The 'music

---

[32] *Selections from the Records of the City of Oxford 1509–1583*, ed. W. H. Turner (Oxford 1880), 299, 394. I owe most of the following information and bibliography on the 'common musicians' to the work of Mr W. R. Loosemore and Professor J. R. Elliott.

[33] W. Woodfill, *Musicians in English Society from Elizabeth to Charles I* (Princeton 1953), 74–108.

[34] References to the waits and musicians in the seventeenth century are found in the following: *Oxford Council Acts 1583–1626*, ed. H. E. Salter (OHS lxxxvii 1928), 42, 151–2; *Oxford Council Acts 1626–65*, ed. M. G. Hobson and H. E. Salter (OHS xcv 1933), 17–18, 48, 55, 79, 89, 189, 413, 416–17, 441, 466–7; *Oxford Council Acts 1665–1701*, ed. M. G. Hobson (OHS new ser. ii 1939), 66, 68, 88, 126–7. These references apply to the entire section and will not be cited individually.

[35] Bodl. MS Twyne–Langbaine 4, fos 105–8; OUA matriculations 1615–47, SP/2/PP, fos 339ʳ, 348ᵛ; Bloxam, *Reg. Magdalen* ii. 191.

nights' of Merton College, Queen's College, and Christ Church seem to have been in February, while that of Lincoln College was in October. As contemporary accounts reveal, these visits to raise money were an opportunity for more general celebrations.[36]

In 1636 the university musicians were employed to play at the royal plays performed at Christ Church on the occasion of the visit of King Charles and Henrietta Maria. They probably provided incidental music between acts as well as fanfares for royal entries. The music for this royal visit was a collaborative effort between London and Oxford musicians. Henry and William Lawes (who composed much of the music for the plays), Davis Mell, and other singers from the Chapel Royal were joined by the Christ Church organist Edward Lowe, Stephen Goodall, chaplain of Christ Church, and 'Mr Coleman', doubtless Simon Coleman, organist of New College.[37]

In later seventeenth-century accounts it is sometimes difficult to distinguish between the city waits and the university musicians, since players occasionally transferred their allegiance between city and university, or else played for both employers. On certain occasions their functions obviously combined: at his visit in 1687, for instance, James II was entertained by 'the wind musick or waits belonging to the city and universitie'.[38]

Despite their role as professional musicians, all these men were forced to supplement their income from other sources. Many of them earned a living by running alehouses or dancing academies in the city, and the association between music and the taverns was always strong. John Baldwin, a city wait of 1603, was licensed for the Bell in 1604; Richard Burren, a city wait in 1628, became a licensed alehouse-keeper in 1631. Among the university musicians John Gerard was similarly licensed in 1629/30, while Richard Creeke ran the Crown and Lute in St Peter le Bailey in 1670/1. Gerard also ran a music shop where he sold books and instruments. The vintner Thomas Wood had a dancing-school at a tavern in High Street in the early 1650s. In 1652 his ex-apprentice John Newman set up a rival establishment in Ship Street. John Bannister, who had visited Oxford in 1665, settled in the city in 1675 in order to teach dancing.[39]

Young gentlemen at the university were able to take advantage of this musical

---

[36] The following refer to various 'music nights' and payments to musicians: Wood, *Life and Times* ii. 75, 479; *Collectanea* i. 264 (James Wilding's account book); *Collectanea* iv. 179 (Thomas Baskerville's account of Oxford); *Diary of Thomas Crosfield*, ed. Boas, 8, 86, 110.

[37] J. R. Elliott and J. Buttrey, 'The royal plays at Christ Church in 1636: a new document', *Theatre Research International* x (1984), 93–106.

[38] Wood, *Life and Times* iii. 230.

[39] Apart from references in n. 34, see *VCH Oxon.* iv. 427, 432–3; Oxford City Arch. N.4.1 (licences 1578–1653): John Jarrett 20 August 1630, Richard Burren 30 September 1631. A valuable source of information on musicians and singing-men of the university is provided by the OUA chancellor's court inventories. The following examples are taken from the years 1634–6: OUA chancellor's ct inventories, Hyp./A/37, fos 168ᵛ, 171ʳ, 184ᵛ (Gollege), 117ʳ (Halwoode), 96ʳ, 110ᶠ, 145ʳ, 151ʳ, 180ᵛ (Polley), 222ʳ, 228ʳ (Gerard); Hyp./A/38, fos 42ᵛ, 52ᵛ (Gerard vs Polley, Halwoode, Stacie, Jones). The inventory of John Gerard or Jarrett (12 October 1635) is ibid. Hyp./B/13/, fo 3. The instruments were valued at a total of £6 13s 4d, the music books 15s.

environment to arrange private tuition for singing and instrumental playing. William Freke, youngest son of Sir Thomas Freke of Shroton, Dorset, had viol lessons from Thomas Gollege during the period 1620–1 while he was studying at St Mary's Hall in Oxford. Freke paid 5s a month for his lessons. In 1621 he bought a viol bow for 2s 6d and a viol for £2 10s 6d.[40] In 1653 Anthony Wood went to an Oxford musician, Charles Griffiths, to learn the violin. He was subsequently taught by John Parker, a university musician, and William James, a dancing-master trained in France. James's school was just outside the north gate of the city.[41]

The practice of professionals and amateurs making music together informally on a regular basis seems to have begun in Oxford around 1642 and to have continued, perhaps with an occasional hiatus, throughout the rest of the century. John Wilson and the organist George Jeffries were among those displaced musicians who played 'in the rooms of gentlemen of the university for the entertainment of each other' during the civil war years. Whether meetings continued between Wilson's departure in 1646 and his return as music professor a decade later is unclear. But after this, as has already been described, the music school was a focus for such activity under the successive direction of Wilson, Lowe, and Goodson.[42]

Wood's records of the various music meetings he attended in the late 1650s and 1660s reveal the close interrelationship between the music school and informal groups which met elsewhere in the city.[43] The most long-standing of these was run by William Ellis, the ejected organist of St John's College. By the time Wood became involved in 1656, weekly meetings were taking place at Ellis's lodgings in Broad Street (on the site of the New Bodleian), first on Thursdays, then on Tuesdays. Members were charged 6d a time, which provided a useful income for the displaced musician. Wood records the membership for 1656 and 1659, noting the distribution of instruments and voices. Among the music masters listed for 1656 were Ellis himself (organ, virginals), Wilson (consort leader, lute), Lowe (organ), Gervace Westcote (viol), and John Parker, Wood's teacher (violin). Graduate members in that year included Wood (MA All Souls, violin) and Thomas Janes (MA Magdalen, theorbo, lute). The younger Kenelm Digby (MA All Souls,

[40] G. W. Prothero, 'A seventeenth-century account book', *EHR* vii (1892), 88–102, especially 92–6. The account book kept for John and Richard Newdigate while they were at Trinity College refers to payments for instrumental lessons and lute strings: 'The undergraduate account book of John and Richard Newdigate, 1618–1621', ed. V. Larminie, *Camden Miscellany* xxx (Camden Soc. 4th ser. xxxix 1990).

[41] Wood, *Life and Times* i. 181–2; D. C. Price, *Patrons and Musicians of the English Renaissance* (Cambridge 1981), 24–6.

[42] Hawkins, *General History of Music*, ii. 680; J. P. Wainwright, 'George Jeffreys' copies of Italian music', *Royal Musical Association Research Chronicle* xxiii (1990), 109–24. Wainwright suggests that the Italian vocal and instrumental music that Jeffreys copied may have been intended for informal performance at the court in Oxford.

[43] For details of these various groups, see Wood, *Life and Times* i. 204–6, 273–5; Bellingham, 'Musical circle of Anthony Wood', 33–54. An autograph poem entitled 'Dr Wilson and his lute at Ellis his meeting' by the young Robert Southwell (later knighted and FRS) of 31 December 1655 predates Wood's first reference: Bodl. MS Eng. poet. f. 6, fos 24–23 (written in reverse order).

violin) and Matthew Hutton (MA Brasenose, viol) were among those whose names appear for 1659.

Most of the music masters dropped out of Ellis's meetings once they had regained their college and cathedral posts, and Wilson and Lowe were busy with the music school. However, meetings certainly went on until 1669, when Wood ceased to attend, and may have continued until Ellis's death in 1679. During the period between about 1656 and 1662 some of the 'scholastical musicians' and music masters who played at Ellis's also met on a regular basis in various colleges on Friday nights. Wood himself may have acted as host for some meetings in 1657/8, and he certainly played at several of those held by Thomas Janes at Magdalen which Westcote also attended. Westcote, a singing master of St John's, was also the owner of a tavern. In 1662 a group of singers began to meet there regularly, forming a catch club that Wood attended for about six months.

The longest-running series of weekly college meetings was organized by Narcissus Marsh, an enthusiastic player of the bass viol. These first took place around 1666 at his rooms in Exeter College and moved to St Alban Hall (on the east side of Merton College) when Marsh became principal there in 1673. Following Marsh's departure in 1678 to take up his position as provost of Trinity College, Dublin, weekly college meetings continued under the guidance of Henry Aldrich at Christ Church.[44]

A great deal of music that was actually played by these various groups still survives.[45] Jeffries, Wilson, Ellis, Lowe, and Hutton were among those who were active in both copying and collecting. Much of the music favoured at these weekly meetings was a very conservative repertory, distinctively for viol ensemble, deriving from the first half of the seventeenth century by composers such as Alfonso Ferrabosco the younger, Coprario, Tomkins, and Jenkins. The younger generation of composers cultivated at Oxford, notably Christopher Simpson and Matthew Locke, while continuing to write music for viols, increasingly gave prominence in upper parts to the violin.

From the late 1650s the instruments of the violin family began to gain in popularity as suitable for gentlemen and not merely common fiddlers. In March 1658 the best violinist in England, Davis Mell, came to Oxford and impressed everyone with his skill. Wood and others from All Souls 'did give him a very handsome entertainment' by way of appreciation. Mell's talent, however, was soon outshone by that of Thomas Baltzar, a German violinist who had mastered the art of polyphonic playing on the violin to an impressive degree. (Their respective abilities can

[44] Wood, *Athenae* iv. 498; Wood, *Life and Times* i. 275; Dublin, Archbishop Marsh Library MS Z2. 2. 3. b, fo 9 (Marsh's diary). For Marsh's experimental interests, see p. 639 below.

[45] R. Charteris, 'Consort music manuscripts in Archbishop Marsh's Library, Dublin', *Royal Musical Association Research Chronicle* xiii (1977), 27–63; R. Charteris, 'Matthew Hutton (1638–1711) and his manuscripts in York Minster Library', *Galpin Society Journal* xxviii (1975), 2–6; P. J. Willets, 'Music from the circle of Anthony Wood at Oxford', *British Music Quarterly* xxiv (1961), 71–5; J. A. Irving, 'Matthew Hutton and York Minster MSS M. 3./1–4 (S)', *Music Review* xliv (1983), 163–77; T. Crawford, 'An unusual consort revealed in an Oxford manuscript', *Chelys* vi (1975–6), 61–8. See also n. 17 above.

perhaps be gauged from the two sets of divisions on 'John come kiss me now' by
the rival musicians published in John Playford's *The Division Violin* (1684); Baltzar's
require much more virtuosity than those of Mell.) In July of the same year, 1658,
Baltzar was hosted by Ellis and played on two occasions at the latter's lodgings,
causing a great sensation with his virtuosity. John Wilkins, warden of Wadham
College, invited Baltzar and other musicians to play in consort at Wadham, in order
to see and hear the musician in action.[46]

In 1656 Wood and his teacher had been the only members of Ellis's group who
played the violin. In 1659 three more graduates were listed as playing the violin,
presumably inspired by Mell and Baltzar, some of whose music was collected for
use at the weekly meetings. This trend is reflected in what is known about the
instruments in the music school collection. By 1675 the collection included two
violins (together costing £15), and the list of the music school's holdings dated
1682 includes a reference to five violins.[47] Local demand encouraged at least one
instrument-maker to set up his business in Oxford. On 26 February 1668/9
William Baker, instrument-maker, was made freeman of the city. Baker's surviving
instruments comprise a violin dated 1683, two violas (one dated 1683), a small viol,
and a cello dated 1672, one of the earliest known to have been made in England.
There is a strong likelihood that the music school violins were the product of
Baker's workshop.[48]

The richness of practical music in Oxford is well documented. Less well known is
the importance of speculative music theory, linked as it was to the mathematical
sciences, medicine, and the study of Greek and Latin authors.[49] Thomas Allen of
Gloucester Hall, sometime university lecturer in mathematics, was responsible for
inspiring enthusiasm for the mathematical sciences among a whole generation of
students during the period 1570 to 1632.[50] St John's College was an important centre for some of the early interest in speculative music theory. Matthew Gwinne,

[46] Wood, *Life and Times* i. 241–2, 256–7; Bellingham, 'Musical circle of Anthony Wood', 62–4;
P. Holman, 'Thomas Baltzar (?1631–1663), the "incomparable *Lubicer* on the violin" ', *Chelys* xiii (1984),
3–38; M. P. Fernandez and P. C. Fernandez, 'Davis Mell, musician and clockmaker and an analysis of
the clockmaking trade in 17th-century London', *Antiquarian Horology* xvi (1987), 602–17.

[47] Crum, 'Early lists', 27. In the terminology of the time a small viola would have been called an alto
violin, a large viola a tenor, and a cello a bass violin—though characteristically tuned a tone lower than
the modern cello. Therefore this reference is doubtless to a full set of different instruments.

[48] For the date of Baker's freedom see Oxford City Arch. 'Hannisters 1662–1699' (L.5.4); Baker's
known instruments appear in the following catalogues: *The Worshipful Company of Musicians: loan exhibition June–July 1904* (Novello 1909), 155–6; Christie's musical instrument sale 22 November 1989, 36; *Shapes
of the Baroque: the historical development of bowed string instruments*, exhibition at the Amsterdam Gallery at
Lincoln Center, 22 March–10 June 1989, presented by W. Monical (American Federation of Violin and
Bow-makers 1989), 76–7. I owe these references to Peter Trevelyan.

[49] For a definition of speculative music theory (harmonic science) and an introduction to the many
topics which it embraced, see J. C. Kassler, *The Science of Music in Britain 1714–1830: a catalogue of writings,
lectures and inventions* (2 vols New York and London 1979) i, pp. xxv–lxii; J. C. Kassler, 'Music as a model
in early science', *History of Science* xx (1982), 103–39. On the sciences in late sixteenth-century Oxford,
see J. McConica, 'Elizabethan Oxford: the collegiate society' in *The Collegiate University*, 716–21.

[50] Feingold, *Mathematicians' Apprenticeship*, 82–3.

physician to Sir Henry Unton, an important patron of music, was in 1582 a regent master and lecturer in music at the college. Gwinne became the first lecturer in physic at Gresham College in London in 1597.[51]

The early interest in music philosophy at St John's College seems to have been closely linked to a concern for the fate of instrumental music in public worship. In 1588 John Case, a physician and fellow of St John's, published his *Apologia musices*, a defence of church music as well as secular performance.[52] The connection between music and medicine was continued by the physician and hermetic philosopher Robert Fludd, who apparently wrote the section on music of his *Utriusque cosmi ... historia* (1617–19) during the years 1592–8 when he was at St John's.[53] Thus there was already a well-established tradition of music philosophy and defence of musical performance at St John's College by the time Laud embarked on his own reform activities.

Laud shared an interest in the philosophical dimension of music with two other St John's men, William Juxon and Christopher Wren senior. Some time around 1616 when Laud was 'newly made' dean of Gloucester, the three men went to Gloucester cathedral and experimented with the whispering gallery there, as appears from Wren's annotations to the published account of this gallery in Francis Bacon's *Sylva sylvarum* (1626).[54]

Music was not only an important branch of mathematics, it was also closely related to philology and the study of ancient authorities in their original language. Among the many manuscripts and books brought back to Oxford from the continent by sixteenth-century scholars were copies of Greek music texts, and these found their way into various college libraries and the Bodleian. Among the Greek music manuscripts donated to the Bodleian by Sir Henry Savile in 1609 were copies of Ptolemy and Aristides Quintilianus. In 1627 Peter Turner, Savilian professor of geometry, was employed by John Selden to translate and collate Greek music manuscripts housed in the Oxford libraries, including copies of Gaudentius and Alypius.[55]

Edmund Chilmead, a Student of Christ Church in the 1630s, was skilled in classics, mathematics, and music. He used his talents to great effect in the study of ancient and modern music theory. In 1636 Chilmead was engaged by the university

---

[51] Wood, *Athenae* ii. 415–18. Gwinne's 'Oratio in laudem musices' (1582) is published in J. Ward, *Lives of the Professors of Gresham College* (London 1740), Appendix, 81–7.

[52] C. B. Schmitt, *John Case and Aristotelianism in Renaissance England* (Kingston and Montreal 1983), 87–8; M. C. Boyd, *Elizabethan Music and Musical Criticism* (Philadelphia 1940, 2nd edn Philadelphia 1962), 28–32; J. W. Binns, 'John Case and the *Praise of Musicke*', *Music and Letters* lv (1974), 444–53.

[53] J. Godwin, *Robert Fludd: hermetic philosopher and surveyor of two worlds* (London 1978), 5–6.

[54] Wren's account of this occasion is in the marginal notes of his copy of the 1631 edition of Bacon's *Sylva*, 46 (Bodl. T 11. 20 Th). Bacon's reference to the whispering place is in the *Sylva*, century 2, experiment 148. See also P. M. Gouk, 'Acoustics in the early Royal Society 1660–1680', *Notes and Records of the Royal Society* xxxvi (1981–2), 161–2.

[55] Bodl. MSS Auct. F.1.2, F.1.3, MSS Selden *supra* 121–2, MS Selden *supra* 108, fos 180, 228; M. Feingold and P. M. Gouk, 'An early critique of Bacon's *Sylva sylvarum*: Edmund Chilmead's treatise on sound', *Annals of Science* xl (1983), 139–57.

to catalogue the Baroccian collection of Greek manuscripts given by William Herbert, earl of Pembroke, in 1629. At about the same time he wrote an essay 'De musica antiqua Graeca' and transcribed three odes of Dionysius, which were all published posthumously by John Fell in 1672. Chilmead also began to prepare a critical edition of Gaudentius' *Isagoge harmonica*. When informed by Selden that Marcus Meibom, a philologist and critic from Holstein, was preparing an edition of Gaudentius along with other ancient Greek and Latin commentators of music, he allowed his notes to be used for this edition. Between 1650 and 1652 Selden acted as the intermediary between Meibom and Gerard Langbaine, keeper of the university archives until his death in 1658, who undertook to provide Meibom with transcripts of the ancient music manuscripts in Oxford.[56]

Charles Butler, initially a chorister at Magdalen College, later music master at Magdalen School, was another Oxford MA who combined music with an interest in philology, grammar, and classical scholarship. He was also an apiarist. Butler's *Feminine Monarchy: or a treatise concerning bees*, published in 1609, was the first book printed in Oxford to contain musical notation, which he subsequently elaborated into a 'bees' madrigal' for four voices, laid out in table-book form. He later went on to publish works on grammar and rhetoric, and his *Principles of Musick, in Singing and Setting* (London 1636). This work, written in Butler's own system of phonetic orthography, reveals his knowledge of ancient, medieval, and modern music theory, and his desire to refute specifically puritan objections to church music.[57]

Another noted Greek scholar and mathematician interested in the study of ancient music theory was John Wallis. Wallis first came to Oxford in 1649 as the Savilian professor of geometry and held the post until his death in 1703. In 1658 he succeeded Langbaine as keeper of the university archives. Although Wallis was obviously interested in music theory for many years, in connection with his work in natural philosophy, his first work on music, a Latin translation of Ptolemy's *Harmonicorum libri*, was not published until 1682. This edition included an appendix dealing with the history of Greek music theory which was used extensively by John Hawkins in his *History of Music* of 1776.[58]

In 1699 the third volume of Wallis's *Opera mathematica* appeared, including his Latin translations of two musical treatises, Porphyry's commentary on Ptolemy, and Bryennius, the last compilation of Greek music theory in the Byzantine period.[59] Wallis's translations remained the standard editions of these texts until well into

[56] Bodl. MS Selden *supra* 109, fos 302, 304ᵛ, 309ᵛ, 313, 325 *et seq.*; Feingold and Gouk, 'Chilmead', 141–5; on Meibom, see Hawkins, *General History of Music* i. 110–11, ii. 642–4; *New Grove* xii. 68–9.

[57] Carpenter, *Music in the Medieval and Renaissance Universities*, 185–6; F. Madan, *The Early Oxford Press* (OHS xxix 1895), 73; *New Grove* iii. 577–8.

[58] *Claudii Ptolemaei harmonicorum libri tres*, ed. John Wallis (Oxford 1682), 'Appendix de veterum harmonica ad hodiernam comparata'; Hawkins, *General History of Music* i *passim* (e.g. 31, 36–8). On Wallis see P. M. Gouk, 'Music in the natural philosophy of the early Royal Society' (London Ph. D. thesis 1982), 233–9.

[59] John Wallis, 'Porphryii in harmonica Ptolemaei commentarius, nunc primum ex codd. MSS (Graece et Latine) editus' in his *Opera mathematica* (3 vols Oxford 1693–9) iii. 183–355; John Wallis, 'Manuelis Bryenni harmonica ex codd. MSS nunc primum edita' ibid. 359–508.

the twentieth century. These works and a series of letters published in the *Philosophical Transactions of the Royal Society* in 1698 established Wallis as a leading expert on music theory.[60] He was also interested in language and grammar, and the teaching of the deaf and dumb. These were topics closely related to music, being concerned with sound and the voice.[61]

Wallis was not the only scholar renowned for his musical expertise in Restoration Oxford. Henry Aldrich, dean of Christ Church from 1689, was an enthusiastic performer, composer, and collector of all types of music, both practical and theoretical. As dean of the college he stipulated that all the singing clerks should have had a suitable training in music before being admitted, thereby ensuring a high standard from the choir. Aldrich himself was not lacking in such skills. In 1672 some verses by John Fell (then dean of Christ Church) spoken before Encaenia were set to music by Aldrich and sung by masters of music of the university.[62] Aldrich's collection of music, which still remains in Christ Church, includes 8,000 pieces of sixteenth- and seventeenth-century music, both English and foreign, particularly Italian. According to Hawkins, Aldrich 'formed a design of writing a history of the science of music' which was never completed. The material which Aldrich gathered included information about different types of musical instrument (the Talbot manuscripts), a mathematical music treatise by Nicholas Mercator, and an unfinished history of music from the Greeks and Hebrews to modern times, possibly by Aldrich himself.[63]

Aldrich was also responsible for encouraging Peter de Walpergen, an immigrant German typefounder in Oxford, to design two different round-note typefaces for music. The first of these typefaces is found in *Musica Oxonienses* (Oxford 1698), while the second is in Wallis's 1699 edition of Ptolemy's *Harmonicorum libri* which was republished along with his translations of Porphyry and Bryennius.[64]

---

[60] John Wallis, 'A question in music lately proposed to Dr Wallis, concerning the division of the monochord, or section of the musical canon', *Philosophical Transactions of the Royal Society* xx (1698), 80–8; 'A letter of Dr John Wallis to Samuel Pepys esquire, relating to some supposed imperfections in an organ' ibid. 249–56; 'A letter of Dr John Wallis to Mr Andrew Fletcher: concerning the strange effects reported of musick in former times' ibid. 297–303.

[61] John Wallis, *Grammatica linguae anglicanae* (London 1652); J. Wallis, *A Defence of the Royal Society ... in Answer to the Cavils of Dr William Holder* (London 1698); see also C. F. Mullett, '"An arte to make the dumbe to speake, the deafe to heare": a seventeenth-century goal', *Journal of the History of Medicine and Allied Sciences* xxvi (1971), 123–49.

[62] Wood, *Life and Times* ii. 248; W. G. Hiscock, *Henry Aldrich of Christ Church* (Oxford 1960), 32–41; S. Wollenberg, 'Music in eighteenth-century Oxford', *Proceedings of the Royal Musical Association* cviii (1981–2), 77; D. Pinto, 'The music of the Hattons', *Royal Music Association Research Chronicle* xxiii (1990), 79–108.

[63] These are in CA MSS 1130, 1187. Hawkins, *General History of Music* ii. 765–6; Gouk, 'Music in the early Royal Society', 268–83. See also A. Baines, 'James Talbot's manuscript', *Galpin Society Journal* i (1948), 9–26; R. Donington, 'James Talbot's manuscript' ibid. iii (1950), 27–45; W. A. Cocks, 'James Talbot's manuscript' ibid. v (1952), 44–7.

[64] Wallis, *Opera mathematica* iii. 1–187; D. W. Krummel, *English Music Printing 1553–1700* (London 1975), 134–7. Hiscock's claim that the types were modelled on Aldrich's own musical hand is based on a misattribution; they are both the work of an anonymous music scribe. I owe this observation to Dr J. Wainwright, who recently completed his Ph. D. thesis 'The musical patronage of Christopher, first Baron Hatton (1605–1670)' (Cambridge 1993).

The men mentioned here as being interested in Greek music theory, notably Chilmead and Wallis, were, along with many of their contemporaries, also involved in the experimental philosophy of the period. Largely due to the influence of Francis Bacon's *Sylva sylvarum* and Marin Mersenne's *Harmonicorum libri* (Paris 1635) and *Harmonie universelle* (Paris 1636–7), in England music from the 1630s onwards began to be treated not only mathematically as a branch of the quadrivium, but also as sound and motion—a branch of physics and dynamics. Oxford became one of the leading centres for natural philosophy during the seventeenth century, and music was an important area for such inquiry.[65]

One of the earliest examples of this interest is 'An examination . . . of the *Natural History*' by Edmund Chilmead, a series of *quaeres* on the second and third centuries of the *Sylva* which are concerned with the nature of sound. In the treatise, written in the mid-1640s, Chilmead revealed his familiarity with the developments in the field of musical acoustics made by Mersenne and his circle. Chilmead also gave the first correct explanation for overtones in a vibrating string. It is clear that scholars such as Chilmead and Butler, the author of *The Principles of Musick*, which also contains references to Mersenne's work, were fully up-to-date with developments in this branch of natural philosophy.[66]

One of the most important groups of natural philosophers in Oxford was that which revolved around John Wilkins, warden of Wadham College between 1648 and 1660. Wilkins, as already noted, was very fond of music; in 1658 he invited Wood and others in Ellis's music group to play with Thomas Baltzar at the college. Members of Wilkins's group included Christopher Wren, Robert Hooke, and John Wallis, who went on to become active members of the Royal Society. Among their many interests was the desire to create a universal language (possibly involving the use of musical notation) and to build an organ which could articulate the sounds of the human voice.[67] In 1653 another member of the group, William Brouncker, published *Renatus Des-Cartes Excellent Compendium of Musick*, with a series of *Animadversions* added to the translation. The *Compendium*, written in 1619, was a popular music theory treatise throughout the seventeenth century in England. It provided some of the mathematical foundations of music in a form readily accessible to musicians and educated amateurs alike.[68] Interest in such subjects extended

[65] On Oxford science see M. Feingold, 'The mathematical sciences and new philosophies', above; R. T. Gunther, *Early Science in Oxford* (15 vols Oxford 1920–67); C. Webster, *The Great Instauration* (London 1975); R. G. Frank, 'John Aubrey, FRS, John Lydall, and science at Commonwealth Oxford', *Notes and Records of the Royal Society* xxvii (1973), 195–217; N. Tyacke, 'Science and religion at Oxford before the civil war' in D. Pennington and K. V. Thomas (eds), *Puritans and Revolutionaries* (Oxford 1978), 73–93; Feingold, *Mathematicians' Apprenticeship*. Information on the Restoration period is also found in K. T. Hoppen, *The Common Scientist in the Seventeenth Century: a study of the Dublin Philosophical Society 1683–1708* (London 1970).

[66] Charles Butler, *The Principles of Musick* (London 1636), 33. See also nn. 55–6 above.

[67] B. J. Shapiro, *John Wilkins 1641–1672* (Berkeley and Los Angeles 1969), 118–47; J. P. Knowlson, *Universal Language Schemes in England and France 1600–1800* (Toronto 1975), 81–4, 95–8.

[68] On Brouncker see Wood, *Fasti* ii. 98–9; *New Grove* iii. 339–40; Gouk, 'Music in the early Royal Society', 134–9.

far beyond the university. Christopher Wren, his father the dean of Windsor, and William Holder, his brother-in-law, all closely connected with Oxford, were interested in acoustics, the teaching of the deaf and dumb, and practical music. William Holder later became sub-dean of the Chapel Royal and in 1694 published his *Treatise on the Natural Grounds and Principles of Harmony* in which he examined music in the context of natural philosophy.[69]

The parallels between the informal groups of natural philosophers and informal groups of musicians who began to meet regularly in Oxford are striking. During the Interregnum Wadham was the principal meeting-place for the natural philosophers, while Ellis's lodgings in Broad Street were the main centre for the musicians, but meetings for both activities also occurred elsewhere in colleges, lodgings, and taverns. Both groups shared the same social mix of gentlemen and practitioners, as well as the emphasis on practical 'exercises' and demonstrations. During a brief period in 1663 Wood himself went to the weekly chemistry lectures of the German physician Peter Stahl as well as continuing his musical commitments.[70]

The connection between music and experimental philosophy at Oxford continued after the Restoration. We know from John Wallis that in 1665 members of the Royal Society moved to Oxford on account of the plague and undertook some experiments on musical strings and pendulums there.[71] As already noted, Marsh was the principal organizer of weekly musical activity among university members until his departure in 1678. It was through Marsh that the discovery of nodes in a vibrating string, made independently by William Noble of Merton College and Thomas Pigot of Wadham College around 1673/4, was made widely known. In 1677 an essay by Marsh on sympathetic vibration was published in Robert Plot's *Natural History of Oxfordshire*. The essay discussed the discovery of the phenomenon in some detail and related it to the sympathetic vibration of strings. Wallis also communicated the discovery of nodes to the editor of the *Philosophical Transactions* published in the same year.[72] Marsh became a founder member of the Dublin Philosophical Society in the early 1680s. In 1682 the Oxford Philosophical Society was founded, including among its members Robert Plot, Wallis, Ralph Bathurst, and Aldrich. Modelled on the Royal Society, the Oxford Philosophical Society held weekly meetings in which various topics were discussed. In 1683 Aldrich is reported to have spoken on the structure of the ear and theories of hearing. Three years later Joshua Walker of Brasenose College, and another member of this society, read a 'Discourse concerning sounds and echoes', an account of his attempts to measure the speed of sound. This may well be identical to his article

[69] Gouk, 'Music in the early Royal Society', 57–8, 284–93; R. L. Colie, 'Dean Wren's marginalia and early science at Oxford', *Bodleian Library Record* vi (1960), 541–51; J. M. Stanley, 'William Holder: his position in seventeenth-century philosophy and music theory' (Cincinnati Ph. D. thesis 1983).

[70] Wood, *Life and Times* i. 475; Webster, *Great Instauration*, 153–78.

[71] T. Birch, *History of the Royal Society of London* (4 vols London 1756–7) ii. 68.

[72] Narcissus Marsh, 'Essay touching the sympathy between lute or viol strings' in R. Plot, *Natural History of Oxfordshire* (Oxford 1677), 288–99; J. Wallis, 'Dr Wallis's letter to the publisher, concerning a new musical discovery', *Philosophical Transactions of the Royal Society* xii (1677), 839–44.

published in the *Philosophical Transactions* of 1698.[73] Sound and acoustics as well as practical music were important subjects to men such as Wallis and Aldrich.

Musical life at Oxford in the seventeenth century was thus rich and varied, involving both professional and amateur activity. It is true that there was no formal training for the music degrees awarded at the university. Yet it is clear that the statutes alone give no indication of the extent to which practical and theoretical musical instruction was actually available for members of the university. At the music school, in college rooms and taverns, there was ample opportunity for the teaching and performance of vocal and instrumental music. A number of informal groups were actively involved in music-making by the 1640s. There was a similar, informal interest in the theoretical side of music among scholars trained in classics, philology, and mathematics. In many cases this interest overlapped with the new experimental philosophy, another subject that had no formal status in the curriculum.

[73] Bodl. MS Ashmole 1810, fo 3, MS Ashmole 1811, fo 23; J. Walker, 'Some experiments concerning sounds', *Philosophical Transactions of the Royal Society* xx (1698), 433–8.

12

Drama

JOHN R. ELLIOTT Jr.

UNLIKE music drama never had an official position in the Oxford curriculum, as it was not considered to have a sufficiently philosophical dimension. But if it lacked a faculty it did not lack students. From the 1540s on, largely following a model provided by Cambridge, drama played an extensive, authorized, role both in college life and in the public life of the university. This role was sometimes recreational, sometimes ceremonial, and sometimes quasi-curricular. We know of two instances in which arts students were required to write a play in order to supplicate for their BA; one of them described the practice as 'bringing a trifle to receive a hood'.[1] Less trifling was the expenditure by the dean and chapter of Christ Church from 1554 onwards for the annual production of two comedies and two tragedies, one of each pair in Latin and the other in Greek, payments regularly recorded in the treasurer's accounts for the next sixty years.[2] Similar allowances of college funds in support of plays, by order of the governing body, are recorded at Magdalen College in 1580 and St John's College in 1582.[3] These formal endorsements of dramatic activities reflect the practical, if not the theoretical, value that drama was deemed to have in the training of young men for public life. For Oxford as for Cambridge humanists, drama was a branch of rhetoric whose educational function was to hone the skills of the future preacher and statesman. As William Gager put it in a letter to John Rainolds in 1592, plays served:

to practyse owre owne style eyther in prose or verse, to be well acquaynted with Seneca or Plautus, [and] honestly to embolden owre pathe; to trye their voyces and confirme their memoryes, to frame their speeche, to conforme them to convenient action; to trye what mettell is in evrye one, and of what disposition thay are of; wherby never any one amongst

---

[1] In 1512 an Edward Watson, college or hall unknown, was admitted to teach in the school of grammar on condition that he write '100 songs (*carmina*) in praise of the university and one comedy (*comediam*)': OUA register G, fo 143. In 1640 Martin Llewellyn of Christ Church presented a play to the dean, Dr Samuel Fell, in order to 'begge degree', an occasion he recorded in a poem printed a few years later: M. Llewellyn, *Men-Miracles with other poemes* (London 1646), 80. This may have been the same play that was scheduled to be performed before King Charles II in Oxford in 1661 (see n. 54 below).

[2] J. McConica, 'Elizabethan Oxford: the collegiate society' in *The Collegiate University*, 652 n. 2; R. E. Alton (ed.), 'The academic drama in Oxford: extracts from the records of four colleges' (Malone Soc. collections v 1959), 62–76. There is no confirmatory evidence, however, that Christ Church ever did perform a play in Greek.

[3] MCA Vice-president's register 1547–1839, fo 42ᵛ; SJM register 1557–91, fo 209ᵛ.

vs, that I knowe, was made the worse, many have byn muche the better, as I dare reporte
me to all the university.[4]

It is important to stress this official encouragement of drama since the influence
of the opponents of play-acting is sometimes exaggerated. At no time in the sixteenth or early seventeenth centuries was drama in Oxford as marginal an activity
for students as it has been for most of the twentieth century. The objections of
opponents such as Stephen Gosson and John Rainolds to 'stage-plays' fell largely
on deaf ears in Oxford, however effective they may have been elsewhere.[5] There
is no evidence that such complaints produced any change in the frequency with
which plays were put on or in the types of plays produced. Nor were the occasional royal or cancellarian decrees prohibiting stage-plays intended to have such
an effect. Leicester's letter to congregation in July 1584, endorsing the reform of
various disorders in the university, approved a ban on professional players but
made an exception for student plays as being 'commendable and greate furderances
of learning', even recommending that they be 'continued at set times and increased,
and the youth of the universitye by good meanes to be incurraged to the decent
and frequent setting fourth of them'.[6] The privy council letter of July 1593 was
similarly directed only at travelling players, and made no mention of student plays.[7]
There was, in fact, a notable increase in the number of play productions in Oxford
during the first two decades of the seventeenth century, at a time when fewer plays
were being produced at Cambridge.

Oxford plays took place principally in those colleges with large numbers of
undergraduates, such as Christ Church, Magdalen, and St John's. They were performed most usually in the college hall (rarely outdoors), and often with the financial support and supervision of the governing body. Many of them were written by
students, most of whose names were not recorded. Some, however, were written
by senior members of the university, who seldom tried to hide their identities,
though they maintained an amateur profile by not usually seeking to publish their
plays (William Gager being a notable exception). From manuscript texts and other
evidence we can gather the names of the principal academic playwrights of the early
seventeenth century: Robert Burton, William Cartwright, Thomas Goffe, and
William Strode of Christ Church; Samuel Bernard, Jasper Fisher, and Peter Heylyn
of Magdalen College; Matthew Gwinne, John Sandsbury, George Wilde, and
Abraham Wright of St John's College. Just as no play written for the professional
stage is known to have been performed by Oxford players, so none of these play-

---

[4] CCCA MS 352, pp. 41–65. The letter is dated 31 July 1592.

[5] J. Barton, 'The king's readers' in *The Collegiate University*, 290–1; McConica, 'Elizabethan Oxford',
652; for an overview see J. A. Barish, *The Antitheatrical Prejudice* (Berkeley and Los Angeles 1981), ch. 4.

[6] OUA register L, fo 242ᵛ.

[7] Ibid. fos 262ʳ⁻ᵛ; P. Williams, 'Elizabethan Oxford: state, church, and university' in *The Collegiate
University*, 404, 427. The privy council letter had been sent to Cambridge at the request of the authorities there, and a copy was sent to Oxford as an afterthought. Similar letters had been sent to Cambridge
in 1575 and 1592. (Information about plays at Cambridge is taken from A. H. Nelson (ed.), *Records of
Early English Drama* (2 vols Toronto 1989).)

wrights is known to have sought further performances of his work outside the university. The only Oxford dramatist who did see a professional production of one of his plays was Cartwright, whose *The Royal Slave* was acted by the Queen's Men at Hampton Court in 1636 by request of the queen herself, though with the university's proviso that Oxford's costumes should not thereafter be worn 'upon any mercenary stage'.[8] By carefully maintaining the distinction between educational drama and the work of 'common players' Oxford managed to preserve its humanist theatrical tradition down to the eve of the civil war.

Not every Oxford play was, of course, educational in the strict sense. Many were written and produced primarily for entertainment, though even these might serve the practical purpose of keeping the students occupied during the long Christmas holidays, when travel elsewhere was difficult and often limited by college statute.[9] The fullest record of such entertainments is preserved in a St John's College manuscript, in the form of an untitled anthology of play-texts with connecting narratives now generally referred to as *The Christmas Prince*. This comprises eight plays written and performed by the students of St John's over the Christmas vacation of 1607–8, on a scale to match the revels of the Inns of Court, on which they are clearly modelled. As at the inns of court, the individual plays marked the stages of a larger festive occasion: the election, coronation, and reign of a Christmas prince, or lord of misrule, who in this year was a bachelor named Thomas Tucker. Performances of the eight plays began as early as 30 November, and continued until Shrovetide. The performance of a ninth play whose text was lost before it could be copied is mentioned, as are three more plays partially written but prevented from performance 'by the shortness of time and want of mony'. Virtually every member of the college was expected to participate in the festivities, since 'it was thought fitt that in so publike a busines euery one should doe something'. Money was initially raised from the senior members, including William Laud who paid 10s, and the balance was paid out of college funds later on.[10] The actors were principally bachelors and undergraduates, and the plays—variously called comedies, tragedies, interludes, 'devices', 'shews', 'mock plays', and 'wassails'—were performed in the hall and open to the public, mainly students from other colleges, some of whom behaved in unruly fashion. Sword-bearing ushers called 'whiflers' were obliged to lock the rowdiest of them in the porter's lodge, and to carry out others who had fainted or been trampled in the crowded hall. On 21 January Christ Church students parodied the St John's offerings with a comedy in their own hall called *Yuletide*, described as 'a medley of Christmas sportes, by which occasion Christmas lords were much jested at'. A counter-attack by St John's was considered but was rendered unnecessary when the dean of Christ Church made a

---

[8] OUA register R, fo 138.

[9] See for example W. H. Stevenson and H. E. Salter, *The Early History of St John's College Oxford* (OHS new ser. i 1939), 149.

[10] SJM Acc. V.E.4, fo 48: 'set on for an end of our Christmas sportes, £vj iijs'.

personal apology. On 13 February, after more work for the whiflers, many broken windows, and two stabbings of actors and spectators, the revels finally ended.[11]

The high spirits on this occasion, tending toward anarchy and even violence, strike us today as more in keeping with a football crowd than a theatre audience, yet they seem to have been taken for granted as part of a holiday ritual. Only one man was brought before the college officials for discipline, the rest of the miscreants being dealt with by the prince's court itself, which devised various imaginative and largely symbolic punishments.[12] The stage dramas were thus overshadowed by the meta-dramatic 'misrule' of the college by the student-prince, whose actions, however, were little more indulgent than those of the college authorities themselves. When President Buckeridge found the hall 'still pestered with the stage and scaffoldes' and filled with snow through the broken windows on the day before Hilary term was to begin, he simply prorogued the term by a week so that more plays could be performed.[13] Oxford's tradition of Christmas revels was considerably older than its tradition of humanist drama, and it remained deeply ingrained in the life of the colleges. The diary of Peter Heylyn tells us that the custom of electing a Christmas prince still flourished at Magdalen throughout the 1620s and 1630s, while at St John's the accounts show regular performances of plays at Christmas, New Year, Twelfth Night, and Candlemas right up to 1641.[14]

The most ambitious dramatic entertainments that Oxford produced, however, came on the occasion of official royal visits, of which there were four between 1566 and 1636. At such times the university as a corporate body became the 'producer' of the plays, in the sense that the vice-chancellor and his deputies oversaw the choice of plays, their financing and furnishing, and their mode of production. These university plays, as they may be called, were all, with one exception, put on in Christ Church hall, both because Christ Church as a royal foundation traditionally acted as host to the sovereign, and because its hall was the largest in either Oxford or indeed Cambridge. Actors in these plays were drawn from all the colleges, though Christ Church men tended to predominate. Occasionally a single college might assume responsibility for the casting of an entire play, as with Magdalen's version of Sophocles' *Ajax* for James I in 1605 or with St John's College's production of George Wilde's *Love's Hospital* for Charles I in 1636. The latter was the only occasion when the royal party ventured out of Christ Church to see a play, which was staged in St John's hall to celebrate the opening of Laud's new quadrangle and was paid for privately by the archbishop himself.[15]

[11] *The Christmas Prince*, ed. F. S. Boas (Malone Soc. reprints, Oxford 1922); for a facsimile of the manuscript, see *The Christmas Prince*, ed. E. J. Richard (Renaissance Latin Drama in England, 1st ser. 11, Hildesheim and New York 1982).

[12] *Christmas Prince*, ed. Boas, 194. On college discipline in general, with examples from St John's, see McConica, 'Elizabethan Oxford', 664–5.

[13] *Christmas Prince*, ed. Boas, 152.

[14] *Memorial of Bishop Waynflete*, ed. J. R. Bloxam (Caxton Soc. xiv 1851), pp. x–xxiv. The earliest reference to a Christmas lord is in the Merton register for 1486: *Registrum annalium Collegii Mertonensis 1483–1521*, ed. H. E. Salter (OHS lxxvi 1923), 94.

[15] The expense sheets survive in PRO SP16/348, no. 85.

Preparations for such royal visits began with an official letter from the chancellor to the vice-chancellor, advising him of the nature of the occasion and requesting him to provide suitable entertainments. The letter generally stressed that it was the university as a whole which was providing the entertainment and that each college and hall, as well as each student (with the exception of poor scholars), was to bear an appropriate share of the financial burden.[16] The chief beneficiary of this stipulation was Christ Church, which was exempted from making even a proportional contribution, in exchange for the use of its facilities. A committee of delegates was then formed to supervise the entertainments and to collect the money to pay for them. Presumably the delegates also made the choice of plays and playwrights, though unfortunately few records of what options they were given and how they made their decisions have survived. All of the plays presented, except for Sophocles' *Ajax*, were written by Oxford men, in most cases fresh for the occasion. The delegates then drew up a list of the valuations of each college's estates and levied a rate against them to pay the costs of the productions. They also levied a rate for each student depending on his status, the sons of earls bearing the heaviest burden, and so on down the social ladder. If this system proved insufficient to meet the actual costs, then it was applied again after the royal guests had departed, a procedure that had to be called into use after the expensive entertainment of Charles I in 1636 which ran to £843, a fraction of the cost of a court masque but a lavish amount for Oxford.[17]

Our principal information on the plays put on for Queen Elizabeth in August 1566 comes from two eye-witness accounts: one by a spectator, John Bereblock, which survives in three manuscript copies, the other by an actor, Miles Windsor, which survives in two significantly different holograph versions. Bereblock's account, in Latin, says little about the content of the plays (none of whose texts survive), but gives a vivid description of how Christ Church hall was fitted out for the occasion.[18] Both the walls and the ceiling were lined with gold panelling to create the effect of an ancient Roman palace (*veteris Romani palatii*). Scaffolds for the audience were placed at one end of the hall and along each of the side walls. Boxes for the more important spectators were built at the top of the scaffolds, while ordinary spectators (*populus*) stood around the stage. This may have been placed at the west end of the hall, opposite the screen, with a throne at the centre for Elizabeth,

[16] See for example Laud's letter of 1636 in W. Laud, *Remains* (2 vols London 1695–1700) ii. 100.

[17] J. R. Elliott Jr and J. Buttrey, 'The royal plays at Christ Church in 1636: a new document', *Theatre Research International* x (1985), 93–109.

[18] Bereblock's account, called *Commentarii siue ephemerae actiones rerum illustrium Oxonii gestarum in adventu serenissimae Principis Elisabethae*, survives in (*a*) Bodl. MS Add. a. 63, fos 1–22; (*b*) Bodl. MS Rawlinson d. 1071, fos 1–25; (*c*) Folger Shakespeare Library MS V.a.109, fos 1–24. Quotations given here are from *a*. All three were copied, probably from a common lost original, soon after the events they describe. Manuscripts *b* and *c* bear dedications to William Brook and William Petre, the last of whom died in 1572. Manuscript *b* also has the signature of Thomas Hearne on the fly-leaf and was used for his edition of the work (in *Historia Vitae et Regni Ricardi II* (Oxford 1729), 253–96). Hearne's edition, but not the original manuscript, was collated with *a* in C. Plummer, *Elizabethan Oxford* (OHS viii 1886), 111–50. The Folger manuscript remains unpublished.

who sat facing the audience.[19] The scenery consisted of classical stage-houses, resembling 'splendid palaces' (*magnifica palatia*), which also served as the actors' dressing-rooms. Bereblock gives short plot synopses of the three plays presented, but fails to mention either their titles or their authors. Miles Windsor's account, in English, survives in two different versions, both now bound into a single manuscript in the Corpus Christi College archives.[20] Windsor lists the three plays as *Marcus Geminus*, a Roman history play in Latin by Toby Matthew of Christ Church; *Palamon and Arcyte*, a two-part play in English, genre unspecified, by Richard Edwards, a former Corpus man now master of the Children of the Chapel; and *Progne*, a Latin tragedy by James Calfhill of Christ Church. Windsor, who played the part of Perithous in Edwards's play, which was a dramatization of Chaucer's 'Knight's Tale', appears not to have attended the other two performances, but provides nevertheless a list of the actors who appeared in all three plays.[21] This includes the name of Toby Matthew, who may be presumed to have acted in his own play, a practice not uncommon in Oxford (Thomas Goffe is known to have acted the leading part in his play *The Courageous Turk* at Christ Church in 1619[22]).

Windsor's most detailed information is naturally about the play that he himself

[19] G. Wickham, *Early English Stages 1300–1660* (3 vols in 4 London and New York 1959–81) i. 357–8; T. J. Manning, 'The staging of plays at Christ Church, Oxford, 1582–92' (Michigan Ph. D. thesis 1972), 66–9. Bereblock's wording is ambiguous: he says that a 'theatrum' was built 'in the upper part of the hall, which looks back on the west ('parte illius superiori, qua occidentem respicit')'. The existence of a screen in Christ Church hall at this time has recently been demonstrated by J. Orrell, 'The theatre at Christ Church, Oxford, in 1605', *Shakespeare Survey* 35 (1982), 129–40.

[20] CCCA MS 257, fos 104–23. This work has been generally misattributed to Thomas Neale, an error originated by a scribe who copied an abridgement of it into what is now Folger Shakespeare Library MS V.a.176, fos 167–74. That manuscript was then copied by Thomas Baker into BL MS Harleian 7033, fos 150–7, which in turn was printed in J. Nichols (ed.), *Progresses of Queen Elizabeth* (3 vols London 1788–1805, 2nd edn London 1823) i. 95–100, and in Plummer, *Elizabethan Oxford*, 195–205, all of whom repeat the misattribution. There can be no doubt that it is by Windsor, however, as the Corpus manuscript is in his hand and bears his initials. The copy of one part of it made by Brian Twyne in 1636 in Bodl. MS Twyne 17, pp. 157–67, clearly acknowledges the source as 'Mr Miles Wyndisores obseruations'. Finally, the narrative includes details of events that took place after the royal visit when the queen stayed at the home of Lord Edward Windsor, Miles's cousin, in Bradenton, Buckinghamshire, events that only Miles Windsor among the actors could have observed. Twyne's transcript of Windsor's account was printed by Anthony Wood in *History of the University* ii. 158–63, without attribution. This is the only version of the longer work hitherto known by scholars. The abridgement of Windsor's narrative found in the Folger manuscript and in its anonymous source, Bodl. MS Twyne 21, fos 792–800, is said by the Folger manuscript scribe to be the work of Richard Stephens, who like Windsor was an undergraduate of Corpus at this time: *Register of the University of Oxford*, ed. C. W. Boase (OHS i 1885), 270. But since the scribe's reference to it as 'an extract drawen oute of a longer treatise made by Mr Neale reader of Hebrew at Oxford' is demonstrably wrong, the attribution of the abridgement to Stephens may be wrong also. The two versions of Windsor's work found in the Corpus manuscript comprise a rough draft (fos 115–23) and a much-shortened fair copy (fos 104–14) transcribed in 1636 by Twyne. The title given to both versions is 'The receiving of the queens majesty into Oxford in 1566'. For details of the Corpus manuscript, see John R. Elliott Jr., 'Queen Elizabeth at Oxford: new light on the royal plays of 1566', *English Literary Renaissance* xviii (1988), 218–29.

[21] Printed in F. S. Boas, *University Drama in the Tudor Age* (Oxford 1914), 105–6, 390–3.

[22] D. Carnegie, 'The identification of the hand of Thomas Goffe, academic dramatist and actor', *The Library* 5th ser. xxvi (1971), 161–5; D. Carnegie, 'Actors' parts and the "Play of Poore" ', *Harvard Library Bulletin* xxx (1982), 6.

performed in, *Palamon and Arcyte*, and its main interest lies in the fact that while on stage he was close enough to the throne to hear the queen's reactions to what she saw. As usual, she was voluble and candid, interrupting the actors and speaking back to them and the audience. The chief victim of her wit was an unfortunate young man named John Dalaper, playing a character called Trevatio, whose function in the play we can only guess as he does not appear in Chaucer's tale.[23] This actor was so nervous in the presence of the queen that he forgot his lines and, after exclaiming 'by the masse and Gotes blutt I am owte', decided to whistle a hornpipe instead. At this the queen cried, 'Goo thy way, Godes pity, what a knave it tis', and Secretary Cecil echoed her words with 'goo thi wayes, thowe arte clir [clear] owte, thowe mayste be lowde to playe the knave in any grownde in England'.[24] Other student–actors fared better. After the play the queen spoke appreciative words to those who played Palamon and Arcyte, and gave rewards of eight angels each to John Rainolds, then aged 17, who played Queen Hippolyta, and to the unnamed boy (possibly Peter Carew, son of George Carew, former dean of Christ Church) who played Lady Emilia, the latter for 'gatheringe her flowers pretelie in the garden and synginge sweetlie "In the Pryme of Maye" '.[25] The queen lent costumes for the plays from her own wardrobe, principally old ones which had belonged to Queen Mary and King Edward VI. This appears to have been common knowledge among the spectators, one of whom ('a stander by'), at the point in the play when Theseus, Emilia, and Perithous all threw mementoes on to Arcyte's funeral pyre, grabbed Windsor's arm and said, 'Godes woundes, will ye burn the King Edward cloake in the fier?' Richard Edwards the author, Windsor, and the queen all remonstrated with the spectator, the queen exclaiming 'what ailyth ye? let the gentleman alone, he playeth his parte'.[26] Whether the 'stander by' was unusually credulous or just seeking publicity is unclear. It seems highly unlikely that the cloak would actually have been burned, but we know that at least one expensive garment was never returned,[27] and that realistic effects were aimed at in other parts of the play. Theseus' hunting-scene, for example, took place outside in the quadrangle with live hounds, the sound of horns and dogs reaching the queen

[23] In Twyne's transcript, and all subsequent published versions based on it, the name of this character is mistakenly spelled 'Trecatio'.

[24] CCCA MS 257, fo 118. In Windsor's fair copy, which was the basis for Twyne's transcript, this passage is awkwardly abridged, with the result that the queen's word 'knave' appears to refer to the character rather than to the actor. This has occasioned some fruitless speculation about the plot of the play; see for example W. Y. Durand, 'Notes on Richard Edwards', *Journal of Germanic Philology* iv (1902), 356–69; and Boas, *University Drama*, 103 n. 1.

[25] CCCA MS 257, fo 110ᵛ. The name of Peter Carew, who was about 14, is on the list of actors; Wood says he had earlier charmed the queen with an oration in Latin and Greek: Wood, *History of the University* ii. 158. The song mentioned by Windsor, along with one other from the play, survives in BL Add. MS 26,737, fos 106ᵛ–108ᵛ. Others assigned to parts by Windsor include one 'Lynhame' (missing from the cast list) as Palamon, and Brian Banes as Arcyte. Rainolds later acknowledged having played Hippolyta but failed to mention his reward by the queen: *The Overthrow of Stage Plays* (Middleburg 1599), 45.

[26] CCCA MS 257, fo 118. Twyne, and hence Wood, mistakenly wrote 'St Edward' for 'King Edward'.

[27] J. Arnold (ed.), *'Lost from Her Majesties back': items of clothing and jewels lost or given away by Queen Elizabeth I between 1561 and 1585* (Costume Soc. extra ser. vii 1980).

through the windows and prompting her to observe that 'those boyes ar readye to leape owte at wyndowe to followe the howndes'.[28] It was at the beginning of this play that the hall staircase collapsed under the weight of would-be spectators, killing three of them. Windsor tells us that 'the quene vnderstandinge thearof sente furthe presentlye my lord chamberlayne and her owne surgions to helpe them'. This official (Lord William Howard) 'when he found that thei were dedd sayde burye them', and after a pause the play was resumed, with the queen laughing 'full hartelye afterwarde at sum of the players'.[29] The queen was not present, due to illness, at the earlier performance of Toby Matthew's 'history', *Marcus Geminus*, a kind of political morality play about Roman conspirators, whose source has yet to be found. According to Bereblock it contained both raucous comic scenes and a crucifixion, though the latter was probably offstage.[30] This is Matthew's only known dramatic work, but he evidently retained his interest in, and respect for, academic drama, for in the 1590s we find him supporting Albericus Gentilis in his controversy over stage-plays with John Rainolds, now opposed to plays, and permitting his son, Sir Toby Matthew, to act in college plays.[31]

We are less fortunate in our information about the plays at Elizabeth's second royal visit to Oxford in September 1592, since the only surviving eye-witness account is that of a Cambridge 'spy', Philip Stringer, who made notes at the time but did not write them up until eleven years later.[32] By that time he had forgotten everything except the names of the two plays acted for the queen and his impression that they were 'but meanly performed'. Anthony Wood, who did not know Stringer's account, could discover even less—'but what they were or how

---

[28] CCCA MS 257, fo 110ᵛ. In Windsor's draft version it is 'the ladyes in the wyndowe cill' who do this (fo 118ᵛ).

[29] Ibid., fo 119ᵛ. Bereblock's account agrees with Windsor's on the matter of the pause. A third account, by a Cambridge man, Nicholas Robinson, says there was no pause at all ('veruntamen non fuit intermissum spectaculum'). Robinson also tells us that Richard Edwards spent two months in Oxford overseeing the production of all three plays: 'Of the actes done at Oxford when the quene's maiestie was there', Folger Shakespeare Library MS V.a.176, fo 159. This manuscript has been printed, from a transcript by Thomas Baker in BL MS Harleian 7033, fos 142–9, in Nichols (ed.), *Progresses of Elizabeth* i. 81–94, and in Plummer, *Elizabethan Oxford*, 173–91.

[30] Bodl. MS Add. a. 63, fos 5–6.

[31] Barton, 'The king's reader', 291; Boas, *University Drama*, 200, 246, 289–90.

[32] Philip Stringer, 'A breife of the entertainment given to Queene Elizabeth at Oxford', Cambridge University Library, Add. MS 34, fos 3ᵛ–9. This is a holograph account by Stringer, fellow of St John's College, Cambridge, written on 3 May 1603 in Cambridge from notes made in Oxford in 1592. Stringer gave the manuscript to Henry Mowtlowe, fellow of King's College, who had accompanied Stringer to Oxford, 'for the use of the university here', with the request that Mowtlowe add his own recollections before giving it to the vice-chancellor. The manuscript also contains an anonymous account, undated and in a different hand, of King James's 1605 visit to Oxford (fos 28–45ᵛ) which may be by Mowtlowe, as the author appears to have been a King's College man. Both accounts were copied by Thomas Baker into BL MS Harleian 7044, fos 97–107, from which they were printed in Nichols (ed.), *Progresses of Elizabeth* iii. 149–60, and J. Nichols (ed.), *Progresses of King James I* (4 vols London 1828) i. 530–59. The 1592 account only is given in Plummer, *Elizabethan Oxford*, 247–61. We do not know how many other Cambridge 'spies' went to Oxford in 1592; in 1605 there were forty of them whose job was 'to view in secret and note the whole event' and then to record their observations in shorthand 'in a table-booke': William Fennor, *Fennors Descriptions* (London 1616), sig. E2ʳ.

applauded, I know not'.[33] From other evidence, however, we know that the plays were Leonard Hutten's Latin comedy *Bellum grammaticale*, not printed until 1635 although originally performed in Christ Church in 1581, now fitted out with two new prologues and an epilogue by William Gager;[34] and Gager's own *Rivales*, a Latin comedy (now lost) first performed for the state visit of the Polish prince pala-tine, Alberto Alasco, in 1583 and, like *Bellum grammaticale*, previously revived as a Shrovetide entertainment in Christ Church a few months before the queen's visit.[35] Beyond the fact that the costumes for these plays were borrowed from the Office of the Revels and that special care was taken to keep order around 'the haule staires', we have no other details of their performance or of the queen's reaction to them.[36] The fact that Christ Church recorded expenses of only £31 2s 2d for the 'stage and towards plaies' suggests that they were indeed more 'meanly' set forth than in 1566, while the use of two plays already in that year's repertory may indicate that insufficient warning of the queen's visit was given for the university to come up with something new.[37]

Such was not the case in 1605 when King James visited Oxford with Queen Anne and the young Prince Henry, an occasion more amply documented than either of his predecessor's entertainments.[38] Four plays were presented in Christ Church for the royal party, three in Latin for the king, all written or adapted by Oxford men, and one in English especially for the queen and prince by the queen's favourite court poet, Samuel Daniel.[39] The three Latin plays seem to have been chosen to demonstrate the three kinds of classical drama as labelled by Vitruvius, and took place on the first three nights of the visit.[40] *Alba*, co-authored by Robert

---

[33] Wood, *History of the University* ii. 248–9.

[34] On the 1581 performance, see McConica, 'Elizabethan Oxford', 719; the prologues and epilogue were printed in Gager's *Meleager* (1593).

[35] Boas, *University Drama*, 181–3.

[36] Kent Archives Office, U269 C1, letter of the vice-chancellor (Nicholas Bond) to the lord trea-surer, 11 September 1592; *Reg. Univ.* ed. Clark i. 231; Plummer, *Elizabethan Oxford*, 271–3.

[37] CA xxii.b.35, fo 97 (disbursement book 1592–3). The committee to 'oversee and provyde for the playes' was not appointed until 17 August. The queen arrived on 22 September: *Reg. Univ.* ed. Clark i. 230.

[38] The three most detailed accounts are: (1) Cambridge University Library, Add. MS 34, fos 28–45ᵛ ('The preparacion at Oxford in August 1605 against the comminge thither of King James . . . together with the things then and there done and the maner thereof'); (2) Anthony Nixon, *Oxfords Triumph* (London 1605); (3) Isaac Wake, *Rex Platonicus* (Oxford 1607). The name of the Cambridge observer is not recorded but may be Henry Mowtlowe (see n. 32); Anthony Nixon was a prolific poet and pam-phleteer with connections among professional playwrights; in 1605 Isaac Wake was a fellow of Merton and public orator of the university.

[39] A fifth play was presented especially for Prince Henry at Magdalen, a comedy written by Douglas Castillion, praelector of Greek: Alton, 'Academic drama', 60. Nothing more is known of this play, though it appears to be referred to in the memoirs of William Ayshcombe, a student at St John's: Huntington Library, MS HM30665, fo 2ᵛ ('the Prince Henry at Magdalen Colledge, where there were likewise playes and orations'). On this manuscript, formerly attributed to John Pym, see *DNB* xvi. 518.

[40] J. Orrell, *The Theatres of Inigo Jones and John Webb* (Cambridge 1985), 30. The university delegates referred to them simply as 'three playes to be made in Lattin. viz ij comodies and a tragedie', but left the 'choyce of actors and pen men to helpe to penn them' to a subcommittee of the heads of Magdalen, New College, and St John's: 'Decrees & orders', OUA WP/Γ/19/1, fo 2ᵛ.

Burton, was a satyr play featuring shepherdesses, hermits, various gods and god-
desses, and a magician. Though its text is now lost, a costume-list survives indicating its classical pastoral setting and Isaac Wake tells us that it made use of a live
flock of wild doves.[41] Next, Magdalen College students presented a version of
Sophocles' tragedy *Ajax flagellifer*, a choice of text possibly influenced by the
designer, Inigo Jones, who owned an Italian edition of Vitruvius giving specific
instructions for the staging of this play in a Roman-style theatre.[42] Finally Matthew
Gwinne of St John's provided an allegorical comedy acted by the students of that
college called *Vertumnus: sive Annus recurrens*, known in English as 'The Year About',
whose whimsical nature may be sampled from the opening words of a lengthy plot
summary preserved in an Inner Temple manuscript:

Vertumnus (god of the yeare) brings forth the foure Seasons, placeth them in their foure
quarters for all the play-while, goeth forth without speache, and streight turnes out the
Calender, apparelled in the tuelf signes; who wondreth seing his foure quarter-lords mett at
once, enquireth the cause of their meeting, which being to shewe their maiesties the sports
of the yeare, they laye the charge on Calender to shewe their force on Man (called
Microcosme or the little world) in his foure ages. To which purpose they ioyne to him the
foure humors: Lustie-blood, Hotspurre, Mallicoly [and] Milksop.[43]

Another observer from Cambridge was characteristically ungracious about all
three of these performances, remarking that *Alba* was 'a pastorall much like one
which I have seene in King's Colledg in Cambridge, but acted farr worse' and that
the king found it tedious; that *Ajax* 'was not acted soe well by many degrees as I
have seene yt in Cambridge' and that it wearied the king; and that at *Vertumnus*
(which lasted until 1 a.m.), in spite of its being 'well and learnedly penned' and
'acted much better then eyther of the other', the king 'fell a sleepe [and] when he
awaked, he would have bene gone, sayinge "I marvell what they thinke mee to be"'.
Even the 'rare devises' attempted by Inigo Jones he dismissed as having accomplished 'very litle to that which was expected'. In this last judgement he seems to
have been joined by the officials of the court, including the lord chamberlain (Lord
Suffolk), who forced Jones and Simon Basil (comptroller of the works, who had
designed the auditorium) to move the king's throne away from a position where it
commanded the best sight-lines to a place where he could be better seen by the
audience. The court's decision, opposed by the university officials who sided with
Jones and Basil, showed their bewilderment over the perspective scenery which

---

[41] For the costume-list, see F. S. Boas and W. W. Greg (eds), 'James I at Oxford in 1605' (Malone
Soc. Collections i pt 3 1909), 247–59. On Burton's authorship of *Alba*, see R. L. Nochimson, 'Robert
Burton's authorship of *Alba*: a lost letter recovered', *Review of English Studies* new ser. xxi (1970), 325–31.
[42] *M. Vitruvii Polionis de Architectura*, ed. Daniello Barbaro (Venice 1567), 256. Jones's annotated copy
is preserved at Chatsworth House: Orrell, *Theatres*, 33 and n. 17.
[43] Inner Temple Library, MS Petyt 538, vol. 43, fo 293. The Latin text of *Vertumnus* was published
by Gwinne in 1607, along with the text of a 'device' called *Tres Sibyllae*, containing the prophecies of
the three witches to Macbeth, spoken by 'three little boyes' to the king outside St John's upon his entry
into Oxford. Gwinne's *Vertumnus* has often been confused with Burton's *Alba*, which according to Isaac
Wake was based on the Ovidian legend of Vertumnus and Pomona.

Jones was using for plays for the first time in England (he had designed his first Whitehall masque only a few months before). The stage was now placed at the west (high-table) end of the hall, and there could be no question of the king sitting on it, as it was raked so that the players seemed to be 'descending a hill'. Instead the king's throne was placed on an 'isle' in the centre of the auditorium with his courtiers seated on benches in front of him and in boxes fastened to the side walls. What they beheld was a 'false wall fayre painted' behind a platform containing 'statelie pillers which pillers would turne about', that is, the *periaktoi* of the ancient Greek theatre.[44] The effect on Oxford spectators was more appreciatively described by Wake:

The cloths and houses of the scene were skilfully changed by means of a machine time and again according to all the necessary places and occasions, so that the whole form of the fabric of the stage suddenly appeared new, to everyone's amazement, not only from day to day for each production, but even in the course of a single performance.[45]

The tragedy of *Ajax* saw the most extensive use of the triangular *periaktoi*, each face of which was painted with a different scene and which were turned by winches located underneath the stage. During this play the audience was shown 'the living image of Troy', a forest scene, and a seascape with tents and ships. The machinery remained in place on the stage throughout the four days ('from day to day for each production') and also furnished the scenes for *Alba*, *Vertumnus*, and the last play, Daniel's *Arcadia Reformed* (later renamed *The Queen's Arcadia*). The text of *Vertumnus* suggests that there must have been five such *periaktoi*, as that play required a central rural scene flanked by four 'houses' for the four seasons, which remained in position throughout the play. The fact that all the plays had similar scenic requirements—a tree for *Alba*, *Vertumnus*, and *Arcadia*, caves and mountains for *Ajax* and *Arcadia*—argues a collaboration between designer and playwright of a kind that would soon transform the nature of English court theatre. While the sceptical Cambridge reporter implies that Jones scarcely deserved the £50 he was paid, other witnesses were aware of the revolutionary visual effects he achieved. If Anthony Nixon can be believed, this included the king, who found the scenery for *Vertumnus* 'so richlie set foorth and beautified, with such curious and quaint conceipts and deuises, as that it made his maiestie pronounce himselfe as muche delighted therewith, as with anie sight (of the like nature) at anie time heretofore presented vnto him'. Nixon reports a similar royal reaction to the 'costly and curious ... deuice' of *Ajax*, but was apparently not present at *Alba*.[46]

The 1605 plays at Christ Church set a precedent for opulence and splendour that was only to be outdone by the entertainment of Charles I in 1636, the last occasion on which plays were presented to a monarch in Oxford. By that time Inigo

[44] Cambridge University Library, Add. MS 34, fos 30–44ᵛ.

[45] Wake, *Rex platonicus*, 46, trans. in Orrell, *Theatres*, 31. A plan of the auditorium has recently been discovered and is reproduced in Orrell, 'The theatre at Christ Church', plate II. On the Cambridge observer, see nn. 32 and 38.

[46] Cambridge University Library, Add. MS 34, fo 44ᵛ; Nixon, *Oxfords Triumph*, sigs B3, C1ᵛ, E1ᵛ.

Jones had become surveyor of the king's works, and had gained thirty years' experience as a designer of masques and plays. On this occasion he appears to have worked with a team of other designers, as the Christ Church accounts mention 'the designers for the sceenes' in the plural, but two other contemporary documents make it clear that Jones was once again the principal architect of the Christ Church stage.[47] By this time he had left his antique *periaktoi* far behind and had mastered the new Italian art of perspective involving the use of flats and grooved shutters, a technique which has best been described by John Orrell:

> The essence of ... [Jones's] stage design ... was the sense of recession given by flat side wings standing one behind another and leading the eye on to the exciting veil of the shutters, which would draw back to reveal yet another series of receding surfaces in the relieves set against the infinity of the backcloth.[48]

What these devices accomplished in Christ Church hall in 1636 has been recorded for us in admiring detail by Brian Twyne, fellow of Corpus and first keeper of the university archives:

> A goodly stage made at Christchurch from the uppar-ende of the hall allmost to the hearth, after the newe fashion with 3 or 4 openinges at ech side thereof, and partitions much resemblinge the deskes in a library, out of which the actors issued forth on ech side, and these partitions they could drawe in at their pleasure uppon a sudden, and thrust out newe in their places according to the nature of the scene, like churches, dwellinge houses, pallaces or the like, which bred great varietie and admiration, and over all, delicate payntinge resemblinge the cloudes and sky cullur etc. At the upper ende, a great fayre shutt of two leaues painted curiously on the outside that opened and shutt together againe without any visible helpe, within which was set forth the embleme of the whole playe in sumptuous manner to behold: therein was the perfect resemblance of the billowes of the sea rollinge vp and downe, and an artificial iland with churches and houses, wauinge vp and downe really and flotinge in the same in one whole peice, the rockes and trees and hilles, in and about the shores thereof, in the playe of the passions calmed; and after that many other fine peices of worke and landscips at sundry openinges thereof did appeare, and their was a chayre came glidinge in uppon the stage without any visible helpe etc. But in the other playe called the Royall Slaue, where within these shutts as [*sic*] a curious temple and the sun shininge on it, there was much more varietie of the scene, and curious prospects of forests and the like, within those great shutts spoken of before, with villages and men visibly appearinge in them goeinge vp and downe here and there, about their businesse etc.[49]

The plays which Twyne is here describing were William Strode's *The Floating Island*, performed on the night of 29 August, and William Cartwright's *The Royal Slave*, acted on the following night. In between, the king and queen were treated to a matinée performance of George Wilde's *Love's Hospital* in St John's hall on 30 August, at Archbishop Laud's expense, of which no description has survived.[50]

---

[47] Elliott and Buttrey, 'Royal plays at Christ Church'; Orrell, *Theatres*, 206–7.

[48] Orrell, *Theatres*, 37.   [49] Bodl. MS Twyne 17, p. 201.

[50] We may guess from the sum of £394 spent on 'the stage and comedy' that it was no ordinary college production, but it is not known whether the court designers were involved. (On Laud's expenses, see n. 15.)

(A fourth play, Jasper Mayne's *The City Match*, was written for the occasion but not performed.)[51] The two Christ Church plays, though written and acted by Oxford men, were in all other respects the product of the king's usual purveyors of court entertainment. The scenery and costumes were provided by the Office of the Works and the Office of the Revels, respectively; the music was written by William and Henry Lawes and performed by the King's Musick and by the Children of the Chapel; the actors were coached by Joseph Taylor, leader of the King's Men at the Globe; a set of candelabra was dismantled in Whitehall Palace and reassembled in Oxford to provide lighting. In contrast to the choice of learned academic plays for King James, all of the 1636 plays were comedies, and all, by royal command, were written in English,[52] confirming William Cartwright's remark in the Epilogue to *The Royal Slave* that

> There's difference 'twixt a colledge and a court;
> The one expecteth science, th'other sport.

Perhaps because of this, *The Floating Island*, a political allegory extolling monarchy, was generally dismissed as incomprehensible by the courtiers, despite its scenic wonders. *The Royal Slave*, however, an exotic romance about a Persian prisoner miraculously rescued from a pagan sacrificial altar, got a warm reception from the entire court, especially the queen, who made a special request to have it performed by her own company, with the Oxford scenery and costumes, at Hampton Court the following January. What she saw both there and in Oxford, however, was not representative of Oxford culture in any sense, but merely an imitation of the usual type of Stuart court entertainments. *The Royal Slave* itself was closely modelled on Phillip Massinger's play *The Bondman*, which had been performed by Lady Elizabeth's company a decade earlier. By this time Oxford royal entertainments had ceased to be displays of learning, and had become instead simple vehicles of flattery. Not surprisingly, there is no report of this king having fallen asleep at any of the performances.

In his letter to the university Chancellor Laud had recommended that the scenery and costumes for the royal plays of 1636 afterward be 'laid up in some place fit', so that 'if any college or hall shall at any time for any play or show that they are willing to set forth, need the use of any, or all of these things, it shall be . . . lawful, and free for them to have and to use them'.[53] This was a generous but quixotic gesture, as it was unlikely that students would know how to use such elaborate fittings or have occasion to do so, even in ordinary times. By 1642 times were no longer ordinary, and although the king was now in residence at Christ Church, there is no evidence of any dramatic entertainments having taken place there during the civil war years.

---

[51] Bodl. MS Twyne 17, p. 194. *The Royal Slave* was published in 1639, *The Floating Island* in 1639. *Love's Hospital* survives in BL Add. MS 14,047. As regards *The Royal Slave*, see K. Sharpe, *Criticism and Compliment: the politics of literature in the England of Charles I* (Cambridge 1987), 47–51.

[52] P. Heylyn, *A Briefe and Moderate Answer* (London 1637), 78.

[53] Laud, *Remains* ii. 100–1.

At the Restoration a revival of the custom of royal dramatic entertainments was contemplated but soon abandoned. Timothy Halton, fellow of Queen's College, tells us that in July 1661 a committee was formed to plan the reception of the new King Charles II in Oxford, and that 'the play is made by Dr Llewellyn'. He then notes, however, that the plan could not be carried out because 'they are so in want of actors'.[54] This undoubtedly means a lack of experienced actors, not just a shortage of potential participants, engendered by a nearly twenty-year gap in dramatic activities in Oxford. While the professional companies in London quickly reorganized at the Restoration, Oxford drama never recovered from this break in its traditions. Charles II returned to Oxford in September 1663, and James II in September 1687, but neither the university nor the Christ Church accounts record any payments for drama. In 1664 Christ Church attempted to revive the custom of Christmas revels by staging a comedy called *The Tricks* by a Student named Richard Rhodes. This, however, according to Wood, led only to extensive damage to the hall and general 'drunkenness and wantonness'. Jasper Mayne, who remembered the events of 1636, tried to encourage the cast by saying 'he liked well an acting student', but the college accounts reveal that this was the last such play to be performed in Christ Church hall, and it was indeed virtually the last student play to be performed in Oxford until the founding of OUDS more than two centuries later.[55]

---

[54] *CSPD 1661–2*, 32. On the playwriting career of Martin Llewellyn, who in 1660 was appointed king's physician and principal of St Mary Hall, see n. 1.

[55] Wood, *Life and Times* ii. 2. The night before the Christ Church performance (7 January 1664), University College put on a play called *The Wit in a Constable* by Henry Glapthorne: ibid.

Appendix

Here are listed the sixty-four plays performed within the University of Oxford before 1642 whose titles are known. The titles are given in chronological order of performance, and are followed by: (1) the name of the author; (2) the genre of the play; (3) the language of the play; (4) the calendar year (New Style) and place of performance; (5) details of the surviving texts (except for classical plays). Only plays with documented productions are listed.

1. KING SOLOMON
Thomas More and others. Comedy. Language unknown. c.1495. Magdalen College School? Text lost.

2. MARY MAGDALEN
John Burgess. Miracle play? Language unknown. 1507. Magdalen College. Text lost.

3. CHRISTUS REDIVIVUS
Nicholas Grimald. Tragicomedy. Latin. c.1541. Brasenose College? Printed text, Cologne 1543.

4. ANDRIA
Terence. Comedy. Latin. c.1559. Trinity College.

5. MARCUS GEMINUS
Toby Matthew. History. Latin. 1566. Christ Church. Text lost.

6. PALAMON AND ARCYTE
Richard Edwards. Comedy. English. 1566. Christ Church. Text lost, except for two songs (BL Add. MS 26,737, fos 106ᵛ–108ᵛ).

7. PROGNE
James Calfhill. Tragedy. Latin. 1566. Christ Church. Text lost.

8. WYLIE BEGUYLIE
Author unknown. Comedy. English. 1567. Merton College. Text lost.

9. EUNUCHUS
Terence. Comedy. Latin. 1567. Merton College.

10. MENAECHMI
Plautus. Comedy. Latin. 1568. Merton College.

11. DAMON AND PYTHIAS
Richard Edwards. Comedy. English. 1568. Merton College. Printed text, London 1571.

12. BELLUM GRAMMATICALE
Leonard Hutten. Comedy. Latin. 1581, 1592. Christ Church. Printed text, London 1635.

13. THE SUPPOSES
Ludovico Ariosto, translated by George Gascoigne. Comedy. English. 1582. Trinity College. Printed text, London 1573.

14. CAESAR INTERFECTUS
Richard Edes. Tragedy. Latin. 1582. Christ Church. Text lost, except for Epilogue (Bodl. MS top. Oxon e. 5).

15. MELEAGER
William Gager. Tragedy. Latin. 1582, 1585, 1592. Christ Church. Printed text, Oxford 1592/3.

16. RIVALES
William Gager. Comedy. Latin. 1583, 1592. Christ Church. Text lost.

17. DIDO
William Gager. Tragedy. Latin. 1583. Christ Church. MS text: CL MS 486.

18. CAPTIVI
Plautus. Comedy. Latin. 1584. Merton College.

19. TANCREDO
Henry Wotton. Tragedy. Language unknown. 1586. Queen's College. Text lost.

20. PHILOTAS
Richard Lateware. Tragedy. Language unknown. c.1588–96. St John's College. Text lost.

21. OCTAVIA
Seneca? Tragedy. Latin. 1591. Christ Church.

22. ULYSSES REDUX
William Gager. Tragedy. Latin. 1592. Christ Church. Printed text, Oxford 1592/3.

23. HIPPOLYTUS
Seneca, with additional scenes by William Gager. Tragedy. Latin. 1592. Christ Church. Printed text of Gager's scenes, published as appendix to no. 22.

24. THE TRAGEDY OF CAESAR AND POMPEY, OR CAESAR'S REVENGE
Author unknown. Tragedy. English. c.1592–6. Trinity College. Printed text, London 1607.

25. ASTIAGES
Author unknown. Tragedy. Language unknown. 1597. St John's College. Text lost.

26. A TWELFTH NIGHT MERRIMENT
Author unknown. Comedy. English. 1603. St John's College. Printed text, London 1893 (under the title NARCISSUS).

27. HIPPOLYTUS
Seneca? Tragedy. Latin? 1604. St John's College. Text lost. Possibly identical to no. 23.

28. LUCRETIA
Author unknown. Tragedy. Language unknown. 1605. St John's College. Text lost.

29. TRES SIBYLLAE
Matthew Gwinne. A 'device'. Latin. 1605. St John's College. Printed text, London 1607, published as appendix to no. 32.

30. ALBA
Robert Burton and others. Pastoral. Latin. 1605. Christ Church. Text lost.

31. AJAX FLAGELLIFER
Sophocles. Tragedy. Latin. 1605. Christ Church.

32. VERTUMNUS: SIVE ANNUS RECURRENS
Matthew Gwinne. Comedy. Latin. 1605. Christ Church. Printed text, London 1607.

33. THE QUEEN'S ARCADIA
Samuel Daniel. Pastoral tragicomedy. English. 1605. Christ Church. Printed text, London 1606.

34. ARA FORTUNAE
Author unknown. A 'device'. Latin. 1607. St John's College. MS text: SJM MS 52. Printed text: *The Christmas Prince*, ed. F. S. Boas (Oxford 1922).

35. SATURNALIA
Author unknown. Interlude. Latin. 1607. St John's College. MS text: SJM MS 52. Printed text: *Christmas Prince*, ed. Boas.

36. PHILOMELA
Author unknown. Tragedy. Latin. 1607. St John's College. MS text: SJM MS 52. Printed text: *Christmas Prince*, ed. Boas.

37. TIME'S COMPLAINT
Author unknown. A 'shew'. English. 1608. St John's College. MS text: SJM MS 52. Printed text: *Christmas Prince*, ed. Boas.

38. SOMNIUM FUNDATORIS
Author unknown. Interlude. Latin? 1608. St John's College. Text lost.

39. THE SEVEN DAYS OF THE WEEK
Author unknown. A 'mock play'. English. 1608. St John's College. MS text: SJM MS 52. Printed text: *Christmas Prince*, ed. Boas.

40. PHILOMATHES
Author unknown. Comedy. Latin. 1608. St John's College. MS text: SJM MS 52. Printed text: *Christmas Prince*, ed. Boas.

41. YULETIDE
Author unknown. Comedy. English? 1608. Christ Church. Text lost.

42. THE FIVE BELLS OF MAGDALEN CHURCH
Author unknown. A 'wassail'. Latin and English. 1608. St John's College. MS text: SJM MS 52. Printed text: *Christmas Prince*, ed. Boas.

43. IRA SEU TUMULUS FORTUNAE
Author unknown. A 'shew'. Latin. 1608. St John's College. MS text: SJM MS 52. Printed text: *Christmas Prince*, ed. Boas.

44. PERIANDER
John Sandsbury. Tragedy. English. 1608. St John's College. MS text: SJM MS 52. Printed text: *Christmas Prince*, ed. Boas.

45. MERCURIUS RUSTICANS
Author unknown. Comedy. Latin. *c.*1610–18. Location unknown. MS text: Bodl. MS Wood d. 18, pt 2.

46. FUIMUS TROES, OR THE TRUE TROJANS
Jasper Fisher. History play. English. *c.*1611–33. Magdalen College. Printed text, London 1633.

47. ORESTES

Thomas Goffe. Tragedy. English. *c.*1613–18. Christ Church. Printed text, London 1632.

48. THE RAGING TURK, OR BAJAZET THE SECOND

Thomas Goffe. Tragedy. English. *c.*1613–18. Christ Church. Printed text, London 1631.

49. SPURIUS

Peter Heylyn. Tragedy. English. 1617. Magdalen College. Text lost.

50. JULIUS ET GONZAGA

Samuel Bernard. Tragedy. Latin. 1617. Magdalen College. Text lost.

51. TECHNOGAMIA, OR THE MARRIAGES OF THE ARTS

Barten Holiday. Comedy. English. 1618, 1621. Christ Church. Printed text, London 1618.

52. ANDRONICUS COMNENUS

Samuel Bernard. Tragedy. Latin. 1618. Magdalen College. Text lost.

53. PHILOSOPHASTER

Robert Burton. Comedy. Latin. 1618. Christ Church. Printed text, London 1862; text and translation, Stanford 1931.

54. PHOCAS

Samuel Bernard. Tragedy. Latin. 1619. Magdalen College. Text lost.

55. THE COURAGEOUS TURK, OR AMURATH THE FIRST

Thomas Goffe. Tragedy. English. 1619. Christ Church. Printed text, London 1632.

56. DOUBLET, BREECHES, AND SHIRT

Peter Heylyn. A 'shew'. English. 1619. Magdalen College. Text lost.

57. THE REFORMATION

Abraham Wright. Comedy. English? *c.*1629–33. St John's College. Text lost.

58. EUMORPHUS SIVE CUPIDO ADULTUS

George Wilde. Comedy. Latin. 1635. St John's College. Printed text, Salzburg 1973.

59. THE COMBAT OF LOVE AND FRIENDSHIP

Robert Mead. Comedy. English. *c.*1634–42. Christ Church. Printed text, London 1654.

60. THE FLOATING ISLAND (also called PASSIONS CALMED and PRUDENTIUS)

William Strode. Tragicomedy. English. 1636. Christ Church. Printed text, London 1655.

61. LOVE'S HOSPITAL

George Wilde. Comedy. English. 1636. St John's College. MS text: BL Add. MS 14,047.

62. THE ROYAL SLAVE (also called THE PERSIAN SLAVE)

William Cartwright. Tragicomedy. English. 1636. Christ Church. Printed text, Oxford 1639.

63. THE CONVERTED ROBBER (also called STONEHENGE)

John Speed? Pastoral. English. 1637. St John's College. MS text: BL Add. MS 14,047.

64. GROBIANA'S NUPTIALS

Charles May. Comedy. English. 1638. St John's College. MS text: Bodl. MS 30 (formerly MS 27,639).

13

Libraries, Books, and Printing

I. G. PHILIP and PAUL MORGAN

THE BODLEIAN LIBRARY

THE Bodleian Library, founded and endowed by Sir Thomas Bodley at the opening of the seventeenth century, was the third university library of Oxford. The first
comprised manuscripts bequeathed to the university early in the fourteenth century by Thomas Cobham, bishop of Worcester, and was housed in the congregation house adjoining the church of St Mary the Virgin which had been built from
funds given by Cobham himself; it provided sufficient space for the university's
collection of manuscripts for over a hundred years. But the gifts made by
Humfrey, duke of Gloucester, between 1439 and his death in 1447 made a larger
building necessary, and as the university was then building its new divinity school,
Duke Humfrey agreed to add an upper floor to which the enlarged university
library could be transferred. Unfortunately the duke died before this project could
be completed, and the building was not finished until 1488.[1] But by the middle of
the sixteenth century this second library had disappeared, the books were dispersed
or destroyed, the original bookcases had been sold, some to Christ Church in
about 1556, and for a time the room was used by the faculty of medicine.[2] So
when Bodley decided in 1598 to set up his 'staffe at the library doore in Oxford'
he had no competition, and those to whom he applied for help had no similar
calls upon their generosity (Cambridge University Library was then in one of its
long periods of inactivity).[3] Bodley's intention was to create not just a private institutional library for the university, but a public library serving the whole commonwealth of learned men.

Bodley, born in 1545, had been taken as a boy to Geneva when his parents

---

This chapter was begun by I. G. Philip, who died in 1985. He drafted the section on the Bodleian
Library, which is based on his *The Bodleian Library in the Seventeenth and Eighteenth Centuries* (Oxford 1983),
where fuller details and references may be found, and outlined or partly wrote other sections. Paul
Morgan has been chiefly responsible for the sections on college libraries and the Oxford book-trade.

[1] Philip, *Bodleian Library*, 5–6; T. H. Aston and Rosamond Faith, 'The endowments of the university
and colleges to *circa* 1348' in *The Early Oxford Schools*, 272–3; S. Gillam, *The Divinity School and Duke
Humfrey's Library at Oxford* (Oxford 1988), ch. 1.

[2] N. R. Ker, 'The provision of books' in *The Collegiate University*, 465–6; Gillam, *The Divinity School*,
51–2.

[3] *The Life of Sir Thomas Bodley written by Himselfe* (Oxford 1647), 15 ('staffe at the library doore'); J. C. T.
Oates, *Cambridge University Library: a history from the beginnings to the copyright act of Queen Anne* (Cambridge
1986), 153.

entered voluntary exile during the reign of Mary. From an early age he studied under the protestant leaders there, particularly Calvin and Beza, and when his family returned to England he matriculated at Magdalen College in 1560, subsequently becoming a fellow of Merton College. In 1576 he decided to leave this academic life having 'waxed desirous to travell beyond the seas, for attayning to the knowledge of sume speciall moderne tongues, and for the encrease of my experience in the mannaginge of affayres'.[4] He devoted the next ten years to service on diplomatic missions for Queen Elizabeth, eventually becoming the English representative in the United Provinces. In 1586 he married a rich widow, Ann Ball of Totnes, and he was able to retire from court employment in 1596, to concentrate in his 'solitude and surcease from the commonwealth affayres' on the refounding of a public library for the university in Duke Humfrey's room.[5] On 23 February 1598 he set out his project in a letter to the vice-chancellor:

Where there hath ben heretofore a publike library in Oxford, which you know is apparent by the rome it self remayning and by your statute records, I will take the charge and cost upon me to reduce it again to his former use, and to make it fitte and handsome with seates and shelfes and deskes and all that may be needed to stirre up other mens benevolence to helpe to furnish it with bookes.[6]

Before the library was officially opened Bodley chose as his librarian Thomas James (1573–1629), Wykehamist and fellow of New College, whose parents, like Bodley's, had fled to the continent in Mary's reign. James, although twenty-eight years younger than Bodley and without personal experience of exile, shared his religious background and theological outlook. His particular interests lay in trying to establish accurate texts of the Christian fathers and to denounce those 'Romish corruptions' which he claimed had been introduced by Roman Catholic editors.[7] This demanded a bibliographical knowledge of both manuscript and printed sources, and fitted in well with his assiduous care as librarian.

The library was officially opened on 8 November 1602, when about 2,000 books had been acquired and classified into the four main divisions of theology, law, medicine, and arts. By 1610 the existing building was full and Bodley financed and supervised the construction of the proscholium with Arts End above it, which not only gave additional space for folios but galleries to house the increasing number of smaller books not large enough to be chained (plate 2). Bodley also had plans for further extensions. Before his death in January 1613 he persuaded the university to rebuild 'those ruinous little rooms' which lay between Arts End and Catte Street and undertook to provide funds for building over the resulting new

---

[4] *Trecentale bodleianum: a memorial volume for the 300th anniversary of the public funeral of Sir Thomas Bodley* (Oxford 1913), 7.

[5] Ibid. 19.

[6] *Letters of Sir Thomas Bodley to the University of Oxford 1598–1611*, ed. G. W. Wheeler (Oxford 1927), 4.

[7] *The Humble Supplication of Thomas James for Reformation of the Ancient Fathers Workes by Papists Sundrie Wayes Depraved* (London [c.1607]).

schools a third storey to afford 'a very large supplement for stowage of bookes' (plate 1).[8]

The building of the new schools began on the day following Bodley's funeral. During the 1630s a western extension over the new convocation house completed those additions which Bodley had in mind and for which he had also left funds (plate 2). There was no further major structural change until the last decade of the seventeenth century.

Although Bodley's original intention had been merely 'to stirre up other mens benevolence' he was soon buying books from his own resources as well as exercising control over those bought from contributions made by his 'store of honourable friends', men like Lord Buckhurst, later earl of Dorset, the earl of Essex, Lord Hunsdon, Sir Walter Ralegh, and the earl of Southampton.[9] From these benefactions Bodley supervised the purchase of books over the whole range of learning then recognized, including Hebrew and other oriental languages, with a small selection of Chinese books as early as 1604. For manuscripts he relied on a group of men who were mainly members of the first Society of Antiquaries: William Camden, Sir Walter Cope, Sir Robert Cotton, and John, Lord Lumley. Their gifts, together with the collections of medieval manuscripts presented by the chapters of Exeter cathedral and St George's, Windsor, established the Bodleian Library as a library for the study of English medieval history. Furthermore, the agreement of 1610 with the Stationers' Company of London, whereby a copy of every book printed by a member of the company was to be presented to the library, introduced into the university's collections a selection of English books, many of which Bodley himself, however, regarded as 'idle bookes and riffe-raffes'.[10] By the time of Thomas James's retirement in 1620 the library's stock amounted to about 16,000 printed books and manuscripts, a collection which attracted scholars from all over Europe, and it then could be said of Bodley that 'his single worke clouds the proud frame of the Ægyptian Library and shames the tedious growth of the wealthy Vatican'.[11]

Thomas James, 'the incomparably industrious and learned bibliothecary of Oxford', composed two catalogues of the library's holdings. The first, published in 1605, was essentially a shelf-list with the books arranged by subject: theology, medicine, law, and arts. The second, published in 1620, was a much larger work describing everything in the growing collections in a single author-catalogue. This volume of 575 pages was the first published alphabetical catalogue of a public library and as such is a landmark in European library history, immediately being used by other libraries and private collectors. It was followed in 1635 by an appendix of accessions compiled by John Rous, librarian from 1620 to 1652, but thereafter until

[8] *Letters of Bodley to the University*, ed. Wheeler, 21; W. D. Macray, *Annals of the Bodleian Library* (Oxford 1868, 2nd edn Oxford 1890), 406–7. Macray prints full transcripts of many documents relevant to this chapter.

[9] F. Madan, 'A survey of Bodleian Library finance', *Bodleian Quarterly Record* viii (1935–7), 10.

[10] *Letters of Sir Thomas Bodley to Thomas James*, ed. G. W. Wheeler (Oxford 1926), 219, 221–2.

[11] Macray, *Annals*, 58; *Life of Bodley*, 'To the reader'.

Thomas Hyde's new catalogue was issued in 1674 readers had to make do with an interleaved copy of the 1620 catalogue, in which successive librarians entered only such books as they thought worthy of record. Bodley himself doubted if books in the vernacular could merit inclusion in either his library or its catalogue, but about 170 English titles were among the 5,000 or so entries in the 1605 catalogue; by 1620 there was a scattering of English works, mostly published after the agreement with the Stationers' Company. The situation was changed by Robert Burton's bequest, in 1640, of his large library which included much in the vernacular. Though John Rous selected about 900 items from Burton's library (the remainder going to Christ Church) some plays and similar popular works were not included in the 1674 catalogue and in fact had to wait some 200 years before being made generally known in the Bodleian catalogue of 1843.[12]

Sir Thomas Bodley's influence in attracting benefactors persisted long after his death; Archbishop Laud followed his example in not only making gifts himself but also persuading others such as Sir Kenelm Digby and William Herbert, earl of Pembroke, to present manuscripts. It was benefactions like these that made necessary the extension, already mentioned, over the new convocation house. Rous had puritan sympathies, as probably did Thomas James, but the library's reputation was such that it was protected both during the royalist control of Oxford during the years 1642–6 and when the city surrendered to General Fairfax, who 'set a good guard of soldiers to preserve the Bodleian Library'.[13] Rous died in 1652 having kept the library open and unmolested for over thirty very chequered years—despite revolution, civil war, and near bankruptcy. Borrowing by the king and loss of rents and bequests had resulted in an empty Bodleian chest by April 1648, but some rents had begun to be received again in 1649 and finances then gradually improved.[14]

As Rous's successor the university approved the appointment of Thomas Barlow, fellow of Queen's College, an encyclopaedic scholar who managed to accommodate his principles to a variety of political circumstances. The situation in 1652 was indeed difficult and it does not seem that Barlow was much in sympathy with those who were then taking an active interest in the library. One of the results of the ascendancy of parliament had been to bring new men to Oxford and to encourage a new generation of scholars to consider more practical aims in education. They wished the library to be more useful and considered that their first need was for a subject-catalogue. Thomas James's old subject-lists were still of some value in the traditional disciplines—his subject-catalogue of arts books, then 'all torne and worne out', had been copied afresh in 1645—but men were now looking for something quite different.[15] The members of the Oxford experimental

---

[12] *The Bodleian Library in the Seventeenth Century: guide to an exhibition held . . . 1951* (Oxford 1951), 14 ('learned bibliothecary'); G. W. Wheeler, *The Earliest Catalogues of the Bodleian Library* (Oxford 1928), 69–80; N. K. Kiessling, *The Library of Robert Burton* (Oxford Bibliographical Soc. new ser. xxii 1988), pp. x–xii; Philip, *Bodleian Library*, 33.

[13] Macray, *Annals*, 101.   [14] Madan, 'Bodleian Library finance', 12–14.

[15] For the recopying of 1645 see *The Bodleian Library Account Book 1613–1646*, ed. G. Hampshire (Oxford Bibliographical Soc. new ser. xxi 1983), 144.

philosophy club, an informal group centred on John Wilkins, warden of Wadham, and Seth Ward, professor of astronomy, had from 1648 been considering the directions in which experimental science might develop and had formulated plans for some preliminary guide to published research. Ward reported to Sir Justinian Isham on 27 February 1652 that:

We have conceived it requisite to examine all the bookes of our public library (everyone takeing his part) and to make a catalogue or index of the matters and that very particularly in philosophy, physic, mathematics and indeed in all other facultyes, that so that greate numbers of bookes may be serviceable and a man may at once see where he may find whatever is there concerneing the argument he is upon.[16]

The classification of knowledge was then very much in the air and less than three weeks after Seth Ward's letter on the experimental philosophy club project, Gerard Langbaine, provost of Queen's College, wrote to explain to John Selden his own view of what was needed and how it might be achieved.

For myself I have engaged a matter of a score of our ablest men in that kind to undertake a thorough survey of our Public Library intending to make a perfect catalogue of all the books according to their severall subjects in severall kinds; and when that's done to incorporate in it all the authors in any of our privat college libraryes which are wanting in the publicque, so as he that desires to know may see at one view what wee have upon any subject.[17]

Some of Langbaine's working papers show that he had worked out a scheme for dividing the library's collections into twenty parts, to be allotted to the twenty helpers. But the next steps were more difficult. Two catalogues written by Langbaine still exist, being his own unfinished contribution and describing less than 300 out of the 650 volumes which were his allocation. His descriptions occupy over 330 quarto pages and in one instance more than three pages are devoted to a subject-analysis of one volume containing two legal commentaries. No evidence has so far come to light to suggest that any of the twenty experts worked within the framework of Langbaine's scheme, though some certainly worked on the bibliography of their own chosen subjects.[18] But their enthusiasm was short-lived— probably these scholars found the mere listing of titles tedious—and the problem of subject-guides in the library was not raised again in the seventeenth century.

Barlow's period of office was notable for the arrival in 1659 of the greatest single benefaction to the Bodleian Library of the seventeenth century: the library of John Selden (died 1654) whose wide interests included law, archaeology, and Hebrew. It numbered about 8,000 printed volumes, some 2,000 fewer than in

[16] H. W. Robinson, 'An unpublished letter of Dr Seth Ward', *Notes and Records of the Royal Society* vii (1949–50), 69.

[17] Bodl. MS Selden *supra* 109, fo 465. See also G. W. Wheeler, 'A projected subject-catalogue', *Bodleian Quarterly Record* iii (1920–2), 193–4.

[18] M. Purver, *The Royal Society: concept and creation* (London 1967), 121–6; R. G. Frank, 'John Aubrey, FRS, John Lydall, and science at Commonwealth Oxford', *Notes and Records of the Royal Society* xxvii (1972–3).

Richard Holdsworth's bequest to Cambridge University Library in 1649. But Selden's library was much richer in manuscripts.[19] Barlow was followed as librarian in 1660 by Thomas Lockey, who claimed in 1664 to have catalogued all Selden's books; he also had plans for a new general catalogue of the library's printed books compiled by fifty masters of arts, but the project came to nothing. In 1665 Lockey retired to a canonry of Christ Church leaving his successor, Thomas Hyde, to produce a new catalogue, ultimately published in 1674. It was a landmark in the history of cataloguing as it was the first that consistently attempted to transcribe titles from title-pages, to distinguish synonymous authors and works, and to add numerous cross-references from translators and editors. By this time there were probably at least 40,000 manuscripts and printed books, the collection having grown from about 5,000 in 1602.[20] The value of Hyde's catalogue was shown by its immediate use in other libraries as a guide to their own collections; the annotated copy of 'Hyde' was the only catalogue available at the Mazarin Library in Paris, for example, down to 1760, while Edmund Gibson added locations to a copy when appointed librarian at Lambeth Palace in 1696. It sold at 19*s*, and until 1692 all new readers at the Bodleian Library had to buy a copy. Hyde, the first orientalist to be librarian, had his labours lightened to some extent, as for most of his period of office relatively few books were received under the arrangements Bodley had made with the Stationers' Company, in spite of complaints from the university. There was no penalty for non-compliance until the third licensing act of 1665. Even so, the recalcitrance of the London printers continued and the proportion of books received did not increase although both Oxford and Cambridge universities made joint efforts to enforce their rights in 1674. In that year Ralph Bathurst, Oxford's vice-chancellor, declared it was easier to wrest his club from Hercules than a book from a London stationer.[21]

Benefactions continued to arrive, such as the manuscripts of Thomas, Lord Fairfax in 1673—he who had protected the library in 1646—and these included the topographical collections of Roger Dodsworth. The bequest of the Anglo-Saxon and Middle English manuscripts of Francis Junius in 1677 brought the Cædmon manuscript of *circa* AD 1000 and the early thirteenth-century *Ormulum*. Thomas Marshall (died 1685), rector of Lincoln College, and Bishop John Fell (died 1686) also bequeathed noteworthy collections, so that by the end of the century the Bodleian Library had indeed become an institution attracting scholars from all over Europe.

Besides the greater names in Sir Thomas Bodley's 'store of honourable friends' there were also many lesser subscribers. In the years from 1600 to 1605 Bodley received in all about £1,700 from benefactors, and with this backing was able to

---

[19] Oates, *Cambridge University Library*, 328.

[20] Macray, *Annals*, 107; Philip, *Bodleian Library*, 48: Wheeler, *Earliest Catalogues*, 21, 57. This calculation follows Wheeler in using a multiplier of two to convert 'volumes' into books.

[21] Philip, *Bodleian Library*, 52–5; Oates, *Cambridge University Library*, 416–24.

employ two of the leading London booksellers, John Norton and John Bill. He seems to have relied largely on Norton's stock and advice, and on his twice-yearly importations from the Frankfurt book fair, while Bill acted more frequently as his travelling agent. In the summer of 1602 Bill was buying for Bodley in Paris, Venice, and nine towns in northern Italy. By June 1603 Bodley was able to declare that Bill 'hath gotten every where what the place would affourd: for his commission was large, his leasure very good, and his paiment sure at home'. In the following year Bill paid a short visit to Spain intending to make a tour of book-trade centres as he had done in Italy, but he got no further than Seville and then had to return home because the 'people's usage towardes all of our nation is so cruel and malicious'.[22] Despite this hostility, which could have been no great surprise, Bill was able to arrange for a considerable consignment to be sent over, many of them, including the now rare first edition of *Don Quixote*, being entered as a gift from the earl of Southampton who gave £100 in 1605. Bodley himself could choose what he wanted from what the booksellers offered to him, but the major selection and range of choice were the result of the highly effective professional operations of his two agents.

After Bodley's death the library ordinances approved by the university on 13 November 1613 came into effect and henceforth the curators were to exercise, theoretically at least, as tight a control over purchases as Bodley had in his lifetime. By library ordinance the librarian was to follow the advice of the curators in all purchases, and the books purchased were to be 'exhibited to the curators at the next visitation, with the price written on the books respectively, which the librarian (in behalf of the trust reposed in him) is to take care is the least possible'. Books asked for by students were to be entered in what would now be called a suggestions book in order that, after professors in the faculty had been consulted and the vice-chancellor had consented, the books might be purchased. Further details were specified in an ordinance of July 1615: the curators were to meet within a week of the arrival of the spring and autumn catalogues from Frankfurt, to decide which books would be creditable or useful and so should be bought for the library.[23]

There are no records of Bodley's personal expenditure on books, but by 1609 he had made known what manner of endowment he proposed for purchases after his time, and in 1610 Thomas James calculated that the proposed Bodleian estate would bring in £62 15s od 'for ever to be employed in books yearely'.[24] This was the sum which the curators had at their disposal for purchases when they took over the administration in 1613 and money of this order was available for book purchases until the outbreak of civil war prevented the collection of rents from some of the Bodleian estates. During the thirty years from 1613 to 1643 the main suppliers of books were major London booksellers engaged in the foreign trade, starting with John Bill, who was succeeded in 1621 by Henry Featherstone and who

[22] *Letters of Bodley to James*, ed. Wheeler, 57, 61, 65, 76, 90, 117, 118.
[23] *Statutes*, trans. Ward, 263, 268. [24] Madan, 'Bodleian Library finance', 10.

was in turn followed by George Thomason in 1632.[25] The main purchases were, as the library ordinances indicated, closely tied to imports from Frankfurt. For several years in the late 1620s book purchases were simply noted in the library accounts as £30 spent 'at the autumn mart' and £20 'at the spring mart', but in the 1630s, when the Thirty Years War had disrupted the Frankfurt market, France and Italy were cited as the source of purchases. Imports from Italy normally came through Robert Martin, while Octavian Pullen, who shared the main supply from 1639 to 1642 with George Thomason, quotes Paris and Lyons as his sources.[26] Nine of Pullen's bills for 1639–40 survive and show that at this time he was submitting priced lists of his foreign purchases from which the librarian made his choice.[27] With few exceptions all the books offered by Pullen were bought by the library.

But this system ended with the civil war. In 1642–3 no rent was received from the library's London property, and in the following years none came from that in Berkshire. Expenditure on books dropped to £12 a year and, since normal trade between Oxford and London was disrupted, there were changes too in the suppliers and the quality of books supplied. The library's meagre resources, soon falling to less than £10 a year for books, were spread among a few booksellers with Oxford connections, particularly Francis Bowman, an Oxford bookseller who migrated to London, Michael Sparke, a London stationer who was a native of Eynsham and partner of the Oxford printer William Turner, and Thomas Robinson, an Oxford bookseller with a shop on the corner of High Street by St Mary's church. The change from the major London to the minor provincial trade is illustrated by a bill for books presented by Robinson in June 1645. This bill comprises twenty-eight items bought for a total of £2 16s 1d, all English publications and, as the price indicates, mainly pamphlets.[28] But more remarkable is the tenor of the pamphlets, for the majority are by puritan writers. At a time when Oxford was still a royal garrison and the seat of a court which revered the memory of Laud, it is surprising to find such a selection of polemical pamphlets in the stock of an Oxford bookseller; and that the library should choose to spend a third of its meagre book allocation on buying a handful of pamphlets of this kind betokens a degree of current awareness which was quite new. This purchase also illustrates the complete breakdown of the arrangement with the Stationers' Company made in 1610 which should have brought in free copies of all London publications.

Though some spectacularly successful purchases were made in the second half of the seventeenth century, the library never had, for a variety of reasons, any very consistent buying policy. No accounts survive for 1647–8, but purchasing remained

---

[25] Bodl. Library records b. 36, nos 4, 7; *Bodleian Account Book 1613–1646*, ed. Hampshire, pp. x, 8, 15, 18, 23–4, 158–61. CCCA MS 492, fo 13 is a substantial fragment of a bill from Featherstone receipted 27 July 1627.

[26] *Bodleian Account Book 1613–1646*, ed. Hampshire, pp. x, 46, 92–3, 96, 105, 125, 131.

[27] Bodl. Library records b. 36, nos 16–25.

[28] Ibid., no. 30; for details see G. Hampshire, 'An unusual Bodleian purchase in 1645', *Bodleian Library Record* x (1978–82).

small in scale until the late 1660s.[29] The reason may have been partly the absorption of the librarian and his small number of staff in the business of dealing with the great scholarly collection of John Selden, which had reached Oxford in 1654. The financial outlook was also discouraging, for the effects of the civil war were long-lasting. The library's loan of £500, made to Charles I in 1642, was never repaid, and in the early 1650s the unpaid rents from the London property amounted to over £200. More rents began to be received in 1660 but the library's capital account had a further setback with the failure of legal action to regain £450 of the money owed by Bodley's defaulting executor, Sir John Bennet.[30] Then, just when conditions were improving, the Great Fire of London destroyed the London property and again no rents were received for several years.

But this was not the whole picture. The university was prepared to use money in other accounts when the cause seemed good, and in the period 1668–72 about £125 a year was spent on books and manuscripts; in these four years the library's total expenditure was consistently more than twice its income and the deficit was regularly made good, the Bodleian chest being empty, by transfers of over £100 a year from the university's schools account, which was supposed to be used to further the activities of the university press.[31] Subventions of this kind were made particularly to finance the purchase of special collections, the first being one of medieval manuscripts formed by Christopher, first Lord Hatton, which the library bought in 1671 through the bookseller Robert Scott, then its principal London agent. It was the first step in acquisitions which within a decade made the library famous as a repository of materials for the study of Anglo-Saxon and early English philology and history.

Meanwhile the library's resources for regular book-buying continued to shrink and some attempt to remedy the position was made by the sale of duplicates. In 1676 Hyde, the librarian, was paid £10 from library funds 'for his paines about the duplicats', and Obadiah Walker, newly elected master of University College, was paid £10 from the vice-chancellor's account 'for his care and pains in prizing the duplicats'.[32] Many of the books sold at this time were probably replaced by copies in the Selden collections. They certainly included some of the earliest donations to the library which had been stamped with the arms of those who gave money for their purchase. The original Bodleian first folio of Shakespeare was also presumably sold, probably in 1676 or at an earlier sale in 1664; but although it was eventually restored, its recovery was an expensive operation, for in 1905 the library had to pay £3,000 to regain its former property.[33]

The sale of duplicates in December 1676 brought in £248, but this had no immediate effect on purchases for, put aside in the library chest, it was borrowed by the

[29] Macray, Annals, 105.

[30] Bodl. Library records e. 8, fo 158ᵛ; see also Bodleian Account Book 1613–1646, ed. Hampshire, pp. vii–viii.

[31] OUA WP/β/21/5, fos 14, 18, 22, 26.

[32] Bodl. Library records c. 28, fo 5ᵛ; OUA WP/β/21/5, fo 46.

[33] E. Craster, History of the Bodleian Library 1845–1945 (Oxford 1952), 179–81.

vice-chancellor in the years 1680–2 when the university urgently needed funds for the building of the Ashmolean Museum. Most of this was repaid in 1685–6 and enabled the library to buy £134-worth of books from Robert Scott in 1687, but purchases of this size could not be repeated and by the 1690s routine expenditure on books dropped to about £10 a year. Thomas Hyde, in his letter of resignation dated 10 March 1701, described his financial problems:

I should have left the library more compleat and better furnished but that the building of the elaboratory [the Ashmolean Museum] did so exhaust the university mony that no books were bought in severall years after it. And at other times when books were sometimes bought, it was (as you well know) never left to me to buy them, the vice-chancellor not allowing me to lay out any university mony. And therefore some have blamed me without cause for not getting all sorts of books.

Hyde went on to explain the procedure he adopted and its negative result:

Before the visitations I did usually spend a month's time in preparing a list of good books to offer to the curators, but I could seldom get them bought, being commongly answered in short that they had no mony. Nay, I have been chid and reproved by the vice-chancellor for offering to put them to so much charge in buying books. These things at last discouraged me from medling in it.[34]

Such scattered records as have survived support Hyde's contention that he was allowed little direct responsibility for book purchase, and the library accounts show that when the curators warned the librarian that they had no money they were usually speaking the truth. This did not, however, deter them from making elaborate plans to purchase desiderata: in November 1684, for example, they ordered 'that the term catalogues at London, the Francfort catalogue, [and] the *Acta eruditorum* in Germania be from time to time, as they come forth, brought into the library'.[35] This sad decline in purchasing was fortunately arrested during the librarianship of Hyde's successor, John Hudson, between 1701 and 1719.

Salaries for the librarian, under-keeper, and janitor to carry out the curators' orders had first call on the available funds and totalled £51 6s 8d after Bodley's death.[36] This sum would have been considered quite inadequate by John Dury (died 1680), a protestant scholar with a wide experience of European libraries who was deputy in charge of books and artefacts at St James's palace between 1650 and 1654.[37] Rather typically he published his thoughts on the subject, considering the status of librarians as far too lowly; his remarks on Oxford are significant in view of his European experience:

I have been informed, that in Oxford (where the most famous librarie now exstant amongst the protestant-Christians is kept,) the setled maintenance of the librarie-keeper is not above fiftie or sixtie pound *per annum*, but . . . if librarie-keepers did understand themselves in the nature of their work, and would make themselvs, as they ought to bee, useful in their places

---

[34] Macray, *Annals*, 170–1.
[35] Bodl. Library records e. 3, fo 9. The *Acta eruditorum* was a periodical started in 1682 at Leipzig.
[36] *Bodleian Account Book 1613–1646*, ed. Hampshire, p. ix.   [37] *DNB*.

in a publick waie, they ought to becom agents for the advancement of universal learning; and to this effect I could wish that their places [should receive] the competent allowance of two hundred pound a year.[38]

About the same time the librarian at Cambridge University was paid £10 a year, with fees.[39]

Annual binding costs were usually under £10, being £4 6s 0d in 1620–1 and £8 2s 0d in 1638–9, for example. Other costs were entertainment expenses for the visitors' dinner, gloves and fees for the vice-chancellor amounting to £17 8s 4d each year between 1614 and 1646, and varying sums for structural repairs, such as £3 16s ½d in 1634–5 for glazing, plumbing, and roof-mending.[40]

In his draft statute Bodley stipulated that senior graduates and bachelors of arts of two years' standing should be admitted to read in the library, and that other bachelors of arts might also be admitted if they came to the library in cap and gown and there demeaned themselves 'with reverence in geving place to their superiours'. Non-members of the university might be admitted if they were likely to be men of influence or benefactors. 'Sonnes of lordes of the parliament' came within this category, 'for of the lordes themselves there may be no question', as did those who 'of their zelous affection to all kinds of good literature have enriched that stoare house with their bountifull giftes'. Students from other universities from whatever country might be given permission by grace of congregation if their proposed studies in the library found favour.[41] When the statute was finally promulgated by convocation in June 1610 undergraduates who were students in civil law of three years' standing and of good repute also qualified as readers.[42]

After Bodley's death successive curatorial ordinances clarified or elaborated the clauses of the original statute. By an ordinance confirmed by convocation in November 1613 'bachelors of arts and all other persons being undergraduates' were enjoined to 'abstain from reading books ill-adapted to their studies', and careful rules of conduct were laid down. Undergraduates and all graduates of inferior order were to 'show due observance and deference to the seniors by giving place to them the moment they see them approaching the bench or bookcase where they are, or else by passing to them, if the case require it, the book which they were previously using'. Any default in such conduct was to be officially recorded by the registrar. The clause about books ill adapted to a particular student's study clearly caused confusion, and a further ordinance of July 1615 explained that bachelors and undergraduates were not to 'roam about from place to place but are diligently to ply their studies in that part of the library wherein the books of the faculty of arts

---

[38] John Dury, *The Reformed Librarie-Keeper* (London 1650), 16–17.

[39] Oates, *Cambridge University Library*, 382.

[40] *Bodleian Account Book 1613–1646*, ed. Hampshire, 13, 41, 99, 117, 148.

[41] *Trecentale bodleianum*, 49–53; see also G. W. Wheeler, 'Sir Thomas Bodley's "Heads of Statutes" ', *Bodleian Quarterly Record* iii (1920–2), 119–21.

[42] *Statutes*, trans. Ward, 254.

(and those alone) are contained'. There was a topographical problem here, for until the 1630s, when the present staircases were built, the entrance to the old library was at the west end, and all those wishing to get to Arts End had perforce to walk the length of Duke Humfrey's Library to reach the books they were permitted to read. The best that could be done was to insist that they were not to roam. One important exception was made: strangers and foreigners admitted as readers who might not qualify as senior graduates were nevertheless specifically exempted from these restrictions on movement.[43]

For the first year of the library's operation, that is from 8 November 1602 to 7 November 1603, Thomas James kept a meticulous register, noting all readers by name and whether they read in the morning or afternoon, or both.[44] The record is no doubt incomplete and inaccurate in parts, but as the first Bodleian reader-census it is a very useful record. It shows, for instance, that the average daily attendance for the whole year was seventeen, but the daily attendance was rising to thirty for the few days of November 1603 included in the record. Attendance in the afternoon was always slightly higher than in the morning. The total number of readers recorded in that first year was 248, of whom twenty were *extranei*, that is non-members of the university admitted by special dispensation, half of whom were graduates of or students from foreign universities. It has been calculated that there were about 540 Oxford graduates then resident and of these 209 are entered in the register as readers; the most regular attenders were graduates of St Edmund Hall, whose number of attendances is twice that of the next college on the list—Exeter. Figures like this are curious and interesting, but may be subject to varying interpretations: constant attendance at the university's library might be evidence of intellectual curiosity or just an indication of an inadequate college library. Foreign students were commonly more constant than the natives, for they were normally in Oxford for a limited period and, having no access to college libraries, had to rely solely on the Bodleian Library.[45] The first foreign student entered as a reader, a French student of civil law, Jean Basire, was admitted on 15 February 1603, three months after the opening of the library, and in a letter written a week later from his lodging at a draper's house, he described with satisfaction how he had been admitted to the public library to work six hours a day.[46] Altogether ten foreign students were admitted as readers in 1603 and twelve in 1604, and the range of nationalities—German, Dutch, Scandinavian, and Swiss—witnesses to the part the library was beginning to play in the advancement of learning in Europe.[47] The library admissions book in fact reveals a regular flow of students from Europe who found the Bodleian Library the best endowed and most accessible for their purpose. The outbreak of the Thirty Years War put a stop to some of the travel, but the Bodleian

---

[43] *Statutes*, trans. Ward, 264 (1613), 269 (1615).

[44] Bodl. MS Bodley 763; see also G. W. Wheeler, 'Readers in the Bodleian, Nov. 8, 1602–Nov. 7, 1603', *Bodleian Quarterly Record* iii (1920–2), 212–18 and Wheeler, *Earliest Catalogues*, 124–34.

[45] Philip, *Bodleian Library*, 20–1.   [46] Bodl. MS Don. c. 171.

[47] For a 'List of persons using the Bodleian 1602–1622' see *Reg. Univ.* ed. Clark, pt 1, 262–82.

records evidence a continuing traffic of academic refugees from Germany and the other war-torn protestant countries of northern Europe. From 1620 to the outbreak of the civil war in England about 350 foreign readers were admitted; half of these were students from Germany, especially from the Palatinate, the Baltic states, and as far east as Prussian Poland. Another major category of foreign readers was those from Holland, including a steady stream of young men who came from Dutch universities to work under John Prideaux, rector of Exeter—the last being Nicholas Heinsius, son of the famous Daniel Heinsius of Leiden, who came on the eve of the civil war in July 1641.[48]

Many of these visitors were energetic young scholars on their way to fame and slightly impatient of local erudition and library regulations. Such a one was Lucas Holsten of Hamburg, who later became Vatican librarian. He was granted a grace to use the library in June 1622 and, as he reported, eagerly ran through the old Latin and Greek codices 'which no-one in that part of the world ever bothers about'; he also studied some of the Greek manuscripts given by Sir Henry Savile in 1620.[49]

The determination of foreign scholars was all the more commendable because they were not unaware of a persistent xenophobia. Johan Friedrich Gronovius, for instance, admitted as a reader in 1639, complained in a letter to the French classical scholar Salmasius that visitors were called 'Frencs dogs'.[50] It must have been particularly galling for Gronovius, born in Hamburg and aspiring to a Dutch professorship, to be so called, but what chiefly irked him was the library regulation which insisted that manuscripts might not be used by anyone not a member of the university unless he brought a master of arts or bachelor of civil law to stand or sit by his side so long as he used the manuscript.[51] As he complained, 'where am I to find men willing to waste time to sit with me for three or four hours studying my finger-nails?'[52] It must have been difficult enough to do this in midsummer, when Gronovius was writing, but in midwinter in an unheated library it must have been well-nigh impossible to persuade anyone to undertake this personal supervision. The curators, however, took the matter seriously and called attention to this requirement of the Bodleian statute in 1641, apparently following the discovery that some pages of a manuscript had been stolen. The curators' action produced a strong protest from eighteen readers, ten of whom were Germans, seven Danes, and one an English medical student.[53] They complained that there were no grounds for suspecting them and thought the fault more probably lay with the librarian's lax administration. However that may be, the signatures of seventeen foreign scholars on this remonstrance gives some measure of the use of the library

---

[48] Bodl. Library records e. 533, fo 172ᵛ; P. R. Sellin, *Daniel Heinsius and Stuart England* (Leiden 1968), 84–7.

[49] Lucas Holsten *Epistolae ad diversos*, ed. J. F. Boissonade (Paris 1817), 10, 124.

[50] *Sylloges epistolarum a viris illustribus scriptarum*, ed. Petrus Burmannus (5 vols Leiden 1727) ii. 594.

[51] *Statutes*, trans. Ward, 248. [52] *Sylloges*, ed. Burmannus ii. 594.

[53] Macray, *Annals*, 94.

by foreign students at this time and, though the numbers fell after the civil war, foreign scholars remained an active and important factor in the library's history.

One of the library's ordinances approved by the university on 13 November 1613 laid down that the librarian had to keep entry-books in which, when any reader ordered a book (that is a manuscript or printed book too small or valuable to be chained with the folios) the shelf-mark and the reader's name had to be recorded.[54] Unfortunately only one complete entry-book from the seventeenth century, for 1648 and 1649, survives. This shows for the first half of 1648 an average of about fifteen readers ordering between them up to about thirty volumes a day.[55] This compares with an earlier report of the chaplain of the Venetian ambassador who visited the library in 1618 and reported that 'one always sees fifteen or twenty gownsmen studying there most attentively and writing down the fruit of their reading'.[56] But it must be admitted that the figures of book-orders for 1648 reflect the persistent work of one who was not a gownsman: David Czernitz of Danzig was the most regular attender, frequently ordering five or six manuscripts a day, steadily working his way through particular groups, especially in the Digby and Laud collections.[57] When Brian Twyne and Thomas James disputed in 1613 about the shelving of manuscripts, James had apparently maintained in self-defence that only two people, Twyne and Thomas Allen, consulted manuscripts in the Bodleian Library.[58] The great donations of the Barocci, Laud, and Digby collections changed all that and it was as a great manuscript repository, particularly of Greek manuscripts, that the library attracted scholars from Europe in the next few decades of the seventeenth century. The library's international reputation, mentioned by John Dury in 1650, continued to grow during the last few decades of the seventeenth century, and its status was well reflected in the description by Humphrey Wanley which was included in editions of Edward Chamberlayne's *Angliae notitia* from 1702: 'The most famous Bodleian Library, that for a noble lightsome fabrick, number of excellent books, choice manuscripts, diversity of languages, liberty of studying, [and] facility of finding any book, equals, if not surpasses, most of the foreign libraries'.[59]

COLLEGE LIBRARIES

The book needs of senior members of the university were met not only by the Bodleian Library, the public library for the scholarly world, but also by their colleges.[60] Benefactions from their members were, in the medieval tradition, the col-

---

[54] *Statutes*, trans. Ward, 266.

[55] Bodl. Library records e. 544, fos 5ʳ–26ʳ; altogether 400 books were ordered in January 1648.

[56] *CSPV 1617–19*, 247. Since the figure for 1618 probably includes those reading only folio works, overall numbers of readers would appear to have increased.

[57] Bodl. Library records e. 544, for example fos 5ʳ–17ʳ.

[58] G. W. Wheeler, ' "Free-access" in 1613', *Bodleian Quarterly Record* iv (1923–5), 197.

[59] Edward Chamberlayne, *Angliae notitia* (London 1669, 20th edn London 1702), 449.

[60] For college and departmental libraries see P. Morgan, *Oxford Libraries Outside the Bodleian* (Oxford 1973, 2nd edn Oxford 1980).

leges' main source of books; substantial bequests and gifts of books to libraries can be estimated at an average of six a decade between 1600 and 1640, rising to over ten during the civil war and Commonwealth and decreasing to about seven after the Restoration.[61] These ranged from the bequest of at least 2,000 volumes— mostly theological—by Archdeacon Philip Bisse to Wadham in 1613, through the 780 surviving vernacular and other works left by Robert Burton to Christ Church in 1640, to much smaller groups such as the six early printed books and his own publications bequeathed by William Prynne to Oriel in 1669.[62] The custom, found in earlier centuries, that on leaving a college a member should give either a single volume or the money to purchase one continued; indeed this practice was laid down as a duty at Christ Church in 1614.[63] In most colleges the names of donors are recorded inside the books, sometimes on specially printed labels.[64] At Christ Church between 1583 and 1636 and at Brasenose College between 1650 and 1764 determining bachelors combined each year to buy a substantial work suitably inscribed with their names, a custom also known at Edinburgh University from 1596.[65] In addition colleges followed the example of the Bodleian Library by start- ing to record gifts in benefactors' registers, All Souls being the earliest in 1604.[66] Christ Church also imitated the Bodleian Library in 1614 in having its newly insti- tuted benefactors' register finely bound, the first college to do so. After the Restoration more colleges adopted this practice, presumably to attract donors by displaying how their gifts would be splendidly recorded. Those at Queen's College and St Edmund Hall have local views of architectural interest incorporated into the decorative capitals.[67]

The medieval practice of maintaining a chained collection of books for reference and an unchained one for loans continued throughout the seventeenth century. Purchases of chains appear at irregular intervals in several college accounts, as at Jesus in 1636, at Lincoln in 1661, between 1632 and 1781 at Brasenose, and between 1685 and 1717 at St Edmund Hall.[68] Special funds for buying books were unusual

[61] These estimates are based on an analysis of Morgan, *Oxford Libraries*; cf. the general remarks in S. Jayne, *Library Catalogues of the English Renaissance* (Berkeley and Los Angeles 1956, 2nd edn Godalming 1983), 17–21. For gifts to medieval college libraries see N. R. Ker, 'Oxford college libraries before 1500' in J. Ijsewijn and J. Paquet (eds), *The Universities in the Late Middle Ages* (Louvain 1978), 301–5 and Ker, 'Provision of books', 447.

[62] Wood, *History of the Colleges and Halls*, 601; Kiessling, *Library of Robert Burton*, pp. xii–xiii; C. L. Shadwell, *Registrum orielense* (2 vols London 1893–1902) i. 152.

[63] W. G. Hiscock, *A Christ Church Miscellany* (Oxford 1946), 6. For this practice at Merton in the thir- teenth century see Ker, 'College libraries before 1500', 302.

[64] *STC* i. 145–53. See also B. N. Lee, *Early Printed Book Labels: a catalogue of dated personal labels and gift labels printed in Britain to the year 1760* (Pinner 1976); for Oxford examples with dates see for instance nos 6, 10, 56.

[65] Morgan, *Oxford Libraries*, 19, 25.

[66] Jayne, *Catalogues*, 18–21; E. Craster, *The History of All Souls College Library*, ed. E. F. Jacob (London 1971), 53.

[67] *Fine Bindings 1500–1700 from Oxford Libraries: catalogue of an exhibition* (Oxford 1968), nos 127–8, 219, 224–6, 231, 233.

[68] C. J. Fordyce and T. M. Knox, 'The library of Jesus College, Oxford', *Proceedings and Papers of the Oxford Bibliographical Society* v (1936–9), 61; V. H. H. Green, *The Commonwealth of Lincoln College 1427–1977*

at the beginning of the seventeenth century, but common by its end. Corpus Christi College enjoyed a bequest of £10 a year for this purpose from 1597, and from 1606 Lincoln allowed admission fees to be spent on books or plate; after the Restoration most colleges made regular allotments from fees, as did Oriel from 1662 and Brasenose from 1669.[69]

The extent of the use made of college libraries is now difficult to determine. A register of books borrowed by fellows between 1665 and 1698 survives at New College and one used at St Edmund Hall from 1666 to 1674 was retained by White Kennett; another for the years 1693–1706 is at Balliol, but such records are few.[70] So far as college manuscripts are concerned the key to their use is Gerard Langbaine, who began cataloguing Greek manuscripts in the Bodleian Library in 1643.[71] He went on to do the same in college libraries, and became the one to whom all scholars turned—and he followed up their inquiries with zest. Thus in 1647 he spent two days in Magdalen College library unsuccessfully dealing with a query from Archbishop Ussher and 'while I was there tumbling amongst their books I light[ed] upon an old English comment upon the psalms, the hymns of the Church and Athanasius's Creed which I presently conjectured (though there be no name to it) to be Wickliff's'.[72] Between 1650 and 1652 Langbaine undertook to provide transcripts of Oxford manuscripts for Marcus Meibom, then compiling his *Antiquae musicae auctores septem*, published at Amsterdam in 1652. For this he employed a team of young graduates, paid from funds held by Bodley's Librarian, to transcribe manuscripts in Magdalen, Balliol, Lincoln, and Trinity Colleges.[73] Langbaine himself, having worked on Barocci and Savile manuscripts for Meibom, went to consult a Ptolemy manuscript in New College. There he 'met with a rub which I cannot yet get removed, [for] they have in New College archives a copy of Ptolemy which they promised me the use of but cannot find the key. Upon a like occasion before they were content to break open the doore and make a new key; and they promise (in case they doe not find that againe) to doe so now.'[74] The work of Langbaine was drawn on by Edward Bernard's *Catalogi librorum manuscriptorum Angliae et Hiberniae* of 1697, which covered Oxford college libraries.

The regulations issued by colleges from time to time to prevent misuse, partic-

(Oxford 1979), 275 n. 5; R. W. Jeffery, 'The bursars' account books', *The Brazen Nose* iv (1924–9), 24–5; A. B. Emden, *An Account of the Chapel and Library Building, St Edmund Hall, Oxford* (Oxford 1932), 24.

[69] J. G. Milne, *The Early History of Corpus Christi College, Oxford* (Oxford 1946), 38; A. Clark, *Lincoln* (London 1898), 61; Morgan, *Oxford Libraries*, 19, 98.

[70] Morgan, *Oxford Libraries*, 90 (New College), 11 (Balliol); the St Edmund Hall register is now with White Kennett's manuscripts in BL Landsdowne MS 697 (cited by Emden, *Account of the Chapel and Library*, 7–8).

[71] *Summary Catalogue of Western Manuscripts in the Bodleian Library* (7 vols 1895–1953) i, p. xxii.

[72] Richard Parr, *The Life of . . . James Usher, late Lord Arch-Bishop of Armagh* (London 1686), 513.

[73] For this scheme, in which John Selden was the intermediary, see Marquardus Gudius, *Epistolae*, ed. Petrus Burmannus (Utrecht 1697), 56–7. Langbaine's reports to Selden on the progress of transcriptions are in Bodl. MS Selden *supra* 109, fos 325 ff.

[74] Bodl. MS Selden *supra* 109, fo 327. For the importance of Langbaine's work see *Summary Catalogue of Western Manuscripts* i, pp. xviii–xxv; his work was not generally available during his lifetime, but a series of his notebooks was purchased by the Bodleian Library after his death in 1658.

ularly the unauthorized removal of books, also provide evidence of how their libraries were used. In 1630 scholars of Queen's College were excluded from their library on penalty of a fine of 12*d*, and a new bar and new keys were provided for the door.[75] At St John's College in 1655 new regulations were issued because 'there have been of late several abuses and disorders in the library tending to the greate discouragement of students [and] yf not tymely prevented to the ruine of the library'. Orders were added to existing rules providing that no one was to be admitted who did not have the president's permission or was not of at least a year's standing, unless a gentleman-commoner, and that no one was to obtain a key except from the president.[76] The detailed orders issued for the library of Magdalen Hall in 1656 typify the regulations which by then were common form in most colleges. They included provision that 'none of what degree or condition soever shall take away any book ... under pain of expulsion from the Hall, excepting the library-keeper', and that only the principal, MAs, BAs, and upper-commoners and undergraduates of three years' standing might study in the library, though any undergraduate could use it on payment of 20*s*. The library was open between 6 a.m. and 6 p.m. in the summer and between 8 a.m. and 4 p.m. in the winter. Upper-commoners paid 10*s* on entrance, MAs 10*s*, BAs 5*s* on graduating, 'for the benefit of the library'.[77] Some colleges introduced more detailed rules, as at Oriel in 1655, when fellow-commoners over 17 years old and having taken the oath were admitted, 'keepinge themselves in those seates where the humanity and philosophy bookes are placed'.[78] It was not unusual for regulations to permit non-members to be admitted to read; at St John's a member had 'to continue with them in the same seate' on pain of a fine of 10*s*.[79] On the other hand the 1665 regulations at Oriel laid down that non-members could be admitted for a fee of 5*s* and the cost of a key.[80]

Thomas James had wanted to provide a separate room in the Bodleian Library for 'the yonguer sort' in 1608, but the proposal was rejected by Sir Thomas Bodley on the grounds of the expense of the extra library-keeper required, so only graduates were admitted during his lifetime.[81] But the statute approved for the library after Bodley's death included among those who were to be admitted as readers two special classes of undergraduate: students in civil law of three years' standing and sons of barons.[82] Anthony Wood 'took [it] to be the happines of his life' when as a new BA he was admitted into Arts End.[83] In his *Microcosmographie*, first published in London in 1628, John Earle, a Merton man, envisaged 'a young gentleman of

[75] *The Diary of Thomas Crosfield*, ed. F. S. Boas (London 1935), 46 (18 August 1630).

[76] J. F. Fuggles, 'A history of the library of St. John's College, Oxford, from the foundation of the college to 1660' (Oxford B. Litt. thesis 1975), 175.

[77] Prefixed to HCA catalogus benefactorum aulae Magdalenae bibliothecae.

[78] *Dean's Register of Oriel*, 334.

[79] Fuggles, 'Library of St. John's College', 175.   [80] *Dean's Register of Oriel*, 334.

[81] *Letters of Bodley to James*, ed. Wheeler, 183; see also P. Morgan, 'Books for "the yonguer sort"', *Antiquarian Book Monthly Review* iii (1976), 117.

[82] *Statutes*, trans. Ward, 254.   [83] Wood, *Life and Times* i. 182.

the university' loitering at the library studying heraldry and genealogy, but not opening his own books in their 'neat silk strings'. It is perhaps significant that when the same author wrote about 'a down-right scholar' and 'a pretender to learning' libraries were not mentioned.[84]

Queen's College had a separate library for tabardars from at least 1625, chiefly supplied by gifts from their own number (some of these books survive).[85] John Harris, a scholar at Trinity College from 1684 to 1688, recorded in his autobiography that:

> there were also in this college a very good collection of philosophy and mathematics books of all kinds, as also of the classicks, placed in a room which we called the *Lower Library*, where every undergraduate had the liberty to go and study as long as he pleased which was a mighty advantage to the house and ought to be imitated by other colleges.[86]

Trinity was apparently the first in a general movement in Harris's time for colleges to provide books in separate rooms or to make special arrangements for undergraduate reading. At Balliol for example money was being spent on a separate room by 1700.[87]

Recreational reading, naturally, was not catered for officially. Anthony Wood wrote in 1668 that 'a little before Christmas, the Christ Church men, yong men, set a library in Short's Coffee Hous in the study ther, *viz*. Rabelais, poems, plaies, etc. One scholar gave a booke of 1*s* and chaine 10*d*.' This was possibly the earliest example of a feature of coffee-houses in Oxford satirically mentioned in Thomas Warton's *Companion to the Guide and a Guide to the Companion* first published about 1760.[88] English literature, however, was not entirely neglected: Brasenose College, for example, in 1675 bought verse by Edmund Spenser, Abraham Cowley, and Katherine Philips, and in 1679 plays by Beaumont and Fletcher.[89] More came, of course, in gifts and bequests such as Robert Burton's to Christ Church, already mentioned, Brian Twyne's to Corpus Christi College in 1644 and Richard Mansfield's to Lincoln College in 1648.[90] Topographical works by authors like Sir William Dugdale, Robert Plot, and Anthony Wood were given to or purchased by most colleges.

Besides libraries in colleges and halls, the seventeenth century saw the beginnings of specialist subject collections in Oxford. A small library was attached to the Savilian chairs of astronomy and geometry from 1619 and was augmented by their successive holders, while both manuscripts and printed books were acquired at the

---

[84] *Character Writings of the Seventeenth Century*, ed. H. Morley (London 1891), 181–2, 185–6, 206–7.

[85] Morgan, *Oxford Libraries*, 109.

[86] M. Maclagan, *Trinity College* (Oxford 1955, rev. edn Oxford 1963), 22, quoting a Trinity College manuscript.

[87] J. Jones, 'The eighteenth-century undergraduates' library', *Balliol College Annual Record* (1980), 61.

[88] Wood, *Life and Times* ii. 147; Thomas Warton, *A Companion to the Guide and a Guide to the Companion: being a complete supplement to all the accounts of Oxford hitherto published* (London n.d.), 9–10.

[89] BNCA library account book 1667–1872.

[90] R. F. Ovenell, *Brian Twyne's Library* (Oxford Bibliographical Soc. new ser. iv 1952), 9–10; Morgan, *Oxford Libraries*, 63.

physic (botanic) garden founded in 1621.[91] At the new Ashmolean Museum 'a handsome room fitted for a library of natural history and philosophy' was mentioned in 1684, as well as a room 'designed for a chymical library to which several books of that argument have been already presented'.[92]

The size of college libraries varied so considerably that generalizations are hazardous. By 1632, for example, Jesus College had only sixty-five manuscripts and about 330 printed books, while in the 1620s New College had 295 manuscripts and about 3,300 printed books.[93] These approximate sizes contrast with the estimated 16,000 manuscripts and printed books already at the Bodleian Library in 1620.[94] Samples of the books that are now on the shelves of Oxford and Cambridge college and departmental libraries suggest several tendencies. At Oxford the imprint dates reveal a steady increase until the 1680s and a decline thereafter, while at Cambridge the decline begins about 1660. At both universities there are more books in Latin printed up to 1640 than in English; the subsequent increase in English imprints was no doubt caused by the large number of controversial tracts that came to the colleges in bequests. Thus numbers of books in English now on the shelves rise from about 10 per cent of those dated 1600 to about 60 per cent of those printed at the close of the century.[95] But it must be borne in mind that a high proportion reached the libraries many years after publication.

Large bequests during the last quarter of the seventeenth century, such as those of Thomas Marshall to Lincoln College in 1685, Sir Leoline Jenkins to Jesus in the same year, Thomas Barlow to Queen's in 1691, and John Fitzwilliam to Magdalen in 1699, besides enriching the libraries' scholarly value caused the perennial problem of shelving to be felt more acutely.[96] Throughout the century additional buildings had had to be erected or adaptations made. To take a few examples, Otho Nicholson's gift in 1613 to Christ Church enabled an older room to be adapted, while at Jesus a separate building was erected between 1621 and 1630 but pulled down in 1640, the presses being stored until reused in the present library, which was completed with a new gallery in 1679.[97] The new shelving in Merton's ancient library may have influenced that chosen for both the Bodleian Library and Christ Church in the reign of James I.[98] The room over the antechapel at St Edmund Hall, built between 1680 and 1690, was the earliest Oxford college to have bookcases backed against a wall, like Arts End in the Bodleian Library, and is believed to be the latest designed for chaining.[99]

[91] Craster, *History of the Bodleian Library*, 183–4; Morgan, *Oxford Libraries*, 167; H. N. Clokie, *An Account of the Herbaria in the Department of Botany in the University of Oxford* (Oxford 1964), 12–13, 16–17.

[92] Chamberlayne, *Angliae notitia* (12th edn London 1684), pt 2, pp. 327–8; see also R. F. Ovenell, *The Ashmolean Museum 1683–1894* (Oxford 1986), 24, 39.

[93] Jayne, *Catalogues*, 71–2, 74.　　　　　　　　　　　　　　[94] Macray, *Annals*, 58.

[95] J. W. Jolliffe (ed.), *Computers and Early Books: report of the LOC project investigating means of compiling a machine-readable union catalogue of pre-1801 books in Oxford, Cambridge and the British Museum* (London 1974), 1–2, 9, 122, (fig. I), 124, (fig.IV).

[96] Morgan, *Oxford Libraries*, 52, 64, 69, 111.

[97] Hiscock, *Christ Church Miscellany*, 6–7; Fordyce and Knox, 'Library of Jesus College', 54–6.

[98] Philip, *Bodleian Library*, 8.　　　　[99] B. H. Streeter, *The Chained Library* (London 1931), 75–6.

During the seventeenth century evidence grows of members of colleges being paid to look after their libraries. From 1599 Christ Church elected a BA as a library-keeper to hold office until he took his master's degree. From 1603 the *custos bibliothecae* at St John's was paid 6*s* 8*d* (later increased by £2) a quarter, to attend for an hour daily. At Brasenose the post was combined with that of *custos jocalium* (keeper of the treasures) and names are recorded from 1614, while the earliest record of a library-keeper at Lincoln is 1641.[100]

A feature of many smaller libraries, such as those in colleges, is the frequency with which new catalogues are compiled; Oxford is no exception and many have survived.[101] For example St John's, Oriel, and Corpus Christi colleges have catalogues from the reign of James I, and New College, Oriel, Magdalen, All Souls, Brasenose, and Jesus from that of Charles I.[102] The first catalogue to be printed was that of Magdalen Hall in 1661, designed by Principal Henry Wilkinson both as an incentive to further reading by his students and as a guide to old members who wished to fill gaps or replace books lost in the civil war; it shows that the hall then owned about 500 volumes, with 646 entries in the catalogue.[103] Colleges also acquired copies of the 1674 Bodleian catalogue of printed books to interleave and annotate with their own holdings; those at Christ Church, Jesus, Merton, and St John's are among those which have survived.[104]

PRESS AND BOOK-TRADE

The seventeenth century saw the real beginning of university printing and publishing in Oxford, developing slowly and almost in parallel to what occurred in Cambridge.[105] Throughout this period certain occupations including printing, bookselling, and bookbinding were reserved for 'privileged persons'; as in university towns generally the book-trade came under close academic control, and was exempt from any other regulations, such as those of guilds or city corporations. The status of privileged person was attained by the formality of matriculating in the university.[106] At the opening of the century Joseph Barnes had been settled near the west end of St Mary's church since 1573 as a bookseller and wine-merchant, and from 1586 as a printer also in consequence of a decree of star cham-

---

[100] Hiscock, *Christ Church Miscellany*, 4; Fuggles, 'Library of St. John's College', 100; *Brasenose Register* ii. 92–4, 110; A. J. Butler, 'The benefactions bestowed on the college', *Brasenose Monographs* i, no. IV, p. 23; G. H. Wakeling, 'History of the college, 1603–1660' ibid. ii pt 1, no. XI, p. 22; Green, *Lincoln College*, 275 n. 2.

[101] Jayne, *Catalogues*, 67–75.

[102] Morgan, *Oxford Libraries*, 9, 23, 40, 53, 70, 94–5, 103, 133; Craster, *All Souls Library*, 59.

[103] Madan, *Oxford Books* no. 2545.

[104] Hiscock, *Christ Church Miscellany*, 14; Morgan, *Oxford Libraries*, 53, 88, 133.

[105] For the history of the university press see H. Carter, *A History of the Oxford University Press* (Oxford 1975). Madan's *Oxford Books* not only describes each book up to 1680 but also includes documents and surveys of the Oxford book-trade and its members. Madan's manuscript notebooks for the period 1681–1713 were transcribed and edited by J. S. G. Simmons as a *Chronological List of Oxford Books 1681–1713*, printed in a limited edition of twelve copies in 1954. For Cambridge see M. H. Black, *Cambridge University Press 1584–1984* (Cambridge 1984), 50–86.

[106] Carter, *Oxford University Press*, 189–90.

ber empowering the university to allow one press with one apprentice.[107] Cambridge University, though, had appointed its own printer ten years earlier.[108] Barnes's type-stock included Greek and Hebrew; among his more significant publications were the first Bodleian catalogue of 1605 and Captain John Smith's *Map of Virginia* in 1612.[109] Barnes regularly used the university arms on the title-pages of his books and described himself as printer to the university, but his activities were in fact independent; the business was his own and he alone bore all the financial hazards. In this independent and to some extent uncontrolled position Barnes in 1617 was succeeded by two printers who shared a press, William Wrench and John Lichfield, the former leaving after only one year, the latter the first representative of a family whose members were styled printers to the university continuously, working with varying efficiency, up to 1749.

The average number of titles printed in Oxford each year over the first three decades of the seventeenth century was thirteen, rising to twenty-eight between 1631 and 1640. During the civil war the great number of tracts produced caused an enormous increase, peaking at 277 in 1643 and then slumping to eight in 1649. For the years 1651 to 1670 the annual average was thirty-two. During the 1670s, the last decade for which figures are available, this rose to thirty-eight.[110]

Until Bishop Fell reorganized university printing after the Restoration, books produced by those styled printers to the university were a matter of individual negotiation. The cost to an Oxford author is well exemplified by surviving documents relating to Nathanael Carpenter's *Geography Delineated*, printed by John Lichfield and William Turner and sold by Henry Cripps in 1624–5. Carpenter, a fellow of Exeter College and a most meticulous person, entered into an agreement with these three tradesmen on 30 July 1624 which stipulated among its detailed arrangements that at least one sheet a week should be printed at a cost of 12s 6d a sheet for 1,250 copies, the usual size of an edition at this time. The total amounts in the end were £47 10s 0d for workmanship and £45 for paper, making a unit cost of approximately 1s 6d. The wholesale price was 3s 4d a copy, just over 100 per cent on prime cost. The final retail price was not specified and no doubt varied, but it was probably about 200 per cent on prime cost, a proportion which Bishop Fell adopted when calculating retail prices for the university press in the late 1660s. Carpenter's book was typographically complex, so the cost of labour formed a comparatively high proportion of the total—over 50 per cent. In more straightforward works the cost of paper was sometimes nearer 75 per cent and this did not decrease substantially until the eighteenth century.[111]

---

[107] Ibid. 22 [108] Black, *Cambridge University Press*, 36.

[109] Madan, *Oxford Books*, nos 264, 365.

[110] These statistics have been calculated by Dr Tim Wales from Madan's *Oxford Books*, and exclude works published by Oxford booksellers but printed at London. They suffer from the disadvantage that much new material has accrued since the publication of Madan's work, although it is unlikely that the inclusion of this would alter the broad trends. Cf. *STC* iii. 210–11.

[111] Madan, *Oxford Books*, no 554; I. G. Philip, 'A seventeenth-century agreement between author and printer', *Bodleian Library Record* x (1978–82), 68–73, based on documents in ECA.

Barnes's successors did less credit to the university and were more obviously uncontrolled, though they had to be licensed like other Oxford tradesmen. This state of affairs became critical in 1627 when the two printers Lichfield and Turner broke up their partnership and established two independent presses, a clear contravention of the decree in star chamber of 1586. This prompted the intervention of Laud as chancellor; in 1632 he regularized the position by obtaining letters patent which gave the university the right to appoint three printers (an amplification of 1633 allowed each to have two presses and two apprentices). But this was the merely mechanical aspect of Laud's ideal of a university press which would print Greek manuscripts, notably those in the Barocci collection which he himself had inspired the third earl of Pembroke to give to the Bodleian Library in 1628. The next extension of Laud's design was a royal charter, obtained in 1636, giving the university the right to print all kinds of books. This grant included the printing of bibles, almanacs, and grammars, formerly the monopoly of the royal printers and the Stationers' Company of London; but the university made little attempt at this stage to enter into competition with the London trade, rapidly surrendering its newly acquired right to the company in return for an annual payment of £200. The immediate effect was that this income made possible the purchase of matrices for Hebrew and Arabic type at Leiden in 1637.[112]

For Laud himself the prime purpose of a university press was to be the production of texts, especially Greek ones, only available in manuscript. The inroads into the monopoly of the London stationers were, however, a useful bargaining counter. In contrast at Cambridge editions of the Bible and Book of Common Prayer were published from 1629.[113] Laud was delighted at progress towards the kind of press he had in mind, but the increase in type available was not always matched by an increased efficiency or discipline in the printers. Lichfield printed the *Ad Corinthios epistola prior* of Pope Clement I in 1633 with the Greek type presented to the university by Sir Henry Savile, a work of genuinely modern scholarship with missing words supplied by the editor printed in red, the earliest use of this method, but the other considerable Greek project of these years, the edition of the chronicle of John Malalas, was frustrated by the 'peevishness or extreme sottishness' of the printer, William Turner, partly caused by lack of payment.[114]

Between the retirement of Joseph Barnes in 1617 and the outbreak of civil war in 1642 there were some other notable publications issued in Oxford: five editions of Robert Burton's *Anatomy of Melancholy*, the Bodleian catalogue of 1620, and the first English translation of the Latin version of Bacon's *Advancement of Learning* in 1640.[115] Yet no further new work of scholarship appeared until, after the outbreak of war, James Ussher, archbishop of Armagh, and Gerard Langbaine, provost of

[112] Carter, *Oxford University Press*, 29–34. During 1636 and 1637 a Latin grammar and three almanacs were published at Oxford: Madan, *Oxford Books*, nos 831, 842, 848, 869.

[113] Black, *Cambridge University Press*, 71–4.

[114] Carter, *Oxford University Press*, 30, 36; Madan, *Oxford Books*, nos 742–3 and ii, pp. 524–5.

[115] Madan, *Oxford Books*, nos. 493, 521, 605, 716, 881, 934.

Queen's College, put learned works to press and ensured fuller use of the university's stock of Greek, Hebrew, and Arabic type. Their achievement was built on Laud's foundations and the range of type was further increased by the purchase of more Hebrew founts in 1655–7 and a large fount of Anglo-Saxon in 1656. The growing stock of exotic types made possible the production of a remarkable series of scholarly books in oriental languages, mathematics, and Anglo-Saxon: Bainbridge's *Canicularia* in 1648, Pocock's *Specimen historiae Arabum* in 1650 and his *Porta Mosis* in 1655, Wallis's *Opera mathematica* (1656–7), and Somner's *Dictionarium saxonico-latino-anglicum* of 1659.[116] But the university's part in these productions did not involve direct responsibility for publication; all these important works printed at Oxford during the Commonwealth were published not by the university but by London or Oxford booksellers.

In 1659 the university took a step towards direct control of the press by appointing an *architypographus*, an academic officer envisaged in Laud's scheme, who could advance money from university funds to booksellers who would undertake to issue those books which the university wished to see published. For such purposes the university was willing to lend its Greek, Hebrew, and Arabic type, but was still unwilling to run any direct risk of loss or to consider the possibility of profit. For ten years the question of some more formal establishment of a learned press on Laud's model was considered at intervals and without effect until in 1668 John Fell, dean of Christ Church and vice-chancellor, persuaded Archbishop Sheldon to agree that the Sheldonian Theatre, his gift to the university, should serve as a printing-house when not required for university ceremonies. Now for the first time the university was to have its own premises for a press and its own equipment. Fell set out his intentions in a letter of 1671 to Isaac Vossius: 'We have it in mind ... to set up in this place a press freed from mercenary artifices, which will serve not so much to make profits for the booksellers as to further the interests and convenience of scholars.'[117] To that end Fell combined with three distinguished partners who took a lease which relieved the university of all responsibility for the press, and with their own money and investments from others in the trade were able to pursue a policy which initiated a heroic age in the history of the press. Fell did his utmost to provide for all aspects of a learned press: he established a regular type-foundry at Oxford and encouraged the setting up of a paper-mill at Wolvercote; his gifts of Syriac, Coptic, and Samaritan founts added to the Old English, Gothic, and Runic acquired from Francis Junius, together with the Hebrew and Arabic bought in 1637, made Oxford second only to the Vatican press in variety of exotic types while, with its five presses, it exceeded in potential scale of operation all but three of the London printers. The 1670s saw the production of the third Bodleian catalogue in 1674, Wood's *Historia universitatis* in the same year, Loggan's *Oxonia*

[116] Carter, *Oxford University Press*, 38–41, 44, 113, 239–40; Madan, *Oxford Books*, nos 2002, 2034, 2277, 2316, 2458.
[117] Leiden, Universiteitsbibliotheek, MS Burm. Cod. Fol. no. 11, ii, fo 62, quoted by Carter, *Oxford University Press*, 61.

illustrata in 1675, Prideaux's *Marmora oxoniensia* in 1676, and Plot's *Oxfordshire* in 1677, works which not only brought fame to the press but added greatly to the reputation of the university.[118] Fell drew up an even more ambitious programme of publication, which was impossible of realization because he commanded neither the finance required nor the means of marketing his products at an economic rate. Years later Arthur Charlett, master of University College, recalled this crucial weakness in the Oxford press: 'the vending of books we never could compasse; the want of vent broke Bishop Fell's body, public spirit, courage, purse and presse'. Nor were these losses significantly offset by profits from bible printings after 1675.[119]

After Fell's death in 1686 his executors made over to the university all his interest in the press and its equipment, and so at last in 1690 a true university press was established. By an agreement made with the Stationers' Company in 1692 the university surrendered the control of the bible press and abandoned the unsuccessful experiment of Fell and his partners of printing schoolbooks, almanacs, and the metrical psalms; the hostility of the stationers in London was thus considerably reduced.[120] The activities of Fell and the effects of his legacy did not pass unnoticed in Cambridge, and probably influenced the reforms begun there by Richard Bentley in 1696.[121]

Both Laud and Fell took a rather ungrateful view of the artificers of the printing trade. Laud believed that 'these mechanic craftsmen for the most part look for profit and saving of labour, caring not at all for beauty of letters or good and seemly workmanship', and Fell similarly feared that the booksellers' desire for profit conflicted with the claims of scholarship.[122] But until 1690, when it was able to establish its own press with Fell's legacy, the university was still to a large extent dependent on the Oxford book-trade for publishing and marketing the scholarly works of its members. Probably no one took more risks on their behalf than the Oxford bookseller Richard Davis. He had been privileged as a university stationer in 1639 and set up as a bookseller in 1645–6. His career lasted until 1685 when he 'shut up his shop windows for debt'; his stock was dispersed in four auctions between 1686 and 1692, the catalogues listing over 40,000 works. Davis's scale of operation as a bookseller far outstripped those of his Oxford rivals, but he was not just a bookseller and made an important contribution to academic publishing in Oxford. In a career lasting forty years he published, or had some share or interest in publishing or reissuing, over 250 items. Though he reissued three books in 1690, his effective career ended in 1685. Many of these works were textbooks, often shared with other local booksellers, sermons, or other minor works of pastoral theology, but his total output included a substantial element of scientific

---

[118] Carter, *Oxford University Press*, 55–8, 67, 74–8, 82–6, 90–1; Madan, *Oxford Books*, nos 2996, 2999, 3035, 3092, 3130.

[119] Carter, *Oxford University Press*, 61–3; HMC *Second Report*, p. 254[b].

[120] Carter, *Oxford University Press*, 105–9.

[121] Black, *Cambridge University Press*, 87–90.   [122] Carter, *Oxford University Press*, 31.

publication.[123] From 1663 to 1684 he published, doubtless at the author's expense, a number of the writings of Robert Boyle and, presumably through Boyle, he was commissioned to produce three numbers of the Royal Society's *Philosophical Transactions* in 1665–6 when the great plague prevented publication in London.[124] His connection with university printers was very close, from the appointment of Samuel Clarke as *architypographus* in 1658 to Clarke's death in 1669. During this period Davis undertook many publications for the university and entered into a bond to repay any money which the university was able to advance; after Fell came into the publishing field Davis continued to take responsibility for many scholarly works which were beyond the resources of the partners. So in 1672 he published Thomas Willis's *De anima brutorum*, 'the first considerable medical work from the Sheldonian press', and in 1679 the third edition, also printed at the Sheldonian press, of the same author's *Pharmaceutice rationalis*.[125] These are instances of Davis taking over the cost and the risk of marketing books which the university delegates were glad to print but lacked the organization to distribute. His growing reputation and confidence are shown in his undertaking with the encouragement of the Royal Society the publication by subscription of an expensive and difficult work, John Wallis's *De algebra* in 1685.[126] But Davis's interests were never solely scientific and one of his major achievements, which strained his resources even more, was the publication in 1679 of an edition of Lyndwood's *Provinciale*, still considered a standard and authoritative text for the study of English canon law, the *editio princeps* of which had been one of the first books printed in Oxford two centuries earlier.[127]

Davis's long and not entirely unsuccessful career can be contrasted with that of Anthony Stephens, a minor figure in the Oxford book world from the same period. Stephens served an apprenticeship in Oxford, being made a freeman and matriculating as a bookseller in 1681. Between 1682 and 1685 he published twenty-one works, but he could not repay the money borrowed to finance these ventures and was sued for debt in 1685. In 1687 his career ended when his stock was seized and valued at £130, a sum comparable with the probate stock value of £100 left by his first master Thomas Gilbert in 1673, the £120 stock value of John Forrest in the same year, and the value of £120 put on John Barnes's stock in the following year. The inventory reveals that publications in which Stephens had a financial interest had not sold, some remaining in quantities of several hundred copies.[128] It is

[123] Wood, *Life and Times* iii. 157; R. Davis, *Catalogus variorum in quavis lingua et facultate insignium* (4 vols London 1686 and Oxford 1686–92). The publication figures quoted were calculated from Madan and E. A. Clough, *A Short-Title Catalogue Arranged Geographically of Books Printed and Distributed in the English Provincial Towns . . . up to . . . 1700* (London 1969), 91–109.

[124] *The Correspondence of Henry Oldenburg*, ed. A. R. Hall and M. B. Hall (13 vols Madison, London, and Philadelphia 1965–86) ii. 563, 579. Cf L. Rostenberg, *Literary, Political, Scientific, Religious and Legal Publishing, Printing and Bookselling in England, 1551–1700* (2 vols New York 1965) ii. 250–1.

[125] Carter, *Oxford University Press*, 43–4; Madan, *Oxford Books*, nos 2953–4, 3239.

[126] John Wallis, *A Proposal about Printing a Treatise of Algebra* (Oxford 1683).

[127] Madan, *Oxford Books*, nos 14, 3221; Carter, *Oxford University Press*, 10–12.

[128] D. G. Vaisey, 'Anthony Stephens: the rise and fall of an Oxford bookseller' in *Studies in the Book Trade in honour of Graham Pollard* (Oxford Bibliographical Soc. new ser. xviii 1975).

interesting that apparently Stephens had no other occupation recorded, unlike many other members of the Oxford book-trade.

Books printed in Oxford before publishers' bindings became the general custom required covering, and binders were well established in the town by the seventeenth century. Some were connected with the book-trade as stationers and printers—for instance William Spire, stationer and bookbinder, who died in 1636—but there were several men supporting themselves entirely by this craft.[129] After the Restoration artistic standards rose in Oxford, as elsewhere in England, and the work of Roger Bartlett in the 1680s and of Richard Sedgley in the 1690s, especially on benefactors' registers, is particularly noteworthy.[130] Scholarly book-collectors of the period, such as Robert Burton or Thomas Barlow, favoured plain calf with a minimum of blind-tooling; vellum or sheep wrap-arounds were in a minority. The Bodleian Library, however, ordered vellum covers for smaller books received in sheets from the Stationers' Company.

It is, of course, impossible to generalize about how much individual dons and students spent on books or the size of personal libraries. The contents of the latter reflect idiosyncratic interests besides what was necessary for study or teaching. For example the inventory of Richard Fysher of Merton College in 1601 lists seventy-two books, some in Italian and French, while in 1607 John Rainolds, president of Corpus Christi College, left well over 2,000 scholarly books.[131] The vernacular books prominent in the collections of Brian Twyne (died 1644), now in Corpus Christi College, and Robert Burton (died 1640), now divided between the Bodleian Library and Christ Church, are exceptional and form a significant proportion of the minority of works in English already discussed.[132] The large library bequeathed by Thomas Barlow (died 1691) to the Bodleian Library and Queen's College shows the widest range of learned interests.[133] At the opening of the seventeenth century John English, a fellow of St John's College who died in 1613, had 518 books—over half of them theological—assessed at £22 10s 3d, roughly equalling in value his clothing, furniture, and personal effects.[134] Also in 1613 Walter Browne of Corpus Christi College left as many as 535 books.[135] These two libraries were well above average, for in the years up to 1640 bequests of books by individuals to their colleges and the inventories of other owners rarely exceeded

[129] S. Gibson, *Abstracts from the Wills and Testamentary Documents of Binders, Printers, and Stationers of Oxford from 1493 to 1638* (London 1907), 21–2, 29–32; N. R. Ker, *Fragments of Medieval Manuscripts used as Pastedowns in Oxford Bindings, with a Survey of Oxford Binding c. 1515–1620* (Oxford Bibliographical Soc. new ser. v 1954), 212–17.

[130] *Fine Bindings 1500–1700*, nos 215, 224–6, 231–2; M. M. Foot, *The Henry Davis Gift: a collection of book-bindings* (2 vols London 1978–83) ii, nos 129, 151 and the references there cited.

[131] Jayne, *Catalogues*, 135, 139; M. H. Curtis, *Oxford and Cambridge in Transition 1558–1642* (Oxford 1959), 285.

[132] Ovenell, *Brian Twyne's Library*, 12–42; Kiessling, *Library of Robert Burton*, pp. viii–ix.

[133] Macray, *Annals*, 157–8; Morgan, *Oxford Libraries*, 111.

[134] Jayne, *Catalogues*, 144; W. C. Costin, 'The inventory of John English, B. C. L., fellow of St John's College', *Oxoniensia* xi–xii (1946–7), 106–16.

[135] Jayne, *Catalogues*, 144 (where he is wrongly styled 'William').

fifty volumes.[136] But later in the century senior members owned considerably larger collections, such as the theological library formed by Richard Allestree which he left for the use of the regius professors of divinity (now administered by Christ Church) or the miscellaneous collection of several hundred works bequeathed to Corpus Christi College by John Roswell in 1684.[137]

These senior scholars probably acquired at least a proportion of their books in Oxford, where undergraduates also presumably bought their necessary textbooks. Thus the very full financial accounts kept by the brothers John and Richard Newdigate while they were at Trinity College reveal the purchase of over fifty books between 1618 and 1620, at a cost in excess of £7 10s 0d.[138] Later in the century Henry Fleming of Queen's College spent £1 11s 0d in 1679 on seven logic, arithmetic, and classics books, including a Euclid, together with two quires of blank paper for 1s, presumably for notes and exercises. In 1689 George Fleming of St Edmund Hall owned ninety-seven books worth £5 10s 6d, of which only a few had been brought with him from his Westmorland home.[139]

Clearly the need for booksellers, and to a lesser extent printers and binders, grew during the seventeenth century, securing Oxford's place as one of the two main centres in England for the book-trade outside London.

[136] Ibid. 133–72 lists over eighty-five benefactions or bequests to Oxford libraries and thirteen inventories attached to wills of Oxford individuals; see also Curtis, *Oxford and Cambridge*, 285–6.

[137] Hiscock, *Christ Church Miscellany*, 14–15; Morgan, *Oxford Libraries*, 39.

[138] Warwicks. RO CR 136, B 602. This information was kindly provided by Dr Vivienne Larminie, who has now published an edition of the Newdigate account book: 'The undergraduate account book of John and Richard Newdigate, 1618–1621', *Camden Miscellany* xxx (Camden Soc. 4th ser. xxxix 1990).

[139] *The Flemings in Oxford* i. 295–6, ii. 273–80.

14

Oxford and the Civil Wars

IAN ROY and DIETRICH REINHART

THE history of Oxford University during the 1640s divides naturally into three parts: the two years before the civil war, the four years of royalist occupation (1642–6), and the immediate post-war years of parliamentary visitation.

The university had been closely associated with the government of the personal rule. Laud had been chancellor, and the colleges and halls had (with some exceptions) responded positively to the new ideas emanating from Whitehall and Lambeth. Through his agents at Oxford and as visitor of six colleges and all the halls by the end of the decade, the archbishop successfully undertook a comprehensive reformation of his alma mater, introducing new statutes, which were to govern the university thereafter, and reasserting its ancient rights. The programme of reform was supervised by the vice-chancellor, usually Laud's nominee, and the proctors, in charge of discipline, who met the heads of houses every week. Richard Zouche, regius professor of civil law and principal of St Alban Hall, Peter Turner of Merton, Savilian professor of geometry and one-time Gresham professor, and Brian Twyne, created keeper of the university archives as a reward for his endeavours in collecting the evidence for the university's case against the town, were Laud's principal assistants. Important changes were made in matters of worship and liturgy in the chapels, some of which were extensively rebuilt, ornamented and beautified to accommodate the new emphasis on ceremony and ritual. The wearing of proper academic dress, especially hats, and the use of Latin was insisted on. Strict control was exercised over the behaviour of the students. The power of the proctors was reinforced: to quell disturbances among the student body, to settle disputes between town and gown, and to regulate the large number of alehouses—which were reduced by two thirds.

In this drive for discipline the archbishop had the enthusiastic support of the king himself. Charles I was, like Laud, a 'great lover of order and decency', and royal munificence in the 1630s towards this favoured seat of learning was considerable. The university press was given new privileges, the university a new charter. The royal visit of 1636 set the seal upon the endeavours of Laud. Regardless of expense, he entertained the king and queen in a setting which was thoroughly reformed, unveiling the most complete and expensive manifestation of the new order in stone and bronze, the splendid Canterbury quadrangle at his old college, St John's. The dons responded by presenting no less than eight volumes of commemorative royal verses during the decade, three in 1633, the year of Laud's promotion to Canterbury. A new programme of building showed that the university was expanding to meet the needs of the increasing numbers who required higher education.[1]

The growth of the colleges and halls in size and wealth, their new building projects, and their reassertion of old privileges inevitably collided with the interests of the city which housed them. Since the town–gown disturbances of the Middle Ages the crown had helped the seat of learning to dominate the city. Now the closest possible association with the royal government, and the presence of Laud and his Oxford protégé Bishop Juxon on the privy council, reinforced the university's claims. The right of the proctors to keep the watches at night and patrol the streets (night-walking, or noctivagation), to appoint the clerk of the market and levy tolls on corn, to try certain cases before its own courts and to take the goods of convicted felons were all enforced. The obligation of the new mayor to swear to uphold the privileges of the academics, in the university church, and to undertake in the same place the annual St Scholastica's day ceremony was insisted on, as was the taking of the mayor's oath in the exchequer chamber at Westminster.

The triumph of these 'innovations' at Oxford had always been, despite the royal ban on disputing them, contentious, and they became even more so in the course of 1640. With the calling of the Short Parliament and the continuing resistance of the Scots giving encouragement to the opponents of the personal rule, the nation— and the university—entered upon what Frewen, the Laudian president of Magdalen, called 'this busy and inquisitive time'.[2] The support which the crown enjoyed from the clergy in the execution of its policies against the Scots, and the convocation of the clergy's promulgation of the canons (the ill-famed 'etcetera' oath had to be taken by university masters as well as the clergy and other office-holders) placed the clerical hierarchy, and so the universities, in the front line of political controversy. That disenchantment with the Laudian regime, perhaps even anticlericalism, was present and growing at Oxford itself during the politically and militarily disastrous summer of 1640 is shown by the willingness of the townsmen, led by Alderman John Nixon, to challenge the university's monopoly of the night watch. Laud took them to court. The town's high steward, the earl of Berkshire, was no match for the archbishop and his powerful allies, and Laud went so far as to scold the councillors publicly for alleged drunkenness at the mayoral elections, a sin against his campaign for 'decency and order' at Oxford. A scare over the mass being openly celebrated at Oxford gave credence to similar criticisms made in the

---

[1] For Laud as chancellor see K. Sharpe, 'Archbishop Laud and the University of Oxford' in H. Lloyd Jones, V. Pearl, and B. Worden (eds), *History and Imagination: essays in honour of H. R. Trevor-Roper* (London 1981); Laud, *Works* v. 267; A. J. Taylor, 'The royal visit to Oxford in 1636', *Oxoniensia* i (1936), 151–8; Madan, *Oxford Books* ii, nos 651, 726, 728, 731, 816, 840, 871, 931.

[2] Edward Hyde, earl of Clarendon, *The History of the Rebellion and Civil Wars in England*, ed. W. D. Macray (6 vols Oxford 1888) ii. 533; Wood, *History of the University* ii. 425–6; *Proceedings of the Short Parliament of 1640*, ed. E. Cope and W. Coates (Camden Soc. 4th ser. xix 1977), 182; *The Short Parliament (1640): diary of Sir Thomas Aston*, ed. J. Maltby (Camden Soc. 4th ser. xxxv 1988), 96.

Short Parliament.[3] University convocation proved reluctant to re-elect in October, for the Long Parliament, the nominee of the court, Secretary of State Sir Francis Windebank, whom it had chosen in March. Instead the celebrated lawyer John Selden, the protégé of the university's high steward, the earl of Pembroke, joined Laud's nominee, the noted diplomat Sir Thomas Roe, at Westminster.[4]

When parliament met in November 1640, the close ties between the university and the government ensured that the former could not long remain immune from attacks on the latter. Dissident academics (such as 'Long Harry' Wilkinson) and resentful townsmen clamoured for revenge as the archbishop's difficulties mounted. The association of Arminianism with popery gave them an opportunity for counter-attack: anti-popery re-emerged in Oxford as elsewhere, and for two years moral panics about Catholic activity were common. In January 1641 the city petitioned the house of lords against the university's control of the market at Oxford, and later showed that it was no longer prepared to put up with its medieval subjection to the university. Gathering at Carfax every night to hear the latest news from London the Oxford citizens, according to Anthony Wood, formed disorderly assemblies in defiance of the university authorities, roughed up passing scholars, and spread rumours and alarms about popish subversion in the city. Catholic citizens were closely watched, by the joint orders of the vice-chancellor and the mayor, and when in early 1642 some gunpowder was found at the Star Inn there was much excitement. The more puritan students interrupted the services of the Laudian rector of St Martin Carfax, Giles Widdowes, and attacked the local maypole.[5]

The debates in the earlier stages of the Long Parliament, associated with the root-and-branch petitioning movement, uncovered deep unease about alleged popish influence in the university. Pluralism and non-residence among academics were complained of to parliament. The London root-and-branch petition of December 1640 referred to 'great corruptions which are in the universities'.[6] Sir Robert Harley, whose son had attended puritan-inclined Magdalen Hall, chaired the committee set up to remedy the abuses of the universities (a subcommittee of the committee for religion). The records of the university were sent for, closely examined—and not returned. While a bill for reform made little progress—the first reading in August 1641 was the last, and the subcommittee ceased to meet until early 1642—local changes did take place, as the mood of the country was reflected at Oxford. The Arminian rearrangement of Magdalen College chapel was condemned, and by April 1641 the communion table there, and at Queen's College, had been placed in the body of the choir, and the walls plainly whitewashed. In

---

[3] *Oxford Council Acts 1626–65*, ed. M. G. Hobson and H. E. Salter (Oxford 1933), 105–6, 363–4; Laud, *Works* v. 295–6; A. Fletcher, *The Outbreak of the English Civil War* (London 1981), 204; Wood, *History of the University* ii. 425, 437.

[4] M. F. Keeler, *The Long Parliament, 1640–1641* (American Philosophical Soc. Philadelphia 1954), 60, 325, 336–7.

[5] Wood, *History of the University* ii. 427–8; Wood, *Life and Times* i. 49.

[6] *The Constitutional Documents of the Puritan Revolution, 1625–1660*, ed. S. R. Gardiner (Oxford 1889, 3rd edn Oxford 1906), 139.

this way some of the leading colleges at Oxford, as at Cambridge, anticipated the wishes of the house of commons, expressed in its orders of September, much as they had hastened to please a previous regime.[7]

The university defended itself not only by publicly conforming to the new trends where possible but by countering the more extreme charges made to parliament. In a rare show of unanimity the heads met to repudiate the suggestion that 'mass was ordinarily said in the university, and frequented by university men, without any control of the governors there'; only Rogers of New Inn Hall dissented.[8] In April 1641 petitions were drafted to king and parliament, defending both episcopacy and cathedral churches, which were among the earliest in the country to indicate some negative reaction to the reforms proposed by parliament. One claimed to have been subscribed by almost all the resident graduates of the university, and nearly a thousand sympathetic gentry, freeholders, and clergy, who had the future welfare of the church at heart. The flow of commemorative verses celebrating royal events again increased in 1641, with volumes published in May and November.[9]

But the principal champion of the university recognized that he could be of no further use to his alma mater. Writing from the Tower on 25 June 1641 Laud resigned his chancellorship.[10] It was a sign of the changing times that convocation should elect on 6 July as his replacement a leading courtier, Philip Herbert, earl of Pembroke, the university's high steward since 1615, who was a well-known opponent of Laud. His elder brother, William, the third earl, had been Laud's predecessor as chancellor, and two of his sons were currently students at Jesus. Convocation no doubt hoped that he would be better able to protect the university he knew well in its time of trial. Many academics felt that the threat facing their institution was no less serious than that to the religious houses in England a century before. As the brilliant young poet and Christ Church Student William Cartwright apostrophized the earl, he would be a 'tried defense' against those who 'trust | To see our schools mingled with abbey dust'.[11] A general assault on the privileges of clerics and academics would undermine the basis of their existence.

[7] *The Journal of Sir Symonds D'Ewes*, ed. W. Notestein (New Haven 1923), 82; *CJ* ii. 155; list of committee members (November 1640) in *The Diary of Henry Townshend of Elmley Lovett, 1640–1663*, ed. J. Willis-Bund (3 vols Worcestershire Historical Soc. 1915–17) i. 16; *The Private Journals of the Long Parliament*, ed. W. Coates, A. Young, and V. Snow (3 vols New Haven 1982–92) i. 350; *Calendar of the Correspondence of the Smyth Family of Ashton Court, 1548–1642*, ed. J. H. Bettey (Bristol Record Soc. xxxv 1982), 172, 198. The records of the university were still with parliament in 1647: Bodl. MS Wood f. 35, fos 144–5. A copy of the bill 'for the better regulating of the universities' is in the Langbaine collection, OUA WP/γ/26/1, fos 499–527.

[8] OUA WP/γ/11/1, fo 1. The president of St John's, who would no doubt have subscribed, was absent; he was probably visiting Laud in the Tower: Laud, *Works* v. 295–8.

[9] OUA SEP V, 3; Wood, *History of the University* ii. 432. Plush and satin bindings for presentation copies of these verses were less costly than the vice-chancellor's trip (with a coach and six) to Hampton Court to deliver the second volume to the king in person: Madan, *Oxford Books* ii. 148–51, nos 964, 965.

[10] Laud, *Works* v. 300; Madan, *Oxford Books* ii, no. 970.

[11] William Cartwright, 'To the right honourable Phillip Earle of Pembroke and Mountgomery . . .' (Oxford 1641); Madan, *Oxford Books* ii, no. 966.

Much would depend on the men Pembroke chose to fill the most responsible positions in the university.

The Herbert family was cultivated and brutish by turns. Handsome, rich, and munificent, the favourites of James I and, for a time, his son, William and Philip were the 'most noble and incomparable, paire of brethren' to whom Shakespeare's first folio was dedicated, and Aubrey described the elder, a notable benefactor of the Bodleian, as 'a most magnificent and brave peer' who 'loved learned men'. But the fourth earl, head of the royal household in succession to his brother, had long been viewed as a moody, middle-aged Hamlet at the court of Charles I. Though the patron of Van Dyck and later Inigo Jones, he was unstable, subject to uncontrollable 'passions', sub-literate, and easily led. He was increasingly at odds with the king, and within a month of his new appointment lost his post at court, characteristically after exchanging blows with a fellow peer in the house of lords. An old enemy of Laud, he had a profound distrust of the Laudian university, which was motivated in part by pique: he had failed by only nine votes to defeat Laud for the chancellorship in 1630, and according to his adversary 'had long gaped for' the post. He revealed his political preferences (and, Charles I would have said, his political mentor) by nominating as his replacement as high steward Lord Saye and Sele, the leading popular party peer and head of the great north Oxfordshire family, whose two sons were influential in Harley's committee and were later to organize the county's petition which accused the university of 'Arminianisme'.[12]

As vice-chancellor Pembroke chose John Prideaux, rector of Exeter and regius professor of divinity, who had backed his candidacy for the chancellorship in 1630 and was known as a moderate episcopalian. He had the further advantage that he was not associated with the old chancellor. But before the end of the year Prideaux had been advanced to the vacant see of Worcester and, although he remained in Oxford until June 1642 and was not involved in the controversy surrounding the bishops at Westminster, his authority was none the less somewhat weakened by Pembroke's decision to appoint, in March 1642, a special lay commissary to preside over the chancellor's court. The new chancellor had apparently been advised, on questionable legal grounds, and in spite of a plea for general exemption by Oxford divines, that Prideaux as a cleric was barred from so acting by the parliamentary statute passed the previous month, for 'disenabling all persons in holy orders to exercise any temporal jurisdiction or authority'. Pembroke chose as his commissary Giles Sweit, principal of St Alban Hall and a civil lawyer. Sweit can be shown to have exercised this office, usually by surrogate, during 1642.[13] After the

[12] Clarendon, *History of the Rebellion* i. 74–5, 345, ii. 539–41; Wood, *History of the University* ii. 535, 630–1; G. Aylmer, *The King's Servants* (London 1961), 61, 70, 92, 126; *Aubrey's Brief Lives*, ed. A. Clark (2 vols Oxford 1898) i. 318; *Reg. Univ.* ed. Clark, pt 20; *Diary of Henry Townshend*, ed. Willis-Bund, 16; *Private Journals*, ed. Coates *et al.* i. 340–1; *LJ* iv. 575.

[13] Wood, *Life and Times* i. 52 n. The university divines' petition to Pembroke must be dated late February or early March 1642, as reference is made to the 'late act', i.e. the clerical disenabling act of 13 February: OUA papers relating to the siege of Oxford, SP/F/40/7 and 8. OUA WP/γ/4/1a; *Constitutional Documents*, ed. Gardiner, 241–2; OUA chancellor's ct papers 25 (1642).

departure of Prideaux in June his other functions as vice-chancellor were per-formed by successive deputies, Robert Pincke and John Tolson. The growing division in the nation prevented a more permanent solution. Charles I believed that Pembroke, counselled by Viscount Saye and Sele, wanted to replace Prideaux with Clayton, a doctor of medicine and head of the college which bore the chancellor's name; in fact it was another layman, the civil lawyer Sir Nathaniel Brent, warden of Merton College, to whom Pembroke had promised the post. The king made clear, through his new adviser and spokesman, Edward Hyde, well versed in Oxford affairs, that he preferred Pembroke to nominate either Mansell or Fell. With the condemnation by parliament of Fell, and the open partisanship of Mansell, however, the chancellor's freedom of choice was limited. The situation remained unresolved until February 1643 when Tolson, a cleric, became vice-chancellor and Sweit ceased to function as commissary.[14]

The taking of sides in the summer of 1642 had not been precipitated at Oxford by the need to subscribe parliament's protestation oath in February. As a loyalty test this oath was designed to uncover Catholics, not—as early as this—potential royalists, and those asked to accept it (males over 18) could do so, whatever their political views, with a good conscience. In general it is impossible to detect in the surviving returns for the university any significance in the presence or absence of a college member when the oath was taken. Of 2,038 listed (including college servants and privileged persons, eleven sick and three 'deliberating') almost a third of the student body was marked absent, but this can be explained as normal wastage at a low point in the academic year; and, as explained elsewhere, as much as a third of the student body was not recorded at all. Additionally, if the age limit for subscription was strictly applied, more than half the undergraduates would have been too young to qualify. Only one ordinary member can be identified as officially demurring.[15] If the members of parliament, who had eagerly voted for the promulgation of the oath throughout England, ever examined the returns from Oxford, which is doubtful, they would have had the clearest refutation of the charge that popery was rampant in the university; no Catholic recusant was unequivocally revealed by the religious test of February 1642. The heads' earlier rebuttal of the accusation can be said to have been vindicated, so long as we accept that the wholesale absence of so many did not conceal any real political or religious objections to the oath.

A partial exception, however, to the apolitical nature of subscription is the response of the heads of houses. Asked to subscribe in advance of their colleges

[14] J. Le Neve, *Fasti Ecclesiae Anglicanae*, ed. T. D. Hardy (3 vols Oxford 1854) iii. 477; letters of Pembroke and his son Philip to Hyde, June–August 1642: *Clarendon State Papers*, ed. R. Scrope and T. Monkhouse (3 vols Oxford 1767–86) ii. 144–9; Wood, *Life and Times* i. 52; OUA WP/γ/4/1b–c. We are grateful to Dr N. Tyacke for help in reconstructing the history of Giles Sweit's commissaryship.

[15] *Oxfordshire Protestation Returns*, ed. C. S. A. Dobson (Oxfordshire Record Soc. xxxvi 1955), 100–19. For under-registration see S. Porter 'University and society', pp. 35, 41, 44 above. According to Wood only James Hyde, cousin of Edward Hyde, fellow of Corpus Christi and later head of Magdalen Hall, refused on principle: Wood, *Fasti* ii. 92; Wood, *History of the University* ii. 438–9.

seven (and one deputy) did so only with qualifications which emphasized their obedience to monarchical authority. Four of the colleges of these 'qualifiers' followed the lead of their head and took the oath with the reservations he had expressed. Known anti-Laudians, such as those who would soon promote the 'Calvinist' petition of the coming summer, were among those so assenting, while Laudian sympathizers and later royalists were willing to take the oath as originally devised. At this level college solidarity prevailed. But the heads were in a more exposed position, had greater political responsibilities and no doubt felt that they should give a lead; their response was an indication of their thinking at this juncture. All the 'qualifiers' were old followers of Laud, and were later to side with the king. They represented the wealthiest and most important colleges, especially if to their number we can add Frewen, president of Magdalen, who, as a busy pluralist, was absent from Oxford at this time. Laud had worked well during the past decade to place, in the most influential posts, men of his own mind.[16]

There are other and clearer signs of growing divisions at Oxford. That the political initiative still lay with the Long Parliament, and that the errors of the government of the personal rule were still uppermost in the minds of its supporters, can be inferred from the petition organized at Oxford in the early summer of 1642. In form similar to the celebrated grand remonstrance of November 1641 the petitioners indicted in detail the Laudian regime of the 1630s under eleven 'heads of the remonstrance', blaming 'their late chancellor' and his book of statutes for altering the traditional balance of power in the government of the university in favour of the heads of house and the archbishop of Canterbury as visitor, at the expense of the masters in convocation and congregation. They urged parliament to annul the statutes and restore 'the ancient liberties and privileges of the said university'. The ninety-two signatories (including twenty-four from Fell's Christ Church) represented the minority view of those who had suffered under Laud and were excluded from the higher reaches of college government.[17]

But the stance of these academic also-rans was increasingly out of tune with majority opinion at Oxford. The revolutionary steps the leaders of the popular party at Westminster had taken to put England in a posture of defence, and the iconoclastic zealotry of some of their followers, began to produce an adverse effect in the country at large, and nowhere more obviously than in Oxford. If the university could boast that it had organized the first petition to parliament in defence of the existing church, with 'bishops, deans, archdeacons, etc.', it was natural that it should share to the full the reaction in favour of the king, which developed nationwide in the summer of 1642. The stream of royal pronouncements printed at York was publicized and, from June, reprinted at Oxford and well received there,

---

[16] *Protestation Returns*, ed. Dobson, 100–1, 104–5. The seven heads are Tolson (Oriel), Fell (Christ Church), Pincke (New), Mansell (Jesus), Baylie (St John's), Sheldon (All Souls), and Potter (Queen's), while the deputy was Richardson (Brasenose). The four colleges following their lead were Christ Church, Jesus, Queen's, and St John's.

[17] Copies of the petition made by Wood: Bodl. MS Bodley 594, fos 137–46, summarized in HMC *Leyborne-Popham MSS*, 4–5.

thus helping to reduce the impact of the parliamentarian propaganda which had held sway previously.[18] It was now the turn of those who could be identified as puritans to feel the weight of popular disapproval as the country drifted towards civil conflict, and in some quarters they were blamed for the division of the nation.

The king's court at York, gathering men, money, and military resources for the coming war in the early summer, was well aware of the sympathy for the royal cause shown in these months by members of the university, and kept in close touch with some of the leading academics. Later Hyde (by then earl of Clarendon) claimed some credit for concocting a plan, with his friend Gilbert Sheldon, warden of All Souls, and probably also Frewen of Magdalen, to send money and plate from Oxford to York.[19] Writing on 7 July Charles reminded the university of his royal 'care and protection of such nurseries of learning' in the past, and asked for loans from colleges and individuals, at 8 per cent interest.[20] Convocation met on 11 July to agree the proposal, and the same day the first payments were made from the university, Savilian mathematical, and Bodleian chests to Richard Chaworth, the special emissary chosen for the delicate task of negotiating these loans. Chaworth was a well-connected ecclesiatical lawyer and close associate of Laud, who had an intimate knowledge of Oxford politics: a Christ Church man of twenty years' standing, he had served as proctor in 1632. As the ground had been carefully prepared, and he had the able assistance of a young fellow of All Souls, Henry Jansen, his mission was soon crowned with success: within a week the king was able to thank the university for the sum of £10,667 14s 3d paid into his war chest.[21] Unlike Cambridge University, which despite the efforts of Oliver Cromwell, one of the MPs for Cambridge town, was able to smuggle to York over £5,000, partly in coin, partly in silverware, Oxford did not at this time send plate, as apparently originally intended. But, according to one report, colleges with few reserves in their chests pawned their plate to raise the necessary money. By whatever means it was accomplished, Oxford University enjoys the distinction of being the first corporate body to lend material assistance to the king for the coming conflict. It stands, with

---

[18] HMC *Leyborne-Popham MSS*, 4, order of the king to Prideaux, 1 July 1642; *Oxford Council Acts 1626–65*, ed. Hobson and Salter, 366; Wood, *Life and Times* i. 49. From January to August 1642 eighteen orders were sent from Charles I to the university to publicize his declarations (from 14 June to have them reprinted by the university printer): OUA register of convocation 1642–7, NEP/*supra*/25, register Sb, pp. 1–8; Madan, *Oxford Books* ii, pp. 160–8, nos 1006–15, 1019–25, 1027, are Oxford-printed or reprinted royalist items, 25 June–19 August 1642.

[19] OUA SP/F/22, and WP/γ/16/1, 6, 8; Clarendon, *History of the Rebellion* ii. 33–2, 409.

[20] OUA siege papers, 1643–4, SP/F/40/1; OUA register Sb, p. 6.

[21] Chaworth was briefly MP for Midhurst, Sussex. He contributed to the university's commemorative verses from 1622 to 1638: Madan, *Oxford Books* ii, nos 498, 650, 726, 870. His first wife was daughter of the earl of Lindsey, the first lord general of the royalist army; his second wife was a Croft, probably of the celebrated courtier family, and she was buried in Christ Church cathedral in 1645: Keeler, *The Long Parliament*, 131; Wood, *Fasti* i. 515; Wood, *City of Oxford* ii. 550. Jansen was equally well connected, the son and heir of a knight who was groom of the bedchamber: Wood, *Athenae* iv. 138. The king's letter of 18 July 1642: OUA siege papers, SP/F/40/34; OUA register Sb, pp. 6–7. See also *CSPD 1641–3*, 359, and *A Narrative by John Ashburnham* (2 vols London 1830) ii, appx, p. iii.

Cambridge, at the head of the contributors to the king's cause in the accounts of the treasurer-at-war.[22]

How this Oxford loan was made up is unclear, for not all the individual contributors can be identified from the college accounts alone. Four heads of college were described as 'backward' in stirring their houses to contribute: Brent at Merton, Radcliffe of Brasenose, Clayton of Pembroke, and Hood of Lincoln. They account for some of the uncertainties, and delayed payments.[23] By contrast, other prominent figures were active in raising this impressive sum, often giving from their own resources. Frewen lent his own and his college's money; Potter was no doubt behind Queen's contribution and he gave £1,000 more a few months later; Fell was probably instrumental in raising a loan from Christ Church, which, because the record of it is lost, may largely account for that part (about £4,000) of the total sum lent the king in July which cannot be certainly identified. Later he was responsible for the further loan of £300 from the university chest, as well as his own gift of £600. John Greaves, fellow of Merton, helped overcome his college's reluctance to contribute, and he eventually gave £400. Tolson, provost of Oriel, provided £766 at about the same time. If we take these later contributions into account the university lent the royalist cause, in the first few months of the war, £14,283.[24]

The response of parliament to Oxford's action was angry and immediate: on 12 July it ordered the arrest of those members of the university it thought most responsible, Fell, Frewen, Potter, and the absentee Prideaux. But, as we have seen, news from the capital travelled fast to Oxford, and by the time parliament's agents arrived in the city the birds had flown. They found even the townsmen uncooperative, and were dismissed with a 'non sunt inventi'.[25] The vice-chancellor had already taken up his duties at Worcester, and Pincke was now acting as pro-vice-chancellor. The university was firmly in the hands of old Laudians, and equally closely tied to the emerging royalist cause. Charles was properly grateful: Oxonians had shown themselves, more forwardly than most, to be 'good subjects' and their timely aid, he wrote, 'we shall never forgett'.[26] He dispatched Sir John Byron's

[22] *A Narrative by John Ashburnham* ii, appx, pp. iii, xxxvi, xxxix; *The Life of the Reverend Dr John Barwick . . . by Dr Peter Barwick* (London 1724), 22–7; J. Twigg, *The University of Cambridge and the English Revolution* (Woodbridge 1990), 70–5; Bodl. MS Clarendon 23, fo 242, the undated notes of a discourse about Oxford, where the hope is expressed that Lord Danby will help pawn the plate; BL MS Harleian 822, fos 582–3, letter from Oxford to Archbishop Ussher, 18 July 1642, now missing, but calendared in the printed catalogue.

[23] J. Twigg, 'College finances', pp. 775–6 below; letters to be sent to the four heads of 'backward' colleges, none of whose houses was an early contributor, are in Bodl. MS Clarendon 23, fo 242; *A Narrative by John Ashburnham* ii, appx, p. vii (entries probably to be dated from early 1643).

[24] Twigg, 'College finances', 775–6; *A Narrative by John Ashburnham* ii, appx, pp. iii, v, vi, ix, x; OUA siege papers, SP/F/40/4; *CSPD 1641–3*, 359; Clarendon, *History of the Rebellion*, ii. 330–1; Wood, *History of the University* ii. 438–9. The university, Bodleian, and Savilian mathematical chests are mentioned in OUA register Sb, pp. 6–7. The Bodleian gave £500, and entered it as a debt every year until 1782: W. D. Macray, *Annals of the Bodleian Library* (Oxford 1868, 2nd edn Oxford 1890), 95–6.

[25] *LJ* v. 208; *Oxford Council Acts 1626–65*, ed. Hobson and Salter, 367; Ussher letter of 18 July 1642 referred to in n. 22 above.

[26] *Royal Letters addressed to Oxford in City Archives*, ed. O. Ogle (Oxford 1892), 260–1; OUA register Sb, p. 7.

troop of horse, the first raised for the king, for their protection. On the way it was worsted at Brackley by superior parliamentarian forces—one of the first cavalry actions of the war—and limped into Oxford at the end of August.

Nevertheless the welcome the troopers received from most of the academic community was unhesitating: Pincke and others found lodgings and stabling for the weary men though it was 'in the dead of the night', and thereafter, as part of a thirty-strong committee, co-operated enthusiastically with the cavaliers billeted for a fortnight in the city. College heads who, like Pincke, had already shown their distaste for parliamentary proceedings by their refusal to take the protestation oath without qualifications in February—Fell, Tolson, Baylie, and Sheldon (Potter and Mansell were absent)—joined the pro-vice-chancellor in this task, together with Frewen, Escott of Wadham, Lawrence of Balliol, and Walker of University College. Pincke, nearly 70 and using his staff of office as a drill sergeant's baton, had already been training a company of over 300 volunteers consisting of scholars, privileged men, and their servants, in Christ Church quadrangle, and some defensive works had been started.[27] Now the students joined the soldiers in military preparations, arming themselves from the college stores, marching in the streets and drilling in New Parks, and 'night and day gall[ing] their hands with mattocks and shovels' to add a half-moon bastion opposite St Giles' church to the existing works. The commissioners of array for the county met at the Star Inn, the heads of house busied themselves to meet the demands of the cavaliers, raising money from the colleges for their maintenance, further fortifications were planned, and more arms (if only bows and arrows) were distributed to loyalists while suspect townsmen were disarmed.[28]

Oxford had already assumed the air of a garrison town for the king, a role it was soon to play. To escape retribution in such an atmosphere Brent and John Wilkinson (Magdalen Hall), among others, fled to London and other safe havens, as did several of the citizens, including the town's two MPs. Identifiable puritans who attempted to stay soon found themselves and their property in danger. Christopher Rogers, principal of New Inn Hall, and his wife were plundered before they left, and the houses of some citizens were attacked. One of the town councillors complained that he had been 'squeezed' in the street by hostile students, and that he had been intimidated by shots fired into his 'backside' (back garden).[29]

When Byron's men departed, on 10 September, a hundred or so fellows and students went with them as volunteers. Among the 'doctors delinquent', as their opponents styled them, were Thomas Read (New College) and John Nourse (Magdalen), both civil lawyers, and Peter Turner of Merton. Where they led,

[27] HMC *Portland MSS* i. 57; John Rushworth, *Historical Collections* (7 vols London 1659–1701) iii pt 1, p. 759; Wood, *Life and Times* i. 52–9. The delegacy consisted of the vice-chancellor, the proctors, ten doctors, and seventeen masters, named in OUA register Sb, pp. 8–10. An inner circle of seven met daily, and hoped to raise £1,000 for Byron's maintenance: OUA siege papers, SP/F/40/37.

[28] HMC *Portland MSS* i. 59; Wood, *Life and Times* i. 55–9.

[29] OUA siege papers, SP/F/40/36 and 37; Wood, *History of the University* ii. 442–9; HMC *House of Lords MSS* xi. 322–33; HMC *Portland MSS* i. 56–8, 59–60.

others enthusiastically followed. The summer's musters at Oxford had 'so besotted' many young men 'with the training and activitie and gayitie' of the soldier's life that, like Anthony Wood's eldest brother, who 'left his gowne at the town's end', they willingly exchanged their books for a musket. Sixty years later the bishop of Llandaff, William Beaw, recalled that as a young fellow of New College he had 'left his studies and advantages' before the battle of Edgehill, 'and went into the king's service, carrying with him of his pupils and other scholars and gentlemen no less than 12'. Five of these seem to have been fellows of the college.[30]

The military careers of some were short-lived. Turner was captured *en route*, and Nourse was killed at Edgehill. Another Oxford acquisition, of much greater importance, was not fully exploited at the battle. The university press, as we have seen, had been busy and effective in printing the king's declarations during the summer, but after the departure of Byron, and the brief parliamentarian occupation, it fell silent; it may even have been deliberately put out of action. With the arrival of the royalist army in the vicinity, however, the press was ordered into battle. As it was firmly believed among the royalists that there would be mass desertion from the opposing ranks if the king could issue a public pardon to those in arms against him, Lichfield was asked to rush into print hundreds of copies of a royal proclamation to this purpose. By dint of much effort, as he later proudly related, he produced them on time. But in the excitement and confusion of the day of Edgehill they were forgotten, and any good effect they might have had was lost.[31]

Oxford itself had been seized by parliament's forces in September. While the university may have been overwhelmingly royalist, the city lay well within the Long Parliament's sphere of influence before the first campaign of the war. It was the constant passage of London troops which had encouraged the first drilling of the academic volunteers in July, and it had become clear in September that Byron's small force would not be able to hold the city against the army being assembled in the capital under the earl of Essex. When the cavaliers withdrew to join the king at Shrewsbury Pincke wrote to Pembroke in appeasing terms to explain his actions, and sent negotiators to the parliamentarian headquarters at Aylesbury. The exposed position of the university was now all too clear; it was the turn of those displeasing to parliament to leave in a hurry. In addition, and disastrously for the future, the daily alarms and excursions were frightening off the students, 'a great part of whom', wrote Pincke, 'are fled away from us, home to their mothers'. Pembroke's reply to Pincke was devastating. The 'unadvised counsels and actions' of the authorities had reduced the university to the straits it was now in. By admitting

[30] Wood, *Life and Times* i. 53, 59–60, 68; P. Young, *Edgehill 1642: the campaign and the battle* (Kineton 1967), 325–8. Beaw went on to serve the tsar of Russia and the king of Sweden: *Walker Revised: being a revision of John Walker's 'Sufferings of the Clergy during the Grand Rebellion 1642–60'*, ed. A. G. Matthews (Oxford 1948), p. xxv.

[31] Clarendon, *History of the Rebellion* ii. 350, 360, 364–5; *Stuart Royal Proclamations*, ed. J. Larkin and P. L. Hughes (2 vols Oxford 1973–83) ii, no. 351; Madan, *Oxford Books* ii, nos. 1043, 1044. Lichfield's own account in verse is in *Musarum Oxoniensium ΕΠΙΒΑΤΗΡΙΑ* (Oxford 1643): Madan, *Oxford Books* ii, no. 1418.

Cavaliers they had made it 'a notorious mark of opposition' to parliament. Those responsible, he was also reported as saying, were 'a pack of corrupt knaves'. He appears to have blamed Samuel Fell particularly for Oxford's plight, and was to harangue him on the subject later. Pembroke took no action to protect the university from the condign punishment about to fall upon it and which he no doubt felt it richly deserved. Parliament's orders to arrest Frewen and Potter now took effect, and Baylie and Pincke were also imprisoned.[32]

It was not their chancellor who came to take charge at Oxford, however, but their steward, Viscount Saye and Sele, the new lord lieutenant of Oxfordshire. As round-head troops occupied the city and the surrounding villages, he led the destruction of the works which had been built, disarmed the colleges, searched New College and Queen's by torchlight and seized plate hidden at Christ Church. He made a bonfire of 'popish' books and pictures, and the statue of the Virgin Mary on the porch of the university church was damaged by the passing soldiers. He was, however, unde-cided what to do with Oxford. At a conference with the heads of house several alter-natives were discussed, and Principal Rogers, among others, advocated placing a garrison there. Saye may well have agreed, and have hoped to make his son, Nathaniel, governor of Oxford; but both town and gown seemed to prefer Bulstrode Whitelocke, the prominent parliamentarian lawyer and local MP, a man unacceptable to him. In cold, wet weather, his troops growing mutinous, and many academics assuring him that the university was in no position to offer further resistance to par-liament, he decided to cut his losses and leave Oxford undefended. It was an 'open city', therefore, when the king's army, after Edgehill, entered it on Saturday 29 October 1642, and a new phase of the university's history began.[33]

Most of the academians had now exchanged the gown for the military coat, and square caps for the helmet; and, with the exception only of those who by old age were rendered unfit for the services of war, or of those who retained their sacred habit as a cloak for their sloth or timidity, all the rest were on guard night and day, ready for any attack, and became intre-pid and well disciplined soldiers for the defence of the city. . . . Oxford recommended itself in a two-fold character, as the seat of the muses, and also of Charles their king.[34]

[32] Pincke's letter and Pembroke's reply are printed in Rushworth, *Historical Collections*, iii pt 2, pp. 11–13; Wood, *Life and Times* i. 59. For the charges against Pembroke in 1643 see OUA siege papers, SP/F/40/8, Bodl. MS Clarendon 21, fo 118, and MS Wood f. 35, fo 123. Pembroke was simply reflect-ing the official line, for on 1 September the commons had concluded that Oxford had become 'a ren-dez-vous for wicked and ill-affected persons': *CJ* ii. 748, 763. This exchange was given great publicity at the time, and has been widely cited since, but while Pembroke's response sounds genuine it may be doubted whether Pincke, who had given the students such a firm lead, would make such a damaging admission about the exodus of students. It is certainly possible that the letters are among the many forgeries of this year concocted, it was commonly said, by broken-down Oxford and Cambridge schol-ars in London ale-houses: see Madan, *Oxford Books* ii, no. 1038, and *Private Journals*, ed. Coates *et al.* i. 165–6, 326, 328–9.

[33] Wood, *Life and Times* i. 60–7; OUA SP/F/21; *The Diary of Bulstrode Whitelocke, 1605–1675*, ed. R. Spalding (Records of Social and Economic History new ser. xiii 1990), 136–7; Christ Church plate, 'which was concealed', was itemized and ordered to be sent to London's Guildhall, where it was pre-sumably melted down for the parliamentary war effort: PRO SP/28/145, fo 259.

[34] Wood, *History of the University* ii. 470, *sub anno* 1644.

Anthony Wood's own experiences as a schoolboy, and those of his family—his brother had run off to join the army, it will be recalled—as well as his inimitable style, give an added flourish to his description of the transformation of the university brought about by the war. If most academics had welcomed Byron's bedraggled remnant in August how much more joyfully would they receive a few months later the king himself at the head of a splendid army, which had been victorious, as the royalists claimed, at Edgehill, and bearing before them the sixty or seventy colours captured from their enemies at the battle. The university assembled at Christ Church to do homage to his majesty, and he was no doubt confirmed in his view that he had no more loyal followers than those at Oxford. The choice of Oxford as the royalist headquarters was largely accidental—the result of the disposition of the rival forces following the encounter at Edgehill. Nevertheless the close contact maintained between the court and the university during the summer, the never-to-be-forgotten willingness of Oxonians to aid the king in his hour of need, and the up-to-date intelligence of the situation at Oxford supplied by refugees and recruits from the university, persuaded his advisers that the city was not only the most convenient quarters for his army but also the place where the necessary supplies would be given ungrudgingly, and Charles I and his followers housed in the most appropriate manner. Oxford had been, after all, the refuge for parliament in 1625, when plague threatened London, and Charles, his sons, and his nephew Prince Rupert had been entertained there royally in 1636.[35]

When it was clear, by mid-November, that a direct assault on the capital by the king's forces would not be successful, and that the war would not be over by Christmas, the conversion of Oxford to the needs of the royalist war effort on a more permanent basis was begun. The first requirement would be space, and here the university's situation in late 1642 was favourable to the invaders. Many of the students had not come up to Oxford for the Michaelmas term, or had returned home when danger threatened; others had enlisted in the king's forces when the war began. There was a sharp fall in the number of matriculants in 1642, and thereafter, for all the years of war and royalist occupation that followed, undergraduates stayed away. The continuance of academic life would depend upon the smaller body of foundationers, and as rents from college estates dried up, college property was destroyed, and conditions worsened in the garrison town, the number of these would be reduced by death, absence elsewhere in the service of the king—or parliament—or self-imposed exile. The activities of fewer than half those who held fellowships during the war years can be traced (see pp. 716–17 below). In January 1644, when rooms were most in demand, a royal proclamation advised the vice-chancellor to send scholars home. Those who did remain would be heavily outnumbered by the cavaliers lodging with them. It has famously been said that 'the university had found Oxford a busy, prosperous borough, and reduced it to a

[35] Wood, *Life and Times* i. 67–8; Taylor, 'The royal visit to Oxford', 151–8.

cluster of lodging houses'; now it was the turn of the university to submit to this role at the hands of a greater power.[36]

While the royalist occupation of Oxford restored to their places a number of senior academics who earlier had fled on the approach of the parliamentarian forces (three heads, Mansell, Sheldon, and Frewen, returned to their respective colleges 'in the rear of the king's army', while Fell, Pincke, Baylie, and Potter were released from parliamentarian custody before Christmas),[37] noted sympathizers with the parliamentarian cause were forced to flee as they had done on the approach of Byron's troop in August. Only Paul Hood of Lincoln stayed on, and even contributed a lukewarm piece to the volume of verses dedicated to the queen in the following year. Rogers, cruelly vindicated in his belief that it was a mistake not to garrison Oxford for parliament, was again compelled to abandon his headship of New Inn Hall, and Wilkinson also left Magdalen Hall. Sir Nathaniel Brent, active in London, did not return to Merton. The halls, without established revenues of their own, depended largely on fee-paying students, who were attracted to one or two well-known teachers. When these disappeared so did the undergraduates. New Inn Hall, although it had recorded 114 members in February 1642, was apparently empty when the royal mint (plate 24) moved in there in January of the following year, and it had no institutional presence thereafter in Oxford. Magdalen Hall declined from the 145 listed for the protestation oath in early 1642 to no more than half that number of adult males resident by June 1643; and no doubt very few of these were students. Gloucester Hall was poor and weak, requisitioned for munitions production, and turned into a guard house in the inner defences, of which it formed part; yet it somehow managed to survive during 1642–4. There were at least a few students at St Edmund Hall in 1645, but rooms at St Mary Hall seem to have been almost entirely requisitioned for cavalier lodgers.[38]

We know roughly the numbers resident in colleges and halls in summer 1643, as a survey was made of adult males liable to work on the defences. No distinction was made between residents and lodgers, so it is not possible to establish how many of these were scholars. In any case numbers fluctuated widely as the war ebbed and flowed outside Oxford's walls, and there was a constant turnover of royalist lodgers, some staying only a term or two in college before moving on. A total of 1,550 were listed as liable to work, roughly half as many as were returned as living in citizens' houses. The colleges, in other words, were making a substantial contribution to the housing of the city's swollen wartime population. A later

[36] *Stuart Royal Proclamations*, ed. Larkin and Hughes, ii, no 470; Madan, *Oxford Books* ii, no. 1514. For the drop in matriculations see S. Porter, 'University and society', pp. 32–3 above; W. A. Pantin, *Oxford Life in Oxford Archives* (Oxford 1972), 118, citing J. R. Green.

[37] Leoline Jenkins, *The Life of Francis Mansell* (London 1854), 9; Wood wrote that Fell, Potter, Baylie, and Frewen returned to Oxford 'a little before Christmas': Wood, *Life and Times* i. 74–5.

[38] Hood, identified as 'backward' in contributing to the king (see p. 695 above), survived all the changes of regime at Oxford, remaining rector of his college from 1620 to 1668: Foster, *Alumni*; Madan, *Oxford Books* ii, no. 1418; *Protestation Returns*, ed. Dobson, 108–12; T. E. Reinhart, 'The parliamentary visitation of Oxford University, 1646–1652' (Brown University Ph.D. thesis 1984), 224, 606; F. Varley, *The Siege of Oxford* (London 1932), ch. 9. For the fate of the halls see pp. 706–7, 727 below.

listing, of 'strangers' only, part of a desperate search for lodgings just before the first meeting of the king's counter-parliament in January 1644, uncovers the situation in two colleges at that time of acute shortage. Lincoln was home to seventy-two, of whom twenty-nine were women and eight children, and Pembroke contained 107, of whom twenty-three were women and five children. Lincoln was a small college, its normal complement of foundationers only seventeen, and the number of fellows appears to have declined to ten or less. Most of the commoners had left (admission fees dropped from a pre-war average of £7–£8 to 6s 3d at most) and after 1642 only one new student matriculated until the return of peace. The college records show that about twenty good rooms were available for rent, and that an equal number of courtiers, officials, and other royalist gentlemen paid in total £13 each term for these. Even some small and inadequate ones were highly priced. Thomas Fuller, forced from his wealthy London parish, said that even the 'second cockloft' at Lincoln College cost him more in seventeen weeks than had seventeen years at Cambridge before the war. The 1644 census shows that perhaps half the 'stranger' residents had their wives, maidservants and grooms, and in some cases their children, with them in wartime Oxford. Pembroke was even more crowded with 'strangers'. It must be the case that at times of maximum occupation, in several colleges and all the halls, the core of academics was outnumbered by three to four times as many temporary lodgers. In some cases there would be more women living in college rooms than scholars.[39]

Little is known about the process of allocating billets in citizens' houses or in half-empty colleges and halls to the king's soldiers and civilian followers, and one can only guess how much was obtained by the 'harbingers' of the royal household, well practised in obtaining accommodation for a large entourage during the progresses of the sovereign, by private treaty between heads of houses and their friends and relatives among the occupying forces, or by the army quartermasters chalking numbers on doors. The royal proclamations on the subject, acknowledging that the city was so 'pestered and straightned' that disease could spread easily, tried in vain to restrict the flow of migrants. But at the same time the king was bound to recognize an obligation to offer protection to those who were 'forced hither from their owne inhabitation, by the insolency and tyranny of the rebels'.[40] There was an attempt to separate the king's men by their calling as well as their status, with space assigned the soldiery, but royal proclamations acknowledged that officers of the army went where they could; distribution of space was often haphazard and certainly inequitable. College rooms were made available mainly to the wealthy and well placed: royalist officers (but not, of course, their rank and file), prominent royal officials, and the cavalier nobility and gentry. They were joined by

[39] Bodl. MS Add. d. 114, fos 17, 85; Lincoln College accounts, computi, 1644. V. H. Green, *The Commonwealth of Lincoln College, 1427–1977* (Oxford 1979), 245.

[40] *Stuart Royal Proclamations*, ed. Larkin and Hughes ii, nos 389 (18 January 1643), 447 (5 October 1643), 470 (15 January 1644); Madan, *Oxford Books* ii, nos 1192, 1461, 1514.

bishops banished from their sees, ejected Cambridge fellows, and clergy deprived of their livings.[41]

Bursars' accounts and college buttery books show such 'strangers' paying (or not paying) for rent of rooms, dinners in hall, and battels supplied as in a sense temporary members of the college for the duration of their stay. Sir Peter Wyche, comptroller of the household, described himself in 1643 as 'commen[salis]' of Exeter College, where he lodged with his family. George Wharton, the royalist astrologer and artilleryman, was said to have been 'esteemed a member of Queen's College' during his service at Oxford, and his friend and colleague, Elias Ashmole, was the only matriculant at Brasenose in 1644.[42]

While the common soldiery were packed into requisitioned houses in the town, and Thomas Fuller found only an expensive attic, luxury accommodation was available—at a price—in the best rooms of some colleges, and Thomas Clayton senior, the master of Pembroke, was able to keep his large house almost empty. It was natural that Jesus should offer lodgings to prominent figures from Wales and the Marches, such as Lord Herbert, the son of the marquess of Worcester, while he stayed in Oxford. This was done, it was said, 'by order from the court'. In 1644 Sir Edward Stradling, from St Donat's in Glamorgan, who had raised a regiment of foot for the king there, died and was buried in the college. Lincoln College was temporary home for officials of the exchequer, once the king had recreated at Oxford the organs of financial administration. Edward Hyde no doubt owed his lodging at All Souls to his friendship with Gilbert Sheldon, the warden. Royalists with Cheshire connections, like Ashmole, tended to congregate around the Mainwarings and Sir Thomas Aston at Brasenose, which had a long-standing connection with the county. Many cavalier gentry found a welcome in those colleges where they had once been students. Colonel Richard Spencer returned to Corpus Christi, where he had matriculated thirty-four years before: he may have moved to Merton, however, for he buried his children in the chapel there. Some of the judges who joined the king took lodgings with citizen-lawyers in the town, but two were housed in colleges, Foster at Wadham and Bankes with Tolson, provost of Oriel. The sons of these prominent cavaliers were almost the only matriculants in the colleges where their fathers lodged: Bankes's eldest son at Oriel, Sir Peter Wyche's at Exeter, and Secretary Nicholas's son at Pembroke.[43]

---

[41] *Stuart Royal Proclamations*, ed. Larkin and Hughes ii, nos 470, 473, especially pp. 1002, 1005. Cambridge scholars were granted degrees by convocation because of 'the distress of that university': OUA register Sb, p. 25; Wood, *Fasti* ii. 79–89, 100. When Frewen, president of Magdalen, was consecrated bishop of Coventry and Lichfield in the college chapel on 28 April 1644, the archbishop of York and the bishops of Winchester, Oxford, Salisbury, Rochester, and Peterborough were in attendance; in the following month an influx of clergy, recently released from London, was noted: *The Life, Diary and Correspondence of Sir William Dugdale*, ed. W. Hamper (London 1827), 65, 67.

[42] *Musarum Oxoniensium ΕΠΙΒΑΤΗΡΙΑ*; Foster, *Alumni*, s.v. Wych and Bankes; Bodl. MS Wood 44, fo 229; QCA liber Pincerna, 1645; BNCA senior bursar's account, 1644–5, junior bursar's account, 1644, buttery books, 1647–8; *The Diary of Elias Ashmole, 1617–1692*, ed. C. H. Josten (5 vols Oxford 1966) i. 20, ii. 350–2.

[43] P. Young and M. Toynbee, *Strangers in Oxford: a sidelight on the first civil war, 1642–1646* (London 1973), 10, 67–8; LCM computi, 1644; *Ashmole*, ed. Josten ii. 350–2; BNCA bursar's accounts, 1644; Jenkins,

Not all lodging arrangements in wartime Oxford were by agreement of both parties; just as private theft—as we shall see—could be used by the soldiery to supplement the authorized contribution paid by the citizens and academics, so royalist officers and courtiers, often themselves unpaid and increasingly desperate, took what they needed by force or fraud. Citizens who had supplied food and lodging on credit ended up with worthless paper tickets; college bursars were left with unpaid bills, or worse. Nicholas Brookes, principal of St Mary Hall, found that rooms there were taken by deception and maintained by violence, and that, to add insult to injury, one of the royalist officers responsible slipped away with his wife before the surrender of the city—no doubt to evade his creditors—and left their 3-year-old daughter 'on the parish', or rather, in this case, with the principal.[44]

The king himself lodged in the deanery at Christ Church, where he had stayed on his last visit. It is not known where Dean Fell and his family found alternative quarters. Oxford's largest and richest college was not only fit for a king, it provided a number of rooms which could easily be converted to royal use. The separate households of the prince of Wales and the duke of York were found space, as were other prominent courtiers, such as the marquess of Hertford on his arrival in early 1643. The great hall was where the king could dine in state, and be seen and heard in public. The young freshman, John Aubrey, 'was wont to see [him] at supper' in the early months of the war. It was an appropriate setting for any ceremonial occasion, such as the official reception of foreign ambassadors, the formal installation of major office-holders, and the inaugural address by Charles I to his parliament in early 1644. The audit house, where hung the portraits of past college dignitaries, accommodated meetings of the council of war, and may have been a room where the privy council (infrequently) met. The 'lords commissioners', delegated by the king to take charge of Oxford in his absence, organized the defence of the royalist capital throughout the war in this room, which also witnessed the surrender of the city in June 1646. But when the vice-chancellor's representatives or delegates from the town council were summoned before it the larger chapter house, sometimes called the council chamber, was used.[45]

The cathedral was the scene for the sermons delivered before the king, some printed by the university press, solemn thanksgivings for victories in the field, at one of which 'the vicechancellor and all the doctors of the universitie were present in their scarlet robes', and other religious services which emphasized the continued use of the Book of Common Prayer. Fashionable weddings and christenings were

Life of Mansell, 10; Wood, *City of Oxford* iii. 252; A. Bott, *The Monuments in Merton College Chapel* (Oxford 1964), 98–100. The judges' lodgings are listed, perhaps in consequence of the January 1643 proclamation, in Bodl. MS Twyne–Langbaine 2, fo 37ᵛ.

[44] See I. Roy, 'The city of Oxford, 1640–1660' in R. C. Richardson (ed.), *Town and Countryside in the English Revolution* (Manchester 1992). Brookes's 1650 petition is in Oxford City Library E/4/6, fo 8.

[45] Varley, *Siege of Oxford*, 48, and ch. 12; *Aubrey's Brief Lives*, ed. O. L. Dick (Harmondsworth 1972), 44. The installation of George Digby as steward of the university on 2 November 1643 was in 'Chancellor's Hall': OUA register Sb, pp. 43–4; BL MS Harleian 6852, fos 82, 162–4; PRO PC/2/53 *passim*; R. L. Poole, *Catalogue of Oxford Portraits* (3 vols OHS 1911–26) iii. 110; *Dugdale's Diary*, ed. Hamper, 90–1; Wood, *Life and Times* i. 95–6.

attended by the king, and elaborate and costly funerals, such as that of his kinsman, Lord D'Aubigny, mortally wounded at Edgehill, displayed the sacred character and dignity of the royal cause. Several monuments in the cathedral testify to
the prominent royalists buried there.[46]

The deanery was rearranged to perpetuate the division in the royal palace
between the king's private quarters and the more formal public rooms, and yeomen
of the guard were stationed at the doors and on the stairs to prevent unauthorized
access.[47] More informally Charles could use the college gardens for exercise, and
walk and talk with his councillors and senior officers or visiting parliamentarian
commissioners. When the queen made her triumphal entry into Oxford in July
1643 she was installed, after her formal reception at Christ Church by the vice-
chancellor and heads of house, and a speech from the public orator, in the warden's lodgings at Merton, vacated by Brent. A way was made through the garden
of one of the canons, Dr Robert Payne, in Christ Church, and Corpus Christi's
'backside', to enable the king privately to visit his wife. Until her departure the following April the queen held court there. Of the peers who abandoned parliament
for a time in the summer of 1643 'the earl of Holland came frequently in the afternoon to Merton College, where the queen lay, and where the king was for the most
part at that time of the day'. Many of her large entourage seemed to have stayed
on after she left: three members of her household were buried in the college chapel,
and the new warden appointed in 1645, as we shall see, still had to compete for
living room with the goods of aristocratic occupants.[48]

Close to the court, as we might expect, were some of the most notable of
Charles's servants: Secretary Nicholas at Pembroke, Jack Ashburnham at Corpus
Christi, Cottington—if only for a term—at Oriel, Culpepper at Merton, while the
royal lifeguards and household staff were billeted on the inhabitants of St Aldates,
opposite Christ Church. The earl of Bristol, and his son, Lord Digby, were at the
other end of town, occupying the president's rooms at Magdalen. Digby had been
a member of the college in the 1620s, along with his future brother-in-law, the fifth

---

[46] BL MS Harleian 965, fos 1–2; Wood, *Life and Times* i. 82, 103–6; Wood, *City of Oxford* ii. 550; PRO
SP/19/125, fos 286–7; *Dugdale's Diary*, ed. Hamper, 81, 84. The monuments to two governors of
Oxford, Pennyman and Gage, were ordered to be defaced by parliament in 1647. Several of the most
splendid memorials to royalists buried in Oxford were post-Restoration. There are monuments or
monumental inscriptions in St Mary the Virgin and Merton College chapel as well as the cathedral.
Varley's *Siege of Oxford*, ch. 12, usefully summarizes a good deal of information on the accommodation
of the king and court.

[47] The council of war in January 1643 placed the guards round the royal apartments and regulated
access to the presence: BL MS Harleian 6851, fos 117, 156, Add. MS 15,750, fos 16–17.

[48] *Dugdale's Diary*, ed. Hamper, 75; *The Diary of Bulstrode Whitelocke*, ed. Spalding, 142; Wood, *Life and
Times* i. 91, 103; Wood, *History of the University* ii. 446; Varley, *Siege of Oxford*, 58–9, from Clarendon, *History
of the Rebellion* vii. 180, 188–9. A register of the marriages, christenings, and burials in Merton College
chapel was kept by the college chaplains during the queen's stay, and later lost (Wood, *Life and Times* i.
130) but some entries are noted ibid. i. 110, and in Bott, *Merton Monuments*, 3–4, 49, 53, 116. The
Restoration petition of Merton's chaplain is supported by an august assemblage of those, many associated with the queen, who had lodged there during the civil war: PRO SP/29/14, fos 129–31. See below,
n. 67, for the entry of Harvey in 1645.

earl of Bedford; when the latter, like Holland, briefly deserted parliament in the summer of 1643 he was lodged at Magdalen.[49]

All the functions of government were to be reproduced at Oxford, as the king endeavoured to make his military headquarters a genuine capital. He invited officials and judges, courtiers and craftsmen, peers and MPs (for the Oxford Parliament), to carry on their duties at Oxford. From early 1643 the law courts, summoned from Westminster, met in the schools, at least for a time. Some of the king's ministers used their college lodgings as offices: Cottington presided over an important committee at Oriel, Hyde transacted some financial business at All Souls. When the parliament was summoned in early 1644, the commons sat in the new convocation house (where chancery had been located earlier), forcing convocation itself back to its old home in the university church, and the lords took over part of the upper schools.[50]

As well as these official bodies, space had to be found for the generality of those who wished—or were forced—to reside close to their sovereign. 'Oxford was then the common refuge and shelter of such persecuted persons', wrote John Fell of the reception of deprived ministers and Cambridge academics in exile, 'so that it never was nor is like to be a more learned university ... nor did ever letters and arms so well consist together, it being an accomplisht academy of both.' It was certainly true that a wide variety of professions, interests, and talents (well represented in the lists of 'strangers' kept in the colleges' buttery books) were attracted to the royalist capital. Unemployed or ousted London heralds, astrologers, booksellers, botanists, stage players, musicians, and artists found billets in the colleges or citizens' houses. William Dugdale, for example, lived with his patron, Lord Hatton, at Hart Hall. Henry Hammond, expelled from his living in Kent, took rooms in his old college, Magdalen, when his friend John Oliver was appointed president in 1644, and kept the press occupied. William Dobson, the sergeant–painter, having lived in several lodgings in the town, at last and surprisingly, in view of the cost and his supposed poverty, took the best rooms in Canterbury quadrangle, St John's, to complete his gallery of royalist portraits. That admired scholar, James Ussher, archbishop of Armagh, found lodgings in the fine new house of Bishop Prideaux in the absence of the owner, and made good use of the 'public library'. The scholarly and artistic achievements of such persons go some way to justify the otherwise misleading image of wartime Oxford presented by Fell.[51]

---

[49] Macleane, Pembroke. 222; OCA buttery book, 1643–44; Wood, Life and Times i. 69; Young and Toynbee, Strangers in Oxford, passim; 'A secret negotiation with Charles I', ed. B. M. Gardiner, Camden Miscellany viii (Camden Soc. new ser. xxxi 1883), 30; Varley, Siege of Oxford, 58–9; Journal of Sir Samuel Luke, ed. I. G. Philip (Oxfordshire Record Soc. xxix 1950), 11.

[50] Royal proclamations on removal of law courts to Oxford: Stuart Royal Proclamations, ed. Larkin and Hughes ii, nos 380, 400, 409, 446, 465; Varley, Siege of Oxford, 31, 48, 52–3; Calendar of the Proceedings of the Committee for the Advance of Money 1642–1656 (London 1888), 1002–3; Wood, Life and Times i. 83; Wood, History of the University ii. 469; OUA register Sb, p. 57.

[51] [John Fell], The life of ... Dr. Thomas Fuller (Oxford 1661), 22; Dugdale's Diary, ed. Hamper, 67–8; John Fell, The life of ... Dr. H. Hammond (Oxford 1661), 27–32; Oxford, SJM, buttery book, 1645; DNB

Charles I himself asked to borrow a book from the Bodleian in December 1645, when he could presumably do little further to galvanize the royalist cause, and had the leisure to study a little French history. But his request was frustrated by the librarian, Rous, whose charge it was to let no book leave the library, however eminent the borrower. The king acquiesced gracefully, as Protector Cromwell was to do later.[52]

Despite the presence of 'many great bishops, and learned doctors, and grave divines' the tone of life in academic halls and gardens in wartime Oxford was distinctly aristocratic and feminine. The colleges (many with desirable and expensive accommodation) were all within the defences and none was more than ten minutes' walk from the royal presence. Such famous ladies (and relicts of the Villiers clan) as the duchess of Buckingham and Lady Grandison, for instance, were to be found at Brasenose and Jesus respectively. The countess of Northampton, her female relatives, and the duchess of Richmond followed the queen to Merton.[53] While colleges were of course well used to catering for many gentle residents, they had less experience of accommodating women and children. Most fellows were unmarried, and senior academics with families had to live outside the college in their own houses. Rooms had to be adapted to this new purpose, and the semi-monastic, male-oriented atmosphere of the academic community was thereby threatened. Some friction resulted. Aubrey's story of the encounter between Ralph Kettell, the elderly president of Trinity, and the ladies who lodged in his college, is well known. Kettell was old-fashioned and eccentric, even by Oxford standards; a formidable figure with 'a terrible gigantic aspect', he was severe on youthful disorders, especially long hair. Teased by one of the ladies of the court, he delivered the crushing retort: 'Your husband and father I bred up here, and I knew your grandfather; I know you to be a gentlewoman, I will not say you are a whore; but gett you gonne for a very woman.'[54]

As well as for lodgings, several of the colleges were requisitioned for other purposes. A cannon foundry was set up in the purlieus of Christ Church. Part of New College was taken over by the ordnance office for the central magazine of arms and munitions. The cloisters quadrangle there was a natural fortress, protected from the weather and unauthorized entry, and guarded by the bell tower at the north-east corner; in the last emergency which troubled Oxford in the period, the invasion of 1651, it was deemed by the garrison a more defensible stronghold than the castle itself, where the new fortifications were as yet incomplete. Other rooms in the college were also used for this purpose, and the mound in the garden was heightened, no doubt to provide a better view for sentinels. Gloucester Hall was

s.v. James Ussher. John Fell, the celebrated son of the then dean of Christ Church, was 18 at the start of the war. He was a junior officer in the university regiment of foot.

[52] Macray, *Annals of the Bodleian Library*, 99–100.

[53] *The Burdens of England* . . . (London 1646), sig. A 2ᵛ; *Brasenose Monographs* ii. xi, p. 31; JCA Mansell's accounts, 1644; PRO SP/29/14, fos 129–31.

[54] *Aubrey's Brief Lives*, ed. Clark ii. 17, 21, 24–5.

taken over by the master of the armouries as a forge for making sword blades. Magdalen College grove became the park for the field artillery of the marching army, well sited to offer space and some protection behind the bulk of the college, with access to the London road and the river, and close to the main arsenal. Craftsmen attached to the artillery train had their workshops close by. The college tower served as a watchtower, from which the king himself could observe the movement of the enemy forces closing on Oxford in the summer of 1644.[55]

The uppermost rooms in the tower of the schools quadrangle were requisitioned for the storage of the townsmens' arms; gunsmiths and metalworkers were employed there to repair arms. County arms were stored in a room in Peckwater Inn. The workshops to provide boots and clothing for the army were set up in the music and astronomy schools; grain and cheese were stockpiled in the law and logic schools; drawbridges were constructed in the rhetoric school and stakes for palisades in Brasenose. Match was stored in part of the old convocation house at St Mary's. In January 1643 the mint arrived in several carts from Shrewsbury and was installed at New Inn Hall. Later that year the task of provisioning colleges was given, in each case, to two of its gentry residents. Some of their more public and well boarded rooms would soon be used to store foodstuffs against a siege.[56]

The fortifications thrown round Oxford, to the building of which the academics made a big contribution, embraced an area large enough to include all the colleges and halls. Those housing military installations, or possessing walls or gardens which were incorporated in the defences, however, were provided with 'courts of guard' (sentry posts): Gloucester Hall, the back of Christ Church, the New College magazine, Wadham College, and, in Magdalen's water walks, 'Dover's peer', an observation post called after the university regiment commanded by the earl of Dover which did guard duty there. The back of Merton, overlooking the flooded Christ Church meadow, was fortified and armed with iron cannon, and the college was ordered by the king to pay for the works around Holywell, where it owned land. But beyond the defences a free-fire zone would have to be created: Oriel's hospital of St Bartholomew lay, a mile to the east, in the path of any hostile approach to the city, and it was progressively destroyed. Made into a pest house for the garrison, its chapel roof was stripped to make lead bullets. At last its buildings were razed and the fine grove of elm trees which shaded them cut down 'least they should be a shelter to the rebells'.[57]

[55] *The Royalist Ordnance Papers 1642–1646*, ed. I. Roy (Oxfordshire Record Soc. xliii 1964 xlix 1975), 19, 25–8, 32, 142, 203, 295, 456, 473; NCA bursar's computi, 1642–3, 1646–7; Wood, *Life and Times* i. 68; Varley, *Siege of Oxford*, 123.

[56] Wood, *Life and Times* i. 70–1, 83–4, iv. 123; Wood, *History of the University* ii. 461 n.; *Royalist Ordnance Papers*, ed. Roy, 19, 25–8, 32; Varley, *Siege of Oxford*, 25. Bodl. MS Add. d. 114, fo 85, note of rooms to be used for storing foodstuffs at All Souls, Brasenose, Lincoln, New, and Wadham colleges and Hart Hall; BL MS Harleian 6804, fo 173, list of commissioners for provisioning strangers [?June 1643].

[57] R. T. Lattey, E. J. S. Parsons, and I. G. Philip, 'A contemporary map of the defences of Oxford in 1644', *Oxoniensia* i (1936); *Oxford Council Acts, 1626–65*, ed. Hobson and Salter, 390–5; Wood, *Life and Times* i. 100; Wood, *City of Oxford* i. 245, ii. 517–18; MCR item 115, Charles I to warden and fellows of

The king also made immediate use of the university in other ways. At the convocation held on All Saints' Day, 1 November 1642—just over a week after the battle of Edgehill—the king's two sons were honoured, and thereafter, in the hectic space of that and the following day, some 400 of his leading supporters were granted degrees by the king's special command, or given leave to have them awarded on a later occasion. Of the thirty-four doctors of civil law Wood commented that 'most were courtiers, nobles and gentlemen', and of the whole process that 'some were so impudent as to thrust themselves (when it grew dark) into the hands of him that presented, to be created, being not at all mentioned in the Catalogue of those that were signed by the king'. The court viewed the Caroline creation, as it came to be called, as an opportunity to reward cheaply the more prominent followers of the king for the help they lent his cause in the early months of the war and especially, among the officers of the army, their conduct at Edgehill. As the grant was by direction of the king no fees were payable to the university. In January 1643 the recently arrived followers of the marquess of Hertford, who had helped to raise troops in the west country, were granted degrees in the same way.[58]

Convocation, in February 1643, perhaps fearing a further deluge of such grants, petitioned the king that it could not replenish its common stock, 'being of late utterly exhausted', nor maintain its academic reputation, if those proceeding to degrees were excused the usual 'moderate fees', and the need to undergo public examination. Aware of the political realities, convocation did not object to the noble and gentry recipients, who had done the university 'much honour in accepting of her favours'. But the 'great multitudes of schollars ... and strangers' so rewarded threatened its livelihood. The king promised moderation, but he would not easily give up a method of conferring honours which had little cost to himself. From February 1643 until his departure from Oxford in April 1646 104 degrees were given out by special command (see table 14.1). Most recipients were those in the royalist army and court; but a number of students who in serving the king had lost the time needed to complete their studies and comply with university regulations were permitted in this way to proceed to their degrees.[59]

The government of the university soon also came to reflect political reality. Chancellor Pembroke had won no new friends at Oxford as one of the parliamentarian negotiators in spring 1643, although he had made amends for his failure to replace Prideaux in the previous summer by nominating Tolson, provost of Oriel, as vice-chancellor. His sharp words about some of the leading dons ('a pack of corrupt knaves') had not been forgotten, and he was siding with the king's enemies; the university petitioned for his removal, and Charles agreed. In October 1643 convocation elected as chancellor the marquess of Hertford, whose followers

Merton, 19 June 1643; 'Oxford church notes, 1643–4', ed. R. Graham, *Collectanea* iv. 123–4; *Royalist Ordnance Papers*, ed. Roy, 187, 468.

[58] Wood, *Fasti* ii. 12–33; Wood, *History of the University* ii. 455.
[59] OUA register Sb, pp. 11–22.

TABLE 14.1 *Oxford creations, 21 February 1643–27 April 1646*

Reason	Number
Royalist officer	20
Member of royal household	5
'Active in king's service'	3
Courtier's recommendation	17
University member losing time because in army	12
University member unable to perform exercises	10
Eligible Cambridge scholar	4*
Reason not readily apparent	33
TOTAL	104

* Another twenty Cambridge scholars were incorporated during this period.

had been so liberally rewarded in January; at the same time the new secretary of state, Lord Digby, replaced Lord Saye as high steward. Digby had long cultivated his Oxford connections, and he had raised a troop of horse from among the student body, which guarded the eastern approaches to the city.[60]

Hertford, one of the king's greatest supporters, had made an important contribution to the successful summer campaign in the west. He was now prominent at Oxford as one of the lords commissioners who governed the city in the king's absence, and as the newly promoted groom of the stole. As chancellor he found he had acquired no sinecure. It is clear that the earlier doubts concerning the holding of office by those in holy orders, consequent on the clerical disenabling act, continued to undermine the authority of the chancellor's court, and the new chancellor was besieged in his rooms in Christ Church by suitors who would normally have taken their cases to court. Nevertheless in 1645 pleadings were resumed after an interval of two years during which little more had been done than listing the goods of deceased academics.[61]

Hertford nominated Pincke as vice-chancellor in November, and kept him in place the following year. The 'present and weighty affaires' of the king were now so intermingled with the business of the university, said Hertford, that no one else would do. Pincke, it will be recalled, was now 70. To assist the work of the vice-chancellor and other university officers convocation had appointed a delegacy of

[60] OUA siege papers, SP/F/40/8, articles exhibited against the earl of Pembroke by the university, February 1643; BL Add. MS 32,093, fos 203–4, Charles I to university, 23 October 1643; OUA register Sb, pp. 15–16, 19, 40, 41–3, 43–4; *Journal of Sir Samuel Luke*, ed. Philip, 11.

[61] In January 1644 Hertford complained to convocation of 'those uncessant clamours that doe dayly accost me': OUA register Sb, pp. 51–2. However, he did have the leisure, like his master, to consult the Bodleian catalogue, for he complained of defects to the librarian: Macray, *Annals of the Bodleian Library*, 98. He was hearing cases in his rooms at Christ Church, October 1645: Oxford City Library E/4/3, fo 28ᵛ. For academic wills see OUA chancellor's ct papers, 25 (1642–4) and 26 (1645–6).

twenty-two in May 1643 consisting of the officers, six heads, six doctors, and seven MAs. By 1644 death had reduced their number to scarcely more than half.[62]

Among the tasks set these delegates was the defence of the privileges of the university. Since the first meeting of the Long Parliament the townsmen had regained control of many areas previously in dispute with the academics, and the mayor and council refused to make their annual homage at the university church. The taxation by the city of those privileged of the university was particularly resented. With the military crisis of spring 1643 out of the way the new delegacy petitioned the lords commissioners to preserve their old immunities. The king's judges, however, delivered a most confusing ruling on the issue, and in September 1644 the commissioners, meeting in the audit house, and with the chancellor among their number, provided no better outcome. The houses of leading academics remained rated with those of the citizens; and the mayor continued to boycott the St Scholastica's day ceremonies. While the city bore the main burden of maintaining the garrison, and in spite of Hertford's and Pincke's value to the royal cause, the privileges of the academics would remain secondary.[63]

Civil war Oxford was overcrowded, insanitary, and dangerous. The large number, and varied character, of the temporary inhabitants, living in cramped conditions, the poor state of the roads, ditches, and gateways—which had long constituted a severe problem for the city, even in the best of times—and the increasingly riotous behaviour of the soldiery made life in the garrison town hazardous. The streams were choked by rubbish, offal, and filth, even dead horses and dogs. Some lanes, for one of which Pembroke College denied responsibility, were impassable. A royal order, in Latin, deplored the 'horror abominabilis' of the pigs and pigsties which blocked the public ways, even close to the king's court. Academics found themselves in a town, previously accounted healthy, in which living conditions were deteriorating and the diseases associated with bad housing, a military presence, and polluted water supplies reached epidemic proportions.[64]

Sickness and death held sway in wartime Oxford. From summer 1643, when 'morbus campestris' (a form of typhus) took hold, there was a huge increase in the number of burials: the pre-war annual average increased sixfold. In the following year plague, unknown at Oxford for some years, began to be recorded; during the summer months the death rate was at crisis levels. All the colleges and six halls contributed to the cost of isolating and relieving plague victims and burying those who died. They were rated according to their presumed wealth, for this as other shared expenses: Christ Church, Magdalen, and New colleges together paid nearly 40 per cent of the whole, the halls, in total, 3.7 per cent. As well as these massive epidemics smallpox was, as usual, endemic in the city. While the garrison soldiery,

---

[62] OUA register Sb, pp. 28, 31–3, 44, 53, 65. For Pincke, born 1573, see *DNB* s.v. Robert Pinck.

[63] *Oxford Council Acts 1626–65*, ed. Hobson and Salter, 374–8, 388–90; Bodl. MS Twyne–Langbaine 2, fos 29, 31–2, 33, 35, 41–2, 47; OUA register Sb, pp. 29–30, and WP/γ/22/1. For a discussion of the town–gown disputes at this time see Roy, 'The city of Oxford, 1640–1660'.

[64] For conditions generally in the garrison see Roy, 'The city of Oxford, 1640–1660'.

and their citizen hosts, probably suffered most, the already diminished academic communities were not immune. Between October 1642 and June 1646 (the surrender to Fairfax) at least twenty-eight college members are known to have died, and the true figure is probably twice as great. The heads of Oriel, Queen's, St Mary Hall, and Trinity, the professor of astronomy, the keeper of the university archives, Brian Twyne, the public orator and one of the proctors, the young poet William Cartwright—all died; several were buried in college chapels, where also, as we have seen, some 'strangers' were interred. The king himself, it was said, 'dropped a tear' at the news of Cartwright's death.[65]

In these dangerous and unpleasant circumstances any semblance of normal life in the colleges must have been hard to sustain. Nor could the usual teaching and regular public examinations be continued. 'Lectures and exercises for the most part ceased, the schools being employed as granaries for the garrison.' Under 1645 Wood noted: 'no Act solemnized this, three years before, or divers after'. Few proceeded to their degrees by examination after the requisite passage of time. Many, as we have seen, were awarded by special edict of the king or chancellor, without fee or examination, because time had been lost on active service, as a military or political reward, or as compensation for loss of Cambridge fellowship or sequestrated living. The figures for those graduating in the normal manner bear out these observations. Where there had been 131 inceptors (candidates preparing for the MA degree) in 1642 there were only forty-two in the following year and twenty-five in 1644. Similarly the number of determiners (newly admitted BAs) in Lent fell from over 200 in 1641 to 107 in 1642, forty in 1644, and thirty-one in 1645.[66]

Yet most heads, and those to whom the government of the university had been entrusted, remained at their posts, though their number was reduced by death. As fellows departed, for whatever reason, most vacancies were filled, although on a diminishing scale as the war intensified; some college communities, as we have seen, existed on a reduced basis or faced imminent dissolution. Where a head was absent for any length of time normal activity, such as elections to fellowships, might be suspended. At Merton both the warden and the sub-warden (Brent and his son-in-law, Edward Corbett) were absent, as the king noted, and deplored, at an early stage; the college was virtually taken over by the queen's entourage in 1643, whose presence was still obtrusive long after she had left. Only a handful of fellows remained, and the butler testified later that the college was suspended at the end of 1643. It was not until 1645 that Brent was replaced by Dr William Harvey,

<hr>

[65] The figures for mortality, from which also the estimates of high morbidity may be assumed, are derived from the six surviving parish registers, now in the Oxfordshire record office. Wood noted a number of academic deaths, *Life and Times* i. 104, 116, 125–6, and burials, *City of Oxford* iii. 198–264. Burials in Christ Church cathedral are noted in Wood, *City of Oxford* ii. 259. On Cartwright see Wood, *Athenae* iii. 69–72, and *DNB*. Ten burials from one college, Jesus, including those of two academics, were recorded in the registers of St Michael. The chancellor's court recorded over twenty wills in the period: OUA chancellor's ct papers 25 and 26, 1642–6. For colleges' contribution for plague relief, 17 July 1644, see BL Add. MS 24,064, fos 10–11.

[66] Wood, *History of the University* ii. 487–8, 475; OUA register of congregation 1634–47, NEP/*supra*/16, register Q, fos 61–3, 92–3, 118–20.

one of the king's physicians. He had been entrusted with the care of the royal children in the first campaign of the war; it was probably the recommendation of his disciples, John Greaves and Charles Scarburgh, two notable early scientists, which helped secure him the wardenship of Merton.[67]

The massive presence of the king and the royal court, and his greatest supporters, including the new chancellor of the university, could not but have an impact on the elections which took place during the royalist occupation, but the royal or cavalier influence is not obvious. To replace a fellow killed in his service the king wrote twice to All Souls in favour of Thomas Standard, noting that two other vacancies needed to be filled. But Standard was not admitted fellow until 1647, and it is doubtful if all the other vacancies were filled. One of the contestants for the warden's place at Merton was Peter Turner, a fellow, Savilian professor of geometry, assistant to Laud in the 1630s, and active royalist. It might be assumed that he had influential friends at court, but when the king asked Hertford, as chancellor, to adjudicate, he found for the popular choice, Harvey.[68]

This disputed election was commented upon in one of the few surviving personal letters written by Oxford academics during the war. Martin Aylworth, fellow of All Souls, writing to Mansell in South Wales—where the principal of Jesus was putting heart into the local cavaliers—at the height of the war, showed that a taste for academic gossip was not diminished by even the keenest adversity. He gave his friend the latest Oxford news: the death of colleagues—Tolson of Oriel, Strode the public orator, the temporary breaking up of his own college, the courting of a young beauty. But his chief topic was the preferment of colleagues, some of them at court. He was apparently not displeased that the fellows of Merton, in spite of their boasting, had passed over one of their own as warden, and had been obliged, as he put it, to cull their prime fruit out of a foreign garden.[69]

As well as the interruption to teaching, study, and examination, Laud's other concern—the observation of dress and ceremony—was neglected. The very face of the university was utterly changed. 'Few there were that went in academical habits or formalities, for all under the age of 60 were upon military duty, and therefore continually wore swords.' The presence of the garrison, and the court, made the maintenance of good order and discipline in the university extremely difficult. 'To speak the truth the soldier spoils the scholar for the most part', John Aubrey's tutor admitted, when he advised him not to return to Oxford. He recommended Leiden instead.[70]

---

[67] The case brought by Edward Greaves in 1651 for the payment of his Linacre lecturership by the college shows that in 1643 Merton was struggling to survive. When Harvey moved in he found the furnishings and goods of the countess of Northampton occupied pride of place: OUA chancellor's ct papers, 27, 1651, bundle 3, nos 5, 7, 19; MCR 1567–1731, pp. 351, 355–6, 357–9. See p. 704 above for evidence of the queen's household's stay at Merton.

[68] Bodl. MS Tanner 340, fo 148, Charles I to All Souls, 2 November 1643. On the Merton election see the references given in the previous note. On Standard's and Turner's careers at Oxford see Reinhart, 'Visitation', 546, 578, 608.

[69] JCA 155, Martin Aylworth to Francis Mansell, 16 December 1644 and 6 May 1645.

[70] Wood, *History of the University* ii. 475, 487; Bodl. MS Aubrey 12, fo 35, William Browne to John Aubrey, 9 September 1645.

Young Anthony Wood was attending the little school in the cloisters tower of New College when the war broke out. The class had to move to a 'dark nasty room' close by, which was cramped and airless; as the college housed the main royalist magazine Wood and the other boys were, it could be said with pardonable exaggeration, sitting on a powder keg. Wood recalled later that his father, 'foresaw that if his sons were not removed from Oxon they would be spoiled. It was a great disturbance to the youth of the citie'. His family eventually sent him to safer quarters at Thame for the duration of the war. The few remaining scholars 'were for the most part, especially such that were young, much debauched, and become idle by their bearing arms and keeping company with rude soldiers. Much of their precious time was lost by being upon the guard night after night', where they learned to drink and swear.[71]

As well as space the king asked for money from the university. College chests were of course empty after his appeal in the summer of 1642, but in January 1643 he revived the original scheme for the loan of college plate. Both sides had, at the beginning of the war, depended heavily on private donations of coin, jewellery, and silver plate, and thereafter the Oxford mint was kept busy melting down the family silver of the cavalier gentry. To this was now added the college plate, to be lent at 8 per cent interest. The royalists valued the plate at 5s an ounce for white and 5s 6d for silver gilt. Having asked the colleges in early January the king sent to convocation on the 25th of the same month to allow the loan of plate from the halls; on the 31st convocation duly agreed. Several colleges still possess the king's letter and the receipt signed by the two masters of the mint at New Inn Hall. If the proportion of white to gilt plate lent was generally similar to that of the seven colleges where the amounts are known (75 : 25 per cent: All Souls, Exeter, Oriel, Queen's, St John's, University, and Wadham), then the total value of the college silver given was roughly £7,000. Magdalen presented the largest amount in weight, but that of All Souls may have been the most valuable contribution, as almost a third of it was silver gilt. That Christ Church, the richest college, had only an average amount to give reflected the earlier removal by the parliamentarians of a substantial part of its collection (see p. 698 above).[72]

But not all the royalists' money-raising devices were legitimate or couched in the polite language the king employed in asking assistance of 'such nurseries of learning' as the Oxford colleges. Within weeks of their first entry in November 1642 two senior officers called on an aged college rent-collector living in St Giles who, as a privileged person, was a member of the university. They had no doubt heard that he was a wealthy man, and probably reputed a puritan. They threatened to blow up the house where he lodged unless he parted with the £300-worth of plate,

[71] Wood, *History of the University* ii. 475, 487.

[72] Varley, *Siege of Oxford*, 35–41 and plate 1, the king's letter to Oriel College, 8 January 1643; OUA register Sb, p. 17, unanimous agreement of convocation, 31 January 1643; Twigg, 'College finances', pp. 775–8 below.

gold, and rings he had in store. He was still vainly hoping to right this wrong when he died three years later.[73]

There were enough able-bodied young men remaining in the colleges for the royalist authorities to suggest, at various times, that a regiment might be raised in the city for home defence from among their number. Some 400, as we have seen, were mustered at the start of the war, in a show of strength designed to deter parliamentarian reprisals. But the academic volunteers (and their arms) then displayed had been dispersed, some to the king's field army (about a tenth of the 1,000 weapons and pieces of armour handed in to the royal stores had been from colleges and their members), and it proved difficult to reassemble a coherent force. In June 1643 convocation was asked to authorize the listing of university men for the city's defence, under an experienced commander, and 400 men were inspected in Christ Church meadow. But while a regiment of townsmen, created at the same time, remained thereafter as part of the garrison, the academic contribution failed to take root. A few months later, perhaps mindful of the assorted arms of all kinds now reposing in his stores, the king suggested to convocation that Colonel John Knightley might recruit a regiment of bowmen, 'sagitarii', from among the body of scholars. But nothing seems to have come of this either, and Knightley was employed elsewhere.[74] Not until the Oxford Parliament, in the spring of 1644, recommended the creation of such auxiliary regiments for royalist garrisons, which would free regular units for service in the field, was the attempt renewed. A regiment of 'scholars and strangers', commanded by a leading royalist councillor, the earl of Dover, was successfully recruited and armed. At its first muster in Magdalen College grove in May 1644 it was 630 strong. The 'academic militia' consisted of separate companies of scholars and strangers, kept strictly independent of the main army, supplied from separate stores, and confined to watching and warding in the city defences. It did, however, sally forth in raids and skirmishes on occasion, and it was publicly commended, and further recruited for, by the king before the end of the year. This may be the basis for Wood's otherwise hyperbolical statement that Charles I preferred to leave his capital in the safe keeping of the academic regiment before any other. As we have noted, it gave its name to the most easterly observation post in the defences—'Dover's peer'—and was still manning the works on the western side of the city in the final siege.[75]

[73] Young and Toynbee, *Strangers in Oxford*, 208–9.

[74] For the personal arms of Oxford academics see *Royalist Ordnance Papers*, ed. Roy, 34, 88, 237; Bodl. MS Twyne–Langbaine 2, fos 26–7; OUA siege papers, SP/F/40/41; BL MS Harleian 6852, fo 67; *Stuart Royal Proclamations*, ed. Larkin and Hughes no. ii, 412. OUA siege papers, SP/F/40/ 13, 16, Colonel Hollyland to command collegians, June 1643; Wood, *History of the University* ii. 465. OUA register Sb, p. 36, royal order on 1,200 bowmen volunteers considered, 17 October 1643.

[75] *Stuart Royal Proclamations*, ed. Larkin and Hughes ii, nos 490, 495, 504; the copy of the 28 April 1644 proclamation (ibid., no. 490) in the university archives bears manuscript notes which describe the regiment in this way: OUA WP/γ/26/1, fo 530; BL MS Harleian 6802, fos 99–100, 134; Bodl. MS Ashmole 36–7, fo 23; *Royalist Ordnance Papers*, ed. Roy, 350, 352, 504; for 'Dover's peer' see n. 57 above. Wood wrote that: 'The generality of the scholars were very loyal to the crown, and did the best and most exact service of any during the time that Oxford was a garrison', and that the king himself held

The garrison, city, and university were brought under tighter military control as the war continued. In April 1645 the royalist governor imposed a loyalty oath on all in the city; responsibility for the subscription of the academics lay with Vice-Chançellor Fell, Baylie of St John's, Potter of Queen's, Sheldon of All Souls, and Hammond. The oath itself was printed by Lichfield, and its condemnation of all the king's enemies as traitors and rebels appears to have been recalled with some bitterness later. Those who were most involved in its circulation were viewed after the war as irreconcilable enemies of parliament: perhaps this was why Wood referred to it in his *History* as 'that bloody Oxford oath'.[76]

The scholars had from the first been more active than the citizens in building the city's defences. Throughout 1643 they worked with a will, if Twyne is to be believed, at their designated stretch of the line. With a third of the able-bodied residing in colleges and halls, on two days out of a six-day week the labour was supplied from academic quarters: on Fridays colleges from Magdalen to St John's, on Saturdays from Pembroke to University, with some of the colleges north of High Street. Such attempts to recruit workmen were, however, increasingly unsuccessful, and in the following year a weekly levy of £40 was imposed on the colleges, according to the agreed rate. Finding money for 'the bulwarks' was eventually just another heavy burden on college finances throughout the war. Those lodgers who refused to pay were ordered to be expelled from the city.[77]

It has been shown that Oxonians in general made a considerable contribution to the royal cause. But the activity of fellows was diverse and often more specialized, as the table 14.2 demonstrates. The overwhelmingly royalist character of their activity can be seen. Forty-five served in the king's forces, as soldiers or chaplains, only three in parliament's. A more significant proportion (30%) managed to stay uncommitted, mostly (as incumbents) by remaining in their country livings; a few took the opportunity to study abroad. While a large number of clerical fellows delivered sermons before the king, only a handful sat in the Westminster Assembly, parliament's main vehicle for church reformation. The military occupation of Oxford no doubt reinforced this royalist bias. Some acted in an official capacity, as royal chaplains (including Sheldon, Radcliffe, and Hammond), or put their

'such an high opinion of the fidelity and courage of his university' that he entrusted his capital mainly to its charge: *History of the University* ii. 470, 478, 486. Robert Mead, a Student of Christ Church and captain in the regiment, was specially commended by the duke of York for an exploit, and rewarded with a DM on the last day before the surrender of Oxford, 23 June 1646: Wood, *History of the University* ii. 478; OUA register Sb, p. 117; Wood, *Fasti* ii. 98.

[76] BL MS Harleian 6852, fos 263–4; Madan *Oxford Books* ii, no. 1764; Wood, *History of the University* ii. 500.

[77] Wood, *Life and Times* i. 72, 89, 100; *Stuart Royal Proclamations*, ed. Larkin and Hughes ii, nos 420, 438. Twyne's note on 8 June 1643 proclamation indicates that the scholars themselves were working principally at Christ Church meadow, New Parks, and about Holywell in June 1643. Madan, *Oxford Books* ii, nos 1807 and 1884 mention the fortifications behind Christ Church in August 1645, and the last-minute improvements to the western line in June 1646; Bodl. MS Add. d. 114, fos 17–18, 20, 65, 75; OUA siege papers, SP/F/40/15, 22, orders to colleges, and amounts charged 1643–44; Bodl. MS Rawlinson d. 399, fo 120, the royal order to college lodgers, 11 May 1644.

TABLE 14.2   Activities of Oxford fellows, 1642–6

Activity	Royalist	Parliamentarian	'Neutral'
Within Oxford			
Degree by royal creation	4		
Collegiate dispensation by king	2		
Preached before king	27		
Published on behalf of king	2		
Royal commemorative verse (1643)	8 (20)*		
Total within Oxford	43		
Outside Oxford			
I. Accompanied king on campaigns	5 (1)		
Royal office	1		
Loss of royal office	3		
II. Member of Westminster Assembly and preacher to parliament		3	
Member of Westminster Assembly		1	
Parliamentary office		1	
Ejected from headship by king		2 (1)	
III. Soldier outside Oxford	36 (2)	1	
Military chaplain	7	1 (1)	
IV. *Benefice in 1642*			
Retained until 1646	20 (4)		24 (5)
Sequestrated by 1646			
Resigned before 1646			2

V. *New living 1642–6*		
(a) Presented by king		
benefice	1	
prebend's stall	5 (3)	
(b) Presented by college/university		
retained	3	
sequestrated	7 (1)	
resigned	3	
(c) Other patron		
retained	7 (4)	
sequestrated	6	
resigned	3	
(d) Intruded by		
Committee for plundered ministers	7 (2)	
Parliament	3 (2)	
		16 (2)
		3
		25
		25
VI. *Fled Oxford*		
Local royalist activity	1	
Became parliamentarian		
Employment	4	
Foreign study	5	
Reason unknown	2 (1)	
Total outside Oxford	89	66
GRAND TOTAL 223	132	66

* Numbers given in brackets represent fellows counted in a different category.

expertise at the disposal of the garrison (Clayton and other physicians looked after the earliest casualties of the war, brought to Oxford). Edward Greaves, fellow of All Souls and appointed a royal physician, published a perceptive analysis of the typhus epidemic of 1643, based no doubt on his observations during the outbreak. A student of mathematics, Richard Rallingson or Rawlinson, a BA of Queen's, earned the thanks of the king himself by drawing a 'scheme or plott' of Oxford's defences. He was allowed to graduate MA, without further fee or lapse of time.[78]

The most notable contribution made by academics was literary and exhortatory. They provided the war poets, preachers, journalists, and apologists for the royalist cause. The college chapels, including the cathedral, were the scene of uplifting sermons, as well as appeals for charity and the publicizing of royal proclamations. As table 14.2 indicates, twenty-seven fellows in holy orders preached before the king, and the university press printed many of their and others' sermons. Prayers were specially composed to intercede for the sovereign and the university in time of danger (May 1644). A substantial number, however, confined their activities on behalf of the king to the care of their parishes, distant from Oxford, until ejected in 1646.

In terms of propaganda the most successful activist was a fellow of All Souls, John Berkenhead, who edited the witty and informative royalist weekly newspaper *Mercurius Aulicus*, which lasted for 118 issues. He was rewarded with the moral philosophy professorship in March 1643. Another All Souls man, Dudley Digges, argued the royalist case with distinction, as did Gerard Langbaine of Queen's. William Cartwright, Henry Berkhead, and Henry Llewelyn were among the verse contributors to the last of the celebratory volumes presented to the king on the arrival of the queen in July 1643. It brought the series of commemorative verses on royal events to a fitting climax. As one observed:

> The birth of princes the chiefe theme hath beene,
> For schollars, now, the safety of the queene.

The verses were contributed by over fifty individuals, including twenty-seven fellows (five of them heads of house and twelve from Christ Church alone) and the university printer.[79]

Leonard Lichfield printed most of the literature produced in defence of the royal cause at Oxford, together with the official declarations and proclamations of the king and his council of war, the lords commissioners, and the high command, con-

---

[78] Reinhart, 'Visitation', 222–9, and accompanying references. *DNB*, s.v. Hammond, Greaves; Bodl. MS Twyne–Langbaine 2, fo 37, the certificate of Oxford physicians, Clayton (master of Pembroke), John Bainbridge (professor of astronomy), and John Saunders (principal of St Mary Hall) that they daily care for the sick [*c.* December 1642]; [E. Greaves], *Morbus epidemius anni 1643* . . . (Oxford [1643]); Madan, *Oxford Books* ii, no. 1502; OUA register Sb, p. 37; Wood, *Fasti* ii. 60. Rallingson's plan is that reprinted in Wood's original Latin version of his history of the university.

[79] For the editor of *Mercurius Aulicus* see P. W. Thomas, *Sir John Berkenhead, 1617–1679: a royalist career in politics and polemics* (Oxford 1969); OUA register Sb, p. 24. Digges is noticed by Wood, *Athenae* iii. 65–6. *Musarum Oxoniensium ΕΠΙΒΑΤΗΡΙΑ* is Madan, *Oxford Books* ii, no. 1418. As well as Cartwright, the Christ Church Student Henry Berkhead penned elegant verses in praise of individual royalists, including the eulogy placed on the monument to Sir Bevil Granville: Madan, *Oxford Books* ii, no. 1436.

tinuing the invaluable work he had begun in June 1642 until the surrender four years later. He was interrupted in October 1644, when the great fire on the west side of the city destroyed his works in Butcher Row; the other Oxford printer, Henry Hall, took over part of the printing of *Mercurius Aulicus* thereafter. Both were owed money by the royalists at the end of the war.[80]

The final siege of the city took place in May and June 1646, after the king himself had departed. The lords commissioners were therefore in charge of the negotiations with Fairfax, and received his representatives in the audit house at Christ Church, where so much of the work of governing Oxford had been done for the past three and a half years. Hertford, the chancellor, was among the leading commissioners; and the delegates named by convocation also ensured that the interests of the university were not forgotten in the negotiations for the surrender. In particular Sheldon and Baylie pressed for greater assurances on the future of the university; it is possibly in connection with their demands that successive drafts of seven articles safeguarding academic freedoms have survived, in the hand of the keeper of the archives, Gerard Langbaine. But in the event the pressing need to conclude the surrender before food and the soldiers' pay ran out meant that no further concessions were made, other than that dons would benefit from the treaty in the matter of compounding, and that their existing rights would be upheld until parliament decided otherwise. No guarantee was given that they would not be subject to reprisals or loss of office, if found to be guilty of aiding the king.[81]

The last weeks of the royalist occupation were particularly miserable. With the arrival of disbanded troops from other fallen strongholds the city became even more crowded and disorderly. The discipline of the garrison soldiery, short of pay and provisions, appears to have broken down; they mutinied, murdered their officers, and threatened the lords commissioners so that for a time they could not meet in the audit house. One regular officer committed some nameless outrage against the vice-chancellor himself. It was no doubt with feelings of some relief, as well as considerable apprehension, that the remaining body of academics watched the cavaliers depart.[82]

For four years the university had made great sacrifices to support the royalist war effort, one of the celebrated succession of lost causes it was to espouse. When the young Anthony Wood came up, at the war's close, he found it empty of scholars and full of roundhead soldiers. To outward view the war had done remarkably little physical damage. The defences had been extensive enough to contain all the colleges; while houses had been demolished to make way for the works and create

---

[80] Sermons printed at Oxford include Madan, *Oxford Books* ii, nos. 1546, 1548, 1590, 1618, 1621, 1624, 1637, 1641, 1655; prayers include Madan, *Oxford Books* ii, no. 1648 (May 1644); for the printing history (including bills unpaid) of *Mercurius Aulicus* see Madan, *Oxford Books* ii, pp. 280, 362–3, 366–7, 491–6.

[81] Varley, *Siege of Oxford*, prints the treaty of 24 June 1646; the seven unadopted articles in Langbaine's hand are in OUA SP/F/39/4–8. Accounts of the negotiations are found in *Dugdale's Diary*, ed. Hamper, 86–92, and Bodl. MS Clarendon 28, fos 98–101.

[82] *Dugdale's Diary*, ed. Hamper, 79, 90–2; Bodl. MS Clarendon 28, fos 98–101; OUA register Sb, pp. 104–5, indignity offered the vice-chancellor, June 1646.

a clear field of fire for the defenders, only some college gardens were affected. The exception, as we have seen, was Oriel's hospital of St Bartholomew's. Even the extensive and fast-moving fire of October 1644, which had destroyed much college-owned property, had spared St Mary Hall, directly in its path. A cannon-ball had fallen against Christ Church Hall during an earlier siege, but the timely surrender in June 1646 preserved the university from bombardment and assault. Wood, however, noted ruin and decay everywhere. 'The colleges were much out of repair by the negligence of soldiers, courtiers and others that lay in them, a few chambers that were the meanest . . . being reserved for scholars use.' Books had been stolen from college libraries, the halls, which had been largely rented out to non-scholars, were 'ruinous', parts of some colleges were almost uninhabitable, and the remaining scholars were indigent. The fabric of Merton, where only a few of the thirty fellows remained at the end of the war, was so dilapidated that the hall lay, in the words of the college register, 'situ et ruinis squalida'. It is clear that the college community was suspended for a time in 1644. Balliol, in the seventeenth century small and poor, had been dissolved early in 1644. All Souls had been temporarily suspended in the same year, and Jesus was to undergo further trials which led to its near dissolution later. While St John's survived, it did so only with the help of a wealthy old member, and was greatly indebted and wholly out of repair. In his imprisonment Laud had dreamt that his old college was ruined, its roof fallen in, and that the church of God, which he had striven to perfect—along with his university—had perished. With the despoliation accompanying four years of civil warfare, and the surrender of his alma mater to the king's enemies, his worst fears, it seemed, were about to be realized. Oxford had backed the losing side, and most fellows, heavily involved in the king's cause, could scarcely expect to keep their places. But Laud himself would not see their downfall. Oxford citizens and academics had witnessed against him, and he had died on the scaffold eighteen months before the army of parliament occupied the city in summer 1646.[83]

With the surrender of the king's headquarters, and the dispersal of the royalist garrison, a new phase in the history of the university opened. As we have seen actual physical damage to college and public buildings and to the libraries was limited; the select band of collegians at the end of the war who had remained in Oxford was 'much augmented' by those returning to their posts, some of whom had been actively involved in the king's cause. Colleges and halls were now free of the combined weight of garrison, court, and royalist refugees (2,000 passes for civilian followers of the king were signed by Fairfax in the days after the surrender),

---

[83] Wood, *History of the University* ii. 488; "Tis said there was more hurt donne by the cavaliers (during their garrison) by way of embezilling and cutting off chaines of bookes, then there was since': *Aubrey's Brief Lives*, ed. Dick, 264. G. C. Brodrick, *Memorials of Merton College* (OHS iv 1885), 87–8; OUA chancellor's ct papers, 27, case of Edward Greaves, 1651, and claim that Merton was suspended at end of 1643; ibid. 28, the case of Balliol's manciple, 1653, refers to the dissolution of the college. Laud's dream is referred to in Sharpe, 'Archbishop Laud and the University of Oxford', 164. Brent and Corbett, warden and sub-warden of Merton, were among those who took part in Laud's trial: Laud, *Works* iv. 194, 220–1, 229.

but several societies were close to bankruptcy, though only one, Balliol, was actually dissolved. Fairfax had wisely set a guard on the Bodleian, having expressed his care for learning; but he had made few concessions to the university in the articles of surrender, and parliament had now to decide what was to be its fate. It was rumoured that Cardinal Mazarin had set aside £40,000 to buy up the Bodleian. Would the treasures of the university suffer the same fate as 'the late king's goods' were to do, through sale and dispersal?[84]

Parliament's first move was to prohibit the university making any new appointments to vacant posts, or entering into new leases of its property.[85] As a corporation the university was to be brought into line with the rest of the nation under parliamentary control, and exposed for the first time to the new arrangements in the government of church and state: 'complying with country committees', the subscriptions to oaths of loyalty and the payment of the monthly tax, ejection from office of 'scandalous ministers' and those deemed 'delinquent', acceptance of the directory of worship and the Presbyterian classis. Those actively aiding the king had forfeited their estates and church land was about to be seized. There was little prospect that leading academics, who had assisted the king from before the beginning of the war, could escape the nemesis that awaited them.

The second move of parliament was to counter the effects on Oxford of four years of royalist propaganda by dispatching seven reliable preachers, headed by Francis Cheynell, the celebrated Presbyterian controversialist, to undertake a programme of godly reformation. A healing dose of right doctrine was to be administered to an institution described by Cheynell in the following year as 'much corrupted'. The university press, whose output had been dwindling for some time, was placed under their control.[86]

The new ministers were mostly familiar with the Oxford scene, though their ties had been severed by either Laudian persecution before the war or royalist occupation during it. Cheynell had been a fellow of Merton until suspended in 1638 for refusing to bow to the altar, and had since risen to prominence as chaplain to the earl of Essex and as the bitter antagonist of William Chillingworth. Edward Reynolds, Henry Cornish, Henry Langley, Robert Harris, Edward Corbett, and Henry Wilkinson, were all well known though often controversial figures in Caroline Oxford. They had all enjoyed advancement in the service of parliament, some becoming sufficiently eminent to have been invited to give sermons before that body; most were members of the Westminster Assembly, and shared the predominant Presbyterianism of the representatives of the clergy there. Henry Wilkinson

[84] OUA SP/E/5/12, petition of the university to Fairfax, undated [1647]; Wood, *Life and Times* i. 128; Wood, *History of the University* ii. 486.

[85] OUA register Sb, p. 124, copy of an order of parliament, 2 July 1646; Wood, *History of the University* ii. 489.

[86] Bodl. MS Wood 35, fo 1, Fell to Langbaine and Brookes, 1 September 1646, mentioning the 'country' committees; OUA register Sb, p. 124, copy of the order of parliament, 16 September 1646; Cheynell's 1647 account is given in Madan, *Oxford Books* ii, no. 1917; order of the house of commons on the press, 14 October 1646: Madan, *Oxford Books* ii, p. 430.

('Long Harry') had been one of the city's lecturers, at the town church at Carfax, before the war, and so served again, with Cornish, from 1647 until the Restoration.[87]

These men dominated the chapels and churches of Oxford for the next few months, also attracting 'doubting brethren' to private devotions and conferences. A meeting-place for this purpose, an inn in the parish of St Peter's-in-the-East, was nicknamed the 'scruple house'. Their sway was challenged, however, both by pockets of residual episcopalianism and by growing sectarian activity among the troops of the garrison. Radical army preachers like Hugh Peter and John Saltmarsh spoke in the university church, which was also the setting for a formal disputation between Cheynell and his chief separatist rival, William Erbery, a chaplain to the forces at Oxford and a graduate of Brasenose. The orthodox ministers had to appeal to Fairfax to recall Erbery, so disturbing was his presence. Wood implies that their main success was with the townsfolk ('especially silly women'), but concedes that some scholars were affected and that former students, particularly from the halls which had once enjoyed a puritan reputation, New Inn and Magdalen, were returning to take advantage of the changed situation at Oxford. Christopher Rogers, Sir Nathaniel Brent, and John Wilkinson, the heads of New Inn Hall, Merton, and Magdalen Hall, who had all been deprived during the war, were restored to their places.[88]

Presbyterian conformity, upheld by the rule of the sword, could be maintained physically, at least for a time, at Oxford. But beyond the limits of the university other forces were being unleashed by the breakdown of traditional authority caused by the war, and the rising tide of radical opinion in the nation as a whole. Reformers from the continent, such as Comenius and Hartlib, who had come to England to take part in a hoped-for reformation, and their English followers such as John Dury and John Milton, attacked what they deemed the gibberish of scholastic divinity and the parrot-like repetition of dead languages. As well as the army preachers, who found themselves in Oxford and took the opportunity to make their views on the subject known, prominent non-academic and non-clerical figures offered their advice on the methods and purpose of university education. William Walwyn, the eloquent Leveller writer, and Gerard Winstanley, the Digger, among many others, advocated a more utilitarian approach to learning. It was at this time that the young George Fox experienced the revelation, as he was walking in the fields, that 'being bred at Oxford or Cambridge was not enough to fit and qualify men to be ministers of Christ'. The reformation of the university was eagerly awaited by a much wider audience in the nation at large than that within the closed world of the Oxford schools.[89]

[87] For each of the Presbyterian ministers see *DNB* and Foster, *Alumni*; J. F. Wilson, *Pulpit in Parliament* (Princeton 1969); *Oxford Council Acts 1626–65*, ed. Hobson and Salter, pp. xi–xii, 148, 155, 293.

[88] Wood, *History of the University* ii. 491, 494–8, 500; Wood, *Athenae* iii. 360–2; A. Laurence, *Parliamentary Army Chaplains, 1642–1651* (Woodbridge 1990), 111–12, 116, 124, 163–6, 170.

[89] Reinhart, 'Visitation', 247; C. Webster, *The Great Instauration* (London 1975); R. L. Greaves, *The Puritan Revolution and Educational Thought: background for reform* (New Brunswick 1969); *The Journal of George Fox*, ed. J. L. Nickalls (London 1975), 7–8.

But those who had led the university through the war, and were still in place in masters' lodgings and professorial chairs, were not prepared to concede defeat. Neither moderate reform nor radical revolution was acceptable to them. Despite the occasional note of resignation, or pessimism concerning the future, detectable in their correspondence, the leading dons took immediate steps to defend their privileges and recover their lost revenue. Two heads were sent to London to lobby parliament (especially John Selden, their remaining MP), and obtain the arrears of rent due from the university's tenants in the capital. Gerard Langbaine and Nicholas Brookes, the heads of Queen's College and St Mary Hall respectively, were granted expenses of £14 to undertake this task. But even with the help of Selden it proved difficult to accomplish. The relevant house of commons committee sat infrequently, and tenants—and others like the London stationers, whose payments to the university for the right to print bibles were in arrears—continued obdurate, taking advantage of the doubts over the claims of the academic authorities.[90]

Not until 1 May 1647 did parliament enact the ordinance which all awaited, for the visitation and reformation of the university of Oxford, and the 'correction of abuses' there.[91] It named the twenty-four visitors charged with this task, headed by Brent, warden of Merton, and appointed a committee of the lords and commons, seventy-eight strong, as a final arbiter and court of appeal. The board of visitors included Cheynell and three of the other ministers recently sent to Oxford, the newly restored heads of hall, MPs with an interest in university affairs, such as William Prynne, and six lawyers from the Inns of Court. It was to hear and determine all matters of complaint and discover—by inquiry upon oath—those who had assisted the king in arms, had not subscribed to the solemn league and covenant and the negative oath, and who had not accepted the new directory of worship.

Unfortunately for the effectiveness of the visitors their most positive actions coincided with two of the gravest political crises of the year. They had no sooner arrived at Oxford when the repercussions of the army's seizure of the king (3–4 June 1647) led to divisions among the forces in the city. Oxford was ringed with troops and there was a minor skirmish between rival parties of soldiers outside All Souls. In contrast, their academic opponents, meeting regularly in convocation to concert their actions, showed unity of purpose and considerable resourcefulness. Led by Fell, still dean of Christ Church and vice-chancellor, the doctors and masters elected on 13 October 1646 a powerful delegacy, which included seven heads and three canons of Christ Church, to co-ordinate their efforts and draw up the case against the visitors.[92]

[90] Madan, *Oxford Books* ii, p. 430; OUA SP/F/26, the university petition, 16 September 1646, to be presented to the house of commons, with Selden's help; Bodl. MS Wood f. 35, fo 1, and OUA WP/γ/16/1, 17, 19, 21, Fell to Langbaine and Brookes, August–September 1646; BL Add. MS 32,093, fos 234–5, 237–8, 239–40, 241–2, Langbaine to Selden, September–November 1646. Both Fell and Langbaine expressed doubts about the future of university education at Oxford in these months. The university appealed to Fairfax to mediate with its tenants: OUA SP/E/5/12.

[91] *Acts and Ordinances of the Interregnum*, ed. C. H. Firth and R. S. Rait (3 vols London 1911) i. 925–7.

[92] OUA register Sb, p. 125; Wood, *History of the University* ii. 501–4, 506–8.

The immediate result of this initiative was the celebrated *Reasons of the Present Judgment of the University of Oxford*, which was approved by a full convocation on 1 June 1647. The legal arguments were put by Richard Zouche, the regius professor of civil law who had assisted in the framing of Laud's statutes, and those dealing with matters of conscience by the regius professor of divinity, Robert Sanderson. The pamphlet addressed the question of obedience to the visitation ordinance of parliament and the earlier enactment of the solemn league and covenant, the negative oath and the Presbyterian directory of worship. Gathered under nine headings, their argument was that submission would be contrary to the oaths they had already taken, those of supremacy and allegiance, and the 1642 protestation oath. Regarding the new ecclesiastical arrangements they stressed the antiquity and legality of episcopacy. They tellingly contrasted the moderate defence of the monarchy and the church, which had characterized parliament's case in 1642, with more recent developments—pamphlet attacks on the king, and the growth of separatism. So far as the validity of the visitation was concerned the authors argued that the king himself was the only authority they could recognize, and if the board claimed, by its commission, to be acting in his name, they cheekily offered to ask the king in person if he approved.[93]

The volume circulated widely in Oxford and London. Gerard Langbaine, the university archivist in succession to Twyne, translated it into Latin for the benefit of the international community of learning, and versions in other languages were published. The several editions, the large print-run, and the many notices of the volume all indicate that the reasoned refusal of the dons found a sympathetic audience among the educated at home and abroad. When, eighteen years later, the whirligig of time had worked its changes, the Cavalier Parliament recalled the document, and sent thanks to the university for its firm stand against the 'usurped powers' then prevailing. The *Reasons* was reprinted again at moments of crisis for the Stuart monarchy. Its main purpose had also been achieved: those who had to answer to the charges put by the visitors thereafter had at their disposal a coherent and well understood case.[94]

Throughout the summer of 1647 the visitors were frustrated at every turn. Their opponents successfully used every form of delaying tactic—such as taking advantage of a misprint in the notice of a meeting—to avoid compliance.[95] To give them greater authority new powers of inquiry were granted, and additions to their responsibilities, to include the seizure and examination of the university's records and the imprisonment of refusers. The former chancellor, Pembroke, was restored to office, and the reflections on his character, which had been made in the patent creating Hertford chancellor in 1643, erased from the record. The board was

---

[93] Wood, *History of the University* ii. 507–8; OUA register Sb, pp. 133–49; Wood's annotated copy of the *Reasons* is Bodl. Wood 514 (31).

[94] Lichfield was paid for printing 1,030 copies: Madan, *Oxford Books* ii, nos 1926–30; Wood, *History of the University* ii. 520–1; *CJ* viii. 623, resolution of the commons, 31 October 1665.

[95] 'July' was mistakenly printed for 'June' in the notice of 24 May 1647: Madan, *Oxford Books* ii, no. 1923; Wood, *History of the University* ii. 511–13.

ordered to sit from day to day, and to keep a register; it did so from September.[96] Sheldon and Hammond were summoned to attend the king as royal chaplains, and this temporarily removed two influential voices from Oxford. But timewasting and prevarication on the part of the academics, the refusal of university officers (including the proctors) to give up keys and insignia, and of the vice-chancellor and the registrar to yield seals and books, led to further delays.[97]

The visitors needed to employ harsher measures. In October Fell was imprisoned in London, and the summons to leading academics to appear before the Oxford committee was immediately followed by orders for them to answer to the ultimate authority, the committee of lords and commons in London.[98] But these more decisive moves were unhappily timed. No sooner had the committee convened at Westminster under the chancellor's chairmanship, in November, than the second political crisis of 1647 interrupted proceedings. The capital was thrown into uproar by the sudden flight of the king from Hampton Court to the Isle of Wight, and once again uncertainty concerning the whereabouts of political authority, and the future shape of events, must have given encouragement to those resisting the will of parliament. The hearings were treated to a display of Pembroke's 'passions'. He 'fell into a great heat' when questioning Fell, and berated him as an incendiary, who had brought 'fyer from hell' into the university. In spite of—or because of—this strong lead from the chairman the committee was divided on whether to deprive Fell and others: the university's MP, Selden, and the parliamentary lawyer, Bulstrode Whitelocke, argued for clemency. They were, however, outvoted and the committee went on to order the removal of Fell, two canons of Christ Church, the defiant proctors, and Baylie of St John's, who was known to have strengthened Hannibal Potter's will to resist when the president of Trinity, a timid man, was standing in for Fell. A week later Potter himself, Radcliffe of Brasenose, and Oliver of Magdalen were dismissed.[99]

In the following month Edward Reynolds, a Presbyterian minister and like two other leading visitors, Brent and Cheynell, a former fellow of Merton, was appointed vice-chancellor by the Lords and Commons, on the recommendation of Pembroke, in place of the still-imprisoned Fell. He would shortly replace him as dean of Christ Church. New proctors were also ordered to take up their duties, and convocation, interrupted since November 1647, was restored to life by the visitors. But while the parliamentary committee issued edicts and the visitors continued to sit daily in Brent's lodgings at Merton to regulate the university's affairs and interrogate the contumacious, there seems to have been little obedience to the orders given. Convocation was very poorly attended when it met again in April,

[96] *Acts and Ordinances*, ed. Firth and Rait i. 995–6, 1001–2; Wood, *History of the University* ii. 513–19; *Register*, ed. Burrows, p. i.

[97] Wood, *History of the University* ii. 520–1, 524–5. Even a head willing to comply could not deliver college records which were under joint custody: OUA SP/E/5/23, Langbaine to the visitors, 10 October 1647.

[98] Wood, *History of the University* ii. 522, 528, 533.

[99] Ibid. 534–5, 545–7; Bodl. MS Wood f. 35, fo 123, Fell to Sheldon, 13 December 1647.

and Fell's wife and children refused to leave the deanery. If Wood is to be believed, 'not a man stirred from his place or removed'. Moreover colleges were continuing to appoint new fellows to vacancies, in spite of parliament's prohibition. The old guard was sufficiently confident to fill two professorial chairs that fell vacant during 1647.[100]

What was required was direct action at Oxford, and a personal visit from the chancellor was agreed. From his seat at Ramsbury, Wiltshire, and accompanied by such local parliamentarian potentates as the two Popham brothers, together with an impressive entourage, Pembroke made a stately progress to Oxford. He was received with all the ceremony that could be mustered on 12 April 1648. Royalist lampoons—eight were published in London and Oxford, one of the wittiest by Berkenhead—made much of his lack of scholarly pretensions, as well as the rather thin assembly of academics which met him at his entrance, and the absence of the university insignia, keys, seals, and beadles' staves, which should have been carried in procession before him. At the convocation which was immediately held degrees were awarded to two of Pembroke's sons and over eighty leading academics drawn from the supporters of the new regime: the many scholars who had returned to New Inn Hall and Magdalen Hall and those from Cambridge, a university already 'reformed', who were looking for advancement in the other place. The realities of power were also acknowledged in the honorary degree conferred on Colonel Kelsey of the garrison.[101]

Harsh measures against the recalcitrant followed. The visitors had already gained access to Christ Church, Mrs Fell, sitting in her chair, being carried out into the great quad by the soldiers. The new appointments could now be implemented. Reynolds entered the deanery, Corbett took Hammond's place as sub-dean, and Rogers was translated from New Inn Hall to a canonry. This forcible entry was thereafter duplicated at several other colleges. The doors at All Souls, Wadham, and Magdalen were broken down to admit those the visitors had appointed: John Palmer, John Wilkins, and the elderly John Wilkinson. The last moved the short distance from Magdalen Hall to the college itself, in place of Oliver, to where he had once been a fellow when Elizabeth reigned. In each case the buttery book was called for, the name of the original incumbent scored out, and the new man entered.[102]

Throughout 1647, despite the uncertainties and actual violence experienced in Oxford as elsewhere, there had been a sharp recovery in the number of new students admitted, if not in the number of degrees awarded, other than by creation.

[100] Wood, *History of the University* ii. 547–9, 558–9; Reinhart, 'Visitation', appx B, records all fellows in place, 1646–52.
[101] OUA register T, 10–12, order of parliament that Pembroke should take possession of his chancellor's place, 8 March 1648, and account of the visit; Wood, *History of the University* ii. 558–74; Wood, *Fasti* ii. 110–18. Printed items ridiculing the visit, and the chancellor, are listed in Madan: the best known, Berkenhead's *News from Pembroke and Montgomery*, is Madan, *Oxford Books* ii, no. 1982. For the nature of the reformation in the other place see Twigg, *University of Cambridge*.
[102] Wood, *History of the University* ii. 557, 563, 568–70.

In the following year, however, the recorded number of matriculants fell markedly. This may reflect the immediate reaction to the displacement of so many established figures in the university and colleges, but perhaps also indicates gaps in the records themselves. The trickle of matriculants during the civil war years did not become a flood until the 1650s, yet there now seems to have been a partial restoration of normal recruitment. Even Balliol, in suspended animation until 1649, matriculated a few students during 1647–8. There was nothing, however, like the number of new undergraduates at the halls, all of which record (except for Magdalen Hall) only a few matriculants in the years 1643–9, that might be expected from our knowledge of the dominant role played by the heads of halls in the visitation. It would of course be returning undergraduates and graduates, rather than freshmen, who would be involved in the sudden reactivation of these houses, and the filling of vacancies elsewhere in 1648; nevertheless their enhanced status did not immediately lead to an increase in numbers.[103]

Resistance to the visitors was being overcome, if necessary by force, in the spring and summer of 1648. In May the London committee pronounced that prevaricating answers were tantamount to non-submission, and ordered the visitors to enforce the changes agreed. A further order required bursars to yield the money in their hands to the new heads. Only worship according to the directory was to be permitted in college chapels. The parliamentary authorities, nationally and locally, assisted in the process of identifying, and proceeding against, those academics who ought not to benefit from the Treaty of Oxford, because they were 'delinquents' in their private capacities, as active followers of the king, royal office-holders, or incumbents whose livings were sequestrated. The canons of Christ Church, for example, at least still had a cathedral to employ them, but otherwise were treated as delinquent. As we have seen their dean, Fell, had long been viewed by parliament as a notorious incendiary; he was deprived of his several offices, but was able to retire to his parsonage in Berkshire, where he died in 1649. In the end, however, few academics were forced to compound for their private estates, presumably because most fell below the limit of £200 in value which qualified for sequestration. Several petitioned to compound, but—with some exceptions—their cases were not proceeded with. It would appear that—taking the case of those who had livings in neighbouring counties, for example—the majority lost both their fellowships and their benefices.[104]

With Fell gone, Pincke dead, and Baylie soon to be deprived, resistance in the early summer of 1648 centred on Sheldon and Hammond, both now banished from the king's presence and under house arrest at Oxford. There was great resort

[103] OUA chancellor's ct papers, 28, 1653 case, states that Balliol was put into commons again about 22 June 1649; Porter, 'University and society', pp. 31–4 above; Wood, *Fasti* ii. 104.

[104] *Acts and Ordinances*, ed. Firth and Rait, 1143; Wood, *History of the University* ii. 576, 586–7. *Register*, ed. Burrows, 22, 88–9, 94–5. For Fell see *DNB* and Wood, *Athenae* iii. 242–3. Baylie, Zouche, and Hood, for example, petitioned to compound; the first two were fined, Hood was not. For other instances see *Walker Revised*, ed. Matthews, 23–35; *Calendar of the Committee for Compounding with Delinquents* (5 vols London 1889–93), 486, 1513, 1523–4, 1528–9, 1549, 1552, 1632, 3257; *CSPD 1645–7*, 486–7.

to both. In May they were ordered to be taken from the university and imprisoned. Eventually they were allowed to retire to the country. They continued to correspond thereafter, and Hammond, charitable to the last, interested his friends in founding scholarships which would enable poor but able boys to have a university education. Another important resister was the sub-warden of Exeter, Henry Tozer. Reputed a 'puritan' for his pious and precise lifestyle, he had been nominated for the Westminster Assembly; but he now preached defiance from his place in the city church at Carfax. Garrison soldiery were used to pull him down from the pulpit, and he was imprisoned in June.[105]

Armed with the orders of the London committee the visitors began the task of summoning all college members to appear before them and make their submission. The visitors' register from mid-May becomes a much fuller, if still imperfect, listing of those summoned, their response—or their non-appearance—and the decision in each case. The notional total of some 463 senior posts in the university—including headships of halls and professorial chairs, and accepting some problematical decisions with regard to members of Christ Church, New College, and St John's—was reduced by the thirty-four which were unfilled in the summer of 1648. As some fellows held more than one position it may be calculated that about 420 academics should have been liable to appear. In fact a rather smaller number, 379, was named in the visitors' register. Their response to the summons is summarized in table 14.3. Only a small minority accepted the authority of the visitors; most either did not attend or gave negative answers of one kind or another—the equivocations which the London committee had instructed those on the spot not to accept. It is noteworthy that the published *Reasons* of the previous year provided the legal and philosophical basis for many refusals. Lists of those not submitting were posted up at college gates and elsewhere, and the garrison soldiery were authorized to expel them from Oxford. It was threatened that those remaining would be prosecuted as spies. By the end of October the process was virtually complete.[106]

But the story does not end there. What has puzzled all historians since, as well as contemporaries hostile to the purge, is that the number of fellows not submitting, and ordered to be expelled their colleges, is greater than those actually expelled. In spite of the refusal of the great majority, half of those listed remained in post; forty-three of these had actually been ordered to leave. That the end result of the actions of the visitors was much less severe than might have been assumed

---

[105] Printed orders of parliament: Madan, *Oxford Books* ii, no. 2000; Wood, *History of the University* ii. 586–9; Bodl. MS Wood f. 35, fo 235; BL MS Harleian 6942, fo 14; *Register*, ed. Burrows, pp. lxxv, cx–cxi, 113, 115; *Calendar of Committee for Compounding*, 1528–9.

[106] *Register*, ed. Burrows, from p. 89; Wood, *History of the University* ii. 587–9, 593, 598–600, 605–6. For a full analysis, by college, of expelled and intruded, see Reinhart, 'Visitation', ch. 6 and appx B. 'For the sake of comparability, special criteria have been devised to identify the "fellows" of Christ Church (which instead of fellows had a small chapter of canons and a large, highly differentiated body of Students) and those of New College and St John's (where since virtually all members of the foundation were fellows, rank alone does not suffice to establish the elite).' Ibid. 527.

TABLE 14.3 *The response to the visitation, 1648*

Response	Fellows	(%)
Submission	45	(11.9)
Refusal to submit	139	(36.7)
Reservations	25	(6.6)
Non-appearance	69	(18.2)
Excuse for absence	4	(1.1)
No record	97	(25.6)
TOTAL	379	(100.0)

from a study of their original decisions may have something to do with the complications of the process, the erratic nature of seventeenth-century bookkeeping, differing interpretations of the non-submitters' responses (in spite of the authorities' warnings on the matter), and the ameliorating factors of college solidarity, nepotism, bribery, and other forms of political or private patronage.

A breakdown of the fate of Oxford fellows by college in table 14.4 shows widely differing experiences. Three houses, Corpus, Wadham, and St John's, suffered a much higher number of expulsions than the rest. At the other end of the scale Merton, Lincoln, Balliol, Queen's, and Trinity suffered least. This had less to do with their political stance in the recent past than the character of the head in 1648, his political connections, the influence of great patrons, and the pragmatic policies being pursued by the colleges. Fell and the canons of Christ Church were termed delinquent by parliament, but that did not prevent most of the Students of the house submitting to the new authorities. His association with Selden may have persuaded Langbaine of Queen's, previously active in resistance, to conform and thus protect his college from intrusion.

Given many such individual and unorthodox responses any simple categorization of submitters and refusers is bound to fail. All that can be said is that fellows in their thirties, with MAs, were more likely to remain in place than those younger and less qualified. Was there a royalist bias in those matriculating on the eve of the civil war and later? There is some correlation between behaviour in 1648 and an earlier political stance only in the case of those who signed the 1642 remonstrance against Archbishop Laud: most surviving signatories conformed. It is noteworthy, however, that a quarter did not.[107]

Royalist commentators were certain that the result of these changes was disastrous. As Fell put it: 'Within the compass of a few weeks an almost general riddance was made of the loyal University of Oxford, in whose room succeeded an illiterate rabble, swept up from the plough-tail, from shops and grammar schools,

[107] Reinhart, 'Visitation', 397–402.

TABLE 14.4 Colleges and fate of Oxford fellows, 1648

College	Expelled	(% across)	Expelled but remained	(% across)	Remained	(% across)	Total	(% across)
All Souls'	17	(50.0)	6	(17.6)	11	(32.4)	34	(100.0)
Balliol	3	(25.0)	—	—	9	(75.0)	12	(100.0)
Brasenose	10	(58.8)	1	(5.9)	6	(35.3)	17	(100.0)
Christ Church	19	(41.3)	3	(6.5)	24	(52.2)	46	(100.0)
Corpus	17	(85.0)	1	(5.0)	2	(10.0)	20	(100.0)
Exeter	8	(50.0)	1	(6.3)	7	(43.8)	16	(100.0)
Jesus	5	(62.5)	1	(12.5)	2	(25.0)	8	(100.0)
Lincoln	1	(11.1)	4	(44.4)	4	(44.4)	9	(100.0)
Magdalen	27	(69.2)	3	(7.7)	9	(23.1)	39	(100.0)
Merton	3	(13.6)	2	(9.1)	17	(77.3)	22	(100.0)
New College	19	(47.5)	7	(17.5)	14	(35.0)	40	(100.0)
Oriel	7	(43.8)	5	(31.3)	4	(25.0)	16	(100.0)
Pembroke	4	(44.4)	—	—	5	(55.6)	9	(100.0)
Queen's	—	—	5	(35.7)	9	(64.3)	14	(100.0)
St John's	30	(81.1)	1	(2.7)	6	(16.2)	37	(100.0)
Trinity	3	(25.0)	3	(25.0)	6	(50.0)	12	(100.0)
University	5	(62.5)	—	—	3	(37.5)	8	(100.0)
Wadham	11	(84.6)	—	—	2	(15.4)	13	(100.0)
Principals of halls	— [1]*	—	—	—	4 [1]	(100)	4 [2]	(100.0)
University professors	1 [6]	(66.6)	—	—	2 [2]	(33.3)	3 [8]	(100.0)
TOTAL	190	(50.1)	43	(11.3)	146	(38.5)	379	(100.0)

* Numbers given in square brackets represent individuals counted in a different category.

and the dregs of the neighbour university.' In the same spirit Wood wrote of the 'scum of Cambridge', men conforming to the puritan authorities even to the extent of keeping their hair short—'the committee cut'—and invading the rival institution. But both had to admit that, if only by accident, or the improper use of political patronage, some good and learned men were intruded.[108]

From July 1648 a committee of thirteen was created by the visitors to vet applications for academic places. Once approved, the candidate's name was ordered to be entered into the college register. In the course of the next few months fifteen heads were intruded and a further 128 fellows. One fifth were promotions within the same college; one third were drawn from another Oxford college or hall. Especially notable was the number from Magdalen Hall and New Inn Hall who obtained fellowships elsewhere. Another third were Cambridge men, with those from Emmanuel making the biggest contribution. Fell and Wood had been correct in noting a migration from the 'neighbour university'. Those intruded were in general younger and less well qualified than those whom they replaced.[109]

The commanding heights of the academic establishment were henceforward occupied by those placed in office by the visitors in 1648. The engagement controversy of 1649, following the declaration of the republic, removed one or two, such as Reynolds and (in 1650) Cheynell, who refused the oath. But the university thereafter was largely the creation of the visitation, and remained in conformity to the new regimes of the 1650s, as the next chapter makes clear. Thus Fairfax and Cromwell were fêted after the suppression of the Burford mutiny in May 1649. John Wilkins typified the university's strength, both in terms of its celebrated contribution to scientific research and in its political and religious connections; he was, after all, Cromwell's brother-in-law. A sustained attempt was made to come to an accommodation with the rival corporation, the city of Oxford, in line with the 'healing and settling' which characterized the policy of the university under its new puritan heads; but that did not prove to be possible. Nevertheless, after a decade of revolutionary turbulence and catastrophic civil conflict, in which it had fully participated, the university was now entered upon the calmer waters of the years which were to follow.

[108] *Register*, ed. Burrows, p. xc; Wood, *History of the University* ii. 573–4; Wood, *Fasti* ii. 106, 110–18.
[109] Reinhart, 'Visitation', 406–17, and tables 6.10, 6.11 and 6.12.

15

Cromwellian Oxford

BLAIR WORDEN

By 1652, when the five years of the parliamentary visitation ended, the resourceful and bitter resistance of Oxford's royalism had been worn down. Few more significant challenges, political or military, had faced the victors of the civil wars. The post-war university, the defeated capital of crown and church, was united against its conquerors, and connected with the wider world of English royalism, by deep political and personal loyalties and by the unwavering commitment to the Book of Common Prayer sustained by Fell, Hammond, Sheldon, and their colleagues. College walls sheltered royalist tutors, royalist servants, and royalist conspirators. In the neighbouring countryside there were landowners closely tied both to the university and to the royal cause. The strategic importance of Oxford survived the city's surrender to parliament—and would persist through the Interregnum, when Oxford was repeatedly the expected target of invading and rebel armies: of Charles II in 1651, of Penruddock in 1655, of Monck and then Lambert in 1660.[1]

Oxford's new puritan rulers experienced a sense of insecurity and isolation which was heightened by the second civil war of 1648, when the university's defiance provoked a more extensive purge than had apparently been intended.[2] Further expulsions followed the coup of 1648–9 which produced the regicide and the rule of the Rump, and which in Oxford as elsewhere diminished such support as the puritans could muster. 'Presbyterian' visitors opposed to the new regime made way for 'Independent' ones supporting it; the king's arms were removed from Oxford's walls and buildings; and 'good affection' to the republic was demanded of candidates not only for academic positions but for posts in the kitchens, butteries, and stables.[3] Those measures, extensive as they were, would

---

[1] Charles II: *CSPD 1651*, 365, 403–4; Penruddock: see p. 768 below; Monck: *Calendar of Clarendon State Papers*, ed. H. Ogle *et al.* (5 vols Oxford 1872–1970) iv. 534; Lambert: R. Hutton, *The Restoration* (Oxford 1985), 116. Among Oxford's principal royalist neighbours were the families of Cope, Stonehouse, Walter, and Falkland.

[2] See especially *Register*, ed. Burrows, 88 ff. For the moderation favoured by some visitors see Henry Wilkinson sr, *Miranda, stupenda* (London 1646), 29; Bodl. MS Wood f. 35, fo 334; OUA register of convocation 1647–59, NEP/*supra*/26, register T, pp. 34–5; Wood, *History of the University* ii. 618. For the isolation and insecurity see *CSPD 1649–50*, 59–60, 69, 175, 248, 303–4, 461–2; *Mercurius Politicus* 14–21 November 1650, 391–2.

[3] In Exeter College the cook was dismissed 'for his misdemeanours and contempt of the authority of parliament' and replaced by one recommended 'for his great suffering and general affection to the authority of parliament'—with what culinary consequences we cannot say: ECA register 1619–1737, fo 42. Cf QCA register R, p. 131; *Register*, ed. Burrows, 170, 236–7, 241–2.

not have tamed the university by themselves. The stability of puritan rule in Oxford was always proportionate to the stability of puritan rule in England; and the most stabilizing event during the parliamentary visitation was not a local but a national one, the final defeat of the royalists by Oliver Cromwell at Worcester in September 1651. The Oxford garrison, whose support had been essential to the previous work of the visitors, was now redundant; the fortifications were slighted;[4] the soldiers and the puritan bosses of Oxfordshire yielded their places on the visitation to civilian heads of house. At last the subjugation of Oxford was complete. In the course of its life the visitation had replaced a majority of the heads, most of the professors and readers, and approximately two hundred fellows. It had also appointed a small army of demys and scholars from which would be drawn the majority of the fellows elected or promoted after the restoration of self-government to the colleges in the 1650s. Until late in that decade, perhaps even on the eve of the Restoration in 1660, the colleges were essentially controlled by men whom the parliamentary visitors had intruded or vetted. The visitation had laid the foundations on which the godly university of the puritan imagination could be built. Never in the history of Oxford has more power been held by its would-be reformers.

Yet even to that power there were limits, as events would show: limits imposed partly by the resilience of the institution, partly by the difficulties of translating puritan ideas into practice, but partly too by the boundaries which had circumscribed the visitors' achievement. The failures of the Cromwellian rule of Oxford were to be as closely related as its successes to the legacy of a visitation which had secured outward conformity to the puritan occupation but which had engendered little support for it. When the visitation required the men who were brought before it—most of them young—to acknowledge its authority, it presented them with a problem of conscience. Could they reconcile submission to the visitors with their political allegiances and with the national and collegiate oaths which they had taken earlier? The handful of puritan zealots submitted gladly; a much larger number refused; but as large too was the number with less certain loyalties who contrived to survive the purge: who were conveniently absent when the visitors summoned them, or who having initially resisted changed their minds, or who offered submissions which they would as willingly retract if the political wind were to alter. Amidst the national turmoil and uncertainties of the late 1640s the population and the opinions of Oxford were too shifting to allow the straightforward classifications that were essential to the smooth operation of the purge, while the information and the machinery of the visitors were too restricted to permit the thorough execution of their decisions. Men who slipped through the visitors' net, remembering their friends among the less fortunate, sometimes succeeded in restoring them to their posts, or, when that endeavour failed, in enabling them to retain their chambers and their commons and even their teaching.

The visitors resisted such backsliding, not without effect, but their efforts were

[4] On the fortification of Oxford in 1649–51 see H. M. Reece, 'The military presence in England, 1649–1660' (Oxford D. Phil. thesis 1981), 131–2.

impeded by the quarrels between them and their masters at Westminster. The parliamentary visitation was essentially Presbyterian, designed to impose on Oxford the Presbyterian rule which had already been thus enforced on Cambridge.[5] Yet when Cambridge was purged there had yet to emerge the rival Independent faction which united congregationalists, New Model officers, and erastian MPs, all groups suspicious of Presbyterian clericalism and intolerance. In the Presbyterian inquisition into the consciences of the royalists at Oxford, the Independents recognized a threat to their own. The MPs John Selden, Bulstrode Whitelocke, Nathaniel Fiennes, Sir John Trevor, and Humphrey Salwey, each a friend to learning and a friend to Oxford, undermined the visitors' work and aided those heads and fellows who opposed, and yet strove to survive, the visitation.[6] Not only could Oxford sometimes turn parliament against the visitors: at other times it could set the visitors against parliament, by encouraging them to identify more readily with the university, where many of them now held high positions, than with the distant and meddlesome committee at Westminster to which the visitors were answerable.

There were in any case pressing reasons for a measure of restraint by the visitors. Even before the purge, the war had gravely depleted the ranks of Oxford's fellows and teachers. The greater the number of visitatorial evictions, the harder it became to find MAs and BAs statutably and intellectually qualified to fill the vacant posts—even when forty or so young men had been brought from Cambridge[7] and when fellowships of All Souls had been showered on soldiers and on the sons of rumpers and regicides. In general—though there were significant exceptions—those of the visitors' appointments who had had least previous experience of Oxford were those who lasted least long in the university and made least impact upon it. The bulk of the intruded fellows were Oxford men with Oxford loyalties. Their principal interests lay less in national politics or in puritan reform than in their studies and their careers—and in those endemic animosities of college life of which the bitter experiences of the war and of the visitation, and the 'many questions and differences about seniority' raised by the purge,[8] had notably enlarged

[5] The Letters and Journals of Robert Baillie, ed. D. Laing (3 vols Edinburgh 1841–2) ii. 386, 393; Wilkinson, Miranda, stupenda; Robert Johnson, Lux et lex (London 1647), 43; Wood, History of the University ii. 543; Register, ed. Burrows, 22.

[6] Selden: see especially John Leland, De rebus Britannicis collectanea, ed. T. Hearne (6 vols Oxford 1715) v. 282–3; Bodl. MS Tanner 456, fos 3, 5; Bodl. MS Rawlinson d. 1070, fos 21–2; Bodl. MS Selden supra 109, fo 335. Selden and Whitelocke: Wood, History of the University ii. 545–6; Bodl. MS Lat. misc. c. 19, pp. 121–2; Bulstrode Whitelocke, Memorials of the English Affairs (London 1682, new edn 4 vols Oxford 1853) iv. 287; Bulstrode Whitelocke, Journal of the Swedish Embassy (2 vols London 1772, new edn London 1855) ii. 492; Contemporaries of Bulstrode Whitelocke, ed. R. Spalding (Oxford 1990), 206; and cf BL Add. MS 37,344, fo 323, with Register, ed. Burrows, 254, 257–8, 372. Selden and Fiennes: Bodl. MS Wood f. 35, fo 144ᵉ⁻ᵛ. Trevor: Walter Pope, Life of Seth Ward (London 1697), 20–2; Seth Ward, De cometis (Oxford 1653), epistle dedicatory. Salwey: Bodl. MS J. Walker c. 9, fos 113, 182, 185 (cf fo 189). For restraining influences among the parliamentary Independents see too Memorials of the Civil War in England from 1646 to 1652, ed. H. Cary (2 vols London 1842) ii. 415; The Humble Petition and Argument of Mr Hotham (London 1651), 8.

[7] The majority of them had been undergraduates at Cambridge in the mid-1640s; about a third of them were from Emmanuel College. My calculations are based on entries in Venn, Alumni.

[8] CA chapter book 1648–88, p. 4; Register, ed. Burrows, 217. The 'differences' were ubiquitous.

the scope. It was not only the rank and file of the newcomers whose puritan commitment was uncertain. Among Oxford's new leaders there arrived, alongside the eager initiators of reform, skilful politicians of more conservative outlook. The basic political divisions of Cromwellian Oxford would primarily arise not between the fresh appointments and those opponents of the purge who had survived it, but among the fresh appointments themselves.

Late in 1649 a new cloud appeared over Oxford that would persist until 1651: the imposition of the Rump's engagement of loyalty to the kingless commonwealth. Yet this new purge, Independent rather than Presbyterian, proved much less extensive than that of 1648. It scarcely reduced the clear majority enjoyed by Presbyterians among Oxford's leading puritans. The university did lose its vicechancellor, Edward Reynolds, but was deprived of only a handful of other members.[9] Widespread evictions were averted largely through the influence of Oliver Cromwell, who was elected chancellor in January 1651.[10] His regard for learning, and his concern to retain moderate and Presbyterian support for the national revolution, were well understood by Oxford's electors.[11] Even so it was the Independents who were his natural allies, and it was to them that he looked as the

---

[9] For Reynolds see *CJ* 14 March 1651; Edmund Ludlow, *A Voyce from the Watch Tower*, ed. A. B. Worden (Camden Soc. 4th ser. xxi 1978), 95; Edward Reynolds, *Death's Advantage* (London 1657), ep. ded. (to the Independent MP John Crewe, whom he thanks for his attempt to have him spared from eviction); Bodl. MS J. Walker c. 8, fo 217ᵛ; *Register*, ed. Burrows, p. xxxvii. The university waged a subtle and defiant campaign against the engagement: OUA register T, p. 84; ibid. vice-chancellor's accounts 1621–66, WP/β/21/4, p. 267; Bodl. MS Wood f. 35, fo 358; Bodl. MS Tanner 56, fos 147, 157; *Memorials*, ed. Cary ii. 240; L. Twells, *The Life of Edward Pocock* (London 1816), 129–38; W. N. Clarke, 'Illustrations of the state of the church during the great rebellion', *Theologian and Ecclesiastic* vi (1848), 221–2. The visitors were reluctant to impose the test (Bodl. MS Wood f. 35, fo 255; WCA MS 4/83), and parliament knew too little about the personnel of Oxford to enforce it without the visitors' co-operation (*Register*, ed. Burrows, 329). Although orders laying down strict arrangements for the imposition of the test were delivered to the colleges (QCA register H, p. 118; WCA MS 4/83), there is firm evidence of only a handful of men either taking or refusing it: QCA MS 2Y/32; BNCA MS A.I.2, fo 74ᵛ; UCA college register 1509–1727, fo 30; *Register*, ed. Burrows, 274 n., 329 (cf ibid. 130 n.); Whitelocke, *Memorials* iii. 153. (The departure from the presidency of St John's of Francis Cheynell, who certainly opposed the engagement, is unlikely to have been principally caused by it: SJM register III, pp. 426–31; *Register*, ed. Burrows, 249.) Possibly the government grasped that the thorough imposition of the engagement in Oxford would be likely to remove not its royalist enemies but its potential allies among the Presbyterians, whose scruples about the test were more severe than those of royalists: *Mercurius Politicus* 1–8 August 1650, 44; *Register*, ed. Burrows, 196. A number of cavaliers who seem to have either taken or evaded the engagement were none the less expelled on other grounds during the period of its imposition. There were, too, many voluntary resignations at that time, some of them perhaps by men who feared to be confronted by the test. See also HMC *De Lisle and Dudley* vi. 472.

[10] W. C. Abbott, *Writings and Speeches of Oliver Cromwell* (4 vols Cambridge Mass. 1937–47) ii. 281, iv. 987. Cf *CJ* 14 March 1651; Wood, *Athenae* iii. 1068 (cf pp. 758–9 below). For Cromwell's election see OUA WP/β/21/4, p. 275; ibid. WP/Y/22/le; ibid. register T, pp. 118, 120, 129–30, 135; *The Diary of Bulstrode Whitelocke 1605–1675*, ed. R. Spalding (Records of Social and Economic History new ser. xiii 1990) 254. Until 1653 Cromwell was ideally suited to fill the influential role of intermediary between government and university that had traditionally been welcomed by Oxford, but that advantage was lost when he became protector: Bodl. MS Add. d. 105, fo 10.

[11] Bodl. MS Wood f. 35, fo 341; Twells, *Life of Pocock*, 131; Wood, *History of the University* ii. 667; cf T. C. Barnard, *Cromwellian Ireland* (Oxford 1975), 198–9. Cromwell made extensive use of his chancellorship to plant and recruit pious young men and to enlarge his following.

principal instruments of reformation in Oxford and in England. In March 1651 Reynolds (whom Cromwell had tried to save from dismissal) was succeeded as dean of Christ Church by John Owen, who had been Cromwell's chaplain and companion on the Irish and Scottish campaigns in 1649–50. The appointment restored Owen to the university from which Laudian ceremonialism had prompted him to withdraw in 1637.[12] From 1652 he would be Cromwell's annual choice as vice-chancellor for five years. Both in Oxford and in the wider nation he was one of 'the two Atlasses and patriarchs of Independency'.[13] The other was Thomas Goodwin, who in January 1650 was appointed by the Rump to the presidency of Magdalen.[14] Through their closeness to Cromwell the two men gave Oxford an influence on the Cromwellian church at least as great as that which it had exerted on the Laudian church before it. Owen and Goodwin, and the party they built in the university, designed or prompted the principal ecclesiastical initiatives of the Interregnum: the system of triers and ejectors; the Cromwellian schemes for a national confession of faith and for the definition of liberty of conscience; the Savoy Conference of 1658.[15]

Upon Cromwell's return to civilian politics after his triumph at Worcester, control of the visitation passed to those puritan heads whom he especially favoured. Owen and Goodwin were two of them. A third was John Conant, rector of Exeter, son-in-law to the evicted vice-chancellor, Edward Reynolds. Like Reynolds, Conant was a Presbyterian who stood out against the Rump's engagement;[16] but Cromwell, who had failed to preserve Reynolds, succeeded in rescuing Conant, who would eventually replace Owen as Cromwell's vice-chancellor.[17] The rise of Conant on the visitation belonged to the national political strategy pursued by Cromwell in the autumn of 1651, when he sought through a series of initiatives to broaden the base of the Commonwealth's support—and when his chief parliamentary ally in that endeavour, his cousin Oliver St John, became chancellor of Cambridge.[18] It was then too that Jonathan Godard, who had been Cromwell's physician on the Scottish campaign, was installed by him as warden of Merton.[19] Godard joined the visitation with Cromwell's brother-in-law Peter French, a recently appointed canon

[12] P. Toon, *God's Statesman: the life and work of John Owen* (Exeter 1971), 9.

[13] Wood, *Athenae* iv. 98.

[14] *CJ* 8 January 1650. Cf Whitelocke, *Memorials* iii. 47; *CSPD 1651*, 30, 214; *Register*, ed. Burrows, 264.

[15] For the origins of the schemes in Oxford see especially *Weekly Intelligencer* 30 March–6 April 1652, 409; Toon, *God's Statesman*, 91, 95, 103; *Diary of Sir Archibald Johnston of Wariston 1650–1654*, ed. D. H. Fleming (Scottish History Soc. 2nd ser. xviii 1919) ii. 246; *Mercurius Politicus* 14–21 October 1658, 922–5; *A True Catalogue or an Account of . . . by whom Richard Cromwell was Proclaimed* (London 1659), 61; cf *Register*, ed. Burrows, 384.

[16] J. Prince, *The Worthies of Devon* (Exeter 1810), 232–3.

[17] For Cromwell and Conant see especially 'The Restoration Visitation of the University of Oxford and its colleges', ed. F. J. Varley, *Camden Miscellany* xviii (Camden Soc. 3rd ser. lxxix 1948), 2; John Conant jr, *The Life of the Reverend and Venerable John Conant*, ed. W. Stanton (London 1823), 22.

[18] B. Worden, *The Rump Parliament 1648–1653* (Cambridge 1974), ch. 13; C. H. Cooper, *Annals of Cambridge* (5 vols Cambridge 1842–53) iii. 448.

[19] MCR Registrum Collegii Mertonensis, pp. 385–7 (cf ibid. pp. 396, 414).

of Christ Church who had taken up office there at about the same time as Owen.[20] Under the protectorate French would become one of the official preachers to Cromwell's council and be given state lodgings in Whitehall.[21]

After French's death in June 1655 his widow, Cromwell's sister Robina, would marry the intruded warden of Wadham, John Wilkins. The marriage solidified Wilkins's power in Oxford,[22] but he had come to the forefront of university politics much earlier, and had played a leading part in the university's resistance to the engagement, which he seems not to have taken.[23] In 1652 Wilkins was appointed to a board of five set up by Cromwell to execute many of the chancellor's duties: the others were Owen, Goodwin, Godard, and French.[24] The group was well balanced. Owen and Goodwin led a radical party in Oxford; Wilkins headed a conservative one; Godard and French seem to have occupied a middle ground, even though they were too often absent from Oxford to exert a consistent influence. John Wilkins and his circle—especially Seth Ward, who had joined him at Wadham, and John Wallis—would influence the political as much as the intellectual history of Cromwellian Oxford, where Wilkins emerged as the chief and eventually victorious rival to Owen in the direction of university policy. The well-documented resolve of Wilkins and his fellow experimental philosophers to avoid the discussion of 'state affairs' at their scientific meetings, and to elevate intellectual inquiry above the divisive passions of the times,[25] should not be taken for political innocence or abstinence. It was the policy of the Wilkins circle to sustain the forms and traditions of the university, to quieten the controversies which puritan reform brought to it, and to uphold Oxford's standing no less among royalists and neutrals than among parliamentarians. The claim made by Thomas Sprat for Wilkins and his friends, that 'it was in good measure by the influence which these gentlemen had over the rest that the university it self, or at least any part of its discipline and order, was saved from ruine', was not empty.[26]

Wilkins's friend the diarist John Evelyn, a devotee of crown and church, approvingly noted Wilkins's aim 'to preserve the universities from the ignorant sacrilegious commander and souldiers'.[27] Yet, unlike Evelyn, Wilkins cannot be called a royalist. A better term for him would be 'monarchist', for until the fall of the pro-

---

[20] CA MS I.B.3, fo 39.

[21] *Perfect Proceedings* 21 March 1655; *Mercurius Politicus* 14–21 June 1655, 5419; *CSPD 1655–6*, 588. For French as a preacher in Oxford see Bodl. MS Don. f. 41, fo 69; *The Diary of John Evelyn*, ed. E. S. De Beer (6 vols Oxford 1955) iii. 104–5.

[22] B. Shapiro, *John Wilkins 1614–1672* (Berkeley and Los Angeles 1969), 111–13.

[23] OUA register T, pp. 84, 97; *CJ* 17 August 1659.   [24] OUA register T, p. 167.

[25] Shapiro, *John Wilkins*, 129–30; Pope, *Life of Seth Ward*, 45–6.

[26] Thomas Sprat, *The History of the Royal Society* (London 1667), 54. Ward and Wallis are frequently seen together in Oxford politics. For their moderating instincts see NCA MS 1073; *Lettere di Henry Stubbe a Thomas Hobbes*, ed. C. Nicastro (Siena 1973), 29. As a Presbyterian, however, Wallis found it less easy to agree with Wilkins and Ward in religion than in politics. Godard's scientific interests drew him close to Wilkins, whose contemporary he had been at Magdalen Hall; See too (for Godard and Ward) Ward's *Ismaelis Bulliandi* (Oxford 1653), ep. ded. For the cohesion of the Wilkins circle see also H. F. Kearney, *Scholars and Gentlemen* (London 1970), 127.

[27] *Diary of John Evelyn*, ed. De Beer iii. 165.

tectorate a Cromwellian monarchy seemed a much stronger possibility than a Stuart restoration, and Wilkins and his friends would certainly have settled for a stable Cromwellian monarchy, provided it distanced itself from its revolutionary origins and disowned its revolutionary supporters. Even so, it was only the exigencies of revolution that lent attraction to the prospect of a Cromwellian monarchy. When in 1659–60 it began to seem that the pre-war forms might be restored after all, Wilkins and his followers gladly transferred their allegiance to the Stuarts.

Wilkins may not have been a royalist under Cromwell, but he had allies who certainly were. They were to be found above all in two colleges, Trinity and Queen's. At Trinity his chief contact was the distinguished physician Ralph Bathurst, who in the Interregnum became vice-president of his college and was among 'the principal and most constant of those who met in Dr Wilkins his lodgings in Wadham College'. During the parliamentary visitation Bathurst had 'thought I had no more to do but to sit still and rest content with whatever befell under a prevailing party'. In the 1650s he had royalists and Anglicans for his 'constant friends and intimate acquaintance' in Oxford.[28] At Queen's the provost Gerard Langbaine, a survivor of the visitation, had long made his commitment to the Stuart monarchy and to episcopacy, and his hatred of puritanism and rebellion, abundantly clear.[29] Yet to Langbaine, keeper of the university archives, friend to Selden and Ussher 'and the great Goliaths of literature', outward deference to the usurpers was a necessary price to pay for the preservation of his university and his college. When a royalist fellow of Queen's urged Langbaine to rally the fellowship in opposition to the visitation, the provost declined, explaining his disagreement with colleagues who 'fly so high upon the point of loyalty and privilege, as if they were ambitious of suffering'.[30] In that spirit he helped to sustain the reputation of a university which, under Cromwellian rule, owed its distinction in secular learning to men out of sympathy with the partisan ambitions of puritanism.[31] Langbaine allied with Wilkins in a skilful and often unobtrusive policy of minimal tactical concession.[32] With John Conant and the five delegates of Cromwell's chancellorship, Langbaine was in the front rank of university politicians in the 1650s. He was the only survivor of civil war Oxford in that company, but behind him stood others—a number of them from Queen's and from its neighbour All Souls—of similar experience and outlook.

Such were the lines of battle in Cromwellian Oxford. We turn next to the course of the conflict.

[28] *DNB*, s.v. Ralph Bathurst; T. Warton, *The Life and Literary Remains of Ralph Bathurst* (London 1761), 202–6. For Wadham and Trinity see also *Register*, ed. Burrows, 337.

[29] See his many publications of the 1640s and early 1650s.

[30] Wood, *Athenae* iii. 446–7; Bodl. MS Wood f. 35, fo 312; Leland, *De rebus Britannicis* v. 283–4. For Langbaine's stoicism see also Bodl. MS Rawlinson letters no. 89, fo 108; QCA MS 423, p. 150.

[31] For that common characteristic of the intellectual fellow-spirits of John Selden in Cromwellian Oxford see Bodl. MS Selden *supra* 109, fo 452.

[32] For the early stages of their collaboration, see OUA WP/a/10/11. A number of politically important university documents of the 1650s are in Langbaine's hand.

To posterity a tension is observable in Cromwell's plans for Oxford and for England. He aimed both to reform and to reconcile. Was not his programme of godly reformation bound to antagonize the interest groups and the moderate opinion he wished to reassure? And if he sought to broaden the base of support for the revolution, must he not restore traditional forms and institutions—and thereby dull the excited sense of providential mission, of building a new Jerusalem, from which the energy of reforming puritanism sprang? The course of Cromwellian politics, in Oxford as outside it, can largely be explained in the terms of that dilemma. Yet Cromwell saw no contradiction. There, as in so much else, he belonged to the mainstream of the puritan tradition: a stream that had run at its most powerful in 1640–1, when puritanism had seemed to speak for a united nation, and when godliness had seemed the natural ally of political stability. The collapse of the Caroline regime had confirmed in puritan minds the identification of instability with the forces of popery and wickedness. Those evils had flourished in pre-war Oxford and Cambridge, and in the continental seminaries to which parents had alternatively sent their sons.[33] Now, Cromwellians hoped, the conquered universities of England—and of Ireland and Scotland—would become nurseries not of heresy and profanity but of orthodoxy and sobriety.[34] To them would fall a task fundamental to the creation of the godly commonwealth: the task of training the pious ministry and magistracy that in turn would puritanize, and so stabilize, the land.

Cromwell could hardly expect Oxford to fulfil that task without firm direction from above. The months after Worcester made it equally plain to him that reform, either of Oxford or of the nation, could not be left to the Rump. The decision of the purged parliament in April 1652 to terminate a visitation which Cromwell's confidants now controlled was a defeat for him.[35] The chancellor responded by urging the Rump to appoint a fresh visitation and, when it resisted, by appointing one of his own.[36] In pursuing that initiative he secured the united if predominantly reluctant acquiescence of the university, which had evidently sensed that a second visitation was inevitable. It asked only that instead of the large and largely alien body of 1647–52 there should now be a smaller one drawn exclusively from Oxford's resident members. That pre-emptive request, expressed in an embassy to London headed by Wilkins, was granted, and we must look for a moment at the composition, and at the scantily documented activities, of the second visitation. A clear majority of its members were Independents: John Owen and Thomas Goodwin, the Atlases of Independency; the Independent sub-warden of All Souls

---

[33] Abbott, *Cromwell* iv. 494. Cf J. B. Mullinger, *The University of Cambridge* (3 vols Cambridge 1873–1911) iii. 204; J. Morgan, *Godly Learning* (Cambridge 1986), 256.

[34] For Ireland and Scotland see *Acts and Ordinances of the Interregnum*, ed. C. H. Firth and R. S. Rait (3 vols London 1911) iii, pp. cxii–cxv; Barnard, *Cromwellian Ireland*, 198–207; F. D. Dow, *Cromwellian Scotland* (Edinburgh 1979), 58, 104, 167, 197.

[35] *CJ* 21 April 1652 (when Cromwell's followers Cornelius Holland and Philip Skippon were the tellers against the proposal to terminate the visitation). See also QCA register H, pp. 338–41.

[36] Bodl. MS Wood f. 35, fos 366–7 (cf Wood, *History of the University* ii. 650–2); also Bodl. MS J. Walker c. 9, fo 195; OUA WP/β/21/4, p. 277. The date of the commission's appointment is unclear: NCA MS 9655, p. 5; UCA college register 1509–1727, fos 32ᵛ–3; OUA SP/E/4, fo 62.

Samuel Basnett; and two of the firmest followers of Owen and Goodwin, both of them members of the congregation which Goodwin gathered in Magdalen: Francis Howell, fellow of that college, and Thankful Owen, the intruded president of St John's, who in later life would edit Goodwin's works and who would be buried beside him.[37] There were only two Presbyterians: John Conant of Exeter, and the president of Corpus Edmund Staunton.[38] The period of the second visitation was the high point of the Independents' power in Oxford, and its opening meetings in June 1653 coincided with their highest hopes of national reformation. The intransigent Rump had been expelled in April; the handpicked assembly of the pious that would become known as Barebones Parliament had been summoned in its place; and the sectarian and destructive character of Barebones, an experiment which would escape from Independent control and provoke a reaction in favour of Presbyterianism, had yet to become evident. In the slim records of the second visitation there can be found the strained and exalted language of that 'high-water mark of Puritanism'.[39]

Yet the policies of the new body proved to be more modest than its vocabulary. Its powers and its ambitions seem to have been abridged by the refusal of the expiring Rump parliament to give it statutory sanction, and by the imposition of a date, apparently towards the end of 1654, beyond which it was not to act. The new commissioners permitted or confirmed the return of all but the most refractory of the colleges to a measure of self-government. In elections to fellowships and scholarships, the visitors mainly contented themselves with vetting candidates already chosen by the colleges, a role analogous to that of the triers in the national church designed by Owen and Goodwin. Even that degree of interference outraged Gerard Langbaine, who told Selden that candidates at Queen's were being vetoed who 'are not known to these visitors to be regenerate'.[40] There was indeed much feeling among puritans that college electors should 'principally look after holynesse'.[41] Yet Langbaine's charge parodied the goals of Owen and Goodwin, who understood the dependence of puritan reform on the maintenance of the university's scholarly esteem, and who, if they ever did overlook that principle in 1653, were recalled to it by the venomous attacks that were directed at the universities in that year, when Oxford was assailed in the prints as a capital both of Aristotelianism and of Antichrist. The second visitation aimed not to challenge the colleges but to co-operate with them, and so to secure the appointment of pious and godly tutors and the provision of godly sermons and godly exercises. That programme, to which we shall return, was vigorously pursued.

[37] For Goodwin's congregation see Wood, *History of the University* ii. 645; Bloxam, *Reg. Magdalen* ii. 146–7.

[38] For the firmness of Staunton's Presbyterianism see 'Illustrations of the state of the church', 127; *Mercurius Politicus* 14–21 November 1650, 391–2.

[39] The phrase is S. R. Gardiner's: *History of the Commonwealth and Protectorate* (4 vols London 1903) ii. 340. The records are in *Register*, ed. Burrows, 356–99.

[40] Bodl. MS Tanner 52, fo 60.

[41] Henry Wilkinson jr, *Three Decades of Sermons lately preached to the University* (Oxford 1660), pt ii, 77.

The establishment of the protectorate under the instrument of government in December 1653 dashed the messianic hopes of that year. The new regime, aware that the extremism which had flourished during the rule of Barebone's had played into the hands of 'some malcontented gain-sayers' in Oxford,[42] anxiously publicized its commitment to the preservation of learning and the universities.[43] Yet Cromwell's dedication to reform persisted. Among the ordinances approved by the protector and his council in 1654 was that of 2 September 'for the carrying on and perfecting of the reformation and regulating of the universities'.[44] The decree introduced yet a third puritan visitation—the last—to Oxford,[45] the second having held its last meeting on the day before the passage of the ordinance. Although some of Cromwell's councillors and some puritan gentry were named to the third visitation, only its resident members took part in it. Most of the visitors on the second commission were reappointed, and the party of Owen and Goodwin—either or both of whom may have drafted the ordinance—remained strong.[46] Even so it was less strong than before, for in accordance with the latitudinarian tendency of the early protectorate the new board included two Presbyterian members of the first visitation who had been omitted from the second: the admittedly ageing president of Trinity Robert Harris and a more forceful figure, the Lady Margaret professor of divinity Henry Wilkinson senior, who had been a dominant figure on that earlier body.

If the balance of power on the third visitation was more even than on the second, the power granted to it was significantly larger, and provoked intense hostility and suspicion within the university. The ordinance, which the protectoral council discussed and passed in haste in the days before the first parliament of the protectorate opened on 3 September, was clumsily worded.[47] In consequence the new body was able to claim rights which the council had evidently not intended for it. Above all the ordinance appeared to bestow on the commission the authority to alter university and college statutes without reference to parliament.[48] The Presbyterians on the third visitation hesitated to assert the prerogatives which had been inadvertently awarded it, but Owen and Goodwin grasped at them. They sensed that, without fresh and bold exertions on their part, the reformation of Oxford would be stillborn. For the passage of time, and the changes in the uni-

---

[42] *Mercurius Politicus* 14–21 September 1654, 3773.

[43] *Certain Passages* 10–17 February 1654, 38; *Moderate Intelligencer* 15–22 March 1654, 1342–3; *Severall Proceedings* 27 April–4 May 1654, 3807. The publicity is unlikely to have been wholly reassuring: cf p. 751 below.

[44] *Acts and Ordinances*, ed. Firth and Rait ii. 1026–9.

[45] Its records are in *Register*, ed. Burrows, 400–39.

[46] Owen had roused controversy by securing election, despite his clerical status, as the university's representative in the parliament of 1654—an election which parliament quashed. Cf *The Works of John Owen*, ed. W. H. Goold (16 vols Edinburgh 1965–8) xiii. 287.

[47] For the council's discussion see *CSPD 1654*, 346. Except where I indicate otherwise, the paragraphs which follow are based on OUA SP/E/4, fos 62 ff. A number of the documents in that collection are printed in Wood's *History of the University*, but in a much less revealing and sometimes misleading form.

[48] For the powers of the visitation see also: *Register*, ed. Burrows, 409, 433, 437; BNCA MS A.I.2, fo 85; *The Correspondence of John Owen*, ed. P. Toon (Cambridge 1970), 102.

versity's population which that would inevitably bring, would erode the gains of the previous two visitations—gains which in any case were all too incomplete.

The persistence of the Independent threat to Oxford was soon evident. Before the new commission set to work, the university could reasonably have expected the protectorate to produce a gradual return to traditional forms. Instead, the dissolution in January 1655 of a parliament which had rejected all Cromwell's legislative initiatives brought a reversal to military rule. Cromwell and his council continued to implement the ordinances which parliament had declined to confirm, the decree for the third visitation among them. Eight days after the dissolution, the visitors aroused fresh alarm. They crushed an attempt by the earl of Pembroke to reassert his right, as visitor of Jesus College, to judge a dispute there: a right which the visitation claimed to have devolved upon itself.[49]

The university was quickly in revolt. The leaders were John Wilkins of Wadham, Gerard Langbaine of Queen's, and Langbaine's friend John Palmer, the intruded warden of All Souls. They took charge of a committee appointed by the university to secure fundamental revision of the ordinance. In memoranda drafted for that purpose they argued that the time for such 'extraordinary courses' as the third visitation was past. In the aftermath of civil war, they conceded, some such body as the first visitation 'might' have been necessary, if only to secure for the victorious cause the political allegiance to which—Wilkins and his friends were careful to acknowledge—it had been and remained entitled. But that allegiance, after all, had now been achieved. Why, asked the memoranda, should the colleges and the university not be left to govern themselves by their statutes? Why should the local visitors not be restored? Admittedly some of the visitors were bishops, whose order had been abolished; but why should the government not meet that difficulty by replacing them, perhaps by holders of high political and legal office? If there must be a third visitation, then let the university choose the resident members of it; let the commission's claim to make and unmake statutes be disavowed; and above all let there be a time limit to the third visitation as there had been to the second. Palmer contributed some especially acid observations. He had sat in the Rump, and he remembered the arguments with which Cromwell had justified its forcible expulsion. Oliver's criticisms of it, Palmer now hinted, could be directed with no less justice at the new visitation, for the 'unlimited and arbitrary power' which the ordinance gave to 'standing visitors', and the authority thus vested in 'a few and private hands', would surely constitute an insuperable temptation to corruption, 'yea even of godly men'.

The visitors were sufficiently alarmed by the rebellion to arrange a meeting with Wilkins's committee. It took place in John Owen's lodgings in Christ Church at 2 p.m. on 9 February. Having submitted its demands, the committee was asked to withdraw to an adjoining room. A long wait was before it, for the visitors, divided among themselves, eventually broke up without informing the university's

---

[49] *Register*, ed. Burrows, 401–2.

representatives that the meeting was over. It was after 9 p.m. when Thankful Owen returned to tell them of the visitors' refusal to 'treate' with them further. The rebels, thwarted in Oxford yet confident of their support there, resolved to take the battle to Whitehall. To that end they approached their colleagues, and Cromwell's associates, Jonathan Godard and Peter French, on whose absence in the capital they blamed the breach. Yet from those mollifying personalities they received, in return, a counsel of caution. Was it necessary, asked Godard and French, to demand the rewriting of an ordinance which—whatever Owen or Goodwin might suppose—no one in London believed to have conveyed the power of making or changing statutes? Was it prudent, at a time when the breakdown of the recent parliament and the mounting evidence of royalist conspiracy had deflected the government from its conciliatory path, to confront the protector's council with evidence of its legislative incompetence? Would not Owen and Goodwin be sure of persuading Cromwell that the resistance to the ordinance had sprung from 'a design to frustrate the reformation of the university', and that 'the leading persons are such as appear least zealous for the interest of religion and the power of godlinesse'?

Wilkins and his friends took the hint. Owen, too, appears to have pulled back; and the university, 'upon confidence that the visitors would use their power with due moderation and discretion . . . let the businesse fall asleep'. For a time that confidence seemed justified. The visitors learned to treat the colleges more delicately, and for a while the university was spared further initiatives towards major reform. Yet if Owen had withdrawn from the attack it was merely to regroup. Striking images survive of his rule as vice-chancellor. We see him plucking down the Terrae-Filius from the stage with his own hands,[50] and, at the time of Penruddock's rising in March 1655, 'riding up and down like a spiritual Abeddon' as he mustered a troop of sixty horsed scholars and struggled to mobilize the neighbouring countryside in the Commonwealth's defence.[51] Such episodes, although they sometimes grew in the telling, are characteristic of an able administrator whose energy outreached his tact.

It was at a 'very thin' delegacy summoned by Owen at short notice on 25 December 1655, a day when some of the absent members were doubtless more merrily engaged, that he and his puritan allies launched a reform programme that would inflame the university in the months ahead.[52] Not all of his proposals were deeply controversial. Those of them which were designed to improve academic dis-

[50] *Register*, ed. Burrows, p. xli.

[51] For Owen's military exertions in response to Penruddock's rising see *Correspondence of John Owen*, ed. Toon, 82–4; ECA MS A.II.10, 20 March 1655; *Perfect Proceedings* 29 March–5 April 1655, 4569. The comparison with Abeddon (= Abaddon? see Revelation 9. 11) is in George Vernon, *A Letter to a Friend concerning some of John Owen's Principles* (London 1670), 13.

[52] For the episodes described in this and the two following paragraphs see OUA SP/E/4, fos 90 ff.; Wood, *History of the University* ii. 668–75; Bodl. MS Eng. hist. c. 310, fos 81ff.; WCA MS 4/116; OUA register T, pp. 279–85; *Register*, ed. Burrows, 411, 415–16, 430, 434; *The Oxford Orations of John Owen*, ed. P. Toon (Callington, Cornwall 1971), 10, 18, 24, 31–2; Vernon, *Letter to a Friend*, 12–13; Pope, *Life of Seth Ward*, ch. 6 (although the last two sources are not to be trusted in detail).

cipline were in some instances scarcely contentious. But Owen had broader aims. He planned to 'new model' convocation, with the purpose of giving more power to himself and to his 'godly and prudent' supporters and less to the regent MAs; to end the frivolity of the annual Act and to change the occasion into 'a serious philosophicall exercise';[53] to shift the balance of teaching away from the colleges towards the university, where he could more easily control it; to set up working parties of puritan fellows and tutors to devise means of guaranteeing the provision of godly worship in the colleges and the punishment of 'such who scoffe at sermons, public ordinances, and ministers'; to ensure 'the election of fellowes that are godly'; and to enforce the neglected parliamentary decree of November 1648 which had eliminated the voting rights, in the university and the colleges alike, of fellows who had survived the visitation without formally submitting to it.

Wilkins and his friends, peaceable by inclination, offered a number of concessions to the vice-chancellor. At least Owen was now attempting to achieve reform through the constitutional machinery of the university rather than through the visitors. Had his programme been more gradually introduced it might have won the university's assent. It might even have passed swiftly had he not combined it with an insistence on ending the compulsory use of caps and hoods. Those 'reliques of popery' had long offended Oxford's 'godly party'. Yet they were, as Wilkins remonstrated, 'things common to us, with almost all the considerable corporations in England'. Wilkins thought Owen's war on 'habits' needless, 'when anyone that pleaseth doth take the liberty to neglect the use of them without control'. No one had been 'troubled' for that omission 'for many years, or like to be'.

The vice-chancellor's reforms were largely rejected by convocation on 10 April 1656. He met his defeat first by withdrawing from Oxford with Thankful Owen and then, fortified by the reflections of that retreat, by threatening on his return to appeal to Cromwell and even to 'make use of the major generall': that is, of either Charles Fleetwood, a close ally of Owen against conservative tendencies within the protectoral regime, or of Fleetwood's no less radical deputy in Oxfordshire, William Packer.[54] Owen also invoked, for the first time since February 1655, the extraordinary powers of the visitation. He succeeded only in dividing it, for the Presbyterian visitors Conant, Harris, and Wilkinson urged a policy of restraint upon Owen. The principal effect of his campaign on the university was a counterproductive one, for 'they who cared not before whether they wore caps or hoods, or not, now immediately procured them', so that by the summer of 1656 'caps were never more in fashion than now'.[55] In his Essex parish the puritan minister Ralph

---

[53] Puritan worry about the Act (like puritan worry about horse-racing) concerned not only morality but order and security: OUA register T, p. 108; Wood, *History of the University* ii. 646, 670; Wood, *Life and Times* i. 175; BNCA MS A.II.46, p. 26; OUA SP/E/4, fo 91ᵛ.

[54] The threat may not have been idle. Fleetwood was 'gallantly entertained' somewhere (we do not know where) in Oxfordshire on his return from Ireland to London in September 1655: *Thurloe State Papers*, ed. T. Birch (7 vols London 1742) iv. 32.

[55] *CSPD 1656–7*, 51. Cf ibid. 288–9, 294; Bodl. MS Tanner 52, fo 98.

Josselin learned that the vice-chancellor's war on 'habits' had made him 'a great scorne'.[56] The days of Owen's regime were numbered.

His decline and fall, like so much else in the politics of Cromwellian Oxford, had a national as well as a local dimension. The process belonged to that conservative reaction which followed the meeting of the second protectorate parliament in September 1656. In the spring of 1657, to Owen's disgust,[57] parliament offered Cromwell a new, more traditional constitution, the humble petition and advice (which he accepted), and the title of king (which he refused). Meanwhile the 'strange irregularity' of the third visitation had come under fierce attack from the house of commons. A parliamentary committee refused to endorse the ordinance of September 1654 on which the authority of the commission rested 'in regard the visitors undertake to make laws against the fundamental laws'. There was little support for the plea of Owen's friend Major-General John Desborough, who told the house that, 'whatever reproach may be cast upon' the visitation, 'it has been a great means to regulate the university, and to purge loose and profane persons'.[58] Parliament resolved that the visitation be terminated in January 1658, a decision to which Cromwell submitted.[59] Owen, ill and exhausted, at odds with the protector, gave up the vice-chancellorship in October 1657, complaining in his farewell oration of 'wrongs and slanders' and of 'many things I have suffered at the hands of men impelled by hate'.[60] His successor was the Presbyterian rector of Exeter, John Conant, whose appointment was greeted with 'a universal shout of a very full congregation'.[61] By now Thomas Goodwin, who in contrast to Owen had supported the introduction of the humble petition and advice and had retained Cromwell's favour, had distanced himself from his fellow 'Atlas of Independency'.[62] Soon the rejected vice-chancellor withdrew from the course of sermons which he and Goodwin had for some years given on Sunday afternoons in the university church, 'and at the same university houre hath set up a lecture in the parish church, it is conceived in opposition, and to draine St Mary's'.[63]

Even so, the visitation was not dead yet. In its last weeks Owen took part in its final battle, one in which the commission may for once have had widespread sup-

[56] *The Diary of Ralph Josselin 1616–1683*, ed. A. Macfarlane (London 1976), 374. Another 'formality' was personally embarrassing to Owen: his own title. The 'title of doctor', he explained when mocked on that account, 'was conferred on me by the university in my absence, and against my consent . . . nor did I use it till some were offended with me . . . for my neglect': *Works of John Owen*, ed. Goold xiii. 302.

[57] Toon, *God's Statesman*, 99–100; cf *Lettere di Henry Stubbe*, ed. Nicastro, 16.

[58] *Diary of Thomas Burton*, ed. J. T. Rutt (4 vols London 1828) ii. 63–4.

[59] *Acts and Ordinances*, ed. Firth and Rait ii. 1139–40. Cf OUA SP/E/4, fos 96–7, 100; Bodl. MS Add. d. 105, fo 9. In the event the visitors enjoyed a brief extension of their authority, apparently with Cromwell's blessing: PRO SP25/78, p. 840; *Register*, ed. Burrows, 437, 439.

[60] *Lettere di Henry Stubbe*, ed. Nicastro, 11; Bodl. MS J. Walker c. 9, fo 188; *Oxford Orations of John Owen*, ed. Toon, 32–3, 41. Cf *Correspondence of John Owen*, ed. Toon, 94; *CSPD 1656–7*, 51.

[61] Conant, *Life of John Conant*, 24; cf Wood, *Life and Times* i. 359.

[62] *Thurloe State Papers*, ed. Birch vi. 539, 558, vii. 561; *CSPD 1656–7*, 318; BL MS Lansdowne 823, fo 35. The differences between Owen and Goodwin which Wood places as early as 1654 are exaggerated, if not imagined, by him.

[63] PRO SP18/158, fo 58, cf Vernon, *Letter to a Friend*, 28.

port in Oxford.[64] Like many reformers before and after them, the visitors resolved to break the system by which fellowships were sold at All Souls and New College. That system, they declared, was 'odiouse to God and all good men', and discouraged 'worthy, godly and deserving persons from appearing to stand in such elections'. In no colleges had the successive visitations made less headway. In both of them the warden and a handful of 'godly and honest fellowes' had struggled to impose order and reform on 'the major parte', only to be consistently outmanœuvred and outvoted.[65] It was in All Souls that battle was now joined, for there, as the visitors recorded, 'it pleased God to load and trouble the conscience' of one of the fellows, who, 'the Lord pursuing his love towards him, with an effectuall worke of grace upon his heart', confessed to having paid £150 for his post the previous year.

Initially Cromwell and his council encouraged the visitors' assault. Yet, as the weeks passed, the council retreated into a cool neutrality, and the reformers discovered how well connected their adversaries were. Although we cannot be certain, one ally is likely to have been particularly helpful to All Souls: the protector's elder son. Richard Cromwell, whom Oliver was tentatively grooming for the succession to the protectoral throne, was elected to succeed him as chancellor in the summer of 1657, when Owen was about to be replaced as vice-chancellor by John Conant. Richard's support for the conservative direction of Cromwellian rule was unmistakable. At the ceremony of his installation as chancellor—a ceremony held not in Oxford but in Whitehall—his escort was John Wilkins, who from the outset established himself as Richard's right-hand man at Oxford.[66] In December 1657, in the midst of the battle between the visitors and All Souls, Richard was added to his father's privy council. There he was given special responsibility for the handling of the dispute, together with that conservative influence on Cromwellian politics Nathaniel Fiennes, who as a patron of New College was unlikely to wish to challenge the system of corrupt elections.[67] Soon the hopes of reforming that system were abandoned, and All Souls proceeded to elect

[64] For the battle see: *Register*, ed. Burrows, 418–34; *CSPD 1657–8*, 181–2, 188, 236, 238, 260, 278–9, and MSS there calendared; WCA MS 4/116. Cf QCA MS 2Y/41; UCA register, fo 32; *CJ* 5 February 1657.

[65] All Souls: *Register*, ed. Burrows, 223–4, 287, 307, 315–16, 321, 336–7, 342; Bodl. MS Wood f. 35, fo 365. (Palmer was a more dutiful warden than has been supposed: ASA MS ccccl(a), fos 117–37.) New College: *Register*, ed. Burrows, 191–2, 210, 217, 226, 235–9, 370, 380–1, 393 (cf ibid. 362–3, 397–8, 403–5, 433–4); *Diary of John Evelyn*, ed. De Beer iii. 108; NCA MS 988, entry at back (cf *Register*, ed. Burrows, 361; *Correspondence of John Owen*, ed. Toon, 121 n.); NCA MS 9665, fo iv and pp. 5, 53; ibid. Long Book 1649, second term, 'to reform the college', and fourth term, 'To the soldiers for watching Dr Vivian's chamber' (cf third term, 'Lieutenant West's chimney'; *Register*, ed. Burrows, 244–5, 370–1, 382–9, 404, 414).

[66] *Mercurius Politicus* 23–30 July 1657, 7955–6; *CSPD 1657–8*, 215, 349; *CSPD 1658–9*, 352; *Memoirs of Edmund Ludlow*, ed. C. H. Firth (2 vols Oxford 1894) ii. 61: Cf *Public Intelligencer* 16 August 1658; OUA WP/β/21/4, pp. 284, 293. In the *Weekly Intelligencer* 24 August 1655, there lies a hint—only a hint—that Cromwell may have contemplated transferring the chancellorship to Richard two years earlier, at a time when a proposal that Cromwell should take the crown was under intensive discussion.

[67] Cf *CJ* 30 December 1656, 23 January 1657 (cf OUA WP/β/21/4, p. 289); *Acts and Ordinances*, ed. Firth and Rait ii. 1077; *Diary of Thomas Burton*, ed. Rutt i. 84, 353–4.

candidates of royalist persuasion.[68] As chancellor, Richard would always favour traditional forms. Early in 1659 a puritan move to introduce yet another visitation was easily seen off by the Wilkins circle.[69] The time of 'extraordinary courses' was over at last.

The conflicts between the visitors and the visited of Cromwellian Oxford are a major portion of its history. Yet they are only a portion of it, and the rivalries that divided Owen and Wilkins are only a portion of its politics. Inevitably there were friendships across the parties and enmities within them. Inevitably a host of skirmishes arose, often parochial and personal, to complicate the principal divisions. In any case, conflict is only one side of the story. The other is co-operation. It concerns issues which united Owen and Wilkins in the university's defence.

The puritans came to reform Oxford, but also to preserve it. With them they brought assumptions about the purpose of a university which were sometimes more conventional than the language which expressed them. Of course, puritans knew how sterile and how dangerous the training of the intellect could be. They knew how depraved was human reason and how empty its vanity.[70] Soon after Owen's appointment at Christ Church the commonwealth's rulers of Ireland reminded him that 'where learning is attained before the work of grace upon the heart, it serves only to make a sharper opposition against the power of godliness'.[71] He scarcely needed the warning, convinced as he was that 'ability of learning and literature' was, without faith and election, 'of no use at all to the end and interest of true wisdom'.[72] Yet Oxford's puritans held the intellect to have its essential uses, so long as it was deployed with 'moderation', as a 'servant' to faith, 'keeping its true distance'.[73] It was essential above all to theology, in Owen's mind 'the queen and mistress of the other branches of learning'.[74] Knowledge of the Bible in its original tongues was essential if the ministers trained at Oxford were 'to give the right sense of scripture to the unlearned'[75]—and if they were to answer those plausible objections with which the sectaries and the sceptics of the puritan revolution were disconcertingly forward in confronting the orthodox clergy.

If theology had the first claim on learning, Owen did not suppose it to have an exclusive one. He gave encouragement to the secular subjects and especially praised the university's 'outstanding mathematicians'.[76] No less than Wilkins was he concerned to strengthen the resources and morale of the university and to preserve a lay base for its support. No less than Wilkins had he reason to be. The civil wars,

---

[68] Cf Wood, *Athenae* iii. 1046.

[69] Bodl. MS Add. d. 105, fos 9–11; Conant, *Life of John Conant*, 28–30; Wood, *Life and Times* i. 268.

[70] For puritan attitudes to learning see Morgan, *Godly Learning*.

[71] *Correspondence of John Owen*, ed. Toon, 51.   [72] *Works of John Owen*, ed. Goold ii. 80.

[73] Henry Wilkinson jr, *Three Decades of Sermons*, pt i, 74; Wilkinson, *A Second Decade of Sermons*, 76–7.

[74] *Oxford Orations of John Owen*, ed. Toon, 15.

[75] *A Modest Reply, in Answer to an Modest plea for an Equal Commonwealth* (London 1659), 4.

[76] *Oxford Orations of John Owen*, ed. Toon, 15, 24–5, 34–5. Cf Bodl. MS Selden *supra* 109, fo 372; *Diary of John Evelyn*, ed. De Beer iii. 105.

as Anthony Wood said, had left Oxford 'exhausted of its treasure', 'deprived of its number of sons'; 'lectures and exercises had for the most part ceased'; 'in a word there was scarce the face of an university left, all things being out of order and disturbed'.[77] Within the spectrum of Oxford politics Owen was a radical figure, but he had no sympathy with those root-and-branch critics of the university who saw in its civil war collapse an opportunity to redesign it on first principles. If the university were to be reformed, he believed, it must first be reconstructed. In the task of reconstruction, which occupied much of his labour, he and Wilkins discovered wide common ground.

During the earlier 1650s the traditional procedures of the university were gradually (even if not always smoothly) restored: the regular provision of lectures, the machineries of matriculation and examination, the rotatory appointment of proctors, the functioning of the chancellor's court, and the performance of the annual Act. A general programme of physical repair was announced by the erection of scaffolding, by the rhythm of hammers, by the smell of fresh paint. Gradually the military flavour of the civil war period—which had been sharpened in the late 1640s by an influx of disbanded soldiers come to study—disappeared, although the memories of war were sustained by the intermittent reappearance of troops in and around the city after the withdrawal of the garrison, and by the maimed ex-soldiers and the refugees from Ireland and Scotland who lingered at the college gates and in the quadrangles to beg relief.[78] Gradually, too, a sense of something like normality returned to the university. Its puritan rulers, sensitive to the popular identification of puritanism with unlettered philistinism, and conscious that the first visitation had purged some of Oxford's most distinguished scholars, were determined to restore, even to improve, its academic standards. Vigorously they enjoined constant attendance at lectures and the regular performance of exercises, attacked such 'gross abuses' as the wining and dining of examiners,[79] and insisted on the classical tongues as the languages of conversation.[80] Whether the puritans pursued those traditional goals more effectively than earlier reformers it is not easy to say, but such glimpses as we have of the educational activity of Cromwellian Oxford are not suggestive of torpor.[81]

---

[77] Register, ed. Burrows, p. lviii.

[78] The evidence of such destitution, as of post-war rebuilding and redecoration, is liberally distributed among the accounts of the university and of the colleges.

[79] OUA NEP/supra/49, ii, fo 157^v; ibid. SP/E/4, fos 88, 102^b; ibid. register T, pp. 280, 283.

[80] Register, ed. Burrows, 249, 266; Bodl. MS Wood f. 35, fo 350; CCCA B/5/1/1, 1653, second term; CA MS I.B.3, p. 72. The parliamentary authorities preferred English as the language of record-keeping: their withdrawal from involvement in the colleges is often marked by a return to Latin in the college records.

[81] The scientific enthusiasms of the 1650s were passed on to undergraduates: OUA NW/3/4, fo 26; ibid. WP/β/21/4, pp. 54, 56; [John Wilkins and Seth Ward], Vindiciae academiarum (London 1654); Walter Charleton, The Immortality of the Human Soul (London 1657), 50. Music was probably the only subject of which the study was slow to revive after the wars: [Wilkins and Ward], Vindiciae academiarum, 29; OUA WP/β/21/4, p. 296; ibid. NW/3/4, p. 226; ibid. register T, p. 292; Bodl. MS Eng. hist. c. 310, fo 84. Pococke and Langbaine worked to establish proper founts for the printing and the study of Hebrew and Arabic: Bodl. MS Selden supra 109, fos 343, 349, 392, 403, 469; OUA WP/β/21/4, pp. 287, 291;

The most pressing problems of reconstruction were the interrelated ones of finance and student numbers. In many colleges financial problems had been created or exacerbated by the difficulty experienced during and after the war of collecting rents and tithes.[82] Only in the later 1650s were fellowships, many of them previously kept vacant to save money, filled as a matter of course. By then, too, other emergency measures of retrenchment had become less frequent. Yet the threat of penury persisted.[83] It troubled the officers not only of the colleges but of the university, which was apparently unable to resume the full payment of professorial salaries until at least 1657.[84] Undergraduate numbers were slow to climb. Although they gradually became respectable, they failed to reach the high levels of the 1630s, a period which, as Owen was uncomfortably aware, had come to seem a golden age of the university.[85] The main burden of numerical decline fell on the halls. Under Laud they had been refuges for puritans. Now that puritans were welcome in the colleges, the halls sought vainly for an alternative role, and in some cases stood close to extinction.

Anxious to revive Oxford's morale, dependent on the traditional institutions of the university for its reconstruction, Owen and his allies were not lightly tempted towards structural reform. Their appetite for change was further curbed by the clamorous national movement for the overhaul of the universities: a movement which reached its first peak amidst the political turmoil of 1653 and its second in that of 1659, years when the very survival of the university seemed in doubt.[86] The movement had some supporters within Oxford—among them the fellow of Lincoln William Sprigge, who owed his appointment there to the 'recommendation' of Oliver Cromwell,[87] and that dextrous trouble-maker of Christ Church

ibid. NW/3/4, p. 240 (cf p. 148); ibid. NEP/*supra*/49, ii, fo 168. Some light on the buying and reading of books in puritan Oxford is cast by: UCA MS Pyx J.J. fasc. 5; OCA MS II.G.9, pp. 25, 123; J. Wells, *Wadham College* (London 1898), 62–3; JCA benefactors' book, pp. 51–8; see also CCCA MS D/3/3 (library catalogue, with some entries probably of the 1650s).

[82] CA MS I.B.3, fo 10; OUA register T, p. 72 (cf JCA shelf 19, bursars' accounts 1631–53, p. 160); ASA MS ccccl(a), fo 117ᵛ (cf JCA MS 155, Ayleworth to Mansell 16 December 1644); NCA MS 988, 31 May 1650; QCA register H, p. 132; MCA MS C.II.4.13, 17 December 1649 and September 1652; UCA 'Duplicate papers relating to the visitation', 20 April 1648.

[83] For the financial difficulties of the colleges see MCR registrum, p. 396; CA MS B.I.3, fo 102; ibid. MS xi, no. 36 (cf no. 26); NCA MS 988, 4 January 1655; *Dean's Register of Oriel*, 331–2; UCA Pyx J.J. fasc. 4 (20 August 1652); ibid. Smith transcripts xi, pp. 140–9; LCM Md. reg. fo 101; H. W. C. Davis and R. Hunt, *A History of Balliol College* (rev. edn Oxford 1973), 126; *Register*, ed. Burrows, 302, 329–30, 374, 386–9. In general, see J. Twigg, 'College Finances 1640–1660'.

[84] OUA register T, pp. 168–9, 234; *Register*, ed. Burrows, 225; Bodl. MS Eng. hist. c. 310, fo 91; *Oxford Orations of John Owen*, ed. Toon, 45; *Correspondence of John Owen*, ed. Toon, 77, cf *CSPD 1657–8*, 365.

[85] *Oxford Orations of John Owen*, ed. Toon, 8. Matriculation procedures were restored in 1650. The matriculations of the decade peaked in 1658. For numbers of undergraduates and the difficulty of assessing them see S. Porter, 'University and society' pp. 31–5, 44. The numbers of high-born students are especially hard to assess, but those of matriculands in the 1650s whose fathers were knights or of higher status are low, averaging around twelve a year (cf Wood's comments in *Life and Times* i. 301).

[86] *Oxford Orations of John Owen*, ed. Toon, 11, 21, 41; *Correspondence of John Owen*, ed. Toon, 64–5; *CSPD 1657–8*, 328. Falls in matriculation figures in 1654 and 1659–60 may be related to the radical scares.

[87] LCM Md. reg. fo 94. Cf R. L. Greaves, 'William Sprigge and the Cromwellian revolution', *Huntington Library Quarterly* xxxiv (1971), 99–113; V. H. H. Green, *The Commonwealth of Lincoln College* (Oxford 1979), 254.

Henry Stubbe, who arrived there as the client of Cromwell's intimate friend Sir Henry Vane.[88] Yet the menace was principally an external and hence a unifying one. The discrete but uniformly hostile demands of John Milton and Samuel Hartlib and John Hall, of William Dell and John Webster, of Quakers and Fifth Monarchists, procured enough hints of support in high places to create profound anxiety.[89] Some visionaries condemned all learning as an enemy to grace and truth, and cast covetous eyes on the endowments of the monkish colleges; others demanded a more utilitarian syllabus; others still recommended the study of Paracelsian medicine or of the mystical effusions of Jacob Boehme.[90]

In Oxford's self-defence the party of Owen and the party of Wilkins joined forces.[91] The attacks of 1653 provoked a spirited vindication of the university's teaching methods by Wilkins's friend Seth Ward, the Savilian professor of astronomy. Owen would certainly have concurred with the distinction drawn by Ward between 'the reall and solid wayes of knowledge' which were followed at Oxford and the 'windy impostures of magick and astrology' favoured by its opponents.[92] In 1654, the two parties combined on behalf of the famous orientalist Edward Pococke, the regius professor of Hebrew and the friend of Langbaine and Selden. Shy of controversy, Pococke was none the less unambiguously royalist and Anglican in his sympathies. Four years earlier his refusal of the Engagement had cost him his canonry of Christ Church. He had however retained his other posts in the university, thanks to a campaign mounted on his behalf by Wilkins and Langbaine.

[88] It is unfortunate that our knowledge of Stubbe's career in Oxford depends so heavily on his self-enlarging accounts of it: see *Lettere di Henry Stubbe*, ed. Nicastro. For other glimpses of that career see *CSPD 1657–8*, 349; OUA register T, pp. 318, 321; Varley, 'Restoration visitation', 17; Wood, *Athenae* iii. 1075–6 (cf UCA MS D.D. 14); Wood, *History of the University* ii. 682–3. Stubbe's influence can perhaps be seen in the discontent of the students of Christ Church expressed in CA MS xi, nos 36, 61 (cf Longleat House, Thynne MS xii, fo 166); *Sundry Things from Severall Heads concerning the University of Oxford* (London 1659).

[89] John Lambert, possibly the most powerful of Cromwell's councillors, took an interest in learning and in the universities and may have been regarded as a favourer of educational experiment: John Webster, *Academiarum examen* (London 1654), ep. ded.; OUA register of convocation 1642–7, NEP/*supra*/25, register Sb, p. 126; Barnard, *Cromwellian Ireland*, 218; Wood, *History of the University* ii. 687; *CSPD 1654*, 346. William Dell, who had married Henry Ireton to Oliver Cromwell's daughter, became master of Gonville and Caius, Cambridge, with the Rump's approval: E. C. Walker, *William Dell: master puritan* (London 1970), 105.

[90] A general account of the agitation may be found in Mullinger, *Cambridge* iii. 371–4, 447–71, 534–7; and see A. G. Debus (ed.), *Science and Education in the Seventeenth Century: the Webster–Ward debate* (London 1970). For the demand for Behmenism see *Original Letters and Papers of State . . . addressed to Oliver Cromwell*, ed. J. Nickolls (London 1743), 99–102. For Quakers and Fifth Monarchists in Oxford: Wood, *Life and Times* i. 190–1, 221, 293 (cf D. Underdown, *Pride's Purge* (Oxford 1971), 350); *CSPD 1658–9*, 148; *Thurloe State Papers*, ed. Birch vi. 187; A. Woolrych, *Commonwealth to Protectorate* (Oxford 1982), 196–7. Even during the earlier protectorate, a time of reaction against radical reform (although also the peak of John Lambert's political influence), the university could not feel sure of the government's commitment to a learned and university-trained ministry: *Mercurius Politicus* 13–20 April 1654, 3429; cf [Wilkins and Ward], *Vindiciae academiarum*, 30; Abbott, *Cromwell* iv. 273.

[91] The university's self-defence: OUA register T, pp. 221–2 (cf [Wilkins and Ward], *Vindiciae Academiarum*, 48), 226–7; Walker, *William Dell*, 132; Bodl. MS Selden *supra* 109, fo 309; Leland, *De rebus Britannicis* v. 291–2.

[92] [Wilkins and Ward], *Vindiciae academiarum*, 36; cf *Oxford Orations of John Owen*, ed. Toon, 35.

On that occasion a petition on Pococke's behalf, hailing him as 'a great ornament to this university', had won unanimous approval in Oxford, even the most zealous puritans among the intruded heads pleading for his survival.

Now, in 1654, Pococke came under threat from another quarter. The commissioners for the ejection of scandalous ministers in Berkshire, where he held a living, proposed to evict him on account of his commitment to the Prayer Book. Owen was shocked. 'Some few men of mean quality and condition, rash, heady, enemies of tithes', he wrote, were 'casting out' Pococke 'on light and trivial pretences'.[93] A delegation of four, consisting of Owen, Wilkins, and Wilkins's lieutenants Seth Ward and John Wallis, journeyed to Berkshire to remonstrate with the commissioners: 'particularly Dr Owen, who endeavoured, with some warmth, to make them sensible of the infinite contempt and reproach which would certainly fall upon them, when it should be said, that they had turned out a man for insufficiency, whom all the learned, not of England only, but of all Europe, so justly admired for his vast knowledge, and extraordinary accomplishments.' The shaken commissioners backed down.[94]

On other fronts too the university defended itself with unified determination. It lobbied resourcefully to protect the study of civil law from the parliamentary criticisms of the protectorate period.[95] It lobbied no less resourcefully to forestall the creation of the college planned by Oliver Cromwell for Durham, a project in which the university saw a prospective rival and which Richard Cromwell, when he succeeded his father as lord protector, gratified Oxford by allowing to sleep.[96] The steersmen of the Durham scheme favoured Baconian principles of educational reform which had their supporters in Oxford, among them three men with powerful patrons outside it: William Sprigge and Robert Wood at Lincoln, both of whom were allocated posts at Durham, and William Petty at Brasenose.[97] Petty's ideas had much in common with those of Samuel Hartlib, who had added an apocalyptic dimension to Bacon's programme.[98] Yet Petty was too often away from Oxford to make much impression on it, while the reaction both of Owen's friends and of the Wilkins circle to Hartlib's proposals was hostile. Hartlib's wish for a post at Oxford was blocked, his utopian schemes ignored.[99]

[93] *Correspondence of John Owen*, ed. Toon, 83.   [94] Twells, *Life of Pocock*, 129–38, 151–75.
[95] OUA register T, p. 252 (cf ibid. register of convocation 1659–71, NEP/*supra*/27, register Ta, p. 50); ibid. SP/E/4, fos 63, 100; Bodl. MS Eng. hist. c. 310, fos 88, 92; Wood, *Life and Times* i. 187; Wood, *History of the University* ii. 667; *CJ* 21–2 November 1656; *CSPD 1657–8*, 272; *Correspondence of John Owen*, ed. Toon, 76–9.
[96] Bodl. MS Add. d. 105, fo 9; OUA WP/β/21/4, p. 305; ibid. register T, pp. 339–42; Conant, *Life of John Conant*, 26–7; Wood, *History of the University* ii. 687–94.
[97] Wood, like Sprigge, owed his appointment at Oxford to external support: LCM Md. reg. fo 91ʳ⁻ᵛ. So did Petty at Brasenose, which unenthusiastically accorded him a privileged status: BNCA MS B.I.D.36, 7 March 1651, 16 July 1658, MS A.I.2, fo 74ᵛ, MS A.II.44, pp. 32, 35; cf OUA register T, p. 73.
[98] Cf Barnard, *Cromwellian Ireland*, 217–18. For Hartlib's ideas see C. Webster, *The Great Instauration* (London 1975).
[99] See e.g. Leland, *De rebus Britannicis* v. 188–9. Hartlib did have friends at Oxford, among them Henry Langley, master of Pembroke (*CSPD 1653–4*, 143; Webster, *Great Instauration*, 193–4); but such radical sympathies as Langley may have possessed are unlikely to have been deeply rooted: Bodl. MS Don. f. 39, fos 166 ff.

Less unified, admittedly, was the university's response to proposals for a new body of statutes to replace the Laudian ones. The idea, which was extensively canvassed in 1649–52 and which secured influential support in parliament,[100] was favoured by Owen as late as 1657, when it had otherwise been generally forgotten.[101] Yet the puritans' objections to the existing statutes seem not to have been fundamental. Their main criticisms were of the political and ecclesiastical loyalties which the Laudian code enjoined, an embarrassing anachronism but one which was widely felt to have been satisfactorily met in 1650–1, when the university declared that no statute 'contrary to the word of God or the law of the land' was binding.[102] Such initiatives as were taken for statutory reform were easily contained by Langbaine. The puritans had no antiquarian expertise to match that of the provost of Queen's or of his friend and fellow royalist the civil lawyer Richard Zouche. Yet in any case statutory reform was low on Owen's agenda. In pursuing his policy of reconstruction he found that the existing statutes, however deficient, were indispensable landmarks. It is characteristic of the puritans' experience that they found themselves more often demanding the observance of existing statutes than proposing new ones.[103]

The puritan rule of Oxford, then, was characterized by institutional caution. It did not, however, lack energy or ambition. Puritans were often indifferent to institutional forms, which were but means to be used or discarded in the pursuit of godly ends. They looked more to good men than to good laws as the instruments of reformation. In Oxford they looked for reformation in three main respects: the definition and inculcation of orthodox doctrine; the preaching and teaching of God's saving word; and the purification of morality.

Since the reformation, it had been the duty of the universities, in John Owen's words, 'to defend, improve, give and add new light unto old truths'.[104] The war against popery had been on one front a war of theology and scholarship, and so it remained. Upon the leading puritans of Cromwellian Oxford there fell, they believed, the responsibilities which had been sustained by the giants of English reformed theology: by Jewel, Abbot, Morton, Ussher, Hall, Davenant, and Prideaux.[105] Owen was among the puritan heads who in their youths had witnessed

[100] OUA NEP/*supra*/49, ii, fos 139–68; ibid. WP/Y/6/2; ibid. WP/β/21/4, pp. 276–7; ibid. SP/E/5, fo 55; ibid. register T, pp. 72–141; QCA register H, p. 116; WCA MS 4/90; Wood, *History of the University* ii. 651–2; HMC *Leyborne–Popham MSS*, 80; *Register*, ed. Burrows, 259, 261, 264; C. E. Mallet, *A History of the University of Oxford* (3 vols London 1924–7) ii. 388 n.; Webster, *Great Instauration*, 194–6, 523–8.

[101] *Correspondence of John Owen*, ed. Toon, 100–1; cf ibid. 50–1.

[102] OUA register T, p. 122; Bodl. MS Wood f. 35, fo 349; Wood, *Life and Times* i. 173–4; Wood, *History of the University* ii. 636–7; NCA MS 9655, p. 9. It was agreed that the existing statutes imposed 'the needless multiplying of sundry oaths': Wood, *Life and Times* i. 297.

[103] *Register*, ed. Burrows, 182, 228, 259, 294, 313; QCA MS 2Y/30; WCA MS 4/116; Richard Mayo, *The Life and Death of Edmund Staunton* (London 1673), 16–17. Cf Bodl. MS Wood f. 35, fo 359; Barnard, *Cromwellian Ireland*, 200.

[104] *Works of John Owen*, ed. Goold xi. 11.

[105] Ibid. xi. 497; *Oxford Orations of John Owen*, ed. Toon, 16; Wilkinson, *Three Decades of Sermons*, pt i, preface; cf Thomas Barlow, *De studio theologiae* (London 1699), 73.

the catastrophic subversion of Calvinist orthodoxy in Laudian Oxford. In recalling that shameful period they found one consoling memory: the resistance which had been led from Exeter College by Prideaux, a figure whose hold on their hearts and minds survived his death in 1650.[106] It was an admiration sharpened by fellow-feeling, for even though political revolution had brought the guardians of Calvinist orthodoxy to power, they felt as beleaguered in the 1650s as Prideaux had done in the 1630s. Throughout England, and across Europe, they observed the alarming advances of Pelagianism, of scepticism, of Epicureanism. Those tendencies did not merely challenge the puritans' theological convictions. By emphasizing ethics above doctrine, they questioned the very primacy of faith.

In the England of the Interregnum they assumed two particularly insidious forms: Arminianism and Socinianism. Both heresies reasserted, in the face of the Calvinist emphasis on the fall and on man's helpless depravity, the dignity of human reason. Arminianism restored the element of free will which the Calvinist version of the doctrine of predestination denied: Socinianism challenged the doctrine of the trinity—although the term was sometimes used more loosely, to describe that movement towards rationalism in theology of which antitrinitarianism was an extreme form. Arminianism and Socinianism alike seemed to the puritan heads of house to exert a perilous attraction on the young of Oxford and of England. In hours snatched between committees and on his journeys to London, Owen in his time as vice-chancellor composed more than half a million words to expose the subtle hypocrisy and the logical fallacies of those soul-destroying tenets.[107] His campaign was fought on two fronts: the first against what he considered to be the Socinian writings of Hugo Grotius and of Grotius' disciple Henry Hammond, whom the parliamentary visitors had expelled from the college which Owen now ruled; the second against the Oxford graduate John Bidle, whose antitrinitarian treatises the protector's council instructed Owen to answer.[108] To Owen's efforts the puritan leaders—Conant, Staunton, Harris, Henry Wilkinson junior, principal of Magdalen Hall, Henry Langley, master of Pembroke, Joshua Hoyle, master of University College, and Lewis du Moulin, Camden professor of history—lent energetic support.[109] Prominent advisers of Cromwell were persuaded to support a scheme to

---

[106] *Register*, ed. Burrows, p. xxx; CA MS I.B.3, p. 5; BNCA MS A.8.13, 12 November 1659; Michael Ogilvy, *Fratres in malo* (Oxford 1660), 29; Henry Wilkinson jr, *Two Treatises* (London 1681), 47; *The Genuine Remains of . . . Dr Thomas Barlow* (London 1693), 181, Bodl. MS Wood f. 45, fo 130.

[107] *Works of John Owen*, ed. Goold xi. 16, xiii. 209, 213, 299. See also Toon, *God's Statesman*, 40, 83; *Oxford Orations of John Owen*, ed. Toon, 16; Macray, *Reg. Magdalen* iv. 91–2.

[108] H. R. Trevor-Roper, *Catholics, Anglicans and Puritans* (London 1987), 224–5; B. Worden, 'Toleration and the Cromwellian protectorate', *Studies in Church History* xxi (1984), 202–5, 219.

[109] Their campaign and their priorities are discernible in: Bodl. MS Rawlinson e. 199, fos 4, 30, 56–8, 114, 151; Bodl. MS Wood f. 45, fo 128 (Wilkinson jr); BL MS Harleian 3998, fos 114–41 (for Conant, cf Bodl. MS Rawlinson c. 945, pp. 361–411, 425–9, 520; Bodl. MS Don. f. 40); Conant, *Life of John Conant*, 13, 18, 20; Wood, *Life and Times* i. 300, 444–5; Robert Harris, *A Brief Discussion of Man's Estate* (London 1653), 65; Wilkinson, *Miranda, stupenda*, 36; Wilkinson, *Three Decades of Sermons*, pt 1, preface and 75, 116, 175, pt 2, 18, 97–8, 162, pt 3, 3, 23, 28; Wilkinson junior's preface to Nicholas Claggett, *The Abuse of God's Grace* (London 1659); Lewis du Moulin, *Paraenesis ad aedificatores* (London 1656); William Fulman, *A Short Appendix to the Life of Edmund Stanton* (London 1673); Bloxam, *Reg. Magdalen* i. 57 n. For

turn St Mary Hall, 'not at present made use of, or endowed', into a research institute where 'tenne godly able men' would compose 'a generall synopsis of the true
reformed protestant religion', and so at last make the rectitude of Calvinist teaching unanswerably plain to England and to Europe.[110] Had the project been executed, St Mary Hall would have offered a shelter to refugee protestant scholars
from the continent, a class to which puritan Oxford was always generous.[111]

True doctrine needed to be defined and defended in print. Yet it was in sermons
that it could be made most vivid and be stamped on the university's young ima-
ginations. Henry Wilkinson junior was warranted in assuring a university congregation in 1660 that 'for these thirteen years past there hath been sermons more
constant, and more practical edifying preaching amongst us, then the oldest alive
can remember ever before in this university'.[112] George Trosse, a tense and devout
undergraduate at puritan Pembroke, would be grateful to have been at Oxford
'when there were so many sermons preached, and so many excellent, orthodox,
and practical divines to preach them'. 'Then', he recalled, 'was religion in its glory
in the university' and, he added tellingly, 'a qualification for respect and advancement'.[113] Philip Henry, at Christ Church under Owen, would remember of that
time that 'serious godliness was in reputation'.[114] The collapse of Oxford puritanism at the Restoration, when in dissenting eyes the university became a 'nursery of Baal's priests',[115] doubtless lent retrospective enchantment to Cromwellian
rule, but the memories of Trosse and Henry were faithful to its essential character. So many sermons were there, so many devotional exercises and biblical discussion groups, that the timetable became overcrowded. A special time was
Thursday afternoon, when the godly would hurry from the exercise at Edmund
Staunton's lodgings in Corpus to catch a similar meeting in Christ Church.[116]

Such gatherings represented the voluntary element of puritan worship. There was
a strenuous element of compulsion too. The university and many of the colleges

the defence of orthodoxy in Oxford see also OUA register T, p. 97; Robert Crosse, *Exercitatio theolog-
ica* (Oxford 1651); Edward Bagshaw, *Dissertationes duae anti-Socinianae* (London 1657); Edward Bagshaw,
A Practicall Discourse concerning God's Decrees (Oxford 1660); John Wallis, *Mens sobria* (Oxford 1657); Henry
Hickman, *Concio de haeresium origine* (Oxford 1659); Henry Hickman, *A Review of the* Certamen epistolare
(Oxford 1659); Henry Hickman, *Laudensum apostosia* (Oxford 1660); *Register*, ed. Burrows, p. lxv; cf *An
Account given to the Parliament by the Ministers sent to Oxford* (London 1647).

[110] BL Add. MS 32,093, fos 399–400. (The amending hand in the document is that of Bulstrode
Whitelocke.) For comparable proposals, see *Perfect Proceedings* 7–14 July 1656, 688; Mullinger, *Cambridge*
iii. 349; John Dury, *An Earnest Plea for Gospel-Communion* (London 1654); Stephen Geree, *The Golden Mean*
(London 1657), 4.

[111] *Oxford Orations of John Owen*, ed. Toon, 36; cf R. Vaughan, *The Protectorate of Oliver Cromwell* (2 vols
London 1839) i. 19. References to grants of money to distressed protestants are scattered though the
accounts of colleges. The puritan preoccupation with the conversion of Jews and Indians was also evident in Oxford.

[112] Wilkinson, *Three Decades of Sermons*, preface; cf ibid. pt 1, 74, 235, pt 3, 33.

[113] *The Life of George Trosse* (London 1714), 81–5.

[114] *An Account of the Life and Death of Mr Philip Henry* (London 1712), 19.

[115] Ludlow, *Voyce from the Watch Tower*, 9.

[116] Wilkinson, *Three Decades of Sermons*, preface; *Life of George Trosse*, 81; Burrows, 335–6; Wood, *History
of the University* ii. 645; Mayo, *Life of Edmund Staunton*, 17.

issued strict orders for courses of preaching and praying; for the 'repetition' before their heads or tutors of the sermons which pupils had heard; and for the catechizing and nightly devotional guidance with which tutors were likewise entrusted.[117] It was the tutors of England's future ministers and magistrates who held the key to the nation's spiritual health, for as Henry Wilkinson reminded them, 'in doing good to one scholar, you may do good to a whole parish or city'.[118]

Yet if the university were to be made fit for God's eyes, the establishment of sound doctrine and worship would not be enough. There must be moral reformation too. The licentiousness and debauchery against which puritans had so long remonstrated must be extinguished. War was waged on alehouses and brothels, on hunting, and on the 'mirth and jollity' of the tennis-court and the bowling-green.[119] Stern injunctions were issued against the 'excess and vanitie' of personal appearance that blossomed in post-war Oxford. The powdering of hair caused particular concern. So did 'exotick garbes', particularly the craze for 'boots and spures and bote-hose-tops' and the 'phantasticall' wearing of ribbons with 'even all the colours of the rainbow' on hats, round waists, on breeches.[120] The distress inflicted on puritans by the university's sartorial iniquities was especially acute in May 1650, a time when England's new rulers were blaming their severe political problems on divine anger and on the national sins that they believed to have provoked it, and when luxurious apparel was felt to offer an insensitive contrast to the current hardship of Oxford's and the nation's poor.[121] If merriment and ostentation must be purged, then so must the monuments of superstition. Images of Christ, of the virgin, and of the saints were taken down from college gates and chapels and chapel windows. Organs were removed from most of the colleges, Christ Church among them, and from St Mary's, where the erection of a 'large' pulpit confirmed the new priorities.[122] There were even attempts to end the use of holy names for churches

[117] *Register*, ed. Burrows, 27, 248, 302, 372, 382, 390, 411–12; Bodl. MS Eng. hist. c. 310, fos 86, 90; OUA SP/E/4, fo 99; Wood, *Life and Times* i. 166; Wood, *History of the University* ii. 656; CA MS I.B.3, pp. 24–5, 62; CCCA MS B/5/1/1: 1649, 1653; LCM Md. reg. fo 94; NCA MS 988: 3 July, 2 August 1650, 8 December 1651, 15 February 1653; WCA MS 2/2, pp. 7–8, 10.

[118] Wilkinson, *Three Decades of Sermons*, pt 2, 78.

[119] OUA register T, pp. 30, 109; Bodl. MS Eng. hist. c. 310, fo 89ᵛ; CCCA MS B/5/1/1, *passim*; NCA MS 988, 31 May 1650 (bowls); Wilkinson, *Three Decades of Sermons*, pt i, 29, 161, 230–1. For the iniquities of tennis: Bodl. MS Wood f. 35, fo 359; OUA SP/E/4, fo 42.

[120] *Register*, ed. Burrows, 294, 313; CA MS I.B.3, pp. 24–5; QCA MS 2Y/30; Wilkinson, *Three Decades of Sermons*, pt 2, 18–19; Wood, *History of the University* ii. 635. The fashion for boots and spurs revived an 'old humor': see M. Curtis, *Oxford and Cambridge in Transition* (Oxford 1959), 144. The story that Vice-chancellor Owen powdered his hair was surely a canard, perhaps concocted by Anthony Wood and George Vernon over a pot of ale: Wood, *Life and Times* i. 221; Vernon, *Letter to a Friend*, 13. Wood's account of Owen's dress, in which the vice-chancellor's informality is taken as vanity, seems equally fanciful.

[121] *Register*, ed. Burrows, 294; Bodl. MS Wood f. 35, fo 359; CA MS I.B.3, pp. 24–5; NCA MS 988 (31 May 1650); Wilkinson, *Three Decades of Sermons*, pt 2, *Second Decade*, 18–19 (on the poor). Cf OUA register T, p. 108, 24 May 1650; B. Worden, 'Oliver Cromwell and the sin of Achan' in D. Beales and G. Best (eds), *History, Society and the Churches* (Cambridge 1985), 131–2; K. Thomas, 'The puritans and adultery' in D. Pennington and K. Thomas (eds), *Puritans and Revolutionaries* (Oxford 1978), 263.

[122] On the policy of demolition see Wood, *History of the University* ii. 648–9; *Register*, ed. Burrows, 114 n.; C. G. Robertson, *All Souls College* (London 1889), 127; *Diary of John Evelyn*, ed. De Beer iii.

and feast days, although, as most puritans seem to have grasped, the Christian nomenclature of Oxford ran too deep to be swiftly eliminated.[123]

The surviving evidence is not of a kind to tell us how systematically the puritan reforms were enforced. Nevertheless such hints as it supplies suggest the accuracy of Wood's recollection that many of the measures were widely observed, at least in those colleges whose heads were sympathetic to them.[124] The regular provision of puritan worship seems particularly likely to have been achieved. By 1655 Owen felt sufficiently pleased with the advances of puritanism to assure the university that never had it 'nourished a greater number of innocent and saintly souls than it does now'.[125] Next year Cromwell told parliament 'that God hath for the ministry a very great seed in the youth of the universities'.[126] The protector's claim would be amply endorsed after 1660 by the contribution which ministers who had been trained at puritan Oxford made to Restoration nonconformity.[127] Yet alongside so pleasing a stock of virtue there remained, as Owen acknowledged, 'very many' who were opposed or indifferent to God's work.[128] It was one thing, conceded the younger Henry Wilkinson, to oblige the young to attend services, another to get them to listen to sermons or to stop them fidgeting and sniggering during prayers.[129]

And how should that not have been so? The failures of puritanism are often conspicuous enough. Yet they can easily be misunderstood or exaggerated. The very frequency of puritan injunctions against wickedness is sometimes interpreted as evidence of their ineffectiveness. It might equally well be evidence that puritans were setting themselves impossible standards, against which their efforts of evangelism could only be judged failures. To one half of their minds the judgement would not have been altogether unwelcome. For puritanism throve as much on the consciousness of failure as on the awareness of success. However distressing the wickedness of the reprobate, its persistence offered puritans the reassurance of a distinctive and collective identity. It was as a 'select number', as the precious separated from the vile, that the godly of Cromwellian Oxford formed gathered churches, met for prayer in college rooms, or were chosen by devout heads for

109. College organs and chapels: CA MS I.B.3, pp. 2, 40; CA MS xii.b.103, pp. 91, 123; Wood, *Life and Times* i. 309 (Merton); Bloxam, *Reg. Magdalen* ii, p. cxv and n. St Mary's: OUA WP/β/21/4, p. 277 (cf ibid. p. 326); ibid. NW/3/4, fos 182, 244; *CSPD 1655–6*, 289.

123 OUA NEP/*supra*/49, ii, fos 140–1; Wood, *Life and Times* i. 174, 197; CCCA B/5/1/1, 'Festu . . . '. Cf for example MCR registrum, p. 385; LCA Md. reg. fo 91ᵛ; Bodl. MS Rawlinson d. 912, fos 1–2; H. E. D. Blakiston, *Trinity College* (London 1898), 142.

124 Wood, *Life and Times* i. 300; Wood, *History of the University* ii. 654. There is evidence of at least intermittent enforcement in CCCA MS B/5/1/1.

125 *Oxford Orations of John Owen*, ed. Toon, 24. Cf ibid. 116; Wilkinson, *Three Decades of Sermons*, pt 2, 76. For a similar claim for Cambridge, see *Perfect Proceedings* 7–14 July 1656, 688.

126 Abbott, *Cromwell* iv. 273. Cf Thomas Harrison, *Threni Hybernici* (London 1659), 19.

127 *Calamy Revised*, ed. A. G. Matthews (Oxford 1934), p. lxi, notes that among the nonconformist ministers whose biographies appear in his volume, Cambridge men outnumber Oxford men by nearly three to two. If we confine our calculations to those of Matthews's ministers who were educated at the universities in the 1650s, we find that Oxford, although still behind Cambridge, is markedly less so.

128 *Works of John Owen*, ed. Goold xi. 11; *Oxford Orations of John Owen*, ed. Toon, 14, 16, 43.

129 Wilkinson, *Three Decades of Sermons*, pt 2, 170.

supplementary divine instruction.[130] The puritans were a community within a community, their friendships extending across the university and stretching too into the town, where the godly party among the citizens submerged their jurisdictional resentments against the university in the cause of common worship.[131]

If the puritans of town and gown acquired a feeling of solidarity, an unsavoury episode of November 1651 suggests that their opponents may likewise have developed a sense of common cause. A gathered congregation in which town and gown were represented was set upon by a gang of scholars and townsmen, who invaded the service, taunted the men, and molested the women. The congregation blamed the episode on the withdrawal of the garrison, 'who were (almost) the onely visible support' of Oxford's godly: the elect could no longer 'adventure out of our houses after day light is downe, without danger of our lives.'[132] A few months later the godly of one (unidentifiable) college, preparing to pluck down an image of Christ from the front gate, found themselves so 'exclaimed against' by 'the neighbours and passers-by' that their exploit had to be delayed until dead of night.[133] It is a measure of the impact of puritan rule on Oxford that the godly would scarcely have felt so exposed by the time of the protectorate. Even so, there is a sense in which they were always a race apart.

Naturally there were disagreements within the puritan community and among its leaders. Above all there was the division between Presbyterians and Independents. Members of both groups were prominent in the national organizations of their movements. The one party wished to impose 'classical presbyteries' on Oxford,[134]

---

[130] *Life of George Trosse*, 81; Conant, *Life of John Conant*, 14.

[131] A key figure in that collaboration was the city father John Nixon, whose contacts with Thomas Goodwin's Magdalen were especially close: MCA MS C.II.4.9, September 1652, 25 November 1652, 23 January 1653; MCA C.II.4.13, 10 December 1652; Bodl. MS Rawlinson d. 715, fo 218. For Nixon see also *Thurloe State Papers*, ed. Birch iv. 595; *Acts and Ordinances*, ed. Firth and Rait ii. 974; OUA SP/E/4, fo 59; Longleat House, Thynne MS xii, fo 162; Wood, *History of the University* ii. 560. For the godly party in the city see also *Register*, ed. Burrows, 354; *Mercurius Veridicus* 14–21 April 1648, 3; UCA 'Duplicate papers', petition of Oxford citizens.

[132] OUA SP/E/4, fos 45, 47, 102ᵃ; *CSPD 1651–2*, 81–2.

[133] Bodl. MS J. Walker c. 9, fo 195. (The year of this letter, which I deduce from internal evidence, cannot be established beyond all doubt.) Cf Robertson, *All Souls College*, 127.

[134] For 'classical presbyteries' see *CJ* 14 March 1660; cf Wilkinson, *Three Decades of Sermons*, pt 3, 24. For Oxford's place in the national Presbyterian network (where a key contact was the London attorney and bookseller Samuel Gellibrand) see Barnard, *Cromwellian Ireland*, 127; OUA register T, pp. 51, 78; Bodl. MS Wood f. 35, fos 128, 140; Wood, *History of the University* ii. 697; Bodl. MS Don. f. 39, fo 212 (visit of the leading Presbyterian minister Simeon Ashe to Oxford). Under the protectorate, as earlier, Presbyterians were eager to provide financial support for godly students who would become ministers—a preoccupation strengthened by their conviction that the status and the attractions of a clerical career had been weakened by the economic damage, the political uncertainties, and the ecclesiastical vacillations of the puritan revolution and by the anticlericalism which it fostered. Edmund Calamy, *The City Remembrancer* (London 1657), ep. ded.; Thomas Case, *Sensuality Dissected* (London 1657), 78 ff.; Christopher Fowler and Simon Ford, *A Sober Answer to an Angry Epistle* (London 1657), 19; [Matthew Poole?], *A Model for the Maintaining of Students* (London 1658); Richard Baxter, *The Crucifying of the World* (London 1658), sig. f. 4; Nathaniel Hardy, *The Olive-Branch* (London 1658), 37; Thomas Watson, *A Plea for Alms* (London 1658), 38–9; *Calendar of the Correspondence of Richard Baxter*, ed. N. H. Keeble and G. F. Nuttall (2 vols Oxford 1991) i. 99, 264–5, 290, 292–3, 326–7, 334, 380, 382, 386; *Mercurius Politicus* 29 October–20 November 1657, 7355, 7388, 7397; *CJ* 22 November 1656.

the other to protect the principle of the voluntarily gathered congregation. Occasionally the debate flared during the Interregnum, and Owen's contribution to it in 1656–7 may have hastened his downfall.[135] Yet for most of the 1650s a truce was observed. The challenge presented by the sects to the very principle of church government, and to the status of the ministry and of ministerial ordinances, persuaded Oxford's Presbyterians and Independents to emphasize those ecclesiastical principles which they held in common. So did the need to meet the shortfall of godly ministers in the parishes, a deficiency which even the combined resources of the two parties would be pressed to rectify. The Pelagian threat brought home to both sides their shared commitment to Calvinist orthodoxy. They were again at one in their determination to secure godly preaching and worship in Oxford, and to purge the university of vice and superstition. From the mounting appreciation of their common priorities there grew close and lasting friendships. The differences between Presbyterians and Independents about issues of national politics were likewise largely suspended in the service of the common puritan cause—at least until that cause began to collapse in 1659. Confident that piety would guarantee loyalty, the puritan rulers of Oxford preferred—almost as much as the Wilkins circle did— to avoid discussion of politics. They subjected the university only to religious, never to political, indoctrination.

The avoidance of political controversy assisted the puritans in their relations not only with each other but with the university at large. There was much in their programme that was not exclusively puritan. Measures designed to correct undergraduates who 'misspend their time and money', and to ensure that the sons of gentlemen studied diligently, were doubtless reassuring to fathers across the political spectrum.[136] Puritanism may have been the creed of a party, but it can also be viewed in a broader light, as a movement that characterized a historical period, a movement that preceded and then transcended the divisions of civil war. The moral and sartorial injunctions imposed by Oxford's puritan rulers often resembled those announced two decades earlier by its Laudian ones.[137] Again, while their enemies might quarrel with many aspects of the puritans' understanding of the duties of a godly ministry, there were pastoral needs and responsibilities which all sides acknowledged. When the royalist chancellor of Cambridge, the earl of Holland,

---

[135] *Lettere di Henry Stubbe*, ed. Nicastro, *passim*; *Works of John Owen*, ed. Goold xiii. 217–18, 299–300. Owen (like Oliver Cromwell) aimed to reconcile Presbyterians and Independents (*Works of John Owen*, ed. Goold xiii. 258, 275, 296), but, again like Cromwell, he did not extend his ecumenicalism to the more clericalist and intolerant Presbyterians, a group which bitterly attacked Owen's Independency in 1656–7—but which was not conspicuous in Oxford. A work of Owen's Oxford ally Lewis du Moulin in 1656, *Paraenesis ad aedificatores*, was hailed by the Cromwellian press as a blow to the more 'severe' Presbyterians (*Mercurius Politicus* 4 September–2 October 1656, 7231, 7275; cf ibid. 26 March—2 April 1657, 7701, and *Works of John Owen*, ed. Goold xiii. 298).

[136] Bodl. MS Wood f. 35, fo 359; Bodl. MS Eng. hist. c. 310, fo 82; CA MS I.B.3, p. 61 (though cf OUA register T, p. 280); Bloxam, *Reg. Magdalen* ii. 284–5. For the likelihood of parental approval see BL Add. MS 37,344, fo 323; *CSPD 1659–60*, 258; *Register*, ed. Burrows, p. xxxiii.

[137] *Register*, ed. Burrows, p. xvi; Mullinger, *Cambridge* iii. 269 n.; K. Sharpe, 'Archbishop Laud and the University of Oxford' in H. Lloyd-Jones, V. Pearl, and B. Worden (eds), *History and Imagination* (London 1981), 146–64.

expressed on the scaffold in 1649 the hope that God would make his university 'a nursery to plant' pious ministers there 'that the souls of the people may receive a great benefit', he voiced sentiments that crossed the civil war divide.[138] So did the earl of Clarendon: in the unexpected tribute in his *History* to the achievements of the puritans in Oxford; in his pleas, as chancellor, for a further reformation of the university at the Restoration; in his dislike of the tendency of Englishmen to educate their children in popish countries abroad.[139] As the 1650s progressed, so Oxford's puritans became increasingly willing to extend the hand of friendship to 'all sober, serious, peaceable royallists', whom they strove to separate from their less virtuous allies.[140]

Even the rigorous Calvinist understanding of the doctrine of predestination, an interpretation which could be so divisive, had its Cavalier as well as its Roundhead adherents—just as it had had them among the most devoted churchmen of the period of the Laudian ascendancy. The royalists of civil war Oxford, who watched in despair as the puritans destroyed the Church of England, none the less contained a party whose Anglicanism was firmly Calvinist in doctrine: the party of Ussher and Prideaux and Prideaux's colleague at Exeter Henry Tozer, all of whom were revered by the puritans of Cromwellian Oxford.[141] Also of that party was Thomas Barlow, who would become a bishop under Charles II. There was no more bitter an opponent of the Roundhead cause or of the post-war visitation than Barlow, who none the less survived the purge to become provost of Queen's on Langbaine's death in 1658.[142] Barlow's doctrinal Calvinism, his hatred of Arminianism and Socinianism, had been unyielding.[143] Like Owen, whose tutor he

[138] Mullinger, *Cambridge* iii. 359.

[139] Edward Hyde, earl of Clarendon, *The History of the Rebellion*, ed. W. D. Macray (6 vols Oxford 1888) iv. 259; OUA register T, p. 82; *A Collection of Several Tracts of the Right Honourable Earl of Clarendon* (London 1727), 313–48. Cromwellian Oxford, remarks Clarendon, 'yielded a harvest of extraordinary good and sound knowledge in all parts of learning; and many who were wickedly introduced [by the puritans] applied themselves to the study of good learning and the practice of virtue'—although Clarendon gives the credit to providence, not to the Cromwellians.

[140] Hickman, *Review of the* Certamen epistolare, ep. ded. Admittedly the hand was extended the more urgently as the puritan cause crumbled and the Restoration approached.

[141] Prideaux: see p. 754 above. Tozer: Bodl. MS Wood f. 35, fos 171ᵛ, 200ᵛ, 316, 320ᵛ; Bodl. MS Rawlinson letters 89, fos 108, 137; *Register*, ed. Burrows, 211, 217; Conant, *Life of John Conant*, 8–9. Ussher: Bodl. MS Eng. hist. c. 310, fos 87ᵛ, 88ᵛ; *Public Intelligencer* 4 April 1658; du Moulin, *Paraenesis ad aedificatores*, preface; Peter Heylyn, *Certamen epistolare* (London 1651), 118, 124–5; *CSPD 1656–7*, 271 (see too Joshua Hoyle, *A Rejoinder to Master Malone's Reply* (Dublin 1641); Bodl. MS Rawlinson letters 52, no. 4). Probably at the instigation of Francis Mansell, and perhaps too at that of the surviving royalist fellow of Jesus James Vaughan, Ussher held dining rights there from 1652, if not earlier, until his death in 1656; but we cannot tell whether he used them, or whether he ever resided in the college during the same period: Bodl. MS DD Jesus College, a. 6–7. For Vaughan: Bodl. MS Selden *supra* 109, fo 450; *Lettere di Henry Stubbe*, ed. Nicastro, 18–19; Pope, *Life of Seth Ward*, 45.

[142] For the intensity of Barlow's royalism see Bodl. MS Wood f. 35 (especially the documents in his hand); QCA MS 423, pp. 55–60; T. Barlow [?], *Pegasus* (London 1647).

[143] *Genuine Remains of . . . Dr Barlow*, 72–83, 122–40, 181; Bodl. MS Tanner 52, fos 212–13; Bodl. MS Rawlinson c. 945, pp. 443–58, 503–16; Thomas Barlow, *De studio theologiae* (London 1699), 48, 55–63; John Prideaux, *Manuductio ad theologiam polemicam* (Oxford 1657), preface; Wilkinson, *Three Decades of Sermons*, pt i, preface; William Sheppard, *Sincerity and Hypocrisy* (Oxford 1658); cf N. L. Matthews, *William Sheppard: Cromwell's law reformer* (Cambridge 1984), 33, 64.

had been at Queen's in the 1630s, Barlow felt that Calvin may well have been right to have the antitrinitarian Michael Servetus burned.[144] And how Barlow shuddered to recall the moment in Laudian Oxford when, at a disputation chaired by Prideaux, the young Gilbert Sheldon had introduced the heresy that the pope was not the Antichrist![145] A client of Barlow among the fellows of Queen's was the 'strict Calvinist' Thomas Tully, like Barlow an Anglican and royalist.[146] He became principal of St Edmund Hall in 1658 and rapidly revived that expiring house by his efficient rule and his energetic fundraising.[147] In the Interregnum, believed John Owen's close ally Lewis du Moulin, Barlow and Tully 'did keep this university of Oxon from being poyson'd with Pelagianism, Socinianism, popery etc.'[148]

Not all of Oxford's rulers, admittedly, welcomed the puritans' insistence on Calvinist orthodoxy. Gerard Langbaine shared the distaste of his friend John Selden for heresy-hunts.[149] The Wilkins circle, who believed that the theological disputes so dear to puritans were weakening the hold of Christianity itself, were sniped at by zealots who described them as 'meer moral men, without the power of godliness', and who accused them of elevating the ethical above the doctrinal content of religion.[150] Yet Wilkins and his friends were at one with the Calvinists in their diagnosis of the spiritual malaise of the time—even if hardly in their recommendations for its cure. Wilkins and Ward lamented the proliferation of 'scepticks', 'epicures', and 'atheists' in terms which might have been Owen's.[151] The moral earnestness of Wilkins and his friends had its puritan dimension. Wilkins devoted strenuous labours to the composition of conventional works on providence and prayer and preaching.[152] He attended John Conant's sermons at St Mary's church together with Ward, who often preached there himself without obligation or reward.[153] The Wadham of Wilkins and Ward, it is true, was a merry as well as a cultivated college. So was the Queen's of Langbaine. Yet amidst the good cheer, the talk of wine and women, the practical jokes, the music and the hunting, we catch glimpses in both colleges of sombre introspection, regular

---

[144] *Genuine Remains of . . . Dr Barlow*, 204 (cf ibid. 241–2); Worden, 'Toleration and the Cromwellian protectorate', 205, 231–2.

[145] *Genuine Remains of . . . Dr Barlow*, 191–2.

[146] Wood, *Athenae* iii. 1055–9; cf QCA Lamplugh papers, 'T.T.'.

[147] Bodl. MS Wood f. 28, fo 306; Bodl. MS Lat. misc. c. 19, pp. 131–2; OUA matriculations 1648–62, SP/37, p. 553; A. B. Emden, 'The Old Library', *St Edmund Hall Magazine* v (1943–8), 39–40; *The Oxinden and Peyton Letters 1642–70*, ed. D. Gardiner (London 1937), 229–30.

[148] Wood, *Athenae* iii. 1058.   [149] Bodl. MS Selden *supra* 109, fos 380, 452.

[150] Pope, *Life of Seth Ward*, 43–4; cf Bodl. MS Don. f. 39, pp. 256–8; Bodl. MS Don. f. 41, pp. 76–8.

[151] John Wilkins, *Ecclesiastes* (London 1656), 12; John Wilkins, *Of the Principles and Duties of Natural Religion* (London 1675), 1; Seth Ward, *A Philosophicall Essay* (Oxford 1655), 1–2, 80; Bodl. MS Don. f. 42, Ward's sermon 8 December 1661 (and see S. Ward, *A Sermon preached before the Peers* (London 1666), 1).

[152] The account of Wilkins's *A Discourse concerning the Beauty of Providence* (London 1649) given in Webster, *Great Instauration*, 29, is misleading.

[153] Conant, *Life of John Conant*, 19; Pope, *Life of Seth Ward*, 22–7. Cf Bodl. MS Rawlinson e. 199, fos 82ᵛ–4; Claggett, *Abuse of God's Grace*, preface by Henry Wilkinson jr.

devotion, troubled prayer—features of religious life to which even the more convivial members of that afflicted generation could be susceptible.[154]

Even so, generations pass. When puritan rule collapsed in 1659–60, it was among young men that royalist enthusiasm was most widely noticed. In their eyes puritanism, the religion under whose sway they had grown up, had been a destructive force, a source of bloodshed and chaos and misery. Oxford was a young community, its youthfulness a source of undisguised regret to its puritan educators, to whom 'young' and 'youth' were almost pejorative terms. They despaired of the lightheadedness of youth, of its 'frothy wit', its perilous indifference to eternal verities.[155] At the first Anglican services to be held openly in Oxford in 1660, the church 'was always full of young people purposely to hear and see the novelty'.[156] The anti-puritan priorities acquired by so many youths of the 1650s would become clear later in the century. Alongside the ranks of future dissenters in Cromwellian Oxford who submitted to its Calvinist teaching, there were large numbers of young men who in the later Stuart age would become leading high churchmen, or who would crow over the executions of the Rye House plotters in 1683 and of Monmouth in 1685, or who would be non-jurors after 1688.[157] There were Tory politicians in the making too. Thanks to the History of Parliament Trust, we can trace the careers of the Oxford men who sat in the house of commons in the later seventeenth century. Although such calculations are fraught with difficulty, there does seem to have been a contrast—not sharp, but perceptible none the less—between the members who had been at Oxford in the Interregnum and those who were there before or after it. The products of the Laudian and of the Restoration university were more likely to be whig than tory: those of Cromwellian Oxford were more likely to be tory than whig.[158]

It was ultimately in the colleges that the battles for the puritan reformation of Oxford were won and lost. George Trosse believed that godliness had flourished

---

[154] For Wadham see Shapiro, *John Wilkins*, 120–2. For Queen's see *CSPD* for the period of the protectorate, s.v. Joseph Williamson (and Williamson's prayer in PRO SP18/205, fos 168–70); Wood, *Life and Times* i. 290.

[155] Wilkinson, *Three Decades of Sermons*, pt 2, no. 1; *Oxford Orations of John Owen*, ed. Toon 16, 32, 43; OUA register T, p. 72. The failure of the university's ban on Francis Osborne's *Advice to a Son* (Oxford 1656, 6th edn Oxford 1658), an injunction which merely boosted its sales in Oxford, confirmed the apprehensions of an older generation, which also lamented the influence of Hobbes on students: George Lawson, *An Examination of the Political Part of Mr Hobbes's Leviathan* (London 1656), preface; John Wallis, *Due Correction for Mr Hobbes* (Oxford 1656). For extreme and despairing comments (by intelligent men) on the spiritual and moral depravity of the youth of the Cromwellian universities see Bodl. MS Rawlinson a. 42, fo 349; Bodl. MS Tanner 52, fo 199; *Oxford Orations of John Owen*, ed. Toon, 5.

[156] Wood, *History of the University* ii. 704.

[157] See for example Bloxam, *Reg. Magdalen* v. 223–9 (cf ibid. 236); John Fitzwilliam, *A Sermon preached at Cottenham near Cambridge* (London 1683); Foster, *Alumni* i. 129 (Nathaniel Bisby). Wadham, Christ Church, and Queen's were especially productive of future high churchmen, for reasons that will emerge.

[158] B. D. Henning (ed.), *The House of Commons 1660–1690* (3 vols London 1983) i. 4, gives the numbers and the allegiances of Oxford's graduates in Restoration parliaments (but does not divide them into generations: here the—inevitably tentative and imprecise—calculations, based on Henning's biographies, have been my own).

in his time there because 'most' of the houses had had 'religious governors'.[159] The heads were indeed the effective rulers of seventeenth-century Oxford, and it was in their colleges and halls that the fate of puritan reform hung in the balance. It is time to make a tour.

The college which came closest to meeting the puritan ideal was the Magdalen of Thomas Goodwin, a house of which puritans had despaired in the time of Laudianism. In his youth, under the inspiration of Richard Sibbes, Goodwin had been a model puritan tutor at Cambridge, inculcating godly principles, winning souls, helping to extend the nation's puritan network. His principal motive in accepting the presidency of Magdalen was 'to bring in young men that were godly, both fellows and scholars, that should serve God in the ministry in after-times.'[160] His gathered congregation drew puritans—Presbyterians and Independents alike— from across Oxford into Magdalen, and supplied energetic preachers to the neigh-bouring parishes. The puritans teaching at Magdalen in the 1650s included the future prominent dissenters John Howe and Theophilus Gale, the university politi-cians James Barron (who would be the editor, with Thankful Owen, of Goodwin's posthumous works) and Francis Howell, the influential tutor Thomas Cracraft, who became Goodwin's vice-president, and the controversialist Henry Hickman, who was the 'stated preacher' of the congregation attended by George Trosse next to Pembroke.[161] The leading puritan divines whose sons were at Magdalen in the 1650s included Edward Reynolds, John Conant, Philip Nye, Sidrach Simpson, John Tombes, and Thomas Fairfax's chaplain Isaac Knight. Of all the colleges, Magdalen supplied the largest number among the ministers who would be ejected from their livings in the 1660s. Not far behind were Exeter and Christ Church.[162] At Exeter John Conant, active in 'new peopling of his college', was an able governor. He revived the high academic and spiritual reputation which the college had enjoyed under Prideaux, whose pupil he had been and on whom he modelled his rule. Puritan exercises and godly conduct were strictly enjoined by Conant, who as vice-chancellor 'used frequently to take his rounds at late hours to ferret the young stu-dents from public and suspected houses'.[163] At Christ Church—not an easy college to govern—Owen waged a vigorous campaign of moral and spiritual reform, as Reynolds had done before him. Like Magdalen, Christ Church boasted a number of Oxford's most influential puritan politicians, among them Henry Wilkinson senior, Henry Cornish, and Ambrose Upton. And like Magdalen's, the puritan

[159] *Life of George Trosse*, 81.

[160] *The Works of Thomas Goodwin* (11 vols London 1861–5) ii, p. xxxi.

[161] *Life of George Trosse*, 81; Hickman, *Concio de haeresium origine*, ep. ded.

[162] My calculations, which are based on the biographical entries in *Calamy Revised*, ed. Matthews, are admittedly an imperfect test of the puritanism of the colleges, especially since not all puritans became nonconformists and not all nonconformists were puritans; but the calculations do reveal clear general patterns. For the contribution of Cromwellian Exeter to Restoration nonconformity see also P. Collinson, *The Elizabethan Puritan Movement* (London 1967), 129.

[163] Conant, *Life of John Conant*, 25. For the spiritual life of Exeter see too *The Correspondence of John Locke*, ed. E. S. De Beer (8 vols Oxford 1976–89) i. 631.

contacts of Christ Church stretched across the university. Most conspicuously they stretched to neighbouring Pembroke, the college of George Trosse, where the Presbyterian Henry Langley was an energetic head.[164]

The house to which Goodwin's Magdalen was most closely linked was naturally Magdalen Hall, whose principal was the Presbyterian Henry Wilkinson junior. Wilkinson believed that the fellows of Magdalen College had been ready to elect him unanimously to their presidency when Goodwin was intruded upon them in 1650. He harboured similar hopes later in the decade, when Goodwin came to yearn for the leisure 'to perfect severall bookes ... contayninge a body of divinity, and without doeing of which he professeth he cannot dye in peace'; but Goodwin stayed in office until 1660.[165] Despite his disappointments Wilkinson was content at the hall, to which, as to the university, he was warmly devoted.[166] As principal he modelled his rule on the godly and expansionist regime of his predecessor John Wilkinson, under whom he had long served, and after whose example he 'took all the ways necessary to make his house flourish with young students'.[167] While he stood no chance of matching the very high numbers of the 1630s, he did enable Magdalen Hall, alone of the halls, to maintain an intake with which an average-sized college would have been pleased.[168] The halls of the mid-century are virtu-ally without records, but if Wilkinson practised what he so often preached at St Mary's church then he must have been a vigilant disciplinarian. At New Inn Hall the rule of Christopher Rogers, who like Goodwin was pastor of a gathered church,[169] was so far as we know untroubled. So were those of Owen's ally Philemon Stephens and the puritan Tobias Garbrand in two barely surviving bod-ies, Hart Hall and Gloucester Hall. Yet it is a question whether Rogers, Stephens, and Garbrand had the personal authority and the administrative gifts on which puritan advance depended.

Certainly not all the puritan heads of college appear to have possessed them. There is little evidence to suggest that St John's under Thankful Owen experienced the reforming impetus injected elsewhere by his friends Goodwin and John Owen, even though a remarkably high number of ministers sent their sons to the college during his reign, and even though the eviction of royalists by the first visitation had been more thorough there than in many houses. Greenwood at Brasenose, the stop-gap vice-chancellor of 1650–2, may likewise have disappointed the hopes of his fellow puritans. At Trinity the regime of Robert Harris, the intimate friend of

---

[164] PCA MS 4/1/1; see also Job Roys, *The Spirit's Touchstone* (London 1657), ep. ded. (to Langley); *Mercurius Politicus* 20–7 January 1659, 192.

[165] Bodl. MS Rawlinson letters 52, no. 90; *Thurloe State Papers*, ed. Birch vi. 539; *CSPD 1659–60*, 400–1.

[166] Bodl. MS Wood f. 45, fos 128–40; Bodl. MS Ballard 46, fos 93–8; Claggett, *Abuse of God's Grace*, preface.

[167] Wood, *Athenae* iv. 285. For the character of Wilkinson's regime see also PRO SP29/11, fo 43; ibid. SP29/14, fo 146; BL Add. MS 11,610, pp. 204–7; Wood, *Life and Times* i. 413–16. Cf OUA regis-ter T, reverse entries, p. 1.

[168] Matriculation figures from Magdalen Hall in the 1650s averaged about twenty a year: in the 1630s they had averaged around fifty a year.

[169] Nickolls, *Original Letters*, 140.

his fellow Presbyterian Henry Wilkinson junior,[170] was more harmonious than puritan. Even at Corpus, where Edmund Staunton, that zealous enemy to vice, 'took great care to introduce and elect into the colledge such as he either saw or heard to have some appearances of grace', the president's mastery of his house was uncertain.[171]

Thus the support of an intruded head, although a necessary condition of puritan reform, was not a sufficient one. Some colleges with new governors were too divided or unsettled for reform to be practicable. Their number probably included Merton, whose warden Jonathan Godard, in any case no zealot, was so often away. At University College neither Joshua Hoyle, nor Francis Johnson who succeeded him in 1654, seem to have imposed his puritan values on a college riddled with debt and with division. The former army chaplain George Marshall at New College, and the admittedly more circumspect reformer John Palmer at All Souls, were easily thwarted.

Two colleges in the Turl were in comparable disarray. The dark and cymric feuds of Jesus College reduced that house to administrative chaos and exposed the intruded principal Jonathan Roberts to charges of embezzlement and eventually to dismissal.[172] In 1638, as a young fellow, Roberts had been expelled by the previous principal Francis Mansell for his 'covetous and worldly inclinations' and for his failure to repay money to the college.[173] Mansell, who had striven to build up the college and to heal its internecine strife, was devoted to the crown and to the Church of England.[174] Yet he contrived to return to Jesus in 1651 and to reside there throughout the Interregnum.[175] His relations with Principal Roberts we can only imagine. At Lincoln College the rector, Paul Hood, was not a puritan appointment. Alone of the heads of 1640 he weathered every storm of the revolution. The butt of unconcealed contempt from his juniors, he was in 1650–1 'articled against by some of the fellows' and 'upbraided' with 'timerousnesse' by the sub-rector, Thankful Owen (who had yet to move to St John's). Hood's crime was his acquiescence in the admission, at parliament's behest, of a group of fellows who had been brought from Cambridge in the cause of reformation, but whose characters proved to have been gravely misjudged. Their drunken and disorderly conduct and

[170] Claggett, *Abuse of God's Grace*, preface; Wilkinson, *Conciones tres*, 175, 184–90; Wilkinson, *Three Decades of Sermons*, preface, pt 3, 74.

[171] Mayo, *Life of Edmund Staunton*, 17–18. Staunton may have had an unfairly bad press in the later Stuart period (see Fulman, *Short Appendix to the Life of Edmund Stanton*; Bodl. MS J. Walker c. 8, fo 247), but the visitation register for the 1650s does not show his rule in a flattering light. His disciplinary endeavours are evident in CCCA MS B5/1/1. For his outlook see also his *Rupes Israelis* (London 1644) and *Phinehas's Zeal* (London 1645).

[172] For that dispute, which surfaces frequently in Burrows, see also OUA WP/a/38/1; T. Richards, 'The puritan visitation of Jesus College', *Transactions of the Honourable Society of Cymmrodorion* (1922–3), passim.

[173] JCA MS 156, 'Dr Mansell's apologie'.

[174] Ibid. MSS 151–2, 155–6; S. L. Jenkins, *The Life of Francis Mansell* (London 1854), 15 ff., cf QCA Lamplugh papers, 'Jesus College case'. For royalism in Jesus see also JCA box 1, no. 1; ibid. bursars' accounts 1631–53, pp. 135, 172.

[175] Bodl. MS DD Jesus College, a. 6–9.

their apoplectic tempers provoked a series of quarrels that brought the fellows to blows in the dining-hall and in the street. The party of William Sprigge and Robert Wood, the educational reformers, seems to have been a scarcely more stabilizing force.[176] In the 1650s Lincoln attracted scarcely more than a quarter of the number of undergraduates it had admitted in the 1630s, a fall far greater than that suffered by any other college.[177] During the later years of the Interregnum a group of fellows led by Nathaniel Crew became increasingly open in its royalist preferences and in its repudiation of the revolution with which the rector had complied. Crew, the future bishop of Durham and benefactor, was probably a protégé of John Wilkins. By 1660 the rector was under Crew's thumb.[178]

If, as puritans hoped, the colleges were to produce a godly ruling class, then not only must they be brought to order under puritan rule; they must also awaken the souls of those pupils who had hitherto lacked the advantages of a puritan upbringing. The sons of royalists must be drawn to Oxford and given puritan tutors and make puritan friends. Here puritanism failed. To apply a simple but revealing measurement, there were only two colleges, the Christ Church of Owen and the Wadham of Wilkins, where we find a significant number of both royalist sons and future dissenters; and even there the two categories rarely overlapped. Wilkins's ability to attract families from across the political spectrum gave his college an undergraduate population half as high again as that of the 1630s, an achievement without rival in Cromwellian Oxford.[179] Yet it was 'especially those then stiled Cavaliers and malignants'—among them the royalist rebel John Penruddock, who was executed in 1655, and the royalist judge David Jenkins—who sent their sons to Wadham,[180] where there were six future bishops to guide them: Wilkins, Ward, Thomas Sprat, William Lloyd, Gilbert Ironside, and Walter Blandford.[181] The wits

---

[176] The principal sources for the quarrels are: *Register*, ed. Burrows; LCM Md. reg.; OUA SP/E/4, fos 41–5; 'Illustrations of the state of the church', 167–8. Lincoln's account books are also useful. See too, for Sprigge, Bodl. MS e. mus. 77, p. 380. V. H. H. Green, 'New light on Rector Hood', *Lincoln College Record* (1979–80), 11–13, revises the assessment of Hood given in Green's *The Commonwealth of Lincoln College* (Oxford 1979).

[177] The college supplied only about seven matriculands a year in the 1650s.

[178] The main source for the conflicts surrounding the rise of Crew is LCM Md. reg. (especially fo 105); see also Wood, *Life and Times* i. 268, 274, 290, 332–3, 362; BL Add. MS 34,769, fo 63. Crew became a fellow soon after Richard Knightley, with whose family both he and Wilkins were closely connected. All three families had links with that of Lord Saye and Sele, who was a patron of the Sprigge family, had influence at the college (Md. reg. fo 99ᵛ), and regarded Cromwell's rule as a lawless usurpation (Bodl. MS Carte 80, fo 749). Saye's grandson, the son of Nathaniel Fiennes, matriculated from Lincoln in 1655.

[179] Matriculations from Wadham were about seventeen a year in the 1630s, twenty-five a year in the 1650s. My principal means of identifying sons of royalists in Cromwellian Oxford has been to compare entries in the university matriculation register and in Foster, *Alumni* with M. A. E. Green, *Calendar of the Committee for Compounding* (5 vols London 1899–1902) and other standard printed sources for the civil wars.

[180] Pope, *Life of Seth Ward*, 28. For Jenkins see W. Wynne, *The Life of Sir Leoline Jenkins* (2 vols London 1724) ii. 643. For Penruddock, cf JCA MS 156, and Henning, *House of Commons* iii. 792.

[181] Lloyd came to Wadham in 1656, after his ordination by Bishop Brownrig, who made Ward precentor of Exeter cathedral in the same year.

Rochester and Sedley were there, as was Christopher Wren until his departure to join the *virtuosi* of All Souls in 1654.

Wadham and Christ Church were among the four colleges with the largest undergraduate populations in the 1650s. The others were Exeter and Queen's. Those four were also the most public-minded of the colleges. Among them they produced three fifths of those MPs of the later seventeenth century who had been at Cromwellian Oxford.[182] Puritan Exeter, which unlike the others had few sons of royalists among its pupils, was likewise alone of the four in producing more whig MPs than tories.[183] Queen's under Langbaine provides a strikingly different picture. There an unusually high proportion of the fellows had managed to survive the post-war purge. Known as the house 'resorted to by all that were cavaliers or of the king's party',[184] its character can be arithmetically illustrated. In the Interregnum it was the college with the largest number of sons of royalists among its pupils; it was the college, ahead even of Christ Church, with the largest number of matriculated undergraduates whose fathers were knights or of higher rank; it was the college which produced most future tory MPs; and there was scarcely a future dissenting minister on its books. Only one other house preserved so distinctly royalist a character: Oriel, a smaller college, where the proportion of sons of royalists was even higher than at Queen's. The royalist provosts Richard Sanders and his successor Robert Saye resisted all visitatorial efforts to puritanize their house with obstinacy, even with insolence.[185] A royalist flavour also survived at Balliol, whose master Henry Savage,[186] parliament's puzzling choice as successor to the intruded puritan George Bradshaw in 1651, had no more love for puritanism or rebellion than had the heads of Queen's and Oriel.[187]

To a large degree, therefore, the puritans and the royalists of Cromwellian Oxford kept themselves apart. The hours of puritan voluntary worship were liable to find royalists at music or at the coffee-houses which sprang up in Oxford during the 1650s.[188] Even more perhaps than the puritan network, the royalist community stretched beyond the colleges into the town, where it included men who had been expelled from the university by the parliamentary visitation. Royalists from within and without the colleges attended the services held on Sundays and holy days in the houses of Thomas Willis and Alderman White. There John Fell administered the sacrament, and there Anglican forms were observed 'with such

[182] My calculation is based on the biographical entries in Henning, *House of Commons*.
[183] There was a comparable dearth of royalist sons at puritan Magdalen.
[184] Henning, *House of Commons* iii. 458–9.
[185] Saye's royalism: PRO SP29/4, fo 216; Bodl. MS Rawlinson c. 421, fo 70; D. Underdown, *Royalist Conspiracy in England* (New Haven 1960), 265. Oriel's royalism and defiance: *Register*, ed. Burrows, 383, 386, 395; Wood, *History of the University* ii. 654 n., cf OUA WP/β/21/4, p. 326.
[186] Davis and Hunt, *History of Balliol College*, 122–30; cf BCA computi 1615–62, Baptist term 1652, gift to 'poore gent. formerly in the k[ing]'s service'.
[187] BCA college register 1514–1682, esp. pp. 263–4; Bodl. MS Rawlinson c. 421, fo 70; Henry Savage, *Balliofergus* (Oxford 1668), ep. ded., 105, 118, 122, 125. Balliol's undergraduate numbers rose promisingly in the earlier 1650s, only to fall again.
[188] *Diary of John Evelyn*, ed. De Beer iii. 106; Wood, *Life and Times* i. 201.

circumstances of primitive devotion and solemnity as was hardly to be paralleled elsewhere during the storm of that persecution'.[189] In 1654 a secret collection was organized in Oxford for distressed bishops in exile,[190] probably by the deposed principal of Jesus, Francis Mansell, and by his protégé Leoline Jenkins. Jenkins lived in the city and taught royalist sons who in happier times would doubtless have been sent to the colleges.[191] Among the contributors to the collection we find, alongside the names of expelled royalists, those of Gerard Langbaine, Thomas Barlow, Thomas Tully, and the future bishop Thomas Lamplugh at Queen's; of rector Hood of Lincoln; and of two veterans of civil war royalism who had survived at All Souls, Martin Aylworth and John Prestwich.

Except perhaps during 1655, when the government's fears of royalist conspiracy were grave, the puritans connived at the survival of Anglican devotion at Oxford. At least the devotees could be more easily kept under watch if they remained in Oxford than if they left it.[192] Under the protectorate the royalists of Oxford appear to have presented no serious threat to the security of the regime. When Penruddock rose in 1655 the colleges seem to have united in sending men and weapons for the troop raised by John Owen in the university's defence.[193] Yet it was a taste for order, not for puritanism, that secured Oxford's loyalty.[194] When that order began to collapse with the fall of the protectorate in 1659, loyalty was rapidly eroded or transferred. In 1660, when the Restoration visitation undid the puritan purge, its work was carried out by heads and fellows who had survived that purge but who now found the new world of the Restoration much more congenial. Among them was Thomas Lamplugh of Queen's, who with his friend Joseph Williamson of the same college found royal favour in 1660. In Lamplugh's papers there survives a document of that year, penned by fellow Oxford royalists, which asks for similar favour to be extended to Seth Ward. During the usurpation, the petitioners remarked, Ward had 'zealously . . . asserted the liberties' of the university 'from those amongst our selves, who have endeavoured to invade them'.[195] In

[189] Wynne, *Life of Sir Leoline Jenkins* i, p. v; Jenkins, *Life of Francis Mansell*, 22–5; Wood, *History of the University* ii. 613; Wood, *Athenae* iv. 194, cf Wood, *Life and Times* i. 161.

[190] JCA MS 154; cf Jenkins, *Life of Francis Mansell*, 23, 26.

[191] Wynne, *Life of Leoline Jenkins* ii. 645–50; JCA MS 153, letter of 12 July 1651; ibid. MS 156.

[192] *Register*, ed. Burrows, p. xlii; cf *Correspondence of John Owen*, ed. Toon, 61–2. For the royalist threat in and around Oxford see Abbott, *Cromwell* iii. 746 (cf ibid. iv. 746); *Mercurius Politicus* 14–21 June 1655, 5419; *Perfect Proceedings* 23 August 1655; *Perfect Account* 23 August 1655; *Certain Passages* 29 August 1655; Bodl. MS Rawlinson a. 27, p. 753.

[193] ECA MS A.II.10, 20 March 1655; JCA bursars' accounts 1651–9: 1655, 'For a pistol . . . ' and 'To the college trooper'; PCA MS 4/1/1, fo 23; OUA register T, pp. 271–2; Green, *Commonwealth of Lincoln College*, 257. It seems that Joseph Williamson of Queen's, who would shortly be taking royalist private pupils to France, was enlisted in the troop; or so I infer from the subsequent badinage in *CSPD 1655*, s.v. Williamson. For expressions of Oxford's outward loyalty to puritan rule see *Musarum Oxoniensum* (Oxford 1654); OUA NW/3/4, fo 66ᵛ; and the services performed for the state in 1653–4 by the royalists Ralph Bathurst (*Register*, ed. Burrows, 389–90) and Richard Zouche (*DNB*, s.v. Zouche).

[194] Wood, *History of the University* ii. 668, records that Owen's troop was raised for the university's 'safety'. For the same priority at other times see ibid. 683–4; Wood, *Life and Times* i. 155, 194–5, 280, 303; OUA register T, p. 72.

[195] QCA Lamplugh papers, companion document to paper dated 19 June 1660.

1644 Ward's refusal to take the solemn league and covenant had led to his expulsion from Cambridge. In 1656 he had been made precentor of Exeter Cathedral by its exiled bishop. Although willing to cooperate with puritan rule and to seek to influence and modify it, he can have shed no tears for its passing. Soon after the Restoration he was denouncing before his king 'the late days of darkness' and the rebellious principles which had produced them.[196] Soon too he reaped his episcopal reward.

Ralph Bathurst, Ward's friend at Trinity, believed that by the eve of the Restoration 'the generality of the university was, for the most part, come about to wish well to the government both of church and state, as by [ancient] law established'.[197] The mounting confidence of monarchist sentiment in the later 1650s can be glimpsed in the election or re-election to fellowships of men who had been purged by the visitation of 1647–52, their return being in some cases assisted by Richard Cromwell.[198] Plainer still was the tendency in elections to headships. On that front the puritans won their last victory in 1657, in a battle fought largely in London. At Jesus College Seth Ward had been proposed 'by the direction of Dr Mansell' as successor to Jonathan Roberts. His candidacy was 'much backed by Wilkins, but not by Owen', whose party secured the appointment instead of Thomas Goodwin's friend, the Independent Francis Howell.[199] Next year, however, Goodwin's bid to have Thomas Cracraft, his vice-president at Magdalen, imposed as president of Trinity was thwarted by the fellows there. They elected William Hawes, who had failed to submit to the parliamentary visitation; when Hawes died soon after, they chose Seth Ward in his place. Trinity had learned the art of proceeding to a swift election before the puritans could interfere.[200] The same tactic was used at Queen's, where Langbaine was instantly replaced by Thomas Barlow in 1658,[201] and at Wadham, where, on the appointment of Wilkins as master of Trinity College Cambridge by Richard Cromwell in 1659, the fellows rapidly named the future bishop Walter Blandford to succeed him.[202] Blandford would be a member of the royalist visitation of 1660. So would Michael Woodward, who during Richard Cromwell's protectorate was made warden of New College 'after a great controversy and difference'.[203]

[196] Seth Ward, *Against Resistance of Lawful Powers* (London 1661), ep. ded., 5, 26–7, 33.

[197] Warton, *Life of Ralph Bathurst*, 206.

[198] Bloxam, *Reg. Magdalen* ii, p. cvii; *Correspondence of John Owen*, ed. Toon, 74–5 (for the year of that letter see CA MS xi.a.15, no. 61); Wood, *Athenae* iii. 881; and see NCA MS 9655, p. 53, for Richard's appointment, as protector, of Edward Reynolds to a visitation of New College.

[199] *Lettere di Henry Stubbe*, ed. Nicastro, 21; Pope, *Life of Seth Ward*, 455–6, cf Bloxam, *Reg. Magdalen* iii. 149. Howell seems to have restored order to the college's finances: JCA bursars' accounts 1651–9, annual signatures. As Roberts remained at Jesus at least until 1658, Howell had to live beside two deposed principals (the other being Mansell): Bodl. MS DD Jesus College a. 8–9 (see especially October–November 1657).

[200] *Thurloe State Papers*, ed. Birch vii. 561; QCA Lamplugh papers, document cited above, p. 768 n. 195; TCA register A, fos 86ᵛ, 88–90; Pope, *Life of Seth Ward*, 47–8.

[201] QCA register H, p. 155.   [202] WCA MS 2/1, pp. 115–16.

[203] NCA MS 9655, fos 45, 53. For the mounting defiance of puritan and Cromwellian rule by New College see NCA MS 9655, fo 51; ibid. MS 1067; ibid. MS 4214 (Long Book 1659: 'service books'). For

In the year before Charles II's return, the stability which Cromwellian rule had given to Oxford disintegrated. England, remarked John Fell with pardonable exaggeration as the chaos grew, was witnessing 'more governments on foot than all Europe has had for centuries of years'.[204] The government of England had reverted to the hands of a divided radical clique, whose rule was unacceptable to the broad body of puritan opinion in the university. In the summer of 1659 Oxford became once more a city under military occupation;[205] royalist conspiracy, now widespread in the nation, penetrated the town and the colleges and won encouragement from the pulpits;[206] the annual Act had to be cancelled;[207] and the heads of house, who during the panic preceding the battle of Worcester in 1651, and again during Penruddock's rising in 1655, had abetted the enlistment of scholars on the government's behalf, now 'stiffly denied' a request by Major-General Desborough and by Owen for a similar show of loyalty.[208] In February 1660 'the news of a free parliament' was greeted in Oxford by bonfires and bellringing, rumps being roasted in Queen's and tossed at the windows of John Palmer, the dying warden of All Souls.[209] In March the Long Parliament, whose return to power extinguished the influence of radicals, dismissed Owen from Christ Church, restored Edward Reynolds to his place, and cancelled all the expulsions, in Oxford and elsewhere, that had been caused by the engagement.[210]

Owen's departure, and that of other Independents in 1659–60, was in the first instance a victory not for royalists but for Presbyterians, who hoped once more for the dominance in Oxford that had eluded them in the 1640s.[211] But the current of royalist feeling bore Presbyterianism before it. In the contest to represent the university in the Convention—the assembly which would restore Charles II—John Fell canvassed openly and tirelessly in the king's cause.[212] Oxford did not merely spurn George Monck's candidate, the Speaker William Lenthall, but turned on those university politicians who had proposed Monck himself in preference to an unambiguously royalist candidate.[213] Soon the puritans were being taunted by the

---

a proposal to re-elect Gilbert Sheldon to the wardenship of All Souls in the spring of 1660 see Longleat House, Thynne MS xii, fos 152, 156.

[204] Longleat House, Thynne MS xii, fo 144.

[205] *CSPD 1659–60*, 52–3, 76, 110, 195; Wood, *Life and Times* i. 288.

[206] *Calendar of Clarendon State Papers*, ed. Ogle iv. 186, 386–7, 399 (cf ibid. 648–9); *CSPD 1659–60*, 242; Wood, *Life and Times* i. 279–80, 368–9; Underdown, *Royalist Conspiracy in England*, 275; Henning, *House of Commons* iii. 493.

[207] OUA register T, pp. 348–9; ibid., register Ta, p. 7.

[208] Wood, *History of the University* ii. 696; PRO SP25/79, p. 438.

[209] Wood, *Life and Times* i. 303–4; Longleat House, Thynne MS xii, fo 150.

[210] *CJ* 3, 12, 13 March 1660. For Reynolds's restoration see also Longleat House, Thynne MS xii, fo 156; CA MS I.B.3, pp. 93–4.

[211] *CJ* 14 March 1660; R. S. Bosher, *The Making of the Restoration Settlement* (London 1951), 127; cf Wood, *History of the University* ii. 697. Departure of other Independents: *CJ* 13 March 1660; Bloxam, *Reg. Magdalen* ii, p. cvii; NCA MS 1067; Bodl. MS Rawlinson d. 912, fo 361.

[212] Longleat House, Thynne MS xii, fos 152–64.

[213] OUA register Ta, pp. 10–12; NCA MS 9655, reverse entries, fo 8; Longleat House, Thynne MS xii, fos 152–64; Wood, *Life and Times* i. 311–13.

erection of maypoles.[214] When the king at last returned in May, Oxford was 'perfectly mad', its rejoicing greater than that of 'any place of its bigness'.[215] Even so, the royalists who rapidly took over the university found it in serious disarray. The political turmoil of the previous year had generated a corresponding disorder in Oxford's academic and administrative life.[216] Its problems were compounded by the absence in London of many leading figures eager to attract royal favour or forestall royal wrath.[217] In July the Act, which Oxford's puritan rulers had so often been unable to hold, was cancelled by its royalist ones on account of 'the present discomposure' of the university.[218]

Cromwellian Oxford is the Oxford of the young Anthony Wood. Had it not been for Wood's antiquarian zest and his preservation of documents, the history of puritan rule could scarcely be written. Even so he can be a misleading guide. That is partly because his grasp of party alignments is uncertain. More fundamentally it is because of his taste for caricature. He misrepresents not only puritans but the royalist survivors whom he despised as time-servers. Sometimes his retrospective accounts of Cromwellian Oxford are less revealing than the notes and diaries which he kept in the 1650s and on which his later compilations drew. Not least, those earlier documents suggest a university less sharply polarized, and more alive to its common humanity, than that portrayed by the older Wood. In the 1650s the high point of Wood's week was the regular musical session where the 'natural and insatiable genie he had to musick' found its outlet. The company with whom he played included intruded puritans, hardened royalists, and a Roman Catholic.[219] In their spirited gatherings a wrong political or ecclesiastical opinion was a less serious offence than a wrong note. Even in a time of revolution, national events may not be the most pressing preoccupation of students and scholars. The partisan loyalties of puritans and royalists, deep and socially divisive as they often were, were time and again softened or sublimated by common enthusiasms, by scholarly collaboration, or by private kindness. The allegiances of church and state did not stop Gerard Langbaine from inviting a Presbyterian colleague to baptize his son 'after the new cut, without godfathers'.[220] They did not stop Ralph Bathurst from calling in his fellow-royalist physician Thomas Willis to help him tend Robert Harris, the elderly puritan head of Trinity, that college where 'there was ever a fair correspondency' between the parties.[221]

Wood's restrospective characterizations distort not only Oxford's past but his own. For all the sour toryism of his maturity, he had not been untouched by the puritan influences around him. The friends of his youth included the intruded

[214] Wood, *Life and Times* i. 314.
[215] Ibid. 317; Wood, *History of the University* ii. 697–8.
[216] CA MS I.B.3, p. 102; ibid. MS D.P. I.B.7, fo 8ᵛ; MCA liber computi 1660.
[217] See for example CA MS xii.b.103, p. 4; NCA MS 1073.
[218] OUA register Ta, p. 17; Wood, *Life and Times* i. 320.
[219] Wood, *Life and Times* i. 173, 204–6, 273–5, 316.   [220] *CSPD 1656–7*, 51.
[221] H. E. D. Blakiston, *Trinity College* (London 1898), 139, 146; cf Bloxam, *Reg. Magdalen* ii. 162, 164.

fellows of Lincoln William Sprigge and John Curteyne, in whose company he would mock the return of Anglican ceremonies at the Restoration.[222] Sprigge and Curteyne, it is true, may have been among the jollier of the Cromwellian newcomers. Yet it is not the frivolous Wood who notes appreciatively the funeral sermon given for his brother Edward by Edward's puritan tutor, the Cromwellian visitor Ralph Button. Button's ministrations, Anthony gratefully observed, had helped Edward 'to make a most religious end', an end which Anthony piously described not as death but as 'falling asleep'.[223] It is not the frivolous Wood who is moved by the death of a friend to compose reflections on the 'fraile estate of man' which are conventionally puritan, even predestinarian.[224] Even in later life, as Oxford seemed to him to sink into sloth and debauchery, Wood could find virtues to remember in the earnestness and energy of Cromwellian rule.[225] That is the serious, even sombre side to Wood. Yet even in the 1650s another side is more commonly visible: that of the cheerful young man who is so often in the alehouse; whose 'silly frolicks' include an expedition to Kingston Bagpuize where he and his friends dressed as poor fiddlers to beg for money; and who was led, blushing, to play the violin before an appreciative and convivial audience at John Wilkins's dinner-table.[226] The glimpses of daily existence disclosed by Wood's youthful diaries confirm what our larger story has suggested: that the puritans made a profound impact on Oxford, and that the more they changed it the more it remained the same.

---

[222] Wood, *Life and Times* i. 281, 378; Bodl. MS Wood f. 44, fos 329–37; ibid. MS Wood f. 45, fos 155, 158.

[223] Wood, *Life and Times* i. 197–8, 200; Edward Wood, *That which may be known to God by the Book of Nature* (Oxford 1656), sig. A2ᵛ, cf *Oxford Orations of John Owen*, ed. Toon, 28.

[224] Bodl. MS Wood f. 45, fo 150.

[225] Wood, *Life and Times* i. 300, 360, 422–3, 465, ii. 212.

[226] Ibid. i. 189–90, 257; cf *Diary of John Evelyn*, ed. De Beer iii. 105–6, 110.

16

College Finances, 1640–1660

JOHN TWIGG

THE conventional view of the financial state of the university and its colleges during the English Revolution is clear enough: a period of widespread prosperity before 1642 was followed by sudden collapse in the wartime years, brought about principally by falling, unpaid, and uncollectable rents, sequestrations, unrenewed leases, neglect of property, plunder, and taxation. Conditions then improved gradually during the rest of the decade and throughout the 1650s, so that the university had almost recovered at the Restoration.[1] Such a verdict is unsurprising. The health of college finances depended largely upon income from property, and their changing fortunes are likely to have been similar to those experienced by landlords in general at this time. The experiences of the Cambridge colleges were similar during the civil war, but several were slow to recover thereafter.[2] Illustrations of the developments at Oxford abound, but more systematic analysis is frustrated by the inadequacy of the archival sources. College accounts of the early modern period, which form our principal source material, are often inconsistent and inscrutable, and there are some substantial gaps in the records of the 1640s.[3] As a result, the present survey is uneven and sometimes impressionistic; however, all the existing evidence supports the broad hypothesis outlined above.[4]

The prosperity of many of the Oxford colleges in the early seventeenth century

I am grateful to the many people who have assisted me in various ways during the researching and writing of this essay: the late Mr T. H. Aston, Professor G. E. Aylmer, Mr H. M. Colvin, Mrs C. M. Dalton, Dr J. R. Glynn, Dr J. H. Jones, Mr J. Newman, Dr D. J. Osler, Mrs B. Parry-Jones, Mr R. Peedell, Mr D. A. Rees, Mr J. S. G. Simmons, Mrs Topliffe, Dr N. Tyacke, Miss R. F. Vyse, and Mrs J. Wells.

[1] These developments are noted briefly by G. E. Aylmer, 'The economics and finances of the colleges and university *c* 1530–1640' in *The Collegiate University*, 557–8.

[2] For Oxford college finances in general see ibid. 521–58; G. D. Duncan, 'The property of Balliol College *c* 1540–*c* 1640' and G. D. Duncan, 'An introduction to the accounts of Corpus Christi College' in *The Collegiate University*, 559–73, 574–96. For landlords in general during the mid seventeenth-century revolution see C. Clay, 'Landlords and estate management in England' in J. Thirsk (ed.), *The Agrarian History of England and Wales* v *1640–1750* (2 pts Cambridge 1984–5) pt 2, pp. 119–32. For the Cambridge colleges see J. D. Twigg, *The University of Cambridge and the English Revolution, 1625–1688* (Woodbridge 1990), 85–6, 137–46, 202–4.

[3] For the difficulties of interpretation in general see Aylmer, 'Economics and finances', 524–9, 532, 545; J. P. D. Dunbabin, 'College estates and wealth 1660–1815' in *The Eighteenth Century*, 270–2.

[4] I regret not having had time to explore the archives of every college, but my experience of colleges at both Oxford and Cambridge suggests that further exploration would not have altered the picture substantially.

has been widely reported and is generally accepted.[5] But such prosperity could be fragile. Merton College is said to have been in a healthy economic position on the eve of the civil war, but at his visitation there in 1638–41 Archbishop Laud expressed concern over the college's lax financial administration.[6] At Lincoln College in 1631 the bursars were made personally liable for college debts contracted during their year of office, after the college had 'beene much damnified' by 'the great negligence of some former bursar'. In 1637 University College required each bursar to have two sponsors to guarantee against any losses he might incur.[7] In a letter to the president of Magdalen College in the mid-1630s the visitor, the bishop of Winchester, counselled that profligacy in times of plenty would leave the college without resources to cope with any 'unhappy accidents, or occasions that may befall [it]', and he offered some sound but very elementary advice about the ordering of its financial affairs, including

First that none of the colledge rents, by any ... negligence or default be suffered to decay, but that all good meanes may be speedily and effectually used, for the getting in of all such debts, as shall at any time be owing and unpaid ... Secondly for your expences, that all provisions for the colledge, may be made at the best rate, that the towne and markett can afford[8]

Such precautions were intended to be a safeguard against corruption as well as mismanagement. Fellows were under strong temptation to enrich themselves rather than their colleges, and the modern concept of college corporate wealth was unknown to them: the purpose of collegiate income in this period was to benefit the fellows by dividing corn rents and the spoils of irregular sources such as entry fines and sales of timber among themselves. If the college made a profit on its annual accounts, the fellows expected the surplus to go into this dividend.[9] Colleges tended not to accumulate large cash reserves against bad years, therefore, and so the balance between prosperity and financial adversity was easily tipped. A striking example of what could happen when negligence and self-interest gained the upper hand is provided by Brasenose College, which was nearly £1,750 in debt by 1643. Here outstanding rents and battels bills had not been collected, college property had been alienated, and there had been irregularities in the issuing of leases, the levying and division of fines, and the calculation of corn rents. Some of

---

    [5] Aylmer, 'Economics and finances', 530–44, 548–50. For individual colleges see for example H. E. D. Blakiston, *Trinity College* (London 1898), 127; W. K. Stride, *Exeter College* (London 1900), 56–8; M. Burrows, *Worthies of All Souls* (London 1874), 110; C. E. Mallet, *A History of the University of Oxford* (3 vols London 1924–7) ii. 202; Costin, *St. John's*, 97; P. Williams, 'From reformation to the era of reform 1530–1850' in J. Buxton and P. Williams (eds), *New College Oxford 1379–1979* (Oxford 1979), 53; V. H. H. Green, *The Commonwealth of Lincoln College 1427–1977* (Oxford 1979), 244.

    [6] G. C. Brodrick, *Memorials of Merton College* (OHS iv 1885), 74 n. 3, 82; B. W. Henderson, *Merton College* (London 1899), 96–7, 102–3, 109–14; *CSPD 1639–40*, 509–10.

    [7] LCM A. 1. 2, fo 71; W. Carr, *University College* (London 1902), 106.

    [8] MCA MS 730(a), fo 91. The manuscript is defective: the list tails off at this point.

    [9] The best explanation of this concept is by C. N. L. Brooke, *A History of Gonville and Caius College* (Woodbridge 1985), 102–3. For corn rents, dividends, and frauds at Oxford see Aylmer, 'Economics and finances', 524, 527–31, 537–40.

the fellows laid the blame squarely at the door of the principal, Samuel Radcliffe, but there must have been collusion among a section of the fellowship for the college's financial condition to have been allowed to sink so low: its debts had been mounting for about eighteen years.[10]

The most immediate consequence of the outbreak of war in the summer of 1642 was the elimination of such limited university and college cash reserves as there were, leaving nothing to fall back on in the hard times to follow. The king asked both universities and their colleges in July 1642 for the loan of as much money as they could send and received an enthusiastic response from Oxford, which apparently produced over £10,000 (including loans from individual college members, which are mostly indistinguishable within their colleges' corporate donations).[11] These contributions, where known, are itemized in table 16.1. Some colleges gave more than ready cash. University College pawned plate; Balliol College voted to pay part of its donation out of caution money; Magdalen College borrowed just over half of its contribution of £1,000 from the president and one of the fellows, to be repaid by selling plate and, if necessary, out of college receipts; St John's College left itself without any money to pay outstanding debts on its new buildings.[12]

In January 1643, the royalists having made their headquarters at Oxford, the king wrote again asking the colleges for the loan of their plate, for which they would be repaid in cash at a set rate per ounce.[13] The idea may have been mooted the previous summer. Certainly some plate was sent from Cambridge in August 1642 and parliament took steps to ensure that none reached the king from Oxford at that time.[14] Lord Saye, commander of the parliamentary force which occupied Oxford in September, confiscated plate from Christ Church and University College because it had been concealed from him, but he allowed the other colleges to keep theirs 'upon condition it should be forthcoming at the parliament's appointment, and not in the least employed against them'.[15]

The colleges' response to the royal request in January was again enthusiastic and

[10] BNCA visitation 1643. Debts due to brewers, bakers, and others were said to comprise about £1,400 of this and only some £350 was due to the college's loan to the king and 'the necessities of the times'. See also G. H. Wakeling, 'The history of the college 1603–1660', *Brasenose Monographs* xi. 61–4.

[11] There is a copy of the royal letter in MCA MS 730(a), fo 96; I. Roy and D. Reinhart, 'Oxford and the civil wars', pp. 694–5 above. But contemporaries also believed that Cambridge had been equally generous, which was very wide of the mark: *CSPD 1641–3*, 359; Edward Hyde, earl of Clarendon, *The History of the Rebellion and Civil Wars in England begun in the year 1641*, ed. W. D. Macray (6 vols Oxford 1888) ii. 409; F. J. Varley, *Cambridge during the Civil War, 1642–6* (Cambridge 1935), 75; Twigg, *University of Cambridge*, 70–1.

[12] Carr, *University College*, 107; BCA treasury book 1637–89, 3–4; BCA plate records 2; MCA MS 730(a), fos 96–7; H. A. Wilson, *Magdalen College* (London 1899), 152; Costin, *St. John's*, 103. All Souls borrowed £300, the amount owed to the college treasury in outstanding debts: Burrows, *Worthies*, 167.

[13] Macleane, *Pembroke*, 127–8; *Dean's Register of Oriel*, 297–8; ECA A. I. 6, fo 30; MCA MS 730(a), fo 97; Wood, *Life and Times* i. 81.

[14] Clarendon, *History of the Rebellion* ii. 330 n. 2, 331; Twigg, *University of Cambridge*, 71–6; Burrows, *Worthies*, 167–8; *CJ* ii. 666–7; *LJ* v. 205, 208.

[15] Wood, *History of the University* ii. 450, 452; Wood, *Life and Times* i. 61–4; Burrows, *Worthies*, 167; Carr, *University College*, 107–8; W. G. Hiscock, *A Christ Church Miscellany* (Oxford 1946), 137–8.

TABLE 16.1 *College contributions to the king, 1642–3*

College	Amount lent (£ s d)
All Souls	654. 14. 3.
Balliol	210
Brasenose	500 + 100 (Christmas 1642)
Christ Church	unknown
Corpus	400
Exeter	310
Jesus	100
Lincoln	unknown
Magdalen	1,000
Merton	400 (probably in the summer)
New College	unknown
Oriel	unknown
Pembroke	8. 17. 0.
Queen's	800
St John's	800
Trinity	200 (November 1642)
University College	150
Wadham	100
Oxford University	860 + 300 (January 1643)
TOTAL	6,893. 11. 3.

Sources: Robertson, *All Souls*, 116–17; Burrows, *Worthies*, 167; ASA c. 265, Jocalia 11; Davis, *Balliol*, 117; Jones, *Balliol*, 103; BCA treasury book 1637–89, 3–4; Wakeling, 'History of the college', 31–2; Butler, 'College plate', 30; BNCA college—loan to Charles I (Hurst, xxxv); BNCA bursarial—money. 1 (Hurst, xxxii); Walker, *Sufferings of the Clergy*, 229–30; Milne, *Corpus Christi*, 70; *Registrum Collegii Exoniensis* ed. C. W. Boase (OHS xxvii 1894), p. cxiv; Stride, *Exeter*, 60; JCA I. arch. 4. 21; Wilson, *Magdalen*, 152; MCA MS 730(a), fos 96ʳ⁻ᵛ; *Register*, ed. Burrows, 252–3, 282–4; Macleane, *Pembroke*, 222; R. H. Hodgkin, *Six Centuries of an Oxford College: a history of the Queen's College 1340–1940* (Oxford 1949), 98; Costin, *St. John's*, 103; Wood, *Life and Times* i. 81, 94 and n., 95; Blakiston, *Trinity*, 131; Carr, *University College*, 107; Wells, *Wadham*, 56; Wood, *History of the University* ii. 439, 458; OUA register Sb, pp. 7, 14; OUA SP/F/40 (41); J. Ashburnham, *A Narrative by John Ashburnham of his attendance on King Charles the first from Oxford to the Scotch army, and from Hampton-Court to the Isle of Wight* (2 vols London 1830) ii, appx, pp. viii–x, xv. The table includes some money given shortly afterwards, for example by Brasenose and Trinity later in 1642, and the donation from Merton, the date of which is unknown but seems to have been at some time during that year. Some private contributions are recorded with these corporate donations. Christ Church is said to have lent the crown £60 in 1645: *CSPD 1645–7*, 149. There is a similar table in T. E. Reinhart, 'The parliamentary visitation of Oxford University, 1646–1652' (Brown University Ph. D. thesis 1984), 199–201, which differs from this in some details.

a large amount was collected, as shown in table 16.2; there were also some individual donations. It appears that every college gave at least some of its silver, although the full details are unclear in a few cases. The university also loaned some plate held (and owned) by it on behalf of the halls.[16] Some was kept back: it was generally accepted, for example, that communion plate should be exempt, as well as items of particular historic value such as founders' donations.[17] There was also some demur: St John's asked the crown 'to assign a considerable parte of this plate to bee coined for the proper use of the college' in paying off its building debts, to which the king assented readily. Pembroke College was rumoured to have hidden some silver, and Corpus Christi College tried to redeem its plate with a money payment.[18] The only open resistance came from Exeter College, which pleaded poverty due to its earlier loan of money and invoked college statutes forbidding the alienation of plate; but the crown's irate response soon brought the college into line. In fact the royal letter of request to the colleges had specifically dispensed with any statutes against such alienation, and there are also examples of colleges selling silver in peacetime to pay for repairs and improvements.[19] The care with which the fellows of Exeter College recorded details of their loan reveals their wholly justifiable anxiety that they would not be repaid, the royal promise to the contrary notwithstanding, and a few other colleges continued to enter their loans of both money and silver in their records long after there was any hope of redress. At All Souls College this continued into the middle of the eighteenth century, presumably as a memorial to the college's loyalty.[20] More significantly, in the short term the colleges found themselves without capital resources at the moment when they were needed most, as the crippling effects of the civil war on their incomes became apparent.

The war soon cut colleges off from many of their properties, whose tenants were either unable to pay their rents or took advantage of the situation to avoid doing so. Colleges exercised direct control of their properties by means of progresses, that is to say visitations, usually during the summer months, to renew leases, hear

[16] The colleges concerned are Corpus Christi, New College, and Pembroke: Wood, *History of the University* ii. 458; Mallet, *University of Oxford* ii. 279 and n. 5, 355 n. 6, 356; C. Oman, 'The college plate' in Buxton and Williams (eds), *New College*, 299–300; J. G. Milne, *The Early History of Corpus Christi College Oxford* (Oxford 1946), 70–3; Fowler, *Corpus*, 200; Macleane, *Pembroke*, 222, 281; D. Macleane, *Pembroke College* (London 1900), 126–7. The university's donation is recorded in OUA register of convocation 1642–7, NEP/*supra*/25, register Sb, p. 7, but the exact amount is not known.

[17] Wood, *Life and Times* i. 94 and n., 95; J. Wells, *Wadham College* (London 1898), 56–7; H. W. C. Davis, *A History of Balliol College* (Oxford 1963), 117; J. H. Jones, *Balliol College: a history 1263–1939* (Oxford 1988), 103; Blakiston, *Trinity*, 132; A. J. Butler, 'The college plate', *Brasenose Monographs* v. 3–7; C. G. Robertson, *All Souls* (London 1899), 222–3; Wilson, *Magdalen*, 154; Stride, *Exeter*, 60; Oman, 'College plate', 300; *Dean's Register of Oriel*, 297–8; ECA A. I. 6, fos 32ʳ⁻ᵛ.

[18] Costin, *St. John's*, 103; Milne, *Corpus Christi*, 70–3; Fowler, *Corpus*, 200; Macleane, *Pembroke*, 222, 281; Macleane, *Pembroke College*, 126–7; Mallet, *University of Oxford* ii. 279 and n. 5.

[19] ECA A. I. 6, fos 30ᵛ⁻3; ECA C. II. 8; Stride, *Exeter*, 60 and n; LCM A. 1. 2, fos 83ᵛ⁻4; *Dean's Register of Oriel*, 296.

[20] ECA A. I. 6, fos 32ᵛ⁻3; ECA C. II. 8; BNCA bursarial—money. 1; Wakeling, 'History of the college', 33–4; BCA benefactions I (1636–76); Robertson, *All Souls*, 117–19; W. Blackstone, *Dissertation on the Accounts of All Souls College Oxford* (London 1898), 17.

TABLE 16.2 *College loans of plate to the king, January 1643* (lb. oz. dwt.)

All Souls	253. 1. 19
Balliol	41. 4. 0
	+67. 5. 8 (April 1643)
Brasenose	121. 2. 15
Christ Church	172. 3. 14
Corpus	unknown
Exeter	246. 5. 1
Jesus	86. 11. 5
Lincoln	47. 2. 5
Magdalen	296. 6. 15
Merton	79. 11. 10
New College	unknown
Oriel	82. 0. 19
Pembroke	unknown
Queen's	193. 3. 1
St John's	224. 12. 0
Trinity	174. 7. 10
University College	61. 6. 5
Wadham	123. 5. 15
TOTAL	2,270. 10. 2

Sources: ASA c. 265, Jocalia 12; Robertson, *All Souls,* 117–19; Burrows, *Worthies,* 173 and n. 3; *Collectanea curiosa,* ed. J. Gutch (2 vols Oxford 1781) i. 227; Davis, *Balliol,* 117, 289–90, 292; Jones, *Balliol,* ch. 10; BCA plate records 2; BCA treasury book 1637–89, 4; Wakeling, 'History of the college', 53; Butler, 'College plate', 24–7; Milne, *Corpus Christi,* 70; Fowler, *Corpus,* 200; Wood, *Life and Times* i. 94 and n., 95; H. C. Moffat, *Old Oxford Plate* (London 1906), p. x; ECA A. I. 6, fos 32ᵛ–3; ECA C. II. 8; Hardy, *Jesus,* 106; Green, *Lincoln,* 246; Wilson, *Magdalen,* 154; MCA MS 730(a), fo 97; Henderson, *Merton,* 119; Oman, 'College plate', 300; Macleane, *Pembroke,* 222, 281; Costin, *St. John's,* 103; Blakiston, *Trinity,* 132; Carr, *University College,* 108; Wells, *Wadham,* 56–7. Table 2 includes some plate from Balliol given subsequently, in April 1643. There is a similar table in Reinhart, 'Parliamentary visitation', 262, which differs from this in some details. For some individual donations see Burrows, *Worthies,* 173–4; ASA c. 265, Jocalia 12; Carr, *University College,* 107–8. Walker claimed that some scholars contributed money at this time, but there is no other evidence of this: Walker, *Sufferings of the Clergy,* 232.

complaints, and generally check that tenants were observing the conditions under which property had been let to them.[21] Many factors might influence the efficacy

[21] The records of the progresses of Michael Woodward, warden of New College, provide an excellent illustration: 'The annual progress of New College by Michael Woodward—warden 1659–1675', ed. G. Eland, *Records of Buckinghamshire* xiii (1934–40), 77–137; 'The progress notes of Warden Woodward round the Oxfordshire estates of New College, Oxford 1659–1675', ed. R. L. Rickard, *Oxford Record Society Publications* xxvii (1949); 'The progress notes of Warden Woodward 1659–1675 and other

of these progresses as an instrument of control, not least the personal abilities of the college officials (usually bursars) who undertook them, but visits had to be made regularly to be truly effective. From the very start of the war progresses were abandoned. All Souls College had visited between two and three major estates a year between the financial years 1638/9 and 1640/1, but only one was visited in 1641/2, and none at all in the years 1642/3 to 1645/6. Progresses were resumed normally in 1646/7, though one Welsh estate did not receive a visit until 1651/2. There were no progresses from Brasenose College in the years 1642/3 to 1644/5; they began again in 1645/6. New College seems to have been similarly disrupted and did not resume normal contact with its estates, many of which were relatively near, until 1646. Jesus College stopped visiting its property in 1642/3 and the accounts contain no further expenditure on progresses until 1649. In general, routine estate management was fully restored by the early 1650s.[22]

Rental income from college properties—the principal component of their income overall—began to fall rapidly from the start of the war. Some impression of this and of its consequences is given in table 16.3, though the surviving accounts are deficient for some of the crucial years of the period, and some of the figures given here are ambiguous and require careful explanation to be understood properly. Precise statistical comparisons are not feasible, for there are significant differences in the accounting procedures used by the individual colleges.

At first sight the colleges' accounts appear somewhat inscrutable, but they are capable of interpretation. The columns for rental income appear particularly confusing, for in several accounts rental income is shown to remain relatively steady throughout the period. This is because only the notional rental income is shown, irrespective of the amounts actually collected. In such cases, the figures for the colleges' total incomes often reflect the real situation more accurately; but even these occasionally repeat the practice of entering only notional receipts, and in such cases the college expenditure accounts, with unpaid rents entered as debits, will show substantial increases despite the many austerity measures introduced by the colleges during the war years. The final columns containing the annual resolutions of the accounts generally demonstrate the outcome.

Allowing for these complications, as well as for individual variations between colleges in the extent to which they were affected, the figures do supply a broad impression of the acute financial crisis which the collapse of college income, especially rental income, brought about. Colleges were running increasingly into debt as their rent arrears mounted. Their economies were always finely balanced and it

17th-century documents relating to the Norfolk property of New College, Oxford', ed. R. L. Rickard, *Norfolk Record Society* xxii (1951), 85–115; 'Progress notes of Warden Woodward for the Wiltshire estates of New College, Oxford 1659–1675', ed. R. L. Rickard, *Wiltshire Archaeological and Natural History Society* xiii (1957).

[22] ASA c. 296, c. 297; BNCA bursar's rolls 1642–8 (all *sub anno*); BNCA A2. 43, 10–11, B1d. 36; NCA 988, entries for 1650 and following years; NCA 3509, 57–9, 4206, 7672, entry for 1646, 7674, entry for 1653, 7675, entry for 1653, 7677, entry for 1655/6, 11,704, letter from Mr Hippsley to Warden Pincke, September 1647; JCA bursar's accounts 1631–53, *sub anno*.

TABLE 16.3 *Colleges' annual accounts (£)*

Financial year	Rental income	Total income	Expenses	Resolution
		ALL SOULS		
1638/9	1,751	2,677	1,697	980
1639/40	1,688	2,291	1,778	513
1640/1	1,776	2,440	1,985	455
1641/2	1,581	2,086	2,343	−257
1642/3	1,717	1,907	1,443	464
1643/4	1,582	1,697	—	—
1644/5	1,774	1,836	—	—
1645/6	1,970	2,606	—	—
1646/7	2,349	2,602	—	—
1647/8	1,330	2,315	3,138	−823
1648/9	—	—	—	—
1649/50	1,304	1,664	2,306	−642
1650/1	—	—	—	—
1651/2	1,793	2,113	2,204	−91
1652/3	1,537	3,217	3,096	121
1653/4	1,342	2,000	1,937	63
1654/5	1,554	2,719	2,915	−196
1655/6	1,779	2,349	2,330	19
1656/7	1,915	2,575	—	—
1657/8	2,240	2,594	2,521	73
1658/9	2,405	3,075	3,030	45
1659/60	2,101	2,603	—	—
1660/1	2,071	2,218	—	—
		BALLIOL		
1638/9	256	515	332	183
1639/40	243	508	271	237
1640/1	241	506	230	276
1641/2	241	481	247	234
1642/3	241	332	208	124
1643/4	241	434	—	—
1644/5	241	—	—	—
1645/6	—	—	—	—
1646/7	—	—	—	—
1647/8	—	—	—	—
1648/9	—	—	—	—
1649/50	—	—	—	—
1650/1	—	—	—	—
1651/2	234	394	319	75

Financial year	Rental income	Total income	Expenses	Resolution
1652/3	234	399	325	74
1653/4	234	398	336	62
1654/5	198	336	286	50
1655/6	198	394	322	72
1656/7	198	414	336	78
1657/8	199	411	339	72
1658/9	198	407	384	23
1659/60	198	380	343	37
1660/1	198	398	332	66
		BRASENOSE		
1638/9	—	1,337	1,307	30
1639/40	—	1,262	1,247	15
1640/1	—	—	—	—
1641/2	—	1,182	1,296	−114
1642/3	869	1,247	1,584	−337
1643/4	1,136	1,495	2,113	−618
1644/5	1,602	2,005	3,005	−1,000
1645/6	2,180	2,647	3,861	−1,214
1646/7	2,620	3,220	4,215	−995
1647/8	2,467	3,102	2,830	272
1648/9	2,106	2,747	2,814	−67
1649/50	2,228	2,931	2,342	589
1650/1	1,546	2,055	1,940	115
1651/2	1,367	1,906	1,868	38
1652/3	1,414	1,820	1,668	152
1653/4	1,362	1,667	1,545	122
1654/5	1,350	1,785	1,755	30
1655/6	1,430	1,892	1,832	60
1656/7	1,368	1,889	1,908	−19
1657/8	1,386	2,013	1,973	40
1658/9	1,349	2,082	2,042	40
1659/60	1,350	1,935	1,977	−42
1660/1	1,363	2,028	2,003	25
		EXETER		
1638/9	—	—	—	—
1639/40	—	578	481	97
1640/1	—	581	494	87
1641/2	—	488	466	22

TABLE 16.3 *cont.*

Financial year	Rental income	Total income	Expenses	Resolution
1642/3	—	598	592	6
1643/4	—	310	306	4
1644/5	—	256	261	−5
1645/6	—	261	242	19
1646/7	—	622	551	71
1647/8	—	—	—	—
1648/9	—	—	—	—
1649/50	—	—	—	—
1650/1	—	—	—	—
1651/2	—	—	—	—
1652/3	—	589	658	−69
1653/4	—	535	625	−90
1654/5	—	508	573	−65
1655/6	—	626	718	−92
1656/7	—	580	688	−108
1657/8	—	—	—	—
1658/9	—	—	—	—
1659/60	—	—	—	—
1660/1	—	—	—	—
		JESUS		
1638/9	—	—	—	—
1639/40	—	746	620	126
1640/1	—	731	631	100
1641/2	—	444	438	6
1642/3	—	95	341	−246
1643/4	—	—	—	—
1644/5	—	—	—	—
1645/6	—	—	—	—
1646/7	—	—	—	—
1647/8	—	—	—	—
1648/9	—	267	353	−86
1649/50	—	110	318	−208
1650/1	—	—	—	—
1651/2	—	—	—	—
1652/3	—	467	417	50
1653/4	—	361	468	−107
1654/5	—	446	415	31
1655/6	—	513	526	−13
1656/7	—	551	537	14

Financial year	Rental income	Total income	Expenses	Resolution
1657/8	—	452	487	−35
1658/9	—	516	519	−3
1659/60	—	—	—	—
1660/1	—	403	393	10

		MAGDALEN		
1638/9	—	3,575	3,204	371
1639/40	—	3,486	3,086	400
1640/1	—	3,439	2,951	488
1641/2	—	3,135	3,028	107
1642/3	—	2,990	2,892	98
1643/4	—	—	—	—
1644/5	—	3,368	3,384	−16
1645/6	—	3,974	3,428	546
1646/7	—	5,348	3,801	1,547
1647/8	—	—	—	—
1648/9	—	4,714	3,345	1,369
1649/50	—	5,126	4,109	1,017
1650/1	—	4,484	4,227	257
1651/2	—	4,502	3,981	521
1652/3	—	4,431	3,890	541
1653/4	—	3,633	3,422	211
1654/5	—	3,915	3,870	45
1655/6	—	4,510	3,940	570
1656/7	—	4,466	4,328	138
1657/8	—	5,221	4,015	1,206
1658/9	—	5,588	4,268	1,320
1659/60	—	4,586	3,993	593
1660/1	—	—	—	—

		NEW COLLEGE		
1638/9	—	—	—	—
1639/40	2,875	4,310	3,458	852
1640/1	2,903	4,156	3,293	863
1641/2	2,085	5,114	3,278	1,836
1642/3	1,861	—	—	—
1643/4	1,059	1,877	2,142	−265
1644/5	—	—	—	—
1645/6	—	—	—	—
1646/7	—	4,803	4,061	742

TABLE 16.3 *cont.*

Financial year	Rental income	Total income	Expenses	Resolution
1647/8	—	—	—	—
1648/9	—	—	3,350	—
1649/50	—	—	3,104	—
1650/1	—	—	—	—
1651/2	—	2,881	—	—
1652/3	2,600	2,837	2,827	10
1653/4	2,782	2,896	2,883	13
1654/5	2,451	2,475	2,439	36
1655/6	2,941	2,977	2,825	152
1656/7	2,842	3,125	2,891	234
1657/8	3,233	3,542	2,809	733
1658/9	2,141	2,685	2,336	349
1659/60	3,119	3,618	3,299	319
1660/1	—	—	—	—

Sources: ASA c. 296, c. 297; BCA computi (1615–62); BNCA bursar's rolls, vols xxi–xxiv; ECA A. II. 10; JCA bursar's accounts 1631–53, 1651–69; MCA libri computi; NCA 7661–7681 (all *sub anno*). Precise amounts are not easily obtained, and sometimes conflicting sums appear; on these occasions I have employed those which seem the most plausible or consistent. Most of the gaps are due to missing accounts, but some are due to the totals for that year not being easily computable. In some colleges the calculations begin and conclude at different dates. The totals are better regarded as relative rather than absolute amounts. The university's accounts show a similar sharp decline in income: OUA WP/β/21/4, *sub anno*.

was impossible for them to reduce expenditure by the same amount as their falling incomes.

Other, more straightforward, evidence confirms this picture. Balliol College blamed its financial difficulties in the later 1660s partly on 'a continuall and irrecoverable losse or defalcation of its most considerable rents, on the borders of Scotland, during the late troubles', which had begun with Charles I's war against the Scots in 1639.[23] Martin Aylworth, the experienced and capable bursar of All Souls College, wrote to Francis Mansell, principal of Jesus College, in December 1644 that: 'Wee are now at our accompts, and all our wealth doth consist in *tribus billis* [arrears]'. All Souls, which owned a good deal of property in parts of southern and eastern England under parliamentary control, had a total debt of £3,468 by 1645/6 and a substantial proportion of the college's income was taken up by

[23] BCA benefactions I (1636–76), loose sheets inserted at front; Henry Savage, *Balliofergus, or a Commentary upon the Foundation, Founders and Affaires, of Balliol Colledge* (Oxford 1668), 24; Davis, *Balliol,* 115. See also Jones, *Balliol,* 103. The arrears recorded in the 1650s are not abnormal, but there are no records of arrears from the 1640s in the college: BCA arrears book (1650–78), 9–24, arrears book (1651–90).

debt repayments.[24] None of the tenants of Jesus College paid in their rents in 1643; and between 1644 and 1648 the college received less than half of what was due from rents, rent charges, and gifts.[25] Christ Church was only able to pay £2,010 of its £4,227 of scheduled disbursements for 1643/4. Outgoings were reduced considerably in the following year, to £3,688, but the college paid out less than £1,300 of this.[26] Oriel College postponed its annual audit on several occasions during the war years and afterwards because its rents had not come in and the accounts could not therefore be completed; by 1645 its financial problems were reckoned to be very serious. Exeter College is known to have had difficulty in collecting its rent arrears, which rose from £39 in 1640/1 to £346 in 1643/4 and £749 in 1645/6. The rent arrears at New College were £575 in 1642 and £4,731 in 1645, rising still higher in the following year.[27] St John's College was owed £1,910 in 1645, and in 1649 its intruded president, Francis Cheynell, pointed out that 'as the fairest part of our college revenues doth arise out of impropriations, it may easily be conjectured how negligent men are in paying ecclesiastical dues now tithes are generally decried by such as take more care to save their purses than their soules'. Magdalen College, despite the appearance of relative prosperity given in the table of its annual accounts, was said to be £1,600 in debt by 1648. Trinity College had rents and battels arrears totalling nearly £1,400 in 1651. Arrears of rent owed to the university increased eightfold between 1642/3 and 1646/7.[28] While the war lasted the colleges had no hope of gathering in many of their outstanding rents on their own, especially those for lands in areas where there was fighting, or which could only be reached by passing through war zones.

There was also parliament's attitude to contend with. In March 1644 the House of Commons ordered university and college tenants to retain their rents until further order. In October it was decided that tenants should pay their rents to their respective county committees. At the same time John Selden, one of the university's representatives in parliament, was instructed to prepare an ordinance for its rents. The ordinance was discussed occasionally during 1645, but did not come to anything at that time.[29] The articles for the surrender of Oxford in June 1646 included the provision that university members were to enjoy

all their rights etc. (except such rents and revenues as have been already taken and received by ordinance of parliament) ... free from sequestrations, fines, taxes, and all other molestations whatsoever for or under colour of anything whatsoever relating to this present war or to the unhappy differences between his majesty and the parliament.[30]

[24] ASA c. 297, *sub anno*; JCA I. arch. 4. 21. The term *tribus billis* is explained in Blackstone, *Accounts of All Souls*, 18.

[25] E. G. Hardy, *Jesus College* (London 1899), 103; JCA Mansell's inventory (1648–9), fos 15–19, 33–42ᵛ.

[26] CA xii. b. 87, xii. b. 88 (both *sub anno*).

[27] *Dean's Register of Oriel*, 297–9, 301–2, 307, 312–13, 320; Stride, *Exeter*, 61; ECA A. II. 10; NCA 1207 (all *sub anno*).

[28] Costin, *St. John's*, 97–102, 107, 113; Wilson, *Magdalen*, 170; Blakiston, *Trinity*, 131; OUA vice-chancellor's accounts 1547–1666, WP/β/21/4 (*sub anno*).

[29] *CJ* iii. 432, 662, iv. 122, 273.

[30] *Register*, ed. Burrows, p. lvi.

Yet some university men remained uneasy. Samuel Fell, dean of Christ Church, wrote after the siege of 'tenants combining with our county committees' to avoid paying their rents, and the university lobbied hard in London for its dues, apparently with some success, for in November the parliamentary committee for the reformation of the university ordered college tenants to pay their arrears and in January 1647 the committee for complaints touching breach of articles ordered tenants to pay rents and arrears as laid down by the articles of surrender.[31] Yet Magdalen College was still awaiting £700 from the committee for Lincolnshire in 1650.[32]

Without official support arrears were likely to remain uncollected for a long while. The difficulties are well illustrated by the experiences of the university in collecting its own rents. In 1644 it empowered attorneys 'to ask demaund require leavy implead sue receive and take all and every the rents and arrerages of rents and other dutyes and services whatsoever', and to re-enter property if necessary to enforce these demands. At that time it was a hollow threat and numerous similar letters of attorney were issued during the following years with little success. It was not until 1649 that the threat of legal action began to recover arrears on any significant scale and the university was still suing for pre-1648 arrears in 1653.[33]

Some of the colleges were also beginning to take a firmer line with their tenants by this time. All Souls College began to seek its arrears soon after the end of the siege, but it is not clear how much success it met with. In 1649 the committee for the advance of money authorized the summoning of two tenants of Exeter College to explain their refusal to pay their arrears; again, the outcome is unknown.[34] New College was enforcing its rights vigorously in 1650 and afterwards, re-entering property on occasion, and Brasenose College also seems to have been more forceful at this time; these processes may well have begun in the late 1640s, but the records at both colleges are deficient for this period. Stern measures did not always achieve the desired result: George Bradshaw, the intruded master of Balliol College, imprisoned the college's tenant at Old Woodstock in Oxfordshire for non-payment of over two and a half years' rent worth about £250, but the tenant died in the Bocardo and so the debt was lost.[35] In some cases it must have been simpler to write the debts off completely or in part. Some colleges had to make deductions from their tenants' rents because of the latter's losses through wartime taxation,

---

[31] OUA WP/γ/16/1/19, WP/γ/16/1/21; Wood, *History of the University* ii. 487; Costin, *St. John's*, 100; SJM register iii, between pp. 376 and 377 (I am grateful to Mr H. M. Colvin for looking up this manuscript source for me); *CSPD 1645–7*, 518. See also OUA WP/γ/16/2/104.

[32] Wilson, *Magdalen*, 170. The committees do not appear to have been irresponsible in looking after college rents. The house of commons ordered a few payments out of the rents to university men exiled during the royalist occupation because of their loyalty to parliament: *CJ* iii. 649, iv. 347, 355, 368, 515.

[33] OUA register Sb, pp. 59, 50x, 57x–8x, 68–9, 93, 96–7, 100–1, 115, 125, 152–5; OUA register of convocation 1647–59, NEP/*supra*/26, register T, pp. 23–4, 26–8, 40–2, 50–3, 61, 75, 78, 83, 85–6, 92, 180.

[34] ASA c. 297, entry for 1646/7; *Calendar of the Proceedings of the Committee for Advance of Money, 1642–1656* (London 1888), 74.

[35] NCA 988; BNCA Bld. 36 (both *sub anno*); BCA lease log book (1588–1850), 138.

free quarter and other war damage. Such deductions were significant, but their full extent cannot be gauged.[36] The extent to which colleges were able to recover their arrears remains a mystery.

Rent collection was rendered even more difficult by sequestrations. Colleges often found the income from their property illegally sequestered because of their tenants' royalism during the civil war. The extent of this problem is also unquantifiable. There are numerous examples of colleges petitioning for their rents, and the petitions appear to have been treated sympathetically in the main. But it was sometimes a protracted procedure—some money was not collected until well into the 1650s—and though the sums detained varied enormously they could be substantial, running into hundreds of pounds.[37]

The visitors appointed by parliament to reform the university after the siege was ended were anxious to rescue rents from sequestrations.[38] But they in turn faced obstructions to rent collection of a new kind, from ejected royalist fellows. A parliamentary ordinance in 1648 ordered tenants to pay their rents only to those heads of house approved by parliament or their designated subordinates, but this order was often ignored.[39] In Wales royalist tenants of Jesus College refused to pay and the ejected principal, Francis Mansell, continued to receive rents after his expulsion. Michael Roberts, who had been intruded into Mansell's place, complained in September 1649 of the difficulty of getting rents from tenants who were determined not to pay, and it was alleged that the college was on the verge of financial collapse.[40] Wadham College was reported in 1649 as having recalcitrant tenants despite the ordinance, and these too may well have been royalists.[41] In May 1648 the visitors ordered the arrest of two ejected fellows of Magdalen College for collecting rents 'in an unstatutable way' which they had not paid to the intruded president, and this diversion of rents persisted for a short while after the two were seized.[42] The bursar at St John's College forbade tenants to pay their rents to the

---

[36] JCA Mansell's inventory (1648–9), fo 42ᵛ; Costin, *St. John's*, 98–101; OUA register T, pp. 23–4, 43, 47, 57, 141, 191; ASA c. 297, entries for 1646/7, 1653/4, 1654/5, 1655/6; *Register*, ed. Burrows, 288. New College, on the other hand, decided in 1651 not to abate any rents because of taxes and assessments unless the college was named in the demands, in keeping with its hard line of the early 1650s: NCA 988, entry of 30 April 1651, and see ibid., entry of 25 March 1650.

[37] For examples of this see *CSPD 1625–49*, 696; *CSPD 1645–7*, 326–7, 484, 501–2, 517–18; *CSPD 1648–9*, 3; *CSPD 1654*, 345; *Calendar of Committee for Advance of Money*, 676, 888–9; *Calendar of the Proceedings of the Committee for Compounding, 1643–1660*, ed. M. A. E. Green (5 vols London 1889–92) 105, 107, 705–6, 718, 765, 915, 1034, 1443, 1528–9, 1549–50, 1595, 1622–3, 1634, 1707–8, 1943, 1998, 2419–20, 2458, 2797–8, 3057, 3223–4; PRO SP 20/1, fos 247, 274, 278, SP 20/8, fos 42, 170, 182, 198, 202, SP 28/347, fo 16; *CJ* iv. 739; *LJ* viii. 584, 600; 'Annual progress', ed. Eland, 89; BNCA A2. 43, pp. 10–11, 16. See also *CJ* iv. 713.

[38] *Register*, ed. Burrows, 109–10.

[39] *LJ* x. 216–17. See also *CJ* vi. 25. The visitors designated certain persons to be bursars and rentgatherers for their colleges in the period before the restoration of college autonomy in elections and government: *Register*, ed. Burrows, 83, 191, 204–5.

[40] *Calendar of Committee for Advance of Money*, 1062; Hardy, *Jesus*, 117; T. Richards, 'The puritan visitation of Jesus College, Oxford, and the principalship of Dr Michael Roberts (1648–1657)', *Transactions of the Honourable Society of Cymmrodorion* (1922–3), 46; *Register*, ed. Burrows, 346; OUA register T, p. 72.

[41] *Calendar of Committee for Advance of Money*, 888.

[42] *Register*, ed. Burrows, 41, 95–7, 119; see also ibid. 83, 111–12.

new college authorities, and the president warned in 1648 that 'I have imprisoned the bursar but cannot prevail with him to pay any debts for what is past or to make any provision for the future'.[43] This was a serious problem for a time, but there is no evidence that it persisted on any significant scale far into the early 1650s.

The reduction of colleges' regular income from rents was accompanied by an equally severe fall in one of their principal irregular sources of income from property: entry or lease fines, which were levied on all tenants when they took up or renewed their leases. These too were of vital importance to college finances, especially in balancing the accounts during difficult years. The number of leases issued varied greatly from one year to the next in peacetime, but renewals were savagely disrupted by the civil war. Brasenose College, which sealed on average just over ten leases a year between 1634/5 and 1639/40, sealed only fourteen in total during the next five years, and none at all in 1646/7 and 1647/8. Then, with normality returning, ninety-six leases were issued in the five years following. A similar pattern can be observed at Christ Church: an average of nearly seventeen renewals annually between 1636 and 1641; a total of only twenty-two in 1642–7; and an annual average of over thirty-two in 1649–52. Balliol College issued only two leases between 1642 and 1649. At Magdalen College the recovery began earlier, in 1646, but there had been considerable disruption there too: an annual average of over thirty-five between 1638 and 1641, falling to an average of under twelve between 1642 and 1645, and fifty-seven renewals in 1646.[44]

The level of a fine was calculated from the rental value of the property concerned, and so the income from fines was normally subject to considerable annual fluctuations depending on which particular leases came up for renewal; but where figures are available the major loss of income during the 1640s due to non-renewal of leases is quite evident.[45] Magdalen College received on average over £651 from lease fines annually in 1638–41; its total income from fines in the next five years was only £625. At Brasenose College the average annual income from fines in the 1630s was £232, falling to under £56 between 1640/1 and 1644/5, and recovering to over £309 between 1645/6 and 1649/50 as the flurry of renewals came in; the annual average remained almost as high throughout the 1650s. Wood commented that the fellows who remained in Oxford at the end of the siege were 'enriched (if

---

[43] Costin, *St. John's*, 106–7.

[44] BNCA A3. 19, 476–505; CA xx. c. 4, 1. b. 1 (both *sub anno*); BCA lease book (1588–1665), 98–101; MCA libri computi (1617–43), *sub anno*. Renewals began at New College in 1646 also: NCA 3509, 58–9. In July 1646 the parliamentary committee for the university ordered that there should be no renewals of leases until further notice, but the university protested and several colleges seem to have paid little attention to the order: Wood, *History of the University* ii. 489; *Register*, ed. Burrows, pp. lix,13–14, 297–8; Costin, *St. John's*, 99.

[45] For further general remarks about fines and how they were calculated see Aylmer, 'Economics and finances', 527–8, 534–5; Dunbabin, 'College estates and wealth', 277. A fine of about one seventh the annual rental value was usual in the 1660s: Dunbabin, 'College estates and wealth', 277. The Balliol College lease log book cited in n. 47 below shows fines set consistently at about one ninth the annual rental value during the fifty years after 1619.

not ejected) within few years after by the many fines and renewing of leases that came in'.[46]

Colleges were by tradition reluctant to raise fines and seem to have resisted the temptation even in this time of crisis. At Brasenose College, where the evidence for 1640–60 is good, higher fines were certainly not imposed. New College did attempt to raise fines in 1650: there was some haggling with the tenants over this, but the threat of not renewing leases, which the college also employed at this time, was a potent one now that the war was over and normal college government had been restored, and the college collected over £1,800 from lease renewals in 1651. No doubt New College was aided in its recovery by the proximity of many of its estates. Balliol College, on the other hand, which had had property in Northumberland damaged in the wars, could not afford to be so forceful when issuing a lease in 1649, the former tenant being unable to renew because his property had been sequestered and the college could do little more than settle for whatever it could get.[47] In cases where property had become run down because of the troubles it was usual to reduce the fine anyway: there are one or two recorded examples of this and there were probably many more instances.[48] In an extremely unusual example, All Souls College granted a tenant 'an easy fine' in 1650 'by reason of his extraordinary respect shewed to the college these troublous times in paying all his rents fully and well without any deduction for taxes, and some rents twice both to the parliament and also to the college'.[49]

The sale of timber produced on college estates provided another important source of irregular income. Tenants were forbidden to fell trees on college properties except occasionally for repairs, and this was in theory strictly regulated by the colleges. The length of time taken by wood to mature meant that colleges could not afford to be profligate in felling trees, but even here fellows did not always act in the colleges' best interests, since the profits from timber sales went to swell their dividends. The bishop of Winchester, visitor of Magdalen College, complained in 1638 of dishonest dealing in this regard: the college had cut down timber ostensibly for building repairs, but more wood had been cut than was needed, and it was of too high a quality. The bishop ordered a halt to all felling except under the clear direction of the president.[50]

The sudden collapse of their other principal sources of income after the outbreak of war tempted colleges to sell timber to meet their urgent needs. In 1643 Robert Heywood, a fellow of Brasenose College, argued that the college should sell

---

[46] MCA libri computi (1617–43), sub anno; BNCA A3. 19, 476–505; Wood, History of the University ii. 488.

[47] BNCA A3. 19, 476–505; NCA 40, entry for 1651; NCA 988, entries for 1650; BCA lease log book (1588–1850), 112–13. In the previous year, however, the college had ordered that all leases were to be for the customary length of twenty-one years and that there was to be no diminution of rents: BCA register (1514–1682), 235.

[48] For example BNCA Bld. 36, entry for 30 September 1653; BCA lease log book (1588–1850), 138–9.

[49] Burrows, Worthies, 205.

[50] MCA MS 730(a), fo 93.

as much timber from its estates as it could possibly spare to pay off its present debts and meet its future needs 'if another winter-garrison, and the distractions of the times continue'. Brasenose may not have made any systematic attempt to follow Heywood's advice, but the evidence is too fragmentary for any clear conclusions to be drawn, and the college perhaps possessed only limited timber reserves. Moreover, comparisons with any 'normal' pattern of wood sales are problematic, since the pattern was so very irregular. When Brasenose raised £67 from wood sales in 1653, the principal and fellows decided to divide all but £15 of the money among themselves, which suggests that they were no longer in great need of such income for general college purposes, an impression confirmed on examining the resolutions of the annual accounts for the early 1650s.[51]

The pressure is more apparent in other cases. Oriel College realized almost £280 from a sale of timber in 1643 'necessitate belli impellente [forced by the needs of war]'.[52] The All Souls College accounts show the college raising similarly large sums from timber sales throughout the two revolutionary decades, but especially in the 1650s: an average of £225 a year was received in this way in twelve recorded years between 1645/6 and 1659/60. All Souls was taking a calculated risk in selling so much timber which it would take a long time to replace, but its financial situation at the time was serious enough to make the risk necessary.[53] Anthony Wood was critical of the intruded warden at New College, George Marshall, who in 1649, he alleged, 'made great havock of the college trees near Stanton St John, in this county, and elsewhere, cutting down about 5,000'. Michael Woodward, who succeeded Marshall in 1658, took a similarly dim view of the proceedings, it appears, and he also thought that a good deal of timber had gone astray during the revolutionary era.[54] But the 1649 felling of trees may well have been to meet urgent debts—the college's financial position at that time is not known—and the evidence of its timber policy in the 1650s indicates watchful husbandry: rights to fell were defined strictly and careful surveys were made of college woods.[55] There was great need for this. The cutting down of wood illegally by tenants was a perennial problem which may have become even worse during the civil war as tenants took advantage of their landlords' difficulties, and the tight estate management which New College is known to have operated from at latest 1650 onwards may have been a

[51] BNCA 1643 visitation: A2. 42, 21–2, A2. 43, 8, A2. 45, fo 6, A2. 46, 4, Bld. 36, entry for 13 December 1653.

[52] *Dean's Register of Oriel*, 309.   [53] ASA c. 337, c. 338, both *sub anno*.

[54] Wood, *History of the University* ii. 622; 'Oxfordshire estates', ed. Rickard, 7, 73; 'Wiltshire estates', ed. Rickard, p. xiv. In *c*.1646 a New College tenant was allowed wood for his fire in return for a loan to the college of £10 'in their necessitie': 'Annual progress', ed. Eland, 84.

[55] NCA 988, entries for 1650 and following years; NCA 7675, entry for 1653/4. The parliamentary visitors were concerned at profligate and unauthorized felling of college timber; in 1648 they ordered those in charge of woods belonging to All Souls and St John's not to cut any woods or underwoods: *Register*, ed. Burrows, 64–5, 108, 136. This may explain the relatively low level of felling by All Souls in 1649/50: ASA c. 337, entry of 1649/50, and see also NCA 7672, entry of 1647. The county committees also seem to have tried to restrain felling: BNCA A2. 43, 11; NCA 814, letter from Warden Pincke, 25 November 1646.

response to it. A college minute in February 1650 referred to the unauthorized loss of 'much timber and other wood which is every day feld and cutt' on one of its estates. Even the utmost diligence could not eradicate the abuse entirely, and Michael Woodward continued to record numerous instances of illegal felling and theft, which may indicate a gap—how avoidable we cannot tell because we cannot judge what the situation was like normally—between what was aimed at and what was achieved. In May 1660 the house of lords had to forbid the felling of trees at two coppices in Northamptonshire belonging to All Souls College, perhaps because the college was unable to restrain the tenants.[56] Woods were also vulnerable to plunder and requisitioning for military purposes and even to sequestration, as well as simple neglect.[57]

From an early stage in the war the colleges had to pay for their defence. Early in September 1642 the university decided to raise £1,000 from them for this purpose, and according to Wood the king asked for a further loan of £2,000 from the university in June 1643, probably for the same end.[58] Payments are recorded in some college accounts of 1642/3, although they were not yet a major burden in most cases.[59] In January 1644 the university was ordered to raise a total of £40 per week for twenty weeks from colleges and halls, and after the order ran out a new weekly rate of £20 was levied. Colleges were assessed for this according to their means.[60] The burdens now became significant: All Souls College's annual contribution rose from less than £19 in 1643/4 to over £53 in the following year. Christ Church spent £260 towards fortifications in 1643/4 and New College just over £123. Magdalen College contributed a total of over £200 between 1643 and 1645. Poorer colleges such as Jesus and Balliol contributed a good deal less in absolute, but not in relative, terms.[61] The demands were short-lived and by 1645/6 had declined sharply, but at their peak they coincided with that period when colleges, their reserves already gone, were first experiencing severe hardship from loss of rents and other sources of income from land.[62] The crown showed awareness of the university's financial plight in June 1643 when, though calling for contributions

[56] NCA 988, entry for 8 February 1650; 'Annual progress', ed. Eland, 83–91; 'Oxfordshire estates', ed. Rickard, passim; 'Wiltshire estates', ed. Rickard, passim; LJ xi. 39.

[57] Calendar of Committee for Compounding, 2797; 'Annual progress', ed. Eland, 89; Costin, St. John's, 102; Dean's Register of Oriel, 309.

[58] Wood, History of the University ii. 448; Wood, Life and Times i. 100–1; OUA register Sb, p.10.

[59] CA xxii. b. 86; ASA c. 296; BCA computi (1615–62); BNCA bursar's rolls, vol. 22 (all sub anno); Jones, Balliol, 101. At Jesus payments connected with the arrival of the royalist army and Oxford fortifications do account to a great extent for the very large annual expenditure that year: JCA bursar's accounts (1631–53), 134–5.

[60] Wood, History of the University ii. 467–8; OUA SP/F/40/21, SP/F/40/30; Dean's Register of Oriel, 299–300.

[61] ASA c. 296; c. 297; CA xii. b. 87; BCA computi (1615–62); NCA 4204; NCA 7668 (all sub anno); Robertson, All Souls, 119; Burrows, Worthies, 176; Wilson, Magdalen, 155; Hardy, Jesus, 103. V. H. H. Green believes the burden on Lincoln to have been trivial but irritating: Lincoln, 246.

[62] The university also had to raise troopers in 1651 and 1655, but the financial outlay was not so great and colleges were starting to recover by then: NCA 988, 4207; BCA computi (1615–62); ASA c. 297 (all sub anno); Wood, Life and Times i. 170; CSPD 1651, 416; Green, Lincoln, 257.

to maintain infantrymen, it insisted that these should come from individual heads of house and fellows, 'not from the publick stock, which we believe to be exhausted already for our ayde', but its own financial needs were pressing.[63]

The financial consequences of the court and the army taking over the colleges for their own use during the royalist occupation cannot be calculated with any accuracy, although the disruption of normal university life is well documented. The Christ Church accounts for 1642/3 show that £600 was spent on receiving the king but this was an extreme example and other college account books are less forthcoming.[64] One of the most significant financial effects of the occupation was the neglect of and damage to college buildings. Anthony Wood admitted that 'the colleges were much out of repair by the negligence of soldiers, courtiers and others that lay in them'.[65] The hall at Merton College was said to be in a sorry state in October 1646. An inventory drawn up at Jesus College in 1649 noted that: 'The principall had more household stuffe in his lodging, but most of it hath bin lost by the meanes of the strangers who lodged in and had the use of it for divers yeares'.[66] Many depredations of this kind were unlikely to find their way into formal college records.

Some visitors also ran up debts to the college butteries or failed to pay room rents, but their general contribution to college income may have been very welcome at that time.[67] The severe reduction in student numbers meant that colleges lost valuable income from chamber rents, significant in some cases though not in others. It was certainly very important to some of the halls, which had to rent their rooms out to townspeople instead.[68] It also affected the university, which derived an important part of its income from graduation fees; and in February 1643 it complained about the large numbers of degrees being awarded by royal mandate for which fees were waived.[69]

[63] Wood, History of the University ii. 464; OUA SP/F/40 (47); ECA A. I. 6, fos 33ᵛ–4. It appears that the colleges paid the money from a levy on the fellows—certainly so at Brasenose and apparently at other colleges, though the accounts are unspecific: BNCA B2a. 78, 24–43, A2. 42, 39; ASA c. 296, c. 297 (both sub anno); Carr, University College, 109–10; Hardy, Jesus, 103.

[64] CA xii. b. 86, sub anno (there are also one or two smaller items).

[65] Wood, History of the University ii. 488. There is a similar description in John Walker, The Sufferings of the Clergy during the Great Rebellion 1642–60 (Oxford and London 1862), 233.

[66] Brodrick, Merton, 89–90; Hardy, Jesus, 114. For other examples of damage and neglect see Davis, Balliol, 116–17; Hardy, Jesus 104; Green, Lincoln 247, 257.

[67] Hardy, Jesus, 104–5; Wakeling, 'History of the college', 36–7; Green, Lincoln, 244; BNCA B2a. 78, 11, 13.

[68] For the halls see Wood, History of the University ii. 488; Walker, Sufferings of the Clergy, 233. Jesus College, which received no chamber rents at all in 1643, did depend on the income to a substantial degree: JCA bursar's accounts (1631–53), passim; Hardy, Jesus, 104. University College received no chamber rents at all in 1644–6: Carr, University College, 109. For the decline in student numbers overall see L. Stone, 'The size and composition of the Oxford student body 1580–1909' in L. Stone (ed.), The University in Society (2 vols Princeton 1974) i. 91. The colleges also lost income from battels, but the figures for income from members not on the foundation are not easily discernible from college accounts: Aylmer, 'Economics and finances', 524. The same problem sometimes attends calculations of chamber rents.

[69] OUA register Sb, pp. 21–2. The university's income from admissions money fell from £73 in 1640/1 to just £3 in 1645/6, and the total for the years 1642/3 to 1645/6 was only £18: OUA WP/β/21/4, schools accounts, sub anno.

The colleges were genuinely afraid of plunder. Robert Pincke, pro-vice-chancellor, wrote to the university's chancellor, the fourth earl of Pembroke, in September 1642 warning that the colleges would be 'ransacked, defaced, demolished' if they were not protected, and several colleges purchased arms and ammunition at the beginning of the war for self-defence. Nearly all of these weapons were called in by the royalist army in 1643.[70] Though there were instances of vandalism and plunder subsequently, these were isolated and insignificant compared to the other problems which the university and colleges had to face. Most of the damage was confined to college chapels, and was done after the parliamentary takeover, largely for religious motives; it could not of course be made good until the Restoration.[71] Plunder proper was rare at any time during the period. Wood alleged that 'the books of some libraries [were] imbeziled', but it is not clear how much weight should be attached to this. The parliamentary visitors accused a fellow of Merton of having taken college goods without permission and having 'gratified courtiers with them, in other howses'.[72]

Wood also accused the intruded fellows of Magdalen College of having plundered a stock of gold left by the founder, and the intruded president of Trinity College of keeping large sums of money found hidden during repairs there. He wrote of plans to break open the Bodley and Savile chests of the university which were abandoned when it was learnt that there was nothing to be found there. Walker alleged that timber for the interrupted building programme at Christ Church had been appropriated by the fellows.[73] Such tales by royalist sympathizers against the intruded regime need to be taken with a pinch of salt. The Trinity College story has been dismissed as improbable: a box of plate was found there in 1648 but put formally into the care of the visitors' delegates in the college.[74] There is no evidence of the stories concerning the university chests and the Christ Church timber, although in the latter case it is not improbable that timber could have been employed for the common good. The account of the gold at Magdalen College is reliable, however, and is confirmed by evidence heard at the chancellor's visitation of the university in 1660. It seems that much of the money was returned.[75]

[70] NCA 7665, entry for 1641/2; NCA 11,704, petition of 7 September 1642; *Oxford Council Acts 1626–1665*, ed. M. G. Hobson and H. E. Salter (OHS xcv 1933), pp. vi–vii; ASA c. 296, entry for 1642/3; Costin, *St. John's*, 102; Hardy, *Jesus*, 103; Brodrick, *Merton*, 84 n. 1; *Royalist Ordnance Papers 1642–1646*, ed. I. Roy (Oxfordshire Record Soc. xliii 1964 xlix 1975), 34, 70, 72, 76, 81, 84, 95.

[71] Costin, *St. John's*, 108–9; Brodrick, *Merton*, 88, 107–8; Wilson, *Magdalen*, 167–8; Hiscock, *Christ Church*, 216; T. Warton, *The Life and Literary Remains of Ralph Bathurst, M. D.* (London 1761), 65–6; *Diary of John Evelyn*, ed. W. Bray (2 vols London 1907, rev. edn London 1966) i. 294; G. Jackson-Stops, 'Gains and losses: the college buildings, 1404–1750' in Buxton and Williams (eds), *New College*, 205–6; *VCH Oxon.* iii. 146; NCA 991. New College housed the garrison's magazine and there is a reference to college windows being broken by ammunition: NCA 7672, entry for 1647; C. Woodforde, *The Stained Glass of New College, Oxford* (Oxford 1951), 14. Other minor incidents of vandalism and damage are recorded in Wood, *Life and Times* i. 64.

[72] Wood, *History of the University* ii. 488; *Register*, ed. Burrows, 252–3, 282–4.

[73] Wood, *History of the University* ii. 623–5; Walker, *Sufferings of the Clergy*, 283–4.

[74] Blakiston, *Trinity*, 139–40; *Register*, ed. Burrows, 81.

[75] Wilson, *Magdalen*, 168–71; 'The Restoration Visitation of the University of Oxford and its Colleges', ed. F. J. Varley, *Camden Miscellany* xviii (Camden Soc. 3rd ser. lxxix 1948), 10–11.

Yet fear of widespread plunder and indeed of the collapse of the university was undoubtedly influential in the decline in the number and value of benefactions received during the two revolutionary decades. This is difficult to quantify, since there is no knowing how much might have been given in endowments under normal conditions, and both university and other educational benefactions had already begun to decline in the decade before the war. The value of new educational benefactions in England as a whole in the 1640s was 27 per cent lower than that of the 1630s, although in the 1650s it recovered to its pre-war level. The sum given to colleges and universities in the 1640s was 41 per cent below that of the previous decade, and in the 1650s it was 58 per cent less. The amount given towards scholarships and fellowships fell by over 57 per cent in the 1640s and was little different in the 1650s.[76]

Some of those who did give remained uneasy. Sir Thomas Roe donated a collection of coins to the Bodleian Library in 1644, 'which I desire may be sent thither, when safely they may, and if these tymes doe not evyve [destroy] both the universitye and librarye'. Lincoln College received a benefaction of £100 from a former fellow in 1645 which was to be spent in various specified ways 'all within two yeares of a setled peace in this kingdome of England'.[77] After the parliamentary purge of the university, political and religious prejudice were added to the existing uncertainty. Jesus College lost about £200 a year which the late bishop of Llandaff had planned to settle on the college because his heirs refused to honour the agreement with the new college administration. A rent charge of £50 a year intended for the college was also lost, as were some tithes. Leoline Jenkins, principal in 1661, commented that 'none will advance any thing to us by way of contribution or benevolence, because they will not care to pay off the debts, that those who were here (only by right of the sword) have contracted, and cast upon us'.[78]

The colleges' response to the changed conditions is another indicator of the severity of their financial problems. Major capital projects such as buildings were largely out of the question. While several colleges had been building during the 1620s and 1630s, the only major projects started during the revolutionary period were the chapel and library of Brasenose College, begun in 1656 and 1657 respectively, and a new refectory with rooms above at St Edmund Hall, constructed in 1659.[79] Work already in progress in 1642 ground to a halt. Jesus College received

[76] Percentages calculated from figures in W. K. Jordan, *Philanthropy in England, 1480–1660* (London 1959), 373. Jordan's figures, based on wills, do not cover the whole range of benefactions, however, and his methods and conclusions have been challenged: see for example M. Feingold, 'Jordan revisited: patterns of charitable giving in sixteenth and seventeenth century England', *History of Education* viii (1979).

[77] J. G. Milne, 'Archbishop Laud and the university collection of coins', *Oxoniensia* i (1936), 160; LCM A. 1. 2, fo 87ᵛ; Green, *Lincoln*, 247.

[78] Hardy, *Jesus*, 92–3; JCA register (1604–24), loose letters at end; William Wynne, *The Life of Sir Leoline Jenkins* (2 vols London 1724) ii. 651. At Brasenose, though, the pattern did not alter from that of the early seventeenth century: A. J. Butler, 'An account of the benefactions bestowed upon the college', *Brasenose Monographs* iv. 23–5.

[79] O. Jewitt, 'On the late, or debased, Gothic buildings of Oxford', *Archaeological Journal* viii (1851), 382–96. For the building at Brasenose and St Edmund Hall see Wakeling, 'History of the college', 59–61;

private donations for a new quadrangle until May 1643, but work on the scheme was abandoned and did not recommence until 1676. The building of the great quadrangle at Christ Church was halted until 1661. A new chapel at University College begun in 1639 was abandoned until the Restoration, but in the mid-1650s a determined effort was made to raise money from private subscriptions to complete the college's hall, which was finished in 1657. A tenement in St Ebbe's parish belonging to Balliol College burned down in October 1644 'and lay un-built for many yeares after'.[80]

Colleges had also to reduce their everyday expenditure, which mainly comprised the maintenance of members on the foundation, and one of the principal means of achieving these cuts was by keeping fellowships vacant and using the profits to pay off college debts. They were helped in this by the ban on free elections during the parliamentary visitation, but the practice had to be approved by the visitors in each case. Specified fellowships were kept vacant for limited periods of time at many colleges well into the 1650s, although the numbers varied greatly.[81] Merton and St John's colleges tried to resist the visitors' insistence that they should maintain full complements of fellows. Francis Cheynell warned the visitors in 1648 when they wished to appoint four new fellows to St John's that: 'The colledge had broken up if I had not taken order for its maintenance upon my owne creditt. This is the fourth week that is running on. Unless there be some speedy course taken, the colledge will dissolve for I am not able to maintaine it upon my purse or creditt.' St John's College was still resistant to the appointment of fellows three years later. Brasenose College decided in January 1646 that although college statutes did not permit them to reduce numbers, fellows elected in future were not to be admitted to the benefits of their offices until peace returned.[82]

Even after the Restoration some colleges were unwilling to fill all their places. Leoline Jenkins complained in 1661 that Jesus College was 'not well able to pay the members that are already stipendary (much less to pay off any considerable part of our debt)'. In the late 1660s Balliol College put forward 'the necessary number of their foundation' as one reason for their inability to pay off their debts contracted during the civil war.[83]

E. W. Allfrey, 'The architectural history of the college', *Brasenose Monographs* iii. 14–24; BNCA A3. 20; BNCA bursarial—money. 1; J. N. D. Kelly, *St Edmund Hall: almost seven hundred years* (Oxford 1989), 41–2. There were some alterations at St John's in 1642–3: *VCH Oxon.* iii. 261–2. I am grateful to Mr J. Newman for correcting some errors in an earlier version of this paragraph.

[80] Jewitt, 'Gothic buildings', 395–6; *VCH Oxon.* iii. 73–6, 232, 274; J. N. L. Baker, *Jesus College, Oxford 1571–1971* (Oxford 1971), 5; JCA uncatalogued notebook, fos 2–4ᵛ *et seq.*; Hiscock, *Christ Church*, 156, 200–3; Carr, *University College*, 120, 208; Wood, *Life and Times* i. 210; BCA lease log book (1588–1850), 62–3.

[81] This is known to have happened at Balliol, Brasenose, Exeter, Jesus, Lincoln, Oriel, Queen's, University, and Wadham; Merton and St John's tried to resist appointments: *Register*, ed. Burrows, 214, 224, 263, 268–9, 288, 293–4, 301–2, 329–31, 341, 346, 363, 366, 371, 386–9, 399; Carr, *University College*, 114, 119; Wells, *Wadham*, 64; BNCA uncatalogued envelope entitled 'Houghton, John 1625'; ECA A. I. 6, fos 44, 49; Davis, *Balliol*, 126; Hardy, *Jesus*, 122; LCM A. I. 2, fos 94, 99, 109, 111ᵛ, 112ᵛ.

[82] Henderson, *Merton*, 133; Costin, *St. John's*, 106–7, 112; BNCA A1. 2, fo 68; Wakeling, 'History of the college', 39.

[83] Wynne, *Leoline Jenkins* ii. 651; BCA benefactions I (1636–76).

Reductions were also made in expenditure on fellows' and scholars' commons, particularly during the civil war. All Souls College had real difficulty in providing for its fellows for a while in 1644, and in 1646 it reduced commons to one meal a day. Oriel College also reduced its commons allowance by half in March 1646; in November the previous year it had decided that fines, instead of being divided among the fellows, were to be applied to maintaining their table. St John's College debated in 1645 whether to 'dissolve their publicke meetings in the hall and everie fellow to provide for his particular as hee could', though it was rescued for a while by a donation of £40.[84] The reduction of commons expenses was suggested at Brasenose College as early as 1643. Fellows at Merton and All Souls colleges were made to move out of college for a while to cut costs. Other colleges such as Jesus and Exeter were also reducing expenditure and allowances for commons at this time. According to Wood, in the halls and some of the colleges 'ale and beer were sold by the penny in their respective butteries', rather than on account.[85] In New College curbs on commons expenditure were introduced in 1651 and 1655, but for other colleges the measures may have been more short-term.[86]

During the royalist occupation colleges were ordered to lay in large stocks of provisions for months ahead, especially during the siege.[87] Although Wood claimed that there was plenty of food still in store when the Oxford garrison surrendered, he also believed that the university was by then 'exhausted of its treasure and . . . little could be procured abroad for its subsistence'. Merton College in March 1646 had to give in a bond of £94 for the purchase of provisions, having no ready money, although it had been able to lay in supplies apparently without problems the previous November. Brasenose College was already heavily in debt to tradesmen at the start of the war and had to sign numerous bonds during the 1640s to buy provisions. Similar debts have been noted at St John's College. Jesus College still owed money to brewers and bakers in 1650, and Leoline Jenkins observed in 1661 that while the college remained in debt 'we must be at the mercy of those who trust us with provisions, as to their fair dealing'. In 1650 the visitors suspended three vacant fellowships and three vacant scholarships at Wadham College for four years to pay off more than £400 owed to brewers, bakers, and others.[88]

[84] JCA I. arch. 4. 21; Burrows, *Worthies*, 177; *Dean's Register of Oriel*, 308–9, 311; Costin, *St. John's*, 100, 107–8.

[85] BNCA visitation 1643; Robertson, *All Souls*, 119; Brodrick, *Merton*, 87; JCA bursar's accounts (1631–53), 130; ECA A. II. 10, *sub anno*; Wood, *History of the University* ii. 488.

[86] NCA 988, entries for 18 August 1651, 4 January 1655; see also 11 January 1655. The curbs of 1655 were brought about by the changing price of corn. The question of corn rents in this period is puzzling. They do not on the surface appear to alter at Brasenose and Exeter, but these may be nominal rather than actual payments: BNCA B2a. 81, A3. 19, 294–5; ECA A. III. 10, *sub anno*. St John's had to fix its commons expenses because it could not rely on its former corn rents: Costin, *St. John's*, 101.

[87] NCA 7668; ASA c. 297 (both *sub anno*); OUA SP/F/40/15; Wood, *History of the University* ii. 472, 476–7, 486–7; Wood, *Life and Times* i. 125; BNCA B2a. 78, 11, 14, 25, 32; Wakeling, 'History of the college', 34–5; Costin, *St. John's*, 102–3; Green, *Lincoln*, 246–7; Brodrick, *Merton*, 89; Burrows, *Worthies*, 176–7.

[88] Wood, *History of the University* ii. 487; Brodrick, *Merton*, 89; Costin, *St. John's*, 100; JCA bursar's accounts (1631–53), entry for 1650; Wynne, *Leoline Jenkins* ii. 651; BNCA college—bond. 5; BNCA college—debts 2–5; BNCA B2a. 78, 33–6, 53, 62; Wells, *Wadham*, 64–5; *Register*, ed. Burrows, 288.

Some colleges had to borrow money during the worst years, though we cannot estimate the extent of this. One was Magdalen College, which did not look to be in particular difficulty from its annual accounts. Some of the college's creditors were tenants, who may have hoped for favourable terms when their leases were renewed. The warden of New College, Robert Pincke, thanked a creditor for a loan which the college paid off in November 1646, 'for the fellowes sake especially, whoe had the benefit of it to keepe them alive heere and together, some of them not having any freind to succour and support them elswhere'.[89]

Once the siege was over a slow return to normal life was possible, but the political problems which beset the university during the parliamentary visitation in the later 1640s greatly delayed this process. Royalist obstruction was the prime cause, preventing the new college governments from taking stock of their financial position or trying to put it to rights. In September 1647 the visitors called in all college documents concerning their 'government or affayres', but this and repeated orders the following April did not meet with much compliance, and in July 1648 the visitors complained of the 'conveyinge away of moneyes, plate, seales, evidences, registers, books of accompt, and other things which concerne the state of the severall colledges contrary to oathes and statutes'.[90]

Obstruction was quite blatant at several colleges. When Daniel Greenwood was intruded as principal of Brasenose College in 1648 and sought the college statutes which were customarily held by the principal, he was told 'that the statute booke was safe, and in such hands as had more right to keepe than had the said doctor'. Greenwood was still trying to recover the statutes in 1651.[91] On occasions the visitors were forced to order the arrest of bursars and other fellows, the breaking open of rooms in the search for documents and even the use of soldiers. None the less the royalists fought a vigorous rearguard action and here as in so many other areas of their operations the visitors had difficulty in enforcing their will.[92] Certainly they had great difficulty in discovering the true financial state of the colleges, and the royalist obstruction may account for some of the gaps in college financial and administrative records of the 1640s.[93]

This, coming on top of the wartime disruption, led to general administrative

[89] MCA libri computi (1617–43), entries for 1644–6; Robertson, *All Souls*, 119; Wilson, *Magdalen*, 157; *Dean's Register of Oriel*, 307; NCA 814, letter of 25 November 1646.

[90] *Register*, ed. Burrows, 1–2, 5, 7–8, 12, 23–4, 161. The warden's plate of New College was taken by the ejected warden, Henry Stringer, who instructed his heirs to return it to the first warden to be properly elected by the college statutes. It was received by Michael Woodward in 1660: NCA 2817.

[91] BNCA uncatalogued file mostly containing letters from Charles II: letter of John Houghton, 31 July 1651. See also *Register*, ed. Burrows, 120.

[92] *Register*, ed. Burrows, 5, 17–18, 20–1, 26, 79–81, 83–4, 88, 95–6, 107–8, 120, 125, 127, 132, 142, 192, 205, 208–12, 222, 228; *Dean's Register of Oriel*, 315, 317–19; Blakiston, *Trinity*, 131; Burrows, *Worthies*, 204–5; Wood, *History of the University* ii. 603; *Calendar of Committee for Advance of Money*, 688; B. J. Shapiro, *John Wilkins, 1614–1672: an intellectual biography* (Berkeley 1969), 83; NCA 1014, 1069, 9751, 481; Mallet, *University of Oxford* ii. 14; Walker, *Sufferings of the Clergy*, 269–72. Corpus Christi did not get many of its estate documents back until 1653; they were returned by the ejected college steward, who received £5 for his 'ingenuous dealing': Fowler, *Corpus*, 228–9.

[93] *Register*, ed. Burrows, p. lxxxiv.

chaos. By 1649, when the visitors permitted colleges to be governed by their own statutes once more, 'all things were in a confusion, and every one did what he thought fit'.[94] Records of formal administrative meetings and decisions at several colleges show that these declined in frequency during the war years, recovering only once the intruded fellows were securely established. The exceptionally high number of meetings at New College in 1650–1 parallels that college's attempts to re-establish its estate administration and reassert its full rights over its tenants.[95] The frequency of the university's wartime meetings did not decrease greatly, despite Wood's lament in 1645/6 that 'The acts . . . are very few or none this year, neither doth any thing material occur in our books.'[96] Nevertheless, evidence of meetings must be handled carefully. The fact that they continued to be held, though less frequently, is noteworthy, but the power of the colleges to implement the decisions reached was another matter. Moreover, we have no way of telling how much important business may have been transacted informally.

The significance of the widespread absence of many college fellows and some heads of house during the civil war and afterwards can be exaggerated, for only a small number of college officers was needed to administer college affairs, and the presence of a head of house was generally required only for particularly important business such as elections to fellowships and the annual audit. Laud's injunctions at Merton College in 1638 had included the requirement that the sub-wardenship be held for one year only so that all the fellows could become acquainted with college business; clearly the sub-warden's was an active position.[97] There were difficulties of course: the bursar's accounts at Jesus College for 1642 record that: 'In the last quarter of this yeare happened the troubles of the universitie, the bursar and most of the societie with the manciple (the principall being away before) left the place, which hath hindered the full evening of the accompt for all the yeare.' There is a note later in the same book that the accounts for 1644–8 were drawn up by the principal and fellows as they happened to be at college, 'for there was no bursar in all that time', and the college remained without one until 1650. Michael Roberts, the intruded principal of Jesus, protested in 1649 that his enforced absence from the college to attend an inquiry in London into allegations that he had been a royalist 'did *ipso facto* break up house-keeping . . . to the great prejudice of that societie', but this was most likely special pleading. There was a fierce quar-

---

[94] Wood, *History of the University* ii. 625.

[95] NCA 988, entries for 1650–1; LCM A. 1. 2, *sub anno*; BNCA A1. 2, fos 65–81ᵛ. There are no entries in the Balliol register between December 1645 and October 1648, when they begin regularly again, but this may be a defect in the records: BCA register (1514–62), 234–5. There is a gap in the Magdalen register for the years 1649–60, perhaps removed: MCA MS 730(a), *sub anno*.

[96] OUA register of convocation 1628–40, NEP/*supra*/24, register R; ibid. register Sb; ibid. register T (all *sub anno*); Wood, *History of the University* ii. 475.

[97] Brodrick, *Merton*, 82. There is a good illustration of a Cambridge college with a largely absentee master in the Interregnum managing more than adequately thanks to a skilful deputy: Brooke, *Gonville and Caius*, 131–40.

rel between politically aligned factions within the college at that time, which is likely to have been a far greater source of disruption.[98]

Moreover, at most colleges the bursar's office was held by fellows in irregular rotation, generally with two bursars functioning at one time, so that everybody learnt how to manage affairs. Some remained in office for long spells and acquired great expertise in the business, but there was usually somebody who could fill the breach in an emergency. St John's College abandoned the practice of two concurrent bursars in 1649/50 for a system whereby a single bursar held office for six months only, but it reverted to tradition the following year, perhaps due to the laxity of one of the men involved in the 1649/50 experiment. The lists of bursars at Balliol and Brasenose colleges show a steady blend of new faces and seasoned men throughout the period. The latter college gained much from the experience of John Houghton, nine times a senior bursar in the years 1646–61. Samuel Lee, who was intruded to a fellowship at Wadham College, is said to have introduced an improved system of account-keeping there. Wood's complaint that the appointment of new fellows at Oriel College in November 1648 meant that 'the whole government of that house was put into the hands of those that knew nothing of it, or the government of any house besides, while the antient fellows ... who understood the business well were passed by' carries weight only if the 'antient fellows' refused to offer their advice to the newcomers.[99]

The personal qualities of office-holders—their integrity as well as aptitude—were important in good times as well as bad. The conditions imposed by the war would have tested even the most able. The bursars of Magdalen College were so confused at the college's audit of 1646 that although they produced nearly £600 received from tenants they were unable to say who had sent the money.[100] Many of the intruded heads were capable and conscientious administrators.[101] Daniel Greenwood at Brasenose College defended his record on financial matters at the 1660 visitation: when he became principal there in 1648, he said, the college was between £12,000 and £13,000 in debt, 'all which I did fully discharge in the space of two or three yeares; and have not onely provided a sufficient stock to lay out

[98] JCA bursar's account (1631–53), 121, 139; Hardy, Jesus, 103, 115; Richards, 'Puritan visitation', 41, 47–50.

[99] Costin, St. John's, 110; BCA computi (1615–62), sub anno; Brasenose College Register 1509–1909 (2 vols in 1 OHS lv 1909) ii. 80, 84; Wakeling, 'History of the college', 55; Wells, Wadham, 79; Wood, History of the University ii. 611. Martin Aylworth, who is said to have been the chief man of business at All Souls from soon after his election to a fellowship in 1611 until his death in 1657, remained at the college: Burrows, Worthies, 190.

[100] Wilson, Magdalen, 157.

[101] See for example Davis, Balliol, 122–3; Wakeling, 'History of the college', 55; Burrows, Worthies, 187–8; John Conant, The Life of the Reverend and Venerable John Conant, DD (London 1823), 11–12, 32–3 (cf the remarks on this source in n. 104 below). John Owen spoke in 1654 of the importance of the intruded heads in restoring the university and ensuring its survival: J. Owen, The Oxford Orations of Dr John Owen, ed. P. Toon (Callington, Cornwall 1971), 15. Michael Roberts of Jesus is an example of an intruded head who may not have matched up to these standards, although the issue is clouded by the bitter faction-fighting within the college during his time there: Richards, 'Puritan visitation'; Hardy, Jesus, 116–20; Register, ed. Burrows, 302–3, 306, 332; Calendar of Committee for Advance of Money, 1066–7.

beforehand for necessaries; but wee have beene able to contribute and lend large summes toward the erecting and furnishing of our new buildings'.[102]

Much of the evidence is partial. On the one hand there is the mud-slinging of royalists who refused to admit good of the intrusions or made them scapegoats for problems beyond their control: for example, at Balliol College, where some of the blame for its impoverishment in the 1660s was put on 'severall injuries it received from severall persons, who were then imposed as gourvenors of the said colledge: together with many arrears of debts from some who were members of the said colledge in those licentious times'.[103] On the other hand there are the eulogistic tendencies of some contemporary biographies: that of John Conant, rector of Exeter College from 1649 to 1662, is a good example, although Conant was undoubtedly a diligent governor.[104] Yet it seems safe to claim that the personal and administrative qualities of the intruded heads and fellows were overall not inferior to those of the men they replaced, and that the most important factors affecting the colleges' financial state were external.

An officer in the parliamentary force which held Oxford briefly in the late summer of 1642 told Anthony Wood 'that the universitie had forfeyted all their estate by their late doeinges and takinge up armes'.[105] In fact there was never any serious threat to university and college property from the Long Parliament or the various republican governments which succeeded it, not even the Barebones Parliament, although many feared it.[106] The university's traditional exemption from parliamentary taxation was lost for a while after the outbreak of war, but with Oxford under royalist control this is unlikely to have had any effect. The exemption was recovered in 1647 and does not appear to have been threatened thereafter.[107] Parliamentary ordinances of the 1640s guaranteed university property and rents, and the only real danger was to Christ Church from the ordinance for selling deans' and chapters' lands which at first contained no specific exemption, although lobbying supplied this in the final version of the ordinance.[108] Cromwell's assurance to the university in May 1649 that the parliament men were not antagonistic towards the academic community 'and were so far from substracting any of their means, that they purposed to add more' only involved augmentations to the

---

[102] BNCA uncatalogued envelope containing Greenwood's reply to the 1660 visitors. There were still some outstanding debts from the 1640s at this time, but they were not very large and John Houghton did not think they could be collected: BNCA bursarial—money. 1; BNCA uncatalogued envelope entitled 'Houghton, John 1625'.

[103] BCA benefactions I (1636–76), loose sheets inserted at front. A similar allegation was made by Michael Woodward concerning New College, here used to explain the college's poor gift to Charles II at his restoration; but it sounds too much like an easy excuse: 'Oxfordshire estates', ed. Rickard, 7.

[104] Conant, *Life of John Conant*, 11–33; ECA A. II. 10.

[105] Wood, *Life and Times* i. 66.

[106] For Barebones and the universities see A. H. Woolrych, *From Commonwealth to Protectorate* (Oxford 1982), 160, 170, 194–8, 233, 245, 340–1, 396; Wood, *Life and Times* i. 294. There were fears of disendowment again in 1659: Dunbabin, 'College estates and wealth', 269.

[107] Aylmer, 'Economics and finances', 557–8; *Acts and Ordinances of the Interregnum, 1642–1660*, ed. C. H. Firth and R. S. Rait (3 vols London 1911) i. 984, 1077; ii. 318, 687, 1095.

[108] Wood, *History of the University* ii. 612–13; *Acts and Ordinances*, ed. Firth and Rait ii. 85.

salaries of the heads of house, but Cromwell was a supporter of the university system as it stood—he was after all chancellor of Oxford—and had no time for the radical schemes for their disendowment which were broadcast at the time.[109] John Owen, the Cromwellian nominee as vice-chancellor, did complain to Sir Thomas Widdrington in 1654 that 'the noble arts, placed dishonourably on the lowest step, and hard-pressed by lack of money, rise with difficulty', but in December of that year he thanked Cromwell for having rescued the university from its recent 'slippery and uncertain' position—possibly referring to the supposed threat of Barebones—and in 1657 he expressed his confidence that the university had emerged intact from all its dangers with its treasury replenished.[110]

Owen was not a wholly impartial spokesman, but the financial chaos and collapse which had so crippled the university in the 1640s had been largely overcome by a combination of careful economies and administration within the university and a period of peace and relative political stability in the country at large. Numbers, and hence fees and incomes from chamber rents, rose after the civil war, and Wood noted of the year 1659 that 'money [was] then stirring, and comming from the new gentlemen'.[111] At the Restoration all college leases and grants since the start of the civil war were legally confirmed, removing a major cause of anxiety.[112] There were bound to be exceptions to the general recovery, just as there had been to the general prosperity before the war. Balliol College, for example, remained in a sorry plight in the 1660s, not helped by the loss of London property in the fire of 1666, and it had to appeal to subscribers to bail the college out. Jesus College also was said to be in a 'shatter'd condition' in 1660, 'in no wise able to support the most just and necessary charges of it; and was almost beyond hopes of recovery', but the college was the victim of a decade of corruption and internal strife quite unique in Oxford during the revolutionary period.[113]

The experiences of the civil war had inflicted a deep psychological shock on college communities. The rigorous financial administration practised during the Restoration period by men such as Michael Woodward of New College and Ralph Bathurst of Trinity College owed much to a new awareness of the vulnerability of their finances, and represents an extension of the methods of the late 1640s and 1650s into more prosperous times after the post-war recovery had been completed.[114] It may also have led to a more mercenary spirit. At New College in

[109] The quotation is from Wood, *History of the University* ii. 619. For a summary of Cromwell's views on learning and the universities see C. H. Firth, *Oliver Cromwell and the Rule of the Puritans in England* (London 1953), 346–9.

[110] *The Correspondence of John Owen (1616–1683)*, ed. P. Toon (Cambridge 1970), 77–9; *The Oxford Orations of John Owen*, ed. Toon, 33–4, 38, 40–5.

[111] Wood, *Life and Times* i. 301, and see 297. For numbers see Stone, 'Size and composition', 91.

[112] *Restoration Visitation*, ed. Varley, pp. vi–vii.

[113] BCA benefactions I (1636–76); Davis, *Balliol*, 143–4; Wynne, *Leoline Jenkins* i, p. viii, and see ii. 651; Richards, 'Puritan visitation'; Hardy, *Jesus*, 116–20.

[114] For Woodward see 'Annual progress', ed. Eland; 'Oxfordshire estates', ed. Rickard; 'Norfolk property', ed. Rickard; 'Wiltshire estates', ed. Rickard. For Bathurst see Blakiston, *Trinity*, 152. In general see also Dunbabin, 'College estates and wealth', 283–4.

December 1660 when the visitor, the bishop of Winchester, asked for a college lease to the widow of the former tenant—who had been a sufferer for the royalist cause—to be renewed at the usual fine, some of the fellows called for the fine to be raised.[115] Perhaps this was a sign of changing times.

[115] NCA 11,704, letter of 8 December 1660.

17

Restoration Oxford and the Remaking of the Protestant Establishment

R. A. BEDDARD

THAT Oxford came to occupy a unique place in the history and affection of the protestant establishment is largely attributable to the long-lived achievements of the Restoration era. Charles II's reign saw not only the recreation of that establishment, as it was to endure well into the nineteenth century, but the swift and permanent return of the university to the centre of the nation's religious and political life after more than a decade of enforced marginalization. At the Restoration, Oxford resumed its old, pre-war, Reformation status, as part of the government of church and state under a reinvigorated, national, protestant monarchy. Yet there was one important change which cut it off from its pre-war past: henceforth, parliament decreed that its work should be confined to conformist protestants. The harsh legislation passed by king, lords, and commons in the early sessions of the Cavalier Parliament marked the final defeat of puritanism after more than a century of troubling the peace and unity of the church.

In 1660 those essential components of historic Anglicanism, episcopacy and liturgy, emerged triumphant from the bitter domestic struggles of English protestantism, along with their accustomed patron, the hereditary Stuart monarchy. The act of uniformity of 1662 defined the state church—the Church of England—as an episcopal institution, staffed by bishops, priests, and deacons who were required to conform to the doctrine and discipline of a revised prayer book. It also erected a church state—the protestant establishment—a system of government in which communicant members of the Church of England held a monopoly of office in education, religion, local and central administration, and the armed forces.[1] It was no accident that in after-ages the exclusively Anglican character of the University of Oxford was widely regarded, and fervently cherished, as the shield and buckler of protestant orthodoxy in the land.

The legislators of the Cavalier Parliament, many of whom had attended Oxford and Cambridge,[2] recognized the vital role which the two national universities would have in underwriting the Anglican ascendancy. Only the universities, and

---

[1] *Statutes of the Realm* v. 364–70: 14 Car. II, c. 4 (1662). For its operation in Oxford see *Restoration Oxford, 1660–1667*, ed. R. A. Beddard (3 vols OHS forthcoming) ii, nos 608–9, 616–17, 619–22.
[2] B. D. Henning (ed.), *The House of Commons 1660–1690* (3 vols London 1983) i. 4–5.

the dons who ran them, could ensure that the legal establishment, enacted at Westminster, became a living and self-perpetuating social reality. Henceforth, they were charged with raising future generations of protestants, loyal to the service of king and church, as the twin guarantors of an immutable Anglican constitution.[3] It was for this reason that the Cavalier MPs insisted that the universities, which were already closed to Catholics, should be barred against dissenters also. By thus denying all nonconformists access to higher education—irrespective of whether they were protestants who objected to episcopacy and liturgy, or Catholics who rejected the royal supremacy and refused to attend the parish church—the sticklers for the Church of England sought to engross political power to themselves. Their known adversaries, whom they opprobriously denominated 'fanatics' and 'papists', were reduced to the rank of second-class citizens: lesser breeds before the law.

Under the authority of the restored monarch, Oxford was called on to function as a powerful regulatory body. Entrusted to safe Anglican hands, the university would, it was hoped, bring peace to a kingdom riven by internal ecclesiastical dissension through its promotion of a shared set of values. None doubted even for a moment that, inspired and led by the faithful remnant of the Cavalier Anglican party, it would rise to this new challenge. In the event, the zeal with which Restoration Oxford undertook its appointed task exceeded all but the most sanguine of Cavalier Anglican expectations, as the loyalist university became, at one and the same time, the eager initiator, dedicated upholder, and grateful beneficiary of a remodelled protestant establishment. In concert with the entire Church of England after 1660, the university acted as a vehicle for religious, social, and political conservatism in the life of the nation.[4]

The key to understanding the religious and political imperatives that moulded the life of the Restoration university is to be found in the Cromwellian Interregnum—in the formation in Oxford of a discreet, but defiant, Cavalier Anglican congregation, which maintained the creed of the civil war university. Centred on John Fell, the son of the deposed royalist vice-chancellor, Samuel Fell, dean of Christ Church,[5] and himself an ejected Student of Christ Church,[6] it met throughout the 1650s in the lodgings of his brother-in-law, Thomas Willis, another staunch church-

---

[3] Preaching on the subject of education Robert South held it necessary to inculcate 'a hatred of rebellion' and a commensurate love of 'obedience and subjection to government', enjoined the receiving of confirmation and holy communion, highlighted the dangers proceeding from 'tender consciences', and vindicated the rites and ceremonies of the Church of England from attack: Robert South, *Sermons preached upon Several Occasions* (7 vols Oxford 1823) iii. 394–5, 402–11.

[4] In 1694 South dedicated the second volume of his sermons to the university, in which he expressly savaged the 'innovating spirit which had been striking at the constitutions of our church', and trusted in the efforts made at Oxford and Cambridge 'to support and recover her declining state'. Ibid. i. 345–7.

[5] Bodl. MS Wood f. 35, fo 123, Vice-Chancellor Samuel Fell to Gilbert Sheldon, London, 13 November 1647; Bodl. MS Tanner 338, fo 74; *Walker Revised: being a revision of John Walker's 'Sufferings of the Clergy during the Grand Rebellion 1642–60'*, ed. A. G. Matthews (Oxford 1948), 28; *Register*, ed. Burrows, 1, 7–8, 10, 14, 20; *Calendar of the Proceedings of the Committee for Compounding, 1643–1660*, ed. M. A. E. Green (5 vols London 1889–92) i. 1528.

[6] Bodl. MS J. Walker c. 8, fos 204ᵛ, 259ᵛ; *Register*, ed. Burrows, 32, 92; Wood, *Athenae* iv. 193.

man, who on leaving Christ Church took up residence in Beam Hall in Merton Street.[7] There Fell was joined by two other Christ Church clerics, ejected Students like himself. The first was Richard Allestree, a favourite of Fell's father, who quickly evolved into an undercover royalist agent, entrusted with carrying messages back and forth across the Channel to the Stuart court.[8] The second was John Dolben, the grand-nephew of Archbishop Williams of York, who, by his marriage to Katharine Sheldon, became the trusted nephew of Warden Sheldon of All Souls.[9] Together they kept up the forbidden offices of the Church of England. The fact that these three young academics chose to take episcopal orders amid the general collapse of episcopacy was a measure of their personal commitment to the old church.[10] At the services which they held every Sunday and weekday the Book of Common Prayer was used, and the surplice worn; holidays, with their vigils, were observed as the Anglican kalendar directed; and the sacrament of the Lord's supper was administered 'according to the Church of England'.

On a Sunday in term time 'about three hundred episcopalians' attended service, the clergy 'admitting none but their confidants'.[11] The large congregation was drawn from the ranks of the ejected dons, who included the president of St John's, Richard Baylie, and the principal of Jesus, Francis Mansell;[12] from the legion of adolescent royalists who continued to attend the university—most notably at Christ Church, Oriel, Queen's, Wadham, and New College, where sympathetic tutors were to be found;[13] and from the unmatriculated royalist youths who were taught privately in the town by ejected scholars like Leoline Jenkins of Jesus College.[14] Such was the solemnity with which Fell, Allestree, and Dolben conducted divine worship that it could 'hardly ... be paralleled otherwhere' in England, occasioning Jenkins to recall later, that 'the church it self might be said to have retir'd to that

[7] R. A. Beddard, 'The Restoration church' in J. R. Jones (ed.), *The Restored Monarchy 1660–1688* (London 1979), 156–7; Bodl. MSS Wood a. 21, fo 76, f. 39, fo 327; MCA 2. 11, fo 16ᵛ; Wood, *Athenae* iii. 1050.

[8] John Fell, *The Life of Richard Allestree* (Oxford 1684, London 1848), 1, 9–12, 18; Worcester College Library MS 54, p. 252; *The Letter-Book of John Viscount Mordaunt 1658–1660*, ed. M. Coate (Camden Soc. 3rd ser. lxix 1945), 16 ff.; Peter Barwick, *The Life of ... Dr. John Barwick* (London 1724), 201–2, 238, 250, 413, 418, 423 ff.; Wood *Athenae* iii. 1269–72; *Register*, ed. Burrows, 30, 32, 92.

[9] R. A. Beddard, 'An unpublished memoir of Archbishop Sheldon', *Bodleian Library Record* x (1978), 40–51; R. A. Beddard, 'The character of a Restoration prelate: Dr John Dolben', *Notes and Queries*, ccxv (1970), 418–21; Longleat House, MS Thynne 12, fo 145; Wood *Athenae* iii. 1050; *Register*, ed. Burrows, 30, 32, 92, 144.

[10] ORO MS Oxf. dioc. papers e. 13, p. 512; Bodl. MS Rawlinson b. 407a, fos 240ᵛ–41.

[11] [Leoline Jenkins], *The Life of Dr Francis Mansell* (privately printed 1845), 22–3.

[12] They remained in Oxford, Baylie and his family living behind the schools, and Mansell in Jesus. Both were considered worthy of promotion by the exiled Stuart court. Bodl. MS DD Jesus College, a. 6–a. 9, *passim*, MS Clarendon 66, fo 299ᵛ; BL MS Egerton 2542, fos 266, 267, 268, 269, 270.

[13] 'Memoirs of the life ... of Dr. Robert South' in South, *Sermons* i, p. v; *Restoration Oxford*, ed. Beddard, iii, appx, no. 13; *Register*, ed. Burrows, 536–7; BL MS Egerton 1634, fo 5ᵛ; Wood, *Life and Times* i. 301.

[14] Jenkins's tutorial establishment, styled 'the little Welsh-Hall', occupied High Street premises belonging to the Cavalier Anglican citizen, Sampson White, who was 'turn'd out of the councell house for his loyalty'. William Wynne, *The Life of Sir Leoline Jenkins* (2 vols London 1724) i. pp. iv–vi; Bodl. MS Wood f. 4, p. 155; JCA MSS 153/1, 154/6; Wood, *Fasti* ii. 231.

... upper chamber' in Willis's house.[15] There can be no denying the highly partisan nature of the enterprise. Besides keeping the liturgy of the Church of England alive, Fell's congregation served as a recruiting ground for the Anglican ministry within the university,[16] formed a convenient centre for the production and dissemination of Cavalier Anglican propaganda[17] and provided a sure source of royalist funding.[18] Its allegiances remained emphatically those of the old order: episcopacy in the church and monarchy in the state.

The future welfare of the university under loyalist auspices was, in a large measure, to depend on this intrepid band of men, who united the residual Cavalier Anglican presence in Cromwellian Oxford with the excluded grandees of their own party: senior academics who had formed the very backbone of the university's resistance to the parliamentary visitation in 1647–8. Of these grandees, two were to attain commanding stature in the restored Anglican hierarchy. They were Gilbert Sheldon, clerk of the closet to Charles I and the ejected warden of All Souls, who became bishop of London in 1660 and archbishop of Canterbury in 1663,[19] and his friend, George Morley, chaplain to Charles I and an ejected canon of Christ Church, who became bishop of Worcester in 1660 and bishop of Winchester in 1662.[20] By remaining in England, safely ensconced in the family of that most committed of royalists, Sir Robert Shirley of Stanton Harold, and pursuing a vigorous policy of Anglican self-preservation, Sheldon established himself as a leader of the intransigent clergy of the Church of England;[21] while Morley, by going into exile to serve as chaplain to Charles II and to his lord chancellor Sir Edward Hyde, turned himself into one of the main channels of communication between the Cavalier Anglicans at home and the Stuart court abroad.[22] Morley's long-standing friendship with Lord Chancellor Hyde (better known by his later title, the earl of Clarendon)[23] made possible the development, from 1660 onwards, of a close and

---

[15] [Jenkins], *Mansell*, 20–2, 25.

[16] R. A. Beddard, 'Bishop Skinner's ordinations, 1646–1662' (unpublished seminar paper); *Restoration Oxford*, ed. Beddard ii, no. 598.

[17] Besides Fell aiding Henry Hammond and others in their publications, members of his congregation, such as Matthew Wren, son of the bishop of Ely, wrote in defence of monarchy against the republican, James Harrington. Bodl. MS Rawlinson d. 316, fos 147–8, MS Tanner 306, fo 371; Matthew Wren, *Monarchy Asserted* (Oxford 1659, 2nd edn Oxford 1660).

[18] JCA MS 154/1–8; Bodl. MS Clarendon 70, fos 196, 205; *Restoration Oxford*, ed. Beddard i, no. 404, iii, appx, no. 26.

[19] *Walker Revised*, ed. Matthews, 23, 76; *Register*, ed. Burrows, pp. xxi, liii, lxiii, lxxx, 20–1, 187–8, 190, 206–7; JCA MS 155/2; Bodl. MS Wood f. 35, fos 65–6, 67, 70, 121, 123, 137, 148; R. A. Beddard, 'Sheldon and Anglican recovery', *Historical Journal* xix (1976), 1005–17.

[20] LPL, Juxon register, fos 182–8[v]; 283[v]–89; *Walker Revised*, ed. Matthews, 24, 377–8; *Register*, ed. Burrows, 20, 134.

[21] See Sheldon's entries regarding the Shirley family in his own bible: Bodl. Bib. Eng. 1648, d. 3.

[22] BL MS Harleian 6942, fos 138 ff.; Bodl. MS Tanner 88, fo 71, MS Rawlinson a. 42, p. 330; R. S. Bosher, *The Making of the Restoration Settlement . . . 1649–1662* (London 1951, rev. edn London 1957), 32, 50, 51, 55, 58, 60 ff.

[23] For clarity he is referred to in the text as Clarendon, though as Sir Edward Hyde he was successively declared lord chancellor of England at Bruges (13 January 1658), created Baron Hyde of Hindon (3 November 1660) and earl of Clarendon (20 April 1661). PRO PC 2/54, pp. 29, 35; *Restoration Oxford*, ed. Beddard iii, appx, nos 41, 44.

effective working relationship between Sheldon, Clarendon, and himself above, and Baylie, Fell, Allestree, and Dolben below. More than anything else, it was this development which ensured that the university would be resettled on the basis of the embattled, wartime, Cavalier Anglican interest.

After the Restoration the Cavalier Anglican academics were well placed to defend the university and its religious and political concerns against almost any eventuality, for they had powerful allies in court and country. At Whitehall, they could count on some of the foremost ministers of the crown, including a string of secretaries of state, stretching from Sir Edward Nicholas in the early 1660s to Sir Leoline Jenkins in the 1680s; most of the bishops of the Church of England, particularly those prelates who were entrusted with running the chapel royal; and a host of lesser government officials. In the country, they possessed many friends, especially among the Cavalier Anglican nobility and parliamentary gentry, not a few of whom were forward in acknowledging their regard for the church and for their alma mater.

The linchpin of this emerging network of clients, patrons, and friends was the indefatigable John Fell, 'a great assertor of the Church of England'.[24] As an academic dedicated to the recovery and advancement of his college and university, Fell believed in the importance of building up good public relations. Over the years he displayed a facility, little short of genius, for cultivating the affection and support of influential churchmen, clerical and lay, as his wide-ranging private correspondence and the impressive social record of his admissions to Christ Church amply attest, for he was 'very sensible how much the publick' was 'concern'd in the education of persons of birth and interest'.[25] 'The very triumph of active virtue', he used his accumulated official powers—decanal, vice-cancellarial, and episcopal—to raise the reputation and authority of the university in the life of the nation, and in the scholarly esteem of continental Europe.[26] It was from his personality, his allegiances, his initiatives, and his industry that so much of the distinctive character and achievements of Restoration Oxford sprang.

The churchmanship professed by Restoration Oxford displayed four invariable characteristics: a high strain of Stuart loyalism, an elevated concept of episcopacy, a single-minded attachment to liturgy, and an intense hatred of 'fanaticism'. Although these elements had been present in the intellectual and religious life of the university during Archbishop Laud's chancellorship, they derived their militancy, as a political creed, from the polarized partisanship of civil war Oxford[27]—

---

[24] BL MS Landsowne 987, fo 56ᵛ.

[25] Bodl. MS Carte 33, fo 92, Dean Fell to the duke of Ormonde, Christ Church, 26 August 1663. The aristocratic character of his admissions can be seen in CA D. P. i. a. 2 and 3, 'Matricula Ecclesiae Christi seu nomina admissorum . . . sub auspiciis doctoris Johannis Fell'. OUA SP 3, fos 1–32.

[26] Bodl. MS Ashmole 1813, fo 244, A. Cunningham to Edward Bernard, Aberdeen, 16 January 1684/5.

[27] For example the university's plea that the Long Parliament protect episcopacy, 'that ancient and apostolicall order'. To the High and Honorable Court of Parliament, the Humble Petition of the Universitie of Oxford (Oxford 1641), 2–3.

a partisanship which had been systematically fostered and deliberately transmitted to new generations of university men by Fell's congregation. It was the indomitable Fell and his Christ Church colleagues who were rightly credited with having 'upheld the arke' of the Cavalier Anglican faith 'in the late times', and it was they who, after 1660, succeeded in stamping their partisan vision of church and state relations on the Restoration university.[28] Their substantial achievement in resettling Oxford on the basis of their party principles enabled the university, for a second time in the century, to rally to the defence of king and church during the exclusion crisis of 1679–81.

The recidivist element in Oxford politics, never wholly in abeyance in the Cromwellian period, became more pronounced in the late 1650s. The vice-chancellorship of Rector Conant of Exeter, a Presbyterian moderate who succeeded the Independent John Owen in October 1657, marked a turning away from the path of radical puritanism, to the manifest relief of the university.[29] The turnabout was detectable in the partial resumption of academic dress after Owen's declared dislike of it;[30] in the rejection of the proposal that parliament should nominate college visitors in place of the discarded bishops of the Church of England;[31] and in outspoken opposition to the foundation of a third university at Durham:[32] convincing evidence of the undiminished strength of Oxford's institutional conservatism. But this was not all. Amid determined moves to petition for their abolition, the parliamentary visitors appear to have given up the ghost of their own accord. It was as if, by silently retiring, they recognized the futility of continuing to sit. The last order recorded in their register was dated 8 April 1658—more than two years before the return of the king.[33]

The final years of the protectorate also saw a change in the pattern of academic elections. Back in the statutory disposal of the colleges, elections tended to favour more traditional types than those intruded by the parliamentary visitors between 1648 and 1652 especially. Heartened by the tendency, a number of ejected dons sought to be elected or readmitted to fellowships.[34] Of greater significance, for they indicated the direction in which affairs were moving, were the four headships that went to known episcopalian and royalist sympathizers: Thomas Barlow, an intimate

---

[28] Bodl. MS Wood f. 39, fo 327, John Aubrey to Anthony Wood, St John the Evangelist's day 1679.

[29] Conant was Richard Cromwell's nominee. OUA register of convocation 1647–59, NEP/*supra*/26, register T, pp. 309–10, 332–3; OUA register of convocation 1659–71, NEP/*supra*/27, register Ta p. 1; John Conant jr, *The Life of . . . John Conant*, ed. W. Stanton (London 1823), 23–4.

[30] Conant, *The Life of John Conant*, 26; Walter Pope, *The Life of . . . Seth [Ward], Lord Bishop of Salisbury* (London 1697), 35; Wood, *Life and Times* i. 359.

[31] Conant, *The Life of John Conant*, 28–30; Wood, *History of the University* ii. 680; *Register*, ed. Burrows, cii–ciii.

[32] OUA register T, pp. 39–42, 'Reasons to be presented in the name of the university . . . against the erecting of an university at Durham'; Conant, *The Life of John Conant*, 26–7; Wood, *History of the University* ii. 694–5.

[33] Wood, *Life and Times* i. 268; Wood, *History of the University* ii. 686; *Register*, ed. Burrows, 439.

[34] *Register*, ed. Burrows, 473, 486, 537, 546, 560 ff.

correspondent of the ejected Cavalier Anglican clerics, Morley, Hammond, and Sanderson, at Queen's in 1657;[35] Michael Woodward, who had contacts with the Stuart court in exile, at New College in 1658;[36] Walter Blandford, chaplain of the Cavalier Lord Lovelace of Hurley, at Wadham in 1659;[37] and, perhaps more striking, in that it involved the election of a relative outsider, Seth Ward at Trinity, again in 1659. Only two years before, Ward, a loyalist fugitive from Cambridge and the chaplain of Bishop Brownrig of Exeter, had narrowly failed to carry the principalship of Jesus, his election having been quashed by Cromwell.[38] The election of such men, freely bestowed on them by their colleagues, reflected the dissatisfaction which the nation felt for the unstable revolutionary regime, as it lurched from one unacceptable alternative to another. More reassuringly for Charles II, it revealed the steady revival of legitimist feeling inside the university.

As the protectorate crumbled, and radical factions began to contend for power in the capital, Oxford found itself once more subjected to military occupation: a recurrence which, for most dons, underlined the political bankruptcy of the republic.[39] It was a development which served to alienate the university still further from its puritan rulers. Quite how far that alienation had proceeded was made clear, in August 1659, by the refusal of the heads to raise a regiment of scholars to defend 'the good old cause', when called on by Major-General Desborough and Dean Owen.[40] In the earlier crises, caused by Charles II's invasion from Scotland in 1651 and Penruddock's rising in Wiltshire in 1655, they had shown no reluctance to succour the state, but had sanctioned the enlisting of a volunteer force.[41] On this occasion their denial stemmed from quite another concern than the basic need to maintain the peace, which had previously been the deciding factor in their minds. With the collapse of Sir George Booth's Cheshire rising on behalf of the king in the late summer of 1659, the extent to which the university, city, and county of Oxford were permeated with royalist sentiment and royalist conspiracy began to be apparent, even to the negligent republican authorities.

[35] QCA register H, pp. 155–8: 15 February 1657; QCL MS 218, fos 116, 166ᵛ, Morley to [Barlow], 'ex Collegio Auriaco Bredae', 24 April and 1 July 1659. Barlow was deemed worthy of preferment by the exiled Stuart court. BL MS Egerton 2542, fos 266, 269.

[36] NCA MS 5061, item 2, 23 November 1658, MS 9655, fos 45, 53. Secretary Nicholas noted Woodward among the 'worthy men to be preferred to dignities in the church' in the event of a restoration. BL MS Egerton 2542, fo 269.

[37] WCA 2/1, pp. 115–16, 5 September 1659 (two days after Wilkins's resignation).

[38] TCA register A, fos 88–9; Pope, Ward, 45–6, 47–8. For Ward's asserting 'the liberties' of the university against 'those amongst ourselves, who have endeavoured to invade them', see QCA MS 521 (Lamplugh papers), published in Restoration Oxford, ed. Beddard i, no. 219 [August 1660]. [John Wilkins and Seth Ward], Vindiciae academiarum (Oxford 1654). For his burgeoning royalism see Beddard, 'The Restoration church', 166–7. Lettere di Henry Stubbe a Thomas Hobbes, ed. O. Nicastro (Siena 1973), 21.

[39] Bodl. MS Rawlinson a. 27, p. 753, 'The quarters of the regiments of horse'; Wood, Life and Times i. 288.

[40] Wood, History of the University ii. 696; PRO SP 25/79, p. 438.

[41] Wood, History of the University ii. 668; OUA register T, pp. 271–2; Oxford City Arch., E.4.6, fo 15, Protector Cromwell to the city, Whitehall, 12 March 1654/5; JCA bursars' accounts 1651–9, sub 1655; ECA MS A. 11. 10, sub 20 March 1655; PCA MS 4/1/1, fo 23; V. H. H. Green, The Commonwealth of Lincoln College 1427–1977 (Oxford 1979), 257.

Besides an extensive network of local Cavalier landowners, the conspirators
included at least one head of house, Provost Saye of Oriel, in whose lodgings (formerly a meeting-place of Charles I's wartime privy council) they regularly met. It
was in the quadrangle of Oriel College that they were instructed to assemble on
receiving the call to arms.[42] Although the Oxford royalists did not rise in support
of Booth, for no summons ever came, several Christ Church scholars, impatient
to act their part, made an attempt to join the Cheshire insurgents, but without success.[43] The failure of the royalist uprising, which had been projected on a national
scale that simply did not materialize, dashed the hopes of the Stuart court for an
immediate restoration: hopes which had encouraged Charles II and Secretary
Nicholas to draw up plans for replenishing the depleted hierarchy of the Church
of England, in which the university and its royalist alumni were to be given pride
of place.[44] The replanting of Christ Church with dependable loyalists—a top priority in the evolving Cavalier Anglican strategy—was so well advanced on paper
that the king had already signed warrants appointing his own chaplain, George
Morley, to the deanery and John Fell to a canonry. As things turned out, these well-
laid plans had only to be postponed, not abandoned.[45]

The royalists' disappointing performance was of short duration. In no time at all
popular reaction to the unwelcome prospect of a renewal of civil war, conjured up
by disputes inside the army, favoured their efforts to restore the king. In particular, it brought them the support of influential Presbyterians, who had grown weary
of 'reformation' being presented to them at a 'pyke's end'.[46] Already, as Ralph
Bathurst of Trinity knowingly observed, 'the generality of the university' had 'come
about to wish well to the government both of church and state as by law established': that is, as it had been constituted under episcopacy and monarchy, before
the Great Rebellion had subverted the rule of law.[47] The conversion of Nathanial
Crew—complete, on his own admission, by 1658—was a case in point. The son
of a Cromwellian lord, and raised a Presbyterian, he had been turned into 'a rot-
ten Cavalier' during his time in puritanical Lincoln, where, as sub-rector to the aged

[42] Bodl. MS Clarendon 65, fos 46, 59; PRO SP 29/4, nos 125, 126. For the college's resistance to
the parliamentary visitors see *Register*, ed. Burrows, 383, 386, 395; OUA WP/B/21/4, p. 326. For the
military wing of the royalist organization in Oxfordshire, Berkshire, and Buckinghamshire, see *Restoration
Oxford*, ed. Beddard iii, appx, no. 31.
[43] Bodl. MS Clarendon 65, fo 129, Mordecai Weare's examination, 3 October 1659, cf ibid., fos 74–7.
[44] BL MS Egerton 2542, fos 265–70ᵛ, Secretary Nicholas's memoranda.
[45] First destined for the mastership of the Savoy, Morley was finally set down for the Christ Church
deanery: ibid. fos 266, 267ᵛ, 268ᵛ, 270ᵛ. On 14/24 July 1659 Morley acknowledged his appointment, and
wrote to Hyde: 'I think you have made a good choyce for the canons of Christ Church': Bodl. MS
Clarendon 62, fo 86ᵛ; *Restoration Oxford*, ed. Beddard iii, appx, no. 35.
[46] Dr Williams's Library, London, Baxter letters IV, fo 69ᵛ, Peter du Moulin to Richard Baxter,
Adisham, 27 September 1659.
[47] T. Warton, *Life and Literary Remains of Ralph Bathurst* (London 1761), 206; John FitzWilliam, *A
Sermon Preach'd at Cotenham, near Cambridge, on the 9th September 1683* (London 1683), 26–7; Wood, *Life and
Times* i. 317.

Rector Hood, he was fast making himself a power in the land.[48] Scarcely less remarkable was the transformation wrought in Henry Foulis, a promising youth of Presbyterian parentage and upbringing. Having rubbed shoulders with the sons of northern Cavaliers, and been tutored by a devout churchman at Queen's, he became an enthusiastic Anglican royalist. It was as such that he was welcomed into the fellowship at Lincoln College by Crew in January 1660.[49] Similar conversions took place throughout the university, as 'every thing visibly tended to the reduction of his sacred majestie, and all persons in their several stations began to make way and prepare for it'.[50]

The resumption in 1659 of fanatical attacks on the universities, as the hives of indolent academic drones and centres of useless clerical learning, helped to push moderate Presbyterians into closer alliance with the devotees of the Church of England, in an attempt to defend the vestiges of a learned protestant ministry.[51] If the price of obtaining ecclesiastical and political stability, and of ensuring decent academic standards, was the acceptance of bishops and liturgy, then it was one which many Presbyterians were prepared to pay. When in July 1659 Robert South, a Student of Christ Church and a member of Fell's Anglican congregation,[52] preached in St Mary's against the reckless folly of fanaticism, and the injury it did to learning, religion, and the ministry, he was warmly congratulated by Oxford's most eminent Presbyterian divine, Edward Reynolds, the father-in-law of Vice-Chancellor Conant.[53] Only months before, South had shown where he thought the future lay by receiving clandestine orders from an Anglican bishop.[54] Also in July 1659 another Westminster Student of Christ Church, Henry Thurman, sent to the press his spirited *Defence of Humane Learning in the Ministry*, in which he denounced 'the haters of humane learning, as irrational, brutish and irreligious persons'.[55] He

---

[48] 'Memoirs of Nathaniel, Lord Crewe', ed. A. Clark, *Camden Miscellany* ix (Camden Soc. new ser. liii 1895) 1–2, 5–6; LCM register II, fos 101ᵛ, 103, 104ᵛ–15; C. E. Whiting, *Nathaniel Crewe Bishop of Durham and his Diocese, 1674–1721* (London 1940), 7–9, 13–23. Wood's personal animus must be discounted in *Life and Times* i. 332–3; cf *Restoration Oxford*, ed. Beddard i, nos 187 (and n. 1), 192–3, 236.

[49] LCM Register II, fo 105. Foulis's *The History of the Wicked Plots and Conspiracies of our Pretended Saints* (London 1662) became a great favourite with the Cavalier Anglicans. BL MS Lansdowne 960, fo 34ᵛ, Andrew Allam to White Kennett, St Edmund Hall, 21 September 1680; Wood, *Athenae* iii. 881.

[50] [John Fell], *The Life of . . . Dr H. Hammond* (London 1661), 208; Wood, *History of the University* ii. 696–8; Stephen Penton, *The Guardian's Instruction* (London 1688), 44.

[51] [Henry Stubbe], *A Light Shining out of Darkness* (London 1659); William Sprigge, *Modest Plan for a Commonwealth*, and *Sundry Things from Severall Hands concerning the University of Oxford* (London 1659); Wood, *History of the University* ii. 695–6; Wood, *Life and Times* i. 293–6. Wood bound many of the items of the controversy together in Bodl. Wood b. 24.

[52] The usurping Dean Owen had threatened South with expulsion and opposed his MA for attending Fell's 'episcopal meetings': 'Memoirs . . . of Dr. Robert South' in South, *Sermons* i, pp. iv–v.

[53] Robert South, *Interest Deposed, and Truth Restored, or a Word in Season delivered in Two Sermons: the first at St. Maryes in Oxford, on the 24th July, 1659* (Oxford 1660, 4th edn London 1678); Wood, *Life and Times* i. 369; Wood, *Athenae* iv. 633.

[54] He was ordained in 1658 'by a regular, though deprived bishop' of the Church of England: 'Memoirs . . . of Dr Robert South' in South, *Sermons* i, p. vii.

[55] Henry Thurman, *A Defence of Humane Learning in the Ministry* (Oxford 1660), epistle dedicatory, Christ Church, 14 July 1659; Wood, *Athenae* iii. 992.

was encouraged to do so by the sole surviving pre-war canon at Christ Church, John Wall. At last, even the most slippery of academic worms were turning against 'godly reformation'.[56]

The recall of what was left of the rebellious Long Parliament (disparagingly styled the Rump) in May 1659 signalled the defeat of the political radicals—an event that was at length brought home to an approving university by the dismissal from Christ Church of the ayatollahs of Independency, Dean Owen and Prebendary Upton, and the reinstatement on 13 March 1660 of two Presbyterian royalists, Edward Reynolds and John Mylles.[57] In 1651 Reynolds and Mylles had refused to take the engagement to the commonwealth, and had consequently been dismissed from their posts for owning their loyalty to Charles II.[58] The seeming victory of Presbyterianism was, however, short-lived. A rapidly disintegrating force in politics, neither it, nor any of the lesser sects, could withstand the floodwaters of Cavalier Anglicanism, which, like a spring tide, rose everywhere 'very high', and quickly inundated Oxford and the adjacent counties.[59]

Early in 1660 these old and newly reclaimed royalists—Cavalier Anglicans and moderate Presbyterians—were given fresh opportunities for action, of a safer kind than that of armed rebellion, which had always magnified fears of republican reprisal leading to last-minute losses of nerve. In February 'about five thousand considerable inhabitants' of Oxfordshire, led by the Cavalier activists Viscount Falkland, James Fiennes, and Sir Anthony Cope, joined in General Monck's call for 'a free parliament' as the best way of asserting 'the fundamental laws of the land' in relation to liberty, property, and religion. Among the demands voiced in their printed *Declaration* was one calling for the profession of 'the true protestant religion', the continuance of 'a lawful succession of godly and able ministers', and the preservation of 'the two universities, and all colledges in or belonging to either of them'.[60] It was a clear endorsement of the need for a settled and academically educated ministry, though as yet the political caution insisted on by the absent king and his advisers prevented the ministry from being identified with that of the episcopal Church of England, to which the local Cavaliers were inseparably wedded by conviction and interest. On 13 February Oxford greeted 'the news of a free parliament' with the ringing of bells and the roasting of 'rumps or tayles of sheep' on

---

[56] Wall, Thurman's dedicatee, had been Morley's tutor, and was the only canon of Christ Church to submit to parliament, though he did so with evident reluctance. *Register*, ed. Burrows, 14, 183, 189, 298; Bodl. MS Tanner 306, fos 374–5, MS J. Walker c. 8, fo 259ᵛ, MS Wood f. 35, fo 173ᵛ; Wood, *History of the University* ii. 605.

[57] *CJ* vii. 872; CA MS D. P. i. a. 11, fo 44ᵛ, 1. B. 3, pp. 93–4.

[58] Reynolds eventually 'subscribed in a quallifyed sence', but that did not save him. Dr Williams's Library, Baxter Letters IV, fos 177, 177ᵛ, H[enry] S[mith] to [Richard Baxter], 12 February 1650/1; *Restoration Oxford*, ed. Beddard iii, appx, nos 20–1; Bodl. MSS Wood f. 41, fo 236ᵛ, f. 35, fo 334, MS Rawlinson b. 407a, fo 84ᵛ, MS J. Walker c. 8, fo 217ᵛ.

[59] *The Thurloe State Papers*, ed. T. Birch (7 vols London 1742) vii. 895.

[60] *The Declaration of the County of Oxon., to His Excellency, the Lord General Monck* (London 1660), § v. It was presented on 13 February: *Restoration Oxford*, ed. Beddard i, no. 2.

bonfires. As a gesture of defiance against the iniquity of the old Cromwellian order and the contempt in which the Rump was held, some of the rumps were insultingly thrown at the windows of Warden Palmer of All Souls, an intruder, who lay dying in the college, but who in his heyday had been accounted 'a great favourite of Oliver' and 'a great rumper'.[61]

The general election of April 1660 for the Convention—the last of the irregular assemblies to be authorized by the moribund republic, and the one which restored Charles II—confirmed the direction in which the country was moving. In Oxford there was a fierce tussle among the voters of town and gown. For the first time since the imposition of the parliamentary visitation the royalists came out into the open, with John Fell and the members of his congregation campaigning vigorously on behalf of the king's partisans.[62] After a resounding royalist victory in the city on the 5th, culminating in the triumphal entry of Fell's friends Lord Falkland and Squire Huxley into Oxford,[63] the much smaller academic constituency, consisting of some 300 doctors and regent masters of the university, faced a four-sided contest on the 12th. The choice lay between, on the one hand, Monck's candidate, Speaker William Lenthall of Burford,[64] and Serjeant Matthew Hale of the neighbouring county of Gloucester, whom Vice-Chancellor Conant espoused[65] and, on the other, two gremial academics, both of whom had come out strongly in favour of recalling the king: the regius professor of medicine, Thomas Clayton junior, a covert episcopalian and a supplier of funds to the Stuart cause,[66] and the civilian, John Mylles, the recently reinstated 'collegiate prebend' of Christ Church, who had barely taken the trouble to disguise his monarchical preferences.[67]

After a hard fight, fought 'with all [the] art and the diligence' that each side could muster, Clayton and Mylles carried the poll. The satisfactory outcome of the royalists' labours prompted Fell to predict that, 'if elections are made at this rate in other places, we shall have reason to hope well of the ensueing parliament'. The

[61] Wood, *Life and Times* i. 303–4. At Palmer's death two All Souls fellows, Thomas Millington and Timothy Baldwyn, both of them covert royalists, put in for the wardenship, though Fell and the Cavaliers speculated (correctly) on Gilbert Sheldon's hoped-for reinstatement: Longleat House, MS Thynne 10, fos 153, 155, 156, 164.

[62] Longleat House, MS Thynne, fos 152–3, 155, John Fell to Thomas Thynne [Oxford], 6 and 15 March [1660].

[63] Ibid., fo 162, Fell to Thynne [Oxford, 7 April 1660]; Oxford City Arch., A.4.4, *sub* 14 and 20 March and 5 April 1660, A.5.7, fos 270, 270ᵛ, 271; Bodl. MS Clarendon 71, fo 240, MS Tanner 102, p. 136.

[64] OUA register Ta, pp. 10, 11–12, Monck to the university, St James's, 27 March and 5 April, Lenthall to same, The Rolls, 3 April 1660; NCA MS 9751, pp. 463–4, Lenthall to New College, The Rolls, 3 April 1660.

[65] J. B. Williams, *Memoirs of the Life . . . of Sir Matthew Hale* (London 1835), 45–6, Vice-Chancellor Conant to Hale, Oxford, 2 April 1660. Hale and Mylles had served as university burgesses in 1659: OUA register T, pp. 332–3.

[66] Longleat House, MS Thynne 10, fos 152, 162. For his subsequent stand on behalf of the church interest in the House of Commons, see Bodl. MS Dep. f. 9 (Bowman's diary), fos 23, 53ᵛ, 63, 65, 79, 83ᵛ, 86. For his role in royalist funding see *Restoration Oxford*, ed. Beddard i, no. 229. MCR 4. 20, pp. 34–5.

[67] Mylles had refused the engagement to be 'true and faithfull to the commonwealth of England' as 'is now established without a king or house of lords': *Register*, ed. Burrows, 274, 317, 489.

reviving independence of the university, not content with returning two royalists to Westminster, rebounded on those misguided colleagues who, 'upon their own score', had sought to make a present of a burgess's seat to Monck. Only the interposition of Vice-Chancellor Conant, who was plainly implicated in the episode, saved his cronies from the humiliation of an official investigation.[68] Their electoral efforts, it should be said, had not been squandered on the lost cause of republicanism, from which they were now as keen as any to distance themselves, but in trying to keep the interest of 'reformed religion' alive by defeating Clayton, whose parental attachment to the Laudian party was well known, and by restraining Mylles, whose moderate brand of Presbyterianism was, in concert with that of Dean Reynolds of Christ Church, reverting to the 'antediluvian Church of England', from which both of them had imprudently strayed.[69]

Flushed with their electoral triumph, the local Cavaliers could afford to be conciliatory to their old opponents. To ensure that fears of a royalist backlash did not hinder the Restoration, the Oxfordshire nobility, gentry, and clergy who had 'adhered to the late king' made a show of goodwill by issuing a manifesto at the end of April. In it they disavowed 'all purpose of revenge, or partial remembrance of things past', and declared their willingness 'to acquiesce in the determinations of ensuing parliaments'.[70] Among the thirty-nine signatories there was a healthy contingent of Cavalier Anglican academics, led by Archbishop Laud's nephew, Richard Baylie, the most senior of the surviving Royalist heads, who in 1648 had lost the presidency of St John's. In 1630 and 1636 Baylie had served as Laud's vice-chancellor.[71] Associated with him were no fewer than four Christ Church men— an ejected canon, Richard Gardiner, and three ejected Students, Fell, Dolben, and Samuel Jackson—and one ejected fellow of New College, John Lamphire.[72] In repudiating thoughts of revenge they acted under instructions from the king that had most probably been conveyed to them by Morley, the dean-designate of Christ Church, who was currently acting as the king's agent in London and the south of England.[73] It was Morley's unenviable commission to curb the expression of excessive episcopalian zeal and allay the remaining doubts of the Presbyterian moder-

[68] Longleat House, MS Thynne 10, fo 164.

[69] Mylles had been instrumental (along with Selden) in protecting the episcopalians of Queen's in the parliamentary visitation: *Restoration Oxford*, ed. Beddard iii, appx, no. 13. Morley accurately reported that Reynolds was 'for a moderate episcopacy': Bodl. MS Clarendon 71, fo 233; *The Flemings in Oxford* i. 132, 138.

[70] *A Declaration of the Nobility, Knights, and Gentry of the County of Oxon., which have adhered to the late King* (London 1660). Wood's copy adds the date, 28 April, to the imprint: Bodl. MS Wood 276A, item 221.

[71] For Baylie's pre-war vice-chancellorship see OUA register of convocation 1628–40, NEP/*supra*/24, register R, fos 130, 150, 156ᵛ–7; A. J. Taylor, 'The royal visit to Oxford in 1636', *Oxoniensia* i (1936), 151–8. For his relationship to Laud: BL MS Sloane 3080, MS Lansdowne 986, fos 62–3; *The History Of The Troubles And Tryal Of ... William Laud*, ed. H. Wharton (London 1695), 455. Baylie had been chaplain to Charles I: OUA *register of convocation 1642–7*, NEP/*supra*/25, register Sb, p. 5.

[72] For a detailed identification of the other signatories, see *Restoration Oxford*, ed. Beddard i, no. 15.

[73] Bodl. MS Carte 30, fo 566, MS Clarendon 71, fo 121; *Reliquiae Baxterianae*, ed. Matthew Sylvester (London 1696), pt ii, pp. 208, 217–18.

ates concerning Charles's intentions towards them.[74] The Oxfordshire manifesto—one of many that appeared across the country—was calculated to promote 'that perfect union', which, it was believed, would not fail 'to bring the nation to a happy settlement' of its disorders by calling in the king.

As Charles II's return grew more and more likely by the day, political confidence increased among the ejected royalist dons. With the king about 'to enter his own', they began to assume that they too might recover the preferment from which they had been 'forceably ejected' for no other reason than that they had loyally refused recognition to the unlawful parliamentary visitation. On 9 April an ejected fellow of New College, Robert Bowman, initiated proceedings to regain his fellowship by bringing his claim before the commissioners for restoring ministers and other unduly sequestered persons.[75] Following the Convention's May Day resolution in favour of restoring the monarchy, a more substantial claimant appeared in the person of the ejected president of Magdalen, John Oliver, Archbishop Laud's former domestic chaplain.[76] On learning of the Rump's tardily obeyed dismissal of the intruded Independent, Thomas Goodwin, Oliver did all he could to canvass his claim to the presidency. Convinced that the law was on his side, he solicited the president of the council of state, Arthur Annesley, for restitution.[77] He was already privately in touch with the senior fellows of the college, who, in the vacancy, were keen to have him back. Though Oliver was most eager to return, he was careful not to prejudice the interest of the ejected royalist fellows by striking a precipitate deal with the existing society.[78] To make sure that he stood fair in the eyes of the king, he opened a correspondence with the Stuart court at Breda, where he had a well-wisher in the person of Lord Chancellor Hyde, his former pupil.[79]

A significant breakthrough occurred on 17 May. As a result of multiple petitions presented to the revived house of lords (a body firmly dominated by Cavaliers), ten ejected fellows of New College were ordered to be restored, including the enterprising Bowman. Two days later the order was carried out by Warden Woodward.[80] On the 18th President Oliver obtained a similar order, which was, again, obeyed with alacrity.[81] Further restitutions were ordered on 22 and 25 May, the beneficiaries being six ejected fellows of Magdalen and the ejected master of University

---

[74] Bodl. MS Clarendon 71, fos 75, 108, 138, 150, 158, 356–61; Bosher, *The Making of the Restoration Settlement*, 105–14, 126–7, 134–5, 138–9.

[75] NCA MS 1069, item 7; *Restoration Oxford*, ed. Beddard i, no. 13; *Register*, ed. Burrows, 49, 55, 92, 144, 527; *Walker Revised*, ed. Matthews, 30.

[76] *Walker Revised*, ed. Matthews, 28, 223; *Register*, ed. Burrows, 10, 21, 95, 96, 105; Bloxam, *Reg. Magdalen* v. 82; *The Flemings in Oxford* i. 133.

[77] *CJ* vii. 823; *Register*, ed. Burrows, 264, 330, 339 ff; *Restoration Oxford*, ed. Beddard i, no. 4.

[78] MCA MS 684 (unfoliated), Nathaniel Chyles to Dr Henry Clerke, Middle Temple, 2 May, Oliver to same, London, 12 May 1660.

[79] Bodl. MS Clarendon 72, fos 206, 207ᵛ, Oliver to Hyde, London, 4 May 1660.

[80] HLRO main papers, 14 and 16 May 1660; *Restoration Oxford*, ed. Beddard i, nos 24, 26; *LJ* xi. 31, 34; NCA MS 1069, 19 May 1660.

[81] HLRO main papers, 18 May 1660; *LJ* xi. 33; *Mercurius Publicus*, no. 21 (17–24 May 1660).

College, Thomas Walker, another of Laud's former chaplains.[82] The flurry of royalist activity was given added impetus on 8 May by the resignation, out of the blue,
of the chancellorship of Oxford by Richard Cromwell, the fallen lord protector.
'Amidst the many examples of the instability and revolutions of humaine affaires'
which surrounded him, he found that he was unable to help either himself or the
university.[83] His resignation activated the half-forgotten royalist chancellor, William
Seymour, marquess of Hertford, to assert his right to govern the university.

On 18 May Lord Hertford wrote directly to the university. He pointedly
reminded the dons that his patent for the chancellorship had been granted to him
for life, and that they were not, as some supposed, free to make a new election,
for the place was legally his.[84] He subsequently forwarded an order of the house
of lords, dated 26 May, restoring him to the exercise of his office, and commanding 'all persons and members of the university . . . to yield obedience' to him.[85] All
of this was as wormwood and gall to Vice-Chancellor Conant and the puritan
heads, but they had, ineluctably, to accept a notorious Cavalier Anglican as their
lawful chancellor. In a meeting of convocation held on 6 June, Hertford was formally readmitted to his place—just two days after he had obtained a supplementary order from the lords, empowering him to restore all heads, fellows, and
officers of the colleges and university who had been 'unjustly put out' of their freeholds.[86] There was no mistaking his intention to restore the university, so far as he
was able, to the state it had been in under Charles I, when it was called on to sow
'the good seedes of religion, loyalty, and learning' throughout his dominions.[87]

Hertford issued his commission for visiting the university on 14 June. His delegates began work at Oriel on the 18th.[88] A month later, on 23 July, they were
superseded by the order for a royal visitation.[89] The overlapping identity of those
named in both commissions ensured that the process of reviewing the academic
body remained in reliable hands. The king's commissioners were loyal episcopalians
to a man.[90] Contrary to what Wood recorded, they sat not for ten weeks but for

---

[82] HLRO main papers, 22 and 25 May 1660; *LJ* xi. 36; UCA register I, fos 20–1, 27, long book, p.
1; *Restoration Oxford*, ed. Beddard i, nos 32–5, 37.

[83] OUA register Ta, p. 15, Cromwell to Vice-Chancellor Conant, Hursley, 8 April 1660.

[84] Ibid., pp. 16–17, Chancellor Hertford to Vice-Chancellor Conant, Essex House, 18 May 1660. His
letters patent ran 'durante vita tua naturali'. OUA register Sb, pp. 42–3, 'diploma cancellarii',
Convocation House, 27 October 1643. Bodl. MS Wood f. 35, fo 370; *Restoration Oxford*, ed. Beddard iii,
appx, no. 6.

[85] *LJ* xi. 42.

[86] OUA register Ta, p. 17; *LJ* xi. 53; Bodl. MS Wood f. 35, fo 369a.

[87] OUA register Sb, p. 40, Charles I to university, Oxford, 23 October 1643, calling on his 'faithfull'
university to elect 'some such nobel personage among the loyall peeres' following the defection of the
earl of Pembroke to the rebels.

[88] NCA MS 1069, unnumbered items, Hertford's commission and his commissioners' summons for
New College to appear before them on 19 May; QCA MS 521; WCA 4/119; for their proceedings see
Restoration Oxford, ed. Beddard i, nos 48, 51–4, 58, 75.

[89] MCA MS 730b, fo 2ᵛ, Charles II to Vice-Chancellor Conant, Whitehall, 13 July; Bodl. MS E museo
246, the original commission; CCA MS 301, fos 161–4ᵛ.

[90] Twelve of Hertford's fourteen commissioners were named by the king in his commission.
Compare the two sets of names in *Restoration Oxford*, ed. Beddard i, nos 48, 104.

above two years, during which time the appointment and qualifications of all mem-bers of the university were thoroughly examined.[91] The commissioners did a good job in reconciling the bulk of the existing university to king and church. Their work was made easier by the voluntary and extensive return to pre-war academic alle-giances, which had either antedated or accompanied Charles II's homecoming, and by the general acquiesence of the intruders. Though death, marriage, preferment, and conversion to the Catholic Church had greatly reduced the number of ejected royalist dons who were eligible to be restored,[92] restorations were authorized right across the face of the university, beginning with professors and officials and extending through college societies from heads of house to domestic servants. Where there were no royalist claimants to be satisfied, the present occupants were confirmed on accepting the king's authority and conforming to local statutes—irre-spective of whether they were lawful appointees who had submitted to the parlia-mentary visitors or had been subsequently and illegally intruded by them.[93]

With Hertford, the victor of Lansdown, back in the seat of authority the Cavalier Anglican strategy moved remorselessly forward.[94] His promotion of honorary degrees proclaimed his intention to raise anew the reputation and status of the 'suf-fering' episcopalian clergy in their efforts to recapture the national establishment. In the three months of failing health left to him, from July to September 1660, the marquess recommended forty-three candidates for degrees: nearly two thirds of them in the faculty of theology—twenty-four DDs and two BDs.[95] The chief recip-ients were the bishops, deans, and prebendaries of the reviving Church of England.[96] Among the rest were heads of house, incumbents of important town livings, and civil lawyers who operated the ecclesiastical courts: individuals who were essential to the re-erection of the protestant establishment. The all-too-short Indian summer of Hertford's reinstated chancellorship set the pattern for his suc-cessors to emulate. They, like him, were to rely upon the advice of Sheldon and Morley, who, for the remainder of their lives, stood resolutely behind the chancel-lor's throne, tirelessly working for the good of king and church.

The election of the lord chancellor of England as Hertford's successor, on 27 October 1660, was the Cavalier Anglicans' master stroke, for not only was Edward Hyde one of the outstanding statesmen of the English seventeenth century, but he was also a man who by family, education, conviction, and service was intimately

---

[91] 'The Restoration Visitation of the University of Oxford and its Colleges', ed. F. J. Varley, *Camden Miscellany* xviii (Camden Soc. 3rd ser. lxxix 1948). Varley's historical introduction is inaccurate and mis-leading, and the text he publishes corrupt and incomplete. Wood, *History of the University* ii. 699–700.

[92] Wood, *History of the University* ii. 701. Bodl. MS Wood f. 35, fos 241, 248, 249, 251, 252, 259, 286.

[93] 'Restoration Visitation', ed. Varley, 7, 9, 22, 24, 26, 28 ff.

[94] His first act was to restore the ejected Cavalier Anglican, Nicholas Strangways, to his Wadham fellowship on 20 June 1660: WCA 4/119, 2/1, p. 119. For his favourable judgement on the degrees and seniority of those Oxonians who had been 'a longe time debarred by ... our late unhappy troubles', see OUA register Ta, pp. 48–9; CCA MS 301, fos 167[r-v].

[95] OUA register Ta, pp. 24, 27, 34, 39, 40, 41, 45.

[96] Ibid., pp. 19, 29, 30, 32, 45.

identified with the university, the monarchy, and the church.[97] In accepting the post Clarendon freely acknowledged that a part of his 'trust' was 'to use all possible endeavours' to increase the number of the university's friends, 'and to lessen the power of those whoe, by the folly and wickednesse of the late ill times, have contracted a prejudice to learning and learned men'.[98] With Sheldon and Morley to guide him, the ascendancy of the Cavalier Anglican interest was assured. For the next seven years Chancellor Clarendon regularly dispensed his patronage in favour of attested royalists and 'orthodox' churchmen.[99] The widespread distribution of Cavalier Anglican dons throughout Oxford, combined with their impressive record of fidelity to king and church, their academic seniority, and their superior connections with the extramural leaders of their party in court and country, did more than offset their numerical weakness. Such advantages allowed them to occupy the high moral ground, to dominate the government of the university, and to carry all before them.

Clarendon's fall from royal favour, his subsequent impeachment, and his sudden flight to France caught Oxford unawares. No longer able 'to be of use' to his academic clients, he wrote from Calais on 7 December 1667, tendering his resignation of the chancellorship, 'to the end that they make choyce of some other person better qualified to assist and protect them'.[100] Fortunately John Fell, as the reigning vice-chancellor, was in a position to act decisively. He was more determined than ever to perpetuate the Cavalier Anglican hold over the university, for he disliked the direction in which court politics were moving under the malign influence of the libertine George Villiers, second duke of Buckingham. Keen to acknowledge the gratitude which the university felt for Sheldon's munificence in building the theatre, and recalling the glorious chancellorship of his hero, William Laud, he summoned convocation, and proposed the archbishop of Canterbury as Clarendon's successor.[101]

On 20 December Gilbert Sheldon was elected without demur.[102] He was the last ecclesiastic to be chosen head of the University of Oxford. However, the snap election created almost as many problems as it solved. Having obtained the chancellorship for Sheldon, Fell was distressed to find that the archbishop would not, after repeated 'importunities', take the office upon him. Age, attendant infirmity, and

---

[97] OUA register Ta, pp. 64–5, 67–8, 69–71; Bodl. MS Ashmole 840, p. 261; *Mercurius Publicus*, no. 47 (15–22 November 1660). These correct the date and amplify the account in Wood, *Life and Times* i. 346–7.

[98] OUA register Ta, p. 100, Chancellor Hyde to university, Worcester House, 12 March 1661.

[99] Ibid., pp. 80–2, 104, 107, 111–12, 122; BL Add. MS 14,269, fos 3–4ᵛ, 5, 9ᵛ, 9*ᵛ, 12ᵛ, 13 ff. He named Sheldon and Morley as the overseers of his will, Rouen, 11 December 1674. Bodl. MS Clarendon 87, fo 239. *Restoration Oxford*, ed. Beddard i, nos 290–2, 329, 348–9, 357, 382, 410, 425–7, 430.

[100] Bodl. MS Clarendon 85, fo 437, Chancellor Clarendon to Vice-Chancellor Fell, Calais, 7/17 December 1667.

[101] Bodl. MS Tanner 338, fo 178, Vice-Chancellor Fell to Chancellor-elect Sheldon [Christ Church], 20 December [1667].

[102] OUA register Ta, pp. 240–1.

existing responsibilities were the reasons given for his declining to be admitted chancellor.[103] Confidentially, Sheldon hinted at what was a more pressing reason for thinking himself 'unfitt . . . to accept of their kindness'—his own loss of royal favour, an occurrence brought about by his continued refusal to make concessions to the dissenters, and his earlier support for the disgraced lord chancellor.[104] Fell felt unavoidably downcast, even rejected, and said so. It was a reproach which the archbishop emphatically repudiated.[105]

For the time being an irregular makeshift arrangement, not sanctioned by the Laudian statutes, was worked out, whereby Sheldon remained chancellor in name, but undertook no business, and the dean, as vice-chancellor, got on with running the university as best he could until a dependable successor could be installed. For Fell it was an unsatisfactory outcome, which laid him open to undeserved charges of personal ambition.[106] Yet, in spite of its drawbacks, the arrangement sufficed to tide the university over an awkward hiatus in its government. It avoided the danger of leaving the chancellorship vacant, just as the long-gathering dislike of Cavalier Anglican policies had erupted at court in demands for a revision of the Restoration settlement in church and state.[107] The stop-gap prevented the king from attempting to strengthen the incoming Cabal administration—a ministry which the Cavalier Anglicans feared for its patronage of comprehension and indulgence. Checkmated by the most loyal of his adherents, Charles was unable to foist on to the university a courtier more in tune with his own tolerationist outlook.

In declining the office for himself, Sheldon had a clear understanding of what Oxford required in a chancellor. It needed a lay grandee, preferably a Cavalier Anglican nobleman of the stature of Hertford, who enjoyed Charles II's respect. In the treacherous years of the Cabal administration it was not an easy combination to come by. In recommending ex-lord lieutenant of Ireland James Butler, duke of Ormonde, to the University on 31 July 1669, he named 'the most fitt person' he could think of for the post.[108] Having incurred the royal displeasure for his unremitting advocacy of Cavalier Anglican policies, Sheldon was careful to relinquish the chancellorship to one whom he knew was 'acceptable to the king', as well as dependable in his churchmanship.[109] He appreciated the necessity of keeping up good relations with the king. After Clarendon's removal from the

---

[103] Ibid., p. 270, Sheldon to Vice-Chancellor Fell, Lambeth House, 31 July 1669; Bodl. MS Eng. letters c. 328, fo 509, Thomas Barlow to Francis Parry, Queen's, 8 January 1668/9.

[104] Bodl. MS Add. c. 308, fo 108ᵛ, Sheldon to Principal [Jenkins], no date; BL Add. MS 19,526, fo 136; Beddard, 'The Restoration church', 170–2. For Sheldon's private strictures on Clarendon's more recent conduct see Beddard, 'Sheldon and Anglican recovery', p. 1010 and nn. 17 and 18.

[105] Bodl. MS Add. c. 308, fo 109, Sheldon to Vice-Chancellor [Fell], Lambeth House, 24 January 1667/8.

[106] BL Add. MS 19,526, fos 160ᵛ–1; Bodl. MS Bodley 594, p. 56; Wood, Life and Times ii. 144–5.

[107] M. Lee, The Cabal (Urbana Ill. 1965), 162–3, 175–6, 197–200.

[108] For the surviving English bishops' appreciation of Ormonde's services to king and church during the Interregnum see Restoration Oxford, ed. Beddard i, no. 20; see also J. C. Beckett, The Cavalier Duke (Belfast 1990), 103.

[109] OUA register Ta, p. 270, Sheldon to Vice-Chancellor Fell, Lambeth House, 31 July 1669.

government, Charles had gone out of his way to assure Ormonde of the continuance of his favour by forestalling any suggestion from England that his own reputation might be damaged by the lord chancellor's fall. Charles knew that he could rely on his loyalty and service, despite 'so declared a friendship' between the two men.[110] Even after deciding to dismiss him from the lieutenancy of Ireland in February 1669 (the result of court intrigue rather than of a change of heart on Charles's part), the king expressed his entire satisfaction with the duke's great services to the crown, as well he might.[111]

From a Cavalier Anglican viewpoint, Ormonde was eminently qualified to be chancellor of Oxford. Of his attachment to the established church there was no doubt. Ever since his upbringing as a protestant had been arranged by James I in the household of the Calvinist archbishop of Canterbury, George Abbot, he had been a staunch member of the Church of England.[112] At his return to Ireland as lord lieutenant in 1662, he had been expected to 'excel the earle of Strafford in his kindnesse to the church'.[113] The support which he unstintingly gave to the infirm protestant episcopate of Ireland had more than answered Cavalier Anglican expectations.[114] 'Besides the eminency of his birth and dignities' he had, Sheldon reminded the electors, 'made himselfe more illustrious by his vertue and meritts, by that constant integrity he hath in all fortunes borne to the king and church, and ... by his love of letters and learned men'. The archbishop undertook that, as his 'quality' would 'dignify their choyce' of him, so 'the duke's affection for them' would 'improve his care over them', and his interest would 'be able at their need to support them'.[115] It is typical of the unchanging allegiances of the Cavalier Anglican creed that Sheldon should nevertheless have emphasized his candidate's good standing with king and church: the lodestars of Restoration Anglicanism. With this degree of clerical stage-management, in which the recommendation of Lambeth House was backed by Vice-Chancellor Fell's accurate sense of timing, the very idea of a competitor appearing against the duke was avoided.[116]

Ormonde's election on 4 August 1669 was a foregone conclusion. It was made sweeter still by Sheldon's valued reassurance of his own personal readiness to serve

[110] Bodl. MS Carte 220, fo 326, Lord Ossory to Ormonde, 4 January 1667/8; BL MS Egerton 2618, fo 115, Charles II to Ormonde, Whitehall, 15 September [1667].

[111] Bodl. MS Carte 50, fo 24, Ormonde to Matthews, Whitehall, 27 March 1669; T. Carte, *The Life of James Duke of Ormond* (6 vols Oxford 1851) v. 103; J. I. McGuire, 'Why was Ormond dismissed in 1669?', *Irish Historical Studies* xviii (1972–3).

[112] In 1620 his mother, Elizabeth Poyntz, had placed him in a Catholic school at Finchley, Middlesex, whence he was deliberately removed and made a royal ward in order to be raised a protestant: Carte, *Ormond* i. 6–11, iv. 483, 526; Lady Burghclere, *The Life of James First Duke of Ormonde* (2 vols London 1912) i. 31–4.

[113] BL Add. MS 29,584, fo 6, Bishop Jeremy Taylor of Derry to Christopher, Lord Hatton, Dublin, 23 November 1661.

[114] In Ireland he was valued 'as one of the chiefest pillars of support' for the protestant establishment. Bodl. MSS Carte 30, fo 685, Dudley Loftus to Ormonde, Dublin, 1 June 1660, 33, fo 532, Archbishop Michael Boyle to same, Dublin, 12 August 1664.

[115] OUA register Ta, p. 270; Bodl. MSS Carte 69, fo 160, 141, fo 99, 147, fo 99.

[116] Bodl. MS Add. d. 105, fo 37, Dr John Wallis to [Robert] Boyle, Oxford, 17 August 1669.

the university on all occasions. Three weeks later Ormonde took the oaths as chancellor in an extraordinary convocation held in Worcester House, Clarendon's former residence. The ceremony provided the opportunity for a show of Church of England strength in what was virtually a party rally, attended by an array of bishops and noblemen, headed, of course, by those immovable Oxonian figures Sheldon and Morley.[117] The duke of Ormonde was to serve Oxford well as chancellor for two whole decades. At his death in 1688 he was succeeded in the chancellorship by two of his grandsons: James Butler, second duke of Ormonde, who served from 1688 until 1715, when as a fully fledged Jacobite he joined James III in exile;[118] and Charles Butler, earl of Arran, who carried on from 1715 to 1758.[119] The Restoration legacy was an enduring one. For almost a century the Butler clan gave sterling service to Oxford.

The Butlers' record of dedication was matched, and sometimes exceeded in length of years, by that of other Cavalier Anglican families of cancellarial rank: in particular, in the descendants of Chancellor Clarendon—from his sons, Henry Hyde, second earl of Clarendon, and Lawrence Hyde, first earl of Rochester, and his grandson, Henry Hyde, second earl of Rochester and fourth earl of Clarendon, who, between them, monopolized the high stewardship of the university from 1686 to 1753,[120] to his great-grandson, Henry Hyde, Viscount Cornbury, burgess of the university from 1732 to 1750;[121] in the collateral kindred of Chancellor Laud—from his nephew by marriage, President Baylie of St John's (1632–48, 1660–7), through Baylie's son-in-law and successor in the presidency, Peter Mews (1667–73), later bishop of Winchester and the statutory visitor of five Oxford colleges (1684–1706), down to President M. J. Routh of Magdalen, who, after an incredible sixty-three years as the head of his college, died in 1854;[122] and in the collateral relatives of Chancellor Sheldon—from his nephew by marriage, John Dolben, Student (1640–8) and canon of Christ Church (1660–6), and, later, as archbishop of York, the visitor of Queen's (1683–6), down to Sir William Dolben, burgess of the university in 1768 and again from 1780 to 1802, both of whom were, like four more, unbroken, and scarcely less distinguished generations of the Dolben family, Old Westminsters and Christ Church men.[123] It was this kind of hereditary academic association within the historic landowning families of England which gave

---

[117] Bishops Henchman of London, Blandford of Oxford, and Dolben of Rochester were also present: OUA register Ta, pp. 271–5.

[118] R. A. Beddard, 'James II and the Catholic challenge', pp. 942, 950–2 below; R. A. Beddard, *A Kingdom without a King* (Oxford 1988), 124, 153–4, 158, 165, 168, 174, 203; G. H. Jones, *The Mainstream of Jacobitism* (Harvard 1954), 103, 106–7; D. Szechi, *Jacobitism and Tory Politics 1710–14* (Edinburgh 1984), 39–40.

[119] OUA register of convocation 1704–30, NEP/*subtus*/31, register Bd, fos 126–7ᵛ.

[120] Bodl. MS Carte 50, fo 372, MS Bodl. 594, fo 58ᵛ; OUA register Bd, fos 59ᵛ–60, 75–75ᵛ.

[121] OUA register of convocation 1730–41, NEP/*subtus*/32, register Be, fos 14, 14ᵛ.

[122] R. D. Middleton, *Dr Routh* (London 1938), 3, 144.

[123] OUA register of convocation 1766–76, NEP/*subtus*/36, register Bi, pp. 42–5; OUA register of convocation 1776–93, NEP/*subtus*/37, register Bk, pp. 112–13; OUA register of convocation 1793–1802, NEP/*subtus*, pp. 577–82; CA D. P. i. a. 15, fos 97ᵛ, 121ᵛ, 130, 133; G. F. Russell Barker and A. H. Stenning, *The Record of Old Westminsters* (2 vols London 1928) i. 274–6.

social cohesion and political solidity to so much of the institutional life of Oxford under the *ancien régime*, and, in the process, helped to perpetuate the ascendancy of the protestant establishment into Victorian times.

Throughout the Restoration period Oxford was particularly blessed in its choice of worthy churchmen to serve as chancellor. They were, without exception, unimpeachable loyalists of the highest moral character, endowed with a genuine love for the established church, and imbued with the Anglican ideal of public service. In this respect Oxford's good fortune stands in marked contrast to the ill fate of Cambridge, where Charles II was forced to intervene no less than twice, in 1674 and again in 1682, to remove the chancellor of the university, and recommend a successor of his choosing.[124] The king's repeated intervention at Cambridge highlights the personal distinction attaching to the chancellors of Oxford in the same period, and the political success of Oxford's Cavalier Anglicans in managing their own affairs.

Christ Church was from the very beginning to occupy a special position in the life not only of Restoration Oxford, but also of the restored Church of England. Because of the unique nature of its foundation by Henry VIII, as a protestant cathedral which doubled as the grandest of all the Oxford colleges, it necessarily stood at the forefront of Cavalier Anglican endeavours to return the university and diocese to pre-war orthodoxy.[125] It set the pattern which the other colleges followed, more or less as the provisions of their local statutes and financial endowments enabled them. Being a cathedral meant that its major appointments were ecclesiastical, and belonged to the crown *pleno jure*. Vacancies in the dean and chapter—its governing body—could, therefore, be supplied at once by the king, without waiting for the royal visitation of the university to start work. Since it had long been known that the deanery and four out of the eight canonries were vacant by the deaths of their lawful incumbents, and had fallen into Charles's immediate gift, they had become the subject of sustained Cavalier Anglican lobbying within the exiled court, intensified, on its return to England, by a new wave of petitions from individual ejected Christ Church royalists, soliciting preferment in their old college. The petitioners, understanding the intricacies of ecclesiastical patronage, addressed themselves, not to the indulgent house of lords, but directly to the Anglican king.[126] Instructively, the Christ Church posts were among the very first dignities of the Church of England to be filled at the Restoration[127]—an acknow-

---

[124] For the removal of the dukes of Buckingham and Monmouth see Bodl. MS Tanner 157, fo 21, Charles II to the University of Cambridge, 11 July 1674; CCCA MS 301, fo 182, same to same, 4 April 1682; QCL MS 521; PRO SP 29/418, nos 173, 177, SP 44/57, p. 48.

[125] Fell maintained that Christ Church was 'not a college properly so called, but a cathedral church': Bodl. MS Wood f. 41, fo 234.

[126] Bodl. MS Clarendon 62, fos 86–7; PRO SP 29/6, nos 6, 25, SP 29/8, no. 79, SP 29/20, no. 116. There were counter-petitions from the intruders: PRO SP 29/6, nos 22, 24.

[127] CA MS xii. b. 103, pp. 43, 56, 57; I. M. Green, *The Re-establishment of the Church of England 1660–1663* (Oxford 1978), 67.

ledgement of the importance which Charles and his pertinacious Cavalier Anglican supporters attached to them.

The king began by naming the new dean early in July 1660. It was a bold move, for the intruded Presbyterian Reynolds, whom the Rump had recently restored to the deanery, had been conspicuous in welcoming him home. His timely conversion had eased the accession of other Presbyterian notables to the king's cause.[128] On signifying his willingness to conform to the Church of England, Reynolds was moved sideways to the wardenship of Merton, to make room for the returning royalist émigré, George Morley.[129] A Calvinist episcopalian with a fine record of uninterrupted service to both Charles I and Charles II, Morley had been earmarked for the deanery prior to Booth's rising in 1659, for the government appreciated the need to have a reliable Cavalier Anglican cleric in the most prestigious permanent post in the university. To support him, Charles advanced to the vacant canonries that valiant triumvirate of Christ Church royalists: Fell, Dolben, and Allestree, who had maintained the cause of church and king in Oxford throughout the Cromwellian Interregnum.[130] They too had been scheduled for promotion by the exiled court. They were now joined by another ejected Christ Church don, Jasper Mayne, who had lost his Studentship and his livings for owning the same loyal cause.[131]

In ignoring the existing 'collegiate prebends', who had been illegally intruded into Christ Church by the usurping authorities, Charles stuck to the letter of the law; as he did at Merton, in disregarding the intruded Cromwellian warden, Jonathan Goddard. In removing Reynolds to Merton, the king created the opportunity to exercise another of the prerogatives of the crown: the right to nominate a warden during the vacancy of the see of Canterbury, the archbishop having, as the visitor of the college, the final say in any election.[132] In this concerted fashion Charles managed simultaneously to stamp his personal authority on two of the greatest colleges of the university, Christ Church and Merton, and open the way for a speedy resumption of Anglican worship in the most public place in Oxford—the cathedral.

As in other cathedral cities, the reappearance of the Anglican authorities was popular. Morley was conducted into the city 'by above 80 horse', mostly Students

---

[128] Bodl. MS Clarendon 72, fos 19, 284, MS Carte 77, fo 635; Sion College, London, register A, fo 204; *Mercurius Publicus*, no. 22 (24–31 May 1660); *Reliquiae Baxterianae*, pt ii, pp. 229, 230, 232, 265, 274, 278, 281–3, 303 ff.

[129] MCA registrum 1567–1731, pp. 419–20; 4. 29, p. 33.

[130] Fell had the grant of Morley's canonry by Charles II's 'immediate warrant': PRO SP 29/8, no. 80. All three of them simultaneously received DDs 'per literas regias': OUA register Ta, p. 57. Sheldon got Morley to put Hyde in mind of his nephew, Dolben: Bodl. MS Clarendon 72, fo 117ᵛ, 'Jeremie Baker' [Morley's royalist code-name] to Hyde, London, 1 May 1660.

[131] BL MS Egerton 2542, fo 270ᵛ; *Walker Revised*, ed. Matthews, 25, 298; *Register*, ed. Burrows, 30–1, 196; Wood, *History of the University* ii. 610. All four were made royal chaplains: PRO SP 29/76, no. 67.

[132] *Statuta Collegii Mertonensis*, ch. 29, De electione custodis; *Restoration Oxford*, ed. Beddard i, no. 84 and n. 3.

of Christ Church. Such a high turn-out, representing approximately 80 per cent of the Student body, was an earnest of the college's affection for his person and for the reviving Church of England. As his cavalcade passed from Magdalen Bridge to Christ Church the streets were lined 'on both sides' by scholars and townsfolk, and his arrival greeted 'with lowd acclamations and ringing of bells', which he correctly supposed was 'an argument of the people's inclination the right way'. On 26 July he was installed dean, and proceeded forthwith to install the new canons. At the close of a busy day he was able to report to Whitehall that he had met with no opposition. 'All the intruders', he wrote, 'are willing to quit theyr possession to us.'[133]

The restored dean and chapter lost no time in instituting a return to pre-war Anglican normality. Having announced their resumption of authority to the college by ordering that the canons' table be re-erected in the hall, they set about reforming the religious discipline and domestic economy of the college.[134] A beginning was made with the reintroduction of the Book of Common Prayer into the cathedral.[135] The number and timing of 'fastinge nights and gaudy dayes' were regulated 'according to the rule of the church and the custome of the colledge'—in other words, according to the Anglican kalendar, which appointed which holy days, vigils, and fasts were to be observed throughout the nation. Instead of the private prayer sessions, held of an evening in tutors' rooms, that had found favour under puritan rule, public Latin prayers were ordered to be said 'constantly att night' in the cathedral, beginning at half past eight.[136] Before the year was out the text of the *Liber precum publicarum in usum ecclesiae cathedralis christi* was once more in print, and on sale to churchmen in and out of Oxford.[137]

In Morley's subsequent absence the work of restoration fell on the broad backs of the dedicated, hardworking, younger canons: Fell, Dolben, and Allestree. Even before their installation as canons, Fell and Dolben had been elected to key college offices; the former as sub-dean, the latter as treasurer.[138] The ascendancy of the old Cavalier triumvirate was sealed on 31 July, when Morley nominated Allestree to act as his proxy during his repeated absences in London, where he was required to assist the equally absent warden of All Souls, Gilbert Sheldon, dean of the chapel royal, in settling the church interest on a firm foundation at court.[139] Between them the three friends, who were very much of one mind when it came to serving the church, were able to give a strong lead to their brethren of the chapter, and, by this means, to the entire college. On 1 August, after an intermission

[133] PRO SP 29/8, no. 64, Dean Morley to John Nicholas [Christ Church], 26 July 1660. BL Add. MS 19,526, fo 44.

[134] CA MS D&C, i. b. 3, p. 101, 27 July 1660.

[135] PRO SP 29/11, no. 27; Bodl. MS Tanner 102, fo 71ᵛ; BL Add. MS 19,521, fo 44ᵛ.

[136] CA MS D&C, i. b. 3, pp. 102–3, 31 July 1660.

[137] *Liber precum publicarum in usum ecclesiae cathedralis christi oxon* (Oxoniae exc. H. Hall, per R. Davis 1660); it was a new edition of the 1615 book. Madan, *Oxford Books* iii. 118–19.

[138] CA MS D&C, i. b. 3, p. 101, 23 July 1660.

[139] Ibid., pp. 101, 103. Dean Fell also nominated Allestree as his proxy: ibid., p. 129.

of twelve years, the monthly communion service was ordered to 'be revived', and the dean and canons enjoined, 'in their turnes', to discourse the members of the college before each celebration—presumably on their Christian duty to receive the sacrament.[140]

By early November 1660 the canons were ready to make a definite return to Anglican ceremonial in the cathedral, where, since their return, the statutory offices of the prayer book had been said, not sung.[141] With the aid of yet another surviving royalist, Edward Lowe, the readmitted former organist and master of the choristers,[142] and the expertise of the repatriated Dallam family of organ-builders, who at the Restoration returned to England from France, the canons reintroduced the distinctive pattern of cathedral worship.[143] The daily services of morning and evening prayer demanded by the Elizabethan act of uniformity were again intoned by singing chaplains, and the more elaborate antiphonal settings of the canticles, psalms, and anthems were sung by a mixed choir of boys' and men's voices, accompanied by the playing of the organ.[144] Surplices, the traditional choir garb of the clergy, students, scholars, lay clerks, and choristers, were ordered to be worn, despite the offence which the retention of this vestigial 'rag of popery' gave to puritan consciences. To make sure that this minimal mark of religious decency was observed, Fell 'kept the dore' of the cathedral, first as sub-dean and later, from 30 November, as dean, following Morley's elevation to the bishopric of Worcester.[145]

In this, as in other areas of Anglican life, the inroads of the Cromwellian regime simply had not lasted long enough to extinguish all memory of the medieval choral tradition, though they had seriously blighted it. Such minor music-making as had gone on in Cromwellian Oxford had been of the instrumental variety. Vocal music had been frowned upon, for no better reason than that it had been 'used in church by the prelaticall partie'.[146] The great revival of 'cathedrall musicke' that occurred after 1660 owed a considerable debt to the deep concern felt by Edward Lowe for the sacred music which he had known and loved 'from his childhood' as a chorister at Salisbury under John Holmes.[147] The encouragement which he received from

[140] Ibid., p. 103. Fell subsequently introduced a weekly communion—a rarity for its day in the Church of England. Bodl. MSS Rawlinson d. 850, fo 306, c. 983, fos 46, 46ᵛ.

[141] Wood, *Life and Times* i. 347.

[142] OUA register Ta, pp. 325 ff; Bodl. MS Rawlinson b. 407a, fo 252; *Restoration Oxford*, ed. Beddard i, no. 295; R. T. Daniel and P. le Huray, *The Sources of English Church Music 1549–1660* (Early English Church Music supp. vol. i pt 2 London 1972), 120–1.

[143] CA MSS xii. b. 103, p. 91, xii. b. 104, p. 14. For Dallam at New College see NCA MS 1195, item 33, MS 989. C. Clutton and A. Niland, *The British Organ* (London 1963), 62 ff.

[144] Wood, *Life and Times* i. 356–8. For satirical verses on the restoration of cathedral worship, appropriately entitled 'Lowe's lamentation' see Bodl. MS Tanner 306, fo 373.

[145] Wood, *History of the University* ii. 698; Wood, *Life and Times* i. 347, 348–9. For protests against the reintroduced surplice see ibid. i. 347, 358–9, 406, 466; Bodl. MS Wood f. 45, fo 155; *Restoration Oxford*, ed. Beddard i, no. 340.

[146] Bodl. MS Wood f. 31, fo 16; Wood, *Life and Times* i. 298–9.

[147] J. Pulver, *A Biographical Dictionary of Old English Music* (London 1927), 309–10; D. H. Robertson, *Sarum Close* (London 1938), 175–6, 184; P. G. le Huray, *Music and the Reformation in England 1549–1660* (London 1967), 162, 224, 227–8, 268, 321, 367.

Dean Fell and from Fell's brother-in-law, Walter Jones, the sub-dean of the chapel royal (where Lowe was retained, along with his better-remembered contemporaries, William Child and Christopher Gibbons, as organist to the king), was amply rewarded.[148] His Oxford publications—*A Short Direction for the Performance of Cathedrall Service*[149] and his *Review* of the same, which was undertaken in response to the 1662 revision of the liturgy[150]—were of lasting value. Basic and essentially practical in conception, these works drew upon the all-but-forgotten repertoire of Tudor church music, particularly on the settings of the Edwardine composer, Merbecke.

Lowe's books helped musicians, whether survivors from the wreckage of the Great Rebellion, or newcomers to the art, to resurrect the magnificent choral tradition associated with the cathedrals and colleges of the protestant establishment, a tradition which remains, three and a half centuries later, the chief glory of the Church of England, having, regrettably, outlived the words of the prayer book that inspired it. The choral foundations of New College and Magdalen eagerly emulated the example of Christ Church 'with the singing of prayers after the most antient way', as did those lesser colleges, like St John's, which had organs, but no choir: 'to which places', Wood tells us, 'the resort of the people ... was infinitely great', as town and gown jostled one another for admission; some out of devotion, others out of idle curiosity.[151] Despite his court duties, Lowe remained on hand to advise colleges other than his own in the technical matter of organ specifications, and to help tune the pitch of their newly built instruments.[152] A kinsman of Clarendon, and one of the first dons to hail the Restoration in Oxford, which he did by staging a concert of assorted vocal and instrumental music on 24 May, 'to congratulate his majestie's safe arrival in his kingdomes', he succeeded John Wilson as professor of music in November 1661, a position he retained for the next twenty years.[153]

The visual break with the puritan past was no less apparent, and scarcely less abrupt. The canons quickly got down to remedying the material legacy of 'the broken times', as the Cromwellian interval in Oxford's history was now contemptuously styled in the university. The care and attention, skill and money, that were lavished on the furnishings and fabric of the cathedral proclaimed the counter-revolutionary shift which the Restoration effected in religion, away from 'fanatical'

---

[148] *The Old Cheque-Book or Book of Remembrance of the Chapel Royal*, ed. E. F. Rimbault (Camden Soc. new ser. iii London 1872), 17, 94, 128, 221–2.

[149] E. L., *A Short Direction for the Performance of Cathedrall Service. Published for the information of such persons, as are ignorant of it, and shall be call'd to officiate in cathedrall, or collegiate churches, where it hath formerly been in use* (Oxford 1661).

[150] E. L., *A Review of some Short Directions formerly printed ... with many useful additions according to the common prayer book, as it is now established* (Oxford 1664), dedicated to Fell's brother-in-law, Walter Jones, sub-dean of the chapel royal, for whom see Beddard (ed.), *Restoration Oxford* i. 11–12.

[151] Wood, *Life and Times* i. 347, 356, 357–8.

[152] NCA MS 989, Warden Woodward's memorandum, 10 March 1662.

[153] Wood, *Life and Times* i. 316. For Wilson, Heather professor of music see ibid. i. 204–5, 212, 233, 257, 420 ff.

licence, back to the formal corporate worship demanded by the doctrine of religious uniformity. The offering up of the common prayer of the church, in liturgy and music, replaced the extempore outpourings of individual nonconformist preachers, who had prayed as the spirit had moved them. The canons were understandably concerned to create the right spiritual environment for public worship; and that, for them, meant recreating the tidy physical world of Anglican religious experience which they had known in the 1630s and early 1640s before the onset of war and usurpation.

Within a matter of months a physical transformation had been effected. As neglect yielded to devotion, the communion table—once again regarded as the holy of holies—was covered with a damask cloth, and placed 'altar-wise' beneath a canopy of state, its handsome silver furniture set off to advantage by the contrasting drapery of a rich hanging dorsal.[154] In the cathedral, as in other college chapels, the practice of bowing towards the east was revived, as a token of respect in God's house.[155] The reverence shown to the east and, even more palpably, the progressive embellishment of the communion table, declared the dean and chapter's resolve to return to decent, pre-war, Laudian standards of worship: standards which clearly exceeded those called for by the canons of 1604. One of the restored canons, Richard Gardiner, a staunch defender of the liturgy and the deputy university orator who had greeted Charles I's entry into Christ Church after the battle of Edgehill, led the way. He took from their hiding-place the finely bound bible and prayer book, with their delicately engraved, matching silver covers, that had graced the communion table before the rebellion.[156] Restored to their familiar position, they were soon joined by new ornaments, which were either given or purchased.

Some of the items came as thank-offerings from the scions of prominent Cavalier Anglican families, who, having survived 'the worst of times' to be admitted to Christ Church, were more than happy to attest their affection for the church in which they worshipped each day as undergraduates. Sir Seymour Shirley, the son and heir of that redoubtable royalist, Sir Robert Shirley, who had sheltered Sheldon during the Cromwellian Interregnum, presented a pair of silver-gilt flagons;[157] Edward Hyde, the youngest of Chancellor Clarendon's sons, and the only one of an age to attend the university, gave a silver-gilt alms dish decorated with the double Tudor rose,[158] while the dean and chapter provided new communion plate—a

[154] CA MS xii. b. 103, p. 91; Wood, *Life and Times* i. 388.

[155] Wood, *Life and Times* i. 370, 445; Bodl. MS Wood f. 31, fo 11.

[156] *Walker Revised*, ed. Matthews, 24, 278; *Register*, ed. Burrows, pp. lxxi, lxxxii, cxii, 10; Wood, *Life and Times* i. 68, 161; Wood, *Athenae*, iii, 921. He was a good friend of Sheldon: BL MS Harleian 6942, fo 121. They were given in 1638 by Canon Henry King, archdeacon of Colchester and afterwards bishop of Chichester: W. G. Hiscock, *A Christ Church Miscellany* (Oxford 1946), 137 and plate 49.

[157] CA D. P. i. a. 2, fo 85; OUA SP 41, p. 11, register Ta, p. 131; *Restoration Oxford*, ed. Beddard ii, no. 536; E. A. Jones, *Catalogue of the Plate of Christ Church Oxford* (Oxford 1939), 4 and plate 3.

[158] CA D. P. i. a. 2, fo 84; OUA SP 41, p. 7, register Ta, p. 129; Jones, *Catalogue*, 1–2 and plate 2; *Restoration Oxford*, ed. Beddard ii no. 536. For the Hydes' generosity in refurbishing Baylie's cathedral, see Bodl., MS Clarendon 80, fo 149 and R. A. Beddard, 'Cathedral furnishings of the Restoration period: a Salisbury inventory of 1685', *Wiltshire Archaeological Magazine* 66 (1971), 148–9.

pair of silver-gilt chalices and patens of *repoussé* workmanship, together with a pair of silver-gilt pricket candlesticks, acquired from the London silversmiths by the 'exchange of old plate' for new.[159] Their action was proof that the modest ideals of 'the beauty of holiness', which Archbishop Laud had championed in the peaceful years of Charles I's personal rule, had not merely survived, but had triumphantly surmounted the rage of iconoclasm, to inform and shape the liturgical usage of the Restoration church.

New sets of prayer books and a large bible for the lectern were obtained; the pulpit cloth and cushions for the communion-rail mended; mats purchased 'for the masters to kneele on' during prayers; candelabra, candles and bell-ropes bought, the latter to ring the long-silent bells of the cathedral; and besoms provided for sweeping the dust of the puritan regime out of church.[160] Much of the damage done by the puritan iconoclasts was irreversible. Nowhere was this more in evidence than in the destruction of the cathedral's wonderful heritage of medieval stained glass, some of which had been trampled underfoot by that unbalanced fanatic Dr Henry Wilkinson, one of the intruded parliamentary prebendaries;[161] while the rest had been ordered by the disapproving dean, the Independent John Owen, to be deployed about the college in mending broken windows.[162]

The impact of wartime controversy over the nature of the Church of England, its government, ministry, and worship, was acutely and abidingly felt in Oxford, where it had been rammed home by the fanatics' forcible takeover of the university, the wholesale expulsion of their opponents, and the deliberate slighting of episcopacy and liturgy. Consequently the parliamentary visitation had engendered a deep-seated loathing of religious 'fanaticism'.[163] As a result of their shared sufferings, the Cavalier Anglicans had been brought to altogether 'stricter notions' of the episcopal character of their church by 1660, and thereafter maintained them 'with more fierceness' than at any time before the troubles.[164] They recognized in the institution of episcopacy the sole guarantor of ecclesiastical order in a church that had been savagely disestablished,[165] and saw in episcopal ordination the *sine qua non* of

[159] CA MS xiii. b. 4, p. 53, 'A noate of the colledge plate, taken February 19, 1661[2]'; Jones, *Catalogue*, 2–3 and plates 2 and 3.

[160] *Restoration Oxford*, ed. Beddard i, nos 295, 304.   [161] Wood, *History of the University* ii. 648–9.

[162] CA D&C i. b. 3, p. 40, order of 2 June 1651. For the paucity of medieval glass in Christ Church see P. A. Newton, 'Stained glass at Oxford' in N. Pevsner and J. Sherwood, *The Buildings of England: Oxfordshire* (London 1974); M. Archer, S. Crewe, and P. Cormack, *English Heritage in Stained Glass: Oxford* (Oxford 1988), 12–15.

[163] It was seen primarily as a 'fanatical visitation' overthrowing the lawful statutes of the university and colleges. *The Privileges of the University of Oxford, in point of Visitation* (Oxford 1647); *Rustica academiae oxoniensis nuper reformatae descriptio, in visitatione fanatica octobris sexto, &c. anno domini 1648*; *Oxonii lachrymae* (London 1649); [Fell], *Hammond*, 50 ff; Bodl. MS J. Walker c. 8, fos 247, 247ᵛ.

[164] Gilbert Burnet, *A History Of My Own Time*, ed. M. J. Routh (6 vols Oxford 1823) i. 237. *Reliquiae Baxterianae*, pt ii, pp. 149, 179.

[165] Allestree asserted the necessity of 'this highest order in the church' in a sermon dedicated to Sheldon, as the acknowledged patron of episcopacy: *A Sermon preached in St Peter's Westminster . . . Jan. 6. 1660* (London 1661); cf Henry Hammond, *Dissertationes quatuor, quibus episcopatus jura ex s. scripturis &*

admission to a ministry that had unaccountably fallen prey to ignorant and presumptuous interlopers.[166] Similarly, their attachment to the Book of Common Prayer had, if anything, grown emotionally deeper and spiritually stronger since its attempted abolition by ordinance of the Long Parliament in 1645.[167]

Because of the religious consolation which the restored royalists unashamedly drew from their continued use of the prayer book, they had little or no sympathy with renewed puritan demands for liturgical 'reform' after the Restoration. Indeed, they were reluctant to admit that the Church of England's liturgy required any modification or improvement. Such was their addiction to the Book of Common Prayer by 1660, that their liturgical conservatism stood in the way of all change. The refusal of Oxford's Cavalier Anglican divines to countenance change operated in contrary directions. As it ruled out making major concessions to puritan scruples, so it disappointed the hopes of Cambridge ritualists, like Bishop Wren and Dean Cosin, to bring the text and ceremonial closer to that of the first Edwardine prayer book of 1549 and the Scottish liturgy of 1637.[168] It also discounted the Calvinist reservations of Thomas Barlow of Queen's, who was unhappy over the wording and content of the offices of baptism, burial, commination, and confirmation. Convinced of the wisdom of sticking to the old ways, they were averse to admitting any innovations that might prejudice a return to pre-war usage. Even Barlow, in submitting his 'Considerations concerneinge the Common Prayer Booke' to the judgement of his superiors, held 'the whole booke to be the best liturgy in the world, especially the communion service, it beeinge allmost impossible that any office penn'd by men (not divinely inspired) should breath more piety, or containe more truth and decency'.[169]

Fell and his associates, including President Baylie of St John's, were not to be reckoned among the 'plain and moderate episcopal men', whom the puritan Richard Baxter believed to harbour thoughts of 'reconciliation and union', as 'a reward to the Presbyterians for bringing in the king'. Far from it, they were intransigent episcopalians of the most dogmatic kind, believing episcopacy to be of the *esse*, not merely of the *bene esse*, of their church.[170] Conscious of their long years of

primaeva antiquitate adstruuntur (London 1651), and Henry Hammond, *A Vindication of the Dissertations* (London 1654).

[166] For Oxford condemnation of the 'pretended orders', or 'none att all', of the Presbyterians, see QCL MS 280, fo 251; ORO Oxf. dioc. papers c. 650, fo 22; *Reliquiae Baxterianae*, pt ii, p. 207. For the background see R. A. Beddard, 'Old priest *versus* new presbyter: Symon Patrick and the controversy over ordination in Cromwellian England' (forthcoming).

[167] Barlow maintained that since no reasons of sin could be objected to 'our liturgy', dissent from it was 'criminall disobedience, and the dissenters schismaticall'. QCL MS 278, fo 274. *Acts and Ordinances of the Interregnum 1642–1660*, ed. C. H. Firth and R. S. Rait (3 vols London 1911) i. 582–607.

[168] For Wren's 'advices' see *Fragmentary Illustrations of the Book of Common Prayer*, ed. W. Jacobson (London 1874), 43–109; Cosin's proposals are in *The Durham Book*, ed. G. J. Cuming (London 1961, 2nd edn Alcuin Club 1975) and G. J. Cuming, 'The making of the Durham Book', *Journal of Ecclesiastical History* v (1955), 60–72; G. Donaldson, *The Making of the Scottish Prayer Book of 1637* (Edinburgh 1954).

[169] QCL MS 279, item 8, 23 September 1661. For Barlow's view of 'the sadd condition of our bleedinge church' in 1657 see *Restoration Oxford*, ed. Beddard iii, appx, no. 28.

[170] *Reliquiae Baxterianae*, pt ii, pp. 229, 207–8, 210.

exclusion from the university, and supremely aware of their efforts in seeking to bind Oxford to king and church, they were opposed to making more concessions than they absolutely had to following Charles II's return. Their uncompromising stance was shared by the Cavalier Anglican gentry, with whom they had forged lasting bonds of friendship, and from whom they were currently receiving support for their highly successful efforts to revive the church in the dioceses and parishes, without waiting for the go-ahead from central government.[171]

The restored Oxford dons stood for pre-war episcopacy and liturgy. They wanted a return to 'sovereign episcopacy' of the prelatical, propertied, diocesan kind, not Primate Ussher's untested model of a 'reduced episcopacy' which, under the pressure of adverse events, the Presbyterians had come ruefully to accept.[172] They also demanded the restoration of the Book of Common Prayer, whole and entire, as they had received it from their forefathers.[173] They took their stand on the unrepealed act of uniformity of 1559, which required its immediate reinstatement. With them actions spoke louder than words, as was demonstrated by the lead which the revived dean and chapter of Christ Church gave to the rest of the university and the restored bishop of Oxford, Robert Skinner, gave to the surrounding diocese. Their intransigence reflected that of their great patron, Gilbert Sheldon, whose promotion in October 1660 to the bishopric of London confirmed his political leadership of the Anglican hierarchy, given the decrepitude of Archbishop Juxon.[174] Even the Calvinist Morley, who had been charged by the king with reconciling the Presbyterians to the church, became convinced of the need to take a tough line if the old church, for which he and his friends had suffered so much, was to be preserved. To him a schism outside the church was preferable to a schism inside the church.[175]

The Savoy Conference of 1661, called to restore 'peace and unity' to the national church by reviewing the prayer book, stuck close to the tenor of the king's warrant, which warned the negotiators on both sides against 'all unnecessary alterations'. The process of revision, in which the conservative-minded Sheldon was well to the fore, left 'all in the old method'; which was just as well, given the widespread reintroduction of the old liturgy that had already taken place at the local level. The revised liturgy was essentially the Jacobean prayer book of 1604 with minor alterations.[176] It was not to be imagined that those ejected clerics, whose

[171] *Reliquiae Baxterianae*, pt ii, pp. 112, 149; Beddard, 'The Restoration church', 156–7, 161–5.

[172] [James Ussher], *The Reduction of Episcopacie unto the Form of Synodical Government received in the Ancient Church* (London 1641).

[173] Representative of academic opinion was the tract written by the ejected royalist don, John Barbon, Λειτουργιά θειοτέρα 'εργία: *or, Liturgie a most Divine Service* (Oxford 1662), aimed against Vavasor Powell, and containing a powerful 'defence of episcopacy' (pp. 149–93).

[174] Bosher, *The Making of the Restoration Settlement*, 180–3.

[175] *A Supplement to Burnet's* History of my Own Time, ed. H. C. Foxcroft (Oxford 1902), 69.

[176] E. C. Ratcliffe, 'The Savoy conference and the revision of the Book of Common Prayer' in G. F. Nuttall and O. Chadwick (eds), *From Uniformity to Unity 1662–1962* (London 1962), 91–148; G. J. Cuming, *A History of Anglican Liturgy* (London 1969, 2nd edn London 1982), 116, 120–1, 123–4; *The Durham Book*, ed. Cuming, pp. xxv–xxvi, 180.

disrupted lives had been sustained by the uninterrupted services of the prayer book in the 1650s, would, on being readmitted to positions of power, be willing to part with them merely to satisfy the objections of their former persecutors, or to humour the personal preferences of a few churchmen. The reinstatement of pre-war episcopacy and liturgy was the best vindication that they and their church could receive for their unshaken attachment to the rule of law.[177] The contradictions which the Cavalier Anglican MPs had recently encountered in the Convention, not least in attempting to settle the personnel of the university, made them the more determined to stand their ground when they knew that circumstances favoured them.[178] Sheldon's increasingly open opposition to the conciliatory policy pursued by Charles II and Clarendon was vastly strengthened as a result of the new general election, which returned a large body of 'cavaliers or the sons of cavaliers' to parliament in the spring of 1661.

The university played its part in augmenting the Cavalier Anglican presence at Westminster by electing, at the behest of Chancellor Clarendon and Bishops Sheldon and Morley, two cast-iron episcopalians to serve as its representatives: Lawrence Hyde, Clarendon's second son, and the solicitor-general, Sir Heneage Finch, the church's chief parliamentary spokesman, both of whom belonged to Fell's Christ Church.[179] It was not for nothing that this long-lived parliament earned the name the Cavalier Parliament. From 1661 until 1679 the Cavalier Anglican leadership of the church could count on its support in the struggle to uphold the legal requirements of uniformity, particularly after its re-enactment in May 1662. In 1663 it was Solicitor-General Finch who, more than any other MP, acted against the king's attempt to break the act of uniformity by proposing religious toleration for dissenters and Catholics. In doing so he took his cue, not from Clarendon, who as the first minister of the crown had to toe the royal line, but from the courageous stand made on behalf of the church in the privy council by Bishop Sheldon in the summer of 1662, just as the new act was coming into force.[180]

The Cavalier Commons' assertion of 'the laws and the religion established, according to the act of uniformity', as 'the most probable means to produce a settled peace and obedience through the kingdom', chimed exactly with the prevalent conservatism of Oxford.[181] There the intransigent divines, believing in the indivisibility of church and state, maintained that 'it was not indulgence which the

[177] *Supplement*, ed. Foxcroft, 69–70.

[178] *CJ* viii. 227, 27 December 1660; 'Restoration Visitation', ed. Varley, 31, 34, 39, 40; OUA register Ta, p. 9 (reverse); *Restoration Oxford*, ed. Beddard i, nos 293, 308.

[179] OUA register Ta, p. 100, Chancellor Hyde to university, Worcester House, 12 March 1661. For the bishops' role, see PRO SP 29/16, nos 66, 67, SP 29/31, nos 2, 26, 30, 31, 59, SP 29/32, nos 8, 19; M. B. Rex, *University Representation in England, 1604–1690* (London 1954), 231–4, 236.

[180] *Mercurius Publicus*, no. 35 (28 August–4 September 1662); Bosher, *The Making of the Restoration Settlement*, 261–4; *Restoration Oxford*, ed. Beddard ii, no. 607; Henning (ed.), *House of Commons* ii. 319.

[181] *CJ* viii. 442–3; D. T. Witcombe, 'The Cavalier house of commons: the session of 1663', *Bulletin of the Institute of Historical Research* 32 (1959), 181–3.

schismaticks desir'd, but empire'.[182] Cromwellian Oxford had demonstrated that by cashiering the pre-eminent loyalists. They had, therefore, every reason to oppose the king's policy of appeasement, and to throw the weight of the university behind the existing legal establishment erected by their parliamentary allies—the worldly wise, intolerant, Cavalier Anglican squires, who knew, as well as they, how necessary it was to keep the enemies of their church under the restraint of the law. Only when faced by the king's moves to favour his Catholic subjects did the Cavalier Commons briefly look towards easing the lot of the protestant dissenters in 1673, but decided to do nothing.

It became the regular practice of the senior members of the university, as of their episcopal rulers, to support the Cavalier Anglican party in the house of commons. So dominant was the Cavalier ideology and interest within the university that when, in January 1674, a sudden by-election was caused by Finch's appointment to the woolsack, as lord keeper, and the dons were somewhat surprisingly left to their own devices to elect a successor, they voted in Thomas Thynne. Though he had not taken a degree, Thynne was an exemplary churchman. Formerly of Christ Church, and a close friend of the dean, he had in the late 1650s been a stalwart of Fell's Cavalier Anglican congregation.[183] Having a Coventry for his mother, and a Finch for his wife, were additional recommendations, showing that he stood in the mainstream of Anglican high churchmanship: a point which was emphasized by his Oxonian suspicion of the court's motives in taking up indulgence in the wake of Clarendon's dismissal.[184] In a smart three-sided contest, on 16 January 1674, Thynne defeated his nearest rival—the court candidate, Sir Christopher Wren, another impeccable churchman and the nephew of Bishop Wren—by 203 votes to 125.[185]

From the late 1660s onwards, Oxford men were fully persuaded 'that the Presbyterians and all nonconformists desire and indeavour the dissolution of this, and the call of another parliament, hopeinge to chuse such members, as may give a toleration (if not a greater incouragement or establishment) of their sect', by tempting the king with what remained of the church lands, as a means of paying off the public debt. Scandalized by 'fanatic' talk of raising money 'out of the churche's ruines', the dons comforted themselves with the knowledge that, while the Cavalier Parliament sat, it would 'never doe an act soe manifestly sacrilegious', and that, even 'if . . . another parliament should indeavor it', the king— 'his sacred majesty, on whose head may the crowne florish'—would 'never consent'

[182] Bishop Parker's History of his Own Time, trans. Thomas Newlin (London 1727), 65.

[183] The pupil of Thomas Lockey and Fell's 'dearest friend', the vital connection of Thynne with the pre-Restoration congregation is missed in Henning (ed.), House of Commons iii. 565. Longleat House, MS Thynne 10, fos 178, 152; CA MS xii. b. 86, fo 83, D. P. i. a. 2, fo 73. For the dean and chapter's congratulations to Finch see HMC Finch MSS ii. 13.

[184] Thynne later complained of his 'hard fortune' at displeasing the court by his principled conduct in parliament: BL Althrop papers, C 5 (unfoliated), Thomas Thynne to Lord Halifax, 12 July 1679.

[185] OUA register of convocation 1671–83, NEP/supra/28, register Tb, pp. 52–5. Wren had also worshipped in Fell's congregation in the 1650s.

to it.[186] For all their distrust of court strategems, shown by their rallying behind Thynne's candidature rather than Wren's, they were as reluctant as ever to think ill of the king himself. As it turned out, their diagnosis of political events was correct. Charles II ultimately did prove more dependable than a parliament dominated by whigs and dissenters.

Central to the stability of Restoration Oxford was the regulation of the all-important faculty of theology: the dynamo that generated so much of the intellectual current that supplied the university with political as well as religious energy after 1662. In matters of doctrine most of its leading theologians—Thomas Barlow, John Hall, Robert South, and William Jane—fitted into the Calvinist tradition which had been established in the university under Elizabeth I, and which, following the rout of 'the epidemical Arminians' in the parliamentary visitation, had been forcibly rehabilitated in the late 1640s.[187] But theirs was not the cancerous Calvinism of the sects. In ecclesiastical discipline and government they heartily conformed to the official liturgical and episcopal priorities of the restored church. Barlow, the most intractable and pugnacious of Oxford Calvinists, reserved his energy to attack the Church of Rome and Socinianism. He extolled the prayer book as 'the best liturgy in the world', condemned the 'fanatique zeale' of those who disdained it, and upheld episcopacy as 'jure apostolico'.[188] He found no difficulty in accepting the bishopric of Lincoln in 1675, any more than Hall, his successor in the Lady Margaret chair of divinity, scrupled to accept that of Bristol in 1691.

As for South and Jane, both of whom belonged to Fell's Christ Church, they were so 'fond of the rites and ceremonies of the church', that they were prepared to do battle for them at every turn, even to the extent of incurring royal displeasure after 1688. They were justly reputed bitter enemies to dissent, and widely esteemed as the harriers of schismatics.[189] Belonging to a younger generation, they did more to influence the long-term outlook of the Oxford clergy than Barlow and Hall, whose unadulterated, iconoclastic, sabbatarian brand of Calvinism seemed theologically irrelevant and politically inapposite in the struggle to assert the identity and authority of the Church of England against a body of hostile domestic dissent—especially after 1689, when dissent was legally tolerated by the state.

Barlow and Hall were not favoured by Sheldon and Clarendon. The archbishop distrusted the extent of their attachment to minimizing Calvinism, with its neurotic

[186] Bodl. MS Eng. letters c. 328, fo 509, Thomas Barlow to F. Parry, Queen's, 8 January 1668/9.

[187] The Restoration dons recognized that previous regius professors of divinity had 'all [been] Calvinists, whither conformist or nonconformist', from Elizabethan times: BL MS Lansdowne 960, fo 41, A. Allam to W. Kennett, St Edmund Hall, 12 December 1681.

[188] QCL MSS 340, p. 1, 279; Bodl. MS Eng. letters c. 328, fo 509, Barlow to Parry, Queen's, 8 January 1668/9.

[189] Jane was 'brought into the colledge' by Morley, and Fell backed South's claims to a Christ Church canonry: BL Add. MS 17,017, fo 163, Morley to Lawrence Hyde, Farnham Castle, 12 May 1680; PRO SP 29/281, no. 58, Fell to Joseph Williamson [Christ Church], 20 December [1670]; CA MS D&C, i. b. 3, pp. 162–3; R. A. Beddard, 'Vincent Alsop and the emancipation of Restoration dissent', *Journal of Ecclesiastical History* xxiv (1973), 163.

aversion to ceremonies, music, and Sunday recreation, and its boundless hatred of popery.[190] There were additional reasons for his dislike of Barlow. He disapproved of his erroneous views on the sacrament of baptism. The provost of Queen's was known to have maintained the invalidity of lay baptism, and had expressed serious reservations regarding the baptismal regeneration of infants, to the extent of doubting that the sacrament was at all necessary to salvation.[191] To doctrinal unorthodoxy he had added political faults. His intimacy during the Interregnum with the freethinking Warden Wilkins of Wadham, who had married into the usurper Cromwell's family, and his friendly dealings with Thomas Hobbes, the defamer of religion and the derider of universities, gave further cause for concern.[192] Perhaps, too, his untimely defection from the Cavalier opposition to the parliamentary visitation of 1647–8, after he had supported it so warmly before, still rankled.[193] Taken together, these objections outweighed Barlow's reputation for erudition, which no one questioned. With Hall, it was his delayed entry into the Anglican ministry, and his strong family ties and enduring friendships with out-and-out Presbyterians, which made Sheldon uneasy.[194]

Neither man owed his tenure of the Lady Margaret chair of divinity to any outside patron, but to the election of his academic peers, the resident theological graduates of the university. Their sequential elections—Barlow's in 1660, after the deprivation of the Presbyterian Henry Wilkinson for nonconformity, and Hall's in 1676, after his predecessor's elevation to the see of Lincoln—bore witness to the unshaken hold of intellectual Calvinism on the mind of Oxford's theologians.[195] Sheldon's efforts to debar Barlow's entry to the episcopate were no more successful than his earlier endeavours had been to impede Hall's election as master of Pembroke College in 1664.[196] The provost had powerful patrons in the persons of the Calvinist Bishop Morley and the two secretaries of state, Sir Joseph Williamson and Sir Henry Coventry, both of whom were Queen's College men, the former an absentee fellow and the latter Barlow's old pupil.[197] Although their influence pre-

---

[190] Bodl. MS Wood f. 31, fos 4, 14. Barlow fanned the belief that the Roman Catholics, the Jesuits especially, had fired London in 1666: Bodl. MS Eng. letters. c. 328, fo 509ᵛ.

[191] QCL MS 278, fos 49 ff., Barlow's 'De paedobaptismo analecta'. He later confessed his reservations insufficient 'to warrant any division or disturbance of the peace of my mother, the Church of England': ibid., fo 34.

[192] BL Add. MS 32,553, fo 22, Barlow to 'my honored freind', T. Hobbes, Queen's, 23 December 1656. *Lettere di Henry Stubbe*, ed. Nicastro, 16–19, 21–5.

[193] [Thomas Barlow], *Pegasus, or the Flying Horse from Oxford. Bringing the proceedings of the visitours and other bedlamites there* (Oxford 1648); Bodl. MS Wood f. 35, fos 37–59ᵛ, 62, 121; *Register*, ed. Burrows, pp. liii, lxxxvii, cxxiii, 74, 89.

[194] Bishop Skinner had recommended his public ordinations in Merton chapel on 2 August 1660, but Hall delayed receiving episcopal ordination until 31 March 1661: ORO MS Oxf. dioc. papers d. 106, fos 1, 5.

[195] OUA register Ta, pp. 2–3 (reverse), 21 September 1660; OUA register Tb, pp. 9–10 (reverse), 24 May 1676; PRO SP 29/445, no. 44.

[196] After the Restoration Sheldon 'protested that so long as he should keep his seat, Barlow should rise no higher then now he was': Bodl. MS Wood f. 31, fo 14; *Restoration Oxford*, ed. Beddard ii, no. 864.

[197] PRO SP 29/370, no. 269, Barlow to Williamson, Oxford, 29 May 1675, owning Williamson's and Morley's efforts for him.

vailed at court, the archbishop showed his disapproval of the appointment by refusing to participate in his consecration as bishop.[198] Hall's elevation to the episcopate had to wait until after the revolution of 1688, when, in notoriously changed circumstances, another and more powerful Calvinist sponsor, William III, nominated him to the see of Bristol in 1691.

Inside the faculty of theology Sheldon had to content himself with disposing crown patronage. In 1661 he persuaded Charles II to prefer the Arminian William Creed to the regius chair of divinity, on the promotion to the episcopate of his friend Robert Sanderson, the restored Cavalier professor, who had long since abandoned Calvinism.[199] On Creed's death in 1663 he again intervened in favour of an Arminian. This time it was for Fell's right-hand man Richard Allestree, canon of Christ Church and the king's chaplain. On both occasions, when a vacancy occurred, Sheldon preferred to make use of the services of an unquestioned Cavalier Anglican don, albeit in Creed's case he had to summon a country parson back to the university.[200] By his adroit deployment of royal patronage Sheldon managed to provide Oxford with an Arminian countervalent to the Calvinism of the Margaret professors. In practice it turned out to be rather more than that, for the regius professor was, because of his superior status as a royal nominee, regarded as the unofficial head of the faculty of theology.

Allestree was called from the cathedral on to the university stage to promote the Cavalier Anglican strategy of returning Oxford to the bosom of the established church. With Christ Church well on the way to recovering its pre-war form, his sponsors felt that a portion of his energy and expertise could be spared for resettling the university on a sound Anglican footing.[201] As regius professor of divinity from 1663 to 1680, he accepted responsibility for the running of his faculty. As well as being the most august of the university's schools, the faculty of theology was unavoidably the one most troubled by the reimposition of uniformity. On entering office, 'he found the university in a ferment', with the controversy over the requirements of conformity rumbling on, and 'a great part' of the faculty's 'growing hopes sufficiently seasoned with ill prepossessions' to be a worry to his superiors, Sheldon and Morley.[202] Such problems were facets of the legacy of vexation bequeathed to churchmen by a decade of sectarian indoctrination and infighting.

It fell to Allestree to wean his graduate charges from Cromwellian heterodoxy by asserting Anglican doctrine. As a resolute episcopalian, dedicated to reestablishing 'that apostolical and divine dignity' of episcopacy in the church for

---

[198] LPL Sheldon register I, fos 146 ff.

[199] William Creed, *The Refuter Refuted* (London 1660), 460–8; *Walker Revised*, ed. Matthews, 24, 33, 256–7, 372; *Register*, ed. Burrows, 94, 47, 50, 91, 114, 132, 198; 'Restoration Visitation', ed. Varley, 1–2; OUA register Ta, p. 120.

[200] Bodl. MS Wood f. 35, fo 316b; *Restoration Oxford*, ed. Beddard ii, no. 460.

[201] Bodl. MS Clarendon 80, fo 198, Bishop Morley to Clarendon, Westminster, 12 September 1663; PRO SP 29/94, no. 40, Allestree to Williamson, 7 March 1664.

[202] Fell, *Allestree*, 29.

whose preservation he had worked in the 1650s, he appreciated the urgency of putting an end to the ecclesiastical wrangling which had so sorely 'disturbed the peace of the last age'.[203] For the next seventeen years he used his authority as 'doctor of the chair'—that is, as the chief moderator (examiner) in the divinity school— to discourage unnecessary clerical contention. Learned and orthodox in his pronouncements, rigorous yet affable in debate, he skilfully intervened, when the need arose, to remind disputants of the rules of the Church of England, as contained in its historic formularies. By the 1680s it was accepted that 'the essentialls and substantialls' of the Church of England, 'as to faith', were 'compriz'd in the Thirty-Nine Articles, liturgy, homilies, book of ordination, and some say canons too': 'a right and good understanding' of which Oxford tutors advised their would-be clerical pupils to strive after.[204]

In silencing the acrimonious differences of opinion inside the theology faculty, Allestree took his stand on Charles II's *Directions concerning Preachers* issued on 14 October 1662. In these the king, as supreme governor of the church, forbade dissension in the pulpit, and explicitly 'admonished' divines not to study 'abstruse and speculative notions' of the kind that had excited theological unrest. More especially, he ordered them to refrain from handling 'the deep points' of election, reprobation, grace, and free will.[205] As volatile left-overs from the damaging quinquarticular controversy that had set Calvinist against Arminian on the eve of the civil war, doctrinal disagreements still had the capacity to divide the clergy and hinder the church from regaining its ascendancy over the people.[206] The king and his ministers rightly regarded fratricidal dispute as politically dangerous; for, as Fell observed, whenever such controversies raged, they quickly 'passed from the schools to the state, and shocked the government and public peace'.[207]

After 1662 the university loyally strove to enforce 'the king's edict' against potential disturbers of the church, irrespective of whether the culprits were Calvinist or Arminian in profession. Mercy was shown to neither. Hauled before the doctors and heads to give an account of their actions, offenders were forced to recant on their knees and beg pardon for their faults. The authorities' aim was to stamp out clerical dissension by punishing disobedience 'to the king's commands'. What they most frowned upon was the use of 'irreverent and unseemly language' in conjunction with 'bold and desperat' theological opinion.[208] They were careful not to pre-

---

[203] Allestree, *A Sermon Preached . . . Jan. 6. 1660*, 2; Worcester College Library, MS 54, p. 252, Barwick, *John Barwick*, 238–9, 242 and note y, 488; Fell, *Allestree*, 11–12.

[204] BL MS Lansdowne 960, fo 34ᵛ, A. Allam to W. Kennett, St Edmund Hall, 21 September 1680.

[205] E. Cardwell, *Documentary Annals of the Reformed Church of England* (2 vols Oxford 1839) ii. 253–9. They were communicated to the province of Canterbury by Archbishop Juxon on 23 October 1662.

[206] For the dons' awareness of the old controversies, see Bodl. MS Locke c. 22, fos 7, 8ᵛ; *Restoration Oxford*, ed. Beddard ii, no. 460.

[207] Fell, *Allestree*, 29.

[208] The university was empowered to act under statute XVI. ix: 'De offensionis et dissensionis materia in concionibus evitanda' of the Laudian statutes: *Laudian Code*, ed. Griffiths, 161. For an example of action against Thomas Smart of St John's and his submission, 17 April 1679 see OUA register Tb, p. 2 (reverse); Wood, *Life and Times* ii. 448.

scribe allegiance to either Calvinism or Arminianism, both of which systems of belief continued to colour the content of non-controversial lectures and sermons within the university, and to claim new adherents.

So it was that Barlow and John Wallis, the Savilian professor of geometry, went on lecturing and preaching according to their Calvinist lights; while Allestree's performances as a preacher and moralist, and those of Thomas Pierce, president of Magdalen, continued to betray their Arminian sentiments. Both sides tacitly acknowledged the limitations placed on them by the king's injunctions, and stopped short of meddling with 'the unfathomable abyss of God's decrees'.[209] Even that unrepentant puritan John Wallis, the former secretary of the Westminster Assembly, and a known adversary of Laudian 'super-conformity', 'purposely waved' the disputing of theological niceties, 'as more tending to disturb the peace of the church, than to promote piety'.[210] The severe disruption inflicted by the puritan revolution on all forms of religious learning had the salutary effect of putting academic conformists, of whatever persuasion, on their best behaviour. In Restoration Oxford ecclesiastical peace was prized as never before.[211]

Theological disputations did not, of course, cease. They remained a regular and valued part of the viva voce process of college teaching and university examining. Academic discipline encouraged undergraduates to frequent the disputes held in college halls, and made graduates attend those held in the schools of the university. Under Allestree's guidance, instead of being allowed to degenerate into *odium theologicum* and clerical sniping, the cutting-edge of theological controversy was turned against 'the most formidable enemies' of the Church of England: the Catholics and dissenters.[212] Thus, not only did the time-honoured exercise of oral disputation continue to impart a decidedly adversarial quality to Anglican divinity, but professorial directives ensured that a major proportion of a theologian's training would be spent in mastering the doctrinal grounds on which the arguments of anti-Catholicism and anti-dissent depended. Roger North, an admirer of Fell's Oxford, remarked with pride how the Restoration clergy were reputed 'the most able in controversie of any in the world ... becaus (as they all abroad allow) they are kept in perpetuall exercise by the papists and sectarys'.[213] He might have added that their penchant for controversy was very much a product of their university education.

---

[209] See N. Tyacke, 'Religious controversy', pp. 601–4 above.

[210] John Wallis, *The Necessity of Regeneration: in two sermons to the University of Oxford* (London 1682), sig. A.

[211] In 1679 the university and Christ Church put off a dispute over the location of university sermons preached by doctors and masters of the college: OUA register Tb, p. 2 (reverse).

[212] Allestree further identified these as Roman Catholics, Genevan (i.e. non-episcopal) Calvinists, Cracovian Socinians, and atheistical 'Hobbists' (the disciples of Thomas Hobbes): Fell, *Allestree*, 28–9. Barlow similarly listed the Anglicans' adversaries as 'pope, presbyter, and phanatick': *The Genuine Remains of ... Dr. Thomas Barlow* (London 1693), 54. For Barlow's opposition to Socinianism see Wood, *Life and Times* ii. 166.

[213] BL Add. MS 32,526, fo 86. For North's admiration of Fell see R. North, *General Preface and Life of Dr John North*, ed. P. Millard (Toronto 1984), 119.

Anti-Catholicism provided much of the life-blood of the restored Church of England. It remained an essential ingredient in the education of the higher Anglican clergy, as it had done in the previous century. It could scarcely have been otherwise, given the growing realization in Britain that continental protestantism, which had been advancing and diversifying in the sixteenth century, was in the seventeenth century in retreat and decline. The walls of the divinity school resounded to repeated protestant denials of papal supremacy, the state of purgatory, the invocation of the saints, a sacrificing priesthood, transubstantiation in the mass, communion under one kind, the use of Latin in the people's liturgy, the merits of good works and the validity of seven sacraments[214]—teachings and practices which lay at the heart of the Catholic faith, as defined by the revivifying Council of Trent.[215] In only one important respect was there any suggestion of relaxing the university's tradition of virulent anti-Catholicism, and that was in faltering confidence in the once-axiomatic identification of the papacy with the Antichrist of the Apocalypse, an identification which had first been shockingly denied in the Oxford schools, in 1628 by that up-and-coming cleric, Gilbert Sheldon, now archbishop of Canterbury and the revered 'patronus munificentissimus' of the university.[216]

Knowledge of the archbishop's views did not, however, stop dogmatic Calvinists, like Provost Barlow and his associate, Thomas Tully, principal of St Edmund Hall, from maintaining the old view of an Antichristian papacy, or from taxing the Church of Rome with formal 'idolatry'.[217] The inordinate fear of popery that characterized the popular religious culture of Restoration England mirrored, albeit in a distorted and vulgarized form, the considered theological judgement of the Oxford clergy that the Church of Rome was at best corrupt, and at worst an obstacle to salvation. So long as the theological faculties of Oxford and Cambridge systematically taught the complete and detailed rejection of Catholic dogma to renewed generations of the Church of England's clergy, the ageing intellectual motor of English anti-Catholicism remained in good repair, and antipopery, as a political force, continued to dominate the collective religious consciousness of the nation—with, on occasion, terrifying and hideous consequences.

When in 1680 Allestree died, Sheldon was already dead. It fell to the Christ Church bishops Compton and Fell as the residuary legatees of Sheldon's policies, to take up where the archbishop had left off. They interceded at court to carry the nomination to the regius chair for their protégé William Jane, canon of Christ Church and of St Paul's, London, a divine whose intellectual formation had, it is

[214] This analysis is based on my forthcoming study of the 'quaestiones in vesperiis et comitiis discutiendae' in the Restoration faculty of theology: OUA register of congregation 1659–69, NEP/ *supra*/ 18, register Qb, fos 173–6, 178, 1680–92, NEP/ *supra*/ 20, register Be, fos 202–4ᵛ.

[215] H. Jedin, *Geschichte des Konzils von Trient* (2 vols Freiburg im Breisgau 1957) ii. 379 ff; M. Bendiscioli, *La riforma cattolica* (Rome 1958); H. O. Evennett, *The Spirit of the Counter-Reformation*, ed. J. Bossy (Cambridge 1968).

[216] For Sheldon's denial, see Beddard, 'Sheldon and Anglican recovery', 1007 n. 10.

[217] In his doctoral exercise in 1660 Barlow had affirmed the question, 'An ecclesia pseudo-catholica romana sit formaliter idolatrica?' OUA register Qb, fo 173. For Barlow's adversaria against the Church of Rome, headed 'de idolatria' and 'de Mariolatria' see QCL MS 230, fos 62, 89.

true, been Calvinistical, but whose liturgical preferences and high church politics were unmistakably those of his Cavalier Anglican backers.[218] Significantly, when Hall resigned the Lady Margaret chair in 1691, his elected successor was Henry Maurice, the learned, high church chaplain of the non-juring Archbishop Sancroft. Maurice was a theologian who had been reared in the school of Fell and Allestree, and had received every encouragement from Sir Leoline Jenkins, during whose principalship he had been a fellow of Jesus College.[219] His claim to fame was that he had, in 1682, published a solid defence of diocesan episcopacy and the early church against the objections of the university's *bête noire* Richard Baxter, a renegade Anglican deacon.[220] Maurice's election by the resident divines of the university indicated the transformation that had taken place in Oxford theology since Barlow's election in 1660.

In the sermons of South and the lectures of Jane Restoration Anglicanism spoke with a new assurance. The 'miraculous' deliverance of the Church of England from its time of troubles had left it with a greater sense of mission. It was able to draw on the reserves of liturgical piety and patristic scholarship accumulated amid the wreckage of the Laudian church by that galaxy of ejected royalist scholars—Ussher, Hammond, Sanderson, Cosin, Taylor, Thorndike, Pearson, Heylyn, Sparrow, Fell, Allestree, Pierce, and Gunning.[221] By building on their very remarkable achievement, and that of the earlier Jacobean and Caroline divines, South and Jane helped to produce a maturer, sturdier, more learned and evidently more attractive synthesis of English protestantism: a religion which, while continuing to deny the claims of Rome and scorn the novelties of dissent, was not afraid to look back beyond the Reformation to the early church for spiritual guidance. If, in the process of retrospection, the Restoration divines came to reappraise the inherited Calvinist formula of *scriptura sola* as no longer adequate for their needs, they also managed to extend the bounds of tolerance within the established church.

By the end of Charles II's reign the Church of England had become a broad-bottomed church, theologically more comprehensive, doctrinally more cohesive, and politically more united than it had been at any time before the civil war. That it was so owed much to the agreed content of theological study and unremitting control which, in Oxford, Creed, Allestree, and Jane, as regius professors of divinity, exercised over the younger members of their faculty. They succeeded in shifting clerical attention away from an arid search into the theological abstractions that had formerly divided them. Instead, they placed the emphasis, fair and square, on practical religion and on what united churchmen against the common foe, whether

[218] Jane, 'of whose abilities' Allestree 'had perfect knowledge', had been granted Allestree's canonry in 1678 in prospect of his succeeding to the chair: PRO SP 44/27, fo 116; Fell, *Allestree*, 16; Wood, *Life and Times* ii. 486; Wood, *Athenae* iv. 643–4.

[219] JCA foundation register, pp. 37, 46, 51, 60. He had been Jenkins's chaplain on his diplomatic mission to Cologne in 1673: OUA register Tb, p. 248; Wood, *Athenae* iv. 326.

[220] Henry Maurice, *A Vindication of the Primitive Church and Diocesan Episcopacy* (London 1682).

[221] Bosher, *The Making of the Restoration Settlement*, chs 1 and 2; J. W. Packer, *The Transformation of Anglicanism 1643–1660* (Manchester 1969), chs 5 and 6.

perceived as international Catholicism or parochial dissent. At the heart of this developing cohesion lay the Book of Common Prayer and the rich fabric of personal piety and devotional literature which grew up around it.[222] The Restoration divines' attachment to liturgical worship in their everyday lives changed Anglicanism from what it had fundamentally been in the past: the religion of one book, the Bible, into what it was to be for the next 300 years, the religion of two books: the Authorized Version of 1611 and the prayer book of 1662.

An indispensable ingredient in this silent and all-embracing development was the acclaimed series of writings associated with the anonymous author of *The Whole Duty of Man*—a best-selling piece of Anglican spiritualia which has traditionally and convincingly been ascribed to Allestree's pen.[223] Although the work was first published at London in 1658, Fell went out of his way to obtain for the university press the printing and publishing rights of the later titles in the series, which he personally saw through the press;[224] just as, after the death of Allestree, he made a point of writing his friend's 'Life', which he published, again in Oxford, as a preface to his collected edition of Allestree's sermons in 1684. A powerful blend of hagiography and Cavalier Anglican polemic, Fell's biography was written in the hope of perpetuating the memory of Allestree's commendable rectitude and timely moderation beyond the grave; very much in the same spirit of religious edification that he had written and published the life of his earlier deceased friend, Henry Hammond, the angelic doctor of Restoration Anglicanism, in 1661.[225] Fell had no doubt as to the importance of Allestree's contribution in bringing orthodoxy to a disordered university and peace to a divided church and nation.

Anthony Wood, that practised observer of the contemporary scene, was quick to discern the lead taken by Christ Church men in shaping the life of Restoration Oxford. Not only did he comment unfavourably, as a disgruntled Mertonian, on Fell's ambition 'to govern the university', but he also noted how, aided by Allestree and abetted by Dolben, the dean was intent on 'reducing the university to that condition as it stood in Laud's time'. It was an intention which Wood, with his lingering puritan sympathies, found 'very ridiculous' to begin with, since, in his opinion, Oxford was 'quite changed ... by the many mutations' it had 'suffered in the broken times'.[226] Nevertheless, his chronicling of subsequent events indicates

---

[222] See the 'dialogue' concerning sin and grace, supposedly taking place in Holy Week 1667 between 'Uranus', an Oxford tutor, and his pupils (perhaps written, and certainly corrected, by Francis Turner, fellow of New College): Bodl. MS Eng. th. d. 52, fos 9, 10ᵛ, 11ᵃ, 17, 54, 79 ff.

[223] C. E. Doble, 'Who wrote "The Whole Duty of Man"?', *Academy* xxii (1882), 348–9, 364–5, 382–3; P. Elmen, 'Richard Allestree and "The Whole Duty of Man"', *The Library* (5th ser. vi 1951), 19–27. For its popularity see C. J. Sommerville, 'On the distribution of religious ... literature in seventeenth-century England', *The Library* (5th ser. xxix 1974), 221–5.

[224] Madan, *Oxford Books* iii. 276–9, 294, 310 ff.; OUA SEP/P/17b/4, items 2, 8, 10, title-pages marked 'Bookes printed at the Theater in Oxford for Dr Fell, Yates, etc.'

[225] Fell maintained that Hammond's life was 'the best of sermons', and had done his best to check his facts: Longleat House, MS Thynne 10, fos 143, 172. For Fell's presentation copy to Barlow see Bodl., 8° B 85 Linc., inscribed 'Lib. Tho. Barlow ex dono authoris'.

[226] Wood, *Life and Times* i. 348–9.

the overall success that crowned Fell's labours. By the time that the dean became vice-chancellor in August 1666, he had, in Clarendon's words, 'shewen himselfe soe able in governing the greatest college', that he seemed, above others, 'fitt to be trusted with the government of the university'. Clarendon did not doubt but that he would 'apply himselfe with the same zeale' in the university, as he had in Christ Church, 'to the incouragement of learning and vertue, and the suppressing vice and disorder'—in the accomplishment of which he promised 'all the assistance' he could give.[227] It was high time to stem the spate of youthful licence, which had broken out on the removal of puritanical constraints, by stressing the obligations of right religion and intellectual study. Yet, before decency and sense could prevail in everyday life, there was a transcendent need to reassert academic authority on the spot, and none was better placed, or better qualified, to do it than the dean of Christ Church.[228]

Animated by a supreme sense of duty, Fell worked hard and long to reintroduce the policies which had made Laud's chancellorship a period of outstanding achievement between 1630 and 1641.[229] He made it his task to pursue a definite programme of Anglican renewal, linked to the steady reform of university discipline, and underpinned by the systematic courting of benefactions on a magnificent scale. The Laudian impulse was evident from start to finish: from the emphasis Fell placed on keeping up 'an uniformity in the external service of God', to his insistence that the provisions of the Laudian statutes be observed in their entirety.[230] 'Four times in a day' he attended 'public service in the cathedral', and twice more he prayed 'at home' in the deanery. It was a routine which won him the admiration of his well-wishers and the derision of his detractors.[231] Neither he, nor Allestree, nor Dolben, allowed university affairs, however pressing, to disrupt the daily round of their devotions. No matter where they were, or what they were doing in Oxford, they always 'ran home to prayers'.[232] There could be no mistaking their priorities. Even the building of the Sheldonian Theatre, for which Fell acted as clerk of the works, was in response to their desire to free the university church from all ceremonies save those of religious worship.[233]

Similarly Fell's regard for all the 'old laws and statutes', by which the pre-war university had been governed before the troubles, soon became a by-word for his

[227] OUA register Ta, p. 219; *Restoration Oxford*, ed. Beddard iii, no. 1027.

[228] Besides being a strict disciplinarian Fell took a close interest in the intellectual life of Christ Church, examining the tutors as to 'what they taught their pupils and what they studied themselves': LPL MS 2564, fo 325.

[229] Fell held that 'there is no pleasure in the world but duty': Bodl. MS Eng. letters d. 195, fo 1, Fell to Lady Pakington [Christ Church], 31 December [1675]; John Fell, *The Character of the Last Daies. A sermon preached before the king* (Oxford 1675), 1.

[230] Vice-Chancellor Fell (Oxford, 28 December 1666) joined with Archbishop Sheldon (Lambeth, 12 December 1666) in licensing the publication of Laud's *A Summarie of Devotions* (Oxford 1667), which had been edited by Richard Baylie.

[231] Bodl. MS Wood f. 39, fo 334; Wood, *Life and Times* i. 348.

[232] Wood, *Life and Times* i. 392.

[233] Bodl. MS Tanner 461, fo 6ᵛ, Sheldon's foundation charter, Lambeth House, 25 May 1669; OUA register Ta, p. 266.

approach to the problem of discipline.[234] As early as the spring of 1662 he was instrumental in getting Clarendon and Sheldon to insist that the colleges return to the proctorial cycle, which Charles I had instituted in 1628, and from which the parliamentary visitors had strayed in 1649.[235] Although Merton and Magdalen had chosen men to serve as proctors, Christ Church and Brasenose—the colleges appointed by 'the rule of the cycle'—successfully challenged the right to elect for the ensuing year.[236] The dean's reputation for performing what he set his mind to inevitably bred petty-minded jealousies in the university. Before entering upon the vice-chancellorship it was rumoured that 'he would be very severe, rigid, and not to be endured'. But this did not deter him from his purpose to do good.[237]

Within days of assuming office, and in plenty of time for the Michaelmas term, Fell issued orders in August 1666 for regulating academic dress in a move to end the 'undecencie and excesse in the apparell of younger scholars'.[238] The sumptuary requirements of the Laudian statutes had been repudiated altogether by the sectaries and widely neglected by the parliamentary intruders, many of whom, having been drafted in from puritan Cambridge, had promiscuously imported the habits of their former university.[239] With characteristic efficiency, Fell furnished the Oxford tailors with detailed printed instructions and precise patterns on which to model their products. He left nothing to chance. The city tailors, as members of one of the privileged companies of tradesmen, were commanded to observe the directives 'with all exactnesse possible', on pain of being fined and ultimately 'discommoned': the penalty whereby they could be denied the lucrative custom of the university.[240]

For Fell, as for Laud, the wearing of the cap and gown appropriate to one's rank was the mark of belonging to a well-ordered and disciplined society, one in which the observance of degree, priority, and place—social as well as academic—was much prized. After the demotic disturbances of the mid-century there was greater reason than ever to strengthen traditional concepts of hierarchy. Moreover, the regulation of academic dress complemented the ecclesiastical authorities' parallel revival of the distinctive 'prelaticall garb' of the clergy: a policy officially endorsed by the king, as supreme governor of the Church of England, who wisely disapproved of the spread of lay attire and secular fashions to the clerical estate.[241]

---

[234] Bodl. MS Tanner 45, fo 103ᵛ, Wood to [Richard Lower], 15 September 1666. Clarendon had recovered 'the originall booke of statutes of the university'. BL Add. MS 14,269, fo 5; OUA register Ta, pp. 82–3; CCCA MS 301, fos 171–2.

[235] OUA WP/γ/25 c. 1, register R, fos 2–4; Bodl. MS Tanner 338, fos 123–4ᵛ, 125–6ᵛ.

[236] MCA registrum 1567–1731, p. 435; *Restoration Oxford*, ed. Beddard ii, nos 550, 555.

[237] Wood, *Life and Times* ii. 83.

[238] OUA register Ta, p. 222, 27 August 1666. For Fell's printed *programma* see Bodl. Wood 276A, item 320.

[239] *Laudian Code*, ed. Griffiths, 143–4; Wood, *Life and Times* i. 148, 268, 300–1, 356, 359, 369.

[240] OUA register Ta, p. 223. For Principal Jenkins's draft, corrected by Fell see QCL MS 506. Bodl. MS Bodley 594, fos 25–6.

[241] For Vice-Chancellor Bathurst's *programma* of 24 November 1674, sparked off by Chancellor Monmouth's signification of Charles's displeasure to Cambridge, see Wood, *Life and Times* ii. 298, 300, 355. PRO SP 29/362, nos 183 and i, 7. Madan, *Oxford Books* iii, no. 3018. Bodl. Wood 276A, item 322.

In 1667 the vice-chancellor turned his attention to the more glaring abuses occasioned by 'coursing' and public-house drinking. He reformed the Lenten disputations in the schools, which, being conducted on a college basis, had given rise to inter-collegiate rivalry and undergraduate disorder on the streets of Oxford. He did not merely rely on proctorial enforcement of vice-cancellarial injunctions, but took to attending the disputes and overseeing the disputants in person. Equally, he spared no pains in 'continually hauling taverns and alehouses' in the town, to the general improvement of discipline, moral and academic. In this he was as fierce as any of his puritan predecessors.[242] His government helped reduce 'the university to that temperament that a man might study and not be thought a dullard, might be sober and yet a conformist, a scholar and yet a Church of England-man'.[243]

Meanwhile, Fell's hatred of irregularity of all kinds—the blame for which he laid firmly at the door of the illegal parliamentary visitation with its disruption of the old order—had reached its symbolic apogee on 25 January 1667. Following the outcome of a delegacy of inquiry into past divergencies from the Laudian statutes, the superior legislative body of the university, the house of convocation, passed a formal condemnation of everything that had been transacted in convocation between 1648 and 1660 'durante tyrannide parliamentaria': during the 'pretended' chancellorships of the rebel fourth earl of Pembroke and the usurpers, Oliver and Richard Cromwell.[244] In the face of the Convention Parliament's express prohibition in 1660, preventing the restored royalists from cancelling the degrees, leases, and other corporate acts made by the university during the Interregnum, the condemnation by the masters and doctors was about as far as the Cavalier Anglican reaction could safely be carried by Fell. Contrary to the protestations of April 1660, forswearing vengeful thoughts and 'partial remembrance' of past injustices, the Cavalier Anglicans had no intention of allowing the university either to forgive, or to forget, what their enemies had inflicted on them.[245]

Fell's greatest achievement was undoubtedly his realization of Archbishop Laud's vision of establishing 'a learned press' in Oxford. Originally envisaged, in 1629, as 'a Greek press' for printing the Greek Barocci manuscripts presented to the Bodleian Library by the third earl of Pembroke, Laud's predecessor as chancellor, the project had done little more than survive as an idea since the archbishop's execution;[246] though a modest step forward had been made in 1658 with the appointment of an *architypographus*, Samuel Clarke.[247] Steeped in the piety of the royalist

---

[242] Bodl. Wood 276A, item 353, Fell's *programma*, 16 February 1667; Wood, *Life and Times* i. 349, ii. 82–3, 100; *Restoration Oxford*, ed. Beddard iii, nos 1089, 1059; Bodl. MS Wood e. 32, fo 17ᵛ.

[243] Penton, *Guardian's Instruction*, 45.

[244] OUA register Ta, pp. 225, 357; *Restoration Oxford*, ed. Beddard iii no. 1084.

[245] *LJ* xi. 41. See p. 814 above.

[246] For the pre-history of the press see H. Carter, *A History of the Oxford University Press* (Oxford 1975), 29–34; for the donation of the Barocci MSS see OUA, register R, fo 9ᵛ.

[247] Strictly speaking, this was a re-election, as he had first been elected on 24 July 1649. OUA register T, pp. 7 (reverse), 325; BL Add. MS 22,905, fo 9, Langbaine to Samuel Clarke, 7 December 1657.

martyrology, and ambitious to revive the university's reputation for learning at home and abroad after the depredations of the Cromwellian era, Fell consciously set out to fulfil the intention of the martyred prelate. He wanted a press that would serve 'the concerns and convenience of scholars' rather than profiteering printers and booksellers[248] and, at the same time, prevent foreign countries—Catholic or protestant—from imposing their wares and 'opinions from their dictates'.[249]

The dean prevailed on Archbishop Sheldon, as Laud's successor both in the primacy of Canterbury and in the chancellorship of Oxford, to permit the use of his theatre for printing when it was not required for academic ceremonies.[250] Foreseeing the expiry of the London stationers' lease of the university's privilege of printing (by which the university had renounced its right to print bibles and prayer books in return for an annual payment of £200), Fell formed a consortium of Oxford friends to 'undertake the whole affair of printing' on behalf of the university. On 22 August 1671 the delegacy of printing recommended to convocation that a lease should be granted to him and his three partners: the business-like principal of Brasenose, Thomas Yate; the eminent civilian, Leoline Jenkins, principal of Jesus; and the highly placed under-secretary of state, Sir Joseph Williamson, an absentee fellow of Queen's. The lease was, in the first instance, to run for three years from Lady day 1672.[251] Having obtained Sheldon's consent, Fell boldly anticipated obtaining the approval of the university. By early 1669 no fewer than five presses had been built and installed in the Theatre, alongside several compositors' frames. Thereafter, the dean sensibly concerned himself 'only in letters': that is, in the provision of type for the press and in the commissioning of copy for publication.[252] Financial management, including marketing, he remitted into the hands of Yate.[253]

Fell's chief agent in procuring types from the continent was the *émigré* royalist clergyman, Thomas Marshall, the prize pupil of the celebrated pioneer of Old English scholarship, Franciscus Junius.[254] Ejected from Lincoln College in 1648 for having borne arms for Charles I, Marshall had subsequently found employment

---

[248] PRO SP 29/413, no. 4, 'An account of the state of the press at Oxford as it now stands', 9 January 1680.

[249] Bodl. MS d'Orville 470, fos 168–9, Fell to Isaac Vossius, Oxonii, 12 March 1670/1 (copy).

[250] Bodl. MS Tanner 461, fo 6ᵛ; Corbet Owen, *Carmen pindaricum in Theatrum Sheldonianum* (Oxford 1669), stanza 19.

[251] PRO SP 29/291, no. 230, Fell and Yate to Jenkins [Oxford], 25 July [1671]; PRO SP 29/292, nos 115–17, 132–3, 164. For later indentures see QCA Z. U. 74 and 75.

[252] Bodl. MS Eng. letters c. 328, fo 513, MS Rawlinson d. 397, fos 132–3, Fell's notes on types, MS Marshall 134, fo 18.

[253] For example Bodl. MS Rawlinson d. 398, fo 159, Yate's bill for Robert Ashborne, bookseller of York.

[254] Marshall was an outstanding linguist, being equally at home in the classical and oriental languages, especially Arabic and Coptic. For his preliminary work on an Old English grammar, the basis of George Hickes's famous *Institutiones* of 1689, see Bodl. MS Marshall 78. E. N. Adams, *Old English Scholarship in England 1566–1800* (Yale 1917), 71–3; D. Douglas, *English Scholars 1660–1730* (London 1939, 2nd edn London 1951), 65–6, 68, 82 ff.; Bodl. MS Auct. d. 3. 18, 'Collectiones psalteriorum graecorum'.

overseas, as chaplain to the English Merchant Adventurers at Dordrecht.[255] From thence, he had attracted the patronage of Sheldon and Morley with the timely dedication to them of the four gospels in Gothic and Anglo-Saxon. In 1668 he became a fellow of Lincoln, and four years later was elected rector of his college.[256] It was primarily through his Dutch contacts that the university press was equipped with an excellent array of Roman, Italic, and Greek types—some of them of the utmost historical and artistic distinction. Later, as a result of Jenkins's presence as plenipotentiary at the Nijmegen peace conferences, the residential services of the German punch-maker Peter de Walpergen were secured.[257] By 1672 a printing-house had been constructed to the east of the Theatre, and foreign compositors recruited with the appropriate technical skills to operate the press. Paper was obtained from Wolvercote mill, just to the north of the city, and from the London paper merchants, who imported supplies from France and Italy.

Not content with procuring the very best types for his press, Fell demonstrated a desire (exceptional for its time in England) to improve the visual appearance of his books by commissioning illustrations from competent engravers.[258] The attraction into the university's service of the Danzig-born, Scottish topographical artist David Loggan, who was retained in 1669 as *publicus academiae sculptor* with a yearly salary of 20s, made possible the production of that instructive pictorial record of Restoration Oxford, the *Oxonia illustrata* of 1675: a fine set of detailed perspective views of the university, its colleges and halls.[259] Soon Oxford could boast other talented 'chalcographers' in metal and wood, most notably the naturalized Dutchman, Michael Burghers, and the Englishmen Robert White and George Edwards.[260]

From all of this it can be seen how dependent Fell was on foreign expertise and foreign technology in realizing Laud's scheme to promote Oxford scholarship in the service of the protestant religion and English letters. Indeed, there is evidence to suggest that, in fostering the learned press, Fell was deliberately measuring his efforts and achievements against the distinguished products of Louis XIV's *imprimerie royale* at the Louvre, in the same way that Sir Thomas Bodley had set out to rival the Vatican Library in Rome.[261] The foundation of the university press, like that of the Bodleian Library,[262] was part of a continuing national protestant

[255] OUA register Sb, pp. 80–1; Mattys Balen, *Beschryvinge der stad Dordrecht* (Dordrecht 1677), 194–5; W. Steven, *The History of the Scottish Church, Rotterdam* (Edinburgh 1833), 300–1, 325–6.

[256] *Restoration Oxford*, ed. Beddard i, no. 448; PRO SP 29/292, no. 116, SP 29/302, no. 28 I, SP 29/303, no. 18; Bodl. MSS Rawlinson d. 317, fos 142, 145, d. 398, fos 132–3, 123.

[257] N. Barker, *The Oxford University Press and the Spread of Learning 1478–1978* (Oxford 1978), 17–19.

[258] In projecting an annotated English bible Fell desired 'all the advantages of print and paper and exterior ornaments': PRO SP 29/305, no. 117, Fell to Jenkins, 11 April [1672]; Bodl. MS Rawlinson d. 398, fos 127, 127*, Fell's draft prospectus.

[259] OUA register Ta, p. 237, 30 March 1669; *Oxonia illustrata* (Oxford at the Theatre 1675).

[260] Barker, *Oxford University Press*, 14, 22–3, 44, 61.

[261] PRO SP 29/305, no. 98, Fell to Williamson, 8 April 1672.

[262] *Letters of Sir Thomas Bodley to Thomas James*, ed. G. W. Wheeler (Oxford 1926), 11; G. W. Wheeler, *The Earliest Catalogues of the Bodleian Library* (Oxford 1928), 57; *pace* I. Philip, *The Bodleian Library in the Seventeenth and Eighteenth Centuries* (Oxford 1983), 2.

strategy aimed at withstanding the encroachment of the counter-reformation.[263] It is not the least of historical paradoxes that, in the theologically antagonistic atmosphere of Restoration Oxford, there was no disguising the electrifying influence of Tridentine Catholicism on the protestantism it sought to combat.

In bringing 'the trade of printing' to Oxford Fell aimed at the 'honour and advantage' of the university and English scholarship. The success of his altruistic endeavours can be seen in some of the earliest books to come from the Sheldonian press.[264] Anthony Wood's two-volume *Historia et antiquitates universitatis oxoniensis*[265] and Thomas Hyde's *Catalogus impressorum librorum bibliothecae bodleianae*,[266] both of them published in 1674, together with Loggan's *Oxonia illustrata* of 1675, were landmarks in Oxford publishing. Each in its unique way enhanced the university's national and international reputation as an ancient, beautiful, and well-endowed seat of learning. For example, the catalogue of Bodley's printed books was to be as useful elsewhere as it was to readers in Oxford.[267] Widely purchased, interleaved and annotated, it served as a catalogue for other libraries of note, private and institutional.[268] John Locke used it for listing his own books[269] and until 1760 it served, with handwritten additions, as the catalogue of the Bibliothèque Mazarine in Paris.[270] It was a use which Fell's partner, Principal Yate, had expressly catered for, having observed at the outset: 'if we print the catalogue, [we are] to do it in a larg letter, larg paper, a larg margent, and on paper [that] will beare inke.'[271] The ambitious scope of Fell's scholarly patronage, ranging from patristics to botany, was ably attested from the outset by the publication in 1672 of William Beveridge's massive *Synodicon*, a collection of Greek canons,[272] and Robert Morison's work on the umbelliferous plants, the first part to appear of a projected *Plantarum historia oxoniensis*: the former dedicated to Archbishop Sheldon, the latter to the duke of

---

[263] For contemporary perceptions, see John Dury, *The Reformed Librarie-Keeper* (London 1650), 16; CCC MS 332, fo 18, John Beale to Christopher Wase, the newly-elected *architypographus*, Yeovil, 21 October 1671; Wood, *Life and Times* ii. 529, where the library is styled 'our Vatican'.

[264] PRO SP 29/293, no. 95; ASL MS 239, fo 641, Fell's autograph first prospectus.

[265] *Historia et antiquitates universitatis oxoniensis* (Oxford at the Theatre 1674), dedicated to 'augustissimo monarchae Carolii', Allestree presenting a copy to the king in July 1674; Fell sent a copy to Chancellor Ormonde.

[266] *Catalogus impressorum librorum bibliothecae bodleianae in academia oxoniensi* (Oxford at the Theatre 1674), dedicated to Archbishop Sheldon.

[267] The university had a number 'printed on royal paper for presents to their friends and patrons', such as King Christian V of Denmark, the Grand Duke Cosimo III de' Medici of Tuscany, Chancellor Ormonde, Lord Keeper Finch, Lord Chief Justice Hale (Selden's executor), Henri Justel, Isaac Vossius, John Evelyn, etc.: CL Evelyn collection, letters B/313, Ralph Bohun to Evelyn [New College 1674].

[268] College librarians used it to locate titles, as Edmund Gibson, the Lambeth librarian, did to find 'very much displac'd' books in the archbishop's library in 1696: Bodl. MS Tanner 24, fo 116; Hiscock, *A Christ Church Miscellany*, 14; P. Morgan, *Oxford Libraries outside the Bodleian* (Oxford 1973, 2nd edn Oxford 1980), 58, 88, 133.

[269] J. Harrison and P. Laslett, *The Library of John Locke* (Oxford Bib. Soc. new ser. xiii 1965), 30–1, 37–8, plates 3 and 4.

[270] Philip, *The Bodleian Library in the Seventeenth and Eighteenth Centuries*, 50.

[271] OUA SEP/P/17b/1/m, Yate's memoranda for the press.

[272] *ΣΥΝΟΔΙΚΟΝ, sive pandectae canones ss. Apostolorum, et conciliorum ab Ecclesia Graeca receptorum* (Oxford at the Theatre 1672). For a unique prospectus see Bodl. MS Junius 7, fo 1.

Ormonde.[273] In Restoration Oxford science as well as theology was highly valued, and more often than not professed by scholars who doubled as divines and scientists.

The effectiveness of the Cavalier Anglicans' protection of the university was demonstrated by its ability to weather the successive crises that assailed church and state relations under the restored monarchy. Despite the enormous degree of intellectual commitment on the part of Oxford to Charles II's rule, the king's ecclesiastical policies were frequently capricious and damaging to the established church, and consequently a source of anxiety to the academic clergy. Yet, secure in the patronage of the Cavalier hierarchy and its well-entrenched, secular allies, the university was able to avoid the worst effects of the king's fitful flirtation with dissent. Repeatedly, between 1660 and 1673, Charles tried to improve the lot of his nonconformist subjects, sometimes by promoting comprehension (church union), and sometimes by offering indulgence (toleration). In each case he strove to widen his political options by freeing dissenters from the penalties imposed by intransigent Anglicanism. Both policies were anathema to Oxford high churchmen.[274] Resolutely attached to the exclusive political and religious power of their church in government and society, they did not wish to abate by one iota the terms of conformity laid down in the 1662 act of uniformity. Any move to free dissenters from the constraints appointed by law, or to lower the requirements for belonging to the church, was met by studied opposition—regardless of the quarter from which it came: royal, ministerial, or parliamentary.

Considering the university's esteemed role as the guardian of Anglican orthodoxy, it was to be expected that the Oxford authorities would view with alarm any attempt by dissenters to encroach on its privileged preserve. Throughout the Restoration period the dons found dissenters uncomfortable neighbours, and kept a close and critical watch on fanatical activity in the town and diocese, lest it prove invasive.[275] In discharging this readily assumed duty they could count on two unfailing assets: their time-honoured position in the local municipal magistracy,[276] and the friendly countenance which they received from their Cavalier Anglican patrons inside official government circles. The first allowed them to prosecute their adversaries virtually at will; the second ensured that their prosecutions would rarely be challenged, even by the crown.

Academic intolerance of dissent declared itself well before the parliamentary re-enactment of uniformity in May 1662. As early as December 1661 Vice-Chancellor Baylie—who, it should be remembered, shared Laud's horror of schism and his

---

[273] *Plantarum umbelliferarum distributio nova, per tabulas cognationis et affinitatis ex libro naturae observata & detecta* (Oxford at the Theatre 1672).

[274] Wood, *Life and Times* i. 465–6. Robert South complained of 'the whole nation' being 'so unsettled': BL Add. MS 4,276, fo 127, South to Jones 19 March 1668/9.

[275] *Restoration Oxford*, ed. Beddard i, no. 327; Wood, *Life and Times* i. 377, 379.

[276] Oxford City Arch. O.5.11, fos 45ᵛ, 47, 47ᵛ, 50 ff; *VCH Oxon.* iv. 339; L. K. J. Glassey, *Politics and the Appointment of Justices of the Peace 1675–1720* (Oxford 1979), 4.

determination to repress it—took a tough line against the unruliness of the local Quakers, a sect which had taken its rise in the Interregnum. By continuing to hold conventicles in competition with church services, Quakers not only offended Anglican decorum, but also threatened to disturb the peace.[277] Having failed by lesser means to curb their lawlessness, Baylie had resort to force. He sent their ring-leader, Richard Bettrice, to Bocardo (the town gaol) in an effort to disrupt their meetings. His action received the fullest approbation of Clarendon as chancellor of the university, even though, as the king's lord chancellor, he was currently pursuing a policy of conciliation towards the more sober dissenters in London.

Clarendon did not mince his words. He told the vice-chancellor to keep the troublemaker in prison, 'till, by the change of his behaviour', he gave good 'reason to believe he has changed his opinions'. Meanwhile, he counselled Baylie to take care that Bocardo did not 'serve him for a chappell by the concourse of his party'. If others undertook 'to succeed him, in encouraging and seducing the rest', then the vice-chancellor would do 'very well to send them to keep Bettrice company'.[278] In May 1662 Matthew Wren, Clarendon's secretary, expressed his master's surprise on hearing the offender was out of gaol, adding that, in the chancellor's judgement, churchmen had sufficient 'instruction from experience' to know Quakers were 'a sort of people upon whom tenderness and lenity doe not at all prevaile'. Furthermore, since the passage of the 1661 act against them, it was 'of absolute necessity to put it severely in execution', in Oxford especially, for 'it would be of very ill example that we should not be able to root them out of an university'.[279] Plainly, the Cavalier Anglicans were determined to prevent their alma mater from being polluted by fanaticism.

The eradication of nonconformity inside the university posed difficulties which could not speedily be overcome. The revival of prayer book services, acceptable though they were in the main, occasioned some withdrawal of support from college chapels, as puritan scruples began to manifest themselves in individual acts of separation. Quite how many refused attendance at Anglican worship it is impossible to say. In extreme cases those with insuperably 'tender consciences' left Oxford altogether; some voluntarily, but many after being formally ejected by the king's commissioners from the places to which they had been 'unduly and illegally admitted' by the defunct parliamentary visitors.[280] Others, reluctant to forfeit an acade-

---

[277] Quakers were seen as an 'unstable people': Wood, *Life and Times* i. 190–1, 280, 293. Dr Williams's Library, Baxter letters III, fo 33. For earlier punitive action in the Oxford region see ORO B.O.Q.M. iv/i/1, fos 1ʳ⁻ᵛ.

[278] Bodl. MS Tanner 338, fo 110; for Bettrice see ORO MS Oxf. dioc. papers, c. 99, fo 238, 'nomina excommunicatorum'; Wood, *Life and Times* i. 190; Joseph Besse, *A Collection Of the Sufferings Of the People called Quakers* (2 vols London 1753) i. 569, 571, 572; *The First Publishers of Truth*, ed. N. Penney (Friends Historical Soc. supplement 1 London [1906]), 206–7, 212–14.

[279] Bodl. MS Tanner 338, fo 135, Matthew Wren to Vice-Chancellor Baylie, 15 May [1662]; *Statutes of the Realm* v. 350–1: 14 Car. II, c. 1; *Restoration Oxford*, ed. Beddard ii, nos 562–3. For Wren see n. 17 above.

[280] E. Calamy, *An Account of the Ministers ... ejected or silenced after the Restoration* (London 1702, 2nd edn 2 vols London 1713) ii. 73; 'Restoration Visitation', ed. Varley, 2 ff.

mic education, took to attending conventicles. They gathered around 'refractory and ill affected' teachers, whether resident in the university, like the Presbyterian John Troughton, an intruded fellow of St John's,[281] or living at some distance from Oxford, like the Independent divine, John Owen, who, since his ejection from the deanery of Christ Church, had retired to his patrimonial estate in nearby Stadhampton, whence he directed the dissenting faction in the college.[282] Before St Bartholomew's day (24 August) 1662, when the new act of uniformity came into force, there could be no 'universal riddance' of nonconformists from the university—though the Cavalier Anglicans did everything they could to lessen the size of the problem.

Whenever possible the king's commissioners, working hand in glove with the restored college authorities, removed those intruded academics who impeded the return of the lawful incumbents. These intruders necessarily included some of the most stiff-necked dissenters. However, when there was no royalist claimant to be restored, the commissioners had perforce to act circumspectly. The fear of incurring parliamentary wrath remained even after they had defeated an attempt to engage the king directly in preserving some whom they had discharged.[283] Aware that, as late as December 1660, the more irreconcilable of the ejected dons were still trying to stir up trouble in the Convention, where they had sympathizers enough to listen to their complaints, the commissioners either gave them time to reconsider their position and conform, or remitted the settlement of their tenure to dependable college heads, such as the dean of Christ Church, President Oliver of Magdalen, or Principal Mansell of Jesus.[284] The heads were, after all, better placed to examine the past irregularities and current views of the individuals concerned, and had the power to demand that their members submit to the local statutes by which their societies were governed.

Although reliable dates for the departure of nonconformists are rarely forthcoming because of the incompleteness of the visitatorial and collegiate record, it is clear that, following the dissolution of the feared Convention and the election of the benign Cavalier Parliament, the restored authorities were able to press ahead with reforming the personnel of their colleges. What Anglican example, persuasion, and exhortation had failed to achieve, punitive action in the shape of censures and dismissals increasingly accomplished. It has been estimated that, prior to 24 August 1662, eleven heads of colleges and halls, thirty-nine fellows (including 'collegiate

[281] Troughton refused the surplice, cut college prayers, and was 'vehemently suspected to seduce some of the younge scholars of the colledge'. 'Restoration Visitation', ed. Varley, 9, 53–5; A. E. Matthews, *Calamy Revised* (Oxford 1934), 494; *Register*, ed. Burrows, 403, 406.

[282] When the militia raided Owen's house they found two ejected heads with him: Johnson of University College and Thankful Owen of St John's: *Restoration Oxford*, ed. Beddard i, no. 327 *The Correspondence of John Owen*, ed. P. Toon (London 1970), 125.

[283] BL MS Egerton 2618, fos 81, 82ᵛ, 83, 84ᵛ, Charles II to his commissioners, Whitehall, 30 July and 1 August 1660; *Restoration Oxford*, ed. Beddard i, nos 135, 157.

[284] 'Restoration Visitation', ed. Varley, 42–3, 19, 33, 48, 52, 53; QCL MS 521 (Lamplugh papers), Mansell's 'expedient' proposed to the king's commissioners [24 August 1660]; JCA foundation register, pp. 2–3.

prebends' of Christ Church) and three chaplains were removed by the king's commissioners or by decision of the colleges.[285] The toll taken of the junior members of the university is less certain. Some were called home by their families, if not immediately, then before they were 'to take those oathes which the statutes require of all proceeders' to degrees.[286] Others withdrew of their own accord, though not always with parental blessing, as was shown by the defection of the future Quaker leader and American proprietor, William Penn, a gentleman-commoner of Christ Church who, much to his father's annoyance, had fallen under the spell of the ejected Dean Owen.[287]

In one area only were the Cavalier Anglicans and their allies powerless to proceed against their adversaries. Where an existing head professed himself a nonconformist, but his title was not challenged by a returning royalist, he could not be touched, at any rate not before 24 August 1662, when persistent refusal to conform to the worship and discipline of the Church of England finally became a criminal offence punishable by 'amotion'. On failure to comply with the demands of the new act of uniformity, which were notably stiffer than those required by its Elizabethan predecessor of 1559, the Cavalier Parliament decreed that each and every defaulter in the university should *ipso facto* be deprived, and his place declared void, 'as if the person so failing were naturally dead'. The major stumbling-block to conformity was the statutory requirement that all academics declare their 'unfeigned assent and consent to all and every thing contained and prescribed in and by ... the Book of Common Prayer', including the revised Anglican ordinal, with its insistence on episcopal ordination.[288]

The cumulative effect of two years of unremitting Anglican attrition paid off. The number of Bartolomean deprivations 'for non-subscription to the Anglican liturgy' was gratifyingly small: three heads of house, four fellows and seven graduate and undergraduate scholars.[289] The heads were Rector Conant of Exeter, who as Richard Cromwell's vice-chancellor had led the university delegation to congratulate Charles II's restoration, and the principals of Magdalen Hall and New Inn Hall, Henry Wilkinson junior and Christopher Rogers.[290] Surrounded by conformists, they had withstood the pressure to conform. Indeed, the Presbyterian Wilkinson had endured several 'chidings' from Chancellor Clarendon, who was incensed that the head of his own undergraduate society should slight the liturgy,

---

[285] Matthews, *Calamy Revised*, p. xiii. Of the displaced heads, Goddard of Merton simply retired to London and was not a nonconformist, and Stephens of Hart Hall died in October 1661.

[286] OUA register Ta, pp. 314–15, 325–6, 330, register Tb, pp. 4, 6, 15.

[287] Penn subscribed the oath of allegiance and the Thirty-nine Articles of Religion, but refused to conform to the liturgy: OUA SP 37, p. 22, SP 41, p. 5; T. Clarkson, *Memoirs of ... William Penn* (2 vols London 1813) i. 10–11; *The Diary of Samuel Pepys*, ed. R. Latham and W. Matthews (11 vols London 1970–83) ii. 206, iii. 17, 73.

[288] *Statutes of the Realm* v. 364–70. For nonconformist difficulties see *Reliquiae Baxterianae*, pt 2, pp. 308–33, 358–60.

[289] Matthews, *Calamy Revised*, 13 corrected in the light of Bodl. MS Tanner 338, fo 411 (seven not six defaulters from New Inn Hall, 8 September 1662); Wood, *Life and Times* i. 453.

[290] Wood, *Life and Times* i. 130, 530–1, 414–15. ECA register 2, fo 59.

and afford protection to 'not only factious, but debauched schollers', that had been turned out of other colleges for nonconformity.[291]

Weeks before Wilkinson and Conant incurred the statutory incapacity the authorities of church and state moved to prevent any disorder that might arise in the town on their deprivation, which they did by severing their links with the citizens whom they had served for many years as lecturers. In May the city council, which was about to be remodelled under the auspices of the 1661 corporation act, discharged Wilkinson from his lectureship at Carfax church.[292] In July Vice-Chancellor Baylie intervened to suppress Conant's lectureship at All Saints. The authorities acted in unison, out of the belief that 'such lectures ... had been fomenters of the late rebellion': a Cavalier Anglican conviction that was highlighted by recent events in Oxford, where they still strove to 'nourish faction' by controverting church doctrine. When questioned by the vice-chancellor and regius professor for preaching an anti-Arminian sermon at All Saints, in which he had disputed the efficacy of baptism as a means of cancelling sin, as taught by the Anglican liturgy, Conant had rejected the authority of 'Common Prayer', maintaining that it was in no way 'authenticke to resolve him in that point'.[293]

By 1662 Conant (who had already been removed from the regius chair of divinity by the king's commissioners) was not simply a Calvinist who objected to the doctrine of baptismal regeneration, but an obstinate Presbyterian. Unlike his fellow Oxonians, Warden Reynolds of Merton and John Wallis of St John's, who had also represented the puritan party called to review the liturgy at the abortive Savoy Conference of 1661, he refused to back down when substantial concessions were unforthcoming from the episcopalian side.[294] A 'presbyter' by conviction, he had been commissioned by the Presbyterian classis at Salisbury in 1652.[295] After a decade spent in the public exercise of his ministry he declined to admit that his vocation was defective, simply for want of episcopal imposition. Having been ordained deacon on the title of his fellowship in 1633, he had in 1652 turned his back on the Anglican ministry. For all that he was the son-in-law of a reclaimed Presbyterian, Warden Reynolds, the newly consecrated bishop of Norwich, Conant remained unmoved by his example—at least until 1670, when, stimulated by the perceived upsurge of popery and 'arbitrary government' associated with the Cabal administration, he threw over his dissent (but not entirely his delinquent nonconformist ways), and sought ordination and preferment from Bishop Reynolds.[296]

[291] Wood, *Life and Times* i. 499. Clarendon had matriculated from Magdalen Hall on 31 January 1622/3: OUA SP 2, fo 297.

[292] Oxford City Arch. A.5.7, fos 299, 309–10; Bodl. MS Wood f. 45, fo 137; C. J. H. Fletcher, *A History of the Church and Parish of St. Martin (Carfax) Oxford* (Oxford 1896), 77–9.

[293] Conant, *The Life of John Conant*, 18. For his Friday lectures at All Saints see BL MS Harleian 3998, fos 114 ff; Wood, *Life and Times* i. 444–5.

[294] 'Restoration Visitation' ed. Varley, 1–2.

[295] Bodl. MS Rawlinson c. 945, fo 425, 'A brief confession of faith made by Dr John Conant, rector of Exon. Coll., when he was ordained. October 28, 1652'; Conant, *The Life of John Conant*, 19.

[296] Conant, *The Life of John Conant*, 32, 33 n., 35. For his later semi-conformity see PRO SP 29/417, no. 136. For Reynolds's consecration see LPL Juxon register, fos 252ᵛ–60.

Almost forty years after receiving deacon's orders, the prodigal son-in-law entered the Anglican priesthood at Norwich on 28 September 1670. Of the university's thirteen Bartolomean deprivees, more than half were in the fullness of time to retrace their steps and become 'after-conformists'.[297]

The bulk of the university's contribution to the body of ministerial nonconformity was made before 'black Bartholomew': the date from which the annals of 'Old Dissent'—of Presbyterian, Independent (Congregationalist), and Anabaptist (Baptist) nonconformity—are conventionally reckoned by dissenting historians. Oxford's dissidents, in common with those of Cambridge, did not wait for the parliamentary axe to fall before relinquishing communion with the established church. If the Cavalier Anglican dons played a crucial role in the re-establishment of the Church of England by returning to Oxford in triumph at the Restoration, as they most assuredly did, then it ought also to be recognized that the local acceptance, and eventual embodiment in law, of their partisan principles played a decisive part in the precipitation of protestant dissent on a scale which ensured its survival as a permanent force in English religious life—despite subsequent and spirited Cavalier Anglican efforts to suppress it.

The ejected nonconformist pastors of Restoration Oxford, like the ejected Catholic priests of Elizabethan Oxford, set about improvising an alternative religious and educational system to that provided by the official establishment:[298] hence the founding of numerous dissenting conventicles (congregations) and academies (schools) which, by perpetuating the nonconformist schism to posterity, were, in the years ahead, severely to puncture the pride of the conformist clergy and earn the undying enmity of the universities. For the next three centuries English protestantism was to be divided between 'church' and 'chapel'. It was a division which owed much to the entrenched beliefs and uncompromising policies of the Cavalier Anglicans, animated as they were by a consuming hatred of schismatics. In the protracted and sometimes vicious struggle that ensued between conformist and nonconformist in Restoration society, the University of Oxford—until so recently the scene of confessional strife, and the enduring repository of wartime episcopalian militancy—consistently supported the intolerant, exclusive, high church wing of the established church, to which it belonged by Cavalier Anglican descent and Cavalier Anglican conviction.

The avidity with which the Oxford dons seized on the principles and practice of monopolistic Anglicanism, after an interruption of almost fourteen years, was truly astonishing; as was the perennial dedication which a large proportion of them brought to the instruction of successive generations in the duty of serving king and

[297] *Restoration Oxford*, ed. Beddard ii, no. 617 and notes.
[298] For the earlier Catholic enterprise see *Letters and Memorialls of Cardinal Allen* (London 1882), ed. T. F. Knox, 52–67; P. Guilday, *The English Catholic Refugees on the Continent 1558–1795* (London 1914), 3–5, 9, 64 ff; A. C. F. Beales, *Education under Penalty* (London 1963), 39 ff; G. Anstruther, *The Seminary Priests ... of England and Wales 1558–1850* (4 vols Great Wakering 1968–77), vols i and ii.

church. In all of this they took their lead from the nucleus of restored Cavalier Anglicans who dominated the government of the university after 1660.[299] As ordained ministers of the Church of England they gladly accepted the legal tests imposed on them by the Cavalier Parliament's act of uniformity, and willingly made them the rule by which they lived their lives. The creed which they professed, and passed on to their pupils, met the provisions of the act exactly. It was, in a word, conformist: religiously exclusive, politically obedient, and socially conservative.

Under the tutelage of Fell and a sequence of vigilant clerical Anglican vice-chancellors, the university became the ideological champion of the restored regime, dedicated to preserving the *status quo* in church and state.[300] As such, it was not only revered by the parochial clergy, but courted by politicians, crown officials, parliament men, and country squires intent on maintaining and raising their family stake in the protestant establishment. They knew full well that a university education, and the contacts and connections made during it, would stand their sons in good stead and enhance their career prospects. The institutional bond between the university and the clerical profession became exceptionally close, as was evidenced by the substantial body of the sons of the clergy who entered the colleges,[301] and, in turn, graduated into the parochial ministry, which in certain parts of the country began to resemble a hereditary caste. The overwhelmingly clerical ambience in which the laity studied at Oxford helped to regain respect for the cloth, and led to the growth of what the Whigs later denounced as 'high episcopal' politics, and the post-1688 generation of anticlerical writers stigmatized as 'priestcraft'.[302]

Throughout the Restoration period the hallmark of Oxford churchmanship was its militant Anglicanism—a doctrinally assertive, politically aggressive, insular brand of protestant episcopalianism, which manifested itself most obviously in two complementary traits: a total refusal to contemplate any relaxation of the act of uniformity and the penal legislation, which together guaranteed the rule of conformity in church and state and an uncompromising hostility to its spiritual rivals, the residual Catholics and mushrooming dissenters, who dared to reject that rule. Under intensive Cavalier Anglican surveillance, the university came to define its public persona primarily in confessional terms. Consequently Restoration Oxford saw itself as the custodian of the Church of England's doctrinal orthodoxy, the upholder of diocesan episcopacy, the asserter of its liturgy, the defender of its legal establishment, the instructor of its clergy, the apologist for the penal laws against

---

[299] The king's commissioners administered the oaths of allegiance and supremacy to all colleges and halls in the opening months of 1661: 'Restoration Visitation', ed. Varley, 4, 7; OUA SP 41 (subscription book 1660–93), *passim*; PRO SP 29/30, no. 72.

[300] The only layman to be elected vice-chancellor in the period was the physician, Dr Henry Clerke, president of Magdalen, who served for two years, 1676–7. OUA register Tb, pp. 152–82. Bloxam, *Reg. Magdalen* v. 154.

[301] Cf table 12.1 in G. V. Bennett, 'University, society and church 1688–1714' in *The Eighteenth Century* 362.

[302] *A Letter from a Person of Quality* (London 1675), 1–2; *Bishop Burnet's History of His Own Time*, ed. M. J. Routh (6 vols Oxford 1823) iv. 378; J. A. I. Champion, *The Pillars of Priestcraft Shaken* (Cambridge 1992), 9, 11, 17 ff.

popery and dissent, the patron of defecting Catholics and reclaimed dissenters, the cherisher of fugitive Huguenots and converted Jews, and—last, but by no means least—as the fountain-head of obedience to the divinely ordained, indefeasible, hereditary Stuart monarchy, under which the university prospered as never before.

Inevitably, given the fissiparous nature of protestantism, the restoration of Anglican conformity was not accepted by all protestants. By building on Oxford's privileged position, as one of only two national universities entrusted with educating the youth of an increasingly populous kingdom, the academics rapidly reestablished their religious and educational reliability in the eyes of the political nation, as was shown by the willingness with which the gentry of the Anglican ascendancy once more sent their sons to Oxford in droves, and continued to add to its collegiate buildings and endowments. Where they fell down, and fell down badly, was in their general failure to attract pupils from discontented puritan families, particularly those associated with the disrupted parliamentarian regime. Though the religious stance of these families varied from occasional conformity to outright separatism, they tended not to send their sons to the university for fear that they would be turned into either conformists, or debauchees, or both.[303] Among dissenters and some of their low church Anglican sympathizers, Restoration Oxford acquired an adverse reputation for combining rigid conformity with loose living—the latter chiefly on account of the mischievous reportage of its rejected nonconformists.[304]

Instead of favouring a university education, as they had done 'before the warr', the 'fanaticks' preferred to 'keep their children at home', where they could be taught by hand-picked, congenial private tutors, drawn from the pool of ejected Restoration dons and dissenting ministers; or, more provokingly, bred them 'in privat schooles', again 'under fanaticks', many of whom were the dispersed relics of the Cromwellian establishments of Oxford and Cambridge.[305] Their teachers included several ex-heads, fellows, and chaplains of Oxford colleges and halls, who, in search of an alternative livelihood, turned to school mastering, as some of the ejected Cavalier Anglican dons had done before them in the Cromwellian Interregnum. Despite the opposition of the Anglican episcopate and the denunciations of the Oxford dons, 'conventicling schools' sprang up to cater for the education of 'fanaticks' sons' and the children of half-hearted conformists.[306]

One such local academy was that at Shilton, outside Bampton, in the west Oxfordshire countryside, founded and run by the Presbyterian scholar Samuel

---

[303] Wood, *Life and Times* i. 301, 388, 423. Clarendon complained that 'too many of our great men are without that affection and zeal for the government of the church ... and having no desire that their children should be better instructed ... must pick some quarrel with our universities': Edward Hyde, earl of Clarendon, *A Brief View and Survey of the Dangerous and Pernicious Errors to Church and State, in Mr. Hobbes's book, entitled Leviathan* (Oxford at the Theatre 1676), 323.

[304] For Wood's contradicting fanatical aspersions see Bodl. MS Ballard 14, fos 17–18, MS Wood f. 31, fo 120; Wood, *History of the University* ii. 703–8.

[305] Wood, *Life and Times* i. 465.   [306] South, *Sermons* iii. 409–11.

Birch, the ejected chaplain of Corpus.[307] His academy became a thriving concern, attracting the interest and support of the socially eminent and politically active puritan families—including the Whartons, Harleys, Harcourts, and Ashley Coopers.[308] Though 'perpetually molested, either by the deputy lieutenants, or the bishops of Oxford, or the gentlemen of Doctors Commons', Birch kept his academy going through thick and thin;[309] which he did by sheltering behind his appointment as chaplain to the sympathetic nobleman, Philip, fourth Baron Wharton.[310] The retraction of the puritans from the university—initially and very largely the result of Cavalier Anglican expulsion but, as time wore on, increasingly the product of deliberate dissenting and low church abstention—was recognized by contemporaries as contributing to the falling number of undergraduates entering Oxford after 1662.[311] A few wealthy puritans, such as Lord Wharton, went so far as to send their sons to study abroad, either in or near the Huguenot academies of France, or at the universities of Leiden and Utrecht in the United Provinces: a practice which attracted outspoken criticism from Fell and Compton.[312]

Given the university's massive commitment to anti-dissent, it was appropriate that the Oxford session of the Cavalier Parliament should produce one of the most draconian pieces of legislation against nonconformity: the five mile act of 1665. It was a statute which was aimed expressly against ministerial dissent—against the ejected, but still busy, nonconformist ministers and preachers who were instilling 'the poisonous principles of schism and rebellion' into the people.[313] In too many places, as in Oxford itself, the ejected had been reluctant to remove from their homes. The bonds of friendship and familiarity linking them to their old congregations and neighbourhoods had not been broken. Their unshaken hold on local society was therefore seen as detrimental to the re-establishment of conformity.[314] In retreat from the plague-ridden metropolis, parliament followed the king and

---

[307] Mansfield College Library, Samuel Birch's manuscript 'Book of prayers', for extracts from which see *Restoration Oxford*, ed. Beddard iii, appx, nos 37–8. Wood, *Life and Times* ii. 477; OUA register T, pp. 267, 268, 270, 271; Matthews, *Calamy Revised*, 56–7.

[308] Bodl. MSS Rawlinson letters 50, fos 17, 94, 138, letters 51, fos 29, 103; Bodl. MS Locke c. 11, fo 231, J[ohn] H[oskins] to Locke, London, 5 February 1679/80.

[309] E. Calamy, *The Nonconformist's Memorial*, ed. S. Palmer (London 1775, 2nd edn 2 vols London 1777) ii. 302–7; W. H. Summers, *History of the Congregational Churches in the Berks, South Oxon and South Bucks Association* (Newbury 1905), 286–7.

[310] ORO MS Oxf. dioc. papers c. 650, fos 20, 22, Dr Henry Aylworth to Bishop Compton of Oxford, Oxford, 28 October and 27 November 1675.

[311] Wood, *Life and Times* i. 301, 423, 465, ii. 1; Bodl. MS Wood f. 31, fo 17ᵛ, cf L. Stone, 'The size and composition of the Oxford student body 1580–1910' in L. Stone (ed.), *The University in Society* (2 vols Princeton 1974) i. 6 (graph 1), 37 ff.

[312] For Wharton's sons see *Restoration Oxford*, ed. Beddard ii, nos 508, 525, 527, 533. Fell complained of the efforts made by 'papists, fanatics, travail'd fops, witts, virtuosi, and atheists . . . to disparage and decry university education, and afraight all persons from sending their children hither': Bodl. MS Rawlinson d. 850, fo 267, Fell to Dean Grenville of Durham, [Oxford], 29 December [1684].

[313] *Statutes of the Realm* v. 575: 17 Car. II, c. 2.

[314] Wood, *Life and Times* i. 499–500. For Thomas Gilbert's hobnobbing with Conant and Cornish at Sir Philip Harcourt's see Bodl. MS Rawlinson letters 53, fo 13.

court into the safety of plague-free Oxford—the only provincial centre which had, since medieval times, accommodated such a large removal from Westminster. The switch of venue suited the savage mood of Clarendon and the bishops, who made the most of their stay in the civil war capital of royalist England, alive, as it was, with wartime memories and partisan fervour. As chancellor of the university, Clarendon arranged for the lodging of the parliament men, who included an unusually high turnout of Cavalier Anglican MPs and a sizeable contingent of Archbishop Sheldon's most reliable episcopal allies.[315]

Resident in the colleges of the university, the Cavalier Anglican MPs instinctively responded to the political and religious imperatives of their surroundings. In an extraordinarily short and felicitous session, they declared their regard for church and state by voting a generous supply to the king and a handsome present to James, duke of York, for his services at sea in the second Anglo-Dutch war, and by enacting the concluding item of the 'Clarendon code' against nonconformity.[316] Addressing themselves to wartime fears of domestic unrest (for there were signs of Dutch attempts to infiltrate the disaffected dissenters),[317] and to well-informed episcopal concern over the strength of municipal dissent (into which Sheldon had just completed a primatial inquiry),[318] the MPs made it a criminal offence for ejected ministers and unlicensed teachers to reside or come within five miles of their previous parish, or of any parliamentary borough. Only by swearing an oath *not* to endeavour to alter the constitution of church and state could the ejected escape banishment from their homes.[319]

The oath—which became known as the Oxford oath—was particularly to the bishops' liking, for it allowed them to distinguish between submissive and truculent dissenters.[320] There was naturally a good deal of socializing among the MPs and more senior Cavalier Anglican dons who, unlike their juniors, stayed on to greet their returning friends and the sons of their friends. It is highly likely that the stipulated limit of five miles, a common enough measurement in legislation, was in this instance a conscious repetition of the order, made in 1648 by the committee of lords and commons for the reformation of the university, to prohibit the deprived Cavalier Anglican dons from living within a five-mile radius of Oxford.[321] That there was actual political collusion between the dons and MPs is proven by the final deed of the Oxford session. In response to a suggestion made by the restored Cavalier, John Lamphire, Camden professor of ancient history, to a sym-

---

[315] *Restoration Oxford*, ed. Beddard iii, nos 938, 941, 944–5, 947–8, 951, 954, 959, 962.

[316] *CJ* viii. 613–25; *LJ* xi. 683–701; C. Robbins, 'The Oxford session of the Long Parliament of Charles II, 9–31 October 1665', *Bulletin of the Institute of Historical Research* xxi (1948), 214–24.

[317] Bodl. MS Eng. letters d. 2, fos 151–3, Clarendon's circular to JPs; PRO SP 29/129, no. 109.

[318] David Wilkins, *Concilia Magnae Britanniae* (4 vols London 1737) iv. 582–4.

[319] In 1666 Conant took the oath 'and about twelve more with him', as did Christopher Rogers, the ejected principal of New Inn Hall: *Reliquiae Baxterianae* iii. 201–5; Matthews, *Calamy Revised*, 414.

[320] For the bishops' implacable zeal in the lords see Bodl. MS Rawlinson a. 130, fo 56, 30 October 1665.

[321] *Register*, ed. Burrows, 178, 1 August 1648; Bodl. MS Wood f. 35, fo 295.

pathetic group of parliament men that included Colonel Giles Strangways,[322] it was moved in the House of Commons on 31 October 1665 that the university should be formally and publicly thanked for its defiance of encroaching usurpation in 1647[323]—the year in which the royalist dons had protested against the authority of the rebellious Long Parliament, and the measures it had undertaken in the name of a subverted Reformation, by publishing their *Judicium* against the hated Solemn League and Covenant.[324]

The Commons' resolution, expressing gratitude to the university for its 'eminent loyalty to his majestie, and his father, of ever blessed memory, in the late rebellion', and for its exemplary resistance to usurpation, provided the dons with proof positive that, whatever hardships they and their church might undergo on account of their allegiance to Charles II, they could safely put their trust in the 'prudent and worthy patriots' of the Cavalier Parliament to defend them.[325] The resolution was conveyed to a specially convened meeting of convocation on 7 November by an acclaimed posse of episcopalians: the two university burgesses, Lawrence Hyde and Solicitor-General Finch, and two civil war veterans, Sir John Berkenhead and Colonel Strangways.[326] In recognition of the amicable accord that obtained between the Cavalier Anglican parliament and the Cavalier Anglican university the vice-chancellor conferred honorary DCLs on Finch and Strangways.[327] The exchange of compliments underlined the political pact between them.

The fall of Clarendon and the rise of Buckingham at court exposed the Church of England to renewed anxieties. In September 1667 the incoming president of St John's, Peter Mews, a long-serving, no-nonsense, Cavalier soldier (who was brought into the presidency to succeed Fell as vice-chancellor between 1669 and 1673),[328] confided his fears to Under-Secretary Williamson on hearing that a 'greate indulgence' was in the offing: 'I hope there is no such thing in designe, but, iff there bee, I dread the issue of it'. His apprehension at the prospect of ecclesiastical change, and the hostility which underlay it, was shared by the rest of the university.[329] As the 1660s turned into the 1670s the king first tried comprehension, and later indulgence, in his search to break out of the political straitjacket imposed on him by intransigent churchmen. In the event, the unofficial negotiations over comprehension in 1668—held under the auspices of the duke of Buckingham, his

---

[322] For Lamphire's Cavalier credentials and the academic rewards given him by the king, Clarendon, and the bishops see *Restoration Oxford*, ed. Beddard i, nos 15 (and n. 29), 24, 31, 189–90, ii, nos 17, 28, 33, 167, 168, 609, 610, and 689. For Strangways see Henning (ed.), *House of Commons* iii. 495–7. D. Underdown, *Royalist Conspiracy in England 1649–1660* (New Haven 1960), 31, 54.

[323] Wood, *Life and Times* ii. 50; *CJ* viii. 617.

[324] *Judicium universitatis Oxon. de solenni liga et foedere* (Oxford 1648). The English version was 'reprinted in 1660 when the king's commissioners sate at Oxon. to reform the universitie'. Bodl. Wood, 514, item 3. OUA register Sb, pp. 133–49.

[325] *CJ* viii. 6.   [326] OUA register Ta, pp. 207–8.

[327] Wood, *Life and Times* ii. 61–2; Wood, *Fasti* ii. 286.

[328] SJM register III, pp. 841–3; PRO SP 44/19, p. 63; OUA register Ta, p. 276, register Tb, p. 22.

[329] PRO SP 29/217, no. 174, Mews to Williamson, Oxford, 26 September 1667.

protégé Bishop Wilkins of Chester, the former intruded warden of Wadham, and Lord Keeper Bridgeman—came to nothing.[330]

Archbishop Sheldon's energetic campaign, waged in parliament and the press, put paid to any concessions to dissenters.[331] Bent on vindicating the existing establishment, he conducted a propaganda war, in which he deployed to devastating effect the pens of his domestic chaplains, Thomas Tomkins and Samuel Parker, fierce episcopalians whom he had recruited from his Oxford colleges: All Souls and Trinity.[332] Their well-reasoned tracts did more than rehearse Cavalier Anglican objections to the danger of pandering to potential rebels. By throwing the charge of heresy and schism into their opponents' camp, they turned the flank of their nonconformist enemies, gave the alarm to their parliamentary allies, and unnerved the low church Anglican proponents of concession—much to the delight of the Oxford dons, who loudly applauded their labours.[333] Looking back on the defeat of his hopes for comprehension, one of the disappointed negotiators, Richard Baxter, confessed his heaviness of heart. What discouraged him most was the unrelenting attitude of the University of Oxford, where 'two such worthy, learned, pious men, as Dr Fell and Dr Allestry' had declared themselves 'against all indulgence and accomodation'. With the dean of Christ Church and regius professor of divinity set against concession, 'who', he lamented, 'can we hope will be for it?'[334] Taking comfort from the wily Sheldon, Fell and his colleagues were more than content to let 'the younckers' of the Cavalier Parliament wreck any attempt to repeal or amend the act of uniformity.[335]

The sort of rapport that existed between the lay Cavalier Anglicans above and their academic allies below was demonstrated at the close of 1669, when Vice-Chancellor Mews exploited a temporary breakthrough of Cavalier Anglican influence at court to assert the letter of the law against Oxford's dissenters. Not content with arresting 'the authors' of an audacious conventicle which, following the lapse of the first conventicle act, had met in the city at Captain Davies's to hear the ejected Presbyterian don, John Troughton, he got the chancellor to complain to

[330] For Thomas Barlow's account of these projects, taken from his autograph notes in Bodl. B. 14. 15. Linc. see J. W. H. Nankivell, 'A survey of the attempts at religious comprehension in the Church of England during the seventeenth century, with special reference to the period from the Restoration to the revolution' (Oxford B. Litt. dissertation 1943). B. Shapiro, *John Wilkins 1614–1672* (Berkeley 1969), 170–5.

[331] N. Sykes, *From Sheldon to Secker* (Cambridge 1959), 71–3.

[332] Tomkins had made his name by publishing *The Rebels Plea* (London 1660) against Baxter, and his *Short Strictures* (London 1661) on Crofton's indictment of the university's *Judicium* of 1647: Wood, *Athenae* iii. 1046–8; Parker, *History of his Own Time*, 323–4, 37–41; Wood, *Athenae* iii. 1646, iv. 225–35.

[333] For Tomkins's presentation copy to Barlow of *The Inconveniences of Toleration* (London 1667) see Bodl. B. 14. 15. Linc., item 19, inscribed 'Lib. T. Barlow e coll. Reg. Oxon. ex dono domini Tomkins, archiepiscopo Cant. a sacris domesticis, amici et authoris. Oct. 10, 1667'.

[334] Dr Williams's Library, Baxter letters III, fo 108, Baxter to John Humfrey [early 1669].

[335] Throughout the ferment of comprehension and indulgence Sheldon insisted on sticking to the letter of the law: 'his majestie's sence is no otherwise knowne than by his publique laws, and by them, therefore, wee are only to bee guided in our dutyes': BL MS Harleian 7377, fo 55ᵛ, Sheldon to Bishop Compton of Oxford, Lambeth House, 21 September 1674.

the king in council.[336] Ormonde begged Charles to consider how important it was for 'the publique good to have that place and seat of learning preserved free from the infection of unsound and seditious principles'.[337] The king listened sympathetically to the complaint, for he, as much as the governors of the university, disliked the idea of a fanatic preacher combining with a Cromwellian soldier to flout the law. He ordered the immediate prosecution of those involved to deter others 'from the like insolency and disobedience of the lawes'.[338]

Mews was instructed to work with the assize judges in bringing the offenders to book, so that the harbourer of the conventicle and its teacher might 'feele the effect of those lawes they have transgrest'. At the same time an unauthorized dame's school kept by the captain's wife was also ordered to be closed, in order to stop Mrs Davies from infusing 'her ill principles' into her scholars, and to vindicate the licensing authority vested in the bishop of Oxford by the act of uniformity.[339] Armed with the privy council's letter 'to suppresse conventicles', the vice-chancellor did a huge amount of ferreting out of dissenters, forcing 'some of them to St Mary's' to attend church service.[340] However, Mews's reign of terror came to an abrupt halt with the promulgation, on 15 March 1672, of the king's declaration of indulgence, granting freedom of worship to dissenters and Catholics alike.

The king's prerogative action—part of his concerted bid for monarchical independence—plunged the university into unaccustomed turmoil, as the emancipated dissenters took out licences from the secretary of state.[341] Although the number of dissenters in the city was 'inconsiderable', the three major sects—Presbyterian, Independent, and Anabaptist—proved unexpectedly 'brisk in Oxon', not least 'because the vice-chancellor had been eager against them'.[342] Leadership was provided by four ejected nonconformist dons: Henry Langley, the former master of Pembroke,[343] Henry Cornish, an intruded canon of Christ Church,[344] John Troughton, an erstwhile fellow of St John's, and Thomas Gilbert, an ex-chaplain of Magdalen.[345] Protected by the king's favour, they returned to their old haunts about the city, much to the disgust of the university authorities.[346] Though Mews

---

[336] Oxford City Arch. o.5.11, fos 111ᵛ, 112, 114.   [337] BL Add. MS 21,092, fo 12.

[338] PRO PC 2/62, fo 92, Whitehall, 31 December 1669.

[339] BL Add. MS 21,092, fos 12, 13, 'A letter from the board to the vice-chancellor of Oxford'; PRO SP 29/272, no. 55.

[340] Bodl. MS Eng. letters c. 328, fo 605, Mrs Anne Saye to F. Parry [Oriel], 10 February 1669/70; PRO SP 29/275, no. 177.

[341] F. Bate, *The Declaration of Indulgence 1672* (London 1908), 76 ff. For the text of Charles's indulgence see *English Historical Documents 1660–1714*, ed. A. Browning (London 1966), 387–8.

[342] Wood, *Life and Times* ii. 244.

[343] *Register*, ed. Burrows, 4, 6, 102, 110, 141, 237; 'Restoration Visitation', ed. Varley, 5, 7, 18, 43; PRO SP 29/320, no. 122, SP 44/38A, p. 31.

[344] Cornish had become 'the voice and soul of schism' in Bicester. *Register*, ed. Burrows, 4, 14, 102, 141 ff.; 'Restoration Visitation', ed. Varley, 2; White Kennett, *Some Remarks on ... Henry Cornish* (London 1699).

[345] For Troughton, see p. 849, n. 281 above. For Gilbert see Matthews, *Calamy Revised*, 221–2; PRO SP 29/320, no. 230, SP 44/38A, p. 50.

[346] They were already closely associated, the first three (together with William Conway, ejected from Magdalen Hall) having formed 'a combination of nonconformist ministers' at Cogges. LPL MS 951/1, fo 113ᵛ, 'Oxford diocese conventicles, 1669'.

was able to prevent the appropriation of the parish church of St Peter le Bailey for nonconformist worship by appealing directly to Under-Secretary Williamson for help, he had to bow to the inevitable and recognize his adversaries' immunity from further prosecution, given the king's declared policy.[347]

The vice-chancellor was powerless to deny dissenters royal licences, eight or nine of which were issued to preachers and meeting-houses in and about Oxford.[348] The rash of meetings that sprang up excited violent undergraduate protest. Having first flocked to the various conventicles 'out of novelty', the junior members soon showed themselves 'something rude' to the 'parlour preachers', who included notorious excommunicates, an Oxford tanner, and an Abingdon miller—the familiar rag-tag and bob-tail ranters of Cromwellian vintage, whom they had been systematically taught to despise.[349] On one occasion Vice-Chancellor Mews was humiliatingly forced to defend from undergraduate ragging a pack of conventiclers, who, as he bitterly complained to Archbishop Sheldon, would have lynched him, had he been in their power.[350] Such were the painful incongruities visited on loyalist Oxford by Charles's wayward policies.

Mercifully for strained Anglican tempers, the Cavalier Parliament made the impecunious king recall his indulgence 'before it was a yeare old'.[351] This time it was Charles's turn to be humiliated by his 'old friends'. Having read him a severe lesson on the supremacy of parliamentary statute and the limitations of his ecclesiastical prerogative, the Cavalier MPs passed the first test act of 1673, which disrupted the detested Cabal administration by driving non-Anglicans from office, including the king's brother, the Catholic James, duke of York.[352] Vice-Chancellor Mews's promotion to the bishopric of Bath and Wells, also in 1673, was one of the earliest pointers to the rehabilitation of the Cavalier Anglican interest at court.[353] Within two years Lord Treasurer Danby, a kinsman of the great Strafford, had effected a *rapprochement* between Whitehall and Lambeth by persuading the king to support his Cavalier Anglican programme. Briefly stated, this was 'to keep up parliament, to raise the old Cavaliers and the church party, and to sacrifice papists and Presbyterians'.[354] Archbishop Sheldon's return to royal favour inaugurated an era

[347] PRO SP 29/305, no. 118, Vice-Chancellor Mews to Williamson, Oxford, 11 April 1672. The bishops were also rendered powerless: 'If ever the bishops were truly stiled overseers surely 'tis now when they may doe little else': Bodl. MS Lister 3, fo 24.

[348] Bate, *Indulgence*, appx vii; G. L. Turner, *Original Records of Early Nonconformity under Persecution and Indulgence* (3 vols London 1911–14) ii. 827–30, 941.

[349] Wood, *Athenae* iv. 406; Dr Williams's Library, Baxter letters II, fo 3, James Penny to Edward Norton, Christ Church, 18 June 1672.

[350] Bodl. MS Add. c. 302, fo 250, Vice-Chancellor Mews to Sheldon, Oxford, 26 June 1672.

[351] Bodl. MS Tanner 102, fo 107.

[352] Beddard, 'The Restoration church', 169. The new test was taken at the quarter sessions by all the university clergy. Oxford City Arch. o.5.12, fos 5ᵛ, 6, 11, 21ᵛ, 23, 24, 28, 29 ff.; Bodl. MS Carte 77, fo 538ᵛ.

[353] PRO SP 44/27, fos 41, 45, 46.

[354] *Selections from the Correspondence of Arthur Capel Earl of Essex 1675–1677*, ed. C. Edwards Pike (Camden Soc. 3rd ser. xxiv 1913), 1, 6. A. Browning, *Thomas Osborne, Earl of Danby . . . 1632–1712* (3 vols Glasgow 1944–51) i. 147–9, 167–73, 191–3, 273–5.

of cordial and beneficial co-operation between the twin authorities of church and state that was to last well into James II's reign. In Oxford there was a welcome resumption of coercive measures against dissent.[355]

Sheldon now had the opportunity to tighten still further his party's hold on Oxford. In December 1675 he secured Fell's nomination as bishop of Oxford from the king, which he did without his client's having to relinquish the deanery of Christ Church, with its assurance of an adequate income and lodgings in the heart of the university.[356] Being allowed to retain the deanery *in commendam* with the see was an unprecedented favour, and indicated not just the esteem in which Fell was personally held at Lambeth and Whitehall, but the significance which Danby's ministry attached to Oxford in the Cavalier Anglican scheme of things.[357] The bishopric, a Tudor creation with poor revenues and a residence ruined in the civil war, occupied a lowly position in the church hierarchy.[358] Despite the attraction of being near the university, it had for too long served as a stepping-stone to higher preferment. Since 1660 there had been a rapid turnover of bishops: Robert Skinner and Walter Blandford had been translated to Worcester in 1663 and 1671 respectively, Nathaniel Crew to Durham in 1674, and Henry Compton to London in 1675. Only the less distinguished William Paul, bishop from 1663 to 1665, had died in office.[359]

With Fell's promotion the diocese gained a firm governor for the next decade, a span of time which encouraged a greater degree of planning and application to duty. More important than the benefits which accrued to the diocese was the fact that the university came under the sustained influence of a scholarly and hard-working bishop of unrivalled Cavalier Anglican repute.[360] It was a move calculated to enhance the episcopalian character of the university, a consideration which never left Sheldon's mind, and one which accorded with Danby's declared aim of raising 'the old Cavaliers and the church party'.[361] Fell's elevation guaranteed that he would be on hand to liaise with Chancellor Ormonde, who was increasingly absent in Ireland, and to direct succeeding vice-chancellors, over whose selection he exercised a virtual veto. In Ormonde's repeated delegations of his cancellarial authority he was always named second after the vice-chancellor, though in practice the latter invariably deferred to his ecclesiastical superior, the bishop.[362] In charge of

---

[355] Oxford City Arch. o.5.11, fos 151, 153, 153ᵛ, o.5.12, fo 1; ORO B.O.Q.M. 1/ii/1, fos 3, 3ᵛ, 6, 6ᵛ.

[356] For Charles II's particular concern for the university and see of Oxford see PRO SP 44/43, p. 64, Sir Joseph Williamson to Fell, Whitehall, 2 December; PRO SP 44/47, pp. 20, 22–3, SP 29/375, no. 178; CA MS D&C, i. b. 3, pp. 202–12.

[357] Bodl. MS Tanner 147, fo 69, Charles II's dispensation, Whitehall, 15 January 1675/6.

[358] In 1675 its value was put at £381 11*s* o*d*: PRO SP 29/381, no. 21. J. C. Cole, 'The building of the second palace at Cuddesdon', *Oxoniensia* xxiv (1959), 49–52, 54.

[359] W. Stubbs, *Registrum Sacrum Anglicanum* (Oxford 1858, 2nd edn Oxford 1897), 124, 126, 127.

[360] He was consecrated on 6 February 1676 in the chapel of Morley's town residence, in Chelsea, by Bishops Compton, Morley, and Dolben and two others: LPL Sheldon register I, fos 176 ff.

[361] Cf HMC *Ormonde MSS* new ser. v. 117, 151–2, 337–8, 347.

[362] OUA NEP/Pyx. A/13, Chancellor Ormonde's commissions of delegation; OUA register Tb, pp. 68, 182–3, register of convocation 1683–93, NEP/*subtus*/29, register Bb, pp. 46–7.

both the university and diocese, Fell was able to guide Oxford through the critical years of no-popery and exclusion, and to ensure that the Church of England dons made a crucial contribution to the rise of the tory party and to the definition of the tory creed.

18

Tory Oxford

R. A. BEDDARD

TRY as it might, the university could not escape the political agitation set in motion by the Popish Plot. The scaremongering associated with Titus Oates's discovery of a supposed Catholic conspiracy against the life of Charles II seriously unhinged protestant minds. Before the end of 1678 Oxford was in the grip of alarmist journalism, much of it subversive in content, inflammatory in tone, and sectarian in origin. As the extraordinary explosion of pamphleteering approached civil war levels of intensity, it inevitably took a heavy toll of intellectual calm and academic study.[1] The numerous taverns and crowded coffee-houses of the town, combined with the recent development of common-room life inside the colleges, facilitated political discussion and the 'prating of news' on an unprecedented scale.[2] The bibliophile, Anthony Wood, an incurable haunter of bookshops, noted that 'nothing but pamphlets are taken into scolars' hands and they buy nothing else'.[3] His own extensive collection of ephemeral tracts and newspapers, now in the Bodleian Library, is a standing testimony to the voraciousness with which Oxford booksellers and readers devoured the outpourings of protestant alarm.[4]

No sooner had the anti-Catholic hysteria of the capital invaded Oxford than there was a sharp revulsion of feeling against individual papists. In the resultant climate of suspicion and recrimination their protestant friends fared little better. They were often cynically accused of being 'popishly affected'. Both categories of men were pointedly ostracized by the rank and file of the Church of England, rather 'as the prelaticall partie' had been ostentatiously shunned 'by the Presbyterians and Independents in the broken times'.[5] The inbred anti-Catholicism of the nation—never far beneath the surface of Restoration politics—became ever more strident and merciless. The local magistracy made good use of the information collected by Bishop Fell in his primary visitation of the diocese in 1676.

---

[1] O. W. Furley, 'The whig exclusionists: pamphlet literature in the exclusion campaign, 1679–81', *Cambridge Historical Journal* xiii (1957), 19–36; W. G. Mason, 'The annual output of Wing-listed titles 1649–1684', *The Library* 5th ser. xxix (1974), 219–20.

[2] For the complaint by Bodley's Librarian of 'very fanatical letters, full of sedition' being sent to Oxford coffee-houses see PRO SP 29/416, no. 120.

[3] Wood, *Life and Times* ii. 429.

[4] His collection occupies Bodl. Wood 422, 424–6. For his acquisition of tracts see Bodl. MS Wood f. 50, fo 11.

[5] Wood, *Life and Times* ii. 421–2, 424, 429, 431, 436–8; Bodl. MSS Wood f. 22, fo 167, d. 19 (2), fo 100.

Suspected recusants were rounded up, indicted at the petty sessions, and bound to 'good behaviour', so that there was little danger of subversion from what was a tiny and cowed minority.[6]

Vice-Chancellor Nicholas, the trimming warden of New College, was particularly active. His officious conduct in arresting the most harmless of Catholics, such as the poverty-stricken William Joyner, a converted pre-war fellow of Magdalen College, was seen by his critics as a bid to curry favour at Westminster in the hope of attracting preferment.[7] Certainly, his anti-Catholic zeal visibly 'laggd when the parliament was prorogued' on 30 December 1678.[8] A more convincing explanation of the vice-chancellor's conduct lay, however, in his understandable desire to keep on the right side of ultra-protestant militancy, and to secure the university from outside interference. Parliament had already, in the previous October and November, voiced its disquiet over the publicly expressed attitudes of some members of the university towards the vexed question of the nation's religion.

The master of the rolls, Sir Harbottle Grimston, one of the most voluble opponents of popery, had complained on the floor of the house of commons of 'the printing of popish books at the theater in Oxon', and, invoking parliamentary privilege, had not hesitated to name their authors.[9] One of the books he arraigned was Obadiah Walker's edition of Sir John Spelman's *Life of Alfred*[10] which, Grimston maintained, was larded with papistical footnotes drawn from explicitly Catholic sources.[11] In point of fact, the master and fellows of University College had undertaken to publish Spelman's work in order to advertise the antiquity of their college, of which Alfred the Great was (erroneously) reputed to be the founder. The underlying purpose of their collaborative enterprise was to recommend the college's appeal for building funds by letting the world know 'that their benefactions' were 'not bestowed on mere drones', but on hard-working, productive scholars.[12]

Among many other alleged infelicities, Walker had dared to assert that the Catholic Alfred, to whom Charles II was fulsomely compared, had shown 'great respect' for the pope as the successor to St Peter. Still more alarming, in the context of growing public concern over the prospect of a 'popish successor' mounting Charles's throne, was his seeming reconciliation of the royal supremacy with papal obedience; for he portrayed Alfred as ruling supreme over the English Church, even after he had been consecrated king in Rome by Pope Leo IV.[13] The master's historical misdemeanours were compounded by his close friendship with

---

[6] Oxford City Arch. o.5.12 (petty sessions roll 1679–1712), fos 9, 12 ff.

[7] Wood, *Life and Times* ii. 424, 427, 432; for Joyner, see R. A. Beddard, 'James II and the Catholic challenge', p. 945 below.

[8] Wood, *Life and Times* ii. 433.   [9] Ibid. 441.

[10] John Spelman, *Aelfredi magni Anglorum regis invictissimi vita tribus libris comprehensa* (Oxford 1678), sig. a^v, pp. 4–7, 70–1; *The Flemings in Oxford* i. 269.

[11] In making use of Richard Smith's *Florum historiae ecclesiasticae gentis Anglorum libri septem* (Paris 1654), Walker called him by his 'popish title', bishop of Chalcedon, as if he owned his spiritual authority. Wood, *Athenae* iii. 384.

[12] UCA Pyx. LL. fasc. 1, pt 2, no. 18; Bodl. MS Ballard 49, fo 26; QCL MS 524, item 5.

[13] Spelman, *Aelfredi magni . . . vita*, 70–1; N. Tyacke, 'Religious controversy', pp. 610, 614 above.

the deceased Catholic propagandist Abraham Woodhead, his former tutor and an earlier convert to the Church of Rome. At his death in May 1678, Woodhead had stood accused of educating young men 'in popish principles' at Hoxton, outside London, while continuing, with Walker's connivance, to draw a fellow's stipend from University College.[14]

Another work which the ultra-protestant Grimston denounced as offensive to protestantism was Anthony Wood's semi-official *Historia et antiquitates universitatis oxoniensis*, 'wherein', it was claimed, 'many unseemly things' were said in derogation of the protestant reformation,[15] despite the book's having been approved of and paid for by Bishop Fell.[16] In each case, it would appear that Grimston had been primed by that Scottish busybody, Gilbert Burnet. In spite of Burnet's having undertaken to write the definitive history of the English reformation (or perhaps because he, as an outsider, had presumed to do so), he was thought by some in Oxford not to have a right understanding of the genius of the English Church.[17]

The truth was that Grimston had long harboured a grudge against University College and its master, on account of his kinsman's uneasy passage through a fellowship election.[18] He had allowed his anger and his ultra-protestant prejudices to be exploited by two self-seeking parliamentarian quondams of the college— clerics who ran with the times: the restless Israel Tongue, Oates's co-informer, and the aggrieved William Shippen, an ambitious Cheshire parson.[19] In 1660 Shippen had lost seniority at the return to the college of the royalist fellows, Walker and Woodhead among them.[20] Each, it seems, nursed a secret desire to settle old scores by supplanting the scholarly Walker as master. Only the timely intercession of a friend in the house of commons saved Walker from the humiliation of being sent for by a messenger.[21] As for the unfortunate Anthony Wood, he underwent a worse fright. As a result of the distant menaces of his would-be parliamentary per-secutors, the vice-chancellor decided to conduct a personal search of Wood's lodg-ings in Merton Street on 1 December for incriminating evidence.[22] Having drawn a blank there, he summoned the distraught suspect before him, and tendered him the oaths of allegiance and supremacy, which Wood took without demur.[23] Obstinate and resentful as he could be, Wood understood the danger of his

[14] Bodl. MS Eng. misc. c. 88, fos 18–19; Wood, *Life and Times* ii. 421; Wood, *Athenae*, iii. 1157.

[15] Wood, *Life and Times* ii. 449.

[16] Fell had supervised the translation of Wood's English text into Latin, paid for it, and printed the whole work on the press at his own charge. Ibid. i. 47, ii. 199–200, 204, 243–4, 247, 259–60, 272–3, 276, 301, 322, iii. 253, iv. 189.

[17] Bodl. MS Wood f. 1 (unfoliated), Anthony Wood to Gilbert Burnet, 5 July 1679 (draft).

[18] UCA Pyx. LL. fasc. 4, nos 4, 5, Grimston to Thomas Walker, The Rolls, 13 January and 22 February 1664/5.

[19] UCA registrum I, fos 27, 27ᵛ, 35ᵛ; *Register*, ed. Burrows, 121, 173, 260; Wood, *Life and Times* ii. 422.

[20] UCA registrum I, fos 39, 39v, 40ᵛ. For the reinstatement of Woodhead and Walker see *Restoration Oxford 1660–1667*, ed. R. A. Beddard (3 vols OHS forthcoming) i, no 186.

[21] Wood, *Life and Times* ii. 421.

[22] Ibid. 424–5.

[23] Bodl. MS Bodley 594, fo vi, Vice-Chancellor Nicholas's certificate, 2 December 1678; Bodl. MS Ballard 46, fo 168.

predicament. Having already been mentioned adversely in parliament, he recognized the need to vindicate his protestantism, all the more so because his greatest benefactor was Ralph Sheldon, the imprisoned Catholic squire of Weston, a man known to have spent a considerable time in Rome.[24]

Anxious to clear the university's good name from the damaging charge of sheltering papists and affording protection to scholars with popish sympathies, the government took remedial action. On 29 January 1679 the king ordered the vice-chancellor to launch an immediate official inquiry. Nicholas promptly obeyed. He called on the heads of colleges and halls, together with the ministers of the central Oxford parishes, to make a return of the names of any Catholics, or suspected Catholics, so that he could inform the council board forthwith.[25] The replies produced but a single name—that of the wretched Wood, who was denounced as a suspected papist by Warden Clayton of Merton, presumably on the grounds of common fame, and of his having been long associated with notorious Catholics.[26] It did not matter that the antiquary's friendships had been formed in the pursuit of his laudable, scholarly objectives, for without the help of Catholic intellectuals and recusant information he could scarcely have got to grips with the history of the university as a Catholic foundation.[27]

Meanwhile the university, which could derive no comfort from the behaviour of parliament, was effectively put on its guard. When it was recalled that Grimston had in 1640 been the chief advocate of Archbishop Laud's impeachment and had subsequently engaged in rebellion against Charles I,[28] and that the parliamentary intruders, Tongue and Shippen, were, after the elapse of eighteen years, still animated by a spite conceived against two reinstated Cavalier academics, loyalists of the calibre of Vice-Chancellor Nicholas had cause to tread warily in their dealings with popery and parliament.[29] Circumstances were not made any easier by the sweeping charge of 'popish affectation' which had plagued the entire university ever since the 1660s—an accusation that stemmed directly from the animosity of those nonconformist dons who, having been ejected from Oxford headships

---

[24] For Ralph Sheldon see Wood's sketch of his life: Bodl. MS Wood f. 51, fos 41–2, MS Tanner 102, fo 67ᵛ; for Sheldon's arrest: BL MS Add. 34,730, fos 3, 32. HMC *Eleventh Report*, appx, pt 2, pp. 232, 234.

[25] OUA WP/a/11/1, p 4, Fell's draft precept from the king's commissioners, 13 February 1678/9. For Charles's commission see PRO SP 44/43, p. 273, Secretary Williamson to Vice-Chancellor Nicholas, Whitehall, 1 February 1679.

[26] 'In Merton Coll: there is only Mr Anthony Wood who hath been suspected to be popishly affected. Tho: Clayton, cust. Coll. Mert.': OUA WP/a/11/1, p. 7. For the negative returns see ibid., pp. 5, 6, 8, 10–28, 30.

[27] The suspicion of popery dogged Wood to the grave. Bodl. MS Tanner 456a, fo 34; R. A. Beddard, 'Bishop Cartwright's death-bed', *Bodleian Library Record* xi (1984), 226–7 and n. 68; R. A. Beddard, 'Two letters from the Tower, 1688', *Notes and Queries* ccxxix (1984), 348–9.

[28] H. R. Trevor-Roper, *Archbishop Laud 1573–1645* (London 1940, 2nd edn, London 1965), 403–4.

[29] Royalists to the core, Walker and Woodhead had been nominated 'delegati pro defensione universitatis' on 1 September 1642, and deprived by the parliamentary visitors, as such, in 1648. OUA register of convocation 1642–7, NEP/supra/25, register Sb, pp. 9–10; *Register*, ed. Burrows, 103, 106, 145, 199, 214, 271.

and fellowships, wilfully traduced their conformist supplanters as crypto-Catholics.[30]

Although the charge had no foundation other than malice, as was shown by the outcome of the vice-chancellor's investigation, it none the less suited the dissenters' whig patrons to make repeated use of it in their partisan efforts to blast the reputation of the academic clergy who, as ardent supporters of the succession of the Catholic James, duke of York, were naturally reckoned among the most implacable of the whigs' opponents.[31] Needless to say, the combined attempts of dissenters and whigs to discredit the university in the esteem of the nation did nothing to endear either party to the dons.[32] It served only to steel their inner resolve to withstand popular pressure for a radical review of the Restoration settlement in church and state.[33] Keen as they were to succour the protestant establishment, they remained averse to the whigs' self-interested promotion of protestant irenicism, and were openly critical of the *de facto* toleration which successive exclusionist parliaments accorded their nonconformist clients, contrary to the laws of the land and in contempt of the Church of England's spiritual discipline.[34]

Even though there was a sizeable contingent of Oxford men among the whig MPs mustered by Shaftesbury to press for the enactment of exclusion,[35] few academics became full-blooded whigs. Initially, a considerable number of scholars were thrown off balance by the violence of popular anti-popery in 1678—the most noteworthy being the master of Pembroke, John Hall, a thorough-paced Calvinist, who had recently been elected Lady Margaret professor of divinity; but the bulk of them, including the temporizing Hall, had within a year or so recovered enough of their political composure not to endanger the highly privileged position of the established church by falling, once more, into the trap of faction.[36] The sense of estrangement from the vast majority of the Oxford clergy had a sobering effect on them, inclining them to moderate the public expression, if not the private strength, of their anti-Catholic convictions.[37] Consequently, the tally of professed whigs

[30] For an early charge by Ralph Button of Christ Church see 'Memoirs of the life . . . of Dr. Robert South' in Robert South, *Sermons preached upon several occasions* (7 vols Oxford 1823) i, pp. vi–vii.

[31] Wood observed that the whigs 'will not send their sons' to the 'popish' university 'for the fear of turning tories': Wood, *Life and Times* iii. 7. See my article, 'A whig view of tory Oxford in 1683', *The Bodleian Library Record*, 15 (1995).

[32] Leopold William Finch's outspoken epistle dedicatory addressed to James, earl of Abingdon, in *The Lives of Illustrious Men. Written in Latin by C. Nepos and done into English by several hands* (Oxford 1684).

[33] For an Oxford attack on protestant fanaticism delivered before the house of commons see William Jane, *A Sermon preached on the day of the Public Fast, April the 11th, 1679* (London 1679), 40–1.

[34] For what Oxford opposed, see H. Horwitz, 'Protestant reconciliation in the exclusion crisis', *Journal of Ecclesiastical History* 15 (1964), 204–16; D. R. Lacey, *Dissent and Parliamentary Politics in England, 1661–1689* (New Brunswick NJ 1969), 121 ff.

[35] B. D. Henning (ed.), *The House of Commons 1660–1690* (3 vols London 1983) i. 4–5, 48–9, 51.

[36] Bodl. MS Tanner 102, fo 120; Wood, *Life and Times* ii. 422; *Letters of Humphrey Prideaux*, ed. E. M. Thompson (Camden Soc. new ser. xv 1875), 62–3.

[37] Oxford's few 'academicall whigs' were 'all jeered' at by the Terrae-Filii in 1683. Wood, *Life and Times* iii. 60.

among the protestant stalwarts of the university was exceedingly small, probably no more than could be counted on the fingers of two hands.

Despite the shock tactics used by Oates and his fellow informers to loosen the traditional attachment of the church to the government of the day; despite the build-up of 'country' feeling in Oxford during the 1670s; and despite the increasing pressure and sophistication of the whig party machine from 1679 to 1681, the unshakeable dynastic conservatism of the dons was politically impressive. In this respect alone, they were significantly—even perilously—out of step with protestant opinion in the country at large: a fact which was to be made much of, both by their enemies in the advancing whig party, and by their friends in the hard-pressed court of Charles II.

The older generation of whig academics belonged to a definite type. They were what, in the overtly partisan years of the exclusion contest, were called 'interval men': dons who, having entered Oxford amid the turmoil of the late 1640s and 1650s,[38] now felt themselves to be undervalued by their Restoration superiors. As individuals, they were of little account, apart that is from three of them: the Savilian professor of geometry and keeper of the university archives, John Wallis, an ex-Presbyterian, who had opposed Laud and Charles I in the 1640s, and had, ever since conforming to the church in 1662, displayed the customary lack of judgement associated with mathematicians in Oxford;[39] 'the Corporean whigg', George Reynell, a disappointed senior fellow of Corpus, who doted on the duke of Monmouth, and whom his detractors esteemed to have been 'always a round-head';[40] and the alienated but as yet unpublished political philosopher, John Locke, a lay Student of Christ Church, whose aversion to the clericalism of the house and abilities as a physician had led him into the employ of the ailing and anticlerical Lord Shaftesbury.[41] Notwithstanding their personal merits, none was in a position to influence academic politics one way or another—not even Wallis, the only whig holding university office. Lacking supporters of the rank of head of house, and denied any prospect of winning support from the body of regent masters, whiggery was condemned to a position of political ineptitude in the rigidly structured and intensely hierarchical life of the university.

Among their juniors, the masters and bachelors of arts, the number of identifiable whigs was remarkably few.[42] As was to be expected, the most active whig fledgelings were the offspring of well-known exclusionist fathers. Such were

---

[38] For the expression see Wood, *Life and Times* i. 357, cf ibid. i. 359, 441.

[39] OUA, register of convocation 1647–59, NEP/*supra*/26, register T, pp. 245–6; Bodl. MS Wood f. 31, fo 14ᵛ; PRO SP 29/33, no. 66; Wood, *Life and Times* ii. 63, 84, 488–9, 491, 507–8, 553, iii. 63, 133, 177; Wood, *Fasti*, ii. 117, 124, 184.

[40] Bodl. MS Tanner 35, fo 66. For Reynell's family see Bodl. MS Ashmole 763, fo 15; Bodl. MS Rawlinson b. 81, fos 18, 30–3; Bodl. MS Add. c. 302, fo 26. Wood, *Life and Times* ii. 422, 431, iii. 60, 106–7; Wood, *Athenae* i. 658.

[41] For their shared anti-episcopal sentiment see Bodl. MS Locke c. 7, fo 72, Shaftesbury to Locke, 20 March 1680; M. Cranston, *John Locke* (London 1957), 93 ff; K. H. D. Haley, *The First Earl of Shaftesbury* (Oxford 1968), 202 ff.

[42] Wood, *Life and Times* ii. 431.

Strange Southby, a probationary fellow of Merton,[43] and John Pratt, a fellow of Wadham:[44] the former the puffed-up son of the whig knight of the shire for Berkshire, Richard Southby,[45] and the latter the loud-mouthed, quarrelsome son of the whig chief serjeant and macebearer of the city of Oxford, Richard Pratt.[46] They responded more to family influence, and to the tenor of life at home, than they did to the prevalent academic toryism about them. Their 'popular and republican arguments' were taken up and amplified by James Parkinson, an able, but impishly opinionated, whig fellow of Lincoln.[47] While the university's exclusionists counted for little individually, collectively they could not be ignored. They were a constant irritant in the eyes of an overwhelmingly conservative community: a community which undoubtedly sharpened the edge of its own tory response to the emergence of a national whig party by being repeatedly called upon to state its local opposition to their contradictory notions of government.[48]

For example, Pratt maddened many by indiscriminately airing his whig opinions. Though a fellow of Wadham, he was currently studying common law at the Inner Temple. It was there that he 'listed himself into the Green Ribbon Club', the London headquarters of the whig party.[49] Unwisely, he made no secret of his whig views on his periodic returns to Oxford, where he soon put tory backs up with his advocacy of what, in the university, were looked on as the 'strange libertys and propertys of the people'.[50] He was one of only three academics that rode out of town to meet the whig duke of Monmouth when he came in search of popular applause in 1680.[51] Pratt's association with the insolent citizenry and, even more, his provocative partisan talk were such that he was openly 'threatened by men of far different discourse and principles to be summoned into convocation, and to have his gown pulled off'.[52] The visceral toryism of the university was confirmed, rather than confounded, by the alacrity with which whig attitudes spread among the more independent townsmen of Oxford—the traditional antagonists of the academics. By the general election of 1681 their slogans had degenerated into cries of 'no universities! no scholars! no clergy! no bishops!', so that 'there was likely to have been some quarrels' between the rival parties of town and gown.[53]

[43] MCR registrum 1567–1731, pp. 534, 539; Wood, *Life and Times*, ii. 511–12.

[44] Wood, *Life and Times* ii. 431, 497–8; Oxford City Arch. B.5.1, fo 207.

[45] Oxford City Arch. B.5.1, fo 277; Wood, *Athenae* iv. 405; Henning (ed.), *House of Commons* ii. 457–8, 597.

[46] Oxford City Arch. B.5.1, fo 117; Wood, *Life and Times* i. 443, ii. 128, 140.

[47] Bodl. MS Wood d. 18, fo 51ᵛ; Wood, *Life and Times* ii. 431.

[48] Wood, *Life and Times* ii. 497–8.

[49] Magdalene College Library, Cambridge, MS Pepys miscellanies 7, fos 489–91; BL MS Harleian 6845, fo 282.

[50] Bodl. MS Wood f. 39, fo 35, Andrew Allam to Wood [St Edmund Hall], 12 November 1680.

[51] Oxford City Arch. B.5.1, fos 185ᵛ–6; Wood, *Life and Times* ii. 496; Bodl. MS Carte 39, fo 214, C[olonel] M[ansell] to the B[ishop of] M[eath], London, 26 September 1680.

[52] Bodl. MS Wood f. 39, fo 35. He prospered after 1688, eventually becoming lord chief justice of king's bench (1718).

[53] Wood, *Life and Times* ii. 513; Bodl. MS Wood f. 39, fos 24ᵛ, 24, Andrew Allam to Wood, St Edmund Hall, 1 October 1680.

If the dons were opposed to making any alteration in the lineal succession of the crown, they were even more hostile to the whigs' meddling with religion. Since most of them were, or were about to become, clergymen, with their sights fixed on moving, sooner or later, into the parochial ministry, they looked askance at the whigs' efforts to relieve dissenters in the second exclusion parliament of 1680, by repealing the 1593 statute against sectaries, and calling for a suspension of all prosecutions against them—developments which would seriously undermine the Anglican monopoly of religion.[54] Influenced by the steadily evolving tory propagandists—prominent among whom were the distinguished Oxonian clerics Thomas Long, George Hickes, Samuel Parker, Thomas Sprat, and Henry Maurice—they became more and more convinced that, under the guise of no-popery, the low church whigs were about to sell out to their political allies, the dissenters, by readmitting their ejected pastors to the already overpopulated ministry of the church.[55]

There was 'much talk and fear' in senior common rooms of 'a comprehension act to bring into church preferments almost all sorts of separatists', and that 'upon very easie terms and subscriptions'.[56] Besides posing a threat to their future livelihood as parsons, such rumours activated the high churchmen's suspicion that the ceremonies, discipline, and doctrine of the Church of England were to be made a bargaining counter, in a bid to buy the electoral support of dissent at the cost of permanently ruining the act of uniformity—the sheet anchor of Anglican conformity and the basis on which the university had functioned since 1662.[57] Academic anxiety was given further food for thought, in December 1680, with the arrival in the Oxford coffee-houses of what purported to be the text of just such a parliamentary bill. Entitled 'The heads of a bill for the uniting his majestie's protestant subjects', it confirmed the dons' worst fears for the welfare of their church and the integrity of the Anglican ministry, for which the low church whigs showed scant respect. The proposed concessions were deemed such as endangered the very being of the established church.[58]

In setting its face against whig demands, the university was given a positive lead by Chancellor Ormonde, backed by the ever-vigilant, never idle, and infinitely resourceful Bishop Fell, his right-hand man in Oxford throughout the exclusion contest. The duke, long revered as the acme of Anglican Cavalier orthodoxy on both sides of St George's Channel, came out strongly in favour of the existing

[54] Dr Williams's Library, MS Morrice P, pp. 274, 280. For the parliamentary initiatives see R. Thomas, 'Comprehension and indulgence' in G. F. Nuttall and O. Chadwick (eds), *From Uniformity to Unity 1662–1962* (London 1962), 223–7.

[55] With the exception of Parker, they all attracted the patronage of Archbishop Sancroft. R. A. Beddard, 'The commission for ecclesiastical promotions, 1681–84: an instrument of tory reaction', *Historical Journal* x (1967), 24, 32–3, 37, 38.

[56] Bodl. MS Wood f. 39, fo 35.   [57] Roger North, *Examen* (London 1740), 346.

[58] Bodl. MS Ballard 70, pp. 48a–51. Wood noted that the heads were 'inclosed in the newsletter that came to Oxon., 12 December *anno* 1680'.

establishment and the inherent rights of James, duke of York.[59] In January 1679 he confided to Fell his resolution to preserve his loyalty, come what may. From Dublin he declared: 'I will thro' all dangers maintain and support the religion of the Church of England as it is this day taught, practised and established by law, and the monarchy and crown of England in a right and lawful succession.'[60] It was a declaration which Fell wholeheartedly endorsed, and one which elicited support from all levels of the university. That Ormonde was heart and soul behind everything the Restoration university stood for was demonstrated by his decision to entrust his 'greatest treasure', his grandson, Lord James Butler, to Fell's safe keeping at Christ Church in January 1679.[61] He was confident that his heir, on whom the future prosperity of the Butler family depended, would be 'confirmed and perfectly instructed in the religion professed, practised and best taught in that university, wherein is comprehended the principles of honour, virtue, and loyalty'.[62]

The two vice-chancellors who successively ruled Oxford from 1679 to 1686 were convinced high churchmen, tories on whom Ormonde and Fell could automatically rely to keep the university steadfastly loyal and free from whig contagion. They were the provost of Queen's, Timothy Halton, who had served Fell faithfully as archdeacon of Oxford since 1675,[63] and the principal of Jesus, John Lloyd, who was valued at Christ Church as 'an honest good man', 'a very fit person' to tighten the university's grip on the magistracy of the town, which had fallen victim to whig opposition.[64] Their backgrounds inspired confidence. Halton, as Barlow's successor at Queen's, numbered Secretary Williamson and Bishops Lamplugh and Compton among his patrons, while Lloyd looked to Secretary Jenkins, his predecessor in the principalship of Jesus, for support and encouragement.[65] As dignified ecclesiastics, holding accumulated preferments in England and Wales, they were concerned to maintain the established church at the height of its power, and had every reason for obeying the sovereign will of its supreme governor.[66] With such single-minded leaders at the helm there was little opportunity for whiggery to disturb the daily discipline of Oxford.

[59] There was more to Ormonde's stance throughout the whig challenge than the political caution detected in J. C. Beckett, *The Cavalier Duke* (Belfast 1990), 116 ff. It was a matter of intense and lifelong conviction. James reciprocated Ormonde's sense of loyalty, being 'a true friend' to him and his, 'which I am sure you deserve from all our family': HMC *Ormonde MSS* v. 359, Windsor, 31 July 1680.

[60] HMC *Ormonde MSS* iv. 306, v. 160–1, Chancellor Ormonde to Bishop Fell, Dublin, 20 January 1678/9, Dublin, 23 July 1679.

[61] Bodl. MS Carte 118, fos 330, 200, Fell to Sir Robert Southwell, 16 February [1679], [Southwell] to Ormonde, 28 June 1679. CA D. P. i. a. 3, fo 19ᵛ; OUA SP 3, p. 21; Bodl. MS Rawlinson d. 397, fo 290ᵛ

[62] HMC *Ormonde MSS* iv. 269, 289, 306, v. 39–40, 141, 156–7, 173, 194–5, 214–15, 217–18, 320, 337–8, 399, 413–14, 417–18, 419, 471.

[63] Ibid. v. 347; Bodl. MS Rawlinson d. 923, fo 233; PRO SP 44/47, p. 8, SP 44/62, p. 305.

[64] BL MS Lansdowne 960, fo 77; *Letters of Humphrey Prideaux*, ed. Thompson, 103, 109, 133.

[65] For Halton see Bodl. MS Rawlinson d. 923, fos 233–4. For Lloyd see JCA foundation register, pp. 33, 40, 70–2.

[66] Halton was prebendary of St David's (1662), archdeacon of Brecknock (1672) and Oxford (1675); Lloyd was precentor (1672) and treasurer of Llandaff (1679). Wood, *Athenae* iv. 520, 870; PRO SP 29/32, no. 76.

To the high church academics and their episcopal patrons in the house of lords, the demands of the whig majority in the house of commons posed a double threat to the safety of the restored regime under which they had prospered for almost twenty years. First, the whigs' demand for James's exclusion affronted Anglican respect for the indefeasible, hereditary, divine right of the House of Stuart, by violating the sacrosanct principle of primogeniture. Secondly, their demand for the legal toleration of protestant dissenters, outside the national establishment, struck at the foundation of the Restoration settlement in church and state, by undermining the hallowed principle of uniformity.[67] Fell sprang instinctively to the defence of Stuart legitimacy and the constitutional framework in which it seemed to him to function best—namely, the intolerant, exclusive, high church protestant establishment erected by his friends and allies in the disbanded Cavalier Parliament.[68] In the deteriorating political climate it was only to be expected that he would look to the members of the university, the greatest clerical corporation in the land, to give a lead to their brethren of the cloth, so that clergymen everywhere might encourage resistance to whig aggression.

It is politically revealing of Oxford's attitude towards the monarchy that, throughout the era of no-popery and exclusion, the salaried divines of the university did not publish a single new book attacking the Church of Rome.[69] Yet, there can be no question that they remained inveterately anti-Catholic in conviction, and continued to instil a horror of Catholic doctrine in the clergy whom they trained and sent into the ministry. Rather than run the risk of jeopardizing their loyalty to the crown or weakening the hereditary succession by appearing to stoke the fires of anti-Catholicism, the authorities decided that dynastic caution was the better part of protestant valour. They had no wish to aggravate the duke of York's plight. With Barlow, the most virulent and stirring of the university's anti-papalists, no longer in Oxford,[70] and the entire academic community becoming increasingly sceptical of the existence of Oates's plot, they contrived by a massive exercise of willpower to stand aloof from the torrent of popular anti-popery.[71] In maintaining an unbroken silence they continued to acknowledge the respect due to the king's *Directions to preachers* to avoid unnecessary controversy. They preferred to take positive measures to bolster the teachings of their own church, rather than negative ones to

---

[67] R. A. Beddard, 'William Sancroft as archbishop of Canterbury, 1677–1691' (Oxford D. Phil. dissertation 1965), 96–103.

[68] He never ceased to regret the dissolution of 24 January 1679: Longleat House, MS Thynne 10, fo 230.

[69] The latest anti-Catholic book from the Theatre was Daniel Brevint's *Saul and Samuel at Endor, or the new waies of salvation and service, which usually temt men to Rome ... truly represented, and refuted* (Oxford 1674).

[70] Barlow published his swingeing attack on *Popery: or, the principles and positions approved by the Church of Rome ... very dangerous to all; and to protestant kings and supreme powers, more especially pernicious,* not in Oxford, but in London in 1679. *The Flemings in Oxford* i. 273.

[71] Wood, *Life and Times,* ii. 419, 452, 457, 462, 465–7, 515; *Letters of Humphrey Prideaux,* ed. Thompson, 70.

savage still further the vilified Church of Rome, which, they concluded, was in no position to harm them.[72]

Fell, active in this as in other spheres, got Rector Marshall of Lincoln, a trusty Calvinist episcopalian, to issue a brief explanation of the prayer book catechism, based on 'the scripture-proofs' which were fundamental to protestant belief.[73] Licensed by Vice-Chancellor Nicholas on 20 March 1679, and printed at the university press, it proved a timely and successful initiative. In a prefatory letter addressed 'to the reader' Marshall argued that the catechism was capable of 'a more diffusive use in the church, than onely to capacitate youth for the rite of confirmation', its original and primary purpose in the life of the national church.[74] Intent on recommending his argument to the widest possible audience, he quoted Archbishop Ussher's opinion, delivered in a sermon preached before James I in 1624, that 'so long as the foundation' was 'unlaid and the first principles untaught, upon which all other doctrine must be builded', the preaching of the clergy, however forceful, was but a lost labour.[75] The quotation from Ussher, a prelate who was universally respected among English protestants, conformist and nonconformist, stressed the true aim of Marshall's undertaking, which was to boost protestantism—but without inciting his countrymen to fresh outbursts of confessional hatred.[76]

Marshall's exposition, a small octavo, was well received in the university and diocese of Oxford, where it was disseminated on Fell's authority.[77] Elsewhere, it came to have quite a vogue among the clergy and adult laity. The preservation of an interleaved copy, with copious manuscript notes (mostly in Latin, but some in Greek) expanding the scriptural references contained in the critical apparatus of the work, shows how educated churchmen, as well as the ordinarily literate, could make use of Marshall's book as a means of opening up the study of Anglican doctrine along strictly scriptural lines.[78] Its wider success was attested by the eleven editions through which it passed between 1679 and 1700: a total which omits the important Welsh translation made by the Jesus College graduate, John Williams, the Welsh incumbent of a London living, which was published at Oxford in 1682 as part of the Restoration Church's drive to improve its standing in Welsh-speaking Wales.[79]

It was natural that Fell, imbued with high notions of 'the office and work of a

---

[72] For official academic censure of Francis Nicholson's 'popish sermon' preached at St Mary's on 20 June 1680 see Wood, *Life and Times* ii. 488–9, 490–1.

[73] For Fell's initiative, see Wood, *Athenae* iv. 171.

[74] Thomas Marshall, *The Catechism set forth in the Book of Common-Prayer, briefly explained by short notes, grounded upon holy scripture* (Oxford at the Theatre 1679), sig. A2: 'To the reader'.

[75] Ibid. sig. a. 3.

[76] Marshall assisted Richard Parr, Ussher's former chaplain, in compiling his *Life of Ussher* (London 1686), a prelate whom he had greatly admired from his student days.

[77] ORO MS Oxf. dioc. papers c. 650, fo 31.   [78] Bodl. 8⁰ Rawlinson 613.

[79] Madan, *Oxford Books* iii. 373; BL Add. MS 4,274, fo 38, Bishop William Lloyd of St Asaph to Bishop Fell, 9 May 1682. For Fell's support for Welsh religious publishing see Bodl. MS Rawlinson d. 317, fos 11, 11ᵛ.

bishop', should also be drawn to patristic scholarship, the bedrock of Christian tradition.[80] His approach to the Fathers was, in common with most scholars of his
generation, dictated by polemical considerations.[81] He was concerned to justify and
maintain the current practice of the Church of England. Above all, he wished to
vindicate the credentials of diocesan episcopacy from what he saw as the exorbitant claims of the bishop of Rome and the mistaken objections of non-episcopal
dissenters. In pressing for the return of 'schismatics' to the established church
within the diocese of Oxford, he was confident that the authentic and abiding
source of unity in God's church was provided by diocesan episcopacy, not by papal
monarchy, and still less by the vagaries of the individual conscience.[82] It was his
desire to represent the Church of England as the golden mean between the unacceptable extremes of popery and 'fanaticism' that made him turn for support to
the testimony of the early church: the church of the patristic era, before the rise
of the papacy to its acknowledged position as the universal ordinary of
Christendom. Fell inevitably found what he was looking for. The more he peered
down the well of Christian antiquity, the more he became convinced that the image
which he saw reflected in the pure waters of the primitive Christian past was one
that accorded most closely with contemporary Anglican practice: that is to say, with
an episcopally organized church, unfettered by Rome.

The most compelling reason which persuaded him to undertake his laborious
edition of the writings of the third-century African father, St Cyprian of Carthage,
was that saint's insistence that the true focus of ecclesiastical unity was to be found
in the episcopal office. Such an authoritative stance by one of the greatest of the
Latin fathers was immensely valued by a harassed latter-day English bishop, whose
overriding concern it was to assert the right of the established church to order the
spiritual welfare of the nation, by virtue of its having retained episcopacy at the
reformation.[83] Fell was so taken with the argument of St Cyprian's treatise, *De
catholicae ecclesiae unitate*, that he published an English translation of the work in 1681
in the conviction that it would impel conventiclers to return to the bosom of the
national church by the sheer strength of its argument. The Cyprianic argument for
the unity of all Christians with their local bishop made it, to his mind, quite 'impossible' for Catholic recusants or protestant nonconformists 'to continue in their
opinions' and divisions.[84] His reading of St Cyprian was so determinately Anglican,

[80] The Christ Church-educated chaplain of Fell, Adam Littleton, had preached at his consecration
maintaining that 'episcopal government was grafted on the apostolical stock, and so is not (as enemies
cavil) a plant, which God hath not planted': *Sixty One Sermons Preached mostly upon Publick Occasions*
(London 1680), 293.

[81] D. C. Douglas, *English Scholars 1660–1730* (London 1939, 2nd edn London 1951), 14, 16, 18–22,
24 ff; F. L. Cross, 'Patristic study at Oxford', *Oxford Society of Historical Theology* (abstract of proceedings
1948–9), 9–10.

[82] Cf Fell's visitation charge to his diocese in 1685: Bodl. MS Tanner 31, fo 156.

[83] For the decidedly anti-papalist context in which Anglican interest in St Cyprian flourished see
Bodl. MS Tanner 290, fos 162–3, Bishop Peter Gunning to Sancroft, 1681, Cf ibid., fos 159, 159ᵛ, 164.

[84] *Of The Unity of the Church: a discourse written a thousand and four hundred and thirty years since, in the time
of Decius the persecuting emperor. By Cyprian bishop of Carthage and martyr. Most usefull for allaying the present heats,
and reconciling the differences among us* (Oxford at the Theatre 1681).

that he saw no incongruity in using the authority of a father of the Catholic Church to promote the fortunes of the protestant Church of England. He was more than content to equate contemporary English Catholics and dissenters with the heretics of St Cyprian's day, the Novatians and Donatists, and to treat them accordingly.

Yet the scrupulous work of collating the different manuscript sources on which his critical edition of the complete text of St Cyprian's writings for the Oxford Press depended was not always as straightforward as Fell would have liked it to be.[85] The *variae lectiones* caused him one insuperable problem. When he encountered a passage in one of the sources of the *De catholicae ecclesiae unitate* which appeared to contradict his partisan belief in an ancient autonomous episcopate, functioning independently of Rome, he was forced to reject, as a later interpolation, the unwelcome 'primacy text', testifying to the acceptance of Petrine authority and the jurisdiction of the supreme pontiff.[86] That he was prepared to insist on the dubiety of the embarrassing passage, which he relegated to the status of a footnote, rather than concede one inch of ground to his Catholic adversaries, betrayed the controversial basis on which he conducted his editorial labours.[87] Even so, the acclaimed folio edition of the *Opera recognita et illustrata per Joannem oxoniensem episcopum* of 1680 marked a further milestone in the history of Oxford patristic scholarship,[88] one which, despite the existence of 'very many excellent uncollated copies' of St Cyprian's works in England, could not have been achieved without considerable international collaboration, for the manuscript sources of the Cyprianic text were scattered across the face of Western Europe.[89] Presented with the wide distribution of the relevant source material, Fell was forced to rein in his religious prejudices and moderate his customary xenophobia in the pursuit of scholarship.

Much the most dramatic and confrontational of the university's encounters with organized whiggery occurred neither in the city of Oxford nor in the county of Oxfordshire, both of which had, in marked contradistinction to the burgeoning toryism of the dons, opted to support exclusion,[90] but in parliament, the main arena of whig ambition. It was through Bishop Fell's presence in the house of lords and, more conspicuously, that of Sir Leoline Jenkins, the junior university burgess, in the house of commons, that conservative academic sentiment was made known to the nation at large. In the protracted debate on the deeply divisive

---

[85] For the textual problems, see 'an advertisement', ibid. 38–40.

[86] *Sancti Cæcilii Cypriani opera recognita & illustrata per Joannem oxoniensem episcopum* (Oxford at the Theatre 1682).

[87] Ibid. 108: cf Fell's text with his notes c and d. For more recent discussion of the *textus receptus* see M. Bévenot, 'St. Cyprian's *De unitate* chap. 4', *Analecta Gregoriana* xi (Rome 1937), 1–65.

[88] For notices see Bodl. MS Tanner 34, fo 139, Marcus Meibomius to Archbishop Sancroft, Hagae Comitis, xiv Cal. Oct. 1683; Bodl. MS Ballard 41, fo 103, Thomas Rawlins to George Ballard, 6 October 1735. Jean le Clerc, *Bibliothèque universelle* xii (1689) 208. *Universal Lexicon* (Leipzig 1735) ix. 510.

[89] Fell, *Sancti Cæcilii Cypriani opera*, 'Praefatio', 5; ASL MS 239, fo 641; Bodl. MSS Eng. letters c. 196, fos 201, 201ᵛ, c. 29, fos 55 ff.; BL Add. MS 4,274, fo 38.

[90] *Letters of Humphrey Prideaux*, ed. Thompson, 75 ff.; *The Flemings in Oxford* i. 298 ff., ii. 65 ff.; A. Crossley, 'Early modern Oxford: city government', *VCH Oxon*. iv. 123–4; Henning (ed.), *House of Commons* i. 356 ff.

issues of James's exclusion and the dissenters' relief from the penal laws, Fell and Jenkins unhesitatingly voiced their opposition to whig demands, and voted consistently with the depressed court interest. Confident that their consciences were clear on the matter, they were not intimidated by the clamour raised by their adversaries.

At once public-spirited and partisan, Fell took his parliamentary duties seriously. He greatly deprecated the dissolution of the Cavalier Parliament and the advent at Westminster of so many 'commonwealths-men and fanatics'.[91] Having done what little he could in the three general elections between 1679 and 1681 to get dependable church-and-state candidates elected in the constituencies of his diocese,[92] he attended all three of the exclusion parliaments in person.[93] In the critical Lords' debate of 15 November 1680 he joined with the majority of peers to throw out the commons' bill of exclusion.[94] After a gruelling sitting that lasted for twelve hours, the bishops—led by the Oxonians, Henry Compton of London and Peter Mews of Bath and Wells—were unanimous in rejecting the bill.[95] After this decisive vote, which settled the parliamentary fate of exclusion, Fell sought to soothe the storm of popular protest by seeking to reunite the political nation behind the existing protestant establishment.

In a cogently worded sermon preached before the Lords on 22 December, he took as his text a verse from St Matthew's Gospel, reminding his countrymen of the desolation that lay in wait for a kingdom divided against itself.[96] In it he fearlessly condemned schism, faction, and rebellion, warned against Shaftesbury's machinations, owned the impossibility of reuniting dissenters to the established church, and stressed the destructive force of religious toleration. In an attempt to calm tempers, he urged the advantages of peace and unity, recalling 'those mad divisions' that had ushered in the Great Rebellion; which, were they to be allowed to return, would, he feared, produce 'the same or worse events'.[97] For all his partisanship, Fell preached Christian reconciliation, not tory vengeance. He wanted sanity, not resentment, to prevail. In the aftermath of the Lords' rejection of exclusion, he appealed to the rank-and-file whigs to abandon the earl of Shaftesbury's dangerous demands and to rally behind the king and bishops by making the most of the laws of the land and the inherent strength of the Church of England.[98]

---

[91] Longleat House, MS Thynne 10, fo 230, Bishop Fell to Thomas Thynne, 27 July [1679].

[92] Bodl. MS top. Oxon. c. 325, fo 15, MS Clarendon 155, fo 39; Wood, *Life and Times* ii. 442–3, 460–1, 519, 544; M. B. Rex, *University Representation in England 1604–1690* (London 1954) 266–70, 280–2.

[93] *LJ* xiii. 309–31, 334, 337–42, 345–417, 420–3, 449 ff.

[94] Wood is mistaken in claiming that Fell 'withdrew himself a little before the commons came up with a bill', as is Hearne, who makes him vote for exclusion: Wood, *Life and Times* ii. 500. Hearne, *Collections* iii. 444; *LJ* xiii. 665; Beddard, 'Sancroft', 97–8.

[95] E. S. De Beer, 'The house of lords in the parliament of 1680', *Bulletin of the Institute of Historical Research* xx (1943–5), 31–2, 37; Narcissus Luttrell, *A Brief Historical Relation of State Affairs* (6 vols Oxford 1857) i. 61.

[96] 'Every kingdom divided against itself is brought to desolation': Matthew 12. 25.

[97] He quoted Ammianus Marcellinus on the way that Julian the Apostate sought to extirpate Christianity by encouraging 'several sects of heretics in their different ways of worship'. John Fell, *A Sermon preached before the house of peers on December 22. 1680. Being the day of solemn humiliation* (Oxford at the Theatre 1680), 5–6, 7–8, 12–14.   [98] Ibid. 5, 19–30.

Sir Leoline Jenkins, a civilian-turned-diplomatist, was labelled 'thrice vile' in his politics by the ex-parliamentarian Shaftesbury, who was only too painfully aware of his opponent's Cavalier Anglican pedigree and outlook.[99] An ejected Oxford Cavalier, who had privately tutored the sons of the loyal Welsh gentry and attended Fell's congregation in the 1650s, Jenkins was a zealous episcopalian, whom Sheldon had got elected to the principalship of Jesus College in 1661.[100] From the moment that he had entered the second exclusion parliament in November 1680 he had opposed the whig party in the house of commons. Dissatisfied with the craven behaviour of his predecessor in the first exclusion parliament,[101] the university had, under Fell's guidance, replaced him with Jenkins, who had but recently returned from Nijmegen.[102] It did so in the knowledge that he could be relied on to represent the university's true feelings at Westminster. A 'great assertor of the divine right of monarchy', he was, along with Fell, 'set in every punctilio of the Church of England'.[103] An exceptionally devout layman, whose name had been canvassed to succeed Sheldon at Canterbury in 1677, his loyalty derived directly from his churchmanship.[104] 'It is from the church I have learnt my duty to the king', he informed the protestant archbishop of Armagh, 'and 'tis to her I shall always endeavour to approve myself'.[105]

Appointed secretary of state by Charles II in April 1680 for the same reason that the university had elected him a burgess, the loyal Jenkins acted as the government's spokesman.[106] He spoke against the exclusion bill at every reading thereafter, and repeatedly advocated, against the 'extremity' of exclusion, the court-sponsored policy of enacting 'expedients', whereby statutory limitations would be placed on the prerogative of a Catholic successor—but to no avail.[107] A strict legitimist, he believed that exclusion would 'change the very essence and being of the monarchy' from a hereditary into an elective one. Holding that 'the government

---

[99] J. R. Jones, 'Shaftesbury's "worthy men": a whig view of the parliament of 1679', *Bulletin of the Institute of Historical Research* xxx (1957), 23.

[100] R. A. Beddard, 'Restoration Oxford and the re-making of the protestant establishment', p. 805 above. JCA foundation register, p. 8. He was Sheldon's protégé: *Restoration Oxford*, ed. Beddard i, no. 375, and R. A. Beddard, 'The character of a Restoration prelate: Dr John Dolben', *Notes and Queries*. ccxv (1970), 419.

[101] For John Edisbury's disappointing performance see A. Browning and D. J. Milne, 'An exclusion bill division list', *Bulletin of the Institute of Historical Research* xxiii (1950), 217 and n. 3, but see also K. Feiling, *A History of the Tory Party, 1640–1714* (Oxford 1959), appx i, p. 495.

[102] Jenkins's and Charles Perrot's commanding lead in the poll on 19 August 1679 (204 and 224 respectively over William Oldys's 104 and James Lane's 45) ruled out a contest in 1681 and 1685. OUA register of convocation 1671–83, NEP/*supra*/28, register Tb, pp. 285–6; PRO SP 29/415, no. 11; Bodl. MS Wood f. 43, fo 2; Wood, *Life and Times* ii. 460–1, 522, iii. 135; *The Flemings in Oxford* i. 298–9.

[103] Gilbert Burnet, *History of My Own Times*, ed. O. Airy (2 vols Oxford 1897) ii. 257.

[104] Beddard, 'Sancroft', 322.

[105] PRO SP 63/341, p. 10, Jenkins to Michael Boyle, lord chancellor of Ireland, Whitehall, 22 May 1680.

[106] PRO PC 2/68, p. 489, SP 44/51, p. 338, Adm. 77/1, no. 43; Luttrell, *Brief Relation* i. 35, 42. For Jenkins's reports to Vice-Chancellor Halton see PRO SP 44/62, pp. 117, 118, 26 October and 6 November 1680.

[107] William Wynne, *The Life of Sir Leoline Jenkins* (2 vols London 1724) i, p. xlii; *Debates Of The House of Commons, from the Year 1667 to the Year 1694*, ed. Anchitel Grey (10 vols London 1679) vii. 403.

had its original not from the people, but from God', he argued that 'when God gives us a king in his wrath it is not in our power to change him'.[108] Having failed to defuse the succession crisis by privately persuading James to return to the church of his 'baptism and education', he pressed the commons to accept him 'as he is'.[109]

Like the rest of Oxford, Jenkins maintained that of the three religious parties of the nation—Roman Catholic, nonconformist, and Anglican—only the Church of England men could provide the realm with political stability. Recalling the services rendered to Charles I by the Cavalier Anglicans, he wrote in a private memorandum, 'I am sure they have deserved much, and have suffer'd much, they are the only people, whose pretensions are founded on the law, and whose principles and form of government strengthen and support monarchy'. Toleration for Catholics was out of the question, for it would be the 'ruining of all'. And as for protestant dissenters, they had either to 'be governed with firm and steady reins', or to be bought by concessions, 'but what those can be that will satisfie, God alone knows'.[110] Clearly, he would have no part in harming the Anglican ascendancy.

Sensing that the tide of public opinion was turning in his favour, and assured of 'all demonstrations of duty and affection' from the university, the king summoned the third exclusion parliament to Oxford in January 1681.[111] The removal from the whig-dominated capital to tory Oxford was seen by both parties as essaying a trial of political wills—a signal that England might once more be on the brink of civil war.[112] However the court fared in the general election, Charles knew, as he told Vice-Chancellor Halton, that he came to 'a place and a body of men that have alwayes manifested a zeale, well becoming their education and abilities, for the true protestant religion, as it is established by law', and that alone guaranteed the loyalty and support he and James needed in the present crisis. Having already made up his mind to stand by the laws of the land, to defend the church, and to reject the clamour for exclusion and toleration, Charles was resolved to break with the whig faction. In sending the whigs packing, he could be confident that they would find no support from a university city which had 'upon all occasions' shown its 'inviolable fidelity' to himself and his father.[113] On 14 March he entered Oxford amid shouts of 'let the king live, and the devill hang up all roundheads: at which', it was reported, 'his majestie smiled and seemed well pleased'.[114] The outcome of the week-long session is well known. Faced with the whigs' refusal to compromise,

---

[108] *Debates*, ed. Grey vii. 418–20.

[109] Wynne, *Jenkins* ii. 690–1, Secretary Jenkins to James, duke of York, 8 December 1680.

[110] Ibid. i, p. xlv, 'What is amiss in the present state of affairs'.

[111] QCA 2. U. 73, Charles II to Vice-Chancellor Halton, Whitehall, 25 January 1680/1; Bodl. MS Perrott 1, fos 91–2; PRO SP 44/53, pp. 536–8.

[112] For the university's preparations to receive king, court, and parliament see OUA register Tb, pp. 281–3, 292–4; HMC *Ormonde MSS* v. 554, 585–6; PRO SP 29/415, no. 46.

[113] QCA 2. U. 73. For the swing of political opinion against the whigs see R. A. Beddard, 'The retreat on toryism', *Wiltshire Archaeological Magazine* 72 (1980), 82–106, and R. A. Beddard, 'An anonymous paper of advice tendered to Charles II in 1680', *Notes and Queries* ccxxiii (1978), 25–30.

[114] Wood, *Life and Times* ii. 527.

and the spectacle of the Lords and Commons at loggerheads, Charles dissolved parliament on 28 March.[115] It was never again to meet during his reign.

The Cavaliers' political ends, and the means which they advocated to secure them, did not vary with the passage of time. Fell and Jenkins were as convinced of the rightness of their cause in the 1680s as they had been in the 1640s. For Fell, 'the preservation of the protestant religion' was wholly dependent upon maintaining the 'established government' in church and state, and that meant adhering to 'the present constitution', regardless of the pressures for change. He was utterly opposed to 'letting in all dissenters' to the Church of England, believing that such a course would destroy ecclesiastical peace, and lead, yet again, to 'the alteration of government' by subverting episcopacy from within. If comprehension was out of the question, so too was indulgence. Toleration would, he argued, be 'destructive of our reformed religion, whether procured by a Lord Clifford' for the benefit of Catholics, or by the whigs for the benefit of dissenters.[116] Good could not come from licensing the endlessly proliferating sects, which grew only at the expense of the church. Although Fell's arguments were drawn at least as much from ecclesiological conviction as they were from political experience, he had necessarily to dwell on the lessons of history in attempting to win over individual exclusionists, since they rejected out of hand his exclusive brand of high church episcopalianism.

In wooing one whig parliamentarian—Sir Richard Newdigate, the Christ Church son of an old Trinity friend of Sheldon's, whom he was intent on retrieving from the snares of exclusion and pan-protestantism—Fell stressed the calamitous outcome of the Great Rebellion.[117] In particular, he cited the triumph of sectarian republicanism and the loss of social privilege that had resulted from violent constitutional change: 'we remember very well the time when blood and rapine put on the mask of godliness and reformation, and we lost our king, our liberty, and property, and religion, by fighting for them'. It had then been the fate of the 'poor Cavaliers' to be 'scandalled with the names of malignants and papists' for defending the integrity of their church, as now, he lamented, they were defamed by whigs and dissenters for the selfsame reason. Yet, the Cavalier Anglicans had been right to resist the remodelling of the church and monarchy in the 1640s, and the tories were right to resist the whigs' blind demands for radical constitutional change forty years on. 'God knows', he protested to Newdigate, 'while we think we pursue our

---

[115] Charles was so satisfied with the reception he had received at Oxford that he transferred the trial of Stephen College from whig-dominated London to Oxford by special commission: PRO SP 44/62, p. 222, Jenkins to Lord Chief Justice North, Whitehall, 23 July 1681. *The Flemings in Oxford* ii. 21–2, 25, 27, 30.

[116] Warwickshire Record Office, MSS Newdigate, CR 136/B 413, Bishop Fell to Sir Richard Newdigate [1681]. For Clifford and toleration see M. Lee, *The Cabal* (Urbana Ill. 1965), 102, 186, 188, 190.

[117] CA D.P.i.b.2, p. 5. Again the link went back to the Interregnum, when Newdigate senior had acted as legal counsel defending Sheldon and the Cavalier university against the parliamentary visitors. Bodl. MS Wood f. 35, fos 141, 141ᵛ, 295; *Register*, ed. Burrows, 207.

safety we may probably leap into irremediable ruin.'[118] He did not want to see a
repeat performance of that earlier tragedy.

Fortunately for him, the bishop was not alone in his reasoning. The bulk of the
political nation, having been once bitten by insatiable faction, was to prove twice
shy of leaping into the dark with the whigs. Fell's uncompromising churchmanship
slotted neatly into the evolving 'Yorkist' strategy, which sought to harness the scattered and as yet disparate conservative forces within propertied society.[119] From
turbulent, sect-ridden Scotland the duke of York let it be known, via his Anglican
domestic chaplain Francis Turner, an academic with close connections with both
of the English universities and with Lambeth palace, that he placed 'his hopes altogether upon ... the Church of England, upon the episcopal party, and mainly
upon the bishops themselves'.[120] To give weight to his words, James did everything in his power, as Charles's high commissioner in Edinburgh, to demonstrate
his concern for the downtrodden episcopalian interest north of the border. In concert with his well-placed Hyde brothers-in-law at court, he urged Archbishop
Sancroft to advise the king 'how mighty safe' he would be 'to stick by his old
friends and the laws'—meaning, of course, the Cavalier Anglicans and the laws
which they had enacted for safeguarding the Anglican constitution in church and
state.[121]

The drawing together of the Catholic duke and protestant bishops in defence of
the legal establishment, as it was currently constituted under the Stuart crown, did
more than soothe the badly frayed nerves of the Church of England; it helped to
fix the rising crescendo of tory sentiment on the firm foundation of old-fashioned,
locally motivated Anglican intolerance: an intolerance which, in spite of having
been temporarily driven out of sight by the whigs' pursuit of protestant reconciliation, had been neither destroyed nor substantially weakened by it, but was securely
rooted in provincial society. The penal laws, which the whigs had failed to repeal,
were intact. They therefore remained what they had always been: a form of political, as well as of religious, control—one which the surviving Cavalier Anglican
prelates and magnates, their clients among the high church clergy and tory
squirearchy, and their supporters among the people, were adept at operating.

Since 1660 these intransigent churchmen had enjoyed episodic success; chiefly
during periods of governmental anxiety, when the king had found it to be to his
advantage to maximize their support for his ministers in parliament, as in the early
years of the Restoration, in 1669–70, and in the mid-1670s. What had been done
before could be done again. The penal code was, moreover, a system of legal

---

[118] Warwickshire Record Office, MSS Newdigate, CR 136/B 413. The king ordered Newdigate's
removal from the commission of the peace: BL Add. MS 34,730, fo 54, Newdigate to Thomas Marriett,
Arbury, 12 January 1679/80.

[119] Beddard, 'Sancroft', pp. iii–v, 14–37, 104 ff.   [120] Bodl. MS Tanner 36, fo 31, 2 June 1681.

[121] Bodl. MS Clarendon 87, fo 331, James, duke of York, to Henry Hyde, second earl of Clarendon,
Edinburgh, 23 November 1681; R. A. Beddard, 'The Restoration church' in J. R. Jones (ed.), *The Restored
Monarchy 1660–1688* (London 1979), 173–4.

repression which, at the parochial level, could easily be turned against the whigs, a significant proportion of whose popular support was recognized at court, no less than in the provinces, as coming from ingrained ideological dissent. All that was required was for the king and his ministers to give the tories leave to discipline law-breakers and trouble-makers. They were more than ready to do the rest. The king's increasing appreciation of the Cavalier Anglicans, as men of proven loyalty 'in the worst of times', and his astute adoption of their rallying-cry of 'the church in danger', elicited a predictably energetic response from the bishop of Oxford and his clerical cohorts as they moved—deliberately, massively, decisively—into forward gear.

The officialdom of Oxfordshire was fully primed for a resurgence of Cavalier Anglican activity. Bishop Fell in the diocese and his opposite number in the county, the king's tory lord lieutenant, James Bertie, earl of Abingdon, were poised to put the laws in execution against their enemies. Both men had, after all, been appointed to office expressly to carry out the high church policies of Lord Treasurer Danby.[122] The effective working partnership which they built up in the period of Charles II's personal rule, between 1681 and 1685, rested as much on their shared Cavalier Anglican faith and an accurate appreciation of their own political interest, as it did on court favour; for Lord Abingdon, like Fell, was descended from impeccably royalist stock—his grandfather and father, the first and second earls of Lindsey, having fought for Charles I on the field of battle.[123] It was their absolute determination to prevent another bout of suicidal war that steeled their resolve to quash the enemies of crown and mitre before events got further out of control.

The dissolution of the Oxford Parliament, followed by the publication of the king's declaration of 8 April 1681, justifying his rejection of all that the whigs stood for, created a climate of political reaction in which Fell and Abingdon were able to rally other conservatives. By appealing over the heads of the whig die-hards to his 'old friends' in the country at large, Charles sidestepped the demand for exclusion, and emancipated from whig intimidation those of his law-abiding subjects who remembered, just as clearly as himself, 'that religion, liberty and property were all lost and gone, when the monarchy was shaken off, and could never be reviv'd till that was restored'.[124] In publicly summoning to his side the powerful emotions of loyalty, religion, and self-preservation, the king sounded the knell of departing whiggery, and cleared the way for the tory reaction, which dominated the closing years of his reign, and provided the platform for his brother's peaceful succession.

The eclipse of parliamentary whiggery brought enormous pastoral benefits to the

---

[122] Beddard, 'Restoration Oxford', above, pp. 860–2; PRO SP 44/29, p. 105, Charles II's commission, Whitehall, 19 March 1674; Wood, *Life and Times* ii. 283.

[123] For Abingdon's political power see Bodl. MSS top. Oxon. c. 325, fos 7, 20–1, 24, 27–8, 30 ff, d. 314, fo 41, MS Clarendon 155, fos 33, 35, MS Eng. misc. c. 75, fo 12. G. E. Cokayne, *The Complete Peerage* (13 vols London 1910–40) viii. 17 ff.

[124] *His Majesties Declaration to all his Loving Subjects, touching the causes & reasons that moved him to dissolve the two last parliaments* (London 1681), 10.

Church of England.[125] The advent of committed tories in the magistracy (the result of a comprehensive purge by the court of the commissions of the peace),[126] and the freeing of the bishops and peers from attendance at parliament (the result of Charles's dispensing with parliament after 1681), allowed the authorities of church and state to reside full time in their jurisdictions, and to give their undivided attention to the problem of nonconformity. Fell, who had held the regular triennial visitations in 1676 and 1679,[127] put the reduction of dissent at the top of his agenda during his third episcopal visitation in 1682, deeming its mere presence in his diocese to be an affront to the authority of an apostolic, 'Cyprianic' bishop.[128] Dissent was doubly offensive to him. It was sinful on account of the heresy and schism it involved, and subversive on account of its political association with whiggery and lawlessness.[129]

In addition to pursuing the published aims of his visitation articles, Fell besought his clergy, as he went the rounds of the Oxfordshire deaneries in the summer of 1682, to help him to win over separatists.[130] He enjoined incumbents to visit absentees in their homes rather than wait for them to come to church of their own free will, which they would never do. They were to confer with them 'concerning those principles of religion and parts of divine worship, wherin they dissent from the orders of the church ... by law established', and to use 'whatsoever powerfull arguments' they could to persuade them to 'a conformity with the said lawes'.[131] The essence of his campaign was to foster obedience—obedience to the formularies of the church and obedience to the laws of the land. Ministers were to make returns of the names of obdurate dissenters, so that he might make 'examples' of them by prosecuting them in the ecclesiastical courts.[132] Further information was collected through the more frequent six-monthly visitations of the archdeacon of Oxford, Provost Halton of Queen's, who, having laid down the burdens of the vice-chancellorship, was also in a position to devote his time and energy to tackling dissent.[133] After the depressing 'times of generall toleration' in the 1670s the ordinary parochial clergy, most of whom shared the intolerant outlook of the university of which they were graduates, were eager to exploit the return of 'a kind aspect towards the church'.[134] Apprised of the potential danger to public peace posed by 'consciences so tender, that a ceremony is deadly offensive, but rebellion is not',

[125] Beddard, 'Sancroft', 104–8, 113–17, 121–6, 197–232.

[126] L. K. J. Glassey, *Politics and the Appointment of Justices of the Peace 1675–1720* (Oxford 1979), 46–58.

[127] ORO MS Oxf. dioc. papers d. 19, fos 1–40ᵛ.

[128] Ibid., d. 20, fos 1–16, c. 430, fos 1–36.

[129] Fell continued his drive against dissent in his 1685 visitation: ORO MS Oxf. dioc. papers d. 708, fos 54–178, d. 20, fos 16ᵛ–29ᵛ.

[130] *Articles of Visitation and Enquiry ... of ... John ... Bishop of Oxford* (Oxford at the Theater 1682).

[131] ORO MS Oxf. dioc. papers c. 430, fo 28, Henry Gregory to Bishop Fell, Middleton Stoney, 8 July 1682.

[132] Ibid., b. 68, fos 9–10ᵛ, Fell's directives, especially no. 2.

[133] For Halton's archidiaconal work see QCA 2. T. 153–60, 170. For his close collaboration with Fell in 1682 see ORO MS Oxf. dioc. papers b. 68, fos 9–12.

[134] ORO MS Oxf. dioc. papers c. 430, fo 27, John Bushell to Fell, Lewknor, 4 July 1682.

they redoubled their pains to heal dangerous divisions and to reform 'mutinous spirites' among their fellow protestants.[135]

The combined efforts of the clergy of the university and the parsons of the parishes to break the hold of dissent on the people, and to keep the impenetrable papist under the lash of the law, were ably seconded by the actions of their lay allies in secular administration.[136] Under the command and patronage of the earl of Abingdon, the deputy lieutenants and justices of the county made it their business to disturb conventicles, to stir up lax constables to do their duty, and to prosecute inveterate conventiclers at the assizes and quarter sessions.[137] The dissenters' meetings were, once again, widely seen as 'the seminaries of sedition and rebellion'—very much as they had been seen by the original framers of the Cavalier Anglican penal code back in the unsettled 1660s.[138] The tory objective was plain. It was to eradicate dissent from the county; or, if that proved impossible, to reduce it to such a parlous state that it would be politically and psychologically incapable of challenging the protestant establishment.

As an intellectual and a pastor, Fell's preference was for persuasion, not force, in the first instance—hence his systematic distribution throughout the diocese of printed copies of St Cyprian's short piece on church unity[139] and Thomas Marshall's exposition of the church catechism.[140] But when arguments failed neither he nor his intolerant tory backers were at all shy of invoking the letter of the law to compel them to conform. Presentments, *ex officio* prosecutions, excommunications, fines, distraint of goods, and imprisonment were the lot of those who refused to relent. Goaded by protracted denials, pastors often turned informer with the bishop's blessing, and inaugurated punitive proceedings. The tory parsons and squires were in bullish mood.[141] They had no qualms about resorting to the use of 'the lancet', prescribed by the law for drawing the monstrous boil of dissent, when 'anodynes and softer usages' had 'proved ineffective'.[142]

The onslaught became so severe that some dissenters in 'the warmest corner' of the diocese fled the county, declaring it 'to be the persecuted shire of England'. Others made over their property to conformist relatives, and stepped out of the way. Even the religiously indifferent and atheistical began to quail, 'partly terrifyed by the paenal lawes, and partly ashamed by so many eyes at this juncture upon

[135] Ibid., fo 30b, Alexander Charnelhouse to Fell, Salford, 7 June 1682.

[136] For example in Oxford city: Oxford City Arch. O.5.12, fos 41, 42ᵛ, 45, 51, 52ʳ⁻ᵛ, 54ᵛ, 55–6ᵛ, 58ʳ⁻ᵛ, 61.

[137] ORO MS Oxf. dioc. papers c. 430, fos 3, 12, 21, Thomas Reynolds to Fell, Aston Rowant, 3 July, George Ashwell to Fell, 22 June 1682; ORO B.O.Q.M. 1/ii/1, fos 41ᵛ, 42.

[138] ORO MS Oxf. dioc. papers c. 430, fo 17, Adam Morton to [George] Ashwell, Drayton, 27 May 1682.

[139] Ibid., fos 21, 24, George Ashwell to Fell, Hanwell, 22 June, Richard Parr to Fell, Ibstone, 10 June 1682.

[140] Ibid., c. 650, fo 31, Edward Jennings to Fell, Little Rollright, 16 August 1682.

[141] Ibid., c. 430, fos 3, 21, 24, 27.

[142] Ibid., fo 30b, Alexander Charnelhouse to Fell, Salford, 7 June 1682.

them'.[143] By late 1683 Archdeacon Halton could count no more than forty-five dissenters in nine of the more populous parishes of Oxford,[144] a city of over 10,000 souls, so successful was the drive for conformity.[145] In this manner, and with these heartening local effects, the last great religious persecution was unleashed on the nation. It was a persecution which brought the realm nearer to total outward conformity than at any time since the collapse of Laudian 'Thorough'.[146] For many an Oxonian the suppression of conventicles, and its counterpart in the improvement in church attendances, constituted the supreme achievement of the halcyon days of Caroline toryism, during which the Cavalier Anglican ideology of a confessional society received a new lease of life.

It was a pastoral achievement which was fondly, and indeed longingly, recalled in the starker, leaner years of the post-revolutionary whig ascendancy, when the dons' cherished act of uniformity was forced by the usurping William of Orange to yield pride of place to the toleration act of 1689:[147] a statute which, in the opinion of Bishop Barlow of Lincoln, granted impunity to dissenters 'against the expresse law of God, of nature, and all', and regardless of their having previously 'ruin'd church and state, and murder'd their kinge'.[148] The toleration act certainly dealt a blow to Anglican church discipline from which it never recovered. Clerical resentment at William III's perverse ecclesiastical policies was to provide much of the dynamic behind the recrudescence of high church toryism in the 1690s;[149] nowhere was this more apparent, or more disconcerting for the government, than in the religiously aggrieved and politically alienated University of Oxford: an Oxford which, for a quarter of a century, had grown accustomed to persecuting religious minorities, regardless of what would nowadays be called human rights.

The publication in London in 1682 of Samuel Johnson's *Julian the Apostate* caused a minor sensation in Oxford.[150] It was not just another vapid exclusionist tract, but a calculated challenge to the university's teaching by an Anglican parson, who unashamedly backed to the hilt the whigs' endeavours to debar 'a popish successor' from the throne. Under the guise of writing an account of the fourth-century Emperor Julian, the apostatized nephew of Constantine the Great who was assassinated in 363, the author compared modern popery to ancient paganism, cast the duke of York in Julian's role as the persecutor of true religion, and asserted that

---

[143] ORO MS Oxf. dioc. papers c. 430, fo 27, John Bushnell to Fell, Lewknor, 4 July 1682.

[144] Halton's replies to Fell's queries: ORO MS Oxf. dioc. papers b. 68, fos 11–12, 6. Cf ibid., c. 430, fos 41, 41ᵛ, 'Nomina recusantium infra dioecesi Oxon. et aliorum'.

[145] For population statistics see *VCH Oxon.* iv. 75–6.

[146] Fell's clergy knew that it was 'the fear of punishment, more than love of God', that made 'many in this juncture of time appeare in our assemblies': ORO MS Oxf. dioc. papers c. 650, fo 27, John Kerie to Fell, Cornwell, 25 April 1682.

[147] *Statutes of the Realm* vi (1819), 74–6: 1 Guil. et Mar. c. 18.

[148] QCL MS 280, fo 251ᵛ, Barlow's autograph 'Adversaria concerneing this act of exemption'. They have been prepared for publication.

[149] G. V. Bennett, *The Tory Crisis in Church and State 1688–1730* (Oxford 1975), chs 1 and 3.

[150] Wood, *Life and Times* iii. 18–19; Luttrell, *Brief Relation* i. 287.

the doctrine of passive obedience, 'when it is taught without any regard to laws, and is prescribed both without law and against law, is not evangelical but Mahumetane, and the very Turkish doctrine of the bow-string', a means of 'wheedling men out of their lives'.[151] Johnson's advocacy of exclusion was shocking enough from 'a church-divine', but he did not stop at that. He had the temerity to sanction active disobedience, to defend resistance and even to condone tyrannicide. Julian's fate was held up for all to see, and his killer, whom Johnson conveniently supposed had been a Christian, exculpated by implication.[152]

Overnight *Julian* became 'the oracle of the cause, the pocket-book of all the party'. In whig-infested London it was carried 'in triumph' to the Royal Exchange and into the coffee-houses of the city, and extolled by the grandees of the whig party, who, in an excess of anticlerical fervour, thanked God that there was one clergyman 'who is not for enslaving the people'.[153] The partisan motive of Johnson's historical disquisition was underlined by the knowledge that he was the chaplain of Lord William Russell, a leading exclusionist and reputed republican.[154] Its publication came not a moment too soon to boost whig morale in the continuing power-struggle with the tories, who, under the direction of three Oxonians— Secretary Jenkins, the duke of Ormonde, and Bishop Compton—and the Cantabrigian Lord Keeper North, had launched an all-out offensive to capture control of the capital.[155]

Adjudged 'a very cunning and malicious piece' of whig propaganda, *Julian the Apostate* particularly scandalized the clergy by its scurrilous lampooning of passive obedience, which was widely revered as 'the doctrine of the cross'.[156] In teaching that subjects had a duty to submit themselves to the higher powers, the established church claimed dominical authority; it was prescribed by Christ Himself, and had been exemplified by his passion and death at the hand of pagan Romans and perfidious Jews. Johnson's book, which 'was much received into the hands of scholars', was incessantly 'talked of and against' in Oxford common rooms.[157] Its refutation became a leitmotiv of academic sermons. Beginning in St Mary's on Act Sunday 1682, one after another of the university's select preachers took Johnson's 'specious arguments to pieces'. Prominent among his assailants were some of Fell's ablest disciples: Henry Aldrich, canon of Christ Church, who, having been the most successful tutor to the noblemen and gentlemen-commoners of the house, was

---

[151] Samuel Johnson, *Julian the Apostate: being a short account of his life . . . together with a comparison of popery and paganism* (London 1682), pp. viii, 88.

[152] Ibid. 61.

[153] [George Hickes], *Jovian. Or, an answer to Julian the Apostate. By a minister of London* (London 1683), sig. B.

[154] For the privy council's examination of the author and printer of *Julian* see PRO SP 29/433, no. 7. For Russell see Bodl. MS. Eng. hist. c. 273, fo 41. Luttrell, *Brief Relation* i. 33, 263, 267–8, 270–1.

[155] D. Ogg, *England in the Reign of Charles II* (2 vols Oxford 1934) ii. 636 ff; J. Levin, *The Charter Controversy in the City of London, 1660–1688* (London 1969).

[156] [Hickes], *Jovian*, sig. B2.

[157] BL MS Lansdowne 937, fo 14ᵛ; Wood, *Life and Times* iii. 18.

being groomed as Fell's successor in the deanery;[158] William Wyatt, Student of Christ Church and, since 1679, public orator of the university;[159] and John Mill, the Greek Testament scholar, who drudged for Fell at the press.[160] Others followed. Scarcely any Oxonian was able to resist 'one or two smart flouts at Julian'.[161]

However, the *coup de grâce* was reserved for yet another of Fell's former clients, George Hickes, a fellow of Lincoln, whose well-grounded churchmanship had been galvanized into full-blown toryism by a spell in rebellious Scotland as chaplain to the duke of Lauderdale, Charles's earlier high commissioner.[162] A popular preacher who was greatly in demand, and a seasoned apologist for the government, Hickes was the darling of the Cavalier Anglican hierarchy and of the university,[163] which had recently, in November 1679, paid him the unusual compliment of creating him a doctor of divinity, *honoris causa*, for his outstanding services to king and church.[164] Since then he had added lustre to his reputation with the publication in 1681 of his sermon, *The True Notion of Persecution Stated*, in which he had not only vindicated the penal laws against dissenters from whig objections, but had also sprung to the defence of passive obedience by insisting that Christianity was 'a suffering religion'. Irrespective of whether 'the supreme power happens to be infidel, idolator, or heretic, and so sets itself against the gospel in general', it was, he maintained, 'the duty of all Christian subjects to suffer', as their Lord and Saviour had suffered, by submitting to the powers that be.[165]

This was exactly what the university authorities wanted to hear, for it showed that their long years of teaching in the service of church and state had not been spent in vain. Passive obedience was, of all the doctrines of the Church of England, the most highly prized by the 'suffering' Cavalier Anglican dons and their academic progeny, among whom Hickes was to be counted, having acted in the early 1660s as servitor to Henry Yerbury, a restored fellow of Magdalen.[166] Hickes, who was sometimes upbraided by the whigs for his education in the university, made it

---

[158] Bodl. MS Tanner 37, fo 244, Fell to Sancroft, 8 February [1681]; W. G. Hiscock, *A Christ Church Miscellany* (Oxford 1946), 17 ff; E. G. W. Bill, *Education at Christ Church Oxford 1660–1800* (Oxford 1988), 240, table 4.3.

[159] OUA register Tb, p. 231, Wyatt's election as public orator, 26 March 1679; Wood, *Life and Times* ii. 446, 495, 518, 527.

[160] John Mill (Milne), later principal of St Edmund Hall (1685). OUA register of congregation 1680–92. NEP/*supra*/20, register Be, fo 122; *The Flemings in Oxford* i. 232, 261, 280, 308 ff, ii. 12, 22, 26 ff; Wood, *Athenae* iv. 528.

[161] BL MS Lansdowne 937, fo 38ᵛ; Wood, *Life and Times* iii. 19.

[162] For the college's licences for his absence see LCM register II, fos 186ᵛ, 187ᵛ, 188. Bodl. MS Eng. misc. e. 4, fos 8, 9, MS Eng. hist. c. 273, fo 15.

[163] Beddard, 'The commission for ecclesiastical promotions, 1681–84', 32–3, 37.

[164] OUA register Tb, p. 246, convocation, 17 November 1679, acting on the chancellor's delegates' letter of 27 October.

[165] George Hickes, *The True Notion of Persecution Stated* (London 1681), 2; Bodl. MS Eng. hist. c. 273, fo 41ᵛ.

[166] Bodl. MS Eng. misc. e. 4, fos 4, 5. For Yerbury see *Register*, ed. Burrows, 44, 90, 114, 137; 'The Restoration Visitation of the University of Oxford and its Colleges', ed. F. J. Varley, *Camden Miscellany* xviii (Camden Soc. 3rd ser. lxxix 1948), 11–12, 22, 56.

a matter of pride that he had been 'bred in Oxford, where passive obedience hath long been the doctrine of the malignant place'. Clearly, his use of the word 'malignant'—the term used by Charles I's rebels to denigrate their loyal opponents—meant that he was only too well aware of the whigs' indebtedness to the subversive ideology of the civil war sects.[167] He was determined to assert the church's teaching against 'ancient and modern fanatical treatises'. For him and his fellow Oxonians, *Julian the Apostate* was but the latest in a long line of such works.[168]

Having been personally attacked by 'Julian' Johnson, Hickes was more than ready to reply to him, which he did in his *Jovian* of 1683.[169] Never having 'read any thing so bold' from a man of Johnson's 'mediocrity' (for though Johnson had studied at Cambridge, he was a mere BA), he marvelled that he had dared to dispute the combined judgement of the house of lords, the Scottish estates, his own University of Cambridge, Secretary Jenkins, and the loyal addressers by still calling for exclusion, when they, who were 'at least as wise, and learned, and as good protestants as himself', were of the opposite opinion. In his preface Hickes placed great reliance on the Lords' vote against exclusion, which had confirmed the king's opposition to the bill. As a law-abiding Oxonian tory, he repeated the words of 'the most learned, and loyal' Sir Leoline Jenkins, university burgess in the two last exclusion parliaments, that 'a bill of exclusion, if it should pass, would change the essence of the monarchy, and make the crown elective'. He urged the moral obligation of the oath of supremacy which, in common with every other cleric, Johnson had sworn to observe. That alone seemed 'to make an act of exclusion unlawful', for the oath was sworn to the king and his lawful heirs, and they, it was well known, succeeded strictly 'according to proximity of blood'.[170]

As for the oft-heard complaint that there was no security against the Catholic James once he succeeded, he pointed out that the whigs had but themselves to blame. 'The truly loyal party' of the Church of England had repeatedly been 'for making of good laws for our security against him', something which the whigs had frustrated by their purblind pursuit of exclusion.[171] It was completely consistent with Hickes's Oxford education that his quarrel with Johnson concerned only the first part of his book, containing his mistaken view of passive obedience in the early church, based as it was on a misreading of the sources for Julian's reign. It did not embrace his adversary's extensive comparison between popery and paganism, with which Hickes declared himself well satisfied, as, indeed, did most of

---

[167] [Hickes], *Jovian*, 227. The word 'malignant', had been specifically applied to the opponents of the parliamentarian cause. See p. 879 above.

[168] [Hickes], *Jovian*, 238.

[169] Hickes wrote his *Jovian* at the request of Archbishop Sancroft, who had preferred him to his London living of All Hallows, Barking by the Tower: Bodl. MS Tanner 37, fo 113, Lauderdale to Sancroft, 5 August 1680. Cf [Hickes] *Julian*, 100.

[170] [Hickes], *Jovian*, preface. For Johnson's academic qualifications see Venn, *Alumni* ii. 481.

[171] For the aborted Anglican-inspired bills for educating the royal children in the protestant religion, and for providing for the continuance of a protestant clergy see Bodl. MS Carte 81, fos 352 ff. HMC *Eleventh Report*, appx, pt 2, pp. 209–10, 220–2.

Johnson's critics. The Oxonians' regard for James's person did not extend to his religion.

Hickes's *Jovian* was instantly recognized and accepted for what it was: a classic statement of Anglican political thought, a tory manifesto second only in importance to the *Patriarcha* of Sir Robert Filmer—a treatise which had been written earlier in the century, and had only belatedly appeared in the press, as a posthumous publication, in 1680.[172] Hickes's book, a work of more substantial scholarship than anything Johnson could attempt, carried the day.[173] It furnished an excellent illustration of the way in which the Cavalier Anglican ethos of Oxford's political divinity, still conditioned by the impact of the Great Rebellion, made a central contribution to the propaganda of the nation-wide tory reaction. For his doughty and seasonable performance Hickes received the ultimate accolade: the unsolicited thanks of the octogenarian Bishop Morley of Winchester, doyen of the Cavalier Anglican hierarchy, who despite his years still took a lively interest in church politics from the fastness of Farnham castle.[174]

In the spring of 1683, just one year after his triumphant return to London from Edinburgh, James decided to pay a state visit to Oxford.[175] Whereas he had previously visited the city in the company of the reigning monarch, either his father or his brother, this time he came in his own right—as the acknowledged heir to the Stuart throne.[176] Keen to stress his dynastic status, he chose to make it a York family occasion, knowing full well that the loyal university could never see enough of the royal family in all its branches. He brought with him his beautiful, but little-known, Italian wife, Maria Beatrice d'Este, and his younger daughter, the Lady Anne, a child of his first marriage to Anne Hyde, Lord Chancellor Clarendon's daughter.[177] The declared purpose of his visit was to show the university to the Catholic duchess, who had never been to Oxford, and to preside over the official celebrations held to mark the opening of the Ashmolean Museum.[178] The visit had, however, a more important, if undeclared, political purpose. It was designed as a means of rallying public opinion even more solidly behind the duke's succession by demonstrating his undiminished respect for the university, as the citadel of the Church of England and the seminary of its bishops and clergy.

---

[172] Archbishop Sancroft had a hand in Edmund Bohun's publication of a reliable text of Filmer's *Patriarcha*: Emmanuel College Library, Cambridge, 335. 5. 20 (Sancroft's annotated copy of the first edition). Bohun also consulted Hickes over his tory propaganda: Bodl. MS Eng. letters c. 12, fos 156–7; G. J. Schochet, 'Sir Robert Filmer: some new bibliographical discoveries', *The Library*, 5th ser. xxvi (1971), 156–60.

[173] *Jovian* reached a second edition in 1683.

[174] Bodl. MS Eng. misc. e. 4, fo 18ᵛ. Charles nominated Hickes dean of Worcester while staying at Winchester on 11 September 1683. Hickes owned Sancroft as the author of his promotion. Bodl. MS Tanner 34, fo 132. PRO SP 44/53, p. 118.

[175] Bodl. MS Wood d. 19(3), fos 53–8ᵛ. Dr Williams's Library MS Morrice P, p. 368. BL MS Lansdowne 937, fos 40–1. Luttrell, *Brief Relation* i. 259–60.

[176] OUA register Tb, pp. 361–2, 364; *Restoration Oxford* ed. Beddard ii, nos 745–7, 749–50, 752, 756.

[177] Oxford City Arch., E.4.5, fo 206ᵛ.

[178] C. H. Josten, *Elias Ashmole 1617–1692* (5 vols Oxford 1966) i. 252–3, iv. 1719–20.

By timing his arrival to coincide with the inauguration of the Ashmolean, an event which could be relied on to bring many of Oxford's distinguished friends to the university, James used the well-publicized opportunity to underpin his progressive rehabilitation in the hearts and minds of the protestant establishment: a process which had begun long before, in November 1679, with his pro-episcopalian administration in Scotland,[179] and was not complete until May 1684 when, after an absence of sixteen years, he re-entered the English privy council, and resumed responsibility for the affairs of the admiralty.[180] With so much depending on the success of the visit, it was carefully planned and faultlessly executed. The academic authorities were concerned to create a good impression, for they realized that the eyes of the nation were upon them, and that James, in common with every prince before him, would value them on the strength of their proven attachment to him.[181]

On 18 May the royal party was met at Sandford by the lord lieutenant at the head of 'more than 100 country gentlemen', and made its entrance into Oxford at the East Gate, where it was waited on by the mayor and corporation, whom Abingdon presented; 'at which time and before, most of the rings of bells in the city and those belonging to the colleges rang for the duke's reception'.[182] Outside St Mary's James was greeted by the vice-chancellor, doctors, and masters. After having 'saluted him with a short Latin oration', the public orator addressed another in English to the duchess; which 'being kindly received', and cheered by the scholars, the procession wound its way to Christ Church through the massed ranks of the bachelors and undergraduates. Beneath Wren's recently completed Tom Tower the dean and chapter welcomed them, and conducted them to their lodgings in the deanery, which Fell, as an appointee of the crown, dutifully made over to them. After a further salutation of verses, spoken to the duke by the youthful earl of Clancartie, a canon commoner and Ormonde's great-nephew,[183] Abingdon 'introduced severall gentlemen of the county to kiss his hand'. That evening the Yorks dined privately in the deanery, at the duke's expense; James proudly acknowledging the fact that his name still stood on the books of Christ Church, where he had been entered by his father in 1642 after the battle of Edgehill.[184]

The next day, a Saturday, began with the presentation of the university delegation, led by Vice-Chancellor Lloyd, 'with the doctors in their scarlet, and proctors in their formalities', who, having congratulated the duke's arrival among them, 'kneeled downe, and kissed his hand'. This duty done, the duke and duchess made a tour of the colleges, where they were warmly received by the heads and fellows.

[179] Beddard, 'Sancroft', 25–30, 118–19.
[180] PRO PC 2/70, p. 1, SP 63/340, p. 30, Adm. 77/2, nos 83, 103, SP 8/1, pt 3, no. 105.
[181] For the arrangements see OUA register Tb, p. 3.
[182] Oxford City Arch., B.5.1, fos 213ᵛ–14.
[183] Bodl. MS Rawlinson d. 397, fo 290ᵛ; Wood, Life and Times iii. 48.
[184] James and his brother Charles, prince of Wales, had been created MAs on 1 November 1642: OUA register Sb, p. 11, 'Creatio Carolina'; Bodl. MS Rawlinson d. 397, fo 289. For their remaining on the battel books see CA X.C. 49, fos 1ᵛ, 2ᵛ, X.C. 55, fo 2ᵛ.

Wherever they went speeches were the order of the day. In many cases the words of welcome were pronounced by the sons and relations of conspicuous 'Yorkist' peers and squires:[185] those initial Anglican tories who, against the odds, had espoused James's cause against his whig opponents, and, in so doing, formed the hub of an unmistakable and increasingly magnetic, 'Yorkist', reversionary interest, which, in the early 1680s, had irresistibly drawn the whole of Oxford into its orbit.[186]

In each college the royal couple made a point of viewing the chapel. Only one college, Pembroke, was not on their itinerary, simply because it 'had no chappell'.[187] At Exeter—once the home of Oxford's leading Calvinists, Prideaux and Conant—James showed something of his old Anglican flair by complaining 'that the communion table stood contrary to the canon', that is east–west, not north–south or altar-wise, as the abortive canons of 1640 had directed.[188] It was a complaint which the high churchmen greatly relished. Although, of course, there was no question of the duke and duchess attending protestant prayers, they kept their Catholicism to themselves, and made sure that no Catholic priest appeared with them in public. So tactful were they not to offend protestant feelings, that their removal to the earl of Clarendon's residence at Cornbury Park for the rest of the weekend obviated any awkwardness that their being in Oxford on a Sunday might otherwise have presented.[189]

At their return on Monday, 21 May, the duke and duchess resumed their tour of the university, taking in the library, divinity school, and theatre, where there was yet another formal reception, before going next door to the Ashmolean Museum.[190] Though the museum had been finished since the end of March, it was not until the beginning of May that the curator, Robert Plot, had furnished the room and arranged 'the rarities', which Ashmole had donated, 'in their distinct cabinets and places'.[191] In the presence of his wife and daughter, and surrounded by 'a great number of earles and lords and other persons of quality', who either belonged to the Yorks' household, 'or came to pay their devotions to them and shew the greatness and sincerity of their zeal to the royal family' after the trials and tribulations of exclusion, James opened the museum amid the greatest display of state that the university could command, and was the guest of honour at the banquet which followed.[192] The visit concluded on 22 May with a solemn convoca-

---

[185] Wood, *Life and Times* iii. 48–51; *London Gazette*, no. 1827 (21–4 May 1683).

[186] For the growth of the secular Yorkist reversionary interest see HMC *Seventh Report*, 480, 30 November 1682.

[187] Wood, *Life and Times* iii. 54. The society worshipped in the adjacent parish church of St Aldate's.

[188] Ibid. 53. Cf canon VII of 1640: E. Cardwell, *Synodalia* (2 vols Oxford 1842) i. 404–5.

[189] BL MS Lansdowne 937, fo 40ᵛ; Wood, *Life and Times* iii. 51.

[190] For Elias Ashmole's benefaction see OUA register Tb, pp. 362–3. Bodl. MS Wood f. 31, fo 141. Edward Chamberlayne, *Angliae Notitia* (London 1684), 325–8.

[191] Bodl. MS Ashmole 1813, fo 14ᵛ, F. Aston to Robert Plot, London, 22 March 1682/3.

[192] BL MS Lansdowne 927, fo 41; Wood, *Life and Times* iii. 54–6.

tion, in which honorary DCLs were conferred on eight noblemen and gentlemen of the duke's Anglican retinue.[193]

The visit was ajudged a resounding success, the royal party meeting with 'all the duty and respect imaginable'.[194] At their farewell, the duke was presented with Wood's *Historia*, and the duchess with Loggan's *Oxonia illustrata* and Plot's *Oxfordshire*. To the Duke's protestant daughter, Anne, the university gave its greatest token of regard—'a fair bible'.[195] As the granddaughter of both King Charles I and Lord Chancellor Clarendon, the god-daughter of Archbishop Sheldon, and the pupil of Bishop Compton, the 18-year-old princess had already acquired a reputation for being a good churchwoman.[196] James's decision to take Anne, a possible future queen, with him to Oxford may have been a deliberate attempt to appeal to Anglican loyalty. Certainly, her dutiful presence in the cathedral at 'morning prayers' was widely noted, and deeply gratifying to churchmen of all shades of opinion. It reminded the older generation of the exemplary devotion with which her grandfather, the royal martyr, had attended Christ Church services in the 1640s.[197] Perhaps, Anne's appearance among them went some way to reassuring protestants of the long-term security of their religion. After all, neither of James's heirs was a Catholic. His elder daughter, Mary, another conspicuous protestant, was married to the Calvinist William of Orange, and Anne was soon to be safely married to the Lutheran Prince George of Denmark.[198]

News of the Rye House conspiracy of June 1683 exploded like a bombshell on Oxford, shattering its sense of well-being.[199] Bishop Fell was aghast at the enormity of the intended crime. He could scarcely credit that even the most desperate of whigs had wickedness enough to contemplate, let alone plot, the assassination of Charles and James. He saw in the merciful delivery of the Stuart princes 'a fresh and most remarkable instance of the divine providence watching over the king and this nation'.[200] Predictably, the university felt itself menaced by this latest of attempted whig atrocities.[201] Having recently played host to the duke of York, it

---

[193] OUA register Tb, pp. 361–2. James also recommended his Anglican chaplain, Thomas White, to be created DD, which was done with Ormonde's approbation: Bodl. MS Bodley 594, pp. 103, 105; Wood, *Fasti* ii. 392.

[194] Bodl. MS Eng. letters d. 72, fo 33ᵛ.   [195] Bodl. MS Wood d. 19(3), fo 54.

[196] For Sheldon's acting as godfather see Bodl. Bib. Eng. 1648. d. 3. For Compton's tutorship see 'Diary of Dr. Edward Lake', ed. G. P. Elliott, *Camden Miscellany* 1 (Camden Soc. xxxix 1847) 7 ff.

[197] See my forthcoming article, 'Bishop Mews's memoir of the royal martyr'.

[198] For the sense of protestant relief at these alliances see F. Sandford, *A Genealogical History Of the Kings of England* (London 1677), 567; Marquise Campana di Cavelli, *Les Derniers Stuarts à Saint Germain en Laye* (2 vols Paris 1871) i. 201–3. R. A. Beddard, 'Wren's mausoleum for Charles I and the cult of the royal martyr' in J. Newman (ed.), *Design and Practice in British Architecture: studies in architectural history presented to Howard Colvin* (London 1984), 37–8.

[199] For the conspiracy see D. J. Milne, 'The results of the Rye House Plot and their influence upon the revolution of 1688', *TRHS* 5th ser. i (1951), 91–108.

[200] BL Add. MS 29,582, fo 17, Fell to Christopher, Viscount Hatton, 5 July [1683].

[201] Monmouth's name, inserted after his stay in the college in 1665, was struck from the Corpus buttery book on 12 July 1683, when it was known that he was implicated in the conspiracy. T. Fowler, *Corpus Christi College* (London 1891), 157.

was not content, as was Cambridge, simply to exchange compliments with the crown.[202] While the other corporations of England presented adulatory addresses to Whitehall, congratulating 'the happy deliverance' of the king and duke 'from the bloody attempts of wicked men',[203] the university heads decided to embark on a more substantial exercise: one that they believed would be of greater service to the king and kingdom, and one 'more suitable' to their professional abilities and to the high political role which, under Cavalier Anglican auspices, Oxford had aspired to fill ever since 1660. By putting itself forward as the moral guardian of society, the university strove, once and for all, to reclaim the crown's deluded subjects from the beguiling but wrong-headed arguments of faction-mongers.

It undertook to 'search into those ill principles' which, it was convinced, had inspired the wicked attempt of the Rye House conspirators, and provided the intellectual basis on which all sowers of sedition, treason, and heresy had hitherto predicated their opposition to the house of Stuart.[204] For the benefit of the nation, the university set about the task of unravelling 'the pretences which gave of late, and may hereafter give, protection and countenance to those designes and practices', that not only threatened to make away with the king's 'sacred person', and that of his heir, but which, were they allowed to go unchecked, would destroy 'the lawes and religion, and most certainly the learning and studies of three flourishing kingdoms'.[205] Urged on by Bishop Fell and Vice-Chancellor Lloyd, neither of whom could put aside their horror of rebellion and regicide, the university expressed its sense of outrage by seeking to exercise its customary teaching *magisterium* on an altogether more ambitious scale than it had done at any time since the Restoration. Having long given the rule to its own members, and, therefore, cumulatively to the clergy who had graduated since 1662, Oxford now essayed to give guidance to the rest of England. In doing so, it had before it the precedent of 1647, when convocation had denounced as pernicious the solemn league and covenant: an act for which the university had been solemnly thanked by the Cavalier Parliament in 1665.[206]

Under the exacting eye of the newly appointed regius professor of divinity, William Jane of Christ Church, those statutory arbiters of protestant orthodoxy—the senior resident doctors of divinity—were called upon to examine virtually the entire output of opposition literature.[207] By measuring the miscellaneous effusions of sedition against the yardstick of Anglican political thought, they systematically located, summarized, and attributed the arguments which the enemies of king and

[202] For the Cambridge University address see David Wilkins, *Concilia Magnae Britanniae* (4 vols London 1737) iv. 607. Luttrell, *Brief Relation* i. 271–2.

[203] [John Oldmixon], *A Complete History of Addresses* (London 1709, 2nd edn London 1710), 60 ff; *London Gazette*, nos 1839 ff. The Oxford corporation addressed under Lord Abingdon's auspices: Oxford City Arch. B.5.1, fos 215, 215ᵛ, 217.

[204] BL Add. MS 29,582, fo 35, Fell to Hatton, 27 July [1683].

[205] PRO SP 29/429, no. 107, item iv, university to Chancellor Ormonde, 21 July 1683.

[206] OUA register Sb, pp. 133–49, 'Judicium academiae oxon. de foedere nationali', convocation, 1 June 1647; Beddard, 'Restoration Oxford', above, pp. 856–7.

[207] Jane was also sub-dean of Christ Church from 1679 to 1683. CA D&C i. b. 3, pp. 233, 237, 241, 244, 247. Bodl. MS Bodley 594, fos 53ᵛ–4, minutes of hebdomadal council, 16 July 1683.

church had repeatedly used to commend their subversive purposes to the people. Such was their white-hot zeal to fix a mark of public disapprobation on the would-be disturbers of their peace that they dispatched their apparently arduous task in a matter of days.[208] The truth was they were fully prepared to discharge the office which the university had put upon them.

After years spent in adjudicating cases of conscience, and in debating the pros and cons of moral, theological, and legal *quaestiones* in the schools, not a few of which had both raised and resolved points of political and ecclesiastical controversy, Jane and his colleagues in the faculty of theology were well equipped to compile what was tantamount to an Anglican version of the Roman *Index librorum prohibitorum*: a schedule of 'damnable doctrines', which listed the titles of the tracts in which they had been found, and gave, so far as was known, the names of their authors.[209] Jane was in his element. Besides having acted as Bishop Compton's licensing chaplain since 1674, which had accustomed him to the business of vetting theological works submitted for publication,[210] the production of loyalist propaganda ran in his family. The son of an Anglican Cavalier who had served as a clerk of the privy council during Charles II's banishment,[211] he had reason to be proud of the fact that his father had been one of the earliest royalists to spring to the defence of Charles I's *Eikon basiliké*, which he did in 1651 with his *Eikon aklastos*—a work that had censured Milton's *Eikonoklastes*, paragraph by paragraph.[212]

In drawing up an inventory of offensive propositions to put before convocation, Jane had four main targets in his sights: whiggery, dissent, Hobbism, and popery. Of these, popery escaped comparatively lightly with the condemnation of just two Jesuit authors, Robert Parsons and Cardinal Bellarmine, for arguing in favour of the popular origin of government and the right of the people to alter the succession on religious grounds.[213] The inclusion of the 'atheist', Thomas Hobbes, was a foregone conclusion, on account of what Clarendon had called his 'false and evil doctrine', compounded of equal measures of pessimism and irreligion.[214] But it was

[208] The doctors took from 16 to 21 July: OUA register Tb, p. 375.

[209] Wood's annotated copy of the printed decree and his listing of the titles help to identify the censured items: Bodl. Wood 423, item 58, MS Wood d. 19(3), fo 60.

[210] The antipathy of Jane to Catholic and dissenting authorities and his hatred of 'the apostate principles of the *Leviathan*' are clear from his *Sermon preached at the Consecration of . . . Henry Compton, Lord Bishop of Oxford . . . December 6. 1674* (London 1675), 4, 8, 19–20, 23–4, 28; Wood, *Life and Times* ii. 412.

[211] PRO PC 2/54, p. 1; Wood, *Athenae* iv. 644; *State Papers collected by Edward, Earl of Clarendon*, ed. R. Scrope and T. Monkhouse (3 vols Oxford 1767–86) iii. 19, 167.

[212] *State Papers*, ed. Scrope and Monkhouse iii. 74, 134; [Joseph Jane], *EIKΩN AKΛAΣTOΣ The Image Unbroaken* (London 1651).

[213] *Judicium et decretum universitatis oxoniensis, latum in convocatione habita julii 21 an. 1683, contra quosdam perniciosos libros et propositiones impias* (Oxford 1683), propositiones 1–3, 5 [*The Judgement and Decree of the University of Oxford past in their Convocation July 21. 1683* (no imprint). It sold for 3d.] OUA register Tb, p. 376. Parsons is cited under his alias, 'Dol[e]man'. Cf Wood's notes in Bodl. Wood 428, item 58.

[214] Edward Hyde, earl of Clarendon, *A Brief View and Survey of the Dangerous and Pernicious Errors to Church and State, in Mr Hobbes's Book, entitled Leviathan* (Oxford at the Theatre 1676), the 'epistle dedicatory' to Charles II, dated from Moulins, 10 May 1673. It was written during the second exile of Clarendon, with the aid of Morley's criticisms, and published after his death by Fell on Sheldon's press. In Oxford the book was 'much commended' even before its publication.

the whigs and their allies, the dissenters, who were the real objects of the exercise. In 1683 they posed the more serious political menace to the *pax Anglicana*. It was their collaboration in seeking to compass the murder of the king and duke of York that had occasioned the university's fears, and it was their immoral principles that fittingly drew most of Oxford's firepower.

One by one, the salient arguments of whiggery were denied: 'civil authority' did not originate in the people; there was no 'mutual compact' between prince and subject; 'tyrants' did not forfeit their right to govern; 'the sovereignty of England' did not reside 'in the three estates' of parliament; the king did not have merely 'a co-ordinate power' with the lords and commons, and could not, in consequence, 'be overruled by the other two';[215] 'possession and strength' did not confer 'a right to govern', any more than 'success in a cause or endeavour proclaims it to be lawful and just';[216] there was no right of resistance, either against 'tyrants', or religious persecutors;[217] 'self-preservation' was not part of the 'fundamental law of nature'; 'the state of nature' was not one of war; Charles I had not been lawfully executed, nor had he been guilty of waging war on his parliament and, thereby, ceased to be king.[218]

If the Oxford decree was intended to be an academic exercise in practical loyalty to the ruling house, even more was it a clerical exercise in exclusive Anglican churchmanship. The political tenets of dissent were anathematized, particularly those of the anti-social Quakers, the violent Fifth Monarchists and the 'trouble-church' Presbyterians. The unlawfulness of oaths was rigorously denied; 'dominion' was not 'founded in grace'; 'the powers of this world' were not 'usurpations upon the prerogative of Jesus Christ'; 'Presbyterian government' was not 'the sceptre of Christ's kingdom'; and 'wicked kings and tyrants' ought not 'to be put to death'.[219] The indictment of such infamous fanatical beliefs was, of course, only to be expected, given the ecclesiastical bias that informed the university's political thinking. To the Oxford mind, moulded as it had been for two decades by the dominant influence of Cavalier Anglicanism, fanaticism constituted the *fons et origo* of whiggery.[220] In the light of the havoc wrought by past sectarian excesses, it was perfectly understandable that the university deprecated wholeheartedly the non-execution of the penal laws against dissenters, and condemned outright the demand for toleration.[221] Seeing beneath the whigs' espousal of pan-protestantism the thinly veiled machinations of faction, the dons did not hesitate to reprove the whigs' latest attempts to promote an association in defence of religion, which—

---

[215] *Judicium et decretum*, propositiones 1–4.

[216] Ibid., propositio 10. This Anglican denial furnished one of the main objections to William of Orange's usurpation of the crown in 1688.

[217] Ibid., propositiones 3, 23, and 8.   [218] Ibid. 7, 11, 26, and 27.

[219] Ibid. 16, 18, 19, 20, and 23.

[220] As early as January 1678 Thomas Sprat, a former fellow of Wadham, and, like South, a canon of Westminster under Dean Dolben, had warned MPs to be alert 'that the same schismatical designs, and antimonarchical principles … may not once more revive': *A Sermon preached before the Honourable House of Commons, January 30th, 1678* (London 1678).

[221] This response to pan-protestant projects lay behind *Judicium et decretum*, propositiones 21 and 22.

revealingly—they bracketed with the Presbyterian solemn league and covenant of 1643.[222]

Historians of party strife have tended to ignore the anti-sectarian content of the decree, when in point of fact it explains the alacrity with which the text was put together, and much of the animus that lay behind it, for Jane and the Oxford censors worked from a familiar, and well prepared, ideological position, which had frequently been expressed in the disputations, lectures, and writings of individual members of the university. What was novel in 1683 was not their findings, but the flamboyance with which they proclaimed them to the outside world. The university authorities had long deplored the deleterious effects which fanaticism had had on the policy of uniformity in the church. Now, the revelation of the Rye House conspiracy persuaded them that it had spilled over into the state, with consequences no less dire. In both areas it seemed that the 'fanatics' were intent on shaking the foundations of government. In their view, whigs and dissenters were not convenient allies who had blundered into co-operation by chance. They were natural blood brothers: antinomians, who had consciously joined forces to subvert the established government of 'sovereign episcopacy' in the church and hereditary monarchy in the state. At base, whiggery was no better than political fanaticism to Oxford's historically minded tories. To many clerics it smacked of the devil.

Yet, there was more to the decree than the public negation of 'damnable doctrines'. It had a positive educational purpose. It affirmed the political content of what had been regularly taught in Oxford since 1660. In the first place, the university's thoughts were for vindicating the honour of almighty God, preserving 'truth in the church', and securing the king as the lord's anointed: concerns which, it felt, would best be served by solemnly restating its conservative creed.[223] In promulgating the decree in a specially summoned convocation, on 21 July 1683, the vice-chancellor, proctors, doctors, and masters set the seal of their approval on 'that most necessary doctrine, which in a manner is the badge and character of the Church of England, of submitting "to every ordinance of man for the lord's sake".' The quotation, it need hardly be said, was taken from holy scripture—from the First Epistle of St Peter.[224] Its inclusion demonstrated the university's desire to impress on a fiercely protestant nation the biblical warranty which the established church had for insisting on the cherished doctrines of passive obedience and non-resistance.[225]

To ensure that the orthodoxy of the university remained inviolate, all professors, tutors, and catechists, who had charge of the education of the young, were commanded to instruct their scholars that 'this submission and obedience' was to be 'clear, absolute, and without exception', to the end that everyone might lead 'a quiet

---

[222] Ibid. 6, 'Licet subditis non modo non consentiente, sed prohibente supremo magistratu in sui et religionis defensionem inire leges, pacisci foedera, coniuratus associationes conflare. *Solennis liga et foedus, nupera associatio.*' For the projected whig association see Haley, *Shaftesbury*, 614–15, 656, 677–8, 680, 687, 692, 694–5, 725.

[223] OUA register Tb, pp. 375–6.   [224] Ibid. 379–80.

[225] J. N. Figgis, *The Divine Right of Kings* (Cambridge 1892, 2nd edn Cambridge 1914), 208 ff.

and peaceable life in all godliness and honesty' under the king, whom God was besought to preserve. In branding the offending propositions 'false, seditious, and impious', the university sought at one and the same time to assert Christian teaching and to uphold the government of church and state, as by law established. It did not doubt that the heterodox notions taught by whigs, dissenters, and papists were 'fitted to deprave good manners, corrupt the minds of unwary men, stir up seditions and tumults, overthrow states and kingdoms, and lead to rebellion, murder of princes, and atheism itself',[226] objectives which cut clean across its own, avowed, moral purposes. Henceforth, members of the university were forbidden to read the books in which the censured propositions appeared, and the books themselves were ordered to be publicly burnt by the university marshal.

Although the heads of house had taken the initiative in deciding to call Oxford's intellectual adversaries to account, they did not have to press a reluctant university into agreeing with them.[227] After Jane had read aloud to convocation the twenty-seven propositions which were to be censured, 'the house … unanimously consented and hum'd' when Vice-Chancellor Lloyd proposed the 'allowance of them': proof that the passage of the decree was not forced through an unwilling assembly by the hebdomadal board, as sometimes was the case in transacting university business. Indeed, some 250 dons—about two thirds of the senior members of the university—had crowded into convocation, keen to demonstrate their solidarity with the Stuart regime. The whigs were noticeably absent; save, that is, for James Parkinson of Lincoln, who, for his brazenness in appearing, came near to being 'hissed out' of the house by his tory colleagues.[228] In the circumstances there were no dissentients from this corporate act of exorcism, aimed at driving the evil spirits of whiggery, dissent, Hobbism, and popery out of the national body politic.

Following the dismissal of convocation a fire was kindled in the schools quadrangle, right outside the Bodleian Library, and 'the pernicious books' consigned to the cleansing flames—to the evident satisfaction of 'scholars of all degrees and qualities' who, standing round the fire, 'gave severall hums' of approval 'whilst they were burning'.[229] Conspicuous among the works that went into the fire were that most reviled of seventeenth-century English books, Thomas Hobbes's *Leviathan*; the Scot George Buchanan's *De jure regni*; the puritan Richard Baxter's *Holy Commonwealth*; the Independent John Owen's *Sermon before the Regicides*; the nonconformist Philip Hunton's *Treatise of Monarchie*; the republican John Milton's 'pieces in defence of the king's murder', especially his *Defensio pro populo anglicano*; the Catholic Robert Bellarmine's *De Conciliis* and *De romano pontifice*; Daniel Whitby's temporizing *Protestant Reconciler*; and that sharp thorn in the flesh of Oxford's clergy, past and present, Samuel Johnson's *Julian the Apostate*. Taken together, they spanned a

[226] OUA register Tb, p. 379.   [227] Bodl. MS Wood d. 19(3), fo 59.
[228] Bodl. MS Bodley 594, fos 53ᵛ–4. Wood specifically noted that John Wallis of St John's and Henry Hill of Corpus were absent: Wood, *Life and Times* iii. 62.
[229] PRO SP 29/429, no. 107, Vice-Chancellor Lloyd to Secretary Jenkins, 22 July 1683; Wood, *Life and Times* iii. 62–3.

century of active opposition to Stuart rule, and indicated the diverse intellectual strands—philosophical, religious, and political—from which that opposition ostensibly derived. It was the Church of England's duty, and therefore the university's privilege, to stand up and contradict such iniquitous and destructive principles.[230]

The university saw to it that its decree received maximum publicity. Latin and English versions of the text were published simultaneously, and a large number of copies printed on Sheldon's press, each carrying the official imprint of the university.[231] A fair copy was dispatched to Ormonde at court on 21 July, with Vice-Chancellor Lloyd's promise that whatever the duke undertook on the Oxonians' behalf would be made good, they being ambitious to approve themselves the true successors of those Cavalier Anglican academics who had stood by the king's father 'in his greatest exigence'.[232] In his dual capacity as chancellor of Oxford and lord steward of the royal household, Ormonde ushered the university delegation into Charles's presence on 24 July.[233] He was delighted to be of assistance in presenting the decree. 'Of all the obligations I have to the famous University of Oxford', he later informed the vice-chancellor, 'there is none I esteem greater than the last, whereby I have been made the instrument of conveying to his majesty her unanimous sentence and judgment against those pernicious positions which have so long infested, and so often involved, these nations in civill, barbarous, and bloody wars and dissensions.' Charles, on having the contents of the decree read out to him, was similarly delighted. He commanded Ormonde to thank 'that learned and ever loyall society' for 'so valuable and seasonable a manifestation of their affection to his person and government', under which, the duke was to assure them, they would 'certainly find all the protection and encouragement' that they deserved and he could give.[234]

Armed with the king's 'gracious acceptance' of the university's outstanding act of homage, Secretary Jenkins arranged for the text of the decree to be printed, a third time, in the eagerly devoured pages of the *London Gazette*,[235] the government newspaper which in the months since the dissolution of the Oxford Parliament he had turned into a formidable organ of tory propaganda.[236] In returning the king's thanks, the secretary of state was confident that, as 'the sound judgment and loyalty of the university' would be of 'great use and for the service of his majesty

---

[230] Milton's and John Goodwin's works, having been 'called in and burnt' by the common hangman in 1660, had also been taken out of the Bodleian Library. Similarly, William Prynne's books against Laud and *juro divino* episcopacy had been removed from the open shelves and 'put in the study in the gallery' of the Bodleian. Bodl. MS Tanner 102, fo 71ᵛ; *The Parliamentary Intelligencer*, no. 37 (3–10 September 1660); Wood, *Life and Times* i. 319.

[231] *Judicium et decretum*, Luttrell, *Brief Relation* i. 271.

[232] The letter was read in convocation, 'quod universorum suffragiis comprobatum erat'. Bodl. MS Carte 69, fo 165, university to Chancellor Ormonde, Convocation House, 21 July 1683.

[233] Wood, *Life and Times* iii. 64.

[234] Bodl. MS Carte 69, fo 162, Chancellor Ormonde to Vice-Chancellor Lloyd, St James's Square, 28 July 1683; OUA register Tb, p. 383.

[235] *London Gazette*, no. 1845 (23–6 July 1683); Dr Williams's Library, MS Morrice P, pp. 372–5; BL MS Sloane 2903, fos 243–7; Cambridge University Library, MS Eee. 12¹²; QCL MS 268, fos 6–11.

[236] Beddard, 'The retreat on toryism', 102–3.

within his realmes', so they would 'redound to the honour of our church, as well as of the university abroad, when the world is informed of this their decree, which will help to wipe off those aspersions that the enemies of our religion and monarchy', meaning the continental Catholics, 'endeavour to fasten upon them'.[237] Overjoyed at Jenkins's enthusiastic signification of the king's approval of their actions, a grateful convocation ordered the secretary's letter to be laid up in the university archives as a lasting record of their service to the crown.[238]

The promulgation of the decree was no empty gesture of defiance on the part of the university, as James Parkinson of Lincoln found to his cost. Previously, the sole member of the university to have suffered in his estate (as distinct from his reputation) for his whig beliefs was Strange Southby of Merton. In August 1679 Southby had been elected probationer fellow of his college, and had subsequently been admitted 'in anno probationis'.[239] He seemed set for an academic career. However, his vociferous advocacy of exclusion during his trial year persuaded the fellows of Merton not to elect him to a perpetual fellowship in January 1681. They cited his 'unpeaceable and otherwise ill behaviour' as the reason for dismissing him: an opaque phrase that barely served to disguise their party political motives for acting as they did.[240] Southby's faults were no secret. They included defaming King Charles I, whom, he claimed, had 'died justly', and 'speaking against the bishops' for having helped to vote down exclusion in the house of lords in November 1680.[241] Despite an appeal to the visitor, and Archbishop Sancroft's plea that every allowance should be made for his extreme youth and regrettable misconduct, the college refused to relent.[242] At a college meeting, held to review Southby's plight, not a single vote was cast in favour of readmitting him to a further period of probation.[243]

There the matter rested until June 1682, when, in response to sworn accusations brought against Southby in congregation, the vice-chancellor formally denied his grace for the MA degree. The denial, a rare enough occurrence in itself, betrayed the increasingly waspish temper of the university. This time his opponents openly acknowledged that his offences were political. He had made it 'his businesse in all companys to speake scandalously of the governement'. In particular, he had presumed to charge both Charles I and Charles II with war guilt, and had attempted to justify 'the murder of the old king', grotesquely maintaining it to be 'a glorious

---

[237] PRO SP 44/68, p. 347, Jenkins to Vice-Chancellor [Lloyd], 26 July 1683.

[238] OUA register of convocation 1683–93, NEP/*subtus*/29, register Bb, p. 1; Bodl. MS Bodley 594, fo 54.

[239] MCR registrum 1567–1731, pp. 534, 539.

[240] Academic insufficiency, probably a side-effect of his activities as 'a green ribband man', was also a charge brought against him. Ibid. 541.

[241] Wood, *Life and Times* ii. 511–12.

[242] For the appeal see Bodl. MS Tanner 339, fo 386. The progress and outcome of his case can be followed in ibid. fos 388, 389, 390, 392, 394.

[243] MCR registrum 1567–1731, p. 541, 30 March 1681; Bodl. MS Tanner 339, fo 394, Warden Clayton to Archbishop Sancroft, Merton, 5 April 1681.

'action' that had been 'done in the face of the nation'.[244] Such reflections on a monarch who was revered by the Church of England as 'a martyr' could not be tolerated.[245] The only wonder is that Southby was allowed to keep his BA degree, and was not stripped of it, as William Prynne had been of his in 1632.[246]

With the decree securely in place from the summer of 1683, the toryism of the rank-and-file dons became rampant. No longer restrained by the fear of outside interference from a militantly whig house of commons, and basking in the plaudits of king and court, they abandoned their tight-lipped silence in the face of repeated political provocation. They were finally free to give vent to their repressed partisan feelings[247] and—infinitely more satisfying—to embark on disciplining their most recalcitrant whig colleague. The Jehu-like ferocity with which the tory fellows of Lincoln drove on their proceedings against their arch-tormentor, James Parkinson, provided the flagging forces of whiggery with an academic martyr and Oxford with a topical *cause célèbre*.[248] A capable scholar and a popular tutor, Parkinson had over the past three years grievously tried the patience of his peers.[249] Encouraged by the fulminations of the decree, they suddenly turned on him as 'a rank stinking whigg', whose opinions, having long played fast and loose with the received wisdom of their church, cried aloud to heaven for reproof.[250]

To begin with, five of the Lincoln fellows lodged a complaint against Parkinson at a college meeting presided over by Rector Marshall. They accused him of 'holding, maintaining, and defendinge' certain 'unwarrantable and seditious principles', and of acting in a manner 'ever esteemed by all honest and well affected persons' to be 'inconsistent with, and destructive of', the government of church and state. Since the university had expressly condemned such dangerous tenets, they argued that it was not possible that 'the same' should 'be permitted to take sanctuary in privat colleges', or that one who 'notoriously abetted any of them' should be 'allowed the opportunity of poysoning others'.[251] Although Marshall heard the complainants out, he did nothing, probably believing that Parkinson's aberrant views fell short of the disciplinary statutes of the college. Thus thwarted, the fellows of Lincoln carried their complaint to Provost Halton of Queen's. In the absence of Vice-Chancellor Lloyd, Halton had, as pro-vice-chancellor, been left in charge of the university.[252]

---

[244] OUA register Be, fo 19ᵛ, congregation, 1 June 1682.

[245] B. S. Stewart, 'The cult of the royal martyr', *Church History* 38 (1969), 175–87; Beddard, 'Wren's mausoleum for Charles I and the cult of the royal martyr', 36–49.

[246] On leaving Merton, Southby migrated to Magdalen Hall, and later fled 'into Holland on the breaking out of the fanatical plot, 1683': Bodl. MS Ballard 46, fo 166ᵛ. Cf W. M. Lamont, *Marginal Prynne 1600–1669* (London 1963), ch. 2; Wood, *Athenae* iii. 844.

[247] See Leopold William Finch's epistle dedicatory cited p. 867, n. 32 above.

[248] The conduct of Parkinson was judged especially culpable, he having been nominated to his fellowship by Bishop Fuller of Lincoln, the college visitor. LCM register II, fos 181ᵛ–2; Wood, *Life and Times* ii. 288.

[249] Bodl. MS Add. d. 105, fo 79, John Wallis to anon., Oxford, 19 September 1683.

[250] Hearne, *Collections* ii. 63.

[251] Bodl. MS Ballard 49, fos 116–17ᵛ, MS Wood d. 18, fo 53ᵛ.

[252] Bodl. MS Wood d. 18, fo 54ᵛ; OUA register Tb, p. 345.

Halton examined both the accusations and Parkinson. On finding the complaints 'proved by the oathes of severall witnesses', he ordered Parkinson to be taken into custody, and did not release him before he had bound him in a bond of £1,000, with two sureties of £500 each, to appear at the approaching assizes on 3 September.[253] One of Parkinson's sureties was the execrated whig townee, Robert Pauling, a notorious conventicler and the intimate of John Locke.[254] With Fell's knowledge and approval, Halton forwarded the sworn affidavits to Secretary Jenkins on 25 August, indicating that the 'crimes' objected against Parkinson could not be taken cognizance of under the existing university statutes.[255] In reply, the secretary of state advised Halton to follow the directions which would be given him by the assize judge. As a hint to the wise, Jenkins observed in passing, that, if, for any reason, the common law did not reach Parkinson's offences, he would none the less deserve expulsion from the university.[256]

In obedience to instructions received from Whitehall, the offender was duly indicted at the Oxford assizes for 'high misdemeanours against the king's crown and dignity'. On 5 September a bill 'for seditious words' was found against him, and Halton was desired, in the king's name, to expel him.[257] It was a request to which the tory pro-vice-chancellor 'readily assented'.[258] The next day the proctorial *bannimus*, proclaiming Parkinson's expulsion, was posted in the public places of the university, and the culprit remitted to the processes of the law.[259] Bishop Fell expressed considerable satisfaction at the outcome, and voiced the sincere hope that the justice done by the university on 'the seditious talker' of Lincoln College, together with the speedy finding of the indictment against him, would satisfy the king. It was also his wish that the example, so clearly and decisively given by Oxford, would 'extend beyond this place'.[260] As Fell realized, the time for half-measures was well and truly passed—though, typically, he did his best to reclaim Parkinson from the error of his ways, rather than abandon him completely.[261]

The most celebrated casualty of the tory reaction in Oxford was, without doubt, John Locke, who forfeited his Christ Church Studentship in 1684 on account of

---

[253] Halton acted on legal advice from Sir Richard Holloway. PRO SP 29/431, no. 6, Halton to Jenkins, Queen's, 29 August 1683.

[254] Fell recommended his removal from the city corporation. Ibid., no. 5. Wood, *Life and Times* ii. 463, 480, 496–7, 541, iii. 72, 145, 155–6, 256, 261, 506–7, iv. 66. For his application for a licence to preach in 1672 see F. Bate, *The Declaration of Indulgence 1672* (London 1908) appx vii, p. xliv.

[255] PRO SP 29/430, nos 164–8, informations sworn against Parkinson by Edward Hopkins, Avery Thompson, Robert Farrow, Thomas Williamson, and William Musson, 23 August 1683.

[256] PRO SP 44/64, p. 83, Jenkins to Provost Halton, Whitehall, 1 September 1683.

[257] Bodl. MS Add. d. 105, fo 79; PRO SP 29/431, no. 112, Philip Burton to Lord Keeper North, Oxford, 6 September 1683.

[258] PRO SP 29/431, no. 113, Halton to Jenkins, Queen's, 6 September 1683.

[259] OUA liber niger procuratorum, fo 102, 'Jacobus Parkinson, artium magister et collegii lincolniensi socius, obverba contumeliosa, malitiose, et seditiose in serenissimum dominum nostrum Carolum secundum prolata, tanquam pacis et publicae tranquillitatis perturbator bannitus. Septembris 6⁰, 1683. Hen. Gandy, procurator senior. Ar. Charlett, procurator junior.'

[260] PRO SP 29/432, no. 20, Fell to Jenkins, 8 September 1683.

[261] Ibid., nos 87, 88, same to same, 22 September [1683]; Parkinson's petition to Charles II for clemency.

his whig affiliations.[262] He had evolved in a quite contrary political direction from that taken by most of his fellow collegians.[263] Having welcomed the Restoration, when he had argued strongly for the royal supremacy and the church's right to impose ceremonies against nonconformist objectors, he had found favour with the restored authorities.[264] He had been appointed a tutor by Dean Fell and had discharged several college offices before turning his back on the Anglican ministry, embracing medicine and entering the household of the earl of Shaftesbury.[265] Under Shaftesbury's influence he developed into a fully fashioned whig, becoming an arch-critic of Filmerian patriarchalism, then all the rage in tory and clerical circles.[266] It was to Locke (and, through him, to John Wallis) that Shaftesbury and his friends had turned in 1681 to find accommodation during the short-lived Oxford Parliament.[267] Despite his careful conduct in Christ Church, where not even the Argus-eyed Fell was able to catch him out, his intimacy with Shaftesbury attracted the fatal attention of the government, which was bent on weeding whigs out of all positions of trust.[268] Even so, it took a direct order from Secretary Sunderland to get Fell to dismiss him from his Studentship in November 1684,[269] by which time he had fled to the safety of the United Provinces.[270]

Locke's expulsion, widely deprecated though it has been by posterity, is all the more understandable when it is recalled that he had only retained his Studentship by virtue of an exercise of the royal prerogative, after refusing to take holy orders.[271] Whatever his later whig inhibitions on the score of over-mighty Stuart kingship, Locke had, like many a liberal after him, taken full advantage of the existing system to obtain Charles II's dispensation from the force of college custom in 1666.[272] The fact that he enjoyed one of the four faculty places reserved at Christ

---

[262] Wood simply states he 'was expell'd for whiggisme': Wood, *Life and Times* iii. 117.

[263] Even so, Locke does not appear to have instilled his vigorous political views into his pupils, John Alford, MP for Midhurst, a mild church-and-state tory, and Sir Charles Berkeley, MP for Gloucester, a lukewarm whig. Henning (ed.), *House of Commons* i. 527, 631 (no notice is taken of Locke's having tutored Berkeley).

[264] Bodl. MSS Locke e. 7, c. 28, fo 1, c. 22, fos 1, 2ᵛ, 3–4, 5 ff.

[265] Ibid., c. 7, fos 212, 214, John Dolben to Locke, Whitehall, 17 May [1661]; CA MS D&C, i. b. 3, pp. 104, 110, 113, 114, 125; H. Kearney, *Scholars and Gentlemen: universities and society in pre-industrial Britain, 1500–1700* (Ithaca 1970), 123–5.

[266] Robert Filmer, *Patriarcha*, ed. P. Laslett (Oxford 1949), introduction.

[267] W. D. Christie, *A Life of Anthony Ashley Cooper, First Earl of Shaftesbury* (2 vols London 1871) ii. 392–401; *The Correspondence of John Locke*, ed. E. S. De Beer (8 vols Oxford 1976–89) ii. 353–5, 357, 360–7, 378, 382.

[268] PRO SP 29/438, nos 77, 82, Fell to Robert, earl of Sunderland, 8 and 16 November 1684.

[269] CL MS 375, item 1, Sunderland to Fell, Whitehall, 11 November 1684; PRO SP 44/57, p. 101.

[270] There, according to the king's envoy, Locke lived 'amongst the worst of our traitors'. C. Price, 'Thomas Chudleigh on John Locke, 1684', *Notes and Queries* cxciv (1949), 519.

[271] PRO SP 44/14, p. 103, Charles II to the dean and chapter of Christ Church, 14 November 1666. *Restoration Oxford*, ed. Beddard iii, no. 1057. Cf Bodl. MS Locke c. 25, fo 11, Locke's draft of a royal dispensation, 14 November 1666.

[272] After the revolution of 1688 Locke, the secularist, favoured parliamentary legislation to exempt fellows and scholars of Oxford and Cambridge colleges from the local statutory obligation to enter Anglican orders: Bodl. MS Locke c. 25, fo 45, endorsed 'Universities, November 1690'.

Church for laymen, as a result of the king's dispensing power, meant, in a period of heightened dynastic loyalty, that his intimacy with Shaftesbury, an absconded traitor, was deemed incompatible with his continued enjoyment of Charles's favour. Although he had not yet published his *Two Treatises of Government*, which were almost certainly drafted as an exclusionist pamphlet,[273] and had wisely removed his papers from Christ Church,[274] he was presumed guilty by association. His flight abroad confirmed the court's opinion of his guilt, so that tories of George Hickes's ilk could only wonder why Fell had 'let the king's bread go to nourish and comfort his majesty's enemies, and the retainers of such great and apparent villains as the late earl of Shaftesbury was'.[275]

Outside Oxford the more avid tories of the Anglican hierarchy ensured that the university's bite was just as effective as its bark by according the decree a status comparable to that enjoyed by the legally enforceable requirements of the church canons and the statute book. Had the majority of the condemned authors still been alive, the authority of the university would undoubtedly have been more widely invoked in the struggle against whiggery and dissent.[276] As it was, it made a significant impact on the clergy. The most eminent of the surviving Anglo-puritan divines, Richard Baxter, made haste to clear himself of the charges of which he stood accused by Oxford's tories.[277] An ejected deacon who, in 1662, had conformed to the established church as a layman, but without renouncing his preaching ministry,[278] Baxter made use of an intermediary to let Fell know that he had long ago retracted his views concerning the co-ordinate powers of the crown in parliament and the political accountability of the monarch.[279] Having fallen foul of his Anglican tory persecutors for persistent conventicling, he was anxious to avoid any further clash with the authorities of church and state.[280] His private representations, while they did not save him from the censure of the university, certainly

---

[273] P. Laslett, 'The English revolution and Locke's *Two Treatises of Government*', *Cambridge Historical Journal* xii (1956), 40–55; R. Ashcroft, *Revolutionary Politics and Locke's* Two Treatises of Government (Princeton 1986), 429–50.

[274] They were removed to James Tyrrell's house at Oakley, near Brill, Buckinghamshire, and to Robert Pauling's house in Oxford: PRO SP 29/428, no. 109; Wood, *Life and Times* iii. 117.

[275] Quoted in Beddard's review of J. Locke, *Epistola de tolerantia*, ed. R. Klibansky and J. W. Gough (Oxford 1968) in *Oriel Record* (1968), 40. Locke used Fell's being overruled by 'positive orders' from Charles II as grounds for his petitioning William III, 'visitor of the said colledg', to restore him in November 1689. CL MS 375, item 3, draft petition.

[276] Owen, the ejected dean of Christ Church, had died the previous month: W. Orme, *Memoirs of the Life, Writings, and Religious Connexions of John Owen* (London 1820, 2nd edn London 1826), 71–2.

[277] London dissenters thought Baxter harshly treated by Oxford, when Grotius, Hooker, and Bilson 'went far beyond' him 'in placing the originall of power in the populacy, and in the doctrine of resistance', and yet had escaped condemnation. Dr Williams's Library, MS Morrice Q, p. 80.

[278] R. Schlatter, *Richard Baxter and Puritan Politics* (New Brunswick 1957), 154; PRO SP 29/421, nos 176, 177.

[279] Dr Williams's Library, Baxter letters IV, fos 61–2; rough draft of a letter which Baxter asked John Humfrey to send to Fell. For Baxter's recantation see PRO SP 29/274, no. 160.

[280] Luttrell, *Brief Relation* i. 230, 237; A. G. Matthews (ed.), *Calamy Revised* (Oxford 1934), 39.

helped to delay the day of reckoning, until the unbridled tory partisanship of James II's reign brought him into king's bench on a charge of treason.[281]

Other younger and more conformable clerics, whose published views conflicted with the findings of the decree, appear to have been initially less intimidated than Baxter. They preferred to brazen matters out—perhaps believing that, as beneficed clergymen, their personal record of conformity would afford them sufficient protection against their censurers. If such was their reasoning, then they were badly mistaken. The very correctness of their behaviour in church, as opposed to the heterodoxy of their publications, made them seem more, not less, dangerous to their superiors, who feared that their ability to mislead churchmen was so much the greater because of their being esteemed orthodox. The cases of two quite different parsons—the one an Oxford doctor of divinity, the other a non-graduate—highlighted the retribution which awaited otherwise respectable clerics who, in presuming to question the existing establishment, broke their canonical oath of obedience by departing from their promise not to endeavour to make changes in church and state. In 1683 the anonymous plea for protestant unity put out by Daniel Whitby, a former fellow of Trinity College and a fervent anti-papalist, raised a storm of protest.[282] His *Protestant Reconciler, humbly pleading for condescention to dissenting brethren* in things indifferent, and, as he thought, 'unnecessary', gave grave offence.[283] His theme was too closely linked in tory minds with the whigs' attempts to improve the lot of protestant dissent not to excite ecclesiastical tempers.[284]

Promptly dubbed 'Whigby' by his adversaries, Whitby's prime offence was held in Oxford to be his adoption of those pleas in favour of 'tenderness and moderation' which the dissenters 'themselvs commonly use';[285] in particular, he had followed them in arrogating to their case the scriptural injunction against offending weaker brethren—an argument which the Anglican authorities had rejected in 1661–2, as evidence of the dissenters' immovable error and remorseless opposition to the Church of England. This, along with his assertion of the unlawfulness of 'impositions' in worship, was unequivocally condemned by the Oxford decree.[286] Cited into the consistory court of Salisbury for publishing a libel, Whitby was forced to recant his errors, to apologize to his superiors, and to engage not to print anything without the approbation of his diocesan or metropolitan: all of which he did publicly before Bishop Ward, the chancellor of the diocese, the cathedral

---

[281] Dr Williams's Library, Baxter letters III, fos 76 ff; Luttrell, *Brief Relation* i. 345, 350; PRO Adm. 77/2, no. 138; F. J. Powicke, *The Reverend Richard Baxter under the Cross 1662–1691* (London 1927), 143 ff.

[282] At Oxford it was quickly fathered on Whitby: BL MS Lansdowne 937, fo 32ᵛ.

[283] *The Protestant Reconciler, humbly pleading for Condescention to Dissenting Brethren, in Things Indifferent and Unnecessary, for the Sake of Peace* (London 1683).

[284] Baxter, an interested party, sought to vindicate Whitby from 'what he is charged with': Dr Williams's Library, Baxter letters IV, fo 62ᵛ.

[285] It was speculated that 'discontent for want of preferment answerable to his expectations' was the underlying motive for Whitby's imprudent performance: BL MS Lansdowne 960, fo 107, Andrew Allam to White Kennett, 29 January 1682/3.

[286] *Judicium et decretum*, propositiones 21 and 22; OUA register Tb, p. 378.

chapter, and an assembly of local clergy, aldermen, and citizens in October 1683.[287] His recantation was quickly communicated to the university, where it greedily 'passed to and fro in manuscript' for everyone to read and gloat over.[288] Even so, the more vehement of his critics—notably the Cantabrigian Bishop Womock of St David's—took some persuading that 'this gentle acquittall' of his was an adequate punishment;[289] and only his subsequent very loyal behaviour got Whitby off a grand jury indictment in September 1685.[290]

Whitby's companion in the lists of heterodoxy, Samuel Bolde, fared less well. He was that recurrent Anglican figure, the clerical traditor, who wilfully betrayed the teaching and discipline of his church, while continuing to pocket its emoluments. As vicar of Shapwick in Dorset, he took the opportunity presented by reading the charitable brief for the relief of the persecuted Huguenots of France to preach against the persecution of domestic dissenters in March 1682. Besides addressing the printed text of his sermon, somewhat provocatively, 'to the consideration of violent and headstrong men', he had the gall to renew the whig MPs' demand for an end to prosecutions on the penal laws, as 'inconvenient and hurtful to the protestant religion'.[291] In response to the outcry that ensued, Bolde aggravated his offences by publishing a further *Plea for Moderation towards Dissenters*, in which he tangentially attacked the stance of the university, by denouncing the 'superfine con-formist' as the greatest enemy of religion, and frontally assaulted its reigning authorities, Hammond, Maurice, and Dodwell, by stricturing their advocacy of the *jus divinum* of episcopacy.[292]

Not content with offering these affronts, Bolde heaped coals of fire on the heads of the dons by commending the 'moderation' of Oxford's black sheep, the latitu-dinarian Bishop Wilkins of Chester, who in the late 1660s had rashly promoted comprehension in the teeth of Sheldon's opposition, and by praising the trouble-some dissenters Baxter and Hickman as 'shining lights in the church of God'.[293] It was all too much for the tory Anglicans to stomach. Although Bolde's publica-tions escaped the notice of the Oxford censors, his fate was harsher than Whitby's. He was brought to heel by a deftly executed pincer exercise, in which his outraged

[287] Dr Williams's Library, MS Morrice P, p. 370; Bodl. MS Tanner 143, fos 253–4ᵛ, 182.

[288] Bodl. MSS Ballard 70, pp. 62–3, 34, fo 18; Dr Williams's Library, MS Morrice P, p. 414.

[289] Bodl. MS Tanner 34, fo 199. In the end Womock confessed himself 'very well satisfied': ibid., fo 226.

[290] Whitby's case may be traced in detail: ibid., fos 133, 141, 182, 199, 226, 240; ibid. 143, fos 117, 153ʳ⁻ᵛ, 223, 232.

[291] Samuel Bolde, *A Sermon Against Persecution. Preached March 26. 1682* (London 1682, 2nd edn London 1682), 26. Barlow commented on the title-page of his copy: 'The execution of our lawes (ecclesiasticall and civil) against nonconformists he miscalls persecution: and railes impotently against all who put those lawes in execution.' Bodl. C. 8 20 Linc., item 17. For the theological exposition of the 'true notion' of persecution, see Hickes, *The True Notion of Persecution Stated*, which upheld the right of church and state to discipline 'heretics'.

[292] Samuel Bolde, *A Plea for Moderation Towards Dissenters; occasioned by the grand-juries presenting the ser-mon against persecution, at the last assizes holden at Sherburn . . . to which is added an answer to the objections com-monly made against that sermon* (London 1682), 42, 16.

[293] Ibid. 7, 35–6.

diocesan, the Oxonian Bishop Gulston of Bristol, co-operated with the Dorsetshire tory gentry to prosecute him in the consistory court and at Sherborne assizes. Condemned to preach three sermons by way of recantation, he was also fined and, when he failed to pay his fine, cast into gaol. Only the demise of his leading prosecutors freed him from further trouble.[294]

By the close of Charles II's reign it was clear that Oxford constituted one of the pillars of the restored monarchy. In the quarter of a century that had elapsed since the Restoration the university had not only regained its place at the heart of the Stuart system of government, but had also demonstrated how effective its counter-revolutionary contribution had been in resettling the realm on the basis of an Anglican constitution that upheld the rule of one king, one faith and one law—the defence of which had led to the formation of the first tory party. When, in the winter of 1685–6, James II embarked on a policy of challenging the concept of a single confessional state, he did much more than loosen the ties of affection which bound the University of Oxford and Church of England to his person. He attacked the principle on which the Restoration settlement rested, and on which much of the vigour of toryism depended. In seeking to free first Catholics, and later dissenters, from the statutory restraints of monopolistic Anglicanism, he injected into the enforced calm of English political life a measure of ecclesiastical disturbance the like of which had not been known since the Great Rebellion. It was a rejection of tory policy with which—long after the unexpected seizure of his throne by William of Orange—Oxford and the Church of England found the very greatest difficulty in coming to terms.

---

[294] Samuel Bolde, *A Sermon Against Persecution . . . now republished; with a brief relation of the prosecutions against the author* (London 1720), 38–48.

19

James II and the Catholic Challenge

R. A. BEDDARD

AT the death of Charles II in 1685 Oxford was solidly Anglican, predominantly high church and imperturbably tory in its religion and politics. Indeed, it remained so well beyond the revolution of 1688, in which the protestant William of Orange forcibly dethroned Charles's successor, the Catholic James II. Yet in the brief interval between the demise of one Stuart king and the deposition of another, the university saw such a challenge to the monopoly of the Church of England and to the academically ordered, religiously uniform, and financially secure way of life which the protestant establishment guaranteed to churchmen, that the political behaviour of the dons, normally submissive, if not actually obsequious to the government of the day, underwent a visible transformation: one which, while insufficient to alter their fundamental loyalty to the house of Stuart and their inherited conservative convictions, was none the less sufficient to push them into otherwise unaccountable acts of defiance against the lord's anointed. Only a few years before, such an extraordinary development would have been unthinkable.[1] There was only one explanation for the sudden upsurge of political discontent and the astounding ideological volte-face which ostensibly accompanied it. It was, of course, the accession to the throne of a powerful and proselytizing Catholic monarch.

Amid the general rejoicing which greeted James II's accession on 6 February 1685, few onlookers could have dreamt that his reign would be so short, or that it would end so violently. In Oxford the ceremonies of the proclamation passed off peacefully.[2] At the first meeting of the privy council in London James promised to follow the example of his brother in showing 'great clemency and tenderness to his people' by endeavouring 'to preserve this government, both in church and state, as it is now by law established'. On the Church of England he set a particular mark of esteem. He acknowledged that its principles were 'for monarchy', and that its members had 'shewed themselves good and loyal subjects'. He therefore promised

---

[1] See R. A. Beddard, 'Tory Oxford', pp. 870–3, 875–902, 905.

[2] Bodl. MS Wood d. 19, pt 3, fos 62–3ᵛ; BL MS Lansdowne 937, fo 64ᵛ, White Kennett's account; Wood, *Life and Times* iii. 127–9; Narcissus Luttrell, *A Brief Historical Relation of State Affairs from September 1678 to April 1714* (6 vols Oxford 1857) i. 329; *London Gazette*, no. 2008 (12–16 February 1685).

to take care 'to defend and support it'.[3] To give substance to his words, he retained the services of his brother's ministers in government office. Foremost among them were his former brothers-in-law, the earls of Clarendon and Rochester, whose long and close association with the University of Oxford had helped to identify them as the leaders of the high church wing of the Church of England.[4] With James's confirmation of tory hegemony the whigs became the most despicable of men.[5]

Gratified by the king's words of favour, the university hastened to congratulate him on his accession. Its loyal address was penned by the regius professor of divinity, William Jane, canon of Christ Church and the framer of the Oxford decree of 1683. In it the vice-chancellor, doctors, and masters protested that they would 'never swerve from the principles of our institution in this place, and our religion by law established in the Church of England', which indispensably bound them 'to bear all faith and true obedience to our sovereign without any restrictions or limitations'.[6] In pledging their undying duty the dons had no inkling that the king would renege on his word, or that they would repent of their promises.

On 27 February the university delegates carried the address to court. Dressed in mourning gowns, and on their knees, they presented their compliments. These James received with obvious pleasure. He told them that 'he was very sensible of the loyaltie of the universitie towards him; and that, as his ancestors had been gratious and kind to them, so he himself would not be backward in it'. Consonant with that part of his accession speech in which he had stressed that he would 'never invade any man's property', he assured them that 'he would endeavour to preserve their liberties and privileges to the utmost'.[7] The vice-chancellor then presented the king with a modest volume of academic verse, dedicated to the memory of his deceased brother.[8] Before returning home the delegates were warned by Lord Chief Justice Jeffreys not to employ the keeper of the university archives, John Wallis, a known whig sympathizer, in 'any trial ... least their cause faire the wors'.[9] A few weeks later, on 2 May, the king rewarded Jane for his services in promoting the

[3] PRO PC 2/71, fos 6ʳ⁻ᵛ, 6 February 1685. The speech was 'made publique' at the request of the privy council, led by the earl of Rochester, and confirmed by the king in parliament on 22 May. R. A. Beddard, 'The church of Salisbury and the accession of James II', *Wiltshire Archaeological Magazine* 67 (1972), 132–3; *London Gazette*, no. 2006 (5–9 February 1685); *The Diary of John Evelyn*, ed. E. S. De Beer (6 vols Oxford 1955) iv. 442–3.

[4] PRO PC 2/71, fos 6, 7, SP 44/56, p. 165, SP 44/69, p. 127; R. Steele, *Tudor and Stuart Proclamations 1485–1714* (2 vols Oxford 1910), nos 3772–3, Whitehall, 6 February 1685.

[5] Bodl. MS Wood d. 19, pt 3, fo 64ᵛ; Wood, *Life and Times* iii. 129–30.

[6] OUA register of convocation 1683–93, NEP/subtus/29, register Bb, pp. 74–5, 21 February 1685; Luttrell, *Brief Relation* i. 333. For the address of Bishop Fell, the chapter of Christ Church and the clergy of Oxford diocese see *London Gazette*, no. 2027 (20–3 April 1685).

[7] Wood, *Life and Times* iii. 133.

[8] *Pietas universitatis oxoniensis in obitum augustissimi et desideratissimi regis Caroli secundi* (Oxford at the Theatre 1685); *The Flemings in Oxford* ii. 135.

[9] Wood, *Life and Times* iii. 133; PRO PC 2/71, fo 74ᵛ. For Wallis's whig sympathies and connections see Bodl. MS Add. d. 105, fos 75, 79, Oxford, 2 October 1682 and 19 September 1683; Bodl. MS Rawlinson letters 53, fos 101, 104; R. A. Beddard, 'Tory Oxford', pp. 868, 896, n. 228, 901 above.

loyalist cause by appointing him dean of Gloucester.[10] There could scarcely have been a more auspicious start to the new reign. King and university seemed to be in perfect political agreement.

In March a whig-inspired attempt to disrupt the accord by sending an anonymous letter to Oxford, addressed to Fell 'by unknown hands', completely backfired. 'Full of canting', and seeking to possess the bishop with the thought that his beloved university 'should be all overwhelm'd with popery', the letter simply confirmed the adverse view which the tories had formed of the whigs as desperate men, 'who live and get their ends by lying'.[11] Even the startling news that Charles II had died a professed papist, which also reached Oxford in March (this time in the form of an anonymous printed tract), did nothing to damage the trust that the university reposed in James's word. As Anthony Wood wrote on his copy, 'few believed it'.[12]

Quite what could be achieved under Anglican tory auspices, when court and country were in agreement, was impressively shown by the results of the general election. Locally, the court candidates made a clean sweep of the city and county as well as of the university.[13] It was part of a tory landslide throughout England and Wales—a dramatic reversal of party fortunes, when set against the growing whig majorities of the last three parliaments.[14] Out of Oxfordshire's nine parliamentary seats five were uncontested in 1685.[15] On 17 March Vice-Chancellor John Lloyd nominated the old members, Secretary Jenkins and Charles Perrot, to serve as university burgesses for a third term. They were chosen without opposition. The doctors and regent masters were well satisfied with their conduct in having opposed exclusion.[16] The nation-wide eclipse of the whig interest ensured that James would meet an Anglican tory parliament at Westminster on 19 May.[17]

Happy to have contributed its talent to the treasury of electoral merit at court, the university went on to celebrate the coronation of James and Mary of Modena, which it did with immense gusto on St George's day. Proceedings began in the morning with the inevitable sermon at St Mary's, at which John Hall, the Lady Margaret professor of divinity and master of Pembroke, preached to a packed

[10] PRO SP 44/57, p. 109, James II's warrant to the clerk of the signet; BL MSS Lansdowne 937, fo 66, 987, fo 185.

[11] Wood, *Life and Times* iii. 134; BL Add. MS 29,582, fo 219, Fell to Christopher, Viscount Hatton, 23 June [1685].

[12] *A True Relation of the Late King's Death* (n.d.). For Anthony Wood's annotated copy, see Bodl. Wood 236, item 4. Luttrell, *Brief Relation* i. 332, 365.

[13] BL Add. MS 29,582, fos 231, 235, 227, Fell to Hatton, 14 and 27 February, 8 March [1685].

[14] R. A. Beddard, 'The retreat on Toryism', *Wiltshire Archaeological Magazine* 73 (1980), 81–106.

[15] B. D. Henning (ed.), *The House of Commons 1660–1690* (3 vols London 1983) i. 356–62.

[16] Ormonde had intervened to recommend his grandson, Ossory, but he was taken off by a writ of summons to the house of lords: BL Add. MS 29,582, fos 239, 241, Fell to Hatton [Oxford], 15 and 21 March [1685]. Bodl. MS Bodley 594, fo 57. OUA register Bb, pp. 75–7, 17 March 1685; *LJ* xiv. 3–4. M. B. Rex, *University Representation in England 1604–90* (London 1954), 296.

[17] BL Add. MS 29,582, fos 227, 241, Fell to Hatton [Oxford], 8 and 21 March [1685]; *Memoirs of Sir John Reresby*, ed. A. Browning (Glasgow 1936), 367; R. H. George, 'Parliamentary elections and electioneering in 1685', *TRHS* 4th ser. xix (1936), 167–95.

congregation. From a notorious low churchman, whose old-fashioned Calvinism had undeservedly earned him the reputation of 'a Presbyterian', it was only to be expected that the occasion would elicit a 'lukewarm, trimming sermon'.[18] Did one not know that the vice-chancellor and heads were above such petty spites, it might almost be supposed that their choice of Hall was dictated by a wish to embarrass him, for he had too long been a thorn in the flesh of the high church party.[19] Yet, for all his mealy-mouthedness, Hall's sermon was not without a defiantly protestant flourish. Having preached to the converted at length, imploring them 'not to hearken in the least after popery', he became characteristically contentious. He so far forgot his manners, as 'to pray for the king that God would open his eyes to see the light' of the reformation, regardless of the fact that James had already seen 'the light', and, finding it repellent, had firmly turned his back on it.[20]

Whatever the awkwardness of the moment, Hall's words were soon forgotten amid the 'great extraordinaries in eating and drinking' that followed in each college.[21] After these apolaustic labours slumber might have seemed desirable, even irresistible. But authority ruled otherwise. Rest was denied to all by the afternoon bell that summoned the university to a solemn convocation.[22] Arrayed in their formalities according to degree, and seated in the Sheldonian Theatre according to rank, the academics were regaled with a panegyric from Public Orator Wyatt, delivered *memoriter*. He was succeeded by two bachelors and nine gentlemen-commoners. After both King James and Queen Mary had been fulsomely saluted *in absentia*, England's patron saint, the coronation rite, the crown imperial, royal power, and 'the Britannic Neptune' were all apostrophized. In between the recitations the theatre resounded with festive music, vocal and instrumental.[23] It was a quintessentially English celebration of the day—well planned, patriotic, and unashamedly domestic.

The university having done its duty from one o'clock 'till near 6 in the evening', the dons and students dispersed to their college bonfires, around which, on bended knee, they drank the renewed health of the king and royal family.[24] The scene at Merton must stand for many others, and makes plain the consciously partisan nature of Oxford's rejoicing. At night Merton tower, high against the southern sky, was ablaze with light from two dozen 'lyncks' burning on the battlements; while below, at the fireside, the sub-warden and fellows, flown with wine and replete with loyalty, officiously consigned to the flames the relics of defeated whiggery. 'The

---

[18] Wood, *Life and Times* iii. 137, 140–1; Bodl: Wood 276A, nos ccclxxiii, ccclxxviii; BL MS Lansdowne 397, fo 65ᵛ.

[19] Ever since the days of Sheldon and Clarendon, Hall had attracted criticism and distrust: see *Restoration Oxford, 1660–1667*, ed. R. A. Beddard (3 vols OHS forthcoming) ii, no. 864.

[20] Wood, *Life and Times* iii. 141.

[21] Bodl. MS Wood f. 45, fo 240, Edward Worseley to Andrew Allam, 27 April 1685; BL MS Lansdowne 397, fo 65ᵛ.

[22] OUA register Bb, p. 81, 23 April 1685; Bodl. Wood 276A, no. ccclxxiii.

[23] *Comitia habita in universitate oxoniensi Ap. 23. an. 1685. Die inaugurationis augustissimi principis Jacobi II. Et gratiosissimae reginae Mariae* (Oxford at the Theatre 1685); Bodl. Wood 276A, no. ccccviii.

[24] Bodl. MS Wood f. 45, fo 240, Worseley to Allam, 27 April 1685; Bodl. MS Wood d. 19, pt 3, fo 67ᵛ.

exclusion bill, black box, and the first and second parts of *The Character of a Popish Successor*—a savage whig attack on James's person and religion—were burnt to the repeated huzzas of the bystanders.[25] Tory jubilation continued unabated for weeks on end.

It was dispelled by the announcement that Charles II's illegitimate son James Scott, the protestant duke of Monmouth, had on 11 June landed at Lyme in Dorset, intent on leading a protestant rebellion against his Catholic uncle.[26] Yet, it was Monmouth's pretensions to the crown that had attracted the scorn of the loyal Mertonians on 23 April in the ritualistic burning of the 'black box'—the legendary box in which, it was claimed, had been found the marriage lines of Charles II and the duke's mother, Lucy Walter.[27] Despite King Charles's denial of the claim before the privy council and nation in 1680, the belief that such a marriage had taken place persisted among the more ill-disposed whigs and sectaries.[28] It eventually led the duke to take the fatal step of proclaiming himself king at Taunton market cross on 20 June.[29] The reaction of the university and its courtly patrons to 'the alarums of a rebellious bastard, that made an attempt to bring war and desolation upon our land, to overturn our laws, to take away our liberties, and to destroy our king', was as swift as it was hostile. They prepared to do battle on behalf of James II.[30]

Within days of Monmouth's landing the king's recruiting officer arrived in Oxford to beat for volunteers.[31] As one of the counties lying between London and the rebels, the strategic importance of Oxfordshire was instantly recognized. On 16 June the lord lieutenant, the earl of Abingdon, was authorized to raise the militia horse and put the foot on general alert.[32] Three days later the king ordered the horse to advance to Reading. Abingdon remained behind, to take care of the city

---

[25] Wood, *Life and Times* iii. 141. For the 'illuminations' at University College, see Bodl. MS Wood f. 45, fo 240; BL MS Lansdowne 937, fos 65ᵛ–6.

[26] BL MS Harleian 6845, fos 251–5; PRO Adm. 77/2 no. 141, newsletter, 13 June 1685; Bodl. MS Wood d. 19, pt 3, fo 73; C. Chenevix Trench, *The Western Rising* (London 1969), 11–16; P. Earle, *Monmouth's Rebels* (London 1977), 16–17; R. Clifton, *The Last Popular Rebellion* (London 1984), 158–60.

[27] For the 'black box' myth, see Robert Ferguson, *Letter to a Person of Honour concerning the Black Box* (London 1680); J. R. Jones, *The First Whigs* (London 1961), 69–70, 80, 82, 126; K. H. D. Haley, *The First Earl of Shaftesbury* (Oxford 1968), 464, 485, 574–5, 577, 579.

[28] PRO PC 2/69, fos 4ᵣ–ᵛ; *His Majesties Declaration to all his Loving Subjects, 2 June 1680*; R. A. Beddard, 'William Sancroft as archbishop of Canterbury, 1677–1691' (Oxford D. Phil. thesis 1965), 87–9.

[29] BL MS Lansdowne 1152, fos 258–61; Steele, *Tudor and Stuart Proclamations*, no. 3793; *Correspondence of the Family of Hatton . . . 1601–1704*, ed. E. M. Thompson (2 vols Camden Soc. new ser. xxii, xxiii 1878) ii. 56, Fell to Hatton [25 June 1685].

[30] *The Correspondence of Henry Hyde, Earl of Clarendon*, ed. J. S. Clarke (2 vols London 1816) i. 175, earl of Rochester's meditations on the death of his daughter, Anne, Lady Ossory, 25 January 1686.

[31] Wood, *Life and Times* iii. 145, 16 June 1685. The town council raised two independent companies of foot soldiers. *Oxford Council Acts, 1665–1701*, ed. M. G. Hobson (OHS new ser. x 1939), 173, order of 26 June 1685.

[32] PRO SP 31/2, p. 7, memorandum of James II's order to the earl of Abingdon, 16 June [1685]. For the measures taken by Abingdon's deputy lieutenants see Bodl. MS top. Oxon. c. 325, fos 43, 55.

and county.[33] To encourage the flow of recruits he promised that volunteers from his own tenantry should have 'their copyholds and leases renewed gratis', if they fell in battle; and, rather than that the king's service should suffer, he pledged his own credit to buy more horses for the militia.[34]

On 20 June the lord lieutenant was commanded to seize all disaffected and suspicious persons that might attempt to join Monmouth's growing army, or seek to comfort the king's enemies by stirring up insurrection. He was particularly instructed to arrest those perennial disturbers of the king's peace, the nonconformist ministers and former rebels against Charles I and II, but few could be found.[35] He had better success when it came to rounding up the leading local exclusionists, whom he unhesitatingly denounced as 'the worst men about the country'.[36] Soon the gaol was overcrowded with whigs and sectaries.[37] These arrests, a precaution which was taken in other counties, did much to stop the contagion of rebellion from spreading among the discontented whig party.[38]

Fearful that the departure of the militia might expose the city to marauding rebel forces, Bishop Fell proposed that the university should take measures to defend itself. It was he, not the vice-chancellor, who took the initiative.[39] With Abingdon's blessing the proposal was put before the king, who approved. To make the necessary arrangements, Fell turned to his old ally at court, the earl of Clarendon, recently promoted to the privy seal. Not only did Clarendon have first-hand knowledge of Oxford and Oxfordshire, he was ideally placed to prosecute university business, both with the king, his brother-in-law, and with the chancellor of Oxford, the septuagenarian duke of Ormonde, whose grandson had married his niece.[40] In deference to Abingdon's office, Fell suggested that his heir, Montagu Bertie, Lord Norreys, should take command of the university forces, along with those scholars whom the earl should approve.[41] That his suggestion sprang from friendship rather than from practical considerations is made clear by the fact that Lord Norreys, then a Student at Christ Church, was a 12-year-old child.[42] Fell's proposal was to raise two troops of horse and six companies of foot, requiring in all some 800 or more

[33] PRO SP 31/2, p. 16, SP 44/56, p. 231, SP 44/164, p. 204, James II to Abingdon, 19 June 1685; Bodl. MS top. Oxon. c. 325, fo 46.

[34] *Clarendon Correspondence*, ed. Clarke i. 135–6, 138, Abingdon to Clarendon, Oxford, 21 and 27 June [1685].

[35] PRO SP 31/2, p. 18, SP 44/164, pp. 210–11, memorandum, 20 June.

[36] Bodl. MS top. Oxon. c. 325, fos 46, 46ᵛ, Abingdon to [Clarendon], and to Secretary Sunderland, Oxford, 21 June 1685 (drafts). *Clarendon Correspondence*, ed. Clarke i. 135, 136.

[37] *Clarendon Correspondence*, ed. Clarke i. 140, Abingdon to Clarendon, Oxford, 29 June 1685; Bodl. MS top. Oxon. c. 325, fo 57, Christian Pauling to Robert Mayot, Oxford, 28 June [1685].

[38] For the national round-up of known suspects, see PRO SP 31/2, p. 18, SP 44/164, pp. 210–11, SP 44/56, p. 248, SP 44/336, p. 147.

[39] Bodl. MS top. Oxon. c. 325, fo 41, Fell to Abingdon [Oxford], 16 June [1685]; *Clarendon Correspondence*, ed. Clarke i. 132, Fell to Clarendon, 20 June 1685.

[40] For Ormonde's avowal of his enduring friendship with Rochester see *Clarendon Correspondence*, ed. Clarke i. 106–7, Dublin, 28 January 1685.

[41] Ibid. i. 133, Fell to Clarendon, 20 June 1685.

[42] Bodl. MS top. Oxon. c. 325, fo 41, Fell to Abingdon [Oxford], 16 June [1685]; Wood, *Athenae* i, p. ciii; Wood, *Life and Times* iii. 59, 148–9, 152.

scholars—a significantly large proportion of the graduate and undergraduate body. A loyalist to the core, he was not a man to do things by halves when it came to upholding 'the old Cavalier interest'.[43]

Solicitous as ever to preserve the jurisdiction of the university, Fell requested that commissions given to its members should come 'immediately from the king', as they had done from Charles I, and not from the lord lieutenant. Besides obtaining this favour from James, Clarendon kept Ormonde informed of the university's every move.[44] On 22 June the chancellor agreed to put off the Act 'till some fitter time', lest a spate of visitors should impede the progress of the king's affairs.[45] On the same day convocation appointed delegates to raise 'a regiment of scholars, and a troop of horse, to secure the universitie and city of Oxon'. The local shortage of horses ruled out the formation of a second troop of cavalry, as Fell had proposed.[46] The delegates included some of the university's most prominent tories: dons such as the respected Jonathan Edwards of Jesus, who had preached a loyal sermon before the whig house of commons at Oxford in 1681;[47] John Massey of Merton, who had just laid down the senior proctorship;[48] and Henry Gandy of Oriel, a fierce opponent of dissent.[49] Within a week they had effectively mobilized the university.

Manpower posed no problems, for there was a rush of adolescent volunteers to fight for the king—much to the consternation of distant parents, who feared, not unreasonably, for the safety of their sons. The supply of arms and ammunition was a different matter, and gave cause for concern. The vice-chancellor and mayor found on inspection that there were 'not above sixe score arms in the hands of both corporations'.[50] Again, it was Fell who came to the rescue. He begged Clarendon, at court, to urge that supplies be sent from the king's stores at Windsor.[51]

By 26 June Lord Norreys's troop had mustered 'above 120' scholars, drawn mostly from Christ Church; while the much-needed troop of horse had enlisted 'about eighty', and expected 'to make them an 100' shortly.[52] By the 27th, the latter was sufficiently well organized to provide a flying detachment of some forty horse to conduct arms from Windsor, under the command of the chancellor of the

[43] *Clarendon Correspondence*, ed. Clarke i. 134, Abingdon to Clarendon, Oxford, 20 June 1685; BL Add. MS 29,582, fos 280, 219, Fell to Hatton, 28 July, 23 June [1685].

[44] *Clarendon Correspondence*, ed. Clarke i. 133, Fell to Clarendon, 20 June 1685.

[45] OUA register Bb, p. 98, Chancellor Ormonde to the university, St James's Square, 22 June 1685; Bodl. MS Bodley 594, fo 57.

[46] OUA register Bb, p. 96, convocation, 22 June 1685. [47] Wood, *Life and Times* iii. 531.

[48] OUA register Bb, pp. 14–15, 45, 82; UCA registrum I, fo 53.

[49] Gandy, also a former proctor, went on to become a non-juror. Wood, *Life and Times* iii. 44, 55, 92, 143, 384–5, 490; G. C. Richards and C. L. Shadwell, *The Provosts and Fellows of Oriel College* (Oxford 1922), 116; J. H. Overton, *The Non-Jurors* (London 1902), 147–52; H. Broxap, *The Later Non-Jurors* (Cambridge 1924), 190–1.

[50] Bodl. MS top. Oxon. c. 325, fo 41, Fell to Abingdon [Oxford], 16 June [1685]. Some parents called their sons home 'least they should beare armes'. Wood, *Life and Times* iii. 156.

[51] *Clarendon Correspondence*, ed. Clarke i. 147, Fell to Clarendon, 14 July 1685.

[52] Bodl. MS top. Oxon. c. 325, fo 49, Abingdon to Clarendon [Oxford, 26 June 1685].

diocese.[53] Clarendon's interposition produced an order from the king to the master of the ordnance, Lord Dartmouth, to issue arms, matchlock muskets, bandoliers, pikes, pistols, and holsters.[54] Soon Abingdon was able to distribute 'the six hundred university arms'. Even then the earl did not relax, but pressed the government to greater efforts, telling Clarendon that he confidently believed 'we shall raise eight hundred or a thousand, if we can get more arms'.[55] In spite of their endeavours there was still a worrying shortage of match.[56]

By 29 June five of the six foot companies were fully operational. They were properly officered, each company having a captain, lieutenant, and cornet, and properly equipped with arms and ammunition. Commissioned under their own hastily improvised colours, they were already regularly exercising.[57] For instance, that captained by Leopold William Finch, an avid Christ Church tory, was drilled twice a day 'in feats of arms' in the quadrangle of All Souls, where he had recently become a fellow.[58] The others exercised separately about the university—on New College bowling green, in Peckwater, and in the quadrangles and groves of Magdalen and Trinity. Only that based on St John's lagged behind the rest.[59] Meanwhile the university horse was put through its paces by both the lord lieutenant and Colonel John Peacocke.[60]

As it transpired, the university forces were not deployed until after Monmouth's defeat at Sedgemoor on 6 July. It was in the aftermath of the rout, while Oxford celebrated the victory with yet more bonfires, that Lord Abingdon called out his academic reserves. Their assignment was to stay the eastward flight of fugitives from the south-west. Under the lord lieutenant's personal command the university horse scoured the Thames valley about Dorchester and Abingdon, and westwards along the Vale of the White Horse to Faringdon. By the 10th it was reckoned safe to lift the blockade.[61] Not wishing to burden the county with needless expense, James ordered the Oxfordshire militia to stand down on the 9th.[62] The bishop

---

[53] Bodl. MS top. Oxon. c. 325, fos 41, 53; BL Add. MS 15,892, fo 226; *Clarendon Correspondence*, ed. Clarke i. 138, 139, Abingdon to Clarendon, Oxford, 27 June, Fell to Clarendon, 27 June [1685].

[54] PRO SP 44/336, p. 145, warrant to Lord Dartmouth, master general of the ordnance, 25 June 1685.

[55] *Clarendon Correspondence*, ed. Clarke i. 140, Abingdon to Clarendon, Oxford, 29 June 1685.

[56] Ibid. i. 147, Fell to Clarendon, 14 July 1685.   [57] Wood, *Life and Times* iii. 146–51.

[58] Finch had merited James's favour 'for some passages that gave offence elsewhere', which he had written in his preface to an edition of *Cornelius Nepos*, reflecting on sectarian fanaticism and the exclusionist parliaments. Bodl. MS Eng. hist. c. 6, fo 122, Arthur Charlett to [George Hickes?], Oxford, 19 January 1686/7; ASA, registrum II, fo 57. His election as fellow had given rise to controversy—see Bodl. MS Tanner 36, fos 182, 184, Archbishop Sancroft to Lord Nottingham, Lambeth House, 2 December 1682, Nottingham to Sancroft, 2 December 1682.

[59] Ormonde made Finch's 'readinesse to serve his majestie' the main reason for recommending his admission as MA in the next Act: OUA register Bb, p. 115, Ormonde to the university, St James's Square, 5 December 1685; Wood, *Life and Times* iii. 146.

[60] For Peacocke of Cumnor, Berkshire, see Bodl. MS top. Oxon. c. 325, fo 63, MS Eng. hist. b. 212, fo 13; *Restoration Oxford*, ed. Beddard i, no. 15 (and n. 16).

[61] PRO SP 31/2, pp. 57–8, Sunderland to Abingdon, Whitehall, 7 July 1685; HMC *Fifteenth Report*, appx, pt 2, pp. 27, 71; Wood, *Life and Times* iii. 151.

[62] PRO SP 31/2, p. 60, James II to Abingdon, Whitehall, 9 July 1685; HMC *Twelfth Report*, appx vii, p. 197, Henry Fleming to Sir Daniel Fleming, 15 July 1685.

and vice-chancellor hourly expected the dimission of their forces, but no order came.[63]

In the interval there was much socializing. On the 20th Lord Abingdon invited the troop of horse to dine with him at Rycote. It was a merry occasion, from which they 'came home well fuz'd'.[64] On the 21st James dismissed the scholars from further military duties, though not before commanding Secretary Sunderland to let the vice-chancellor know that he was 'very well satisfied' with the zeal they had shown for his service.[65] Vice-Chancellor Lloyd received his thanks more substantially, in March 1686, when James nominated him to the see of St David's.[66] With the excitements of war fast receding, Oxford once again became 'mighty quiet'.[67]

In retrospect, Monmouth's rebellion marked a watershed in the unfolding of James II's domestic policies, and in the way in which his protestant subjects viewed his motives and objectives. It convinced the king of his vulnerability for, though savagely quelled, the rebellion had exposed his military weakness 'against false titles and fanaticks'. His army had been too small and scattered to be instantly effective against invasion, and the militia had been too antiquated and fumbling to defend him against revolt. He therefore resolved to keep his newly raised regiments (thereby doubling the size of the army to just under 19,000), and to retain the services of those Catholic officers (fewer than a hundred) that he had commissioned during the emergency.

His decision to maintain a standing army was fraught with political danger. Worse still, his retention of 'popish officers' contravened the provisions of the test act: an action that was judged provocative by legally minded civilian protestants. It added religious disquiet and legal grievance to growing political distrust within the protestant establishment. At Oxford Anthony Wood sensed the danger, and strongly hinted that there would be trouble when James's 'loyal parliament' reassembled in November 1685. During the long vacation he heard that 'some sober men' of the Church of England, as well as dissenters generally, were already saying that the standing army was 'to be kept in pay ... to bring in popery and arbitrary government'.[68] Wood's hint at trouble in store was amply borne out by

---

[63] *Hatton Correspondence*, ed. Thompson ii. 58–9, Fell to Hatton [Oxford], 12 July [1685]; Wood, *Life and Times* iii. 152; OUA register Bb, p. 96.

[64] Wood, *Life and Times* iii. 152; C. Oman, *All Souls College* (London 1891), 227.

[65] PRO SP 31/2, p. 71, Secretary Sunderland to Vice-Chancellor Lloyd, 21 July 1685.

[66] Ibid., SP 44/53, p. 188, James II to the clerk of the signet attending, 19 March 1686. Lloyd was consecrated on 17 October 1686, but scarcely lived to enjoy his bishopric. LPL Sancroft register I, pp. 148–56; PRO SP 44/53, pp. 188, 198, 480, SP 44/57, pp. 147, 164.

[67] *The Flemings in Oxford* ii. 138, Henry Fleming to Sir Daniel Fleming, Oxford, 15 July; *Clarendon Correspondence*, ed. Clarke i. 147, Fell to Clarendon, 14 July; *Hatton Correspondence*, ed. Thompson ii. 58–9, Fell to Hatton, 28 June [1685].

[68] Humphrey Prideaux of Christ Church remarked that after the routing of rebellion 'we have now got a standeing army, a thing the nation hath long been jealous of; but I hope ye king will noe otherwise use it then to secure our peace'. *Letters of Humphrey Prideaux ... to John Ellis ... 1674–1722*, ed. E. M. Thompson (Camden Soc. new ser. xv 1875), 142–3, Oxford, 9 July 1685; Wood, *Life and Times* iii. 154, 157; *Diary of John Evelyn*, ed. De Beer iv. 488–9.

events. The second session of James's one and only parliament proved as troublesome as the first session had been trouble-free. The bone of contention was popery. The tories denounced James's employment of Catholics. The opposition began in the lower chamber and spread to the lords where, notwithstanding James's presence in the house, it reached ugly proportions. The Anglican bishops, who were fully prepared for a showdown, joined in the lords' outright condemnation of the king's Catholicizing stance. Bishop Compton acted as their spokesman.[69] He took his stand on the test acts, as the legal defences of protestantism. Any attempts to set aside the sacramental test for office would, he argued, endanger 'the whole civil and religious constitution of the realm'.[70]

Confronted by his erstwhile allies, who were adamant in rejecting even a modicum of relief for Catholics of proven loyalty, James saw that it was time to try to do without them. Unless he did something for his co-religionists, it was clear that they would be kept in the position of second-class citizens, and that was to him intolerable. On 20 November he prorogued parliament 'to the amazement of all people'.[71] Having already dismissed the marquess of Halifax from court,[72] he removed Bishop Compton from the privy council and from his post as dean of the chapel royal in December.[73] The university bore a part in his disgrace in that, after the deaths of Archbishop Dolben of York in April and Fell in July 1686, Compton was the most prominent Oxonian in the protestant episcopate, and, as such, was owned by many of Oxford's leading dons as their greatest patron.[74] Without James's radical reappraisal of his God-given duty as a Catholic monarch to aid his Catholic subjects, and his galling disappointment with the Anglican tory parliament, the Catholic challenge to the protestant establishment would never have materialized at Oxford (or, for that matter, in any other part of the kingdom) in the way that it did.[75] Denied the preferred, parliamentary, statutory means of attaining his aims, James relied more and more on his extra-parliamentary prerogative powers as king to accomplish what he wanted. These powers he had already used to benefit his co-religionists. On 27 February he had put a stop to prosecu-

---

[69] Beddard, 'Sancroft', 132–6; *The Autobiography of Sir John Bramston*, ed. Lord Braybrooke (Camden Soc. xxxii 1845), 217; *Memoirs of Sir John Reresby*, ed. Browning, 395–6.

[70] For Compton's 'watchfulness for the security of the Church of England', see *The Life of . . . Dr. Henry Compton Late Lord Bishop of London* (London n.d.), 15–16.

[71] *CJ* ix. 761; *LJ* xiv. 88; Wood, *Life and Times* iii. 170.

[72] H. C. Foxcroft, *The Life and Letters of . . . George Savile . . . First Marquis of Halifax* (2 vols London 1898) i. 448–51; PRO SP 8/3, no. 159, SP 31/1, no. 134.

[73] PRO PC 2/71, fo 93, Whitehall, 23 December 1685. Bishop Crew of Durham was admitted, as dean of chapel, to the privy council on 8 January 1686: ibid., fo 95. Bodl. MS Ballard 12, fo 15, [Dr George Hickes] to Arthur Charlett, 15 November 1685; Luttrell, *Brief Relation* i. 368; HMC *Twelfth Report*, appx vii, p. 198, Sir Christopher Musgrave to Sir Daniel Fleming, 26 December 1685.

[74] Although Compton had matriculated at Queen's, Oxford (1654), and had taken his MA (1661) at Cambridge (incorporated at Oxford 1666), he had become identified with Christ Church, first as a canon (1669) and subsequently as bishop of Oxford (1674–5). *The Life of . . . Dr. Henry Compton*, 2–4. OUA register of congregation 1659–69, NEP/*supra*/18, register Qb, fo 90ᵛ; CA DC i. b. 3, pp. 188–96, D. P. i. a. 2 (Fell's autograph matricula), *sub* 7 April 1677.

[75] R. A. Beddard, *A Kingdom without a King* (Oxford 1988), 14–15.

tions on the recusancy statutes,[76] and on 23 November he had empowered Catholic officers to retain commissions in the army.[77] In the face of such resolute royal action his protestant opponents were powerless.

Although James 'heartily' declared his wish 'that all the people of our dominions were members of the Catholic Church', he had no desire to impose Catholicism on an unwilling nation, any more than he intended to erect a military tyranny in the place of a lawful monarchy.[78] Unlike his cousin of France, Louis XIV, James abhorred the forcing of conscience and disliked religious persecution. What he most wanted was to secure equality before the law for his fellow Catholics. He wished to enable them to worship in public, educate their sons at Oxford and Cambridge, and enter politics, the civil service, and the armed forces, just as churchmen did.

Modest though this sounds to modern ears, four generations on from the achievement of Catholic emancipation in the nineteenth century, at the time his objectives struck fear and dread into the hearts of many Englishmen. Given the nature and extent of their anti-Catholic convictions, most protestants could not shake off the inbred notion of a 'popish plot' against English liberties.[79] They tended automatically to interpret James's actions as so many steps towards the forcible conversion of England to popery. The king was, of course, undeterred by such fantasies. An ardent convert, James saw that, if the plight of Catholics was permanently to be improved, it would be necessary to give them access to higher education at Oxford and Cambridge.

The king was the driving force behind successive Catholic attempts to secure a footing in the universities. Yet, he did not act alone. Right from the start he could count on the help of a group of Catholic converts inside Oxford: established dons who, by quitting the church of their baptism and seeking to be reconciled to the Catholic Church, provided him with important local support. In one college at least they formed a ready-made base on which to build his hopes for the future. That college was University College, 'the antientest seminary of learning, not only in the University of Oxford, but in this whole nation'.[80]

In terms of the individuals involved there were two distinct, yet overlapping and complementary, phases to the Catholic challenge that was mounted in Oxford: the one lay, the other clerical. The first phase, which began in late 1685, was

---

[76] PRO SP 44/335, pp. 504–6, James II's warrants to the justices of assize and gaol delivery for the midland, northern, western, home, Norfolk, and Oxford circuits, etc.

[77] PRO SP 44/336, pp. 280–4, warrant to the attorney-general to prepare a bill to pass the great seal containing a pardon and dispensation to seventy-one Catholic officers.

[78] *His Majesty's Gracious Declaration to all his Loving Subjects for Liberty of Conscience*, Whitehall, 4 April 1687, reprinted in E. Cardwell, *Documentary Annals of the Reformed Church of England* (2 vols Oxford 1839) ii. 309.

[79] R. A. Beddard, 'The protestant succession' in R. A. Beddard (ed.), *The Revolutions of 1688* (Oxford 1991), 3–6.

[80] Bodl. MS Ballard 49, fo 26.

dominated by Catholic laymen, mainly converts from the ranks of the Church of England's ministry. It was centred on the gremial academic Obadiah Walker, a former protestant clergyman and, since 1676, the much-respected master of University College.[81] The second phase, which began in late 1687, was dominated by cradle Catholics, chiefly secular and regular priests educated, not in Oxford, but in the continental colleges of the English Catholic diaspora: at Douai, St Omer, Paris, Rome, and Valladolid. It was centred on 'a Sorbonist', Bonaventure Giffard, the son of an old recusant family of Staffordshire, who, in 1688, became titular bishop of Madaura *in partibus infidelium*, vicar apostolic of the midland district, and president of Magdalen College.[82]

The advent of Catholicism in 1685 was gradual and piecemeal. Once again, the defeat of Monmouth marks a turning-point. As part of the victory celebrations Nathaniel Boyse, fellow of University College, preached a thanksgiving sermon at St Mary's on 26 July, in which he let fall 'many things savouring of popery'. He was promptly delated to the vice-chancellor by Gilbert Ironside, warden of Wadham, who acted at the instigation of the visiting bishop of St Asaph, William Lloyd, a noted controversialist and bitter enemy of the Church of Rome.[83] Like two other 'popishly affected' senior members of his college before him—Timothy Nourse in 1673 and Francis Nicholson in 1680[84]—the conduct of Boyse was severely censured by authority. On 1 August he was made to recant his views before the vice-chancellor and doctors.[85]

Scarcely had this untoward incident been dealt with than Obadiah Walker, the head of Boyse's college, published a life of Christ.[86] To begin with the book sold well, and was warmly received as a work of piety which combined patristic insight

---

[81] An ejected royalist fellow, who had been restored to his fellowship in 1660, Obadiah Walker was unanimously elected master of his college on 22 June 1676. UCA registrum I, fos 39[r-v], 49[v]–50, Pyx DD fasc. 3, n. 6. Bodl. MS J. Walker c. 8, fos 208[v], 270[v], 271[r-v], MS Ballard 1, fo 56[v], MSS Wood f. 31, fo 254, Wood f. 35, fos 249, 286[v]. *Restoration Oxford*, ed. Beddard i, no. 186.

[82] For Bonaventure Giffard (DD, Sorbonne 1678), see Archivio Segreto Vaticano, secretaria brevia apostolicorum 1769, fo 3, James II to Pope Innocent XI, Whitehall, 25 November 1687. J. Gillow, *A Literary and Biographical History . . . of the English Catholics* (5 vols London 1885) ii. 454–6; W. M. Brady, *The Episcopal Succession in England, Scotland, and Ireland A.D. 1400 to 1875* (3 vols Rome 1876–7) iii. 203; G. Anstruther, *The Seminary Priests: a dictionary of the secular clergy of England and Wales 1558–1850* (4 vols Great Wakering 1968–77) iii. 67–75.

[83] Wood, *Life and Times* iii. 152, 155, 156. For Boyse (Boys, Boyce, Bois) see UCA registrum I, fos 46[v], 48[r-v], Pyx DD fasc. 3, n. 6; Bodl. MS Wood d. 1, fo 17[v]; Wood, *Athenae* i, pp. lxxv, xcviii, iii. 1160, iv. 440; HMC *Twelfth Report*, appx vii, pp. 199–200.

[84] For Nourse, see UCA registrum I, fos 29[v], 36[v], 48[v], Pyx LL. 6, n. 9–13, letters between Nourse and Richard Clayton, 1672–3; Wood, *Life and Times* ii. 276; Wood, *Athenae*, iv. 448–9; *Letters of Humphrey Prideaux* ed. Thompson, 31. For Nicholson see Wood, *Life and Times* ii. 488–91; Wood, *Athenae*, iv. 449–50.

[85] OUA register Bb, fos 1, 1[v] (reverse).

[86] *An Historical Narration of the Life and Death of Our Lord Jesus Christ. In two parts* (Oxford at the Theatre 1685). Though anonymous, the book was immediately ascribed to Walker. It was priced at 5 shillings: *The Flemings in Oxford* ii. 141, Henry Fleming to Sir Daniel Fleming, Oxford, 12 September 1685. There are, however, grounds for thinking that Abraham Woodhead was the true author: M. Slusser, 'Abraham Woodhead (1608–78): some research notes, chiefly about his writings', *Recusant History* 15 (1979–81), 406, 414.

with scriptural exegesis in the best tradition of high church scholarship.[87] Upon closer inspection it seemed less commendable. It struck some of his colleagues in the faculty of theology that certain passages in it were doctrinally unsound. They were those passages relating to the high honour which historic Christianity accords to the person and theological status of the Blessed Virgin Mary as the Mother of God, and to the Petrine claims to primacy among the apostles.[88] Even to hint at the immaculate conception and papal supremacy was enough to give doctrinal palpitations to the Oxford doctors. Being systematically trained to detect and refute anything that remotely smacked of popery, their response was predictably hostile and shrill.

That the book had been printed 'at the Theater', on Fell's protestant press, encouraged them to make an issue of the matter, for they clearly felt that the university's good name as the citadel of protestant orthodoxy had been sullied. What made matters worse was the fact that before the work had gone to the press it had been vetted by the regius professor of divinity, William Jane. With the concurrence of Bishop Fell, he had made a number of 'deletions and corrections' to the manuscript. All of this was done privately; not to spare Walker's feelings, but to avoid attracting the attention of Whitehall. A public reprimand to the head of another house was out of the question when his unique fault was that he inclined to the king's religion. Walker, however, remained defiant. Unwilling to submit to protestant censorship, he printed the text as it had originally stood.[89] Fell was mortally offended.[90] The vice-chancellor, Timothy Halton, provost of Queen's, being 'govern'd by Dr. Fell', refused to let the matter drop. On 1 October he sent the bedels 'to forbid the booksellers to sell any' of the master's books, Walker having 'dispersed all the copies ... among the booksellers in Oxford'.[91]

It was clear that the 69-year-old Walker was not a man to be browbeaten by his juniors in the university. He was already in touch with the vicar apostolic, John Leyburn, bishop of Adrumetum, whom Pope Innocent XI had recently sent from Rome to take care of the depleted Catholic community.[92] A former secretary to Cardinal Howard, the protector of England, Leyburn was aware of the wretched

---

[87] *The Flemings in Oxford* ii. 142, Henry Fleming to Sir Daniel Fleming, Queen's, 21 November 1685; HMC *Twelfth Report*, appx vii, p. 198; Bodl. MS Smith 47, fo 42, Edward Bernard to Thomas Smith, Oxford, 18 October 1685.

[88] *An Historical Narration of the Life and Death of Our Lord Jesus Christ*, sections 9 (pp. 11, 12) and 255 (p. 191).

[89] Wood, *Athenae* iii. 1160; Wood, *Life and Times* iii. 164–5; HMC *Twelfth Report*, appx vii, p. 199, [Thomas Smith, bishop of Carlisle, to Sir Daniel Fleming, Rose Castle, 27 April 1686]. I am grateful to Dr N. Tyacke for information on this subject.

[90] Fell removed Walker from his will as a lessee of the university's privilege of printing: OUA chancellor's ct, Wills F/Hyp./B/25, fo 23, 11 June 1686. Cf chancellor's ct papers, 1687/84/19–20.

[91] Wood, *Life and Times* iii. 164–5; Halton only consented to act as vice-chancellor under pressure from Bishop Compton: Bodl. MS Rawlinson d. 923, fo 234, Compton to Halton, 2 May 1685 (copy); OUA register Bb, p. 105, Ormonde to the university, Windsor, September 1685.

[92] West. CA A 34, pp. 931 ff; B. Navarra, *Filippo Michele Ellis Segni e la sua diocesi nei primi decenni del '700* (Rome 1973), 51; PRO 31/9/100A, fo 331; B. Hemphill, *The Early Vicars Apostolic of England 1685–1750* (London 1954), 7–12.

state to which English Catholicism had been reduced by more than a century of proscription and persecution.[93] By the 1680s, Catholics constituted less than 1 per cent of the total population of England and Wales. Besides doing his utmost to succour the remnant of the faithful, Leyburn was solicitous to win proselytes from the Church of England.[94] How else could he increase the number of Catholics?

On his arrival in England Leyburn had been allotted lodgings at court, including an apartment at Somerset House, the residence of the Catholic queen dowager, Catherine of Braganza, widow of Charles II. It was there that he set up his headquarters and there that he conferred with Obadiah Walker. Independent evidence dating from the 1670s suggests a previous connection between the concealed Catholics of University College and Somerset House.[95] This is hardly surprising for, well before James II's accession, Catherine's court had enjoyed immunity from the operation of English law under the provisions of her marriage settlement. One article of the treaty agreed between Charles II and Alfonso VI of Portugal in 1661 had guaranteed to the queen the full and free exercise of her religion.[96] In the context of widespread religious hostility it was to be expected that Somerset House, with its Catholic chapel served by Portuguese Capuchins and English and Irish Benedictines, would become a haven for the faithful in and around the capital. After Leyburn's arrival, and the opening of the Catholic chapel royal to the public, it developed into a rallying-place for converts and catechumens, as well as for practising Catholics.[97]

The Oxford converts turned to the Catholic monarch for protection against the menaces of Vice-Chancellor Halton. Making the most of their contacts at Somerset House, Walker and his fellow converts—of whom Boyse was the first to break cover—appealed to the king himself. By 13 October Nathaniel Boyse was at

[93] For Bishop Leyburn (MA, Sorbonne 1646), see Archivio Segreto Vaticano, secretaria brevium apostolicorum 1769, fos 13, 14; Gillow, History of the English Catholics iv. 232–7; Brady, Episcopal Succession iii. 140–1; D. A. Bellenger, English and Welsh Priests 1558–1800 (Downside 1984), 82, 209; Archivio, Venerabile Collegio Inglese, Rome, liber 283, p. 44; Paris, Bibliothèque Nationale, MS Latin 9154, fo 76; R. A. Beddard, 'A relic of Stuart popery: prayers for Queen Mary Beatrice, anno 1688', Bodleian Library Record viii (1971), 274–5; T. A. Birrell, 'English Catholics without a bishop 1655–1672', Recusant History 4 (1957–8), 171–2.

[94] For Leyburn's pastoral zeal see T. B. Trappes-Lomax, 'Bishop Leyburn's visitation in 1687', Newsletter for Students of Recusant History iv (1962); Beddard, A Kingdom without a King, 15–16; HMC Downshire MSS i, pt i, pp. 258, 278, 281.

[95] Timothy Nourse admitted attending mass at Somerset House, ostensibly 'to heare the musick', when answering the charge that he had become a Catholic: UCA Pyx LL. 6, n. 9, Nourse to Richard Clayton, Paris, 6 September 1672. He was deprived of his fellowship on 5 January 1674: UCA registrum I, fo 48ᵛ.

[96] Bodl. MS Clarendon 76, fos 41ᵛ–2, 51ᵛ, 'Treaty of marriage with Portugall 1661[2]' (draft). See also Colleccao dos Tratados, Convencoes, Contratos e Actos Publicos, ed. J. F. Borges de Castro (30 vols Lisbon 1856–79) ix. 210–18; Grande Enciclopédia Portuguesa e Brasileira (Lisbon, n.d.) vi. 286 ff.

[97] Charles II had attempted to restrict access to the queen's chapel in 1678, and in 1680 had ordered her to remove to St James's. In 1685 she returned, as queen dowager, to Somerset House: Steele, Tudor and Stuart Proclamations, no. 3671, Whitehall, 6 December 1678; Marquise Campana di Cavelli, Les Derniers Stuarts à Saint Germain en Laye (2 vols Paris 1871) ii. 36; The Diary of John Evelyn, ed. De Beer iv. 433; Wood, Life and Times iii. 172, 177; A. S. Barnes, 'Catholic chapels royal under the Stuart kings', The Downside Review, new ser. i (1901), 158–65, 232–49, ii (1902), 39–55.

Whitehall, where he was admitted to an audience with the king. James spoke cordially to Boyse, telling him that 'he had seen and read the sermon of his' which the university had censured, and that he 'was well pleased with it', esteeming it to be 'an ingenious discourse and well pen'd'. Furthermore, he had seen the *Life of Christ* produced by Walker. That, too, he praised, as 'a very good book' (which, incidentally, it is). He 'wondred how any one' should 'find fault with it'. The warmth of Boyse's welcome at court spelled disaster for the university's attempts to keep a tight grip on its internal religious affairs.[98]

Between the autumn of 1685 and the spring of 1686, the period during which the king's revised objectives began to take shape, the identity of Walker's band of converts became clear. Alongside the assertive Boyse there was his slightly older colleague, Thomas Deane, fellow and Greek lecturer of University College,[99] and a young fellow of Brasenose, John Barnard, the grandson of Archbishop Laud's Arminian chaplain and biographer, Peter Heylyn.[100] Less than half Walker's age, they were known in Oxford as the master's 'three disciples'. Wood also credited Walker with 'a half' disciple in John Massey, sub-warden of Merton; even though his conversion occurred later, in October 1686, and largely as a result of the efforts of Bishop Leyburn and the Jesuits.[101]

Walker, Boyse, Deane, and Massey shared a common background. They were, or had been, members of University College. A born teacher, Walker naturally evolved into an active and successful proselytizer after his conversion.[102] His role in gaining the younger men to Catholicism was pivotal. While still a tutor he had turned his three pupils, Boyse, Deane, and Massey, into lifelong friends. Long after they had graduated they continued to look up to him. It was under his influence that they became Catholics, rather as he had received his earliest impulse towards Catholicism from his own former tutor, Abraham Woodhead, a quiet, energetic scholar who, after 1660, was recognized as 'the most ingenious and solid writer of the whole Roman party' in England.[103] Although Woodhead had ceased to reside

---

[98] Wood, *Life and Times* iii. 165–6.

[99] Thomas Deane (MA 1676) declared his conversion about the same time as Walker, 'whose creature and convert he was'. He contributed two titles to Walker's Catholic press. Wood, *Athenae* iv. 450–1; Wood, *Life and Times* iii. 176, 177, 183, 184, 213, 214 ff. UCA registrum I, fos 53ᵛ, 54, bursar's book, 1688–9 (rough draft) *sub* Deane.

[100] John Barnard (MA 1683) had been elected fellow of Brasenose from Lincoln College on 24 June 1681. He took the additional name of Augustine on his reception into the Roman Church: LCM, Rector Marshall's admissions book, p. 17; BNCA registrum B, fo 122; Bodl. MS Wood d. 1, fo 16; Wood, *Life and Times* iii. 183, 184, 186, 207, 213–15, 217, 219, 245, 287, 296, 340; Wood, *Athenae* iv. 610; Wood, *Fasti*, ii. 372.

[101] Wood, *Life and Times* iii. 177, 189, 190; MCA registrum 1567–1731, pp. 563, 564, 566.

[102] London, Dr Williams's Library, MS Morrice P, p. 532; HMC *Downshire MSS* i, pt 1, p. 175, Bishop Francis Turner of Ely to Sir William Trumbull, Ely House, 29 May 1686; Hearne, *Collections* viii. 264. Not all of the attempts by Walker at conversion were so successful. He failed to win over his friend and collegian, John Radcliffe, the eminent physician. [William Pittis], *Dr. Radcliffe's Life and Letters* (London 1715, 4th edn Dublin 1724), 16–20.

[103] An ejected royalist, Woodhead was also restored to his fellowship at University College in 1660 at the same time as Walker: ORO MS Oxf. dioc. papers, e. 13, pp. 183, 197; Bodl. MS J. Walker c. 8,

in University College, he maintained his links with the college until 1678, and kept up an intimate friendship with Walker until his death.[104]

The recurrent pattern of academic relationships—of pupil and tutor—is a reminder that tutorial succession can, in conducive circumstances, be a strong force for perpetuating religious attitudes and private allegiances in university life. It was by this means that the undercover transmission of Catholicism continued for over three decades inside the walls of University College until, with the accession of a Catholic monarch, it burst into the open. In that small, close-structured, friendly community, safe from prying eyes, the streams of tutorial and confessional influence repeatedly converged to pass on the *depositum fidei*; it was handed down from tutor to pupil, even to the third and fourth generation of those who, at their admission to the college, had not known the faith of their forefathers.

The conversion of two of Walker's fellows was made easier by the fact that Boyse and Deane were inseparable friends. From the day of their joint matriculation, on 19 October 1669, their academic careers had proceeded in tandem.[105] As for Massey, though he had migrated to nearby Merton, he had begun life in Oxford as Walker's servitor back in 1666.[106] At first sight Barnard appears to be at a tangent to the rest; but not so. He, no less than the trio from University College, had fallen under the older man's spell and shared his antiquarian and historical interests. Walker was an attractive figure, notwithstanding his love of solitude. Upright, learned, cultured, enthusiastic and industrious, he had a gift for inspiring the academically ambitious. His attractive qualities survived even his election to the headship of his college: a rare achievement.[107]

The range of Walker's intellectual interests helped him in this. Reared in *literae humaniores*, he had made a specific study of logic, oratory, rhetoric, and grammar, to which he added divinity—moral and exegetical—geography, history, and numismatics, on which subjects he wrote and published authoritatively.[108] He was in every way 'best qualified for the advancement and direction of collegiate and academicall studies', as his close collaboration with Fell had attested.[109] It was his

---

fos 208ᵛ, 270ᵛ, 271ʳ⁻ᵛ, MS Ballard 1, fo 56ᵛ, MS Wood f. 35, fo 252; Wood, *Athenae* iii. 1157; *Register*, ed. Burrows, 199, 214, 271, 556; *Restoration Oxford*, ed. Beddard i, no. 186.

[104] Woodhead continued to draw his fellow's stipend from his restitution in 1660 until 1678: UCA general account books (1632–67, 1668–1706) and buttery books (1674, 1677). For his high regard for Walker, whom he made one of his executors, see BL Add. MS 43,377, fos 53, 55.

[105] OUA SP 3 (matriculation register 1662–93), p. 343; Bodl. MS Wood d. 1, fo 17ᵛ; UCA registrum admissionum, p. iv (19 October 1669).

[106] OUA SP 3, p. 341, 16 March 1666; UCA registrum admissionum, p. ii; MCA registrum 1567–1731, pp. 563–4; Bodl. MS Wood d. 1, fo 74ᵛ; Wood, *Life and Times* iii. 189, 197.

[107] Walker was reckoned 'neither proud nor covetous' even by his protestant critics: W. Smith, *Annals of University College* (Oxford 1728), 258.

[108] For Walker's publications, see Wood, *Athenae* iv. 442–4 and *DNB*, which accounts need to be revised in the light of Slusser, 'Abraham Woodhead (1608–78)', 406–22. For evidence of Walker's theological and historical interests, see Bodl. MS Rawlinson d. 377, fos 146–53, 154ᵛ, 155–8, 159, 161, MS Rawlinson b. 158, and MS Ballard 5, fo 52.

[109] Bodl. MS Ballard 21, fo 106: 'The character of Obadiah Walker by R[ichard] R[eeve], a Romish priest', which served as the basis of Wood's sympathetic account of Walker in the *Athenae*. For

knowledge of the continent that particularly fascinated others, for he was, by Oxford standards, exceptionally well travelled. As an ejected royalist in the 1650s and, again, as a readmitted fellow with repeated leave of absence in the 1660s, he had spent much time in those incomparable centres of civilization, Rome and Paris.[110] There was a cosmopolitan air about him. His observation of 'divers communities' abroad, and his 'conversation with their most eminent directors and professors', set him apart from most dons with their 'meer home-bred education'.[111] It was probably his repeated sojourns in Italy and France, as much as the example of Woodhead and the accumulating maturity of age, that reinforced his long-nurtured aesthetic and devotional inclinations to Catholicism. Of one thing we may be sure. His brave acknowledgement of his conversion was the product of careful reflection, as it needed to be in a country which viewed the reconciliation of a native protestant to the Catholic Church as an act of treason.[112]

Walker spent most of January 1686 in London, having been 'sent for up to the cabal of papists at Somerset-hous'. There he was 'severall times' closeted with Bishop Leyburn. The purpose of summoning him to court was 'to perswade him to declare', and to plan the measures that would be required to protect him and his companions. On his return to college he left off attending chapel prayers. Boyse and Deane acted more circumspectly. They continued to attend the statutory services throughout Lent, but stayed 'in the outer chapel'. Their stalls remained unoccupied. Both they and Barnard were conspicuous by their absence from the Anglican communion on Easter day.

Scarcely had Walker begun, in March, to confide in 'some of his friends that he was a Roman Catholic', than the news was made public by the French *Gazette*.[113] Considering English fear of France and growing national concern over Louis XIV's persecution of the Huguenots, the manner of announcing Walker's conversion was at once sensational and intimidating.[114] As if to add insult to injury, it was also given out that the master was 'building a chapel to sing mass'—a revelation which some outraged dons wrongly took to mean that he had received Catholic orders.[115] The news scandalized an already suspicious and fearful people. 'It was discoursed

examples of Walker's co-operation with Fell in securing the Arundel marbles and establishing the Ashmolean Museum, see Bodl. MS Ballard 9, fo 9, Walker to John Evelyn, University College, 24 September 1667, and Fell to [Evelyn], 26 April 1676; Bodl. MS Rawlinson c. 912, fo 670, 'Propositions sent to my lord bishop of Oxford (by Mr. Walker, master of University College) from Mr. Ashmole, 30 September 1682'.

[110] UCA registrum I, fos 42, 42b^r-v; Bodl. MS Ballard 5, fo 56, Edmund Gibson to Arthur Charlett, 18 July 1694; Wood, *Athenae* iv. 437–8.

[111] Bodl. MS Ballard 21, fo 106.

[112] J. A. Williams, 'English Catholicism under Charles II: the legal position', *Recusant History* 7 (1963–4), 123–43, especially p. 129.

[113] Wood, *Life and Times* iii. 176–7, 181, 182, 183; Luttrell, *Brief Relation* i. 369, 373.

[114] For the linkage of anti-Catholic and anti-French sentiment and the rising tide of Francophobia in Restoration society, see R. A. Beddard, 'The protestant succession', in R. A. Beddard (ed.), *The Revolutions of 1688*, 2–10.

[115] Wood, *Life and Times* iii. 182, 186; HMC *Twelfth Report*, appx vii, p. 200, Bishop Thomas Smith of Carlisle, quoting John Mill, principal of St Edmund Hall.

of over all the nation', and gave 'great offence' to high and low alike.[116] Whereas churchmen were understandably alarmed and thrown on to the defensive, their enemies, the dissenters, were triumphant, and did their best to proclaim 'that all the university were papists', which was very far from the truth, as they must have known.[117]

The defections were undoubtedly an early and valuable *coup de théâtre* for Catholic propaganda, which was just beginning to emerge under court sponsorship. Even so, the huge outcry at the loss of Walker, Boyse, Deane, and Barnard—shortly to be followed by that of Massey—cannot be explained by reference to their number, but has to be set against the overriding consideration that was in everybody's mind: namely, that protestant England was now ruled by a Catholicizing king. Individual conversions had, of course, happened at Oxford before, but none had been caught in the blaze of publicity that attended those of 1686.[118] The critical difference in 1686 was that, by then, 'all people expected popery to be introduced' apace, as a result of the king's stand on the Catholic officers and his dismissal of the Anglican tory parliament.[119]

Moreover, it was feared that they were the first trickle in James's expected flood of converts, who would ruin the Church of England. Their appearance together at Oxford, which of all places was regarded as the staunchest of protestant redoubts, seemed to give colour to the dissenting and whig accusation (hitherto frowned upon) that the high church clergy contained a significant phalanx of 'tantivies', or covert 'church papists', just waiting for a safe opportunity to ride post-haste for Rome. It should be remembered that Walker and 'his disciples' were not merely revolted churchmen, but renegade clergymen of the Church of England.[120] That made the desertions look infinitely more sinister than they were. As for Walker, the instigator of the conversions, he was singled out as the arch-villain. It was held inconceivable that he, a respected academic in Oxford since 1660, could have been 'turned' while in the university. Implausible as it may now seem, he was thought to have been 'a concealed papist' for '30 yeares or thereabout'—a Catholic 'sleeper', who, at his return from exile in Catholic Europe, had been infiltrated into Oxford with the design of 'perverting' other Oxonians to popery, and so subverting the protestant establishment from within.[121]

---

[116] HMC *Twelfth Report*, appx vii, p. 199, Bishop Smith to Fleming, Rose Castle, 27 April 1686.

[117] Wood, *Life and Times* iii. 177, cf p. 137.

[118] For example Walter Harris, who resigned his New College fellowship in 1673; Richard Gastrel, 'an Oxford schollar'; Richard Durston, probably of New Inn Hall; Thomas Kingsley (Kyngsmyll) of Magdalen, and Richard Reeve, master of Magdalen College School (1670–3). Wood, *Life and Times* ii. 269–70, 275, 280, 401, 431; Archivio Venerabile Collegio Inglese, Rome, liber 283, pp. 16, 39.

[119] Wood, *Life and Times* iii. 176, 177–8; *The Diary of John Evelyn*, ed. De Beer iv. 510.

[120] For the protestant orders of Walker, Boyse, Deane, and Barnard, see ORO MSS Oxf. dioc. papers e. 13, pp. 350, 446; e. 15, pp. 81, 94; 73; 171, d. 106, fos 74, 79; 71ᵛ; 99.

[121] Wood, *Life and Times* iii. 182. For earlier instances of Walker's being 'suspected to be a papist' see HMC *Twelfth Report*, appx vii, p. 150, Thomas Dixon to Sir Daniel Fleming [Queen's College], 27 November 1678; Wood, *Life and Times* ii. 346, 350, 421–2, 449, 488–9, 491.

It was not until May that the practical impact of the 'publique defection' of Walker and his colleagues was brought home to the university authorities. Only then were the implications of having a nucleus of Catholic dons resident in Oxford fully grasped. In that month the master of University College received two letters patent from King James: a dispensation and a licence. The former allowed him and his fellow converts to keep their college posts;[122] the latter permitted him to print and publish Catholic works.[123] At court it was hoped that these two documents would provide an adequate base from which to launch a bid for converts inside and out-side Oxford. James's dispensation of 3 May 1686 was amply drawn. Its effect on the established academic and Anglican discipline of the university was devastating. At a stroke it set aside the requirements of the 1662 act of uniformity and the restrictions imposed on Catholics by the whole body of penal legislation that had been enacted by parliament since the first year of Elizabeth's reign.

Access to the royal court, which from first to last was the converts' lifeline, was kept open by a clause specifically enabling them 'to travail to the cittyes of London and Westminster, and come and remayn in our presence, or in the presence of our royall consort the queen, or of Katherine, queen dowager of England, or in our court':[124] a privilege hitherto denied to Catholics, unless individually sanctioned by a signed order from the lords of the privy council.[125] Over the next two years Walker had frequent recourse to his political and ecclesiastical superiors in the cap-ital for advice and support. Their aid underwrote his own schemes and helped to counter those of his enemies in the university.[126]

That Walker was not to be a token Catholic, but to be of real service to the king and the Catholic cause he espoused, was revealed by the ambitious tenor of the licence granted to him by James to print, reprint, publish, and sell certain, named, Catholic books, 'without incurring any penalty, loss, or disability whatsoever'. The grant to Walker and his assigns was to run for twenty-one years. The schedule of short titles annexed to the licence indicated the immense scale of the project: some thirty-six titles were listed. The annual output eventually hoped for was enormous, an upper limit of 20,000 copies being set on the print run for any one book in any

[122] James II's warrant to the attorney-general to prepare a bill granting them a royal licence and dis-pensation had been issued on 25 March 1686, after having been held up by stiff Anglican opposition within the administration: PRO SP 44/336, pp. 417–20; *The Diary of John Evelyn*, ed. De Beer iv. 509–10, 512.

[123] PRO SP 44/337, pp. 22–3, 24–6, warrants for granting a royal licence under the great seal, and a dispensation for printing and selling titles contained in the foregoing warrant, notwithstanding any former statutes, 1 May 1686.

[124] UCA registrum I, fos 55ᵛ–6, James II's letters patent, Westminster, 3 May 1686 (registered copy); BNCA registrum B, fos 132–3, 'The king's dispensation for Mr Bernard'. For Archbishop Sancroft's autograph copies of the 'docquet', see Bodl. MSS Tanner 460, fo 53ᵛ, Tanner 338, fo 262, Tanner 30, fos 48ʳ–ᵛ; Dr Williams's Library, MS Morrice P, p. 533; HMC *Downshire MSS* i, pt i, 162; HMC *Twelfth Report*, appx vii, p. 199.

[125] James lost no time in issuing such licences—see PRO PC 2/71, fos 10ᵛ, 11, 13, 14, 18 ff.

[126] Wood, *Life and Times* iii. 165–6, 171, 176–7; *The Diary of John Evelyn*, ed. De Beer iv. 519; Bodl. MS Ballard 23, fo 52ᵛ, S. Gardiner to [Arthur Charlett, Cambridge], 3 May 1687; HMC *Downshire MSS* i, pt i, 187, [Gilbert Dolben?] to Sir William Trumbull, 24 June 1686.

one year.[127] James, who was wildly over-optimistic when it came to predicting the potential for conversions, expected Walker to make a massive contribution to the missionary effort. The master's unrivalled knowledge of the workings of the Oxford press, gained during his time as Fell's assistant, marked him out for such an undertaking.[128] Along with Henry Hills, the king's printer in London, he was expected to provide the back-up of printed propaganda that would be required to put a reorganized English mission under Bishop Leyburn into forward gear.[129]

Proof that King James was behind the carefully planned move to open an Oxford branch of the Catholic propaganda machine is provided by his having personally paid the official costs of issuing the two seals to Walker.[130] It would, however, be wrong to see Walker as a passive tool in the hands of his superiors, for he had actively promoted these developments. Just as James's dispensation to the Oxford converts acknowledges that it was issued 'att theyr humble suite',[131] so an examination of the titles scheduled for publication in Oxford discloses the extent to which Walker participated in the planning of the project. Only he and his ex-pupil and current collaborator, Francis Nicholson, an earlier convert from University College, were in a position to have furnished the king's secretariat with the titles of works extracted from Abraham Woodhead's unpublished literary remains.[132] Since Woodhead's death, which occurred amid the anti-Catholic hysteria unleashed by the Popish Plot, the bulk of his extensive manuscript collections had been deposited for safe keeping at Weld House, in London, in the custody of the Spanish ambassador, Don Pedro Ronquillo.[133] There they remained safe and sound, shielded from protestant confiscation by Ronquillo's diplomatic status, until

---

[127] HMC *Downshire MSS* i, pt i, p 173, Owen Wynne to Trumbull, London, 24 May 1686; Bodl. MS Tanner 146, fo 103.

[128] OUA register of convocation 1659–71, NEP/*supra*/27, register Ta, fo 253, Walker's nomination as 'delegatum pro re typographica', 5 October 1668; *The First Minute Book of the Delegates of the Oxford University Press 1668–1756* ed. S. Gibson and J. Johnson (Oxford Bib. Soc. 1943), 4–12, 61; M. Barker, *The Oxford University Press and the Spread of Learning 1478–1978* (Oxford 1978), 24, 25, 62; Wood, *Life and Times* ii. 172–3, 204.

[129] For Henry Hills, himself a Catholic convert, whom James appointed printer to the royal household and chapel, see PRO SP 44/336, pp. 339–41, 375–80, SP 44/336, p. 361, SP 44/71, p. 283, SP 44/337, p. 120; Dr Williams's Library, MS Morrice P, pp. 520–1; *The Diary of John Evelyn*, ed. De Beer iv. 503–4; Beddard, *A Kingdom without a King*, 43.

[130] *Money received and paid for Secret Services of Charles II and James II*, ed. J. Y. Akerman (Camden Soc. lii, 1851), 141.

[131] UCA registrum I, fo 55.

[132] For the titles, see *Collectanea curiosa*, ed. J. Gutch (2 vols Oxford 1781) i. 288–9. For Sancroft's copy of the schedule see Bodl. MS Tanner 460, fo 54; Yorkshire Archaeological Society Library, Leeds, MS 45, Francis Nicholson's 'Life of Abraham Woodhead'.

[133] Ronquillo, Carlos II's ambassador to the court of St James, was a leading patron of the English Mission, and a well-known collector of manuscripts, most of which perished in the sack of Weld (Wild) House in the Revolution of 1688. For Ronquillo, see Gregorio Leti, *Il Teatro Brittanico o vero Historia Della Grande Brettagna* (5 vols Amsterdam 1684) ii. 511; *Correspondencia entre dos embajadores. Don Pedro Ronquillo y el Marqués de Cogolludo, 1689–1691*, ed. G. M. Gamazo (2 vols Madrid 1951).

Nicholson, acting as Walker's agent, retrieved some of the more relevant items to print in Oxford.[134]

Everything now turned on the master of University College. His top priority was not immediately one of publishing propaganda, but of establishing a place of worship. Nor was this a decision of his making, but a duty imposed on him by the very nature of Catholicism as a religious cult. It was essential to erect a Catholic altar in the university in order to establish Catholic worship, for among Catholics the *cultus Dei* took precedence over all else. As the marquess of Halifax remarked, whereas protestants 'generally place their religion in the pulpit', Catholics centred 'theirs upon the altar'.[135] Even the sacramental emphasis that was discernible in the churchmanship of Restoration Oxford was slight in comparison with Roman practice.

Anticipating the vehement protest that would undoubtedly attend the public inauguration of Catholic worship in the university, the master acted with extreme caution, preferring an incremental rather than a provocative approach. In the spring of 1686 he opened 'a garret ch[amber]' in the master's lodgings as a makeshift oratory. Finding this inadequate and inconvenient for the purpose, he next procured the key to a downstairs room in the south-east corner of the quadrangle, whose occupant was absent from Oxford, and 'furnish'd and adorned the same in manner and fashion of a Romish oratory or chappel'. It was soon crowded 'on Sundays and holy days' by a motley congregation, composed of senior and junior members of University College, a growing band of academic converts drawn from other colleges and a contingent of officers and men from the Catholic earl of Peterborough's regiment quartered in the town. By the summer the single room was 'proving too small to receive their congregation and such other persons as they were willing ... to admit as spectators'.[136] The Catholic dons had after all to think of attracting converts, and facilitating attendance at services was an obvious way of doing that.

Before finally resolving the problem of accommodation the master obtained a mandate from the king. It was read out by Boyse at a college meeting. In it James empowered Walker to turn whatever room or rooms he wanted into a Catholic chapel. He pitched on 'two vacant ground chambers', next to his own lodgings, one of which was already in his hands.[137] These would, he thought, make a decent-sized chapel, once he had removed 'the partitions, studys, and bedrooms, and lay[d] them all in common'. The fellows, the majority of whom remained doggedly

---

[134] The patronage of the Catholic mission by Ronquillo brought violent retribution in December 1688, when the protestant mob sacked his embassy: Beddard, *A Kingdom without a King*, 43, 44, 54, 75, 88, 102–3, 106, 119, 173, 175, 188, 192, 195.

[135] Foxcroft, *Halifax* i. 467, Halifax to the earl of Chesterfield, 20 July 1686.

[136] Bodl. MS Ballard 16, fo 15, 'The college's answer to Mr Walker['s] plea made in the house of commons' after the revolution of 1688 (William Smith's copy).

[137] PRO SP 44/56, p. 344, Secretary Sunderland to Walker, Windsor, 15 August 1686. Cf Bodl. MS Ballard 49, fo 27.

protestant, 'were the willinger to give connivance, or be passive in the matter', albeit it went 'very much against all our minds and inclinations', because they 'had been some time under an apprehension' that their Catholic colleagues 'would have seised upon our public chappel for the same use'.[138] Against the authority of the master, armed with the king's warrant, there was little that they could do, either individually or collectively. Walker 'opened his chappell for publick mass' on 15 August 1686.[139] The date was significant. It was the feast of the assumption of Our Lady—a Marian feast that had been officially excised from the liturgy of the Church of England in 1549, as part of the deliberate protestantization of the nation's religion.

At first the converts, as devout laymen, could do no more than 'sing mattins and vespers' daily from the divine office.[140] With the raising of a public altar and the arrival of a permanent priest to minister to them matters were significantly improved. Henceforth, they were able publicly to participate in the sacramental life of the church in a way which had been denied to generations of English Catholics since the schism with Rome. At Walker's invitation the chapel was served by priests of the Society of Jesus, Edward Humberston and Joseph Wakeman being successively deputed to act as chaplains. Products of the Jesuit college at St Omer, they had recently been sent over from Liège to join the local residence of St Mary.[141] It was in keeping with the master's keen sense of mission that he called in the counter-reformation Jesuit order, with its fine educational record and avidly evangelizing outlook. In his eyes these assets more than outweighed the animosity felt for the society among English protestants.[142]

Based on this centrally located chapel, which they were encouraged to look upon as 'wholly belong[ing]' to them, the Jesuit fathers soon reckoned themselves to be 'in a very hopeful way' of saving souls, finding 'good custom' in town and gown.[143] In addition to their customary instruction of the faithful, given in frequent sermons and addresses, they held weekly catechizing sessions on Sunday afternoons for the

[138] Bodl. MS Ballard 16, fo 15.

[139] Wood, *Life and Times* iii. 194. Within a month his chapel was beset by 'the rabble' of the town, 'in so much that some soldiers at mass were forced to come out and quiet them'. Ibid. iii. 196; Wood, *Athenae* iv. 439–40.

[140] HMC *Twelfth Report*, appx vii, p. 200, [Bishop Thomas Smith of Carlisle] to Fleming, Rose Castle, 3 June 1686.

[141] For Edward Humberston (alias Hall) SJ, and Joseph Wakeman SJ, see *St. Omers and Bruges Colleges, 1593–1773*, ed. G. Holt (Catholic Record Soc. lxix 1979), 140, 273, and *The English Jesuits 1650–1829: a biographical dictionary*, ed. G. Holt (Catholic Record Soc. lxx 1984), 124, 255; Bellenger, *English and Welsh Priests*, 74, 118; Wood, *Life and Times* iii. 276, 285, 298. The number of officiating priests was quickly exaggerated: *The Ellis Correspondence*, ed. G. A. Ellis (2 vols London 1829) i. 55.

[142] For a general account of the society's activities under James II, see B. Basset, *The English Jesuits from Campion to Martindale* (London 1967), 256–61. Anglicans had a special hatred of 'the Jesuits, with their plotts and designes', whom they knew were being deployed by Louis XIV in his drive to convert the Huguenots of Languedoc and the Dauphiné: PRO Adm. 77/2, no. 144, newsletter [London], 8 October 1685; Dr Williams's Library, MS Morrice Q, p. 314; Bodl. MS Smith 48, p. 253, Sir Charles Cotton to [Thomas Smith], Stratton, 30 June 1687; *The Diary of John Evelyn*, ed. De Beer iv. 486.

[143] *Records of the English Province of the Society of Jesus . . . in the 16th and 17th centuries*, ed. H. Foley (7 vols London 1877–83) v. 956, Henry Pelham (*vere* Warren) SJ, to [Fr John Clare?], Oxford, 2 May 1690.

benefit of inquiring protestants.[144] On 28 January 1687 Walker underpinned their endeavours by extracting a further mandate from the king, who commanded the sequestration of the revenue of a vacant fellowship as a means of defraying the cost of maintaining a full-time Catholic chaplain in the college.[145]

Walker was undeterred by his critics. Sure in his allegiance to the Catholic Church and to the Catholic king, he embarked on a policy of blatant Catholic imperialism. He tried to build up a party in the university, as he had done previously in his college, by obtaining posts for Catholics and Catholic sympathizers, on whom he could rely to support the king's forward policies.[146] Faced by the immovable hostility of Oxford, as things stood only death could open opportunities for him to advance his protégés. Not for the last time in academic reckoning, it was a clear case of while there was death there was hope. The deaths, in turn, of the heads of Christ Church, All Souls, and Magdalen, and the retirement of White's lecturer in moral philosophy, found him equipped with a candidate ready and waiting for royal patronage.[147]

In December 1686 he obtained the deanery of Christ Church for 'his quondam servitour', John Massey of Merton, having refused it for himself;[148] in January 1687 he secured *per literas regias* the election of his devotee, John Barnard of Brasenose, to the lectureship in moral philosophy.[149] In the same month he narrowly missed netting the wardenship of All Souls by putting in 'too late' for his friend and fellow collegian, Robert Plot, author of *The Natural History of Oxfordshire*. Plot had dithered on the brink of conversion for some time, and now promised 'he would declare' himself, 'if he could get it'.[150] Unluckily for him, his havering until the last minute robbed him of the king's recommendation, which went instead to the well-connected Leopold William Finch who, like Massey, had been a leading light in marshalling the university's troops against the ill-fated duke of Monmouth in the summer of 1685.[151]

---

[144] Wood, *Life and Times* iii. 223. Cf, *Records of the English Province*, ed. Foley v. 956–7.

[145] PRO SP 44/57, p. 153, James II to University College, 28 January 1687.

[146] Wood, *Life and Times* iii. 209. Such a policy of preferment was in fact advocated by an anonymous paper of advice—see BL Add. MS 32,095, fos 243–6ᵛ, 'Some considerations concerning the obstructions that have hitherto hindred the reduction of the universities to the Catholicke religion'.

[147] Fell died on 10 July 1686, Warden Jeames on 5 January 1687, and President Clerke on 24 March 1687. William Halton of Queen's had statutorily retired as White's lecturer. Wood, *Life and Times* iii. 191–2, 216, 207; HMC *Twelfth Report*, appx vii, pp. 199, 202.

[148] Dr Williams's Library, London, MS Morrice Q, p. 59; PRO SP 44/57, p. 148, James II's warrant to the clerk of the signet attending, 13 December 1686. For Sancroft's copy of Massey's dispensation see Bodl. MS Tanner 30, fos 162–3ᵛ; Wood, *Life and Times* iii. 197–8, 200–1; HMC *Ormonde MSS*, new ser. viii. 348.

[149] OUA register Bb, fos 1ᵛ–2 (reverse), James II to the vice-chancellor and electors to the moral philosophy lecture, Whitehall, 1 January 1687. Barnard was elected on 28 March following, Massey being one of the statutory electors as dean of Christ Church.

[150] Wood, *Life and Times*, iii. 208; Bodl. MS Ballard 23, fo 227, John Laughton to Arthur Charlett, Trinity College [Cambridge], 18 April 1687. Walker was also suspected of underhand dealings with Miles Stapylton, fellow of All Souls. Bodl. MS Tanner 30, fo 171, George Clarke to [Henry Maurice?], All Souls, 4 January 1686/7.

[151] PRO SP 44/57, p. 152, James II to All Souls College, 15 January 1686, Adm. 77/3, no. 56,

It is more than likely that Walker also had a hand in the intensely unpopular promotion of Samuel Parker to the see of Oxford, in succession to Fell, in August 1686.[152] A high-flying tory propagandist, who adhered to court policies, Archdeacon Parker had gained notoriety in the early 1680s for opposing Archbishop Sancroft, his diocesan, and for befriending the recusant families of Kent.[153] Walker had long enjoyed intimate ties with the Catholic Haleses, from just outside Canterbury. Their son and heir, a gentleman-commoner of University College, had recently followed the example of his father, Sir Edward Hales, and his tutor, Boyse, in publicly embracing the Catholic Church in 1685.[154] Deep in the king's counsels, and in close touch with Walker, Hales senior had been instrumental in procuring the judicial ruling upholding the crown's dispensing power: a prerogative power which James repeatedly exercised on behalf of Oxford's Catholics, beginning with the converts from University College—the Hales family college. The lines linking the royal court with Walker, and Walker with Hales, are too well documented for them to be coincidental. They were joint beneficiaries of the case of Godden *versus* Hales, in 1686: a collusive action brought to free all English Catholics from the restrictions of the test acts and the terror of the penal laws.[155]

The appointment of Samuel Parker as bishop of Oxford and of John Massey as dean of Christ Church demands greater attention than it has hitherto received. Not only did it announce the king's resolve to bring the university into line with his decision to improve the standing of his co-religionists, it also provides the key to a correct understanding of the university's growing resistance to his policies. For too long the role of Christ Church has been underestimated in the growth of opposition to James II. Content to repeat the view of Macaulay and Bloxam (itself uncritically adopted from contemporary literary propaganda, much of which emanated from Magdalen), historians have dwelt on the independent stand made

newsletter, London, 18 January 1686; ASA appeals and visitors' injunctions I, item 63, L. W. Finch to Sancroft, All Souls, 1 February 1686/7, registrum I, fos 63–4ᵛ. See also p. 914 above; Bodl. MS Eng. hist. c. 6, fos 122, 122ᵛ. Finch's election as warden also occasioned controversy—see Bodl. MS Tanner 340, fo 426, Sir Thomas Clarges's draft confirmation of his election.

[152] PRO SP 44/57, p. 130, James II's *congé d'élire* to the dean and chapter of Christ Church, Windsor, 21 August 1686; CA D&C. i. b. 3, p. 258, letter recommendatory and *congé* 'under our signet', Westminster, 9 September 1686.

[153] Beddard, 'Sancroft', 61–2, 64–5, 178–89, 234–5.

[154] An opponent of exclusion who had fallen under suspicion of harbouring 'popish' sympathies in 1679, Sir Edward Hales, third baronet, of St Stephen's, Kent was, as an open Catholic, among the first officers to be dispensed from the penalties of anti-Catholic legislation. *Debates of the House of Commons from the Year 1667 to the Year 1694*, ed. Anchitel Grey (10 vols London 1769) viii. 17–18; PRO SP 44/336, pp. 280–4; Beddard, *A Kingdom without a King*, 32, 34, 38, 47, 54, 91, 93, 97, 99–100, 109, 158, 162, 164, 170, 194. For Sir Edward's son, also Edward (m. 24 June 1684) see UCA registrum admissionum, p. 8. The younger Edward's tutor was Boyse: Bodl. MS Ballard 16, fo 15.

[155] For the test case of Godden *versus* Hales (1686), see *State Trials*, ed. T. B. Howell (21 vols London 1809–14) xi. 1195–9; Luttrell, *Brief Relation* i. 380, 382; J. R. Tanner, *English Constitutional Conflicts of the Seventeenth Century 1603–1689* (Cambridge 1928), 253–4 and appx viii.

by Magdalen College as the hub of Oxford opposition, when, in reality, that was but part of a larger, more comprehensive, Anglican campaign.[156]

Magdalen's early show of resistance to royal interference, spirited though it was, was quickly hijacked by Christ Church malcontents: careerist clerics of the Church of England, who, by the spring of 1687, were well seasoned in the arts of opposition, and, by dint of their grand outside contacts, were in a position to instil political vigour into a college campaign that was beginning to show signs of flagging. It was Christ Church, as the largest, wealthiest, and most politically aware of the colleges of the beleaguered protestant establishment, that was both the source and sustainer of ecclesiastical and academic opposition to James's pro-Catholic measures in Oxford. Accurately described by Archbishop Sancroft as the 'most flourishing society' in the university, and one that 'hath bred vast number of worthy persons fitt for any station' in the Church of England, Christ Church was the first casualty of James's break with his 'old friends', the high church tories.[157]

Already, under Fell, Christ Church had come out strongly against advancing Catholicism. Fell had personally denied Walker access to the university press, so that to print his first overtly Catholic work—Abraham Woodhead's *Two Discourses concerning the Adoration of Our Blessed Saviour in the Holy Eucharist*—he was forced to use Leonard Lichfield's printing house.[158] Even then, care was taken to acquire by subterfuge uncorrected proofs from Lichfield's press, in order that some of the Christ Church clergy might secretly undertake a speedy counterblast to Woodhead's pieces; thus making Walker go to the added expense of setting up his own press in University College so as to safeguard the initiative in the war of words between Rome and Canterbury.[159] Again, it was Christ Church men who, as university preachers, took the lead in denouncing the claims of the Catholic Church from St Mary's pulpit.[160] Their strenuous efforts, and those of their London brethren, caused the king to reissue his brother's *Directions concerning Preachers* in March 1686.[161] But, whereas under Charles II these had been used to silence the controversy between Calvinists and Arminians at Oxford, under James II they were

[156] Lord Macaulay, *The History of England from the accession of James the Second*, ed. C. H. Firth (6 vols London 1913) ii. 938–42, 948–55; *Magdalen College and King James II 1686–1688*, ed. J. R. Bloxam (OHS vi 1886), pp. viii ff.

[157] Bodl. MS Tanner 30, fo 93, Sancroft to James II, 29 July 1686 (draft).

[158] For Fell's latest denunciation of 'the furious malice of papists', see his 1685 visitation charge to the clergy of his diocese: Bodl. MS Tanner 31, fo 156. The imprint reads 'At Oxford printed *anno* 1687', but it was actually printed by Leonard Lichfield the third, for whom see H. R. Plomer, *A Dictionary of the Printers and Booksellers . . . in England . . . from 1668 to 1725* (London 1922, reprinted 1968), 188. Wood, *Athenae* iv. 440, Wood, *Life and Times* iii. 198, 202.

[159] Wood, *Life and Times* iii. 209, 217–8, 220; Edmund Calamy, *An Abridgment Of Mr. Baxter's History Of His Life and Times* (London 1702, 2nd edn 2 vols London 1713), 1. 377–9; HMC *Twelfth Report*, appx vii, p. 202.

[160] Wood *Life and Times* iii. 169, 183; cf Luttrell, *Brief Relation* i. 362.

[161] PRO SP 44/57, pp. 119–20, James II to the archbishops of Canterbury and York, 5 March 1686. For Charles II's *Directions concerning preachers*, Whitehall, 14 October 1662, see Cardwell, *Documentary Annals of the Reformed Church of England* ii. 255–9; Luttrell, *Brief Relation* i. 373.

used to muzzle the expression of anti-Catholic conviction, which constituted a major part of seventeenth-century Anglicanism.[162] Denied an outlet in the university church, the anti-Catholicism of Christ Church reared its head in the convocation house, where, in April, the retiring senior proctor, William Breach of Christ Church, boldly 'blamed some scholars for leaving their religion for that of Rome'.[163]

Walker, ever watchful of his enemies, kept Whitehall informed of untoward events. On hearing in May that his *Directions* had been flouted by George Tullie, a visiting university preacher, the king decided to make an example of him. Tullie's attack on the doctrine and worship of the Catholic Church, as being worse than the 'idolatry' practised by heathendom,[164] was seen by James as an attack on himself—an attempt 'to begett in the minds of his hearers an evill opinion of us and our government by insinuating feares and jealousies', and to stir up discontent that might 'lead them into disobedience, schisme, and rebellion'. He demanded that Tullie's ecclesiastical superiors, the dean and chapter of York, should suspend him from preaching altogether, which they did on 18 June.[165]

On 15 July James, still apprehensive of pulpit disturbances, established the hated commission for ecclesiastical affairs to oversee the Church of England and 'to take cognisance of all defaults in both universities'.[166] Intimidated by these latest developments, Vice-Chancellor Halton commanded the Christ Church preachers 'not to inveigh against popery' in the pulpit, lest they be called to account in London.[167] He was wise to do so, for the commissioners lost little time in signalling that they meant business. In September they suspended Bishop Compton from his diocese for refusing to check anti-Catholic sermons in London, many of them preached by Oxford graduates who duplicated his militant protestantism.[168]

---

[162] Bishop Trelawny, formerly of Christ Church, warned his clergy against traducing Catholics, for if 'they preach'd that the papists were cruel, oppressing, and such as could not keep their word with heretiques, they did insinuate to the ignorant people that the king, being a papist, he ought to be dreaded under all those characters': PRO SP 31/3, fo 70, Bishop Jonathan Trelawny to Secretary Sunderland, Trelaune, 21 May 1686.

[163] Wood, *Life and Times* iii. 183.

[164] George Tullie, *A Discourse concerning the Worship of Images. Preached before the University of Oxford on the 24th of May, 1686* (London 1689), 2, 28. It was printed by Tullie after the revolution of 1688, and dedicated to Bishop Compton of London, whose Christ Church chaplain, Zaccheus Isham, licensed it for the press on 7 April 1689.

[165] As sub-dean of York, Tullie was subject to the jurisdiction of the archbishop of York, but the exercise of this fell, *sede vacante*, to the dean and chapter following the death of Archbishop John Dolben: York Minster Library, dean and chapter archives, D 1, nos 1, 2, 4, 5.

[166] Bodl. MSS Tanner 30, fos 73–6, 460, fos 23–6, James II's letters patent, 15 July 1686; PRO C. 66/3286, SP 44/337, pp. 68–74; Luttrell, *Brief Relation* i. 384–5; Wood, *Life and Times* iii. 193–4; Beddard, 'Sancroft', 142–4.

[167] Halton's warning was to Thomas Newey, MA, of Christ Church: Wood, *Life and Times* iv. 193. For the recantation of Thomas Edwards, chaplain of Christ Church, 2 December 1687, for an offensive sermon, see OUA register Bb, fos 2, 2ᵛ (reverse).

[168] *An Exact Account of the Whole Proceedings against . . . Henry Lord Bishop of London, before the Lord Chancellor, and the other Ecclesiastical Commissioners* (London 1688); *A True Narrative of all the Proceedings . . . In the Council-Chamber at White-hall, by the Lords Commissioners appointed by His Majesty to inspect Ecclesiastical Affairs* (London 1689); E. Carpenter, *The Protestant Bishop* (London 1956), 85–100; A. T. Hart, *The Life and Times of John Sharp* (London 1949), 93–8.

The irrepressible anti-Catholicism of Christ Church, though it sprang naturally from a college that had been refounded by Henry VIII to become the seat of the local protestant bishop,[169] invited the king to discipline what was, after all, a royal foundation by giving it a Catholic head; hence Massey's appointment. The need to discourage anti-popery in the university similarly dictated Parker's elevation to the bishopric of Oxford, as it did his nomination to the presidency of Magdalen College in 1687. On Fell's death the eminent preacher, Robert South, had been the odds-on favourite to succeed him as bishop.[170] An Old Westminster and Christ Church man, a distinguished high church divine, a client of the Hydes, and a canon of the cathedral, he had 'stood fair' for the see, until a report that he had privately vilified Walker cost him the king's favour.[171] Though Archbishop Sancroft continued to press South's claims to the bishopric, and similarly advocated the merits of two Christ Church parsons, George Hooper, rector of Lambeth, and William Wigan, vicar of Kensington, for the deanery, it was to no purpose.[172] Truth to tell, the archbishop and his allies had had their day.

Events in Oxford mirrored events at court, where the earls of Clarendon and Rochester had lost ground to the Catholics and ultra-tories, Clarendon making way for Tyrconnell in Dublin, and Rochester for Sunderland at Whitehall. Sancroft had already been banished the court for declining to sit on the commission for ecclesiastical affairs.[173] The manner of Rochester's dismissal from government was particularly resented in academic circles. He was removed from the treasury only after refusing to become a Catholic, and after submitting to 'a conference' arranged for him by the king, in which 'the point of religion' was debated.[174] Significantly, the debate was between two Catholic priests chosen by James, Thomas Godden and Bonaventure Giffard, the one a doctor of divinity of Lisbon,[175] the other of the Sorbonne,[176] and two protestant clergymen chosen by Rochester, William Jane,

---

[169] J. E. A. Dawson, 'The Foundation of Christ Church, Oxford, and Trinity College, Cambridge, in 1546', *Bulletin of the Institute of Historical Research* lvii (1984), 210–11.

[170] Bodl. MS Tanner 30, fo 93, Archbishop Sancroft to James II, 29 July 1686 (draft).

[171] South protested to his Anglican patrons, in vain, against the report: ibid. fos 109, 109ᵛ, Robert South to Sancroft, Caversham, 26 August 1686; *Clarendon Correspondence*, ed. Clarke i. 175–6, South to the earl of Rochester, Caversham, 29 August 1686; Wood, *Life and Times* iv. 195.

[172] Bodl. MS Tanner 30, fo 93.

[173] Beddard, 'Sancroft', 57–67, 138–48.

[174] West. CA OB/IV/137; BL Add. MS 15,892, fos 226, 321, 363, 408; [William Jane], *A Relation of a Conference before His Majesty and the Earl of Rochester* [London 1722].

[175] Godden (*vere* Tilden, or Tylden), BA (Cambridge 1642), DD (Lisbon 1660), the former president of the English College at Lisbon, was chaplain and almoner to the dowager Queen Catherine at Somerset House. *Registers of the Catholic Chapels Royal, i. Marriages*, ed. J. C. M. Weale (Catholic Record Soc. xxxviii London 1941), 10, 17, 18, 19, 20, 29. Luttrell, *Brief Relation* i. 391; T. Baker, *History of the College of St. John the Evangelist, Cambridge*, ed. J. E. B. Mayor (2 vols Cambridge 1869) i. 515–16; Wood, *Athenae* iv. 93, 674.

[176] For Giffard's education at Douai and Paris, see *Douai College Documents 1639–1794*, ed. P. R. Harris (Catholic Record Soc. xliii London 1972), 24, 27, 37 ff.; *The Register Book of St Gregory's College, Paris, 1667–1786*, ed. E. H. Burton (Catholic Record Soc. xix London 1917), 101–5; Paris, Bibliothèque Nationale, MSS Latin 9155, fo 95, 15440, p. 262.

dean of Gloucester, and Symon Patrick, dean of Peterborough, both of them Christ Church doctors of divinity.[177]

Fell's inopportune death was little short of a disaster for Christ Church, the university, and diocese.[178] It deprived Oxford of its great leader at a time when its official patron, Chancellor Ormonde, had retired from court, superannuated and bowed with family grief. Though the duke took up residence at Cornbury Park, Clarendon's residence in the Oxfordshire countryside, it was clear that, remote from Whitehall, he could do little to stem the tide of Catholic influence.[179] Nor was it any less apparent to churchmen that they could expect no help from Bishop Parker, a notorious erastian timeserver.[180] Still, all was not lost. There were other, if lesser, clerical figures willing to take up the struggle against Rome.

Massey's promotion to the deanery of Christ Church infuriated an already aggrieved body of canons and students. That a total outsider, a junior and a renegade protestant deacon turned papist, should be foisted on them, the most august foundation in the university, jarred every fibre of their corporate being. Further afield, the appointment alarmed the clerical estate generally, for, unique among university societies, Christ Church was both a college and an Anglican cathedral.[181] Although the office of dean was an ecclesiastical dignity, not a cure of souls, the alienation of one of the plum preferments of the Church of England to a Catholic convert brought home to the protestant clergy the extent to which intrusive popery endangered the settled constitution of church and state. Moreover, it confirmed the suspicions harboured by many lay folk of James's total untrustworthiness.

It is misleading to conclude with contemporary strangers, who knew nothing of the inner conflict of loyalties that wracked the chapter of Christ Church, that the canons merely complied with James's will.[182] Nominated by James on 15 December, Massey had, it is true, been promptly installed by the sub-dean, Henry

---

[177] Though Symon Patrick was a Cantabrigian, he incorporated his BD via Christ Church on 27 June 1666 and took his DD from there on 3 July 1666. OUA register Qb, fos 68, 106, 135. BL MS Lansdowne 987, fo 294. Wood, *Fasti*, ii. 292.

[178] Fell's death was accounted 'an extraordinary losse at this time'. *The Diary of John Evelyn*, ed. De Beer iv. 519. Bodl. MS Tanner 30, fo 3, Bishop William Llyod of St Asaph to Sancroft, 17 July 1686. *To the Memory of . . . John, Lord Bishop of Oxford, and Dean of Christ Church. A pindarick ode* [London 1686].

[179] Yet, Ormonde remained in favour, and retained the offices of lord steward of the royal household and privy counsellor. PRO PC 2/71, fo 32ᵛ, Adm. 77/2, no. 134, SP 44/336, pp. 40, 63, 74, 170ff. Bodl. MS Carte 40, fos 375, 424; Wood, *Life and Times* iii. 179–80; T. Carte, *The Life of James Duke of Ormond* (6 vols Oxford 1851) iv. 678–80.

[180] It was widely thought that Parker was 'resolved to sacrifice to his ambition', and the more so when he published his subversive *Reasons for Abrogating the Test imposed upon All Members of Parliament Anno 1678. Octob. 30* (London 1687). Bodl. MS Ballard 12, fo 27, [George Hickes] to Charlett, 14 May 1687; BL Add. MS 36,707, fo 20, George Smalridge to James Harrington [April 1688], BL MS Lansdowne 937, fos 94, 97.

[181] 'I am afraid the preferment of Mr Massey will be a temptation to others to forsake our religion in hopes of preferment, and that some in Christ Church may out of fear and flattery bee too compliant with him': Bodl. MS Ballard 12, fo 19, Hickes to Charlett, 3 January 1686/7.

[182] G. V. Bennett speaks of 'the craven submission of Christ Church' in his 'Loyalist Oxford and the revolution' in *The Eighteenth Century*, 18.

Aldrich. This took place in the cathedral on 29 December in a ceremony punctuated by the reading of the king's dispensation, excusing him 'from comming to prayers, receiving the sacrament, taking of all oathes, and other duties belonging to him as deane'. While the 'many yong scholars and townsmen', present on that occasion, were laughing and 'making a May-game' of it, Wood remarked that 'the canons looked grave' enough.[183] They had every reason. The dispensation made a nonsense of decanal responsibilities. Since, according to their lights, to disobey the king would be criminal and sinful, they obeyed; but this did not prevent them from subsequently attempting to invalidate the appointment. Theirs was, at best, a 'half complyance'.[184]

Led by Aldrich, who, as sub-dean and *censor theologiae*, was rapidly assuming the mantle of being Fell's successor in the college,[185] the resident canons drew up a formal certificate on 20 January 1687, attesting Massey's failure to take the oath of supremacy decreed by the 1559 act of parliament, and sought to prosecute him as a popish recusant by initiating proceedings in the court of king's bench.[186] However their bid to activate the law against the intruder quickly came to an abrupt halt. On 6 February James ordered the court to discharge all proceedings.[187] The outcome of their protestation illustrated the futility of his subjects even offering to restrain the king by due process of law. To appeal to the crown against an item of royal policy was almost bound to be self-defeating in a system of personal monarchy. The law of protestant England did not envisage a Catholic king succeeding to the throne, and, consequently, did not provide a remedy for any difficulties that might arise from such an occurrence, which was one reason why the whigs had all along demanded the exclusion of 'a popish successor'.

Saddled with a dean whom they heartily detested, the members of Christ Church did everything they could to give him a rough ride. Unlike that of the master of University College, Massey's position in Christ Church was extremely precarious, for he lacked internal support. As dean he presided, rather than ruled, over his unhappy college, which explains why it was that he continued to frequent the Catholic 'club' that met 'every night in Walker's lodgings', off the High.[188] There is evidence that he encountered hostility at every level of college life: the undergraduates were insolent and unruly, the Students patronizing and insubordinate, the canons jealous and quarrelsome.[189] Even without the solid phalanx of

---

[183] CA D&C. i. b. 3, pp. 272–9; BL Add. MS 32,523, fo 61; Wood, *Life and Times* iii. 201–2.

[184] Even so, it was held to have 'betray'd (in part) the merits of the cause': Bodl. MS Ballard 23, fo 22, John Laughton to Arthur Charlett, Trinity College, Cambridge, 18 April 1687.

[185] CA D&C. i. b. 3, pp. 253, 255, 271, 284, 300; ORO, MS Oxf. dioc. papers d. 106, fo 68; *The Diary of John Evelyn*, ed. De Beer iv. 519. In the university he was also appointed to several offices *vice* Fell: OUA register Bb, fos 135, 144.

[186] Bodl. MS Tanner 460, fo 57: the original certificate. Surrey RO, MS Midleton 1248/1/217, Henry Aldrich to the barrister, St John Brodrick, 16 January 1687.

[187] Bodl. MS Tanner 460, fo 58; PRO SP 44/337, pp. 188–9, James II's warrant to Sir Samuel Astry, clerk of the crown in the court of king's bench, 6 February 1687.

[188] Wood, *Life and Times* iii. 213.

[189] BL Add. MS 36,707, fo 21, Thomas Newey to James Harrington [Christ Church], 5 April 1688; Bodl. MS Eng. hist. c. 6, fo 122ᵛ.

disapproving noblemen and gentlemen-commoners, whose parents had hastily removed them from Christ Church 'for feare of popery' blighting their prospects of heaven and earth, the remaining members of the college were more than a match for their isolated dean.[190] As for the university's treatment of Massey, it ignored him as far as it safely could, and pointedly withheld the doctorate that by custom was bestowed on incoming heads of house.[191] Only during the royal visit of September 1687 was there a semblance of social amity and academic normality in the functioning of Christ Church, and that did not survive James's departure.[192]

Even more than Walker, Massey remained dependent on the king. Already in May of the same year James had had to intervene to support him in a domestic squabble. He vindicated the dean's right to appoint a chapter clerk, as his predecessors had done. He also authorized the sequestration into his hands of funds from a vacant college chaplaincy. These were to be applied to 'such uses' as the king appointed.[193] In January the identical formula had been employed at University College to warrant the maintenance of a Catholic chaplain from collegiate revenues.[194] Massey, who was not without spirit, had earlier succeeded in turning 'the old refectory' of the former Canterbury College into a Catholic oratory, and, emulating Walker, had called on the Jesuit fathers to serve the altar.[195]

James, solicitous as ever to further the cause of true religion, provided Massey with additional funds. On 25 May he remitted to him the half-year's profits accruing from the vacancy of the deanery since Fell's death. At the same time he excused him from having to account to the chapter for his receipts.[196] It was this *ex gratia* payment which gave rise to Wood's report that Walker 'goes snips' with Massey in the decanal revenues, a portion of which appears to have been assigned to cover the considerable expense of erecting and operating an independent Catholic press in Oxford. Such an ill-considered diversion of the 'profits which were once Dr. Fell's', away from the Church of England to the Church of Rome, must have rubbed salt into the gaping wound opened by Massey's presence in Christ Church.[197]

It is hardly surprising that Aldrich and a small hand-picked team of Christ Church Students dedicated their learning and labour to attacking Walker's publica-

---

[190] For the flight from Christ Church and the falling number of matriculands, see Wood, *Life and Times* iii. 202, 209, 215, 221–2, 257; OUA matriculation register, pp. 29–34, register of congregation 1680–92, NEP/*supra*/20, register Be, fos 170ᵛ–3.

[191] Massey's mandamus for a DD was ignored by the university: Bodl. MS Ballard 12, fo 27, [Hickes] to Charlett, 14 May 1687; *Hatton Correspondence*, ed. Thompson i. 405; Luttrell, *Brief Relation* i. 404. Barnard's mandate for a DCL was also ignored: Wood, *Life and Times* iv. 215.

[192] OUA register Bb, pp. 169–73; Bodl. MS Smith 47, fo 46.

[193] PRO SP 44/57, p. 166, James II to Dean Massey, Windsor, 25 May 1687.

[194] See p. 927 above.

[195] 'The new chappell' is also described as having been 'formerly the dean's woodhouse'. Bodl. MS Rawlinson letters 91, fo 54; *The Records of the English Province*, ed. Foley v. 956; *Dialogue between a Churchman and a Dissenter* (London 1689); Wood, *Life and Times* iii. 215.

[196] PRO SP 44/57, p. 166.   [197] Wood, *Life and Times* iii. 201–2.

tions.[198] They included two future Church of England bishops, George Smalridge and Francis Atterbury, and the versatile lawyer and antiquary, James Harrington. As the heirs of Fell's indomitable protestantism, they leapt to the defence of the university's honour.[199] Their greatest fear was that Walker's papistical effusions might pass in the outside world as 'the universities judgement'.[200] To contradict the persistent rumour, which the protestant dissenters disseminated and the Catholics did nothing to deny, that 'Oxford converts came in by whole shoals, and all the university were just ready to declare' themselves Catholics, it was, Aldrich argued, imperative that Woodhead's tracts 'should receive an answer from the same place, from whence they had defy'd the Church of England'.[201]

So it transpired, to the king's intense annoyance, that 'the zealous Church of England men ... seing that Mr. Walker would cut their throats at home, were resolved to answer whatsoever he published'.[202] Set on by Sub-Dean Aldrich, who himself delivered the opening thrust, Christ Church produced a series of anonymous ripostes to the publications of their most 'potent enemy', Walker.[203] In launching their counter-attack they had the backing of Vice-Chancellor Venn, who readily gave the university's imprimatur to their writings.[204] Their appearance in print was applauded by the parochial clergy, who hung on their every word,[205] while the agitated dons of Cambridge ordered their works by the dozen, as an antidote to the endeavours of their own proselytizers.[206] Arthur Charlett of Trinity, the self-appointed settler of troubled Anglican consciences, was kept busy supplying their propaganda needs.[207]

Nor was the Oxford counter-attack physically confined to Oxford. It fed the greater controversy that was raging in the capital.[208] Recruited by Compton to the battalion of anti-Catholic writers in London, none of Christ Church's sons was more tireless, nor more valiant in laying about him, than Fell's confessed admirer,

[198] By May 1687 it was believed in London 'that things are put in a method' at Oxford for the 'speedy' answering of Walker's books: Bodl. MS Ballard 3, fo 3, William Wake to Arthur Charlett, 14 May 1687; Wood, *Athenae* iv. 652–3; W. G. Hiscock, *Henry Aldrich of Christ Church 1648–1710* (London 1960), 2, 44–5.

[199] [Francis Atterbury], *Answer to Some Considerations on the Spirit of Martin Luther and the Original of the Reformation. Lately printed at Oxford* (Oxford 1687), preface.

[200] [Henry Aldrich], *A Reply to Two Discourses. Lately printed at Oxford concerning the adoration of our blessed saviour, in the holy eucharist* (Oxford 1687), 2.

[201] Ibid., 'To the reader'.   [202] Wood, *Life and Times* iii. 217–18.

[203] [George Smalridge], *Animadversions on the Eight Theses ... in a Discourse entitl'd Church-Government. Part V. Lately printed at Oxford* (Oxford 1687), 1; Wood, *Athenae* iv. 652–3.

[204] Venn gave his imprimatur to Aldrich on 19 May, to Smalridge on 2 June and to Atterbury on 29 July 1687.

[205] Bodl. MS Ballard 12, fos 21ᵛ, 29, Dr George Hickes to Arthur Charlett, Worcester, 11 February 1686/7, 9 June 1687; Bodl. MS Ballard 30, fo 12, Abraham Campion to Charlett, Monk's Risborough, 24 February 1687/8; Macaulay, *History of England*, ed. Firth ii. 956.

[206] At Cambridge the Oxford replies were 'greedily snatcht' up. Bodl. MS Ballard 23, fos 11, 9, 13ᵛ, John Laughton to Arthur Charlett [Cambridge], 27 June, 6 June, 19 December 1687.

[207] Wood, *Life and Times* iii. 245.

[208] *A Catalogue of the Collection of Tracts for and against Popery*, ed. T. Jones (Chetham Soc. xlviii lxiv 1859 1865); E. Carpenter, *Thomas Tenison* (London 1948), 43–64; R. A. Beddard, 'The unexpected whig revolution of 1688' in Beddard (ed.), *The Revolutions of 1688*, 48, 67–70.

William Wake, the future archbishop of Canterbury.[209] Having recently returned from Paris, where he had witnessed Louis XIV's persecution of the Huguenots at first hand, he appeared to be the long-awaited David raised by providence to slay the Roman Goliath. His outstanding performance earned him the undying gratitude of the protestant hierarchy, foremost among whom stood the Oxonians: Bishop Ken of Bath and Wells, Bishop Frampton of Gloucester, and George Hickes, dean of Worcester.[210] They, together with Wake's friends in Christ Church, encouraged him to assail the claims of international Catholicism, whether voiced by Bishop Bossuet in France or by Master Walker in England.[211]

The opposition of Christ Church—in common with that of the Church of England in general—came to a head with the declaration of indulgence of 4 April 1687. The averseness shown by the Anglican tory nobles and squires in complying with an increasingly Catholicized court caused James to embark on the wholesale dismissal of recalcitrant churchmen from office.[212] Relying upon his prerogative, he attempted to fashion an alternative power-base to that represented by an exclusive Anglican establishment. He not only granted protestant dissenters, as well as Catholics, the right to worship in public, he allowed them to enter public office.[213] Despite the renewal of the promise to protect the Church of England, the royal initiative was widely regarded as a ploy to humble the established church. This was the view taken by Archbishop Sancroft and the majority of his suffragans.[214] Yet James knew that the support of Catholics and dissenters was not enough. He needed to win over as many churchmen as he could if he was to procure a 'tolerationist' parliament which would give him the statutory approval that he sought. He therefore exploited the presence in the protestant episcopate of a number of ultra-tories to sow division among churchmen.[215]

Bishop Parker of Oxford was tailor-made to act on behalf of the court.

[209] That Compton resented 'the behaviour of the Romish priests', which, he maintained, constrained the protestant ministers 'to say more in this particular, for the settling of men's minds, than otherwise they would do', see Bodl. MS Tanner 31, fo 268. CL Arch. W. Epist. 17, fo 7, Fell to Wake, 12 March [1686]. Dr. Williams's Library MS Morrice Q, p. 117; Bodl. MS Rawlinson d. 399, fo 11; N. Sykes, *William Wake Archbishop of Canterbury 1657–1737* (2 vols Cambridge 1957) i. 20–28; W. J. Sparrow Simpson, *A Study of Bossuet* (London 1937), 121–3.

[210] CL Arch. W. Epist. 17, fos 20, 14, 12, Thomas Ken to Wake, 20 July, Robert Frampton to Wake, Gloucester, 18 December, George Hickes to Wake, Worcester, 9 July 1687.

[211] The bishop of Meaux's *Exposition of the Doctrine of the Catholic Church* had gone through several English translations and editions, including three since 1685 (Bodleian Library copies: Linc. c. 11. 2 (iii); Vet. A3 f. 800; Vet. A3 e. 1793). F. Cabrol, 'Bossuet, ses relations avec l'Angleterre', *Revue d'histoire ecclésiastique* xxvii (1931), 550–3; V. Verlaque, *Bibliographie raisonnée des œuvres de Bossuet* (Paris 1908), 4–7, 14–15, 23.

[212] G. F. Duckett, *Penal Laws and the Test Act* (2 vols London 1882–3), *passim*; L. K. J. Glassey, *Politics and the Appointment of Justices of the Peace 1675–1720* (Oxford 1973), 77–93.

[213] For the dissenters, see R. A. Beddard, 'Vincent Alsop and the emancipation of Restoration dissent', *Journal of Ecclesiastical History* xxiv (1973), 173–84. For the Catholics, see J. Miller, *Popery and Politics in England 1660–1688* (Cambridge 1973), 208–9 and appx 3.

[214] The declaration was looked on as part of a malevolent court stratagem: Beddard, 'Sancroft', 149–50.

[215] For the emergence of the ultra-tory threat, see R. A. Beddard, 'Bishop Cartwright's death-bed', *Bodleian Library Record* xi (1984), 220–2.

Regardless of the harmful implications of indulgence, Parker demanded that the clergy of his diocese present an address of thanks to the king for his repeated promise of protection.[216] At a meeting of his clergy in the university church on 30 May the senior ecclesiastic present was William Jane, an unbending traditionalist. As dean of Gloucester, he had already sided with his diocesan, Bishop Frampton, another Christ Church man, in refusing to address. Back in Oxford, he came out strongly against complying with Parker's demand.[217] Convinced that Parker, like the king, intended to provoke 'a fatal division among the clergy', he maintained that they should not separate from their metropolitan and 'the majority of the clergy'. To do so, he told them, would be to 'forfeit our reputation with the nobility, gentry and commonalty of our communion', many of whom had lost office rather than concur in the designs of the court. Jane carried the day. The clergy agreed not to address.[218] The argument for solidarity with the lay leaders of their church was conclusive. It was one which the academic authorities fully respected, as had been demonstrated by Chancellor Ormonde's pointed nomination of Lord Clarendon to the vacant stewardship of the university, even as he was being dismissed from the vice-royalty of Ireland in January 1687.[219]

Throughout Oxford the signs of Catholic infiltration were plain to see. Before 1687 was out no fewer than eight of the colleges had felt the direct impact of Catholicism, and a ninth, Queen's, was vicariously concerned in the suspensions of Tullie and Compton.[220] University and Christ Church had Catholic heads; University, Brasenose, Trinity, Magdalen, and All Souls had converted fellows; and Balliol had a solitary undergraduate convert.[221] Exeter College, though untroubled by converts, underwent a notable challenge from Lord Petre, the Catholic scion of a former benefactor of the college and the kinsman of Edward Petre, the king's Jesuit confessor.[222] In 1686–7 he spied his opportunity to reclaim his ancestor's

[216] Bodl. MS Rawlinson d. 843, fos 113, 114, MS Rawlinson letters 94, fo 290, Thomas Castillion to Bishop Turner of Ely, New College, 1 June [1687]; Dr Williams's Library, MS Morrice Q, pp. 107, 114; *The Diary of John Evelyn*, ed. De Beer iv. 553–4; Luttrell, *Brief Relation* i. 405, 408; Wood, *Life and Times* iii. 220.

[217] Bodl. MS Rawlinson letters 91, fos 66–7, William Sherwin (overwritten Charles Worcester) to Thomas Turner, 31 May [1687]; BL MS Lansdowne 937, fo 90ᵛ, White Kennett's account.

[218] BL Add. MS 21,092, fo 23, MS Lansdowne 1024, fo 50ᵛ; *A Reply to the Reasons of the Oxford-Clergy against Addressing. Publish'd with allowance* (London 1687), 13–17; *A Copy of an Address to the King by the Bishop of Oxon, to be subscribed by the clergy of his diocess* (London 1687), 1–2.

[219] OUA register Bb, pp. 142–4, 5 January 1687; Bodl. MS Carte 217, fo 272, Vice-Chancellor Venn to Gascoigne, Oxford, 22 November 1686. For Clarendon's interest in the Oxford press and in the case of Magdalen College, see his autograph transcription of some of the relevant documents: MS Carte 198, fos 78, 80–1ᵛ, 82–7ᵛ. *Clarendon Correspondence*, ed. Clarke i. 173, 188.

[220] For the links of Tullie and Compton with Queen's see J. R. Magrath, *The Queen's College* (2 vols Oxford 1931) ii. 55, 270.

[221] In addition to Walker, Massey, Boyse, Deane, and Barnard, they were Stephen Hunt (Trinity), Robert Charnock (Magdalen), Matthew Tindall (All Souls), and Clarke (Balliol). Wood, *Life and Times* iii. 75, 77, 182, 213, 215, 218, 255, 264, 291, 303; PRO SP 44/57, p. 129, SP 44/56, p. 349; TCA miscellanea I, fo 126, Samuel Dugard to Dr Ralph Bathurst, 15 January 1687; BL MS Lansdowne 937, fo 95; Bodl MS Smith 141, fos 17, 20, 21, 32ᵛ, 37; *Hatton Correspondence*, ed. Thompson i. 319–20.

[222] ECA register 1619–1737, fos 78ᵛ–9; Bodl. MS Ballard 25, fo 98.

benefaction for the benefit of his co-religionists.[223] The rector and fellows were hard put to it to defeat his claim, and had to brave a hearing before the ecclesiastical commission.[224] Had they not been successful, Petre might well have endangered the funding of protestant education in the university.

Alone of the colleges, Walker's University College dared to institute an active policy of Catholic recruitment in its undergraduate admissions,[225] but that was sufficient to conjure up protestant nightmares, and reinforced parental reluctance to keep their boys at Oxford, or to send them there in the first place. Falling numbers meant, then as now, a fall in fee income—a development which did nothing to improve frayed academic tempers, or to lessen confessional jealousies.[226] In June 1687, and again in June 1688, the celebration of the Act was put off, it being thought 'not fit as the times now stand'.[227] The underlying fears were religious: first, that the participants, the Terrae-Filii especially, could not be controlled and might 'bring the university into danger' by reflecting 'upon the papists and proceedings in the nation'; and secondly, that 'the great resort of preists and Jesuits' to Oxford would occasion their 'picking holes in the divinity disputations', which were bound to contain specifically anti-Catholic *quaestiones*. In either event there was no knowing what might ensue. Ormonde twice cancelled the Act, the university holding it inappropriate 'to be merry and cheerfull . . . when the Church of England is endeavoured to be over-clouded'.[228]

Of all the trials and tribulations endured by the university none was more protracted, more embittered, and more profoundly upsetting than that which Magdalen experienced at the hands of the Catholic king and his advisers. An oft-told tale, it scarcely requires detailed recapitulation.[229] However, various points need to be made with respect to the king's religious aims, which evolved in response to the increasing politicization of the fellows' opposition, rather than from deliberate malice aforethought on James's part, as has been assumed by too many historians.[230]

On the death of President Clerke, in March 1687, James's ambition was to replace him with one who would be 'favourable to his religion'.[231] The fact was

---

[223] For the earlier history of the Petrean foundation at Exeter College (1616) see ECA F. IV. 7, F. IV. 5/5.

[224] Bodl. MS Rawlinson d. 365, fos 12, 13, 13ᵛ, 14, 2 December 1686–17 February 1687; ECA F. IV. 5/li, ii, 2i, 4, 6, 7.

[225] Dr Williams's Library, MS Morrice P, p. 532; UCA registrum admissionum, pp. 8, 9.

[226] In the town trade slumped 'because of the paucity of scholars frighted away for feare of popery': Wood, *Life and Times* iii. 209.

[227] OUA, register Bb, pp. 160, 198, 23 June 1687, 25 June 1688; Bodl. MS Carte 131B, fo 234.

[228] Wood, *Life and Times* iii. 221–2. Walker had opposed its cancellation in 1688. *The Ellis Correspondence*, ed. Ellis ii. 4.

[229] Most recently by L. Brockliss, G. Harriss, and A. Macintyre, *Magdalen College and the Crown: essays for the tercentenary of the restoration of the college 1688* (Oxford 1988).

[230] The assumption that James intended right from the start to take over Magdalen entirely for Catholics does not square either with the detailed history of his dealings with the college, or with his approach to University College, Brasenose, and Christ Church.

[231] So Bishop Parker informed Thomas Smith, fellow of Magdalen College: Bodl. MS Smith 141, fo 11ᵛ.

well known at court, and discouraged several eligible internal candidates from standing for the presidency—including Princess Anne's domestic chaplain, John Younger,[232] and the erudite loyalist scholar, Thomas Smith.[233] The college visitor, Bishop Mews of Winchester, put forward Bishop Levinz of Sodor and Man, a quondam fellow, and he duly received 'both the unanimous votes and desires of the whole society to bee their president'.[234] But, on hearing that James had issued his mandamus on 5 April in favour of Anthony Farmer, an incorporated Cantabrigian, Levinz withdrew. Despite the ineligibility of Farmer, for he had never belonged to the foundation of either Magdalen or New College, and his being suspected in religion,[235] Levinz declined 'to contest his majesty's mandate'.[236] The fellows, backed by the visitor, petitioned the king against Farmer, as being statutably incapable of succeeding Clerke.[237] Their entreaties met with a denial from Lord President Sunderland, who haughtily told them that his master 'expects to bee obeyed'.[238]

In the long and complex dispute which followed, confessional and political rivalries, rather than legal and constitutional niceties, governed the resistance of the fellows, just as they informed the demands of the king. For James, much was at stake. His nomination of Farmer—made the day after his declaration of universal toleration—was a test of his new policy. For most of the fellows, it seemed about as good an opportunity as any college was ever likely to get to make a stand against further Catholic encroachment in Oxford. Between Levinz's abrupt withdrawal and Sunderland's deliberately delayed message from the king, the fellows 'were put to their shifts' to find an alternative candidate.[239] Determined to oppose the royal nominee, they fixed on one of themselves: John Hough, a fellow of the college since 1674.

An academic nonentity in comparison with Pierce and Clerke, his two predecessors as president, Hough had the supreme and, the fellows gambled, invincible

[232] Lady Shuttleworth, the daughter of the deceased president, had informed Younger, then in waiting at court as chaplain to Princess Anne, of her father's death, so that he might make an interest for himself at London. He chose not to do so: Bodl. MS Smith 141, fo 11; Wood, *Life and Times* iii. 216.

[233] Smith refused 'the conditions' which were attached to the preferment, when he consulted Bishop Parker: Bodl. MS Smith 141, fo 12. For Archbishop Sancroft's copy of 'Dr Thomas Smith's account of his behaviour in the affairs of Magdalen College', see Bodl. MS Tanner 29, fos 85, 86ᵛ–7, 88–9, 90–2, 93–104ᵛ, 105–12.

[234] Bodl. MS Rawlinson letters 94, fo 195, Baptist Levinz, bishop of Sodor and Man, to Archbishop Sancroft, Bishopscourt, Isle of Man, 27 October 1688; MCA MS 418, p. 483, Peter Mews, bishop of Winchester, to Secretary Sunderland, Farnham Castle, 8 April 1687.

[235] Though supported by the Catholic interest, Farmer's rumoured conversion remains open to question. He was a co-operative tory loyalist, who had 'in nupera rebellione pro rege ultra arma suscepisse': MCA MS 249, fo 83, MS 730b (vice-president's register, 1661–1776), fos 45–6, MS 418, p. 481; Dr Williams's Library, MS Morrice Q, p. 93; PRO SP 44/57, p. 163, James II to Magdalen College, 5 April 1687.

[236] Bodl. MS Rawlinson letters 94, fo 195.

[237] PRO SP 44/56, pp. 369, 370, Sunderland to Mews, 16 and 21 April 1687; Bodl. MS Smith 141, fos 14ʳ⁻ᵛ, vice-president and fellows' petition to James II, 10 April 1687; MCA MS 418, p. 484.

[238] Bodl. MS Smith 141, fos 15, 16, 13 April 1687.

[239] PRO PC 2/72, fos 1ᵛ–2ᵛ; Hearne, *Collections* xi. 411.

qualification of being the chancellor's favourite chaplain.[240] With Hough to lead them, they felt confident of Ormonde's support and of the countenance of his friends inside and outside the university.[241] It is inconceivable that Aldrich was not consulted in the choice of candidate. As the local confidant of the Butler family, the former tutor of Ormonde's grandson and heir, Lord Ossory, and the pace-maker of Oxford opposition, he undertook to fortify the college's resolve to resist the court whatever the cost.[242] In this he was assisted by his crony, Henry Smyth, canon of Christ Church.[243] They knew that the duke had already shown his willingness to oppose 'popish aggression' in the affairs of the London Charterhouse, of which he was a governor.[244] Thus, though the vice-president and three senior fellows of Magdalen were for deferring the election called for 15 April, and going back to the king to avoid confrontation, their advice was brushed aside by intemperate juniors amid 'hot debates', in which 'horrible rude reflexions' were 'made upon the king's authority'. The loyal Thomas Smith was appalled, and protested 'that the spirit of Ferguson', the Presbyterian plotter, had got among them.[245] The election went ahead none the less. After a taxing meeting of the governing body, of almost five hours' duration, Hough was elected by a substantial majority. He left immediately for Farnham Castle, the residence of the bishop of Winchester. The next day he obtained his admittance to the presidency from the visitor, only hours before Sunderland's letter arrived at Farnham to forbid it.[246] While Bishop Mews privately confided to the college delegation 'that hee admired their courage',[247] the chancellor and university publicly demonstrated where their sympathies lay by conferring a doctorate on Hough as the acknowledged 'president of St Mary Magdalen College in Oxford'.[248] Their action was rendered more impressive by their studied refusal to grant higher degrees to the court's clients, protestant and Catholic.[249]

[240] J. Wilmot, *The Life of the Rev. John Hough* (London 1812), 4; Dr Williams's Library, MS Morrice Q, p. 93; Bodl. MS Smith 141, fo 18, MS Bodley 594, p. 117; Hearne, *Collections* i. 187, 288.

[241] Bodl. MS Smith 141, fo 18; MCA MS 418, p. 487, President Hough and the fellows' petition to Chancellor Ormonde, Magdalen College, 19 April 1687. For evidence that Hough kept Ormonde abreast of events at Magdalen, see BL Add. MS 21,092, fos 20–1ᵛ.

[242] Aldrich's care of his pupil had earned him his Christ Church canonry, for the obtaining of which he had solicited Lord Ossory's aid: Bodl. MS Carte 70, fo 464, MS Carte 69, fo 495. BL Add. MS 28,875, fos 71, 74; CA D. P. i. a. 12, fo 14.

[243] *Memoirs of Thomas, Earl of Ailesbury* [ed. W. E. Buckley] (2 vols Roxburghe Club Westminster 1890) i. 168.

[244] Ormonde had joined in the governors' refusal to admit the Catholic Andrew Popham, a suffering loyalist, to a pensioner's place in the Charterhouse. PRO SP 44/53, pp. 476, 474, SP 44/337, pp. 210–16; Dr Williams's Library, MS Morrice Q, p. 49; Carte, *Ormond* iv. 682–4.

[245] MCA MS 730b, fo 46; Bodl. MS Smith 141, fo 16ᵛ. For Robert Ferguson, who was soon to be concerned in dethroning James II, see Beddard, *A Kingdom without a King*, 21, 22, 27, 183.

[246] MCA MS 730b, fo 47, 17 April 1687, MS 418, p. 485, Bishop Peter Mews to Sunderland, Farnham Castle, 17 April 1687.

[247] Bodl. MS Smith 141, fos 17ᵛ–18; Dr Williams's Library, MS Morrice Q, p. 94.

[248] OUA register Bb, p. 156, Ormonde to Vice-Chancellor Venn, St James's Square, 18 June 1687; MCA MS 730b, fo 47.

[249] The court backed down over conferring degrees on the clients of Lord Chancellor Jeffreys and Bishop Parker: PRO SP 44/56, p. 385, Sunderland to Vice-Chancellor Venn, Windsor, 19 September 1687; Bodl. MS Ballard 21, fo 10, MS Rawlinson letters 91, fo 54; HMC *Downshire MSS* i, pt 1, p. 251; Luttrell, *Brief Relation* i. 414.

Traditionally treated by its apologists as a classic case of passive obedience,[250] Magdalen's disobedience was no such thing. Its parade of statutory rectitude masked active defiance, as Thomas Smith recognized at the time.[251] Had the fellows refused to elect Farmer, and then been content to suffer the consequences, theirs might have been a genuine instance of passive obedience, for as Dean Hickes observed 'non-resistance is alwayes a duty, and non-compliance very often is'.[252] But they did not. They proceeded, contrary to the king's express command, to elect not his, but another candidate.[253] Their act was totally at odds with the Oxford decree of 1683, which condemned unreservedly the proposition that 'there lies no obligation upon Christians to passive obedience when the prince commands anything against the laws of our country'.[254]

The fellows' disobedience brought them before the ecclesiastical commission, where, after implausibly pleading the authority of their statutes against the king's prerogative, and boastfully asserting their conscientious observance of the founder's statutes, which in the past they had ignored when it suited them, Hough's election was pronounced null and void.[255] To the weeks of wilful opposition that then ensued, during which the king abandoned Farmer[256] and imposed the protestant Bishop Parker on the college as president,[257] there could be but one outcome, given the intransigence on both sides: the expulsion not only of Hough, but of all the disobedient fellows from the college.[258] It was a development which James had never foreseen, nor intended, but of which, in his anger, he took full advantage.

Over and above the 'traitorous and pernicious counsel' which the king may have been given when the vacancy first occurred, and the malice which Sunderland consistently displayed towards the college, matters could not have come to the sorry pass that they did without Hough's decision to carry resistance to extremes. To him, defiance seemed the only means of halting the Catholic advance. In his own words: 'we have a religion to defend . . . The papists have already got Christ Church

---

[250] Bennett, 'Loyalist Oxford and the revolution', 18.

[251] Smith contended throughout 'that the king's authority (as hath hitherto been believed and practised) supersedes the obligation of the statute', which had certainly been the case in the two previous elections to the presidentship: Pierce in 1661 and Clerke in 1672. *Restoration Oxford*, ed. Beddard ii, no. 502; MCA MS 730a, fos 104, 174, MS 730b, fo 1; Bodl. MS Tanner 29, fo 91ᵛ, MS Smith 141, fo 27.

[252] Bodl. MS Ballard 12, fo 25, [George Hickes] to Charlett, 4 May 1687.

[253] Smith consulted the local civilian, Henry Aylworth, chancellor of the diocese of Oxford, who firmly opined that the king's mandate for another 'had in it the force of an inhibition' with respect to the college's proceeding to an election of its own: Bodl. MS Smith 141, fo 20ᵛ.

[254] *Judicium et decretum universitatis oxoniensis latum in convocatione habita julii 21 an. 1683, contra quosdam perniciosos libros et propositiones impias* (Oxford 1683).

[255] MCA MS 908/26, Robert Almont's account; Bodl. MS Rawlinson d. 365, fos 20, 20ᵛ, 21, 21ᵛ, 23.

[256] Bloxam, *Magdalen and James II*, 79–80. He does not print 'Mr Anthony Farmer's vindication from the false, scandalous, and pretended allegations against him by the vice-president and deputed fellows . . . to . . . the lords commissioners ecclesiasticall', which (plausibly) makes out that his opponents had deliberately blackened his character. MCA MS 249, fos 78–86.

[257] PRO SP 44/57, p. 177, James II to the fellows of Magdalen College, Windsor, 14 August 1687. For the king's personal insistence on Bishop Parker's election, see PRO SP 31/2, pp. 39 ff, SP 44/56, p. 384.

[258] Wood, *Life and Times* iii. 249–50; Bloxam, *Magdalen and James II*, 204–5.

and University College: the present struggle is for Magdalen, and they threaten that in a short time they will have the rest.' Consequently, it became his aim to conduct the college's campaign, so as 'to let the world see that they *take* it from us, and that we do not *give* it up'.[259] In Oxford, as all over England, protestant paranoia quickened the pace of resistance, as Hough and his supporters inexorably pushed James into taking severer measures against them. College piety apart, it would be politically naïve to underestimate the extent to which the fellows of Magdalen had turned 'malcontents and muttineers'.[260] That they had previously been conspicuous 'in deffence of the crown' against Monmouth and 'in the greate affaire of the succession' against the whigs, and felt that they deserved James's gratitude and favour, made their resentment of the king's 'interference' all the more implacable.[261]

In making their stand against the court they received encouragement from many quarters: from 'several great men at London', including the whig lawyer Sir John Maynard,[262] from Cambridge admirers,[263] and, nearer home, from Aldrich and Smyth of Christ Church, without whose surreptitious support of Hough the loyal earl of Ailesbury was convinced that 'this pretended bully for the liberties and privileges' of the college 'had submitted at court'.[264] The seemingly harsh sentence of the ecclesiastical commissioners in adding to the punishment of the ejected fellows by incapacitating them, if laymen, from holy orders, and, if clerics, from preferment,[265] had the effect of turning them into protestant heroes—confessors who had lost everything for the sake of their faith.[266] Significantly, it was the Christ Church bishops, such as Frampton of Gloucester and Trelawny of Bristol, who ignored the sentence of incapacity by boldly admitting them to benefices in their

---

[259] MCA MS 421 (Holden papers, unfoliated), J[ohn] H[ough] to Henry Holden, Magdalen College, 31 October 1687 (emphasis added); Bloxam, *Magdalen and James II*, 105, Hough to his cousin, 9 October [1687]; *Memoirs of Thomas, Earl of Ailesbury*, [ed. Buckley] i. 167; Bodl. MS Smith 141, fos 25ʳ⁻ᵛ. The attempt to whitewash Sunderland's conduct is unconvincing in J. P. Kenyon, *Robert Spencer, Earl of Sunderland 1641–1702* (London 1958), 154 and n.

[260] James believed 'it was a confederacy to be stubborn only to draw an odium upon their prince': *The Life of James the Second*, ed. J. S. Clarke (2 vols London 1816) ii. 123–4; Bodl. MS Smith 141, fos 27, 28ᵛ, 32; Bloxam, *Magdalen and James II*, 239.

[261] MCA MS 418, p. 483, Mews to Sunderland, Farnham Castle, 8 April 1687; Bodl. MS Smith 141, fo 16ᵛ.

[262] D. R. Lacey, *Dissent and Parliamentary Politics in England 1661–1689* (New Brunswick NJ 1969), 423. Maynard was soon to distinguish himself as a leading Williamite revolutionary in the whigs' bid to dethrone James II: R. A. Beddard, 'The unexpected whig revolution of 1688' in Beddard (ed.), *The Revolutions of 1688*, 37, 38, 39, 66, 69, 99.

[263] Bodl. MS Ballard 23, fos 9, 24, John Laughton to Arthur Charlett, 27 June and 4 July 1687.

[264] *Memoirs of Thomas, Earl of Ailesbury* [ed. Buckley] i. 168.

[265] Bodl. MS Rawlinson d. 365, fos 23–24ᵛ; MCA MS 730b, fo 48, ecclesiastical commissioners' order, 10 December 1687; CL Arch. W. Epist. 17, fo 25, Bishop Thomas Ken of Bath and Wells to William Wake, 28 December 1687.

[266] Hough magnified their 'ruine' and the fact that 'there are many gapeing for our places'. MCA MS 421 (unfoliated), Hough to Henry Holden, Magdalen College, 31 October 1687 (Bloxam's text is faulty, and the letter is wrongly ascribed to Holden); Bodl. MS Smith 141, fo 25ᵛ; Henry Fairfax, *An Impartial Relation of the Whole Proceedings against Magdalen College* (London 1688).

dioceses,[267] and a tory ally of the Hydes, Sir Thomas Clarges,[268] who took the lead in stirring up the charity of the protestant nobility for the relief of the 'poor deprivees'.[269]

Although the king had been warned 'not to touch the freehold of the clergy' on the grounds that, if he pinched them, the clergy could be relied on to 'return it fourfold—as was found in the sequel', there was no deflecting him.[270] Lulled into a false sense of security by the sweeping ejection of his opponents, James cast caution to the winds. He set about packing the vacant fellowships and demyships with Catholics. Almost to a man they were products of the English colleges of Catholic Europe, not of protestant Oxford.[271] He began on 11 November by nominating William Joyner, a pre-war fellow who had lost his fellowship because of his conversion to Rome,[272] and Job Allibone, the Douai-educated brother of the Catholic judge, Sir Richard Allibone.[273] On 31 December he ordered ten more Catholics to be admitted.[274] Many more followed in the new year.[275]

The recipients of the king's grace ranged from senior Catholic figures, such as James's Benedictine chaplain, Thomas Augustine Constable,[276] and the Jesuit dogmatic theologian, Thomas Fairfax,[277] to converts of recent vintage, such as John Christmas, rector of Cornard Parva in Suffolk,[278] and John Dryden, the second son

[267] MCA MS 370b, fos 54ᵛ, 55, LCD/4 (draft libri computi, 1648–97); BL Add. MS 34,502, fo 133ᵛ, Don Pedro Ronquillo to Carlos II of Spain, London, 27 September 1688; *The Life of Robert Frampton Bishop of Gloucester*, ed. T. Simpson Evans (London 1876), 154–8.

[268] Clarges had laid the 'opportunity to doe some good' for them at dinner with Lords Halifax, Weymouth, and Nottingham at Kensington House: Bodl. MS top. Oxon. c. 325, fo 71ᵛ, Sir Thomas Clarges to [John] Moore, domestic chaplain to the earl of Abingdon, 23 November 1687. For Clarges' espousal of the university cause, see Longleat, MS Thynne 12, fo 275, Clarges to Lord Weymouth, 23 April 1687.

[269] Mary, princess of Orange, demonstrated her sympathy for the protestant cause by contributing £200 to their relief: Bodl. MS Smith 141, fo 28.

[270] *Memoirs of Thomas, Earl of Ailesbury* [ed. Buckley] i. 169.

[271] BL MS Lansdowne 937, fo 94ᵛ. For the vital importance of these foundations for the survival of English Catholicism see P. Guilday, *The English Catholic Refugees on the Continent 1558–1795* (London 1914), 63 ff.; A. C. F. Beales, *Education under Penalty* (London 1963), 115–57.

[272] Bodl. MS Smith 141, fo 25ᵛ. For William Joyner (alias Lyde), see PRO SP 44/56, p. 392, SP 44/57, pp. 184–6, 194; Wood, *Athenae* iv. 587; Wood, *Fasti* ii. 57; Wood, *Life and Times* ii. 427, 432–3, iii. 121, 173–4, 250, 258, 259, 523, 525, 531.

[273] PRO SP 44/56, p. 392, SP 44/57, pp. 184–6; *Douai Diaries 1598–1654*, ed. E. H. Burton and L. J. Williams (Catholic Record Soc. x xi 1910–11) ii. 516, 522; *Douai College Documents 1639–1794*, ed. P. R. Harris (Catholic Record Soc. xliii 1972), 34; Wood, *Life and Times* ii. 142, iii. 523, 525.

[274] Bloxam, *Magdalen and James II*, 225–31.

[275] Ibid. 232, 235, 236, 238, 239–40; MCA MS 730b, fos 52, 53; BL MS Lansdowne 937, fo 94ᵛ; Luttrell, *Brief Relation* i. 425.

[276] For Thomas Constable (alias Thomas Augustine), OSB, see PRO SP 44/57, p. 196, James II to President Samuel Parker, 24 February 1688; H. N. Birt, *Obit Book of the English Benedictines 1600–1912* (Edinburgh 1913), 73–4.

[277] PRO SP 44/57, pp. 185–6, 193, 194, SP 31/4, fo 8; Holt, *The English Jesuits 1650–1829*, 90; B. Basset, *The English Jesuits from Campion to Martindale*, 259, 296.

[278] PRO SP 31/4, fo 8, SP 44/57, p. 193; James II to President Samuel Parker, 31 December 1687; Anstruther, *The Seminary Priests 1558–1850* ii. 254.

of the poet laureate, who was himself a distinguished convert.[279] To begin with, not all of James's nominees had been Catholics. Some were undoubtedly protestants from Cavalier Anglican families, like Thomas Higgons, the nephew of Dean Grenville of Durham.[280] In this phase of the changeover the king relied on Parker to admit his protégés to the foundation and, during Parker's illness, on Robert Charnock, the converted fellow whom he nominated vice-president on 7 January 1688.[281]

In March the death of Parker made room for a Catholic president. Acting on Sunderland's proposal that 'one of the new prelates' appointed by Pope Innocent XI to oversee the Church in England should be put in charge of the college,[282] James named the vicar apostolic of the midland district, Bonaventure Giffard, bishop-elect of Madaura, on 28 March.[283] The royal mandate was received by Charnock and the fellows with 'great gladness of heart'.[284] Parker's demise having removed the last obstacle to the celebration of mass, the vice-president seized the college chapel for Catholic worship.[285] He was evidently apprised of the king's plan to make Magdalen the seat of the newly constituted midland district, a vast area stretching from the Thames to the Humber and from the Marches of Wales to the coast of East Anglia,[286] with the existing medieval chapel serving as Bishop Giffard's pro-cathedral. His action was the unique instance of physical aggression against Oxford protestantism. It sent a shiver of horror down the spine of the Church of England.

Magdalen's future as a Catholic seminary was finally assured, or so it seemed, on 4 June, when the king committed to Giffard 'the full and sole power' of making and dismissing members of the foundation, 'according to the statutes of the founder'. He was also empowered to choose college officers.[287] With his arrival in

---

[279] PRO SP 44/57 p. 193, SP 31/4, fo 8; J. Welch, *The List of the Queen's Scholars of . . . Westminster*, ed. C. B. Phillimore (London 1852), 204; T. A. Birrell, 'James Maurus Corker and Dryden's conversion', *English Studies* 54 (1973), 461–8; J. A. Winn, *John Dryden and His World* (London 1987), 415, 436, 626 n.

[280] Thomas Higgons was the son of Sir Bevil Higgons. As a demy he submitted to Parker's presidency and was promoted fellow. PRO SP 44/57, pp. 184–6, James II to the commissioners for visiting Magdalen College, 11, 12, 13 November 1687. For the Grenville family see *Restoration Oxford*, ed. Beddard i, no. 73 (and n. 4). Bodl. MS Tanner 30, fo 86, Sir Thomas Higgons to Sancroft, Westminster, 21 July 1686.

[281] PRO SP 44/57, p. 194, James II to President Parker, 7 January 1688; *Memoirs of Thomas, Earl of Ailesbury* [ed. Buckley] i. 168.

[282] 'Estratti delle lettere de Monsignor d'Adda, nunzio apostolico', 9 April 1688, printed in J. Mackintosh, *History of the Revolution in England in 1688* (London 1834), 652–3. Pope Innocent XI had charged D'Adda with the task of dividing England into four vicariates: Archivio Segreto Vaticano, secretaria brevium apostolicorum 1769, fo 10ᵛ.

[283] PRO SP 44/57, p. 201, James II to the vice-president and fellows of Magdalen College, 28 March 1688. The king had named Giffard as one of the three new bishops required 'ad propagationem religionis catholicae in hoc regno nostro': Archivio Segreto Vaticano, secretaria brevium apostolicorum 1769, fo 3, James II to Innocent XI, Whitehall, 25 November 1687.

[284] MCA MS 730b, fos 53, 54; Luttrell, *Brief Relation* i. 430, 435, 445.

[285] Luttrell, *Brief Relation* i. 436; Bodl. MS Smith 141, fos 31, 32ᵛ; HMC *Hastings MSS*, ii. 183.

[286] Hemphill, *The Early Vicars Apostolic of England 1685–1750*, 16–26 and map.

[287] PRO SP 44/57, p. 205, James II to President Giffard, 4 June 1688; MCA MS 730b, fos 54ʳ⁻ᵛ; BL MS Lansdowne 937, fo 97.

the college on 15 June, Magdalen was well on the way to becoming the 'new St Omers' which protestants later complained it had become.[288] Between 5 and 9 July he admitted five fellows—all of them Catholic priests, three of whom had taught as professors of theology and philosophy at Douai—proof of his determination to honour Waynflete's original intention to found a Catholic seminary.[289] As a bishop, Giffard was soon at work, presiding at high mass, preaching and confirming, and planning the itinerary of his coming episcopal visitation of the midland district.[290] Knowing that the direction of his college was in reliable Catholic hands, he left Oxford on 11 August to begin the arduous task of Catholic evangelization for which he had been appointed.[291]

The Catholic cause in Oxford, insubstantial as it yet was in size, had made astonishing progress in the first three and half years of James's reign. Only four years before, the Catholic religion had barely maintained a furtive presence in the city, that 'citadel, or principal bulwark of heresy', as the Jesuits described Oxford.[292] By the summer of 1688 its position had been transformed, for it was fast acquiring the wherewithal to launch a counter-reformation offensive. It possessed three public chapels, a printing press, salaried priests and academics, the makings of a seminary, and a resident bishop: testimony to the unstinted patronage of the king and to the unswerving dedication of his Catholic supporters. That Giffard's arrival coincided with a four-month vacancy in the see of Oxford served but to highlight the king's ecclesiastical priorities. When, in July 1688, James got round to filling the vacant protestant bishopric, he took care to appoint a cleric who, like Parker, favoured his policy of religious toleration: Timothy Hall, whose sole recommendation was that he had been one of the very few London incumbents to read the declaration of indulgence from the pulpit of his church.[293] James clearly expected

[288] There was talk of boys 'bred up under Poulton the Jesuit, at the Savoy', being 'elected kings scholars, and sent to Maudlin', on the analogy of Queen Elizabeth's scholars from protestant Westminster being sent to Christ Church and Trinity, Cambridge: Luttrell, *Brief Relation* i. 426; Bodl. MS Smith 141, p. 32. For Catholic designs on Magdalen School, see Wood, *Life and Times* iii. 253; *Parliamentary Debates*, ed. Grey ix. 12.

[289] The professors were Robert Jones, Edward Birtwistle (alias Howarden), and Andrew Giffard, brother of Bishop Giffard: MCA MS 730b, fos 53–4. Bodl. MS Smith 141, fo 32ᵛ; Bloxam, *Magdalen and James II*, 247; Anstruther, *The Seminary Priests* iii. 69, 119, 220; 94–5, 207; 65–7, 228. Bellenger, *English and Welsh Priests*, 77, 40, 64.

[290] HMC *Twelfth Report*, appx vii, p. 212, H. Fleming to Sir Daniel Fleming, Oxford, 29 July 1688; Wood, *Life and Times* iii. 269, 271–2.

[291] 'Reverendus dominus praeses profectus in missionem': MCA MS 730b, fo 54ᵛ; Beddard, *A Kingdom without a King*, 15–16. Giffard's resolute stance in Oxford cannot be reconciled with Kenyon's portrayal of him as being 'in favour of a temporising policy' in religion: J. P. Kenyan (ed.), *The Stuart Constitution 1603–1688*, (Cambridge 1966), 454.

[292] *Records of the English Province*, ed. Foley v. 954, annual letter of the Society of Jesus, 1684–5.

[293] PRO SP 44/53, p. 207, James II to the clerk of the signet attending, Windsor, 26 July 1688; CA D&C. i. b. 3, pp. 290–8; LPL Sancroft register I, fos 184–9; Dr Williams's Library, MS Morrice Q, pp. 260, 261; Luttrell, *Brief Relation* i. 440; Wood, *Life and Times* iii. 273; *Hatton Correspondence*, ed. Thompson ii. 89. Again, the university showed its dislike of James's choice by withholding a doctorate of divinity from Hall: Luttrell, *Brief Relation* i. 457.

Oxford to provide a home base for the English Mission, and to that end all else was subordinated.

Protestant Oxford was appalled at the onset of Catholic militancy. Such was the depth of academic despondency that not even the fillip of a royal visit, with its attendant junketings, was able to retrieve steadily deteriorating relations with the court. While James's presence in Oxford in September 1687 revealed an unshaken respect for his person, it did not dispel the prevailing sense of grievance.[294] Despite the senior proctor's publicly expressed hope, or rather plea, 'that his majesty would be good to *Ecclesia Anglicana*', the king failed to allay protestant anxiety.[295] Yet, apart from his over-publicized tirade against the fellows of Magdalen, he had been affable enough, and had sought to persuade, not hector, the university authorities into accepting his *de facto* toleration.

On taking his leave, James had ventured to deliver a short homily, commending the Christian virtues of 'love and charitie' to his hosts. He desired that there should be 'a right understanding' between his protestant and Catholic subjects, based on an equal service to the crown. He besought them that their eye should not be evil because he did good to all his people. Recalling 'that in the king my father's time the Church of England's men and the Catholicks loved each other', he observed, with regret, that 'now there is gotten a spirit among you which is quite contrary'.[296] Only in private was he less than placatory. In conversation with the vice-chancellor on the vexed matter of Oxford books published against his religion, he was heard to remark 'that the Church of England men were his only enemys'.[297] Whatever good his visit may have done was quickly undone by the fate which subsequently overtook Magdalen College. In the aftermath of that divisive event James's plea for religious tolerance and mutual forbearing sounded hollow indeed to many churchmen.

The so-called 'ruine' of Magdalen College was of national, not merely of domestic, Oxford, importance. It showed the lengths to which James was prepared to go in order to promote his religion. Whatever the rights and wrongs of the fellows' resistance, the proceedings taken against them irreversibly damaged James's reputation and made him 'many enemys'. The punishment of the fellows and the transformation of Magdalen into 'a Romish college' completed protestant disgust with the court's 'arbitrary' measures.[298] That such occurrences should take place in the very heartland of the English reformation brought home to James's former tory friends what his whig adversaries had long ago realized: that, as the laws stood, a

---

[294] For the royal visit, see OUA register Bb, pp. 169–73. Bodl. MS Wood d. 19, pt 3, fos 81 ff; *The Flemings in Oxford* ii. 204–6; *London Gazette*, no. 2275 (5–8 September 1687); HMC *Downshire MSS* i, pt 1, p. 261; Luttrell, *Brief Relation* i. 411; Wood, *Life and Times* iii. 232–3.

[295] Wood, *Life and Times* iii. 235.

[296] Ibid. 233, 238–9; Bodl. MS Smith 47, fo 46ᵛ, MS Rawlinson letters 91, fo 54; *Hatton Correspondence*, ed. Thompson ii. 72.

[297] Vice-Chancellor Ironside replied 'that none of them were for the bill of exclusion': Bodl. MS Ballard 21, fo 12, Thomas Sykes to [Arthur Charlett], 9 September 1687.

[298] Bodl. MS Smith 141, fos 27ʳ⁻ᵛ; Clarke, *Life of James the Second* ii. 119–24; *Memoirs of Thomas, Earl of Ailesbury* [ed. Buckley] i. 167–9.

Catholic monarch could not be trusted to respect either the property or institutions of protestant England.

The religious, legal, and political issues raised by the case of Magdalen College stimulated a radical re-examination by the clergy and laity of the Church of England of 'the measures of obedience', so that Englishmen who 'had been accustomed', by their education in Fell's Oxford, 'to take it for granted that kings were all absolute', now began to think that it might be 'lawfull' to put 'a stop to the king's proceedings'. From the winter of 1687 the doctrines of passive obedience and non-resistance, which for more than a century had been the distinguishing marks of the high churchman's regard for the sovereign prince, were in retreat. By the time that James decided to prosecute the seven bishops for refusing to order the publication of his second declaration of indulgence in the summer of 1688, it was plain to many protestants that matters could not continue as they were, and 'that men who rode post over precipices would either in a little time break their necks, or they would come to their journey's end'.[299]

Throughout 1688 Vice-Chancellor Ironside was uncompromising in his hostility to the Catholic presence in Oxford. He refused to matriculate the intruded Catholic priests and scholars, and denied them the right to wear gowns. At the beginning of Trinity term he declined to attend the St Mark's day sermon, which was normally preached at Magdalen, not caring to hear Fr Fairfax's 'e[u]logies on the Virgin Mary'. Instead, he appointed a protestant to preach before him in the university church.[300] Anxious to avoid harmful complaints at court, he was even-handed in his exercise of discipline, especially in cases where the plaintiffs were Catholic and the defendants protestant.[301] Although the university stayed generally calm under his prudent rule, there were signs that dynastic disenchantment with 'a popish successor' was again setting in, and on a much larger scale than in the 1670s. This time tories as well as whigs were affected. The recurrent bouts of anti-Catholic protest among undergraduates, the tensions between gownsmen and soldiers, the Oxfordshire gentry's refusal to back a parliamentary repeal of the test act, and the Oxford clergy's boycott of the king's declaration of indulgence—serious pointers though they were to the massive growth of opposition to James's policies—were of less consequence in the political life of a hereditary monarchy than the despair that gripped the university and nation in 1688, as the prospect of an upset to the protestant succession became a distinct possibility. The fear was that the birth of a Catholic prince of Wales would seal the fate of protestant England by consigning it for ever to a line of Catholic kings.[302]

Within days of the announcement of Mary Beatrice's being with child 'a scatter'd libell' was picked up by the butler of All Souls, implying that there was a plot

[299] R. A. Beddard, 'Observations of a London clergyman on the revolution of 1688–9: being an excerpt from the autobiography of Dr. William Wake', *Guildhall Miscellany* ii (1967), 406–17.

[300] Wood, *Life and Times* iii. 265; OUA chancellor's ct papers, 9 April 1688.

[301] OUA registrum curiae cancellarii, 1685–1691, fos 9ᵛ–11; chancellor's ct papers, 1688/13/1.

[302] Beddard, *A Kingdom without a King*, 11–13, 17.

to foist an impostor on the kingdom. On 29 January, the official day of thanks-giving for the queen's pregnancy, 'no bells in Oxford range but Christ Church and Magdalen College'. The same happened at the birth of Prince James Francis Edward on 10 June. Whereas a solemn *Te deum* was sung in Magdalen chapel and in Dean Massey's oratory at Christ Church, and the bells of both foundations rang out in celebration of the happy delivery, the rest of Oxford—that is to say, protes-tant Oxford—remained sullenly silent. 'Noe colleges or halls besides took any notice of the birth . . . either by bonfier or ringing of bells—knowing full well that if he lives he is to be bred up a papist and so consequently the crowne of England and popish religion will never part'.[303]

That the king and university were further apart than ever was confirmed three days later by the dispatch of a writ of *quo warranto* against the university's charter.[304] The summons was based on alleged infringement by the university press of the privileges of the king's printer in London. It was, of course, a Catholic ruse to throttle the publication of protestant propaganda. Not even the conjoined inter-vention of the earl of Clarendon as high steward, Lord Chancellor Jeffreys, and Vice-Chancellor Ironside in the legal process was able to defeat Henry Hills's deter-mination to suppress the Church of England's 'seditious pamphletts'.[305]

There was no clearer demonstration of the university's deep distrust of the king than the speed and resolution with which it moved to elect a successor to Chancellor Ormonde in July 1688. The identity of purpose that had been forged between Aldrich and Hough in the contest over Magdalen ensured that the Butler connection, which had served Oxford so effectively since 1669, would continue, and with it the high church leadership that had been established at the Restoration. 'Having early notice' of the chancellor's death on 21 July 'by the care of Dr Hough', the university was able to forestall the intrusion of a courtier.[306] The next day Ironside called a convocation for the morning of 23 July, by which time the defend-ers of the university's residual independence were ready to act. Aldrich threw the force of the Christ Church political machine behind his old pupil, the new duke of Ormonde, grandson of the deceased chancellor.

Though other names—those of Clarendon, Nottingham, and Halifax among

---

[303] Wood, *Life and Times* iii. 255, 268. The libel may have been *Mr. Partridges Wonderful Predictions, pro anno 1688* [London 1687/8]. Notwithstanding factious rumours of a fraudulent birth, the university pro-duced its customary volume of congratulatory verses, to which the Catholic converts, John Augustine Barnard and Thomas Deane, contributed: *Strenae natalitiae academiae oxoniensis in celsissimum principem* (Oxford 1688). Dr Williams's Library, MS Morrice Q, p. 239; Bodl. MS Wood d. 4, p. 338; *Clarendon Correspondence*, ed. Clarke ii. 156; *Ellis Correspondence*, ed. Ellis i. 373.

[304] For the summons of the Catholic sheriff of Oxford, Sir Henry Browne, to the university on 13 June 1688 to answer the writ see Bodl. MS Carte 131B, fo 242. Bodl. MS Ballard 12, fo 35, Dr George Hickes to [Arthur Charlett], 18 June 1688. The university took legal advice, see OUA WP/13/21/5, fo 95, register Bb, pp. 195–6.

[305] OUA register Bb, pp. 234–5, Vice-Chancellor Ironside to Ormonde, Wadham College, 18 June 1688.

[306] Luttrell, *Brief Relation* i. 452; *Hatton Correspondence*, ed. Thompson ii. 89.

them—were bruited, Ormonde was elected.[307] Aldrich's care was well bestowed, for only hours later Ironside received the king's mandamus in favour of Lord Chancellor Jeffreys.[308] As a newcomer to the political stage, but one whose firmness in the protestant religion was vouched for by Aldrich, the duke was the best choice in the circumstances. His election expressed the university's satisfaction with his grandfather's espousal of its interest and signified that its stance of opposition to the Catholic challenge remained unchanged.[309] His sponsors knew that, despite his youthful lack of experience, he could count on the support of his relatives by marriage, the earls of Clarendon and Rochester—which is exactly what happened.

Ormonde's election was, as Rochester informed him, 'the highest testimoniall which that source of our church should shew of their affiance in his honour and of his dareing to defend them'. Aware that he would require guidance in his difficult station, the earl confided 'that he would better succeed therein if, by the friendshipp of Dr Jane or Dr Aldrigge, he were privately informed what discision to make on things that were publickly represented unto him'. Even so, he cautioned him against getting embroiled in 'heat' or 'applause', which 'would soone make him passe for the head of a party', and cripple his influence at court. It was important that he should retain his independent reputation for the benefit of the university.[310] As a fly politician, Rochester instinctively knew, as did his friend George Hickes, that, if the university and Church of England were to escape disaster, they had 'need of the wisdom of the serpent' and 'the innocency of the dove'.[311]

Yet Ormonde's position was not secure even after his election; *en route* for Windsor with the chancellor-elect, Rochester received a message that James 'was much displeased' at the university's choice of Ormonde, and 'that he would not have him accept of it'. At this the duke turned back. The earl went on alone to Windsor to remonstrate with James.[312] Relying on their old familiarity, he played his trump card—the deserts of kinship and loyalty. He stressed the duke's being 'near ally'd to two great peers who were the support of the crown' in the worst of times: Ormonde's grandfather, the deceased first duke, and Rochester's father, Lord Chancellor Clarendon, the flowers of Cavalier loyalty. The implication was

---

[307] OUA register Bb, fo 204, 23 July 1688; BL Add. MS 41,805, fo 34. For the second duke's owning Aldrich's part in his election see Bodl. MS Carte 217, fo 280, Ormonde to Aldrich, Kingston Hall, 24 July 1688; G. W. Keeton, *Lord Chancellor Jeffreys and the Stuart Cause* (London 1965), 444.

[308] Bodl. MS Carte 217, fo 277; *Ellis Correspondence*, ed. Ellis i. 76–7, 79. For the vice-chancellor's letter excusing the non-election of Lord Chancellor Jeffreys see *Clarendon Correspondence*, ed. Clarke ii. 490–1, Ironside to Jeffreys [Oxford, 25 July 1688]; Luttrell, *Brief Relation* i. 452; Wood, *Life and Times* iii. 373.

[309] Warden Finch wrote of 'the happyness' of the university's 'being a long time supported by his [the first duke's] excellent conduct': Bodl. MS Carte 217, fo 277, L. W. Finch to Ormonde, Longleat, 28 July 1688. For an appreciative obituary of the first duke see the *London Gazette*, no. 2367 (23–6 July 1688).

[310] Bodl. MS Carte 69, fos 497, 500ᵛ, earl of Rochester's memorandum concerning Ormonde's exercise of the chancellorship, headed 'Station of Chancellour for Oxford'. For his profession of regard for the new duke see ibid., fo 470, Rochester to Sir Robert Southwell, New Park, 7 August 1688.

[311] Bodl. MS Ballard 12, fo 19, Hickes to Charlett, 3 January 1686/7.

[312] *Clarendon Correspondence*, ed. Clarke ii. 183; *Ellis Correspondence* ed. Ellis ii. 76.

that the king might yet have need of Ormonde and his kind. James relented. Temporarily abstracted from the concerns of religion, he listened to the arguments of his brother-in-law. Still smarting from the acquittal of the seven bishops, he perhaps sensed in this latest contradiction an opportunity to mend relations with the leaders of the Anglican tory party.[313] On 13 August Ormonde accepted the chancellorship with James's blessing, and assured Vice-Chancellor Ironside that he would 'on all occasions' serve the university 'to the utmost' of his power.[314]

Unfortunately for the king, his gesture of goodwill—like all the others that followed—came too late to rally Oxford behind him, as he prepared to oppose the invasion of Dutch William.[315] By late September Oxford was full of men 'waiting for good news' of the prince of Orange's coming.[316] Caught unawares, James had actively to seek a *rapprochement* with the Church of England. On 24 September Clarendon undertook (somewhat rashly as it turned out) that churchmen would 'behave themselves like honest men', in spite of their having been 'severely used of late'.[317] His promise led to a series of audiences in which the protestant bishops spelled out their conditions for political reconciliation. They amounted to a complete rehabilitation of the Anglican tory interest and an end to the Catholic challenge. High on the agenda of their discussions were demands for breaking the ecclesiastical commission, the withdrawal of dispensations in the universities, the restoration of the president and fellows of Magdalen, and the inhibition of the vicars apostolic.[318]

In putting Magdalen College at the forefront of the nation's grievances the bishops were at one with the prince of Orange.[319] Unbeknown to them, William's declaration from The Hague, stating his reasons for coming over, had denounced the expulsion of the fellows from their freeholds as an unprecedented infringement of the rights of property, 'contrary to law, and to that express provision of *magna*

---

[313] The election was greatly applauded by high church tories: Bodl. MS Ballard 12, fo 38ᵛ, [Hickes to Charlett], 30 July 1688; Bodl. MS Ballard 34, fos 124, 126, Henry Box and R[ichard] R[ichmond] to Charlett, 24 July and 6 August 1688.

[314] OUA register Bb, fo 204, Ormonde to Vice-Chancellor Ironside, Windsor, 13 August [1688]. He had already, before learning of the king's dislike, acknowledged the university's election to be 'a great obligation upon mee, who was but a few years since a member of it': Bodl. MS Carte 217, fo 279, Ormonde to Vice-Chancellor Ironside [Kingston Hall], 24 July 1688. For his installation see Bodl. MS Bodl. 594, p. 121. Luttrell, *Brief Relation* i. 456.

[315] R. A. Beddard, 'The loyalist opposition in the Interregnum', *Bulletin of the Institute of Historical Research* 90 (1967), 102.

[316] Wood, *Life and Times* iii. 278.   [317] *Clarendon Correspondence*, ed. Clarke ii. 189.

[318] For the episcopal demands in general see Beddard, 'Sancroft', 159–67; *Collectanea curiosa*, ed. Gutch i. 410–13; BL MS Lansdowne 1024, fo 51; *An Account of the Late Proposals of the Archbishop of Canterbury, with some other Bishops to his Majesty* (London 1688).

[319] 'That your majesty will be graciously pleased that no dispensation may be granted, or continued, by vertue whereof any person not duly qualified by law hath been, or may be put into any place, office, or preferment in church, or state, or in the universities, or continued in the same, especially such as have cure of souls annext to them; and in particular that you will be graciously pleased to restore the president and fellows of S. Mary Magdalen College in Oxford.' Bodl. MS Tanner 28, fo 187ᵛ, Sancroft's autograph paper of advice to James II; Bodl. MS Smith 141, fo 34.

charta, that no man shall lose his life, or goods, but by the law of the land'.[320] Keen to win back the support of his 'old friends' as a means of strengthening his position in the approaching dynastic contest, James capitulated to the bishops' demands. He reversed his policies. On 30 September he restored Compton to his diocese;[321] on 5 October he broke the ecclesiastical commission;[322] on 11 October he ordered Bishop Mews to restore President Hough and the protestant fellows, 'having declared his resolution to preserve the Church of England in all its rights and immunitties'.[323] In a last show of concern for his co-religionists the king took care to ensure that his Magdalen clients, including Bishop Giffard, had time allowed them to quit the premises.[324] When, on 20 October, Mews entered Oxford it was more like a royal triumph than a college visitation. He was escorted in by a vast cavalcade of gentry from Oxfordshire and 'the adjacent counties', and was 'received by the doctors in their scarlett': it was, of course, an expression of protestant solidarity.[325] Five days later he restored the ejected fellows and demies, 'to the satisfaction of the whole university', and to that 'of the whole kingdom'.[326]

James's concessions did not quiet the 'great frett' in which town and gown had been since 1687. If anything, they served to heighten unrest by liberating the pent-up forces of anti-Catholicism. With the removal of royal protection the Catholic community was once again at the mercy of its protestant enemies. On 5 November—the day on which William of Orange landed in Tor Bay—the university was treated to a fiery anti-Catholic sermon at St Mary's, 'shewing the bloodyness of the conspiracy' of 1605. That night Wood noted more bonfires 'at colleges and in the streets' than he had ever seen before. They were lit 'in spite to the papists'.[327] Though James called for volunteers to fight William, none stirred in Oxford save Catholics.[328] The contrast to the rush to arms which had attended the

---

[320] Beddard, *A Kingdom without a King*, 127, William of Orange's First Declaration issued from The Hague, 10 October 1688 (new style).

[321] Bodl. MS Rawlinson d. 365, fo 32ᵛ, MS Don. c. 38, fo 296.

[322] PRO PC 2/72, fo 160, order-in-council; Dr Williams's Library, MS Morrice Q, p. 303.

[323] PRO SP 44/56, p. 452, Sunderland to Bishop Mews, 11 October 1688; Bodl. MS Carte 198, fo 68; *Autobiography of Sir John Bramston*, ed. Braybrooke, 322.

[324] MCA MS 730b, fo 58, Sunderland to Bishop Mews, Whitehall, 13 October 1688; Bodl. MS Don. c. 38, fo 313.

[325] Bloxam, *Magdalen and James II*, 254, 256, 25 October 1688. President Hough entertained the visitor, Bishop Mews, Sub-Dean Aldrich, and the canons of Christ Church, as well as several heads of houses, to dinner to mark his 'restoration': Wood, *Life and Times* iii. 533. For the university's rejoicing see OUA WP/13/21/5 (vice-chancellors' accounts, 1666–97), fo 95.

[326] MCA MS 730b, fos 57–8, 'negotium visitationis', BB/2, 25 October 1688; Bodl. MS Smith 141, fos 34ᵛ–5ᵛ. As a mark of favour, James allowed the restored fellows to defray the expenses of their resettlement from college rents: PRO SP 44/97, p. 5, Secretary Middleton to Bishop Mews, 28 October 1688; *An Account of the Late Visitation ... by ... Peter Ld Bish. of Winton* (London 1688); Surrey RO MS Midleton 1248/1/211, Francis Atterbury to St John Brodrick, 26 October 1688.

[327] Bodl. MS Carte 131B, fo 234, Vice-Chancellor Ironside to Ormonde, Wadham College, 18 June 1688; Wood, *Life and Times* iii. 281.

[328] Several Catholic academics, including Charnock, Barnard, Hales, and Dryden, volunteered to fight for the king against William of Orange in response to a summons from the Catholic sheriff of Oxfordshire, Sir Henry Browne: PRO SP 44/166, p. 4, SP 44/165, pp. 141–4; Wood, *Life and Times* iii. 280–1.

outbreak of Monmouth's rebellion in 1685 could not have been stronger.[329] For the present the fighting spirit had been knocked out of Oxford toryism. The Catholic challenge, while it had not destroyed the university's loyalty to King James, had completely anaesthetized it. As a result, political apathy prevailed over military duty—with fatal consequences for James's kingship. The minimal movement that did occur was in the opposite direction. There was a westward seepage of townsmen and academics out of Oxford towards the prince's advancing army.[330] They were led by the tory earl of Abingdon, who had the dubious distinction of being the first peer to join William's camp.[331]

The Oxford Catholics, not wishing to stay until disaster overtook them, dismantled their chapels, shut down their press, put their books in store, drew in their money, and made ready for flight. Following James's military retreat from Salisbury on 27 November they fled to London to be near a king who was powerless to protect them. For most of them the capital proved to be but a staging-post on their flight overseas, to Ireland and the continent. For those whose misfortune it was to be caught in the tightening net of protestant vigilanteism a worse fate awaited them. They were manhandled and imprisoned. Reviled as traitors for their respective parts in subverting the laws of protestant England, Obadiah Walker was sent to the Tower and Bishop Giffard to Newgate prison. Dean Massey, a no less desirable catch, managed to make good his escape to France disguised as a trooper.[332]

So ended the Catholic challenge amid political calamity, religious turmoil, and personal suffering. When, in the fullness of time, and after far-reaching changes in the law, the Catholic Church was readmitted to the university in the course of the nineteenth century, it returned, not in response to a renewal of royal patronage, but by virtue of its abiding spiritual and intellectual appeal to the hearts and minds of Englishmen who yearned to be united to the one, holy, catholic, and apostolic church: the church which St Gregory the Great and St Augustine of Canterbury had brought to England's shores in 597, and the church of which James II and his Catholic collaborators between 1685 and 1688 were not altogether unworthy members.

[329] 'When Monmouth's rebellion brake out there was, every day almost, a duke, earl, or lord, with company, passing thro' Oxford and making a hurry over all the nation. No man stirs yet.' Wood, *Life and Times* iii. 281. See pp. 911–16 above. Cf PRO SP 8/3, no. 140; James II to William of Orange, 19 June 1685.

[330] Wood, *Life and Times* iii. 282, 283–4, 286–7.   [331] Beddard, *A Kingdom without a King*, 30–1.

[332] Ibid. 47, 158, 162, 164; Bodl. MSS Don. c. 38, fo 297, Don. c. 39, fo 54, MS Clarendon 90, fo 42; Dr Williams's Library, MS Morrice Q, p. 632; BL MS Harleian 6852, fo 402, Add. MS 32,095, fo 303; Wood, *Life and Times* iii. 299, 333, 346; *Hatton Correspondence*, ed. Thompson ii. 98, 124; *CJ* x. 275; Gilbert Burnet, *History of His Own Time*, ed. M. J. Routh (Oxford 1823, 2nd edn 6 vols Oxford 1833) iii. 346, 360; *A Dialogue between Father Gifford, the late Popish President of Maudlin, and Obadiah Walker, Master of University, upon their New Colledge Preferment in Newgate* (n.p. 1689).

Index